THE VICTORIA HISTORY
OF THE
COUNTIES OF ENGLAND

———

A HISTORY OF
SOMERSET

VOLUME IV

THE VICTORIA HISTORY
OF THE
COUNTIES OF ENGLAND

EDITED BY C. R. ELRINGTON

THE UNIVERSITY OF LONDON
INSTITUTE OF
HISTORICAL RESEARCH

Oxford University Press

OXFORD   LONDON   GLASGOW
NEW YORK   TORONTO   MELBOURNE   WELLINGTON
KUALA LUMPUR   SINGAPORE   JAKARTA   HONG KONG   TOKYO
DELHI   BOMBAY   CALCUTTA   MADRAS   KARACHI
NAIROBI   DAR ES SALAAM   CAPE TOWN

© *University of London 1978*

ISBN 0 19 722747 3

*Printed in Great Britain
at the University Press, Oxford
by Eric Buckley
Printer to the University*

INSCRIBED TO THE

MEMORY OF HER LATE MAJESTY

QUEEN VICTORIA

WHO GRACIOUSLY GAVE THE TITLE TO

AND ACCEPTED THE DEDICATION

OF THIS HISTORY

CREWKERNE FROM THE AIR, 1974

A HISTORY OF THE COUNTY OF

SOMERSET

EDITED BY R. W. DUNNING

VOLUME IV

PUBLISHED FOR

THE INSTITUTE OF HISTORICAL RESEARCH

BY

OXFORD UNIVERSITY PRESS

1978

Distributed by Oxford University Press until 1 January 1981
thereafter by Dawsons of Pall Mall

CONTENTS OF VOLUME FOUR

		PAGE
Dedication	. . . .	v
Contents	. . . .	ix
List of Illustrations	. . . .	xi
List of Maps and Plans	. . . .	xiii
Editorial Note	. . . .	xv
Classes of Documents in the Public Record Office used	. . . . .	xvii
Somerset Record Office Accumulations	. . . . . .	xviii
Note on Abbreviations	. . . .	xix
Somerset Record Society Publications	. . . . . .	xx
Topography	Architectural descriptions prepared in collaboration with A. P. BAGGS	
Crewkerne Hundred . . .	By R. W. DUNNING . . .	1
Crewkerne	By R. W. DUNNING and R. J. E. BUSH .	4
Hinton St. George . . .	By R. W. DUNNING . . .	38
Merriott	By R. J. E. BUSH . . .	52
Misterton	,, . .	62
Wayford	,, . .	68
Martock Hundred . . .	,, . .	76
Martock	,, . .	78
South Petherton Hundred . .	By R. W. DUNNING . .	111
Barrington . . .	,, . .	113
Chaffcombe . . .	By R. J. E. BUSH . .	121
Chillington . . .	By R. W. DUNNING . .	128
Cricket St. Thomas . .	By R. J. E. BUSH . .	133
Cudworth . . .	By R. W. DUNNING . .	141
Dinnington . . .	,, . .	147
Dowlish Wake . .	By R. J. E. BUSH . .	151
Knowle St. Giles . .	,, . .	156
Lopen . . .	By R. W. DUNNING . .	163
South Petherton . .	,, . .	170
Seavington St. Mary . .	,, . .	198
Seavington St. Michael . .	,, . .	205
Shepton Beauchamp . .	By R. J. E. BUSH . .	210
Wambrook . . .	,, . .	222
Whitestaunton . . .	,, . .	231
Index	By R. W. DUNNING . .	239

LIST OF ILLUSTRATIONS

Thanks are rendered to the following for permission to reproduce material in their possession and for the loan of photographs: Somerset Archaeological and Natural History Society (illustrations marked S.A.S.), the Royal Commission on Historical Monuments (England) (marked N.M.R.), Aerofilms Limited, Dr. D. Chapman, Mr. J. C. F. Prideaux-Brune, and Mr. W. Vaux. Photographs dated 1977 are by A. P. Baggs.

Crewkerne from the air. Photograph by Aerofilms Limited, 1974 . . . *frontispiece*

Merriott church from the south-west. Photograph, 1977 . . . . *facing page* 16

Crewkerne church from the south-west. Photograph, 1977 . . . . ,, 16

Martock church: the roof, before restoration (N.M.R.) . . . . ,, 17

Hinton St. George church: interior, with the tomb of Sir Anthony Poulett (d. 1600). Photograph, 1977 . . . . ,, 17

Hinton St. George:

    Hinton House from the west, 1725. Drawing by Edmund Prideaux (N.M.R.) . ,, 32

    Hinton House from the south-west. Photograph, 1977 . . . . ,, 32

    Hinton House: the south front. Photograph, 1977 . . . . . ,, 32

Misterton: Manor Farm. Photograph, 1977 . . . . . . ,, 33

South Petherton: Wigborough Manor. Photograph, 1977 . . . . ,, 33

Wayford Manor. Photograph, 1977 . . . . ,, 33

Chaffcombe: Avishays. Photograph, 1977 . . . . . . ,, 33

Martock: the Parrett Works. Engraving, *c.* 1900 . . . . . ,, 48

Crewkerne: factory in Abbey Street. Photograph, 1977 . . . . ,, 48

Hinton St. George: the Fives Wall. Photograph, 1977 . . . . . ,, 49

Martock: Railway Hotel. Photograph, 1977 . . . . . . ,, 49

Martock: school-house. Photograph, 1977 . . . . . . ,, 49

Hinton St. George: view north-east to Ham Hill. Photograph 1977 . . . ,, 64

Hollow Ways in the Yeovil Sands, at the cross-roads west of Shepton Beauchamp. Photograph, 1977 . . . . ,, 64

Shepton Beauchamp: drawing, with plan, of the Rectory House, 1874 (S.A.S.) . . ,, 65

Merriott: Moorlands House. Photograph, 1977 . . . . . . ,, 65

Barrington Court. Photograph, *c.* 1900 (S.A.S.) . . . . . ,, 144

Cricket St. Thomas: Cricket House. Water-colour, 1849 (S.A.S.) . . . ,, 144

Crewkerne: the Abbey. Water-colour by John Buckler, 1831 (S.A.S.) . . . ,, 145

South Petherton: King Ina's Palace. Water-colour by W. W. Wheatley, 1851 (S.A.S.) . ,, 145

Martock: the former chapel at Milton. Photograph, 1977 . . . . ,, 145

Martock: the Treasurer's House. Photograph, 1977 . . . . . ,, 145

Whitestaunton: manor-house and church. Photograph, 1977 . . . . ,, 160

Dowlish Wake: manor-house and church. Photograph, 1977 . . . . ,, 160

Cricket St. Thomas church from the south-east. Water-colour by John Buckler, 1843 (S.A.S.) . . . . ,, 161

Barrington church from the north-east. Photograph, 1977 . . . . ,, 161

Knowle St. Giles church from the south-east. Water-colour by John Buckler, 1832 (S.A.S.) . . . . ,, 161

Chillington church from the south-west. Photograph, 1977 . . . . ,, 161

South Petherton church from the north-west. Photograph, 1977 . . . ,, 192

Shepton Beauchamp church: the base of the former north tower. Photograph, 1977 . ,, 192

Merriott: Bow Mill. Photograph, 1977 . . . . ,, 193

Dowlish Wake: the Dower House. Photograph, 1977 . . . . . ,, 193

LIST OF ILLUSTRATIONS

South Petherton: Stratton Farm. Photograph, 1977 . . . . . *facing page* 193

Merriott: Manor Farm. Photograph, 1977 . . . . . . ,, 193

Martock:

    The market-place with the market house and obelisk. Photograph, 1977 . . ,, 208

    The church from the south-east. Photograph, 1977 . . . . . ,, 208

South Petherton: Hayes End Farm, Granary. Photograph, 1977 . . . ,, 209

Barrington Court: barns in vernacular style in reinforced concrete. Photograph, 1977 . ,, 209

Seavington St. Mary: the village carpenter and wheelwright. Photograph, 1903 . . ,, 209

LIST OF MAPS AND PLANS

The maps and street plans were drawn by Millicent B. Thompson of the Somerset County Planning Office from drafts by R. W. Dunning and R. J. E. Bush, the two street plans being based on the Ordnance Survey with the sanction of the Controller of H.M. Stationery Office, Crown Copyright reserved. The coat of arms was drawn by Patricia A. Tattersfield and the two house plans by A. P. Baggs. The church plans were drawn by Rodney Beeton from surveys by A. P. Baggs.

Crewkerne hundred	page 2
Crewkerne c. 1842	,, 6
Crewkerne street plan 1977	,, 7
Crewkerne U.D. arms	,, 28
Hinton House, plan showing development	,, 43
Martock hundred	,, 76
Martock 1824	,, 80
Martock church	,, 105
South Petherton hundred	,, 110
Barrington church	,, 119
Cudworth church	,, 146
Southern parishes in South Petherton hundred	,, 158
South Petherton street plan	,, 173
South Petherton church	,, 193
Northern parishes in South Petherton hundred	,, 200
Seavington St. Michael church	,, 209
Shepton Beauchamp church	,, 220
Whitestaunton House, plan showing the medieval building and its later development	,, 233

EDITORIAL NOTE

THE PRESENT volume is the second to be produced as a result of the partnership between the Somerset County Council and the University of London. An account of that partnership is given in the Editorial Note to Volume III, which was published in 1974. In that year the responsibility for the *Victoria History of Somerset*, which had until then been borne by a special sub-committee under the chairmanship of Colonel C. T. Mitford-Slade, was assigned to the Libraries (from 1977 the Libraries and Museums) Sub-Committee of the County Council's Education and Cultural Services Committee. From 1974 until 1977, when the compilation of the present volume was completed, the sub-committee's chairman was Dr. A. W. G. Court. The University's appreciation of the way in which the Somerset County Council has met and continues to meet the expenses of compiling and editing the *History* of the county is here most sincerely recorded.

Of the many people who have helped in the preparation of this volume the names of those who were concerned with particular parishes are recorded in the footnotes to the accounts of those parishes; they are thanked warmly for their help. The keeper of the records of the Duchy of Cornwall, Mr. R. J. R. Arundell, Mr. W. S. Blake, and Major H. Hussey are thanked for making available the records in their possession, and the help of Canon F. Bussby, Messrs. G. D. and M. Roper, Mr. A. Sabin, and Miss Dorothy Stroud in providing access to, respectively, Winchester Cathedral Library, the Forde Abbey Cartulary, Bristol Cathedral Library, and the manuscripts in Sir John Soane's Museum is gratefully acknowledged. Among the public libraries and record offices to whose librarians or archivists and their staff the thanks of the *History* are offered for their sympathetic and patient co-operation, special mention must be made of the Somerset Record Office.

The structure and aims of the *History* as a whole are outlined in the *General Introduction* (1970).

LIST OF CLASSES OF DOCUMENTS
IN THE PUBLIC RECORD OFFICE
USED IN THIS VOLUME
WITH THEIR CLASS NUMBERS

Chancery

		Proceedings
C	1	Early
C	2	Series I
C	3	Series II
C	5	Bridges
C	7	Hamilton
C	8	Mitford
C	22	Country Depositions
C	24	Town Depositions
C	54	Close Rolls
C	66	Patent Rolls
C	78	Decree Rolls
C	88	Chancery Files (Tower and Rolls Chapel), Records upon Outlawries
		Inquisitions post mortem
C	132	Series I, Hen. III
C	133	Edw. I
C	134	Edw. II
C	135	Edw. III
C	136	Ric. II
C	137	Hen. IV
C	139	Hen. VI
C	140	Edw. IV and V
C	141	Ric. III
C	142	Series II
C	145	Miscellaneous Inquisitions
C	260	Chancery Files (Tower and Rolls Chapel), Recorda

Court of Common Pleas

C.P. 25 (1)	Feet of Fines, Series I
C.P. 25 (2)	Series II
C.P. 43	Recovery Rolls

Exchequer, Treasury of Receipt

E 41	Deeds, Series AA

Exchequer, King's Remembrancer

E 117	Church Goods
E 134	Depositions taken by Commission
E 149	Inquisitions post mortem, Series I
E 150	Series II
E 152	Enrolments of Inquisitions
E 178	Special Commissions of Enquiry
E 179	Subsidy Rolls

Exchequer, Augmentation Office

E 310	Particulars for Leases
E 315	Miscellaneous Books
E 317	Parliamentary Surveys, Commonwealth
E 318	Particulars for Grants
E 321	Proceedings
E 326	Ancient Deeds, Series B
E 328	Series BB

Exchequer, First Fruits and Tenths Office

E 331	Bishops' Certificates of Institution

Registry of Friendly Societies

F.S. 1	Rules and Amendments, Series I

Home Office

H.O. 107	Census Papers, 1851 Census
H.O. 129	Census Papers, 1851 Census: Ecclesiastical Returns

Justices Itinerant, Assize and Gaol Delivery Justices, etc.

J.I. 1	Eyre Rolls, Assize Rolls, etc.

Exchequer, Office of the Auditors of Land Revenue

L.R. 2	Miscellaneous Books
L.R. 3	Court Rolls

Map Room

M.P.E.	Maps and Plans

Prerogative Court of Canterbury

Prob. 11	Registered Copies of Wills proved in P.C.C.

Registrar General

R.G. 4	Non-parochial Registers
R.G. 9	Census Returns, 1861
R.G. 10	Census Returns, 1871

Court of Requests

Req. 2	Proceedings

Special Collections

S.C. 2	Court Rolls
S.C. 6	Ministers' Accounts
S.C. 12	Rentals and Surveys, Portfolios

State Paper Office

S.P. 16	State Papers Domestic, Eliz. 1

Court of Star Chamber

Sta. Cha. 2	Proceedings

Tithe Redemption Office

Tithe 1	Boundary Awards

War Office

W.O. 30	Miscellaneous

SELECT LIST OF ACCUMULATIONS
IN THE SOMERSET RECORD OFFICE

Deposited Collections

DD/AB	Marquess of Ailesbury
AS	Lord Ashburton
BC	Battiscombe of Silchester
BD	Baker and Duke of Ilminster (solicitors)
CA	Vaughan-Lee family of Dillington
CAK	Canning and Kyrke of Chard (solicitors)
CC	Church Commissioners
CGS	Crewkerne Grammar School
CN	Clarke, Lukin, and Newton of Chard (solicitors)
ED	Estate Duty copy wills
EDS	Department of Education and Science
EM	Eames of Chard
GB	Gibbs family of Barrow Gurney
GRY	St. George Gray of Martock
HA	Hall family of Cricket St. Thomas
HI	Hippisley family of Ston Easton
HK	Hoskyns family of North Perrott
HKE	Hake of Swindon
HLM	Helyar family of Poundisford
JP	Jonas and Parke of Salisbury (solicitors)
KW	King, Wilkinson, and Co. of Taunton (surveyors)
LC	Louch, Wilmott, and Clarke of Langport (solicitors)
LV	Love of Williton
MR	Donne family of Crewkerne
NA	National Trust
PE	Peters family of South Petherton
PH	Phelips family of Montacute
PI	Pretor-Pinney family of Somerton Erleigh
PLE	Poole and Co. of South Petherton (solicitors)
PM	Portman family of Orchard Portman
PO	Popham family of Hunstrete
POt	Popham family of Hunstrete (Thring deposit)
PR	Parsons family of Misterton
PT	Earl Poulett of Hinton St. George
PTR	Proctor and Horden of Chard (solicitors)
SAS	Somerset Archaeological Society
SB	Sparks and Blake of Crewkerne (solicitors)
SF	Sanford family of Nynehead
SFR	Society of Friends
SH	Lord Strachie of Sutton Court
SP	Sheppard family of Taunton
SPK	Speke family of Jordans
SS	Sotheby and Co. (Poulett MSS.)
TH	Thring family of Alford
TMP	Temperley of Merriott (Whitley MSS.)
V	Vernacular Architecture Group
WHh	Walker-Heneage family of East Coker
WI	Somerset Federation of Women's Institutes
WM	Wells Museum
WN	Welman family of Poundisford
WO	Trevelyan family of Nettlecombe
WY	Wyndham family of Orchard Wyndham

S/HR	Poole and Co. of South Petherton (solicitors)
HY	Halliday of Leicester
X/LT	H. Little of Isleworth
MEY	Mrs. E. Morey
SAB	A. Sabin of Bristol
SR	Somerset Record Society
BR/gm	Glyn, Mills, and Co.
py	Perry of Brighton (solicitors)
D/P/	Parish Collections
D/PC/	Parish Council Collections
D/PS/ilm	Ilminster petty sessions

Diocesan Records

D/D/B reg	bishops' registers
B returns	benefice returns
Bg	exchanges of glebe
Bo	ordination papers
C	petitions for faculties
Ca	act books
Cd	deposition books
Cm	marriage licences
Ct	wills
Ol	licence books
Ppb	prebendal peculiars
Rg	glebe terriers
Rm	meeting-house licences
Rr	bishops' transcripts
V	diocesan books
Vc	visitation acts
V returns	visitation returns

Quarter Sessions Records

CR	Inclosure awards
Q/AH	County Map (Highways)
REl	land tax assessments
REr	electoral registers
RL	victuallers' recognizances
RR	recusants' lands, meeting-house licences
RUp	deposited plans
SR	sessions rolls

County Council Records

C/C	property deeds
E	education department

Other Deposits

D/G/Y	Yeovil poor-law union
N/spc	South Petherton and Crewkerne Methodist Records
T/ilm	Turnpike trusts, Ilminster
yeo	Yeovil
T/PH/hsy	photostats, Hussey family of Crewkerne
ptr	Proctor and Horden of Crewkerne (solicitors)
vch	Victoria History of Somerset

NOTE ON ABBREVIATIONS

Among the abbreviations and short titles used the following may require elucidation.

Bk. of Fairs	*Authentic Account published by the King's Authority, of all the Fairs in England and Wales* (5th edn. London, 1767)
Bristol R.O.	Bristol City Record Office
Collinson, *Hist. Som.*	J. Collinson, *The History and Antiquities of the County of Somerset* (3 vols. Bath, 1791)
County Gazette Dir. (1840)	*General Directory for the County of Somerset, presented to the subscribers to the County Gazette* (Taunton, 1840)
Cornw. R.O.	Cornwall Record Office
D.C.O.	Duchy of Cornwall Office
D.R.O.	Dorset Record Office
Devon R.O.	Devon Record Office
Dioc. Dir.	*Bath and Wells Diocesan Directory* (*and Almanack*) (1908–) (Almanack discontinued 1948)
Dioc. Kal.	(*New*) *Bath and Wells Diocesan Kalendar* (1888–1907)
E. Devon R.O.	Exeter and East Devon Record Office
Glos. R.O.	Gloucestershire Record Office
H.M.C. Wells	Historical Manuscripts Commission, Series 12, *Calendar of the Manuscripts of the Dean and Chapter of Wells* (2 vols. 1907, 1914)
Hutchins, *Hist. Dors.*	J. Hutchins, *The History and Antiquities of the County of Dorset* (3rd edn. 4 vols. London, 1861–70)
Mdx. R.O.	Middlesex Record Office
Proc. Som. Arch. Soc.	*Proceedings of the Somersetshire Archaeological and Natural History Society* (from 1968 *Somerset Archaeology and Natural History*)
Pulman, *Bk. of the Axe*	G. P. R. Pulman, *The Book of the Axe* (4th edn. London, 1875, repr. Bath, 1969)
Rep. Som. Cong. Union (1896)	*Annual Report of the Somerset Congregational Union and of the Evangelist Society presented at the One-Hundredth Anniversary* (Wellington, 1896)
S. & D. N. & Q.	*Somerset and Dorset Notes and Queries*
S.R.O.	Somerset Record Office
S.R.S.	*Somerset Record Society* (for list of publications see p. xx)
Salisbury Dioc. R.O.	Salisbury Diocesan Record Office
Som. Incumbents, ed. Weaver	*Somerset Incumbents*, ed. F. W. Weaver (Bristol, 1889)
Som. Wills, ed. Brown	*Abstracts of Somersetshire Wills etc., copied from the Manuscript Collections of the late Revd. F. Brown* (6 vols. priv. print. 1887–90)
W.R.O.	Wiltshire Record Office

LIST OF
SOMERSET RECORD SOCIETY PUBLICATIONS
USED IN THIS VOLUME

i	*Bishop Drokensford's Register, 1309–27* (1887)
ii	*Somerset Chantries, 1548* (1888)
iii	*Kirby's Quest* (1889)
iv	*Pre-Reformation Churchwardens' Accounts* (1890)
vi	*Pedes Finium, 1196–1307* (1892)
vii	*Cartularies of Bath Priory* (1893)
viii	*Cartularies of Bruton and Montacute Priories* (1894)
ix & x	*Register of Ralph de Salopia, 1327–63* (1896)
xi	*Somersetshire Pleas, c. 1200–56* (1897)
xii	*Pedes Finium, 1307–46* (1898)
xiii	*Registers of Bishop Giffard, 1265–66, and Bishop Bowett, 1401–7* (1899)
xiv	*Cartularies of Muchelney and Athelney Abbeys* (1899)
xv	*Gerard's Survey of Somerset, 1633* (1900)
xvi	*Somerset Wills, 1383–1500* (1901)
xvii	*Pedes Finium, 1347–90* (1902)
xviii	*Bellum Civile* (1902)
xix	*Somerset Wills, 1501–30* (1903)
xx	*Certificate of Musters, 1569* (1904)
xxi	*Somerset Wills, 1531–58* (1905)
xxii	*Pedes Finium, 1399–1485* (1906)
xxiii	*Quarter Sessions Records, 1607–25* (1907)
xxiv	*Quarter Sessions Records, 1625–39* (1908)
xxvi	*Feodary of Glastonbury Abbey* (1910)
xxvii	*Star Chamber Proceedings, Henry VII and Henry VIII* (1911)
xxviii	*Quarter Sessions Records, 1646–60* (1912)
xxix & xxx	*Register of Bishop Bubwith, 1407–24* (1913–14)
xxxi & xxxii	*Register of Bishop Stafford, 1425–43* (1915–16)
xxxiv	*Quarter Sessions Records, 1666–76* (1919)
xxxv	*Two Beauchamp Registers* (1920)
xxxvi	*Somersetshire Pleas, 1255–72* (1921)
xxxvii	*Life of Bishop Kidder* (1924)
xl	*Medieval Wills from Wells, 1543–6, 1554–6* (1925)
xli	*Somersetshire Pleas, 1272–9* (1926)
xlii	*Muchelney Memoranda* (1927)
xliii	*Collectanea II* (1928)
xliv	*Somersetshire Pleas, 1280* (1929)
xlvii	*Wulfric of Haselbury* (1933)
xlix & l	*Register of Bishop Bekynton, 1443–65* (1934–5)
li	*Somerset Enrolled Deeds* (1936)
lii	*Registers of Bishop Stillington and Bishop Fox, 1466–94* (1937)
liv	*Registers of Bishop King and Bishop de Castello, 1496–1518* (1938)
lv	*Bishops' Registers, 1518–59* (1940)
lxvii	*Sales of Wards, 1603–41* (1965)
lxx	*Bridgwater Borough Archives, 1468–85* (1971)
lxxi	*Somerset Assize Orders, 1640–59* (1971)
Extra Series	*Some Somerset Manors* (1931)

CREWKERNE HUNDRED

T HE SMALL hundred of Crewkerne is a compact area on the southern boundary of the county at the eastern end of the Windwhistle ridge with a complex geological structure. Its irregular and often dramatic landscape has much in common with north Dorset, from which it was originally divided by the river Axe. The great parish of Crewkerne was a royal Saxon estate which once incorporated all but two of the later parishes into which the hundred was divided, though the town itself was never large, and looked southwards into Dorset rather than north and west into Somerset for most of its trade.

The hundred was formed by 1084. At its head was the royal manor of Crewkerne itself together with its church estate and the parishes of Hinton St. George, Merriott, and Seaborough (now Dors.).[1] Misterton and Wayford then formed part of Crewkerne. The tithings of Crewkerne parish varied during the course of time and for differing purposes, but in 1599 included two 'towns' known as Guyan and Bonevile, evidently medieval freeholds, the second of which was almost certainly part of Crewkerne and not a separate settlement.[2] The hundred remained so constituted until the 19th century.[3]

Ownership of the hundred evidently followed the manor until its division in the 16th century. The 'foreign hundred' was given by William de Reviers (d. 1217) to his daughter Mary on her marriage to Robert de Courtenay, and thence descended through the Courtenay family.[4] In 1556 ownership was divided, and a survey of 1599 recognized the existence of several lords, but subsequent enfranchisements within the manor evidently extinguished some claims to the hundred.[5] The Vivians certainly claimed their ⅛ share of the hundred in 1608,[6] and the Trelawneys at least retained manorial rights until 1613,[7] but the Pouletts alone continued to exercise jurisdiction, in 1666 in respect of their ¼ share and by the beginning of the 19th century the whole hundred.[8]

The only court roll to be found is a fragment dating from 1585–7, the court apparently held jointly by Amias Poulett and William Mohun.[9] Court books survive for 1651–77, 1703–10, and 1715–26.[10] In 1514–15 the lord held two lawdays and eight other courts for the hundred,[11] and in 1526–7 two lawdays and ten other sessions.[12] A similar pattern continued at least until 1545.[13] In 1599 the twice-yearly lawdays were attended by freeholders called 'hundreders' and the three-week courts by the customary tenants. Hinton and Merriott had by that time achieved some independence, for Hinton's tithingman and four posts were obliged to do suit only on two occasions during the year, and the Merriott tithingman and posts had only to attend the Easter

[1] V.C.H. Som. i. 532; R. W. Eyton, Dom. Studies, Som. ii. 21–2. Seaborough was transferred to Dorset in 1896 and is thus reserved for treatment under that county.

[2] S.R.O., T/PH/hsy, survey 1599. Geoffrey, succeeded by John Guyan, held ⅛ fee in Crewkerne in 1303 and 1346 (Feud. Aids, iv. 316–17, 339); the Bonvilles, lords of Clapton, also had a freehold estate in Crewkerne in the 1480s (Cal. Fine R. 1471–85, 284) which they still held in 1599 by knight service (S.R.O., T/PH/hsy, survey 1599).

[3] S.R.S. iii. 318.

[4] G. Oliver, Monasticon Dioecesis Exoniensis, 343–5; Plac. de Quo Warr. (Rec. Com.), 693; see below, p. 11.

[5] S.R.O., T/PH/hsy, survey 1599.

[6] Cornw. R.O. 22 M/T/2/6; D.D.G.R. 725.

[7] E. Devon R.O., CR 675.

[8] C.P. 43/334 rot. 199; C.P. 43/887 rot. 21.

[9] Sherborne School, MS. A 29B; S. & D. N. & Q. xxiii. 215. The occurrence of William Mohun (d. 1587) as joint lord and reference to the death of Stephen Mitchell, a tenant (d. 1585: S.R.O., D/P/crew 2/1/1), provide the dating evidence.

[10] Penes Countess Poulett, Jersey.

[11] E. Devon R.O., CR 528.

[12] S.C. 6/Hen. VIII/6174.

[13] Ibid. 6173.

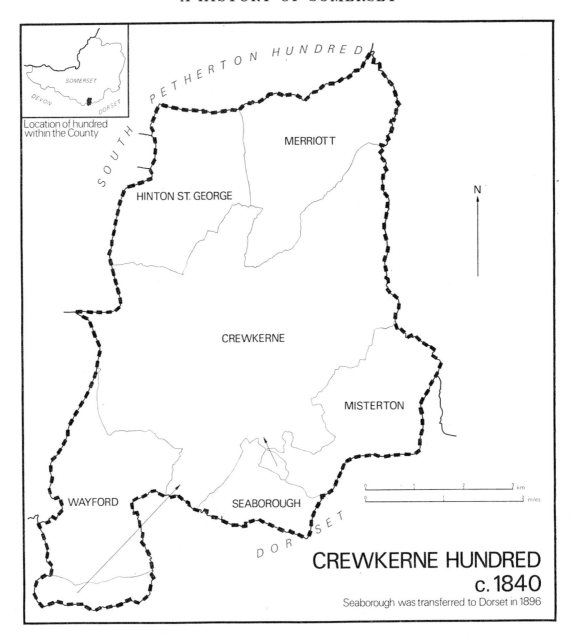

Location of hundred
within the County

CREWKERNE HUNDRED
c. 1840
Seaborough was transferred to Dorset in 1896

and Michaelmas lawdays to do royal suit and were not obliged to make presentments.[14] The jurisdiction then claimed was over waifs and strays, felons' goods, and the assizes of bread and of ale.

By the 17th century the court was held annually in October, on the same day as the Crewkerne manor court, and made orders for highways, bridges, and Crewkerne farming administration.

Until the 17th century the hundred was represented at the sheriff's tourn, held also for adjoining hundreds, on Ham Hill at Easter and Michaelmas.[15] By 1652 these had been 'much discontinued',[16] though the churchwardens of Hinton paid money to their tithingman in 1646–7 either for his expenses at the tourn or for the amercement for non-attendance, the parish register was similarly paid in 1656–7, and amercements are recorded until 1670.[17]

[14] S.R.O., T/PH/hsy, survey 1599.
[15] *Cal. Pat.* 1553–4, 259.

[16] E 317/Somerset 11.
[17] S.R.O., D/P/hin.g 4/1/1.

Hundred courts were maintained by the Pouletts apparently until the 19th century. In 1785 the Michaelmas court leet met at 10 a.m. on 19 October,[18] and jurisdiction was still claimed in 1805.[19] In the 1680s the court met in the church house.[20]

In 1526–7 the officers of the court were two stewards, one of whom was Amias Poulett, and an under-steward.[21] A hundred bailiff was still in office in 1851.[22]

[18] S.R.O., DD/PT, box 41, proposal bk. 1780 etc.
[19] C.P. 43/887 rot. 21.
[20] S.R.O., DD/SS, bdle. 54.

[21] S.C. 6/Hen. VIII/6174.
[22] *Crewkerne in 1851* (statistical table etc. in church).

CREWKERNE

THE TOWN of Crewkerne lies within a large parish on the southern boundary of the county and hundred.[1] Its church was a minster,[2] serving as the mother church of a Saxon royal estate in existence by the end of the 9th century; an estate whose boundaries were clearly marked by the river Axe in the south and the river Parrett on the east, but less obviously by streams in the north, one of which virtually touched the village of Merriott, the 'boundary gate' on the road to Crewkerne from the north.[3] The western boundary bears marks of later origin in its regularity and its failure to follow any natural feature.[4]

The creation of independent parochial units around the dependent chapels of the minster at Wayford, Seaborough, and Misterton from the 13th century[5] considerably reduced the area of the *parochia* served directly by the parish church, and radically altered its southern boundary. The eastern limit was similarly modified in the late 13th century by the emergence of Eastham as an independent parish,[6] but returned to its ancient line when the living was consolidated with Crewkerne in the 20th century. The northern boundary was less easily defined because the manor of Crewkerne possessed land at Shutteroaks in Merriott parish, and because Furland, a tithe-free area within Crewkerne parish, was almost certainly within the medieval field-system of Hinton St. George.[7] The Crewkerne tithe award thus omitted both Furland and part of Hinton Park since it also paid no tithe, so that the parish in 1842 was thought to comprise 4,667 a., together with 205 a. at Eastham.[8] In 1901 the area of the parish was 5,331 a.[9]

The ancient town lay below the eastern end of the Windwhistle ridge, in a coombe just above the 200 ft. contour, sheltered from the north-east by Bincombe Hill, possibly the 'cruc' which gave the town its name.[10] The church occupies a position at the end of a small plateau above the town centre,[11] very like that of South Petherton. To the north and east of the town the gentle contours on the heavily-faulted Yeovil Sands and limestone,[12] generally falling towards Merriott and the Parrett, provided the main stretches of meadow land, concentrated at Furringdons in the north-east. In the 16th and early 17th centuries there is some evidence of water meadows in the area.[13] To the south and west the more irregular and dramatic landscape, cut by a stream flowing south through Hewish and Clapton to the Axe, rises to over 600 ft. in the south at Henley and to over 775 ft. in the extreme north-west. The complicated geological formation of the Windwhistle ridge, including clay, flints, chalk, and greensand, provided a source for stone, sand, lime, marl, and clay for farmers, builders, and brick makers.[14]

Place-name evidence as well as the irregularity of the fields suggests that much of this hilly land was wooded in early times. Henley, Growley, Putelegh, Wyteley, Venley, and Laymore indicate woodland and woodland clearings; and scrubland survived in the west of the parish at Blackmoor, Ridge Hill, Ridge wood, Shave, and Croft in 1315. The common at Roundham was then partially moorland.[15] A park was created at Clapton by the 13th century[16] and another at Furringdons by the 16th, the latter then divided between Cow park and Knight's park.[17] During the 18th and early 19th centuries the Pouletts encouraged tree planting on their holdings at Tuncombe, Coombe, and Misterton, and also increased the timber around Hinton Park.[18]

The original parish included not only the central settlement of Crewkerne itself but villages and hamlets within a radius of some four miles. Eastham and Seaborough became the centres of separate estates before 1086,[19] and the former achieved ecclesiastical independence in 1295.[20] Seaborough continued to pay dues to Crewkerne and to bury its dead at the mother church until the 18th century,[21] but its transfer to Dorset in 1896 precludes further study. Eastham's development as a separate village was unsuccessful: its church was a ruin by the 16th century,[22] indicating earlier depopulation. Wayford and Misterton, like Seaborough,

---

[1] This article was completed in 1976.

[2] *Proc. Som. Arch. Soc.* cxx. 63–7.

[3] E. Ekwall, *Dict. Eng. Place-names.* The hamlet of Merriottsford was in Crewkerne in the 13th century (Devon R.O., TD 51, pp. 191–2; *Cal. Inq. Misc.* i, p. 264) but the boundary was altered in 1934 by a transfer of land to Merriott (County of Somerset (Merriott-Crewkerne) Order, 1934). For dispute over the Misterton-Crewkerne boundary 1839–42 see Tithe 1/30.

[4] A detached area including Laymore was transferred to Wayford in 1885: Local Govt. Board Order 16,420.

[5] *Proc. Som. Arch. Soc.* cxx. 63–7.

[6] Ibid. The parish of Eastham is here considered part of Crewkerne.

[7] E. Devon R.O., CR 550; S.R.O., D/P/crew 4/1/1–2, 13/1/1–2; tithe award; *Cal. Close,* 1346–9, 399–400.

[8] S.R.O., tithe award.   [9] *V.C.H. Som.* ii. 343.

[10] Ekwall, *Dict. Eng. Place-names.*

[11] The area to the south was quarried: B.L. Add MS. 49359, f. 74v. (1315); S.R.O., D/P/crew 4/1/1 (1636–8).

[12] Geol. Surv. Map 1″, solid and drift, sheet 312 (1958 edn.).

[13] E. Devon R.O., CR 550; S.R.O., DD/SS, bdle. 54

(1610). There was some continuous watering at Eastham in the late 18th cent.: S.R.O., DD/PRN, map of Misterton 1770.

[14] *S.R.S.* iv. 189 (lime 1459–60); S.R.O., DD/PT, box 12 (stone, gravel, marl 1618); D/P/crew 4/1/1 (sand 1628–63); DD/SS, bdle. 55 (marl 1778); T/PH/ptr, Wood's map of Crewkerne 1841; *V.C.H. Som.* ii. 353 (brick).

[15] B.L. Add. MS. 49359, ff. 74, 77; Devon R.O., TD 51, p. 186. There is an earthwork at Henley: *Proc. Som. Arch. Soc.* xxxvii. 13.

[16] Devon R.O., TD 51, pp. 187–8; S.R.O., D/P/crew 2/1/1 (1612, 1649), 4/1/1 (1628).

[17] E. Devon R.O., CR 550; S.R.O., DD/PT, box 22B (1815). Called Park close by 1778 (DD/SS, bdle. 55; tithe award).

[18] S.R.O., DD/SS, bdles. 56–7; DD/PT, boxes 12, 21A; DD/SB (C/3034), map of Crewkerne *c.* 1770 (copy 1835).   [19] *V.C.H. Som.* i. 445, 477.

[20] S.R.O., D/D/B reg 1 (loose inside cover): dues of Crewkerne minster; *Proc. Som. Arch. Soc.* cxx. 64.

[21] *Proc. Som. Arch. Soc.* cxx. 63.

[22] E 310/23/127 no. 90.

acknowledged ecclesiastical links with Crewkerne until the early 19th century, though Wayford was otherwise independent by the 13th century. Only Misterton remained in obvious economic dependence on its near and larger neighbour.

The smaller hamlets remaining within Crewkerne parish include the early valley settlements of Coombe, Tuncombe, and Clapton, the former yielding a hoard of 4th-century Roman coins;[23] Furland, Croft, Henley, and Hewish, whose names indicate early stages of cultivation and settlement; and Woolminstone, occurring in 1236 as Wulureston,[24] recalling either an early settler or the fauna of the former woodland.[25] At least until the 16th century Woolminstone and Hewish seem to have been the largest of these hamlets, and with Clapton continued so in the 20th century.[26] A green is referred to at Woolminstone in 1752.[27] Furland, Coombe, Henley, and Tuncombe became the sites of substantial farmsteads. In 1327 the first had 7 tax payers, 6 men were mustered in 1539, and there were 8 holdings there in 1653.[28] A consolidated farm, Furland farm, was created there by William Hussey between 1787 and 1789.[29] Coombe, known from its proximity to St. Reyne's chapel as Coombe St. Reyne in the early 13th century,[30] was detached from Crewkerne manor in 1541 and became part of the Poulett estate.[31] By the end of the 16th century it had developed into a single consolidated farmstead.[32] Croft, apparently divided into two holdings in the mid 13th century and known as Craft St. Reyne and Countess's Craft,[33] lay in the extreme north-west of the parish. Croft castle, traditionally the site of a medieval stronghold,[34] lies to the east of earthworks which may well represent the hamlet of Croft, on the northern slopes of Windwhistle. Croft was another part of the manor sold to the Pouletts in 1541.[35] There were 6 tax payers there, and 6 at Coombe in 1327,[36] but by 1539 the name Craft as a village or hamlet had disappeared.[37]

In 1599 it was clearly stated that there was no intercommoning between the tithings in the parish.[38] The manors of Crewkerne Magna and Crewkerne Parva, the former including Hewish and Woolminstone,[39] shared three common arable fields, but there is no evidence for open fields at Clapton or Henley, and only a group of furlongs and cultures at Eastham in the late 13th century.[40] The very independence of these settlements outside the main manor, however, at least implies some measure of separate agricultural development. The north and south fields of Crewkerne occur in the mid 13th

century,[41] and north, south, and west fields, shared between the two Crewkerne manors, by the early 16th.[42] In the later 16th century these were known as north, south, and east, evidence of some reorganization. North field was north-west of the town, between Tuncombe and the mill stream beside North Street. It was later known variously as North-west, West, or Cuckoo field. South field, known in 1609 as West Southfield,[43] and later as Higher or South-west field, was bounded by Marsh common and Folly and Henley farms, and by the boundary with Misterton. East field, the largest of the three, and subsequently called North-east or Lower field, adjoined the town on its eastern side. The Severalls estate, later Lower Severalls, was carved out of it in the 17th century.[44]

The principal areas of common meadow and pasture were at Roundham and Marsh, with a small meadow at Blacknell. The lord of the manor had 50 a. of pasture at 'Rowenham' in 1315[45] and let the grazing in the early 16th century.[46] It was inclosed in 1823.[47] Traces of it survive in the hamlet of Roundham, the houses built on the waste at the edge of the common beside the Chard road. Marsh common adjoined Roundham common to the south-east, running into the valley now occupied by the railway. This tract was also inclosed in 1823.

Crewkerne was described in the 16th century as 'a thorough fare betwixt London and Exeter',[48] and its position on that route was the key to its prosperity in subsequent centuries. This was, however, only one of the roads which converged on the town, fanning out southwards into Dorset with direct links to Lyme Regis, Bridport, and Dorchester, and northwards to Merriott and Somerton.[49] Two roads were outside this pattern, the most important linking Roundham with Misterton, by-passing the town on the south-west. In the late 18th century it was known as Portway Lane between Roundham and Maiden Beech Tree,[50] and thereafter as Lang Lane.[51] Its present width is an indication of its former status as the main coach route between Taunton and Bridport in the 1790s.[52] A parallel route further south-west, through Hewish and over Shave Hill, has the appearance of a prehistoric ridgeway.

The chronology of the turnpikes emphasizes the relative importance of Crewkerne's roads. The London–Exeter route from Haselbury Bridge on the eastern boundary through the town to Lady's Down on St. Rayn's Hill, was adopted by a trust based at Chard in 1753, but was taken over by

23 *V.C.H. Som.* i. 362.
24 *S.R.S.* vi. 85.
25 Ekwall, *Dict. Eng. Place-names* s.v. Woolley.
26 *S.R.S.* iii. 155–7; xx. 26–30; E. Devon R.O., CR 550; *L. & P. Hen. VIII*, xiv (1), p. 289.
27 S.R.O., DD/PT, box 15.
28 *S.R.S.* iii. 157; S.R.O., D/P/crew 4/1/1.
29 S.R.O., D/P/crew 4/1/2.
30 *S.R.S.* xii. 21; xvii. 24–5.
31 S.C. 6/Hen. VIII/6179; *L. & P. Hen. VIII*, xvi, p. 420.
32 S.R.O., D/P/crew 2/1/1.
33 S.R.O., D/D/B reg 1: dues of Crewkerne minster.
34 See below, p. 11.
35 S.C. 6/Hen. VIII/6179; *L. & P. Hen. VIII*, xvi, p. 420.
36 *S.R.S.* iii. 155.
37 *L. & P. Hen. VIII*, xiv (1), p. 289.
38 S.R.O., T/PH/hsy, survey 1599.

39 E. Devon R.O., CR 550.
40 S.R.O., D/D/B reg 1: dues of Crewkerne minster.
41 Devon R.O., TD 51, pp. 190–1, 200.
42 E. Devon R.O., CR 550; S.C. 6/Hen. VIII/6177, 6179.
43 S.R.O., T/PH/vch 11.
44 Reconstruction based on S.R.O., DD/PT, box 47 (copy survey 16th century), T/PH/hsy (survey 1599), DD/SB 38/1, and leases and other surveys in DD/PT and DD/SS.
45 B.L. Add. MS. 49359, f. 74.
46 S.C. 6/Hen. VIII/6174.
47 S.R.O., CR 26.   48 *S.R.S.* ii. 8.
49 S.R.O., T/PH/hsy, map of rectory estate 1772.
50 Mayden Bench trees 1630–3, Maiden Beach 1732, Maiden Bench cross 1746 (S.R.O., D/P/crew 2/1/1; DD/SS, bdle. 55; DD/CGS 3/1).
51 S.R.O., T/PH/hsy, map 1772.
52 S.R.O., DD/PT, box 21A.

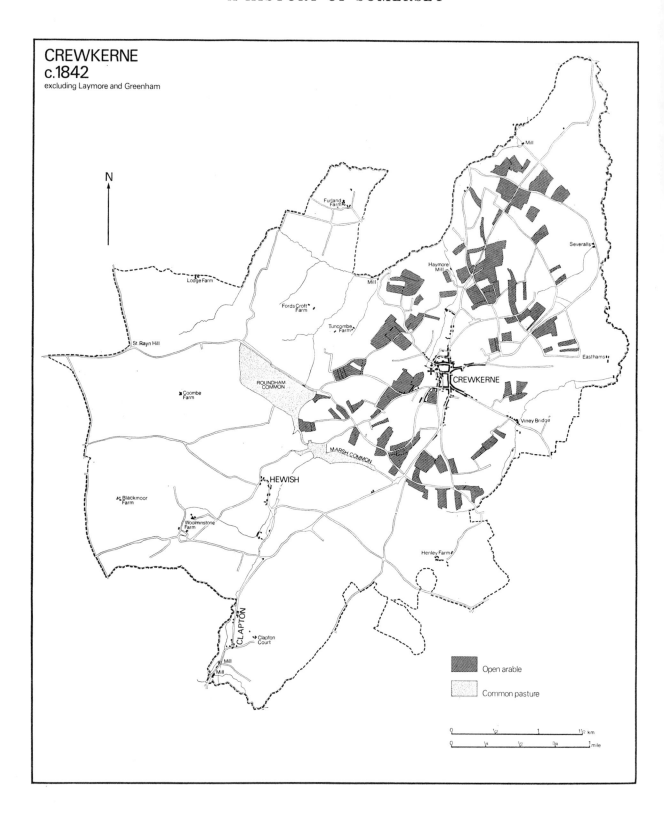

CREWKERNE
c.1842
excluding Laymore and Greenham

N

Furland Farm

Lodge Farm

Fords Croft Farm

Tuncombe Farm

Mill

Haymore Mill

Severalls

St. Rayn Hill

ROUNDHAM COMMON

Coombe Farm

Easthams

CREWKERNE

Viney Bridge

MARSH COMMON

HEWISH

Blackmoor Farm

Woolminstone Farm

Henley Farm

CLAPTON

Clapton Court

Mill

Mill

Open arable

Common pasture

0   ½   1   1½ km
0   ¼   ½   ¾   1 mile

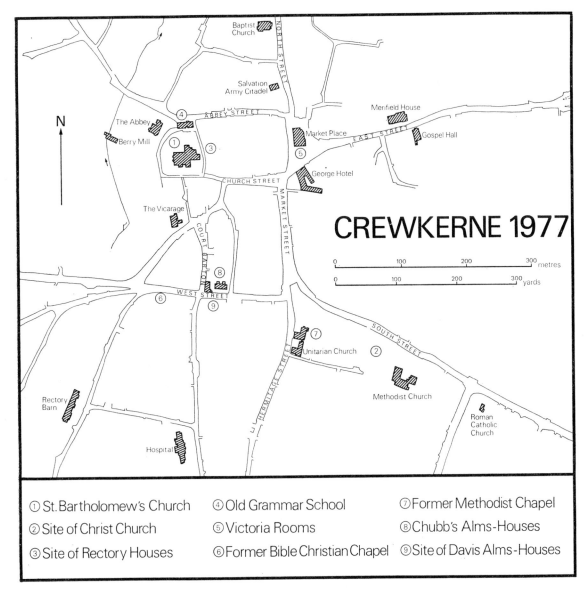

CREWKERNE 1977

① St.Bartholomew's Church   ④ Old Grammar School   ⑦ Former Methodist Chapel

② Site of Christ Church   ⑤ Victoria Rooms   ⑧ Chubb's Alms-Houses

③ Site of Rectory Houses   ⑥ Former Bible Christian Chapel   ⑨ Site of Davis Alms-Houses

the Crewkerne trust in 1825.[53] The Crewkerne trust, established in 1765, immediately adopted the main north–south routes from Ilchester and Taunton via Provost (or Prophet's) Lane in Stoke sub Hamdon and Lopen Head to Misterton, Clapton, and the Dorset ports. Also taken over at the same time was the Portway route from Roundham and the tortuous road to Hinton St. George through Furland.[54] Extensions in 1825 brought in Furringdons Lane from Haselbury to Merriott. The most obvious road improvements were the realignment of the Chard road west of the town north of its original course along Lyewater, and Gouldsbrook Terrace, the new road into Goulds Barton, both done before 1841,[55] and improvements on the same road east of the town at Clammer Hill,[56] by Easthams toll gate, and at Haselbury Bridge.[57]

The principal bridge in the parish was over the

Axe at Clapton. It was said to be 'fallen into great decay' in 1629.[58] There was a washing-place for sheep near by in 1652.[59]

The London and South-Western railway, constructed in 1860 well south of the town, caused a road diversion at Hewish and involved the sale of the remaining piece of Marsh common.[60] Crewkerne station lies in Misterton parish, but dwellings near it in Crewkerne owe their position entirely to the railway.

The tortuous convergence of even the main roads on the present market place indicates that the original street pattern has been modified in antiquity. Properties between church and market place belonged until the 19th century, with a single exception, to the rectory estate, suggesting that the whole area was once an open space, occupied in part by churchyard and in part by an enlarged market

[53] S.R.O., D/T/yeo.
[54] Crewkerne Turnpike Act, 5 Geo. III, c. 61 (Priv. Act).
[55] S.R.O., T/PH/hsy, map 1772; T/PH/ptr, map 1841; tithe award. Known as New Road in 1831 (table at end of D/P/crew 4/1/3).
[56] Hollow way at Clammor hill, 1649 (S.R.O., D/P/crew

4/1/1).
[57] S.R.O., Q/RUp 99, 102; list of toll gates in DD/PT, box 22A (accts. 1826–7) and DD/X/SF (1839).
[58] S.R.S. xxiv. 95.
[59] S.R.O., DD/PT, box 40, acct. bk. June 1652.
[60] S.R.O., D/P/crew 9/1/1.

area.[61] The division of the rectory into portions in the late 13th century and the erection of clergy houses east of the church in consequence, may have been the occasion for the encroachment.

From the market place, the south side of which was known as Fore Street from the 16th century to the late 18th,[62] streets radiated to the cardinal points. East Street was so called at the end of the 13th century;[63] South Street, including the present Market Street, occurs in 1548;[64] and the north street in 1584.[65] Westwards from the market place, leading to Hinton St. George and beyond, was Carter Street, a name perhaps indicating its function as an early trade route and so called by 1539.[66] In more genteel times it became the residential Abbey Street after the rebuilding of the parsonage house c. 1846. The name Church Street has been found only from 1727,[67] and a possible earlier alternative is 'Scole strete', occurring in the mid 13th century.[68] New Court Lane evidently lay east of the church, between Carter and Church streets, and was probably so called because of one of the clergy houses there in the late 15th century.[69] The 18th-century Cross Tree Street or Cross Street, so called after a tree standing there in 1640, was at the southern end of Market Street at the junction with Hermitage and West streets.[70]

The growth of population and trade extended the built-up area and changed street names. Pig Market Street, possibly at the north end of the market place towards Bincombe Lane, occurs in 1680;[71] Oxen Lane (but perhaps referring to the former manor-house complex and not to the town's market) in 1740;[72] and Sheep Market Street (the 20th-century Market Street) by 1772, possibly as a result of the establishment of a sheep market in 1753.[73] Almshouse Street was the 18th-century name for West Street after the founding of the Davis alms-houses there, though the name Chard Street occurs and West Street continued.[74] Hermitage Street is also an 18th-century name in recognition of the 'cottage called Hermitage' standing there in 1540–1.[75]

The irregular street pattern south of the church marks the site of the manor-house and farm complex. The house itself disappeared in the later Middle Ages. By 1526 a barn and barton were let to James Gold (d. 1530), and his widow Margaret later leased closes called Court Barton and Court Orchard.[76] By 1619 their tenancy had produced the alternative name of Gould's Orchard and later Gould's Barton.[77] The property was developed for housing in the 18th century: Court Barton had become a street by 1738 and a new cottage stood in a garden in Oxen Lane by 1740.[78] There was still open ground on the west of the site in the 1830s,[79] and it remained undeveloped until the erection of houses in Gould's Orchard c. 1838 and Gouldsbrook Terrace and Gould's Cottage by 1841, the latter replaced by Gouldsbrook House or Hall c. 1870. Gould's Square, so called by 1859, also recalls the 16th-century tenants.[80]

In the later 18th and early 19th centuries the built-up area of the town was extended, notably along South Street towards Viney Bridge, with infilling along North Street, Hermitage Street, and Lyewater.[81] In 1831 the district of South Street and Viney Bridge housed 550 people from a total of 3,789 for the whole parish, followed by 397 in Hermitage Street and 317 at North Street and Ashlands.[82] Expansion continued generally southwards between Hermitage and South streets in the 20th century, notably on the Severalls estate in the 1920s and in later developments in the same area.

The town centre has a considerable number of Georgian and early Victorian buildings or frontages in the local yellow limestone which reflect both the town's prosperity in that period and its subsequent immunity from later wholesale development. There remain, however, a few earlier buildings such as Candle Cottage and the White Hart, both in East Street, which date from the 15th century, and no. 15 Market Square, formerly the Red Lion inn, which probably belongs to the early sixteenth.[83] Other, evidently substantial, houses such as White Hall in North Street and Sergers Court, are known from written sources,[84] in addition to the manor- and clergy houses. The later 16th and 17th centuries are represented not only by buildings of public or manor-house status like the church hall, formerly the Grammar School, erected in 1636,[85] or Merifield House, partly of 1661 and 1679; there are also substantial dwellings further from the town centre such as Townsend House, East Street, and parts of the Old Parsonage Guest House, Barn Street. Seventeenth-century inventories of town properties describe three-unit houses of hall, kitchen, and buttery with added shops, together with specialist outhouses or warehouses connected with particular trades.[86] The house of John James, apothecary, was evidently more substantial, having five rooms on the first floor including a study and fore chamber above shop, kitchen, brewhouse, and cellar, with an attic floor.[87]

Buildings of the 18th and early 19th centuries

---

[61] S.R.O., T/PH/hsy, map 1772; see frontispiece.
[62] *S.R.S.* ii. 176; S.R.O., DD/CGS 3/1; MS. contract bk. *penes* Maj. H. Hussey, Maincombe, Crewkerne; see plan, p. 7.
[63] Forde Abbey, Cart. p. 398.   [64] *S.R.S.* ii. 176.
[65] S.R.O., D/P/crew 2/1/1.
[66] S.C. 6/Hen. VIII/6177.
[67] S.R.O., DD/SS, bdles. 53, 55.
[68] S.R.O., D/D/B reg 1: dues of Crewkerne minster. Part of the churchyard wall on the south led to School street.
[69] S.R.O., DD/HKE 1/1; DD/SB 49/3; *S.R.S.* lv, p. 62.
[70] Cornw. R.O. 22M/DT/42/6; S.R.O., D/P/crew 4/1/2; DD/SB 38/1; DD/SS, bdle. 56; ex inf. Mr. W. B. Harwood, Crewkerne.
[71] Cornw. R.O. 22M/DT/42/6.
[72] S.R.O., DD/SS, bdle. 57.
[73] S.R.O., T/PH/hsy, map 1772; *Sherborne Mercury*, 25 June 1753.

[74] S.R.O., T/PH/hsy, map 1772; DD/SS, bdle. 54; DD/X/HAW; see below, p. 37.
[75] S.C. 6/Hen. VIII/6179; S.R.O., DD/SS, bdles. 53–5.
[76] S.C. 6/Hen. VIII/6174; E. Devon R.O., CR 550.
[77] S.R.O., DD/PT, box 12 (1647); DD/SS, bdle. 57 (1740).
[78] S.R.O., DD/PT, box 23; DD/SS, bdle. 57.
[79] S.R.O., DD/SB 35/7.
[80] Harrison, Harrod, & Co., *Dir. Som.* (1859); P.O. *Dir. Som.* (1861, 1866, 1875). Gould's Orchard 'lately erected' in 1838: S.R.O., DD/X/HAW.
[81] S.R.O., T/PH/hsy, map 1772; DD/SB (C/3034), map c. 1770; DD/SAS, map c. 1820; tithe award.
[82] S.R.O., D/P/crew 4/1/3, printed table of population.
[83] S.R.O., DD/V.
[84] E. Devon R.O., CR 550; S.R.O., DD/PT, box 22A.
[85] R. G. Bartelot, *Hist. Crewkerne School*, 46–7.
[86] S.R.O., DD/SP inventory, 1644; ibid. boxes 11–12 (1680, 1686).   [87] S.R.O., DD/SP, box 11 (1677).

are much more in evidence, especially in Church and Abbey streets, where frontages have been largely untouched. The elegant proportions of houses in Market Square are matched by no. 17 Market Street, a five-bay building with a segmental pediment over its central door. Datable buildings of the period include part of the Swan inn, said to be 'newly built' in 1774, the King's Arms inn, 'newly erected' in 1782, no. 26 Abbey Street, built as a school-house in 1828 by Richard Carver, then of Bridgwater, to the designs of John Patch of Crewkerne, and the National Westminster Bank, Market Street, of 1838.[88] Residential development later in the century included both Hermitage Terrace (1879) and the villas of Mount Pleasant. A more significant and characteristic feature of the town is the industrial buildings. These occur both in the centre of the town, in Abbey Street,[89] and also on the outskirts, notably at Viney Bridge and South Street, usually accompanied by terraced housing for employees. The County Mail Office, South Street, with its windows in round-headed recesses, also belongs to the mid 19th century, the period of much of the factory-building activity.

Farm-houses and cottages in the surrounding hamlets date from the 17th and 18th centuries, though an exception is Higher Farm, Woolminstone, which has a traditional plan with internal chimney and cross-passage, and in origin may belong to the 16th century. Inventories of the 1630s and 1640s show three- and four-unit houses of two storeys, with occasional larger ones such as that of George Merifield of Woolminstone, yeoman, with hall, kitchen, buttery, parlour, and entrance porch.[90] Woolminstone Farm, the same property but evidently much extended to the north in the later 17th century, in 1751 included hall, a great parlour, two studies, and a porch, with four chambers above as only part of the house.[91] The present house is of local rubble with internal and gable chimneys, and has a reset doorway dated 1617, with the initials of John Daubeney[92] beneath the arms of Merifield.

Buildings of the early 18th century range from Hewish Manor Farm, in traditional style but with later additions, to the symmetrical Clapton Dairy Farm and the long, two-storeyed Lower Severalls, where traces of avenues mark the house as a superior residence. Middle Farm, Hewish, though with a 17th-century datestone, was reconstructed in the 19th century. Coombe, a 20th-century complex of houses, farm- and dairy-buildings almost industrial in scale, has at its centre an imposing ashlar farm-house of the mid 19th century with pillared entrance. On the edge of the parish, on an elevated site in the

south-west corner of Hinton Park, is Warren House, in 1976 in ruins. It is of brick, and evidently originated in the late 17th century as a hunting lodge within the warren of the Poulett estate.[93]

Cockfighting, fives, and visits of travelling players provided regular amusements in the 17th century.[94] A chapter of the Order of Gregorians was formed in 1744 and a music club, founded in 1748, held an annual feast and was known as the Orphean club by 1762.[95] There was a monthly ball at the George inn by 1753.[96] In 1768 three grand 'Ridotto' balls were held at the town hall which 'was formed into a grand garden and illuminated after the manner of Vauxhall', and a Crewkerne Assembly was held regularly at the George during the winter.[97] Travelling theatre companies visited regularly between 1813 and 1820 and between 1831 and 1881, usually performing at the town hall.[98] A Literary and Scientific Institution was formed in 1849, and in 1850 its 100 members were entertained by the choral class run by the church organist and the Crewkerne Philharmonic Society.[99] From 1851 there were music and reading rooms at the town hall.[1]

A race course at Roundham, successor to courses at Haselbury Plucknett and West Chinnock, was used intermittently between 1906 and 1922.[2] A bowling club was formed in 1910 and tennis courts and a bowling green were opened at Severalls in 1923. A recreation ground at Higher Bincombe was presented to the town in 1924 and another at Henhays purchased in 1951.[3] A swimming pool was opened at Viney Bridge in 1935 and closed in 1952.[4] A town band was formed in 1923. 'The People's Perfect Picture Palace' showed silent films at the Victoria Hall during the First World War, and the present Palace Cinema in West Street was opened in 1922.[5]

The George inn on the south side of Market Square occurs by 1541 and has a continuous history since.[6] The Swan or White Swan, at the junction of Market Square and Church Street, was larger in the 17th and 18th centuries.[7] In 1696 the town's inns offered 54 beds and stabling for 130 horses.[8] By 1735 there were 22 licensed victuallers in the parish, 25 by 1740, and 35 by 1751.[9] Among the leading houses were the Green Dragon or Antelope, the Bell, and the White Hart or Gun belonging to the grammar school estate, and the Swan, the Nag's Head, and the Red Lion, adjoining each other on the west side of the market place, all belonging to the rectory estate.[10] The number of inns fell towards the end of the 18th century, but new ones were established outside the town, including the

[88] Western Flying Post, 4 July 1774; S.R.O., DD/SB 25/4; DD/DN 65; DD/CGS 2/2, 9/1; DD/X/SF.
[89] See plate facing p. 48.
[90] S.R.O., DD/SP, inventory 1646.
[91] S.R.O., DD/PT, box 24A.
[92] Ibid. box 23.   [93] S.R.O., DD/V.
[94] S.R.O., DD/CGS 3/1; D/P/crew 4/1/1.
[95] S. & D. N. & Q. xvi. 143; Sherborne Mercury, 4 June, 13 July 1745, 21 July 1746, 14 Nov. 1748, 25 Oct. 1756, 2 Nov. 1762.
[96] Sherborne Mercury, 4 Dec. 1749, 15 Jan. 1753.
[97] Ibid. 20 June, 4 July, 10 Oct., 14 Nov. 1768.
[98] Ex inf. Mr. W. B. Harwood from theatre bills penes Miss W. Starke; Victoria and Albert Mus., Enthoven Colln., Peter Davey MSS.
[99] Hunt & Co., Dir. Som. (1850); United Counties

Miscellany, suppl. Mar. 1850: ex inf. Mrs. P. Andrew, Crewkerne.
[1] Pulman's Weekly News, 13 Dec. 1881; Somerset County Gazette, 29 Dec. 1900.
[2] Ex inf. Mr. Harwood.
[3] Ibid.; S.R.O., D/P/crew 23/10.
[4] Ex inf. Mr. Harwood.
[5] Ibid.; County Mail, 25 Feb. 1970.
[6] E. Devon R.O., CR 550; S.R.O., T/PH/hsy, survey 1599; DD/CGS 3/1; Cornw. R.O. 22M/DT/42/6. See W. G. Willis-Watson, The Inns of Crewkerne (repr. from Pulman's Weekly News, 1935).
[7] S.R.O., D/P/crew 4/1/1.
[8] W.O. 30/48.   [9] S.R.O., Q/RL.
[10] S.R.O., DD/CGS 1/4, 16–20, 2/2, 3/1; DD/SB 49/3; Hants R.O., CC/59493.

Blue Boy at Clapton, so named by 1819 but traceable back to 1780, and the Blue Ball at Roundham, successor by 1770 to the Bottle.[11] The George, the Swan, the Nag's Head, and the White Hart were the survivors of the town's ancient inns in 1976.

A friendly society was formed in 1815.[12] This or another based at the White Hart, was said to have been dissolved c. 1862,[13] but was perhaps re-formed in 1864 and continued as the Royal Old Blue friendly society at least until 1899.[14] Another society was formed in connexion with the Baptist chapel.[15] Branches of national benefit societies paraded together in the town at least until 1930.[16]

In 1548 the whole parish contained 1,000 communicants,[17] and in 1563 there were 250 households.[18] In 1801 the population amounted to 2,576 and within the next century gradually doubled.[19] Thereafter the number fell until the 1950s, and recovered to 5,285 only in 1971.[20]

Crewkerne's position on the London–Exeter road[21] rather than its own importance brought visitors to the town. Catherine of Aragon stayed at one of the parsonage houses for a night in 1501 on her way from Devon to London for her marriage to Arthur, Prince of Wales.[22] Justices of gaol delivery met there instead of at Ilchester in 1543, 1544, and 1547.[23] Gaps in the parish registers in 1643–4 and the absence of churchwardens' accounts for the years 1642–5 are evidence of the disruption caused in the town during the Civil War.[24] Continuous accounts of the grammar school trustees for the period indicate not only the presence of troops but also the financial demands made by both sides in turn. The monthly contributions payable to the hundred constable were increased by special levies for troops in the area.[25] Royalist armies met near the town in June 1643 before proceeding to Taunton and eventually to Lansdown.[26] Exactly a year later Essex was expected at Crewkerne on his way to Cornwall.[27] In September 1644 Prince Maurice was ordered to stay there, and the king was awaited in the town.[28] Early in 1645 troops under Goring were in the neighbourhood, and a substantial party was routed there by Col. Holborne.[29] In July the New Model army under Fairfax spent a night in the town before the battle of Langport.[30] After the fighting was over the school trustees found themselves paying for the 'British Army' and for the removal of the quay at Lyme Regis (Dors.).[31] A number of local gentry and townsmen, including John Merifield, John Bonville of Clapton, and John Bragg were fined for their support of the royalists.[32]

Royalists under Penruddocke came through the town after proclaiming Charles II in Dorset in 1655,[33] but Crewkerne was probably unsympathetic and rang the church bells in 1659 when Attorney General Prideaux passed by.[34] Nearly forty people from the parish were implicated in Monmouth's rebellion, and a number of townsmen bought pardons.[35] Ten executions took place in the town,[36] and the parish found itself supporting soldiers discharged by Col. Kirk.[37] William of Orange passed through the town in 1688.[38]

Thomas Hutchins, post master at Crewkerne by 1619 until after 1631, organized between London and Plymouth the first profitable postal system.[39]

MANORS AND OTHER ESTATES. The manor of *CREWKERNE* formed part of the ancient demesne of the kings of Wessex. It was left by King Alfred (d. 899) to his younger son Ethelweard (d. 922), but evidently reverted to the Crown of Wessex in 937.[40] It was held in 1066 by Eddeva, whom Round identified with Edith 'Swan's neck', mistress of King Harold, and after the Conquest by William I.[41] In 1177 the property was held by Richard de Reviers (II), earl of Devon (d. 1162), and it may have been among estates granted to his grandfather, Richard de Reviers (I) (d. 1107), by Henry I and inherited by his father Baldwin (d. 1155), the first earl.[42] From Richard it passed to his sons Baldwin (d. 1188) and Richard (III) (d. 1193), and then to his brother William, earl of Devon and lord of the Isle (d. 1217), who received lands called the manor of Crewkerne out of dower in 1202. The property was subject to a fee-farm rent of £80 a year.[43]

William had a son, Baldwin, and two daughters. According to a later history of Forde abbey, partially confirmed by contemporary official sources, William gave to his elder daughter Joan, on her marriage with William de Briwere (d. 1232–3), 50 librates of land variously described as at 'Craft' in

[11] S.R.O., Q/RL; DD/PT, box 39, survey.
[12] M. Fuller, *West-Country Friendly Socs.* 161.
[13] Ibid. 141.
[14] Taunton Castle, Tite Colln.
[15] Ibid.
[16] Fuller, *West-Country Friendly Socs.* 100.
[17] *S.R.S.* ii. 8.
[18] B.L. Harl. MS. 594, f. 56.
[19] *V.C.H. Som.* ii. 343.
[20] Census.
[21] *S.R.S.* ii. 8.
[22] *Letters and Papers Richard III and Henry VII*, ed. J. Gairdner (Rolls Ser.), i. 406–7.
[23] *L. & P. Hen. VIII*, xviii, p. 68; xx (1), pp. 313, 319; *Cal. Pat. 1547–8*, 74.
[24] *S.R.S.* xxviii, pp. xxxvi, 14–15; S.R.O., D/P/crew 2/1/1, 4/1/1.
[25] S.R.O., DD/CGS 3/1.
[26] *S.R.S.* xviii. 46; Hist. MSS. Com. 29, *13th Rep. II, Portland* ii. 712.
[27] *Cal. S.P. Dom. 1625–49*, 516; Hist. MSS. Com. 3, *4th Rep.* 296.
[28] *Cal. S.P. Dom. 1644*, 534; Hist. MSS. Com. 39, *15th Rep. II, Hodgkin*, 101.
[29] *Cal. S.P. Dom. 1644–5*, 506, 544; *Cal. Cttee. for Money*, iii. 1333; S.R.O., DD/SH 107.

[30] D. Underdown, *Som. in Civil War and Interregnum*, 100; Hist. MSS. Com. 29, *13th Rep. II, Portland* ii. 232.
[31] S.R.O., DD/CGS 3/1.
[32] *Cal. Cttee. for Compounding*, ii. 1047, 1243, 1408; *Cal. Cttee. for Money*, ii. 1101, 1105.
[33] *S.R.S.* lxxi, p. 69; *Cal. S.P. Dom. 1655*, 234.
[34] S.R.O., D/P/crew 4/1/1.
[35] B.L. Add. MS. 30077, ff. 36v.–37; *Cal. S.P. Dom. 1686–7*, 45, 49, 104, 196, 440; *1687–9*, 234.
[36] R. Locke, *Western Rebellion* (1782), 7.
[37] S.R.O., D/P/crew 4/1/1.
[38] *V.C.H. Som.* ii. 231; Hist. MSS. Com. 25, *12th Rep. VII, Le Fleming*, 224.
[39] *Cal. S.P. Dom. 1623–5*, 117; *1630–1*, 269, 367; *Acts of P.C. 1623–5*, 37–8, 153; J. Crofts, *Packhorse, Waggon, and Post*, 99–101.
[40] Finberg, *Early Charters of Wessex*, 126; W. G. Searle, *Anglo-Saxon Bishops, Kings, and Nobles*, 343. Alfred's will was dated between 873 and 888.
[41] *V.C.H. Som.* i. 398, 439.
[42] *Pipe R. 1177* (P.R.S. xxvi), 24; *Complete Peerage*, s.v. Devon.
[43] *Rot. de Ob. et Fin.* (Rec. Com.), 235; *Rot. Lit. Pat.* (Rec. Com.), 19, 32; *Pipe R. 1205* (P.R.S. n.s. xix), 140; *Complete Peerage*, iv. 313–14.

the manor of Crewkerne and *de castris*, together with the advowson of the church or churches.[44] The younger daughter Mary, wife of Robert de Courtenay (d. 1242), received an estate again variously described as the chace (*chaseam*) of Crewkerne or as the whole residue of the manor of Crewkerne, with the foreign hundred and the chace.[45]

Joan granted part of her estate to William de Lisle in 1249, by virtue of which William's son John held the advowson in 1272 and half of four mills and the market in 1274.[46] She also granted lands in Hewish to Christchurch priory (Hants) in 1256.[47] At her death without issue *c.* 1272 there was a disputed succession, eventually decided in favour of Isabel de Forz, countess of Devon and Aumale, great-granddaughter and heir of William de Reviers, who laid claim to properties including those given to Christchurch priory and to the de Lisle family.[48] In 1282 she granted 'her whole manor' to Agnes, daughter of Robert de Monceaux, subject for her own life to the payment of the £80 fee-farm rent.[49] On Isabel's death in 1293 Agnes was still in possession, but Sir Hugh de Courtenay, then a minor but successor to the Courtenay interest through his great-grandmother Mary de Reviers, was declared to be Isabel's heir.[50]

That part of the Reviers estate granted to Mary de Reviers and her husband Robert de Courtenay descended to their son John (d. 1274), and was described as a manor and included the hundred but only half the market and four mills, then shared with the de Lisles.[51] By 1280 market and mills were shared with Isabel de Forz.[52] John Courtenay was succeeded by his son Sir Hugh (d. 1292), whose estate was described as half the manor of Crewkerne and similarly included half-shares in four mills and the markets.[53] His son, also Sir Hugh, succeeded as a minor, and his estates were held in wardship first by Sir William de Fiennes and, between 1294 and 1297, by the Crown.[54] On the death of Agnes de Monceaux *c.* 1315 Courtenay acquired her half of the manor, and on his death in 1340 the united property descended to his son Hugh (d. 1377), whose widow Margaret (d. 1391) succeeded under a settlement made in 1341.[55] Margaret's heir was her grandson, Edward Courtenay, earl of Devon (d. 1419), from whom the manor passed through successive generations to Hugh (d. 1422), Thomas (d. 1458), and Thomas, earls of Devon. The last leased the manor to William Haddesfeld for the life of the lessee in 1458 and the earl was attainted and executed in 1461.[56]

Licence was given for Henry Courtenay, brother of the attainted earl, to enter on the manor in 1461, but this was evidently revoked and in 1462 the estate was granted to the king's uncle, William Neville, earl of Kent (d. 1463), with remainder failing male heirs to George Neville, bishop of Exeter, and others for twelve years. In 1463 Edward IV gave the reversion after the twelve years to his brother George Plantagenet, duke of Clarence, on whose attainder and death in 1478 the manor again reverted to the Crown.[57] In 1484 it was granted by Richard III to Sir Richard Radcliffe, killed at Bosworth, and in 1485 by Henry VII to Edward Courtenay, a distant cousin of the former earls, on his creation as earl of Devon. Edward surrendered the patent in 1490 in favour of Joan, sister of Thomas Courtenay, earl of Devon (d. 1461), and her husband Sir William Knyvett.[58] On Joan's death in 1501 her son by an earlier marriage, Charles Clifford, was disinherited in favour of Edward Courtenay, earl of Devon.[59] On Edward's death in 1509 it was again confiscated.[60] In 1512 the manor was granted to Catherine, widow of William Courtenay, but passed in 1516–17, before her death, to her son Henry (cr. marquess of Exeter 1525), who was attainted and executed in 1539.[61] From Henry's death the estate was usually described as the manors of *CREWKERNE MAGNA, CREWKERNE PARVA, AND MISTERTON*. Crewkerne returned to Crown ownership in 1539 until Edward Courtenay, son of the attainted marquess, was created earl of Devon, and given the manors in fee tail in 1553.[62] He died unmarried in 1556 when the estate was divided between the descendants of the four sisters of his great-grandfather, Edward Courtenay, earl of Devon (d. 1509), Florence, Isabel, Elizabeth, and Maud.[63]

Florence, wife of John Trelawney, was represented by her grandson, John Trelawney (d. 1563), from whom a quarter descended to his son John (d. 1568), and thereafter in turn to his grandsons John (d. 1569) and Sir Jonathan Trelawney (d. 1604).[64] John Trelawney, son of the last, enfranchised his portions in 1618 and the Trelawney lordship came to an end.[65]

The second quarter was inherited by Sir Reynold Mohun (d. 1567), great-grandson of Isabel, wife of William Mohun. Sir Reynold's son William (d. 1587) was succeeded by his son, Sir Reynold Mohun, Bt. (d. 1639), who enfranchised most of the shares in his quarter in 1610.[66] John Mohun, Lord Mohun (d. 1641), son of Sir Reynold, sold what was claimed to be half the manor to John,

[44] G. Oliver, *Monasticon Dioecesis Exoniensis*, 343–5; *Close R.* 1231–4, 198; *Complete Peerage*, s.v. Devon.
[45] Oliver, *Mon. Exon.* 343–5; *Cal. Inq. p.m.* ii, p. 52; *Complete Peerage*, s.v. Devon.
[46] *S.R.S.* vi. 134; xxxvi. 173–4; C 133/6/1.
[47] B.L. Cott. MS. Tib. D. vi, ff. 178–178v.
[48] *S.R.S.* xxxvi. 166–7, 173–4, 178–9, 181–2; *Complete Peerage*, s.v. Devon.
[49] *Cal. Pat.* 1292–1301, 53.
[50] Ibid. 1292–1301, 53; 1313–17, 268.
[51] C 133/6/1.
[52] *Plac. De Quo Warr.* (Rec. Com.), 693.
[53] C 133/62/7.   [54] S.C. 6/1127/16.
[55] *Cal. Inq. p.m.* viii, p. 196; *Cal. Pat.* 1340–3, 282; C 136/70.
[56] *Complete Peerage*, s.v. Devon; *Feud. Aids*, vi. 504; *Cal. Pat.* 1422–9, 108; C 139/169/38; C 140/67/46;

C 145/325.
[57] *Cal. Pat.* 1461–7, 70, 225–7, 331; 1467–77, 457–8, 529–30.
[58] Ibid. 1476–85, 472; 1485–94, 28–9, 305–6.
[59] *Cal. Inq. p.m. Hen. VII*, ii, pp. 250–1; *L. & P. Hen. VIII*, i (1), pp. 404–5.
[60] *Complete Peerage*, s.v. Devon.
[61] *L. & P. Hen. VIII*, i, p. 521; E 315/34, f. 107; E 150/928/18.
[62] *Cal. Pat.* 1547–8, 173; 1553–4, 256–7.
[63] Ibid. 1555–7, 164.
[64] C 142/138/24; C 142/282/82; J. L. Vivian, *Visit. Cornw.* 475; *S.R.S.* lxvii, p. 207.
[65] e.g. S.R.O., DD/PT, boxes 12, 23, leases 20 June 1618; DD/SS, bdle. 57, lease 20 June 1618.
[66] C 142/150/186; Vivian, *Visit. Cornw.* 324–5; S.R.O., DD/PT, boxes 12, 17, 23, leases 1 Sept. 1610.

Lord Poulett, in 1633, although Warwick, Lord Mohun (d. 1665), was still enfranchising lands there in 1664.[67]

The claims of the third sister Maud, wife of Sir John Arundel, had descended to her great-grandson Alexander Arundel (d. 1563), who was succeeded by his nephew John. In 1580 John sold his quarter of the manors to Sir Amias Poulett (d. 1588), from whom it descended through the Poulett family with the manor of Hinton St. George until the 'fourths' were enfranchised in 1810 and 1811.[68] The claim to the lordship by the earls Poulett, mentioned in 1923,[69] has persisted to the present day.

The fourth sister Elizabeth married John Trethurf and her title to the remaining quarter descended as eighths to the two daughters of her son Thomas (d. 1529). Of these Elizabeth married John (I) Vivian of Trelowarren (d. 1562), the eighth passing to their son John (II) (d. 1577),[70] and then to the latter's second son Hannibal Vivian (d. 1610). Hannibal leased the eighth for 21 years to his son Francis (later Sir Francis) Vivian in 1608, who enfranchised most of the property in 1612.[71] The title apparently passed in turn to Sir Francis's son and grandson, Sir Richard (d. 1665) and Sir Vyell Vivian (d. 1697), Bts., who occur as lords until 1684.[72] The final eighth descended to Margaret Trethurf (d. 1576). Her son Peter (d. 1606), by Edward Courtenay of Landrake (Cornw.), was followed in turn by his sons John (d. 1615) and Edward Courtenay (d. 1622), who were jointly enfranchising their Crewkerne shares in 1611.[73] In 1617 Edward Courtenay leased his part of the manor to Samuel Berd, a Crewkerne yeoman, who was granting long leases of eighths in the following year.[74] Edward's son, Sir Peter Courtenay, and Alice his wife, however, were executing enfranchisements until at least 1652,[75] although their lordship does not occur thereafter.

A dilapidated dovecot was mentioned in 1292 and repairs were made to the great chamber, hall, the chamber beyond the gate, the grange, and various outbuildings of the lord between 1294 and 1297.[76] The manor-house and garden were valued at 40d. and the dovecot at 2s. in 1341, and new barn doors were made in 1396.[77] By the 16th century the house had disappeared, but its site was still recognized, to the south of the church, in closes called Court Barton and Court Orchard. Within the latter in 1599 stood 'an old house of stone which sometime

it should seem was a chapel'.[78] A barn next Court Barton and a small yard were let by 1526 and not long afterwards Margaret Gold or Gould was tenant of Court Barton, Court Orchard, and a house called the Sheerehall there.[79] The 'builded house called the Sheerehall'[80] and other parts of the demesne site continued in being during the early 17th century, though the hall had probably been demolished by 1677 when Lord Poulett leased a quarter share in the rent of a close of land called Sheerehall.[81] A pound survived on the site until after 1772.[82]

The manor of *EASTHAM*, later known as *EASTHAMS*, was held in 1066 with the king's manor of Crewkerne by Godwin, the king's reeve. By 1086 it had been separated from Crewkerne, the overlordship having passed to Robert, count of Mortain, and, like that of Cricket St. Thomas, descended through the Lovel and Seymour families with the manor of Castle Cary.[83] The overlordship was last mentioned in 1377 when it was held by Nicholas Seymour.[84]

By 1086 the terre-tenancy had been granted to Turstin, from whom probably descended a Turstin of Eastham who occurred as a 12th-century witness.[85] In 1223 Andrew of Misterton and John of Eastham may have beeen lords of Eastham manor.[86] An undated precedent produced in a lawsuit of 1312, but perhaps relating to the mid 13th century, refers to John, possibly the above John of Eastham, a former owner of both manor and advowson, being succeeded by his son Roger.[87] In 1295 the manor was held by Thomas Asshelond and William of Cricket.[88] By 1296 Thomas's half had passed to Geoffrey de Asshelond, who also occurred as lord in 1303.[89] Geoffrey was succeeded by his son Ives, who held the half between 1316 and 1320.[90] Ives was father of Thomas and Alice but no evidence has been found that either succeeded him.[91] A reversionary right to Asshelond property in Eastham had descended to John Wouburne by 1329, although William de Asshelond was lord of a half in 1346.[92] The Asshelond estate was held in 1316 under the lord of Crewkerne manor and may have merged with it by 1428.[93] Certainly lands known as Easthams, lying north of the later manor of Eastham, were subsequently held under Crewkerne.

The half held by the Cricket family descended from William of Cricket (d. c. 1313) during his

[67] *Complete Peerage*, s.v. Mohun; S.R.O., DD/SS, bdle., 54, conveyance 23 Oct. 1633; DD/PT, box 23, lease 20 Jan. 1663/4.
[68] C 142/138/23; Vivian, *Visit. Cornw.* 6; S.R.O., DD/SS, bdle. 56, conveyance 21 Dec. 1580; DD/SB 38/1.
[69] *Kelly's Dir. Som.* (1923).
[70] C 142/165/159; C 142/180/22; Vivian, *Visit. Cornw.* 529.
[71] C 142/180/22; C 142/325/178; Vivian, *Visit. Cornw.* 529; Cornw. R.O., D.D.G.R. 725; S.R.O., DD/PT, box 23, leases 20 July 1612, 17 Feb. 1664/5; copy of ct. roll 6 Nov. 1623.
[72] Cornw. R.O. 22M/DT/42/6; Vivian, *Visit. Cornw.* 529; G.E.C. *Baronetage*, ii. 228–9.
[73] C 142/173/22; C 142/378/133; *S.R.S.* lxvii, pp. 169–70; Vivian, *Visit. Cornw.* 117; S.R.O., DD/PT, boxes 11, 23.
[74] S.R.O., DD/PT, box 22B.
[75] Ibid. box 24A, lease.
[76] C 133/62/7; S.C. 6/1127/16.
[77] C 135/260/3; B.L. Add. Ch. 64321.
[78] S.R.O., T/PH/hsy, survey 1599.

[79] S.C. 6/Hen. VIII/6174; E. Devon R.O., CR 550.
[80] S.R.O., T/PH/hsy, survey 1599.
[81] C 142/422/15; *S.R.S.* lxvii, p. 103; S.R.O., DD/PT, box 12, Bayly to Daubeney, 1647; DD/SS, bdle. 53, Poulett to Hodges.
[82] S.R.O., T/PH/hsy, map of rectory estate 1772; DD/SB (C/3034), map of Crewkerne parish c. 1770 (copy 1835).
[83] *V.C.H. Som.* i. 477.
[84] *Cal. Inq. p.m.* xiv, pp. 281, 342.
[85] *V.C.H. Som.* i. 477; Forde Abbey, Cart. p. 465.
[86] *Cur. Reg. R.* xi, p. 275.
[87] *Year Bk.* 5 Edw. II (Selden Soc. xi), 212.
[88] S.R.O., D/D/B reg 1: dues of Crewkerne minster.
[89] *S.R.S.* vi. 295–6; *Feud. Aids*, iv. 316–17.
[90] *Feud. Aids*, iv. 331; *S.R.S.* xii. 83–5. John de Asshetone, probably a misreading for Asshelond, jointly held the advowson of Eastham chapel in 1310, but his relationship to Ives is not clear: *S.R.S.* xii. 19; cf. ibid. vi. 325.
[91] *S.R.S.* xii. 85.
[92] Ibid. 84, 137; *Feud. Aids*, iv. 339.
[93] *Feud. Aids*, iv. 331, 339.

lifetime to his son Michael, who occurred as lord by 1299 until at least 1331.[94] In 1325 William Sinclair claimed rights to Michael's Eastham lands and by 1346 was lord of the former Cricket half.[95] Lettice Sinclair, widow of this William or his namesake, who had held the manor jointly with her former husband, died in 1377 and was succeeded by her son John, then a minor.[96] There followed a succession of owners named John Sinclair during the 15th century, the last of whom, described as son and heir of John Sinclair the younger, settled the manor on trustees in 1479.[97] The manor was mistakenly seized by John Hayes at the same time as he entered on Crewkerne for the king, and Hayes presented to Eastham chapel in 1493.[98] By 1500 rights to the manor had passed to Anne and Joan Copplestone, widows, who in that year conveyed the manor to Sir Reynold Bray (d. 1503), Bray also having obtained or tried to obtain a grant from John Hayes.[99] Bray was succeeded by his nephew Edmund Bray, Lord Bray, whose title to the manor was challenged by John Lacy (d. 1529), nephew of the last John Sinclair, claiming that he had been disseised by Hayes.[1] Lacy successfully evicted Bray c. 1511 and presented to the chapel in 1517 and 1526.[2] Other rights in the manor were claimed in 1510 by William Sandys, Lord Sandys of the Vine, husband of Sir Reynold Bray's half-sister Margery.[3] John Lacy was succeeded by his son Thomas and grandson James Lacy who, having been evicted by Lord Bray, took the manor back by force in 1529. Counter attacks in 1530 and 1531 and protracted lawsuits secured the manor for Bray.[4] In 1532 Lord Bray conveyed the estate to Sir Edward Seymour who sold it in 1535 to Thomas Yorke of Ramsbury (Wilts.), and Yorke still held it three years later.[5] Thereafter the descent is not clear; in 1554 the assignee of Robert Hungerford presented an incumbent to the chapel and Hungerford claimed the manor in 1555–6.[6]

By 1575 the lordship was again held by the Sandys family. In that year a grantee of William, Lord Sandys of the Vine, presented to Eastham chapel and in 1578 Walter Sandys sold the manor to Robert Freke of Iwerne Courtney (Dors.), a transaction confirmed by Lord Sandys in 1585.[7] On Robert's death in 1592 he was succeeded by his four sons, who jointly conveyed the estate to their cousin Francis Freke of Crewkerne and to John his son.[8] In 1617 John Freke settled the manor on his son William, reserving a life interest to himself, but

William combined with his father's mortgagee, John Freke of Hilton (Dors.), to gain possession.[9] By 1692 the property had descended from William to his son Edward, who in the following year settled it on his four sons and two daughters.[10] The manor was apparently being offered for sale in 1694 and was probably purchased by John Poole of Chillington (d. c. 1715), whose widow Mary presented to Eastham chapel in 1734.[11] By 1736 it had descended to Mary Poole's son-in-law Caleb King, a Crewkerne grocer (d. 1759), who by his will divided his lands equally between his son-in-law, John Genest, and his daughters Margaret, wife of Hugh Yeatman, and Christian King.[12]

The third of the manor left to Christian King was subsequently divided equally between her seven children by William Corfield of Taunton. Their representatives and assignees jointly conveyed their third to William Hoskins of North Perrott in 1803. The share inherited by John Genest (d. c. 1766) passed in turn to his son Peter and granddaughter Sophia, wife of Jasper Parratt, who in 1810 also sold their third to William Hoskins.[13] The final share, inherited by Hugh Yeatman (d. 1783), was left to his niece Mary Slade Yeatman, her husband, Nathaniel Dalton, and their daughter Mary Slade Dalton. In 1804 these three conveyed their third to Thomas Graham of Lincoln's Inn, probably acting as a trustee, and this share seems also to have passed to the Hoskins family.[14]

William Hoskins (d. 1813) was succeeded in turn by his sons William (d. 1863) and the Revd. Henry Hoskins (d. 1876). From Henry the manor descended through successive generations to H. W. Hoskyns (d. 1904), H. W. P. Hoskyns (d. 1921), and H. W. W. Hoskyns.[15] The farm was purchased from the last-named as an investment c. 1950 but it is doubtful whether the lordship was included in the sale.[16]

The manor-house, mentioned in 1296, was described as 'new built' in 1694 when it included a small earthen-floored hall, two small butteries within the hall, a large kitchen, a place for tubs and dairy, a brewhouse, a 'bad barn', and a stall.[17] In 1768 as Easthams Farm it was adapted by Hugh Yeatman as a smallpox inoculation centre and continued to be so used in the following year.[18] Its present name, Higher Easthams, was used by the 19th century to distinguish it from Lower Easthams farm to the north.[19] The kitchen and outhouses, described as newly built in 1694, survive as the

[94] S.R.S. xii. 19, 70, 101–4, 107, 157–8; Devon R.O., TD 51, p. 180.
[95] S.R.S. x, p. 528; xii. 102–4; Feud. Aids, iv. 339.
[96] Cal. Inq. p.m. xiv, pp. 281, 342; Cal. Fine R. 1369–77, 176.
[97] S.R.S. xxii. 67; xxix, p. 238; xxxi, p. 66; lii, pp. 6, 78; Cat. Anct. D. vi, C 4822.
[98] Sta. Cha. 2/34/12; S.R.S. lii, p. 185.
[99] Cat. Anct. D. vi, C 4651, 5745; C 1/279/46.
[1] C 1/279/46; Sta. Cha. 2/34/12; C 142/50/33.
[2] S.R.S. liv, p. 186; lv, p. 43.
[3] C.P. 25(2)/51/358/2 Hen. VIII Mich.; C 54/378 no. 30.
[4] Sta. Cha. 2/34/12; 2/25/326; S.R.S. xxvii. 112–19.
[5] L. & P. Hen. VIII, v, p. 1154; E 41/217; E 328/201; C.P. 25(2)/36/239/30 Hen. VIII Mich.
[6] S.R.S. lv, p. 133; C 24/35/19.
[7] S.R.O., D/D/B reg 15; DD/PH 225/74; C.P. 25(2)/206/27 Eliz. I Hil.
[8] S.R.O., DD/PH 225/74; Hutchins, Hist. Dors. iv. 86. In 1611 John Freke granted a rent-charge of £30

a year from the manor to the Revd. William Owsley. Assigned to Humphrey Hody in 1629, it was paid until its redemption by the lord from John Hody Chichester in 1810: DD/PH 225/74; DD/HK, box 1, conveyance 2 June 1810.
[9] S.R.O., DD/PH 225/74; Cal. S.P. Dom. 1648–9, 381.
[10] S.R.O., DD/PH 61; 225/74; D/D/B reg 24.
[11] S.R.O., DD/PH 224/48, 51–4, 68; D/D/B reg 26.
[12] S.R.O., DD/S/WI 57; DD/HK, box 1, deeds of Eastham; D/D/B reg 26.
[13] S.R.O., DD/HK, box 1, deeds of Eastham; DD/S/WI 57.
[14] S.R.O., DD/S/WI 60; Burke, Land. Gent. (1914), 158.
[15] Burke, Land. Gent. (1952), 1288–9.
[16] Ex inf. Mr. G. T. R. Thomas, Easthams.
[17] S.R.S. vi. 295–6; S.R.O., DD/PH 224/68; 225/50.
[18] Sherborne Mercury, 22 Feb. 1768, 3 Apr. 1769.
[19] H.O. 107/1928.

service wing to a large farmhouse of the later 19th century.

The overlordship of the manor of *CLAPTON* was described in 1281 as $\frac{1}{3}$ fee of the little fee of Mortain,[20] and had probably been held at the Conquest by Robert, count of Mortain. The overlordship seems to have descended with the Mortain manor of Bickenhall, held in 1086 by William de L'Estre from whom it had passed by about 1260 to Joan, daughter of another William de L'Estre, who married Robert de Paveley (d. 1274).[21] Paveley held $\frac{1}{2}$ fee in Clapton at his death and it passed to his son John (d. 1281).[22] John's widow Eve successfully claimed the overlordship as her dower in 1287 and by 1303 it was held by John de Bykenhulle, identified with John son of John and Eve de Paveley.[23] The tenure was not mentioned again until 1484 when it was held by John son of Thomas Rodney, who occurred as overlord in 1493.[24] By 1551 and subsequently the manor was held of the king in chief.[25]

In the late 12th century the terre-tenancy was evidently held by William de Durville, who was succeeded by his son Eustace.[26] In 1208 Eustace gave half of Clapton to Christine, widow of Ralph Wake,[27] although this subdivision does not recur. Eustace de Durville had conveyed the manor to Alice de Vaux before 1212, in which year it was held by her son Robert, although her ownership was again recorded in 1214.[28] By 1228 the manor had passed to Baldwin of Clapton who was continuing as lord there in 1252.[29] Robert of Clapton was mentioned in 1254 and the estate was held in 1281 by John of Clapton (d. 1287) and in 1303 for $\frac{1}{4}$ fee by Roger of Clapton.[30] John of Clapton held $\frac{1}{4}$ fee there in 1346, Robert of Clapton owned land in Crewkerne in 1364, and Walter Clapton, mentioned between 1365 and 1386, held $\frac{1}{8}$ fee at Clapton in 1377.[31] By 1412 the manor had descended to Richard Clapton, whose heirs seems to have been Ralph Maloisell and Joan his wife, possibly Richard's daughter.[32] By 1428 Ralph had been succeeded by his brother William Maloisell, who was living in 1435.[33] From Maloisell the manor passed to John Bonville of Clapton, who was mentioned in 1454 and described in a non-contemporary source as husband of Alice, daughter of Richard Clapton.[34] A John Bonville died in 1484 and was

succeeded in turn by his son and grandson, John (d. 1493) and John (d. 1551).[35] From the second the manor passed successively to his sons Thomas (d. 1565) and Richard.[36] Richard mortgaged the manor in 1607 and had been succeeded before 1637 by his son or grandson, John Bonville.[37] A John Bonville held it in 1657 and another sold it in 1667 to Sir Andrew Henley, Bt. (d. 1675), who was succeeded in turn by his sons Sir Robert (d. *c.* 1689) and Sir Andrew Henley.[38] Sir Andrew conveyed the manor to his son-in-law Carleton Whitelock in 1700, and he sold it in the following year to Henry Palmer (d. *c.* 1715) of Henley. Palmer left it to his son Henry (d. 1740), whose heir was his cousin Joseph Palmer of Drimpton in Broadwindsor (Dors.).[39] From Joseph Palmer the manor passed in 1772–3 to John Perkins of Clapton (d. 1791) who left it jointly to his nephews Hugh Perkins Lowman and Robert Lowman.[40] Hugh became sole proprietor in 1795–6 and was succeeded by John Perkins Lowman between 1811 and 1813.[41] The estate was purchased from the Lowmans in 1866 by John Bryant Phelps, who had married into the Lowman family.[42] It was acquired in 1873 by Edward Tanner, owner in 1901, held between 1907 and 1923 by F. T. Wrigley, and by 1927 by Maj. A. E. L. Craven.[43] The property was purchased from Maj. Craven in 1950 by Mr. G. and Mr. L. Martineau, the last-named holding it in 1976.[44]

The site of Clapton manor-house was probably occupied by the Clapton family in the early 13th century. John Bonville refers to his 'household stuff' there in 1551 and the house was known as Clapton Farm in 1715 and 1731, and as Clapton Court by 1791.[45] It is a large gabled house, standing in well-planted gardens, mostly of 20th-century creation, with a small park. The house incorporates a long 17th-century range which has been extended to the north and east at various times in the 18th and 19th centuries. A single-storey outbuilding NW. of the house bears the date 1813 and the initials of J. P. Lowman.

The manor of *HENLEY* was held in 1222 by Richard de L'Estre for $\frac{1}{2}$ fee, when he sold it to Agnes de Windsor, widow of Richard de Esse.[46] From her it evidently descended to John de Asshe who, in 1280, brought an assize of *mort d'ancestor* against Nicholas le Frye for $\frac{2}{3}$ of the manor.[47]

[20] *Cal. Inq. p.m.* ii, p. 399.
[21] *Proc. Som. Arch. Soc.* xl. 180–1; *Cal. Inq. p.m.* ii, p. 52; *V.C.H. Som.* i. 476.
[22] *Cal. Inq. p.m.* ii, pp. 52, 231.
[23] Ibid. p. 399; *Feud. Aids*, iv. 316–17; *Proc. Som. Arch. Soc.* xl. 181–2.
[24] C 141/2/17; *Cal. Inq. p.m. Hen. VII*, iii, pp. 350–1.
[25] C 142/94/85.
[26] *Cur. Reg. R.* vi. 378–9; xi, pp. 53–4.
[27] *Rot. Chart.* (Rec. Com.), 182–3.
[28] *Cur. Reg. R.* vi. 349, 378–9; vii. 280–1.
[29] *S.R.S.* vi. 70–1; xi, p. 322; Devon R.O., TD 51, pp. 192–4. A settlement of 1236 between members of the Vaux family specifically excludes Clapton: *S.R.S.* vi. 367.
[30] Devon R.O., TD 51, pp. 189–90; *Cal. Inq. p.m.* ii, pp. 231, 399; *Feud. Aids*, iv. 316–17. In 1316 Seaborough (Dors. formerly Som.) and Clapton were stated to be held by Agnes de Rochford and Walter atte Barre. The Rochfords held Seaborough and the Barres are linked with Clapton mill.
[31] *Feud. Aids*, iv. 339; *S.R.S.* xvii. 54, 60, 95–6; *Cal. Inq. p.m.* xiv, p. 321; *Cal. Close*, 1377–81, 15; 1385–9, 246.
[32] *Feud. Aids*, vi. 507; C 137/89/13; *Cal. Close*, 1413–19, 71.
[33] *Feud. Aids*, iv. 382; *Cal. Close*, 1413–19, 71; *S.R.S.* xxii. 86–7.
[34] *Cal. Close*, 1447–54, 516; *Visits. Som.* 1531, 1573, ed. F. W. Weaver, 96.
[35] C 141/2/17; *Cal. Fine R.* 1471–85, 284; *Cal. Inq. p.m. Hen. VII*, iii, pp. 350–1; C 142/94/85.
[36] C 142/94/85; C 142/143/19.
[37] *S.R.S.* li, p. 179; C.P. 25 (2)/715/13 Chas. I East.
[38] C.P. 25(2)/593/1657 Trin.; C.P. 25(2)/716/19 Chas. II Trin.; G.E.C. *Baronetage*, iii. 69.
[39] S.R.O., DD/HKE 1/6, 10.
[40] S.R.O., D/P/crew 13/2/4; DD/SB 33/1; Hutchins, *Hist. Dors.* iv. 440.
[41] S.R.O., D/P/crew 13/2/6–9.
[42] Sale cat. Clapton Ct. estate, 1881, *penes* Mr. C. G. Lockyer, Clapton Mills; Pulman, *Bk. of the Axe*, 347; Morris & Co. *Dir. Som.* (1872).
[43] S.R.O., Q/REr; *Kelly's Dir. Som.* (1927); sale cat. Clapton Ct. estate, 1897, *penes* Mr. Lockyer.
[44] Ex inf. Mr. L. Martineau, Clapton Court.
[45] *S.R.S.* xxi. 122; S.R.O., DD/HKE 1/6, 10; Hutchins, *Hist. Dors.* iv. 440.
[46] *S.R.S.* vi. 44; *Cur. Reg. R.* x, p. 116.
[47] *S.R.S.* xliv. 33–4.

John de Asshe may possibly be the John of Henley who held the estate for ¼ fee in 1292.[48] By 1346 the manor was owned by Nicholas le Duyn and his wife Alice, and it may be the ¼ fee in Crewkerne held in 1377 by Robert Montague.[49] Thereafter it evidently continued in the Montague family, for William Montague (d. 1489) was described as of Henley between 1460 and 1473 and in 1483 he settled the manor on his son William (d. 1484) and his son's wife Florence for their lives.[50] The second William was succeeded by his son Robert, although in 1490 John Wyke received a grant of ⅓ of the manor, evidently held in dower by Florence Montague, William's widow, and by his death in 1517 Wyke held the whole estate.[51] The manor had been settled on John Wyke's younger sons, John and Robert, but it passed in 1534 to Thomas Wyke with reversion to Richard Wyke of Nynehead. Thomas leased the manor for his own life to Robert Merifield who acquired in 1557 a 41-year reversionary lease which Richard Wyke had made to Arthur Disshe a year earlier. Merifield assigned the lease to Sir Hugh Poulett in 1557, and the lease on Thomas Wyke's life to Christopher Sampford in 1559.[52] In 1577 Richard Wyke (d. 1590) settled the manor on himself and his wife for their lives and in 1579 leased it to his younger sons Henry, Richard, and William. Henry and Richard assigned their rights in 1601 and 1603 to their eldest brother John (d. 1622).[53] The fee, however, evidently passed to his brother Henry, whose daughters and coheirs, Barbara, Averyn, and Elizabeth, sold their shares to Robert Henley of Henley between 1632 and 1636.[54]

Robert Henley (d. 1656) was succeeded by his son Sir Andrew Henley, Bt., from whom it descended with the manor of Clapton until sold by Carleton Whitelock to John, Lord Poulett, in 1700.[55] The manor continued to be held by the Poulett family with that of Hinton St. George until the Henley estate was sold in 1911.[56] It has been owned since 1946 by Imperial Chemical Industries.[57]

Henley manor-house, now known as Henley Manor, was mentioned in 1473 when an oratory was licensed for mass there.[58] The present house surrounds three sides of a courtyard which is open to the south. The northern range is possibly of late medieval origin, but has been much altered. The eastern range, which incorporates features which suggest it was the earlier hall range, now appears to be of c. 1700, possibly the result of remodelling on its purchase by Lord Poulett.[59] The western range is of the later 16th or early 17th century and may have been built as lodgings.

Lands at Hewish were evidently among those granted to William Briwere (d. 1233) in marriage with Joan daughter of William de Reviers. In 1256 Joan granted 3½ virgates and a ferling of land in Hewish to the priory of Christchurch (Hants), to found a chantry for the souls of herself and her parents.[60] These lands were among those which Isabel de Forz tried to recover, without success, in 1272.[61] The estate was retained by the priory until the Dissolution and was sold in 1545 to Roger Long of London.[62] Long conveyed the property to William Johnson of Hinton St. George in 1547, and he sold it in 1557 to Robert and Elizabeth Merifield of Crewkerne.[63] Robert was succeeded by John Merifield (d. 1581), whose estate was described as the manor of *HEWISH* on the death of John's son Robert in 1608.[64] The estate passed through successive generations to John (d. 1623), John (d. 1666), Robert (d. 1686), and John Merifield (d. 1695).[65] The manor was then left equally between the sisters of the last John Merifield: Susanna wife of William Merifield (d. 1728) of Woolminstone and Alice (d. 1739) wife of John Donne a Crewkerne grocer. Disputes within the family led to a private Act of Parliament for settling the estate and to the physical subdivision of the manor into three parts under successive partitions of 1740 and 1745.[66]

One third was granted to William Merifield of Woolminstone, son of William and Susanna, and was sold in 1752 to Henry Hele, M.D., of Salisbury (d. 1778). Hele's executors conveyed it to William Gray of Crewkerne, who sold it to John, Earl Poulett, in 1809, after which it merged with the other Poulett lands in Crewkerne.[67] Another third passed to John Donne of Crewkerne (d. 1768), son of John and Alice, and descended successively to his son James (d. 1783) and granddaughter Anna Maria Susanna (d. 1856), wife of the Revd. George Donisthorpe. She left the estate jointly to her distant cousins Benjamin J. M. Donne (d. 1928), and his sister Elizabeth (d. 1897), wife of Henry Parsons of Misterton.[68] The third was not mentioned thereafter. The final share was inherited by Mary, widow of Robert Merifield of Shaftesbury (Dors.) (d. 1739), who was half-brother of John (d. 1695), and to her son Matthew. Mary released her share to Matthew Merifield (d. 1782) in 1750, and it evidently passed to Matthew's brother-in-law, Peter Battiscombe of Bridport (Dors.) (d. 1798), and then to Peter's son Robert of Windsor (Berks.) (d. 1839). Subsequently it descended to Robert's son, the Revd. Richard Battiscombe of Hacton in Upminster (Essex) (d. 1873), and was last recorded in 1876 when it was held by the latter's son Robert Charles Battiscombe.[69]

The property known as Merifield House on the north side of East Street was occupied by the lords

[48] *Cal. Inq. p.m.* iii, p. 26.
[49] *S.R.S.* xii. 234; *Cal. Inq. p.m.* xiv, pp. 320–1.
[50] *Cal. Fine R.* 1452–61, 261; *S.R.S.* lii, pp. 100–1; Wedgwood, *Hist. Parl. Biogs.* s.v. Montague; C 141/1/16.
[51] C 141/1/16; C.P. 25(1)/202/42; C 142/43/49.
[52] Deeds *penes* Mrs. G. Shaw, Merifield House, Bower Hinton, Martock, in 1950.
[53] S.R.O., DD/SF 243, 439; DD/SS, bdles. 18, 57; D/P/crew 2/1/1.
[54] S.R.O., DD/SS, bdle. 18; *S.R.S.* li, p. 197.
[55] S.R.O., DD/SS, bdle. 18; G.E.C. *Baronetage*, iii. 69.
[56] S.R.O., DD/SS, bdle. 18; DD/SAS C/2273, 1/C 18.2.
[57] Ex inf. Mr. M. E. Hutchinson, Henley Manor.
[58] *S.R.S.* lii, pp. 100–1.

[59] See above.
[60] B.L. Cott. MS. Tib. D. vi, ff. 178–178v.; *Close R. 1231–4*, 198.   [61] *S.R.S.* xxxvi. 166–7.
[62] Dugdale, *Mon.* vi. 307; *L. & P. Hen. VIII*, xx (2), pp. 228–9.
[63] *Cal. Pat.* 1547–8, 11; S.R.O., DD/MR 7.
[64] *Som. Wills*, ed. Brown, iii. 82; S.R.O., DD/MR 1.
[65] C 142/403/68; S.R.O., DD/PT, box 17, will of John Merifield 1695; DD/MR 71.
[66] D.R.O., D 257/E 1; S.R.O., DD/BC 86, 89.
[67] S.R.O., DD/PT, box 13, conveyance 6 May 1809; box 21A, abstr. of title 1794.
[68] S.R.O., DD/MR 4–6, 71.
[69] S.R.O., DD/BC 90–105; Hutchins, *Hist. Dors.* ii. 241; iii. 56.

of Hewish manor by 1608. On James Donne's death in 1783 the house was physically divided between his two daughters, but was reunited by 1802 in the hands of the sole survivor, Mrs. A. M. S. Donisthorpe.[70] The central block, with panelled front and a recessed Doric doorcase, is of the early 19th century, but is attached on the east to the remains of a 17th-century house, the front section rebuilt in the later 19th century, but bearing the dates 1661 and 1679 and the Merifield arms. To the west is a wing of one storey dated 1901. There is a terraced garden surrounded by a brick wall with a late-17th-century garden house. Gate piers and railings of the 19th century on the street front flank an 18th-century wrought-iron gate surmounted by the Merifield arms.

Among properties owned by Forde abbey at the Dissolution were lands called Laymore, which were granted to Richard (later Sir Richard) Pollard with the site of the abbey in 1540.[71] The grant did not include all the land called Laymore, for some was sold in 1545 to Guy Bonville of Street in Winsham and John Preston of Cricket St. Thomas.[72] Subsequently these lands with others in Thorncombe and Broadwindsor (Dors.) came to be regarded as a single estate called Laymore and Southcombe.[73] Sir Richard's son, Sir John Pollard, sold the estate in 1572 to Sir Amias Poulett,[74] and he conveyed it to William Rosewell, solicitor-general. Rosewell's son, Sir Henry, sold it in 1649 to Sir Edmund Prideaux (d. 1659). By 1692, during the tenure of Sir Edmund's son Edmund Prideaux (d. 1702) it was known as the manor of *LAYMORE*.[75] From Edmund it passed to his daughter Margaret (d. 1709), wife of Francis Gwyn (d. 1734), and thence in turn to their sons Edward Prideaux (d. c. 1736) and Francis Gwyn (d. 1752). The last left it to his distant cousin, John Fraunceis (d. 1789) of Combe Florey, who assumed the name of Gwyn, and was succeeded by his son John Fraunceis Gwyn (d. 1846). In 1847 Gwyn's trustees sold the manor to George Frederick Miles, who conveyed it in 1865 to Jane, widow of William Bertram Evans.[76] It was not mentioned thereafter.

The grant of Crewkerne rectory to the chapter of Winchester in 1547 was followed by several years of confusion. The former rector of the first portion had let his estate for nine years to one H. Creike in 1546–7.[77] By 1548 the three occupiers were Sir William Herbert, Edward Horsey, and Thomas Freke, the second described as a scholar, the last as a clerk.[78] By 1557 John Berde, a Crewkerne draper, was leasing the first and second portions,[79] and his

widow continued his interest in the first at least until 1568, though much of it was sub-let to Robert Hawkins, clerk.[80]

Meanwhile in 1562 Robert Freke of the Inner Temple, later of Iwerne Courtney (Dors.), had taken an immediate lease from the Winchester chapter of the second and third portions for 21 years and a similar reversionary lease of the first portion from 1573.[81] But confusion continued: the churchwardens in a suit in 1567 thought that Winchester college, not the chapter, was involved; and the chapter, aware of previous occupiers of their estate, provided for a rent rebate in the event of their tenant's eviction.[82] The second portion was not formally surrendered until 1564–5.[83]

Robert Freke continued in possession of the whole parsonage from 1573 until his death in 1592, and was succeeded by his son Sir Thomas.[84] In 1612 it passed to Sir Henry Hawley of Buckland Sororum, who ten years later assigned his interest to Henry Poulett of Hinton St. George (d. c. 1633), probably his wife's nephew.[85] It then passed to another Henry, probably son of the first.[86] On the confiscation of cathedral property in 1650 the estate was divided between Elizabeth Poulett, spinster, who took the manorial rights, and Richard Jeane and Thomas Biddell who bought the parsonage house and demesne lands.[87]

Anthony Poulett of Torrell's Preston in Milverton was granted a lease on the old terms for 21 years in 1660, and was followed in 1680 by Richard Cutts, a Middle Temple lawyer, acting as trustee for his daughter Elizabeth, Poulett's sole executrix.[88] From 1684 to 1708 it was held by Elizabeth's husband Andrews Warner of Badmondesfield, Wickhambrook (Suff.), and from then until 1764 by members of the Godwin or Goodwin family of Weeke (Hants) or their trustees.[89] From 1764 the occupier was Nicholas Baconnean, a Winchester surgeon, who by 1767 had assigned his interest to William Hussey of Salisbury.[90]

Hussey, M.P. for New Salisbury, who purchased the freehold in 1801,[91] died in 1813, leaving the rectory to his great-nephew John (1789–1848). It passed to John's son Thomas (d. 1894), and then to Augustus Henry Hussey (d. 1934), Thomas's nephew. On his death the estate descended to Capt. (later Major) H. Hussey, owner in 1976.[92]

In 1599 the rectory estate comprised the tithes of the whole parish and nearly 500 a. of land.[93] A survey of 1650 enumerated just over 494 a., let with the tithes for £52 8s.[94] The land alone was said to be worth over £372 on improvement and

[70] S.R.O., DD/MR 6.
[71] L. & P. Hen. VIII, xv, pp. 409–10.
[72] Ibid. xx (2), 117, 120.   [73] D.R.O., D 55/T 60.
[74] Cal. Pat. 1572–3, p. 402.
[75] D.R.O., D 55/T 61; Hutchins, Hist. Dors. iv. 527–8.
[76] S.R.O., DD/CN 8/1; D.R.O., D 55/T 60–76; Hutchins, Hist. Dors. iv. 527–8.
[77] Winchester Cath. Libr., John Chace's Bk. f. 100v.
[78] L. & P. Hen. VIII, xiv, p. 75; S.R.S. ii. 8; lv, p. 166.
[79] S.R.S. xxi. 206; G.E.C. Baronetage, iii. 69–70.
[80] S.R.O., D/D/Cd 12; C 3/41/29.
[81] Winchester Cath. Libr., Ledger Bk. V, f. 11v.
[82] C 3/41/29; Ledger Bk. V, f. 11v.
[83] John Chace's Bk. f. 100v.
[84] Hutchins, Hist. Dors. iv. 86; John Chace's Bk. f. 100v.; Ledger Bk. VI, f. 1.

[85] Ledger Bk. XI, ff. 11, 66; XII, ff. 13v., 51, 85; C 3/427/63; Complete Peerage, s.v. Poulett.
[86] Ledger Bk. XII, f. 116v.; Hants R.O., CC/59493.
[87] C 54/3575 no. 6; C 54/3576 no. 3.
[88] Ledger Bk. XIV, f. 51; XVI, f. 6; XIX, f. 41.
[89] Ibid. XX, f. 38; XXII, f. 52; XXIII, f. 16v.; XXIV, f. 52; XXV, f. 47; XXVI, f. 31v.; XXVII, f. 31v.; XXVIII, f. 76; XXIX, f. 91; S.R.O., DD/HKE 1/1; V.C.H. Hants, iii. 452; S.R.O., DD/AS, box 29.
[90] Ledger Bk. XXX, f. 78; XXXI, ff. 18v., 149v., 180v.; XXXII, f. 288; XXXIII, ff. 184, 233; surrender, 1767, penes Maj. H. Hussey.   [91] Ex inf. Maj. Hussey.
[92] S.R.O., DD/SB 25/4 (abstr. of title 1880); M.I. in Crewkerne ch.; Som. Country Houses and Villages (1931–2), s.v. Maincombe.
[93] S.R.O., T/PH/hsy, survey 1599.
[94] Hants R.O., CC/59493.

MERRIOTT CHURCH FROM THE SOUTH-WEST

CREWKERNE CHURCH FROM THE SOUTH-WEST

MARTOCK CHURCH: THE ROOF, BEFORE RESTORATION

HINTON ST. GEORGE CHURCH: INTERIOR, WITH THE TOMB OF
SIR ANTHONY POULETT (d. 1600)

the tithes a further £400. The sales in 1650 realized £1,177.[95] After the Restoration the ancient rent was resumed, but from 1680 the farmer contributed £80 a year as salary for the curate.[96] In the 1740s, however, it was said that the chapter of Winchester 'runs (sic) away with the parsonage and starve the curates by their salaries and leave others to make up their deficiencies'.[97] In 1765 the value was £453 9s., and in 1772 the parsonage land comprised 507 a.[98]

In 1765 the tithes claimed in different parts of the parish varied. The town and Furland paid all tithes, great and small, and Coombe paid 'all sorts of tithes' except hay from Blackmoor farm. From Misterton came tithes of corn and sheep only, and from Hewish, Woolminstone, and Clapton tithes of corn, hay, sheep, and beasts, though part of the Hewish hay tithes was commuted for a modus of 1d. an acre. There were also tithes worth £4 from part of Wayford, and from Oathill tithes of corn and hay and a modus 'for the part', worth £4 10s.[99] By 1842 the tithes in the parish were commuted for £1,300. Moduses had been negotiated in some numbers, and were defended in a lawsuit between John Hussey and Earl Poulett over the tithes of Hinton park, part of Crewkerne parish but not so shown on the tithe map.[1] There were moduses of 8d. for every milch cow, 1d. an acre for stock meadow and other small pieces of grass, small sums for mills, and larger sums for Coldharbour farm and the four holdings owned by Earl Poulett in and near Hinton park.[2]

Most of the property, based on the parsonage house, was let to the Budd family from 1758,[3] and the whole in 1842 covered 499 a.[4] Some additional property at Furland, apparently acquired in the 18th century,[5] was sold c. 1922, and the rectory estate comprised c. 400 a. in 1976.[6]

Two parsonage houses survived the 16th century. One stood on the east side of the churchyard in 1650,[7] and may have been partially demolished in 1785.[8] The other was the medieval house, later replaced by the Abbey, which was usually occupied by tenant farmers. That house was demolished in 1846, and its successor became the residence of the owners of the estate.[9] In 1903–4 the family moved to a large house called Maincombe which they had built on high ground to the west of the town. It is of Pinhoe brick with Bath stone dressings in a debased Georgian style by Charles Benson of Yeovil, and a feature of its design was four towers.[10] Much of the house was demolished c. 1948 after occupation by troops during the Second World War.[11] The estate also contained two barns in 1650,[12] described as Parsonage and Blackhall barns. A floor and a half of the latter was let with a 40-a. farm in 1814,[13] and the former, together with a little barn apparently adjoining, was leased with the main farm. Parsonage Barn, of local stone with three porches, apparently dates from the 18th or possibly from the late 17th century. Opposite the barn a house called the Parsonage or the Old Parsonage Guest House was evidently acquired and altered by John Hussey (d. 1848) as a dwelling for the largest tenant when the parsonage house west of the church became uninhabitable.[14]

Lands in Crewkerne which had formed the endowment of the chantry chapel of the Virgin in Crewkerne churchyard were granted in 1549 to Robert Wood of London.[15] It was probably these lands which by the early 17th century had passed to John Pyne (d. 1607) of Curry Mallet and were settled by him on his son Thomas Pyne (d. 1609) of Merriott. At Thomas's death the estate was known as the manor of *CREWKERNE CHANTRY* and was held in socage of the manor of Stanton Lacy (Salop.).[16] From Thomas the property descended through successive generations of the family to John (d. 1679), Charles (d. 1715), and John Pyne (d. 1764) of Curry Mallet.[17] John Pyne of Charlton Mackrell, son of the last, sold the lands to the tenants in 1769 and 1770[18] and the manor was not mentioned thereafter.

ECONOMIC HISTORY. Crewkerne was evidently a place of some importance in the late Saxon period, but although its topographical position gave it a long history of trade with the south coast, its urban development cannot be traced until the 16th century with any certainty. Not until the 19th century did its manufactures, notably webbing and sailcloth, claim more of the labour market than agriculture, the dominant feature of an extensive and prosperous parish.

AGRICULTURE. Crewkerne was an estate which T.R.E. Earl Godwin and his sons had held, but by 1086 it was divided: Eastham and Seaborough had become separate holdings, the latter in the possession of the bishop of Salisbury, and the church estate had passed to the abbey of St. Stephen, Caen (Calvados).[19] All, however, remained within the ancient parish. The main manor, as a royal possession, did not pay geld and the number of hides it contained is not recorded; but there was land for 40 ploughs. The church estate measured 10 hides, and Eastham 2 hides. Hides and plough teams corresponded except on the main manor, where the land for 40 ploughs had only 20 teams.

The demesne of Crewkerne manor, which then included both Misterton and Wayford, had only 5 ploughs; Eastham was wholly in demesne, but the church estate comprised a demesne farm of 2 hides, 4½ hides occupied by peasant farmers, and a 3-hide property held by a knight, half of which was sub-let.

[95] C 54/3575 no. 6; C 54/3576 no. 3.
[96] Ledger Bk. XIX, f. 41.   [97] S.R.O., DD/SH 107.
[98] S.R.O., T/PH/hsy, rectory map 1772 (orig. *penes* Maj. Hussey); DD/SB 49/3.
[99] S.R.O., DD/SB 49/3.
[1] S.R.O., tithe award; DD/PT, boxes 22A, 37.
[2] S.R.O., tithe award.
[3] S.R.O., DD/HKE 1/3; leases *penes* Maj. Hussey.
[4] S.R.O., tithe award.   [5] S.R.O., Q/RE.
[6] Ex inf. Maj. Hussey.   [7] Hants R.O., CC/59493.
[8] Contract Bk. *penes* Maj. Hussey.
[9] S.R.O., DD/HKE 1/3.

[10] *Som. Country Houses and Villages* (1931–2); ex inf. Maj. Hussey. S.R.O., D/P/crew 23/10 says 1906.
[11] Ex inf. Maj. Hussey.   [12] Hants R.O., CC/59493.
[13] Lease *penes* Maj. Hussey.
[14] The arms over the front door are those of John Hussey and his wife.
[15] *Cal. Pat.* 1549–51, 97.   [16] *S.R.S.* lxvii, p. 51.
[17] S.R.O., DD/CN 72; DD/TH, box 5, abstr. of title 1770.
[18] S.R.O., DD/TH, box 5, agreement 27 Nov. 1769; conveyance 5 Oct. 1770.
[19] *V.C.H. Som.* i. 439, 445, 470, 477.

Stock on the demesne farms was dominated by sheep, with 400 on the main manor and 175 on the church estate. There were 64 she-goats on the main manor and a total of 65 pigs in the parish.

As many as 176 people are recorded on Crewkerne manor, the church estate, and Eastham together, an indication of the existence of more than one dependent settlement of peasant origin. The main manor alone had 42 villeins and 45 bordars, and there were 11 villeins, 2 coliberts, and 17 bordars among the church estate tenants. A dozen *servi* were found on the Crewkerne demesne, and one each at Eastham, on the church demesne, and on the knight's demesne. In the 13th century Misterton, Wayford, and Oathill among the 'outliers' had none but tenant farmers,[20] and Woolminstone and Hewish still bore the same character in the 16th century.[21] A *nativus* was found at Hewish at least until 1530.[22]

Accounts and extents dating from 1267 to the beginning of the 16th century do not relate always to the whole manor of Crewkerne, and differ so widely in character that generalizations are impossible. The earliest account, for the manor of 'Craft and Cruk'', the possession of Isabel de Forz, covers the years 1267–8.[23] Nearly half the income was from rents, including some from Misterton, from the farm of markets, mills, and land, from customary aids, church scot and chevage, and perquisites of courts. The demesne arable that year covered 286 a. and was given over to wheat ($108\frac{1}{2}$ a.), oats (84 a.), rye (49 a.), barley (24 a.), and beans (21 a.).[24] Sales of grain were small, but two-thirds of the total of 150 qr. of oats, half new grain and some brought from Honiton (Devon), were consumed by the horses of the countess Isabel's retinue on their journeys to other estates. The sheep flock accounted for sales of 297 large fleeces, 42 sheepskins, 134 lambskins, and 173 cheeses. Other livestock included 24 oxen, 14 cows, and 84 pigs.

The staff of the farm were a hayward, a gardener, three ploughmen, a shepherd, a cowherd, a carter, and a swineherd, with a keeper of beasts and a 'darye' for half a year, an extra carter for harvest, and two women to milk ewes for 17 weeks. Beyond regular services 15 boonworkers ploughed the fallow during that year, 45 reaped the wheat, and 43 the oats.

An extent of lands lately held by John de Courtenay in 1274 in the manor of Crewkerne revealed the strength of villeinage there. The property was valued at £29 2s. 11d., and was evidently that known as the 'chase' of Crewkerne.[25] The demesne was small, only 80 a. of arable then under crop, 12 a. of meadow, and a small amount of shared and common pasture. Two-thirds of the income was from rents of free tenants and villeins, including the customs and services of 22 villeins in Misterton and 13 in Craft and Woolminstone.[26] An extent of Courtenay lands in 1292 referred expressly to a half of the manor of Crewkerne, and was valued at £47 11s. 8d.[27]

The minority of the Courtenay heir and the death of Isabel de Forz in 1293 brought most of the estate into the hands of a Crown-appointed farmer. Accounts of the property between 1292 and 1297 include customary rents which contributed more than a quarter of the total income of £91 6s. $5\frac{1}{2}$d. in 1295–6.[28] There were common renders of hens at Martinmas called church scot from 19 tenants and of cash at Michaelmas for chevage and feudal aids. More unusual were 12 ewes coming from Misterton at Whitsun, 5s. from Craft known as 'bakselver', 5s. 3d. from the sale of 28 slabs of iron, recalling the Domesday renders from Seaborough,[29] and 2s. 6d. rent at Michaelmas called 'skotmust'.

Customary works had largely been commuted, with the exception of mowing at Misterton, the mills, fair, and market were let to farm, and conversion to cash was evident policy. In 1295–6 almost half the demesne arable (346 a.) was fallow,[30] and most of the remainder was shared between wheat and oats, though seed had to be purchased since all had been sold in the previous year. The costs of ploughing, sowing, haymaking, and harvest were only slightly less than the sales of works during the year, though a handsome profit was made on the grain. The demesne sheep flock had been entirely abandoned, and the only livestock in 1296 were two horses and ten oxen. The farm staff had, of necessity, decreased in number to a hayward, a carter, a ploughman, and a drover.[31]

With the return of Courtenay control and the death of Agnes de Monceaux, occupier of the de Forz property, the demesne farm reached its greatest extent in the early 14th century. In 1315 it comprised 281 a. of arable in Crewkerne and 217 a. in Craft, with 45 a. of meadow, 55 a. of pasture mostly at Roundham, 50 a. of alder wood, 155 a. of wood, and 35 a. of thorn scrub.[32] The total value of the tenanted property was £49 8s. $4\frac{1}{2}$d. in terms of cash income, comprising rents of over £26 and commuted works of nearly £19. There were sixteen freeholdings of which three were held by charter and one at will, mostly in return for suit at the three-week court. The two most substantial tenants were Robert le Tort with a virgate and 23 a., and Robert of Potteford holding half of two mills and rents of six marks. Fifteen tenants grouped together held each a ferling or $\frac{1}{2}$ ferling in return for services at haymaking, harvest, and cider making, moving the lord's sheepfold from field to field, helping at sheep washing, and holding office as reeve, tithingman, bedel, hayward, ploughman, or granger (*berubrittarius*). Richard le Borgh, the leading villein, had particular charge of the sheepfold. A group of nineteen tenants, with holdings of similar size and paying rents, aids, cider, and chickens, owed ploughing and sowing duties. There were some 34 cottage holdings, 9 miscellaneous tenants including the prior of Christchurch with 5 virgates and 14 sub-tenants; and finally a group of 33 holders, 23 with a virgate each, involved in extensive works including sheep washing, mowing, and sowing 'gavelsed'. In this group the rents amounted to £4 15s. 7d. and the works were worth £15 3s. $9\frac{1}{2}$d.

The last reference to tenancies in the 14th century

---

[20] *Proc. Som. Arch. Soc.* cxx.
[21] E. Devon R.O., CR 550.
[22] Ibid.
[23] Bodl. MS. Top. Gen. d. 20.
[24] *Proc. Som. Arch. Soc.* cxx.
[25] C 133/6/1; Oliver, *Mon. Exon.* 343–5.
[26] C 133/6/1.
[27] C 133/62/7.
[28] S.C. 6/1127/16.
[29] *V.C.H. Som.* i. 445.
[30] Compare 335 a. in 1292: C 133/6/1.
[31] Also called a second ploughman.
[32] B.L. Add. MS. 49359, ff. 74–78v.

is incomplete, but there were in 1341 35 free tenants and 23 villeins on a moiety of the manor.[33]
Cash received from the property in 1392–3 was
£97 13s. 8d.[34] and the net value in the following
year was £194 4s. 4½d.[35] Already it is likely that the
demesne was let, and it was certainly so by the early
16th century. By that time the estate was divided
for administrative purposes between the 'manors'
of Misterton, Crewkerne Magna, and Crewkerne
Parva. Between 1524 and 1545 the two items of
account to show an increase were perquisites of
the manor court, held for all three 'manors' together,
and the arrears on Crewkerne Magna.[36] Actual
cash income varied between £74 and £113 on
Crewkerne Magna and between £57 and £60 on
Crewkerne Parva, where arrears were negligible.
The main income in both was rents: just over £70
on Crewkerne Magna until the sale of Upcroft and
Coombe to Sir Hugh Poulett in 1541, when they
fell to just under £55; and nearly £60 on Crewkerne
Parva. The income from Crewkerne Magna included
rents from shambles, stalls, shops, and tolls in the
market place and from tenants in Hewish and
Woolminstone. Rents on Crewkerne Parva came
similarly from town as well as parish.

In the later 16th century Crewkerne manor
covered about 2,600 a., including some 420 a. at
Woolminstone, 180 a. at Coombe, 140 a. at Hewish,
and 70 a. at Clapton. There were 8 freeholders and
103 customary tenants, excluding those at Misterton
and Ashcombe in Wayford. Of these one tenant,
Magdalene Partridge, held nearly 300 a., of which
120 a. lay in Woolminstone, and Agnes Stembridge
occupied 122 a. No other tenement exceeded 100 a.
and, apart from cottagers, most holdings were
between 10 a. and 40 a. each. Common pasture was
evidently allotted on the larger tenements in units
of 22 sheep for each, and on holdings of 6 a. or
less for two kine and a bullock each on Roundham,
giving total commoning by the tenants for 683
sheep, 60 kine, and 30 bullocks. Over 300 a. at
Furringdons had been parcelled out in closes of
between 10 a. and 39 a. each, and the former
demesne at Craft had evidently been divided since
1541 into ten allotments of between 20 a. and 28 a.
each.[37] By 1599 the manorial area had shrunk to
just over 2,200 a. It was then 'very good and fruitful
for corn, pasture, and meadow'. Roundham common then comprised 80 a. and was pastured by the
cottagers between Holyrood day (14 Sept.) and
Christmas. The first crop of a common meadow
called Corymead was taken by the tenants, who
thereafter pastured there between Lammas and
Christmas. The tithings of Crewkerne Magna and
Parva were free to pasture the common fields in
summer with as many cattle as they could support
in winter, and sheep pasture in the common fields
had been increased to 90 sheep for each tenement.[38]
In 1658 presentments for depasturing involved
5,980 sheep, and in 1663 c. 4,000.[39]

The granting of 3,000-year leases by the lords of
fractions of tenements started in 1599 and continued until at least 1665, although it was principally carried out between 1610 and 1618. The
quarter retained by the Pouletts was generally
leased to tenants for terms of 21 years, although
some leases for 99 years or lives and copyhold
transactions have been noted. The long leaseholds
so granted encouraged the creation of larger
holdings, particularly from the 18th century.

Of the lesser manors and freeholds the rectory
estate of nearly 500 a. was by far the largest.
Eastham manor had an area of 125 a. in 1693,
little changed from its extent of 106 a. in 1295.[40] In
1694 it was 'as fine a thing of the bigness as England
can afford', with new buildings and well-watered
land, the best worth 40s. an acre and none less than
20s.[41] The Clapton estate was somewhat larger, at
least 190 a. in 1715; Henley manor was 200 a. let to
26 tenants in 1699, and Hewish manor comprised c.
166 a. at its partition in 1740.[42] Another estate centred
on Woolminstone was gradually accumulated by a
branch of the Merifield family during the 17th and
18th centuries, and amounted to 513 a. in 1752.

In 1796 426 a. of Woolminstone property were
purchased by the Pouletts[43] and were added to
a growing estate which in the late 18th and 19th
centuries dominated the rural areas in the north
and west of the parish. The family had held lands
known as Upcroft and Coombe from 1541 and
added Henley to this in 1700. Although they
disposed of their quarter interest in about 1,500 a.
in 1810–11,[44] by 1820 they held 2,228 a. in the
parish, including Woolminstone (458 a.), Henley
(473 a.), Coombe (636 a.), and Fordscroft (198 a.).
The largest estate in 1839 was still that of the
Pouletts, although it had fallen in size to 1,765 a.
It was followed by the Husseys with c. 500 a.,
Clapton Court with 251 a., the Donisthorpe lands
of 226 a., and seven other holdings of over 100 a.
each. The three principal Poulett farms of Coombe,
Woolminstone, and Henley accounted for over
a third of the parish's total area.[45] By 1851 there
were 7 farms of 300 a. or more and a further 8 over
100 a., the farmers in the parish then employing
just over 300 labourers.[46]

The extent of the three open arable fields in
Crewkerne manor had been diminished by inclosure
by the late 16th century, and the process continued
into the 19th century, evidently by private agreement. Those fields were worked only by the tenants
of the manors of Crewkerne Magna and Parva.
The outlying hamlets of Coombe, Woolminstone,
Hewish, Clapton, and possibly Henley and Eastham
may have had their own field systems, but the fields
must have been inclosed by the late 16th century,
and surviving names do not permit their reconstruction.[47] Some few strips survived in 1886: at
Boscombe, Broadshord, Long Strings, Butts, and
Wire Pits in the former East field, Saunders Piece in

[33] C 135/62/4.   [34] B.L. Add. Ch. 13972.
[35] E. Devon R.O., CR 531.
[36] S.C. 6/Hen. VIII/6174–6181; see also an acct. for
1514–15: E. Devon R.O., CR 528.
[37] S.R.O., DD/PT, box 47, survey n.d.
[38] S.R.O., T/PH/hsy, survey 1599.
[39] Ct. bks. 1651–77, penes Countess Poulett, Jersey,
sub Crewkerne hundred.
[40] S.R.O., DD/PH 61; D/D/B reg 1: Crewkerne dues,

inside front cover.
[41] S.R.O., DD/PH 224/68.
[42] S.R.O., DD/HKE 1/10; DD/SS, bdle. 18; DD/PT,
box 23 (partition 1740).
[43] S.R.O., DD/PT, box 21A, abstr. of title.
[44] S.R.O., DD/SB 38/1.
[45] S.R.O., tithe award.   [46] H.O. 107/1928.
[47] S.R.O., T/PH/hsy, survey 1599; DD/PT, box 47,
survey n.d.

the North field, and at Bush field in South field, but these had been inclosed by 1931.[48] Common pasture of 90 a. at Roundham and Marsh was inclosed in 1823 by Act of Parliament. Sale allotments accounted for 47 a., more than half, Lord Poulett received 7½ a., and John Hussey and his tenants of the rectory manor 29 a.[49]

A detailed statement of the farming of Woolminstone survives. Of a total of 382 a., 152 a. were arable. Nearly a third was devoted to wheat in 1820, 27 a. to barley, 22 a. to clover and oats, 15½ a. to turnips, 15 a. to oats alone, and smaller areas to beans, ever grass, and White Dutch marl, with 19 a. lying fallow. There were 180 sheep in 1820, when 200 lambs were shorn, and 260 sheep with lambs in 1822; and dairy cows, plough oxen, horses, and young stock 'bred for plough and pail' were grazed on a total of just over 220 a. of meadow and pasture.[50] Crewkerne, like many other places, was affected by a fall in the value of land in the early 19th century. One farmer indicated in 1816 that the fixed rents, particularly on estates held under trustees, would drive his fellows to ruin, dairy lands having lost a third, good arable a half, and grazing lands two fifths of their former values. Poor arable land could then no longer be cultivated since the income from crops would not cover the cost of sowing and much had been laid down to grass.[51] Coombe farm was considered a model unit in the mid 19th century with the most modern machinery, including Chandler's liquid-manure drill, one of Hornsby's drills, a drying kiln for corn, a bone-crushing mill powered by water, and 'scarifiers' and pressers. The farmer had introduced a three-year rotation system of two root crops followed by wheat, and on his 700 a. had 40 Devon cows and 500 breeding Dorset ewes, besides other sheep.[52]

In 1839 the parish was almost equally divided between arable and grass, with 132 a. of wood. By 1905, however, there was nearly twice as much meadow and pasture as arable, although mixed as well as dairy farming has continued to the present day.[53] The Pouletts sold their 640-a. Henley estate in 1911 and some 900 a., including Fordscroft, Coombe, and Lower Coombe farms, were conveyed to the University of Oxford in 1941.[54] In 1939 there were eight farms with over 150 a. each.[55] In 1976 the parish was primarily devoted to grazing livestock, predominantly dairy, and Coombe farm specialized in milk products, especially cheese.

Henley Manor farm of 440 a. was one of five farms in the country used by I.C.I. for the investigation and demonstration of agricultural methods.[56]

TRADE AND INDUSTRY. The existence at Crewkerne of a market and of a pre-Conquest mint during the reigns of Ethelred II and Cnut[57] at least implies a concentration of population for the purposes of trade, but the absence of any evidence of significant urban organization thereafter suggests a decline common to other Somerset towns of the 11th century.[58] Medieval accounts and rentals survive for estates whose property was largely concentrated in the outlying parts of the parish, and only occasional occupation-names and the foundation of the fair bear witness to any development in urban settlement and trade. A family of goldsmiths, active in the 13th and early 14th centuries, was evidently prominent in local affairs.[59] Single references in the later Middle Ages to a chapman, a draper, a dyer, a glover, a hooper, a mercer, a tailor, a weaver, and a whittawer, while evidently involving a concentration on the clothing trade, are not enough to suggest any significant volume of business, though a link with Bridport in 1318,[60] and obvious business connexions outside the parish in the 15th century are indicated.[61] The habit of including occupations in the parish registers of the 16th century onwards certainly reveals a continuing concentration on cloth. Most significant in the 16th century is the appearance of two French weavers, one a linen worker, in the 1560s,[62] and a gradual widening of manufactures thereafter to include felt, fustian, white yarn, bone lace, and finally, by the end of the 17th century, serge.[63]

Associated trades in the same period included clothiers, drapers, a dyer, a fuller, haberdashers, hatters, a hosier, mercers, a milliner, ropers, and tailors.[64] During that period, too, the professions were represented by three attornies, two apothecaries, two doctors, including Daubeney Turberville of Wayford well known as an eye specialist in the 1650s,[65] an organ-maker, practising his craft at Lyme Regis in 1551,[66] a gardener, and a continuing succession of goldsmiths.[67] Prominent among local suppliers to Lord Poulett was John Greenway, variously described as merchant and grocer,[68] who in the early months of 1653 sold his customer such luxuries as capers, olives, spice, and sugar for the table, stockings, silk, fustian, cheyney, galoon,

[48] O.S. Map 6″, Som. LXXXVIII. NE. SE., LXXXIX. NW. SW., XCII. NW., Dors. XIX. NE. (1931 edn.); Char. Com. files.
[49] S.R.O., CR 26. [50] S.R.O., DD/PT, box 37.
[51] Agric. State of Kingdom (Bd. of Agric. 1816), ii. 9.
[52] T.D. Acland and W. Sturge, The Farming of Som. 1851), 70–1.
[53] S.R.O., tithe award; statistics supplied by the then Bd. of Agric. 1905.
[54] S.R.O., DD/SAS, C/2273, 1/C/8.2; sale cat., University Estate, 1958. [55] Kelly's Dir. Som. (1939).
[56] Ex inf. Mr. M. E. Hutchinson.
[57] Anglo-Saxon Coins, ed. R. H. M. Dolley, 146; G. C. Brooke, English Coins, 71; Sylloge of Coins of the British Isles, 7, no. 120; 13, nos. 298–301.
[58] Dom. Geog. SW. England, ed. H. C. Darby and R. Welldon Finn, 201–2, 204–5.
[59] C 133/6/1; B.L. Add. MS. 49359, f. 74v.; Forde Abbey, Cart. pp. 386–90; Devon R.O., TD 51, pp. 186–96, 199–200; S.R.S. xi, pp. 86, 115; xii. 64; xliv. 247; Hist. MSS. Com. 5, 6th Rep., Bridport, p. 488.

[60] Hist. MSS. Com. 5, 6th Rep., Bridport, p. 488.
[61] B.L. Add. MS. 49359, f. 76v.; Devon R.O., TD 51, pp. 194–5; S.R.S. xi, p. 143; xvii. 41; Cal. Pat. 1416–22, 352; 1422–9, 371; 1441–6, 8, 378; 1467–77, 380.
[62] Robert the Frenchman alias Robert Cartall d. 1573; another Frenchman d. 1567: S.R.O., D/P/crew 2/1/1.
[63] S.R.O., D/P/crew 2/1/1; DD/PT, boxes 22B, 23; DD/SS, bdle. 57; DD/SP, boxes 12–13; S.R.S. xxiii. 84.
[64] S.R.O., DD/SS, bdles. 53–5, 57; DD/PT, boxes 12, 22B, 23, 24A, 40; DD/SP, boxes 11, 14; D/D/Cm; D/P/crew 2/1/1; Cornw. R.O. 22M/DT/42/6; S.R.S. xxiv. 21; xxvii. 114; Cal. Pat. 1553–4, 424, 454; 1554–5, 140; Cal. S.P. Dom. 1625–49, 478.
[65] Munic. Rec. Dorchester, ed. C. H. Mayo, 520; S.R.O., D/P/hin. g 4/1/1, sub anno 1678–9.
[66] C 24/35/19; S.R.O., D/P/crew 2/1/1; Grove's Dict. of Music and Musicians, ed. Bloom (5th edn.), vii. 187, sub Robartt.
[67] S.R.O., D/P/crew 2/1/1, 2/1/3, 4/1/1; DD/SS, bdles. 53, 55; S.R.S. xxiii. 227; M.I. to Sweet fam. in ch.
[68] S.R.O., DD/PT, boxes 22B, 24A, 40.

ribbon, buttons, whalebone thread, and trimming to clothe family and household, and pitch, tar, tallow, linseed oil, white lead, and books of gold leaf for use in the garden and for decorating the new rooms at Hinton House.[69] Greenway and four fellow tradesmen issued tokens between 1666 and 1670.[70]

The geographical position of the town on the London road to the south-west had an important bearing on its economy, and by the 1580s the town was a regular post stage.[71] Travellers requiring help from the parish, using both the London road and the road from the south coast, became a serious charge at the end of the 17th century. There were as many as 297 in 1659, 360 in 1675, 282 in 1687, and 785 in 1693, the last number including 536 seamen, 128 soldiers, and 67 'Dutchmen'.[72] Several inns, catering both for travellers and attenders at the market, have continuous histories from the 16th or 17th centuries, most notably the George, first mentioned in a rental no later than 1541.[73] Other prominent inns of the 17th century were the Green Dragon (formerly the Cock) in Fore Street, the Gun in East Street, the Swan, and the Red Lion, followed by the Angel, the Ship, the Lamb, and the Labour in Vain.[74]

During the early 18th century clothing appears to have continued as the dominant industry in the town, particularly in the Foster and Tyler families, the latter insuring textile mills in 1730 and 1740.[75] Sergemakers occur regularly between 1720 and 1761,[76] a dyer, two linen-weavers, and a woolbroker in 1704, a haberdasher and hosier in 1724, a bodice maker and worsted-comber in 1726, and a woolcomber in 1765.[77] Other trades represented include an engraver in 1701, a basket maker, silver-wire drawer, and rope maker in 1704, a tanner in 1727, and peruke makers in 1730 and 1751.[78] The Fitchett family were prominent tallow chandlers and soap-boilers between 1704 and 1764.[79]

Girth-web weavers had come to the parish by 1698[80] and the allied manufacturers of webbing, sailcloth, hair-seating, and later shirts eventually came to dominate the 19th-century labour market. The first factory was probably established in 1789 at Viney Bridge by Samuel Sparks (d. 1827), a Crewkerne solicitor, and Bartholomew Gidley (d. 1812–13). A bleaching or 'bucking' house was built there, and the same firm had a spinning house in Hermitage Street.[81] In 1797 the partners issued tokens from their 'linen and woollen girth web manufactory'. There were two other factories by 1823, William Dummet's in East Street (moved to North Street by 1840) and William French's in Carter Street.

Robert Bird had established himself in Church Street by 1840, had moved to Sheep Market Street by 1842 in partnership with Thomas Matthews, and, again alone, had his factory with 180 hands in South Street by 1850.[82] Tail mill was acquired c. 1825 by Richard Hayward (d. 1852), a sailcloth maker of West Chinnock, and by 1840 it was being run by one of his sons. Another son developed a London outlet for the firm's products, and 132 workers were employed at Tail mill by 1851.[83] After a dispute in 1868 the Hayward business was divided between two firms: R. Hayward and Company took over the Coker works in North Street and Greenham mill, and Richard Hayward and Sons continued at Tail mill, both producing canvas and sailcloth. The Haywards left Tail mill in 1929, selling their goodwill and trademarks to a Scottish firm.[84] Greenham, a sailcloth mill by 1840 and used for flax and tow spinning by 1851, was sold in 1931, although R. Hayward and Company were continuing at the Coker works in 1939.[85]

Henry Holman (d. 1858) took over the former Sparks factory at Viney Bridge by 1830,[86] and Thomas Matthews and Sons at Poples Well and Sheep Market Street added curled hair and hair seating to their manufacture of girth-webs. John Wall Row had also set up a sailcloth factory in North Street by 1850.[87] Thomas Matthews, who had discontinued his factory by 1883, was apparently succeeded by Samuel Laycock and Sons, and by 1883 Arthur Hart had taken over Holman's Viney Bridge works. Robert Bird and Company survived in South Street until 1931, and the factory of Arthur Hart and Son at Viney Bridge was, in 1976, the home of Crewkerne Textiles, uniting the former Hart, Hayward, and Bird companies. The firm was acquired in 1976 by Bridport-Gundry, net makers.[88]

The present factory includes a range of buildings beside the stream dating from the late 18th and early 19th centuries, including one bearing the letters 'S & G' and the date 1793.

In 1872 the West Somerset and Devon Shirt Manufacturing Company started in Market Street and had moved to Abbey Street by 1875. Another factory was added in North Street in 1880 and the firm had about 600 employees in 1897. By 1939 it had taken over Southcombe's shirt factory in North Street and from 1950 occupied the former works of Robert Bird and Company. In 1953 the business was purchased by Van Heusens of Taunton, but it closed in 1976. The Abbey Street factory was occupied from 1953 by 'Bonsoir' shirt and pyjama makers.[89]

By c. 1797 other miscellaneous trades and

[69] S.R.O., DD/PT, box 40.　[70] Taunton, Som. Co. Mus.
[71] Hist. MSS. Com. 73, *Exeter*, p. 65; ibid. 9, *Salisbury*, xiv, p. 79; xv, p. 170.　[72] S.R.O., D/P/crew 4/1/1.
[73] E. Devon R.O., CR 550. There was also then a cottage called the Star; S.R.O., T/PH/hsy, survey 1599; DD/CGS 1/4, 16–20, 2/2, 3/1; C 78/1156/89; Cornw. R.O. 22M/DT/42/6.
[74] S.R.O., D/P/crew 4/1/1; DD/CGS 1/4, 16–20, 2/2, 3/1; DD/SP, box 12 (1686).
[75] *S. & D. N. & Q.* xxx. 183.
[76] S.R.O., DD/SS, bdles. 53, 55–7.
[77] S.R.O., D/P/crew 2/1/3; DD/SS, bdles. 53, 56–7; DD/PT, box 24A.
[78] S.R.O., DD/PT, box 23; D/P/crew 2/1/3; DD/SS, bdle. 56; Q/RL.　[79] S.R.O., D/P/crew 2/1/3.
[80] S.R.O., DD/HK, box 1, conveyance 25 Dec. 1701.

[81] S.R.O., DD/SB 38/1; *Univ. Brit. Dir.* ii.
[82] Pigot, *Nat. Com. Dir.* (1822–3, 1842); *County Gazette Dir.* (1840); Hunt & Co. *Dir. Som.* (1850); H.O. 107/1928.
[83] S.R.O., D/P/crew 13/1/2; *County Gazette Dir.* (1840); *Som. Year Bk.* (1936), 95–7; H.O. 107/1928.
[84] *Som. Year Bk.* (1936), 95–7.
[85] *County Gazette Dir.* (1840); H.O. 107/1928; deeds of Greenham mill *penes* Messrs. Sparks and Blake, Crewkerne; *Kelly's Dir. Som.* (1939).
[86] S.R.O., DD/SB 26/1.
[87] Hunt & Co. *Dir. Som.* (1850).
[88] *P.O. Dir. Som.* (1875); *Kelly's Dir. Som.* (1883–1931); *Crewkerne Official Guide* (n.d. c. 1972); *Western Gazette*, 1 July 1976.
[89] *P.O. Dir. Som.* (1875); *Kelly's Dir. Som.* (1906–39); ex inf. Mr. W. B. Harwood, Crewkerne.

manufactures had developed in the town, including maltsters, vintners, clockmakers, a printer, a breeches maker, ironmongers, and three butter factors.[90] Apart from the 22 per cent of the working population employed in the sailcloth industry, there were in 1851 about 140 glovers, mainly female outworkers supplying factories elsewhere, 82 female dress makers, and 76 boot and shoe makers. The principal shoemaker, William Lucy in South Street, had a work force of eleven under him and the Public Benefit Boot Company was still flourishing in 1910.[91] Other minor industries represented in 1851 included basket, straw-bonnet, sieve, and trunk makers.[92] There were brick and tile works in North Street in 1841, at Furringdons in 1854, and at Henley in 1886, a fourth at Maiden Beech surviving until 1939.[93] An industrial estate was established in 1958 at Blacknell Lane and on adjacent sites at Cropmead, and a smaller area on the former mill and brewery sites in North Street. Industries represented include a foundry firm specializing in nickel and chrome castings and horticultural engineers.[94] In 1976 Tail mill housed Merriott Mouldings Limited, a plastics moulding company.

A bank was opened by Hoskins, Gray, Hoskins, and Company in the late 18th century. It was joined by another, next to the George inn, founded in 1806 by Sparks and Gidley, the sailcloth makers, and in 1810 by a third, established by Robert Perham and Thomas Phelps, butter factors, which took over the Hoskins bank in 1816. The Sparks bank suspended payment in 1829, owing to over-speculation in the lace and sailcloth industries, and both the surviving banks were assimilated by Stuckey's bank in the same year. Perham, Phelps, and their banking partner from 1821, Peter Smith Payne, were butter factors who were prominent among others with financial interests in trade through Lyme Regis with ports further east.[95]

The town's professional men in the 19th century included 5 attorneys, 4 surgeons, and 2 auctioneers in 1823, 6 surgeons by 1830, and 7 by 1840. Also by 1830 there were 2 chemists, 2 perfumiers and hairdressers, 2 veterinary surgeons, and by 1840 a land surveyor and 3 printers and booksellers.[96] The most prominent printer and bookseller was G. P. R. Pulman (d. 1880). Between 1849 and 1851 he issued the *United Counties Miscellany*, was editor of the *Yeovil Times*, in 1857 founded *Pulman's Weekly News and Advertiser*, a paper continuing in 1976, and wrote a local history, the *Book of the Axe*.[97] The *County Mail*, an advertisement newssheet, was started in the town by James Wheatley in 1878 and was still issued in 1976.[98]

MARKETS AND FAIR. In 1086 a market at Crewkerne paid £4.[99] In 1267–8 it was let to farm with a mill and other properties, and in 1274, when shared between John de Courtenay and John de Lisle, it was worth £5.[1] Twenty years later, when linked with the fair and still held in halves, it was worth £6 13s. 4d.[2] One half was sub-let by 1315 for £3 6s. 8d.[3] By 1504 the tolls of the market were let with shambles, stalls, and shops in the market place for £4 13s. 4d., a figure which remained constant at least until 1545.[4] From 1511 the whole, which apparently also included the profits of the fair, was let by the Crown to Sylvester Stewkley. Stewkley later assigned his lease to Sir Richard Sackville, though William Glover and William Anston of Crewkerne claimed 'by inheritance' and took the profits.[5]

By the end of the 16th century the market was held every Saturday. It was said to be 'well served and furnished with all kinds of wares and victuals out of all parts of the county'. With the fair it was worth £40, but the office of portreeve, the collector of rents, hitherto in the gift of the lord, had been let by copy for lives for £4 13s. 4d.[6] The market itself was let during the 17th century, from 1663 until 1694 or later to John Marder.[7] By 1699, the property was worth £90 a year. Three quarters were held in fee and the remainder for three lives; the tenant in fee was Carleton Whitelock, son-in-law to Sir Andrew Henley.[8] The Pouletts, who owned the remaining quarter share, seem to have bought up the rest c. 1742, when they leased the tolls and profits of all markets and fairs for seven years for £140.[9] Sheep markets for ten weeks in the Spring of 1749 were worth £27 12s. 6d., and lettings from the shambles and outstandings were at the annual rate of £88 10s. Lessees included 37 butchers and 49 traders in the stalls, both in the market place and under the market house, among them two bakers from South Petherton and one from Cerne Abbas (Dors.).[10] In 1787 fairs and markets were let together for ten years for £90.[11]

In 1811 Earl Poulett sold the market and fair rights to William Gray, a Crewkerne banker, for £3,716.[12] On Gray's death in 1817 they passed to his great-nephew John Gray Draper (d. 1843) and then to John's son William. In 1898 William Gray Draper sold his interest to a group of local men who formed the Crewkerne Fair and Markets Company. This company, which rented and later purchased a site for the stock market off West Street, in 1956 sold the Victoria Hall to the Urban District Council, retaining in 1976 only the right to hold the annual fair in the centre of the town.[13]

[90] *Univ. Brit. Dir.* ii.
[91] H.O. 107/1928; *Kelly's Dir. Som.* (1910).
[92] H.O. 107/1928.
[93] S.R.O., T/PH/ptr, map 1841; D/P/crew 4/1/14–16; O.S. Map 6″, Dors. XIX. NE. (1886 edn.); *Kelly's Dir. Som.* (1939).
[94] *Crewkerne Official Guide* (n.d. *c.* 1972); local information.
[95] *Univ. Brit. Dir.* ii; P. T. Saunders, *Stuckey's Bank*, 48, 50, 52–3; S.R.O., DD/SB 38/1; ex inf. Mr. M. D. Costen, Bristol.
[96] Pigot, *Nat. Com. Dir.* (1822–3, 1830); *County Gazette Dir.* (1840).
[97] *Selected Poems in the Som. Dialect*, Som. Folk Ser. i (1921), 46; *Pulman's Weekly News*, 10 Feb. 1880.
[98] Ex inf. Mr. Harwood.   [99] *V.C.H. Som.* i. 439.

[1] Bodl. MS. Top. Gen. d. 20; C 133/6/1.
[2] C 133/62/7; S.C. 6/1127/6.
[3] B.L. Add. MS. 49359, f. 74.
[4] E. Devon R.O., CR 528; S.C. 6/Hen. VIII/6183.
[5] E 321/24/92.
[6] S.R.O., T/PH/hsy, survey 1599.
[7] S.R.O., D/P/crew 4/1/1.
[8] S.R.O., DD/SS, bdle. 18.
[9] S.R.O., DD/PT, box 23.
[10] Ibid. In 1708 traders included an Evershot (Dors.) shoemaker and a Shepton Mallet stocking-maker: S.R.O., Q/SR 247/3, 257/7.
[11] S.R.O., DD/PT, box 21.
[12] S.R.O., DD/SB 38/1; Crewkerne Fair and Markets Co., abstr. of title; ex inf. Mr. P. S. Horden, Crewkerne.
[13] MSS. *penes* Crewkerne Fair and Markets Co.

In 1820 the market and fair together were rated at £80 and in 1824 the income from tolls was £19 1s.[14] In 1830 the market was said to be a good one for corn and 'other marketable articles', and there were extra sales in April and May for sheep and cattle.[15] By 1840 the Saturday market specialized in corn, meat, and vegetables, and there was also another on Wednesdays.[16] By the early 1850s both Wednesday and Saturday had been established as market days; there were 'great markets' on alternate Saturdays for corn, cattle, and flax, with sheep markets 'numerously attended' in April and May, September, and October.[17] Monthly sheep and cattle sales were held regularly by the 1870s, and by the late 1890s these were held on Tuesdays.[18] At the turn of the century they were transferred from the market place to a sale yard off West Street. By the beginning of the First World War markets were held only on alternate Tuesdays, with monthly stock sales, a practice which continued until c. 1956, when stock sales ceased.[19] During the 1970s Crewkerne became a centre for Fine Art sales.

By 1511 there were shambles and shops in the market place associated with the market and fair.[20] Leland described 'a pretty cross environed with small pillars', and 'a pretty town house' which stood in the market place[21] between the cross on the south and the town well on the north. By 1541 the house was let to the churchwardens.[22] In 1660 the central block was let to John Serry, barber surgeon, while the wardens continued to pay rent for a quarter, sub-letting it to the tenant of the market.[23] The fourth quarter was let from 1684 to a merchant, subject to its use as a court house.[24] The building continued to be let in parts until c. 1742, when it was probably rebuilt.[25] A lease of the house in 1787 offered it as a silk factory.[26]

The mid-18th-century market house or town hall was raised on arches and was reached by a wide staircase. A 'south piazza' was added in 1836 after the demolition of the shambles. One of the rooms was used in the mid 19th century for depositing flax sent for sale. This building was extensively remodelled and the arches filled by Charles Benson of Yeovil in 1900 to create the Victoria Hall and a number of shops and offices.[27]

An annual fair on St. Bartholomew's day (24 August) was established probably in the 1270s.[28] It was evidently let with the market during the Middle Ages, and was described as a 'great fair' in 1599.[29] Its date was changed in 1753 to 4 September, and

in 1767 was said to be noted for horses, bullocks, linen drapery, cheese, and 'toys'.[30] Sheep, horses, bullocks, and cheese were its specialities a century later, and it was unrivalled in the county as a pleasure fair.[31] By this time it lasted for two days, and the sale of its rights to the Crewkerne Fair and Markets Company in 1898 included hurdles to pen at least 60 dozen sheep. The growth of the weekly cattle market in the early 20th century gradually confined the fair to pleasure, though in 1974 stalls and sideshows occupied the market place and Market Street and spilled over into Church Street and the western end of East Street. Early in the century there was also a regular Whitsun fair, evidently held like other travelling shows on the Fair Field or Chubbs Lawn, on the south side of West Street.[32]

MILLS. In 1086 there were six mills in Crewkerne, four on the principal manor, one on the rectory estate, and one on Eastham manor.[33] Only that at Eastham can positively be identified. By the 13th century there were at least eight, and possibly nine, but it is not clear which had 11th-century sites.

Eastham mill, part of Eastham manor, was in 1296 occupied by Alice of the mills.[34] In 1320 it was leased to Richard Lough and it was probably this mill, with a dovecot and 22 a., which was held by Robert Lough in 1361.[35] Richard and Alice Pruet held it in 1426 and it was sometimes described as two mills at various dates from 1597.[36] In 1693 the water-grist mill with a malt mill was occupied by Richard Sherlock the elder.[37] The mill and mill-house were known as Pikers mill c. 1820, but were disused by 1842.[38] The mill stood about 250 yds. SSE. of Higher Easthams Farm, the former manor-house, its site marked by an overgrown stone wall. The mill was evidently overshot, driven by a leat running east along the contour.

In 1228 a mill at Clapton, formerly held by Walter le Despenser, was exchanged by his widow Agatha with Baldwin of Clapton, then lord of Clapton manor.[39] Baldwin let the mill to Adam Rys, burgess of Taunton. Rys was succeeded by his sister, Avice de la Barre. She sold it to William de Lo, clerk, who conveyed it to Walter Boce in 1263. In the same year Boce obtained the right to divert water from the river Axe to drive the mill.[40] This source of water seems to identify the property with the present Clapton mills which in 1976 were still partly driven by a leat fed from the Axe.

[14] S.R.O., D/P/crew 13/1/1; MSS. penes Crewkerne Fair and Markets Co.
[15] Pigot, Nat. Com. Dir. (1830).
[16] County Gazette Dir. (1840).
[17] Crewkerne in 1851 (statistical table etc. in church).
[18] P.O. Dir. Som. (1875); Kelly's Dir. Som. (1889, 1897); ex inf. Mr. Horden.
[19] Kelly's Dir. Som. (1914, 1939); ex inf. Mr. Horden.
[20] E 321/24/92; S.C. 6/Hen. VIII/6174; E. Devon R.O., CR 528.
[21] Leland, Itin. ed. Toulmin Smith, i. 160.
[22] E. Devon R.O., CR 550; S.R.O., T/PH/hsy, survey 1599; see below, p. 31.
[23] S.R.O., DD/SS, bdle. 54; D/P/crew 4/1/1.
[24] S.R.O., DD/SS, bdles. 53–4.
[25] S.R.O., DD/PT, box 23. Crewkerne in 1851 says c. 1732, but the premises were still being let in quarters in 1741: S.R.O., DD/PT, box 23.
[26] S.R.O., DD/PT, box 21.
[27] Crewkerne in 1851; date on building; Crewkerne

Fair and Markets Co., minute bk. 1898–1918.
[28] It was certainly in existence in 1280, but does not occur with the market in the account of 1267–8 nor in the extent of 1274: Plac. de Quo Warr. (Rec. Com.), 693; Bodl. MS. Top. Gen. d. 20; C 133/6/1.
[29] S.R.O., T/PH/hsy, survey 1599.
[30] Sherborne Mercury, 25 June 1753; Proc. Som. Arch. Soc. lxxxii. 128–9; Bk. of Fairs.
[31] Pigot, Nat. Com. Dir. (1830); County Gazette Dir. (1840); Proc. Som. Arch. Soc. lxxxii. 128–9.
[32] Ex inf. Mr. Horden.
[33] V.C.H. Som. i. 439, 470, 477.
[34] S.R.S. vi. 295–6.   [35] Ibid. xii. 84, 103; xv. 48.
[36] e.g. C.P. 25(2)/207/39 Eliz. I East.; C.P. (25)2/346/9 Jas. I East.; C.P. 25(2)/869/4 Wm. & Mary East.; C.P. 25(2)/869/5 Wm. & Mary Mich.   [37] S.R.O., DD/PH 61.
[38] S.R.O., DD/HK, box 1; DD/SAS, map c. 1820; tithe award. In 1976 the site was known as Pigs mill.
[39] S.R.S. vi. 70–1.
[40] Devon R.O., TD 51 pp. 183–4, 190, 192–8.

Subsequently the mill appears to have been held with Crewkerne manor. It was occupied as a corn mill by Roger Longdon between 1530 and 1541 and was granted by copy in 1553 to Robert Merifield.[41] One Pynnye of Clapton mill was mentioned in 1588, by 1599 the mill was held by John Hitchcock, and in 1625 it was bought by Robert Hitchcock, a Clapton tanner.[42] It was called Langdon's mill in the 1640s and 1650s, and Lower mill when held in 1658 and 1660 by John Palmer. Occupied by Edward Cossins from 1660, it passed c. 1680 to John Palmer (d. 1696), and then to his son John.[43] The mill was worked by the Palmer family until c. 1824, followed by George Trenchard, who owned it in 1827, and William Trenchard before 1842.[44] By 1852 it had been acquired by the Lowmans, lords of Clapton manor, and their last tenant, Robert Lockyer, miller and corn merchant, bought the mill in 1901. The family owned it in 1975.[45] The present mill was built c. 1875 and is powered by two streams, one from the Axe and the other from the mill stream through Clapton, carried on pillars to drive an overshot wheel, 21 ft. in diameter, constructed by Thomas of Beaminster (Dors.) in 1864. In 1976 the mill had three pairs of millstones, a roller mill, and a cubing plant.[46]

A second mill at Clapton was held with Clapton manor by 1607 and was probably that mill occupied by John Elford between 1653 and 1663.[47] It was occupied in 1743 by Thomas Guppy,[48] by Richard Cannicott between 1828 and 1845, and by members of the Tucker family until 1861.[49] Soon afterwards the mill, on the west side of the road through Clapton, ceased to grind and was converted to a farm-house held with Clapton Court and known as Court Farm. The mill building survives.

In 1272 Roger de Putford held half of two mills in Crewkerne.[50] They were sold by him to Agnes de Monceaux in 1296, and in 1315 were identified as Paddokeslake mill (in Misterton) and 'Cotemylle', having been given in 1309 to endow the chantry of the Virgin in Crewkerne churchyard.[51] 'Courtesmyll' was mentioned in 1527 and formed part of the lands of the chapel at its dissolution in 1548, when it was occupied by Richard Hull.[52] In 1549 the mill was sold to Robert Wood of the Inner Temple, London, and it was probably one of the two water-grist mills which formed part of the manor of

Crewkerne Chantry in 1572 and 1671.[53] The mill was held between 1742 and 1780 by Adam Martin, under the name of Viney mill, and from 1780 by Roger Cossins.[54] The property was acquired by Sparks and Gidley for webbing manufacture in 1789, when the mill buildings, some yards south of the Lyme Regis road, were incorporated into the expanded Viney Bridge mills.[55]

Bery or Bury mill occurs in 1274. It was then treated separately from four other mills held with Crewkerne manor, and may thus have been of recent foundation.[56] By 1541 it was held by Margaret Gold, widow, under the manor of Crewkerne Parva.[57] John Vanner held it as copyhold from 1563 until after 1599.[58] By 1611 the mill was owned by John Freke of Crewkerne, who assigned his interest to John Daubeney of Woolminstone (d. 1625) in 1619.[59] John Daubeney the younger was still holding it in 1647.[60] By 1677 it had passed to William Hodges of Crewkerne, but its name changed to Whitepot or Whiteford mill. A succession of tenants included Jasper Fone from 1788 until at least 1842.[61] It was known as Town, Whiteford, or Carey mill in 1842 and Bury mills in 1850, by the latter year having been sub-let by Fone's trustees, but it evidently ceased to grind soon after 1860.[62] The mill building west of the church was in 1976 a dwelling-house known as Whitford Mill. The mill leat and mill-pond, which formerly drove an overshot wheel, survived.

A windmill was held at his death c. 1281 by Thomas Trivet under John de Horsey, and then passed to his son William.[63] Fields on the northern slopes of a hill east of North Street and south of Tetts Lane were known as Windmill and may indicate the site.[64]

Tail mill, called the 'Tayle' in 1292, was probably named after the family of Hubert le Taile of Merriott mentioned in 1225.[65] It was held at farm under Crewkerne manor between 1294 and 1297 and was worth 30s. in 1315.[66] It was held by William Mitchell in 1548 and by him or his namesake in 1599.[67] The premises were sold to Henry Elliott in 1632 as a 'late' water-grist mill. 'The house of Henry Elliott called Tayle mill' was a nonconformist preaching place in 1669,[68] and the Elliott family were still occupiers in 1737. It was held from 1760 by successive members of the Parker family.

[41] E. Devon R.O., CR 550; S.R.O., DD/PT, box 47, survey n.d.
[42] S.R.O., D/P/crew 2/1/1; T/PH/hsy, survey 1599; Cornw. R.O. 22M/DT/42/6.
[43] S.R.O., D/P/crew 4/1/1; DD/HKE 1/3.
[44] S.R.O., D/P/crew 13/1/1–3; DD/SB 38/1; DD/BD 46; Q/RE; tithe award.
[45] S.R.O., D/P/crew 13/1/2; Hunt & Co. Dir. Som. (1850); P.O. Dir. Som. (1866); Morris & Co. Dir. Som. (1872); ex inf. Mr. C. G. Lockyer, Clapton.
[46] Ex inf. Mr. Lockyer.
[47] S.R.S. li, p. 179; S.R.O., D/P/crew 4/1/1.
[48] S.R.O., DD/HKE 1/6, 10.
[49] S.R.O., D/P/crew 13/2/10; Q/REr, box 9; Hunt & Co. Dir. Som. (1850); Slater, Nat. Com. Dir. (1852–3); Harrison, Harrod, & Co. Dir. Som. (1859); P.O. Dir. Som. (1861).
[50] S.R.S. xxxvi. 166–7.
[51] Ibid. vi. 297–8; B.L. Add. MS. 49359, f. 74.
[52] S.R.S. ii. 176.
[53] Cal. Pat. 1549–51, 97; C.P. 25(2)/204/14 & 15 Eliz. I Mich; C.P. 43/352 rot. 177.
[54] S.R.O., D/P/crew 13/2/2–9; DD/PT, box 39, survey 1770; DD/MR 32.

[55] S.R.O., DD/MR 32; DD/SB 7/2; DD/PRN, map of Misterton 1770; O.S. Map 6″, Som. LXXXIX. SW. (1886 edn.).
[56] C 133/6/1.
[57] C 133/62/7; E. Devon R.O., CR 550.
[58] S.R.O., DD/PT, box 47, survey n.d.; T/PH/hsy, survey 1599.
[59] S.R.O., DD/MR 25.
[60] S.R.S. lxvii, p. 103; DD/PT, box 12, partition 1647.
[61] S.R.O., DD/SS, bdle. 53; D/P/crew 13/2/1–9; DD/PT, box 39, survey 1770.
[62] Pigot, Nat. Com. Dir. (1842); Hunt & Co. Dir. Som. (1850); Morris & Co. Dir. Som. (1872); S.R.O., tithe award; D/P/crew 4/3/1, 13/1/3.
[63] Cal. Inq. p.m. ii, p. 238; Cal. Fine R. 1272–1307, 144.
[64] S.R.O., tithe award.
[65] S.R.S. xi, p. 50; C 133/62/7.
[66] C 133/62/7; S.C. 6/1127/16; B.L. Add. MS. 49359, f. 74.
[67] S.R.O., DD/PT, box 47, survey n.d.; T/PH/hsy, survey 1599.
[68] S.R.O., DD/SS, bdles. 53–4; A. Gordon, Freedom after Ejection, 91, 333.

George Parker sold the mill c. 1825 to Richard Hayward, when the mill was converted to the manufacture of sailcloth and flax and tow spinning.[69] Merriott Mouldings Ltd. was established there in 1938. The earliest buildings probably date from the late 18th and early 19th centuries, and are of stone with brick voussoirs to the windows. To the north is the base for a chimney, presumably connected with a large steam engine, and several more buildings, mostly of one storey, which were probably erected in the later 19th century as weaving sheds.

Hewish mill was mentioned in 1292, but by 1294 it had been 'totally destroyed'.[70] John Browning had a corn-mill there c. 1530–41 and from 1583 until 1618 it was held by Peter Downham as a copyhold.[71] Peter's son, John, bought a long lease of part of the mill in 1618, and assigned it in 1635 to his son, also John.[72] This son, a worsted-maker from Glastonbury, assigned his interest to Robert Ford of Hawkchurch (Devon), whose father, James Ford, took long leases of the rest of the mill in 1637 and 1638. The property was then known as Downham's mill and was occupied by James Downham. In 1668 Robert Ford assigned the mill to Richard Minterne of Meerhay, Beaminster (Dors.), and in 1701 John Minterne settled it on his daughter, Joan, and her husband John Whitehead, a miller from Netherbury (Dors.). The Whiteheads sold it in 1705 to Tristram Palmer of Montacute, mill carpenter, who assigned it in the following year to the tenant from 1684, John Rowsell of Merriott.[73] Thomas Rowsell owned and occupied the mill, again known as Hewish mill, by 1730, and from his brother Henry, a mill carpenter of Merriott, it passed in 1737 to William White, then the tenant. In 1766 White conveyed the mill to his son Robert, on Robert's marriage, in return for a lease of a newly-built house and stable beside the mill, the use of an oat-meal mill and drying house, and a payment of 1s. a sack for oats produced by him as an 'out sheller'.[74]

In 1793 the mill was destroyed by fire. Robert Hull of Dowlish Wake rebuilt it in the same year and assigned it in 1795 to John Bartlett, a Merriott miller.[75] In 1812 Bartlett agreed that the tenant of Coombe farm might pond back the water at night to drive a recently-built threshing mill and machine.[76] By 1829 the mill had been purchased by Lord Poulett, and was leased with Coombe farm.[77] In 1840 Job Ireland was miller at Hewish followed by John Manley in 1850.[78] The Manleys continued to work the mill until it became a farm in 1925; it has since been known as Hewish Mill farm. The mill-house, evidently that built after the fire in

1793, lies at the southern end of Hewish village and the leat, mill-pond, and sluice survived in 1976. The overshot mill-wheel was removed during the Second World War.[79]

Coombe mill and Dunnings mill, valued in 1292 at 6s. and 16s. 8d. respectively, were held at farm under Crewkerne manor between 1294 and 1297. In 1315 a house with half of Dunnings mill and 2 a. of land produced 15s.[80] Neither has been subsequently traced, although Coombe mill probably lay near the present Coombe farm.

A mill and lands in Crewkerne and adjacent parishes were leased by Thomas and Parnell de Baa to John and Alice Crosse in 1353,[81] but have not been subsequently traced.

In 1484 John Lisle and Avice his wife granted to Henry and Isabel Burnel their interest for Avice's life in a mill in Crewkerne.[82] On Isabel's death in 1524 her possessions included a water-mill which passed to her son John and was sold by him to Humphrey Walrond in 1541.[83] Its site has not been identified.

Henry Lede held a grain mill c. 1530–41, which had passed by 1599 to Thomas Hawkins.[84] References in 1578 to John Hill of Hewish, miller, and in 1581 to one Hill at Hawkins mill, suggest that the property may have been a second mill at Hewish.[85] Atkins or Atkings mill, mentioned between 1653 and 1658, may possibly be the same mill under a corrupt name.[86]

In 1571 John Draper and Elizabeth his wife held lands which included a water-mill.[87] The property was still held by John Draper in 1599, and was described as formerly held by the heirs of Downham,[88] possibly ancestors of the later millers at Hewish.

A water-mill probably in Crewkerne was owned in 1606 by Robert Hody (d. 1610) and evidently passed to his son John, who sold it in 1639 to Robert Bowditch.[89] Its later descent has not been noted.

Two mills to the west of North Street were held by Richard Sherlock in the late 17th century. One of these, on the site later occupied by the Coker sailcloth works, was described in 1707 as a paper mill. It was called Hemp Mill in 1770, and in 1811 was the site of a former 'balling' mill.[90] Apart from its water supply all traces have been destroyed. The second mill lay c. ½ mile to the north at Haymore, possibly the Whites mill of the period 1530–41, perpetuated by the field name White Mill or Bowdens Mill.[91] In 1704 the site was occupied by a water-grist mill. Richard Sherlock

[69] S.R.O., D/P/crew 2/1/3, 13/2/2–9; Q/RE; *County Gazette Dir.* (1840); *P.O. Dir. Som.* (1861, 1866, 1875); *Kelly's Dir. Som.* (1883–1902).
[70] C 133/62/7; S.C. 6/1127/16.
[71] E. Devon R.O., CR 550; S.R.O., DD/PT, boxes 22B (deeds of Hewish mill), 47, survey n.d.; T/PH/hsy, survey 1599.
[72] S.R.O., DD/PT, box 22B; DD/SS, bdle. 54.
[73] S.R.O., DD/PT, box 22B; D/P/crew 4/1/1. A reference to George Rowsell of Hewish mill in 1654 suggests an earlier date for family occupation: S.R.O., D/P/crew 2/1/2. [74] S.R.O., DD/PT, boxes 17, 22B.
[75] Ibid. box 21A.
[76] Ibid. box 13, conveyance 1812.
[77] S.R.O., D/P/crew 4/1/2.
[78] *County Gazette Dir.* (1840); Hunt & Co. *Dir. Som.* (1850); *Kelly's Dir. Som.* (1894).

[79] *Kelly's Dir. Som.* (1902–23): ex inf. Mr. H. Stoodley, Crewkerne.
[80] C 133/62/7; S.C. 6/1127/16; B.L. Add. MS. 49359, f. 74.
[81] *S.R.S.* xvii. 24–5. [82] Ibid. xxii. 155.
[83] C 142/41/17; C.P. 25(2)/36/240/32 Hen. VIII East.
[84] E. Devon R.O., CR 550; S.R.O., T/PH/hsy, survey 1599. [85] S.R.O., D/P/crew 2/1/1. [86] Ibid. 4/1/1.
[87] C.P. 25(2)/204/13 Eliz. I Hil.
[88] S.R.O., DD/PT, box 47, survey n.d.; T/PH/hsy, survey 1599.
[89] C.P. 25(2)/345/4 Jas. I East.; C.P. 43/227 rot. 14; C 142/525/163.
[90] S.R.O., DD/SS, bdle, 55; DD/SB 38/1, 48/1.
[91] E. Devon R.O., CR 550; S.R.O., DD/PT, box 22A, lease 1811.

was dead by 1704 and his lands were subsequently divided between his two daughters, Ann wife of the Revd. Amos Martin of Crewkerne, and Elizabeth wife of John Clarke. Clarke took a lease on the mill in 1704 but the premises passed *c.* 1707 to Ann Martin. They had been sold by 1719 to Osborne Thomas, and were known as Haymore mills by 1759 when they were owned by Thomas Templeman of Merriott. They passed *c.* 1760 to Osborne Templeman, who conveyed them *c.* 1778 to John Phelps, descending *c.* 1787 to Thomas Phelps, described *c.* 1797 as a miller, and as a butter merchant by 1811.[92] The Phelps family continued as owners at least until 1852 and successive millers worked it until *c.* 1890.[93]

A third mill on former Sherlock land, probably a water-grist mill, occupied the site of the later Ashlands brewery, also on the west side of North Street. It was held by Henry Marsh between 1761 and 1800 and was known in 1770 as Marshes mill.[94]

Shutteroaks mill occurs in 1748.[95] Its name was changed to No Place mill in 1785, corrupted by the early 19th century to New Place.[96] The Edgars, occupiers since 1788, were still at the mill in 1828, and were succeeded by a number of different families until *c.* 1874.[97] In 1976 the site, just south of the northern parish boundary near Shutteroaks bridge, was occupied by a 20th-century house known as New Place Mill with remains of the mill dam and mill leat.

A paper mill and watercourse were mentioned at the northern end of four closes at Maincombe in 1714.[98] This may possibly represent an earlier reference to New Place mill, or another mill site to the west of it. A further paper mill, in South field, was mentioned in 1723 and 1741, but has not been located.[99]

Stray references to milling activity in the parish include a millward of Furland in 1359, a water-grist mill held by Richard Braine, clerk, in 1633, a mill called Palmers mill in North field in 1715, and Cottens mill in 1741.[1]

LOCAL GOVERNMENT AND PUBLIC SERVICES. The royal manor of Crewkerne T.R.E. included in Wayford, Misterton, Eastham, and Seaborough settlements which subsequently achieved measures of independence as units of secular administration, though they all, with the exception of Eastham, retained the ancient ecclesiastical links with the central mother church. Within the ancient parish from the 16th century units of local government varied. In 1539 for the purposes of a muster the parish comprised the tithings of Crewkerne, Misterton, Woolminstone and Coombe, Furland, and Hewish, while Clapton was linked with the otherwise independent Seaborough.[2] For a similar purpose thirty years later the six tithings were Crewkerne, Misterton, Clapton, Hewish, Woolminstone, and Furland.[3] Tithingmen present at a hundred court *c.* 1586 represented Misterton, Hewish, Eastham, and the two Crewkerne manors, Crewkerne Prima and Crewkerne Secunda.[4] A manorial survey of 1599 divided the property between Crewkerne Magna, Crewkerne Parva, Misterton, Woolminstone, Coombe, Clapton, and Hewish,[5] but by the mid 17th century Crewkerne was divided into three tithings, first, second, and third, together with Woolminstone, Clapton, Hewish, Coombe, Misterton, Furland, and Eastham.[6] By the mid 18th century the same area was divided for tax purposes between the tithings of Town, Misterton, Woolminstone, Coombe, Clapton, Hewish, and Furland.[7]

Manorial jurisdiction claimed in 1280 covered Crewkerne and Misterton but excluded the more ancient members of the royal manor, Wayford, Seaborough, and Eastham. The exact rights are difficult to distinguish from those of the hundred, but the assize of bread and ale, then shared between joint lords, was linked with the market and fair in the vill.[8] Hundred and manor were distinct in 1274, but were apparently administered together in the 1290s and in 1315,[9] although only financial records and not court rolls survive. In the later 14th century the manor courts were attached to one half of the Courtenay estate in Crewkerne, the hundred courts to the other.[10] By the early 16th century the two jurisdictions were quite separate, the manor having two lawdays and six other courts in 1514–15, increased to ten other courts in 1526–7.[11]

Income in the 16th century from strays, fines, heriots, and trespass, and a successful case against the Crown for ownership of a felon's goods, imply a much wider jurisdiction than that claimed in 1280.[12] The division of the manor after 1556 and enfranchisement of properties on three of the four quarters *c.* 1600, effectively put an end to courts for those estates, though in 1599 courts baron for customary tenants were said to meet at need, a court of survey for the Trelawney share was held in 1613, and copies from the Trelawney and Vivian shares survive for 1609 and 1624 respectively.[13] The remaining fourth part of the manor held by the Poulett family continued unenfranchised until 1810–11, and was administered as a single manor. The conveyance of 1578 claimed to include a fourth

[92] S.R.O., D/P/crew 13/2/1–9; DD/SS, bdle. 55 (lease 1723); *Sherborne Mercury*, 25 June 1759; *Univ. Brit. Dir.* ii; S.R.O., DD/SB 38/1.
[93] S.R.O., tithe award; D/P/crew 13/1/2; Harrison, Harrod, & Co. *Dir. Som.* (1859); *P.O. Dir. Som.* (1861, 1875); *Kelly's Dir. Som.* (1883–94).
[94] S.R.O., D/P/crew 13/2/3–4; DD/PT, box 39, survey 1770.
[95] S.R.O., DD/PT, box 44, rental 1748.
[96] S.R.O., D/P/crew 13/2/6–9.
[97] S.R.O., DD/SB 38/1; D/P/crew 4/1/2, 4/3/1; tithe award; *County Gazette Dir.* (1840); Slater, *Nat. Com. Dir.* (1852–3); Harrison, Harrod, & Co. *Dir. Som.* (1859); *P.O. Dir. Som.* (1861–75); Morris & Co. *Dir. Som.* (1872).
[98] Extract of court baron *penes* Maj. Hussey.

[99] S.R.O., DD/SS, bdles. 53, 55.
[1] *Cal. Pat.* 1358–61, 229; S.R.O., D/P/crew 2/1/1; DD/SS, bdle. 54; DD/PT, box 22B, lease 1715, copy will 1741.   [2] *L. & P. Hen. VIII*, xiv (1), p. 289.
[3] *S.R.S.* xx. 23–31.
[4] Sherborne School, MS. A 29B.
[5] S.R.O., T/PH/hsy, survey 1599.
[6] Ct. bks. *penes* Countess Poulett, Jersey.
[7] S.R.O., Q/RE.
[8] *Plac. de Quo Warr.* (Rec. Com.), 693.
[9] C 133/6/1; S.C. 6/1127/16; B.L. Add. MS. 49359, f. 74.   [10] C 135/62/4; C 135/260/3.
[11] E. Devon R.O., CR 528; S.C. 6/Hen. VIII/6174.
[12] S.C. 6/Hen. VIII/6174–99; *Cal. S.P. Dom.* 1547–80, 72.
[13] E. Devon R.O., CR 675; S.R.O., DD/TH, box 4.

share of courts leet and view of frankpledge,[14] and sessions in the 17th century were described as courts baron and views of frankpledge.[15] An extract survives for 1617 and court books for 1651–77.[16] Between 1677 and 1703 the sessions were divided, tenancy business remaining with the court baron and all other matters being transferred to the town court. Court books of the 'manor baron' survive for 1703–10 and 1715–27, and extracts until 1785.[17] The 'town leet court', held on the same day as the manor and hundred courts by the 18th century, appointed two constables and dealt with nuisances and the examination of butter weights and bread within the town. Court books survive for 1703–10 and 1715–26.

Sessions in 1684 were held in the church house.[18] In October 1785 the 'town leet court' was held at noon after a session of the hundred court and was followed by a 'manor baron' at 4 pm.[19] The leet is said to have continued until the mid 19th century.[20] The manor court acquired a new 'shillyngstole' for offenders in 1514–15.[21]

No rolls and only one extract have been found from the first roll of the court of Sir Reynold Bray (d. 1503) for the manor of Eastham. The extract probably belongs to the year 1500.[22]

The first and third portioners of the rectory, sharing the same steward, reckoned perquisites of court among their income.[23] The chapter of Winchester reserved the courts leet and baron of the first portion from their first surviving lease of the property made in 1562, and the lessee was obliged to find food and lodging for seven men and seven horses for two days and nights while courts were in session.[24] Lessees from 1617 also kept courts, and extracts survive of entries and surrenders before courts baron between 1714 and 1800. Enfranchisements took place by 1814 and the courts thereafter ceased to exist.[25]

The chantry priests of the two main chantries included perquisites of court in their income in 1535.[26] There were certainly copyhold tenants belonging to the chantry of the Virgin in the churchyard, and the estate after the Dissolution was known as the manor of Crewkerne Chantry, though no court rolls have been found.[27]

In 1599 it was recalled that in the past the lords of the manor chose a portreeve, whose duties were to collect and gather the profits of markets and fairs.[28] The office had by that time ceased to exist because the markets and fairs had been let to farm. How far such an office implies a measure of urban government is uncertain, but Robert the portreeve occurs in 1272, Robert the provost in 1280, and bailiffs of Crewkerne at the end of the 13th century.[29] There is no further trace of similar officers until the

bailiff and the constable were involved in an affray at Eastham in 1531.[30]

By the early 17th century collective decisions were being made at meetings of townsmen, presided over by the constable. Town clerks, who occur from 1573,[31] may well have had duties in respect of this body. The townsmen approved payments to an Irishman in 1627, were concerned with the erection of a workhouse in 1631, fixed rates in 1638–9 and 1668, and approved the sale of a seat in church in 1658. In the 1650s the accounts of the churchwardens were approved by two constables and up to 18 other signatories, and the tradition continued into the 1670s. In 1691 there were several 'parish meetings' of townsmen.[32]

The role of the grammar school trustees was of importance in the development of collective government during the same period. At least from 1577 the trustees included 'six of the most discreetest men of the town',[33] and from the early 17th century they gave the town financial support. They lent money during plague, gave to the poor in hard times, advanced cash to buy fire buckets in 1626, and contributed substantially when the bridewell was partially converted to a workhouse and a cage and pillory were erected in 1630–1. In 1638 the trustees were hosts at a meeting to settle a dispute over the choice of churchwardens.[34]

Poor-relief was administered in the 18th century by four overseers through monthly meetings, decisions of which were usually signed by up to a dozen people. Meetings were first called vestries in 1747. A policy begun in 1724 gave the parish possession of property and goods of all paupers, and those receiving parish pay were divided between 'constant payers' and those having 'free gifts'. Expenditure in the early 18th century was almost evenly shared between the two groups. Payment for medical care was strictly controlled, but patients were sent to hospital in Bath and Exeter in 1758 and an apothecary or surgeon was retained from 1759. A pauper tailor was employed by the parish from 1763.[35]

A workhouse, first suggested in 1756 in face of growing expenditure on the poor, was not established until 1767. In January 1779 it had 67 inmates, and continued in use until the parish became part of the Chard poor-law union in 1836. It was then sold, together with other parish poorhouses. The workhouse stood in Hermitage Street, and the poorhouses there and in Goulds Barton.[36]

By 1782 the churchwardens had responsibility for the housing and maintenance of a fire engine, which was regularly 'played' on Shrove Tuesday, Whit Monday, and 5 November each year. In the 1780s it was kept in the shambles, but by 1820

[14] S.R.O., DD/SS, bdles. 54, 56.
[15] Ct. bks. *penes* Countess Poulett.
[16] S.R.O., DD/SS, bdles. 53, 55, 57; ct. bks. *penes* Countess Poulett.
[17] Ct. bks. *penes* Countess Poulett.
[18] S.R.O., DD/SS, bdle. 54.
[19] S.R.O., DD/PT, box 41, proposal bk.
[20] Pigot, *Nat. Com. Dir.* (1830, 1840, 1852–3).
[21] E. Devon R.O., CR 528.
[22] *Cat. Anct. D.* vi, C 5737.
[23] *Valor Eccl.* (Rec. Com.), i. 163.
[24] Winchester Cath. Libr., Ledger Bk. V, f. 11v.
[25] Ibid. Ledger Bks. *passim*; MSS. *penes* Maj. Hussey; S.R.O., DD/HKE 1/1, 1/3; DD/SB 49/3.

[26] *Valor Eccl.* (Rec. Com.), i. 163.
[27] *S.R.S.* ii. 6. Courts were apparently held to *c.* 1770: S.R.O., DD/S/HR, box 9; DD/TH, box 5.
[28] S.R.O., T/PH/hsy, survey 1599.
[29] *S.R.S.* xxxvi. 178–9; xliv. 247; Forde Abbey, Cart. p. 399.
[30] *S.R.S.* xxvii. 113.
[31] S.R.O., D/P/crew 2/1/1.
[32] Ibid. 4/1/1.
[33] S.R.O., DD/CGS 1/1.
[34] Ibid. 3/1; *S.R.S.* xxiv. 139.
[35] S.R.O., D/P/crew 13/2/1–7.
[36] Ibid. 13/2/3–7, 15–18; DD/SB 9/2, 35/7.

was stored in the church porch.[37] The wardens also maintained the town pumps.

In the early years of the 19th century the vestry, comprising the minister and some fifteen members, continued to administer the town and parish through two wardens and four overseers. A salaried assistant overseer was not appointed until 1843, and one of the wardens was chosen by the minister from 1841. From the late 1830s improvements were made for public benefit, including the enclosure of the churchyard, and in 1842 the sum of £400 was borrowed to help emigrants to be chosen by a committee.[38]

The growth of population and the consequent pressure on the work of the vestry is marked by increase in local government bodies. A lighting committee was formed in 1838, from 1848 the parish was divided into districts for nuisance removal, from 1851 the vestry conducted regular elections for the office of surveyor of the highways, and from 1853 the town constable was salaried.

CREWKERNE URBAN DISTRICT COUNCIL. *Or, a lion rampant azure between three torteaux; on a chief ermine a pale sable, thereon three swords in pile, points downwards, proper, pommels and hilts of the first*

A Board of Health was formed in 1854, and a Drainage District in 1866. Special committees of the vestry dealt with nuisances from 1858, finance from 1862, and sanitary matters from 1868. A Burial Board was formed in 1872.[39] Crewkerne urban district was established in 1894 to administer the town, the remainder of the ancient parish becoming the civil parish of West Crewkerne. In 1974 urban district and parish became part of the enlarged Yeovil District.

Until 1871 the vestry met at various places in the town, first in the church and thereafter at one of the larger inns or at the National schools. In 1858 and regularly from 1871 it met at the town hall, where the overseers had permanent use of a room.[40]

Stocks stood in the market place next to the shambles by 1772, and the town had a blind house by the 1830s.[41] A fire engine was bought by the vestry and a brigade newly organized in 1876.[42] The town was lighted by gas in 1837.[43] A voluntary

hospital established by Robert Bird in 1867 in South Street, in a converted factory, was replaced by the present building opened in 1904.[44]

The trustees of the grammar school from 1703 but not earlier used a seal which bears the legend SIGILLUM CROKORNIENSIS in a scroll above a castle. It has been variously interpreted as formerly a corporate seal of the town or as a device linking the grammar school with the Holy Trinity chantry and the Templars, previous owners of part of the school estate.[45]

CHURCH. The church of Crewkerne was a minster[46] of Saxon origin, probably founded by one of the royal owners of the estate, and its territory extended over the later parishes of Misterton, Wayford, and Seaborough (Dors.). Chapels at those places and at Eastham depended on Crewkerne as their mother church, but during the course of time acquired varying degrees of independence. The position of each dependency is set out in a statement of dues, dating in its present form largely from the mid 13th century, before the benefice of Crewkerne was divided into portions, apparently between 1272 and 1282.[47]

At the Conquest the church, with 10 hides of land and all the tithes of its 'territory', was given by William I to the abbey of St. Stephen, Caen (Calvados).[48] The abbey seems to have lost possession by Henry I's time,[49] and by the early 13th century the church had evidently been reunited with the manor. William de Reviers (d. 1217) gave the advowson of the church or churches to his elder daughter Joan on her marriage to William Briwere (d. 1233).[50] Joan's grant of property to William de Lisle in 1249 seems to have included the advowson, and in 1272 Isabel de Forz, countess of Aumale and great-granddaughter of William de Reviers, successfully reclaimed it from John de Lisle, then a minor.[51] Subsequently Isabel granted her property for life to Agnes de Monceaux, and Agnes evidently acted as patron of the divided rectory.[52] On her death c. 1315 the patronage passed to the Courtenays, successively owners of the manor with some interruptions, until 1547.

As a minster serving a wide area the church had probably been the base for a community of clergy, but such a group was apparently dispersed before or at the Conquest.[53] By the 13th century the benefice had become a sole rectory.[54] Between 1272 and 1282, however, the living was divided into three portions, the only such arrangement in the county.[55] The first and largest portion was also called the portion of the rector, the second that of the deacon,

[37] S.R.O., D/P/crew 4/1/2.
[38] Ibid. 9/1/1.
[39] Ibid. 9/1/2; DD/X/HAW.
[40] S.R.O., D/P/crew 9/1/1–3.
[41] Ibid. 4/1/4; T/PH/hsy, map of Crewkerne rectory manor 1772 (original, by S. Donne, *penes* Maj. Hussey).
[42] S.R.O., D/P/crew 23/10.
[43] *Kelly's Dir. Som.* (1883); S.R.O., T/PH/ptr, map of Crewkerne 1841 (original *penes* Messrs. Proctor and Horden, Crewkerne, by John Wood).
[44] S.R.O., D/P/crew 23/10; Messrs. Sparks and Blake, Crewkerne, deeds register.
[45] S.R.O., DD/CGS 1/1; R. G. Bartelot, *Hist. Crewkerne School*, 31–2; Pulman, *Bk. of the Axe*, 339.
[46] Devon R.O., TD 51, (Courtenay Cart.), at end.

[47] *S.R.S.* xxxvi. 166–7, 173–4; *Cal. Pat. 1292–1301*, 53.
[48] Dugdale, *Mon.* vi. 1070; *V.C.H. Som.* i. 406, 470. Confirmed in 1096–7: *Reg. Regum Anglo-Norm.* ii, p. 404.
[49] Dugdale, *Mon.* vi. 1071–2.
[50] Oliver, *Mon. Exon.* 343–5; *Close R. 1231–4*, 198.
[51] *S.R.S.* vi. 134; xxxvi. 166–7, 173–4, 178–9, 181–2; *Cal. Pat. 1292–1301*, 53; *S. & D. N. & Q.* xx. 36.
[52] *Cal. Pat. 1307–13*, 183.
[53] No priests were mentioned at Domesday: *V.C.H. Som.* i. 470.
[54] Forde Abbey, Cart. p. 479; Devon R.O., TD 51, pp. 181–2, 191–2; *Close R. 1231–4*, 384–5; *S.R.S.* vi. 110; xi, p. 168; xxxvi. 166–7, 173–4.
[55] *S.R.S.* xxxvi. 166–7, 173–4; *Cal. Pat. 1292–1301*, 53; *V.C.H. Som.* ii. 21.

the third that of the subdeacon,[56] an arrangement which may be an echo of Crewkerne's former collegiate status. The deacon's portion survived as a name until the 15th century,[57] and the two deacons or clerks of the 16th century were perhaps similar survivals.[58]

The sole rectory was supported by a substantial estate[59] and also by tithes payable from the whole *parochia* of the former minster. By the mid 13th century the heart of the territory, most of the later parish of Crewkerne, yielded tithes of all kinds, paid solely to the mother church. The establishment of chapels at Wayford, Seaborough, Misterton, and Eastham had by the 13th century diverted some revenue elsewhere, but links still remained. The people of Ashcombe and Bere in Wayford still paid all tithes and oblations to Crewkerne and a few tenants at Seaborough also owed tithes to the mother church, but annual offerings at the dedication festival and burial at Crewkerne were the sole obligations of the people of Misterton, Wayford, and Oathill, and burial rights alone were reserved from the people of Seaborough and Eastham. Henley tenants were treated like the people of Misterton, but the lord, his family, and chief servants were considered part of Crewkerne. In 1295 previous arrangements for Eastham were modified to give the portioners of Crewkerne half the tithes of 106 a. of land in exchange for yielding burial rights.[60] Misterton and Wayford continued to send their dead to Crewkerne until the 18th century.[61]

In 1547, in return for some property in Wiltshire taken by the Crown, the chapter of Winchester was given, *inter alia*, the advowson of the three portions of Crewkerne rectory, with licence to appropriate the then vacant first portion and the other two when they fell vacant, and to endow a vicarage.[62] For more than a decade there was evidently confusion over the benefice: it is not known when the two remaining rectors ceased to serve, though Edward Horsey esquire, captain of the Isle of Wight, who surrendered the second portion in 1564–5, may perhaps be identified as the scholar appointed in 1539.[63] A Crown presentation to the sole rectory in 1557 was evidently of no effect, but no vicarage was ever ordained.[64] Leases of the rectory from 1562 required the farmers to provide for the cure and they continued to do so well into the 17th century,[65] but from 1680 onwards the curate was chosen by the chapter of Winchester.[66] The chapter's choice was often exercised in favour

of men with Winchester connexions until 1908 when the patronage was exchanged with the Lord Chancellor, patron in 1976.[67] The benefice, augmented by endowment, became a vicarage in 1868.[68]

The value of the minster estate in 1086 was £11.[69] In 1291 the first portion was taxed at £33 6s. 8d., the second at £10 13s. 4d., and the third at £6 13s. 4d.,[70] though an extent of 1315 put the figures much higher, at £66 13s. 4d., £26 13s. 4d., and £20[71] and a statement also of the 14th century gave the first portioner £40 and agreed with the two lower figures.[72] In 1535 the clear value of the first portion was £55 12s. 11½d., the second £20, and the third £10 1s. 6d. The chapel at Misterton seems to have been annexed to the third portion.[73]

In 1535 the value of tithes and oblations of the first portion was £44, of the second £16 5s. 1d., and of the third £3 7s. 0d. Glebe land, tenants' rents, and perquisites of court were worth respectively £10 7s. 8d., £2 17s. 0d., and £6 9s. 8d. All three portioners received small rents from the lord of the manor and the first two also from the abbot of Forde (Dors.).[74]

Each of the three portioners presumably had a residence, and that of the third rector was in need of repair in 1557.[75] The third rector's association with New Court and the presence of New Court Lane near the churchyard suggests its close proximity,[76] and the one recognized clergy house stood in 1650 on the east side of the churchyard.[77] A second, probably the largest, and associated with the first portion of the rectory, was already in lay hands by 1547 and subsequently became the centre of the parsonage estate; it was occupied in the 17th and 18th centuries by tenant farmers.[78] It was a substantial house of the 14th century, the hall entered by a porch and lit by a tall 15th-century window. A long cross-wing to the south had its principal rooms on the first floor with a small annexe, possibly for a chapel, against the gable wall.[79] This house was replaced in 1846 by a house in similar style known as the Abbey, which incorporates a traceried window of the former building.[80]

Under the arrangements for the vicarage in 1547 the incumbent was to be assigned a 'suitable dwelling' and a pension of £18 until the second and third portions should be vacant, when these were to be taken instead.[81] The curates appointed on the failure of the scheme seem to have been paid £10 in 1575[82] but by 1651, when there was a sole curate, the value was £30.[83] It was increased between 1649 and 1659,[84] and from 1680 the lessee of the

[56] Devon R.O., TD 51, at end; B.L. Add. MS. 49359, f. 74.

[57] *Cal. Pat.* 1476–85, 165; *S.R.S.* lii, p. 82.

[58] S.R.O., D/P/crew 2/1/1, 4/1/1.

[59] *V.C.H. Som.* i. 470; see above, p. 16.

[60] S.R.O., D/D/B reg 1; *Proc. Som. Arch. Soc.* cxx.

[61] The last Seaborough burial at Crewkerne was in 1734: S.R.O., D/P/crew 2/1/3.

[62] *Cal. Pat.* 1547–8, 25.

[63] *L. & P. Hen. VIII*, xiv, p. 75; Winchester Cath. Libr., John Chace's Bk. f. 100v.

[64] *Cal. Pat.* 1557–8, 248.

[65] Winchester Cath. Libr., Ledger Bks.; S.R.O., D/P/crew 2/1/1; D/D/Ca 73; D/D/Vc box 9 (1634); Hants R.O., CC/59493 (Parl. Survey 1650).

[66] Winchester Cath. Libr., Ledger Bk. XIX, f. 41.

[67] *Lond. Gaz.* 6 Oct. 1908.

[68] Pulman, *Bk. of the Axe*, 281.

[69] *V.C.H. Som.* i. 470.

[70] *Tax. Eccl.* (Rec. Com.), 199.

[71] B.L. Add. MS. 49359, f. 74.

[72] Devon R.O., TD 51, at end.

[73] *Valor Eccl.* (Rec. Com.), i. 163.

[74] Ibid.

[75] S.R.O., D/D/Ca 27.

[76] S.R.O., D/D/B reg 12, f. 41v.; DD/HKE 1/1; MSS. *penes* Maj. Hussey, ct. baron 1714. New Court appears as Newcok in *S.R.S.* lv, p. 62.

[77] Hants R.O., CC/59493.

[78] Ibid.; S.R.O., T/PH/hsy, map 1772; MSS. *penes* Maj. Hussey.

[79] B.L. Add. MS. 36381, ff. 101–101v; see plate facing p. 145.

[80] See above, p. 17.

[81] *Cal. Pat.* 1547–8, 25.

[82] *S. & D. N. & Q.* xiv. 32.

[83] Lambeth Palace MSS., COMM.V/1.

[84] Ibid. COMM.VIb/2.

rectorial estate was paying £80 a year.[85] In 1812 the benefice was augmented with £600 by Parliamentary grant and there were further augmentations of £200 in 1820 and £400 in 1833.[86] By 1851 the income from other sources beyond fees and the lay rector's contribution was £50.[87] The Ecclesiastical Commissioners added a further grant of £111 yearly in 1870,[88] and by 1884 the value of the benefice had risen to £300.[89]

At least from the middle of the 17th century no house was provided for the curate, and in 1650 Jacob Tomkins was renting a house from the farmer of the rectory containing four lower rooms, two upper rooms, and a small garden.[90] This house he continued to occupy after he had been removed from the curacy.[91] In 1815 the curate declared there was no glebe house and that he lived in a hired lodging.[92] A proposal in 1832 to build a dwelling was evidently not proceeded with, but a house was erected on Constitution Hill c. 1840.[93] It was extended in 1862–3 and again in 1882, on both occasions by J. M. Allen.[94] The house was sold in 1947 and was replaced by the former Gouldsbrook Hall, a 19th-century building in Gouldsbrook Terrace.[95]

The valuable portions of the rectory attracted distinguished incumbents, many of whom had close connexions with the Courtenays and with Devon. Robert Pyl (1328 at least until 1352) was at the time in Sir Hugh Courtenay's household.[96] Walter Collys (1422–7) was a lawyer well beneficed in Devon and later became a diplomat. His successor, Thomas Hendyman, a theologian and a former chancellor of Oxford University, remained at Crewkerne only six months, exchanging with John Odelande or Wodelond (1428–72), a canonist and another Exeter clerk.[97] John Combe (1472–96) also held high office in Exeter, but may have been a native of Crewkerne and is considered to have founded the grammar school.[98]

The second portion was twice used for the benefit of Courtenay's younger sons, when Philip Courtenay was appointed in 1362 and John in 1431–5, both having only the first tonsure.[99] Andrew Lanvyan (1428–c. 1431) was registrar of the bishop of Bath and Wells.[1] The same portion was later held by Richard Surland (1479–1509), subdean of the chapels royal, followed by Christopher Plummer (1509–c. 1536), chaplain successively to Queen Elizabeth of York, Henry VIII, and Queen Catherine of Aragon. For opposing the king's divorce Plummer

was attainted and lodged in the Tower in 1534, but was pardoned two years later.[2]

The most distinguished occupant of the third portion was John Stafford (1422–7), subsequently Bishop of Bath and Wells and Archbishop of Canterbury, who while holding Crewkerne was also Treasurer of England. Thomas Kent, appointed in 1443, having recently lectured in canon law in Italy, was clerk of the Council from 1444 and under-constable of England from 1445. His successor William Hoper (1446–54) was also a distinguished lawyer and considerable pluralist.[3]

The 16th-century curates after the appropriation of the portions are obscure. William Pyers and John Toller were both deprived in 1554 for being married, though the former said Mass while under suspension.[4] William Robyns (c. 1577–c. 1586) was also rector of Eastham.[5] Most of the other curates until the 1640s are unidentifiable, often serving for very short periods.[6] John Norris, serving c. 1596, was later presented in court for not holding a cure, but it was found that he had retired to Clapton because he was 'not well able to see and read divine service'.[7] In contrast, however, John Fuller held one of the two curacies from c. 1595 until his death in 1642.[8]

Jacob Tomkins, sole minister by 1646, continued until 1660, when the parish secured his removal. He is regarded as an after-conformist and subsequently held the living of Misterton.[9] Daniel Ballowe, curate from 1683, was 'very insolent' to Bishop Kidder when the bishop discovered he was also holding the curacy of Chard in 1692 and 'plied between the two market towns . . . and . . . designed to keep them both'.[10] Nathaniel Forster (1720–52), formerly a minor canon at Winchester, combined the livings of Misterton and Crewkerne.[11] James Taggart (1753–75) was also a Winchester minor canon, and his successor Robert Hoadley Ashe, D.D. (1775–1826), was the son of a Winchester prebendary and also for a time (1780–87) master of the grammar school.[12]

From the mid 15th century the parish was normally served by two parochial chaplains,[13] in 1532 described respectively as curate and stipendiary,[14] in addition to the two chantry chaplains. In a Chancery suit in 1567 the wardens claimed that 'time out of mind . . . two priests or ministers at the best' had been found to serve the cure. They further stated that the then lessee had only appointed one priest for the previous six years.[15] Leases of the rectory from 1562 onwards required the farmers to

[85] Winchester Cath. Libr., Ledger Bks. passim.
[86] S.R.O., D/D/B return 1815; Hodgson, *Queen Anne's Bounty* (1845), pp. ccxviii, ccxli; Pulman, *Bk. of the Axe*, 281.
[87] H.O. 129/318/4/8/14.
[88] *Lond. Gaz.* 18 Feb. 1870, 912.
[89] S.R.O., D/P/crew 23/10.
[90] Hants R.O., CC/59493.
[91] S.R.O., D/P/crew 4/1/1.
[92] S.R.O., D/D/B return 1815.
[93] Cornw. R.O. 22M/DE344/8: S.R.O., T/PH/ptr, Wood's map of Crewkerne 1841.
[94] S.R.O., D/P/crew 23/10.
[95] Ibid.
[96] *S.R.S.* ix, pp. 72–3, 106, 178.
[97] Ibid. xxxi, p. 62; *Cal. Papal Regs.* viii. 163; ix, p. 56; Emden, *Biog. Reg. Univ. Oxford.*
[98] R. G. Bartelot, *Hist. Crewkerne Sch.* 5–10; N. Orme, *Education in the West of Eng. 1066–1548*, 131–2.
[99] *S.R.S.* x, p. 766; xxxi, p. 95.

[1] Ibid. xxxii, p. 285.
[2] Emden, *Biog. Reg. Univ. Oxford.*
[3] Ibid.
[4] S.R.O., D/D/Ca 22; D/D/Vc 66, f. 9v.
[5] S.R.O., D/D/Ca 54, 73.
[6] S.R.O., D/P/crew 2/1/1, 4/1/1; *Som. Incumbents*, ed. Weaver.
[7] *S.R.S.* xliii. 68, 106.
[8] S.R.O., D/P/crew 2/1/1, 4/1/1.
[9] Ibid.
[10] *S.R.S.* xxxvii. 86.
[11] Foster, *Alumni Oxonienses.*
[12] *D.N.B.*; Bartelot, *Hist. Crewkerne Sch.*, 71.
[13] *S.R.S.* xxi. 207; xlix, pp. 141, 399; lii, p. 28; S.R.O., D/D/Vc 5; D/D/Vc 66, f. 9v.; D/D/Ca 54, 57, 73; D/P/crew 2/1/1. A *lector epistolarum* was absenting himself from service in 1548: S.R.O., D/D/Ca 17.
[14] S.R.O., D/D/Vc 20.
[15] C 3/41/29.

provide two suitable curates and two deacons or clerks 'to serve at the said parsonages and portions and to administer the sacraments to the parishioners there',[16] and certainly from the 1570s onwards two clergymen, one known as the curate, the other as the preacher, jointly served the parish until *c.* 1640.[17] The claim for two ministers was raised unsuccessfully in 1658.[18]

The two 'deacons or clerks', perhaps representing the second and third portions of the old parsonage, seem to have emerged at the same time, distinguished as town and parish clerks.[19] By 1625 each was paid by the parish, but their duties remain unknown until 1648 when the parish clerk also began to care for the clock and chimes, from 1661 when he made register entries, and from 1666 when he cared for the bells and kept the *Book of Martyrs*.[20] The town clerk's duties may have been connected with the meetings of the townsmen.[21]

In 1554 a man from Hinton St. George publicly contradicted a preacher who was declaring the doctrine of transubstantiation.[22] In 1574 there was action against 'immoderate long peals' of bells both on Sundays and holidays.[23] Two years later one of the curates was suspended for refusing to publish a sentence of excommunication against the archdeacon of Taunton 'by reason of trouble of mind'.[24] In 1577 there were complaints about the lack of quarterly sermons and the two curates, evidently suspected of ignorance, were required to repeat by heart chapters from the Epistle to the Romans.[25] From the 1580s onwards a succession of preachers established a tradition of puritanism in the parish, actively fostered by the trustees of the grammar school. In 1610 the trustees paid 'for the preacher's diet for twenty exercises' and from 1614 until at least 1620 supported a regular preacher and later rewarded visitors.[26] The farmer of the rectory was obliged to pay the preachers for regular monthly and quarterly sermons under the terms of his lease of 1617.[27] Complaints against strange preachers in 1629 probably marked the beginning of episcopal opposition to the less regular preachings.[28]

By the 1630s the Holy Communion was celebrated monthly, and a total of 220 quarts of sack was purchased for 18 services in 1635–6. In 1635 the wardens complied with the bishop's regulations for railing the communion table, covering the font, providing a desk for the *Book of Martyrs*, and purchasing a hood for the minister. After a hiatus in their accounts, 1642–5, the wardens listed in their storehouse the rails taken from the communion table and the remains of the church organ. Heavy spending on

glass in 1647–8 suggests further destruction, and purchase of a bason for baptisms in 1648 the temporary disuse of the font. Before the Restoration, in 1659, the communion table was taken back into the 'old place', and the bason was sold in 1662, though the former organ loft continued to be occupied by grammar school master and pupils. After the Restoration celebrations of the Holy Communion were usually held quarterly.[29]

By the 1770s there were 'generally about 70 communicants',[30] and in 1815 two services, each with sermon, were held every Sunday.[31] By 1833 the incumbent had introduced services on Wednesdays and Fridays in Lent and daily services in Passion Week.[32] Ten years later there were three services each Sunday, two with sermons; one of the sermons was supported by public subscription.[33] The incumbent involved in these changes was obliged in 1845 to cease his use of the surplice in the pulpit.[34] In 1851 the congregation on Census Sunday was 918 in the morning (including 316 Sunday-school children), 323 in the afternoon, and 946 in the evening.[35] By 1855 the Holy Communion was celebrated monthly and on special occasions, and by 1870 four sermons were delivered each Sunday.[36]

The church has a long musical tradition. A singing man occurs in 1585, and a 'singing man of the church' in 1621.[37] An organ was endowed in 1592, but was dismantled and melted down by 1646.[38] Orchestra and singers were replaced by an organ in 1823, and from 1828 the organist also taught children to sing.[39] A new organ installed in 1865, replaced in 1906, was said to be 'designed by somebody who never saw the church' and was accompanied by a choir 'anything but first class'.[40]

In August 1544 the churchwardens leased from the manor a plot of land 'to build a church house', and from November of the same year held the plot, in the market place between the high cross on the south and the town well on the north.[41] An undated manor rental shows the wardens paying rent for a 'cottage' next to the market cross called the 'town house'.[42] The wardens continued to pay rent until 1658 and contributed towards its maintenance at least until 1688. Parts were used for storage or for temporary lodging.[43] Items of repair in the 17th century include wattle and daub, suggesting a timber-framed building. The roof was tiled.[44]

There was a chantry of the Virgin in the church by 1253–4, and by 1315 it was worth 100s.[45] Its patronage was in the hands of the Courtenays and their successors as patrons of the rectory.[46] In 1535 its clear value was £4 18s. 4d.,[47] and in 1546 its

16 Winchester Cath. Libr., Ledger Bk. V, f. 11v.
17 S.R.O., D/P/crew 2/1/1; D/D/Vc 58.
18 *Cal. S.P. Dom.* 1658–9, 146.
19 S.R.O., D/P/crew 2/1/1, 4/1/1.
20 Ibid. 4/1/1.
21 See above, p. 27.
22 S.R.O., D/D/Ca 22.
23 Ibid. 53.
24 Ibid. 54.
25 Ibid. 57, 73.
26 S.R.O., DD/CGS 3/1.
27 Winchester Cath. Libr., Ledger Bk. XI, f. 66.
28 S.R.O., D/D/Ca 266.
29 S.R.O., D/P/crew 4/1/1.
30 S.R.O., D/D/V Dioc. bk. 1776.
31 S.R.O., D/D/B return 1815.
32 Ibid. D/D/V return 1833.
33 Ibid. 1843.

34 *Pulman's Weekly News*, 24 Dec. 1924.
35 H.O. 129/318/4/8/14.
36 S.R.O., D/D/V returns 1855, 1870.
37 S.R.O., D/P/crew 2/1/1.
38 *Som. Wills*, ed. Brown, v. 39; S.R.O., D/P/crew 4/1/1; DD/CGS 3/1.
39 S.R.O., D/P/crew 4/1/2.
40 Ibid. 9/1/1; *Western Gazette*, 6 Oct. 1865.
41 S.R.O., T/PH/hsy, survey 1599; S.C. 6/Hen. VIII/6183.
42 E. Devon R.O., CR 550.
43 S.R.O., D/P/crew 4/1/1; DD/CGS 1/3.
44 S.R.O., D/P/crew 4/1/1.
45 Devon R.O., TD 51, pp. 187–90; B.L. Add. MS. 49359, f. 74.
46 *S.R.S.* x, p. 513; xiii, p. 57; xxxi, p. 3; liv, p. 19; lv, p. 29.
47 *Valor Eccl.* (Rec. Com.), i. 163.

plate and ornaments were nominally worth 33s. 4d., though its silver chalice (26s. 8d.) had been sold four years previously 'of necessity'.[48] The last priest was pensioned.[49]

In 1549 the property, including a capital messuage and land, was sold to Laurence Hyde of London, who re-sold it to Sir Hugh Poulett. Poulett conveyed the holding, worth £4 4s., to James Downham of Chillington in 1550.[50] In 1574 some of the property, described as concealed, was granted by the Crown to John and William Marshe of London.[51]

By 1315 2 a. of land in Crewkerne were held for the provision of 10 lb. of wax for St. Edmund's altar, presumably within the church.[52] By 1514 rent was paid for land at Furringdons called 'Oblighacr'' and 'Gambeleacr'' to the first and second portioners of the rectory to provide bread and wine for celebrations at the high altar.[53] A close in Merriott by 1548 gave support for obits, and rents in Crewkerne found lamps and lights.[54] The obit lands were granted to Laurence Hyde in 1549, and the rents were leased to Henry Middlemore in 1572.[55]

Bequests to the fraternity of the Trinity or to the Trinity altar in the church occur between 1508 and 1534.[56] The property of this guild or fraternity, often known as a former chantry,[57] formed much of the endowment of the grammar school said to have been founded in 1499 by a former rector.[58] In 1548 the clear value of the school property was £8 1s. 3d.[59]

The church of *ST. BARTHOLOMEW* is a large building in local Ham stone. It comprises a chancel with double north aisle, a central tower with transepts, an aisled and clerestoreyed nave, and a south porch. A sacristy stood at the east end of the chancel, approached by doors on either side of the high altar, and a vestry is said to have stood on the north side.[60] Both were apparently destroyed in the 19th century. Part of a late-13th-century arch incorporated in the east wall of the south transept suggests that there was a church of cruciform plan by that time, and the west wall of the nave includes walling, of unknown date, evidence for an earlier nave of the same length but with narrower aisles. It may in fact only be contemporary with the crossing arches which are probably early 15th century. In all its other features the church is the product of a major rebuilding of the late 15th or early 16th century. The presence of royal chaplains as rectors between 1479 and c. 1536 may explain both the splendour of the building and some elements of the design, like the twin turrets on the west front, which are unlikely to be of local origin.[61] There is a tradition of vaults beneath the building containing a crowned king and queen.[62]

The Purbeck marble font, of Norman pillared design, is the earliest item of furniture. Before the Reformation there was a figure of St. Michael in the 'midst' of the church.[63] The screen occupied the east side of the crossing, supported by grotesques including a Green Man, and the rood beam was on the west side. The nave roof is supported on angel capitals, and the Woolminstone chapel roof is richly panelled. There is a memorial brass to Thomas Golde (d. 1525) in the chancel. Galleries were built at the west end early in the 17th century, and 'hanging' or 'trap' seats were added to the pews.[64] The galleries had been removed before 1809–11 when the nave was re-pewed and galleries erected at the east end of the north and south aisles and at the west end of the nave.[65] Plans to erect side galleries in the 1840s, drawn by Sampson Kempthorne of London, were not proceeded with, partly on aesthetic grounds,[66] but an arch for a private pew was made over the south porch.[67] The vestry in the south transept had a new screen and panelling by J. M. Allen in 1853–5.[68] Extensive alterations in 1864–5 included the removal of the eastern nave galleries and re-seating.[69] Restoration beginning in 1887 included opening the south porch, renewal of pews, removal of the pulpit from its central position, and lowering the floor.[70] The chancel was restored by the lay rector in 1899–1900, and the remainder of the church refurnished at various times until 1914.[71] The west window was reglazed by A. K. Nicholson in 1930.

There are eight bells: (i) and (ii) 1894, Taylor of Loughborough; (iii) and (iv) 1820, John Kingston of Bridgwater; (v) to (vii) 1894, Taylor; (viii) 1767, Thomas Bayley of Bridgwater.[72] The plate consists of a cup and cover of 1608 by John Freke of Crewkerne, and another of 1609. There is a dish or silver plate dated 1683 by 'F.S.'. The parish also has a flagon of 1847.[73] The registers begin in 1558, but there are gaps in 1643–4 and 1647–8.[74]

There was an anchoress's cell at the church. In the late 12th century Odolina, anchoress of Crewkerne, provided information on the life of St. Wulfric of Haselbury,[75] in 1459 an anchoress had been enclosed within the church for 'many years',[76] and a third received a bequest in 1523.[77] A 'little cell' still stood at the west end of the church in the 1630s,[78] and was maintained at parish expense. The churchwardens replaced stone tiles and crests

---

[48] E 117/8.   [49] *S.R.S.* ii, p. xx.

[50] Ibid. 177; li, pp. 39–40; *Cal. Pat.* 1548–9, 286.

[51] *Cal. Pat.* 1572–5, p. 323.

[52] B.L. Add. MS. 49359, f. 78v.

[53] E. Devon R.O., CR 528; S.C. 6/Hen. VIII/6174.

[54] *S.R.S.* ii. 8, 180.

[55] *Cal. Pat.* 1548–9, 286; 1569–72, pp. 389–90.

[56] *S.R.S.* xix. 120–1; *Wells Wills*, ed. F. W. Weaver, 64–6.   [57] *S.R.S.* ii. 7.

[58] Ibid. 7, 180; Bartelot, *Hist. Crewkerne Sch.*, 13–22.

[59] *S.R.S.* ii. 7.

[60] *Arch. Jnl.* xi. 146.

[61] e.g. Bath Abbey or the Tudor Royal chapels; see plate facing p. 16. Perhaps by William Smyth c. 1475–90: J. H. Harvey, *Eng. Medieval Architects*.

[62] *S. & D. N. & Q.* xix. 90–1.

[63] *S.R.S.* xix. 224.

[64] S.R.O., D/P/crew 4/1/1.

[65] Ibid. 4/1/2, 6/1/1; Pulman, *Bk. of the Axe*, 304. The west gallery was by J. Kemshead of London.

[66] S.R.O., D/P/crew 4/1/7, 9/1/1 (*sub annis* 1842, 1846).

[67] Ibid. 9/1/1 *sub anno* 1847.

[68] Ibid. 4/1/3, 6/1/2.

[69] Ibid. 9/1/1 *sub annis* 1864–5; Pulman, *Bk. of the Axe*, 304.

[70] S.R.O., D/P/crew 6/1/1, 23/10.

[71] Ibid. 23/10; some of the work was done by Bligh Bond.

[72] S.R.O., DD/SAS CH 16/1.

[73] S.R.O., D/P/crew 4/1/1; *Proc. Som. Arch. Soc.* xliv. 16–17.

[74] S.R.O., D/P/crew 2/1/1–30.

[75] *S.R.S.* xlvii, p. 90.

[76] Ibid. xlix, p. 333.

[77] Ibid. xix. 224.

[78] Ibid. xv. 67.

Hinton House from the West, 1725

Hinton House from the South-west

Hinton House: the South Front

HINTON ST. GEORGE

WAYFORD MANOR

CHAFFCOMBE: AVISHAYS

MISTERTON: MANOR FARM

SOUTH PETHERTON: WIGBOROUGH MANOR

in 1629, set up a chimney in 1639, and provided a new carved fireplace in 1678. It was still standing in 1700.[79]

In 1402 a monk of Forde elected to lead the life of a hermit in a house also on the west side of the church, within the churchyard, 'constructed for such a person to dwell in'.[80] This may be the hermitage of St. Edmund for which indulgence was promised to effect maintenance in 1441.[81] Like the anchoress, the hermit was given money and a pair of sheets under a will of 1523.[82] From 1539–40 a cottage called 'Hermytage' was being let by the lord of the manor,[83] and in 1564 it was granted by the Crown to William Gryce, the queen's servant, and Anthony Forster of Cumnor (Berks.).[84] In 1590 it was sold to William Typper and other Crown agents, and by 1599 Magdalene Partridge occupied the chapel of St. Edmund, bishop, and some land belonging to it, as tenant of the manor.[85] The hermitage was still standing in 1633 'not far' from the anchoress's house at the west end of the church.[86]

The chantry of Our Lady in the churchyard was founded under licence of 1309 by Agnes de Monceaux to celebrate daily for the souls of Isabel de Forz, countess of Aumale, and of her ancestors. It was to be endowed with property in Crewkerne, Hewish, and Misterton.[87] The chapel was described as newly built in 1315,[88] and the first priest seems to have been appointed in 1316.[89]

Patronage of the chantry descended in the Courtenay family and their successors: George Neville, bishop of Exeter, and others presented in 1464 after the attainder of Thomas, earl of Devon,[90] and by 1469 the rights had passed to Sir William Knyvett through his wife Joan, the late earl's sister and heir.[91]

The chantry was dissolved in 1548, when its estate produced £4 14s. 10d.[92] The plate and ornaments had already been valued at 35s., and the lead on the chapel roof at £6 13s. 4d.[93] The chantry house, occupied by John Michell, the former chantry priest, then aged 80, was sold to John Whytehorne and John Bayly of Chard,[94] though most of the estate went in the following year to Robert Wood of the Inner Temple.[95] In 1615 the chantry house was owned by William Owsley (d. 1620).[96] The remainder of the estate seems to have become the manor of Crewkerne Chantry.

A chapel dedicated to St. Reyne or Ranus stood near the road between Crewkerne and Chard at the eastern end of the Windwhistle ridge, comple-menting on its western end another, dedicated to St. White or Candida.[97] St. Reyne's chapel was certainly built by the late 13th century,[98] and survived until the late 15th.[99] By the 1630s the site was that of a beacon.[1]

Some waste ground in Woolminstone was known in 1610 as Chappelhaye, and may perhaps have been the site of a chapel.[2]

A chapel of ease, later known as *CHRIST-CHURCH*, on the west side of South Street, was opened in 1854. Nearly half the cost was borne by William Hoskyns of North Perrott who, together with William Sparks, provided an endowment of £40 for the minister and a repair fund.[3] Hoskyns's motive was not only to provide church accommodation for the poor, but also 'to prevent the architectural beauty of the interior of the parish church from being in a great measure destroyed by the erection of side galleries'.[4] The building, designed by J. M. Allen in the Perpendicular style, was of Ham stone, and comprised a chancel, nave with north aisle and north porch, and a turret with one bell. The church was closed and in 1975 demolished.[5]

A building was erected by subscription at Hewish in 1868 to serve as a schoolroom on weekdays and as a chapel of ease on Sundays.[6] It became a mission room only after the closure of the school.[7] The church of the *GOOD SHEPHERD* is a plain stone building of one room with a porch.

In 1223 there was a dispute between William Briwere the younger on the one hand and Andrew of Misterton and John of Eastham on the other concerning presentation to the 'church' of Misterton and Eastham.[8] Eastham chapel had also been linked with the church of 'C' in an undated dispute.[9] Exactly what the link with Misterton implies is not clear since it is the first datable reference to a church in either place, though the separation of the estate at Eastham within the main manor of Crewkerne by 1066 at least argues for an earlier ecclesiastical foundation there than at the less well-developed Misterton. The dispute of 1223 may suggest by that time a sole benefice shared between the two communities, Eastham already perhaps beginning to revert to little more than private manorial status.

Whatever independence the manor acquired in early times was not shared by the church at Eastham, which was a chapel of Crewkerne. In 1295, however, it acquired burial rights, in return for which its rector yielded half the tithes of specified lands.[10] Thereafter, though the incumbent retained the title of rector, the church was variously described

[79] S.R.O., D/P/crew 4/1/1.
[80] *S.R.S.* xiii, pp. 36–7.
[81] Ibid. xlix, p. 18.
[82] Ibid. xix. 224.
[83] S.C. 6/Hen VIII/6179.
[84] *Cal. Pat.* 1563–6, p. 67.
[85] C 66/1362; S.R.O., T/PH/hsy, survey 1599.
[86] *S.R.S.* xv. 67.
[87] *Cal. Pat.* 1307–13, 183; *Inq. ad quod damnum* (Rec. Com.), 239. For an earlier attempt at foundation in 1308–9 see *Inq. ad quod damnum*, 223.
[88] B.L. Add. MS. 49359, f. 74v.
[89] *S.R.S.* i. 106.
[90] Ibid. xlix, p. 426.
[91] Ibid. lii, p. 160; liv, pp. 19–20.
[92] Ibid. ii. 6, 176.
[93] E 117/8; E 117/12 no. 21; *S.R.S.* ii. 6.
[94] *Cal. Pat.* 1547–8, 285.

[95] Ibid. 1549–51, 97.
[96] C 145/535/22.
[97] *Proc. Som. Arch. Soc.* xxxvii. 40–59.
[98] Hook Manor, Donhead St. Andrew, Arundell MSS. G 588; S.R.O., D/D/B reg 1, Crewkerne dues; *Proc. Som. Arch. Soc.* cxx.
[99] W. Worcestre, *Itineraries*, ed. Harvey, 123.
[1] *S.R.S.* xv. 69.
[2] S.R.O., DD/PT, boxes 12, 23: lease 1 Feb. 1612.
[3] Char. Com. files; S.R.O., D/P/crew 9/1/1 *sub anno* 1851.
[4] S.R.O., D/P/crew 9/1/1, 23/10.
[5] Ibid. 9/1/1; local information.
[6] Pulman, *Bk. of the Axe*, 319.
[7] S.R.O., D/P/crew 9/1/2.
[8] *Cur. Reg. R.* xi, p. 275.
[9] *Year Bk.* 5 Edw. II (Selden Soc. xi), 212.
[10] *Proc. Som. Arch. Soc.* cxx.

as a chapel,[11] a chapel with cure,[12] and a free chapel.[13] By c. 1548, however, the benefice was evidently a sinecure, for the chapel was described as a ruin and its property occupied by the rector of Wayford.[14] In 1572 it was evidently regarded as a chantry and was let by the Crown.[15]

The patronage seems to have descended with the ownership of Eastham manor throughout most of the Middle Ages, though under an agreement of 1309 the Asshetones (recte Asshelonds) and the Crickets agreed to alternate presentations.[16] Appointments in 1447 and 1463 were made by the bishop through lapse.[17] The Sinclairs did not dispose of the advowson in 1479,[18] and in 1493 it was exercised by John Hayes.[19] John Lacy died in 1529 leaving the advowson to his son Thomas.[20] Conveyances of the manor in 1538 and 1585 also included the advowson of the 'church and free chapel' and the advowson of the vicarage.[21] The second, a quitclaim from William, Lord Sandys, to Robert Freke, began the Freke interest in the estate, though the family did not apparently exercise the right of patronage of what was still legally a rectory until 1624. In the meantime William Paris alias Court presented by grant of Robert Hungerford in 1554, Elizabeth, widow of William Orchard late of Compton Valence (Dors.) in her own right in 1573, Roger Garvys by grant of William, Lord Sandys, in 1575, and Richard Braine, clerk, in 1622.[22]

The Frekes were patrons in 1660 and 1692, though the bishop collated in 1683. Mary Poole, widow, succeeded to the advowson by 1734, and Caleb King, grocer and merchant, by 1736. The bishop again presented by lapse in 1791.[23] At the next vacancy in 1836 the patron was William Hoskyns of Marylebone (Mdx.)[24] and thereafter the advowson was owned by trustees headed first by Thomas Hoskyns of Haselbury Plucknett and then by his nephew the Revd. Charles Thomas Hoskyns of North Perrott.[25] The Hoskynses ceded their patronage when the living was united with Crewkerne in 1925.

In 1535 the rectory was valued at 66s. 8d. net, and comprised glebe worth 3s. 4d. and predial tithes of 63s. 4d.[26] In 1572 the same property was worth £10.[27] By 1694 the incumbent, insisting on payment of tithes in kind, made £12 or £14, though some of his immediate predecessors had apparently been content with a modus of c. £5.[28]

The gross tithe rent-charge on the tithing or rectory of Eastham in 1840 was £35 17s. 6d.[29]

The small benefice did not attract well-known clergy even during the Middle Ages: there was at least one deprivation for failing to take priest's orders,[30] and the bishop had to collate twice during the 15th century because of lapse.[31] In 1554 the rector, found to be married and newly in deacon's orders, was deprived.[32] The first identifiable rector thereafter, Hugh Atkins, rector 1660–82, was also rector of North Perrott, and his successors all held livings elsewhere, usually within the diocese, until the time of James Draper, rector 1791–1836, who was assistant curate of Crewkerne and also served at Misterton. From 1866 the rectory was always held with the living of Crewkerne, and was united with it in 1925.[33]

About 1548 the chapel was said to be ruined, though its cemetery remained.[34] There was 'no church there' by 1575,[35] though a description of the estate of Eastham in 1693 included a field 'where the chapel stands',[36] and the foundations were still said to be discernible in the 19th century.[37] A fragment of stone in the parish church is said to have come from the site.

ROMAN CATHOLICISM. A few individuals, mostly women, were reported as recusants between 1593 and 1626, three of them members of the Bonville family of Clapton.[38] St. Peter's church, in South Street, was erected in 1935. The parish is served from Chard.[39]

PROTESTANT NONCONFORMITY. In 1662 a Crewkerne Quaker was in trouble for refusing tithe.[40] A regular Quaker meeting, established by 1668,[41] continued, despite persecution in the 1680s,[42] and a new meeting-house was in use from 1725. Licences for worship in private houses between 1737 and 1743 suggest that the group had become small.[43] The meeting-house was still in existence in 1747, but it had apparently been sold and the cause abandoned by 1756.[44]

James Stevenson, minister and physician, who had been ejected from Martock in 1662, lived and probably taught in the town for two years from 1665;[45] and in 1669 three more ejected ministers, Robert Pinney, Jeremiah French, and John Westley,

---

[11] S.R.S. i. 165; xlix, pp. 387–8.
[12] Ibid. x, pp. 528, 614.
[13] Ibid. lii, p. 185.
[14] E 310/23/127 no. 90.
[15] Cal. Pat. 1569–72, pp. 389–90.
[16] S.R.S. xii. 19, 85.
[17] Ibid. xlix, pp. 78, 387–8.
[18] Cat. Anct. D. vi, C 4822.
[19] S.R.S. lii, p. 185.
[20] C 142/50/33.
[21] C.P. 25(2)/36/239/30 Hen. VIII Mich.; C.P. 25(2)/206/27 Eliz. I Hil.
[22] Som. Incumbents, ed. Weaver.
[23] Ibid.
[24] S.R.O., D/D/B reg 34.
[25] Ibid. 39–42.
[26] Valor Eccl. (Rec. Com.), i. 167.
[27] Cal. Pat. 1569–72, pp. 389–90.
[28] S.R.O., DD/PH 224/48.
[29] S.R.O., tithe award.
[30] S.R.S. i. 165.

[31] Ibid. xlix, pp. 78, 387–8.
[32] S.R.O., D/D/Vc 66, f. 12v.
[33] S.R.O., D/D/Bo.
[34] E 310/23/127 no. 90.
[35] S. & D. N. & Q. xiv. 33.
[36] S.R.O., DD/PH 61.
[37] Pulman, Bk. of the Axe, 244 n.
[38] S.R.O., D/D/Ca 175, 244; Recusant Roll 2 (Cath. Rec. Soc. lvii), 141.
[39] Cath. Dir. (1976).
[40] J. Besse, Sufferings of the . . . Quakers, i. 592.
[41] S.R.O., DD/SFR 1/1.
[42] Besse, Sufferings, i. 604–5, 649; J. Whiting, Persecution Exposed (1715), 63, 84, 112; S.R.O., D/P/crew 4/1/1, sub annis 1676, 1684.
[43] S.R.O., Q/RR, meeting-house lics. 1725, 1737, 1738, 1741, 1743.
[44] S.R.O., DD/SFR 1/3.
[45] J. Murch, Presbyterian and General Baptist Church in West of England (1835), 240–1.

were teaching in and near the town, one at Tail mill.[46] Two Presbyterian groups and a teacher were licensed in 1672, one group meeting in the house of John Serry, barber-surgeon, and a further group and their teacher occur in 1673.[47] In 1684 some 'fanatics' at Crewkerne welcomed the arrival of the recently released nonconformist John Trenchard.[48] Three licences, one for 'the public meeting-house' probably in Hermitage Street and two others for private houses, indicate the strength of Presbyterianism under the leadership of John Pinney from 1689.[49] By 1718 Robert Knight, the Presbyterian minister, had a following of 250 people.[50]

The cause continued, apparently becoming Unitarian in theology during the 18th century, though still occasionally called Presbyterian.[51] In 1752 and 1758 two houses at Clapton were also licensed for worship in the same cause. A building called 'the meeting-house' was licensed for Presbyterians in 1761, though this may well refer to the present Unitarian chapel in Hermitage Street, built in 1733 and otherwise unaccounted for.[52] There were said to be 'many' Presbyterians in the town in 1776,[53] though the congregation was described as Unitarian three years earlier.[54] In 1851 the church, described as the Presbyterian meeting-house but of Unitarian persuasion, was without a minister, and no service was held on Census Sunday, though the average general congregation was normally 40 on Sunday mornings.[55]

The Unitarian and Free Christian chapel in Hermitage Street is a plain building in local stone with round-headed mullioned and transomed windows. The dates 1733, 1811, and 1900 over the door indicate foundation and subsequent alterations.

The origins of the Baptists are difficult to trace before the erection of a chapel in North Street in 1820, though worship may have started in private houses licensed in 1808 or 1810.[56] The congregation was Particular Baptist.[57] On Census Sunday 1851 attenders including Sunday-school children totalled 300 in the morning, 200 in the afternoon, and 350 in the evening, in sum rather less than the Sunday average of 960.[58]

The chapel in North Street is a large building of 1880 in local rubble with rusticated quoins. The symmetrical main front has a central pediment, forming a gallery bay, supported on pilasters flanked by pedimented entrance porches. The adjoining manse is a plain symmetrical stone building of the early 19th century.

Followers of Joanna Southcott met in Crewkerne

c. 1811 and found support in the incumbent, Dr. Ashe, who was subsequently lampooned for his views.[59] Their place of meeting is unknown.

About 1821 the Crewkerne Mission was established by itinerant Bible Christian preachers from Dorset and Devon, and by 1824 there were 15 people 'on trial' as potential members of the West Buckland circuit.[60] Later in the year the original circuit was divided and Crewkerne, with 15 full members and 19 'on trial', became for a time the head of a new one. A chapel 'in the possession of people called Arminian Bible Christians' was licensed in 1825,[61] and between 1829 and 1833 services were also held at Woolminstone.[62] During the same period the cause at Crewkerne declined and the chapel was evidently closed in 1831. Another building, known as Ebenezer chapel, in Hermitage Street,[63] was rented and fitted out in 1835–6 but was given up in 1838. No further meetings were held until 1849, but within a year the movement had achieved a membership of 30. Both the period of the closure and the speed of recovery suggest that members changed their allegiance to and from the Wesleyans.[64]

In 1851 the Bible Christians were occupying a room in Chard or West Street erected in 1850, and on Census Sunday the afternoon congregation was 100 and the evening 88 strong.[65] The room was replaced by a chapel in West Street in 1872[66] and by another in Hermitage Street in 1890.[67] This chapel became the head of the United Methodist circuit in 1907 but was absorbed into the former Wesleyan South Petherton and Crewkerne circuit in 1954. The chapel, closed in 1962, is a plain stone building with a gallery.[68]

Wesleyan Methodism was established in the town by 1831 but was apparently strengthened by a secession from the Bible Christians, for a substantial congregation appeared suddenly in 1833.[69] By 1834 the cause had 77 members, the largest society in the South Petherton circuit. Between 1836 and 1864 there was also a small society at Hewish.[70] In the late 1840s membership was over 50 and on Census Sunday 1851 the congregation was 102 in the morning and 90 in the evening.[71] The afternoon service in a private cottage at Hewish was attended by 40, though the annual average was lower.[72]

A chapel in South Street, on the site of a cottage acquired for the purpose in 1828 (possibly by Bible Christians before secession), was completed in 1832.[73] A schoolroom was added in 1864.[74] Both were replaced in 1874 by the present building, of

[46] A. Gordon, *Freedom after Ejection*, 91, 333; T. G. Crippen, *Nonconformity in Som.* (Som. Arch. Soc. Libr., Taunton Castle).
[47] *Cal. S.P. Dom.* 1672, 376, 379, 678; 1672–3, 426.
[48] Ibid. 1683–4, 285–6.
[49] S.R.O., Q/RR; DD/SB 33/4; *Letters of John Pinney 1679–99*, ed. G. F. Nuttall, 6, 62–3, 66, 82, 87–8, 95.
[50] Murch, *Presbyterian and General Baptist Ch.* 241; Crippen, *Nonconf. in Som.*
[51] Murch, *Presbyterian and General Baptist Ch.* 242; London, Dr. Williams' Libr., Thompson's List, 1773.
[52] S.R.O., Q/RR.
[53] S.R.O., D/D/V Dioc. bk.
[54] London, Dr. Williams' Libr., Thompson's List, 1773. For William Blake and his father, successively ministers, see *D.N.B.*
[55] H.O. 129/318/4/8/17.
[56] S.R.O., D/D/Rm, box 2; *Western Baptist Assoc. Letters, 1769–1823*.
[57] Char. Com. files.
[58] H.O. 129/318/4/8/19.
[59] Pulman, *Bk. of the Axe*, 295.
[60] *Arminian Mag.*, Jan. 1826; S.R.O., D/N/spc 31.
[61] S.R.O., D/D/Rm, box 2.
[62] S.R.O., D/N/spc 31.
[63] R.G. 4/1419.
[64] S.R.O., D/N/spc 31.
[65] H.O. 129/318/4/8/18.
[66] Pulman, *Bk. of the Axe*, 326. In 1976 it was known as 33 and 35 West Street.
[67] *Kelly's Dir. Som.* (1902). S.R.O., D/P/crew 23/10 says 1891.
[68] S.R.O., D/N/spc box 3, plans.
[69] London, New Coll. L 53/3/109; S.R.O., D/N/spc 2.
[70] S.R.O., D/N/spc 2.
[71] E. Devon R.O. 64/2/9/1B; H.O. 129/318/4/8/16.
[72] H.O. 129/318/4/8/20.
[73] Char. Com. files; Pulman, *Bk. of the Axe*, 326.
[74] Char. Com. files.

Ham stone in the Decorated style, with a large stone spire on its north-west corner. Schoolrooms were added in 1907.[75]

In 1851 there was one other sect whose precise origins in the town are unknown, but which could have been among the groups meeting in West Street, East Street, Clerks Barton, and at unspecified addresses between 1846 and 1850.[76] By 1851 a group of Latter Day Saints was meeting in a private house in South Street, evidently near Viney Bridge, where there were congregations of 17 in the morning, 28 in the afternoon with 5 Sunday-school children, and 35 in the evening.[77] The subsequent history of the group is unknown.

In 1859 a group of Plymouth Brethren opened a place of worship in East Street on a site occupied by their Gospel Hall in 1976.[78]

The Salvation Army began meetings in a private house in Rose Lane in 1884. Shortly afterwards they moved to a hall in Oxen Lane which they occupied for 70 years. The present hall in North Street was opened in 1959.[79]

EDUCATION. In 1703 Roger Cossins, a Crewkerne engraver, left rents to maintain six local boys at an English school in the town, the boys to be appointed by the warden and feoffees of the grammar school. An income of £3 12s. a year was paid from 1717. A gift of £50 was made in 1762 by Elizabeth Cookson to educate children of the town, and this produced a further £2 10s. a year. In 1822 these sums were being paid to a master who in return taught twelve children to read. Additional payments were required for teaching writing or arithmetic.[80] From 1855 no payments were made and funds of £4 a year were accumulated until 1878.[81] In 1710 Martha Minterne of Crewkerne gave lands from which £5 was paid to teach eight poor children. In 1822 this sum was paid to the sexton's daughter for the purpose, as was £8 8s. a year to J. C. Warr from 1870 to 1877.[82] Charity monies of £9 12s. a year were paid to a single endowed school for 20 girls in 1835, although the endowment was not mentioned thereafter.[83] These were probably the charity and infants' schools which in 1840 and 1842 lay in Church Lane and Church Street respectively.[84] The three educational charities were consolidated under a Scheme of 1878 and had a total income of £23 18s. 9d. in the following year and accumulated funds of £224 14s. 2d. The monies were to be applied in the payment of fees at elementary schools, awarding small scholarships or prizes, and in providing an exhibition for three years at the grammar school. No prizes were given after 1883, but otherwise the Scheme was put into effect.[85]

In 1835 there were 7 private infant schools for 121 children and 4 other day-schools which, with the 2 endowed schools, took 150 children. There were also 4 Sunday schools: one founded in 1820 attached to the parish church with 172 children; one reputedly established in 1796 by the Unitarians for 20 boys; the Baptist school started in 1820, with 180 children; and a Methodist Sunday school in South Street with 202 children, held since 1831.[86]

The two older charity schools were probably replaced by the National Schools built in 1847 in West Street.[87] A new infant department was built further down West Street in 1871, and in 1883 there was accommodation for 680 and an average attendance of 521.[88] Numbers were 485 in 1889 and 591 in 1897.[89] In 1903 there was a total staff of 21, 673 children on the books, and average attendances of 582. The premises were then also used by the Sunday schools, a men's club, the female friendly society, and by Volunteers as a drill hall.[90] Subsequently numbers fell greatly and were 304 in 1935 and 225 by 1946. In 1970 the former infant school of 1871 became St. Bartholomew's infant schools, and in 1972 one of the two First Schools in the comprehensive system. There were 175 children on the books in 1975.[91] The school built in 1847 was closed in 1970 and has since been used as a community centre and youth club.

In 1875 a School Board was formed for the united district of Crewkerne and Wayford and a school for 130 children was built in North Street in 1877.[92] There were 146 on the books in 1889 and the school was enlarged in 1897 for 240 children, including infants, and again in 1903 to take 360 pupils. Average attendances fell from 210 in 1905 to 181 in 1915, and 90 in 1935.[93] In 1946 it became a County secondary modern school, with 148 pupils, and so remained until c. 1959 when it was converted to a Church of England junior school. From 1970 it was known as Ashlands School. In 1972 it became a First School and in 1975 it had 200 pupils.[94]

The School Board also established a school at Clapton in 1878 to serve West Crewkerne, Wayford, and Seaborough. It was attended by 130 children in 1883. Numbers attending were 102 in 1915, 88 in 1935, and 51 in 1946.[95] The school closed in 1970 when most of the pupils were moved to Ashlands School.[96]

Maiden Beech Secondary Modern School was built in Lyme Road c. 1958 to accommodate 300 children. Under the comprehensive plan of 1972 it became a Middle School and in 1975 had 512 pupils.[97]

[75] Datestones on building; C 54/17656. The chapel was commenced in 1872.
[76] S.R.O., Q/RR; D/D/Rm, box 2.
[77] H.O. 129/318/4/8/15.
[78] Pulman, Bk. of the Axe, 326; deeds penes Messrs. Sparks and Blake, Crewkerne.
[79] Official Record of the Crewkerne Corps, ex inf. Mrs. Capt. S. Hunt, Yeovil.
[80] 9th Rep. Com. Char. H.C. 258, pp. 496–8 (1823), ix.
[81] S.R.O., DD/X/HAW; Schs. Inquiry Com. xiv. 264–5.
[82] 9th Rep. Com. Char. 498; S.R.O., DD/X/HAW.
[83] Educ. Enquiry Abstract, H.C. 62 (1835), xlii.
[84] County Gazette Dir. (1840); Pigot, Nat. Com. Dir. 1842).
[85] S.R.O., DD/X/HAW.
[86] Educ. Enquiry Abstract, H.C. 62 (1835), xlii; ex inf. Mr. W. B. Harwood.
[87] S.R.O., D/P/crew 18/7/1; Char. Com. files. The link is established by the payment of Cossins' charity to the National Schools until 1865: S.R.O., DD/X/HAW.
[88] Char. Com. files; Kelly's Dir. Som. (1883); Pulman, Bk. of the Axe, 319.
[89] Kelly's Dir. Som. (1889, 1897).
[90] Char. Com. files; S.R.O., C/E, box 26.
[91] Kelly's Dir. Som. (1906–35); S.R.O. Schs. Lists.
[92] Kelly's Dir. Som. (1883).
[93] Ibid. (1889–1935); S.R.O. Schs. Lists.
[94] S.R.O. Schs. Lists.
[95] Kelly's Dir. Som. (1883–1935); S.R.O. Schs. Lists.
[96] S.R.O., C/E, box 96.
[97] S.R.O. Schs. Lists.

Wadham Comprehensive School north of the Yeovil road was opened in 1972, replacing the existing secondary schools of Crewkerne and Ilminster. Numbers on the roll were 662 in 1975.[98] It is an extensive, flat-roofed complex generally of two storeys.

The Wesleyans built a mixed day-school at South Street in 1880, evidently replacing their existing Sunday school, and the former had attendances of 85 in 1883. It was enlarged in 1887 although the day-school had apparently been discontinued by 1897.[99] A building erected by subscription at Hewish in 1868 served as a school-room on week-days and a chapel of ease on Sundays.[1] It was referred to as a school in 1870 but, apart from the mention of a school-chapel there in 1906,[2] no other reference to its educational use has been noted.

Roger Beard, an accountant, kept a writing school in the town in 1751, which may have survived c. 1797 as Mr. Beard's English boarding school. A ladies' boarding school run by Miss Coombs also occurred c. 1797.[3] By 1822 there were three private boarding schools, two in South Street and one in Church Street.[4] The numbers of private boarding and day-schools had risen to seven by 1852, and in 1872 there were four such girls' schools and a commercial school in East Street.[5] There were only two private schools by 1906, and one, the Crawford House school for girls in East Street, in 1939.[6] St. Martin's boarding and day preparatory school, at present in Abbey Street, was evacuated to the town in 1939, and Bincombe School, founded in 1946, was closed in 1957.[7]

CHARITIES FOR THE POOR. There was evidently some form of financial support for the poor by the 1570s, for the death is recorded of an alms-woman of the town.[8] By will dated 1617 Matthew Chubb of Dorchester (Dors.) gave £100 for the maintenance of the alms-house in Crewkerne which he had 'procured to be built', the sum to be paid out of money owed to him by the Crown which he had advanced for the rebuilding of Dorchester.[9] The exact date of foundation is unknown, though an inscription visible in the early 19th century was read as 1604.[10] For some years after Chubb's death in 1617 the maintenance of the foundation was uncertain, and in 1624 and 1630 money was paid by the grammar school trustees, on the first occasion 'for making of a deed for the assurance of the alms-house to Mistress Chubb'.[11] In 1631 the house, its garden, and a sum of £100 for maintenance, were formally handed over to trustees.[12]

The alms-house, later known as the Old Alms-house, was for 8 people, 7 from Crewkerne and 1 from Misterton.[13] Both the grammar school

trustees and the churchwardens contributed to the maintenance of the fabric, the wardens making repairs 'by the consent of the town' in 1652, mending the 'chimney-hearth' in 1657, and repaying the alms-house warden a debt he had incurred in 1665.[14]

By the 1720s the alms-house possessed land near Henley and a rent-charge of £4 from land in Seaborough (Dors.).[15] By the 1820s this property produced £7 13s. 6d. a year, which kept the house in repair and provided a small quarterly distribution to the 8 residents, then generally women, chosen by the overseers. The doles were supplemented by extra cash at need and occasionally by the provision of spin thread.[16]

By will proved 1844 Jane Hawkesley gave the residue of her estate to be invested, providing doles on Christmas Eve for the residents. In 1869 the sum totalled £10 11s. 6d.[17] A further gift of £200 under the will of Mrs. Anna Maria Donisthorpe (d. 1856) was invested for similar distribution on 1 January.[18] George Slade Jolliffe, by will proved 1894, gave £1,500 to provide quarterly doles for the residents and a like sum to erect an additional building to house 4 more from 1897.[19]

Smaller sums were given for alms-people by Mary Ann Gapper (d. 1869), Mrs. Ann Wheadon (d. 1881), and Sarah Woodcock (will proved 1892), and they and the proceeds of the Jubilee Fund (1888) were amalgamated by a Scheme in 1896 under the title of the Alms-house Charities of Matthew Chubb and Others. The combined income was £125 11s. 8d. for the support of 8 and later of 12 people of over 60, at the rate of at least 3s. a week. A further reorganization took place in 1966 after the demolition of the Davis Alms-houses to create the New Alms-house and the Alms-house Charities of Matthew Chubb and Others Scheme, under which the charities were administered in 1976.[20]

The original building in Court Barton comprised 4 dwellings of 2 storeys each with two rooms in a symmetrical stone house, the entrances arranged in pairs. The additional block, built at right angles facing West Street, was designed by George Vialls of Crewkerne in similar style.[21]

The so-called New Alms-house in West Street, standing opposite the end of Matthew Chubb's Alms-house, was founded under the will of Mary Davis, spinster, dated 1707. Property in Crewkerne and Blackmoor farm in Woolminstone was given in trust after the deaths of her sister and aunt, the town property to be converted into an alms-house for 6 poor old men and 6 poor old women of Crewkerne and Woolminstone. The sum of £4 was also to be distributed on 1 January to 80 poor chosen by the trustees. By 1718 the life interests

[98] Ibid. For the history of the former Crewkerne grammar school see V.C.H. Som. ii. 453–5.
[99] Kelly's Dir. Som. (1883–97).
[1] Pulman, Bk. of the Axe, 319.
[2] S.R.O., D/P/crew 9/1/2; Kelly's Dir. Som. (1906).
[3] Sherborne Mercury, 29 July 1751; Univ. Brit. Dir. ii.
[4] Pigot, Nat. Com. Dir. (1822–3).
[5] Slater, Nat. Com. Dir. (1852–3); Morris & Co. Dir. Som. (1872).
[6] Kelly's Dir. Som. (1906–39).
[7] S.R.O., D/P/crew 23/10; ex inf. Lt. Col. A.E.F. Dowse-Brenan, Merriott, and Maj. R.A. Russell, Drimpton.

[8] S.R.O., D/P/crew 2/1/1.
[9] Prob 11/130 (P.C.C. 74 Weldon).
[10] B.L. Add. MS. 36381, f. 100.
[11] S.R.O., DD/CGS 3/1.
[12] 9th Rep. Com. Char. H.C. 258, pp. 494–5 (1823), ix.
[13] Ibid.
[14] S.R.O., D/P/crew 4/1/1; DD/CGS 3/1.
[15] 9th Rep. Com. Char. p. 495.
[16] Ibid. p. 496.
[17] Char. Com. files; S.R.O., D/P/crew 17/3/3.
[18] S.R.O., D/P/crew 4/1/3, p. 317.
[19] Char. Com. files.   [20] Ibid.
[21] B.L. Add. MS. 36381, f. 100; Char. Com. files.

had ceased, and the charity probably came into being under a decree of 1719.[22]

By 1866 the income of £132 from the farm and a building next to the alms-house was applied in payments of 3s. a week to the 12 occupants, with coals in winter; £4 was distributed yearly to the 80 poor. By the 1950s the income was slightly less, but the accommodation was still for 12 people. In 1961 the property, then unfit for dwellings, was sold to the urban district council and demolished.[23] The income of the charity was amalgamated with that of the Old Alms-houses under a Scheme of 1966, providing a total of 8 dwellings, 6 for people from Crewkerne, 1 from Misterton, and 1 from Woolminstone or West Crewkerne.[24]

The alms-houses were in a single-storeyed building of 9 bays, the central 3 forming a pedimented section with Tuscan pilasters, and each group of 3 having a pedimented door flanked on each side by a window.[25]

In 1876 Robert Bird established a trust for the benefit of old weavers employed in his factory, and provided 6 cottages in South Street and a capital sum of £1,080 for their maintenance, together with doles to the occupants. Under a Scheme of 1953 the benefits of the trust were extended to any resident in or near Crewkerne, though preference was still to be given to employees. In 1957–8 the 'cottage homes' (nos. 3–13 South Street) were modernized to accommodate 5 people, with a communal room. They were sold for a road-widening scheme in 1973 and were replaced by 5 bungalows in Bird's Close.[26]

About 1710 Martha Minterne settled land in trust, the income to be distributed yearly at Candlemas in sums of 3s. each to poor people of Crewkerne.

By 1879 the money, about £24 a year, was given on 14 February, and for some 15 years had been limited to residents in the town tithing. By 1895 it was worth £15 and in 1961 £22 10s.[27] It was administered by the urban district council in succession to the parish overseers until local government reorganization in 1974.[28]

By 1719 an estate at Greenham was charged in the name of Mrs. Jane Reynolds's Charity with payment of £3, to be distributed to paupers not in constant relief. In that year 68 people were relieved.[29] By 1759 the income had risen to £4, and in 1776 it was agreed that £3 should go to people from Crewkerne and £1 to those from Hewish, in units of a shilling.[30] The money was distributed on Easter Monday. The urban district council continued payments in succession to the parish officers until local government reorganization in 1974.[31]

By will dated 1730 William Budd of Crewkerne settled £20 in trust for loans to 'honest industrious persons . . . of Crewkerne' for periods of 4 years each.[32] In 1961 the capital sum was c. £31,[33] and was administered by the urban district council.

William Sharlock of Hereford, by will dated 1786, settled £100 stock in trust for distribution in shillings on St. Thomas's Day.[34] By 1867 the doles were given on 1 January.[35] In 1874 the income of £3 12s. was distributed to 72 people.[36] In 1967 the income was £3 and was administered like Minterne's, Reynolds's, and Budd's by the local authority.[37]

On the death of Miss Marianne Wills of Exeter (d. 1863) and in her name her brother settled £200 stock in trust for distribution, half in bread and half in Bibles yearly on 1 January to residents of the parish.[38] Bibles were given at least until 1927.[39] In 1967 the value of the charity was £5.[40]

HINTON ST. GEORGE

THE HILL-TOP (hēa-tun) village of Hinton St. George occupies a prominent position on a north facing scarp at the north-western corner of Crewkerne hundred. It lies in the centre of its roughly rectangular parish, which is nearly 2 miles long and just over a mile wide. In 1901 the parish measured 1,572 a.[1] Much of its western boundary was probably altered by the extension of Hinton park into Dinnington, but its northern limit, also the boundary of the hundred, follows the course of the Lopen brook and, like the limits of Dinnington and its neighbours, ignores the line of the Foss Way. Part of the eastern boundary follows the course of a road, and at its less regular southern end

coincides with water courses. Its southern boundary has no apparent physical basis.

Most of the parish lies on Yeovil Sands, providing arable, meadow, and pasture in the northern valley below the 250 ft. scarp and forming an undulating terrain to the south, rising to 450 ft. in Paddocks plantation and to over 375 ft. to the west on the Dinnington boundary. Clay and limestone are revealed by a fault bisecting the southern half of the parish. Bricks were made in the parish in the 17th century,[2] and Brick Kiln Close survived as a field-name near the southern boundary in the late 18th century.[3] There seem to have been at least three stone quarries in the 14th century, almost certainly

[22] 9th Rep. Com. Char. pp. 491–4.
[23] Char. Com. files; The Times, 31 May 1961.
[24] Char. Com. files.
[25] B.L. Add. MS. 36381, f. 100.
[26] Char. Com. files.
[27] 9th Rep. Com. Char. p. 498; Char. Com. files.
[28] S.R.O., DD/X/HAW; ex inf. Mr. L. G. Watson, S. Petherton.
[29] S.R.O., D/P/crew 13/2/1.
[30] Ibid. 13/2/1–5.
[31] S.R.O., DD/X/HAW; ex inf. Mr. Watson.
[32] S.R.O., DD/HKE 1/6; D/P/crew 4/1/3.

[33] Char. Com. files.
[34] S.R.O., DD/X/HAW.   [35] Ibid.
[36] S.R.O., D/P/crew 9/1/2.
[37] Char. Com. files; ex inf. Mr. Watson.
[38] S.R.O., D/P/crew 9/1/1; Char. Com. files.
[39] S.R.O., DD/X/HAW.
[40] Char. Com. files.
[1] V.C.H. Som. ii. 343. This article was completed in 1976.
[2] See below.
[3] S.R.O., DD/SAS (C/212), map of Hinton Park c. 1800.

located in the open arable West field, later part of Hinton park.[4] Park quarry and Keeper's quarry were still being used in the early 19th century, together with others at Crimbleford Knap and Stockbridge.[5] Marl was dug in the parish in the 17th century.[6] Water rising in Hinton park drove mills at Dinnington and Kingstone before returning to the parish to drive Hinton mill on the Lopen border. Another supply was brought to Hinton house in the 1650s through lead and alder pipes both for domestic use and for a fountain.[7]

Before the end of the 18th century the village consisted of regular tenements lying either side of a single street. Its eastern end, where several roads converged, was known as Townsend by 1716.[8] North of Townsend, but perhaps once including it, was a green, mentioned in 1523.[9] At the western end of the village stood the church and the manor-house, some distance respectively north and south of the street where it curved gently southwards off the line of its hitherto direct course. The centre of the village was marked by a late-medieval cross, bearing on its shaft a figure said to be St. John the Baptist and surmounted by an 18th-century ball finial. The cross divided Hinton (later High) Street, on the east from Fore or West Street.[10] Northwards from the cross was a way serving the church and the fields. About 1798 New Road was formed taking traffic for Dinnington in an arc to the north of the church when Earl Poulett extended the grounds of Hinton House across the line of Fore Street, blocking its western exit.

The village east of the cross, with its regular plots and a surviving southern rear access known as the Lane by 1717 and Back Lane by 1745,[11] is characteristic of a medieval planned settlement. Teapot Lane was the name given in the 19th century to South Street, the northern part of the Crewkerne road between Townsend and Back Lane. Gas Lane was so named from the late 19th century. It linked Back Lane and the rear entrance of Hinton House with West Street.

A mile south-west of the main village lay the hamlet of Craft or Hintonscraft, first traceable c. 1280.[12] It continued as a settlement until the mid 18th century when extensions to the park absorbed the last individual holdings. Its one surviving house, Oaklands, is part of the complex of Hinton Park farm.

Craft was probably a relatively late settlement for it had no separate arable fields. The holding of the Carent family, evidently centred on the hamlet, was distributed evenly throughout the three open fields of the parish.[13] West field, south-west of the village, lay in the area later occupied by the park, and was probably divided from South field by the road between Craft and Hinton. Traces of North field remained in the names of closes below the

scarp in the 19th century, when land towards Merriott had come to be known as East field, a more rational name for what remained of South field when the park was extended in the 16th century. The name East field occurs in 1569 when the open-field system in the parish was fast coming to an end.[14]

The growth of the park between the 16th and the end of the 18th centuries radically altered the road pattern of the parish. Before that time its main elements were the east–west route along the scarp where the village lay, traceable north-east through Merriott to Ham Hill, and the medieval highway or 'old church way' from the village south-west through Craft to the Windwhistle ridge.[15] The absence of ecclesiastical and tenurial links with Crewkerne is reflected in the indirectness of the roads to the south-east, which, like those below the scarp in the north, are little more than extended field routes. Perhaps the most significant in the north was the road to Hinton mill and Lopen, called Whyetway in the 1520s.[16]

Each stage in the extension of the park was marked by the modification of this pattern. Part of the road along the ridge west of the village was moved northwards in 1766.[17] A new road, largely outside the parish, from Harford's Lodge to Roundham common, was projected in 1765 and finished by 1772, thus completing the encirclement of the park at its greatest extent.[18] The medieval road through Craft to Hinton was then closed to public traffic. The diversion of the village street to the north of the church was accompanied by the closure of footpaths across the park including one representing the westward route from the village towards Kingstone and Ilminster and known as the coach road, the route taken by the predecessor of the Taunton–Bridport coach.[19]

Despite the existence of this coach route the parish roads were virtually untouched by turnpikes. The Foss between Lopen and Dinnington, with its extension to the top of Warren hill skirting the south-western boundary, was taken over by the Ilminster trust in 1823. The projected extension of the Crewkerne trust over the route between Merriott and Hinton Cross in 1825 was not proceeded with.[20]

The south-west of the parish has probably always been wooded. The Denebaud holding in the mid 14th century included woodland called Whatlegh, probably some of the extensive Domesday woodland.[21] There was also a wood called Warener in the 1360s, probably developed into the Old Warren of the 17th century.[22] The name Whatlegh itself suggests a woodland clearing, and Fursyempnet in the same area implies other previous vegetation. Moorland attached to the Forde abbey holding in Craft perhaps refers to the higher land on the southern boundary.[23]

4 C 136/66/8; *Cal. Close*, 1346–9, 399.
5 S.R.O., DD/PT, boxes 8 (waywardens' accts.), 50; D/P/hin. g 14/5/1.   6 S.R.O., D/P/hin. g 4/1/1, p. 179.
7 S.R.O., DD/PT, box 40, acct. bk. 1651–5.
8 Ibid. box 29.   9 S.R.O., DD/SS, bdle. 2.
10 S.R.O., DD/PT, boxes 26, 28, 49; D/P/hin. g 14/5/1.
11 S.R.O., DD/PT, box 29; DD/SS, bdle. 25.
12 Forde Abbey, Cart. pp. 379–80.
13 *Cal. Close*, 1346–9, 399 (where south and west fields are reversed); C 136/66/8.
14 S.R.O., DD/PT, box 2,
15 Ibid.; DD/SS, bdle. 1.

16 S.R.O., DD/SS, bdle. 1.
17 S.R.O., DD/PT, boxes 26, 29.
18 5 Geo. III c. 61 (Priv. Act); S.R.O., T/PH/hsy, map of Crewkerne rectory 1772; DD/PT, box 28 ('lately made' in 1795).
19 S.R.O., Q/SR, Easter 1798; DD/PT, box 50, planting bk.; DD/SS, bdle. 4; *Taunton Courier*, 29 Aug. 1821.
20 25 Geo. III, c. 60 (Priv. Act) and 6 Geo. IV, c. 159 (Local and Personal); S.R.O., Q/AH, map.
21 C 136/66/8; *V.C.H. Som.* i. 507.
22 C 136/66/8; S.R.O., DD/PT, box 40, acct. bk. 1651–5.
23 Forde Abbey, Cart. pp. 378–9.

Woodland increased with the development of the park. An earlier park, called Sopernepark, seems to have been part of North field by 1347.[24] By 1561 a park called Hinton park or Upcroft had been formed, which by 1569 was 4 miles in compass.[25] It spread westwards, its pale enclosing part of the 'manor' of Hill in Chillington,[26] and grew through exchanges with tenants in the 1560s.[27] Work on the estate in the 1650s included levelling hedges and taking in fields, planting hawthorn around the perimeter and making other lengths of hedge around the old Warren, the last an area evidently taken in from Dinnington parish.[28] A New Park mentioned in 1718 perhaps involved further additions.[29] By then there were two lodges marking entrances, one referred to as new in 1654. At the other, the White Lodge, a girl was said to have been cured of the King's Evil by the duke of Monmouth in 1680.[30]

In 1766 Earl Poulett moved the Hinton–Dinnington road northwards to improve the western side of Hinton House. The remaining tenants undertook not to plant trees or erect buildings to obstruct the view. Probably the statue of Diana, standing on a Ham stone pedestal and once surrounded by a double circle of lime trees at the end of Fore Park, dates from this period.[31] Further west, by the end of the century, oaks and thorns were planted around 'Old Diana', evidently another statue, from which six walks radiated; and further south a carriage drive was planned beyond Craft lane.[32] Kent suggested improvements at the turn of the century to match the remodelling of the house. Two ponds at Craft were to become a large lake and belts of trees were to be planted to screen the encircling roads. Much of this work was not carried out.[33]

Deer, mentioned in the 16th century,[34] were evidently introduced in a new deer park by 1802,[35] and further extensive planting and ornamentation continued between 1812 and 1817. A wide variety of trees raised in Dinnington parish was planted, new 'American clumps' were established near the house, and drives improved.[36] Within the next few years, however, the park was broken up into agricultural holdings,[37] and by 1839 only some 184 a. of a total of 753 a. were retained for plantations, ponds, and the gardens and lawns near the house.[38]

Apart from Hinton House the most important domestic building is the Priory, at the centre of the village. At its east end it has a small chapel on the first floor, having an open roof with cusped trusses and a 14th-century window with the head of a saint in the topmost light. This building seems to have been added to the parlour of an earlier house.

The present structure, although showing no features earlier than the 16th century,[39] yet retains a medieval plan with central hall heated by a fireplace in a side wall. The house was extended to the west in the 17th and 18th centuries, and by ranges of farm buildings reaching the street in the late 19th century. At least from the late 17th century it was known as the Home Tenement, its present name stemming from late-19th-century antiquarianism. The presence of the chapel, indicating an owner of some prominence, suggests that the property may have belonged either to Monkton Farleigh priory or, less likely, to the Carent family.[40]

Most of the larger houses in the village centre appear to be of 17th- or early 18th-century origin and are normally of three-roomed plan with internal stack against passage entry. Old Farm, West Street, has a lateral stack and may be earlier. There are marked traces of 19th-century infilling and villa creation, and of 20th-century rebuilding which has consciously retained the form and proportion of earlier structures.

There were at least three inns in Hinton in the late 17th century, one quartering soldiers by 1661.[41] By the 1680s one was known as the White Hart, another as the George.[42] The third was probably the Crown, which occurs by 1712.[43] The Crown and the George, occupying two halves of a house at the cross, facing down the main street, were both let to members of the Tett family during the 18th century, though the Beck family occupied the George for the same period.[44] On Richard Beck's retirement in 1788 the George was described as 'well accustomed and commands a very extensive business in the wine and brandy trade'.[45] Perhaps at this date the George and Crown were united, and so remained until it was burnt down in 1960.[46]

By 1735 there were seven licensed victuallers and a maltster in the parish.[47] Apart from the George and the Crown there was the White Hart which continued until at least 1795 but had ceased to trade by 1814.[48] The Hare and Hounds was so named by 1770, but changed its title c. 1824 to the Poulett Arms, still in business in 1976.[49] The other unnamed inns ceased to trade before the end of the 18th century.

There was a friendly society at Hinton, though its date of origin is unknown.[50] It met on the first Tuesday in June, but was discontinued c. 1900.[51] A cricket club was established by 1827 but moved to Stoke a few years later.[52] The village is noted for its Punkie night celebrations, dating from at least 1877, when children with turnip lanterns recall

[24] *Cal. Close*, 1346–9, 399.
[25] *Cal. Pat.* 1560–63, p. 71; *S.R.S.* xx. 31.
[26] S.R.O., DD/PT, box 10A.
[27] S.R.O., DD/SS, bdle. 1; DD/PT, box 2.
[28] S.R.O., DD/PT, acct. bk. 1651–5. Lord Poulett paid tithe for the warren to the 'parson' of Dinnington.
[29] S.R.O., D/P/hin. g 14/5/1.
[30] S.R.O., DD/PT, box 40, acct. bk.; *Bibliotheca Somersetensis*, ed. E. Green.
[31] S.R.O., DD/PT, boxes 26, 29.
[32] S.R.O., DD/SAS (C/212), map of Hinton Park c. 1800.
[33] S.R.O., DD/PT, map of Poulett estates 1796.
[34] *V.C.H. Som.* ii. 568.
[35] S.R.O., DD/SS, bdle. 4.
[36] S.R.O., DD/PT, box 50, planting bk.
[37] Ibid. box 40, bk. of contracts, 1819.

[38] S.R.O., tithe award.
[39] Smoke-blackened timbers are said to have been seen in the roof during restoration c. 1950.
[40] See below, p. 44.
[41] S.R.O., D/P/hin. g 4/1/1, pp. 105, 125, 189, 266.
[42] Ibid. p. 254; DD/SS, bdle. 25.
[43] S.R.O., DD/PT, box 26.
[44] Ibid. boxes 26, 28.
[45] *Western Flying Post*, 5 Jan. 1789.
[46] S.R.O., Q/RL; local information.
[47] S.R.O., Q/RL.
[48] S.R.O., DD/PT, box 44 (rent bk.); D/P/hin. g 13/2/6.
[49] S.R.O., Q/RL.
[50] Ex inf. Mr. F. James, Salisbury. It is not mentioned in M. Fuller, *West-Country Friendly Socs.*
[51] S.R.O., DD/SAS PR 54/10: W.I. hist. 1933.
[52] S.R.O., DD/LV 8.

(according to one tradition) the search for the men of Hinton returning late from Chiselborough fair.[53] The Men's Reading Room was presented to the village by Earl Poulett in 1906; the village hall in the recreation field was built in 1960. Coal gas was manufactured on the Poulett estate by 1883 and converted to petrol gas in 1912.[54]

The population in 1971 was less than half the peak of 1831 when it stood at 850. This total represented a considerable rise from 575 in 1801 and was followed by notable falls in the decades after 1841 and 1891. In 1901 the total was 477 and after a small increase in the next decade, has since fallen to 413 in 1971.[55]

Hinton was seriously affected by the Civil War, largely because of the Poulett influence on the Royalist side. The house was held unsuccessfully against the Parliamentary trained bands in 1642, though Hertford came through later in the year.[56] The German professional, Colonel Vandruske, fighting for Parliament, was there in 1643, and royalist troops were quartered in the village in 1644.[57] Their opponents returned in 1645, and General Massey's *Truth Discovered* was dated from there in 1646.[58] Hinton House itself was evidently damaged but Lord Poulett seems to have recovered possession in 1648,[59] though a detachment of troops continued to be quartered in the parish until 1661.[60] Lord Poulett himself paid the farmer of Coombe farm the cost of preserving shears and coulters in the time of the wars.[61]

In 1685 the overseers gave money to 'poor people of the parish in their wants in the time of the Rebellion'.[62] Six men of the parish were in Monmouth's army.[63]

Henry Cuff, Regius professor of Greek at Oxford 1590-7 and secretary to the Earl of Essex, was born at Hinton in 1563 and was executed for treason in 1601.[64] Henry Fowler (1858-1933), the lexicographer, lived at Hinton when working on the *Oxford English Dictionary*.[65]

MANOR AND OTHER ESTATES. Like many of the properties of the king's thegn Aelfstan of Boscombe (Wilts.), tenant T.R.E., Hinton passed by 1086 to William, count of Eu.[66] Elsewhere the counts of Eu continued to hold the overlordship of their estates until the beginning of the 13th century, when they gave place to the earls Marshal.[67] Hinton certainly was theirs before 1233, though the property of Richard Marshal, earl of Pembroke (d. 1234), was then under attack.[68] The overlord-

ship passed to his heirs and descended like the 'probable' barony of Chepstow, the manor being held, not without challenge, of Chepstow castle. It was, however, held of the Crown in 1246 when the earldom of Pembroke reverted to royal hands on the death of Anselm Marshal (d. 1245),[69] but passed subsequently with the office of Earl Marshal to Anselm's eldest sister and coheir Maud, countess of Norfolk (d. 1248), and thus to the Bigods. After the death of Roger Bigod, earl of Norfolk, in 1306[70] the overlordship was inherited by Thomas of Brotherton, fifth son of Edward I, and then on his death in 1338 by his eldest daughter Margaret (cr. duchess of Norfolk 1397, d. 1399).[71] Unsuccessful claims to the property were made by the Crown in 1347-8, 1352, 1362, and 1391 in favour of the owner of the manor of Hampstead Marshall (Berks.),[72] but it remained with the successors of Thomas of Brotherton, and in 1428 was held by John Mowbray, duke of Norfolk (d. 1432), great-grandson of Duchess Margaret. The last reference to overlordship was in 1497 when it was claimed by Elizabeth, duchess of Norfolk, widow of the last Mowbray duke.[73]

The early history of the terre tenancy is uncertain until the 1220s, though 17th- and 18th-century historians, the second citing an unidentified 'ancient charter', refer to a John and George Powtrell as owners in the reigns of Richard I and John.[74] A Powtrell heiress is by these historians said to have brought the estate to her husband John Gifford, and as late as 1540 Sir Hugh Poulett was described as 'kinsman and heir of John Gifford'.[75] In contrast, the early history of the rectory suggests that by 1220 the property was owned by Robert de Barnevill.[76] The former link between rectory and manor was confirmed in 1540.[77]

Robert de Barnevill had certainly ceased to hold Hinton by 1241, and he may have been only a life tenant. A possible heir, Ralph de Barnevill, was a Marshal tenant at Hilmarton (Wilts.) in the same year.[78] But already by 1233 the king committed to Theobald de Engleskevill during pleasure the land in Hinton of Philip Denebaud, an adherent of the rebellious Richard Marshal, earl of Pembroke, a grant soon afterwards cancelled in favour of Nicholas of St. Brides.[79] Custody of Robert de Barnevill's land was still being disputed in 1242-3.[80]

Philip Denebaud, who also possessed property at Portskewet (Mon.), near Chepstow, and who is said to have married Alice, daughter and heir of John Gifford, evidently recovered the estate. He gave half to his eldest son William on William's marriage, and later half to his third son Hamon.[81]

[53] Ex inf. Mr. James.
[54] *Kelly's Dir. Som.* (1883); S.R.O., DD/PT file.
[55] *Census.*
[56] D. Underdown, *Som. in the Civil War and Interregnum,* 41, 43.
[57] *Diary of Richard Symonds* (Camd. Soc. 1st ser. lxxiv), 110-14; S.R.O., DD/CGS 3/1; D/P/hin. g 2/1/1: burials of four soldiers including one from Sussex. For Vandruske see Underdown, op. cit. 82.
[58] S.R.O., D/P/hin. g 2/1/1: burial 1 Nov. 1645.
[59] *Cal. Cttee. for Compounding,* ii. 1052-3.
[60] S.R.O., D/P/hin. g 4/1/1, pp. 55, 67, 105; DD/PT, box 40, acct. bk. week ending 17 Mar. 1654/5.
[61] S.R.O., DD/PT, box 40, acct. bk. May 1652.
[62] S.R.O., D/P/hin. g 4/1/1, p. 253.
[63] B.L. Add. MS. 30077, f. 37.   [64] *D.N.B.*
[65] Local information.
[66] *V.C.H. Som.* i. 507.

[67] Ibid. iii. 167; *V.C.H. Hants,* iv. 52-3.
[68] *Complete Peerage; Close R.* 1231-4, 345.
[69] *Cal. Inq. p.m.* i, p. 14.
[70] *Feud. Aids,* iv. 316.
[71] C 260/110/21A; *Feud. Aids,* iv. 339; *Cal. Inq. p.m.* viii, pp. 507-8; *Cal. Close,* 1396-9, 318-19.
[72] C 260/110/21A; *Cal. Inq. Misc.* iii, p. 8; *Cal. Inq. p.m.* viii, pp. 507-8; x, pp. 63-5; xi, p. 201.
[73] *Cal. Inq. p.m. Hen. VII,* iii, pp. 552-3.
[74] *S.R.S.* xv. 88-9; Collinson, *Hist. Som.* ii. 166.
[75] *H.M.C. Wells,* ii. 252.
[76] Ibid. i. 474; *S.R.S.* vii, pp. 22-3; *Cart. St. Bartholomew's,* ed. N. J. Kerling, p. 150.
[77] *H.M.C. Wells,* ii. 252.
[78] *S.R.S.* xi, p. 177; *Bk. of Fees,* i. 724; *V.C.H. Wilts.* ix. 57.   [79] *Close R.* 1231-4, 345, 349.
[80] *S.R.S.* xi, p. 177.
[81] *Cal. Inq. p.m.* i, p. 14.

William died before his father and was succeeded by his son Philip, a minor,[82] who apparently remained in occupation until at least 1303.[83] Meanwhile Hamon had died while returning from the Holy Land c. 1282, leaving his son William as his heir.[84] William Denebaud, probably the same man, occurs in 1303 as grantee of lands by Philip Denebaud,[85] and by 1307 he was evidently the principal occupier in Hinton.[86]

William was still alive in 1317,[87] but by 1346 was succeeded by Thomas, and Thomas on his death in 1362 by his son John, a minor.[88] John came of age in 1371 but died in 1390 leaving another John as his heir.[89] In the dispute which arose concerning the tenure lasting until 1398 John's holding was described as half the manor, though this was evidently an error for half a fee.[90]

John died in 1429 leaving a daughter, Elizabeth, then or shortly afterwards married to William Poulett or Paulet.[91] Thus began the connexion with that family which lasted for nearly five centuries and a half. William died in 1488, apparently very old.[92] His widow survived until 1497, though their son, Sir Amias, had been in actual possession since 1487.[93] Amias, soldier and public servant,[94] seems to have retired to Chaffcombe before his death in 1538, when he was succeeded by his eldest son Sir Hugh (d. 1573),[95] also a soldier and governor of Jersey.[96] His son, Sir Amias (d. 1588), best known as keeper of Mary, Queen of Scots, succeeded him, and was himself succeeded by his second son Sir Anthony (d. 1600). Anthony's son John was raised to the peerage in 1627 as Baron Poulett, and was fined for his support of the Royalist cause.[97] After his death in 1649 the manor descended with the barony, which became an earldom in 1706, until 1973 when the 8th and last Earl Poulett died childless and the earldom was extinguished. By the time of his death the earl had sold most of his property in Hinton, but retained the lordship of the manor.[98]

By the end of the 14th century the manor-house stood in a complex of farm buildings including two stables, an oxhouse, at least one barn, a pigsty, and a dovecot. Margaret Denebaud's share of the house on her husband's death in 1390 included a 'messuage' in a court called the 'gustenchamber' on the east side of the hall, with rooms above and below between the chamber and a gateway by the hall, together with areas adjoining a great porch. The complex also included gardens to the north and south of a court, a lower garden, and various bartons.[99] The house was evidently rebuilt by Sir Amias Poulett, occupier between 1487 and 1538. It was described in the 1540s as 'a right goodly manor place of freestone, with two goodly high towers embattled in the inner court'.[1] In the 17th century the house was considered by Thomas Gerard 'ancient yet very stately and of curious building',[2] and by Cosmo, Grand Duke of Tuscany, a visitor in the 1660s, as 'very different from the common style'.[3]

The medieval house occupied the area of the south-west corner of the present building and was of conventional plan, having a central hall with porch and oriel to the west, service rooms to the north and north-east, and a parlour cross-wing on the south. In the later 16th century a central entrance porch was built between the oriel and the old porch, which became a second oriel, and new wings of ten bays were built out from each end of the front to enclose a forecourt.[4] By this time there may also have been a small courtyard, which was probably of medieval origin, to the east of the hall.[5]

About 1630 the parlour cross-wing was extended eastwards and a new south front, which has pedimented windows and a pierced-quatrefoil frieze, was erected. It is of two storeys and has an irregular 3-2-4 arrangement of the bays reflecting the three-roomed plan of the interior.[6] The ground floor rooms have contemporary panelling and that on the west a moulded plaster ceiling with central oval set in a field of strapwork which is dated 1636. A leaden plaque on the south front bears the arms of the 1st Lord Poulett (d. 1649) and of his wife Elizabeth (Kenn).

During the 1650s the 2nd Lord Poulett erected a 'banqueting house' in his bowling green, and made other extensive alterations and improvements including a new hall, chambers, and porch, much of the work being in brick.[7] Repairs at the same time were carried out in several other rooms and courts. In 1664-5 tax was paid on 47 hearths.[8]

In the late 17th or early 18th century the west front was lengthened by the addition of detached blocks of seven bays which were placed to the north and south of the ends of the later-16th-century wings.[9] Matthew Brettingham was working at Hinton in the mid 18th century[10] and he may have been responsible for additions which connected

---

[82] Cal. Inq. p.m. i, p. 14.
[83] S.R.S. vi. 325-6, 390-1; Feud. Aids, iv. 316.
[84] Cal. Inq. p.m. iii, p. 381.
[85] S.R.S. vi. 325-6.   [86] Cal. Inq. p.m. iv, p. 298.
[87] S.R.S. xii. 117.
[88] Feud. Aids, iv. 339; Cal. Inq. p.m. xi, p. 201.
[89] C 260/110/21A; C 136/66/8; Cal. Inq. p.m. xiii, pp. 51-2; xvi, pp. 396-9.
[90] Cal. Close, 1396-9, 318-19; Feud. Aids, iv. 383.
[91] Cal. Close, 1429-35, 8; C. Franklyn, A Genealogical History of Paulet, 60.
[92] S.R.S. extra series, 240.
[93] Cal. Inq. p.m. Hen. VII, iii, pp. 552-3.
[94] D.N.B.
[95] S.R.S. xxi. 40; C 142/61/14.   [96] D.N.B.
[97] Cal. Cttee. for Compounding, ii. 1051-3; T. G. Barnes, Somerset, 1629-40, 36-9; Complete Peerage.
[98] Sale cats., University Estate and Hinton St. George Estate, 1958, 1968; ex inf. Mr. S. G. Lawrence, Crewkerne.
[99] C 136/66/8.
[1] Leland, Itin. ed. Toulmin Smith, i. 160.

[2] S.R.S. xv. 88-9.
[3] Proc. Som. Arch. Soc. xvii. 63-9.
[4] The plans of the house at this stage are in Sir John Soane's Mus., Drawer VI, File 3 ff. 1v, 5, 8v. The drawings are dated 1796 but must be copies of older plans and depict features not shown on Soane's own survey drawings of the same year. The 17th-cent. drawing (copy) in B.L. Add. MS 33767B, f. 16 is demonstrably inaccurate.
[5] Leland, Itin. ed. Toulmin Smith, i. 160 mentions the inner court; see plan.
[6] The design is closely related to that of Ashton Court and Brympton D'Evercy, the former mentioned in 1629, the latter probably before 1642. The families at all three were inter-related, and the origin of the design is fairly certainly derived from Serlio's Bk. of Architecture (1619). See above, plate facing p. 32.
[7] S.R.O., DD/PT, box 40, accts.
[8] Dwelly, Hearth Tax, 133.
[9] See plate facing p. 32.
[10] See Brettingham's acct. bk. for 1747-64 quoted in H.M. Colvin, Biog. Dict. Eng. Architects, 1660-1840.

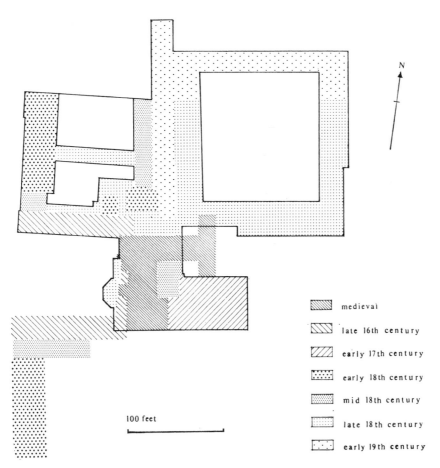

N

medieval

late 16th century

early 17th century

early 18th century

mid 18th century

late 18th century

early 19th century

100 feet

PLAN OF HINTON HOUSE showing its development. The outline is that of the mid 19th century.

the detached blocks to the house and lesser buildings to their east which formed on the north a kitchen court and on the south a stable court.[11] To Brettingham may also be attributed work within the main house including the remodelling of the first floor of the early-17th-century range and the creation of a main staircase in the former open court to the east of the medieval hall. In 1796 Earl Poulett employed (Sir) John Soane to prepare drawings for the remodelling of the house.[12]

Soane's plans provided for the demolition of everything on the south side of the old western court and the creation of a new stable court, incorporating a riding-house, to the north-east of the house, which balances in the southern elevation the remodelled kitchen court. Both ranges have two storeys above basements, sashed windows, and embattled parapets, and are partly faced in stone carved to resemble cobbling.[13] The west front of the hall range was to be demolished and replaced by a central octagonal entrance hall with a staircase on the south; the 18th-century stair was to be removed and the space it occupied used to enlarge

the hall. The work was started in 1797 and Soane's designs were followed closely although a surveyor called Felton was employed to supervise the work, and Soane's plans of that year for remodelling the south front[14] were not adopted. No other designs for decoration at Hinton by Soane survive and it is probable that he had ceased to be Poulett's architect before the work had progressed that far.

By 1801 James Wyatt was working at the house[15] and the interiors of the new work, which are mostly in a flat Gothic style, are probably by him. He also prepared designs for a new entrance hall which would approach the centre of the house from the north along the open passage between the kitchen and stable courts,[16] but this had not been built by 1812 when J. Kemshead produced alternative designs.[17] The surviving entrance with its Gothic *porte cochère* may have been by (Sir) Jeffry Wyatt (Wyatville).[18]

These were probably the last major alterations to the house until its sale and division from the late 1960s into small houses, beginning with the stable court. Many new floors, doorways, and walls

[11] A view from the west was published in Collinson, *Hist. Som.* ii, opp. p. 165. It shows a single-storied building at the north end of the west front which is not shown on the key plan because its dimensions are unknown.
[12] Sir John Soane's Mus., Drawer VI, File 3 and related acct. bk. Soane submitted his bill, for £163 9s. 6d., in Jan. 1798.
[13] Possibly to match work described in 1736 by John Loveday of Caversham (quoted C. G. Winn, *The Pouletts of Hinton St. George* (1976), 130), and noted earlier by

Dr. Thomas Fuller as 'shaped double-ways' or 'like the dowel of a cartwheel': ibid.; S.R.O., DD/SH 107.
[14] Sir John Soane's Mus., Drawer VI, File 3 and Yale Univ., British Art Centre, B1975.2.420.
[15] Designs for interiors dated 1801 are at Yale Univ., British Art Centre, B1975.2.410–11.
[16] Ibid. B1975.2.407–8.   [17] Ibid. B1975.2.419.
[18] James Wyatt died in 1813 and in the following year Jeffry exhibited a design for a Grand Entrance to Hinton House at the Royal Academy.

were inserted and formerly blind windows were opened, but the general appearance of the exterior was preserved.

In 1303 Walter de Stoke was returned as owner of land in Hinton under the Earl Marshal,[19] and by 1316 he was succeeded by Richard de Clare.[20] No location of the estate was given, though its later descent makes clear that it probably centred on the hamlet of Craft or Hintonscraft. Forde abbey had become owner of property there in the later 13th century, and the confirmation of its title by Hamon and later (1317) by William Denebaud suggests that the land had originally come from their estates.[21] The origin of Walter de Stoke's holding is not known, though he is probably the Walter son of Luke de Stoke who conveyed some meadow to Master Richard de Clare, clerk, in 1320;[22] and the same Walter who, after Richard, was given a life interest in a substantial property in Hinton and 'Northcraft by Crewkerne', by John de Carent in 1324.[23] Richard de Clare's interest continued until 1325.[24]

By that time the Carent family had established themselves. In 1343 William, son and heir of William Carent, occupied the estate.[25] He died in 1346 leaving a young son, also William, and an estate of 74 a. and rents.[26] Though not described as a manor, courts were evidently held. William, the son and heir, died c. 1422. Succeeding members of the family had their principal residence at Toomer in Henstridge, but continued in possession of the estate at Craft until 1560, when Leonard Carent of Winterbourne Gunner (Wilts.), a younger son of Sir William Carent of Toomer, sold it to Sir Hugh Poulett for £160.[27]

A second estate was held by the Warre family. In 1320 a Matthew Warre first occurs as a witness to a grant in Hinton.[28] By 1327 he was one of the most substantial taxpayers in the parish.[29] A William Warre had a small holding on the Carent estate,[30] and a possible successor, John Warre, died in 1349 in occupation of 1 a. held of William Carent's heir, 6 a. of the countess marshal, and 4 virgates of Thomas Denebaud, later described as 76 a. of arable and 3 a. of meadow and pasture.[31] Richard, his son, proved his age and succeeded in 1368,[32] and was still in occupation in 1399.[33] The property then descended to John Warre of Hestercombe, and thence to his son Richard (d. 1465)[34] and to his

grandson Sir Richard (d. c. 1482).[35] On the death of Sir Richard's widow Joan in 1499 the property passed to Sir Richard Warre of Chipley (d. 1532).[36] The estate in 1499 was described as the manor of *CRAFTEWARRE*, held of Sir Amias Poulett by unknown service.[37] Thomas Warre of Hestercombe, who succeeded his father Richard, died ten years later.[38] His son Richard sold the estate to Sir Hugh Poulett in 1568 for £80.[39]

At his death in 1334 Henry le Guldene held some 50 a. of land at Hentonescraft, most of it as tenant of Thomas Denebaud though 10 a. of Alan de Cudworth.[40] Much of this estate seems to have been accumulated from 1324 onwards.[41] It descended to Alan's son Alan, then a minor.[42] This Alan died in 1361 leaving part of his property to his daughter Avice (d. 1420), wife of Stephen Derby.[43] Their son Robert died without issue in 1421–2.[44] In 1466 land in Hentonescraft was settled on William Cowdrey and his wife Avice, daughter of Joan the sister and heir of Thomas Gulden.[45] Cowdrey was followed by his son William (d. 1498), whose heir was his son Morgan, a minor. The property, including land in Dorset, was for a time in the hands of Morgan's stepfather, Sir Morgan Kidwelly (d. 1505).[46] The later descent of the property has not been traced.

About 1220 Robert de Barnevill granted the church of Hinton to St. Bartholomew's hospital, London.[47] On 1 August in that same year the hospital acquired a share of the tithes and the site for a barn.[48] In 1341 a house and 4 a. of land were added.[49] By the 16th century the estate of the 'Fryerney' had been modified: it then comprised half the tithe corn of the parish, the site of a barn, 1 a. of arable, and 3 a. of meadow.[50]

Under an agreement made in 1546 the Crown in 1547 granted to the City of London the rectory and advowson of Hinton, with right to appropriate.[51] The revival of St. Bartholomew's hospital and the previous grant to Sir Hugh Poulett of the advowson nullified the arrangement and the hospital continued in occupation of a share of tithes and the land, though Sir Amias Poulett apparently leased the holding from c. 1582.[52] His successors certainly farmed the tithes from the 1670s, and in 1699 Lord Poulett leased a parcel of ground measuring 43 ft. by 18 ft. called 'the Fryerny of George Hinton . . . whereon one thatched tenement lately

[19] *Feud. Aids*, iv. 316.
[20] Ibid. 331.
[21] Forde Abbey, Cart. pp. 378–83.
[22] S.R.O., DD/PT box 10.
[23] *S.R.S.* xii. 92.
[24] S.R.O., DD/PT box 10. [25] Ibid.
[26] *Cal. Inq. p.m.* viii, pp. 507–8; *Cal. Fine R.* 1347–56, 32, 34, 246; *Cal. Close*, 1346–9, 400; *Cal. Pat.* 1348–50, 159.
[27] S.R.O., DD/PT, boxes 10, 10A, 11; *S.R.S.* li, p. 58; *Feud. Aids*, iv. 428; Hutchins, *Hist. Dors.* iv. 112.
[28] S.R.O., DD/PT, box 10.
[29] *S.R.S.* iii. 156.
[30] S.R.O., DD/PT, box 1.
[31] *Cal. Inq. p.m.* x, pp. 63–5; *Cal. Fine R.* 1347–56, 361.
[32] *Cal. Inq. p.m.* xii, pp. 244–5.
[33] *S.R.S.* xvii. 176.
[34] Ibid. xvi. 207–8.
[35] Collinson, *Hist. Som.* iii. 261.
[36] *Cal. Inq. p.m. Hen. VII*, ii, pp. 207–8; *Cal. Fine R.* 1485–1509, 271–2; S.R.O., DD/SF 434–5, 2124.
[37] *Cal. Inq. p.m. Hen. VII*, ii, pp. 207–8.

[38] C 142/66/74.
[39] *S.R.S.* li, p. 80; S.R.O., DD/PT, box 10A.
[40] *Cal. Inq. p.m.* vii, p. 414; *Cal. Close*, 1333–7, 251.
[41] *S.R.S.* xii. 96, 100, 137–8.
[42] *Cal. Inq. p.m.* vii, p. 414; xiv, p. 179; *Cal. Inq. Misc.* iii, p. 228; *Cal. Fine R.* 1356–68, 341.
[43] *Cal. Close*, 1419–22, 161; 1422–29, 237; Hutchins, *Hist. Dors.* i. 283.
[44] *Cal. Close*, 1419–22, 161, Hutchins, *Hist. Dors.* i. 282.
[45] *Cal. Inq. p.m. Hen. VII*, iii, pp. 553–4; *S.R.S.* xxii. 208. [46] *Cal. Inq. p.m. Hen. VII*, iii, p. 79.
[47] *Cart. St. Bartholomew's*, ed. Kerling, p. 150; *H.M.C. Wells*, i. 479.
[48] St. Bartholomew's Hospital, MS. charter 1119; *S.R.S.* vii, pp. 22–3.
[49] *Cart. St. Bartholomew's*, p. 150.
[50] St. Bartholomew's Hospital, Cartulary (HC/2/1b) f. 590. The statement was 'examined' by Sir Hugh Poulett (d. 1573).
[51] *L. & P. Hen. VIII*, xxi(2), pp. 414–16.
[52] *H.M.C. Wells*, ii. 252, 255; S.R.O., DD/SAS PR 54/10.

stood'.[53] By 1848 the hospital's land was 'blended with the estate of the lessee',[54] and it was sold to Earl Poulett in 1869.[55]

In 1227 Thomas le Ostricer sold to the prior of Monkton Farleigh (Wilts.) ½ virgate in the parish.[56] In 1492 the then prior granted the reversion of the tenancy held by John Draper to Sir Amias Poulett.[57] In 1525–6 and at the dissolution of the priory in 1536 the value of the property, in the second year described as a messuage, was 10s.[58] Charles Blount, Lord Mountjoy, had licence in 1545 to alienate the holding, lately occupied by Sir Amias Poulett, to his successor Sir Hugh Poulett.[59] It was then presumably absorbed into the Poulett estates.

ECONOMIC HISTORY. In 1086 the estate at Hinton was assessed for 13 hides, with land for 12 ploughs. The demesne farm measured 5 hides, with 4 ploughs, and was worked by 5 serfs; 16 villeins and 24 bordars worked the remainder with 10 ploughs. The demesne farm supported 36 head of cattle, 44 swine, and 190 sheep, there were 60 a. of meadow, and woodland measuring a league by half a league. Since 1066 the value of the estate had risen from £12 to £15.[60]

By the mid 14th century, when the holding was divided between the Carents and the Denebauds, a three-field pattern of open-field agriculture is revealed comprising North, West, and South fields, meadow land in the north of the parish, and pasture and woodland in the south. The Carent demesne estate in 1347 comprised just over 60 a. of arable, 9½ a. of meadow, 4 a. of separable pasture, and a small piece of oak wood. West field was then under wheat and rye, North field under oats and beans, and South field partly fallow and partly newly-broken, though there was a small plot there 'which can be sown each year'. Other areas of pasture could be sold 'when the fields in which they lie are opened'. There were 21 tenants on the Carent estate, with holdings varying in size between ⅓ virgate and ¼ messuage in return for suit of court, heriots, and commuted works, together with 4 *nativi* holding bondage land but paying cash for rents and works.[61]

A survey of the Denebaud estate in 1362 reveals a similar general pattern. There were 180 a. of arable, of which two-thirds were sown each year; 20 a. of grassland in severalty for hay and thereafter in common, common of pasture worth 12s., and some additional pasturage, together with a little wood. The manor complex was not described, but there were 2 dovecots, and 2 gardens were worth little in that year because the apple trees had been

blown down.[62] A much greater manor complex was described in 1387 when Margaret Denebaud was assigned 75 a. of arable, 10 a. of meadow, and quantities of pasture and wood as her dower.[63]

From the 16th century onwards the economy was dominated by the expansion of the Poulett estate through the absorption of medieval freeholdings and the consolidation of the demesne, against a background of inclosure which by 1600 and probably some years earlier had brought open-field arable cultivation to an end, leaving only the three common meadows, Honeymead, Broadmead, and Westmead, under ancient usage.[64] Purchase of the Craft estates of the Warres and the Carents was accompanied in the 1560s by the disappearance of other free tenants of the manor, the Gerards and the Estmonds, also holders in Craft.[65] Exchanges of land between the lord and his tenants allowed the lord to consolidate holdings in Eastmead and also around Craft, one tenant at Craft receiving licence to inclose and another having pasturage for oxen and cows in the park in lieu of a better settlement.[66] The open East (formerly South) and North fields were only small closes by 1569, though there was still open arable at Berdon, possibly once part of South field, in 1560.[67] Evidence in a court case referring to people coming from the meadows 'a milking' provides a rare glimpse of farming practice.[68]

Accounts of the Poulett estate in the early 1650s[69] refer to the purchase of cattle at Chard fair, of sheep from the fair at Martinstown, now Winterborne St. Martin (Dors.), and of horses from Wales, and of the sale of fat cattle in London. The demesne flock was 150 sheep and 26 lambs in 1652; 2 cwt. of cherry trees were brought from London in the same year, and turkeys were among the livestock on the estate. Much hay was made in the park and harvest in 1652 and other years demanded 2 dozen pairs of gloves for the reapers. Canvas was bought in 1652 for a winnowing fan. A carrier living in the village in 1635[70] travelled to London each week until the 1650s,[71] and a Hounslow waggoner was buried there in 1636.[72] In the 1670s Hinton was the scene of at least one petty sessional meeting.[73]

Important features of 18th-century Hinton are the disappearance of copyholds, the gradual development of consolidated tenant holdings, and extensions to the park. In the late 17th century there were just under 30 copyholds in the manor and just under 50 held by lease.[74] Conversion of all to leaseholds had been accomplished by 1796.[75] Eight tenant holdings were of 30 a. and more, the largest being the 64-a. farm of Bernard Hutchins (d. 1728), who by 1715 had increased his holding to over 100 a.[76] Some of the same land formed part of

[53] S.R.O., DD/PT, box 23.
[54] St. Bartholomew's Hospital, Maps of Landed Estates, 1848 (EO 3/5).
[55] Ex inf. Miss N. J. Kerling, archivist to St. Bartholomew's Hospital. The date 1860 is given in S.R.O., DD/SAS PR 54/10.
[56] *S.R.S.* vi. 56.
[57] E 315/33/27.
[58] Dugdale, *Mon.* vi. 30, 32.
[59] *L. & P. Hen. VIII*, xx. p. 311.
[60] *V.C.H. Som.* i. 507.
[61] S.C. 12/14/36; S.R.O., DD/PT, box 1; *Cal. Close,* 1346–9, 400.
[62] C 135/166/15.
[63] C 136/66/8.
[64] S.R.O., DD/PT, box 2, ct. rolls 1569–71; DD/SS, bdle. 1, ct. roll 1564.
[65] S.R.O., DD/PT, box 1.
[66] Ibid. box 2, ct. roll 1565.
[67] Ibid. box 2, ct. roll 1560.
[68] S.R.O., D/D/Cd 15, 6 July 1574.
[69] S.R.O., DD/PT, box 40, acct. bk. 1651–5.
[70] *Cal. S.P. Dom.* 1635, 512.
[71] S.R.O., DD/PT, box 40, acct. bk. 1651–5.
[72] S.R.O., D/P/hin. g 2/1/1.
[73] *S.R.S.* xxxiv. 122, 144.
[74] S.R.O., DD/PT, box 46, survey.
[75] Ibid., box 44, survey.
[76] Ibid. box 27, survey *c.* 1712; box 43, survey 1715.

a similar holding amassed by Colonel John Helliar in the second half of the century, probably based on Manor Farm,[77] and by his death in 1792 it amounted to over 250 a.[78] Both men were closely connected with the Pouletts: Hutchins left some of his freehold property outside Hinton to Vere Poulett and Helliar served as Earl Poulett's steward.[79]

In 1765 there were only 6 tenant farms of over 30 a., and two years later two of these had disappeared.[80] Among the smaller ones was the Home Tenement, later known as the Priory, a copyhold property traceable from the 1650s when it was held by the Prowse family.[81] More small holdings were absorbed as the Pouletts extended their park. New areas had been added at least since the mid 17th century,[82] but between 1765 and 1773 Earl Poulett's holding in the parish increased from 824 a. to 904 a.;[83] by 1839 that part of the park in Hinton was 753 a., more than half the earl's holding of 1,215 a. in the whole parish.[84] Small holdings in Craft were gradually taken in hand throughout the century so that by 1780 a considerable part of the hamlet had evidently disappeared, though even so late as 1800 several of its small closes remained.[85] The surviving dwellings formed the nucleus of the farm known by 1819 as Brown's and later as Croft farm. The largest and oldest house, evidently the only one to survive, was by 1968 known as Oaklands and formed part of Hinton Park farm.[86] Extensions of the park northwards and westwards were made with little or no disturbance of dwellings in 1766[87] and again in the late 1790s, though several roads were realigned or even abandoned. Landscaping and planting in connexion with these works continued until at least 1817.[88]

Details of farming practice and of other employment in the 18th century are scarce. The park itself was not exclusively ornamental: the old Park was divided for convenient letting in 1744,[89] Colonel Helliar kept cattle there in the 1780s,[90] and in 1783 a dairyman leased 21 milking cows and a dairy house at Craft for a year, with the right to graze the after grass on the lawn next to the Old Park and in other nearby fields. He was to receive feed for 11 calves, take 315 faggots, and have all the milk and the calves for a rent of £110 5s.[91] Just over 27 a. of common meadow survived at Westmead until 1793.[92]

References in the 17th century to flax, flax yarn, hemp, and looms, to a flaxdresser in 1682, and to a worsted comber in the 1690s suggest the presence of some cloth manufacture,[93] and 'linmen' occur c. 1760 and just after the turn of the century.[94] A family of mercers occupied the Priory from 1687.[95] There is otherwise the usual collection of plumber, maltster, blacksmith, tailor, and carpenter, with such additions as cooks, gardeners, and a barber who owed much of their livelihood to employment in the Poulett household and estate. There was also at least one shop. Three men from London settled in Hinton or acquired holdings there at the end of the century: John Healy, a City silk merchant, leased the Home Tenement from 1780, Joseph Rendall left his trade as a paper-stainer in Soho to become a yeoman farmer in 1783, and John Donne, a nurseryman from Millbank, Westminster, leased houses and a field in 1800.[96]

Whether as a direct result of the expansion of the park into Craft or of a general population increase, cottages were put up in some numbers from the 1740s, mostly on the green at the east end of the village in addition to those already standing around its edge.[97] At least three dwellings were built on the waste elsewhere in 1812, a house and five cottages went up in 1814, and a block of four tenements became six dwellings in 1818, all largely through the enterprise of Thomas Beagley, Earl Poulett's steward.[98]

In the mid 18th century the manorial rents of Hinton amounted to less than £44.[99] By 1819–20, after the complete conversion to leaseholds, the sum had increased to £643.[1] The death in 1792 of the estate steward provided the opportunity to rearrange farming units.[2] Three substantial holdings, Brown's, Lodge, and Poulett's farms, were created by 1825, the second mostly outside the parish but including much of the park.[3] Brown's, later Croft, farm, with 372 a., was the largest unit in 1839, followed by the present Manor farm (153 a.) and Lodge farm (133 a. in the parish). Of these only Manor farm-house stood in the village along with the smaller but longer-established holdings of Old, Tett's, Priory, and Bicknell's (later Brown's) farms.[4] By 1851 the larger farms had increased in size: Croft farm was 407 a. with 11 labourers, Manor farm 350 a. with 13 labourers, Lodge farm 280 a. with 12 labourers, and Samuel Palmer's farm 100 a. with 8 labourers. Bridge farm had emerged with 27 a.[5] A century later, when the Poulett estate was sold, some significant changes had taken place. Croft and Lodge farms had been

[77] S.R.O., DD/PT, box 29, deed 15 May 1758.
[78] S.R.O., D/P/hin. g 13/2/3, rates; M.I. in church.
[79] V.C.H. Som. iii. 206; S.R.O., DD/PT, box 44, rent bk.; M.I. in church.
[80] S.R.O., D/P/hin. g 13/2/3.
[81] S.R.O., DD/PT, box 46, survey; D/P/hin. g 4/1/1, p. 84.
[82] S.R.O., DD/PT, box 40, acct. bk; D/P/hin. g 13/2/2, rate 1697.
[83] S.R.O., DD/PT, box 44, survey 1792–6; D/P/hin. g 13/2/3, rates.   [84] S.R.O., tithe award.
[85] S.R.O., DD/PT, box 17 (Moore to Poulett 1730); box 44, bk. of rents 1743, chief rent bk. 1780; DD/SS, bdle. 24 ('plot where house 'lately stood'); DD/SAS (C/212), map of park c. 1798–1812.
[86] S.R.O., DD/PT, box 40, bk. of contracts 1819; sale cat., Hinton St. George Estate, 1968.
[87] S.R.O., DD/PT, box 26, Rendle to Poulett; ibid., box 29.
[88] Ibid., box 50, planting bk. 1812–17; map of Poulett estates, 1796; Q/SR, Easter 1798, road diversion.
[89] Sherborne Mercury, 3 Jan. 1744.
[90] S.R.O., DD/PT, box 44, rent bk. 1780, p. 16.
[91] Ibid. box 28, Poulett to Chick.
[92] Ibid. box 26.
[93] S.R.O., DD/SS, bdles. 24–5; DD/SP, box 12, inventories 1685, 1686; DD/SP inventories, 1634, 1635, 1640(2), 1641.
[94] S.R.O., DD/PT, boxes 28–9, 36.
[95] S.R.O., DD/SS, bdle. 25.
[96] S.R.O., DD/PT, box 28.
[97] Ibid., boxes 26, 28–9; DD/SS, bdles. 24–5, 28.
[98] S.R.O., DD/PT, boxes 36, 49.
[99] Ibid. box 44, rents and disbursements, 1743.
[1] Ibid. box 14.
[2] S.R.O., D/P/hin. g 13/2/3.
[3] S.R.O., DD/PT, box 36 (lease to Darby, 1825) and box 40 (bk. of contracts 1819).
[4] S.R.O., tithe award.
[5] H.O. 107/1928.

joined to create Hinton Park farm with 713 a.; Manor farm had been divided and the older 'village' farms were again revived, sometimes with land at a distance from the farm buildings and in more than one block. There were thus 6 farms measuring between 122 a. and 56 a. in size.[6] By this time Earl Poulett owned virtually the whole of the parish.

Tithe accounts of the early 19th century suggest a preponderance of arable not borne out by the tithe award of 1839, but probably the result of the large number of moduses by then negotiated. Of the arable crops c. 1819 wheat predominated, followed by potatoes, barley, and turnips. Beans, clover, vetches, flax, and hemp were cultivated in smaller quantities. The cider tithe in 1819 amounted to 256 hogsheads; and in 1834 as many as 23 a. of flax were grown.[7] In 1905 permanent grass covered 594 a., arable 249 a., and woodland 111 a.[8] Since 1968 much of the wood has been felled, and farming is mixed.

About half the population was engaged in agriculture in 1821,[9] and Hinton House and estate gave employment to many. Some thirty people were normally employed on the home farm and grounds c. 1806–8, increased to over forty during harvest.[10] The domestic staff in 1837 totalled 24 and the garden employed a further ten.[11] In 1851 as many as 22 people were resident in the house including the earl and his family.[12] Among trades practised in the village in the mid 19th century, 44 women and girls took in gloving, a common occupation of the poor in the area; but the presence of 14 dressmakers, 7 tailors, and 2 milliners reflects the importance of Hinton House to the village economy. The prosperity of the parish is also suggested by the appearance of villa residences. Hinton's 'pleasing air of comfort and respectability' in 1840 was conveyed as much by these dwellings as by its 2 inns and 8 shops, including a bookseller and stationer; and it was an eminently suitable base for Messrs. Guy and Stubbs, land surveyors, whose clerk Benjamin Love, the son of a local carpenter and later occupant of one of the villas, was by 1883 steward of large estates in Wiltshire and Hampshire as well as a land agent with much local business.[13]

During the two World Wars Hinton House was requisitioned: in the 1914–18 war it became a military hospital and from 1939 to 1945 it was occupied by two girls' schools. Its sale and subsequent conversion into many dwellings from c. 1970 has ensured that 'comfort and respectability' characterized the community in the 1970s. The estate itself was sold in two parts. Most of the Poulett holding in the parish, apart from the mansion, the former park, and a few houses, was sold in 1941 to the University of Oxford, and was subsequently dispersed in 1958.[14] The remainder of the property was sold by Earl Poulett in 1968.[15]

In 1632 John, Lord Poulett, was licensed to have two annual fairs at Hinton, one on St. George's day (23 April) and the morrow, and one on 14 and 15 September.[16] No further trace of the September fair has been found, but the Spring fair, where lemons and figs were purchased in 1654,[17] continued until c. 1947.[18] At the beginning of the 20th century cattle and sheep were sold in High Street and amusement stalls stood at the Cross and in Church Street. In 1912 the fair moved to the field by the Rectory.[19] Cattle continued to be sold at least until 1933.[20] In the 1930s there remained the memory of a June 'gooseberry' fair.[21]

There were two mills at Hinton in 1086, worth 7s. 6d.[22] By 1347 a mill called 'Dounemill' belonged to the Carent estate,[23] and perhaps stood near Craft. There was also a mill on the Denebaud estate, worth 30s. in 1362.[24] A mill occurs in 1552, occupied by the Baily family.[25] From 1678 Hinton mill, standing just in Hinton parish but near the village of Lopen and driven by Lopen brook, has a continuous history as part of the Poulett estate, almost certainly in succession to the Denebaud holding. From that time at least until 1796 it was occupied by members of the Cable family.[26] By 1866 the occupiers were spinning and weaving flax for sailcloth, but had evidently ceased production by 1883.[27] In 1958 the mill-house, an early-19th-century brick-fronted building, was part of a small holding.[28]

LOCAL GOVERNMENT. Court rolls for the manor of Hinton survive intermittently for the period 1523 to 1561 and are complete for the decade after 1563.[29] There are court books for the whole Poulett estate for 1651–77, 1679, 1703–10, and 1715–27.[30] Extracts survive for 1685, 1706, 1716, 1726, 1737, and 1786.[31] A list of fourteen 'tithing houses or plots', drawn up at the Michaelmas court in 1814, indicates the regular appointment of tithingmen until 1838.[32] Sessions were described either as 'manor courts' or 'manor courts leet' in the 16th century, though the 17th- and 18th-century extracts are from courts baron. In the 16th century the court met twice a year, in spring and autumn, and in the 17th and 18th centuries once; no place of meeting is known.[33] The only regular officer of the court seems to have

[6] Sale cat., University Estate, 1958.
[7] S.R.O., DD/PT, box 7.
[8] Statistics supplied by the then Bd. of Agric. 1905.
[9] C. & J. Greenwood, *Som. Delineated.*
[10] S.R.O., DD/PT, box 50, wages acct.
[11] Ibid. box 45.
[12] H.O. 107/1928.
[13] *County Gazette Dir.* (1840); H.O. 107/1928; *P.O. Dir. Som.* (1866); *Kelly's Dir. Som.* (1883, 1894); S.R.O., DD/X/MAR.
[14] Sale cat., University Estate, 1958.
[15] Sale cat., Hinton St. George Estate, 1968.
[16] C 66/2598, no. 18.
[17] S.R.O., DD/PT, box 40, acct. bk. 1651–5.
[18] Local information.
[19] Ex inf. Mr. F. James, Salisbury.
[20] S.R.O., DD/SAS PR 54/10.   [21] Ibid.

[22] *V.C.H. Som.* i. 507.
[23] S.C. 12/14/36; *Cal. Close*, 1346–9, 400; S.R.O., DD/PT, box 1.
[24] C 135/166/15.
[25] S.R.O., DD/PT, box 2.
[26] Ibid. boxes 28–9; DD/SS, bdles. 24–5; D/P/hin. g 4/1/2.
[27] *P.O. Dir. Som.* (1866); *Kelly's Dir. Som.* (1883). The earlier entry is to be found under Lopen.
[28] Sale cat., Hinton St. George Estate, 1968.
[29] S.R.O., DD/PT, boxes 1 and 2; DD/SS, bdle. 1.
[30] S.R.O., DD/SAS (C/2072) (1679); *penes* Countess Poulett, Jersey.
[31] S.R.O., DD/SS, bdle. 25; DD/PT, boxes 26, 28–9, 31.
[32] S.R.O., D/P/hin. g 13/2/6, at beginning. There is an earlier list in DD/PT, box 44.
[33] S.R.O., DD/SS, bdle. 4.

been the hayward, chosen each year in the autumn in regular rotation. In 1569 two men were chosen as surveyors of the highways. To the usual concerns about strays, under-tenants, broken hedges, and blocked ditches were added in the 1560s orders for the provision of 'mantells' or chimneys in houses and 'stercovers' in barns.[34] A dangerous dog was reported in 1523.[35]

A court was held on the Carent estate in the 14th century. Only one roll has survived, when the property was in Crown hands in 1347,[36] but tenants in 1343 and 1388 held land by suit twice a year.[37] Both a reeve and a bailiff were mentioned in 1347.[38]

From the 17th century the offices of church-warden and overseer were filled by rotation in respect of holdings. Accounts survive from 1633.[39] A parish constable occurs by 1640 and two surveyors of highways in 1636 and regularly from 1658.[40] Highway accounts exist for the periods 1693–1774 and 1803–32.[41] In 1639 the parishioners agreed to a monthly vestry meeting 'for ordering and setting right of parish business'.[42] From the 1660s onwards a group of six or eight men with the rector signed the overseers' accounts and evidently conducted most of the parish business, 'nominating and appointing' the wardens and 'nominating' the overseers.[43] In the 18th century often only one warden was chosen, and the number of signatories to the accounts varied more widely. Parish meetings were held in one or other of the village inns in the 1680s and 1690s,[44] and in the 18th and 19th centuries were followed by dinners.

By the 1670s the overseers were contributing towards house repairs, rent, nursing, boarding out children, apprentices, and clothing, the money raised not only by rates but by the rent of a garden, the sale of apples growing in a marlpit, and sundry gifts. From 1697 none was to have relief 'but those who come publicly to the church and make their condition known'.[45] Paupers continued to wear badges at least until 1790.[46] Cottages in various parts of the village were rented from 1693 to house the poor, and in the late 1780s one of these stood at Pithill.[47] Cottages continued to be rented for the poor from Earl Poulett until the parish became part of the Chard poor-law union in 1836.[48] At the same time the rents of other paupers were paid in increasing sums.

The prosperity of the parish permitted the overseers to exercise unusual generosity. Special cash grants were made during the hard winter of 1691–2; a cot was given for a young boy in 1715; a flax shop was repaired for a distempered woman in 1726. Much money was spent on medical attention including treatment for eyes at Salisbury in 1678–9 and travel to hospital in Bridgwater in 1831–2. Paupers were first inoculated in 1772 and an apothecary was permanently retained for their care from 1787. Work was provided on parish roads in the early 19th century, and in the 1830s 'engines' were purchased 'for the use of those who wish to learn gloving'. Two men were assisted in their passage to Newfoundland in 1830.[49]

The overseers also maintained a round house or lock-up which in 1830 was used to store a pauper's goods and two years later held the pauper herself.[50] The building stands on the green.

The waywardens were particularly active in the early 19th century when parish paupers were employed on the roads. Earl Poulett, owner of all the local quarries, was nominated for office as waywarden each year between 1808 and 1832, often accompanied by his bailiff.[51]

CHURCH. The benefice of Hinton is a rectory, though from the early 13th century a proportion of the tithes was appropriated. Before 1 August 1220 Robert de Barnevill, describing himself as patron, granted the church of Hinton 'so far as pertains to a lay person' to St. Bartholomew's hospital, London, 'towards the maintenance of priests there ministering'.[52] By another charter Robert granted the patronage to the preceptor of St. Bartholomew's.[53] The patronage was then granted by the preceptor to Jocelin, bishop of Bath,[54] who, perhaps in exchange, on 1 August 1220 gave to the hospital the tithe of sheaves 'of the church estate (*de dominica ecclesie*)', half the tithe of all other sheaves belonging to the church, all the tithe hay from Robert de Barnevill's demesne, and 2 a. of land for the site of a barn.[55]

The patronage was exercised by successive bishops, or by the Crown during vacancies,[56] until it was transferred to Sir Hugh Poulett on the ground that the advowson had once belonged to the manor 'but had come into the hands of the bishops of Bath and Wells by lapse and had been in their possession a long time'.[57] The patronage descended through successive members of the Poulett family until the death of the 8th earl in 1973.

The benefice was valued in 1291 at £6 13s. 4d.[58] In 1532 the rectorial income was said to be £10, and in 1535 £13 13s. 3d.[59] About 1668 its reputed value was £100,[60] and in 1831 the net income was £197.[61] The gross income in 1851 was £214.[62]

34 S.R.O., DD/SS, bdle. 1 (1564).
35 Ibid. bdle. 1 (1523).
36 S.C. 2/198/49.
37 S.R.O., DD/PT, box 10, deeds 1343, 1388.
38 S.C. 2/198/49.
39 S.R.O., D/P/hin. g 4/1/1–2, 13/2/2–6. Only one overseer appointed between 1742 and 1757 and for one or two years earlier; only one warden appointed in many years between 1728 and 1762.
40 S.R.O., D/P/hin. g 4/1/1, pp. 15, 31, 98.
41 S.R.O., D/P/hin. g 14/5/1; DD/PT, box 8.
42 S.R.O., D/P/hin. g 4/1/1, p. 26.
43 Ibid. e.g. pp. 126, 148; 13/2/2, *sub anno* 1697.
44 Ibid. 4/1/1, pp. 254, 266.
45 Ibid. 13/2/2.
46 Ibid. 13/2/3.
47 Ibid. 4/1/1, p. 268; DD/PT, box 44, rent bks. 1747,

1780.
48 *Poor Law Com. 2nd Rep.* p. 547.
49 S.R.O., D/P/hin. g 13/2/2–6.
50 Ibid. 13/2/6.
51 S.R.O., DD/PT, box 8.
52 *H.M.C. Wells*, i. 479.
53 *Cart. St. Bartholomew's*, ed. Kerling, p. 150.
54 *H.M.C. Wells*, i. 474.
55 *Cart. St. Bartholomew's*, p. 150; *S.R.S.* vii, pp. 22–3; St. Bartholomew's Hosp. MS. charter 1119.
56 e.g. *Cal. Pat. 1327–30*, 418.
57 *H.M.C. Wells*, ii. 252, 255.
58 *Tax. Eccl.* (Rec. Com), 199; *S.R.S.* ix, p. 40.
59 S.R.O., D/D/Vc 20; *Valor Eccl.* (Rec. Com.), i. 164.
60 S.R.O., D/D/Vc 24.
61 *Rep. Com. Eccl. Revenues*, pp. 140–1.
62 H.O. 129/318/4/5/6.

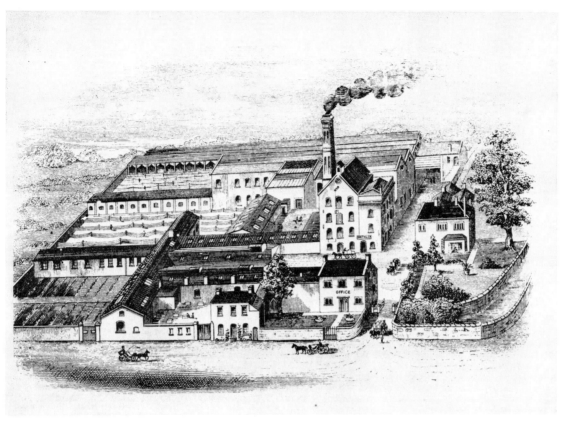

MARTOCK: PARRETT WORKS, *c.* 1900

CREWKERNE: FACTORY IN ABBEY STREET

MARTOCK: RAILWAY HOTEL

MARTOCK: SCHOOL-HOUSE

HINTON ST. GEORGE: THE FIVES WALL

The tithes granted to St. Bartholomew's hospital in 1220 and apparently assessed in 1336 at £13 6s. 8d.[63] were reckoned by the time of Sir Hugh Poulett (d. 1573) as half the tithe corn of the parish;[64] and this remained the hospital's share in the 17th century.[65] The rector's tithe was worth over £5 12s. 6d. in 1535.[66] Lord Poulett was evidently leasing the tithes of the hospital by 1672, and the total value of tithes 'due to Earl Poulett' in the early 19th century varied between £150 in 1810 and £189 10s. 9d. in 1819.[67] A rent-charge of £171 for the rector's share and £60 for St. Bartholomew's share was agreed in 1839, the latter in respect of 360 a. of arable.[68]

By 1839 a wide variety of moduses was payable: 3d. for each cow, a shoulder of veal for every calf killed in the owner's house, a tithe of the sale price of weaned calves, ½d. for reared calves, 1d. for colts, 3d. an acre for ancient meadow, 1d. for gardens, and eggs at Easter. A modus of £6 10s. covered the tithes for most of the park and 6s. 8d. was paid for the mill.

The rectorial glebe was worth less than £3 in 1535.[69] Evidence produced in 1635 claimed that 'within the memory of man' over 40 a. had been alienated, resulting in the extinction of many of the families of those responsible,[70] and the glebe terrier of 1626, listing 14 a. of arable, 1 a. of meadow, and the first share of a further acre, included none of the alienated land.[71] In 1839 the area of glebe was nearly 15 a.[72] All this had been sold by 1975.[73]

Among the properties of the benefice alienated before 1635 and presumably before 1626 was the 'ancient parsonage house' and the site of the parson's pigeon house.[74] In 1626 the parsonage house was described as adjoining the churchyard. Near it was an outhouse 'called a kitchen, with a loft over it'.[75] There were also two barns, one nearby and the other in the middle of the village.[76] This substantial house, having seven hearths in 1664,[77] was found to be insecure, and in 1839 it was demolished and the present house was built 'nearly on the site' of the old, with an enlarged garden, stable, and coach-house.[78] It was completed in 1841 and is a substantial Ham stone structure decorated with simple pilasters.

Several of the medieval rectors had interests outside the parish. Master William le Mercer, rector

by 1311 to 1321 and evidently an Irishman, became dean of Dunwich in 1321;[79] Thomas Foston was licensed in 1402 to study for two years at the request of the abbot of Leicester;[80] and John Marsley, rector 1435–9, was a member of Bishop Stafford's household.[81] There was both a curate and a chantry chaplain in 1532.[82] John Poulett, rector 1552–68 and a younger son of the patron, held three benefices and lived in Jersey, where the Pouletts governed.[83] Edmund Peacham, rector 1587–1614, was imprisoned in the Tower for libelling Bishop Montagu before the High Commission, and was later deprived of his orders and found guilty of treason in 1615.[84] Under Richard Gove, rector from 1618, Holy Communion was celebrated frequently, as many as nine times in a year including four times around Easter, the vestry in 1639 levying a rate of 2d. from every communicant to pay for the bread and wine.[85] The Communion table was railed in 1635–6, and a rate was levied to buy an organ two years later.[86] Gove was ejected from the living c. 1650, and was replaced by Presbyterian ministers[87] under whom in 1665 the wardens were described as 'ruling elders of Hinton Church'.[88] By the 1670s Communion was celebrated only four times a year.[89]

The rectors during the 18th century were normally resident, though from 1779 they held the livings of Seavington St. Michael and Dinnington.[90] In 1776 there were c. 20 communicants.[91] Henry Stambury, rector 1789–1838, took two services each Sunday by 1815, with monthly celebrations of Holy Communion.[92] In 1851 the estimated congregation was 450 in the morning, including 100 Sunday-school children, 520 in the afternoon with 120 children, and 150 at the evening Sunday school.[93] By 1870 Sunday services were held in the morning and evening, both with sermon, and celebrations on the first Sunday in each month and at the chief festivals.[94] From 1913 the benefice was held with Dinnington.[95]

Nothing is known of a chantry beyond the existence of a chantry priest in 1532.[96]

The church of *ST. GEORGE*, so dedicated by the early 13th century,[97] was apparently consecrated on 6 February in an unknown year.[98] It is of Ham stone and comprises a chancel with north vestry and chapel, a nave with north transept forming the

[63] *Cart. St. Bartholomew's*, p. 150.
[64] St. Bartholomew's Hosp., Cartulary (HC 2/1b) f. 590.
[65] S.R.O., D/D/Rg 307.
[66] *Valor Eccl.* (Rec. Com.), i. 164. Glebe and predial tithes are undifferentiated.
[67] S.R.O., D/P/hin. g 4/1/1, rates; DD/PT, box 7.
[68] S.R.O., tithe award.
[69] *Valor Eccl.* (Rec. Com.), i. 164.
[70] S.P. 16/290, 21.
[71] S.R.O., D/D/Rg 307.
[72] S.R.O., tithe award; St. Bartholomew's Hosp., EO 3/5, Maps of the Landed Estates, 1848.
[73] Ex inf. Diocesan Office, Wells.
[74] S.P. 16/290, 21.
[75] S.R.O., D/D/Rg 307.
[76] This second barn may have belonged to St. Bartholomew's.
[77] Dwelly, *Hearth Tax*, 133.
[78] S.R.O., D/P/hin. g 2/1/3. Completed 1841 at a cost of £2,000: par. rec. 'log' bk.
[79] *Cal. Papal Reg.* ii. 173, 197.
[80] *S.R.S.* xiii, p. 29.
[81] *Cal. Papal Reg.* ix. 62.

[82] S.R.O., D/D/Vc 20.
[83] Corpus Christi Coll. Cambridge, MS. 97.
[84] *D.N.B.; Cal. S.P. Dom.* 1611–18, 263, 279.
[85] S.R.O., D/P/hin. g 4/1/1, pp. 7, 18, 26. There was also a levy for church loaves until 1648 (ibid. pp. 3, 53). For Gove see *D.N.B.*; *S.R.S.* xxiii. 297; S.R.O., Q/SR 37(1), 33; D/D/Cd 72; *Calamy Revised*, ed. Matthews.
[86] S.R.O., D/P/hin. g 4/1/1, pp. 18, 42.
[87] He published the first of his 11 tracts from East Coker in 1650: E. Green, *Bibliotheca Somersetensis*. For Hallet see *D.N.B.*, and for Loader S.R.O., D/P/hin. g 4/1/1, pp. 84, 89, and DD/SS, bdle. 25 (deed 28 June 1671, Strode *et al.* to Poulett).
[88] S.R.O., DD/PT, box 40, acct. bk. 14 Nov. 1655.
[89] S.R.O., D/P/hin. g 4/1/1, p. 187.
[90] S.R.O., D/P/sea. ml 2/1/1.
[91] S.R.O., D/D/V Dioc. bk.
[92] S.R.O., D/D/B return 1815.
[93] H.O. 129/318/4/5/6.
[94] S.R.O., D/D/V return 1870.
[95] *Dioc. Dir.*
[96] S.R.O., D/D/Vc 20.
[97] *H.M.C. Wells*, i. 474, 479; *S.R.S.* vii, pp. 22–3.
[98] *S.R.S.* xlii, pp. xi, 129.

Poulett pew, connected with the north chapel, a south aisle and south porch, and a western tower. Masons' marks on the fabric date from the earlier 13th century and are identical with some found at Wells cathedral,[99] though the main details of the fabric are of the 15th and 16th centuries. The font was originally in a plain 13th-century style, but decoration was added in the mid 15th century, incorporating the Poulett arms. The tower was evidently planned or under construction in 1486.[1]

The north transept was remodelled c. 1814 by James Wyatt to create a private pew above the Poulett vault.[2] Pew and chapel together contain family monuments dating from that of Sir Amias Poulett (d. 1538), and including that of his grandson Sir Amias (d. 1588), removed from St. Martin-in-the-Fields, London, in 1728.[3] Earlier monuments elsewhere in the church include a tomb-chest at the entrance to the former transept, with a figure of an armoured knight, assigned in the 17th century to an unknown member of the Denebaud family,[4] and a late-15th-century brass of John Chudderle and his wife.[5]

At least until 1812 the vestry room was an area formed by a screen across the eastern end of the chancel, with entrance doors at each side of the altar.[6] This room had been repaired and the pulpit and 'reading seat' moved in 1790.[7] A vestry was added on the north side of the chancel in 1815, its entrance from the church being an adapted window embrasure.[8] Much of the furniture in the church dates from 1903 and 1924; the pulpit was erected in 1912 and the pews in 1924.[9] The royal arms in Coade stone, by Coade and Sealy of London, are dated 1812. The armorial glass in the church in the 1640s has disappeared.[10] Mural monuments in the nave and aisle include several to members of the Poulett family and their retainers of the 18th and 19th centuries. The gilded weathercock on the top of the tower stair turret was made by Thomas Bayley of Bridgwater in 1756.[11]

There are six bells: (i) 1922, Taylor of Loughborough; (ii) 1828, Kingston of Bridgwater; (iii) 1756, Bayley, Street, and Co., Bridgwater; (iv) 1624, Wiseman of Montacute; (v) 1783, Davis; (vi) 1624, Wiseman.[12] The plate comprises a cup of 1815 and paten and plate of 1813.[13] These replaced a chalice and plate given by Anne, Lady Poulett, in 1665 and a silver tankard acquired in exchange for

an old silver chalice and cover in 1689.[14] The registers date from 1632, though there is a gap between 1647 and the appointment of a parish register in 1653.[15]

NONCONFORMITY. A group of Presbyterians was meeting in a house under the leadership of John Langdale, ejected minister of Cricket St. Thomas, in 1673.[16] A house was licensed for use in 1811.[17] Bible Christians visited the village in 1824; a preacher addressed 'about 200' but was then arrested.[18] A room was licensed in 1845, with no denomination specified.[19] It may have been either for Wesleyan Methodists or for Brethren, both of whom were established by 1851. A Wesleyan group was formed by 1843 and had a membership of 11 in 1849 and 18 in 1864.[20] In 1851 it still met in a private room, and its evening congregation was 20 strong.[21] No separate chapel was erected, but services continued in premises in Teapot Lane, later South Street, until shortly before 1926.[22]

By 1851 a cottage was being used by the Brethren, who held services for 30 on Sunday afternoons under the leadership of a 'minister' from Merriott.[23] A chapel was built on the north side of High Street by Dr. Newberry, son of a former rector.[24] It is a plain building of Ham stone with a tiled roof, and was described as new in 1875.[25] It was closed c. 1972.[26]

There is a tradition of a meeting-house on the green, closed before the end of the 19th century.[27] It may be connected with followers of Joanna Southcott who are said to have worshipped in the parish.[28]

EDUCATION. In 1818 it was reported that a school had been established by Earl Poulett's ancestors; 10 boys were then taught free by a master paid by the family and provided with a house. Other children, presumably boys, were received at the school on payment of 3d. weekly.[29] It is not known how long this school had existed. Henry Cuff (b. 1563) is said to have been taught at a grammar school in the village;[30] there was certainly a schoolmaster there by 1642–3, and in 1652 a woman was paid by Lord Poulett for teaching a pauper child.[31] Barnaby Hanning of Hinton was described as a schoolmaster in 1742,[32] and 10 boys were being

[99] Proc. Som. Arch. Soc. xciv. 126.
[1] S.R.S. xvi. 263.
[2] E. Devon R.O., MS. 46: J. Davidson, 'Som. Church Notes'; Yale Univ., British Art Centre, Wyatt plans.
[3] See plate facing p. 17.
[4] Diary of Richard Symonds (Camd. Soc. 1st. ser. lxxiv), 112.
[5] Thomas Warre (d. 1542), owner of Craft, married Christine Chydlegh: C 142/66/74.
[6] Gent. Mag. 1812, pt. 2, 418.
[7] S.R.O., D/P/hin. g 4/1/2.
[8] Inscription.
[9] Par. rec., log bk.
[10] Diary of Richard Symonds, 110–14.
[11] S.R.O., D/P/hin. g 4/1/3.
[12] S.R.O., DD/SAS CH 16, 16/1.
[13] Proc. Som. Arch. Soc. xlv. 143.
[14] S.R.O., D/P/hin. g 4/1/1.
[15] Ibid. 2/1/1–7.
[16] Cal. S.P. Dom. 1672–3, 426; Calamy Revised, ed. Matthews.
[17] S.R.O., D/D/Rm, box 2.

[18] S.R.O., D/N/spc 31; ex inf. Mr. M. D. Costen, Bristol.
[19] S.R.O., D/D/Rm, box 2.
[20] S.R.O., D/N/spc 2.
[21] H.O. 129/318/4/5/8. Another return for a Wesleyan chapel, filed as H.O. 129/318/4/5/7 and marked 'not in list' must refer to some other Hinton.
[22] S.R.O., DD/SAS PR 54/10; D/N/spc, circuit plans 1923, 1926.
[23] H.O. 129/318/4/5/9.
[24] Ex inf. Mr. F. James, Salisbury.
[25] Kelly's County Topog. (1875), 279.
[26] Ex inf. Mr. E. Arnold, Merriott.
[27] S.R.O., DD/SAS PR 54/10.
[28] Pulman, Bk. of the Axe, 295.
[29] Digest of Returns to Sel. Cttee. on Educ. of Poor, H.C. 224 (1819), ix(2).
[30] D.N.B.
[31] S.R.O., D/P/hin. g 4/1/1, p. 43; DD/PT, box 40, acct. bk.
[32] S.R.O., DD/PT, box 29, lease Poulett to Hanning.

taught in the parish in 1786, possibly under the terms of a will of 1733.[33]

A charity school for boys and girls, possibly the same as the foregoing, is recorded in 1776.[34] From 1797 until 1823 the salaried assistant overseer was paid for instructing poor children in the catechism on Sundays.[35] Several schools were established in the 1820s and 1830s providing instruction at parents' expense: two for infants taking 16 boys and 12 girls; two day-schools for 30 boys and 15 girls; and a boarding school for 14 girls, possibly the one said to have been housed at the Priory.[36] By 1825 there was a Sunday school for 20 boys and 20 girls.[37] Another, started in 1831 and supported by the National Society and by subscription, was held in a room in the churchyard opened in 1833.[38] By 1835 it had 20 boys and 40 girls, and was still open in 1840.[39] By 1840 there were at least two private schools, one for boys, the other for girls either daily or boarding.[40] At least one private school continued until the 1880s.[41]

In 1850 the present school, affiliated to the National Society, was settled in trust by Earl Poulett.[42] It was supported in the late 19th century by grants, by a voluntary rate, and by local efforts. It had accommodation for 228 children, though average attendance was less than half that number.[43] During the 20th century attendances fell, standing at 52 in 1946. In 1949 the school accepted voluntary controlled status, and from 1972 took children only from the 5–9 age range, the older pupils travelling to schools in Crewkerne. In 1975 there were 54 children on the register.[44] Hinton St. George First School stands on the south side of West Street. It is a substantial Ham stone building with a tiled roof, providing in 1903 two classrooms and a house for the teacher. A distinguishing feature is a slim bellcot surmounted by a cross.

CHARITIES FOR THE POOR. An alms-house had been established by 1636,[45] housing 4 people who received 10d. a week.[46] Under the will of the first Lord Poulett (d. 1649) additional lodgings were to be built to bring the total of inmates to 6, each to receive 12d. a week and a frieze gown once a year.[47] During the 1650s 8 inmates received 12d. a week, and each year kersey and blue baize.[48] The number of occupiers was increased to 10 by John, 4th Earl Poulett (d. 1819), but the 5th earl reduced it to nine.[49]

In 1823 it was reported that the establishment was 'scarcely' a regular alms-house, but comprised 'little tenements close together' of which the Pouletts 'granted a permissive occupation from time to time, according to their pleasure'. Each occupier then received 12d. a week and a serge coat or gown each Whitsunday.[50] In 1872 the present alms-houses were erected in Back Lane by Lady Augusta Poulett on land given by her nephew, the 6th earl,[51] and until her death in 1888 the earl continued to pay each occupier 12d. a week, though gowns were no longer supplied. The previous houses, apparently standing by the church path off West Street, were abandoned.[52]

Lady Augusta Poulett also bequeathed £1,000 for the benefit of the alms-house people, increasing their pay to 2s. a week. The two charities were consolidated under a Scheme of 1911, creating the Poulett Alms-house Charity, with trustees who included the owner of the Poulett estate. Nine alms-people were to be chosen from residents of good character. The income of £52 14s. 8d. from investments was to provide not less than 2s. weekly pay for each inmate.[53]

By 1950 Chard rural district council was renting 7 of the dwellings, but under a Scheme of 1964 2 representatives of the Local Authority and Earl Poulett or his nominee became the sole trustees.[54] The premises were later modernized, and the occupants have since contributed towards the loans raised for the purpose.[55]

The alms-house, of local stone, occupies three sides of a grassed quadrangle on the north side of Back Lane, providing 9 single-storeyed dwellings.

By will dated 1728 Bernard Hutchins gave a rent-charge of £41 12s. on land at Hill in Chillington to provide 2s. weekly, on Mondays, for eight poor families to be chosen by Lord Hinton or his heirs (as owners of the land thereafter) or by the rector, churchwardens, and overseers.[56] The terms of the bequest were carried out by successive earls until the early 19th century. By 1823, however, payment was made on Wednesdays, and from 1817 onwards was made to 32 people each month, 8 each week.[57]

Under a Scheme of 1928 the charity was placed under the administration of the Poulett Alms-house trustees, its terms to be the original weekly distribution to 8 poor families.[58] This Scheme was amended in 1967 to give the benefit to the poor in general but especially to poor residents of Hinton.[59]

Colonel John Helliar (d. 1792) devised land in Merriott, the rent to be distributed on St. Thomas's Day (21 Dec.) in shoes and stockings for poor

[33] *Abs. of Rtns. of Char. Donations, 1787–8*, H.C. 511 (1816), xvi.
[34] S.R.O., D/D/V Dioc. bk.
[35] S.R.O., D/P/hin. g 13/2/4–6.
[36] *Educ. Enquiry Abstract*, H.C. 62 (1835), xlii.
[37] *Ann. Rep. B. & W. Dioc. Assoc. S.P.C.K.* (1825–6).
[38] *Educ. Enquiry Abstract* (1835); S.R.O., DD/PT, box 36: expenditure 'about the new school room'; E. Devon R.O., MS 46: J. Davidson 'Som. Church Notes', printed sermon.
[39] *Educ. Enquiry Abstract* (1835); S.R.O., D/D/V return 1840.
[40] *County Gazette Dir.* (1840).
[41] *Kelly's Dir. Som.* (1883).
[42] Char. Com. file. Log bks. date from 1918: ex inf. the headmistress.
[43] S.R.O., C/E, box 27; *Returns of Schs.* [C. 7529] H.C. (1894), lxv.
[44] S.R.O., *Schs. Lists.*
[45] S.R.O. D/P/hin. g 2/1/1, burial of Elizabeth Anthony 'the Blackmoore of the Alms-house'.
[46] *9th Rep. Com. Char.* H.C. 258, p. 500 (1823), ix.
[47] Ibid.
[48] S.R.O., DD/PT, box 40, acct. bk. e.g. 1 Dec. 1654.
[49] *9th Rep. Com. Char.* p. 500.
[50] Ibid.
[51] Inscription on building; Char. Com. files.
[52] S.R.O., DD/SAS PR 54/10.
[53] Char. Com. files.
[54] Ibid.
[55] Ex inf. the clerk, Mr. K. P. Gee, Yeovil.
[56] *9th Rep. Com. Char.* p. 499.
[57] S.R.O., DD/PT, box 9, acct. bk. 1817–54; box 49, acct. 1797; Char. Com. files.
[58] Char. Com. files.
[59] Ibid.

children.[60] In 1967 the income of £12 bought 6 pairs of shoes. In 1975 the charity was similarly distributed in shoes.[61]

Richard Bicknell (d. 1822) bequeathed £50 in trust to provide bread for the poor on Old Christmas Day (6 Jan.). In 1970 there was an income of £1 5s., and in 1976 it was distributed in half loaves of bread to the elderly.[62]

Thomas Beagley (d. 1826) bequeathed the interest on £500 to be given in blankets on 14 January each year. In 1974 the income of £10.85 was distributed in blankets.[63]

MERRIOTT

THE PARISH of Merriott[1] lies 2 miles north of Crewkerne and is traditionally known as Little Ireland. The distinctive dialect, dark hair, and dark complexions of its natives gave rise to unsubstantiated traditions of an Irish colonization.[2] The parish extends over 3 miles from NE. to SW. and 2 miles from east to west at its widest point. The long SE. boundary with Chiselborough, West Chinnock, and Crewkerne is marked by the river Parrett or by one of its tributaries; the northern boundary follows the Lopen brook. It is bounded on the west by Hinton St. George and Furland in Crewkerne. Its roughly triangular shape enclosed an area of 1,750 a. in 1901. The civil parish was increased to 2,760 a. in 1933 by the addition of lands in the north of Crewkerne, and reduced to 2,711 a. by the return of 49 a. to Crewkerne in 1934.[3]

From over 250 ft. on Eggwood Hill in the west, the NE. slope of which was ancient woodland, and near Shutteroak House (Schitrock in 1268)[4] in the south, the ground falls away towards the stream and river beds which bound the parish. The NW. corner lies on loam and flints and provided the principal areas of meadow and pasture in the Middle Ages; field names such as Stoneridge and Longmoor witness to its poor arable potential. Most of the remainder is Yeovil Sands with areas of limestone in the south of the village and clay in the north around Hacking Pit (Haukenesputte in 1375),[5] where marl was evidently dug.[6] A quarry was supplying gravel between 1810 and 1817.[7] The richness of the soil encouraged the development of market gardening from the 18th century. Apart from the streams that bound it, the parish is watered by a brook which cuts off the southern part centred on Marks Barn and Shutteroak houses. It was known as Birdines (1556) or Bardones (1557) water from the field-name Beadon, and drove both Billing's and Court mills.[8]

The village is close to the centre of the SW. boundary apparently at the crossing of two old routes. One runs along a low ridge from West Chinnock across the Parrett at Bow bridge to Hinton St. George; the other from Chiselborough (and perhaps Martock) in the NE. to Crewkerne in the south. Both routes, the first represented by Church (formerly Higher) Street, the second by Lower Street, Shiremoor Hill, and Townsend, have been diverted in the area of the crossing and form a triangle, completed by Broadway, around the former open field called Hitchen or Landshare. The present importance of Broadway (mentioned as Langebradeweye c. 1300)[9] as the principal route through the parish from Lopen Head can be dated at least from its adoption in 1765 by the Crewkerne Turnpike trust.[10] The name Newchester Cross at the junction of Church Lane and Broadway is probably derived from 'Newchurchyard Crose', mentioned in 1608.[11] There were also boundary marks called Eggwoods Cross, recorded in 1571, and Slades Cross, robbed for its stone in 1576.[12]

All the older (pre-1750) buildings lie east of the parish church in Church Street and along Lower Street. The SW. end of Lower Street was known in the 19th century as the Borough,[13] which may suggest a focal point and a possible site for the medieval fair. Both streets contain relatively large numbers of small farms, sometimes with 17th-century houses but often with 18th- and 19th-century dwellings of traditional form and characteristically having a small yard and barn behind the house. Many of the houses have mullioned stone windows, some certainly reset, of a variety of patterns and in three instances they occur on dated buildings (1663, 1729, and 1766), illustrating the persistence of this tradition in the parish. Of the later village houses the so-called Manor House is the most prominent. It has a late-18th-century front of three bays with an extension of one bay to the east. In the 19th century large numbers of cottages were built, both singly and in terraces, particularly in Broadway and towards the SW. end of Lower Street, often filling gaps in the older street frontages. Many, presumably the smaller ones, have been demolished but some, including some short terraces of double-fronted houses, remain. Some were probably built to replace the 24 destroyed in a village fire in 1811.[14] The Hitchen 'triangle' remained largely undeveloped, except for the frontage

[60] 9th Rep. Com. Char. p. 501; M.I. in ch.
[61] Char. Com. files; ex inf. the rector, the Revd. P. Swinbank.
[62] Char. Com files; charity board in church; ex inf. the rector.
[63] Char. Com. files; ex inf. the rector.
[1] The name means 'boundary gate': E. Ekwall, Oxf. Dict. of Eng. Place-names. This article was completed in 1977.
[2] R. Bathgate and R. Munn, Merriott, its Ch. and Par. (1961).   [3] Census, 1901, 1931, 1951.
[4] S.R.S. xxxvi. 19. The word in origin may be a stream name, cf. E. Ekwall, Eng. River-names, 362–4.

[5] Cal. Close, 1374–7, 263–5.
[6] Geol. Surv. Map 1″, solid and drift, sheet 312 (1958 edn.).
[7] S.R.O., DD/PT, box 8.
[8] S.R.O., DD/TMP, box 6, ct. bks.
[9] Cat. Anct. D. iii, C 3001.
[10] Crewkerne Turnpike Act, 5 Geo. III, c. 61 (Priv. Act).
[11] S.R.O., DD/TMP, box 6, ct. bks.
[12] Ibid.   [13] H.O. 107/1928.
[14] Taunton Courier, 18 Apr. 1811. An earlier fire may account for a Merriott church brief in 1687: S. & D. N. & Q. ii. 67.

to the main streets, until the mid 20th century. Much of this area has since been taken for housing development.

The southern part of the parish comprised some freeholds held under Crewkerne Parva and Merriott manors by the names Shutteroaks, Ashlands, and Ashwell (Ashwell's gate occurs c. 1300).[15] Shutteroak House is an early-18th-century house of two storeys with a symmetrical front of seven bays, which has mullioned and transomed windows. The area of Bow mill had been settled by the 14th century and later, probably 18th-century, development included Eggwood House on the western boundary and Sockety Farm, north of the village. Sockety is a later-18th-century house with stone gables and a red-brick front. Waterloo Farm, north of Sockety, is c. 1820. Moorlands, a large late-19th-century house in the 16th-century Gothic style, was built on the western edge of the village by Sir G. Gilbert Scott.[16] Marks Barn House is a large gabled building of c. 1900. Green Nap, a hamlet to the NE. of the village, is linked to Townsend by 20th-century infilling.

The open arable fields in the Middle Ages seem to have stretched across the parish south of Eggwood to the millstream, including the village itself, with extensions by the 14th century further north to Niddons (Netherdon in 1285) and Stoneridge (Stondonrygge in 1400). There is no evidence for secondary field systems at Bow or on the farms south of the millstream. The increase in arable was at the expense of woodland in the 13th century, though Eggwood survived into the 15th century, with a park at its eastern end.[17] Common meadow lay beside the streams on the parish boundaries in the north and west: Elyngham (Yelinghame in 1556) and Elepolesham in 1285, Ham by 1375, and Levermore and Fenbryage Lake by 1400.[18] All these probably occupied the areas later known as Longmoor, Ham, and part of Niddons. Common pasture in 1285 was located at Garstune and Slapusweye or Slopeshulle, probably beside the road leading north from the church called Sandy Hole.[19]

There were at least three village alehouses by 1594 and all were ordered to close after 8.00 p.m. from 1603.[20] An inn called the Rose and Crown was mentioned in 1619[21] and the present King's Head in Church Lane by 1745. The Bell and George inns both occurred in 1770 and both closed in 1958.[22] The Half Moon stood at Green Nap in 1842 and the present Swan inn in Lower Street by 1866.[23] A Working Men's Institute, built in Lower Street in 1884 by Major R. H. Hayward of Shutteroaks, probably for his employees at Tail

mill, was continuing in 1977.[24] Friendly societies called the Victoria club and the Women's club were mentioned in 1887, when the Claxton Friendly society, named after a former vicar, was formed. In 1889 the Merriott Permanent Friendly society was established at the Working Men's Institute and there were also coal and provident clubs, and a clothing club which continued until 1936.[25] The Working Men's Friendly society was still meeting in 1939.[26] A parish hall at the northern end of Broadway was given in 1924 by Robert Blake of Marks Barn House, and a recreation ground was established in the same year as a war memorial. The Working Men's Institute has been used by the Merriott Social Club since 1975.[27]

There were some 785 inhabitants in 1619, of whom 170 were adolescents, and 401 communicants at Easter that year.[28] The population had risen to 1,017 by 1801 and to 1,212 in 1821, and was stabilized at just under 1,500 in the years 1831–71. There followed a steady decline to 1,116 in 1931. Since the Second World War there has been a gradual rise from 1,327 in 1951 to 1,495 in 1971.[29] The persistence and paucity of surnames in the parish led by the early 17th century to the adoption of nicknames such as curlhead, noghead, and boneback, a custom which continued into the early 20th century.[30]

Twenty men from the parish were in Monmouth's army in 1685 and John Templeman of Merriott was pardoned for his involvement in the following year.[31]

Robert FitzHarding (d. 1170) of Bristol, son and brother of successive lords of the manor and founder of St. Augustine's abbey, Bristol, was probably born in the parish.[32] Charles Price (1776–1853), physician to William IV and son of the vicar, was born in the parish.[33]

MANORS AND OTHER ESTATES. At the time of the Conquest the later manor of *MERRIOTT* formed two estates. One of seven hides was then held 'in parage' by Lewin and Bristward and by 1086 had been granted to the count of Mortain, under whom it was occupied by Dodeman. The second estate, of five hides, occupied in 1066 by Godwin, had passed by 1086 to Harding son of Eadnoth the staller.[34] Later these two holdings were combined under the ownership of Harding's descendants, their identities surviving in the division of the overlordship. The Mortain overlordship, described as 1½ fee by 1197, passed from Robert, count of Mortain (d. 1090), to his son William, whose lands were forfeited to the Crown

[15] *Cat. Anct. D.* iii, C 3001; E. Devon R.O., CR 550; S.R.O., DD/TMP, box 6, ct. bks.
[16] Devon R.O. 74B/MP 239; see below, plate facing p. 65.
[17] Adam de Domerham, *Hist. de rebus gestis Glaston.* ed. Hearne (1727), i, p. xc; C 137/89/12.
[18] C 133/42/6; *Cal. Close,* 1374–7, 263–5; D.R.O., D 124, box 97, partition, 1400; S.R.O., DD/TMP, box 6, ct. bks.
[19] *Cal. Close,* 1279–88, 321.
[20] S.R.O., DD/TMP, box 6, ct. bks.
[21] S.R.O., Q/RL.
[22] S.R.O., DD/TMP, box 4, ct. papers; Q/RL; ex inf. Mr. W. B. Harwood.
[23] S.R.O., tithe award; *P.O. Dir. Som.* (1866).

[24] *Kelly's Dir. Som.* (1906).
[25] S.R.O., D/P/mer 1/6/1, 23/1; Taunton Castle, Tite Colln. 116/22, Permanent Friendly Soc. rules, 1889.
[26] *Kelly's Dir. Som.* (1939).
[27] Ibid.; Char. Com. files; local information.
[28] S.R.O., DD/TMP, box 6, tithe bk. The figure of 785 may not include young children.
[29] *V.C.H. Som.* ii. 343; *Census,* 1911–71.
[30] S.R.O., DD/TMP, box 6, tithe bks.; R. Bathgate and R. Munn, *Merriott, its Ch. and Par.* (1961).
[31] B.L. Add. MS. 30077, f. 37; *Cal. S.P. Dom.* 1686–7, 101.
[32] *D.N.B.*
[33] F. Boase, *Mod. Eng. Biog.*
[34] *V.C.H. Som.* i. 477, 523.

in 1106. The other estate, evidently held under the honor of Gloucester by 1201, was described variously as 1 or 1½ fee.[35] The overlordship continued to be held jointly under both honors until at least 1285.[36] Thereafter, although a fee was claimed by the holders of the Gloucester honor as late as 1400, the Crown acted as overlord of the whole estate which was stated to be held in chief.[37]

The manor evidently passed from Harding son of Eadnoth, or Harding de Meriet, to his son Nicholas FitzHarding (d. by 1171), followed by his grandson Henry de Meriet (d. by 1192).[38] Nicholas de Meriet (d. by 1229) inherited his father's lands in 1212, and in 1229 was succeeded by his son Hugh (d. c. 1236).[39] From Hugh's son Nicholas (d. c. 1258) the manor passed in turn to Nicholas's son John (d. 1285), and grandson, also John. The last succeeded as a minor and received his lands in 1297.[40] On his death in 1308 he was followed successively by his sons John (d. by 1322) and George (d. 1328).[41] From George's son, Sir John de Meriet (d. 1369), the manor descended to his son Sir John (d. 1391), and subsequently to the latter's daughter Elizabeth, wife of Urry Seymour.[42] On Elizabeth's death without issue c. 1395 the estate was inherited jointly by her cousins Elizabeth and Margaret d'Aumale, granddaughters of George de Meriet (d. 1328) and wives of Sir Humphrey Stafford and Sir William Bonville (d. 1408) respectively.[43] Under a partition of 1397 the manor was allotted to Bonville[44] and passed eventually to his grandson William Bonville (d. 1412).[45] William was succeeded by his brother John (d. 1427), whose heir was his first cousin, William Bonville, Lord Bonville, executed in 1461.[46] Lord Bonville's widow, Catherine, received a grant of the manor in 1461, and was succeeded by her daughter Cecily (d. 1530), married first to Thomas Grey, marquess of Dorset (d. 1501), and secondly to Henry Stafford, earl of Wiltshire (d. 1523).[47] Thereafter the manor was inherited by Cecily's son Thomas Grey, marquess of Dorset (d. 1530), whose son Henry (cr. duke of Suffolk 1551) was attainted in 1554, when his estates were seized by the Crown.[48]

The manor was granted in 1554 to William Rice and Barbara his wife and a reversionary lease for 2,000 years, failing the heirs of William and Barbara, was made to Sir Jerome Bowes in 1575.[49] The lease

was surrendered in 1577 and a new term of 200 years in reversion was made on similar terms to Ralph Bowes in 1580.[50] Ralph secured a grant of the fee from the Rices in 1585, subject to an annuity for their lives of £50.[51] Bowes sold the manor to James Hooper in 1587, and he purchased interests held by John Strangways in the same year.[52] James Hooper (d. 1598) left the manor to his nephew Henry Hooper, who enfranchised much of the estate and granted parts of the manor by three conveyances to Robert Gough between 1605 and 1608 and the rest to John Wyke in 1609 and 1611. John Gough had succeeded Robert by 1614, and in 1623 bought John Wyke's interest from his daughters: Rebecca wife of Thomas Brookes and Frances wife of Thomas Greenwood.[53]

The manor had been heavily mortgaged by the Hoopers and by 1611 until at least 1625 courts were held by its three or four 'farmers'.[54] John Gough (d. 1635) was followed by his son Robert who sold the estate to John Pitt of Norton sub Hamdon in 1669. Pitt conveyed it in 1686 to Thomas Rodbard, a London fishmonger, who left it to his nephew John Rodbard (d. 1744) of Merriott.[55] John was succeeded by his son Henry Rodbard (d. 1792), who left four illegitimate children, the eldest, John Butcher, assuming the name of Rodbard. The last married a bigamist and his children by her did not inherit, the manor passing to his brother William Butcher (later Rodbard) (d. 1843) of West Coker.[56] After William's death the estate was held jointly by his sister Mary, widow of Silvester Prior Bean (d. 1797), and his niece Charlotte, wife of Edward Whitley (d. 1878).

On Mary Bean's death in 1849 her share descended in turn to her son Reginald Henry Bean (later Rodbard) (d. 1848) and grandson John Rodbard Rodbard (d. 1887). Reginald Henry (d. 1889), son of the last, was succeeded by his sisters Emma (d. 1905) and Frances Sarah, wife of Robert Danger (d. 1895).[57] In 1906 the manor was partitioned between the joint lords, the lordship passing to the Whitleys, and Frances's estate was split up and sold after her death in 1930.[58]

The other half of the manor was inherited on the death of Edward Whitley (later Rodbard) by his son Edward William Rodbard Rodbard (d. 1884). Rodbard left it to his uncle, the Revd. H. C. Whitley (d. 1902), whose son H. E. Whitley

[35] *Red Bk. Exch.* (Rolls Ser.), i. 101, 155, 166, 546, 608; *Pipe R.* 1202 (P.R.S. N.S. xv), 282; Sanders, *Eng. Baronies,* 14. [36] *Cal. Inq. p.m.* ii, pp. 341–2.
[37] Ibid. v, p. 28; *Cal. Inq. Misc.* vii, p. 270; *Cal. Pat.* 1281–92, 173.
[38] *Proc. Som. Arch. Soc.* xxviii. 100–4.
[39] *Pipe R.* 1212 (P.R.S. N.S. xxx), 119, 223; *Cal. Inq. p.m.* i, p. 2.
[40] *Cal. Inq. p.m.* ii, pp. 341–2; *Plac. Abbrev.* (Rec. Com.), 293.
[41] *Proc. Som. Arch. Soc.* xxviii. 104–24; *Cal. Inq. p.m.* vii, p. 119.
[42] *Cal. Inq. p.m.* xii, pp. 376–7; *Proc. Som. Arch. Soc.* xxviii. 126–64. [43] *Proc. Som. Arch. Soc.* xxviii. 164–7.
[44] *S.R.S.* xvii. 169; *Cal. Close,* 1422–9, 93–4.
[45] *Complete Peerage,* s.v. Bonville.
[46] Ibid.; *Cal. Close,* 1422–9, 93–4.
[47] *Cal. Pat.* 1467–77, 456; *Complete Peerage,* s.v. Bonville. A grant of the manor to William Claxton in 1484, in the king's hands for the treason of John Bevyn, a Bonville trustee, was probably reversed after 1485: *Cal. Pat.* 1476–85, 427.

[48] *Cal. Pat.* 1553–4, 259; *Complete Peerage,* s.vv. Dorset, Suffolk.
[49] *Cal. Pat.* 1553–4, 259; 1572–5, 500.
[50] S.R.O., DD/SB 47/1. The grant to Bowes in 1580 was subject to a rent-charge of £50 12s. 1d. to the Crown. By the 17th century the rent had been acquired by the Strangways family, later earls of Ilchester. At the partition of the manor in 1906 it was apportioned to Mrs. Danger and extinguished by her in 1925 for £850 paid to the earl of Ilchester: S.R.O., DD/SB 47/1, 42/3, and box 51, draft, 5 June 1925.
[51] C.P. 25(2)/206/ 27 Eliz. I Hil.; C 142/285/124.
[52] S.R.O., DD/SB 31/3.
[53] Ibid. 38/3; *S.R.S.* li, pp. 183–4.
[54] S.R.O., DD/TMP, box 1, assignment, 17 Oct. 1616; box 6, ct. bks.
[55] *Som. Wills,* ed. Brown, ii. 60; S.R.O., DD/SB 47/1; DD/TMP, box 1, conveyance, 23 July 1686.
[56] S.R.O., DD/SB 9/2; DD/TMP, box 4, copy will of William Rodbard, 1844; box 5, separation papers.
[57] S.R.O., DD/SB 49/7 and box 53, pedigree.
[58] Ibid. 50/1.

(d. 1919) received the entire lordship and half the lands when the estate was partitioned in 1906. He was succeeded by his son H. H. Whitley of Canada. The lands were sold in 1920 although the lordship is believed to continue in the family.[59]

The gardens, curtilages, and dovecot of the manor-house were mentioned in 1285, and the eastern grange of the house, byre, pig-stye by the high chamber, and garden in 1375.[60] In the 17th and 18th centuries two capital messuages called the Upper and Lower farms were held with the manor and lay near to one another.[61] Their site has not been traced and it is not certain that they represent the medieval manor-house, traditionally located north of the church where ploughing has revealed building-stone and fire-damaged debris.[62] The property known as the Manor House at Townsend was the home of the Whitley family before they inherited the lordship.[63]

The appropriation of the rectory by Muchelney abbey before 1392 and the endowment of a vicarage created a separate rectorial estate which remained in the hands of the monks until Muchelney's dissolution in 1538.[64] It was then granted to Edward Seymour, earl of Hertford, who exchanged it with the king for other lands in 1542.[65] Henry VIII granted the rectory to the chapter of Bristol in the same year, and the chapter continued to hold it until succeeded in the 19th century by the Ecclesiastical (now Church) Commissioners.[66] It was described in leases from the later 17th century as a manor.[67]

The advowson was valued at £20 in 1285[68] and the rectory estate was held at farm by 1535 at a rent of £12 1s., a figure which continued unchanged until the 19th century. Early lessees included Sir Amias Poulett (d. 1538) and the families of Pitt (1537–67), Carew, Dawes (1619–72), and Merifield of Woolminstone in Crewkerne (1672–94).[69] In 1619 the estate comprised a house, 90 a. of land, and a tithe barn valued at £50; and in 1649 65½ a. worth £45 a year.[70] In 1764 the house, barn, and 85 a. of land were sub-let for £140.[71] The rectory was leased to Joan Abraham of Purtington, Winsham, in 1694, and she was followed in turn by her son William, of Merriott, in 1708, and grandson Samuel Abraham in 1729. The last was succeeded by his widow Susannah in 1736, and her second husband Henry Fry, lessee from 1743. The estate passed in 1778 to Elizabeth Fry of Chard, and in 1792 by will to Peter Dowding. Dowding died in 1844, leaving his estates in trust for his daughter Elizabeth, wife of the Revd. Adolphus Kent, the lessees being Dowding's executor, Frederick Dowding of Bath (d. 1861), and

Frederick's executor, H. H. Burne of Bath. Burne established his title in Chancery in 1869 and under an agreement of 1876 the rectory was partitioned. The Ecclesiastical Commissioners received 5 a. and a tithe rent-charge of £181 1s., with liability to repair the chancel, and Burne purchased the rectory farm of nearly 74 a. and a tithe rent-charge of £18 19s.[72] In 1764 the rector claimed tithes of all corn and of water-meadows below the water mark.[73] The tithes were commuted for £180 in 1842.[74]

The rectory house may have become the vicarage house at the appropriation. The rectory farm stands at the junction of Ashwell Lane and Broadway. Described in 1806 as built of stone and slate in two bays, it included a dairy, back-kitchen, a newly-built thatched barn, and a malthouse. The farmhouse and barn were burnt down in 1812 and the present house and barton built.[75] The rectory tithe barn, standing opposite the church in Church Lane, was mentioned in 1325 and described in 1619 as formerly greater but reduced to one bay.[76] In 1910 it was granted to the vicar by the Ecclesiastical Commissioners and restored, and has been devoted since 1913 to church purposes.[77]

Bow mill, a house, and a carucate of land were granted by Sir John de Meriet (d. 1391) to John Canon of Lopen and Isabel his wife, for their lives, in 1373.[78] Canon subsequently acquired the fee; by 1381 he was dead, and in 1383 the property had passed to Isabel's second husband, Richard Slade, who still held it in 1399.[79] An interest or possibly tenancy may later have passed to Richard's daughter and heir Edith, wife of William Boef, who held lands in the parish in 1433.[80] In 1400, however, an estate described as Bow mill, Crepe, and 'Northton' was partitioned between the joint lords of Merriott, Sir William Bonville and Sir Humphrey Stafford.[81] The Bonville share was thereafter held with the capital manor, the Stafford interest descending to the Strangways family with the manor of Kingsdon Cary,[82] being described in 1559 and 1563 as the manor of *MERRIOTT AND BOWMILL*.[83] A lease by the joint owners was made in 1546, but after 1563 the Strangways holding seems to have been terminated in favour of the capital manor and their rights were ceded to the principal lord by John Strangways in 1587.[84]

John Bevyn of Lufton granted a house, lands, and water-mill to Thomas Lyte of Merriott, which were evidently sold c. 1573 to John Pyne (d. 1607) of Merriott and Curry Mallet.[85] In 1595 the estate was settled on John's son Thomas Pyne (d. 1609) and Thomas's wife Amy, and was described in 1609 as Court Place and Court mills.[86] Thomas's widow

[59] S.R.O., DD/SB, 48/3; box 51, abstr. of title, 1920; DD/TMP, file.
[60] C 133/42/6; *S.R.S.* xlix, pp. 284–5.
[61] S.R.O., DD/SB 42/2; DD/TMP, box 7, survey, n.d.
[62] R. Bathgate and R. Munn, *Merriott, its Ch. and Par.*
[63] S.R.O., tithe award.
[64] *H.M.C. Wells*, ii. 22; *Valor Eccl.* (Rec. Com.), i. 194.
[65] *L. & P. Hen. VIII*, xiii(1), p. 64; E 318/box 13/573.
[66] *L. & P. Hen. VIII*, xvii, pp. 638–9; Bristol R.O., DC/E/31/6.   [67] Bristol R.O., DC/E/31/1.
[68] C 133/42/6.
[69] S.R.O., DD/X/SAB; Bristol R.O., DC/E/31/1.
[70] S.R.O., DD/X/SAB.   [71] Par. rec. survey, 1764.
[72] Bristol R.O., DC/E/31/1, 6.
[73] Par. rec. survey, 1764.

[74] S.R.O., tithe award.
[75] Bristol R.O., DC/E/31/3–4.
[76] Adam de Domerham, *Hist. Glaston.* i. 211–12.
[77] S.R.O., D/P/mer 9/1/3.
[78] *Cal. Pat.* 1370–4, 359.
[79] Ibid. 1381–5, 280; D.R.O., D 124, indenture, 6 Jan. 1398/9.   [80] *S.R.S.* xxii. 86.
[81] D.R.O., D 124, box 97, partition, 20 May 1400.
[82] *V.C.H. Som.* iii. 115.
[83] E 326/12924; C 142/136/7.
[84] S.R.O., DD/SB 31/3.
[85] C 54/434 no. 57; *Proc. Som. Arch. Soc.* xxviii. 97-8; S.R.O., DD/TMP, box 6, ct. bk.
[86] *Som. Wills*, ed. Brown, i. 3–4; *Visits. Som.* 1531, 1573, ed. F. W. Weaver, 66–7; *S.R.S.* lxvii, p. 51.

still held it in 1620–1, but it subsequently reverted to John Pyne's second son Hugh (d. 1628) and passed to Hugh's son Arthur (d. 1639).[87] As the manor of *MERRIOTT* it was inherited by Arthur's sister Christabel (d. *c.* 1662), wife of Sir Edmund Wyndham, Bt., of Kentsford in St. Decumans (d. 1683). Sir Edmund was succeeded by his grandson Edmund Wyndham, who died childless in 1698, and was followed by his widow Mary (d. 1713–14).[88] Much of the land was sold in 1703 to pay her husband's debts and the remainder left to her brother Sir John Trevelyan, Bt. (d. 1755), of Nettlecombe. From Sir John it passed in turn to his son Sir George (d. 1768) and grandson Sir John Trevelyan (d. 1828).[89] The manor was mentioned in 1793[90] but not thereafter.

ECONOMIC HISTORY. The two Domesday estates in Merriott paid geld for a total of 12 hides. Half the Mortain holding was held in demesne with 2 ploughs and 6 serfs and half by 10 villeins and 6 bordars with 4 ploughs. There were 25 a. of meadow, and pasture ½ league in length and breadth. Livestock comprised 35 sheep, 15 swine, 10 head of cattle, and a riding-horse. Half Harding's land, gelding for 5 hides, was demesne with 2 ploughs and 2 serfs and the remainder was worked by 9 villeins and 6 bordars with 2 ploughs. There was meadow land of 10 a. and 3 furlongs of pasture with a single riding-horse, but no mention was made of woodland under either estate. The Mortain property had increased in value from £4 to £7 since the Conquest, while Harding's had fallen from £5 to £4.[91]

The manor, probably comprising the two Domesday estates, was valued in 1285 at £51 14s. 3d. and included larder dues at Martinmas, church scot, Peter's Pence, two aids, including one on flax, and rents of geese and capons. The demesne then totalled 411 a. of arable, 43 a. of meadow, unspecified amounts of pasture in Eggwood park, Garstune, and Slapusweye, with profits on timber and alderwood. The dower assigned in that year included rents from 6 free and 32 customary tenants.[92] The value of the manor was given as £41 7s. 4d. in 1308 but may not have included a further grant of dower in that year assessed at £22 8s. 3½d.[93] The lands held by John de Meriet in 1311 were supposed to be worth £100 a year, although those occupied by George de Meriet at his death in 1328 produced only £14.[94] The manor was diminished by the grant to John Canon of the estate centred on Bow mill, which in 1381 included

nearly 100 a. of land and 6s. rent,[95] and the remainder of the manor was valued at £40 in 1400.[96]

At least six freeholds had been created by the 13th century,[97] particularly in the area known as Ashlands on the southern border with Crewkerne, but most were small. One held by the Ashland family was described in 1312 as a house and virgate of land, the oldest part of their inheritance, and was probably the estate from which they took their name.[98] Part of the family's lands there descended with a share in Eastham manor, Crewkerne, through the families of Guldene and Kidwelly, passing to the Pouletts in the early 16th century, when they were known as 'Darbies'.[99] Part of the Ashland family estate was held of the Order of St. John of Jerusalem in 1334 and the 16th century, suggesting a connexion with the Order's property in Lopen.[1] Some 100 a. in Ashlands descended from John Heyron (d. 1501) to his son John (d. 1507), and in the 16th century was divided between the families of Sydenham and Rosse.[2]

The manor continued relatively intact with 63 tenants in 1525 and 1566–7. In the latter year the tenants were holding 918 a. and paying rents of £46 1s. 11¾d. Three tenants had holdings of 60 a. but apart from cottagers most farms were of 20 a. to 40 a.[3] The major change came during the lordship of Henry Hooper, who between 1604 and 1608 conveyed much of the manor to his tenants. Fee farm rents were to be paid on enfranchised property and suit to both manor court and mill was reserved.[4] The size of tenements later decreased and at the sale of the manor in 1669 there were 60 reserved tenancies sharing 120 a. between them; the rest were cottagers and all tenants paid a total of £10 17s. 10d. in rent.[5] The demesne holdings comprised Bow farm and mills with 105 a., Chescombe farm (probably Manor farm in Lower Street) with 43 a., and 109 a. at Furringdons in Crewkerne.[6] By 1690 there were 68 freeholders and 55 lease- and copy-holders.[7]

The Wyndham manor had 26 tenants in 1693 paying rents of £11 1s. 7d., and was also fragmented. By 1703 130 a. had been sold and a further 22½ a. by 1706.[8] By 1729 there were 74 a. divided between 7 tenements, of which 3 were in hand, and rents amounted only to £1 5s. 2d.[9] The remainder of the estate had probably been sold off by the early 19th century.

The manor had a rental of £26 in 1800, although this did not include the manor farm and Bow mills with lands of 268 a. held with a further 110 a. in Crewkerne.[10] Most of the small holdings had been conveyed away by the early 19th century with the

[87] *Cal. Cttee. for Compounding*, ii. 965; *V.C.H. Som.* iii. 43.
[88] S.R.O., DD/TMP, box 5, deeds of manor.
[89] *Som. Wills*, ed. Brown, ii. 43–4.
[90] S.R.O., DD/TMP, box 2, lease, 29 Sept. 1793.
[91] *V.C.H. Som.* i. 477.
[92] C 133/42/6.
[93] *Proc. Som. Arch. Soc.* xxviii. 107; *Cal. Close, 1307–13*, 28–9.
[94] *Cal. Close, 1307–13*, 301; *Proc. Som. Arch. Soc.* xxviii. 123.
[95] *Cal. Pat. 1377–81*, 615.
[96] *Cal. Inq. Misc.* vii, p. 270.
[97] *Cal. Close, 1279–88*, 321.
[98] *Cal. Inq. p.m.* v, pp. 226–7.
[99] Ibid. vii, p. 414; *Cal. Inq. p.m. Hen. VII*, iii, pp.

79, 553–4; E 315/385; S.R.O., DD/TMP, box 6, ct. bks. Stephen Derby married Avice Guldene (d. 1420): see above, p. 44.
[1] *Cal. Inq. p.m.* vii, p. 414; E. Devon R.O., CR 550.
[2] *Cal. Inq. p.m.* iii, pp. 446–7; S.R.O., DD/TMP, box 6, ct. bks.
[3] E 315/385; S.R.O., DD/TMP, box 6, survey, 1566–7.
[4] e.g. S.R.O., DD/TMP, boxes 1, 2, 5–7, enfranchisements.
[5] S.R.O., DD/SB 42/3; DD/X/SPK, survey, n.d.
[6] S.R.O., DD/SB 47/1.
[7] S.R.O., DD/TMP, box 4, rental, 1690.
[8] Ibid. lease, 5 May 1693; DD/WO, box 5, deeds of manor.
[9] S.R.O., DD/TMP, box 4, letter, 21 Apr. 1729.
[10] Ibid. box 7, schedule, 1800.

exception of cottages in the village. There were 67 of these held on monthly tenancies in 1844 and 26 were advertised for sale in 1845.[11] By 1881 there were 30 cottagers but in 1906 only 15 remained. At the partition of the manor in 1906 Higher farm had 50 a. and Bow mills 64 a.[12]

The former open-field pattern cannot be recovered in detail. The field names Wodfurlonge and Beredon (later Beadon) which occur in 1285 suggest woodland clearance, and there are references in 1375 to cleared land in the area of Eggwood. By 1285 the area to the north of Eggwood at Netherdon (later Niddons) was arable, as was Clayhill to the east of the park by 1308.[13] The names West field, to the west of the village as far as the parish boundary, and Middle field, in the north of the parish,[14] suggest a later and more simplified field system. Stoneridge in the north-east of the parish lay within an area called East field in 1571.[15] All former open fields were probably inclosed during the 15th or early 16th centuries with the exception of Hitchen or Landshare. All tenants were ordered to maintain the hedges around the cornfield called Hychyns in 1559 and 1561.[16] This was gradually eroded by piecemeal inclosure but was in part farmed in strips until the 19th century.[17] The meadow allotments within Ham, one of the common meadows, were described in the 16th century as mark doles or noble doles, and the flooding of water meadows was mentioned in 1764.[18]

The farming pattern in 1842 was dominated by the 278 a. held by William Rodbard, including Manor farm of 193 a. and Bow mills of 48 a. John Templeman owned 156 a., and Sockety farm of 84 a. was wholly occupied by minor tenants; William Fitchett Cuff held Moorlands with 88 a., and Susannah Whitley the 'Manor House' with 86 a., both sub-let in small units.[19] In 1851 Manor farm totalled 227 a., Moorlands 200 a., and in 1867 there were only these two large farms in the parish.[20] Manor or Merriott farm had decreased to 140 a. by 1870, and there were five other farms with between 50 a. and 100 a.[21] The continuing number of small holdings, 23 farms in 1889 and 20 in 1939,[22] is a reflection of the richness of the Merriott soil, and the area devoted to arable remained relatively stable between 1842 and 1905.[23] The parish continues to be devoted to both arable and dairy farming.

In 1375 the garden and nursery ('noresire') of the manor-house were large enough to be subdivided for a grant of dower.[24] Tithes paid in 1634 and 1679 on cabbages, carrots, roots, hops, apples, pears, and gardens suggest that the gardening tradition was well established in the parish.[25] The Whitley family, later lords of the manor, occurred as gardeners from 1718,[26] and Reginald Whitley, the vicar's son, moved his nursery business from Merriott to Brompton (Mdx.) between 1785 and 1791.[27] Gardeners and nurserymen were mentioned regularly from the later 18th century, and in 1833 market gardens and grounds planted with potatoes amounted to 196 a.[28] In 1867 the vicar commented that many of his parishioners bought an acre or two of the 'very rich land' with borrowed money, and throughout the summer the women and children tended the gardens and picked peas, while the husbands hawked the vegetables around the country.[29] The number of market gardeners fell from 27 in 1861 to 22 in 1866, and 18 in 1889. By 1939 there were only five.[30]

The largest nursery was owned in 1831 by John Webber, succeeded by his son W. W. Webber in 1846.[31] The Webbers were bought out in 1852 by John Scott (d. 1886), who published several editions of his 'Orchardist', an extensive catalogue and handbook, and opened a nursery and retail shop in Yeovil.[32] Before Scott's death the business fell into financial difficulties and was taken over by his mortgagees. Its fortunes had been restored by 1923 when it was sold to R. J. Wallis, and it was continuing as John Scott and Company in 1977.[33]

Fullers and dyers were referred to in 1575 and 1581,[34] a woollen draper in 1674 and 1693,[35] and clothiers in 1665 and 1697.[36] There were some fustian-weavers, coverlet-weavers, sack-weavers, and rope-makers in the 17th century, and fustian was being sent to London in 1608.[37] The raw material, hemp, was being grown in quantity at that time.[38] Other minor activities included tobacco-pipe making in 1676 and 1707.[39]

The employment pattern over the last 150 years has been affected by Tail mill, adjacent to the village but lying in Crewkerne. Formerly manufacturing sailcloth, it has been occupied since 1938 by a plastics company. In 1851 nearly 80 persons were engaged in the flax and sailcloth industry, although some of those may have worked

11 S.R.O., DD/SB 31/5.
12 Ibid. box 51, particular, 1881; box 53, partition, 1906.
13 C 133/42/6; Cal. Close, 1374–7, 263–5; C 134/4/6.
14 S.R.O., tithe award.
15 S.R.O., DD/TMP, box 6, ct. bk.
16 Ibid. box 6, ct. bks.
17 S.R.O., tithe award.
18 S.R.O., DD/TMP, box 6, ct. bks.; par. rec. survey, 1764.
19 S.R.O., tithe award.
20 H.O. 107/1928; Rep. Com. Children and Women in Agric. [4202–I], pp. 468–9, H.C. (1868–9), xiii.
21 S.R.O., DD/TMP, box 7, sewer rate bk. 1870.
22 Kelly's Dir. Som. (1889, 1939).
23 S.R.O., tithe award; statistics supplied by the then Bd. of Agric. 1905.
24 Cal. Close, 1374–7, 263–5.
25 S.R.O., D/D/Rg 313; DD/TMP, box 6, lease, 24 June 1679.
26 S.R.O., DD/TMP, box 3, conveyance, 26 Mar. 1718.

27 Ibid. box 1, bond, 10 Apr. 1785; box 2, deed, 21 Apr. 1791.
28 Ibid. box 4, ct. papers.
29 Rep. Com. Children and Women in Agric. [4202–I], pp. 467–9, H.C. (1868–9), xiii.
30 P.O. Dir. Som. (1861, 1866); Kelly's Dir. Som. (1889, 1939).
31 S.R.O., DD/SB 1/3, 22/8.
32 Ibid. 1/6, 2/7.
33 Ibid. 1/4–6.
34 S.R.O., DD/TMP, box 6, ct. bks.
35 Ibid. box 2, deed to lead fine, 10 Jan. 1673/4; DD/SP, box 13, inventory of George Gough, 1693.
36 S.R.O., DD/TMP, box 7, deed, 27 Mar. 1665; D.R.O., LL 395.
37 S.R.O., DD/TMP, box 2, lease, 20 July 1605; box 5, lease, Oct. 1606, 24 Oct. 1607, 21 May 1659; box 6, tithe bks.
38 Ibid., box 6, tithe bks.; D/D/Cd 57, 19 Nov. 1622.
39 S.R.O., DD/TMP, box 2, lease, 26 Oct. 1676; box 3, conveyance, 1 Feb. 1706/7.

at other factories in Crewkerne. Gloving as a cottage industry then occupied 95 women and girls in the parish.[40]

A fair was held at Merriott in 1243–4 when Nicholas de Meriet was summoned for unjustly taking tolls from Exeter men.[41] The fair was taken into the king's hands in 1279–80 and was valued at 6s. 8d. in 1285.[42] In 1328 George de Meriet tried to reclaim it from the Crown, stating that it had been held by his ancestors from Friday before the Ascension until the morrow of the same feast. It was then worth 12d. a year,[43] but is not mentioned again.

MILLS. There were four mills in 1086, three on Dodeman's holding paying 30s. and one on Harding's paying 5s.[44] The dower assigned to Margaret de Meriet in 1308 included a mill valued at 13s. 4d., and the dower of Maud de Meriet in 1375 part of the rent from 'Lockesmille', possibly Bow mill.[45] In the same year a freehold water-mill was held under the Meriets for ¼ fee,[46] possibly the one later known as Court mill.

Bow mill, granted to John Canon in 1373, had in 1400 a great gate, hall and adjoining chambers, solar, kitchen, bakery, furnace, dovecot, stable, byre, and waggon house.[47] It was leased in halves in 1546 to James Bagge (d. c. 1557), servant of the marquess of Dorset, and to Elizabeth Hooper (d. c. 1560) and her son James.[48] The mill leat was illicitly diverted in 1572 and the mill seems to have been worked by the Sweetland family by 1561 until at least 1583.[49] It was still held in halves and described as two mills in 1587 and all tenants owed suit of multure. The lessees had to grind all grain which the lord required for his household at Merriott.[50] The Hooper lords of the manor occupied the mill-house until its sale to John Gough in 1616, leasing the mill separately by 1602 to Joseph Starr, from whom it was known for a time as Starr's mill.[51] The mill descended with the manor and was included in John Pitt's purchase in 1669.[52] By 1726 there were three water-corn-mills which passed from Robert Parker to Francis Buckland in 1751.[53] The premises were leased to Isaac Hayward in 1791, succeeded by Jesse Hopkins, a Martock miller, who held them until 1848. Members of the Patch family then held the property until 1896, during whose tenure much of the mill was burnt c. 1862 and rebuilt.[54] The premises were evidently not used as a commercial mill after 1896,[55] although the mill-wheel and leat both survived in 1977. The house and mill form one building which is probably of later-17th-century origin, although the mill, which is at the north end, may have been rebuilt after the 19th-century fire. The former house may have been the site of a private chapel licensed for use by William Boef and his family in 1457.[56]

Court mill, so called by 1573, formed part of the estate held by Thomas Lyte from 1543–4.[57] In 1556 the tenant, William Burd, was convicted of felony and his goods, including an old brass furnace and an iron bar for the mill, were bought by Thomas Lyte.[58] The mill was held by members of the Lock family by 1866 and in 1906, but ceased to grind shortly before the Second World War.[59] The mill-house lies south of Lower Street and is probably late 17th or early 18th century in date.

William Ashe built a mill behind his tenement in 1555, known as Berdons mill in 1558. In 1560 Ashe was forbidden to pond back the water in his leat, also used by Court mill, and Thomas Lyte was allowed to pull up Ashe's flood hatches and remove any obstructions.[60] It was later known as Billing's mill after William Billing, mentioned as miller in 1717. The French family occupied the mill during the years 1794–1840 and 1889–1931, and it was worked until c. 1962.[61] The mill-house stands on the north side of Ashwell Lane at the west end of the village, flanked by the stone-lined mill-leat.

LOCAL GOVERNMENT. In 1280 John de Meriet claimed infangthief, frankpledge, gallows, and assizes of bread and of ale, though the jurors of Crewkerne and South Petherton hundreds said that only infangthief and the assizes had been exercised, that thieves ought to be hanged at the gallows of the lord of the hundred, and that de Meriet had only pecuniary rights in the assizes and had no pillory.[62] There is no further medieval evidence of these claims, but the manor court in the 16th century heard business which included pleas of debt and trespass, confiscation of felons' and fugitives' goods (1556, 1625–6), and millers charging excessive tolls.[63] In 1599 the Merriott tithingman and posts or jurymen had only to attend the hundred courts at Easter and Michaelmas and were not required to make presentments, apparently justification enough for Merriott to be called a liberty between 1571 and 1576, a claim obviously with medieval origins.[64]

Court books survive for the years 1555–61, 1568–84, 1593–5, 1602–3, 1610–26,[65] 1728–57,[66] and fairly complete series of court papers for 1674,[67] 1725–56,

[40] H.O. 107/1928.
[41] *Plac. Abbrev.* (Rec. Com.), 121–2.
[42] *Cal. Chanc. Wts.* i. 193; C 133/42/6.
[43] *Cal. Inq. p.m.* vii, pp. 144–5.
[44] *V.C.H. Som.* i. 477, 523.
[45] *Cal. Close,* 1307–13, 28–9; 1374–7, 263–5.
[46] *Cal. Inq. p.m.* xiv, p. 188.
[47] D.R.O., D 124, box 97, partition, 20 May 1400.
[48] Ibid., lease, 1 July 1546; S.R.O., DD/TMP, box 6, ct. bks.   [49] S.R.O., DD/TMP, box 6, ct. bks.
[50] Ibid. box 1, lease, 1 Nov. 1587. The phrase 'from the Buddle at Beck's door upwards', applied to suit of multure, is unexplained.
[51] Ibid. box 6, tithe bks.; conveyance, 10 Oct. 1616.
[52] Ibid. box 7, schedule, n.d.
[53] S.R.O., DD/SB 29/5, 33/4.
[54] Ibid. 29/5, 31/1, 35/4, 50/10.
[55] Ibid. 50/10, 11; box 51, letter, 15 Sept. 1906.
[56] *S.R.S.* xlix, pp. 284–5.
[57] S.R.O., DD/TMP, box 6, ct. bks.
[58] Ibid.
[59] *P.O. Dir. Som.* (1866–75); *Kelly's Dir. Som.* (1883–1906); local information.
[60] S.R.O., DD/TMP, box 6, ct. bks.
[61] Ibid. box 4, ct. paper, 14 Oct. 1794; box 6, conveyance, 26 Sept. 1717; tithe award; *Kelly's Dir. Som.* (1889–1931); local information.
[62] J. I. 1/759 rot. 17d. Two hides in Harding's Merriott estate were geld-free in 1086: *V.C.H. Som.* i. 532.
[63] S.R.O., DD/TMP, box 6, ct. bks.
[64] Ibid.; S.R.O., T/PH/hsy, survey 1599.
[65] S.R.O., DD/TMP, box 6.
[66] S.R.O., DD/SAS C/99.
[67] S.R.O., DD/SB 31/6.

1783–1918.[68] Courts, described usually in the 16th century as courts leet and view of frankpledge and from the 18th century as courts leet alone, were held twice, and sometimes thrice, a year until the 18th century, when a single court was held, from 1745 at the King's Head inn. Refusal by some jurymen to serve on the homage in 1802 led to distress for their fines and the hope that 'the firmness displayed by Mr. Rodbard will reduce the delinquents to reason'. The homage, in turn, frustrated an attempt by the steward to establish a biennial court in 1849. A hayward, mentioned in 1370[69] and sometimes described as keeper of hedges, and a tithingman were appointed from the 16th century. From 1831 a constable's staff, handcuffs, and later the key to the stocks were mentioned. In 1834 and 1839 there were 2 tithingmen. There were 2 haywards by 1834, 4 in 1854, 3 in 1856, and 2 from 1859, called bailiffs and haywards from 1877.

Court business in the later 16th and early 17th century included the presentment of petty larceny, punishment in the pillory and stocks (1571), continuous prosecution of immoral under-tenants, the playing of unlawful games, and even absence from church (1560, 1582). Particular emphasis on scouring ditches and maintaining roads and houses continued into the 20th century, the vestry deferring to the court leet in matters of public nuisance in 1854.[70]

No evidence has been found of courts being held for the manor of Merriott rectory, but 17th- and 18th-century leases reserved the right of the chapter of Bristol to hold 'a court and survey' at will.[71] No court rolls survive for the Trevelyan manor of Merriott although suit of court was demanded of tenants as late as 1773.[72]

There were two churchwardens from 1554 and posts or sidesmen were mentioned in that year and in 1599.[73] Two sidesmen occurred in 1634 and two overseers of the poor from 1642.[74] The vestry appointed salaried parish surgeons regularly between 1781 and 1836, mole catchers in 1782 and 1820 on seven-year contracts, and 2 salaried overseers in 1794–5. From 1842 it nominated 2 waywardens, 2 overseers, and an assistant waywarden and rate-collector. The surgeons were not to deal with confinements, fractures, or venereal disease.[75] No paupers were to be relieved unless they attended church to receive their pay in 1783, or unless they wore a badge in 1792. Vegetables were bought for resale to the poor in 1801 and from 1820 no relief was paid to paupers keeping a pig. Between 1842 and 1847 the churchwardens raised money for pauper emigration.[76]

A poorhouse, probably in Broadway, was mentioned in 1786 and rebuilt after a fire in 1790. Two additional houses were built for the poor in Hitchen in 1793 and others adjoining the existing poorhouse in 1795 and 1807. All these houses were ordered to be sold in 1836,[77] although the overseers still owned six cottages in two groups at Broadway in 1842.[78] The parish joined the Chard poor-law union in 1836.[79] A lock-up or round house, built of Ham hill stone with stone tiles, survives near Manor Farm. It was mentioned in 1911 when it had not been used for many years.[80]

CHURCH. A parson and chaplain of Merriott occur between 1171 and 1192.[81] The patronage of the rectory descended with the lordship of the main manor until 1377, though the Crown presented in 1314 and 1318 during minorities[82] and also in 1390. In 1377 Sir John de Meriet sold the advowson and 1 a. of land to John Harewell, bishop of Bath and Wells.[83] In 1378 the bishop gave it for the maintenance of the vicars, boys, choristers, and other ministers of Wells cathedral.[84] In 1383 Harewell planned to charge the rectory with 25 marks to endow a chantry for the Black Prince, presumably in Wells cathedral, and for a yearly distribution to the choristers. It proved, however, impracticable to impose the charge. The bishop, therefore, gave the advowson and land to Muchelney abbey in 1385,[85] with licence to appropriate the rectory on the death or resignation of the rector in return for a pension of 6s. 8d.[86] The appropriation had taken place by 1392.[87] Thereafter the advowson of the vicarage remained in the hands of Muchelney until the surrender of the abbey to the Crown in 1538, and since 1542 it has belonged to the chapter of Bristol.[88] A grant of one turn was made to Sir Nicholas Wadham in 1517 for unexplained reasons and the Crown presented in 1660.[89]

The rectory was valued at £13 6s. 8d. in 1291[90] and in 1325 there were crops on 32 a., and tithes, rents, and offerings worth 23s. 4d., the whole valued with stock at £21 6s. 4d.[91] The rector in 1384 was said to share the profits with Muchelney abbey[92] but the benefice could not support the charge of 25 marks planned in 1383.[93]

The vicarage was valued at £6 13s. 4d. in 1445 and £12 4s. 8d. in 1535.[94] The living was temporarily augmented with £20 a year in 1658 and had a reputed value of £70 c. 1668.[95] The net income was £312 in 1831 and £324 8s. 11¼d. in 1851.[96]

[68] S.R.O., DD/TMP, boxes 2 and 4; DD/SB, box 51.
[69] D.R.O., D 124, box 16, acct. 1369–70.
[70] S.R.O., D/P/mer 9/1/2.
[71] Bristol R.O., DC/E/31/1.
[72] S.R.O., DD/TMP, box 2, lease, 24 June 1773.
[73] S.R.O., D/D/Ca 22; T/PH/hsy, survey 1599.
[74] S.R.O., D/D/Rg 313; *Som. Protestation Returns*, ed. A. J. Howard and T. L. Stoate, 42.
[75] S.R.O., D/P/mer 9/1/1–2.
[76] Ibid.
[77] Ibid.
[78] S.R.O., tithe award.
[79] *Poor Law Com. 2nd Rep.* p. 547.
[80] S.R.O., DD/SB, box 51, letter, 17 May 1911.
[81] Adam de Domerham, *Hist. Glaston.* i, pp. lxxxix–xc.
[82] *S.R.S.* i. 165; *Cal. Pat.* 1313–17, 95; 1317–21, 219; 1388–92, 187.
[83] *Cal. Pat.* 1377–81, 12; *S.R.S.* xvii. 92.

[84] *Cal. Pat.* 1377–81, 184.
[85] Ibid. 1381–5, 281–2, 581; 1385–9, 6.
[86] *Cal. Papal L.* v. 17.
[87] *H.M.C. Wells*, ii. 22.
[88] *L. & P. Hen. VIII*, xvii, pp. 638–9.
[89] *S.R.S.* xlii, p. 59; lv, p. 16; *Som. Incumbents*, ed. Weaver.
[90] *Tax. Eccl.* (Rec. Com.), 199.
[91] S.R.O., D/D/B reg. 1, f. 226b; printed Adam de Domerham, *Hist. Glaston.* i. 211–12.
[92] *The Metrop. Visit. of William Courtenay, 1381–96*, ed. J. H. Dahmus, 36–7, 141–4.
[93] *Cal. Pat.* 1381–5, 581.
[94] *S.R.S.* xlix, p. 33; *Valor Eccl.* (Rec. Com.), i. 165.
[95] Lambeth Palace MSS., COMM. VIb/2; S.R.O., D/D/Vc 24.
[96] *Rep. Com. Eccl. Revenues*, pp. 144–5; par. rec., valuation, 1851.

Part of the tithes of the demesne, formerly held by Roger, archdeacon of Winchester, were given by Nicholas de Meriet to Bruton priory together with Lopen chapel c. 1209.[97] A dispute over payment in 1339 was settled by 120s. damages, but by 1400 a pension of 21s. was paid in lieu.[98] The remainder of the tithes were let to the parochial chaplain in the absence of the rector in 1325 for 10s. a year.[99] They were valued in 1535 at £10 19s. 2d. and in 1608–9 included those on fustian sent to London and thread delivered to yarn washers.[1] The vicar refused composition money for wool from the lord of the manor in 1617, claiming that he was shearing his sheep out of the parish.[2] In 1634, apart from more usual tithes, 1d. was paid for every garden and a tenth of all rents paid by strangers for land in the parish. Amongst other titheable produce was hemp, flax, hops, and honey, and the tithe hay on certain specified meadows.[3] In 1679 the vicar leased to the lord of the manor for three years all tithes from the latter's lands except those on hemp, flax, carrots, and turnips for £6 a year. The excepted produce was tithed at between 5s. and 2s. an acre.[4] An agreement by the inhabitants to compound for all tithes from 1816 was rescinded after only two years.[5] The tithes were commuted in 1842 for a rent-charge of £393.[6]

Between 1171 and 1192 grazing and the right to gather underwood were granted by the lord to the parson, and between 1236 and 1258 leave to inclose some glebe and the right to place in Eggwood park as many animals as the lord.[7] The glebe totalled 15 a. in 1613, the same lands were extended at 14 a. in 1842, and had fallen to 5 a. by 1939.[8] There were 5 a. in 1975.[9]

The parsonage house may have been used by the vicars after appropriation. A barn was mentioned in 1325, and in 1613 the property then held by the vicar included a house, barn, stable, stall, malthouse, and orchard.[10] The house was rebuilt in 1776 and enlarged in 1852.[11]

Philip Bernardini, son of a Florentine banker and rector 1313–31, received successive licences for absence between 1325 and 1331.[12] His successor, Thomas de London, rector 1331–3, owed 100 marks to two Florentine merchants in 1332, one of whom was Peter Bernardini.[13] Robert de Samborne, rector until 1362, was a monk from Glastonbury abbey and John Stacy, vicar from 1521 until at least 1554, held the living with that of South Bradon.[14] In 1618 Alexander Atkins, vicar 1576–1626, was described by his parishioners as 'most contentious and quarrelsome'. He had demanded more than his just tithes, refused communion to those in arrears, and insulted them from the pulpit.[15] Robert Marks, vicar 1626–57, held the benefice with South Petherton, and his successor, John Greenway, vicar 1657–78, survived the Restoration.[16] Theophilus Powel, vicar 1719–31, held the living with Backwell, and Thomas Price, vicar 1775–1832, with Fivehead and Swell.[17]

In 1557 the church was without a silver-gilt cross and spoon, a pyx, and incense boat, sold without the parish's consent.[18] In 1620, after a church ale with bear- and bull-baiting, a churchwarden was accused of using the communion cup to serve 'alehouse beer' at the bear stake.[19] The curate in 1632 was alleged to have been so drunk that 'he would have cut off some of his hand to give unto his dog'.[20] In 1815 services were held once every Sunday, and twice by 1827.[21] On Census Sunday 1851 the average congregation was 115 in the morning and 140 in the afternoon, including 40 Sunday-school pupils at each service.[22] By 1870 Holy Communion was celebrated monthly.[23] Cottage services were held at Boozer Pit by 1887, and by 1890 in Broadway until at least 1891.[24]

The figure of the Virgin and the lights of the High Cross, Our Lady, and St. Catherine were mentioned in 1538.[25] Parcels of land called the church house, referred to in 1566–7, suggest the former existence of such a building.[26] The old rectory tithe barn has been used for parish meetings since 1913.[27]

The parish church of *ALL SAINTS*, so dedicated by the mid 13th century,[28] is built of rubble and ashlar and has a chancel with north and south chapels, aisled nave with south porch, and west tower. The earliest surviving feature is the tower which has thick walls tapering externally. Its date is not certain but its arch may be of the later 13th century and the parapet, semi-octagonal south vice, buttresses, and west doorway and window are all additions of the 15th or earlier 16th century. Also of that date are the porch and the three western bays of the nave and aisles. The old chancel, which was perhaps 14th century and had no side chapels,[29] was demolished by faculty of 1860, and the nave was extended one bay eastwards and the new chancel and chapels were added to designs by Benjamin Ferrey. The nave roof was renewed, probably at this time, and the entire church was refurnished.

[97] *S.R.S.* viii, p. 39.
[98] Ibid. vii, p. 151.
[99] S.R.O. D/D/B reg. 1, f. 226b.
[1] *Valor Eccl.* (Rec. Com.), i. 165.
[2] S.R.O., D/D/Cd 47.
[3] S.R.O., D/D/Rg 313.
[4] S.R.O., DD/TMP, box 6, lease 24 June 1679.
[5] Par. rec. determination 26 May 1817.
[6] S.R.O., tithe award.
[7] Adam de Domerham, *Hist. Glaston.* i, pp. lxxxix–xci.
[8] S.R.O., D/D/Rg 313; tithe award; *Kelly's Dir. Som.* (1939).
[9] Ex inf. Dioc. Office.
[10] S.R.O., D/D/B reg. 1, f. 226b; D/D/Rg 313.
[11] S.R.O., D/P/mer 3/2/1; DD/SB 27/2.
[12] *Cal. Pat.* 1324–7, 19, 49; 1327–30, 376, 380; *S.R.S.* i. 246, 286–7; ix, pp. 7, 72.
[13] *Cal. Close,* 1330–3, 535.
[14] Emden, *Biog. Reg. Univ. Oxford,* iii. 1635; S.R.O., D/D/Vc 20; D/D/Ca 22.

[15] S.R.O., DD/TMP, box 6, articles 1618; and tithe bks.; D/D/Cd 47.
[16] *Walker Revised,* ed. Matthews, 316; *Som. Incumbents,* ed. Weaver; Lambeth Palace MSS., COMM. III/6 p. 40.
[17] Foster, *Alumni Oxon.*
[18] S.R.O., D/D/Ca 22, 27.
[19] S.R.O., DD/TMP, box 6, tithe bk. The 'play day' mentioned in 1618 may relate to the church ale: ibid.
[20] S.R.O., D/D/Ca 282.
[21] S.R.O., D/D/B returns 1815; D/D/V returns 1827.
[22] H.O. 129/318/4/7/21.
[23] S.R.O., D/D/V returns 1870.
[24] S.R.O., D/P/mer 1/6/1.
[25] S.R.O., DD/X/SR C/403, copy will of Wm. Slade.
[26] S.R.O., DD/TMP, box 6, ct. bk.
[27] S.R.O., D/P/mer 9/1/3.
[28] Adam de Domerham, *Hist. Glaston.* i, p. xc. See above, plate facing p. 16.
[29] Photograph in ch.

Three galleries, put up in 1830, were then removed,[30] and a leaden heart-case was then found in the north wall of the chancel.[31] A carved stone in the vestry wall, bearing figures identified as fighting cocks, has been attributed to the 12th century. A similar date has been claimed for a cross-head with a representation of the crucifixion.[32]

There are six bells: (i) 1733, Thomas Bilbie; (ii) 1827, John Kingston; (iii) 1732, Bilbie; (iv) 1733, Bilbie; (v) 1784, George Davis; (vi) 1955, Taylor of Loughborough.[33] The plate is of the 19th century. The registers date from 1646 and are complete.[34]

NONCONFORMITY. The ejected ministers of Cricket St. Thomas and Heathfield with three others had dissenting congregations of 160 in 1669,[35] and a Presbyterian minister, John Turner, was using a house in 1672.[36] Nonconformist meetings were registered in 1703 and 1705. From 1750 a single house was used by Presbyterians, Anabaptists, and Methodists, but from 1753 by Methodists alone.[37] A Wesleyan meeting was started in 1811 with 13 members, and in 1851 had bought a site for the chapel built in Lower Street in 1857. Attendances were 29 at evening service on Census Sunday, and the chapel was still in use in 1977.[38] Further dissenting licences were issued for houses in 1810, 1826, and 1846.[39]

A congregation of Baptists was formed in 1839 by William Hebditch and the Union or Unity chapel was opened in 1841. On Census Sunday 1851 there were attendances of 32 at the afternoon service and 57 at the Sunday school. A Baptist and Independent chapel in Lower Street was opened in 1878.[40] It was in ruins in 1903, and the Baptist Union surrendered its interest in 1911. The building continued in use as a Congregational chapel, but was subsequently closed and sold in 1964.[41] It has since been extended and in 1977 was used by a squash rackets club.

The Brethren met in the parish from 1846 and opened Broadway chapel in 1847. On Census Sunday 1851 there were congregations of 45 in the morning and 120 in the evening.[42] The cause still continued in 1977.

A Four-Square Gospel Mission hall, built in 1937,[43] was continuing in 1977 as the Elim Pentecostal church.

EDUCATION. For some years the vicar, Alexander Atkins (1576–1626), had a school, and in 1618

taught at least nine boys.[44] A schoolmaster is mentioned in 1739.[45] There was a day-school for 20–30 children in 1819, and 55 by 1825–6, and the Sunday school had 100 in 1825–6.[46] A building for the Sunday school was erected in 1834, and in 1835 had 160 pupils supported by voluntary contributions. Also in 1835 there were two infant schools with 32 children and two day-schools for about 70 boys, all charging fees. The 'farm barton school', evidently held at Manor Farm, was mentioned in 1836.[47]

The Sunday-school room was used as a National day school by 1861. A School Board was formed in 1875 and an infants Board school for 145 children was built in 1876. The former National school then became a mixed Board school, accommodating 120 children.[48] The schools had an average attendance of 242 in 1894 and 265 in 1903.[49] Total attendances fell from 266 to 171 in 1915, 125 in 1935, and 104 in 1946. In 1972 the two buildings were designated a First School, for pupils between five and nine years old, under the comprehensive system centred on Crewkerne. There were 93 children there in 1975.[50]

CHARITIES FOR THE POOR. James Hooper (d. 1598), lord of the manor, left £100 as 'a stock' for the poor of the parish.[51] To this sum Robert Gough added £20, paid over with £3 interest by his representatives in 1713,[52] and Robert England gave £100, probably before 1800. In 1807 the money was lent on security to local men, and the interest of £12 3s. distributed to the second poor on St. Thomas's day (21 December). The funds were ordered to be invested in 1845 and interest of £10 10s. was being distributed as before in 1872.[53] In 1933 tickets for clothing worth £8 15s. were given on St. Thomas's day, but in 1974 the income of £11 was used to purchase hymn books.[54]

Sarah Woodcock (d. 1892), of West Chinnock, left £500 to the vicar and churchwardens, the interest to provide coal, particularly at Christmas, for poor people under the age of 60. In 1933 the income of £12 16s. 4d. was given in coal and in 1967 from £24 9s. 3d. interest, £10 8s. was distributed in cash. A similar bequest of £500 was made by Elizabeth Adams Brown (d. 1904), the interest to be devoted to the deserving poor aged over 60. The income was £15 18s. 8d. in 1933 and £24 9s. 9d. in 1967, distributed in cash. In 1974 the Woodcock and Brown charities, with a total income of £49, were given to 62 people over 60 at 75p each.[55]

[30] S.R.O., D/P/mer 9/1/2.
[31] Now in County Mus. Taunton, identified with that of Mary, first wife of Sir John de Meriet of Hestercombe, d. by 1300: R. Bathgate and R. Munn, *Merriott, its Ch. and Par.* (1961).
[32] *Proc. Som. Arch. Soc.* xxxvii. 36–8; lxvii, pp. xl–xli.
[33] S.R.O., DD/SAS CH 16.
[34] *Proc. Som. Arch. Soc.* xlv. 145; S.R.O., D/P/mer 2/1/1.
[35] T. G. Crippen, *Nonconformity in Som.* (Som. Arch. Soc. Libr. Taunton Castle).
[36] *Cal. S.P. Dom.* 1672, 237, 240.
[37] S.R.O., Q/RR, meeting-house lics.; D/D/Rm, box 2.
[38] H.O. 129/318/4/7/11; D/N/spc 1.
[39] S.R.O., D/D/Rm, box 2.
[40] *Rep. Som. Cong. Union* (1896); H.O. 129/318/4/7/12; Char. Com. files.   [41] Char. Com. files.
[42] H.O. 129/318/4/7/13; G. H. Lang, *God at Work on his own Lines*, 35.
[43] *Kelly's Dir. Som.* (1939).
[44] S.R.O., D/D/Cd 47; DD/TMP, box 6, tithe bk.
[45] S.R.O., DD/TMP, box 4, ct. papers.
[46] *Digest of Returns to Sel. Cttee. on Educ. of Poor*, H.C. 224 (1819), ix (2); *Rep. B. & W. Dioc. Assoc. S.P.C.K.* (1825–6); *Educ. Enquiry Abstract*, H.C. 62 (1835), xlii.
[47] S.R.O., D/P/mer 9/1/2.
[48] *P.O. Dir. Som.* (1861); *Kelly's Dir. Som.* (1889); S.R.O., C/E, box 27.
[49] *Returns of Schs.* [C. 7529] H.C. (1894), lxv; S.R.O., C/E, box 27.
[50] S.R.O., *Schs. Lists.*
[51] *Som. Wills*, ed. Brown, ii. 104.
[52] S.R.O., DD/X/SPK, receipt, 1713.
[53] S.R.O., D/P/mer 9/1/2; 17/3/1.
[54] Char. Com. files.   [55] Ibid.

MISTERTON

THE PARISH of Misterton lies immediately south-east of Crewkerne, its name, a contraction of 'Minsterton', indicating its former dependence on the mother-church of that town.[1] The village is sited about 1½ mile from Crewkerne on the main road to Dorchester. It has an area of 1,361 a. and extends for 2½ miles from NE. to SW. and up to 1½ mile from NW. to SE. The NE. boundary with North Perrott is marked by the river Parrett and the remainder of the eastern and part of the southern boundaries with South Perrott and Mosterton (both Dors.) are formed by a tributary of the same river known at successive points along its course as Brimble Water, Misterton Water, and South Perrott Water. The parish adjoins Seaborough (Dors. formerly Som.) to the SW. and has an irregular and evidently later western boundary with Crewkerne.[2]

The south of the parish is dominated by Knowle hill, which rises to 587 ft. The land falls away to 250 ft. in the area of the village and below 150 ft. on the northern boundary with the Parrett. The centre of the parish lies mainly on Inferior Oolite with clay in the NW. The SW. is principally undifferentiated 'head' with Yeovil Sands and small outcrops of Upper Greensand and Gault.[3] A number of limekilns and quarries, generally disused by 1903, were formerly worked in the SE. of the parish.[4] Apart from the Parrett and the stream along the boundary the principal water is the mill stream which rises in the SW. and flows NE. through the village, formerly powering mills at the present Mill Farm before flowing into the Parrett on the NE. boundary.

The most important route through the parish is the main Crewkerne–Dorchester road, turnpiked by the Crewkerne trust in 1765, which runs south as Station Road to Misterton cross roads, where it turns E. and then SE., continuing as Middle Street through the village and subsequently to South Perrott. It was along this road that the village developed, extending east from the neighbourhood of the church. Earthworks south of the 'Manor House' suggest shrinkage of settlement in this area. At the eastern end of the village expansion had taken place along Silver Street to the NE. by the 17th century. South-east of the village is a second cross roads where a turnpike gate and toll house were sited by 1770, still standing in 1903.[5] The road leading thence south to Mosterton and eventually to Bridport (Dors.) leaves the parish over Bluntsmoor bridge and was also turnpiked in 1765; the route north across the Parrett at Gray Abbey bridge (called Ree bridge in 1770) to North Perrott was adopted in 1825. From 1765 the Crewkerne trust

had responsibility for a road west from Misterton cross roads over Cathole bridge to Roundham in Crewkerne and eventually to Chard.[6] Church Lane, running south to the church from Misterton cross roads, was diverted away from the 'Manor House' grounds in 1831 and a western access to Manor Farm in front of the 'Manor House' was replaced by one from the north.[7] Within the village Unity, formerly Clarks, Lane runs north, taking its name from Unity Cottages, built in 1866,[8] and Silver Street extends NE. from Middle Street, turning east to join the North Perrott road. From the west end of the village Knowle Lane runs south, then SW. to meet the Mosterton–Hewish lane in Crewkerne, which crosses the SW. corner of the parish. From Knowle Lane Ducks Field Lane runs across the Mosterton road at Ducks Field Crossing and continues to Seaborough. Green, Rose, Melancholy, and Swan lanes are all field access tracks.

Older Ham-stone building survives mainly around the church, along the west side of Silver Street, and beside the stream to the north and west, and there are a number of farm-houses of traditional 17th-century type in the two latter areas. Most surviving housing along Middle Street, linking the earlier development, is 19th century in date. At the NW. approach to the village the opening of Crewkerne station in 1860 on the Salisbury–Exeter line,[9] running east–west across the parish to the north of the village, has resulted in almost continuous development from Misterton cross roads along Station Road to Crewkerne. Most 20th-century building has been concentrated between Silver Street and the North Perrott road and in 1976 was continuing in that area. All the early farm sites lay within the village. Well Spring Farm, east of the village on the Dorchester road, had been built by 1886;[10] Langley Farm in the west and Knowle Farm in the south of the parish are both 20th century.

Except for its eastern part, most of the parish was occupied by open arable fields, although their extents can be only approximately traced.[11] North of the village lay North field, south of the village South field, including Middle and Colebrooke furlongs, and possibly SE. of the village was East or Middle field, including the later Little and Lathalon fields. It was probably North field that by 1606 had been divided into the three fields of Nethertown and the remainder which in the same year formed the two fields of Overtown.[12] The name South field survives in a number of closes in the extreme SW. of the parish, but these may refer to Henley farm in Crewkerne which is bounded on the south by a 'hook' of Misterton land. The former

[1] E. Ekwall, *Oxford Dict. of Eng. Place-names*, 328. This article was completed in 1976.
[2] Tithe 1/30.
[3] Geol. Surv. Map 1″, solid and drift, sheet 312 (1958 edn.).
[4] O.S. Map 6″, Som. XCIII. NW. (1903 edn.).
[5] Ibid; Crewkerne Turnpike Act, 5 Geo. III c. 61 (Priv. Act); S.R.O., DD/PT, box 39, survey bk. 1770.
[6] Crewkerne Turnpike Acts, 5 Geo. III c. 61 (Priv. Act); 6 Geo. IV c. 159 (Local and Personal); S.R.O., DD/PRN, map of Misterton, 1770.

[7] S.R.O., Q/SR Epiph. 1831; DD/PRN, map of Misterton, 1770.
[8] O.S. Map 6″, Som. XCIII. NW. (1886 edn.); tablet on Unity Cottages.
[9] D. St. J. Thomas, *A Regional History of the Railways of Great Britain*, i. 33–4.
[10] O.S. Map 6″, Som. XCIII. NW. (1886 edn.).
[11] S.R.O., T/PH/hsy; DD/PT, box 47, survey, n.d.; tithe award.
[12] S.R.O., D/D/Rg 314.

open meadow and pasture in the east and NE. of the parish evidently once included a large low-lying area known as Marsh and a smaller tract between the Mill stream and Rose Lane called Eastbrooks. New Closes, to the NW. of the Mill stream, were probably also medieval meadow and pasture.

In 1672 the churchwardens paid for a warrant 'to warn away the new innkeeper'.[13] The 'little ale house going to South Perrott' occurred in 1729 and was probably the White Swan, mentioned in 1737.[14] The house shortened its name to the Swan by the late 18th century,[15] and in 1976 still stood on the south side of the road at the SE. limit of the village. The George was mentioned in 1770 and the Four Alls, which occupied part of the present Hillview Riding Stables in Middle Street, occurred from 1835–6 and had been converted to a reading room by 1903.[16] The New Inn was referred to in 1837–8, evidently lying in Silver Street, and the Globe Inn, standing in 1976 on the north side of Middle Street beside the mill stream, was mentioned in 1866.[17] The Masons' Arms at the northern end of Silver Street had opened by 1872 and was continuing in 1909, although the building was subsequently demolished. The Queen, later the Queen's Hotel, was opened in 1886 and stands beside the railway station on the northern parish boundary.[18] The number of inns mentioned from the 19th century reflects the importance to the village of traffic between Crewkerne and Dorchester. The churchyard contains a gravestone erected by subscription to the memory of Mary Gear (d. 1876) 'for the faithful discharge of her duties as messenger and errand woman between the village and Crewkerne'.[19]

A male Friendly Society occurs between 1881 and 1913, and its female counterpart between 1895 and 1902.[20] A 'house of help' was started c. 1902 by C. J. H. Locke, vicar 1901–14, for young girls who were 'homeless, rescued from bad surroundings, totally destitute, or those who need a helping hand'. It continued until 1909.[21] A War Memorial recreation ground was established in 1921 to the north of the village in Unity Lane.[22]

There were 40 households at Misterton in 1563.[23] The population was 368 in 1801 and remained fairly constant until it rose to 460 in 1831 and thereafter, gradually, to 556 in 1861. A slight fall to 588 in 1871 was followed by a sharp increase to 670 in 1881, probably the result of an influx of country people into the Crewkerne district during the agricultural depression. Subsequently the population was relatively stable, but fell from 681 in 1901 to 522 in 1931. Since the Second World War there has been a slow but steady rise to 530 in 1951 and 590 in 1971.[24]

The Revd. Arthur Collier (1680–1732), a writer of metaphysical and religious works, inherited the 'Manor House' estate from his mother, and may have lived and worked in the parish.[25] Helen Mathers (1853–1920), authoress of *Comin' thro' the Rye* and other novels, was born at Old Court and wrote some of her books there.[26]

MANOR AND OTHER ESTATES. Misterton was part of Crewkerne manor in the Middle Ages.[27] A manor of *MISTERTON* was mentioned from 1465 until at least 1611, purely as a fiscal convenience, though no manorial administration distinct from that of Crewkerne ever developed.[28]

In the late 13th century the lord of Crewkerne granted two virgates of land to John and Joan Michel, formerly tenanted by Alexander de Wottesdone, to be held by them and their male heirs, and in default to revert to Crewkerne manor. This was evidently the holding whose fee passed to the Spoure family, later of Trebartha, Northill (Cornw.), by grant of 1399 and which was known during the Middle Ages as 'Sporisplace'.[29] Philip Spoure was succeeded by his son, William Spoure of Misterton, whose son Thomas married the heir of Trebartha and subsequently moved to Cornwall. Their grandson, Thomas Spoure, had a son Henry (d. 1603), who leased the estate to his brother Digory for three years in 1585. By 1599 it had been sold to Robert Merifield (d. 1608), who was succeeded by his son Edward (d. 1645).[30] Thereafter the property passed to the Hallett family of Misterton, probably through Katherine wife of Barnaby Hallett. Her son, Merifield Hallett (d. 1718), apparently held it by 1660, and was followed in turn by his brother Barnaby (d. 1724) and niece Grace (d. 1761–2), wife of William Cox of Crewkerne.[31] Her son, the Revd. William Cox (d. 1781–2), was succeeded by his son, the Revd. William Trevelyan Cox (d. 1812), and grandson, William Hody Cox (d. 1834), successively of Chedington Court (Dors.).[32] The son of the last, William Trevelyan Cox, sold the Misterton house to the Revd. Burges Lambert (d. 1843), whose son, William Charles Lambert, conveyed it to Viscount Portman in 1870.[33] During the 19th century it was usually known as Misterton Lodge, but by 1931 it had been given its present

[13] S.R.O., D/P/mis 4/1/1.
[14] S.R.O., DD/PT, box 44, rental, 1729; DD/SS, bdle. 56, lease, 29 July 1737.
[15] S.R.O., DD/SS, bdle. 54, lease, 26 Dec. 1740; DD/PT, box 22B, partition, 1773; tithe award.
[16] S.R.O., Q/RL, 1770; Q/REr, 1835–6; O.S. Map 1/2,500, Som. XCIII. 1 (1903 edn.).
[17] S.R.O., Q/REr, 1837–8; E. J. King, *Years Beyond Memory*, 115; *P.O. Dir. Som.* (1866).
[18] S.R.O., DD/SB, box 20, petty sessions lic. bks.
[19] M.I. in chyd.
[20] S.R.O., DD/X/LCM.
[21] *Dioc. Kal.* (1901–7); *Dioc. Dir.* (1908–20).
[22] Char. Com. files.
[23] B. L. Harl. MS. 594, f. 56.
[24] *V.C.H. Som.* ii. 343; *Census*, 1911–71.
[25] *D.N.B.*; S.R.O., DD/SS, bdle. 54, lease, 30 Sept. 1697.
[26] King, *Years Beyond Memory*, 40; *Wessex Life*, Nov. 1969; W. G. W. Watson, *Chronolog. Hist. of Som.* (Som. Folk Ser. xxii), 230.
[27] *Cal. Inq. p.m.* ii, p. 52; *Bk. of Fees*, iv. 331.
[28] C 140 33/38; C 142/325/178.
[29] Devon R.O., TD 51, pp. 180–1, in which the original grant to the Michels is endorsed 'Spurre tenet'; *Proc. Som. Arch. Soc.* cxx. 64.
[30] *Proc. Som. Arch. Soc.* lxxxv. 70–1; J. L. Vivian, *Visit. Cornw.* 430; *Cat. Anct. D.* vi, C 7805; S.R.O., T/PH/hsy, survey of Crewkerne manor, 1599.
[31] S.R.O., D/P/mis 2/1/1; DD/SB 35/6; *Wessex Life*, Nov. 1969.
[32] Hutchins, *Hist. Dors.* ii. 88–9; S.R.O., D/P/mis 2/1/3–5; Foster, *Alumni Oxon.*
[33] *Proc. Som. Arch. Soc.* lxxxv. 70–1; Venn, *Alumni Cantab.* s.v. Lambert.

name, Old Court, by Major A. A. Crossley, who purchased it from Lord Portman in 1924.[34] Since that time it has passed through a number of different hands and been subdivided into separate dwellings.

The old house, which is depicted in a drawing of c. 1700,[35] comprised a north–south central range with end wings, that on the north being partly occupied by a barn. This plan still underlies the existing house, the southern range having been the service wing and that on the north, rebuilt in the 18th century, stables and outhouses. A new block was added in the centre of the south front in the 19th century to provide more spacious family rooms.

An estate emerged during the 17th century based on the union of several leasehold properties and farmed initially from Manor farm and later from the 'Manor House'. The nucleus of the property was probably created by William Curry (d. 1644–5), succeeded by his son Thomas (d. 1663).[36] Thence it passed to William Elsdon, possibly husband of Thomas's widow, and between 1671 and 1674 to Ann Curry, who married the Revd. Arthur Collier (d. 1697) of Steeple Langford (Wilts.) in 1675. The son of the last, another Revd. Arthur Collier (d. 1732), was succeeded by Genevra Collier, widow, possibly his sister-in-law.[37] By 1743 the lands had passed to Margaret Collier, widow of Arthur, in which year she mortgaged them to Sir Edward Smyth. Smyth or his representatives foreclosed on the mortgage and in 1756 sold the estate to Thomas Hallett of Henley, Crewkerne (d. 1789). Hallett left the lands to John Hallett of Whitelackington (d. 1838), probably his nephew, subject to a life interest in the house for his widow Mary (d. 1790). On John's death the property was inherited by his widow, Maximilla (d. 1845), who in 1840 conveyed it to her son William (d. 1845), reserving to herself a life interest in the house. Thereafter it was held by William's widow, Sarah, until her death in 1855.[38] In 1856 the property was sold to W. C. Lambert who conveyed it to Lord Portman in 1871. Stripped of its lands, the house was purchased by the Portman agent, Henry Parsons (d. 1897), whose son, R. M. P. Parsons, was still holding it in 1932.[39] In 1976 the property was occupied as three distinct dwellings. An L-shaped portion of a 17th-century house became the service wing for a mid-18th-century house with five-bay fronts to the north and south. Additions to the west of the older range and in its angle were made in 1878.[40] To the south of the house is a large sunken walled garden, probably of 18th-century origin.[41] Manor Farm,[42] possibly the former capital messuage of the estate, is a substantial early-17th-century house built on an L-shaped plan with two storeys and gable chimney-stacks. Later in the

17th century the interior was remodelled and a porch with room above was added in the centre of the main front. Extensive farm buildings, mainly 19th century in date, have been converted into dwellings.

ECONOMIC HISTORY. Misterton evidently lay under the tenurial and economic influence of Crewkerne throughout the Middle Ages. The whole parish was included within Crewkerne manor, the services and customary payments of its 22 villeins being valued at 30s. in 1274.[43] All that distinguished it from the parent settlement was a render of twelve ewes at Whitsun known as 'Hock ewe', recorded from 1292. Customary payments in wheat at the winter sowing and barley at the Lenten sowing were also being made by 1295.[44]

The only early freehold, later centred on Old Court, probably had its origin in a grant of two virgates c. 1300, which included common pasture for eight oxen in Crewkerne manor. The property conveyed to the Spoure family in 1399 was relatively small, having an area estimated at 50 a. in 1599 and at 100 a. a few years later.[45]

By the 15th century Misterton was being treated as an individual manor for fiscal purposes, valued at £20 10s. in 1484, although all court business continued to be transacted at Crewkerne.[46] Its net income totalled £36 11s. 6d. between 1515 and 1545, the only expenses being the 10s. paid annually to the reeve.[47] In 1599 there were 33 copyhold tenants holding nearly 1,450 a., paying rents of £36 14s. 3d., and one freeholder with 100 a. The two largest holdings of 90 a. and 86 a. were occupied by John Norris and Hugh Farnham respectively, both members of two of the oldest yeoman families in the parish. Of the remainder, 18 tenants had between 40 a. and 60 a. and 8 between 20 a. and 40 a.[48]

As at Crewkerne the subdivision of the manor led in the earlier 17th century to the progressive enfranchisement under 3,000-year leases of ¾ of each holding, the remaining ¼ being retained by the Poulett family and let out on 99-year leases for lives until sold to the tenants in 1810–11.[49] This acquisition of land by the farmers resulted in the creation of larger units and many more small-holdings. The principal estate was amassed by the Curry family and, when held in 1789 by John Hallet, contained at least 257 a. centred on the 'Manor House'.[50] The Poulett quarter of the manor produced rents of £160 10s. 1½d. in 1729 from 35 leasehold tenants and 3 copyholders. This figure fell to £115 12s. 11d. from 25 tenants by 1749, and rose slightly to £117 10s. 4d. in 1780.[51] By 1840 the Hallett property had grown to 402 a., of which 380 a. were leased to the occupier of Manor farm. There were only two other extensive

[34] P.O. Dir. Som. (1861, 1875); Kelly's Dir. Som. (1931); S.R.O., DD/SAS, C/2273, 1.C. 18. 3.
[35] Cornw. R.O., FS 3/93/1–5.
[36] Som. Wills, ed. Brown, iii. 62; iv. 72; S.R.O., D/P/mis 13/2/1.
[37] S.R.O., D/P/mis 4/1/1; DD/SS, bdles. 54, 57; Q/RE 1766; M.I. in ch.
[38] S.R.O., DD/SB 35/6, abstract of title to Hallett estate; M.I. in ch.
[39] Som. Country Houses and Villages (1931–2), 33.
[40] Ibid.
[41] Copy of old sketch in ho.
[42] See plate facing p. 33.
[43] C 133/6/1.
[44] C 133/62/7; S.C. 6/1127/6.
[45] S.R.O., T/PH/hsy, survey, 1599; DD/PT, box 47, survey, n.d.
[46] Cal. Pat. 1476–85, 472.
[47] E. Devon R.O., CR 528; S.C. 6/Hen. VIII/6183.
[48] S.R.O., T/PH/hsy, survey, 1599.
[49] e.g. S.R.O., DD/HK, box 3; DD/SS, bdles. 53–7; DD/SB 35/6, 38/1.
[50] S.R.O., DD/PT, box 21, leases, 14 Sept., 9 Nov. 1789.
[51] S.R.O., DD/PT, box 44, rentals, 1729, 1749, 1780.

Hinton St. George: View North-east to Ham Hill

Hollow Ways in the Yeovil Sands, at the Cross-roads West of Shepton Beauchamp

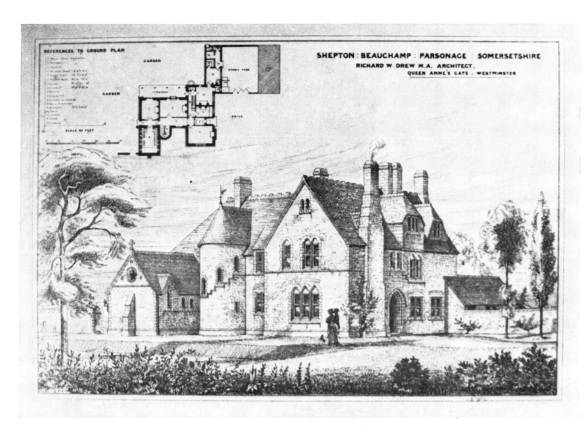

SHEPTON BEAUCHAMP: THE RECTORY HOUSE, 1874

MERRIOTT: MOORLANDS HOUSE

holdings: lands retained by Lord Poulett of 148 a. and Maria Lowman's property of 141 a., and there were three other farms of over 50 a.[52]

There were 12 farmers in the parish by 1861, 11 in 1883, and only 6 between 1894 and 1919. Subsequently the number of farms increased to 10 in 1931, and in 1939 there were 3 of over 150 a. and 10 others.[53]

The three open fields of the late 16th century, North, South, and Middle or East fields, then totalled 593 a., although a further 71 a. were then described as recently inclosed, and other arable areas in South field and meadow and pasture in New Closes, Marsh, and Eastbrooks had evidently been inclosed not long before.[54] By 1606 the fields had been subdivided and open arable comprised the three fields of Nethertown and the two fields of Overtown.[55] Enfranchisement during the 17th century encouraged the allotment of open arable, and by 1770 there were only 39½ a. in four fields, the largest being North field with 28½ a.; there were a further 5 a. of meadow in Winterfield common meadow.[56] The amount of open arable had fallen to 36 a. by 1840 and the remaining strips were inclosed during the 19th century.[57] In 1840 there were 577 a. of arable and 702 a. of meadow and pasture, and by 1905 there was more than twice as much grassland as arable.[58]

Misterton's proximity to Crewkerne led to the development of small-scale industry. Tallow chandlers and soapboilers occurred in 1566, 1706, 1728, and 1732,[59] and clothiers, sergeweavers, and woolstaplers regularly from 1678. The clothing trade occupied some of the leading families in the parish, including the Farnhams, Daubeneys, and Brices.[60] A fishmonger, probably supplying Crewkerne market, was mentioned between 1694 and 1699, and a sack-cloth maker of 1705 was evidently linked with the same trade there.[61] Weavers were common in the earlier 19th century and there were 47 in the parish in 1851. In the latter year there were also twenty glovers, two tinmen, a girth manufacturer, and a dog-breaker.[62] The opening of the railway in 1860 and the siting of Crewkerne station within the parish led to a number of the railway employees moving into the village and also to the development of trading depots around the station site itself. Bradford and Sons and the Somerset Trading Company, both dealers in coal, timber, and slate, had premises there by 1894. They had been joined by two oil traders and the West of England Sack Hiring Company by 1914; in 1939 there were four cattle-food manufacturers and a corn merchant.[63] Other trades referred to included a gravestone cutter, John Potter (d. 1880), whose handiwork is

perpetuated in the churchyard, an accountant in 1882, a 'professor' of music in 1885, a haulier in 1902, and an estate agent in 1906.[64] A firm making 'poultry, pigeon, and cage-bird appliances, rope, twine, and nets' had opened by 1914 and was installed by 1923 in the Enterprise works, specializing in the manufacture of sports nets.[65] The Misterton egg-packing station occupied an extensive site east of the village in 1976.

A mill known as Paddokeslake was mentioned in 1292.[66] In 1548 half of this mill formed part of the endowment of the chantry of the Virgin in Crewkerne churchyard, when it was occupied by William Ash, and in 1549 it was sold to Robert Wood of London.[67] It continued to be occupied by the Ash family until at least 1611–12, when 3,000-year leases of ¼ of the mill were purchased.[68] By 1618 it had passed to Henry Palmer, who then took a further 3,000-year lease on ½ of the mill. The remaining ¼ continued to be leased under the Poulett family until 1811.[69] The ownership descended to the Lidden family, bought out in 1694 by Barnaby Hallett, who sold it in 1699 to Ralph Gillingham (d. 1729) of Yetminster (Dors.), who subsequently became the Misterton miller.[70] The Gillinghams held the mill until another Ralph (d. 1802) left it to his nephew William Daubeny. By 1811 the existing mill, called Gillingham's mill, had been demolished, and in 1819 Daubeny leased the site to John Hopkins Brice, miller, on condition that Brice should build a stone mill-house and a flour mill with all necessary machinery. This had been completed by 1821 when a further agreement was drawn up for the building of a dwelling-house and bakehouse oven.[71] Brice was still there in 1840, although the premises were occupied in 1851 by Thomas Stembridge.[72] Robert Lawrence was miller there between 1861 and 1894, and Henry Newberry, also a farmer and cattle dealer, between 1897 and 1902. The mill had evidently ceased operating by 1906[73] and since that time has been known as Mill Farm. The present mill building is probably that built by Brice c. 1820.

LOCAL GOVERNMENT. Although it was a distinct civil and ecclesiastical parish, Misterton was a tithing within Crewkerne manor. No courts appear to have been held for Misterton but in 1599 a reeve was elected at Michaelmas by the homage of Misterton and Crewkerne Parva to collect the rents for both tithings.[74] 'The four men' of Misterton appear to have taken administrative decisions c. 1600.[75]

The parish had two churchwardens by 1576

[52] S.R.O., tithe award.
[53] P.O. Dir. Som. (1861); Kelly's Dir. Som. (1883–1939).
[54] S.R.O., DD/PT, box 47, survey, n.d.
[55] S.R.O., D/D/Rg 314.
[56] S.R.O., DD/PT, box 39, survey, 1770.
[57] S.R.O., tithe award; O.S. Map 6″, Som. XCIII. NW. (1886 edn.).
[58] S.R.O., tithe award; statistics supplied by the then Bd. of Agric. 1905.
[59] S.R.O., D/P/mis 2/1/1 sub anno 1566; DD/SS, bdle. 53, lease, 29 Sept. 1706; 57, lease, 20 Nov. 1732; DD/PT, box 24A, conveyance, 23 March 1727/8.
[60] e.g. S.R.O., DD/SS, bdles. 54, 55; D/P/mis 2/1/1 sub annis 1692, 1735; DD/HK, box 3.
[61] S.R.O., DD/HK, box 3; DD/PR 75.

[62] S.R.O., D/P/mis 2/1/8; H.O. 107/1860.
[63] Kelly's Dir. Som. (1804–1939).
[64] S.R.O., D/P/mis 2/1/8; M.I. in chyd.; Kelly's Dir. Som. (1902–6).
[65] Kelly's Dir. Som. (1914–23).
[66] Cal. Inq. p.m. iii, pp. 23 ff.
[67] S.R.S. ii. 176; Cal. Pat. 1549–51, 97.
[68] S.R.O., D/P/mis 2/1/1 sub anno 1567; T/PH/hsy, survey, 1599; DD/HK, box 3.
[69] S.R.O., DD/HK, box 3; DD/SB 38/1.
[70] S.R.O., DD/HK, box 3.   [71] Ibid.; DD/SB 38/1.
[72] S.R.O., tithe award; H.O. 107/1860.
[73] P.O. Dir. Som. (1861); Kelly's Dir. Som. (1883–1906).
[74] S.R.O., T/PH/hsy, survey, 1599.
[75] S.R.O., D/D/Cd 47, 24 Sept. 1616.

and until 1704, two sidesmen in 1628 and 1634, two overseers of the poor by 1644, and two way-wardens by 1659.[76] A single churchwarden was appointed from 1705, replaced in 1754 by a man serving as a salaried deputy churchwarden and overseer, an appointment which continued until 1810. Thereafter a people's warden and a vicar's warden were nominated. The 19th-century vestry appointed two overseers of the poor, one way-warden, and, in 1852, two constables. The officers were augmented by a salaried waywarden from 1843 and a salaried overseer from 1844.[77]

In addition to normal items of expenditure the churchwardens were frequently charged for high-way repairs in the 17th century and also for re-lieving the large number of travellers, which rose to 130 in 1668, and 138 in 1675.[78] From 1687 no further payments were to be made to travellers, for killing vermin, or for briefs.[79]

Poorhouses were mentioned in 1683.[80] In 1840 the poorhouses stood at the western end of the village in Silver Street. In 1845 the vestry agreed to lease them, and the houses were last mentioned in 1853.[81] They survived in 1976 as converted dwelling-houses. The parish joined the Chard poor-law union in 1836.[82]

CHURCH. The existence of a chapel (later church) of Misterton may be presumed from at least the mid 13th century, when tithes and other dues were payable by the parishioners to the mother church of Crewkerne.[83] The incumbents, known by that time, most unusually, as *rectores curati*, had acquired both glebe and a share of the tithes.[84] By 1317 they were admitted by the bishop and not by the rector of Crewkerne, even though the chapel was a depen-dency of the mother church. Until the 15th century they were appointed by successive members of the Courtenay family as patrons of Crewkerne.[85] Between 1428 and 1517 the curacy was apparently suppressed and annexed to the third or sub-deacon's portion of Crewkerne rectory.[86] It was probably served by curates acting for the normally absentee rectors, but after the suppression of the rectory of Crewkerne in the mid 16th century the incumbents of Misterton, again known as *rectores curati*,[87] were appointed and paid by the lessees of the Crewkerne rectory estate. In 1633 the patron-age was disputed and the farmer of Crewkerne rectory and two Crown nominees were involved.[88]

Henry Masters was instituted in 1633 but during his tenure Nathaniel Nosse obtained letters patent as 'rector curate' in 1634. Nosse, however, was never instituted and Masters occurs as rector between 1637 and 1642, trying vainly in 1641 to establish his claim also to the advowson.[89] From 1661, when the Crown presented, incumbents have been called vicars.[90] Later the patronage was exercised like that of Crewkerne, in 1681 by the farmer of the rectory and thereafter by the Winchester chapter. In 1908 the gift was transferred from the chapter to the Lord Chancellor, patron in 1976.[91] The living was suspended in 1971 and was served with Hasel-bury Plucknett and North Perrott in 1976.

The church was valued at 5 marks in 1315 and 1377.[92] In 1575 the curate's stipend was £10.[93] He was obliged to pay £3 a year from his tithe income c. 1600 to relieve travellers and for other 'necessary uses'.[94] The benefice was augmented in 1658, in 1733 by the then incumbent, Nathaniel Forster, and in 1784 by Mrs. J. Perceval's trustees.[95] In 1733 the stipend from the third portion of Crew-kerne was said to provide £49 11s.[96] The value was c. £170 in 1815, of which £40 was to be paid to an assistant curate. By 1827 it had risen to 'under £300' and the curate's stipend to £140.[97] The net income was given as £162 in 1831.[98] The living was again augmented in 1858, by £500, and was worth £196 in 1861.[99]

In the 13th century the 'rector curate' received from most of the parish tithes of wax and honey, apples and other fruit, leeks, onions, grass, and 'other things' from all but cottars, the personal tithes of cottars, tithes of servants' wages, and the sheaves of his own glebe. Tenants and cottars of 'Sporis-place', a freehold centred on Old Court, paid half the tithe of lambs and wool to Misterton and half to Crewkerne.[1] In the time of Mark Winter, curate 1585–1607, composition payments were levied on hemp, apples, kine, and calves.[2] Custo-mary moduses payable to the vicar in the earlier 19th century included 8d. for a cow and calf, 3d. for tithe hay from every piece of ground of 24 a., 1s. for the fall of a colt, 1d. for a garden, and 1d. for a cock. At the commutation of tithes in 1840 £205 was awarded to the impropriator of Crewkerne rectory for the great tithes and £70 to the vicar of Misterton.[3]

Glebe land in 1606 comprised 28¼ a. in the open fields and 8 a. in closes, and totalled 33 a. in 1840.[4] The figure had fallen to 22 a. by 1883, rose to

[76] S.R.O., D/P/mis 4/1/1.
[77] Ibid.; D/D/Ca 54; D/D/Vc, box 9, consignation bk. 1634; D/D/Rg 314; *9th Rep. Com. Char.* 502.
[78] S.R.O., D/P/mis 4/1/1–2; 9/1/1.
[79] Ibid. 4/1/1.
[80] Ibid.
[81] S.R.O., tithe award; D/P/mis 9/1/1.
[82] *Poor Law Com. 2nd Rep.* p. 547.
[83] *Proc. Som. Arch. Soc.* cxx, 63–7, based on S.R.O., D/D/B reg 1, description of dues payable to Crewkerne, loose in front cover.
[84] Ibid.; *S.R.S.* xxix, pp. 94, 168; B.L. Add. MS. 49359, f. 74.
[85] *S.R.S.* i. 123; *Som. Incumbents*, ed. Weaver.
[86] B.L. Add. Roll 64327; *Valor Eccl.* (Rec. Com.), i. 163. The last institution recorded was in 1428: *S.R.S.* xxxi. 62.
[87] S.R.O., D/P/mis 2/1/1.
[88] C 3/427/63.
[89] Ibid.; S.R.O., D/P/mis 2/1/1; D/D/Vc, box 9, con-

signation bk. 1623; *Som. Incumbents*, ed. Weaver; *Som. Protestation Returns* ed. A. J. Howard and T. L. Stoate, 42.
[90] S.R.O., D/D/B reg 20, f. 95; 25, f. 10.
[91] S.R.O., D/D/B reg 20, ff. 6, 95; 22, f. 40; 25, ff. 10, 40; 27, f. 36; *Lond. Gaz.* 6 Oct. 1908.
[92] B.L. Add. MS. 49359, f. 74; *Cal. Inq. p.m.* xiv, p. 321.
[93] S.R.O., D/D/Cd 47, 24 Sept. 1616.
[94] *S. & D. N. & Q.* xiv. 31.
[95] Lambeth Palace MSS., COMM. VIb/1; Hodgson, *Queen Anne's Bounty.*
[96] S.R.O., DD/SH 107.
[97] S.R.O., D/D/B reg 20, f. 95; D/D/V return 1827.
[98] *Rep. Com. Eccl. Revenues*, pp. 146–7.
[99] Hodgson, *Queen Anne's Bounty*, p. xlii; *P.O. Dir. Som.* (1861).
[1] *Proc. Som. Arch. Soc.* cxx. 65.
[2] S.R.O., D/D/Cd 47, 24 Sept. 1616.
[3] S.R.O., tithe award.
[4] Ibid.; D/D/Rg 314.

62 a. between 1889 and 1923, and dropped to 4½ a. between 1931 and 1939.[5] There were 2 a. of glebe in 1976.[6]

A parsonage house was mentioned in 1606 and was described as 'ancient' in 1628, when it included a hall with chamber over, a buttery with a kitchen and chamber over, a barn adjoining the kitchen, and a pigstye, garden, and orchard.[7] Its dilapidation was regularly mentioned between 1800 and 1806, and it was described in 1815 as 'a mere hovel' occupied by paupers in which no minister had lived for 120 years.[8] In 1840 it was referred to as a cottage let for £5 a year, and in 1861 it was purchased by the lessee, W. C. Lambert of Old Court, demolished, and the site used to extend the churchyard.[9] In 1859 £500 was raised by mortgaging the glebe and tithes to build a new parsonage house south of the village.[10] This had been converted to a private dwelling by 1976.

Of the incumbents William Gregory, rector from 1350, and Richard Abbot, rector 1410–14, were both acolytes at their institutions.[11] Thomas Vyall, curate, was accused of fornication in 1528 and Robert Bearde of serving the cure without licence in 1576.[12] Richard Baylie, rector curate 1607–25, held the living with Eastham, Crewkerne.[13] Henry Masters, rector from 1633, was 'kept out' until c. 1636 by Nathaniel Nosse, former master of Chard grammar school, who obtained letters patent as rector curate in 1634, although Nosse was never instituted and Masters occurs as rector between 1637 and 1642.[14] The benefice was probably held with Crewkerne during the Interregnum by Jacob Tomkins, vicar 1661–80.[15] Faithful Ashe, vicar 1708–20, occupied the vicarage with Seaborough, and Nathaniel Forster, vicar 1720–52, successively with Stawley and Whitchurch Canonicorum (Dors.).[16] Robert Hoadley Ashe, vicar 1775–1826, was perpetual curate of Crewkerne and master of Crewkerne grammar school, and his successor, Richard Lowe, vicar 1826–52, also held the benefice with that of Crewkerne, but lived in 1827 at Leamington (Warw.).[17]

A lecturer was mentioned in 1653, Holy Communion was being celebrated thrice yearly in 1662, and petitions were presented by the parishioners in 1667 and 1668, apparently vainly, to obtain a resident minister. Sunday services were held alternately in the morning and evening between 1827 and 1840.[18] Two services, one with sermon, were held in 1843, and Holy Communion was celebrated four times a year. By 1870 there were two Sunday sermons and Communion was administered on about eight occasions.[19]

In 1548 the churchwardens held 1 a. of land to maintain a light in the chapel. A lease of the land was granted to Henry Middlemore in 1572, and the freehold was then sold to Percival Gunston of Aske (Yorks. N.R.).[20]

The church of *ST. LEONARD*, so dedicated by 1530,[21] stands at the western end of the village, in Church Lane. The former church comprised chancel, nave, north and south aisles, and south porch, with a bellcot at the junction of nave and chancel. A gallery for the singers was built at their expense and by voluntary contributions in 1772. The chancel was rebuilt in 1811–12 and the church re-roofed in 1822. A private pew or room behind the pulpit was appropriated to the owner of Old Court in 1825. The building was evidently too small for the parish and in 1837 plans were prepared for extending the church to the north to provide additional seats. The decision to rebuild the church was taken in order to obtain a grant from the Diocesan Building Society.[22]

The present church was designed by Sampson Kempthorne of London and built in 1840.[23] It has a chancel, north vestry, nave with gallery, south porch, and a bellcot at its western end.

There are two bells: (i) uninscribed; (ii) Llewellins and James, Bristol, 1908. In 1975 gramophone records of bell ringing were being broadcast from the bellcot and the second bell was stored in the gallery.[24] The plate includes a cup and cover bearing the Exeter hall mark and dated 1635.[25] The registers date from 1558 but were evidently poorly kept during the years 1643–9.[26]

NONCONFORMITY. The churchwardens visited Chard to present papists in 1678.[27] Quakers in the parish were gaoled for not paying tithes in 1659 and for failing to attend church in 1662.[28] Further fines on five persons, probably Quakers, were levied by the churchwardens for non-attendance between 1682 and 1684.[29] A Quaker burial ground had been established at Cathole mead adjoining the south side of the road to Roundham, Crewkerne, by 1705, which probably served the Crewkerne congregation. It was abandoned between 1777 and 1840.[30]

Several houses were licensed in the early 18th century.[31] Baptists from the parish were worshipping at Yeovil by 1720, but the Methodists began a cause in 1754 and Presbyterians in 1760.[32] Bible Christians came in 1824 and registered a private house for worship in 1825.[33] None seems to have survived for long.

[5] *Kelly's Dir. Som.* (1883–1939).
[6] Ex inf. Dioc. Secretary.
[7] S.R.O., D/D/Rg 314.
[8] S.R.O., D/P/mis 4/1/2; D/D/B return 1815.
[9] S.R.O., D/D/V return 1840; D/P/mis 9/1/1.
[10] S.R.O., DD/SB 22/4.
[11] *S.R.S.* x, p. 601; xxix, p. 94.
[12] S.R.O., D/D/Ca 4, f. 26; D/D/Ca 54.
[13] S.R.O., D/D/Vc, box 9, consignation bk. 1623; D/P/mis 2/1/1; *Som. Incumbents*, ed. Weaver.
[14] C 3/427/63; S.R.O., D/P/mis 2/1/1; D/D/Vc 58.
[15] *Som. Incumbents*, ed. Weaver.
[16] Ibid. 430, 440; Foster, *Alumni Oxon.*; S.R.O., D/D/B reg. 25, ff. 10, 40.
[17] *D.N.B.* s.v. Ashe; Venn, *Alumni Cantab.*; S.R.O., D/D/V return 1827.

[18] S.R.O., D/P/mis 2/1/1, 4/1/1; D/D/V returns 1827, 1833, 1840.
[19] S.R.O., D/D/V returns 1843, 1870.
[20] *S.R.S.* ii. 8, 180; *Cal. Pat.* 1569–72, pp. 332, 389.
[21] *Wells Wills*, ed. F. W. Weaver, 65.
[22] S.R.O., D/P/mis 4/1/2, 6/1/2.   [23] Ibid. 6/1/2.
[24] S.R.O., DD/SAS CH 16.
[25] *Proc. Som. Arch. Soc.* xlv. 145.
[26] S.R.O., D/P/mis 2/1/1–9.
[27] S.R.O., D/P/mis 4/1/1.
[28] J. Besse, *Sufferings of the . . . Quakers*, i. 585, 590.
[29] S.R.O., D/P/mis 4/1/1.
[30] Ibid. 2/1/1 *sub anno* 1705; DD/SFR 4/1; tithe award.
[31] S.R.O., Q/RR, meeting-house lics. issued in 1700, 1707 (2), 1723.   [32] Ibid.
[33] S.R.O., D/N/spc 31; D/D/Rm, box 2.

In 1866 the Baptists built a mission chapel on the south side of Middle Street, still in use in 1976. A Wesleyan mission chapel was opened on the north side of the main street near the school in 1891. It was closed in 1931, and in 1976 used as the Women's Institute hall.[34]

EDUCATION. About 1565 the curate was teaching Misterton boys their 'A.B.C. book'.[35] In 1819 the vicar paid for the instruction of such children as he could gather together,[36] and by 1835 there was a mixed day-school with 14 children and two Sunday schools with 40, all supported by subscription.[37] The day-school was probably that kept in 1851 in a house in Middle Street where the vestry met from 1861. A schoolmistress was recorded in the parish in 1861.[38]

The decision to build a National school and teacher's house was taken in 1870 and these were completed in 1874 on glebe land on the south side of Middle Street.[39] Average attendance was 113 in 1883, and in 1895 a new classroom was added and the infants' room enlarged.[40] Thereafter attendances rose from 108 in 1894 to 141 in 1899, and in 1905 there were 5 teachers.[41] Later numbers fell sharply to 74 in 1915, 59 in 1935, and 58 in 1946. From 1972 children over nine went to Crewkerne, and in 1975 there were 48 pupils in the books.[42]

CHARITIES FOR THE POOR. William Owsley (d. 1630), rector of Shepton Beauchamp, left £45 to be accumulated from his rent from the manor of Eastham, Crewkerne, to buy land in Misterton on which was to be built a hospital for four poor men.[43] There is no evidence that these intentions were carried out but Owsley's name is traditionally linked with the purchase in 1644 by the parish officers of half Willdens tenement and 50 a. of land for £200.[44] In 1823 the endowment comprised 20½ a. of land. It produced £38 14s. 6d. which was distributed twice yearly to the second poor.[45] The income has not changed since that time. It amounted to £39 in 1970, when it was distributed to poor people by the parish council.[46]

William Norris of Finchley (Mdx.) (d. 1895) left in trust the income from £500 railway stock, half to be paid equally to five of the 'oldest and most deserving' women, preferably those not receiving poor relief, 3/10 to the poor of the parish generally, and the rest to the costs of maintaining his father's grave. The bequest was subject to a life-interest still in being in 1906. In 1974 the income was 59p. from stock valued at £11.49 and was not distributed.[47]

WAYFORD

THE PARISH of Wayford lies on the southern boundary of the county, 3 miles south-west from Crewkerne and 8 miles east from Chard. It is bordered on the west and north-west by Winsham, on the east by Crewkerne, and on the south by Broadwindsor (Dors.) and Thorncome (Dors., formerly Devon). It had an area of 1,457 a. until a detached part of Crewkerne near Greenham was added in 1885 to give it a total extent of 1,955 a.[1] In 1966 more than half the civil parish south of the river Axe was transferred to Broadwindsor, leaving an area of 996 a.[2]

The ancient parish was divided by the Axe which meanders from east to west. Northwards from the river the ground rises steeply from 250 ft. to 760 ft., the parish narrowing to form a finger of land over successive bands of grit and chert beds, lower chalk, and clay with flints. Southwards the land rises more gradually to 450 ft. on the silts and marls of the Pennard Sands with river gravel around Oathill in the east and alluvium by the river.[3] At least four limekilns were being worked in the north of the parish in 1886, each with associated quarries, and there was a gravel quarry north-west of Oathill.[4] The south of the parish is watered by two streams flowing north to the Axe. Procers Lake, probably known as Holelake in the 13th century,[5] may once have formed the boundary between Bere and Oathill. The other stream marks part of the eastern boundary of the parish. In the north there are springs near the village and a shallow stream in the west flowing south from Ashcombe to the Axe. This brook was probably 'the water of Essche' in which a man drowned in 1225.[6]

Wayford's status as a chapelry within the parish of Crewkerne, and the differing dues payable to the mother church from the four main settlements of Ashcombe, Bere, Oathill, and Wayford, suggest both that the boundary with Crewkerne may be dated to the period of the creation of Wayford manor in the late 11th century, and that Wayford and Oathill were the two main settlements by the mid 13th century if not much earlier.[7] And, since Ashcombe and Bere did not pay dues in the mid 13th century to Wayford church, it seems likely that these settlements originated before the building of the church there, itself first referred to in 1266.[8] This chronology of development is supported by

[34] Char. Com. files; *Kelly's Dir. Som.* (1894, 1906); S.R.O., D/N/spc, box 3: circuit plans; C/2473.
[35] S.R.O., D/D/Cd 47, 24 Sept. 1616.
[36] *Digest of Returns to Sel. Cttee. on Educ. of Poor*, H.C. 224 (1819), ix (2).
[37] *Educ. Enquiry Abstract*, H.C. 62 (1835), xlii.
[38] S.R.O., tithe award; H.O. 107/1860; S.R.O., D/P/mis 9/1/1; *P.O. Dir. Som.* (1861).
[39] S.R.O., D/P/mis 9/1/1; DD/EDS 6116; *P.O. Dir. Som.* (1875).
[40] *Kelly's Dir. Som.* (1883, 1897), S.R.O., D/P/mis 18/8/1.
[41] *Returns of Schs.* [C. 7529], H.C. (1894), lxv; (1899), lxv (2); S.R.O., *Schs. Lists.*
[42] S.R.O., *Schs. Lists.*
[43] Prob. 11/157 (P.C.C. 59 Scroope).
[44] *9th Rep. Com. Char.* H.C. 258, pp. 502–3 (1823), ix.
[45] Ibid.
[46] Char. Com. files.
[47] Ibid.
[1] *Census*, 1881; Local Govt. Bd. Order 16,420, 25 Mar. 1885. This article was completed in 1975.
[2] *Census*, 1971.
[3] Geol. Surv. Map 1″, solid and drift, sheet 312 (1958 edn.).
[4] O.S. Map 6″, Som. XCII.NE., XCII.SE. (1886 edn.).
[5] Forde Abbey, Cart. pp. 541, 544–5.
[6] *S.R.S.* xi, p. 322.
[7] *Proc. Som. Arch. Soc.* cxx. 63–7.
[8] *S.R.S.* xiii, p. 10.

place-names, which indicate a river crossing and cultivation in contrast to woodland clearings.[9] Oathill was divided in the 13th century between Up Oathill and Nether Oathill, probably representing the present Oathill Farm and Oathill Stables; Greenham occurs as Gryndeham or Grinneham and Horn Ash probably as Horne in the same period.[10] Higher farm (formerly Hill Barn), Higher Bere Chapel farm, and Manor farm are creations of the late 19th century.

Wayford is the largest settlement, straggling along a hillside road, Park Lane, commanding views of the Axe and Pilsdon Pen (Dors.). Most of the houses are of 19th-century origin but two, Manor Dairy Farm and a cottage east of the church, have traditional early-17th-century plans with internal chimneys. The village street, running west from Townsend,[11] lies on a direct route from Clapton through Ashcombe to Winsham, but may have been disused at an early date through the formation of a park west of the village. The principal roads cut through the south of the parish. The Crewkerne–Lyme Regis route runs through Oathill and Horn Ash, and was adopted by the Crewkerne Turnpike trust in 1765.[12] The Winsham–Broadwindsor (Dors.) road crosses it at Horn Ash. It was turnpiked by the Chard trustees in 1829.[13] One earlier route linked Lower Bere Chapel Farm with Forde abbey along the Axe, and another passed Ashcombe and led southwards across the river.[14]

Wayford village apparently had two medieval open fields in the north-east corner of the parish. Later, North, Higher, and South fields, and Middle and Gurdhayes furlongs, were mentioned in 1610.[15] A former open arable system is also suggested at Ashcombe, where Elfurland, Witforlang, and Rodfurlang occur in 1235, and Tidley furlong as a field name in 1842.[16] Further areas of arable lay north and north-east of Ashcombe in the earlier 19th century, while meadow land lay principally along both banks of the Axe and beside its tributary along the eastern boundary. Pasture land included the site of the former park, west of the village. This was known as Welmans Park in 1562, and as 'Bakers park called Welmans park' in 1607, and is represented by fields called Higher, Middle, and Lower Park in 1842.[17]

There were two licensed victuallers in the parish in 1735, three in 1751, and one in 1763. None occurs in 1770 or subsequently until 1875, when a beer retailer sold his wares from the house known by 1939 as the Greyhound inn. This closed after the Second World War.[18]

The parish had a population of 162 in 1801, which rose to 224 in 1821 and 238 in 1851. Thereafter it fell to 191 in 1861, rising again to 224 in 1881. After the extension of the civil parish in 1885 the total rose to 367 in 1891, and to 385 in 1911, but subsequently fell steadily to 285 in 1931. By 1951 the numbers had risen to 296 although they dropped to 233 by 1961. The reduction in the size of the civil parish in 1966 left Wayford with a population of 127 in 1971.[19]

In 1685 four men from Wayford tithing and four from Oathill were in the duke of Monmouth's army at Sedgemoor.[20]

Dr. Daubeney Turberville (1612–96), physician, was born at Wayford, and owned and occupied the manor-house. He was known principally as an eye-specialist and was consulted by Pepys and Princess Anne.[21]

MANORS AND OTHER ESTATES. Wayford was apparently included within the royal manor of Crewkerne T.R.W. Overlordship was claimed in 1227 by Walter Foliot, probably because he was guardian of William of Wayford, the terre tenant, custody of whose Devon estates had been held before 1218–19 by Thomas Foliot, Walter's father.[22] This wardship had no doubt been granted to the Foliots by the earls of Devon, lords of Crewkerne manor and, as holders of the honor of Plympton (Devon), overlords of the Foliots in Devon.[23] The Foliots' title to Wayford evidently descended to Robert Foliot (d. c. 1245), whose daughter and heir Ellen married Ralph de Gorges.[24] Ellen was succeeded in turn by her sons William (d. 1294) and Thomas (d. 1305), the second being overlord in 1303.[25] No later references to this tenure have been noted and the overlordship reverted to the earls of Devon as lords of Crewkerne by 1528 until at least 1615.[26] The overlordship was not referred to thereafter.

The terre tenancy had been created by 1200 when William of Wayford held lands there.[27] William acknowledged that he held ½ fee in Wayford and Bere in 1227,[28] and was probably succeeded in turn by his sons Walter and Baldwin of Wayford (fl. 1243–69). Baldwin was patron of the living in 1266 and was described as lord of *WAYFORD* manor in 1269.[29] In 1280 Baldwin's widow claimed dower against Richard de Portesye and his wife Scolace, the latter apparently being Baldwin's heir, and it was probably she, as Scolace of Wayford, who occurs as lady of the manor between 1303 and

[9] E. Ekwall, *Oxf. Dict. Eng. Place-names*, 478.
[10] Forde Abbey, Cart. pp. 270, 526, 528, 531–4, 545.
[11] Also called Borough Cross in 1610 and 1839: D.R.O., LL 388; S.R.O., DD/SB 33/6.
[12] Crewkerne Turnpike Act, 5 Geo. III, c. 61 (Priv. Act).
[13] Chard Turnpike Act, 10 Geo. IV, c. xciii (Local and Personal).
[14] Forde Abbey, Cart. pp. 529–30, 541; Pulman, *Bk. of the Axe*, 356. [15] D.R.O., LL 388.
[16] *S.R.S.* vi. 86–7; S.R.O., tithe award.
[17] Prob. 11/48 (P.C.C. 21 Morrison); *Cal. Antrobus Deeds* (Wilts. A.N.H.S. Rec. Branch, iii), 84; S.R.O., tithe award.
[18] S.R.O., Q/RL; *P.O. Dir. Som.* (1875); *Kelly's Dir. Som.* (1883–1939); O.S. Map 6″, Som. XCII. NE. (1886 edn.); local information.

[19] *V.C.H. Som.* ii. 343; *Census*, 1911–71.
[20] B.L. Add MS. 30077, f. 37. [21] *D.N.B.*
[22] *S.R.S.* vi. 66; *Devon and Cwll. N. & Q.* xx. 343.
[23] *Bk. of Fees*, ii. 766.
[24] *Close R.* 1242–7, 307, 328; *Trans. Devon Assoc.* lxxiii. 150; W. Pole, *Description of Devon*, 335.
[25] *Cal. Inq. p.m.* iii, p. 149; iv, pp. 199–200; *Feud. Aids*, iv. 317.
[26] C 142/80/159; C 142/512/197.
[27] *Rot. de Ob. et Fin.* (Rec. Com.), 274; *Cur. Reg. R.* iv, p. 292.
[28] *S.R.S.* vi. 66.
[29] *Bk. of Fees*, ii. 766; *Proc. Som. Arch. Soc.* lxxxii. 204; *S.R.S.* xiii, p. 10; *Cal. Pat.* 1266–72, 401; Forde Abbey, Cart. pp. 528, 544–5, 551. The wife of William of Wayford was named Scolace: Forde Abbey, Cart. p. 551.

1316.[30] The manor had apparently passed by 1327 to John Bernard, who still held it in 1346, although John Aleyn presented to the rectory between 1339 and 1344.[31] Robert Blanford's family, patrons in 1403 and 1406, were said to have obtained the manor by marriage with the Wayford heirs; John Blanford owned ½ fee there in 1428, and Robert Blanford was patron in 1430 and 1431.[32] The manor is said to have passed from William Blanford to his son William, and thereafter to his grandson Thomas Blanford.[33] Thomas's daughter and heir Eleanor married Robert Pauncefoot of Amesbury (Wilts.), and their only child Elizabeth (d. 1528) brought the manor to her husband James Daubeney.[34] It then descended thus through successive generations of the Daubeney family: Giles (I) (d. 1559), Hugh (d. 1565), and Giles Daubeney (II) (d. 1630).[35] In 1624 Giles (II) mortgaged a third of the manor, without the manor-house and demesnes, to William Norris, a Wayford yeoman, and conveyed the fee to him in 1627.[36] This third apparently descended to Robert Norris, a Wayford miller, who held it 1672–93, and by 1725 to Matthew Norris, a Crewkerne innkeeper. The lands comprising the third had been sold before 1725 to six occupiers.[37] The lordship was not mentioned thereafter.

Giles Daubeney (II) granted a life interest in the manor to his son and daughter-in-law, James (d. 1615) and Elizabeth Daubeney. Elizabeth, who married secondly William Keymer of Pendomer, probably still held it in 1653 when, as a widow, she presented to the rectory.[38] The reversion of the remaining two-thirds of the manor was apparently conveyed to the Braggs of Sadborow, Thorncombe (Dors. formerly Devon). The purchaser was probably Richard Bragg (d. 1643), who had acquired a single presentation to the rectory in 1627.[39] He was followed in turn by his son Richard (d. 1649) and nephew William (II) (d. 1713).[40] The second occurs as lord in 1672 and from him the two-thirds descended successively to his grandsons William (IV) (d. 1726) and John (I) (d. 1749), sons of William Bragg (III) (d. 1702). John Bragg (I) left the estate to his son John (II) (d. 1786), by whose time most of the lands had been enfranchised.[41] Lordship of the manor was claimed by the Pinney family of Blackdown in Broadwindsor (Dors.), as owners of the manor-house, between 1861 and 1883 but was not mentioned thereafter.[42]

The Daubeneys kept the manor-house and demesne, disposing of the lordship. From Giles Daubeney (d. 1630) the property apparently passed to his son Hugh (d. 1662), who devised the house to his widow Elizabeth (d. c. 1664).[43] It was later inherited by their nephew, Dr. Daubeney Turberville (d. 1696), who granted it to his brother-in-law, Gregory Gibbs (d. c. 1680). Thence it descended to Gregory's son Hugh Daubeney Gibbs (d. 1695), whose residuary legatee was his niece Ann Grimstead.[44] The property was acquired c. 1700 by Samuel Pitt (d. 1729) of Cricket Malherbie, also owner of the advowson, but by 1755 he had sold the estate to Azariah Pinney of Bettiscombe (Dors.) (d. 1760).[45] Azariah was succeeded by his cousin John Frederick Pinney (d. 1762).[46] Thereafter the house apparently passed successively to another cousin, John Pinney of Blackdown (d. 1771–2), to his son John (d. 1819), and to his grandson John Azariah Pinney.[47] Between 1839 and 1845 it was bought by Samuel Hood, Lord Bridport (d. 1868), whose son Alexander Nelson Hood, Viscount Bridport, sold it in 1899 to L. I. Baker (d. 1931).[48] It passed to Baker's son, H. L. P. Baker (d. 1966), and was then sold to Mr. R. L. Goffe, the present owner.[49]

The central range of the house, which has a hall on the ground floor, is of medieval origin, and has an arch-braced truss of its original roof *in situ*.[50] This range was remodelled and a central porch and one, and probably two, flanking wings added to the south side c. 1600. The upper storey of the porch bears the Daubeney arms and is supported on fluted columns. Parts of three moulded plaster ceilings and an ornamental fireplace, dated 1602, survive inside. By the late 19th century there was no western (service) wing, and c. 1900 one was added to designs by Ernest George which restored the symmetry of the south front. Adjoining the NE. corner of the house are two ranges of outbuildings. The northern one is probably of the 17th century but incorporates a 14th-century window.

The manor of *BERE*, including the estate of *OATHILL*, both held under Wayford manor, were occupied in the late 12th century by Robert Burnel (I), who made grants therefrom before 1203 to Forde abbey.[51] He was succeeded in turn by his son Ralph and grandson Robert Burnel (II) (fl. 1235–48/9).[52] The estate continued in the Burnels, and was known as *BERE NEXT WAYFORD* in 1388. It was then held jointly by Tristram Burnel and Alice his wife. As the manor of *BERE BURNEL AND OATHILL* it passed in 1491, on Henry Burnel's death, to his son John.[53] In 1530 John Burnel and his wife Dorothy sold the manor of

[30] *S.R.S.* xliv. 43–4, 126; *Feud. Aids*, iv. 317, 331.
[31] *S.R.S.* iii. 156; ix, pp. 360, 367; x, pp. 433, 509; *Feud. Aids*, 339.
[32] *S.R.S.* xiii, pp. 38, 66; xv. 70; xxxi, pp. 75, 117–18; *Feud. Aids*, iv. 382.
[33] *S.R.S.* xv. 70.
[34] Ibid.; *Visits. Som. 1531, 1573*, ed. F. W. Weaver, 58; C 142/80/159.
[35] C 142/80/159; C 142/119/152; C 142/141/16; S.R.O., D/D/Rr 434.
[36] D.R.O., LL 387.
[37] Ibid. 382, 384.
[38] Ibid. 374, 387, 388; D.R.O., D 104, grant of presentation, 19 July 1627; Lambeth Palace MSS., COMM. III/3, p. 3 (3rd nos.).
[39] D.R.O., D 104, grant of presentation, 19 July 1627; LL 31, pedigree of Bragg family.
[40] D.R.O., LL 31.
[41] Ibid. 31, 358, 379, 381–2.
[42] *P.O. Dir. Som.* (1861–75); *Kelly's Dir. Som.* (1883).

[43] S.R.O., D/D/Rr 434; *Som. Wills*, ed. Brown, iv. 60–1.
[44] Prob. 11/457 (P.C.C. 50 Noel), will of Hugh Daubeney Gibbs; C 22/79/13; C 22/79/25; C 22/79/37; C 5/166/102.
[45] C 22/79/25; D.R.O., LL 381, endorsement on conveyance, 15 Dec. 1725; S.R.O., D/D/C, petition for faculty, 13 Aug. 1755; M.I. in ch.
[46] *S. & D. N. & Q.* viii. 345–6; M.I. in ch.
[47] *S. & D. N. & Q.* ix. 351; S.R.O., D/P/wa 4/1/1; M.I. in ch.
[48] S.R.O., D/P/wa 4/1/1; DD/SAS (C/2273/1) B.14.1; *Country Life*, lxxvi. 336; *Complete Peerage*, s.v. Bridport; M.I. in churchyard.
[49] Ex inf. Mrs. R. L. Goffe.
[50] See plate facing p. 33.
[51] *Rot. Chart.* (Rec. Com.), 112; *Cal. Chart. R. 1300–26*, 208; Forde Abbey, Cart. pp. 268–70, 528–30, 541.
[52] Forde Abbey, Cart. pp. 277, 526–7; *S.R.S.* vi. 90, 97, 372.
[53] *S.R.S.* xvii. 135; C 142/6/18.

BERE ALIAS OATHILL to William (later Sir William) Portman of Orchard Portman (d. 1557), who was succeeded by his son Sir Henry (d. 1591) and grandson Sir John Portman, Bt. (d. 1612).[54] John left the manor for life to his widow Anne (d. 1651–2), married secondly to Thomas Neville, and ownership passed with the title successively to his sons Henry (d. 1622), John (d. 1622), Hugh (d. 1632), and William Portman (d. 1645).[55] From William the manor passed to his son William (d. 1690), who devised it to his cousin Henry Seymour, later Henry Portman (d. 1727). Henry left it to his cousin William Berkeley of Pylle, later William Berkeley Portman (d. 1737). Thence it descended through successive generations to Henry William Berkeley Portman (d. 1761), Henry William Portman (d. 1796), Edward Berkeley Portman (I) (d. 1823), Edward Berkeley Portman (II) (cr. Viscount Portman 1873, d. 1888), Henry William Berkeley, 2nd Viscount (d. 1919), and Henry Berkeley, 3rd Viscount (d. 1923).[56] After the death of the last the title passed to his brother, Claud Berkeley, 4th Viscount, and in 1924 the estate was split up and sold.[57] No reference to the sale of the lordship of the manor has been traced. Presumably it passed to the present viscount.

The manor-house, now known as Lower Bere Chapel Farm, is a 17th-century house on an internal chimney and cross-passage plan, with 19th- and 20th-century additions on the east. The name of the farm, recorded in 1737, and a piscina discovered in 1863 suggest that it formerly contained a private oratory.[58]

The estates in Bere and Oathill acquired by Forde abbey in the 12th and 13th centuries from the Burnels and from Savary de Vaux, who had received his lands from Robert Burnel, apparently lay in the south-west of the parish, where the ground was tithe free in the 19th century.[59] The abbey kept the land until the Dissolution.[60] By 1556 certain estates in Oathill which had passed to Thomas Duporte were granted to Leonard Tucker, and in 1566 Duporte sold other lands in Oathill Grange, Oathill, and Crewkerne, together with their tithes, to William Westofer.[61] In 1581 Leonard Tucker sold 80 a. in Oathill to Sir Henry Portman. They then descended with Bere alias Oathill manor.[62]

A free tenement at *ASHCOMBE* was held by Alexander of Ashcombe, whose widow's dower was disputed in 1225 by Robert de Courtenay and Richard of Ashcombe. Alexander's daughter Alice sub-let 81½ a. at Ashcombe in 1235 and, as wife of Warresius son of Reynold, held land in Crewkerne in 1243. Her husband was probably the Warresius

of Ashcombe who occurs as a free suitor to Crewkerne hundred in 1243.[63] Ashcombe manor was held by 1303 with that of Crewkerne and so continued, being occupied by the Greenways in the late 16th century.[64] Three-quarters of the estate was evidently enfranchised during the 17th century, and in 1711 the farm was held by Richard Norris of Netherhay, Broadwindsor (Dors.). By 1719 the property had passed to Elizabeth Bragg (d. 1719) of Sadborow, whose family owned Wayford manor.[65] Elizabeth used the estate to endow charity schools in Wayford and Thorncombe and on her death the farm descended to Dr. Claver Morris (d. 1727) of Wells, who had married Molly Bragg (d. 1725) of Sadborow in 1703.[66] Morris was succeeded by his daughter Elizabeth (d. 1760), wife of John Burland (d. 1746) of Steyning, Stogumber, and then by her son John (later Sir John) Burland (d. 1776), baron of the Exchequer, who took a lease of the remaining quarter of Ashcombe from the lord of Crewkerne manor in 1760.[67] Sir John left the farm to his son John Berkeley Burland (d. 1804), who devised it to his first cousin Mary Anne, daughter of Dr. Claver Morris Burland and wife of James Lloyd Harris (d. 1815–16) of Uley (Glos.).[68] Three-quarters of the farm passed to Harris's son John Burland Harris, who later assumed the surname Burland, of New Court, Newent (Glos.), and sold it to Alexander Nelson Hood (cr. Viscount Bridport 1868) in 1866. James Lloyd Harris purchased the fee of the quarter held under Crewkerne manor in 1812 and left it to his daughter Honoria, wife of William Spencer Palmer, who conveyed it to Hood in 1867.[69] The farm continued with the Wayford manor-house estate until the Bridport lands were sold in 1895.[70] The present Ashcombe farm-house replaced a former building, described in 1883 as recently burnt down.[71]

ECONOMIC HISTORY. Both topographically and economically the parish is divided by the river Axe. Both areas were included within Crewkerne manor T. R. W. and thus no 11th-century valuation has been recovered. The capital manor, lying north over the river and described in 1280 as a house, two carucates, 6 a. of meadow, and 40s. rent,[72] never occupied more than about a third of the parish's total area. It was valued at £25 in 1528, based on a rental of £17 18s. 5d.[73] and by 1565 was worth just over £29.[74] Ashcombe farm, the only other significant settlement north of the Axe, totalled 81½ a. in 1235 and included 142 a. in 1599.[75] South of the river the grants to Forde abbey by the

[54] C.P. 25(2)/35/237/22 Hen. VIII Mich.; C 142/108/94; C 142/229/101; *S.R.S.* lxvii, p. 141.
[55] C 142/406/67; G.E.C. *Baronetage*, i. 90.
[56] G.E.C. *Baronetage*, i. 90–1; Burke, *Peerage* (1967), 2024; Hutchins, *Hist. Dors.* i. 256.
[57] Burke, *Peerage* (1967), 2024–5; S.R.O., DD/KW 15.
[58] C.P. 43/750 rot. 23; Pulman, *Bk. of the Axe*, 355.
[59] Forde Abbey, Cart. pp. 270, 277, 524–30, 539, 541; S.R.O., tithe award.
[60] *Valor Eccl.* (Rec. Com.), ii. 299.
[61] *Cal. Pat.* 1555–7, 7; 1563–6, p. 416.
[62] *S.R.S.* li, pp. 128–9; C 142/406/67.
[63] *S.R.S.* vi. 86–7; xi, pp. 86, 167, 322.
[64] *Bk. of Fees*, iv. 316–17, 339; *Cal. Pat.* 1313–17, 267; S.R.O., D/D/Rr 434, burial of Ursula Greenway of Ashcombe, 29 Nov. 1598; T/PH/hsy, survey of Crewkerne manor, 1599.
[65] C 7/244/10; S.R.O., D/P/wa 2/1/1.
[66] *9th Rep. Com. Char.* H.C. 258, p. 505 (1823), ix; S.R.O., DD/WM 1/112; *Diary of a West Country Physician*, ed. E. Hobhouse, 13–14.
[67] Hutchins, *Hist. Dors.* i. 257; S.R.O., DD/SS, bdle. 54.
[68] *S. & D. N. & Q.* iii. 269; S.R.O., D/P/wa 4/1/1.
[69] S.R.O., DD/BR/an 5; DD/SB 38/1; Burke, *Peerage* (1949), 255.
[70] S.R.O., DD/SAS (C/2273/1) B. 14. 1.
[71] S.R.O., DD/HA 11.
[72] *V.C.H. Som.* i. 439; *S.R.S.* xliv. 43–4.
[73] C 142/80/159.
[74] C 142/141/16.
[75] *S.R.S.* vi. 86–7; S.R.O., T/PH/hsy, survey of Crewkerne, 1599.

Burnels from the 12th century divided Bere and Oathill between secular and ecclesiastical jurisdictions and led to disputes over their respective boundaries.[76] The Burnel manor of Bere and Oathill was valued at £17 in 1491 and the Forde abbey holding at Up Oathill and Bere produced £14 15s. 8d. in 1535.[77] By the late 16th century most of the parish south of the Axe had passed to the Portman family, the former Burnel manor being worth £17 2s. in 1591 and £10 2s. in 1613. The late abbey lands, called 'Whitelandes, Pluckynscrofte, and Whyteyate' in 1556, were valued at £1 for 100 a. in 1613.[78]

The capital manor was split in the early 17th century, William Norris receiving a third of 69 a. besides his divided third share of copyhold and leasehold lands belonging to the manor.[79] The thirds that passed to the Braggs were held in 1719 by 31 tenants paying rents of £11 0s. 3d.,[80] but both tenants and rents fell in number during the 18th century as tenements were sold off. In 1725 there were 24 tenants, by 1734 11 paying £5 17s. 2d., c. 1775 3 holding 24 a. for 23s. 11d. In 1778 the manor head rents amounted only to 16s. 11d.[81] Most surviving Bragg leases were for 99 years or lives and in respect of relatively small holdings. The chief exception was one of 67½ a. in 1769 to the occupier of Ashcombe, which was for 8 years at a rent of £60.[82]

During the 17th and 18th centuries the manor-house and its attached lands remained undivided and in 1698, together with lands in Chillington, they were valued at about £2,000.[83] The neighbouring estate of Ashcombe comprised 210 a. in 1711, then valued at £2,500, but its extent had fallen to 140 a. in 1778.[84] Thereafter it increased in area to 181 a. c. 1787, and to 200 a. in 1809.[85] The Portman estate at Bere and Oathill yielded rents of £10 17s. 10d. c. 1738, and £9 2s. 11d. in 1816.[86] The largest unit in 1766 was Bere Chapel farm of 316 a.; the remaining 350 a., called Oathill manor, was let to 7 tenants in units varying from 93 a. to 15½ a. Apart from Bere Chapel farm, which by 1760 was let for 7 years at £110, the tenements were held on leases for 99 years or lives. In 1837 3 farms were let at £335 and 14 smaller tenements, evidently at Oathill, paid rents of £14 11s. 11d.[87]

By 1842 the parish had 1,015 a. of meadow and pasture, 355 a. of arable, and 90 a. of wood and waste. The relative proportion of grassland to arable was almost the same in 1905.[88] The largest holding in the parish in 1842 was the former manor-house, then known as Wayford farm, with 447 a., owned by Lord Bridport. Bere Chapel and Oathill (later known as Oathill Dairy) farms totalled

424 a. under the Portmans, and Ashcombe 180 a. Wayford Manor farm, the farm-house lying between the church and the rectory house, comprised 173 a. and included the present Manor Dairy farm. A second Oathill farm of 63 a. was the later Oathill Dairy farm.[89] By 1851 the picture had not altered much, although the total area farmed from the manor-house had increased to 550 a.[90] The acquisition in 1866 of Ashcombe farm by Lord Bridport extended his total holding to 689 a., and by 1883 he had created Hill Barn farm with 125 a. out of the manor-house estate, on the site of outbuildings and labourers' cottages.[91] The three farms constituted the Bridport estate in Wayford when sold in 1895; a total of 646 a. then yielded £840 a year in rents.[92] During the later 19th century Lord Portman bought lands north of the Axe, including Manor farm and Manor Dairy farm. He divided Bere Chapel farm into two, and built Higher Bere Chapel farm in 1897. By 1924 the Portman estate at Wayford totalled 768 a., including Higher Bere Chapel (190 a.), Lower Bere Chapel (174 a.), Oathill farm (193 a.), and Oathill Dairy farm (60 a.).[93] Since 1924 Oathill Dairy farm, later called Lower Oathill farm, has become Oathill Stables and by 1975 the areas of Higher and Lower Bere Chapel farms had increased to 330 a. and 303 a. respectively.[94] Within Wayford village Middle farm was built opposite the manor-house, now Wayford Manor, and with Ashcombe, Higher farm (formerly Hill Barn), Manor farm, and Manor Dairy farm, comprised those holdings north of the Axe in 1976.

Lands then recently inclosed in North field were mentioned in 1610, and others were referred to as parcel of the common field of Wayford in 1652.[95] These appear to be remnants of a field system which had already largely disappeared, perhaps during the Middle Ages.

Agriculture was the principal occupation, although a girth web weaver occurs in 1637 and a weaver in 1657.[96] A dyehouse apparently stood on the banks of the Axe before 1766, giving its name to Dyehouse bridge.[97] In 1851 there were four glovers, two dressmakers, and a 'newswoman' in the parish.[98] Four people were then employed in factory work, probably at the flax and tow spinning mills at Greenham. The owner of the factory, James Haydon, then lived at Greenham House in Wayford.[99] In 1868 the population consisted 'entirely of farmers and their labourers'.[1] A road contractor was mentioned in 1919 and a haulage contractor in 1939; by the latter year a café had opened at Horn Ash.[2]

A mill forming part of the manor was mentioned

[76] Forde Abbey, Cart. pp. 268–77, 526–30; *Bracton's Note Bk.* ed. Maitland, i. 168–9.
[77] C 142/6/18; *Valor Eccl.* (Rec. Com.), ii. 299.
[78] C 142/229/101; *S.R.S.* lxvii, p. 141; *Cal. Pat.* 1555–7, 5.
[79] D.R.O., LL 387.
[80] Ibid. 357.
[81] D.R.O., D 104 8495, 8497; LL 358.
[82] D.R.O., LL 375, 377–80, 383, 385.
[83] C 5/166/102.
[84] C 7/244/10; S.R.O., DD/WM 1/112; DD/SAS C/14/18/2.
[85] S.R.O., DD/PT, box 41, proposal bk.; DD/SAS C/14/15.
[86] S.R.O., DD/PM, box 8, rentals.
[87] Ibid. boxes 9, 16, 24.

[88] S.R.O., tithe award; statistics supplied by the then Bd. of Agric. 1905.
[89] S.R.O., tithe award.
[90] H.O. 107/1928.
[91] Ibid.; S.R.O., DD/HA 10, 11.
[92] S.R.O., DD/SAS, C/2273/1, B.14.1.
[93] S.R.O., DD/KW 15.
[94] Ex inf. Mr. E. G. Cox, Wayford.
[95] D.R.O., LL 388; C 8/87/126.
[96] S.R.O., DD/SP, inventories, 1637/69; Prob. 11/266 (P.C.C. 1657/289).
[97] S.R.O., DD/PM, box 24.
[98] H.O. 107/1928.
[99] Ibid.
[1] Char. Com. files.
[2] *Kelly's Dir. Som.* (1919, 1939).

in 1528 and described as a water-mill from 1530.[3] This was probably the water grist mill called Keymer's mill, named after the early-17th-century lord of the manor, which was leased in 1675 and again in 1694 to Robert Norris. The lord repaired the wheels, cogs, 'roungs', and stones in return for the collection of the manor rents by the miller.[4] The property was still held by Norris c. 1719 but as 'the mill tenement' had passed to Henry Symonds by 1734.[5] It is not mentioned thereafter. The field-names Mill meadow, on the north side of Dunsham Lane in the north-east of the parish, and Gills Mill, south-east of the village and north of the River Axe, suggest approximate and alternative sites for the mill.[6]

LOCAL GOVERNMENT. Ashcombe was a separate tithing within Crewkerne manor in 1599 and was later considered to form part of Coombe tithing in Crewkerne. Oathill tithing, which comprised the whole parish south of the Axe, was often stated to lie in Crewkerne parish and included the settlement at Bere and part of Greenham.[7]

No court rolls have survived for the manors of Wayford, Bere, or Oathill. The court of Wayford manor was mentioned in 1610 and a court baron in 1698, suit of court being demanded of lessees in 1716.[8] Courts for the manor of Bere alias Oathill continued until at least 1804.[9]

There were two churchwardens in 1596, one in 1670 and 1674, and one overseer in the last year.[10] A constable was mentioned in 1709. During the 19th century the vestry appointed two church-wardens, two overseers, a waywarden, and, in 1889, an assistant overseer to collect the rates.[11]

The parishioners took the reversion of a cottage for use as a parish house in 1672, probably for paupers. In 1778 the parish officers were renting two other properties.[12] The parish joined the Chard poor-law union in 1836.[13]

CHURCH. A chapel at Wayford was first mentioned in 1266, when an incumbent was presented by the lord of the manor.[14] The chapel, with cure of souls, was a daughter to Crewkerne, though the incumbent was always styled rector, and in the Middle Ages the tenants of Wayford and Oathill with their households were obliged to attend Crewkerne church on Crewkerne's dedication feast, St. Bartholomew's day (24 August).[15] By 1684 and until 1750 this dependence was acknowledged by laying the

key of the north door of the church on the altar at Crewkerne on the first Sunday after Michaelmas, then called 'dedication Sunday', and paying 4d. The custom was evidently revived between 1818–19 and 1833–4, except that the ceremony took place on Easter Sunday and the payment was 1s.[16]

The advowson descended with the lordship of the manor, the bishop collating by lapse in 1424 and 1463.[17] William Larder presented in 1624 by grant from William Keymer and Elizabeth his wife, widow of James Daubeney. A single turn was granted in 1627 by William Keymer to Richard Bragg, but this was not apparently exercised.[18] William Norris acquired one turn in three with the third of Wayford manor which he purchased in 1627, although he did not exercise the right.[19] The remaining two turns descended with the manor-house estate to Dr. Daubeney Turberville (d. 1696), who left his share of the advowson to Robert son of Israel Sayer of London.[20] By 1700 it had been acquired by William Bragg (II) of Sadborow, who sold his two-thirds to Samuel Pitt of Cricket Malherbie.[21] The next vacancy occurred in 1725, but the nominee of Jane Pitt, daughter-in-law of Samuel Pitt, was opposed by William Bragg's grandson, William (IV), evidently unaware of the conveyance to the Pitt family. Bragg tried to obtain the remaining third from Matthew Norris of Crewkerne, heir of William Norris, and the six purchasers of lands forming one third of the manor, but to avoid dispute eventually quitclaimed the next turn to Jane Pitt who duly presented.[22] The third held by the Norris family was not mentioned again. Mary Pitt, great-niece and heir of Samuel, married Thomas Sergison c. 1732, and he presented in 1751.[23] By 1755 the advowson had been sold to Azariah Pinney and thereafter it descended with the manor-house estate until at least 1835.[24] By 1854 the patronage had been acquired by John Hosegood of Chulmleigh (Devon), by 1857 passed to John Alexander of Newbury (Berks.), and by 1880 to A. D. Smith of Edinburgh and Mrs. M. G. Bewley.[25] Mrs. Bewley was still patron in 1907 but by 1913 the advowson had been granted to the bishop of Bath and Wells. The bishop ceded his right to the Lord Chancellor when the benefice was united with Crewkerne in 1971.[26]

In 1535 the rectory was worth 93s. 4d.[27] By c. 1668 the living had a reputed value of £50, which had risen by 1816 to £195 and fallen to £132 net by 1831.[28] By the mid 13th century all tenants except cottars paid tithe to Crewkerne rectory from Wayford and Oathill, together with the farmer at

[3] C 142/80/159; C.P. 25 (2)/35/237/22 Hen. VIII Mich.; C 142/141/16.
[4] D.R.O., LL 380.
[5] Ibid. 357, 8495.
[6] S.R.O., tithe award.
[7] S.R.O., T/PH/hsy, survey of Crewkerne manor, 1599; Pulman, *Bk. of the Axe*, 358n.; S.R.O., DD/PM, box 16, Oathill leases, 1766–1804.
[8] D.R.O., LL 379, 383, 388.
[9] S.R.O., DD/PM, box 16, lease, 11 June 1804.
[10] S.R.O., D/D/Rr 434; *Dir. Som.* ed. Dwelly, ii. 77, 253.
[11] S.R.O., D/P/wa 4/1/1.
[12] D.R.O., LL 358, 376, 384, 8497.
[13] *Poor Law Com. 2nd Rep.* p. 547.
[14] *S.R.S.* xiii, p. 10.
[15] *Proc. Som. Arch. Soc.* cxx. 65.

[16] S.R.O., D/P/wa 4/1/1.
[17] *S.R.S.* xxx, p. 449; xlix, p. 385.
[18] *Som. Incumbents*, ed. Weaver.
[19] D.R.O., LL 387.
[20] Lambeth Palace MSS., COMM. III/3, p. 3 (3rd nos.); Prob 11/431 (P.C.C. 1696/82).
[21] *Som. Incumbents*, ed. Weaver; D.R.O., LL 381.
[22] D.R.O., LL 381–2.
[23] S.R.O., DD/BR/rw, box 2, release, 10 Dec. 1756; D/D/B reg. 27; *Hist. Parl., Commons, 1754–90*, iii. 421.
[24] S.R.O., D/D/C, petns. for faculties, 1755; S.R.O., D/D/B reg. 32–3; *Rep. Com. Eccl. Revenues*, pp. 156–7.
[25] S.R.O., D/D/B reg. 37, 40.
[26] *Dioc. Kal.* (1888–1907); *Dioc. Dir.* (1908–71).
[27] *Valor Eccl.* (Rec. Com.), i. 166.
[28] S.R.O., D/D/Vc 24; D/D/B return 1816; *Rep. Com. Eccl. Revenues*, pp. 156–7.

Ashcombe. The rector of Wayford presumably had the tithe of cottars, and by 1636 tithe from three cottages and about 10 a. in Oathill tithing.[29] In 1535 the rector's predial tithes were worth 16s. 8d., tithes of sheep and lambs 33s. 4d., and oblations and personal tithes 20s.[30] Grants of land in Bere and Oathill to Forde abbey had included the tithes issuing from them, and these estates were later considered to be tithe free. In the early 19th century the impropriator of Crewkerne rectory held the tithes of the remaining lands in Oathill tithing, of Ashcombe, and of a few scattered fields north and east of Wayford village. Bere Chapel farm then paid a modus of £2 8s. 10d. to Crewkerne in lieu of tithes and was the only property in the parish which did not render to the rector of Wayford a modus of 8d. for every milch cow. The tithes were commuted in 1842 when the rector was awarded a rent-charge of £140 12s., and John Hussey, as impropriator of Crewkerne, £102 8s. 10d.[31]

The glebe was worth 23s. 4d. in 1535 and in 1606 comprised two cottages and 27 a.[32] The rector exchanged 2 a. for a further 6 a. with Azariah Pinney in 1756.[33] The area of the glebe was given as 26½ a. in 1842, 25 a. in 1939, and had all been sold by 1977.[34]

The former parsonage house, described in 1606 as a mansion with barn, garden, and orchard, lies east of the church on the south side of the lane through the village.[35] In 1816 it was described by the non-resident rector as 'too small for my large family', and in 1827 was undergoing repairs for the reception of the curate.[36] It was replaced by a house built c. 1965 and sold in 1977.[37]

The benefice did not attract graduate incumbents before the 17th century, the earliest being Edmund Giffard or Jeffard, rector 1611–24, who held it in plurality with Bettiscombe (Dors.).[38] It is not known whether Giffard's successor, Thomas Browne, rector 1624 until at least 1640, was deprived, but Richard Sharp, rector 1653–1701, survived the Restoration and held the benefice with those of Stawley and Bathealton.[39] Henry Layng, rector 1701–12, was also vicar of Winsham, canon of Wells, and rector of Potsgrove and Battlesden (Beds.).[40] The tradition of non-residence continued into the 19th century. Maurice Uphill Hopkins, rector 1793–1819, lived at Stoke Abbott (Dors.), while his assistant curate was vicar of Winsham. Hopkins's successor, Richard Symes Cox, rector 1819–45, although resident, also served Burton Bradstock and North Poorton (both Dors.).[41] G. R. G. Norris, rector 1936–8, held the living with that of Crewkerne and his successors until 1965 with that of Seaborough (Dors. formerly Som.). Thereafter the living was served by a resident curate-in-charge until the union with Crewkerne in 1971.[42]

In the Middle Ages the farmer of Ashcombe had the use of 1 a. land belonging to the lord of Wayford manor for taking his turn in providing the holy loaf for Wayford church.[43] Between the late 17th and early 19th centuries Holy Communion was generally celebrated three or four times a year.[44] The chapelyard was not used for burials until 1718 when, with the consent of the bishop and the incumbent of Crewkerne, the first interment took place.[45] The chapel, like the church of Cricket St. Thomas, was apparently used for clandestine marriages in the 18th century. Between 1721 and 1741 28 couples of whom neither party was resident at Wayford were married there, and a further six in 1752–3.[46] In 1790 it was agreed to supplement the cost of teaching the choir and repairing the instruments from the church rate. Among the instruments provided were bass and tenor viols, treble and tenor violins, and a flute.[47] The Bullen family, tenants of the manor-house in the 19th century, according to their monument 'had charge of the music of the church, even when that music was of stringed instruments'.[48] Services were held once on Sundays between 1827 and 1855, generally in the mornings and afternoons alternately, and in 1855 Holy Communion was administered monthly.[49] On Census Sunday 1851 there were congregations of 50 and Sunday-school attendances of 16 at both the morning and afternoon services.[50] By 1870 there were two sermons every Sunday, although Communion celebrations had fallen to eight a year. The then churchwarden complained that he and the rector had tried to get a new church built, but had failed because 'the landowners don't come forward as they ought'.[51] In 1883 ¼ a. of land was purchased for a cemetery, lying east of Townsend on the south side of Dunsham Lane, and a mortuary chapel was built there in 1884.[52]

The church of *ST. MICHAEL* lies in the centre of the village. It is a small plain stone structure, mostly rendered, comprising chancel, north vestry, nave, north aisle, south porch, and western bell turret. The chancel and nave are of later-13th-century origin. Part of the south wall was rebuilt, to incorporate a new window, when the porch was added in the 17th century. In 1800 the 'front' of the church, possibly part of the north wall, had to be rebuilt. The chancel fell down in 1846 and was rebuilt, apparently reusing or copying the original features. In 1725 a western gallery was inserted and rebuilt in 1739 and 1800.[53] The vestry was added in the 19th century. The timber north

[29] S.R.O., D/D/Rg 327; *Proc. Som. Arch. Soc.* cxx. 65.
[30] *Valor Eccl.* (Rec. Com.), i. 166.
[31] Forde Abbey, Cart. pp. 529–30; S.R.O., tithe award.
[32] *Valor Eccl.* (Rec. Com.), i. 166; S.R.O., D/D/Rg 327.
[33] S.R.O., D/D/C, petns. for faculties, 1755.
[34] S.R.O., tithe award; *Kelly's Dir. Som.* (1939); ex inf. Diocesan office.
[35] S.R.O., D/D/Rg 327.
[36] S.R.O., D/D/B return 1816; D/D/V return 1827.
[37] Ex inf. the vicar of Crewkerne.
[38] *Som. Incumbents*, ed. Weaver; Foster, *Alumni Oxon.*
[39] *Som. Incumbents*, ed. Weaver; S.R.O., D/D/Rr 434; Lambeth Palace MSS., COMM. III/3 p. 3 (3rd nos.).
[40] *Som. Incumbents*, ed. Weaver; Foster, *Alumni Oxon.*
[41] S.R.O., D/D/B return 1815; D/D/V returns 1827, 1833.
[42] *Dioc. Dir.* (1936–72).
[43] *Proc. Som. Arch. Soc.* cxx. 65.
[44] S.R.O., D/P/wa 4/1/1.
[45] Ibid. 2/1/1.
[46] Ibid.
[47] Ibid. 4/1/1.
[48] M.I. in ch.
[49] S.R.O., D/D/V returns 1827, 1833, 1840, 1843, 1855.
[50] H.O. 129/318/4/1/1.
[51] S.R.O., D/D/V return 1870.
[52] S.R.O., D/D/B reg. 40.
[53] S.R.O., D/P/wa 4/1/1; Pulman, *Bk. of the Axe*, 360.

arcade is contemporary with the roofs but the aisle walls may be of 19th-century origin.

The bell turret was reconstructed in 1737 and the two bells are dated 1744 and 1790.[54] The plate includes a cup and cover of 1570.[55] The registers date from 1704 and are complete.[56]

NONCONFORMITY. Robert Riche was presented as a recusant in 1612 and 1623.[57] It was claimed in 1669 that there were 200 'hearers' attending five ejected ministers preaching at Wayford,[58] but there is no subsequent evidence for nonconformity in the parish.

EDUCATION. Elizabeth Bragg (d. 1719) of Sadborow, by will left 50s. a year charged on Ashcombe farm to teach 8 poor children.[59] The school opened in 1719, and in 1822 the parish clerk taught the children reading and religion.[60] In 1819 there were also schools for 41 boys and girls.[61] By 1835 numbers in the two day-schools had fallen to 14 and the Bragg bequest had been diverted to them. There was also a Sunday school for 26 children supported by voluntary contributions.[62] There was no permanent school building in 1865, and in 1873 it was proposed to unite Wayford with Crewkerne for educational purposes and to build a school at Clapton. The Wayford school, called a dame school, with an average attendance of 20, was succeeded by the Crewkerne and Wayford Board school, opened in 1878. Under a Scheme of 1879 a third of the Bragg and Turberville charities (see below) was to be for education for Wayford children who attended a public elementary school in sums of £1 for each child. Under an Order of 1905 the charity was known as Turberville's Educational Foundation.[63]

CHARITIES FOR THE POOR. Dr. Daubeney Turberville (d. 1696) left £100 in trust to purchase land, the rent to be applied to the unrelieved poor. Twelve acres in Mosterton (Dors.) were bought, and the money, usually £15 or £14 10s., was distributed at Christmas to the second poor. The rent fell in the early 19th century to £10 but by 1865 was £20.[64] In 1863 the trustees applied to divert up to one third of the income to the parish school, an action approved in 1866 since there were few second poor then in Wayford. Under a Scheme of 1879 two-thirds was to be applied to the benefit of 'deserving and necessitous persons' and the remainder used for education. In 1892 the income was applied in gifts to 28 poor persons and in 1938 29 heads of families and 16 children received a total of £10. The income amounted to £30 in 1965, distributed as before.[65]

[54] S.R.O., D/P/wa 2/1/1, 4/1/1; DD/SAS CH 16.
[55] *Proc. Som. Arch. Soc.* xlv. 148.
[56] S.R.O., D/P/wa 2/1/1-5.
[57] S.R.O., D/D/Ca 175, 235; *S.R.S.* xliii. 75.
[58] T. G. Crippen, *Nonconformity in Som.* (Som. Arch. Soc. Libr. Taunton Castle).
[59] *9th Rep. Com. Char.* H.C. 258, p. 505 (1823), ix.
[60] Ibid.; S.R.O., D/P/wa 2/1/1.

[61] *Digest of Returns to Sel. Cttee. on Educ. of Poor,* H.C. 224 (1819), ix (2).
[62] *Educ. Enquiry Abstract,* H.C. 62 (1835), xlii. A house formerly a school occurs in 1851: H.O. 107/1928.
[63] Char. Com. files.
[64] *9th Rep. Com. Char.* H.C. 258, pp. 504-5 (1823), ix.
[65] Char. Com. files.

MARTOCK HUNDRED

THE HUNDRED of Martock was conterminous with the manor and ancient parish of Martock and had its origin in the pre-Conquest royal estate which may originally have included Muchelney and part of Tintinhull.[1] It was first mentioned in 1225 when it included the tithings of Ash, Bower Hinton, Coat, and Stapleton.[2] Of the other tithings in the hundred Witcombe occurs in 1243, Hurst, Long Load, and Milton in 1284–6, and Newton (grouped with Hurst) and

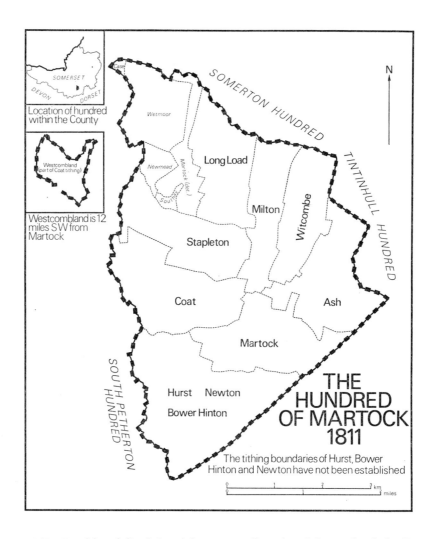

Westcombland (in Buckland St. Mary) in 1327.[3] In 1652 Martock, Ash, Bower Hinton, Coat, Stapleton, Witcombe, and possibly Milton, paid customary dues to the lord.[4] The hundred still included Westcombland in 1841, although by that date Bower Hinton and Hurst had been grouped together and Newton was no longer recorded.[5]

The ownership of the hundred was seldom mentioned but it evidently descended

[1] V.C.H. Som. iii. 38, 255.
[2] S.R.S. xi, p. 57.
[3] Ibid. iii. 130–2; xi, p. 291; Feud. Aids, iv. 282–3.

[4] E 317/Somerset 11. Coat occurs twice, probably in error for Milton and Coat.
[5] S.R.S. iii. 310, 325.

with the capital manor of Martock.[6] No court rolls have been traced. In 1661 the court house, thereafter the free grammar school, was reserved four times a year for holding the hundred and manor courts.[7] By 1475 the sheriff's tourn was being held on Ham Hill, where the tourns for adjacent hundreds also met. It had been 'much discontinued' by 1652.[8]

The office of bedel of the hundred between 1477 and 1537 was leased by the lord of Martock manor with the common bakehouse and the tolls of markets and fairs, and was held from 1505 by the bailiff of Martock manor.[9] Two constables of the hundred were mentioned in 1553.[10]

[6] C 142/25/31; S.R.O., D/P/mart 18/1/1; DD/WY, map of Martock, 1811.

[7] S.R.O., D/P/mart 18/1/1.

[8] D.C.O., roll 300; E 317/Somerset 11.

[9] S.C. 6/Hen. VII/1236; S.C. 6/Hen. VIII/3044.

[10] Sta. Cha. 3/2/11.

MARTOCK

THE ANCIENT parish of Martock, with ten tithings, is one of the largest in the county. It lies 5 miles north of Crewkerne, 3 miles south of Somerton, and 4 miles south-west of Ilchester. Probably in origin a royal Saxon estate, it had its own market and fair from the 13th century and, with the expansion of river traffic, it became a significant trading centre, although constituting a group of individual settlements which looked chiefly to agriculture for their support. In 1633 it was noted as being 'seated in the fattest place of the earth of this county, especially for arable, which makes the inhabitants so fat in their purses'.[1] With the break-up of the capital manor, which had begun as early as the 13th century, there remained no substantial estate to dominate the parish and thus no resident gentry. The farmers ruled Martock, as a 17th-century writer noted. He described them as 'wealthy and substantial men though none of the best bred, which is the cause their neighbours slander them with the title of clowns; but they care not much for that, knowing they have money in their purses to make them gentlemen when they are fit for that degree'.[2] With the expansion of the clothing trade in the 18th century and the establishment of a number of manufacturing concerns in the 19th, Martock became and has remained an industrial centre somewhat at variance with its rural environment.

The ancient parish was probably once triangular in shape, bounded by the Yeo (called locally Load river in 1417)[3] to the north, the Parrett to the south-west, and the Foss Way to the south-east. By the 10th century the north-western extremity had become the parish of Muchelney and the north-eastern part of Tintinhull.[4] Thereafter the parish stretched 5¼ miles from north to south and 3½ miles from east to west, and measured 7,226 a. In 1895 the civil parishes of Ash (comprising the former tithings of Ash, Milton, and Witcombe) of 1,959 a. and Long Load of 1,451 a. were created.[5]

The highest ground lies in the south part of the parish, rising above 200 ft. at Halletts Hill, and east of the centre, where it climbs to 189 ft. at Ash. The higher areas lie principally on the silts and marls of the Pennard Sands, with some Lower Lias in the north-east and an outcrop of Yeovil Sands between Cripple and Ringwell hills on the south. They were chiefly devoted to arable and constituted the open fields of the various settlements. Between the two higher regions a shallow valley carries Mady mill stream and Hinton Meads brook from east to west to join the river Parrett, and dwellings in this part of Martock are still subject to periodic flooding. The remainder of the parish, beside the Parrett to the west and the Yeo to the north, is alluvium below the 50 ft. contour, and those areas formed the medieval pastures and meadows.[6] The low-lying ground has always relied much on artificial drainage, a medieval feature being the 'lakes' into which many of the ditches ran, particularly in the north around Long Load.

The principal route through the parish runs from Crewkerne in the south, enters the parish from the Foss Way between Halletts and Ringwell hills, and meanders north through Bower Hinton, Hurst, across Hurst Bow, through Martock, Stapleton, and Long Load, crossing the Yeo at Load Bridge and continuing north to Long Sutton and Somerton. A road from Gawbridge Bow across the Parrett in the west, linking with roads from Kingsbury Episcopi and East Lambrook, runs east through Coat, Stapleton, and Ash to meet the Foss Way at Tintinhull Forts (called Tintinhull Forches in 1692),[7] continuing to Tintinhull and Yeovil. With East Street, running east from the centre of Martock and then south-east to Cart Gate on the Foss, those roads were adopted by the Martock turnpike trust at its formation in 1760–1.[8] The link with South Petherton from Carys mill bridge over the Parrett in the south-west to Hurst Bow was similarly adopted in 1802–3.[9] Turnpike gates towards the west end of Coat and north end of Long Load had been built by 1811, and a toll gate and cottage at the cross-roads south of Long Load by 1815.[10] The Foss Way, forming the whole of the south-eastern boundary of the parish, was known as the Dyed or Dead Way by 1697.[11]

There are two major bridges in the parish. Gawbridge Bow occurs in 1243 as Gavelbrig.[12] During the Civil War it was removed by the Parliamentary forces for military reasons[13] and between 1648 and 1677 was repeatedly presented, with Load Bridge, as a county bridge requiring repair.[14] Load Bridge was mentioned in 1338[15] and is a late-medieval bridge of five arches. The centre arch has been renewed, probably to repair similar military damage.

A branch of the Bristol and Exeter railway, linking Taunton and Yeovil, and passing west–east through the centre of the parish, was completed as far as Martock station in 1849, but was not opened until the line was extended to Hendford near Yeovil in 1853. Both line and station were closed in 1964.[16]

Martock, the site of the church, was the primary settlement, and the strength both of the capital manor and of ecclesiastical patronage prevented the

---

[1] *S.R.S.* xv. 123. This article was completed in 1974.
[2] *S.R.S.* xv. 123.
[3] Winchester Coll. Mun. 12862.
[4] *V.C.H. Som.* iii. 38,255.
[5] *Census*, 1901; Local Govt. Bd. Order 32,210.
[6] Geol. Surv. Map 1″, solid and drift, sheet 312 (1958 edn.).
[7] S.R.O., DD/PLE, box 50, conveyance, 10 June 1692.
[8] Martock Turnpike Act, 1 Geo. III, c. 29 (Priv. Act.).
[9] Martock Turnpike Act, 43 Geo. III, c. 26 (Local and Personal).
[10] S.R.O., DD/WY, map of Martock 1811; Winchester Coll. Mun., map of Long Load 1815.
[11] S.R.O., D/P/mart 14/5/1.
[12] *S.R.S.* xi, p. 309.   [13] Ibid. lxxi, p. 36.
[14] Ibid. xxviii. 54, 157, 193, 210, 234–5; xxxiv. 205–6, 222; lxxi, pp. 22–3, 36–7, 38.
[15] *Cal. Pat.* 1338–40, 78.
[16] D. St. John Thomas, *Regional Hist. of the Railways of Great Britain*, ii. 176–7.

subsidiary hamlets from acquiring parochial status until the 19th century. The hamlets generally preserve their plans as nucleated or linear settlements surrounded by the former open fields, with a few outlying 19th-century farms built subsequent to inclosure.

LONG LOAD, recorded as Lade in the later 12th century,[17] developed along a spur above the 50-ft. contour on both sides of the main road north to Somerton, the street being built-up for about a mile to the south of Load Bridge. The three former open arable fields were on the higher ground and occupied the whole tithing south of the village. Church Hay field (North field in 1551, Chapelhayfield in 1646) and Littlefield (South field in 1551) lay to the west of the street, and Mare field (East field in 1551, Mearefield in 1646) to the east of it.[18] The low-lying areas in the north-west of the tithing beside the Yeo were occupied by the three 'moors' or common pastures, Outmoor, Foremoor (both so named in 1551), and Rottenham (Rodenham in 1379, Ratnam in 1556).[19] Meadow land lay at Barland (Berelond in 1505) and Gosham (so called in 1440) in the north beside the Yeo, and at Mare mead, north-east of Mare field.[20]

From the church in the centre of the village Load Lane (Churchey Lane in 1507, West drove in 1636)[21] runs west to Muchelney, formerly giving access to the 'moors' in the north. South of the village Wetmoor Lane (Wottewey in 1388, Whetweys Wey in 1561, Whettens Lane in 1690)[22] runs west to join Load Lane, serving common pastures outside the tithing, including Wetmoor in the north-west corner of the parish. The southern limit of the tithing is marked by a cross-roads called Yarley Nap in 1811, formerly the site of a toll gate. The road to the west was known as Southay Lane by 1740 and to the east, leading to Milton, as Paynes Lane by 1886.[23] Both were called Yalwey in 1506 (Yalwaies Waye in 1559, Yollowe Way in 1597).[24]

The irregular western boundary of the tithing between Load and Wetmoor lanes was probably formed by allotment following inclosure between Martock and Load tithings.[25] Withybeds lining the north-western boundary of the tithing and surrounding Rottenham were known locally as 'werbers' or 'weerbeares' by the 17th century.[26]

Stathes or wharves on the Yeo north of the village were mentioned in 1448 and 1552,[27] and the field name 'Coleplott', sited by the river in 1672,[28] suggests one of the principal commodities landed. The firm of Stuckey and Bagehot of Langport had a coal-yard north of the river in Long Load's Kingsmoor allotment in 1824, and there was a salthouse there in 1841.[29] South of the bridge and on the west side of the street stood the Bridgehouse, mentioned in 1379 and held in 1420 by the rent of 1 lb. of wax.[30] It was occupied by John Bradford, boatman, in 1485–6, and continued to be held by the Bradfords until at least 1668.[31] By 1776 the site was occupied by a stable and coal barton.[32] The principal farms all lie along the main street, although settlement on the highway waste along the south side of Load Lane had started by 1647.[33]

It is noticeable that whereas lias predominates in the older buildings along the northern half of the street, the use of Ham stone increases towards the south. There are several 17th- and 18th-century buildings, mostly on the west side of the street and few of any size, but most of the houses are 19th-century. There are some 18th- and 19th-century buildings in Load Lane, much of which has more recently been developed as a chalet and caravan site.

MILTON tithing, formerly known as Milton Fauconberg or Falconbridge, lies east of Long Load; as 'Middleton' it occurs from 1284–6.[34] The hamlet is strung out along a lane running north from the Gawbridge–Tintinhull road to a cross-roads. Thence lanes run west to Long Load, east to Witcombe, and north to the former open fields. Former common meadow and pasture, Milton Leaze and Milton mead, lie on the lower ground in the north beside the Yeo. Three open arable fields were mentioned in 1318: West field (North field in 1608, North or Lower field by 1786) lay immediately north of the village, East field (Middlefield in 1786) east of the village, and Rycroft (Highcroft field in 1786) south and south-east of the village.[35] Fields called Loxhill immediately north of the settlement mark the site of Lockeshull, a hamlet in 1268, and referred to as a manor in 1348.[36]

Milton and Manor farms, the two principal farms in the tithing, lie at the northern end of the village, and at its southern extremity Court cottage, formerly the manorial chapel, stands next to the old pound and probably adjoins the site of the former manor-house. Fields in the south of the tithing (and also in the south-west of Ash tithing) called Gildons were evidently once linked with a capital messuage of that name recorded from 1554.[37] The principal farm-houses are of the 17th century and there are a few smaller 18th- and 19th-century houses.

WITCOMBE tithing, east from Milton, occurs in 1243 as 'Wythicumbe',[38] and like Milton extends north to the Yeo and south to the Gawbridge–Tintinhull road. From this road Witcombe Lane, later Witcombe drove, runs north to the Yeo and over Witcombe bridge to the Martock allotments in Kingsmoor. There was a bridge at Witcombe

17 *S. & D. N. & Q.* xxi. 91. Called Long Load or sometimes Load St. Mary to distinguish it from Little Load in the adjacent parish of Long Sutton.
18 Winchester Coll. Mun. 12845, 23053; map 1815.
19 Ibid. 12845, 12863.
20 Ibid. 12844, 12864; S.R.O., CR 102.
21 Winchester Coll. Mun. 12864, 12908.
22 Ibid. 12862, 12870, 12911.
23 S.R.O., D/P/mart 14/5/1; O.S. Map 6″, Som. LXXXII. NW. (1886 edn.).
24 Winchester Coll. Mun. 12845, 12864, 23046.
25 S.R.O., DD/SAS, map of Martock 1824; D/P/mart 20/1/2.
26 Winchester Coll. Mun. 23053.
27 Ibid. 12862–3.
28 Ibid. 23055.
29 S.R.O., D/P/mart 13/1/1; tithe award.
30 Winchester Coll. Mun. 12862–3.
31 Ibid. 12863, 23055.
32 Ibid. 21429A.
33 Ibid. 23053.
34 *Feud. Aids*, iv. 282.
35 S.R.O., DD/S/HY, box 6; CR 97; S.C. 2/198/64; D.R.O., D 203/C 10.
36 *S.R.S.* xxxvi. 22–3; S.R.O., DD/X/HY, box 6, grant 16 Nov. 1348.
37 S.R.O., DD/SAS, map of Martock 1824.
38 *S.R.S.* xi, p. 291.

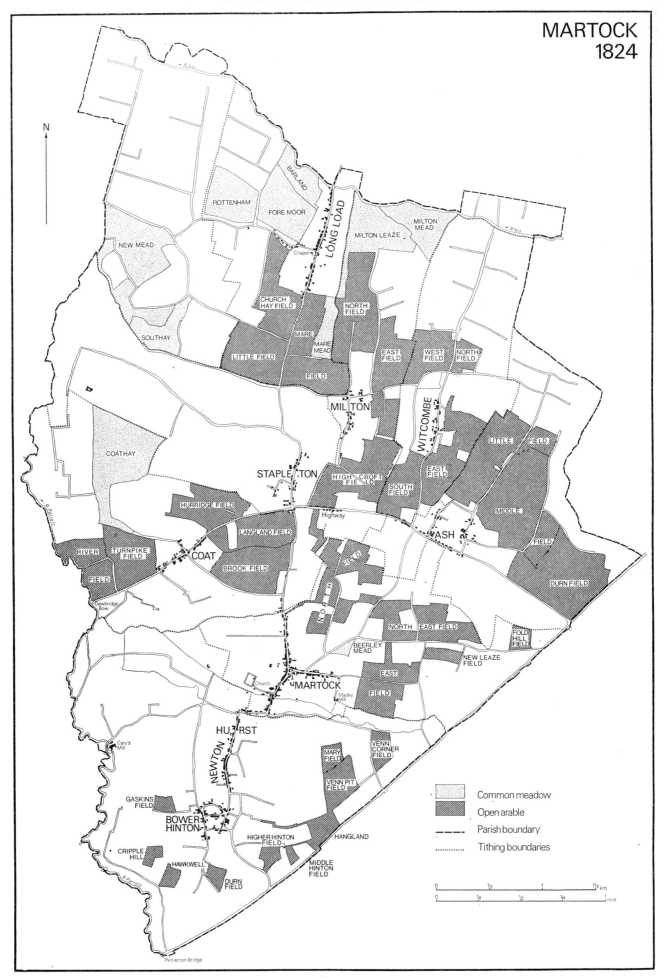

MARTOCK
1824

N

ROTTENHAM

BARLAND

FORE MOOR

LONG LOAD

MILTON LEAZE

MILTON MEAD

Chapel

NEW MEAD

CHURCH HAY FIELD

NORTH FIELD

SOUTHAY

MARE

MARE MEAD

EAST FIELD

WEST FIELD

NORTH FIELD

LITTLE FIELD

FIELD

MILTON

WITCOMBE

LITTLE FIELD

COATHAY

STAPLETON

HIGH CROFT FIELD

SOUTH FIELD

EAST FIELD

HURRIDGE FIELD

Highway

MIDDLE FIELD

RIVER FIELD

TURNPIKE FIELD

COAT

LANGLAND FIELD

ASH

BROOK FIELD

NORTH FIELD

DURN FIELD

Gawbridge Bow

NORTH EAST FIELD

FOLD HILL FIELD

BEERLEY MEAD

NEW LEAZE FIELD

Church

MARTOCK

Madey Mill

EAST FIELD

HURST

NEWTON

VENN CORNER FIELD

Cary's Mill

MARY FIELD

VENN PIT FIELD

GASKINS FIELD

BOWER HINTON

HIGHER HINTON FIELD

HANGLAND

CRIPPLE HILL

HAWKWELL

DURN FIELD

MIDDLE HINTON FIELD

R Parrett

Petherton Bridge

Common meadow

Open arable

Parish boundary

Tithing boundaries

0   ½   1   1½ km
0   ¼   ½   ¾   1 mile

giving access to Kingsmoor by 1543, and one there and at Milton by the late 16th century, also used by Ash tithing, for which the inhabitants paid rent to the lord of Somerton manor.[39] Witcombe bridge and its gate continued to be presented at Kingsmoor court until 1757.[40]

Lanes and droves give access to fields east and west of Witcombe Lane. Meadows and pastures, as at Milton, lie in the north towards the river. Of the four 18th-century open arable fields, West and North fields, on either side of Witcombe Lane north of the village, were probably once a single field in a three-field system; South and East fields occupied the whole tithing east and south of the village.[41] The village itself lies along Witcombe Lane and is the only area of settlement in the tithing. Witcombe Manor farm, the former manor-house of Witcombe and Coat, is on the west side of the lane. The principal houses are of 17th-century origin with stone-mullioned windows and some with thatched roofs. Smaller 18th- and 19th-century houses are scattered along the main street but there has been almost no modern development.

ASH tithing occupies the north-eastern corner of the ancient parish, extending irregularly south of the Gawbridge–Tintinhull road, and was mentioned as 'Esse' in 1225.[42] The village lies along and north of the road, although formerly comprising two hamlets on parallel lanes running north. The western settlement represented the manor of Ash Boulogne and the eastern that of Pykesash. Later development has taken place along the main road, linking the two hamlets and extending west to the 19th-century church and school. Apart from one lane running south-west to Martock most of the tracks are field droves. Meadow and pasture land lined the northern and western boundaries in the lower areas of the tithing. The medieval fields lay 'towards Ilchester', 'towards Tintinhull', and 'above the town'.[43] Littlefield (North field in 1622 and 1704) lay north of the village, Middle field north-east, and Durnfield (East field in 1622 and 1704) to the east.[44] With the exception of Durnfield farm, a 19th-century creation in the inclosed fields, all the farm-houses lie in the village. Fields called Maynes in the south-east of the tithing, south of the Gawbridge–Tintinhull road, evidently represent lands held by Robert Mayne in the later 14th century and called Ashmaynes in 1563 and 1596.[45]

There is a scatter of older houses, mostly of the 18th and 19th centuries, along the main road, but the main concentration of early buildings, including perhaps six of the 17th century, is along Burrough Street to the east. There is also an estate of 20th-century houses at the south end of this street, some modern infilling along the main street, particularly on the south side, and a Local Authority estate to the west of the village. Ash House has a main front

of *c.* 1700 with mullioned and transomed windows and is built to an L-shaped plan. It was extended and refitted in the earlier 19th century.

STAPLETON tithing, recorded in 1195,[46] stretches west from Milton to a stream marking the western boundary of Martock parish, abutting south on Coat and north on Southay Lane. The south-western boundary is formed by the Gawbridge–Tintinhull road, from which at Stapleton Cross (formerly Towns End) the road to Long Load and Somerton runs north through the village. Town Tree Lane runs west, then north-west, formerly served the fields, and from 1239 was a right-of-way to Muchelney abbey.[47] West Street, so named in 1737,[48] runs west from the centre of the hamlet to serve fields in that direction.

Open arable was restricted to the higher ground in the eastern half of the tithing: East field lay east of the road to Load in the north-east corner, North field lay west of the road between Southay and Town Tree lanes, and West field was immediately west of the village.[49] A large area in the south of the tithing called Lords field may represent former demesne arable or possibly a park mentioned in 1670. In the western half of the tithing, towards the Parrett, pastures lay along both sides of Town Tree Lane, and beside the stream forming the western boundary of the parish lay Stapleton mead.[50] There in the early 19th century Stapleton Mead Farm was built.[51] Stapleton manor-house lay in the middle of the village, north-west of the junction of the main road and West Street.

The concentration of houses, most of which are small and close to the street, is around the cross-roads. A few are of 17th- and 18th-century origin but most were built or remodelled in the 19th century. Stapleton House was built in the late 18th century, perhaps as a farm-house, and enlarged to the west and aggrandized *c.* 1825.

COAT tithing, mentioned in 1225,[52] lies south of Stapleton, extending from the Parrett in the west to beyond the Martock–Somerton road in the east. The road to Tintinhull crosses the tithing from Gawbridge to Stapleton Cross, passing through the village, and Coat Road runs south-east from the village cross-roads to the former Martock station. The fourth arm of this cross-roads, Cripple Street, heads north-west towards Coathay, the former common pasture of the tithing, and Coat mead, once common meadow, in the west beside the Parrett. Open arable lay east, north, and west of the village: to the west, and north from Gawbridge, lay River field and Goar or Turnpike field (together called Middle field in 1555), to the north lay Thornhill, to the north-east Hurridge field, and east, and south of the Gawbridge–Tintinhull road, lay Langland (Langland and Down in 1555) and Brook or Lavers fields (Brookfurlong in 1555),[53] the

[39] S.C. 2/198/35; S.R.O., D/D/Cd 130; DD/PO 13.
[40] D.R.O., D 124, box 18, Kingsmoor ct. bks. 1732–56, 1757–96.
[41] S.R.O., DD/PLE, box 50, conveyance 2 May 1775; CR 97.
[42] *S.R.S.* xi, p. 57.
[43] *H.M.C. Wells*, i. 451–2.
[44] S.R.O., CR 97; DD/PLE, box 47, lease 3 May 1704; box 49, lease 9 Mar. 1621/2. Durnfield derives its name from Long and Short Durden furlongs in East field, mentioned in 1622.

[45] S.R.O., DD/S/HY, box 6, confirmation 8 May 1356, grant 5 Oct. 1371; C 142/135/24; C 2/Eliz. I/R 2/5.
[46] *Pipe R.* 1195 (P.R.S. N.S. vi), 233.
[47] *S.R.S.* xiv, pp. 66–9.
[48] S.R.O., D/P/mart 2/1/3.
[49] S.R.O., DD/S/HR, map of Stapleton 1774.
[50] Ibid.; DD/S/HY, box 3, ct. roll 25 Oct. 1670.
[51] S.R.O., DD/S/HR, map of Stapleton 1774; DD/SAS, map of Martock 1824.
[52] *S.R.S.* xi, p. 57.
[53] L.R. 2/202; S.R.O., CR 97.

last two being separated by Dead Brook (so called in 1675).[54] In the south-west of the tithing beside the Parrett is Sash hill, formerly Says hill, and probably held by John de Say in the 14th century.[55] The village lies principally along the Gawbridge–Tintinhull road east and west of the cross-roads. All the farms are in the village and the pound lies a little east of the cross-roads on the south side of the main road. A common bakehouse and oven were built to the east of 'the cross' in 1461.[56]

The village is notable for the number of substantial farm-houses which dominate the south-western end of the street. Most are of the later 17th or early 18th centuries and several have plans which incorporate rooms additional to the three-roomed type which is traditional in the area. There are also a number of two-storeyed barns with a tall loading bay against one end.

Coat tithing includes the buildings south of Stapleton Cross, comprising four shops in 1824,[57] and shares with Milton a hamlet called Highway by 1604.[58] Highway grew up along the side of the Gawbridge–Tintinhull road between Stapleton Cross and Ash and was sometimes called Stapleton Highway. The main settlement of Martock has extended north into Coat to cover the medieval hamlet of Limbury, recorded in the 13th century and as a personal name in 1366,[59] which lay in the south-east of the tithing, south of Coat Lane and west of North Street. The name survived in fields there in the early 19th century.[60] The later settlement of the site was due principally to the coming of the railway and the development of an industrial estate around the railway station.

The tithings of *HURST*, mentioned in 1281,[61] and *BOWER HINTON*, which occurs as 'Hanton Mertoc' in 1225 and 'Burhenton' in 1280,[62] are physically inseparable. Together they occupy the whole southern end of the parish beyond Coat and Martock tithings, from which they are divided by Mady mill stream and Hinton Meads brook. The Foss Way borders the tithings along the south-east and thence the main road through the parish runs north-west, entering Bower Hinton at Jordans Hole (recorded in 1734).[63] The principal settlement lies along this road and on three lanes running west from it: Blind Lane (so called in 1555),[64] Middle Street, and Higher Street. A fourth lane runs north along the western edge of the village to form a simple grid pattern. Droves run east and west from the village to serve the former open fields. The main street continues north through Newton and Hurst to Hurst Bow (mentioned in 1727),[65] spanning Hinton Meads brook. From the bridge a road runs east, leaving the parish by Carys mill bridge over the Parrett. From this road other droves run north-west and south to serve the fields.

The open arable fields lay on the higher ground, Hurst and Bower Hinton evidently sharing one field system. East field (North-east field in 1644, Church Path field in 1758) lay east of Hurst, north of Dimmocks Lane, and north-west of the Foss Way; South field (South-east field in 1644, Middle field in 1758) occupied the area south of Gastons and Dimmocks lanes, bounded by South Leaze drove in the south-west and by the Foss Way; West field (Millfield in 1736) lay west of Hurst and Newton between the road to Carys mill bridge on the north and Gastons Lane on the south.[66] Common meadow lay on the lower ground, principally at Hinton mead and Ham in the extreme north-west of the tithings beside the Parrett and the brooks. Pasture was shared at Wetmoor and in small areas such as Hills. Inscribed stones formerly marking the ownership and site of strips have been found in areas once part of South field.[67]

The centre of the original settlement at Bower Hinton apparently lay at the junction of the main street with Blind Lane and Middle Street, marked by a small green and a group of trees known as Park Trees in 1690. The trees belonged to the lord of Martock and are now known as Pair Trees, from which one of the adjacent farms takes its name.[68] The tithing pound lies opposite the west end of Middle Street and all the farm-houses and farm buildings lie in the village. Sparrow's Electrical Engineering factory, formerly the Somerset Wheel and Wagon Company, lies at the entrance to the village in the south-east.

Between Ralphs Lane in the south and Goggs Pool Lane (Gogs Pool gutter was mentioned in 1752)[69] and the turning east to Lovers Grove in the north lies the medieval hamlet and tithing of Newton, mentioned in 1327.[70] This represents early infilling along the main street between Bower Hinton and Hurst with over 40 cottages on equal plots of $\frac{1}{2}$ a. each.[71] Cottages at Hozen Hole (Ozen Hole in 1555, Osinghole in 1644, Lowzie Hole in 1714),[72] north of Hurst Bow at the west end of Water Street, were included in Newton tithing by 1555 and may have been built on the waste at a similar date.[73] There has been a glove factory in this area since the earlier 19th century.[74] Newton tithing was mortgaged as a unit in 1628 and was mentioned as a topographical area as late as 1827.[75]

Hurst hamlet lies between Goggs Pool Lane in the south and Hurst Bow in the north, and is restricted to dwellings along the main street. A field west of the settlement called Rack Close and the 'cloth hall' at Hurst Barton support the many references to Hurst clothiers in the 18th and early 19th centuries. That part of Bower Hinton which contains the older houses lies in the south along the main road close to the top of the hill and

---

[54] S.R.O., D/P/mart 14/5/1.
[55] *S.R.S.* xii. 87–8; *Cal. Pat.* 1343–5, 87.
[56] S.C. 6/Hen. VII/1236.
[57] S.R.O., DD/SAS, map of Martock 1824.
[58] S.R.O., D/P/mart 2/1/1.
[59] *S.R.S.* xiv, p. 84; *Cal. Pat.* 1364–7, 318.
[60] S.R.O., DD/SAS, map of Martock 1824.
[61] *Cal. Close, 1279–88*, 88.
[62] *S.R.S.* xi, p. 57; xliv. 218–19.
[63] S.R.O., D/P/mart 14/5/2.
[64] L.R. 2/202.
[65] S.R.O., D/P/mart 14/5/2.

[66] L.R. 2/202; S.R.O., DD/MR 92; DD/S/HR, box 20, mar. settl. 16 May 1758; CR 102; D.R.O., D 203/B 84.
[67] L.R. 2/202; ex inf. Mr. P. J. Palmer, Bower Hinton.
[68] S.R.O., DD/MR 33, copy mar. settl. 16 Apr. 1690.
[69] S.R.O., D/P/mart 14/5/3.
[70] *S.R.S.* iii. 130.
[71] L.R. 2/202.
[72] Ibid.; S.R.O., DD/MR 92; D/P/mart 2/1/3.
[73] L.R. 2/202.
[74] S.R.O., DD/SAS, map of Martock 1824; tithe award.
[75] Lancs. R.O., DD/Cl 259; S.R.O., DD/S/HR, box 49, conveyance 19 Dec. 1827.

along Middle and Higher Streets. There are six or seven 17th-century houses, most of which were or still are associated with farms. One, now called Bower House but formerly the Red Lion inn, has plasterwork in a first-floor room dated 1632. In this area there are also a number of other 18th- and 19th-century houses, but the main 19th-century expansion was down the main street to connect with Hurst, houses in the former tithing of Newton being then mostly rebuilt. Most of these houses are smaller and terraced, one notable gap having been filled within recent years. Hurst contains a number of later-17th- and earlier-18th-century houses of traditional plan, some of which have canted bay-windows. Most of the street is infilled with smaller houses of the 19th century.

At Cary mill bridge a medieval mill or mills expanded during the 19th century to form the nucleus of an industrial complex called the Parrett Works, used in 1976 principally for warehousing. The surviving buildings are irregularly arranged around several yards with the mill stream at the western edge and are of various dates. Most are of two storeys and probably 19th century. The principal exception is an early-18th-century mill of four storeys which abuts the northern wheel house. Immediately to its south there is a boiler house with a tall square chimney of the later 19th century. To the north of the road there is a short terrace of later-19th-century houses, presumably built for workers.

The tithing of *MARTOCK* lies east of the centre of the parish, bounded on the north by Coat, Stapleton, Milton, Witcombe, and Ash, and divided from Bower Hinton and Hurst in the south by a stream. The main street runs east from Hurst Bow as Water Street, so called by 1728 from its propensity to flood.[76] It then turns north as Church Street across Pigs Bow, mentioned in 1729,[77] to the church and market house, and continues as North Street, so named in 1761.[78] At the junction of Church and Water streets a lane formerly called Crowdway crosses the stream at Frickers bridge (Friggers Bow in 1811), described as 'new' in 1780,[79] and heads eastwards towards Stoke sub Hamdon. East Street runs east from the market house through the Green to link up with a network of droves and lanes serving the former open fields. From East Street Summer Lane, so called in 1730,[80] runs north-east, continuing as Beerly (or Barley) Road to Ash, with further field droves branching from it.

The open-field system was disrupted at an early date by piecemeal inclosure. North field (called West field in 1732 and Steps field, the name of one of its furlongs, in 1785) lay north of the town and west of Beerly Road; North-east field (often called East field or Middle field) lay west of Beerly Road, being divided by Foldhill Lane from East field (formerly South field), which extended south to Madey mill stream.[81] Common meadow and pasture

lay detached in the low-lying area in the north-west of the parish.[82]

The north end of Church Street has a few substantial houses of the mid 18th to mid 19th century. The south end and the east of Water Street have none earlier than the mid 19th century, but there are one or two earlier houses of a more substantial character at the west end of Water Street. East street has a scatter from the 17th to the 19th century. Those of the 17th century include several of note, including Yew Trees, which has the usual 3-roomed ground plan with a two-storeyed bay-window to the central room. The main area of council housing and other modern development lies north-east along Summer Lane and Beerly Road. In North Street 17th-century houses are limited to an area immediately north of the market house and to two isolated examples, nos. 85-7, 97, 99, further away from the centre, and a farm-house on the west side at the northern limit of Martock tithing. There are no 18th-century buildings of note, but during the 19th century both sides of the frontage from the market house to the stream came to be built up almost continuously, mostly with small houses which form irregular terraces. There is also a group of mid- to late-19th-century houses around the former railway station. Development beyond the station into Coat tithing has largely taken place during the 20th century and some houses and a shopping precinct have been built on fields behind the street frontage. Further building was in progress in 1974.

A small freehold, later a manor, called Fenn or Fenns, first mentioned in 1243,[83] lay in the extreme south-east of the tithing beside the Foss Way, its name surviving in fields called Venns and Venn bridge.

Licences to sell ale in Long Load manor were granted in 1490, 1556, and 1557, and a victualler occurs at Coat in 1607.[84] The oldest inn is probably the George in Church Street, mentioned by name in 1631 and possibly referred to in 1617 when the inhabitants petitioned for the closure of all taverns except 'the Inn' and two other alehouses.[85] Another alehouse licence was requested in 1627, so that the inhabitants could refresh themselves when coming to church from a distance, and the former common bakehouse had become the Bell inn by 1689.[86] There were 4 licensed victuallers in 1732 and, by 1744, 14, of whom 2 lived at Hurst, 2 at Stapleton, and one at Long Load; in 1748 one lived at Ash.[87] The White Hart by the market house was recorded by name in 1736, and both it and the George were regularly used by the vestry, friendly societies, and other parochial bodies.[88] The former Red Lion inn at Bower Hinton was licensed by 1795 and closed c. 1970.[89] The Freemasons Arms at Ash and the Old Wheelwrights Arms, which became the Crown inn by 1889, at Long Load both occur in 1841, and the Royal Marine at Coat, 'recently' closed in

[76] S.R.O. D/P/mart 2/1/3.
[77] Ibid. 14/5/2; DD/WY, map of Martock 1811.
[78] S.R.O. D/P/mart 14/5/3.
[79] Ibid. 2/1/5; DD/WY, map of Martock 1811. The name may be linked with the burial of Joseph Frickar, mason, at Martock on 25 Sept. 1770.
[80] S.R.O., D/P/mart 14/5/2.
[81] L.R. 2/202; S.R.O., DD/PLE, box 50, conveyance 12 Oct. 1785; D.R.O., D 102/T 34.

[82] L.R. 2/202; S.R.O., CR 102.
[83] *S.R.S.* xi, p. 319.
[84] Winchester Coll. Mun. 12863, 12845; S.R.O., D/P/mart 2/1/1.
[85] S.R.O., D/D/Cd 130; *S.R.S.* xxx, p. 72.
[86] S.R.O., Q/SR 58/i/4; DD/SB 5/2.
[87] S.R.O., Q/RL.   [88] S.R.O., D/P/mart 13/2/3.
[89] S.R.O., DD/PLE, box 92, mortgage 6 Mar. 1834; Q/RL; local information.

1973, was mentioned in 1861.[90] Beer houses listed in 1840 included the Butchers Arms and Farmers Arms in North Street, the Carpenters Arms in East Street, and the Ropers Arms in Water Street.[91] The Railway Hotel followed the building of the railway in 1849, the Stapleton Cross inn, closed since the Second World War, occurred in 1886, and by 1939 there were the Nags Head and the White Horse both in East Street, and the Bakers Arms in North Street, the last having closed c. 1973.[92] The present Rose and Crown inn at Bower Hinton was a former beer house.

Martock Friendly Society, known also as the Martock Benefit Society, the Martock Men's Club, or the Old George Club, was established in 1800 and met on Whit Monday, initially at the White Hart, later moving to the George. It was disbanded c. 1912.[93] A female friendly society meeting at the George was set up in 1806 and was holding its anniversary on Whit Tuesday in 1900.[94] The Bower Hinton Male Benefit Society met by 1863 on Whit Tuesday and was continuing in 1882. In 1882 a female friendly society met at Bower Hinton on Whit Wednesday.[95] The Martock Farmers' and Tradesmen's Friendly Society, founded probably in 1853, met at the White Hart in 1863 and 1893.[96]

The social life of Martock was enlivened by such events as a concert at the school house in 1744 and by visits from travelling players recorded twice in 1773.[97] There was a music teacher in the parish by 1830 and the Martock Agricultural Society, founded in 1837, held annual ploughing matches.[98] A New Year tradesmen's ball at the George inn was a regular feature by 1864, in which year Wildman's theatre and the Lyric Opera Company performed at the White Hart assembly rooms.[99] The Martock brass band and a literary institute had been founded by 1889 and the annual flower show of the Horticultural Society, which still continues, was first held in the same year.[1] The Martock flower show committee in conjunction with the Countess de Belleroche raised money to build a hangar on Bower Hinton farm in 1911 for D. G. Gilmour, 'the first airman to fly an aeroplane over this part of the country'.[2] A Constitutional Club was mentioned in 1896, a Conservative Club in 1909, and Short Range Rifle and Liberal clubs in 1910.[3]

Martock had 136 tax payers in 1327, of whom 22 each came from Bower Hinton and Stapleton, 19 from Coat, 15 from Hurst with Newton, 13 from Martock, 12 each from Milton, Long Load, and Ash, and 9 from Witcombe.[4] By 1548 there were 903 communicants, and in 1563 the parish included 253 households, of which 24 were at Stapleton and 26 at Long Load.[5] In 1791 the parish had a population of nearly 2,000 in 377 houses. Of these houses 102 were at Martock, 54 at Hurst, 46 at Long Load, 44 at Coat, and 40 at Bower Hinton. There were 34 in Ash, 22 each in Milton and Stapleton, and 13 in Witcombe.[6] From 2,102 in 1811 the population rose steadily to 3,154 in 1851 and 3,155 in 1861. Thereafter it fell gradually to 2,571 in 1911, but remained constant at over 2,600 between 1911 and 1931. After the Second World War the total rose only slightly, with 2,846 in 1951 and 2,825 in 1961, before reaching 3,359 in 1971. Individual figures for Ash and Long Load in the 20th century show the former rising to 418 in 1921, falling to 395 in 1961, and rising again to 417 in 1971; and Long Load declining from 217 in 1911 to 186 in 1931, with subsequent increases to 200 in 1961 and to 239 in 1971.[7]

John de Langton, treasurer of Wells and chancellor of England, returned to the 'court at Martock', now the Treasurer's House, in 1297 to receive the King's seal kept there during his absence.[8] Robert Patton Adams, born at Martock in 1831, became solicitor-general of Tasmania.[9] Thomas Farnaby (d. 1647) taught in the parish from 1605 as Thomas 'Bainrafe', an anagram of his surname. He later moved to London and became an educationist of European reputation.[10]

MANORS. The manor of *MARTOCK* was held in 1066 by Queen Edith, wife of Edward the Confessor. After the Conquest it passed to the Crown and in the late 11th or early 12th century it was granted to Eustace, count of Boulogne.[11] Eustace settled his lands on his daughter Maud, wife of Stephen, later King of England (d. 1154), and the manor passed to her son William, Count of Boulogne (d. 1159).[12] William granted it to his cousin Pharamus of Boulogne (d. 1183–4), grandson of Eustace's illegitimate son Geoffrey.[13] Pharamus's daughter Sibyl, wife of Ingram de Fiennes (d. 1189), held it in 1199, and by 1206 it had descended to her son William (I).[14] Probably on his death and during the minority of his heir it formed part of the dower of Queen Berengaria.[15] From 1209 it was

---

[90] S.R.O., tithe award; *Kelly's Dir. Som.* (1889); local information.

[91] *County Gazette Dir.* (1840).

[92] O.S. Map 6", Som. LXXXII. NW. (1886 edn.); *Kelly's Dir. Som.* (1939); local information.

[93] S.R.O., Q/R, Friendly Soc. returns; M. Fuller, *West-Country Friendly Socs.* 141; *Western Gazette*, 6 June 1863.

[94] S.R.O., Q/R, Friendly Soc. returns; *Palmer's Weekly News*, 7 June 1900.

[95] *Western Gazette*, 6 June 1863; *Palmer's Weekly News*, 6 June 1882.

[96] *Western Gazette*, 6 June 1863; *Western Advertiser*, 28 June, 1893.

[97] *Sherborne Mercury*, 21, 28 Aug. 1744; S.R.O., DD/X/RED, diary of Elias Taylor, 3 Feb., 1 Mar. 1773. The latter reference was supplied by Mrs. D. F. H. Valentine, Martock.

[98] Pigot, *Nat. Com. Dir.* (1830); *Western Gazette*, 19 Nov. 1864.

[99] *Western Gazette*, 16 Jan., 23 Apr. 1864.

[1] *Som. County Gazette*, 2 Sept. 1893; *Kelly's Dir. Som.* (1889).

[2] Plaque from hangar in market house; par. cncl. mins. 1939–46, 25 June 1941. The hangar had been sold by 1941.

[3] S.R.O., D/P/mart 9/1/1, Apr. 1896; par. cncl. mins. 1905–16, 30 Sept. 1909; *Kelly's Dir. Som.* (1910).

[4] *S.R.S.* iii. 129–32.

[5] Ibid. ii. 111; B.L. Harl. MS. 594, f. 50.

[6] Collinson, *Hist. Som.* iii. 2–3.

[7] *V.C.H. Som.* ii. 347; Census, 1911–71.

[8] *Cal. Close*, 1296–1302, 24; *D.N.B.*

[9] *People of the Period*, ed. A. T. C. Pratt (1897).

[10] *D.N.B.*

[11] *V.C.H. Som.* i. 440; *Cart. Antiq.* (P.R.S. n.s. xvii), 17.

[12] Sanders, *Eng. Baronies*, 151.

[13] *Complete Peerage*, xi. 479; *Cart. Antiq.* (P.R.S. n.s. xvii), 17.

[14] *Genealogist*, n.s. xii. 148; *Pipe R.* 1199 (P.R.S. n.s. x), 237; *Rot. Litt. Claus.* (Rec. Com.), i. 68.

[15] *Cal. Papal Regs.* i. 33, 42.

in the hands of the Crown, but William de Fiennes (II) was given seisin in 1216.[16] William still held it in 1230 but by 1244 his son Ingram de Fiennes (d. *c.* 1270) had inherited it.[17] In 1270 Walter de Fiennes leased it to Eleanor, wife of the Lord Edward,[18] and in 1275 William de Fiennes (III) made a further lease to Eleanor, then queen.[19]

William (III) (d. 1302) was succeeded by his son John, who leased the manor for life to Benet de Folsham in 1328.[20] The manor was confiscated by the Crown in 1337, in consequence of John's connexions with France, and committed to the custody of William Montacute, earl of Salisbury (d. 1344), who received the manor in fee in 1340.[21] In 1362 William's son, also William (d. 1397), successfully resisted an attempt by Robert de Fiennes, constable of France, to secure the manor and in 1394 granted the reversion to Sir John Beaufort (cr. earl of Somerset 1397, d. 1410).[22] It was inherited in turn by Beaufort's sons, Henry (d. 1418) and John (cr. duke of Somerset 1443, d. 1444), the latter being succeeded by his daughter Margaret, countess of Richmond.[23] She was deprived of her lands in 1484, though a life interest was retained by her fourth husband, Thomas Stanley, earl of Derby (d. 1504). The reversion was granted to John, Lord Scrope.[24] On the accession of Margaret's son as Henry VII her lands were restored to her, and, on her death in 1509, the manor passed to her grandson Henry VIII.[25]

In 1525 the king granted Martock to his illegitimate son Henry, duke of Richmond (d. 1536), after whose death it reverted to the Crown.[26] A grant was made in 1539 to Thomas, duke of Norfolk, for life with remainder to Charles Brandon, duke of Suffolk (d. 1545), the latter being succeeded in turn by his sons Henry (d. 1551) and Charles (d. 1551).[27] The last left three daughters and coheirs, between whose representatives the Suffolk estates were divided in 1563, Martock falling to William Stanley, Lord Monteagle (d. 1581), grandson of Charles.[28] Monteagle's daughter Elizabeth carried the manor to her husband Edward Parker, Lord Morley (d. 1618), from whom it was seized by the Crown in 1592 for debt.[29] The reversion, evidently subject to Crown leases, was granted in 1603 to William, Lord Morley and Monteagle (d.

1622), Edward's son, although a further Crown lease for 41 years was made in 1609–10 to James Gilbert.[30] In 1637 William's son Henry conveyed the manor, apparently in three parts, to William Strode of Barrington, George Strode, and Sir Henry Compton.[31] Compton conveyed his share to his son-in-law Richard, Viscount Lumley, in 1640.[32]

After a protracted law suit, Lord Morley agreed in 1642 to repay the purchase money for the manor, believing that he had a buyer in Lord Poulett, but found that 'none will purchase land in such distracted times'.[33] In 1646 the shares of Compton and Sir George Strode were sequested but it was discovered in 1652 that William Strode (d. 1666) had been enjoying the profits of the whole manor.[34] Strode's title passed to his son William (d. 1695), and grandson William (d. 1746), the last selling to Zachary Bayly of Shepton Mallet *c.* 1724.[35] Bayly sold the lordship to two brothers, Henry and John Slade of Ash, in 1759.[36] In 1779 Henry left his share to John who, by will of 1781, gave it to his daughter Ann Slade, lord in 1793.[37] George Slade occurs as lord in 1798, but by 1811 the manor had evidently been purchased by Robert Goodden of Over Compton (Dors.) (d. 1829), whose family was formerly resident in Martock.[38] Robert was succeeded by his brother Wyndham Goodden (d. 1839) and subsequently by Wyndham's son John (d. 1883).[39] On John's death his son J. R. P. Goodden sold the lordship to Walter Leach (d. 1906), whose nephew Robert (d. 1958) was followed by the latter's son, Robert Leach of Largo, Florida, U.S.A., lord in 1974.[40]

In 1633 Robert Wills of Martock purchased lands from Lord Morley and Monteagle, including the church- or school-house and the moated manor-house of the former capital manor, which were thereafter known as the manor of *MARTOCK*.[41] Wills's son, also Robert, died in 1659, and was succeeded by his sister Alice, wife of John Colston of Hurst, Martock, who settled the estate on their daughter Alice and her husband Robert Merifield of Crewkerne (d. 1686).[42] Thereafter it passed to Robert's son John (d. 1695), whose widow Joan, married secondly to Robert Knight, still held it in 1730. On her death it was inherited jointly by her two nephews, John son of John and Alice Donne and William son of William and Susanna Merifield.

[16] *Pipe R.* 1209 (P.R.S. N.S. xxiv), 102; ibid. 1210 (P.R.S. N.S. xxvi), 72; *Rot. Litt. Claus.* (Rec. Com.), i. 278.

[17] *Pipe R.* 1230 (P.R.S. N.S. iv), 54; *Bk. of Fees*, ii. 1156; Sanders, *Eng. Baronies*, 142.

[18] *Cal. Pat.* 1266–72, 459.

[19] *Cal. Chart. R.* 1257–1300, 190–1.

[20] *Cal. Inq. p.m.* iv, p. 60; *Cal. Pat.* 1327–30, 267.

[21] *Cal. Fine R.* 1337–47, 43; *Cal. Pat.* 1338–40, 434; *Cal. Inq. p.m.* viii, p. 387.

[22] *S.R.S.* xvii. 195; *Cal. Pat.* 1391–6, 351; *Cal. Close*, 1396–9, 153; *Complete Peerage*, s.v. Salisbury.

[23] *Cal. Pat.* 1408–13, 307; 1441–6, 349; *Feud. Aids*, iv. 389, 426; *Complete Peerage*, s.v. Somerset.

[24] *Complete Peerage*, x. 827; *Cal. Pat.* 1476–85, 501.

[25] *Complete Peerage*, x. 827; C 142/25/31.

[26] *L. & P. Hen. VIII*, iv (1), p. 673; C 142/82/94.

[27] *L. & P. Hen. VIII*, xiv (1), p. 263; *Cal. Pat.* 1560–3, 557–8; *Complete Peerage*, s.v. Suffolk.

[28] *Cal. Pat.* 1560–3, 489–90, 557–8; *Complete Peerage*, s.v. Monteagle.

[29] *Complete Peerage*, s.vv. Monteagle, Morley.

[30] *Cal. S.P. Dom.* 1603–10, 51; C 66/1811; *Complete Peerage*, s.v. Morley; C 142/441/16.

[31] *Complete Peerage*, s.vv. Morley and Monteagle; C 34/3172 m. 38.

[32] C.P. 43/229 rot. 10.

[33] *Hist. MSS. Com.* 4, *5th Rep.*, p. 26.

[34] *Cal. Cttee. for Compounding*, i. 541–2.

[35] S.R.O., DD/X/PAR 1.

[36] S.R.O., DD/GRY, C/1030, enfranchisement 26 Mar. 1793.

[37] Ibid.

[38] Deeds of Bridge House, Water St., Martock, *penes* Mr. F. J. Banfield, Martock; S.R.O., DD/WY, map of Martock 1811.

[39] Burke, *Land. Gent.* (1894), i. 781; S.R.O., DD/PLE, box 104, abstr. of title 1883; sale cat. 1883.

[40] *Western Gazette* (3rd edn.), 22 June 1883; S.R.O., DD/PLE, box 48, requisitions on title 1911; ex inf. Mr. A. H. Lovegrove, Yeovil.

[41] S.R.O., DD/MR 92.

[42] Ibid. 33, lease 19 Mar. 1661/2, settlement 25 Oct. 1667; 97.

William Merifield sold his half to John Donne (d. 1768) of Crewkerne in 1743,[43] and James Donne (d. 1783), son of John, ordered in his will that his Martock lands should be sold.[44] The manor has not been traced thereafter.

The manor-house, dovecot, and garden, valued at 16s. 8d. in 1302,[45] all lay within the moated area of nearly 2 a. west of the churchyard. By 1506 the pasture within the moat was let and the dovecot was ruinous.[46] Lord Morley and Monteagle leased the mansion and manor-house, called Court House, to Anthony Parsons of Martock c. 1592, and Parsons assigned it to Francis Dyer of Sharpham Park in 1613. After Dyer's death in 1615 his widow married Barnaby Leigh of Shorwell (I.W.) and the lease was assigned to Edward Cheeke in 1619, and to Bray Vincent (d. 1642), a Martock clothier, in the same year.[47] In 1633 Vincent occupied a part of the house 'almost all let to ruin'.[48] The court-house formerly held by Vincent was mentioned in 1699, and the court-house 'moated round with water' after 1730,[49] but these references may relate to the small building which stands on the eastern edge of the moated area and bears a stone inscribed 'Robert Wills, 1659'.

'The Manor House' in Church Street, built probably in 1679, was the home of the Goodden family before they acquired the manor in the early 19th century, and was probably so named after its occupants purchased the lordship. It was burnt down in 1879 but rebuilt.[50]

A chaplain was celebrating in the lord's chapel by 1294.[51] In 1334 it was licensed for divine service,[52] and before 1411 rents supported a chantry there.[53] By 1506 a chantry had been established there for the souls of the second son of Humphrey Stafford, duke of Buckingham, Thomas Stanley, earl of Derby, and for Margaret, countess of Richmond. It was then stated that the 'Chapel Close' had been annexed to the chantry since 1481 to provide wine and wax.[54] The chaplain in 1548 was paid partly from the manor and partly by the inhabitants in the form of churchyard wheat.[55] The last incumbent, Stephen Nurse, evidently remained in the parish until his death in 1571.[56] The chapel, dedicated to the Virgin by 1411 and standing near the manor-house, was pulled down c. 1541 and sold. By 1595 a building called Stoneheald, later Stonehill or Stoneley, House had been erected there,[57] its name suggesting the possible re-use of materials from the demolished chapel. The house was last mentioned in 1706.[58]

The treasurers of Wells cathedral exchanged the church of Evercreech with the bishop of Bath for half the rectory of Martock in 1226.[59] This they continued to hold until it was transferred in 1849 to the Ecclesiastical (now the Church) Commissioners.[60] The treasurer's holding was valued at £33 6s. 8d. in 1291 and at £30 17s. 11d. in 1334.[61] As owner of the greatest portion of the church he was deemed liable to repair the chancel and its ornaments by 1322.[62]

Before 1535 the estate and tithes had been leased; in 1539 to Christopher Newton of Westminster, assigned before 1568 to one Baily.[63] A lease was granted to the Crown in 1602, which in turn sub-let to Roger Townsend of London and Humphrey Flint of Cheshunt (Herts.). This lease was assigned in 1624 to Sir William Ashton of St. Martin-in-the-Fields (Mdx.). He was succeeded by his son William (d. 1651), who left it to his brother Robert Ashton.[64] It passed from Robert to William Ashton c. 1688, and he held it until the lease expired in 1701.[65] In 1701 the treasurer, Ralph Barker, leased the estate to his brothers, Francis and Robert Barker of London, who by 1726 had been succeeded by Robert's son and son-in-law, Robert Barker and Francis Hurdd of London. In 1726 Robert Barker sold his half share to Hurdd, who in 1742 granted it to his mortgagees, Elizabeth Hudson and Nathaniel Pix. It was known as the manor of *MARTOCK RECTORY* by 1741.[66] From c. 1748 it was held by one Lee, possibly Barnabas Eveleigh Leigh, then lord of Stapleton manor.[67] A new lease was made to Sarah Hope of Maidstone in 1767 with covenants to repair the chancel of the church and to entertain the treasurer or his agent for two nights and a day every quarter.[68] A lease was made to Sarah Hope's devisees in 1789, it was held in 1805 by Edward Hill of Whitton in Twickenham (Mdx.), and two leases under similar terms were granted in 1813 and 1821 to the Revd. Elias Taylor of Shapwick.[69] Taylor (d. 1827) left the estate to his grandson William Robert Warry (d. 1873), whose executors continued to administer the manor until 1883,[70] when the property reverted to the present lords, the Church Commissioners.[71]

The rectorial tithes held by the treasurer in 1226 comprised those on hay, cash offerings, cows, wool, lambs, cheese, and eggs at Easter.[72] In 1334 tithes

[43] S.R.O., DD/MR 33, conveyance 15 Jan. 1729/30; 71, genealogical notes; 95.
[44] Ibid. 71, genealogical notes, copy will of James Donne.
[45] G. W. Saunders, *Hundred of Martock* (1935), 106.
[46] S.C. 6/Hen. VII/1236.
[47] S.R.O., DD/MR 92, cover of ct. bk.; *Som. Wills*, ed. Brown, vi. 61.
[48] *S.R.S.* xv. 126; S.R.O., D/P/mart 2/1/1.
[49] S.R.O., DD/MR 33, 95.
[50] S.R.O., DD/SAS, map of Martock 1824; D/P/mart 3/2/3; 13/2/5, 6; Saunders, *Hund. of Martock*, 11. Date stone, 1679, H. & E. G. on gable.
[51] S.C. 6/1127/16.
[52] *S.R.S.* ix. pp. 179–80.
[53] C 137/80/44.
[54] *S.R.S.* xlix, p. 136; S.C. 6/Hen. VII/1236.
[55] *S.R.S.* ii. 110–11, 293–4.
[56] S.R.O., D/P/mart 2/1/1.
[57] C 137/80/44; *S.R.S.* ii. 110–11, 293–4; S.R.O., DD/MR 92; D.R.O., D 203/B 87.

[58] S.R.O., DD/MR 33.
[59] *H.M.C. Wells*, i. 36–7, 51.
[60] S.R.O., D/P/mart 1/7/1.
[61] *Tax. Eccl.* (Rec. Com.), 197; *Feud. Aids*, iv. 403; E 179/169/14.
[62] *S.R.S.* i. 202.
[63] *H.M.C. Wells*, ii. 251; S.R.O., D/D/Ca 40.
[64] Deeds of rectory *penes* J. Stevens Cox, St. Peter Port, Guernsey; Lambeth Palace MSS., COMM. XIIa/1/198–206; *Visit. Beds.* (Harl. Soc. xix), 76–7.
[65] S.R.O., D/P/mart 13/2/1–2.
[66] S.R.O., D/P/mart 13/2/3; DD/SB 5/1, 5/3; DD/CC 209907.
[67] S.R.O., D/P/mart 13/2/3.
[68] S.R.O., DD/CC 5072–3.
[69] Ibid. 5075–6; DD/SB 38/3.
[70] Burke, *Land. Gent.* (1937), 2372; S.R.O., DD/CC 5077–8, 209909.
[71] S.R.O., DD/CC 209909.
[72] *H.M.C. Wells*, i. 36–7.

of corn were valued at £10 13s. 9d., those of milk at £2, and oblations and small tithes (evidently not then appropriated to the vicar) at £12 16s. 8d.[73] In 1650 the rector's tithe on corn, grain, hemp, and flax produced £245, and that of wool, lambs, and hay £55. From the 16th to the 19th centuries the collection of the treasurer's tithes was leased with the rectorial estate. A tithe rent-charge of £799 15s. was granted to the lessee in 1841.[74]

There was a parsonage house and a dovecot in 1226.[75] In 1262 the treasurer purchased a plot of land 80 ft. long and 40 ft. broad on the east side of his 'barton' and in 1293–4 spent money on a 'new hall'.[76] The chamber over the chief gate was referred to in 1482.[77] The house, known in the early 19th century as Martock Priory and only recently as the Treasurer's House, was evidently leased with the manor of Martock Rectory and sub-let. It was sold to H. St. George Gray (d. 1963) in 1942, and was left by Mrs. Gray to the National Trust in 1970.[78] At the centre of the present building are the almost complete hall and cross-wing range of a medieval house. The cross-wing has on its first floor a west window of the later 13th century, which may have lit the solar, whilst the hall is probably that described as 'new' in 1293–4, perhaps the result of a rebuilding or remodelling of an older predecessor. In the late 15th or early 16th century a kitchen range was built alongside, projecting west beyond the solar, and the hall was reroofed. At about the same time the ground floor of the solar range was remodelled, a fire-place being inserted, new windows were put into the west wall, and a gateway was built adjacent to the road. In the post-medieval period the building was sub-divided and additional cottages were built to the north and east. Those to the north, which abutted the hall gable, have now been demolished, and the latter form the kitchens of the reunited house.

The abbey of Mont St. Michel (Manche) had an interest in the rectory from 1156 and established its claim to one half in 1226.[79] The estate was administered by the abbey's daughter house, Otterton priory (Devon).[80] In 1414 the property was taken by the Crown as alien and was granted in 1461 to Syon abbey (Mdx.); Syon continued to hold it until the Dissolution.[81] By 1479 the property was known as the manor of MARTOCK PRIORY.[82]

A Crown lease of the 'rectory and church', probably half the great tithes, was sold to John Ellis in 1569 and assigned to Leonard Doddington

in 1581.[83] By 1601 Sir Robert Cecil (cr. earl of Salisbury 1605) had bought the fee and in 1602 let the tithes and shares in the tithe barn.[84] Half the great tithes, held under the Crown, continued in the hands of the earls of Salisbury until 1788 when most were sold off to the owners.[85] William Wood, a Martock clothier, bought half the tithes on all the arable lands in Stapleton tithing in 1790, and conveyed them to the lords of Stapleton manor in 1797, but most were acquired in smaller lots.[86] In 1841 15 private owners were awarded rent-charges totalling £182 11s. 10¼d., the principal owner being William Robert Warry, who received £100 5s.[87]

The lands of the manor of Martock Priory were probably fragmented at the Dissolution, but property in Coat and Martock formerly of Syon abbey was in 1543 granted by the Crown to Humphrey Collis and sold by him to Richard Buckland of Martock (d. 1557).[88] These lands passed successively to Richard's nephews John (d. 1563) and Thomas (d. 1584) of West Harptree, and then to Thomas's son Francis (d. 1642).[89] John Buckland of West Harptree (d. 1678), son of Francis, left his 'manor of Martock' to his daughter Elizabeth (d. 1697), wife of John Bluet (d. c. 1700), who died without issue.[90] The lands then passed to Buckland's cousin, Charles Buckland of Lewes (Suss.).[91] The latter's son John died without issue and the property devolved on Maurice Buckland (d. 1710), whose son Maurice held it in 1741.[92] The estate has not been noted thereafter.

The manor of STAPLETON was probably subinfeudated before the grant of Martock manor to Eustace, count of Boulogne. It was held in the later 12th century by Sir Robert de St. Clare (I), passing in 1195 to his son William, and by 1212 to the latter's brother Geoffrey de St. Clare.[93] Geoffrey held it by the serjeanty of holding or carrying a towel (manutergium) before the queen at Easter or, later in the 13th century, alternatively of providing a serjeant for the king's army.[94] By 1308 the towel was to be so held at Easter, Whitsunday, Christmas, and at the Coronation, but by 1336 the tenure was reduced to the petty serjeanty of finding an armed horseman for the king.[95] From 1359 it was held in chief for ½ knight's fee.[96]

The manor passed to Geoffrey's son Robert de St. Clare (II) in 1223, and later to Robert (III) (d. 1308).[97] The latter was succeeded by his grandson Robert (V) (d. 1336), son of Robert (IV), and then by his great-grandson Robert (VI) (d. 1359).[98]

[73] E 179/169/14.
[74] S.R.O., tithe award.
[75] B.L. Add. Ch. 19067; H.M.C. Wells, i. 36–7.
[76] H.M.C. Wells, i. 446; S.C. 6/972/30.
[77] Saunders, Hund. of Martock, 111.
[78] S.R.O., DD/CC 209907. The building is described as Martock Priory in 1850: Taunton Castle, Braikenridge Colln., watercolours by W. W. Wheatley; Proc. Som. Arch. Soc. cxiv. 122.
[79] Cal. Doc. France, ed. Round, pp. 268–9; H.M.C. Wells, i. 36–7, 51, 449, 452. See below, plate facing p. 145.
[80] Tax. Eccl. (Rec. Com.), 197.
[81] Cal. Pat. 1461–7, 97; Valor Eccl. (Rec. Com.), i. 425.
[82] Saunders, Hund. of Martock, 108.
[83] Cal. Pat. 1572–5, p. 301; C 66/1260.
[84] D.R.O., D 396, box 1, survey bk. c. 1602; Hist. MSS. Com. 9, Salisbury, xi, pp. 302, 333, 390; xii, pp. 35, 54; Cal. S.P. Dom. 1601–3, 260.

[85] e.g. S.R.O., DD/PLE, box 49, conveyance 6 Aug. 1804; box 50, conveyance 3 July 1788; D/P/mart 13/2/5.
[86] S.R.O., DD/S/HR, box 2, conveyance 27 May 1790; box 45, conveyance 4 July 1797.
[87] S.R.O., tithe award.
[88] L. & P. Hen. VIII, xviii (1), pp. 196–7; C 142/114/39.
[89] C 142/114/39; Cal. Pat. 1560–3, 145; C 142/135/24; C 142/206/30; S.R.O., DD/SAS, Brown wills.
[90] S.R.O., DD/SAS, Brown wills; DD/SF 948.
[91] S.R.O., DD/SF 948.
[92] S.R.O., DD/SH 107.
[93] S.R.S. xiv. 66–7; Pipe R. 1195 (P.R.S. N.S. vi), 233; Bk. of Fees, i. 84–5, 262.
[94] Bk. of Fees, i. 84–5; Cal. Inq. Misc. i, p. 142.
[95] Cal. Inq. p.m. v, p. 66; viii, pp. 23–4.
[96] Ibid. x, pp. 443–4.
[97] Ex. e Rot. Fin. (Rec. Com.), i. 97; Cur. Reg. R. xii, pp. 20–1; Feud. Aids, iv. 282; Cal. Inq. p.m. v, p. 66.
[98] Cal. Inq. p.m. v, p. 66; viii, pp. 23–4.

Robert (VI) was succeeded by his son Richard St. Clare (d. 1362),[99] who settled the reversion on William Bonville (d. 1408).[1] Bonville's grandson William, Lord Bonville (d. 1461), inherited it in 1408 and it later passed to his great-granddaughter Cecily, wife successively of Thomas, marquess of Dorset (d. 1501), and Henry, earl of Wiltshire (d. 1523).[2] Thence it descended in turn to her son and grandson, Thomas, marquess of Dorset (d. 1530), and Henry, duke of Suffolk, until the latter's attainder and execution in 1554.[3]

The manor was granted in 1563 to William Rosewell (d. 1566), solicitor-general, who was succeeded in turn by his sons Parry (d. 1573) and William (d. 1593).[4] In 1586 the last mortgaged Stapleton to William Every (I), and in 1594 William Rosewell's widow Ann and her second husband, John Davies, sold it to Every's son and grandson, John and William (II) (d. 1652) of Cothay, Kittisford.[5] A claim by Sir Henry Rosewell, William's son, was finally released in 1622.[6] John Every of Cothay (d. 1679), grandson of William (II), left the manor to his sister Ann, wife of John Leigh (d. 1688) of Northcourt, Shorwell (I.W.).[7] John Leigh was followed by his son John, and by 1743 by Barnabas Eveleigh Leigh, who was succeeded by his uncle, John Leigh (d. 1772).[8] John's five daughters and coheirs together sold the manor in 1796 to Thomas Richards of Evershot (Dors.) and William Haggett Richards of Kingsbury Episcopi, between whom it was divided.[9]

Thomas Richards (I) (d. 1827) left his half equally between his sons William (d. 1835) and Thomas (II) (d. 1866). The lands were partitioned in 1857, William's daughter Ellanette, wife of John Glyde of Yeovil, receiving 159 a. and Thomas (II) and his son Thomas (III) 185 a. including Stapleton Mead farm.[10] William Haggett Richards (d. 1860) of Stapleton House left his half to his three sons E. E., W. H., and J. W. Richards.[11] The manor is not referred to thereafter.

There was probably a manor-house by the late 13th century, when Robert de St. Clare (III) had a chapel 'in his courtyard', and a garden and dovecot were mentioned in 1308 and 1336.[12] In 1336 the manor-house complex included two chambers by the chapel on the north side of the hall with a solar next to the chapel, a newly-built house opposite the chambers on the west, a little chamber by the same house on the east, a chamber over the gate on the south, a bakehouse, middlehouse, and dairyhouse, with an oxhouse by the highway.[13] In 1525 the site of the manor and dovecot with 55½ a. of land were leased to Robert Dyer, and in 1563 John Fanstone took a lease of the court-house, dovecot, and lands of 6½ a., then occupied by John Dyer.[14] It was probably this court-house that Joan Lavor held in Stapleton manor in 1645, when she surrendered the kitchen, kitchen chamber, and half the northern entry to her son John. A house 'late Lavours called Court House' occurs in 1821.[15] This site on the north-west corner of Stapleton Street and West Street,[16] is now a field and probably represents the position of the medieval house.

In the late 13th century the rector of Martock and the abbey of Mont St. Michel held a virgate of arable and 3 a. of meadow of the gift of the 'old' Robert de St. Clare, in return for maintaining a chantry in the chapel of Stapleton.[17] Robert de St. Clare (V) had licence to hear divine service there in 1334, and in 1525 a customary tenant of the manor supplied wax for use there.[18] From 1535 the chapel was evidently annexed to Martock vicarage.[19]

Between 1154 and 1184 Pharamus of Boulogne as lord of Martock manor granted to the Knights Templar lands in Lade[20] later known as the manor of *LONG LOAD*. On the suppression of the order the manor was given to the Hospitallers in 1332 and by 1338 was regarded as a member of the preceptory of Temple Combe.[21] The order was suppressed in 1540 and in 1551 the Crown granted the manor to Winchester college, owners in 1974.[22]

A ruined house on the property, probably the manor-house, occurs in 1338.[23] It is not mentioned thereafter.

Richard of Boulogne, probably member of a cadet branch of the principal lords of Martock, held a free tenement at Ash between 1254 and 1286.[24] Lands there are referred to in 1288-9 as 'Essebolon',[25] subsequently known as the manor of *ASH BOULOGNE*, and in 1306 the estate was granted by Pauline of Boulogne to Peter of Boulogne, probably her son. It then comprised a house, two carucates, and rents,[26] and was evidently held by Peter in 1310.[27] John of Boulogne occurs in 1318 as holding lands in Milton,[28] but land in Ash seems to have descended through Peter's daughter Joan to Hugh Paveley by 1388.[29] In 1421 Richard Paveley recovered dower in Ash Boulogne,[30] and in 1430

[99] *Cal. Pat.* 1350-4, 119; *Cal. Inq. p.m.* x, pp. 443-4.
[1] *Cal. Pat.* 1358-61, 429; *Cal. Inq. p.m.* xii, p. 233; xiii, pp. 62, 177-8; *Cal. Close*, 1369-74, 491.
[2] *Cal. Pat.* 1408-13, 115, 147; *Complete Peerage*, s.vv. Dorset, Wiltshire.
[3] C 142/53/4; *Complete Peerage*, s.vv. Dorset, Suffolk.
[4] C 142/143/22; C 142/163/14; C 142/237/126.
[5] *Palaeography, Genealogy, and Topography*, ed. H. R. Moulton (1930), 231.
[6] Ibid. 232; C.P. 25(2)/347/19 Jas. I Hil.
[7] *Proc. Som. Arch. Soc.* lviii. 66; Hutchins, *Hist. Dors.* iii. 746-7; *Som. Wills*, ed. Brown, i. 20, 76; S.R.O., DD/BR/we, C/325, lease 31 Dec. 1675; DD/X/WE, C/546, lease 29 Sept. 1691.
[8] C.P. 43/443 rot. 10; *V.C.H. Hants*, v. 280; Burke, *Commoners*, ii. 599.
[9] Burke, *Commoners*, ii. 599; S.R.O., C/C 2/2.
[10] S.R.O., C/C 2/2.
[11] Ibid. SH 4.
[12] C 134/10/9; C 135/47/15.
[13] *Cal. Inq. p.m.* viii, p. 45.
[14] E 315/385; E 310/23/127 no. 36.

[15] S.R.O., DD/S/HY, box 3, ct. bk. 21 Oct. 1645; DD/S/HR, box 19, partition 2 Oct. 1821.
[16] S.R.O., DD/S/HR, survey and map, Stapleton manor 1774.
[17] *Cal. Inq. Misc.* i, p. 142.
[18] *S.R.S.* ix, p. 181; E 315/385.
[19] *Valor Eccl.* (Rec. Com.), i. 199, 225.
[20] *S. & D. N. & Q.* xxi. 91.
[21] *Cal. Close*, 1330-3, 514; *Hospitallers in Eng.* (Camd. Soc. 1st ser. lxv), 184.
[22] *Cal. Pat.* 1550-3, 160; ex inf. the archivist, Winchester Coll.
[23] *Hospitallers in Eng.* 184.
[24] *S.R.S.* xi, pp. 438-9; xxxvi. 22-3; *Feud. Aids*, iv. 282.
[25] *S.R.S.* vi. 277.
[26] Ibid. 348-9.
[27] Ibid. xii. 20. The reference to Pauline Asch in 1316 probably relates to Pauline of Boulogne at an earlier date: *Feud. Aids*, iv. 327.
[28] S.R.O., DD/S/HY, box 6, grant 18 Dec. 1318.
[29] *Pedigrees from the Plea Rolls*, ed. Wrottesley, 172.
[30] *S.R.S.* xxii. 57.

sold the manor to Hugh Kene, his wife Agnes, and their son William. On the death of William in 1467 it passed to his son Anthony Kene.[31] Later it was acquired by the Hody family, William Hody of Pilsdon (Dors.) (d. 1535) settling it on his son Richard (d. 1536) in 1524.[32] Thereafter it descended to Richard's son William and, in turn, to William's sons Henry and Richard Hody.[33] In 1621 Richard's widow Grace and her two daughters sold it to their cousin John Hody, who evidently enfranchised it in the following year.[34] 'Ash Boulogne', a house with traditional passage-entry plan of the 17th century, remodelled in the 18th century, is said to represent the former manor-house.

Joan widow of Richard Pyke (I) received a life grant of lands in Ash and Loxhill from her son Richard (II) (later Sir Richard) in 1309,[35] probably part of an estate formerly held by her husband. In 1333 the property comprised 3 houses, a mill, 1½ carucate, and 18 a. of meadow in Ash Boulogne, and in 1348 included the manor of *LOXHILL* with a carucate.[36] Sir Richard's son, Richard (III), had succeeded by 1356, and the latter's son, John Pyke, by 1371, the estate being described in 1372 as the manor of *ASSHEPYK* with its members of Witcombe and Loxhill.[37] In 1382 John's widow, Isabel (d. 1411), granted a life interest in her lands in Loxhill to her brother-in-law Hugh Pyke, who was holding court for the manor of Ash Boulogne in 1406, and in 1412 Hugh held lands in *PYKESASH*, thereafter the name of the manor.[38] He was still holding the manor in 1434, and it was later settled on his son Thomas and the latter's wife Alice. It was held under the principal manor of Martock in 1499 and 1608.[39]

Alice (d. 1499), married secondly to William Montague, surrendered her interest to her son John Pyke the elder, who granted it to his brother John Pyke the younger in 1496.[40] Part of the estate was then settled on John Pyke the elder (d. 1520–1) and the whole manor eventually came to his son William (d. 1523) and grandson Robert Pyke (d. 1531).[41] In 1551 Robert's son Thomas (d. 1555) settled the manor on his daughter Elizabeth and her intended husband Richard Broughton of Basildon (Berks.).[42] Broughton quitclaimed the manor to John Popham in 1563, and Elizabeth's second husband, James Leigh alias Reynolds, conveyed it to Popham in 1568.[43] Elizabeth, married thirdly to Anthony Stracheleigh, continued to claim an interest in the

estate but Sir John Popham, attorney-general, died seised of the manor in 1607.[44] His son Francis Popham (d. 1644) was followed successively by his younger son Alexander (d. 1669), and then by Alexander's son Sir Francis (d. 1674). Sir Francis left the manor to his son Alexander Popham of Littlecote in Ramsbury (Wilts.) (d. 1705). The last was succeeded by his uncle Alexander, and later by the latter's son Francis Popham, who in 1727 sold the manor to Andrew Napper of Tintinhull (d. 1770). Andrew's son Edward Berkeley Napier (d. 1799) was followed in turn by his son Gerard Martin Berkeley Napier (d. 1820) and grandson Edward Berkeley Napier.[45] The last sold it to Augustus Langdon of London in 1835, who conveyed it to John Batten of Yeovil in 1839.[46] Much of the lands were then enfranchised, although a customary payment of £2, formerly paid to the lord of Pykesash, was still being made to Manor farm in Ash in 1910.[47] No manor-house has been traced, although the above reference to Manor Farm, a house with traditional plan and passage entry of the 17th century, may indicate that it was the former capital messuage.

Lands in Witcombe were held with the manor of Pykesash by 1316.[48] John Popham, lord of Pykesash, granted lands in Witcombe to James Leigh alias Reynolds in 1576, and James in 1588 conveyed the manor of *WITCOMBE* to James Elliott of West Monkton.[49] John Elliott in 1600 conveyed the manor to John Every and his son William.[50] Later the manor descended with that of Stapleton.

A second manor of *WITCOMBE* emerged in the 15th century from the holding of the Witcombe family, who occupied lands in the hamlet from the 13th century.[51] John Witcombe (d. 1527), son of John, settled the manor on his brother William in 1521,[52] and William was still granting leases on it in 1550.[53] Sir Edward Rogers of Cannington purchased lands known as the manor of *COAT* from William Hody and his son Richard in 1555 and evidently acquired Witcombe at about the same time. At his death in 1568 Sir Edward held the manor or manors of *WITCOMBE AND COAT*, which passed in turn to his son Sir George (d. 1582) and grandson Edward Rogers (d. 1627).[54] Edward was succeeded by his son Sir Francis (d. 1638), who settled the estate on his daughter Ann.[55] She conveyed it to her uncle Henry Rogers in 1663.[56] Henry died childless in 1672, the manor passing by

[31] *Cal. Close*, 1429–35, 58, 117, 130–1; *S.R.S.* xv. 208–9.
[32] C 142/58/33; C 142/58/34; Hutchins, *Hist. Dors.* ii. 233.
[33] Hutchins, *Hist. Dors.* ii. 233; S.R.O., DD/GB 45.
[34] S.R.O., DD/GB 45; DD/MR 38, conveyance 6 Mar. 1621/2; DD/PLE, box 49, conveyance 9 Mar. 1621/2.   [35] *S.R.S.* xii. 12.
[36] Ibid. 168; S.R.O., DD/S/HY, box 6, grant 16 Nov. 1348.
[37] S.R.O., DD/S/HY, box 6, confirmation 8 May 1356, grant 5 Oct. 1371, power of attorney 30 July 1372.
[38] Ibid. grants 10 Dec. 1382, 7 Jan. 1405/6; *S.R.S.* xvi. 44.
[39] *Cal. Inq. p.m. Hen. VII*, ii, pp. 187–8; C 142/303/128.
[40] *S.R.S.* xxii. 191; *Cal. Inq. p.m. Hen. VII*, ii, pp. 187–8.
[41] C 142/41/26; C 142/52/115.
[42] C 142/108/120.
[43] C.P. 25(2)/204/5 Eliz. I East.; C.P. 25(2)/204/10

Eliz. I Hil.
[44] E 134/5 Chas. I Trin./10; C 142/303/128.
[45] S.R.O., DD/PLE, box 52, conveyance 4 Apr. 1840; box 92, assignment 20 Feb. 1836.
[46] Ibid. box 92, conveyance 4 Apr. 1842; box 103, conveyance 12 Aug. 1839.
[47] Ibid. box 47, sale cat. 14 Nov. 1910.
[48] S.R.O., DD/S/HY, box 6, deeds of Witcombe.
[49] *Palaeography, Genealogy, and Topography*, ed. Moulton, 230–1.
[50] Ibid.; E 134/5 Chas. I Trin./10.
[51] *S.R.S.* vi. 205–6, 291–2; xxxvi. 57–8; xli. 137–8, 147, 221.
[52] *S.R.S.* xix. 262–3; E 150/915/6.
[53] *S.R.S.* xxvii. 273–86.
[54] C 142/148/28; C 142/197/52; C 142/440/91.
[55] *S.R.S.* lxvii, pp. 144–6; C 142/486/114. In 1639 Witcombe manor was held under Pykesash and Coat under Says Bonville: *S.R.S.* lxvii. 144–5.
[56] S.R.O., DD/PLE, box 50, conveyance 2 May 1710, with schedule of title deeds.

1709 to his great-nephew Sir John St. Barbe (d. 1723),[57] although it was also claimed by Henry's nephew, Alexander Popham, between 1697 and 1703.[58] Sir John left his estates to his cousin Humphrey Sydenham (d. 1757) of Higher Combe in Dulverton, and Humphrey's widow Grace was granting leases in 1758.[59] She assigned the manor to her son St. Barbe Sydenham in 1764, and in 1781 he settled it in marriage on his daughter Catherine and Lewis Dymock Grosvenor Tregonwell. In 1811 Tregonwell and his son St. Barbe sold it to Robert Leach (d. 1837) of Witcombe, and Leach's trustees conveyed it to Thomas Coggan of Bower Hinton and his sister-in-law Ann Coggan, widow of a Martock butcher. Thomas died in 1840, leaving his share to Ann, on whose death in 1843 the estate was fragmented.[60]

The manor-house, occupied in 1672 by John Fry, was sold in 1710 by Sir John St. Barbe to Robert Leach of Thorn Coffin and his son Robert. Robert Leach of Witcombe (d. 1780) left it to his cousin Robert Leach, a cordwainer of Ash, who reunited it with the manor in 1811.[61] A long 17th-century house, it was known in 1974 as Witcombe Manor Farm.

John le Jew and Joan his wife held lands in Coat in 1290 and John was a free tenant of ½ virgate in Martock manor in 1302.[62] He received a life grant of lands in Martock from Nicholas le Jew in 1321 and either he or a namesake occurs as a witness in 1332.[63] By 1336 he had been succeeded by William le Jew, probably his son. His lands were settled on John of Pilsdon (Dors.) for life with remainder to John Jew, son of William, and Alice daughter of John of Pilsdon and their joint issue.[64] John's successor, also John, occurs from 1378 and held lands in Martock and Coat in 1412.[65] On John's death c. 1416 his ultimate heir was his daughter Elizabeth (d. 1473), wife successively of Sir John Hody of Stowell (d. 1441–2) and Robert Cappes (will dated 1475).[66] From Elizabeth the Coat lands passed in turn to her son John Hody (d. 1497) and his son Andrew (d. 1517), who held them of the manor of Says Bonville.[67] Andrew's son and grandson, William and Richard Hody, sold the estate as the manor of *COAT* to Sir Edward Rogers in 1555, and it then descended with Rogers's manor of Witcombe.[68]

John de Say occurs as holding lands in Martock between 1321 and 1343.[69] His lands apparently descended to Sir Edmund Arundel, probably in right of Arundel's wife Sibyl, daughter of William Montacute, earl of Salisbury.[70] The Arundels' daughter Elizabeth (d. c. 1385) was married secondly to Sir John de Meriet (d. 1391), and his cousins and coheirs were Elizabeth and Margaret, daughters of Sir William d'Aumale.[71]

Elizabeth married first Sir John Mautravers (d. 1386) and in 1386 they held half an estate in Martock, Long Load, and 'Hull'.[72] She was married second to Sir Humphrey Stafford of Southwick (Wilts.) (d. 1413), and in 1391 they held half the manors of Martock and Load called *SAYES*.[73] The property continued in the Stafford family until the death of Humphrey Stafford, earl of Devon, in 1469, when it passed to his cousin and coheir Eleanor (d. 1501), wife of Thomas Strangways (d. 1484) of Stinsford (Dors.).[74] Her son Henry (d. 1504) was succeeded by his son Sir Giles (d. 1547) and great-grandson Sir Giles Strangways (d. 1562).[75] During the tenure of the last the manor became known as *MARTOCK SAYES*.[76] In 1586 Sir Giles's son John sold it to Ralph Hurding of Long Bredy (Dors.), and Ralph's son Henry conveyed it in 1621 to Nicholas Putt of Coombe in Gittisham (Devon).[77] Nicholas's son William was declared a lunatic in 1662 and the manor passed to his son, Sir Thomas Putt, Bt. (d. 1686).[78] His son, another Sir Thomas (d. 1721), left his estates to a cousin, Raymundo Putt (d. 1757), and Raymundo's son Thomas held the manor in 1759.[79] It is not subsequently mentioned.

Margaret, the other daughter of Sir William d'Aumale, married Sir William Bonville, to whom in 1385 Sir John de Meriet granted a house and land in Martock, Load, and 'Hull',[80] representing the second half of the Say estate. On Bonville's death in 1408 the property was called *SAYES PLACE*, but was subsequently known from its holders as the manor of *SAYS BONVILLE*.[81] It descended with the manor of Stapleton until granted by the Crown to Richard Dennys in 1561. Dennys sold it to Nicholas Halswell (d. 1564) in 1562.[82] Nicholas's son Robert (d. 1570) was succeeded by Sir Nicholas Halswell, but there is no further reference to the manor until 1694, by which date it had passed to Sir Thomas Putt, who held it with the other half of the Say estate. It may be the 'manor of Long Load' held by Raymundo Putt in 1755, probably purchased by Winchester college

---

[57] C.P. 25(2)/480/14 & 15 Chas. II Trin.; C.P.25(2)/962/8 Anne Trin.; W. Berry, *County Genealogies of Hampshire* (1883), 2.
[58] S.R.O., DD/PO 9, lease of lands in manor of Witcombe and Coat 12 Apr. 1697, warranting lessee against persons claiming under will of Henry Rogers; DD/POt 41, mortgage 22 May 1703.
[59] W. Berry, *County Genealogies of Hampshire* (1883), 2; S.R.O., DD/PLE, box 50, lease 16 Oct. 1758.
[60] S.R.O., DD/PLE, box 50, conveyances 12 June 1811, 18 Oct. 1837; box 84, wills of Thomas and James Coggan.
[61] Glos. R.O., D 1799/M 59; S.R.O., DD/PLE, box 50, conveyance 2 May 1710, will of Robert Leach 1780, conveyance 12 June 1811.
[62] S.R.S. vi. 278; C 133/105/3.
[63] S.R.S. xii. 89; H.M.C. Wells, i. 495.
[64] S.R.S. xii. 190–1, 193–4.
[65] Hutchins, *Hist. Dors.* ii. 228; *Feud. Aids,* vi. 506.
[66] Hutchins, *Hist. Dors.* ii. 228–9, 233.

[67] Ibid.; *Cal. Inq. p.m. Hen. VII*, ii, pp. 55–6; E 315/385.
[68] Hutchins, *Hist. Dors.* ii. 233; C.P. 25(2)/657/1 & 2 Philip & Mary East.
[69] S.R.S. xii. 87–8; *Cal. Pat.* 1343–5, 87.
[70] S.C. 6/Hen. VII/1236.
[71] *Proc. Som. Arch. Soc.* xxviii, ped. facing p. 101.
[72] Ibid.; *Cal. Close*, 1385–9, 164–5.
[73] S.R.S. xvii. 146–7.
[74] Hutchins, *Hist. Dors.* ii. 662.
[75] Ibid.; *Cal. Pat.* 1494–1509, 543.
[76] D.R.O., D 124, box 141, ct. roll; box 16, survey 1558.
[77] Ibid. box 86, conveyance 10 Oct. 1586; C 3/403/14; C.P. 25(2)/347/19 Jas. I Mich.
[78] C 142/524/37; *Complete Baronetage*, iv. 36.
[79] C.P. 43/705 rot. 253.
[80] *Proc. Som. Arch. Soc.* xxviii, ped. facing p. 101; S.R.S. xvii. 128.
[81] C 137/68/42; *Cal. Close*, 1500–09, 163–6.
[82] *Cal. Pat.* 1560–3, p. 305; Devon R.O. 1077 M/5/7; C 142/141/18.

in that year.[83] It is not mentioned thereafter, nor has any reference to a manor-house connected with either half been found.

Lands in Martock were held in 1243 and 1254 by Walter de Fauconberg, who had been succeeded before 1267 by Sir Peter de Fauconberg.[84] In 1286 Peter held 'the greater part' of the vill of Middleton, known by 1327 as the manor of *MILTON FAUCONBERG*, later as *MILTON FAWCON-BRIDGE*, and held of the manor of Martock as ½ knight's fee.[85] Peter had been succeeded before 1309 by William de Fauconberg (d. before 1333), who held the manor jointly with his wife Maud (d. 1349).[86] It then passed in turn to their son Robert, to Peter de Fauconberg (d. 1349), probably a younger son, and later to a cousin, Thomas Loterel.[87] By 1385 it was held by Thomas Beaupyne, a Bristol merchant, who then conveyed it to Sir Matthew Gournay (d. 1406).[88] Matthew's widow Philippe carried it to her third husband Sir John Tiptoft (d. 1443); and on Tiptoft's death it passed to the duchy of Cornwall which had earlier acquired a reversionary interest.[89] The manor was granted in 1445 to Edmund Beaufort, marquess of Dorset, and his male heirs, but was resumed by the Crown in 1449.[90] Henry Holand, duke of Exeter, was appointed keeper for ten years in 1450, but it was regained in 1452 by Edmund Beaufort, duke of Somerset (d. 1455).[91] The manor subsequently passed to the duke's widow in 1456, and in 1457 to her son Henry, duke of Somerset (d. 1464).[92] On his death Milton was granted to George, duke of Clarence, but, like Stoke sub Hamdon, was reunited with the duchy of Cornwall, though held between 1482 and 1495 by William Herbert, earl of Huntingdon.[93]

Thereafter the manor was held by the Crown until 1557 when it was granted to Thomas Marrowe.[94] In the following year Marrowe sold it to Sir Thomas Dyer (d. 1565), whose son Edward was enfranchising lands there in 1570.[95] Edward still held the manor in 1594–5, but it was regained by the duchy of Cornwall after 1603 'when the tenements were again reduced to copyhold'.[96] During the Interregnum the manor was sold in 1651 to Richard Bovett of Taunton, reverting to the duchy at the Restoration.[97] The duchy held the manor in 1974.

There was probably a manor-house by 1287.[98] In 1545 the manor-house, occupied by Alice, widow of John Witcombe, was leased by the Crown to Paul Gressham.[99] A house and two closes called 'Guyldons', formerly occupied by William Witcombe, were granted by the Crown to William Beltes and Christopher Draper in 1554.[1] These were probably sold to Richard Buckland who held a capital messuage called 'Guyldons' at his death in 1557.[2] Richard left his Martock property to his nephew John Buckland (d. 1563), who settled his lands on himself and his wife Thomasine in 1561.[3] Thomasine married secondly Thomas Turbeville, from whom Isabel, widow of William Witcombe, was trying to recover her widow's estate in the copyhold in 1568. Turbeville claimed that William Witcombe had forfeited his copy for non-residence and that the property had been assigned by Turbeville to Robert Goodman.[4] The manor-house is not subsequently mentioned, but may have descended with the rectory lands held by the Buckland family.

In 1287 Peter de Fauconberg had licence to build a chapel and maintain a chaplain in his manor of Milton Fauconberg, 'because of his distance from the church and the floods between'.[5] The chapel can be identified with Court Cottage, immediately north of the former pound and south of the present village of Milton. It was built in the late 13th century and modified in the 15th century. A floor was subsequently inserted and the building was converted for domestic use, with various modifications of the 16th to 19th centuries. Undulations in the adjacent Court Field may suggest the site of the former manor-house.

Lands in Milton were held with the manor of Yeovilton by William Bonville (cr. Lord Bonville 1449), who settled them on his daughter Elizabeth and her husband William Tailboys (d. 1464).[6] They later descended with Yeovilton manor, being known as the manor of *MILTON* by 1516 and the manor of *MILTON FAWCONBRIDGE* in 1586.[7] The tenants owed suit of court to Yeovilton in 1674, and the lands totalled 96 a. in 1615 and about 54 a. in 1689.[8]

Robert de la Fenne, in succession to Hugh de la Fenne his father, held a free tenement at *FENNE* by 1275 and had the right to stray beasts there.[9] Robert still held a virgate of land there in 1302, but was evidently dead by 1315 when his daughter Margery's share in the estate was granted by her husband John de Morbathe to their son Henry.[10] In 1338 Henry and Christine his wife held the lands which later descended to Roger Flemyng and his wife Christine (probably widow of Henry de Morbathe), and to their daughter Joan, wife of

[83] C 142/154/86; C.P. 25(2)/898/6 Wm. and Mary Mich.; Winchester Coll. Mun. 12853.

[84] *S.R.S.* xi, pp. 292, 440–1; xxxvi. 15.

[85] *Feud. Aids*, iv. 282; *Cal. Pat.* 1327–30, 75.

[86] *S.R.S.* xii. 11; *Cal. Close*, 1333–7, 3; *Cal. Inq. p.m.* ix, p. 176.

[87] *Cal. Close*, 1333–7, 3; *Cal. Inq. p.m.* ix, p. 176.

[88] *Cal. Close*, 1385–9, 79.

[89] C 139/110/45; *Rot. Parl.* (Rec. Com.), iv. 141.

[90] *Cal. Pat.* 1441–6, 324; *Rot. Parl.* (Rec. Com.), v. 446.

[91] *Cal. Fine R.* 1445–52, 175, 182–3, 238; *Cal. Pat.* 1452–61, 18, 28.

[92] C 139/160/38; *Cal. Fine R.* 1452–62, 154; *Cal. Pat.* 1452–61, 390.

[93] *Cal. Pat.* 1461–7, 362; *V.C.H. Som.* iii. 239.

[94] *Cal. Pat.* 1555–7, 540–1.

[95] Ibid. 1557–8, 327; C 142/142/64; C 142/242/35; C 142/278/180.

[96] C 142/279/453; L.R. 2/207.

[97] D.C.O., Particulars and Contracts for sale of duchy revenues, 90.

[98] *H.M.C. Wells*, i. 450.

[99] *L. & P. Hen. VIII*, xx(1), p. 423.

[1] *Cal. Pat.* 1553–4, 336–8.

[2] C 142/114/39.

[3] *Cal. Pat.* 1560–3, 145.

[4] Req. 2/88/51.

[5] *H.M.C. Wells*, i. 450.

[6] *Cal. Inq. p.m. Hen. VII*, i, p. 299; *Complete Peerage*, s.v. Kyme.

[7] C 142/31/41; C 142/216/23. For descent of Yeovilton see *V.C.H. Som.* iii. 169.

[8] S.R.O., DD/PH 60; DD/WHh 1013.

[9] *S.R.S.* xli. 6–7; xliv. 155; *Rot. Hund.* (Rec. Com.), ii. 139; *H.M.C. Wells*, ii. 570. Grace de la Fenne was murdered at Martock in 1243: *S.R.S.* xi, p. 319.

[10] C 134/105/3; *H.M.C. Wells*, ii. 589.

Thomas Puf or Pyf.[11] Thomas and Joan granted them to Hugh and Margery Paveley in 1373, but by 1402 Hugh was dead and Margery had married Roland Rake.[12] In 1413 Margery Rake, widow, granted her estate to the chapter of Wells for the maintenance of the vicars choral there. In return masses were to be said daily in the cathedral for the souls of her parents and her two husbands.[13] By 1506 courts for the estate were being held with those for Haythorn, a small estate owned by the vicars in the adjacent parish of Kingsbury Episcopi, and the united properties became known as the manor of *FENNS AND HAYTHORN*.[14] During the Interregnum the manor passed into the hands of Ann Popham, but was regained by the vicars at the Restoration. At that time Fenns was extended at 60 a. and Haythorn at 26 a.[15] The manor passed to the present lords, the Church (formerly the Ecclesiastical) Commissioners, on their establishment in 1857.

Deeds were dated at Fenns from 1275, although a manor-house was not expressly mentioned until 1413.[16] A close called Hayes on the east side of the manor-house was mentioned in 1737, and its 'former' site was referred to in 1819.[17] It may, however, have been demolished before 1650 when the court baron was being held in a barn there.[18]

ECONOMIC HISTORY. The scattered nature of settlement in the parish created a number of self-contained communities which, although united in a single ecclesiastical unit until the 19th century, retained much of their individual identity. Agriculture formed the main basis of the economy, supported by a market from the 13th century, until cloth manufacture developed in the 18th century and engineering in the nineteenth. Industrial sites have been restricted to Bower Hinton, Hurst, and Martock, now continuously built up, and to the isolated Parrett Works; the rest of the parish has remained agrarian in character.

AGRICULTURE. The agrarian pattern of the parish was based partly on its tithings, most of which developed their own field systems, and partly on the manors, of which the largest, Martock, included the tithings of Martock, Bower Hinton, Hurst, Newton, and part of Coat. The development of these individual settlements is described below. Only with the decline or disappearance of the medieval manorial units during the 18th and early 19th centuries is it possible to describe more general developments in farming activity, though Ash, Milton, and Witcombe were united in their claims to pasturage in Kingsmoor, across the Parrett to the north, and one crop, beans, seems to have been characteristic of the whole parish. There

was a saying, recorded in the 18th century, 'take a Martock man by the collar and shake him, and you will hear the beans rattle in his belly'.[19]

Martock. The manor of Martock contained 38 hides in 1086, although it had gelded for only 13 T.R.E., and had land for 40 ploughs. The demesne accounted for 8 hides on which were 3 ploughs, 6 serfs, and 14 coliberts, and the remaining 30 hides were farmed by 65 villeins and 24 bordars with 28 ploughs. Stock included 36 swine and 284 sheep. There were 50 a. of meadow, pasture measuring a square league, and woodland a league long by two furlongs wide. A fishery worth 5s. was later leased with the two mills.[20] The render of the manor was £70 by tale and it was believed that it would have yielded £5 more if the bishop of Winchester had 'borne witness'. This additional sum probably represented the rectory estate. To the manor had been added 4 hides at Oakley in Chilthorne Domer, although the connexion is not mentioned thereafter. Two hides on this estate paid 50s. to Martock manor and the other two hides 40s. From the former manor were taken away $1\frac{1}{4}$ hide at Compton Durville in South Petherton and $1\frac{1}{2}$ hide at Westcombland in Buckland St. Mary,[21] although the latter estate continued to be regarded as part of the hundred and parish until the earlier 19th century.[22]

While the manor was still in the hands of the Crown Stapleton was probably granted to the St. Clare family, and in the 12th and 13th centuries under the Boulognes and their successors the subinfeudation of Long Load, Ash with Witcombe, and Milton Fauconberg took place.

The issues of the capital manor between Christmas 1205 and Michaelmas 1206 were £24 and the value was £40 a year by 1210–12.[23] It fell to £26 13s. 4d. in 1244 but, probably because of the market established in 1247, soared to £200 in 1275.[24] Net income from the manor totalled over £113 in 1293–4.[25] By 1284–6 5 small freeholds had been created in the manor, 4 of which together rendered 39s.,[26] and by 1302 there were 7 freeholds. In 1302 there were 77 life tenants; 6 men held one virgate each, 3 held $\frac{3}{4}$, 42 held $\frac{1}{2}$, 3 held $\frac{1}{3}$, and 16 held a quarter; and there were 41 cottars. Total rents and works were valued at £73 4s. $6\frac{1}{2}d$. The customary tenants were also obliged to make certain renders: 'Lukefyne', on St. Luke's day, church scot at Michaelmas in wheat, 67 lambs, called 'greslamb' in 1294,[27] at Midsummer, 112 capons and 100 hens at Martinmas, and 'Scotmust'. Two tenants paid rents in wax and chevage of boys was worth 5s. 6d. The demesne then included 447 a. of arable, $27\frac{1}{2}$ a. of meadow, and two pastures in severalty, and the whole manor was extended at £145 1s. $6\frac{1}{2}d$.[28]

The manor appears to be undervalued in 1344 at £113 14s. $4\frac{1}{4}d$. The demesne arable had then shrunk to 277 a., the meadow to 15 a., assized rents

[11] *H.M.C. Wells*, ii. 604–5, 632.
[12] Ibid. ii. 632–3, 654; *Feud. Aids*, vi. 506.
[13] *Cal. Pat.* 1413–16, 105; S.R.O., DD/CC 131910a/8.
[14] S.R.O., DD/CC 131910a/10, 131913a/8.
[15] S.R.O., DD/POt 151, survey 1658.
[16] *H.M.C. Wells*, ii. 570; *Cal. Pat.* 1413–16, 105.
[17] S.R.O., DD/CC 115341/5, 115348/2.
[18] Ibid. 116013.
[19] S.R.O., DD/SH 116.
[20] *Cal. Pat.* 1364–7, 92; *Cal. Close*, 1364–8, 489.

[21] *V.C.H. Som.* i. 440, 514.
[22] *Census*, 1841; S.R.O., tithe award.
[23] *Pipe R.* 1206 (P.R.S. N.S. xx), 126, 129; *Red Bk. Exch.* ii. 547.
[24] *Bk. of Fees*, ii. 1156; *Cal. Chart. R.* 1257–1300, 190–1.
[25] S.C. 6/1127/16.
[26] *Feud. Aids*. iv. 282–3.
[27] S.C. 6/1127/16.
[28] Saunders, *Hund. of Martock*, 103–7. A similar payment to 'Lukefyne' was made at Lopen.

had fallen to £48 10s. 2½d., and the value of works had been halved since 1302. The only increase in value was from the farm of demesne meadow and pasture.[29] A sum of £200 a year charged on the manor as security in 1355 and 1365[30] suggests undervaluing in the extents, as do the size of pensions granted from the manor to adherents of the earls of Salisbury between 1366 and 1371.[31] The stated income from the manor had risen only to £126 17s. 4d. by 1484.[32]

By 1508 the value of the manor was £181 0s. 8d. net. Assized rents totalled £51 2s. 8½d., with moveable and new rents adding a further £9 8s. 2d. Moveable rents included the earlier customary payments and other rents paid in geese, gloves, pepper, wax, cider, and, for a fishery at 'Bolewere' from Muchelney abbey, 26 sticks of eels. Labour services had all been commuted for money payments of £53 2s. 11d. Seed corn produced by threshing works was known as 'suleacresede' and carriage labour included the conveyance of timber from Westcombland and charcoal thence and from Neroche forest. A distinction between services due from cottars and sub-cottars was also made.[33]

There was a slight fall in income during the earlier 16th century, the clear value of the manor being given as £159 11s. 7¼d. in the period 1543–6, and the rents and perquisites totalled £174 16s. 3d. in 1555.[34] There were then in Martock tithing 7 free and 58 customary tenants, in Bower Hinton 1 free and 29 customary, in Hurst 5 free and 23 customary, in Newton 34 customary, and in Coat 1 free and 22 customary (the last including three tenants of Westcombland in Buckland St. Mary). Services due from five free tenants in Martock tithing included scouring the manor's half of Gawbridge pool and the stream to Madey mill, and the maintenance of the highway between Martock and Bower Hinton, but these were no longer performed in 1555.

The manor, excluding commons and wastes, then comprised about 3,160 a. with a further 96 a. at Westcombland.[35] Most of this land was sold by the Lords Morley and Monteagle in the earlier 17th century, the residue, 710 a. valued at £112, being conveyed with the lordship in 1637.[36] Subsequent lords enfranchised further lands, particularly William Strode c. 1720, Zachary Bayly c. 1740, and the Slades during the later 18th century.[37] Shortly before the manor was sold to Bayly there were 87 tenants holding 669 a. and paying rents of £39 2s. 8d.[38] Towards the end of Bayly's tenure c. 1755 the area had fallen to 156 a. in the hands of 74 tenants rendering lord's rents totalling £17 9s. 2¼d. This did not, however, include a further £31 12s. 1d. in quit-rents and £6 0s. 8d. in 'manor' rents.[39] By 1883 the manor consisted only of the Market House,

quit- and lord's rents of £29 11s. 11½d., with the tolls of the market and fair.[40]

Lands of about 115 a., including the manor- and church houses, were bought from Lord Morley and Monteagle by Robert Wills in 1633.[41] This estate, also known as the manor of Martock, had grown to about 180 a. by 1644 and to about 270 a. by 1730.[42] Soon after 1730 it was valued at £179 6s. but was subsequently dispersed.[43]

Fenns, which lay in Martock tithing but evidently enjoyed no common rights over Martock fields, comprised 15 a. of land and 4 a. of meadow in 1275.[44] In 1444–5 there were 10 tenants paying rents of £9 1s. 6d.,[45] but by 1515–16 rents had fallen to £7 7s. and by 1650 to £6 10s. from 7 copyhold tenants holding 59 a. of pasture.[46] The rental rose again to £7 7s. in 1658 but had fallen to £6 13s. 8d. by about 1750, when 4 of the tenants were leaseholders.[47] The area remained the same, being estimated at 56 a. c. 1850.[48] In 1444–5 the estate included 4 'sesters' in Chestermead at Ilchester for which 4s. a year was paid, but the meadow was under water at the time of mowing.[49]

Martock manor, comprehending the tithings of Martock, Bower Hinton, Hurst, Newton, and Coat, had three open-field systems. The inclosure of South and East fields in Martock tithing had recently begun in 1555[50] and evidently continued during the 17th and 18th centuries. Bower Hinton and Hurst had a common field system by the 15th century, new inclosures in East and West fields were recorded in 1555, and a 'recent' inclosure there was mentioned in 1720.[51] There were two open fields in Coat called Rogersham and Hetfurlong in 1243. These have not been identified within the three-field system which had developed by 1555.[52] Meadow land within the manor lay principally in Bower Hinton at Westover and Eastover meads, Averland (Overlands in 1841), and Hinton mead; in Coat at Coat mead and Coat Hay; and for Martock tithing at New mead and Southay, detached in the north-west of the parish, and in Bower (later Bow) and Corn meads, parts of which had been recently inclosed in 1555. Pasture land, other than over the open arable fields, was generally shared with other manors, principally at Wetmoor (Wattemore in 1254), Louseham, and Case. Grazing rights there were also held by Long Load and by Muchelney abbey, and in 1462 rents paid for laying birds' nets within the lord's warren at Wetmoor, Southay, Bower mead, and New mead were divided between the lord of Martock and the abbot of Muchelney.[53] Similarly Wetmoor and Louseham with the chase of beasts in New mead were leased to the tenants of Coat in 1496, and licences to fish, hawk, and fowl there, were granted to the same tenants in

29 E 149/9/24.
30 Cal. Close, 1354–60, 181–2; Cal. Pat. 1364–7, 177.
31 Cal. Pat. 1364–7, 318; 1367–70, 364; 1370–4, 97.
32 Ibid. 1476–85, 501.
33 S.C. 6/Hen. VII/1237.
34 S.C. 6/Hen. VIII/3049, 3052; L.R. 2/202.
35 L.R. 2/202.
36 C 54/3172 m. 38.
37 e.g. S.R.O., DD/SAS, C/77/19, enfranchisement 4 Aug. 1720; DD/PLE, box 50, enfranchisements 1740; DD/S/HR, box 2, enfranchisement 22 Oct. 1763.
38 S.R.O., DD/WY, box 85, rental c. 1739.
39 S.R.O., DD/PH 165.
40 S.R.O., DD/PLE, box 104, sale cat. 1883.

41 D.R.O., D 203/B 87.
42 S.R.O., DD/MR 33, settlement 15 Jan. 1729/30; 92.
43 Ibid. 95.   44 S.R.S. xli. 6–7
45 S.R.O., DD/CC 131910a/8.
46 Ibid. 131910a/10; 131913a/5; 16013.
47 S.R.O., DD/POt 151; DD/CC 116014.
48 S.R.O., DD/CC 115997.
49 Ibid. 131910a/8.
50 L.R. 2/202.
51 S.C. 6/972/18, which lists all Martock field systems, refers to 'Hyntonfeld' but not to Hurst; L.R. 2/202; S.R.O., DD/X/PAR 2, will of Thomas Rodbard 1720.
52 S.R.S. vi. 120; L.R. 2/202.
53 S.C. 6/Hen. VII/1237; S.R.O., tithe award.

1541 and 1550.[54] Parliamentary inclosure within Martock manor began in 1810 at Coat when River field and Turnpike field of 100 a. were allotted, and in 1826 the remaining open fields in Martock, Bower Hinton, Hurst, and Coat, with Wetmoor, Louseham, and Case, were inclosed. They amounted to 596 a. arable, 424 a. meadow, 2 a. pasture, and a further 535 a. at Wetmoor shared between Martock and Muchelney.[55]

Stapleton. The manor was valued at £40 in 1219,[56] and by 1308 the estate was worth £21 1s. 8¾d. The demesne included 210 a. of arable, 45 a. of meadow, and two pastures, one 'newly' inclosed, of 25½ a. One freeholder held three ¼-virgate plots, 17 men held one virgate, and six ¼ virgate, and there were 13 cottars. Their works and rents were worth £11 3s. 4¾d.[57] By 1336 the income from the manor had fallen to £14 17s. 4d., demesne arable had been reduced to 120 a., demesne meadow to 40 a., and the value of works had dropped.[58] Dower granted in that year included 53 a. of arable in 11 furlongs and 13½ a. of meadow.[59] By 1359 the manorial value had fallen slightly, but included customary renders similar to those of the main manor of Martock. Thirteen lambs were given at Midsummer, church scot of 21 capons and 43 hens was paid at Martinmas, and 11½ geese at Lammas, worth a total of 14s. 8½d. There were also two withy beds valued at 6s. 8d.[60] By 1525 the rental of the manor derived from 34 customary tenants had risen to over £30 issuing from 644 a. in Stapleton, with additional lands in Wearne and West Chinnock. Customary works or sums in lieu had lapsed and demesne lands, including the site of the manor-house, had been let.[61] Among manorial customs in 1565 women with widow's estate who remarried were to retain for each half yardland tenement a chamber within the house, 1 a. each of wheat and beans, ½ a. meadow of the 'second beast acres', common pasture for one beast, and grass for one beast from the common meadow. Apart from the provision of a chamber the quantities were halved for a farthing-land tenement.[62]

The manor was sold for £1,119 in 1563 and in 1654 had a rental of £37 13s. 1d. paid by 47 tenants.[63] In 1774 the manor had an extent of 842 a. composed of 18 tenements on leases for lives and 20 in hand.[64] Evidently leases were not being renewed so that a higher value could be placed on the estate when sold in 1796. The area of the property remained the same when partitioned between the two branches of the Richards family, Thomas Richards receiving 432 a. and William Haggett Richards 410 a.[65] The

two estates continued relatively intact until 1868 when the Glydes sold off most of their share.[66]

Stapleton had open arable in eleven furlongs by 1336.[67] A three-field system based on the cultivation of wheat and beans was in operation in 1642 and 30 years later the fields were being broken for pasture by agreement between the tenants.[68] Orders restricting grazing in the stubble fields and common meadow by horses and fowls were made in 1642, sheep were not to feed in the droves or fallow field without a keeper, and pigs were not to wander at large.[69] After the breach of Stapleton mead in 1674 tenants were only allowed to graze horses there if they had pasture for four beasts.[70] Parts of Green-moor were described as lately inclosed in 1642 and 1680, and grass haywards and tenants of beast leazes in the meadow were required to take the preys in 1679.[71] The remainder of the common fields and meadows were evidently inclosed during the 18th century, with the exception of 33 a. in East field still open in 1774 but probably allotted by 1790.[72]

Long Load. The manor was described as 10 librates and one virgate in the later 12th century.[73] In 1338 it was worth £14 5s., and included the demesne of 100 a. arable and 12 a. meadow. Assized rents produced 100s. a year and customary works of the *nativi* 31s. 8d.[74] Receipts had risen to £24 3s. 4¼d. by 1426–7 but by 1505 the rental stood at £17 1s. and in 1550–1 the total income from the manor was only £17 6s. 4d.[75] There were 1 free and 33 customary tenants in 1440, although the number of customary tenants had increased to 48 in 1505, consolidation of holdings again reducing this number to 26 in 1551.[76] The rental continued relatively stable during the 17th century, though during the Civil War and Interregnum considerable arrears accumulated.[77]

The pattern of farming was evidently one of gradual encroachment on the commons. The manor included about 145 a. of inclosed lands in 1551, of which 34 a. were then in hand.[78] By 1815, four years before the parliamentary inclosure, the manor amounted to 355 a., just over half the total area of the tithing, the remainder of which was divided between lands attached to the duchy of Cornwall's estate in Milton (110 a.), freeholders (70 a.), and commons and waste (123 a.).[79]

Long Load's arable fields continued relatively unchanged at least from the 16th until the early 19th century and had a rotation system based on wheat, beans, and fallow in the 16th and 17th centuries.[80] In the 17th century the manor court annually

[54] S.C. 6/Hen. VII/1237; L.R. 2/202.
[55] S.R.O., CR 97, 102.
[56] *Bk. of Fees,* i. 262; ii. 1384.
[57] C 134/10/9.
[58] C 135/47/15.
[59] C 135/49/18.
[60] C 135/148/10. An abrupt drop in assize rents from £4 8s. 6d. to £1 18s. 6d. in an inquisition of 1368 is probably a scribal error: C 135/203/2.
[61] E 315/385.
[62] C 3/85/46.
[63] *Cal. Pat.* 1560–3, pp. 571–2; S.R.O., DD/SF 355.
[64] S.R.O., DD/S/HR, survey in roll.
[65] S.R.O., C/C 2/2, conveyance 7 May 1801; DD/S/HR, box 19, partition 2 Oct. 1821.
[66] S.R.O., D/P/mart 5/3/1; C/C 2/2.
[67] C 135/49/18.
[68] S.R.O., DD/S/HY, box 3, ct. roll 26 Apr. 1642, 17 Oct. 1672.

[69] Ibid. 26 Apr. 1642, 11 Oct. 1642.
[70] Ibid. 19 Apr. 1675. Tenants of a half yardland had to pay 1s. each to repair the lower drove in 1674, and the meadow breach was again on St. Martin's day by 1683: ibid. 19 May 1674, 9 Oct. 1683.
[71] Ibid. 11 Oct. 1642, 13 May 1679, 1 May 1680.
[72] S.R.O., DD/S/HR, survey 1774; box 2, conveyance 27 May 1790.
[73] *S. & D. N. & Q.* xxi. 91.
[74] *Hospitallers in England* (Camd. Soc. 1st. ser. lxv), 184.
[75] Winchester Coll. Mun. 12862, 12864, 12875.
[76] Ibid. 12844–5, 12864.
[77] Ibid. 23053, 23055.
[78] Ibid. 12845.
[79] Ibid. map of Long Load 1815.
[80] Ibid. map of Long Load 1815; ibid. 12845, 12910.

granted to the lord the right to certain foreleazes and ridge-ends in Mare field for pasture, and in 1725 grazing in the stubble fields was computed as 3 a. to each horse and 1 a. to 3 sheep or a bullock.[81] The manor had an ancient right of common over the pastures known as Prestmoor and Wetmoor which divided Martock from Muchelney. In 1254 William de la Lade agreed with Muchelney abbey for his pasture in Wetmoor and the abbey's in Prestmoor, and a similar agreement was made in 1258 between the abbot and the lords of Long Load, when Prestmoor was ditched and thereafter deemed to lie within Muchelney parish.[82] Long Load also had rights in the adjacent commons of Louseham and Case, the cause of disagreements in 1505, again in 1562, when Winchester college sued the lord of Martock for molesting the tenants, and in 1567 when the Load tenants were excluded from Case.[83] The three pastures within Long Load tithing, Foremoor, Outmoor, and Rottenham, and the meadows of Barland and Gosham were enjoyed without such external interference. Barland inclosures were being made in 1507, although moves to inclose the other 'moors' in 1674 evidently did not proceed.[84] In 1552 Outmoor was being pastured by 37 tenants holding 204½ beast leazes.[85] In 1740 the lord of Martock again excluded Long Load from Wetmoor, impounded cattle, and levied 10s. on each beast 'as an acknowledgement of our being trespassers on the rights of Martock and Muchelney'. An attempt to inclose Wetmoor by Act of Parliament was made by Martock manor tenants in 1766, supported by such Load tenants 'as can keep a large stock and oppress their neighbours'.[86] In 1776 it was stated that the soil was 'remarkably deep, rich and good'. The arable was 'equal to any in the county', and the meadows were 'very fine', but lay near the river and were subject to floods which rotted the sheep and did the tenants 'a deal of hurt'. Outmoor was inclosed shortly before 1776 when ½ a. was allotted for each beast leaze.[87] The 3 open fields and Barland and Mare meadows, totalling 278 a., were inclosed in 1819.[88]

Tenants in 1552 were required to keep their animals in the withy beds until the breach of Outmoor, and in 1553 to keep only 3 sheep for each acre held within the manor between St. Luke's day (18 October) and the Exaltation of the Cross (14 September). In 1556 the driving of cattle over Barland and Rottenham was forbidden, and three years later tenants were allowed winter pasture in both areas according to their holdings, paupers with no land having grazing for a horse or mare.[89] In 1564 Foremoor was temporarily divided into 2-furlong closes to prevent the straying of sheep, and in 1567 tenants were allowed to keep only one

gander and not more than 4 geese.[90] In 1591 pigs were allowed to wander without a keeper only in the 'open season' from the breach of the fields until St. Luke's day, and overcommoning in 1653 incurred a fine of 5s. per bullock.[91] Strays unclaimed for a year and a day were to be sold by the lord from 1655, and at the breach of Foremoor in 1671 all beasts were to be removed within four hours.[92]

Ash. Of the two estates in Ash, Ash Boulogne comprised in 1432 7 houses, 2 carucates, 40 a. of meadow, and 20 a. of pasture.[93] Pykesash in 1309 had a house, 2 virgates of land, and 20 a. of meadow, and was valued at £27 a year in 1499.[94] By *c.* 1710 the Pykesash rental stood at £19 12s. 2d. with two bushels of wheat from Jeanes's tenement, and continued thus in 1726.[95] When Pykesash manor was sold in 1835 it had 431 a. of land, and chief rents of £3 3s. 6d. due from the manor of Witcombe and Coat formed part of its income in 1839.[96]

Ash had a three-field arable system by 1273.[97] Lands granted to Robert Mayne towards the south of the tithing were probably inclosed in the 14th century,[98] but otherwise the medieval field pattern continued relatively intact. Meadow lands at Longmead and Yellowmead, mentioned in 1622, were later consolidated as Ash mead, and both meadow and pasture had evidently been inclosed before the Act which allotted the three arable fields of 284 a. in 1810.[99]

Witcombe. The hamlet was treated regularly during the 14th century as a member of Pykesash manor, lands there being held directly of the lords of that manor.[1] During the 13th century, however, a prominent family of freeholders occurs who took their name from the tithing. In 1249 John of Witcombe granted 2¾ virgates to Walter of Witcombe, and in 1263 Pharamus of Witcombe conveyed 2 messuages and ½ virgate to Robert son of the same Walter.[2] The link with Ash and the use of the forename Pharamus, borne by the lord of Martock manor, Pharamus of Boulogne (d. 1183–4), suggests that the portion of Witcombe attached to Ash Boulogne was subinfeudated by the Boulogne family to a cadet branch which took its name from the holding.[3] Litigation in 1278 indicates that the estate was fragmented between Pharamus of Witcombe and his cousins, the four sons of Walter of Witcombe.[4] In 1347 it was claimed that a corrupt taxation assessment on the hamlet, resulting in Witcombe being taxed more heavily than Martock, had caused the depopulation of the tithing, all the inhabitants having left, with the exception of 5 poor men and the mesne tenants.[5]

Of the 2 manorial estates within Witcombe tithing, that held with Stapleton manor had a rental of £7 a year in 1629, and by 1654 4 freeholders and

[81] Winchester Coll. Mun. 23053, 6 May 1650, 18 May 1653, 10 Apr. 1654, 23 Apr. 1655; ibid. 12878; 12898.
[82] *S.R.S.* xiv, pp. 60–1.
[83] Winchester Coll. Mun. 12854, 12864, 12872.
[84] Ibid. 12862, 12877–8.
[85] Ibid. 12845.
[86] Ibid. 12880–2.
[87] Ibid. 21429a.
[88] S.R.O., D/P/mart 20/1/2.
[89] Winchester Coll. Mun. 12845.
[90] Ibid. 12870, 12872.
[91] Ibid. 12872, 23053.
[92] Ibid. 23053, 23055.
[93] *S.R.S.* xxii. 84.

[94] Ibid. xii. 12; *Cal. Inq. p.m. Hen. VII,* ii, pp. 187–8.
[95] S.R.O., DD/PO 50; DD/POt 120, 135.
[96] S.R.O., DD/PLE, box 92, conveyance 30 Dec. 1835; box 103, conveyance 12 Aug. 1839.
[97] *H.M.C. Wells,* i. 451–2.
[98] S.R.O., DD/S/HY, box 6.
[99] S.R.O., DD/MR 38; DD/SAS, map of Martock 1824; CR 97.
[1] S.R.O., DD/S/HY, box 6, deeds of Witcombe.
[2] *S.R.S.* vi. 140, 205–6.
[3] Ibid. 205–6. A reference to a Pharamus of Boulogne in the area in 1270 supports this view: ibid. xxxvi. 122–3.
[4] Ibid. vi. 291–2; xli. 137–8, 147, 221.
[5] *Cal. Pat.* 1345–8, 466.

13 leaseholders were paying rents of over £9.[6] The manor of Witcombe and Coat had an income of £25 9s. in 1604–5 derived from 23 tenants, and was stated to be worth £5 10s. 'by office' in 1639.[7] In 1672 the manor had an area of 494 a., including 40 a. in Ilchester, Broadway, Kingsbury Episcopi, and Crewkerne, held by 22 tenants rendering £22 11s. 9d. Perquisites considerably increased the value of the estate, for the total income in 1678 amounted to £115 15s. 5d.[8] The manor-house was sold off with 82 a. in 1710 and the manor with a further 116 a. in 1837 for £5,500.[9]

Witcombe evidently had an open-field system by 1359. Pasture in Oxleaze and meadow in the Hams were mentioned in 1316, as was meadow in Lynhull, now Lionels, in 1359, by which time the inclosure of Hams had begun.[10] Meadow in Shaldron (then Chaldron) mead was recorded in 1629, when lands in 6 furlongs in West field were listed.[11] Of 4 open arable fields enumerated in 1710 part were described in 1775 as being inclosed and laid down to pasture,[12] probably closes north of East field and north-east of the village. The remainder of the four arable fields, totalling 164 a., were inclosed by Act of Parliament in 1810.[13]

Milton. The manor of Milton Fauconberg did not include the whole tithing of Milton, part of which was held by Richard of Boulogne in 1284–6 with his manor of Ash.[14] In turn the lords of Milton acquired a house and 20 a. in Long Load from the Crown in 1329, and by 1349 also held a house and a virgate in Ash and other lands in Wearne near Langport.[15] The manor had an income of £13 13s. 1¾d. in 1442–3 and £21 16s. 6d. by 1456–7.[16] In the latter year the gross income of £25 1s. 9d. was made up of rents of £20 10s. 10d. (nearly half derived from lands in Long Load, Ash, Gildons, and overland in Milton) and the farm of pasture in 'Northmoor', Whatton, Newmead, 'Westlongedole', and elsewhere. Expenses included the repair of a fishery.[17] By 1476–7 receipts had risen slightly, due to increased pasture rents.[18] The value of the manor varied little from that time until the mid 16th century,[19] but increased fines brought the profit to £24 19s. 6d. in 1544–5.[20] During Elizabeth I's reign the manor 'was altogether dismembered, the most of the tenements granted in fee simple, the royalties remaining in her Majesty but the most of the rent suspended'.[21]

In 1610 the manor comprised 476 a. and rents of £24 13s. 8d.[22] In 1619 that part of Milton held with Yeovilton manor was extended at 96 a. held by 4 tenants paying 77s. 6d.[23] By 1650 there were 25 copyhold tenants and the rents and royalties, including felons' goods, hawking, and hunting, amounted to £23 7s. 3d.[24] At this time widows' estate in respect of one yardland consisted of a chamber in the house, 3 a. of wheat, 3 a. of beans, the first shear of 1 a. of meadow, 2 kine leazes in the commons, ⅓ of the fruit of orchards, firing, and running for one pig in the garden. Unlike Stapleton's custom, however, she was to lose her chamber if she remarried.[25] By 1776 the manor was valued at £454 2s. 3d., in 1784 £528, and by 1798 £598 7s.[26]

Milton tithing's three-field system, recorded in 1318, survived until the 19th century.[27] Inclosure of meadow and pasture appears to have taken place east of North field where fields called Newleaze and Hams occur. In the north former areas of meadow called 'Westlongedole' and 'Outmead' and pasture called Northmoor were divided into two triangular areas known as Milton Leaze and Milton mead.[28] In 1776 it was stated that, as in Ash and Long Load, a three-year arable rotation based on wheat and beans was still followed, and that the tenants never sowed turnips, barley, or clover. The soil was then described as 'fine, rich land', many of the tenants never manured their grounds, and others laid only 3–5 cartloads of dung to the acre. Some having sown wheat never harrowed it until the following spring and then only with a light harrow. The farmers were castigated for mismanagement and not improving the land, they kept few sheep which they never folded, and their oxen were 'poor, stunted things', eight being required to pull a plough normally drawn by six.[29] The duchy of Cornwall desired inclosure at Milton in 1798 but it was not until 1810 that the three arable fields, comprising 212 a., were inclosed by Act of Parliament.[30] Milton mead, however, was still divided into dole strips in 1841.[31]

Ash, Witcombe, and Milton all claimed pasture for sheep and horses in Kingsmoor, across the Parrett to the north. In the mid 16th century access to it was gained by means of Witcombe and Milton bridges, and c. 1583 it was claimed that the lord of Kingsmoor 'hath great wrong offered' him by the grazing of Martock sheep.[32] The lord of Somerton manor required 38s. 8d. a year for the grazing in 1555, and in 1631 the vicar of Somerton was claiming a proportion of tithe wool from Martock men appropriate to the length of time their beasts were grazing on Kingsmoor.[33] Suit to Kingsmoor court was paid by the three tithings at least until 1796,[34] and men from Martock were commonly amerced there

[6] E 134/5 Chas. I Trin./10; S.R.O., DD/SF 355.
[7] S.R.O., DD/BR/bn 10; *S.R.S.* lxvii, pp. 144–5.
[8] Glos. R.O., D 1799/M 59, L 12.
[9] S.R.O., DD/PLE, box 50, conveyances 2 May 1710, 24 Apr. 1837.
[10] S.R.O., DD/S/HY, box 6, deeds of Witcombe; *Palaeography, Genealogy, and Topography*, ed. H. R. Moulton, 231.
[11] S.R.O., D/D/Ct, K, will of William Keele 1629.
[12] S.R.O., DD/PLE, box 50, conveyance 2 May 1710, mar. settl. 10 Oct. 1775.
[13] S.R.O., CR 97.
[14] *Feud. Aids.* iv. 282.
[15] *Cal. Inq. p.m.* ix, p. 176. The Long Load property had been seized by the Crown from William the Marshal or de la Lade by reason of Jewry in 1291: *Cal. Inq. Misc.* i, p. 446.
[16] S.C. 6/974/9; S.C. 6/1095/7.
[17] S.C. 6/1095/7.
[18] S.C. 6/1123/3.
[19] S.C. 6/Hen. VIII/3034.
[20] S.C. 6/Hen. VIII/3036.
[21] L.R. 2/207.
[22] D.C.O., survey 1610.
[23] S.R.O., DD/PH 60.
[24] E 317/33.
[25] Ibid.
[26] D.C.O., surveys 1776, 1798.
[27] S.R.O., DD/S/HY, box 6; CR 97.
[28] D.C.O., survey 1610; S.C. 6/1123/3; E 317/33.
[29] D.C.O., survey 1776.
[30] D.C.O., survey 1798; S.R.O., CR 97.
[31] S.R.O., tithe award.
[32] S.R.O., DD/PO 13; D/D/Cd 130; *S.R.S.* lxix, p. 29.
[33] S.R.O., D/D/Cd 130.
[34] S.R.O., DD/PO 13; D.R.O., D 124, box 18, Kingsmoor ct. bks. 1732–96.

during the 18th century for breaking bounds with their sheep. An order to erect a gate at the north end of Witcombe bridge in 1750 took seven years to enforce and between 1757 and 1764 James Williams of Long Load was repeatedly fined for driving his wagons across the moor. Another tenant was fined in 1791 for stocking the moor with 36 sheep above the 159 for which he had grazing rights.[35] The moor was inclosed in 1806 when 47 a. in a rectangular area opposite Witcombe were allotted to Martock.[36]

Of the two estates held at one time by John de Say Martock Sayes had a rental of over £8 between 1508–9 and 1521–2.[37] In 1558 it comprised 91 a. held by 16 tenants paying £8 14s. 6d. No heriots were charged because the manor was 'all demesne land'. The estate lay principally in Long Load and to a lesser extent in Coat, with smaller portions in Martock and Bower Hinton.[38] Says Bonville in 1525 totalled 70 a. held by 5 tenants at will in Long Load, 1 freehold and 4 copyhold tenants in Coat, and 5 copyhold tenants in Martock, rendering a total of £7 10s. 6d.[39] In 1775 Raymundo Putt's 'manor of Long Load', evidently derived from lands in both manors, was held by 8 tenants paying £4 12s.[40]

With the decline, and in some cases disappearance, of the medieval manorial estates a number of larger freeholds were built up during the 18th and early 19th centuries. By 1824 there were three estates in the parish of over 400 a. The largest was that of Robert Goodden, totalling 462 a. and centred on the 'Manor House' and Manor farm in Martock tithing. The Napier estate of 428 a. was based on Pykesash manor, while that of William Cole Wood of 405 a., reflecting its piecemeal acquisition, was distributed throughout the parish. Thomas Richards and John Whitehead Richards between them held 673 a. in Stapleton, but there was no other holding over 250 a. Within individual tithings there were several farms of over 100 a. in extent: 4 in Bower Hinton and Hurst, 2 in Ash, and one each in Coat and Martock.[41] By 1841 the Goodden, Richards, and Wood holdings had increased, accounting between them for nearly 2,000 a., Ann Coggan and George Slade held 279 a. and 242 a. respectively, and there were a further 6 landowners with over 100 a.[42]

With the completion of inclosure the usual consolidation of farming units took place from the mid 19th century. In the former open fields 3 new farms were created: Stapleton Mead farm in Stapleton (96 a. in 1868), Hillside (now Hills) farm in

Martock (87 a. in 1888, 131 a. in 1900), and Durnfield farm in Ash (38 a. in 1864, 135 a. in 1912).[43] The larger estates began to be split up and sold, the Goodden lands amounting to 500 a. being dispersed in 1883.[44] By 1939 there were 14 farms of over 150 a., of which 5 lay at Long Load and 3 at Milton.[45] In the south of the parish Bower Hinton farm, which had 123 a. in 1889, gradually accumulated lands from the former open fields and comprised 200 a. in 1974.[46] The crops cultivated during the 19th and earlier 20th centuries, as in the Middle Ages, were generally wheat and beans with some flax,[47] but an increasing proportion of the land was given over to pasture. In 1841 there were 4,204 a. of meadow and pasture compared with 2,161 a. of arable.[48] By 1905 the area of permanent grass had grown to 5,332 a. and that of arable shrunk to 1,073 a.[49] In Long Load the 1905 arable accounted for less than one eighth of the farmland,[50] and grassland continued to predominate in 1974.

TRADE AND INDUSTRY. As a market town by the 13th century Martock became a trading as well as an agricultural centre. Evidence for medieval occupations is slight. A weaver occurs in 1560, a tailor in 1603, a draper in 1613, and a linen draper in 1654.[51] Clothmakers, dyers, and sergemakers are often found in the later 17th century, and in the 18th a number of clothiers established family concerns which survived for several generations.

William Cole was described as a clothier from 1728 until his death in 1762, his wife's family, the Hillyards, being linked with fulling interests in Taunton.[52] His only daughter married William Wood (d. 1801), probably son of a Martock linenclothmaker, and their son, William Cole Wood, became the most prominent tradesman and landowner resident in the parish.[53] In 1796 he held a workshop and 76 a. of land in Bower Hinton and Hurst, but by 1841 had increased this to 680 a. and shortly before 1849 built Ashfield House.[54] The Patten family of Hurst and Bower Hinton, occurring as clothiers from 1733, married into the Adams family, also clothiers.[55] The Hamlyns are recorded as stocking-makers and clothiers in the mid 18th century as were the Palmers and Butlers in the later 18th and early 19th centuries.[56] In the 18th century these families and others in allied trades formed a merchant class within the parish, marrying within their own ranks, and subsequently involving themselves in more 'respectable' occupations. Thus in the 19th century the Adamses became solicitors and wine merchants, and the Westcotes turned to

[35] D.R.O., D 124, box 18, Kingsmoor ct. bks. 1732–96.
[36] S.R.O., CR 45.
[37] D.R.O., D 124, box 11, accts. 1508–9, 1517–18, 1521–2.
[38] Ibid. box 16, survey 1558.
[39] E 315/385.　　[40] Winchester Coll. Mun. 12853.
[41] S.R.O., D/P/mart 13/1/1.
[42] S.R.O., tithe award.
[43] S.R.O., C/C 2/2, SH 4; DD/PLE, box 104, sale cat. 1912.
[44] S.R.O., DD/PLE, box 104, sale cat. 1883.
[45] Kelly's Dir. Som. (1939).
[46] Ex inf. Mr. P. J. Palmer.
[47] Kelly's Dir. Som. (1883).
[48] S.R.O., tithe award.
[49] Statistics supplied by the then Bd. of Agric. 1905.
[50] Ibid.

[51] Req. 2/157/270; S.R.O., D/P/mart 2/1/1; DD/JL 59 a, b, c, conveyance 5 July 1654.
[52] S.R.O., DD/PLE, box 47, conveyance 27 Jan. 1727/8; D/P/mart 2/1/5.
[53] S.R.O., D/P/mart 2/1/5, 9; DD/S/HR, box 7, mar. settl. 5 Sept. 1772. George Wood, linenclothmaker, occurs 1777–81: S.R.O., DD/SAS, C/77, 19; DD/BR/py, C/492, bdle. 19.
[54] S.R.O., DD/PLE, box 47, mar. settl. 9 July 1796, disentailing deed 2 July 1849; tithe award.
[55] S.R.O., DD/X/PAR 2, conveyance 3 Oct. 1733; DD/BR/py, C/516, bdle. 31; D/P/mart 2/1/3, 5, recording burials of John Adams 1749, William Adams 1770, George Adams 1798, all clothiers.
[56] S.R.O., DD/MR 38; DD/SAS, C/77, 19; DD/S/HR, box 39, mortgage 12 Mar. 1759; box 49, conveyance 19 Dec. 1827; D/P/mart 2/1/3–8.

medicine. Families like the Woods sent their sons to public schools and often left the area.[57] The commitment to clothing and similar trades was still evident in 1851 when there were 41 dressmakers, 16 tailors, 6 wool-sorters, 7 seamstresses, 5 hand-loom weavers, 3 staymakers, 2 fellmongers, and 2 wool-staplers.[58]

A glover was mentioned at Martock in 1655 but glovemakers occur regularly only from the early 19th century.[59] The parish was linked with Stoke sub Hamdon as a production centre and up to 1826 the two were producing 500 dozen beaver gloves a week. The importation of French gloves, however, reduced the demand and, like Yeovil, Martock turned to making kid gloves. By 1830 the manufacture had been 'much reduced' and a year later production from Martock and Stoke had fallen to 50 dozen a week.[60] A recovery had evidently taken place by 1851 when there were 567 women in the parish engaged in gloving, a figure which dwarfed that of any other occupation.[61] Many of these women worked in their own homes but there were always a number of small factories. There were still three of these in 1911, although making mainly silk or fabric gloves,[62] and in 1974 Burfield and Company, the Martock Glove Company, and Seager Brothers were still operating in the parish.

By 1857 the West of England Engineering and Coker Canvas Company had acquired the old Cary's mill site, renamed the Parrett Works, and were producing mining, horizontal, high-pressure, and condensing engines, traction engines, threshing machines, water wheels, corn-mills, flax and spinning machinery, power looms, and Parsons' patent iron and wooden wheels.[63] By 1861 the company had been taken over by George Parsons, who exhibited his patent wheels at the International Exhibition of 1862, and subsequently extended the range of products to include yarns and canvas.[64] A new power-loom shed was opened in 1866.[65] Economic pressures forced the company to discontinue yarn and canvas making and in 1869 it went into liquidation.[66] By 1875 the works had been taken over by two firms: William Sibley's West of England Engineering Company, millwrights and iron and brass founders, and G. H. Smith, makers of Napier matting, blind and sash cords, rope and twine.[67] Sibley's continued there in 1923 but had gone by 1931, leaving Smith's, who were still operating there in 1941.[68] In 1974 the premises were held by West of England Warehouses and

used also by Somervale Foods and Somerset Joinery.

William Sparrow, formerly of the Parrett Works, founded the Somerset Wheel and Wagon Company at Bower Hinton in 1868.[69] The firm was trading as William Sparrow Limited, agricultural engineers, in 1974. James Paull, formerly a seedsman and corn factor in the parish, had established his sack and oil-covering factory by 1872 and in 1889 specialized in making tents and marquees.[70] As Yeo Brothers, Paull, and Company the firm was continuing at the Orient Tent Works in 1974. Another prominent business still operating in Martock is Harry Hebditch Limited, founded c. 1907 to make poultry appliances, who in 1974 manufactured a wide range of sheds, greenhouses, garages, and chalets.[71] Yandle and Sons, timber merchants at Hurst, were wheelwrights at Coat in 1894 and builders and wheelwrights at Hurst by 1906.[72] Between 1883 and 1917 Martock had its own newspaper, *Palmer's Weekly News*, established by M. A. Palmer at the Atlas printing office in Water Street.[73]

The varied nature of trade within the parish is shown by references to a cutler in 1719, a currier in 1720, a tallow-chandler and a roper in 1723, a brush maker in 1728, a stockingmaker in 1738, a stay-maker in 1748, a hosier in 1751, a salter in 1755, a peruke maker in 1762, a tobacconist and a collar-maker in 1772, a fellmonger in 1779, a soapboiler in 1792, and a gunsmith in 1794.[74] An enterprising local clockmaker, Thomas Stocker, started a clock and watch club in 1808. The 21 members met at the George Inn, paying Stocker monthly subscriptions until sufficient money had accumulated for a silver watch at £4 4s. or a clock and case at £5 5s.[75]

A basket maker was mentioned in 1813 and in 1830 there were 2 rope and twine makers, 2 ironmongers, a tallow chandler, staymaker, 2 maltsters, and 2 straw-hat makers. The professional classes were then represented by 2 attorneys and 5 surgeons.[76] By 1839 the manufacture of sailcloth, bricks and tiles, and cheese had been introduced, and the growing population found need of a hairdresser, a veterinary surgeon, and a china and glass dealer.[77] In 1842 there were 7 grocers and drapers, in 1852 an earthenware dealer, and in 1861 an architect and a tinplate worker.[78] Branches of Stuckey's bank and the London and South Western bank opened in 1863, followed before 1875 by the Wiltshire and Dorset Banking Company.[79] A herbalist had established himself by 1875, and 2

[57] A. L. Humphreys, *Som. Parishes*, 465; local information.   [58] H.O. 107/1930.
[59] S.R.O., D/P/mart 2/1/2, 8.
[60] W. Hull, *History of the Glove Trade* (1834), 69–73; Pigot, *Nat. Com. Dir.* (1830).
[61] H.O. 107/1930.
[62] *V.C.H. Som.* ii. 428.
[63] *Pulman's Weekly News and Advertiser*, 31 Dec. 1857. See above, plate facing p. 48.
[64] *P.O. Dir. Som.* (1861, 1866).
[65] *Western Gazette*, Mar. 1866. A works band had been formed by 1863 when Parsons lent a steam engine to help the parish celebrate the marriage of the Prince of Wales: ibid. 7 Mar. 1863.
[66] *Pulman's Weekly News and Advertiser*, 9 June 1868; S.R.O., DD/X/LIV, C/1971.
[67] *P.O. Dir. Som.* (1875).
[68] *Kelly's Dir. Som.* (1923, 1931); S.R.O., DD/X/LIV, C/1971.
[69] Local information; *Kelly's Dir. Som.* (1883).

[70] Morris and Co. *Dir. Som.* (1872); *Kelly's Dir. Som.* (1889).
[71] *Kelly's Dir. Som.* (1910); ex inf. Mr. R. Hebditch, Martock.
[72] *Kelly's Dir. Som.* (1894–1939).
[73] L. E. J. Brooke, *Som. Newspapers, 1725–1960*, 60.
[74] S.R.O., DD/GRY, C/1030, assignment 31 July 1719, deed 3 Apr. 1723; D/P/mart 2/1/3–5; DD/SAS, SE 27A/11, will of R. Bayley 1738; Q/RL, 1762, 1772; DD/JP, box 3, bond 16 Sept. 1779; DD/PLE, box 47, will of Thomas Hamlyn 1792; R.G. 4/1556.
[75] *S. & D. N. & Q.* xxiv. 39–40. Stocker (d. 1817) lived at Providence Cottage, now Hurst Manor.
[76] S.R.O., D/P/mart 2/1/8; Pigot, *Nat. Com. Dir.* (1830).
[77] Robson, *Com. Dir.* (1839).
[78] Pigot, *Nat. Com. Dir.* (1842); Slater, *Nat. Com. Dir.* (1852–3); *P.O. Dir. Som.* (1861).
[79] *Western Gazette*, 17 Oct. 1863, 7 Nov. 1863; *P.O. Dir. Som.* (1875).

photographers and a cardboard-box maker by 1894.[80] There was a jeweller by 1910, a rabbit-skin dealer and a dentist by 1931, and wireless engineers by 1939.[81]

Although no main road passed through the town, in 1830 carriers connected regularly with Yeovil, Crewkerne, Langport, Taunton, Bridport, and Bristol, and in 1839 5 London coaches ran daily through it.[82] The opening of the railway in 1849 reduced the demand for coach services and by 1852 these ran only to Yeovil. Although the carriers had then extended their links to Bridgwater and London,[83] the railway, until 1906 the main route between London, Yeovil, and Taunton, continued as the principal outlet for goods and passengers. As in many rural areas of Somerset, the closure of the railway in 1964 and the dearth of alternative public transport has severely restricted the travel of those without cars.

MARKET AND FAIR. Ingram de Fiennes procured a grant of a weekly market on Tuesdays within his manor of Martock in 1247. By 1294 the market and common oven were let at farm for 73s. 4d. and by 1302 the tolls of the market and perquisites of a fair were worth 6s. 8d.[84] In 1378–9 the tolls were let together with the common oven and office of bedel of the hundred, and by 1506 the tolls were held by the manor bailiff.[85] A new lease of the tolls of grain and cattle was granted in 1531 and was still held in 1555.[86] Evidently the market was discontinued during the 17th and earlier 18th centuries until 1753, when the prices charged by hucksters and bakers in the parish decided the vestry on setting up a Wednesday market for the sale of 'corn and other things'. The vestry also agreed to indemnify anyone prosecuted for selling goods in the market and ordered a house to be built at the Cross to keep corn dry on market days.[87] In 1755 an anonymous message found at the church ordered the vicar to 'see that the market is put up again very soon', and by 1791 the market was being held on Wednesdays and Saturdays.[88] These were continuing as market days in 1840, principally for the sale of meat, but by 1889 had been changed to the last Monday in every month.[89] Between 1906 and 1931 the market was replaced by an auction sale every other Tuesday, and from 1931 at least until 1939 this was held on alternate Mondays in a field near the station.[90]

A fair held on St. Lawrence's day (10 August)

was in being by 1302.[91] A Taunton mercer had a stall at the fair in 1682[92] and the tolls continued to be held with the bakehouse during the 18th century, although the market had been discontinued. By 1767 the fair day had been altered to 21 August and was principally used for the sale of pigs and by pedlars.[93] The fair was for cattle during the 19th century and in 1893 it lasted for two days: the first devoted to the sale of cattle in Mr. Farrant's barton; the second was a pleasure fair in the Market Square and on the Green.[94] The fair was held on 21 August in 1939[95] but does not seem to have survived the Second World War. An unsuccessful attempt to revive it was made in August 1974.

The present market house may be that built by order of the vestry c. 1753, although it was attributed in 1791 to the Slades, who purchased the manor in 1759. In 1791 the butchers' shambles occupied the ground floor with an assembly room above it.[96] The ownership of the building continued in the lords of the manor until 1883. The tolls of the fair were then sold with the lordship, but the Goodden family retained the market house until 1954 when it was sold to the Parish Council.[97] The building was restored and reopened in 1960–1.[98]

MILLS. There were 2 mills within the manor in 1086 paying 35s.[99] These probably correspond with the 2 long-established mill sites in the parish: Walter's mill, later Cary's mill, and finally the Parrett Works, and Madey mill. The two were let for £12 in 1293–4, and in 1302 they were valued at 60s.[1] Both were leased to Ralph de Middleney in 1339,[2] and in 1364 they were let with suit due from the bondsmen of Martock and a fishery.[3] In 1507 one of the mills, known since 1364 as Walter's mill, possibly after a 13th-century miller,[4] was let by copyhold for £10 13s. 4d. The other mill, known from the 14th century as Madey mill, was held in 1507 by copy for a rent of £5.[5] Both mills were in the same occupations in 1537 and both were leased in 1539 to Robert Pullman for £13 a year, the latter still occupying them in 1555.[6]

Walter's mill was granted by copy to William Gardner in 1592, with the grist and toll of the lord's tenants.[7] It was enfranchised in 1627, the freehold passing to Sir Thomas Brudenell and Milicent Herenden.[8] Thereafter the descent is not clear but the mill was tenanted by John Sealy, miller, c. 1704–42, and Thomas Gould, 1750–8, and was described in 1750 as two copyhold water grist mills

[80] P.O. Dir. Som. (1875); Kelly's Dir. Som. (1894).
[81] Kelly's Dir. Som. (1910–39).
[82] Pigot, Nat. Com. Dir. (1830); Robson, Com. Dir. (1839).
[83] Slater, Nat. Com. Dir. (1852–3).
[84] Cal. Chart. R. 1226–57, 315; S.C. 6/1127/16; Saunders, Hund. of Martock, 106.
[85] S.C. 6/Hen. VII/1237.
[86] L.R. 2/202.
[87] S.R.O., D/P/mart 13/2/4. Strachey stated c. 1740 that there was 'now scarce any market left': DD/SH 107.
[88] S.R.O., D/P/mart 13/2/4; Collinson, Hist. Som. iii. 2.
[89] County Gazette Dir. (1840); Kelly's Dir. Som. (1889).
[90] Kelly's Dir. Som. (1906–39); Saunders, Hund. of Martock, 7.
[91] Saunders, Hund. of Martock, 106.
[92] S.R.O., Q/SR 151/7.

[93] S.R.O., DD/WY, box 85, rental, 18th cent.; Bk. of Fairs.
[94] Robson, Com. Dir. (1839); Kelly's Dir. Som. (1889); Som. County Gazette, 26 Aug. 1893.
[95] Kelly's Dir. Som. (1939); local information.
[96] Collinson, Hist. Som. iii. 2.
[97] Western Gazette, 22 June 1883; par. cncl. mins. 1949–56.   [98] Tablet in upper room.
[99] V.C.H. Som. i. 440.
[1] S.C. 6/1127/16; Saunders, Hund. of Martock, 104.
[2] Cal. Pat. 1338–40, 299.
[3] Ibid. 1364–7, 92; Cal. Close, 1364–8, 489.
[4] S.R.S. xi, p. 66.
[5] S.C. 6/Hen. VII/1236. The Tylers, tenants of Madey mill, covenanted in 1507 to supply 'cogges and rogges': ibid.
[6] S.C. 6/Hen. VIII/3044; L.R. 2/202; Req. 2/85/8.
[7] E 178/1970.
[8] S.R.O., DD/X/FRC, conveyance 26 May 1627.

and a malt mill called Walter's mill.[9] From c. 1758 it was owned by Thomas Cary and John Bull, and occupied c. 1758–63 by a tenant. Thereafter the Carys occupied the premises themselves until 1789, and again between c. 1794 and 1840.[10] One of the mills had become a snuff mill by 1811, and in 1838 Henry Cary (d. 1840) was occupying two houses and a warehouse on the site and R. B. Hansford a house and mill.[11] There were two mills in 1841, the snuff mill occupied by Cary's widow and the other by Thomas Leach.[12] Cary's mill was unoccupied in 1853, but by 1857 the site had become the Parrett Works.[13]

By 1592 Madey mill with a horse mill was held by the Gould family[14] and Barnard Gould was still in occupation when it passed with Martock manor to William Strode in 1637.[15] It continued in the family for a time, but in 1717 it was let to James Hurd the younger, and was then described as a watermill and malt mill.[16] Hurd bought the freehold in 1740 and sold it in the same year to Thomas Hopkins, then a Martock huckster and baker.[17] During the earlier 19th century the Hopkins family became the most prominent milling family in the area, holding not only Madey mill, but also Clapton mills in Crewkerne, Gawbridge mills in Kingsbury Episcopi, and other mills in Stoke sub Hamdon, Merriott, and Hook and Maiden Newton (Dors.).[18] Thomas Hopkins leased the mill to his son John in 1773 and conveyed it to him in 1778. From John Hopkins (d. 1800) it passed in 1802 to his son Jesse (d. 1848), who built a new dwelling-house with other buildings and installed a steam engine. The premises were left to William Culliford Hopkins of Stoke sub Hamdon and in 1865 were owned by William Hopkins of Gawbridge. The property then comprised a steam and water corn mill, with boiler house, bakehouse, and oven, 3 pairs of stones, a water wheel, and wire and dressing machines.[19]

The present mill is probably of late-17th-century origin but has been much enlarged on the north and west. The surviving iron wheel, made by Sparrow of Martock, is overshot, the water being conveyed to it by a built-up leat along the valley side, but the arrangement of the mill building suggests that it was designed for an undershot wheel fed at a lower level. The mill-house is c. 1800, presumably built by Jesse Hopkins, and there is a 19th-century granary of three storeys.

There was a windmill in Stapleton manor valued at 5s. in 1308 and at 6s. 8d. in 1336.[20] It does not appear in extents of 1359 and 1368.[21]

A windmill near the highway in Long Load manor held with 1 a. of land for 2s. a year was in decay in 1386. The land was then leased with the reversion of a further acre called the 'Shoveled-acre'.[22] Inclosed bondland in the fields called 'Mil-acre' and 'Sholdacre' was recorded in 1505,[23] but the mill was not mentioned again and the site has not been traced.

Two fulling mills in Martock manor were described as totally waste by 1506.[24] They may perhaps be associated with two fields called Dye House lying on either side of Hinton Meads brook immediately south-east of Madey mill.[25] A house called the Dye House, however, formed part of the manor of Martock Sayes in 1558[26] and the fulling mills site may lie elsewhere.

A mill and mill-house, held with a newly-built house and 32 a. of copyhold land, formed part of that manor of Milton which was held with Yeovilton manor. It was occupied by John Casse in 1619, subsequently by Mary Casse, and between 1682 and 1689 by Valentine Cousins and Anne Cooth.[27] Its site and subsequent history have not been traced.

A close called Windmill of 7¾ a. in Martock was mentioned in 1692 and called formerly Windmill now Fire Beacon in 1816.[28] This may possibly be identified with fields called Great Beacon and Beacon on the northern boundary of Martock tithing on the west side of Bearly Road[29] and may indicate a former windmill site.

LOCAL GOVERNMENT. It may be assumed that the jurisdiction of the capital manor of Martock formerly covered the whole of the ancient parish and also the tithing of Westcombland, reckoned under Coat but locally in Buckland St. Mary.[30] This was modified by subinfeudation and by 1275 the taking of felons' goods was claimed by the bailiff of Martock and strays were being claimed by the lords of Stapleton, Ash Boulogne, Milton, Long Load, and Fenns.[31]

No court rolls for the capital manor have been traced. Between 1506 and 1537 3 lawdays and 4 other courts were held each year.[32] In 1661 courts for the hundred and manor were being held quarterly in the school-house, and suit of court was required of a lessee in 1763.[33] The court baron and

[9] S.R.O., D/P/mart 13/2/2–4; DD/X/MEY, bond 1 Nov. 1750.
[10] S.R.O., D/P/mart 13/2/4–6.
[11] S.R.O., DD/WY, map of Martock 1811; D/P/mart 13/1/2.
[12] S.R.O., tithe award.
[13] *Western Gazette*, 20 Feb. 1953; *Pulman's Weekly News and Advertiser*, 31 Dec. 1857; see above, plate facing p. 48.
[14] E 178/1970.
[15] C 54/3172 m. 38.
[16] S.R.O., DD/X/MEY, copy 1 May 1717.
[17] Ibid. conveyances 11 Apr. 1740, 23 Mar. 1740/1, agreement 9 Dec. 1740.
[18] Ibid. conveyance 13 Oct. 1802, release 17 June 1848, insurance cert. 22 July 1865; DD/ED 147/875. Hook mill was held in 1831 by Theophilus Bartlett, Jesse Hopkins's brother-in-law.
[19] S.R.O., DD/X/MEY, deeds of Madey mill.

[20] C 134/10/9; *Cal. Inq. p.m.* viii, p. 45; C 135/47/15.
[21] C 135/148/10; C 135/203/3.
[22] Winchester Coll. Mun. 12862. A reference to a windmill in 'la Lade' in 1277 may relate to Long Load: *S.R.S.* xli. 93–4.
[23] Winchester Coll. Mun. 12864.
[24] S.C. 6/Hen. VII/1236.
[25] S.R.O., DD/SAS, C/212, map of Martock 1824.
[26] D.R.O., D 124, box 16, survey 1558.
[27] S.R.O., DD/PH 60; DD/WHh 1013.
[28] S.R.O., DD/PLE, conveyances 10 June 1692, 21 Sept. 1816.
[29] S.R.O., DD/SAS, C/212, map of Martock 1824.
[30] See above, p. 76.
[31] *Rot. Hund.* (Rec. Com.), ii. 139.
[32] S.C. 6/Hen. VII/1236; S.C. 6/Hen. VIII/3044.
[33] S.R.O., D/P/mart 18/1/1; DD/S/HR, box 2, lease 22 Oct. 1763.

view of frankpledge were referred to in 1844 and there was evidently a court leet held in October until at least 1852.[34] From the 15th century a salary of £5 a year was paid to the tenant serving as reeve and rent collector, although by 1506 the office was served by the bailiff of the manor. In the same year the hayward of Whaddon was paid for the execution of his office.[35]

Courts baron for the Wills manor of Martock for 1656–7 have been found. Business was then wholly tenurial. Suit of court was still required of a tenant in 1739.[36]

A court book for the manor of Martock Rectory covers the years 1742, 1821–80, although the last formal session was held in 1827. Business transacted related only to tenancies and no manorial officers were appointed.[37] Court rolls for the manor of Martock Priory are extant for 1479, 1482, and 1489; the courts were concerned in some detail with the disrepair of tenements and outbuildings. A reeve, bailiff, and steward were all mentioned, but not apparently appointed by the court.[38]

Court books for Stapleton manor have been found for 1640–56 and 1665–83, with presentments continuing to 1685.[39] Sessions, described variously as courts or courts baron, were usually held twice a year in spring and autumn, probably at the Court House.[40] They were concerned principally with ditch scouring, drove repair, and breaches of grazing and other customs. A hayward was appointed between 1665 and 1682, and grass haywards occur in 1679–80. Two surveyors were occasionally elected (1671–2, 1681).

Court rolls and books for Long Load survive for the years 1379, 1384–8, for many years in the 15th and 16th centuries, and continuously from 1551 to 1923.[41] Sessions were usually held twice a year until the 17th century and thereafter once a year, being described as courts or courts leet for Hockday and Michaelmas terms, sometimes with view of frankpledge. During the 17th and 18th centuries they were generally called courts, with the addition of a view of frankpledge when officers were appointed. Thereafter they were termed courts leet and courts baron until 1873, and courts baron until 1923. The court was probably held in the priest's house during the 16th century, for it was described as the former court-house in 1607. In 1608 it was suggested that the court be held in 'Mr. Brayne's house'.[42] The tenants complained in 1740 that they had not had a proper court for years and that the lord of Martock was requiring them to do homage in his court, had leased Long Load's game, and that their ditches and lakes had not been scoured for want of duly appointed officers.[43] Court business

was chiefly concerned with ditch, drove, and drainage work, the maintenance of foot-bridges, repairs to houses, and breach of grazing customs. Manorial officers included a hayward (1379–1923), who by 1608 had the use of the 'hayward's leaze' during his term of office, and after 1774 served as long as the inhabitants wished. There were also two haywards serving for Outmoor in 1565.[44] A tithing-man was appointed between 1413 and 1809,[45] and a reeve was elected during the years 1442–1507. Two constables were regularly appointed from 1553 to 1809 and made presentments, and a herdsman, elected in 1647 and mentioned in 1671, had to give notice of taking the prey over the commons. Other officers appointed by the courts included overseers to repair banks around the commons (1595), affeerers (1653–70), and viewers (1689).

A single manor court for Ash Boulogne in 1546 was concerned with tenurial business and decayed buildings.[46] Suit of court was demanded of lessees within the manor of Pykesash until 1704, and of Witcombe and Coat until 1793.[47] Court records for that manor of Witcombe held with Stapleton manor survive for 1640–3 and 1665, the sessions being termed courts or manor courts baron.[48]

Court rolls for the manor of Martock Sayes are extant for 1521–3, and 1543–4, the courts being concerned chiefly with the repair of tenements.[49] Suit of court was required of tenants to the combined manors of Martock Sayes and Says Bonville until at least 1760.[50]

Court rolls and books for the manor of Milton Falconbridge survive for 1540–1,[51] and for several years in the 17th century;[52] from 1670 to 1883 the series is fairly complete.[53] Courts were held twice yearly by 1456–7[54] but only annually in the late 18th and 19th centuries. Two leet lawdays were mentioned in 1476–7[55] and courts were usually known in the 16th and 17th centuries as courts, courts baron, or courts leet, sometimes with view of frankpledge. A tithingman and a hayward were regularly appointed from the 17th century, a reeve was elected in 1679, and a grass hayward by 1795. Two grass haywards served between 1802 and 1869, and the last hayward was presented in 1874. Courts were held in John Lavor's house in 1650.[56]

Court rolls for the manor of Fenns, later Fenns and Haythorn, have been traced for 1506 and 1689–1865.[57] Described simply as courts in 1506 and as courts baron from 1689, sessions were evidently held only when required by tenancy changes. In 1650 the court was held in a barn at Fenns,[58] but by 1785 usually in the common hall of the vicars choral at Wells. No manorial officers were appointed by the courts and, apart from an order to scour

[34] S.R.O., DD/PLE, box 104, abstract of title 1883; Slater, *Nat. Com. Dir.* (1852–3).
[35] S.C. 6/Hen. VII/1236.
[36] S.R.O., DD/MR 34, lease 29 Sept. 1739; 92.
[37] S.R.O., DD/CC 209907.
[38] S.C. 2/198/60, printed in Saunders, *Hund. of Martock*, 108–13.
[39] S.R.O., DD/S/HY, box 3.
[40] Ibid., ct. bk. 21 Oct. 1645.
[41] Winchester Coll. Mun. 12845, 12865–74, 23046–69.
[42] Ibid. 13107, 13145.
[43] Ibid. 12879.
[44] Ibid. 12872, 12933, 13145.
[45] Ibid. 23046.   [46] L.R. 3/123.

[47] S.R.O., DD/PLE, box 47, lease 3 May 1704; DD/S/HR, box 29, lease 17 Oct. 1793.
[48] S.R.O., DD/S/HY, box 3.
[49] D.R.O., D 124, box 18, composite ct. roll; box 141, composite ct. roll.
[50] S.R.O., DD/JP, box 3, lease 24 Apr. 1760.
[51] S.C. 2/198/61.
[52] S.C. 2/198/64–5; D.C.O., ct. bks.
[53] D.C.O., ct. bks.
[54] S.C. 6/1095/7.
[55] S.C. 6/1123/3.
[56] E 317/33.
[57] S.R.O., DD/CC 131913a/8, 116015–17.
[58] Ibid. 116013.

ditches in 1506, business was entirely concerned with tenancies.

Churchwardens are mentioned in 1349, posts or sidesmen occur in 1554, and from 1598 there have always been two churchwardens.[59] Four overseers of the poor occur between 1675 and 1843. There were 5 in 1844 and 8 between 1871 and 1894.[60] Two waywardens served from 1675, increasing to 3 in 1689, to 6 in 1729–30; they dropped to 4 between 1731 and 1740, and to 3 from 1741. Four were appointed from 1842, one in 1871, and 2 from 1883 to 1894.[61] Two parish constables were mentioned between 1678 and 1753. In 1844 one paid constable was appointed, with 3 part-time, and between 1854 and 1871 2 paid constables were elected.[62]

By the later 17th century the 4 overseers were each assigned a particular area of the parish. A 'parish house', rented from the lord by 1680 and repaired for the accommodation of the poor in 1725, may possibly be distinguished from 'the church house', repaired for the same purposes in 1730.[63] In 1730 the overseers were ordered to 'seize' a house at Highway for the use of the parish, and in 1735 a workhouse was rented, a master appointed, and each overseer was paid £12 towards maintaining the establishment. Paupers refusing to enter the workhouse received no relief, a vestry committee of 6 was ordered to inspect the house weekly, and a doctor was appointed to tend the poor housed there. In 1742 the Nonconformist members of the vestry succeeded in voting its closure, the paupers were farmed out to other households in the parish at up to 18d. each a week, and the beds and cooking utensils distributed to the needy.[64]

Occupiers of property who became a burden on the rates were required to assign their houses to the parish if they wished to receive relief. Such surrenders were made in 1742 and 1751 and houses were similarly acquired at Load by 1755, in North Street in 1759, and at Ash by 1763. This policy continued into the 19th century, paupers being accommodated whenever a vacancy arose.[65] Use of the 'parish house' continued, one inmate in 1753 being allowed a pair of shoes if she took another female pauper into bed with her. Orphaned children were sent to Betty Locock's house where a dame school was held. Nine children there contracted smallpox in 1758 and a year later the parish paid for the conversion of her loft to house more. There was insufficient accommodation in the parish in 1786, when the vestry agreed to rent or build another poorhouse.[66]

Efforts were made to start a workhouse at Hurst in 1760, and near Shepton Mead bridge in 1789. Land was purchased in Water Street in 1796 for the same purpose, but orders for the building to start in 1799 and 1805 may never have taken effect.[67] In 1824 there were 3 poorhouses in Martock, one in Water Street opposite the present Bridge House, one at the west end of Ash, and a third at Highway.[68] The parish became part of the Yeovil poor-law union in 1836 and two years later the properties accumulated by the parish were sold: a cottage at Milton, three in Ash, two in Coat, and one in Water Street.[69] Two further cottages in North Street and one at Coat were ordered to be sold in 1854.[70]

Badges were introduced in 1722 and poor children were taught to weave dowlas between 1751 and 1768.[71] In 1842 sums were raised to fit out paupers for emigration to Tasmania and similar subsidies were proposed in 1848.[72] Officers later appointed by the vestry included a salaried assistant overseer to collect rates (1836–84), between 4 and 6 lighting inspectors (1875–82), and an inspector of waterworks (1890).[73]

The first fire engine was bought by the vestry in 1755, and a second in 1807, both stored in the Market House in 1891.[74] A fire brigade, formed in 1874, acquired an outbuilding at Manor Farm in 1930 to house a motor fire engine bought in the previous year.[75] A playing field south of Water Street at Frickers bridge was bought in 1951, with money given for a War memorial. The field was converted to a public recreation ground in 1954.[76]

The housing of the poor caused the vestry, and later the parish council, the greatest concern, particularly at Ash. There in the winter of 1863 13 people had to sleep in one room and there was much illness due to unsatisfactory drainage.[77] In 1906 740 of the 'working classes' occupied 212 houses with only one or two bedrooms each and the cottages, and especially their bedrooms, were 'generally insanitary'. The first council houses in the parish were built at Coat in 1913.[78]

CHURCH. Martock church, in the centre of a large pre-Conquest estate, was probably a minster of royal foundation. It was first mentioned in 1156 when it was confirmed as a possession of the abbey of Mont St. Michel (Manche).[79] The bishop of Winchester, 'having long possessed it', restored it to the abbey in 1176–8, but it was acquired by the bishop of Bath by 1190–1, the abbey receiving pensions in return.[80] In 1226 the bishop divided the income: half was returned to Mont St. Michel in exchange for the patronage, and the other half was assigned to the treasurer of Wells cathedral, subject to an annual pension to Merton priory (Surr.).[81]

The bishop of Winchester appointed a vicar before 1176–8, and Mont St. Michel or its daughter house at Otterton (Devon) were patrons thereafter

[59] Cal. Inq. p.m. ix, p. 176.
[60] S.R.O., D/P/mart 9/1/1; 13/2/1–6.
[61] Ibid. 9/1/1; 14/5/1–4.
[62] Ibid. 9/1/1; 13/2/1, 4.
[63] Ibid. 13/2/1–3.
[64] Ibid. 13/2/3; 14/5/2.
[65] Ibid. 13/2/3–5.
[66] Ibid. 13/2/4, 5.
[67] Ibid. 13/2/5.
[68] S.R.O., DD/SAS, map of Martock 1824.
[69] Poor Law Com. 2nd Rep. p. 550; sale cat. 1838, penes Mr. F. J. Banfield, Bridge House, Martock.
[70] S.R.O., D/P/mart 9/1/1.
[71] Ibid. 13/2/1–4.
[72] Ibid. 9/1/1.
[73] Ibid.
[74] S.R.O., D/P/mart 4/1/1; 9/1/1; 13/2/6.
[75] Ibid. 9/1/1; par. cncl. mins. 1925–33.
[76] Par. cncl. mins. 1949–56.
[77] Western Gazette, 19 Nov. 1864.
[78] Par. cncl. mins. 1905–15, 30 Aug. 1906, 27 Feb. 1913.
[79] Cal. Doc. France, ed. Round, pp. 268–9.
[80] Ibid., pp. 276–8; Proc. Som. Arch. Soc. xix. 95.
[81] H.M.C. Wells, i. 36–7, 51, 449, 452; Topographer and Genealogist, i. 195. The pension was part of a larger one payable by Otterton to the treasurers.

until 1226.[82] From that date the advowson belonged to the treasurer of Wells or his grantees.[83] Thomas Owen presented in 1654,[84] the bishop in 1663, 1696, and 1708, and the chapter of Wells in 1692 during vacancies.[85] The bishop became patron between 1883 and 1888.[86]

The vicar's portion was worth £5 in 1291.[87] It had risen by 1535 to £15 9s. 10½d. net, deductions including the salary of a chaplain at Stapleton.[88] The vicarage was valued at £80 in 1650 but by the following year stood at £40 when the living was augmented with a further £80, subsequently reduced to £60 between 1655 and 1657.[89] This augmentation was removed at the Restoration and the value c. 1668 was £50.[90] The living was again augmented in 1733 with £230 to Martock and £200 to Long Load, private benefactors contributing. A further £200 was added to Long Load in 1789.[91] By 1831 the net value had risen to £270, but by 1851 the gross income of over £426 was reduced to £199 net.[92]

Oblations and small tithes were valued at £12 16s. 8d. in 1334,[93] and had risen to £21 14s. 9d. by 1535, including 2s. from Westcombland in Buckland St. Mary in lieu of tithes.[94] In 1606 the vicar was receiving tithes of calves, colts, pigs, fruit, and gardens.[95] During the period 1657–61 tithes were sometimes rendered in kind and sometimes compounded.[96] Until 1721 they were let, but thereafter the vicar received compositions in cash which amounted to £102 by 1733. In 1763 he was paid 1s. for the fall of a colt, 6d. for the fall of a calf if reared, but a tenth of the price if sold and the left shoulder if killed. He also received 2d. for a cow, 5s. for each acre of potatoes, a tenth of the sale price of turnips, and 1s. for a hogshead of apples, 4 hogsheads in 20 being allowed for fallings and rakings on account of the duty on cider. Moduses were paid for the two mills. In 1764 cow whit was discontinued as the amount was so small, and the charge on apples was varied with the cider duty.[97] The tithes were valued at £104 in 1823–4, but the tithe of apples alone was worth £334 in 1836.[98] In 1841 the vicar's tithes were commuted for £316.[99]

About 24 a. and 5 leazes in Coat Hay were given as glebe by the rector, Ralph Barker (d. 1708), and c. 1720 the glebe was let for c. £25.[1] A further acre was given by the then rector in 1720, and one Pittard gave Pittard's Close of 2½ a. in 1728.[2] Some 26 a. in Coat and 2½ leazes in Coat Hay were bought with augmentation money in 1733 and were let in 1764 for £40 10s., of which £20 was devoted to Long Load chapel.[3] The vicar was allotted 38 a. under inclosure awards of 1819 and 1826.[4] In 1841 the glebe lands totalled over 77 a., and in 1849 83 a., including the churchyards.[5] Small sales reduced the glebe to 63 a. in 1889 and 53 a. in 1944, but there were 59 a. in 1974.[6]

The former vicarage house stands at the corner of Church Street opposite the Church House and immediately west of the Treasurer's House. The vicar's house was described in 1639 as having a hall, hall chamber, and parlour, with two chambers over the parlour, an old kitchen, buttery, old stables, and lands partly walled about.[7] It has been suggested that the vicar then occupied the Treasurer's House, of which this might be a description.[8] In 1738 the vicar reserved the parlour and room above for his own use and sub-let the remainder to two other occupiers.[9] In 1815 the house was tenanted by the daughter of a former vicar, although the incumbent was again resident there by 1824.[10] The property was sold in 1875[11] and was known first as the Old Vicarage and, in 1974, as Pattenden.

A new vicarage house was built west of Church Street and south of the mill brook in 1874,[12] and was occupied by the vicar in 1974.

John Southwood, vicar by 1532 until 1543, held the vicarage of St. Cuthbert's, Wells, in plurality.[13] George Spraggett, vicar by 1552, was deprived for being married in 1554, but was subsequently restored.[14] Thomas Curtis, vicar 1625–45, was fined for adultery and drunkenness by the Court of High Commission in 1639.[15] Amos Walrond, vicar 1645–7, was ejected by the Presbyterians and became secretary to Lord Hertford at Oxford.[16] James Stevenson, vicar 1654–62, had fought in Ireland in 1641 and subsequently studied medicine at Leyden. He practised in succession to his son between 1656 and his removal.[17] Thomas Bowyer, vicar 1708–63, was the first to propose the institution of public infirmaries.[18] G. W. Saunders, vicar 1917–52, was also treasurer of Wells between 1940 and 1955, and wrote a history of the parish.[19]

[82] Cal. Doc. France, ed. Round, pp. 277–9; Proc. Som. Arch. Soc. xix. 95. The pension payable by the vicars was increased to 15 marks in the period 1195–1200, and to 20 marks in 1200.
[83] H.M.C. Wells, i. 51; S.R.S. lv, pp. 36, 102; Som. Incumbents, ed. Weaver.
[84] Lambeth Palace MSS., COMM. III/3, p. 232.
[85] Som. Incumbents, ed. Weaver.
[86] Kelly's Dir. Som. (1883, 1888).
[87] Tax. Eccl. (Rec. Com.), 197.
[88] Valor Eccl. (Rec. Com.), i. 133.
[89] Lambeth Palace MSS., COMM. XIIa/1/198–206, V/1, VIb/2, VII/1.
[90] S.R.O., D/D/Vc 24.
[91] Hodgson, Queen Anne's Bounty.
[92] Rep. Com. Eccl. Revenues, pp. 144–5; H.O. 129/319/3/1/1.
[93] E 179/169/14.
[94] Valor Eccl. (Rec. Com), i. 133.
[95] S.R.O., D/P/mart 3/1/1.
[96] E 134/13 Chas. II Mich./43.
[97] S.R.O., D/P/mart 3/2/12.   [98] Ibid. 3/2/4, 8.
[99] S.R.O., tithe award.
[1] S.R.O., D/P/mart 3/1/2, 3/2/12; tithe award.

[2] S.R.O., D/P/mart 3/1/2.
[3] Ibid. 3/2/12.
[4] Ibid. 20/1/2, 3.
[5] S.R.O., tithe award; D/P/mart 1/7/1.
[6] Kelly's Dir. Som. (1889); parochial diary penes the vicar; ex inf. Dioc. Office.
[7] S.R.O., D/D/Rg 222.
[8] Saunders, Hund. of Martock, 14.
[9] S.R.O., D/P/mart 3/2/12.
[10] Ibid. 3/2/3; D/D/B return 1815.
[11] Conveyance, 13 Sept. 1875, penes Newman, Paynter, & Co., Solicitors, Yeovil.
[12] S.R.O., D/P/mart 3/4/1; Lond. Gaz. 19 Dec. 1873, p. 6035.
[13] Emden, Biog. Reg. Univ. Oxford; H.M.C. Wells, ii. 108; Som. Incumbents, ed. Weaver.
[14] S.R.O., D/D/Vc 66, f. 16v.; Cambridge, Corpus Christi Coll., MS. 97.
[15] Cal. S.P. Dom. 1639–40, 289.
[16] Walker Revised, ed. Matthews.
[17] Lambeth Palace MSS., COMM. V/1; Calamy Revised, ed. Matthews.
[18] Bath Chronicle, 4 Aug. 1763; M.I. in ch.
[19] Crockford; Saunders, Hund. of Martock.

There were three chaplains serving in the parish in 1450 and 1468,[20] and by 1532 there was a curate and five other priests.[21] The vicar was required to find two priests in 1548, one in the parish church and one in Stapleton chapel.[22] There were only 5 communicants in 1776, the small number being attributed to nonconformist influence.[23] In 1815 the vicar was living at Bath, but there were prayers and a sermon twice on Sundays at Martock and once at Long Load, and prayers at Martock on Wednesdays and Fridays.[24] By 1827 the vicar was resident and in 1831 was employing two assistant curates.[25] Holy Communion was administered monthly and on feast days in 1843,[26] and on Census Sunday in 1851 there were congregations of 475 in the morning and 826 in the afternoon, including Sunday-school pupils.[27] In 1870 there were monthly celebrations of Holy Communion.[28]

An organ was first mentioned in 1534,[29] and in 1591 money was left to the choristers.[30] There was 'a large pair of organs' in 1644,[31] but these were evidently destroyed 'in Oliver's time'. In 1742 an 'organistical party' defeated nonconformist opposition to purchase a new instrument rather than repair the old.[32] The organ was rebuilt in 1798, probably replaced in 1805, and restored in 1930–1.[33]

In 1325 John de Say gave a toft and 20 a. for a chaplain to celebrate in the church in honour of the Virgin and for the souls of himself and his family.[34] It was probably this chantry which in 1546 possessed goods valued at 6s. 8d.[35] At its dissolution in 1548 it had only a tin chalice and ornaments worth 2s. Lands in Wimborne Minster (Dors.), after deductions, then produced £6 3s. 8d.[36] These lands, with the priest's house in Martock, were granted to Sherborne grammar school (Dors.) in 1550.[37] The priest's house was in 1974 called the Chantry, on the south side of Church Street behind a 19th-century block, incorporating a chemist's shop.[38] A short range of building, including one 15th-century open truss in its roof and a 14th-century doorway, may have been the hall of an early house. Beyond and in line with this range there are buildings of the 18th century.

In 1489 the treasurer of Wells granted a lease of 26½ a. to maintain a chaplain celebrating at St. Thomas's altar in the church. In 1548 the clear value of this grant was 53s. 4d. a year, but there was then no chaplain and no goods.[39] The lands were sold in 1549.[40]

In 1527 John Witcombe left lands in Martock to build a house for a chantry priest who was to keep an obit in the parish church for the souls of himself and his family.[41] No subsequent reference to this chantry has been traced.

In the 13th century William Sclavine of Coat was to keep a light burning at night in a mortuary chapel in the church in partial return for a grant of land in Martock from the abbot of Mont St. Michel.[42] A tenement in Ash was charged in 1349 with maintaining three lamps in the church.[43] In 1527 John Witcombe left money and cloth for gowns to 'five poor men in the worship of the five wounds of Christ',[44] and these may be the brethren or brotherhood of Martock church mentioned between 1541 and 1545.[45] A tenement called 'the brethernehedd land' occurs in 1555.[46] In 1548 8d. a year was paid from land in Pykesash for a lamp in the church.[47]

The former school-house, originally the court house, was bought from the trustees of the grammar school by the vicar, E. A. Salmon, in 1871, and conveyed by him to the parish in 1888.[48] It was later used for parochial meetings and, more recently, to house a branch of the County Library. It was sold in 1975.

The church of *ALL SAINTS* stands at the centre of Martock tithing west of the Market House. It is built mostly of ashlar and has a chancel with north and south chapels, aisled and clerestoried nave with north and south porches, and west tower.[49] The mid-13th-century east wall of the chancel is the earliest surviving feature in the building although it may represent the lengthening of an earlier chancel. By the early 14th century there was a south transept, of which only the south wall remains, and the church probably conformed to the common cruciform plan with a central tower. By the later 15th century when the west tower was added, the nave was probably aisled. It then had 4 bays which are reflected in the layout of the south aisle wall. Early in the 16th century the present arcades of 6 bays and the north aisle were built, perhaps following the removal of a central tower, and the clerestoried nave was covered with a richly-carved and painted roof. This is dated 1513 and its maintenance has been a constant burden on the parish since at least 1755.[50] Also in the early 16th century the east end was reconstructed and the chapels with their two-bay arcades were added. Other structural features of this period include the south porch and a stair turret in the north aisle wall to the rood loft. The east wall of the chancel was rebuilt in 1883.[51]

In a recess in the south aisle is a female Ham-stone

20 *S.R.S.* xlix, pp. 136, 396.
21 S.R.O., D/D/Vc 20.
22 *S.R.S.* ii. 111.
23 S.R.O., D/D/V Dioc. bk. 1776.
24 S.R.O., D/D/B return 1815.
25 S.R.O., D/D/V return 1827; *Rep. Com. Eccl. Revenues*, pp. 144–5.
26 S.R.O., D/D/V return 1843.
27 H.O. 129/319/3/1/1.
28 S.R.O., D/D/V return 1870.
29 *Wells Wills*, ed. Weaver, 152.
30 *Som. Wills*, ed. Brown, ii 59.
31 *Diary of Richard Symonds* (Camd. Soc. 1st ser. lxxiv), 102–5.
32 Winchester Coll. Mun. 12886, 12888; S.R.O., D/P/mart 4/1/1; *Sherborne Mercury*, 21 and 28 Aug. 1744.
33 S.R.O., D/P/mart 4/1/1; Saunders, *Hund. of Martock*, 34–8.
34 *Cal. Pat.* 1324–7, 132.

35 E 117/8/23B.
36 *S.R.S.* ii. 293–4.
37 *Cal. Pat.* 1549–51, 192–3.
38 *S. & D. N. & Q.* xxiii. 149–50; Saunders, *Hund. of Martock*, 17–18.
39 *S.R.S.* ii. 109–10, 293–4.
40 *Cal. Pat.* 1548–9, 286–91.
41 *S.R.S.* xix. 262–6.
42 G. Oliver, *Monasticon Diocesis Exoniensis*, 257.
43 *Cal. Inq. p.m.* ix, p. 176.
44 *S.R.S.* xix. 263.
45 Ibid. xl. 28, 124; S.R.O., DD/SAS, SE 30, ff. 16, 22, 31.
46 *S.R.S.* xxi. 179–80.   47 *S.R.S.* ii. 111, 295.
48 Schedule of deeds in parochial diary *penes* the vicar. See plate facing p. 49.
49 See plates facing pp. 16, 17.
50 Pevsner, *South and West Som.* 231–2.
51 S.R.O., D/P/mart 8/4/1.

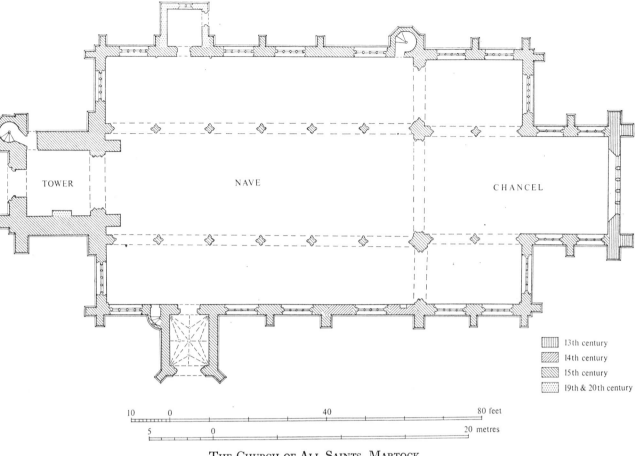

TOWER

NAVE

CHANCEL

▦	13th century
▨	14th century
▧	15th century
▦	19th & 20th century

10   0   40   80 feet

5   0   20 metres

THE CHURCH OF ALL SAINTS, MARTOCK

effigy of *c.* 1315, possibly representing a member of the Fiennes family.[52] Externally there are traces of 7 scratch or mass dials on the south wall, and one buttress on the north side has footholds cut in it to aid the recovery of fives balls from the leads when the game was played there in the 18th century.[53] Gateways to the churchyard to the east and south-west are dated 1625 and 1627. There are 8 bells: (i–iv) 1902, J. Warner and Sons, London; (v) 1657, Robert Austen (II); (vi) *c.* 1500, probably by a Dorset founder; (vii) 1614, Robert Wiseman; (viii) 1877, Llewellins and James, Bristol.[54] The plate includes a paten and flagon of 1758 by R. Cox and two cups of 1861.[55] The parish registers date from 1558 and are complete.[56]

By 1535 the vicar of Martock paid a chaplain to serve Stapleton chapel.[57] By 1548 a light there was supported by 1 a. of meadow in Stapleton.[58]

The chapel was said to be annexed to the vicarage

in 1625,[59] although in 1678 John Fanstone of Downton (Wilts.), grandson of a former lessee of Stapleton court-house, conveyed the chapel and its yard with some land to the lord of Stapleton manor.[60] The chapelry continued to form part of the title of Martock vicarage until 1798, although the chapel had probably then been demolished.[61]

A chaplain at Long Load occurs in 1418, and another, Thomas Colles, in 1494,[62] but none was named in 1548.[63] Chapel and lands were sold in 1549 to a local man, Robert Dyer, probably acting for the inhabitants.[64] Services were evidently continued, though Dyer's grandson was accused of preventing the minister or reader from conducting them.[65] By 1607 the chapel was owned by the lords of Long Load manor.[66]

In 1657–8 there was an attempt to create an independent chapelry, and during the later years of the Interregnum it was served principally by

[52] *Proc. Som. Arch. Soc.* lxiii. 18.
[53] S.R.O., D/P/mart 4/1/1.
[54] S.R.O., DD/SAS CH 16.
[55] *Proc. Som. Arch. Soc.* xliv. 178–9.
[56] S.R.O., D/P/mart 2/1/1.
[57] *Valor Eccl.* (Rec. Com.), i. 199, 225.
[58] *S.R.S.* ii. 294.   [59] E 331/Bath and Wells/2.
[60] E 310/23/127 no. 36; lease 23 May 1678 *penes* Mr. J. S. Cox, St. Peter Port, Guernsey.
[61] S.R.O., D/D/B reg. 32, p. 167. The chapel is not marked on the Stapleton manor map of 1774: S.R.O., DD/S/HR.

[62] Winchester Coll. Mun. 12862–3. Clarice 'atte Church' occurs at Long Load in 1327: *S.R.S.* iii. 131.
[63] *S.R.S.* ii. 110, 296. Saunders, *Hund. of Martock*, 98, mistakenly attributes a Martock stipendiary priest to this chapel.
[64] *Cal. Pat.* 1548–9, 286–91; Winchester Coll. Mun. 13153. A Crown lease of the chapel and lands, then occupied by the inhabitants of Long Load, for 31 years was made in 1572 to Hen. Middlemore, probably in error: *Cal. Pat.* 1569–72, 389–90; E 310/23/127 no. 90.
[65] Winchester Coll. Mun. 13153.
[66] Ibid. 13107.

Edward Stacy, but also by itinerant preachers, including an Anabaptist mason, paid by collections among the inhabitants.[67] From c. 1720 the vicar of Martock held services fortnightly in return for the use of land given by the inhabitants;[68] and from 1733, after augmentation arranged by the vicar, the assistant curate of Martock held a service every Sunday.[69] Weekly sermons and quarterly celebrations of the Holy Communion were held in the early 19th century.[70] On Census Sunday 1851 the afternoon service was attended by a congregation of 113 adults and 47 Sunday-school pupils.[71]

Long Load was created a separate ecclesiastical parish in 1867. The vicar of Martock was patron and the first perpetual curate was the former assistant curate of Martock.[72] From 1957 it was held in plurality with Ash, but in 1972 the living was divided, Long Load being joined with Long Sutton.[73]

The chapel was supported by rents worth 16d. in 1548.[74] Its income was augmented with £20 a year in 1655,[75] and with £200 in 1733 and again in 1789.[76] By 1851 tithes, glebe, and fees produced £47, less than the salary of the curate.[77] An endowment of £200 from the Common Fund was made in 1873,[78] and there were still 4 a. of glebe in 1974.[79]

A church house or priest's house, the responsibility of the tenants of Long Load manor, was ordered to be repaired between 1494 and 1571.[80] In 1607 it was said to have been once called 'the court house' but was then called the 'priest house'.[81] It may possibly be the house held by the parish in 1815 which stood on the north side of the chapel yard.[82] A parsonage house was evidently acquired c. 1852 and was enlarged in 1865.[83] It was sold after amalgamation with Long Sutton.

By 1418 the chapel was dedicated to the Virgin, but a field called Mawdlyn Forde belonging to it in 1548 suggests a different patron saint.[84] In 1791 the building was described as small and ruinous. It measured 53 ft. by 17 ft., contained 10 pews and a gallery, and had a wooden turret at its west end with a clock and 2 bells.[85] It was evidently 'pulled down' in 1796 and presumably rebuilt soon after.[86] A faculty for demolition was granted in 1854.[87]

CHRIST CHURCH, Long Load, was completed in 1856 to the designs of C. E. Giles. It is in the Early English style and comprises chancel, nave, south porch, and a turret with a bell. The Jacobean pulpit survives from the former chapels, and a cup and salver dated 1825.[88] The first baptismal register begins in 1731, its earliest information being drawn from family bibles. Marriage and burial registers survive from 1749.[89]

A chapel was completed at Ash in 1841, and the three tithings of Ash, Milton, and Witcombe were created a separate ecclesiastical parish in 1845.[90] The living was held as a vicarage until 1957 and, after being linked with Long Load between then and 1972, it is held with the vicarage at Martock. Initially endowed with 4 a. and £690 in investments, it was augmented with £200 by Queen Anne's Bounty in 1850 and with £250 from the Common Fund in 1873.[91]

In 1843 two Sunday sermons were normally preached and Holy Communion was administered four times a year.[92] On Census Sunday 1851 there were congregations of 138 in the morning and 300 in the evening, with a Sunday-school attendance of 62.[93] Holy Communion was celebrated monthly by 1870.[94]

The chapel, later church, of the HOLY, ETERNAL, AND UNDIVIDED TRINITY originally comprised a simple rectangular stone building, designed by Sampson Kempthorne, to which a chancel was added in 1889, a porch in 1913, and a western tower as a peace memorial in 1920.[95] The tower contains 6 bells, 3 by Mears and Stainbank installed in 1921 and 3 acquired in 1946.[96] The plate is modern, and the registers are complete from 1841.[97]

NONCONFORMITY. Thomas Budd, formerly vicar of Montacute and Kingsbury Episcopi, had settled at Ash by 1655 and become a Quaker. There in 1657 he held two meetings in his orchard, the first attended by 700–800 people and the second by c. 200, both addressed by Thomas Salthouse, an itinerant Quaker preacher. The first gathering was broken up by five priests, including the vicar, James Stevenson, with 'a great company of rude people with long staves and pikes', and the second by soldiers. Budd and Salthouse were both arrested but subsequently released.[98] Budd was again imprisoned in 1661 for refusing the Oath of Allegiance and died in Ilchester gaol in 1670.[99] Richard

[67] Cal. S.P. Dom. 1655–6, 72; 1657–8, 82, 375; E134/13 Chas. II Mich./43. John Squibb of Load, clerk, mentioned in 1656, evidently served the chapel: S.R.S. xxviii. 286.
[68] Winchester Coll. Mun. 12890A–12904.
[69] Tablet in ch.; S.R.O., D/P/mart 3/1/12; Winchester Coll. Mun. 12890A.
[70] S.R.O., D/D/V returns 1827, 1840, 1843.
[71] H.O. 129/319/3/1/2.
[72] Lond. Gaz. 23 Aug. 1867, p. 4698; S.R.O., D/D/B reg. 39, p. 104.
[73] Parochial diary penes the vicar of Martock.
[74] S.R.S. ii. 110, 296.
[75] Cal. S.P. Dom. 1655–6, 72.
[76] Tablet in ch.; S.R.O., D/P/mart 3/1/12; Aug. Livings, 1703–1815, H.C. 115 (1813–14), xii.
[77] H.O. 129/319/3/1/2.
[78] Lond. Gaz. 21 Feb. 1873, p. 735.
[79] Ex inf. Dioc. Office.
[80] Winchester Coll. Mun. 12862, 12845, 12870.
[81] Ibid. 13107.   [82] Ibid. survey 1815.
[83] Par. rec., vestry bk. 1851–1951.
[84] Winchester Coll. Mun. 12863; S.R.S. ii. 296.

[85] Collinson, Hist. Som. iii. 11.
[86] S.R.O., D/P/l.ld 2/1/1.
[87] S.R.O., D/D/Ca 444.
[88] Proc. Som. Arch. Soc. xliv. 178.
[89] S.R.O., D/P/l.ld 2/1/1–6.
[90] H.O. 129/319/3/1/3; par. rec., vestry bk. 1841–1970; Lond. Gaz. 19 Dec. 1845, p. 7244.
[91] Par. rec., vestry bk. 1841–1970; Livings Aug. Q.A.B. H.C. 122 (1867), liv; Lond. Gaz. 21 Feb. 1873, p. 737.
[92] S.R.O., D/D/V return 1843.
[93] H.O. 129/319/3/1/3.
[94] S.R.O., D/D/V return 1870.
[95] Par. rec., vestry bk. 1841–1970; H. M. Colvin, Dict. Eng. Architects.
[96] Par. rec., vestry bk.
[97] Proc. Som. Arch. Soc. xliv. 174; registers penes the vicar.
[98] S.R.O., DD/SFR 8/2; Q/SR 95/ii/54–6; Besse, Sufferings of the Quakers, i. 578–82; Freedom after Ejection, ed. A. Gordon, 224.
[99] S.R.O., DD/SFR 8/1. Thomas Budd is often confused with a Presbyterian preacher of the same name, probably his son, for whom see below.

Wall, the vicar, was distraining Quakers' goods for attending a Yeovil meeting in 1670.[1]

An Anabaptist mason preached at Long Load during the Interregnum. Members of the sect were recorded there c. 1720, and houses in Martock were licensed for their meetings in 1737 and 1747.[2]

By 1669 there were five Presbyterian preachers in the parish: Henry Butler, ejected from Yeovil, John Dyer, John Bush, ejected from Langport and Huish Episcopi, John Turner, ejected from Cricket Malherbie, and Thomas Grove, ejected from Kilmersdon.[3] In 1672 James Stevenson, ejected from Martock vicarage in 1662, having preached for a time in Crewkerne, returned to preach in Martock, continuing until his death in 1685.[4] Another Presbyterian, William Cooper, ejected from St. Olave's, Southwark (Lond.), was licensed to preach in his own house at Long Load in 1672, and two other houses, one at Load, were similarly registered in the same year.[5] George Bisse, owner of one of the houses, complained that in 1680 he was threatened with arrest and that his house was haunted on Sundays by armed soldiers hoping 'to convict him for a conventicle'.[6] Thomas Budd from Barrington, probably son of the Quaker, evidently succeeded Stevenson as the principal Presbyterian preacher in the parish. He was ministering in Kingsbury Episcopi by 1681 and in Martock by 1685,[7] and occurs with three other itinerant Presbyterian ministers in 1690–1.[8]

It was probably the Presbyterians who licensed Andrew Westcott's house, now the Clerk's House in Pound Lane, in 1699, for in 1701 the 'new-built house in Andrew Westcott's orchard' was registered and subsequently became known as Pound Lane Chapel.[9] By 1722 this chapel had been endowed with 40s. a year for a teacher or preacher and was probably served by Mr. Hallett, 'a modern Calvinist' and an ordained Presbyterian minister, from 1717 until at least 1735, when he had a congregation of 400.[10] The congregation was subsequently described as Independent. By 1774 the activities of Lady Huntingdon's preachers in South Petherton had reduced the attendance at Pound Lane to 100 with only 30 communicants.[11] During the late 18th and early 19th centuries the chapel was attended by people from as far afield as Hardington Mandeville, Isle Abbotts, Pitney, and Donyatt.[12] George White-field preached in the chapel and the Somerset Independents held their annual meetings there in 1797, 1809, and 1825.[13] In 1851 the chapel, which seated 500, was attended by 150 on Census Sunday morning,[14] but during the later 19th century many of the remaining members removed to Bower Hinton Chapel, Pound Lane being served first by a preacher of the Particular Baptists and then by a Baptist layman.[15] Evening services continued to be held until 1905, and morning services until 1908. The chapel was demolished in 1913 and the stone used to repair the wall around the graveyard, which still survives.[16]

The chapel was 'barn-like' with a steeply-thatched roof and square latticed windows, and a gallery supported on wooden pillars ran round three sides.[17]

Twelve houses were licensed for nonconformist meetings between 1689 and 1700, including dwellings at Hurst, Newton, Coat, and Long Load, and seven by Presbyterians between 1742 and 1755, including two at Load.[18] Presbyterians in the parish were still said to be numerous in 1776.[19] The strength of nonconformity is witnessed by the 'dissenting party' voting for the closure of a work-house in the vestry in 1742.[20]

Two licences for Methodist groups were issued in 1747 and one in 1752,[21] and a meeting at Bower Hinton was established by the Revd. Christopher Hull c. 1788, although the register starts two years later.[22] A former member of Lady Huntingdon's college, he 'preached in barns, cottages, and open air, both here and in the adjacent villages and towns'. The present chapel and manse were built in 1791 and Hull continued as minister until his death in 1814.[23] In 1824 the minister registered a house in Long Load for worship, and in 1827 a house at Newton was bought to augment the minister's stipend.[24] The Revd. G. H. Cossins, minister 1830–66, 'a unique and godly man', established the meeting as an Independent (Congregational) chapel.[25] It was known as the Ebenezer chapel by 1837 and in 1851 the Census Sunday services were attended by 95 in the morning, 150 in the evening, and by 37 Sunday-school pupils.[26] A schoolroom was built (1866–8), classrooms added and, between 1887 and 1893, the chapel was enlarged.[27] There were 6 Congregational lay preachers in Martock

[1] S.R.O., DD/SFR 8/1; D/D/Rm 1/9.
[2] Winchester Coll. Mun. 12902; E 134/13 Chas. II Mich./43; S.R.O. D/P/mart 3/2/12; Q/RR, meeting-house lics. Edward Damer licensed his house at Bower Hinton for Anabaptists in 1737, Presbyterians in 1747, and Methodists in 1752: Q/RR, meeting-house lics.
[3] G. L. Turner, Rec. Early Nonconf. ii. 1108–9.
[4] Ibid.; Cal. S.P. Dom. 1672, 298; J. Murch, Presbyterian and General Baptist Churches in W. of Eng. 240–1; S.R.O., D/P/mart/2/1/3.
[5] G. L. Turner, Rec. Early Nonconf. ii. 1108–9; Cal. S.P. Dom. 1672, 298–9, 677.
[6] Cal. S.P. Dom. 1680–1, 688–9. Bisse, evidently the lay leader of the Martock Presbyterians, was arrested on suspicion after the Monmouth rebellion and purchased his pardon.
[7] Cal. S.P. Dom. 1672, 293; R.G. 4/2055.
[8] Freedom after Ejection, 92. The others were Mr. Light, Mr. Bishop, and Mr. Gatchell.
[9] S.R.O., Q/RR, meeting-house lics. 'Martock meeting-house' is mentioned in Budd's register in 1692 and John Gardner of Martock, minister, occurs there in 1693–7: R.G. 4/2055.

[10] Saunders, Hund. of Martock, 56.
[11] Ibid. 57.   [12] R.G. 4/1556.
[13] Rep. Som. Cong. Union (1896), 45.
[14] H.O. 129/319/3/1/5.
[15] Saunders, Hund. of Martock, 58; Rep. Som. Cong. Union (1896), 45.
[16] Saunders, Hund. of Martock, 58; par. cncl. mins.
[17] Saunders, Hund. of Martock, 58, plate facing p. 54.
[18] S.R.O., Q/RR, meeting-house lics.
[19] S.R.O., D/D/V Dioc. bk. 1776.
[20] S.R.O., D/P/mart/13/2/3.
[21] S.R.O., Q/RR, meeting-house lics.
[22] R.G. 4/1420.
[23] Rep. Som. Cong. Union (1896), 45; Saunders, Hund. of Martock, 57. Hull was successful in influencing his former opponent, Dr. Thomas Coke, curate of South Petherton: Rep. Som. Cong. Union (1896), 45; D.N.B.; J. Vickers, Thomas Coke, 24–5.
[24] S.R.O., D/D/Rm, box 6; DD/S/HR, box 49, conveyance 19 Dec. 1827.
[25] Rep. Som. Cong. Union (1896), 46.
[26] Lond. Gaz. 13 Sept. 1837, p.2249; H.O. 129/319/3/1/6.
[27] Rep. Som. Cong. Union (1896), 46.

in 1896.[28] The name of the chapel was changed to the Martock United Reformed church in 1973.

Of eight houses licensed for nonconformist worship between 1807 and 1835, two were Independent (one at Long Load in 1816), and of the others, two were at Bower Hinton (1815, 1825) and one each at Ash (1827), Coat (1829), and Milton (1835).[29] Wesleyans occur at Bower Hinton during the years between 1811 and 1828, at Ash between 1811 and 1838, at Martock between 1828 and 1858, and at Coat in 1832. The Ash congregation moved to Long Sutton.[30] A possible Arminian congregation in 1826, inferred from a reference to a school in that year, has not been traced.[31]

A Wesleyan chapel was built at Long Load in 1855 and closed in 1960.[32] Another in North Street, Martock, was built in 1868 and a Sunday school for 31 girls and 34 boys was formed in the following year. A new schoolroom was started in 1876. The present chapel on the same site was built in 1886.[33]

The Brethren met in the later 19th century at a chapel in Highway on the site of a former poorhouse, and in 1893 built the present Gospel Hall in Church Street.[34]

EDUCATION. It is possible that Stephen Nurse (d. 1571), formerly a chantry priest at the manorhouse chapel, may have been responsible for starting a free school in the parish.[35] John Atkins, formerly of Taunton, was licensed to teach Latin and English in Martock in 1583, and subsequent licences to teach Latin or grammar were granted in 1592 to John Priddell, in 1604 to Simon Sturtevant, in 1605 to Thomas 'Bainrafe', in 1609 to John Gardner, and in 1633 to Thomas Farnham.[36] Sturtevant and Farnham were both graduates. 'Bainrafe' can be identified as Thomas Farnaby (d. 1647).[37] The parish house was also known as the school house by 1644, and there was then also a house for a schoolmaster.[38] In 1646 Charles Darby, the ejected vicar of Montacute, was appointed master and in 1662 became the first master of the grammar school endowed by William Strode.[39]

There was a teacher of infants at Long Load in 1567.[40] Elementary education is again recorded in 1612, when Edward Fry was presented for teaching an English school while unlicensed.[41] Two men were licensed to teach in the parish in 1633 and Thomas Payne, schoolmaster, was mentioned in 1695.[42] Regular payments to women for schooling

pauper children were made by the overseers of the poor during the later 18th century.[43] In 1818 there were a day-school taught by the parish clerk for 50 boys, paid for by the parents, two Sunday schools on Bell's system for 285 children, and a Dissenting Sunday school in Long Load for 47.[44] By 1826 the vicar had established a day-school, probably the school which in 1833 had 50 infant pupils and was supported by subscriptions and parental contributions. Also in 1833 there were 2 schools for 80 boys and one for 40 girls, all private, and 4 Sunday schools: 2 run by the Church of England for 300 children, one Independent, and one Arminian, the last 2 having attendances of 50 each. There were also several dame schools for very young children.[45] There were 4 dame schools by 1846, of which 2 were at Long Load, with 81 paying pupils.[46] In 1868 there were 14 schools in the parish, including an evening-school. There were then 126 pupils on the books of the evening-school, all over 12, with an average attendance of 80, though girls of school age could spare little time from gloving.[47]

A National school at Martock was built by public subscription in 1846 on the south side of Church Street.[48] By 1850 it was run as both a commercial and National school and had 66 boys and 51 girls.[49] The building could accommodate 236 in 1894, but 183 was the average attendance.[50] By 1903 attendances had fallen slightly to 172. The two rooms were used almost every night for parochial activities, including band and choir practices, and temperance and friendly-society meetings.[51] From 1908–9 only boys and infants were taken and numbers fell to 122 in 1914–15 and to 96 in 1934–5. Known as Martock Junior school from 1940, junior boys and infants only were taken from 1945, and junior boys and girls from 1950. A drop in numbers to 77 in 1944–5 was followed by a rise to 106 in 1954–5 and a slight fall to 94 in 1964–5 and to 91 in 1969.[52]

A schoolhouse at Bower Hinton which was in existence in 1837 was assigned to the vicar and churchwardens in 1872, and became the National school there.[53] The school was evidently rebuilt c. 1870 with accommodation for 200 pupils. It had average attendances of 125 in 1889, and 128 by 1894.[54] In 1903 there were 132 children on the books although only 103 attended. There were two rooms, one of which was occupied by the infants. The schoolrooms there were also used for parochial activities.[55] From 1908–9 only girls and infants

[28] *Rep. Som. Cong. Union* (1896), 7.
[29] S.R.O., D/D/Rm, boxes 2 and 6; Q/RR, meetinghouse lics.
[30] S.R.O., D/N/spc 1, 2.
[31] *Rep. B. & W. Dioc. Assoc. S.P.C.K.* (1825–6).
[32] *Kelly's Dir. Som.* (1939); S.R.O., D/N/spc, box 3.
[33] S.R.O., D/N/spc 23–5; foundation stones.
[34] Ex inf. Mr. Gordon Maynard, Ash; date stone on Gospel Hall.
[35] Nurse lived in the parish until his death: S.R.O., D/P/mart 2/1/1.
[36] S.R.O., D/D/ol 8, 12, 18; D/D/Vc 58, 68.
[37] *D.N.B*; see above, p. 84.
[38] S.R.O., DD/MR 92.
[39] Bodl. MS. C.C.C. 390/2; *Calamy Revised*, ed. Matthews. For subsequent history of Strode's grammar school see *V.C.H. Som.* ii. 458–9.
[40] Winchester Coll. Mun. 12871.
[41] S.R.O., D/D/Ca 177.
[42] S.R.O., D/D/Vc 58; DD/S/HR, box 47, lease for a

year 30 Dec. 1695.
[43] S.R.O., D/P/mart 13/2/4–5.
[44] *Digest of Returns to Sel. Cttee. on Educ. of Poor*, H.C. 224 (1819), ix (2).
[45] *Rep. B. & W. Dioc. Assoc. S.P.C.K.* (1825–6); *Educ. Enquiry Abstract*, H.C. 62 (1835), xlii.
[46] *Church Sch. Inquiry, 1846–7*.
[47] *Rep. Com. on Children and Women in Agric.* [4202–I], p. 474, H.C. (1868–9), xiii.
[48] Tablet on building; schedule of deeds in parochial diary, *penes* the vicar. The site was obtained in 1840.
[49] *Mins. of Educ. Cttee. of Council, 1850* [1357], p. 215, H.C. (1850–1).
[50] *Returns of Schs.* [C. 7529], H.C. (1894), lxv.
[51] S.R.O., C/E 27.
[52] S.R.O., *Schs. Lists*.
[53] Schedule of deeds in parochial diary, *penes* the vicar.
[54] *Kelly's Dir. Som.* (1889); *Returns of Schs.* [C. 7529] H.C. (1894), lxv.
[55] S.R.O., C/E 27.

were taken, the school being administered with Martock National school, which accommodated the boys. Numbers rose to 140 in 1914–15 and fell to 112 in 1934–5. It became a junior school from 1940 and since 1950 has been given over to infants, being known as the Bower Hinton Infants school. Numbers, which had dropped to 45 in 1944–5, rose rapidly to 72 in 1954–5, 118 in 1964–5, and to 121 in 1969.[56] A new school was opened in Elmleigh Road in 1975 to replace those at Martock and Bower Hinton.

Ash Sunday school, attended by 121 in 1846, was then receiving a grant from the National Society.[57] Ash Church of England school was built in 1846 for 90 children and had an average attendance of 80 in 1889.[58] An infants' department was added in 1892, giving two rooms with accommodation for 112, and, in 1894, an average attendance of 90.[59] In 1903 there were 88 children on the books and attendances of 70.[60] Numbers fell gradually to 62 in 1934–5 and it became a junior school from 1943. Thereafter numbers generally continued below 45, but had risen to 53 in 1969.[61]

In 1836 Samuel Dyer of Long Load, having formerly set aside £300 to augment the salaries of the teachers in Long Load Sunday school, purchased 5½ a. of land in Aller, the income to be devoted by trustees to the same purpose. In 1866 the vicar of Martock, who was from 1867 also vicar of Long Load, and churchwardens became the trustees and the income was then £14.[62] The Sunday school at Load was attended by 109 pupils in 1846, and a permanent schoolroom was built in 1854.[63] In 1865 the vicar of Martock proposed that the income should be diverted from the Sunday school to found a day-school, and a Church of England school was evidently started soon after.[64] Average attendances of 41 in 1889 fell to 26 in 1903.[65] Subsequently described as a National Voluntary school, attendances remained steady at 36 between 1904–5 and 1914–15. The school took only juniors from 1921 and numbers dropped to 14 in 1934–5, rising to 23 in 1954–5. The school was closed in 1961.[66]

CHARITIES FOR THE POOR. John Goodden of Bower Hinton (d. 1722) left by will 11½ a. of

arable in Martock fields, the income to be distributed in bread every Sunday to people from Bower Hinton, Hurst, and Martock tithings not in receipt of poor-relief. The charity was to be administered by the vicar and churchwardens and in 1789 the earl of Salisbury granted to them his half of the great tithes payable from the charity lands. The lands were producing £11 a year in 1822, and on the inclosure of Martock fields in 1826 9 a. were allotted to the charity. Money received for lands bought by the railway company was used to acquire additional closes, and in 1867 the charity held 9½ a. let for £26 a year. In 1895 attendance at afternoon service in the parish church was required of all recipients of the bread.[67] The income stood at £40 in 1962.[68]

A charity established by the will of Elizabeth Hopkins producing £2 a year for the poor of the parish had been lost by 1822.[69]

By deed of 1852 Mary Leach (d. 1852) gave £300 in trust to the vicar and churchwardens, payable after the death of herself and her husband (d. 1860), to be divided after the repair of family monuments at Martock, amongst the poor of the parish. Between 1862 and 1865 it produced about £9 a year.[70] In 1895 the income of £8 15s. 6d. was paid to the church clothing club. In 1976 it was £8·16 which was combined with the Wood charity, called the Martock Charity and Coal Club, and distributed to the poor at Christmas.[71]

Ann Leaves, by will proved 1876, left £300 to the overseers the income for the poor of Martock, Hurst, and Bower Hinton tithings in coals, clothing, or both. In 1895 the income was £7 11s. 4d., distributed before Christmas in cards for coal or clothing to the value of 2s. 6d. each. The charity was taken over by the parish council in 1906 and, because of war-time rationing, was being distributed in cash in 1947.[72] The income was £6 17s. 8d. in 1962 and £6·88 in 1976.[73]

Half an acre of orchard in Bower Hinton was conveyed to the vicar and churchwardens by Mrs. M. A. Wood in 1878 for the general benefit of the church clothing club. In 1895 the charity was worth £1 15s a year, used according to the donor's intentions.[74] By 1976 the income had shrunk to £0·76 a year and was administered with the Martock Charity and Coal Club.[75]

[56] S.R.O., *Schs. Lists*.
[57] *Church Sch. Inquiry, 1846–7*.
[58] *Kelly's Dir. Som.* (1889).
[59] S.R.O., C/E 26; *Returns of Schs.* [C. 7529] H.C. (1894), lxv.
[60] S.R.O., C/E 26.   [61] S.R.O., *Schs. Lists*.
[62] Char. Com. files; D/P/l.ld 18/1/1.
[63] *Church Sch. Inquiry, 1846–7* S.R.O., D/P/l.ld 18/1/1.
[64] S.R.O., D/P/l.ld 18/1/1; *Kelly's Dir. Som.* (1889).
[65] *Kelly's Dir. Som.* (1889); S.R.O., C/E 27.
[66] S.R.O., *Schs. Lists*; S.R.O., C/E, box 64.

[67] *9th Rep. Com. Char.* H.C. 258, p. 532 (1823), ix; Char. Com. files.
[68] Par. cncl. mins. 1961–8, 28 Mar. 1962.
[69] *9th Rep. Com. Char.* 532.
[70] Char. Com. files.
[71] Par. cncl. mins. 1894–1905; ex inf. the Clerk, Martock parish council.
[72] Par. cncl. mins. 1894–1905; Char. Com. files.
[73] Par. cncl. mins. 1961–8; ex inf. Mrs. Barbara Thomas, Martock.
[74] Char. Com. files; par. cncl. mins. 1894–1905.
[75] Ex inf. the Revd. P. N. H. Coney.

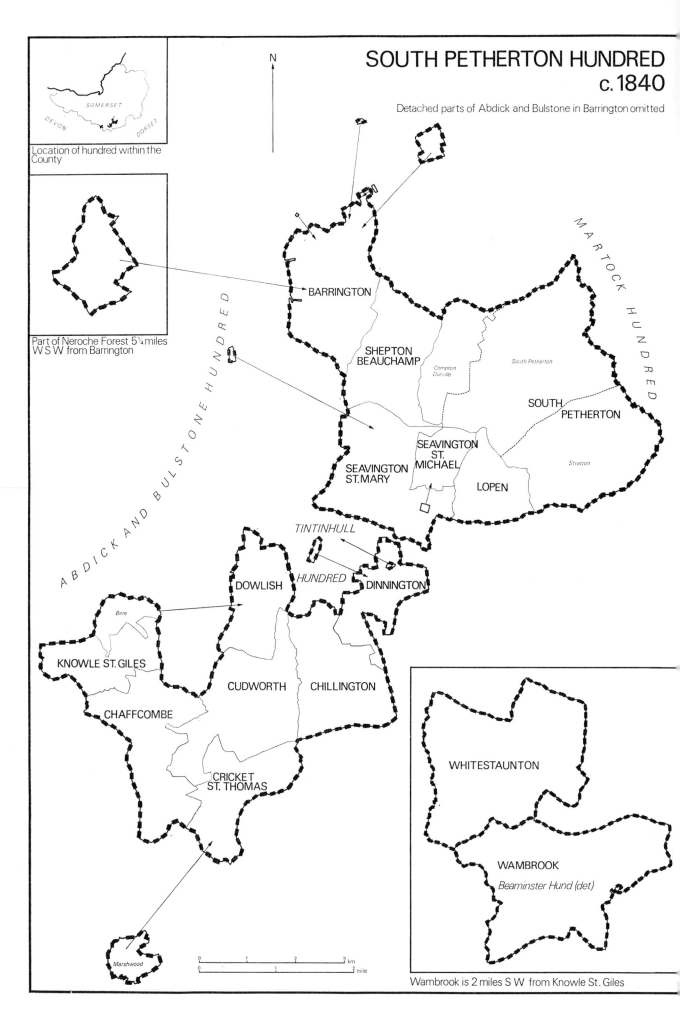

SOUTH PETHERTON HUNDRED
c.1840

Detached parts of Abdick and Bulstone in Barrington omitted

N

SOMERSET

DEVON   *DORSET*

Location of hundred within the County

Part of Neroche Forest 5¼ miles W S W from Barrington

ABDICK AND BULSTONE HUNDRED

MARTOCK HUNDRED

BARRINGTON

SHEPTON BEAUCHAMP

Compton Durville

South Petherton

SOUTH PETHERTON

SEAVINGTON ST. MICHAEL

SEAVINGTON ST. MARY

LOPEN

Stratton

TINTINHULL

DOWLISH

HUNDRED

DINNINGTON

Bere

KNOWLE ST. GILES

CUDWORTH

CHILLINGTON

CHAFFCOMBE

CRICKET ST. THOMAS

Marshwood

0   1   2   3 km
0   1   2 mile

WHITESTAUNTON

WAMBROOK

Beaminster Hund (det)

Wambrook is 2 miles S W from Knowle St. Giles

SOUTH PETHERTON
HUNDRED

THE HUNDRED lies in the southern area of the county, stretching in a south-westerly band along the line of the Foss Way from the upper reaches of the river Parrett to the Windwhistle ridge, and including Whitestaunton on the boundary with Devon. The soils in the north are mostly fertile Yeovil Sands with extensive arable, still in parts undivided by hedges. The wooded southern areas lie on poorer soils with less evidence of open-field cultivation and where pasture has always been predominant. The parishes themselves are mostly small and irregular, with a mixture of nucleated and scattered settlements, the latter in the south often originating in woodland clearings. The predominantly agrarian economy was varied from the 17th century onwards especially at Lopen by the manufacture of coarse cloth and of rope from locally-grown hemp and flax.

The hundred was created by 1084 around the pre-Conquest royal estate of South Petherton and its members.[1] By 1212 it included Shepton Beauchamp and Lopen,[2] by 1225 Whitestaunton,[3] and by 1242–3 Cudworth, Dowlish Wake, Westcombland in Buckland St. Mary, and probably Hurcott in Seavington St. Mary.[4] By 1286 the hundred had almost achieved its fullest extent: South Petherton, with its separate tithings or hamlets of Compton Durville, Great and Little Stratton, and Wigborough, and the tithings or hamlets of Barrington, Chaffcombe, Chillington, Cudworth with Worth, Dinnington, Dowlish Wake, Knowle St. Giles, Lopen, Seavington Dennis, Seavington Vaux, Shepton Beauchamp, Upton (in Seavington St. Mary), White-staunton, and Street and Leigh in Winsham.[5] Cricket St. Thomas, Dommett (in Buckland St. Mary but adjoining the 'island' of Barrington in Neroche forest), and South Illeigh in Knowle were included by 1303,[6] but the last two were not separately enumerated in 1327[7] or 1334[8] though South Harp tithing in South Petherton seems to have replaced Wigborough and Little Stratton. Westcombland formed part of Martock hundred by 1327, but the Forde abbey estates in Winsham, possibly comprised in the earlier properties of Street and Leigh, included Fordebrigge, now Bridge, by 1334[9] and Whatley by 1343.[10] The hundred remained so constituted until the 19th century.[11] Wambrook, in the hundred of Beaminster and Redborne, Dorset, was transferred to Somerset in 1896 and is here treated with the Somerset hundred which it adjoins.

The hundred belonged to the Crown but was claimed by Philip Daubeney (d. 1236) in virtue of his possession of South Petherton manor.[12] The Crown seized it from Ralph Daubeney in 1280 but restored it to him ten years later.[13] Ownership thereafter

[1] V.C.H. Som. i. 534.
[2] Bk. of Fees, i. 86.
[3] S.R.S. xi, p. 57.
[4] Ibid. pp. 317–20. Rent was paid to the hundred by the abbot of Athelney in 1535: Valor Eccl. (Rec. Com.), i. 206.
[5] Feud. Aids, iv. 283–4.
[6] Ibid. 315.
[7] S.R.S. iii. 196–200.

[8] Subsidy of 1334, ed. R. Glasscock, 275.
[9] S.R.S. iii. 131–2; Forde Abbey, Cart. p. 488.
[10] C 260/142/8; Year Bk. 17 Edw. III (Rolls Ser.), 567; ibid. 18–19 Edw. III (Rolls Ser.), 249, 251.
[11] S.R.O., DD/HI, box 9; S.R.S. iii. 327–8; xx. 36.
[12] Plac. de Quo Warr. (Rec. Com.), ii. 127–8.
[13] Cal. Pat. 1272–81, 401; 1281–92, 376; Cal. Close, 1288–96, 337.

belonged to the owners of the main manor of South Petherton until the jurisdiction lapsed in the 19th century. Suit from Seavington Abbots, Seavington Dennis, Dinnington, and Chaffcombe tithings was withdrawn by the earls of Gloucester *c.* 1262,[14] and the Crown still retained those tithings in right of the honor of Gloucester in 1435.[15]

By 1305 a distinction was made between the hundred *intrinsecum*, probably the tithing of South Petherton alone, and the hundred *forinsecum*.[16] Three lawdays, at Hilary, Hockday, and Michaelmas, were held in the mid 15th century,[17] four in the 16th century,[18] and three in 1618–19.[19] In the mid 17th century hundred business was heard in the manor court.[20] Court records survive as an extract for 1445 and for 1618–19.[21]

Philip Daubeney (d. 1236) released all tenants of Bruton priory from suit to the hundred,[22] and Gloucester honor properties and Forde abbey tenants were similarly relieved, the first by illegal withdrawal *c.* 1262, the latter by grant in 1347.[23] By the 1570s there was 'no money paid, nor yet waifed or strayed goods' at the court, but tithingmen except from Shepton Beauchamp were sworn.[24] In 1668, under title of the manor court leet and view of frankpledge, two millers were fined for refusal to appear with their measures, and the tithingmen of Whitestaunton and Cricket St. Thomas were absent.[25] The manor court in 1618 presented that the hundred should provide a cucking stool.[26] Barrington parish continued to pay for release of suit until 1697.[27] No further direct evidence of the court's activity has been traced.

A bedel was appointed by the hundred *forinsecum* by 1386.[28] A hundred bailiff occurs by 1665,[29] and he preceded the manor bailiff in the manor court from 1684 until the offices were combined in 1781.[30] There was an attempt to revive the hundred court in the early 19th century in combination with the manor (hitherto described as vill and manor court),[31] and the offices of constable and steward of the hundred occur until 1868–9 and 1872 respectively.[32]

The hundred was represented at the sheriff's tourn on Ham Hill, held once a year at Hocktide in the late 15th century and by 1575 at Hocktide and Michaelmas.[33] By 1652 tourns were held at Easter and Michaelmas for the hundreds of South Petherton, Crewkerne, Houndsborough, Coker, and Martock, but were then 'much discontinued and few fines or amercements levied for divers years past'.[34] The tourns were evidently revived, and Barrington parish continued payments to the courts until 1697.[35]

[14] *Rot Hund.* (Rec. Com.), ii. 127–8; *S.R.S.* xliv. 343. The Crown claimed damages in 1275 for 13 years; Richard, earl of Gloucester, d. 1262.
[15] C 260/195/18; *Cal. Pat.* 1388–92, 332; 1429–36, 466.
[16] C 133/120/2; C 136/44/1.
[17] Forde Abbey, Cart. pp. 505–9.
[18] S.R.O., DD/X/LT, copy custumal, Shepton Beauchamp 1575.
[19] Hook Manor, Donhead St. Andrew, Arundell MSS., ct. bk. 21.
[20] S.R.O., DD/PE 6, *sub anno* 1668.
[21] Forde Abbey, Cart. pp. 502–4; Arundell MSS., ct. bk. 21.
[22] *S.R.S.* viii, p. 35; *Cal. Pat.* 1388–92, 148.
[23] *Rot. Hund.* (Rec. Com.), ii. 127–8; Forde Abbey, Cart.

pp. 501–4.
[24] S.R.O., DD/X/LT.
[25] S.R.O., DD/PE 6.
[26] Arundell MSS., ct. bk. 21.
[27] S.R.O., D/P/barr 13/2/1.
[28] C 136/44/1.
[29] Arundell MSS., acct. bk. 24.
[30] S.R.O., DD/PE 6.
[31] Ibid. at end: draft summons to 'hundred and manor court' at 'usual place'.
[32] S.R.O., D/PS/ilm, box 1; *P.O. Dir. Som.* (1861); Morris and Co. *Dir. Som.* (1872).
[33] Bradford Central Libr., Swinton MSS., acct. Shepton Beauchamp, 1481–2; S.R.O., DD/X/LT.
[34] E 317/Somerset 11.
[35] S.R.O., D/P/barr 13/2/1.

BARRINGTON

MOST OF the ancient parish of Barrington was in the north of the hundred of South Petherton, with a detached area in Neroche forest lying about 5 miles to the south-west. Although not adjoining South Petherton parish the two were closely linked throughout the Middle Ages, and the least rational boundary is that with Shepton Beauchamp which links Barrington with the remainder of the hundred. The boundaries with the Stocklinches, Puckington, and Isle Brewers are former or present roads, and a stream divides Barrington from Kingsbury Episcopi in the north-east. Islands of Puckington intruded into the parish and village until the end of the 19th century, deriving from a 14th-century grant of property to a chantry, and giving rise to the name Little Puckington as part of the eastern end of the village street.[1] The estimated area of the parish in 1839 was 1,565 a.[2] In 1885 nearly 478 a. forming the detached portion in Neroche were transferred to Broadway, and in 1886 the detached parts of Barrington in Westmoor (88 a.) were added to Curry Rivel and Drayton. Barrington absorbed parts of Curry Rivel, Isle Brewers, and Puckington (c. 64 a.) so that the area of the civil parish in 1886 was 1,158 a.[3]

The village street follows the 100 ft. contour and marks both the geological and the physical division of the parish. To the north, where the land slopes gradually away to the alluvium of Westmoor, below the 15 ft. contour, marls and clays were cultivated in three open fields, East, Middle, and West, divided from each other by the long narrow stretches of Broad mead and Lunmoor.[4] Fields called Brickway there suggest a commercial use for the clay. To the south of the village the scarp of Winsmoor hill rises abruptly to a plateau of Yeovil and Pennard sands, and then to a junction bed of limestone rich in fossils. A limekiln, gravel pits, and a quarry were worked in the 19th and 20th centuries.[5] The plateau, also arable, was divided between the southern stretches of West field on Hackpen and Hangerland, where ridge and furrow survive, and the 19th-century Higher field, where banks and not hedges continue to divide the consolidated furlongs.[6]

The village is largely concentrated in a single street with the Barrington Court complex standing alone to the north-east. The Court is successor to a medieval manor-house, and is surrounded by substantial demesnes consolidated by the 17th century.[7] The church, standing above the street, lies almost at the opposite end of the village. A grid pattern of

roads and droves served the fields both north and south, only Ruskway Lane becoming of any importance after the creation of the canal basin at Westport. The canal also gave rise to a settlement on former common pasture at the edge of Westmoor at Nidons or Knighton.[8] The village street was turnpiked by the Ilminster trust in 1823, together with Ruskway Lane as far as Westport. A toll-house was built at the junction of the two roads.[9]

Most of the timber in the parish until the 17th century came from Neroche,[10] but there was a little coppice and furze near the village at the same period. Wood then cut for mill timbers, rafters, and ladders included oak, elm, ash, and maple, and there were apples and plums in orchards and apples in hedgerows.[11]

The value of the common land in Neroche may have played a part in the prosperity of the parish as reflected in its earliest buildings. The Priory (only so called c. 1880), Knapp House, and Vinces are superior medieval buildings, the first dating from the late 14th century, the others from the late fifteenth. They and Allenbury Cottage are examples of houses built or improved at a time when other villages seem to have spent lavishly on their churches.[12] All retain some evidence of having had open halls with cruck roofs, and have had later ceilings and fireplaces inserted. The Priory also has a self-contained wing at its west end which, though later used as a court room, may have been built to house an older generation of the occupier's family.[13] At the other end of the village Easons is a substantial 17th-century house of ashlar, partly rebuilt in 1715 and remodelled in the late 18th century. Its original wooden screen bears traces of painted floral decoration.[14] Several other houses in the village street, built of local rubble and often thatched, are of 17th-century origin, their very survival and the presence of small cottages in Water Street and Copse Shoot indicating the relative poverty of the smallholder and cottager in the 19th century.

Barrington Friendly Society was founded in 1807 and was dissolved in 1945. Originally open to men alone, it admitted women from 1912. It had 145 members in 1879 but by 1912 there were only 66. The Feast Day was originally the last Tuesday in May, but was later changed to 4 June.[15] A brass band was associated with the society by 1862.[16]

An inn called the Victoria was licensed in 1839. It became the Royal Oak in 1854 and remained so called in 1973.[17] A second inn, on the corner of

---

[1] This article was completed in 1973.
[2] S.R.O., tithe award.
[3] S.R.O., D/P/barr 13/1/3.
[4] S.R.O., DD/SB, map 1808; tithe award; E 310/23/127/90.
[5] O.S. Map 6″, Som. LXXXI. SW. (1886 edn.); *Proc. Som. Arch. Soc.* lxvii. 72–5. The field-name Whitefields also suggests the presence of lime: S.R.O., tithe award.
[6] S.R.O., tithe award; Devon R.O. 1077M/5/7, 6/11.
[7] S.R.O., DD/PH 127. For Roman remains in the area: *Proc. Som. Arch. Soc.* lix. 79–84.

[8] S.R.O., tithe award.
[9] S.R.O., D/T/ilm; Devon R.O. 1077M/6/11.
[10] E 134/22–3 Eliz. I/Mich. 11.
[11] Devon R.O. 1077M/5/7.
[12] S.R.O., DD/V, Langport R.D.
[13] Ibid.
[14] Ibid.
[15] M. Fuller, *West-Country Friendly Socs.* passim; S.R.O., D/P/barr 23/1–2.
[16] *Pulman's Weekly News*, 30 May 1862; Fuller, *West-Country Friendly Socs.* pl. xii.
[17] S.R.O., D/PS/ilm, box 1.

Gibbs Lane and the main street, was there by 1839.[18]

King John was at Barrington in 1207.[19] When the Strodes lived there in the 17th century Barrington Court was the centre of their political activities as opponents of Ship Money, as government supporters during the Commonwealth, and as opponents again in the 1680s when they entertained the duke of Monmouth and supported the Protestant cause.[20] Ten men were accused of complicity in Monmouth's rebellion in 1685.[21]

The population was 374 in 1801.[22] It increased until the 1840s, and in 1841 was 596, including 66 at Nidon, formerly extra-parochial and then recently taken into the parish. Despite gradual decline the figure remained at over 500 until 1871, but the closure of the Westport canal, emigration to the United States and Canada, and removal to South Wales brought the total down rapidly. By the 1930s the figure had risen again, to over 400, and has subsequently remained stable, with 402 in 1971.[23]

MANOR AND OTHER ESTATES. The manor of *BARRINGTON* belonged to the Crown T.R.E., and while not expressly mentioned in 1086 was almost certainly included in the royal manor of South Petherton.[24] Described variously as a manor and a hamlet it descended in the Daubeney family like the manor of South Petherton until 1483, when it was confiscated on the attainder of Giles Daubeney, later Lord Daubeney (d. 1508), for his part in the duke of Buckingham's rebellion.[25] It was, like South Petherton, held briefly by the Crown and in 1484 was granted to Ralph Neville, Lord Neville, later earl of Westmorland (d. 1499).[26] Daubeney recovered his lands in 1485. His son Henry, created earl of Bridgwater in 1538, died without heirs ten years later leaving Barrington to his widow for life with remainder, probably under mortgage, to Sir Thomas Arundell.[27] The countess herself was attainted in 1542. On Arundell's attainder in 1552 the lordship, manor, and park were granted by the Crown to Henry Grey, duke of Suffolk.[28] Almost immediately Suffolk sold the property to William Clifton, a London merchant (d. 1564).[29] He was succeeded by his son Sir John (d. 1593),[30] and by his grandson Gervase, Lord Clifton (d. 1618). Gervase sold the manor to his brother-in-law Sir Thomas Phelips in 1605.[31] Phelips died in 1618.

One of his sons, also Thomas (cr. Bt. 1619), in serious financial difficulties, mortgaged the manor to William Strode and Hugh Pyne in 1620 and to his brother-in-law, Arthur Farwell of Bishop's Hull, in 1621.[32] The Phelipses later claimed that Strode entered lands worth £350 a year after Sir Thomas had failed to repay his first debt, but that the manor had passed to the second mortgagee, Arthur Farwell.[33]

Farwell died in 1625 leaving his son Arthur a minor.[34] In 1631 Sir William Ogle, later Viscount Ogle, of Stoke Charity (Hants) (d. 1682), stepfather and guardian of Sir Thomas Phelips's son Thomas, acquired the manor to the use of Thomas Phelips.[35] Ogle, Phelips, and Farwell in 1642 sold the property to Richard (later Sir Richard) Cholmeley of Bicton (Devon).[36] Sir Thomas Putt, Bt., of Coombe in Gittisham (Devon), married Ursula, Cholmeley's coheir, and the manor was settled on them in 1665.[37]

The Putt family retained the manor until the 20th century. Sir Thomas was succeeded in 1686 by his son Thomas, who died without issue in 1721.[38] Raymundo Putt, his cousin, inherited the property and continued in possession until 1757.[39] Thomas (d. 1787), probably his son, was followed after a ten-year minority successively by his three children Raymundo (d. 1812), the Revd. Thomas, B.D. (d. 1844), and Margaretta (d. 1846), wife of the Revd. Henry Marker of Aylesbeare (Devon).[40] The Revd. T. J. Marker of Coombe (d. 1854), son of Margaretta, was succeeded by his son Richard (1835–1916). Richard's son R. J. Marker died in 1914, and his heir on his death was his grandson R. R. K. Marker (1908–61).[41] The family trustees sold the estate, amounting to 810 a., in 1918, but the lordship was not apparently included in the sale.[42]

The capital messuage and demesnes, which may have been that part of the manor first mortgaged by Sir Thomas Phelips, were again mortgaged and in 1625 sold to William Strode (I) (d. 1666).[43] They were settled on Strode's son William in 1656,[44] though the family's title to the estate was later said to be 'so bad that when he [Strode] was to take up £1,500 to pay his sister's portion the lawyers could find no title sufficient to adventure so much money upon'.[45] William Strode (II) died in 1695; his son William (III) dying childless in 1746 was succeeded by his sister Jane, wife of Robert Austen of Tenterden (Kent).[46] Their son Sir Edward Austen, of Boxley Abbey (Kent), sold

18 S.R.O., tithe award.
19 *Rot. Litt. Pat.* (Rec. Com.), 75.
20 *Cal. S.P. Dom.* 1636–7, 222, 401, 522; 1625–49, 548; 1661–2, 145; 1680–1, 514; Hist. MSS. Com. 51, *Leyborne-Popham*, 157; T. G. Barnes, *Somerset 1629–40*, 222–5.
21 B.L. Add. MS. 30077, ff. 34–5.
22 *V.C.H. Som.* ii. 348.
23 Ibid.; *Census*; S.R.O., C/E 92.
24 *V.C.H. Som.* i. 493; R. W. Eyton, *Dom. Studies, Som.* i. 75 n.
25 *Cal. Pat.* 1476–85, 427; *Complete Peerage* s.v. Daubeney.
26 *Cal. Pat.* 1476–85, 373, 427.
27 E 326/8868. The mortgage was arranged in 1543.
28 *Cal. Pat.* 1550–3, 240; E 318/36/1987.
29 *Cal. Pat.* 1550–3, 416; Devon R.O. 1077M/5/7; C 142/140/158.
30 C 142/237/131.   31 C.P. 25(2)/345/3 Jas. I Mich.

32 Devon R.O. 1077M/5/7; S.R.O., DD/PH 127; C 142/417/28; *S.R.S.* lxvii, pp. 19–20.
33 S.R.O., DD/PH 127.
34 *S.R.S.* lxvii, pp. 19–20.
35 Devon R.O. 1077M/5/7; S.R.O., DD/PH 127.
36 Devon R.O. 1077M/5/7.
37 Devon R.O. 1077M/5/1, 5/7.
38 G.E.C. *Baronetage*, iv. 367.
39 Act to enable Reymunds Putt . . . ., 4 Geo. II, c. 30 (Priv. Act); Devon R.O., bishop's transcripts 192.
40 Devon R.O. 1077M/4/2–9; Burke, *Land. Gent.* (1952), 1698–9; M.I. in Gittisham ch.
41 Devon R.O. 1077M, pedigree in file; M.I. in Gittisham ch.
42 Devon R.O. 547B/P1726.
43 S.R.O., DD/PH 127.
44 Ibid.; *Proc. Som. Arch. Soc.* xxx. 69.
45 S.R.O., DD/PH 127.
46 S.R.O., DD/SAS SE 27; DD/NA.

the house and some 100 a. to Thomas Harvard of Thorney in 1756,[47] and the property passed to the Hanning family in 1786–7 through the marriage of Thomas's daughter Susannah to John Hanning.[48] John was succeeded by his son William (d. 1834) in 1803, and by his grandson John Lee (Hanning) Lee (d. 1874).[49] By 1827 the property was known as Court Farm, and by 1847 was divided into two holdings, known as the Upper and Lower parts of Barrington Court, each of just over 104 a., though then held by the same tenant.[50] Lee sold the farms and house to J. W. Peters of South Petherton (d. 1858); Peters left the estate to his nephew William Parsons (Peters), also of South Petherton.[51] He died in 1902 leaving a son W. P. Peters.[52] In 1905 the property was acquired for the National Trust by Miss J. L. Woodward of Clevedon,[53] and since 1920 has been leased to the Lyle family.

The medieval manor-house complex, including a 'demesne court' or farm-yard by 1235,[54] lay to the north and east of the present house.[55] By the late 14th century the house included not only a hall with a two-storeyed solar wing to the east, but a new two-storeyed addition on the north side, together with kitchens,[56] a chapel, and farm buildings including a gatehouse, a great barn, an ox-shed with lofts (*alte camere*), a straw-house, and a pig-stye, the whole surrounded by a series of ditches.[57]

The present house, usually known as Court Farm until the late 19th century and since then as Barrington Court, entirely replaced the medieval complex.[58] The building, of Ham stone ashlar, has usually been ascribed to Henry Daubeney, earl of Bridgwater (d. 1548), is said to have been put up c. 1514 when he came of age, and is thought to have been influenced in its design by advanced Renaissance details seen in France either when his father was ambassador (but not after 1500) or through his own presence at the Field of Cloth of Gold (1520).[59] If these influences make the accepted dating doubtful Daubeney's subsequent career makes any other in his lifetime unlikely. His interests were centred on the Court and the army, but from the 1530s the sales of his estates and his heavy expenses in acquiring an earldom, though he had no children, mark the beginnings of decline, completed in 1541 by the implication of his wife in the fall of the Howards. In 1543 he yielded all but a life interest in Barrington itself, and by 1547 he almost certainly had but one house, South Perrott (Dors.), his only known residence since 1535.[60]

Leland makes no mention of a house though he

came very near, and the property was described on purchase in 1552 only as a 'lordship, manor, and park'.[61] The purchaser at the time, William Clifton, was a Norwich man and a London merchant who had already invested in other property in the county.[62] Still living in London in 1557, he was certainly resident at Barrington in 1559 and died there in 1564.[63] The porch of the house, which is studded with a series of masons' marks, has been considered an addition of c. 1560–70,[64] but those same marks occur over the whole house, indicating construction in one phase and suggesting that the new purchaser of the estate, William Clifton, may have been the builder.

Assuming the porch to be part of the original design, the house is E-shaped, having a main range containing the hall and buttery divided by a screens passage, and long projecting wings, with staircases in square projections between them and the main range. The style is similar to that of several large houses built in East Anglia in the mid and later 16th century.[65] The twisted finials and ogee caps, the octagonal buttresses to the gables, and the four-centred heads below the transoms of the main windows have local parallels of a similar date at Melbury, Clifton Maybank, Parnham, and other houses in Dorset, the hallmarks of local masons, perhaps creating the notion of a house standing unfinished for a long period.[66]

Until c. 1920, when the stable block was converted to a dwelling, there was a porch at the west side of the house bearing arms which were probably used by William Clifton.[67] Inside there are no original decorations and fittings, the earliest being two overmantels dating from the Strode occupation. William Strode (I) 'bestowed money and labour to restore it to its pristine beauty' before 1633,[68] and his son claimed to have spent £3,000 on it before 1677, presumably largely on the brick stable block of 1674.[69] About 1825 half the house was 'almost completely destroyed' and remained virtually gutted, part being used as a cider cellar. There were suggestions c. 1905 that it should be pulled down and rebuilt elsewhere.[70] Between 1920 and 1925 the house was restored and the stable block converted into a dwelling by Forbes and Tate. Barrington Court is now furnished with the collection of panelling and interior fittings made by Col. A. A. Lyle.[71]

Gardens to the west of the house were laid out after 1920 to the designs of Gertrude Jekyll and include a building known as 'bustalls', a 19th-century

47 S.R.O., DD/NA.
48 S.R.O., DD/CA, introduction to list.
49 Ibid.; D/P/barr 4/1/1, 13/2/2.
50 S.R.O., DD/CA 168.
51 Proc. Som. Arch. Soc. xxiii. 26–9; S.R.O., DD/NA.
52 S.R.O., DD/NA.
53 S. & D. N. & Q. ix. 332–3; xii. 164.
54 Cal. Chart. R. 1226–57, 203.
55 Proc. Som. Arch. Soc. lxxi. 90.
56 There is reference to the north kitchen.
57 C 136/44/1. The chapel was licensed, evidently a renewal, in 1415: S.R.S. xxix, p. 203.
58 S.R.O., D/P/barr 4/1/1; see below, plate facing p. 144.
59 Proc. Som. Arch. Soc. xi. 20; xxiii. 28; xxxvii. 41; lxvii, pp. xxxi–xxxiii; lxxi. 88–92; Country Life, 17 Sept. 1904, 17 and 24 Mar. 1928. But C. J. Richardson thought it was built by the Cliftons: Studies from Old English Manors, 4th ser. (1848).
60 L. & P. Hen. VIII, passim.

61 Cal. Pat. 1550–3, 416.
62 L. & P. Hen. VIII xxi(2), p. 168. He acquired other properties later.
63 Cal. Pat. 1555–7, 345; 1558–60, 236; C 142/140/158.
64 Proc. Som. Arch. Soc. lxvii, pp. xxxi–xxxiii.
65 Ibid. There are other parallels in Clifton's native East Anglia including Kentwell Hall (Suff.) and Channons (Norf.).
66 Proc. Som. Arch. Soc. lxxi. 88–92.
67 The arms, apparently a fess fusilly between escallops, are elements in the arms of the Clifton family: Visits. Notts. 1569–1614 (Harl. Soc. iv), 16–18. Photograph of porch in Country Life, 17 Sept. 1904.
68 S.R.S. xv. 119.
69 S.R.O., DD/PH 127; the date occurs on rainwater heads.
70 Proc. Som. Arch. Soc. xxxvii. 41–2; S. & D. N. & Q. ix. 332–5.
71 National Trust, Guide.

cattle shed.[72] Further from the house, largely on the north and west, stand the home farm and tenants' houses, forming a complete 'manor place' inspired by the work of the Arts and Crafts movement. To the south of the house are the remains of the park, formed by 1483.[73] At its largest in the 16th century it was described variously as one or two miles in compass.[74]

The rectory of Barrington, described as the tithing corn, chapel, and farm, were let by the abbot of Bruton to Sir Thomas and George Speke on a lease for 60 years in 1532.[75] In 1549 the chapter of Bristol, successors of the canons of Bruton, let the reversion of this lease to John Norys of West Monkton and Christopher Samford of Halberton (Devon).[76] Two years later Norys and Samford assigned their rights to Sir Hugh Poulett.[77] The Pouletts appear to have leased the rectory until 1788 though usually sub-letting the tithes.[78] These were worth £96 in 1619 and £120 in 1650.[79] In 1667 they were let for £100, and in 1787 for £115.[80] From 1788 the chapter of Bristol leased the property to the Hannings: John Hanning was succeeded in 1800 by William Hanning.[81] The lease by the chapter to John Lee Lee in 1835 was for £15 3s. 4d. a year including land tax,[82] though the rent-charge in lieu of tithes was fixed at £396 6s. in 1839.[83] The lease reverted to the Ecclesiastical Commissioners before 1895.[84]

Philip Daubeney (d. 1236) gave to the canons of Bruton his grange at Barrington.[85] There seems to have been a barn on rectory property in 1619,[86] though the 18th-century leases do not expressly mention one. A barn certainly stood on the north side of the churchyard until 1871 when it was demolished and its site consecrated for burials.[87]

In 1301 Gilbert de Knovill was licensed to give land and rent to support a chantry in Puckington church.[88] By 1571 the former chantry estate in Barrington, occupied by the rector of Puckington and considered part of Puckington parish, amounted to 76 a.[89] In that year it was granted to Henry Middlemore. The subsequent descent of the property has not been traced.

ECONOMIC HISTORY. Barrington may well have been included in the Domesday estate of South Petherton, and the earliest separate occurrence of it is in 1292 when the property of Ralph Daubeney there, variously then and later described as a hamlet

or manor, was valued at £18 17s. The demesne farm then comprised the manor-house, garden, and dovecot, 142½ a. of arable and 45 a. of meadow, very close to the area of Court farm in the 19th century.[90] Rents of free and customary tenants accounted for £11 10s. 4d., works were valued at 6s. 6d., and chevage at 2s. In 1305 Ellis Daubeney's property comprised slightly less arable and meadow but included pasture, apparently some held in common, and the remainder in closes.[91]

Thirteenth-century land transactions reveal a number of local families including the Lortys and the Durvilles holding estates in the parish, usually amounting to a carucate or less.[92] From 1364 some land was alienated for a chantry at South Petherton, and rents from it were still paid in 1552 when they were owned by Francis Hastings, earl of Huntingdon.[93] In the same year the net value of the manor was only £7 9s. Rents of free and customary tenants together were worth nearly £56, but the chantry rent was £40.[94]

From the early 17th century the parish was without a resident lord, though the Strodes were dominant as owners of the former demesne, and the Pouletts were farmers of the parsonage. In the early 17th century there were over 80 customary lifehold tenants, the largest holdings by 1635 those of William Royce (60 a.) and Thomas Pitterd (57 a.).[95] There were also 'conventionary tenants', 12 in number in 1641, who held leases for 99 years on two or three lives. These included three tenants who between them shared 185 a. of land in Neroche forest. In 1635 there were also three freeholdings, including parcels in Dommett and Swell. Sir George Speke paid rent of 28s. 8d. and owed suit of court twice a year for an estate which may have included the house known from the late 19th century as the Priory.[96] Speke's property had been held by his family at least since 1544,[97] and in 1637 was worth between £5 and £6.[98] Part was leased to the Bicknell family, and in 1601 'Farmer' Bicknell held 100 a.[99] William followed by Arthur Bicknell were leading rate-payers in the parish between 1627 and 1644. The Spekes continued their interest until the end of the 17th century.[1]

The economy was affected by the disafforestation of parts of Neroche forest. Barrington manor claimed an interest there at Cleyhill and Barrington hill, in some 1,200 a. Division took place c. 1631 when part was allotted to the lord of the manor and part to customary tenants. Some inclosure for

[72] B. Massingham, *Gertrude Jekyll*, 37.
[73] *Cal. Pat.* 1476-85, 373.
[74] *S.R.S.* xx. 42-3; xxvii. 293-4; *V.C.H. Som.* ii. 568.
[75] S.R.O., DD/PT, box 10A.
[76] Ibid. box 22B.
[77] Ibid.
[78] Bristol R.O., DC/E/24/1, 3.
[79] S.R.O., DD/X/SAB (Bristol Cath. Chetwynd survey f. 16 and Parl. survey f. 200).
[80] S.R.O., DD/SS, bdle. 4; DD/PT, box 12.
[81] Bristol R.O., DC/E/24/3; S.R.O., DD/CA 82.
[82] S.R.O., DD/CA 83; Bristol R.O., DC/E/24/3.
[83] S.R.O., tithe award.
[84] S.R.O., D/P/barr 13/1/4.
[85] *S.R.S.* viii, p. 35; *Cal. Pat.* 1388-92, 148.
[86] S.R.O., DD/X/SAB (Bristol Cath. Chetwynd survey f. 16, but the MS is defective).
[87] S.R.O., tithe award; D/P/barr 8/3/1; Bristol R.O., DC/E/31/5.

[88] *Cal. Pat.* 1292-1301, 582; 1301-7, 3.
[89] E 310/23/127 no. 90.
[90] C 133/61/23; S.R.O., tithe award.
[91] C 133/120/2.
[92] *S.R.S.* vi. 14, 156, 260; viii, p. 38; xiv, p. 38; xxxvi. 90; xliv. 265; *Cal. Inq. p.m.* iv, p. 252; *Cal. Pat.* 1307-13, 411; *Cal. Fine R.* 1307-19, 69; *Cal. Chanc. R.* 1277-1326, 100.
[93] *Cal. Pat.* 1361-4, 484; 1408-13; 287; *Cal. Inq. p.m. Hen. VII,* i, pp. 196, 533; C 142/25/22; C 142/70/1; E 318/36/1987.
[94] Devon R.O. 1077M/5/7: rental 1635, schedule 1641; S.R.O., D/P/barr 13/2/1.
[95] Devon R.O. 1077M/5/7.
[96] *S.R.S.* xl. 27.
[97] Ibid. lxvii, p. 58.
[98] S.R.O., DD/HI, box 9.
[99] S.R.O., D/P/barr 13/2/1.
[1] Ibid.

wheat had already taken place, and cattle, sheep, and pigs had been grazed, though a century earlier the whole area had been under the control of the manor hayward.[2] The Crown retained some 200 a. at least until 1638,[3] and claims for commonage continued for at least another twenty years. The 'king's part of the forest' was referred to as late as 1701.[4] New Park, later King's Park farm, was established there by 1688.[5] Venner's farm, owned in 1757 by Kingsford Venner, was known by that name in 1786.[6] It was then predominantly 'rough' grassland (128 a.), with 27 a. of arable.

By 1787 the largest rate-payer was John Hanning, owner of the manor-house and demesnes and farmer of the tithes.[7] These last had recently been let for £115, slightly under their apparent value. Quit-rents at the same period totalled £54 10s. 1½d.[8] By the late 1790s the most substantial tenant farmers were the Eason, Rossiter, and Royce families, each of whom had farms of c. 50 a.[9]

Nearly 500 a. were subject to tithes in the main part of the parish by the later 18th century, not including the farm attached to the manor-house. In 1778 grassland accounted for 202 a., wheat for 147 a., and beans for 94 a. The remainder was divided between potatoes (22 a.), flax (12 a.), barley (8 a.), hemp (5½ a.), and peas (2 a.). Cider produced £12 in tithe, cows £2 15s., and sheep c. £2.[10] In 1786 there were 94 a. of beans, 88 a. of Lent grain, and 74 a. of winter wheat, followed by 49 a. fallow, and 20 a. of flax. In that year most of the flax was grown in 15 strips in West field, most of the beans in 73 strips in Middle field, and most of the Lent grain in 61 strips in Higher, Hanging Land, and Hackpen fields.[11] These arable fields, eight in number, were continuously in tillage at the beginning of the 19th century, and the holdings were well scattered.[12] The titheable area in 1839, virtually the whole parish, comprised 813 a. of arable, 667 a. of meadow and pasture, and 80 a. of orchards and gardens.[13]

Parliamentary inclosure affected the detached part of the parish in Neroche forest, and parts of West moor. Small areas were inclosed and added to the old fields on and around Barrington hill in 1833 under Act of 1830.[14] West moor, inclosed in 1838 under Act of 1833, gave just over 108 a. to Barrington in 25 units, mostly for pasture.[15] Open-field tillage continued in large parts of the parish until the end of the 19th century: land in East, Middle, and Higher fields was still extensively cultivated as

strips in 1879,[16] and some strips survived at least until 1918.[17]

The manor estate contained nearly 1,139 a. in the ancient parish in 1895, and included 44 cottages. The largest single holding on it was New House farm (121 a.).[18] Barrington Court farm, held of the Peters family, was larger, amounting to 192 a. Venners and Barrington Hill farms, both in the area transferred to Broadway in 1885, comprised 230 a. and 106 a. respectively.[19] The sale of the manor in 1918 involved about 832 a., comprising 5 farms, 7 small holdings, 47 cottages, and accommodation land.[20]

The parish seems to have suffered at the end of the 19th century not only from the general agricultural depression but also from the closure of the Westport canal. It is impossible to assess the benefit the parish derived from Messrs. Stuckey and Bagehot's wharves and coal yard established at the northern boundary of Barrington in 1840, but a local petition against closure was rejected in 1880, five years after the canal had ceased business.[21] The decline in population at the end of the century was ascribed in part to young men finding no work in agriculture and seeking employment in Glamorgan coal mines.[22] By 1897, however, alternative employment was to be found in a factory at the east end of the village making linen collars, which continued in production until the late 1920s.[23] Gloving was also a common occupation.[24] Flax and hemp were extensively cultivated in the 19th century;[25] the southern part of the parish remains largely arable, the northern principally under grass.

There was a water-mill on the demesne estate by 1292, worth then 6s. 8d.[26] In 1440 Elizabeth, widow of John Daubeney (d. 1409), held land in dower including 'Mulfurlong', said to be near the site of the mill.[27] A mill was farmed for 10s. in 1552.[28] In 1601 there were said to be three water-mills on the manor,[29] and three mills 'new let' were part of the demesne estate in 1656.[30] They have not been traced further, but presumably lay on the stream which flows near the present Barrington Court, where a water-wheel operated c. 1910.[31]

LOCAL GOVERNMENT. There was doubt in the 1580s about the exact status of Barrington, but a witness claimed that in the time of Henry Daubeney, earl of Bridgwater (d. 1548), the manor was represented by a separate homage at courts held

[2] E 134/22–3 Eliz. I/Mich. 11; S.R.O., D/D/Cd 81 (1635), where inclosure had taken place '4 or 5' years earlier. It was said to have been done 'about 7 years ago' in 1638: Cal. S.P. Dom. 1638–9, 192.
[3] Cal. S.P. Dom. 1638, 192.
[4] V.C.H. Som. ii. 563; S.R.O., D/P/barr 13/2/1.
[5] S.R.O., D/P/barr 13/2/1; DD/LC, box 27/6; Devon R.O. 1077M/4/4.
[6] S.R.O., D/P/barr 13/2/2; Devon R.O. 1077M/4/4; Bristol R.O. DC/E/24/4.
[7] S.R.O., D/P/barr 14/5/1.
[8] S.R.O., DD/PT, boxes 12, 17. In 1786 they were assessed at £104 gross, £48 net: Bristol R.O. DC/E/24/4.
[9] Devon R.O. 1077M/2/10.
[10] S.R.O., D/P/barr 13/2/2, 14/5/1; DD/PT, box 37; Devon R.O. 1077M/2/10, 6/11.
[11] S.R.O., DD/PT, box 37; Bristol R.O., DC/E/24/4.
[12] Devon R.O. 1077M/6/11.
[13] S.R.O., tithe award.
[14] S.R.O., CR 107.

[15] Ibid. 101.
[16] S.R.O., D/P/barr 4/3/1, 13/1/3.
[17] O.S. Map 6", Som. LXXXI. SW., SE. (1886 edn.); S.R.O., T/PH/u.
[18] S.R.O., D/P/barr 13/1/4.
[19] Ibid. 13/1/3; DD/SAS PR 463/2.
[20] Devon R.O. 547B/P1726.
[21] J. Hadfield, Canals of SW. England (1967), 87, 91; S.R.O., D/P/barr 4/1/1.
[22] S.R.O., D/P/barr 23/6.
[23] Kelly's Dir. Som. (1897, 1927).
[24] Harrison, Harrod & Co., Dir. (1859).
[25] Ibid.; P.O. Dir. Som. (1861–75); Kelly's Dir. Som. (1883–97).
[26] C 133/61/23.
[27] C 139/104/41.
[28] E 318/36/1987.
[29] C.P. 25(2)/207/43 & 44 Eliz. I Mich.
[30] S.R.O., DD/PH 127.
[31] Local information.

for all the neighbouring Daubeney estates at South Petherton. Other witnesses mentioned a separate bailiff for Barrington.[32] The manor court seems to have continued of comparatively little consequence, owing at least in part to the absence of lords. Extracts from courts variously described as courts leet, courts baron, manor courts, and views of frank-pledge, survive for 1641, 1652–3, 1657, 1705, and 1734.[33] Courts were held until 1914.[34] Before that time its functions were limited to the receipt of rents and the provision of posts and gates. In the late 17th century the offices of tithingman and hayward were held together in annual rotation by presentment of the Michaelmas leet jury.[35] The tenant of a cottage in the mid 19th century was excused lord's rent in return for ringing the church bell 'to give notice of the steward's arrival to hold the court'.[36] The courts were then said to have been held in the Priory.

At least from 1625 parish affairs were under the control of two and occasionally of three overseers and two churchwardens.[37] Waywardens were active from 1697 and surveyors of the highways as necessary.[38] From the late 17th century overseers held office in rotation. From 1798 one overseer was to be paid $1\frac{1}{2}$ guinea for the whole year; the other was said to be paid $\frac{1}{2}$ guinea or himself serve the winter half-year.[39] In 1833 the overseers were paid £4 'as a slight remuneration for executing the office'. A salaried 'acting overseer' was appointed in 1834.[40] By 1690 there was a monthly parish meeting; by the end of the 18th century it was called a vestry and usually comprised three or four members.[41]

From the 17th century badged paupers received house rent, and payments in cash were supplemented by payments for a nurse, the repair of a man's chimney, and the provision of clothing and food.[42] Beans, potatoes, and barley were bought in 1801 and from 1800 the overseers paid for a girls' schooling.[43] On one occasion, in 1701, the overseers also paid for fencing the common fields. The waywardens in 1697 provided a direction post at 'Hucker's Plot'.[44]

By the mid 19th century the churchwardens dominated parish affairs. They paid the salary of the assistant overseer in 1848–9 and again from 1853 to 1864, and also found money for the constable in 1858–9. Both wardens were nominated by the vestry at least until 1868, though the minister was usually chairman from 1859.[45] In 1868 the vestry business was divided; the March meeting thereafter dealt with civil matters not necessarily under the minister, while the April meeting was exclusively ecclesiastical. Overseers and waywardens were elected annually until 1894.[46]

In 1811 the vestry agreed to rent a house for use as a poorhouse.[47] From 1819 this house was rented by the wardens directly from the lord of the manor.[48] The parish became part of the Langport poor-law union in 1836,[49] but the poorhouse was already rented out for other purposes.[50] It was sold in 1838.[51] The house stood on the south side of Court Road at its western end, and in 1973 was a store.

CHURCH. Part of a capital found embedded in the tower is evidence of a building of the earlier 13th century, though the earliest reference to a church occurs as late as 1240–1. In that year the 'risk and inconvenience' of taking corpses to the mother church at South Petherton induced the bishop, after disputes between the inhabitants and the rectors, the canons of Bruton, to consecrate a burial ground at Barrington, provided that the church remained a dependent chapelry.[52] The canons of Bruton were charged with finding chaplains to serve the cure, and remained so charged until the Dissolution.[53] In 1542 the newly-created chapter of Bristol succeeded to the rectory,[54] and retained the patronage until 1885, though the lessees of the tithes usually appointed and paid the chaplains in the 17th and early 18th centuries. In 1885 the chapter exchanged the advowson with Mrs. Eliza Coles (d. 1897) of Shepton Beauchamp and her son, Canon V. S. S. Coles (d. 1929), gave it in 1913 to the Community of the Resurrection, Mirfield (Yorks. W.R.), patrons in 1973, with the suggestion that he or his sister should be consulted 'if occasion should arise'.[55] The benefice, an augmented curacy from 1751, remained a perpetual curacy until 1968. From 1963 it was held with Puckington.[56]

By 1574 the curate was receiving £6 13s. 8d. a year supplemented by 40s. tabling.[57] A further 10 marks was given annually under the will of Sir Anthony Poulett (d. 1600) for preaching four times yearly.[58] In the 1650s Lord Poulett was paying a curate to serve both Barrington and Chillington for £30 a year.[59] In the 18th century the curate of Barrington was paid half that sum, and any assistants received the same.[60] The stipend was augmented in 1750 by £200 each from Dr. Henry Waterland, prebendary of Bristol and rector of Wrington, and from Queen Anne's Bounty. A further £200 was given by lot in 1792. In 1812 £100 from Edward Combe and £100 from the Pincombe trustees were met by a Parliamentary

[32] E 134/22–3 Eliz. I Mich./11.
[33] Devon R.O. 1077M/5/7, 6/11; *penes* Countess Poulett, Jersey (1657). Presentments were extant for 1787–1822 when the Devon R.O. list was compiled but could not be found in 1973.
[34] Devon R.O. 1077M/6/11; par. cncl. min. bk.
[35] S.R.O., D/P/barr 13/2/1.
[36] Ibid. 23/4.
[37] Ibid. 13/2/1–3.
[38] Ibid. 14/5/1.
[39] Ibid. 13/2/2.
[40] Ibid. 13/2/3.
[41] Ibid. 4/1/1, 13/2/2.
[42] Ibid. 13/2/1.
[43] Ibid. 13/2/2.
[44] Ibid. 13/2/1.

[45] Ibid. 4/1/1.
[46] Ibid. 9/1/1.
[47] Ibid. 13/2/2.
[48] Ibid. 13/10/2.
[49] *Poor Law Com. 2nd Rep.* p. 548.
[50] S.R.O., D/P/barr 13/2/3.
[51] S.R.O., D/PS/ilm, box 16.
[52] *S.R.S.* vii, pp. 31–2; viii, p. 38; xiv, p. 38.
[53] *Cal. Papal Regs.* v. 326; *S.R.S.* viii, p. 41.
[54] *L. & P. Hen. VIII*, xvii, p. 638.
[55] S.R.O., D/P/she.b 1/1/1; ex inf. the Librarian, Community of the Resurrection.   [56] *Dioc. Dir*
[57] *S. & D. N. & Q.* xiv. 65.
[58] S.R.O., DD/X/SAB.
[59] S.R.O., DD/PT, box 40, accts.
[60] S.R.O., D/D/Bo; D/D/V Dioc. bk.

grant of £300, and in 1817 a further gift of £100 from Edward Combe, then curate, was matched by the chapter of Bristol and another Parliamentary grant of £300. The last sum was used to purchase just over 12 a. in Somerton in 1818, which was sold in 1877.[61] In 1815 the value of the living was said to be £69, in 1831 £84, and in 1851 £80, £15 coming from endowments and the remainder from land.[62] In 1948 there were 29 a. of glebe situated in Combe St. Nicholas, and the same property was held in 1974.[63]

John Smythe (occurs 1627–34), preached fortnightly though apparently without licence in 1630.[71] Hugh Mere signed the Protestation, and is said to have been imprisoned.[72] John Vaigge combined the curacy with that of Chillington from 1650 to 1655, and was succeeded by a Mr. Crane.[73] Both lived in Chillington. After a vacancy in 1663 the cure was held by John Tyce (d. 1667) who lived at Seavington Abbots.[74] The rapid succession of curates and assistants in the 18th century was at least partly due to the small stipend and lack of a house.

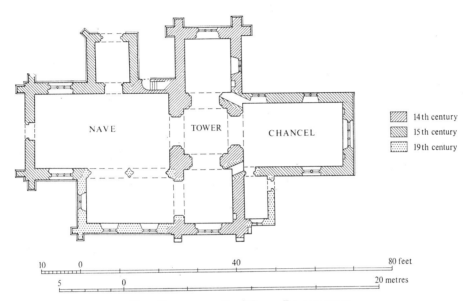

THE CHURCH OF ST. MARY, BARRINGTON

In 1240–1 the parishioners were declared by the bishop to be responsible for finding the chaplain a new house should his own come within the new churchyard boundary.[64] A house was provided for the curate in 1619[65] but there was none by 1815.[66] Joseph Hamlet, curate 1885–1926, lived at first in the clergy house at Shepton Beauchamp, but by 1914 in the Cottage in Barrington.[67] In 1918 he bought a house called Reeveleys, in 1973 known as the Glebe House.[68] This was sold when the benefice was linked with Puckington.

Many of the incumbents combined the curacy with other livings. Leonard Stevenson, B.Th., described as 'rector of Puckington and Barrington', was pardoned for some unknown offence in 1547.[69] William Southeye, curate in 1574 and for the previous seven years, was also prebendary of Cudworth and rector of Puckington and South Bradon.[70] John Meacham, presumably assistant curate to

Edward Combe, curate 1810–48, lived at his family home at Earnshill House; he also served as assistant curate of Isle Brewers,[75] and in 1835 was rector of Donyatt and Earnshill, the second a sinecure, and perpetual curate of Drayton.[76] He was succeeded by James Stratton Coles (1848–72) who held the living with Shepton Beauchamp.[77] Under him the parish began its high church tradition, which was continued under Arthur Lethbridge and Joseph Hamlet (d. 1926) both trained and influenced by Canon Coles.[78] Hamlet served on the Langport Rural District Council and Board of Guardians from 1901 until his death.[79]

The chancel of the church was reported to be in ruins in 1547, and there was no processional in 1557.[80] In 1815 services were held alternately morning and evening.[81] Two services were held by 1851 and on Census Sunday there were congregations of 175 in the morning, including 93 Sunday-

61 Hodgson, *Queen Anne's Bounty*; S.R.O., DD/PI 10/5.
62 S.R.O., D/D/B return 1815; *Rep. Com. Eccl. Revenues*, pp. 126–7; H.O. 129/317/3/11/17.
63 *Crockford*; ex inf. Diocesan office.
64 *S.R.S.* vii, pp. 31–2; xiv, p. 38.
65 S.R.O., DD/X/SAB, Chetwynd survey f. 16.
66 S.R.O., D/D/B return 1815.
67 *Kelly's Dir. Som.* (1914).
68 S.R.O., DD/SAS PR 55; D/P/barr 8/3/5; T/PH/u.
69 *Cal. Pat.* 1548–9, 143.
70 *S. & D. N. & Q.* xiv. 31, 65.
71 S.R.O., D/D/Ca 274; D/P/barr 13/2/1.

72 *Walker Revised*, ed. Matthews.
73 S.R.O., DD/PT, box 40, accts.
74 S.R.O., D/P/barr 13/2/1; DD/SP, inventory 1667.
75 S.R.O., D/D/B return 1815; D/D/V return 1827.
76 *Rep. Com. Eccl. Revenues*, pp. 152–3.
77 Venn, *Alumni Cantab.*
78 R. W. Dunning, 'Nineteenth-Century Parochial Sources', *Studies in Church History*, xi. 305–6.
79 S.R.O., DD/SAS PR 55: Chairman of R.D.C. 1913–26, Bd. of Guardians 1916–26.
80 S.R.O., D/D/Ca 17, 27.
81 S.R.O., D/D/B return 1815.

school pupils, and 254 in the afternoon (with 100 pupils).[82] By 1870 Holy Communion was celebrated fortnightly.[83] Vestments and ornaments were introduced under Arthur Lethbridge, curate 1878–83.[84]

The church of *ST. MARY*[85] is built of coursed Ham stone rubble and ashlar and has a chancel with south vestry, central tower with transepts, and nave with north porch and south aisle. The crossing with its short octagonal tower, the chancel and transepts were built in the late 13th century and retain many of their original features including window tracery and, in the south transept and chancel, piscinas. The chancel windows were, however, replaced in the 15th century and, perhaps at the same time, the tower was heightened and embattled, squints were cut from the transepts to the chancel, and the nave was rebuilt. The new nave, which can be little if any larger than its predecessor, has both western and northern entrances, the latter with a porch decorated with shafts and an ogee cresting above the doorway. The south aisle, of two bays, and the vestry were added in 1860–1 by J. M. Allen of Crewkerne during extensive restoration which included rebuilding the lower part of the tower stair and the renewal of the roofs.[86] An opponent of the scheme said that the church was 'inconsiderately pulled to pieces . . . the interior entirely demolished and denuded . . . so that nothing whatever was left . . . but the naked walls'.[87] A gallery at the west end of the nave, erected in 1819, was dismantled at the time, and a new pulpit and font provided.[88] The windows each side of the chancel are by C. E. Kempe.[89]

The church has six bells: (i and ii) 1894, Taylor of Loughborough; (iii) 1869, Warner; (iv) no inscription; (v) 1743, Thomas Bilbie; (vi) 1894, Taylor.[90] The plate includes a cup and cover by 'I.P.' dated 1573, a paten of 1723, given by Mrs. Anne Strode, a flagon of 1724, given by William Strode (III) her husband; and a chalice and paten of 1877–8 of late-medieval design.[91] The registers date from 1653 but are incomplete; they include marriages celebrated outside the parish between 1668 and 1747.[92]

ROMAN CATHOLICISM. In 1585 a man was 'vehemently suspected of papistry' for having service books, a crucifix, and a private altar in his house, though they had recently been destroyed at the order of the lord of the manor.[93]

PROTESTANT NONCONFORMITY. Thomas Budd was living at Barrington when licensed as a Presbyterian preacher in 1672.[94] Thomasin Budd's house was licensed for worship in 1689 and other premises were used successively by dissenters until at least 1718.[95] Budd was described as minister at Barrington at his marriage in 1690 but as Presbyterian teacher of Burrow in Kingsbury at his death in 1722.[96] A house was licensed for Presbyterians in 1752 and another ten years later.[97] There were 10 Presbyterians and an Anabaptist in the parish in 1776.[98] Two rooms were used, probably by Presbyterians, from 1799.[99] In 1850 another house was licensed for Independents. It had accommodation for 100 and the evening congregation on Census Sunday 1851 numbered eighty.[1]

Wesleyan Methodists[2] were established in 1808 and in 1841 there were 11 members.[3] A decision by the circuit preachers to close the preaching place was flouted by the members in 1847, and in 1851 it was decided by the circuit to provide a preacher 'when they have a preaching place'.[4] A chapel was erected in 1859.[5] It was closed in 1965, and in 1973 was used as an artist's studio.

Public collections were taken at meetings of Bible Christians in 1825 and again in 1844.[6] A small congregation, formed in 1845, had 4 members in 1850 when it ceased to exist.[7]

EDUCATION. From 1800 the overseers paid fees for the education of a pauper girl, presumably in Barrington.[8] By 1818 there were two day-schools for 45 children and a Sunday school for 50 children.[9] By 1825 the Sunday school had 54 pupils.[10] Ten years later there was a day-school for 40 children supported by parents' payments, and a Sunday school for 51 children with an endowment under the will of Elizabeth Eason.[11] The Sunday school had 55 pupils in 1846–7.[12]

The National school, later Barrington Voluntary Controlled school, apparently derived from the endowment of Elizabeth Eason (d. 1830), and is said to have been built *c.* 1840.[13] It remained under the control of trustees until 1903.[14] In 1884 it was reported as 'quite the weakest' school the Diocesan Inspector had to examine.[15] Attendance was always its greatest problem, especially during the blackberrying season, and the attendance officer admitted in 1900 that he was too frightened of Barrington people to enforce the law.[16] In 1903 there were

---

[82] H.O. 129/317/3/11/17.
[83] S.R.O., D/D/V return 1870.
[84] S.R.O., D/P/barr 2/5/1, 4/3/2, 9/1/1.
[85] See below, plate facing p. 161.
[86] The work involved the demolition of a south porch. It was carried out by Maurice Davis of Langport.
[87] Devon R.O. 1077M/6/11.
[88] S.R.O., D/P/barr 4/1/1, 8/3/1–2.
[89] Ibid. 8/3/1, 9/1/1.
[90] S.R.O., DD/SAS CH 16.
[91] *Proc. Som. Arch. Soc.* xlv. 26–7; lix. 75; S.R.O., D/P/barr 2/1/1.   [92] S.R.O., D/P/barr 2/1/1–8.
[93] S.R.O., D/D/Ca 73.
[94] *Cal. S.P. Dom.* 1672, 293. See *Calamy Revised*, ed. Matthews, s.v. Hickman.
[95] S.R.O., Q/RR; D/P/barr 2/1/2.
[96] S.R.O., D/P/barr 2/1/1.
[97] S.R.O., Q/RR; D/D/V Dioc. bk.
[98] S.R.O., D/D/V Dioc. bk.

[99] S.R.O., D/D/Rm, box 1, vol. 3, 236.
[1] H.O. 129/317/3/11/18.
[2] The house of Henry Hutchings in 'Berrington' was used by Methodists in 1748. This may be Burrington: S.R.O., Q/RR.
[3] S.R.O., D/N/spc 1, 2.   [4] Ibid. 27.
[5] Inscr. on building.
[6] S.R.O., D/N/spc 31, 32.
[7] Ibid. 32.
[8] S.R.O., D/P/barr 13/2/2.
[9] *Digest of Returns to Sel. Cttee. on Educ. of Poor* H.C. 224 (1819), ix (2).
[10] *Rep. B. & W. Dioc. Assoc. S.P.C.K.* (1825–6).
[11] *Educ. Enquiry Abstract*, H.C. 62 (1835), xlii; see below.
[12] *Church Sch. Inquiry, 1846–7.*
[13] S.R.O., C/E 26. The date 1848 is also given: *Kelly's Dir. Som.*
[14] S.R.O., C/E 26.
[15] Ibid. 92: log bk.   [16] Ibid.

70 children on the books, and evening classes were held.[17] By 1906–7 the average attendance was 63 when there were 122 children on the books.[18] The average in 1938 was 25 out of 96 on the register.[19] From 1972 the school took pupils in the 5–9 age range, older children travelling to Middle School at Ilminster. In 1973 there were 42 children on the books.[20]

Elizabeth Eason of South Petherton, spinster, by will gave £1,000 in trust for a school for boys and girls.[21] The income was just under £40 at the end of the 19th century, part of which had been used to provide gardens for the school.[22] Under a Scheme of 1927 the income was to be used for the maintenance and repair of the school buildings, to support children in secondary or further education, and for social and physical training.[23] The income of c. £150 in 1976 was distributed in grants for school uniforms and for travelling expenses to attend evening classes.

CHARITIES FOR THE POOR. By will dated 1829 Mrs. Mary England devised the sum of £122 13s. 6d., the income to be applied equally by the vicar and churchwardens to the relief of the poor of Kingsbury Episcopi and Barrington.[24] In the 1840s the charity was distributed in coal, shop tickets, blankets, sheets, or calico for shirts, but twenty years later coal and cash only were given.[25] From 1895 the accounts were rendered to the parish meeting, though the churchwardens remained trustees.[26] Coal was still purchased in 1950 and there were 88 recipients in that year. By 1953–4 cash vouchers were issued[27] and by 1973 payments were made in cash.[28]

CHAFFCOMBE

THE PARISH of Chaffcombe lies 2 miles northeast of Chard and nearly 3 miles south-west of Ilminster, and had an area of 1,106 a. in 1901.[1] It is irregular in shape, extending for nearly 2¼ miles from north to south, and between 1½ mile and less than ½ mile from east to west. It is bounded on the north by Knowle St. Giles and Cricket Malherbie, on the east by Cudworth, on the south by Cricket St. Thomas and Winsham, and on the west by Chard.

The parish is on the western slopes of the Windwhistle ridge overlooking Chard, the ground falling from over 600 ft. on its eastern boundary to 200 ft. by the old Chard reservoir. The highest land, above Lidmarsh, is clay with flints, below which run successive north–south bands of chalk and Upper Greensand. The north-west of the parish is on the Middle Lias.[2] Small streams run through the parish, at Chaffcombe Gate farm and Chaffcombe village in the north, and at Lidmarsh and Avishays in the centre. There are natural springs in the area of Kingston Well farm in the extreme south.

The Domesday manor of Chaffcombe was formed from four separate estates,[3] suggesting a pattern of scattered settlement in the area in the 11th century. Chaffcombe village, the centre of the principal holding, lies along a small stream in a sheltered valley. It includes the church and the site of a medieval manor-house at its east end, the other manor-house, later Court Farm, to the south, and the rectory house to the west, all on higher ground above the village. There is now a spread of older houses, mostly of the 18th and 19th centuries, along the village street, and there has been more recent infilling of the gaps, mostly in the last 20 years. A secondary settlement in the south at Lidmarsh occurs by 1170.[4] There was a capital messuage and at least one house there by 1227[5] and the hamlet seems to have developed around a tract of waste. It remained a substantial collection of cottages until after 1840,[6] and probably represents the centre of one or more of the subsidiary Domesday holdings. Lidmarsh is now a small and scattered settlement of small houses, most of which are of 19th-century origin. Hecstanes, later Hynkestones well or Kingston well, occurs early in the 13th century, Avishays and Oakenhead emerged as freeholds in the fourteenth.[7]

The heavily-wooded terrain, particularly in the north, probably accounts for the tortuous road pattern, the result of piecemeal cutting, imparking, and inclosure over a long period. A grant of free warren in the 13th century[8] and the formation of Chaffcombe Park, later Park Wood, by the 15th,[9] was followed by the creation of a park around a new house at Avishays in the 18th century[10] and around Chaffcombe House and Ashton in the twentieth.[11] Common pasture at Chaffcombe Common in the north-west, at Whitemoor Hill above Avishays, and at Huckers (or Hawkers) Hill or Oakey Common on the Chard road at the end of Mals Mead Lane near Chard Elm, effectively

---

[17] S.R.O., C/E 26.
[18] *Bd. of Educ., List 21, 1908* (H.M.S.O.), 408.
[19] Ibid. 1938, 345.
[20] S.R.O., *Schs. Lists.*
[21] S.R.O., DD/PE 11.
[22] *Returns of Schs.* [C. 7529] H.C. (1894), lxv; S.R.O., C/E 26; D/P/barr 9/1/1.
[23] Ex inf. the clerk, Mr. B. Law, Puckington.
[24] S.R.O., D/P/barr 17/6/1.
[25] Ibid. 4/1/1.
[26] Ibid. 9/1/1.
[27] Ibid. 17/6/1.
[28] Ex inf. the vicar, the Revd. F. W. Cornell.

[1] S.R.O., tithe award; *Census* (1901). This article was completed in 1973.
[2] Geol. Surv. Map 1″, drift, sheet 311 (1957 edn.).
[3] *V.C.H. Som.* i. 446.
[4] *Pipe R.* 1170 (P.R.S. xv), 117.
[5] *S.R.S.* vi. 55–6.   [6] S.R.O., tithe award.
[7] Forde Abbey, Cart. pp. 511–12; *Cal. Inq. p.m.* xiii, p. 16; xiv, pp. 391–2.
[8] *Cal. Chart. R.* 1257–1300, 76.
[9] Parkmede occurs in 1444 and Park Lane in 1530: S.R.O., DD/PT, box 1, rental and ct. roll extract.
[10] See below, p. 126.
[11] Local information.

divided the parish.[12] The principal road, between Chard and Crewkerne, cuts the parish in the south, and part of the Foss Way forms a small section of the south-eastern boundary with Cricket St. Thomas. A route through Lidmarsh to Chaffcombe village and thence to Knowle St. Giles has evidently been diverted, partly by the creation of Avishays park and partly by the formation of Chaffcombe Gate farm.

There were licensed victuallers in the parish in 1751 and 1756[13] and a public house at the west end of the village in 1842.[14] The Happy Return, originally at Chard Elm and subsequently at the junction of Mals Mead Lane and the Chard–Crewkerne road, first occurs in 1859[15] and was closed in 1965.[16]

The parish had 12 households in 1612.[17] The population was 165 in 1801 and then rose gradually to 288 in 1841. After a slight recession to 246 in 1861 it rose again to 280 in 1871. There followed a decline to 192 in 1891.[18] Between 1901 and 1921 the numbers remained steady at around 230, but since that time the population has again decreased, to 176 in 1961 and 159 in 1971.[19]

Four parishioners were reported to have joined the Monmouth rebellion in 1685.[20]

MANORS AND OTHER ESTATES. In 1066 Chaffcombe comprised four estates, two held 'in parage' by two thegns and a further two held similarly by two other thegns. By 1086 these estates had been combined and granted to Geoffrey, bishop of Coutances, under whom they were held 'for one manor' by Ralph the red.[21] This Ralph can be identified with Ralph le (or de) Sor whose family became the principal tenants of the honor of Gloucester in that county and in Somerset.[22] Chaffcombe was also held of that honor. The manor's suit to South Petherton hundred court was withdrawn c. 1262 by Richard, earl of Gloucester (d. 1262).[23] His grandson Gilbert held the overlordship at his death in 1314.[24] It subsequently passed to Gilbert's brother-in-law Hugh le Despenser (d. 1349),[25] and was still held of the honor of Gloucester at least until 1600 though counter-claims were made in the interval.[26]

Ralph le Sor was succeeded as tenant by his son Otes (fl. 1088–1126),[27] and then by Jordan le Sor by 1166.[28] John (I) le Sor, stated to be son of Otes, probably held the manor c. 1176–7, and subinfeudated it to his cousin Richard de Morewell.[29] A claim to the overlordship, however, continued in the Sor family and their successors. Another John, who occurs between 1194 and 1205,[30] was succeeded before 1227 by Robert le Sor (d. by 1241).[31] His widow Gwenllian married Nicholas son of Roger, who held the estate until 1255 when it was inherited by William le Sor, son of John (III) and probably nephew of Robert.[32] William was followed by John (IV) le Sor (d. c. 1296–7)[33] and thereafter by Ela la Sor, probably his daughter, wife of William de Esthalle. She conveyed the Sor estates in Somerset to Sir Richard de Rodney in 1306.[34] Sir Richard was adjudged to be overlord of Chaffcombe in 1316 and the Rodneys again claimed the overlordship in 1498 as of their manor of Backwell.[35] Their title was finally disallowed in 1600 in favour of the honor of Gloucester.[36]

Richard de Morewell, to whom the manor had been granted by John (I) le Sor, subinfeudated it further to Alan de Furneaux for 20s. a year, and before 1189 had assigned this rent to Forde abbey (Dors.).[37] By virtue of this grant the abbey continued to claim lordship over the terre tenants. It was the abbey which granted dower in a moiety of the manor in 1270,[38] and further claims to the overlordship of the manor were made by the abbot up to 1390.[39] Agreements with the tenants of both moieties for the payment of rent were made in 1429 and 1430.[40] No reference to these payments has been noted after 1444.[41]

Alan de Furneaux or Geoffrey his son evidently conveyed the terre tenancy to Oliver Avenel (d. c. 1226).[42] On Avenel's death the manor was divided between his two daughters, Margaret and Emme,[43] and was not reunited until the early 17th century.

Margaret married first Warin de Noneton and then Philip de Cauntelo,[44] the latter being in possession by 1267.[45] By 1286 this half had descended to Margaret's son Baudry de Noneton (d. c. 1310)[46] who left a daughter and heir Margery, wife of Robert de Pudele.[47] By 1314 it had passed to

---

[12] S.R.O., tithe award; DD/X/AD (H/368), conveyance 27 Mar. 1726; Devon R.O. 281 M/E 422.
[13] S.R.O., Q/RL.
[14] S.R.O., DD/SAS (C/909), 135/2, sale poster, 8 June 1842; tithe award.   [15] S.R.O., D/PS/ilm, box 1.
[16] Local information.
[17] S.R.O., DD/HI, box 9, hundred papers.
[18] V.C.H. Som. ii. 348.   [19] Ibid.; Census, 1911–71.
[20] B.L. Add. MS. 30077, f. 35.
[21] V.C.H. Som. i. 446.
[22] 'Sor' means 'reddish' and of five Domesday manors held by Ralph four were occupied by the Sor family in the later 13th cent.
[23] Rot. Hund. (Rec. Com.), ii. 127.
[24] Cal. Inq. p.m. v, p. 337; Cal. Close, 1313–18, 136.
[25] Cal. Inq. p.m. ix, p. 339; Cal. Close, 1349–54, 35.
[26] C 142/259/97.
[27] Trans. Bristol & Glos. Arch. Soc. xiv. 295; xxxi. 22.
[28] Red Bk. Exch. (Rolls Ser.), i. 288. The descent follows that of 14 or 15 fees held of the honor of Gloucester, represented in Somerset by Backwell and Claverham.
[29] Forde Abbey, Cart. p. 514; Pipe R. 1176 (P.R.S. xxv), 126, 159; ibid. 1177 (P.R.S. xxvi), 22, 43.
[30] Pipe R. 1194 (P.R.S. N.S. v), 194; ibid. 1205 (P.R.S. N.S. xix), 92.

[31] S.R.S. vi. 52. Robert le Sor had licence to marry Gwenllian, sister of Hoeli, in 1232 (Pat. R. 1225–32, 506). She had married again by 1241, although described as former wife of John le Sor (S.R.S. xi, pp. 127–8).
[32] S.R.S. xi, pp. 127–8; Close R. 1254–6, 192–3; Forde Abbey, Cart. pp. 517–18.
[33] Cal. Fine R. 1272–1307, 383.
[34] Cal. Chart. R. 1257–1300, 151; S.R.S. vi. 341.
[35] Forde Abbey, Cart. pp. 513–14; Cal. Inq. p.m. Hen. VII, iii, pp. 552–3.
[36] C 142/259/97.
[37] Forde Abbey, Cart. pp. 514–15; Cart. Antiq. (P.R.S. N.S. xxxiii), 162–4.
[38] Forde Abbey, Cart. pp. 519–20.
[39] Feud. Aids, iv. 283; Cal. Inq. p.m. iii, p. 104; C 136/66/8.
[40] Forde Abbey, Cart. p. 521.
[41] S.R.O., DD/PT, box 1, rental, 1444.
[42] Forde Abbey, Cart. pp. 515–17; Ex. e Rot. Fin. i. 138–9.
[43] C.P. 40/17 m. 517.
[44] Ibid.; S.R.S., extra ser. 125–6.
[45] Cal. Chart. R. 1257–1300, 76.
[46] Feud. Aids. iv. 283; Cal. Inq. p.m. v, p. 110.
[47] Cal. Inq. p.m. v, p. 110.

Ralph of Stocklinch, who still held it in 1327,[48] and by 1344 to Roger of Stocklinch.[49] In 1390 John Denebaud, son of Thomas (d. 1362),[50] died holding this estate, evidently in right of his grandmother Joan Stocklinch, wife of William Denebaud.[51] John's son, also John, who was involved in two armed conflicts over lands in Chaffcombe, one with the lord of the other estate,[52] died in 1429.[53] His widow Florence was in possession in 1431,[54] and ownership then passed to their daughter Elizabeth (d. 1497), wife of William Poulett (d. 1488).[55] Sir Amias Poulett, son of Elizabeth, who died at Chaffcombe in 1538, was succeeded in turn by his son Sir Hugh (d. 1573) and grandson Sir Amias (d. 1588).[56] The property passed from the last to his son Anthony (d. 1600), whose son John purchased the other half of the manor in 1613.[57]

Emme Avenel (d. c. 1253), holder of the other half of the manor, married Jordan de Lisle, who owned lands in Chaffcombe in 1235.[58] Their son Walter, dead by 1269, was succeeded in turn by his son William de Lisle (d. c. 1294) and grand-daughter Idony, wife of Hugh de Beauchamp, who presented to the rectory in 1349.[59] From Idony the property passed to John,[60] probably her son, and to his son William Beauchamp (d. 1419–20).[61] William's son John was lord in 1420[62] but by 1461 the patronage and presumably the estate had passed to John (I) Buller of Wood in Knowle St. Giles.[63] John's grandfather or great-grandfather Nicholas Buller is believed to have married John Beauchamp's daughter and heir,[64] and his father Thomas Buller had an interest in Chaffcombe between 1386 and 1410.[65] John (I) died in 1485 and was succeeded by his grandson Alexander (d. 1526), son of John (II) Buller.[66] From Alexander ownership descended in turn to John (III), John (IV) (d. 1592), John (V) (d. 1599), and John (VI).[67] In 1612 the last sold it to trustees[68] who in the next year conveyed it to John Poulett,[69] thus reuniting the two halves of the manor.

The identity of the halves as individual manors was preserved by the Pouletts under the names of *CHAFFCOMBE BULLER* and *CHAFF-COMBE POULETT*, administered separately until the 18th century.[70] The estate descended with the manor of Hinton St. George in the Poulett

family until 1913 when the Chaffcombe lands and the advowson, but not the lordship, were sold to Holliday Hartley of Chaffcombe House.[71] The Hartley estate was divided and sold in 1923.[72] The lordship, not mentioned after the first sale, has apparently continued in the Poulett family.

The manor-house linked with the Poulett half of the manor was leased to Robert Cuffe of Donyatt in 1542.[73] Cuffe assigned the lease to Richard Cogan of Chard in 1544, and his widow Agnes (d. 1549–50) left it to her son John.[74] By 1565 John Cogan had allowed the house, bakery, dairyhouse, and stables to fall into decay,[75] and soon after he assigned the lease to Peter Bryce.[76] In 1599 it was leased by the lord to his son Amias Poulett, who surrendered it in 1615 to his brother John, then lord.[77] It is not mentioned thereafter and was evidently demolished. The site of the house is not precisely known but local tradition places it immediately north-west from the church.

The manor-house attached to Chaffcombe Buller was mentioned in 1294 and treated as leasehold by 1640.[78] It was known as the Court House from the late 17th century[79] and as Court Farm it continued to be held as part of the Poulett and subsequently Hartley estates until 1923, when it was bought by the tenant, F. Wilmington.[80] The latter sold it to R. S. J. Gould in 1945, and his son Mr. C. R. Gould has held it since 1972.[81] The present building is part of an apparently substantial 15th-century house. A traceried window survives on the first floor with unidentified coats of arms on the labels.

A hamlet at Lidmarsh is first recorded as Libbemersa in 1170[82] and Forde abbey received grants of rent and small amounts of land there in the 13th century.[83] The overlordship of these was claimed by the earl of Gloucester in 1315 but was awarded to the heirs of John le Sor in the following year.[84] It is doubtful whether there was a single dominant estate there in the 13th century, but a part of the hamlet may have formed an element of the $\frac{1}{2}$ fee at Cudworth and Knowle St. Giles held in 1303 and 1316 by Matthew de Esse and Humphrey de Kail, and in 1346 by de Kail alone.[85] At his death in 1348 William Kail held a messuage and 30 a. of land in Lidmarsh under Robert FitzPayn which passed to his son John (d. 1384).[86] John also held

[48] Ibid. p. 337.
[49] *S.R.S.* ix, pp. 409, 502. He died probably soon after (*Cal. Close, 1343–6*, 182).
[50] *Cal. Inq. p.m.* xiii, p. 15.
[51] C 136/66/8; *S.R.S.* xii. 117; *Visits. Som.* ed. F. W. Weaver (1885), 20.
[52] *Cal. Pat.* 1408–13, 180; 1416–22, 271–2; *Cal. Inq. Misc.* vii, pp. 346–7.
[53] *Cal. Close 1429–35*, 8; C. Franklyn, *A Genealogical History of Paulet etc.*, 6.
[54] *Cal. Pat.* 1416–22, 271–2; *Feud. Aids*, iv. 432.
[55] *Cal. Inq. p.m. Hen. VII*, iii, pp. 552–3; *S.R.S. extra ser.* 240.   [56] *S.R.S.* xxi. 40; C 142/61/14.
[57] *S.R.S.* li, pp. 190–1; see below.
[58] *Cal. Inq. p.m.* i, p. 66; *S.R.S.* vi. 96.
[59] *S.R.S.* x, p. 577; xxxvi. 94; *Cal. Inq. p.m.* iii, p. 104.
[60] *S.R.S.* xvii. 112; xxxv. 87.
[61] Ibid. xiii, pp. 25–6, 28; xxix, p. 99; *Cal. Close, 1381–5*, 423; *Cal. Inq. p.m.* (Rec. Com.), iv. 42.
[62] *Cal. Inq. Misc.* vii, pp. 346–7.
[63] *S.R.S.* xlix, p. 356.
[64] *Visits. Som.* ed. F. W. Weaver, 12–13; *Visits. Cornw. 1620* (Harl. Soc., ix), 24–5; *S.R.S.* xv. 145.
[65] *S.R.S.* xvii. 128; *Cal. Pat.* 1408–13, 180.

[66] *Cal. Inq. p.m. Hen. VII*, i, p. 66; *S.R.S.* xix. 249.
[67] *S.R.S.* xix. 249; *Visits. Som.* ed. F. W. Weaver, 12–13; C 142/232/42.
[68] S.R.O., DD/SS, bdle. 30.
[69] Ibid.; *S.R.S.* li, pp. 190–1.
[70] S.R.O., DD/PT, box 46, survey (17th cent.); box 43, survey, 1716.
[71] Sale cat. 1923, *penes* Mr. J. G. Vincent, Knowle St. Giles; *Kelly's Dir. Som.* (1914–23).
[72] Sale cat. 1923, *penes* Mr. J. G. Vincent.
[73] S.R.O., DD/SS, bdle. 30.
[74] Req. 2/226/15; *S.R.S.* xxi. 83–4, 109.
[75] S.R.O., DD/PT, box 2.
[76] Req. 2/226/15.
[77] S.R.O., DD/SS, bdle. 30.
[78] *Cal. Inq. p.m.* iii, p. 104; S.R.O., DD/SS, bdle. 30.
[79] S.R.O., DD/PT, box 46, survey, 17th cent.
[80] Sale cat. 1923, *penes* Mr. J. G. Vincent.
[81] Ex inf. Mr. C. R. Gould, Chaffcombe.
[82] *Pipe R.* 1170 (P.R.S. xv), 117.
[83] Forde Abbey, Cart. pp. 510–12.
[84] Ibid. pp. 513–14; see above.
[85] *Feud. Aids*, iv. 315, 331, 337.
[86] *Cal. Inq. p.m.* xiii, p. 16; xiv, pp. 391–2.

20 a. of pasture in Aveneleseigh, later *AVISHAYS*. In 1385 John's widow received in dower 20 a. of land at Okenehede and 10 a. at Lidmarsh in respect of these lands, then stated to be parcel of Cudworth manor.[87] Thomas Kail (d. 1394), son of John, was succeeded in turn by his sister Idony (d. 1401), wife of John Poulett, and her sons John and Thomas. Both sons died in 1413 and the lands, then totalling 100 a. in Aveneleseygh and 20 a. in Lidmarsh, reverted to a feoffee, John Kaynes (d. 1420).[88] The latter's daughter Joan (d. 1462), wife successively of Sir John Speke and Hugh Champernowne, (d. 1482) was succeeded by her grandson, John son of John Speke.[89] William Speke, described as of Avishays in 1506, was followed by his son Thomas and grandson John Speke.[90] By 1530 the estate was held as a freehold under Chaffcombe manor.[91] John Speke's sister Joan and her husband Thomas Sydenham had livery of the Speke lands in Chaffcombe in 1537,[92] and their son Richard Sydenham conveyed the property to John (I) Browne of Frampton (Dors.) in 1559.[93] The premises evidently passed by successive sons to Sir John (II) Browne (d. 1627), John (III) (d. 1659), and John (IV) (d. 1670). They were then inherited by the uncle of the last, George Browne (d. 1677), followed in turn by his sons George and Robert.[94] In 1697 Avishays was sold by Robert Browne to his tenant Elias Sealy of Chaffcombe (d. 1715), to whose family the estate had been leased since Sir John (II) Browne's time.[95] Sealy was succeeded by his son Samuel (d. 1742), whose only surviving child Sarah married James Marwood (d. 1767) of Widworthy (Devon).[96] Under the will of Sarah Marwood (d. 1797) Avishays was to be held jointly by her daughters as long as her only son, James Thomas Benedictus Marwood (d. 1811), continued insane.[97] On his death the Marwood estates were divided between the four daughters, Avishays passing to Sarah Bridget (d. 1821), wife successively of Henry Stevens and John Inglett Fortescue, and subsequently to her sister Mary (d. 1831), wife of the Revd. George Notley of Combe Sydenham.[98] Thereafter it descended to her great-nephew William Warry Elton who sold it to Edward Clarke (d. 1895), a Chard solicitor, in 1859.[99] From that date the property continued to change hands with some frequency, and in 1973 was owned by Mr. James Verner.

The house is of brick with stone dressings and appears to be of the 18th century, but the east side of the main building incorporates part of an earlier-17th-century house which was refronted in the last years of the same century when an eastern courtyard with coach house, stables, and brewhouse were laid out.[1] The courtyard was further enclosed on the north by a kitchen wing, added in the earlier 18th century, and in 1745[2] the main range was extended southwards and doubled in depth by the addition of new principal rooms behind a symmetrical west front of seven bays. More service rooms were added on the north in the 19th century and a conservatory, presumably of similar date, on the south-east was removed in the twentieth century. There is a large walled garden to the south-east and on the hill to the east a small embattled structure of the 19th century, known as the Castle, serves as both eye-catcher and water tower. There are extensive farm buildings of the 19th and 20th centuries to the north of the house.

Oakenhead, mentioned in 1385, formed part of the Avishays estate in 1394 and was held as a freehold of Chaffcombe manor by Joan, widow of Sir Thomas Brook, at her death in 1437.[3] It was inherited by her son Sir Thomas Brook (d. 1439)[4] and evidently passed to her grandson Edward, Lord Cobham (d. 1464).[5] It continued in the Brook family, descending by successive heirs, Lords Cobham, to John (d. 1512), Thomas (d. 1529), George (d. 1558), and William (d. 1597).[6] On the attainder of Henry, Lord Cobham, son of the last, in 1603 the estate evidently passed with other Brook lands to Charles Blount, earl of Devonshire (d. 1606), and subsequently to the latter's illegitimate son Mountjoy Blount, later Lord Mountjoy.[7] Mountjoy sold the property to John Lambert in 1624, in whose family it continued until its settlement in 1656 on Jeffery Pysing (d. 1706) of Winsham and his intended wife Elizabeth Lambert.[8] Their son Hugh (d. 1714) was succeeded by his son Jeffery (d. 1735) and grandson Hugh.[9] The last conveyed it to Jennings Darby in 1743 and sold it to John Notley in 1750.[10] Oakenhead was held by George Notley in 1800 and sold in 1829 by Edward Elton of Greenway (Devon) to Henry Hoste Henley of Leigh in Winsham.[11] By 1830 the farmhouse had been demolished and by 1839 the lands had been absorbed by Henry John Henley's farm at Kingston Well.[12]

Forde abbey owned a small property in the south of the parish linked with the grange at Street in Winsham and known in the 16th century as Hynkestones Well alias Heckestonwill. A William de Hecstanes witnessed an abbey charter in the early 13th century.[13] It was leased with the grange and properties in Dorset to Richard Pollard in 1539

[87] *Cal. Inq. p.m.* xiv, pp. 391–2.
[88] C 136/84/7; C 136/93/33; *Cal. Close*, 1413–19, 28–9; *S.R.S.* xxii. 55–6. The name of the estate is presumably derived from Oliver Avenel, lord of Chaffcombe: see above.
[89] *Cal. Close*, 1461–8, 127; C 140/7/13; C 140/84/32.
[90] S.R.O., DD/SS, bdle. 19; *L. & P. Hen. VIII*, xii(2), 83.
[91] S.R.O., DD/PT, box 1.
[92] *L. & P. Hen. VIII*, xii(2), 83.
[93] C.P. 25(2)/204/2 Eliz. I Hil.; S.R.O., DD/SS, bdle. 1.
[94] Hutchins, *Hist. Dors.* ii. 298.
[95] Devon R.O. 281 M/T 375–6; S.R.O., D/P/chaf 2/1/1.
[96] S.R.O., D/P/chaf 2/1/1; Devon R.O. 281 M/T 384–6; *The Genealogist* (New Ser.), ii. 20–21.
[97] Devon R.O. 281 M/F 2, 8, 20; E 15; *The Genealogist* (New Ser.), ii. 20–21.

[98] Burke, *Land. Gent.* (1914), 607.
[99] Burke, *Peerage* (1949), 707; E. Walford, *County Families of U.K.* (1892), 201; M.I. in chyd.
[1] See plate facing p. 33.
[2] Date on rainwater heads.
[3] *Cal. Inq. p.m.* xiv, pp. 391–2; ibid. (Rec. Com.), iv. 180; C 136/84/7.
[4] *Cal. Inq. p.m.* (Rec. Com.), iv. 187; *S.R.S.* xxii. 194.
[5] S.R.O., DD/PT, box 1; *Complete Peerage*, iii. 346–7.
[6] *Complete Peerage*, iii. 346–7; S.R.O., DD/PT, box 1.
[7] *Complete Peerage*, ix. 343 ff.; Devon R.O. 281 M/E 422, covenant to produce deeds, 1830.
[8] Devon R.O. 281 M/E 422; S.R.O., D/P/wins 2/1/1.
[9] S.R.O., D/P/wins 2/1/1.
[10] Devon R.O. 281 M/E 422.   [11] Ibid.
[12] Ibid.; S.R.O., tithe award.
[13] Forde Abbey, Cart. pp. 511–12.

for 21 years, and then in 1545 its reversion was sold to John Preston of Cricket St. Thomas.[14] The name has not been traced thereafter until the early 19th century as a farm known as Hinkstones Well or Kingston Well, then on the Henley estate, suggesting a descent from the 16th century with the manor of Street and Leigh through the Dewport and Henley families.[15]

ECONOMIC HISTORY. By 1086, after combination, a demesne holding of more than 3 hides out of a total of 4 hides and 3½ virgates had been created. Stock on the farm amounted to 8 head of cattle, 24 swine, and 65 sheep. The two smallest holdings, both occupied by villeins and with two plough teams for a total of only 1¾ hide, probably lay in the south of the parish around a settlement at Lidmarsh. The total value of the property was 60s.[16] It was twice subinfeudated in the late 12th century, first for 10s. a year and then for 20s.[17] In the later 13th century it was valued at 40s.[18] and between 1314 and 1414 at twice that sum,[19] but the true value was probably closer to 106s. 8d., the assessment of the Denebaud half in 1390.[20] By 1444 the rents for one half amounted to £8 8s. 1d. a year.[21]

No reference has been found to open-field cultivation. In 1420 the Beauchamp family complained that John Denebaud had illegally inclosed a 2-a. plot of pasture with a fence and a hedge of thorn and brambles.[22] A rental of 1444 shows that apart from small tracts of pasture and moorland the manor lay almost wholly in closes, one substantial piece of arable called le Sarte suggesting its origin as an assart.[23] The demesne lands held with one half of the manor by William de Lisle in 1294 comprised a house and garden, 30 a. of arable land, 4 a. meadow and pasture, and 20 a. of underwood.[24] By the 16th century the few references to demesne are to isolated closes leased to tenants.[25] In 1542 the Pouletts leased 77½ a. with Chaffcombe Poulett manor-house[26] and in the 17th century 10 a. were held with Court Farm.[27] In neither case, however, was the land recorded as former demesne.

Domesday recorded woodland measuring 8 furlongs square[28] which probably lay on and around Sprays Hill in the north-east of the parish. A wood called 'Rivelos' was claimed in 1275 to have formed part of the Avenel inheritance,[29] and 'Rokewoode' and 'Ryvelhose' occur in 1419.[30] The lord's wood was leased to tenants by 1443[31] and timber

was taken there without licence in 1531.[32] 'Lumbardes wood' of 31 a. was leased with Chaffcombe Poulett manor-house in 1542,[33] and it was presented in 1564 that under-tenants had caused much damage to the lord's wood.[34]

Philip de Cauntelo received a grant of free warren in his demesne lands of Chaffcombe in 1267.[35] Chaffcome Park was part of Chaffcombe Buller, when it contained 40 a., and in 1582 it was leased with Woodhouse in Knowle St. Giles.[36] In 1613 it was sold to the Pouletts with the manor of Chaffcombe Buller[37] and between 1650 and 1759 was held under lease by the Lumbard family.[38] On the expiry of the last lease the park was retained in the hands of the lord and in 1765 was stocked with Poulett cattle.[39]

One half of the manor included 4 houses and 4 bovates in 1390[40] and in 1444 the same property had 9 tenants holding 5 cottages and 2 other tenements, including lands of Old Auster. The manor pound was then divided between four of the tenants and three of these were evidently supplying hurdles in lieu of works.[41] In 1443 mention is made of the non-payment of hurdlesilver for 18 years.[42] Between 1553 and 1560 the administration of the Poulett halves of the manors of Chaffcombe and Knowle St. Giles, together with Illeigh farm in Knowle, was combined[43] and thereafter Chaffcombe manor was considered to include much of Knowle. The problems of the divided manor occasionally caused confusion, as in 1569 when Poulett claimed half the price of a stray sheep presented in John Buller's court.[44] A lease of the Poulett manor-house for 90 years was granted in 1542 and by the end of the 16th century conversion from copyhold tenure to leases for 99 years or 3 lives had begun.[45] The reunion of the two Chaffcombe halves in 1613 resulted in an estate of some 615 a., although this included lands in Knowle St. Giles.[46] About half the holdings were then leased, and conversion to leasehold continued during the 18th century.[47] In 1716, excluding Illeigh in Knowle, there were 2 freeholders, 26 copyholders, and 24 leaseholders, the last two classes holding nearly 500 a. between them and the total rental standing at £22 7s. 9d. Most of the farming units were small: only two over 35 a., of which one was Chaffcombe Park and the other a farm of 71 a.[48] Covenants to plant trees, particularly oaks, form a regular feature of Poulett leases in the late 17th and earlier 18th centuries.[49]

Chaffcombe common is mentioned in 1553

---

[14] S.R.O., DD/SAS PR 495; L. & P. Hen. VIII, xx, p. 120.
[15] C 142/234/51; C 142/488/55; C.P. 25(2)/207/39 Eliz. I, East.; S.R.O., tithe award; O.S. Map 1", sheet 21 (1st edn.).
[16] V.C.H. Som. i. 446.
[17] Forde Abbey, Cart. pp. 514–15.
[18] Cal. Inq. p.m. i, p. 66; iii, p. 104.
[19] Ibid. v, p. 337; Cal. Close, 1349–54, 35; Cal. Inq. Misc. vii, p. 269.
[20] C 136/66/8.
[21] S.R.O., DD/PT, box 1.
[22] Cal. Inq. Misc. vii, pp. 346–7.
[23] S.R.O., DD/PT, box 1.
[24] Cal. Inq. p.m. iii, p. 104.
[25] e.g. S.R.O., DD/SS, bdle. 1, lease, 25 Nov. 1562.
[26] Ibid. bdle. 30.   [27] Ibid.
[28] V.C.H. Som. i. 446.
[29] C.P. 40/17 m. 57.
[30] Cal. Inq. Misc. vii, pp. 346–7.
[31] S.R.O., DD/SS, bdle. 3.

[32] S.R.O., DD/PT, box 1.
[33] S.R.O., DD/SS, bdle. 30.
[34] Ibid. bdle. 1.
[35] Cal. Chart. R. 1257–1300, 76.
[36] S.R.O., DD/SS, bdle. 31.
[37] S.R.S. li, pp. 190–1.
[38] S.R.O., DD/SS, bdle. 30, leases 1 Feb. 1649/50, 17 Oct. 1682; DD/PT, box 41, rental, 1754. The last occupier, John Charlwood, had married Joan Lumbard.
[39] S.R.O., DD/PT, box 41, rental, 1754.
[40] C 136/66/8.
[41] S.R.O., DD/PT, box 1.
[42] S.R.O., DD/SS, bdle. 3.
[43] Ibid. bdle. 1; DD/PT, boxes 1, 46 (survey c. 1665).
[44] S.R.O., DD/PT, box 2.
[45] S.R.O., DD/SS, bdle. 30.
[46] S.R.O., DD/PT, box 46, survey c. 1665.
[47] Ibid. box 46, surveys c. 1665, 1716.
[48] Ibid. survey, 1716.
[49] Ibid. box 20; DD/SS, bdles. 29, 30.

when it was overstocked by the tenants, and it was agreed by the lords of both halves of the manor in 1564 that sheep should be pastured there only between the feasts of St. Andrew (30 Nov.) and Lady Day (25 Mar.).[50] In the 18th century it was suggested that the tenants of the manor, who would otherwise suffer under a parliamentary inclosure, might be granted liberty to inclose the commons themselves.[51] A reference to land lately inclosed from the common in 1812, adjoining 'New close',[52] suggests that inclosure was then proceeding piecemeal. Between 1818 and 1824 the occupiers of estates totalling nearly 530 a., including the owner of Avishays, had rights over Chaffcombe common,[53] but by 1839 the inclosure of the whole common had been completed.[54] Common pasture on 'Hyemore', Whitemoor Hill, and Huckers Hill was mentioned in 1571.[55] The first of these has not been identified, but Cold Harbour cottage at the western approach to Avishays and built by 1700, had formerly stood on Whitemoor Hill common and the name survived as Whitemoor Lane and in closes north-east of Avishays.[56] In 1726 and 1740 an annual rent of 2s. called the Plashett or Plashnett rent, payable within 20 days of Michaelmas, was rendered by the commoners of Whitemoor Hill, Lidmarsh, and Chard Heathfield.[57] Huckers Hill common is probably Hawkers Hill otherwise Oakey common, of which 6 a. was described as recently inclosed in 1830.[58] Much of Lidmarsh was evidently common pasture and again appears to have been privately inclosed by tenants during the 18th century.[59]

Avishays formed the largest freehold in the parish. In 1413 it included 120 a. of which 20 a. lay in Lidmarsh,[60] and a further 60 a. may probably be assigned to Walscombe in Chard.[61] In 1697 the home estate include 40 a. at Avishays and 24 a. at Lidmarsh.[62] The Sealys and Marwoods bought some more land during the 18th century and the acquisition of the lease of Cold Harbour cottage in 1729 to form the western lodge[63] probably gives the approximate date at which the park around the house was laid out.

Formerly the largest farm in the parish, Chaffcombe Gate was created by the Pouletts in the late 18th or early 19th century and had an acreage of 208 a. in 1819,[64] a significant portion of their estate in the parish which totalled 425 a. in 1839. The Henley estate of 230 a. then included Kingston Well farm of 117 a. and substantial property at Lidmarsh; Avishays had increased to 185 a. and

between them these three holdings accounted for 90 per cent of the parish. Tolleys farm at Lidmarsh then had 81 a., and Kennel House near Avishays 64 a.[65]

At the time of the tithe commutation the parish included 311 a. of arable, 467 a. of meadow and pasture, and 117 a. of woodland.[66] By 1905 the amount of arable had fallen to 212 a., the grassland rising to 633 a. and woodland to 132 a.[67] The former Poulett estate was broken up in 1923, when the farms passed into private hands, particularly those of the Vincent family of Knowle St. Giles, Poulett tenant farmers from the 18th century.[68] During the 20th century there has been a diminution in the size of the larger holdings and a corresponding increase in the extent of the smaller farms. Thus in 1973 Court Farm had been extended to 85 a., whereas Avishays had dropped to 150 a. and Chaffcombe Gate to 125 a. The agriculture of the parish continues to be both dairy and arable.[69]

Although the parish has always been dependent principally on agriculture for its economy, there were links with the clothing and gloving industries, presumably by virtue of the parish's proximity to Chard and Ilminster. A weaver is mentioned in 1700, a clothworker in 1741,[70] and a hand-loom weaver of sailcloth in 1851. In 1851 there were 23 female glovers.[71]

LOCAL GOVERNMENT. There were separate courts for each half of Chaffcombe manor, but rolls survive only for Chaffcombe Poulett for the years 1523, 1530–2, 1552–3, 1560–72,[72] 1651–77, 1703–10, 1715–26.[73] Courts continued after the reunification of the manor in 1613, and by 1651 a single court only was held. The courts for the Poulett half of Knowle St. Giles manor had been united with those for Chaffcombe Poulett by 1560, but suit of court to Chaffcombe Buller was required of a tenant in 1776.[74] In the 16th century the manor court met usually twice each year in spring and autumn, being known simply as the manor court or the court leet. Pleas of debt and trespass occur at one court in 1572. No reference to the appointment of manorial officers has been noted.

There were usually two churchwardens in the late 16th and 17th centuries.[75] It was agreed in 1737 that the rector should nominate one.[76] Vestry minutes from 1850 show the appointment of two overseers, two waywardens (one only from 1861),

[50] S.R.O., DD/SS, bdle. 1.
[51] S.R.O., DD/PT, box 43, undated note in survey, 1716.
[52] Ibid. box 20.
[53] S.R.O., DD/SAS, (C/909), 9/3.
[54] S.R.O., tithe award.
[55] S.R.O., DD/PT, box 2.
[56] Devon R.O. 281 M/T 382–3, 396; S.R.O., tithe award; O.S. Map 6″, Som. LXXXVIII SW. (1931 edn.).
[57] S.R.O., DD/X/AD (H/368), conveyance, 27 Mar. 1726; Devon R.O. 281 M/T 384–5.
[58] Devon R.O. 281 M/E 422.
[59] Ibid. T 398, 562, 564.
[60] Cal. Close, 1413–19, 28–9.
[61] Devon R.O. 281 M/T 375–6.
[62] Ibid.
[63] Devon R.O., 281 M/T 398, 562, 564; DD/X/AD, (H/368), conveyance, 27 Mar. 1726. The freehold of Cold Harbour was purchased in 1741 (Devon R.O. 281

M/T 396).
[64] S.R.O., DD/PT, box 40, bk. of maps. Chaffcombe Gate farm was by tradition built of stone from the former Woodhouse Farm in Knowle, burnt down in 1806 (ex inf. Mr. J. G. Vincent). Chaffcombe Gate was mentioned in 1752 (S.R.O., DD/SS, bdle. 4, proposal bk.).
[65] S.R.O., tithe award.
[66] Ibid.
[67] Statistics supplied by the then Bd. of Agric. 1905.
[68] Ex inf. Mr. J. G. Vincent.
[69] Ex inf. Messrs. C. R. Gould, J. W. H. Verner of Avishays, and J. G. Vincent.
[70] Devon R.O. 281 M/T 382, 396.
[71] H.O. 107/1928.
[72] S.R.O., DD/SS, bdle. 1; DD/PT, boxes 1, 2.
[73] Ct. bks. penes Countess Poulett, Jersey.
[74] S.R.O., DD/PT, box 20, lease, 2 Jan. 1776.
[75] S.R.O., D/D/Rr 83.
[76] S.R.O., D/P/chaf 2/1/1.

and a churchwarden. From 1863 one of the overseers was salaried.[77]

A workhouse or poorhouse at Lidmarsh was sold in 1837, the parish having become part of the Chard poor-law union in the previous year.[78]

CHURCH. A rector of Chaffcombe occurs *c.* 1187.[79] The advowson was held with the manor by 1275 when its ownership was in dispute between the lords of the two halves,[80] and similar disputes took place in 1344 and 1402.[81] After the reunification of the manor the advowson continued in the hands of the Pouletts. William Morryn of Knowle St. Giles presented in 1545 by grant of Sir Hugh Poulett,[82] and the bishop by lapse in 1696.[83] In 1913 the patronage passed with the Poulett estate to Holliday Hartley.[84] Between 1923 and 1931 it was conveyed to the Diocesan Board of Finance, the present patron.[85] The benefice was united with the livings of Knowle St. Giles and Cricket Malherbie in 1941.[86]

The church was not mentioned in the taxation of 1291, but the rectory, valued at £8 13s. 4d. in 1445,[87] was exempted from tax in 1517 for poverty.[88] Its gross income had risen to £9 18s. 4d. by 1535[89] and to £40 by 1651.[90] The living was augmented by grants in the 1650s,[91] and was worth £60 by *c.* 1668.[92] It fell to £45 in 1727[93] and to £43 17s. *c.* 1785.[94] The net income was £143 in 1831[95] and 1840,[96] and £165 in 1866.[97]

In 1535 the predial tithes were valued at 19s. 8d., the tithes of sheep and lambs at 26s. 8d., and oblations and personal tithes at 35s.[98] The tithes were leased to Earl Poulett in 1819 for a rent of £126, and were commuted for a tithe rent-charge of £160 in 1839.[99]

The glebe lands, worth £3 6s. 8d. in 1535,[1] totalled 22 a. in 1606 and 1637.[2] They amounted to 28 a. in 1819 when they were leased with the parsonage house for £50 a year.[3] The extent of the glebe remained the same until the sale of all but 4½ a. between 1894 and 1914.[4] No further glebe had been sold by 1972.[5]

The parsonage house was described in 1606 as a mansion, barn, and stable with three little gardens.[6] The building was said to be unfit for residence in 1835.[7] It continued to be used as a farmhouse until its sale between 1894 and 1914.[8] The building, known as the Old Rectory, is generally of stone with a thatched roof. It has an original two-roomed plan with later extensions. The interior has a number of 17th-century features, including a staircase with turned balusters, and there is a cruck roof. A large stone rectory house, built near the church in 1886,[9] housed the incumbent in 1973.

John Clawsey, rector from 1545, was deprived for marriage in 1554 but was restored in Elizabeth I's reign.[10] Edward Middleton, rector 1568–1609, was a former fellow of New College, Oxford, and for 2½ years employed curates to serve in his stead.[11] Peter Cox, rector 1642–?, 1662–95, was ejected during the Interregnum when the church was served by Joseph Shallett by 1648, and then by Robert Pinney from 1658.[12] Cox was reinstated at the Restoration and held Lympsham in plurality.[13] Most of the incumbents since that time have been graduates.[14] Richard Abraham, rector 1789–1822, held the living with that of Ilminster, and Charles Penny, D.D., rector 1848–75, was headmaster of Crewkerne grammar school throughout his incumbency.[15] The lack of any satisfactory parsonage house during most of the 19th century resulted in a succession of non-resident parsons and the curates they employed. The curate in 1827 lived in Chard and also served Cudworth.[16] Curates under Dr. Penny were generally Second Masters at Crewkerne School.[17] It was only when the new rectory was built in 1886 that resident incumbents returned to the parish.

In 1577 the parishioners had only two sermons in a year.[18] The churchwardens were twice presented for not electing a parish clerk in 1623.[19] There were only eight communicants in 1776.[20] One service was held every Sunday in 1827, and by 1840 two, with at least four celebrations of Holy Communion annually, although the parish had reverted to a single Sunday service and sermon by 1843.[21] The advent of a new rector in 1848 resulted in a return to two Sunday services and Holy Communion eight times a year.[22] Census Sunday 1851 produced congregations of 32 in the morning and 90 in the afternoon.[23]

The fraternity of St. Saviour was mentioned in

[77] Ibid. 13/2/1.
[78] Ibid.; D/PS/ilm, box 16; tithe award.
[79] *H.M.C. Wells,* i. 46.
[80] C.P. 40/17 m. 57.
[81] *S.R.S.* ix, p. 409; xiii, pp. 25–6, 28.
[82] S.R.O., D/D/B reg. 13, f. 25.
[83] *Som. Incumbents,* ed. Weaver.
[84] Sale cat. 1923, *penes* Mr. J. G. Vincent.
[85] *Kelly's Dir. Som.* (1923, 1931).
[86] *Crockford.*
[87] *S.R.S.* xlix, p. 33.
[88] Ibid. liv, p. 187.
[89] *Valor Eccl.* (Rec. Com.), i. 166.
[90] Lambeth Palace MSS., COMM V/1.
[91] Ibid. VIb/2.
[92] S.R.O., D/D/Vc 24.
[93] S.R.O., D/D/V Dioc. bk. 1727.
[94] S.R.O., D/P b.on s 23/17.
[95] *Rep. Com. Eccl. Revenues,* pp. 130–1.
[96] *County Gazette Dir.* (1840).
[97] *P.O. Dir. Som.* (1866).
[98] *Valor Eccl.* (Rec. Com.), i. 166.
[99] S.R.O., DD/PT, box 20; tithe award.
[1] *Valor Eccl.* (Rec. Com.), i. 166.

[2] S.R.O., D/D/Rg 293.
[3] S.R.O. DD/PT, box 20.
[4] S.R.O., tithe award; *Kelly's Dir. Som.* (1894, 1914).
[5] Ex inf. the rector, the Revd. W. F. E. Smith.
[6] S.R.O., D/D/Rg 293.
[7] *Rep. Com. Eccl. Revenues,* pp. 156–7.
[8] *Kelly's Dir. Som.* (1894, 1914).
[9] S.R.O. D/P/chaf 13/2/1; *Kelly's Dir. Som.* (1889).
[10] *S.R.S.* lv, p. 124.
[11] Foster, *Alumni Oxon.; S. & D. N. & Q.* xiv. 32.
[12] *Som. Incumbents,* ed. Weaver; *Calamy Revised,* ed. Matthews; *Walker Revised,* ed. Matthews; Lambeth Palace MSS., COMM III/7, 54; VIb/2.
[13] *Som. Incumbents,* ed. Weaver.
[14] Foster, *Alumni Oxon.;* Venn, *Alumni Cantab.*
[15] R. G. Bartelot, *Hist. Crewkerne Sch.* 72.
[16] S.R.O., D/D/V return 1827.
[17] Bartelot, *Hist. Crewkerne Sch.* 72.
[18] S.R.O., D/D/Ca 57.
[19] *S.R.S.* xliii. 67, 105, 134.
[20] S.R.O., D/D/V Dioc. bk.
[21] S.R.O., D/D/V returns 1827, 1840, 1843.
[22] H.O. 129/318/2/6/10.
[23] Ibid.

1531[24] and in 1548 there was £3 9s. 4d. in cash for the maintenance of lights.[25]

The church of *ST. MICHAEL AND ALL ANGELS*, formerly dedicated to St. Michael alone, stands at the eastern end of the village, set back well above the road. It is built of ashlar and has a chancel with north vestry, nave with north aisle and south porch, and west tower. The body of the church was rebuilt to the designs of J. M. Allen in 1858, the north vestry added in 1877, and the tower largely reconstructed in 1882.[26] The nave and chancel of the old church were probably 14th century or earlier, and the three-stage tower was added in the 15th century. The windows of the nave were partly renewed early in the 16th century, those of the south wall of the chancel in the 17th or 18th centuries.[27] The new church may have followed the plan of its predecessor but the features were not copied and are now in a plain 15th-century style.

The plate includes a cup of 1574 by 'M.H.'[28] There are six bells: (i) 1970, Whitechapel foundry; (ii and iii) 1898, Mears and Stainbank; (iv) 1921, Mears and Stainbank; (v) medieval, Exeter foundry; (vi) 1733, William Knight of Closworth.[29] The registers date from 1678 and are complete from 1681.[30]

NONCONFORMITY.

A house was licensed for dissenting meetings in 1704,[31] and an Anabaptist was living in the parish in 1776.[32] Two rooms were licensed for dissenters in 1799.[33] Bible Christians were meeting at Lidmarsh from 1831 and had eight members in the following year. An attempt to establish a cause at Chaffcombe failed in 1834–5 and the Lidmarsh group seems to have disappeared a year earlier.[34] Independents from Chard used a house from 1844.[35]

EDUCATION.

In 1754 a schoolmaster was paid by the Marwoods of Avishays for teaching children to write.[36] The parish had a Sunday school in 1819 supported by Mrs. Fortescue of Avishays in which 30–40 children were taught.[37] This was financed by subscriptions in 1835, in 1846 had a salaried master and mistress and two unpaid mistresses,[38] and by 1851 was maintained at the sole expense of the rector.[39]

A School Board was formed in 1876 and a school was built in the village in 1878.[40] By 1883 the average attendance was 32.[41] An additional schoolroom was built in 1893 and the attendance rose to 39 in the following year and to 63 in 1900.[42] The school was 'in good order and very well taught' in 1903. At that date there were two teachers and a rented teacher's house; the school building was also used for parish meetings and the Sunday school.[43] By 1908 it was a County School with 77 children on the books and an average attendance of 49.[44] The numbers on the books fell to 51 in 1921, and from 50 in 1938 to 31 in 1949.[45] The school, then known as Chaffcombe County Junior School, was closed in 1959 and the pupils transferred to Chard.[46]

CHARITIES FOR THE POOR.

In 1787–8 a sum of £10 vested in Mrs. Marwood of Avishays was producing 8s. a year which was paid to the poor. The name of the donor was then supposed to have been a Mr. James but no details of the charity's foundation have been found.[47] In 1824 the capital, which with accumulated interest had increased to £13 10s., was stated to have been in the hands of the churchwardens for many years and the income distributed to the second poor.[48] The charity had been lost by 1866.[49]

CHILLINGTON

THE PARISH of Chillington, on the northern slope of Windwhistle ridge, measured 882 a. in 1839 and 925 a. in 1901.[1] It occupies a roughly triangular area whose base is the clay and chalk ridge stretching from St. Rayn hill in the east to Windwhistle in the west. Its western boundary with Cudworth is formed by a stream rising in Chillington Down called Stretford water, which flows due north to Dowlish Wake. The eastern boundary is irregular, marked in part by streams and in part by the Ilminster–Crewkerne road, described in the 13th century as the road leading to the chapel of St. Rayn.[2]

The parish is crossed by a network of narrow lanes, the only direct route linking Dinnington with

---

[24] *Wells Wills*, ed. Weaver, 66.
[25] *S.R.S.* ii. 13.
[26] S.R.O., D/P/chaf 13/2/1.
[27] Taunton Castle, Braikenridge Colln. drawing by Buckler.   [28] *Proc. Som. Arch. Soc.* xlv. 139.
[29] List in tower; S.R.O., DD/SAS, CH 16.
[30] S.R.O., D/P/chaf 2/1/1–4.
[31] S.R.O., Q/RR, meeting-house lics.
[32] S.R.O., D/D/V Dioc. bk.
[33] S.R.O., D/D/Rm 2.
[34] S.R.O., D/N/spc 31.
[35] S.R.O., D/D/Rm 2.
[36] S.R.O., DD/SAS (C/909), 4.
[37] *Digest of Returns to Sel. Cttee. on Educ. of Poor*, H.C. 224 (1819) ix (2).
[38] *Educ. Enquiry Abstract*, H.C. 62 (1835), xlii; *Church Sch. Inquiry, 1846–7*.
[39] H.O. 129/318/2/6/10.

[40] *Kelly's Dir. Som.* (1883).   [41] Ibid.
[42] S.R.O., C/E 26; *Returns of Schs.* [C. 7529] H.C. (1894), lxv; ibid. [Cd. 315] H.C. (1900), lv (2).
[43] S.R.O., C/E 26.
[44] *Bd. of Educ. List 21*, 1908 (H.M.S.O.), 409.
[45] S.R.O., C/E, box 5; *Bd. of Educ. List 21*, 1938 (H.M.S.O.), 346.
[46] S.R.O., C/E, box 5.
[47] *Char. Donations, 1787–8*, H.C. 511 (1816), xvi. The will of George James of Chaffcombe was proved in 1607 (*Taunton Wills* (Index Libr. xlv), 255).
[48] *12th Rep. Com. Char.* H.C. 358, pp. 420–1 (1825), x.
[49] Char. Com. files.
[1] S.R.O., tithe award; *V.C.H. Som.* ii. 348. This article was completed in 1974.
[2] Hook Manor, Donhead St. Andrew, Arundell MSS. deeds, general series, 588.

Windwhistle being known as Fisherway Lane.[3] In Dinnington this appears to be the continuation of the Foss Way. The name Stretford water given to the boundary stream with Cudworth implies the proximity of the Foss, and the discovery of Roman coins and part of a lead coffin north of Lower Chillington and coins and a bronze torc near Chillington Down suggest that the Foss ran on or near the line of the Dinnington–Windwhistle route rather than via Ludney Lane and Oldway Lane through Cudworth.[4]

The main settlement in the parish is known as Lower Chillington, on the Yeovil Sands in the undulating valley, and comprises the church on an elevated and possibly prehistoric site, the old manor-house, and two large farm-houses. In the late 19th century there were also several cottages.[5] Chibley farm, further north on silts and marls, may also, in view of its site, be of similar antiquity, and certainly existed by 1305.[6] Hill farm, to the east, represents a small hamlet established at least by the early 15th century.[7] Higher Chillington, in the south-west, developed probably in the 18th century from cottages built on encroachments on the edge of the common on Chillington Down. By the 1970s it housed most of the population.

The extent and position of the common fields may be roughly determined by the position of the sands and marls in the northern half of the parish, between Stretford water and Hill farm. Land called Blacklands north of Hill farm and others to the south of it still bore traces of open-field arable in the 18th century.[8] Woodland just below the highest ground in the south, as in Cudworth, was a significant feature of the parish.

The surviving farm-houses are the only substantial dwellings in the parish with the exception of Old Manor-house. These include Hill Farm which dates from the 17th century and is of three-roomed plan. Lord Hinton, when leasing the farm in 1735, reserved to himself the parlour and chamber above.[9] A smaller, two-roomed, house there was divided in 1744 between the two sons of the owner, one having the kitchen end, the other the hall and entry.[10] Inventories of two other properties of the 17th century show houses with three-roomed plan, one having four and the other three rooms above.[11] Sheephouse Farm is a large mid-18th-century house of stone and thatch, with pedimented door-case and a stair with turned balusters. It has a contemporary dairy wing. Manor Farm is probably earlier but has extensive 19th-century alterations.

Chillington chapelry had 20 households in 1563,[12] and there were said to be half that number in 1601

and c. 1660.[13] Between 1801 and 1841 the population rose from 216 to 321, but after remaining stable for thirty years fell by half by 1901. After a slight increase during the First World War, the total continued to fall; it was 82 in 1961 and 87 in 1971.[14]

Elias Osborn (1643–1720), a Quaker preacher, was born in Chillington.[15]

MANOR AND OTHER ESTATE. Chillington, usually known until the 16th century as a hamlet, was a member of the manor of South Petherton, and descended with that manor in the Daubeney family.[16] It was confiscated in 1483 on Giles Daubeney's implication in Buckingham's rebellion, and was assigned for the payment of Buckingham's debts.[17] In 1485 it was granted to John Howard, duke of Norfolk (d. 1485).[18] Daubeney recovered the property on the accession of Henry VII, and at his death in 1508 left a life interest in what was described as the manor of *CHILLINGTON* to his widow.[19] He was succeeded by his son Henry (cr. earl of Bridgwater 1538, d. 1548), who sold the manor to Edward Seymour, earl of Hertford, later duke of Somerset, in 1540.[20] On Somerset's attainder in 1552 the manor passed to the Crown, where it remained until 1570 when it was granted to Thomas Wentworth, Lord Wentworth (d. 1584).[21] The Seymours, in the person of Edward, earl of Hertford (d. 1621), recovered the manor in 1582,[22] though James Daubeney, descendant of a younger brother of Giles, Lord Daubeney, held half the manor of Hertford at his death in 1613, presumably in succession to his grandfather who held property in the parish in 1510.[23] The manor descended to William Seymour (cr. marquess of Hertford 1641, duke of Somerset 1660). He died in 1660 and was succeeded by his grandson William (d. 1671) and then by his own second son John (d. 1675). On John's death without issue the estate passed to Elizabeth (d. 1697), wife of Thomas Bruce, earl of Ailesbury.[24]

Charles Bruce, Lord Bruce, their eldest son, was still in possession of the manor in 1705,[25] but by 1741, and probably by 1736, the manor had passed to George Speke (IV).[26] Speke died in 1753 and his trustees sold the manor before 1766 to the Revd. George Notley (d. 1768) of Cricket St. Thomas.[27] The property passed to his son, also the Revd. George (d. 1831),[28] and then successively to his grandsons George and James Thomas Benedictus (d. 1851), both of Combe Sydenham in Stogumber.[29] James was followed successively by his sons George (d. 1855), James T. B. (d. 1872), and Marwood (d.

[3] O.S. Map 6″, Som. LXXXVIII. SE., SW. (1886 edn.).
[4] *V.C.H. Som.* i. 360; *S. & D. N. & Q.* xiv. 335.
[5] O.S. Map 6″, Som. LXXXVIII. SE., SW. (1886 edn.).
[6] *Cal. Inq. p.m.* iv, p. 221.
[7] C 137/79/42.
[8] S.R.O., DD/SS, bdles. 19–20; Bristol R.O. DC/E/24/4.
[9] S.R.O., DD/PT, box 22B.
[10] S.R.O., DD/SS, bdle. 19.
[11] S.R.O., DD/SP, inventories, 1645, 1669/14.
[12] B.L., Harl. MS. 594, f. 56.
[13] S.R.O. DD/HI, boxes 9, 10.
[14] *V.C.H. Som.* ii. 348; *Census.*
[15] *D.N.B.*
[16] e.g. *Cal. Chart. R.* 1226–57, 142.

[17] *Cal. Pat.* 1476–85, 497.
[18] Ibid.
[19] C 142/25/22.
[20] E 326/11706; C 142/115/38.
[21] *Cal. Pat.* 1569–72, pp. 306–7.
[22] S.R.O., T/PH/pat; C 66/1218.
[23] C 142/512/197; S.R.O., DD/X/TU (C/294).
[24] *Complete Peerage*, s.v. Ailesbury.
[25] S.R.O., DD/SS, bdle. 20; DD/PT, box 21.
[26] S.R.O., DD/SS, bdle. 20.
[27] S.R.O., DD/CA 2; DD/PT, box 21.
[28] S.R.O., D/P/chill 2/1/2–4.
[29] Foster, *Alumni Oxon.*; M.I. in Chillington ch.; S.R.O., D/P/chill 2/1/1; D/P/stogm 2/1/6, 12; Burke, *Land. Gent.* (1851), i. 942.

1903).[30] Marwood Notley's son Marmion died in 1904, and the lordship passed with c. 50 a. of land, to his widow Anne, who in 1905 married C. F. Sweet of Monksilver.[31] Anne sold the lordship and land in 1942 to the University of Oxford. The property, then planted as copse, was sold in 1958 to Cdr. Patten Thomas of Lower Shiplake (Oxon.), who died in possession in 1973.[32]

A house known as Old Manor-house may originally have been built by the Notleys. It is a late-18th- or early-19th-century house, formerly thatched, with brick gable ends. An older house may have stood in the garden, and there are late-18th-century buildings including a coach-house opposite.

The tithes of the parish, part of the rectory of South Petherton, were let by Bruton abbey and their successors the chapter of Bristol. From 1532 the lessees were Thomas and George Speke, though by 1552 Sir Hugh Poulett was in actual occupation.[33] The Pouletts remained farmers of the tithes and of a small piece of glebe until 1802, when they purchased the freehold.[34] In 1786 the tithes and glebe together were valued at £74 6s. 9d. gross and £27 8s. 5d. net.[35] In 1839 the glebe had been absorbed into the Poulett estate and the tithes were commuted to a rent-charge of £237.[36] In 1786 there was a tithe barn 'almost in ruins', apparently in the village of Lower Chillington. The glebe then comprised 7 a. south of Chibley farm.[37]

ECONOMIC HISTORY. The whole estate at Chillington was divided at least by the end of the 13th century into separate and substantial tenant holdings, and its probable origin as a detached estate and member of South Petherton in the 11th century or earlier may suggest that there was never any demesne holding there. The income at the end of the 13th century came largely from assessed rents from freeholders and villeins together, and amounted to £7 in 1292, £5 0s. 6d. in 1294, and £5 12s. 6¼d. in 1305.[38] Underwood in the first two years produced a few shillings and court perquisites 2s. The substantial tenant holdings included 1½ virgate shared by two men in 1232,[39] and John Wake's tenement called Chubbeleye, represented later by Chibley farm, in 1305.[40] By the end of the 14th century the tenants included several families of importance in the area such as the Bullers, the Kayneses, and the Lindes;[41] Thomas Kaynes, for example, held 80 a. of pasture.[42] Pasture and wood seem, from the slight surviving evidence, to have been of the greatest importance in the parish.[43]

The value of the property had risen comparatively little by the end of the 15th century, assessed rents being fixed by 1493–4 at £12 10s. 11½d.[44] Before 1548 an estate of 40 a. of meadow and pasture helped to support three priests at Ilminster.[45] The land was granted in 1557 to Thomas Powle and John Slade.[46]

Among the substantial tenants in the early 16th century were the Spekes. William Speke of Avishays in Chaffcombe held an estate called Chubleys, probably Chibley, in 1506.[47] It was settled with other properties on his granddaughter Joan, wife of Thomas Sydenham, in 1537,[48] but in 1560 it passed to the Brownes of Frampton (Dors.).[49] For the next hundred years it was leased to the Hutchinses, but Bernard Hutchins (d. 1728) apparently acquired the freehold, and at his death left the property to Vere Poulett (later 3rd Earl Poulett, d. 1788).[50] By that time the land was centred on Ludney farm in Kingstone, with fields in both parishes.

By 1766 the Pouletts had acquired further properties including Hill and Sheephouse farms, which made them the largest landowners in the parish.[51] Vere and Anne Poulett acquired interests in Sheephouse farm in 1749;[52] Hill farm, like Sheephouse farm held by the Poole family in the late 16th and early 17th centuries,[53] came to John Poulett, Lord Hinton (later 2nd Earl Poulett, d. 1764) by 1735.[54] By 1786 the Pouletts held 473 a., and early in the 19th century the total rental was worth £425.[55] In contrast the rental of the manor was small. In 1650 and 1671 it amounted to 27s. 1d. from freeholders, £4 6s. 4d. from leaseholders, and £6 14s. 6d. from copyholders, though arrears were then high and the chief rent from the Browne holding had remained unpaid for eleven years.[56] By 1766 the Notleys, in the persons of John and the Revd. George Notley, virtually shared the remainder of the parish.[57] By 1786 their estate amounted to c. 235 a.[58]

The two largest farming units at the end of the 18th century were Hill farm (177 a.) and Thomas Poole's holding of the Revd. George Notley, later part of Manor farm. Poole also held Chibley farm (44 a.) of Earl Poulett. One named farm later absorbed into other holdings was Hocombe (Oakham) farm, held of the Read family.[59] Grazing and milk production were the most profitable aspects of farming. Of seven surviving inventories dated between 1634 and 1669 two included flocks of sheep and another two equipment for cheese-making. Roger Bragge (d. 1669) left goods and stock worth over £127, including 6 cows, 3 young bullocks, and 47 sheep. Robert West (d. 1645), assessed in 1641

[30] S.R.O., D/P/stogm 2/1/6, 12; M.I. Monksilver chyd.
[31] Ex inf. Cdr. Patten Thomas.
[32] Sale Cat. University Estate; ex inf. Miss Chapman, Chillington.
[33] S.R.O., DD/PT, boxes 10A, 23.
[34] Bristol R.O., DC/E/24/7.
[35] Bristol R.O., DC/E/24/4.
[36] S.R.O., tithe award.
[37] Bristol R.O., DC/E/24/4.
[38] C 133/61/23; C 133/68/5; C 133/120/2.
[39] Curia Reg. R. xiv, pp. 491–2.
[40] Cal. Inq. p.m. iv, p. 221.
[41] C 136/44/1.
[42] Cal. Close, 1374–7, 40; Cal. Inq. p.m. xiv, p. 3.
[43] C 133/120/2; Cal. Close, 1374–7, 40.
[44] Bradford Central Libr., Swinton MSS.

[45] S.R.S. ii. 136.
[46] B.M. Harl. MS. 606, ff. 57–58v.; Cal. Pat. 1555–7, 494.
[47] S.R.O., DD/SS, bdle. 19.
[48] Ibid., bdle. 12; L. & P. Hen. VIII, xii(2), p. 83.
[49] C.P. 25(2)/204/2 Eliz. I. Hil.
[50] S.R.O., DD/SS, bdles. 19–20; DD/PT, box 16.
[51] S.R.O., Q/RE.
[52] S.R.O., DD/PT, boxes 15, 17, 21, 27.
[53] Ibid., boxes 15, 17, 27.
[54] Ibid., boxes 15, 22B; DD/SS, bdles. 19–20.
[55] Bristol R.O., DC/E/24/4; S.R.O., DD/PT, boxes 14, 44.
[56] Wilts. R.O., 192/38A; S.R.O., DD/AB 14.
[57] S.R.O., Q/RE.
[58] Bristol R.O., DC/E/24/4.
[59] Ibid.

among the prosperous farmers of the parish,[60] had 30 sheep, 3 cows, a heifer, and a bull. The possessions of Judith Marshall (d. 1640) included 19 lb. of flax and £200 in cash.[61] Field names surviving to the end of the 18th century included Flaxland Orchard, Hemphay, and Rackhay.[62]

Grazing developed further in the 18th century as common arable lands were inclosed. Blacklands, north of Hill farm, was still held in common in 1692, and it seems likely that at the same date some strips survived in former common fields known as Upfield, Wheatfield (or Whitefield), Little field, and Parrock field.[63] Some common remained at least until 1715, and there were a few uninclosed parcels in 1736.[64] Some of the last to be inclosed were 13 a. on the Hill, still arable in 1786, and 30 a. of common on Chillington Down, taken by the Notleys for pasture.[65] Water meadows were developed in the north of the parish on Chibley farm by Anne Poulett in 1742. The land involved, known as Bruffalongs, was evidently once arable.[66] In 1754, on the same farm, Poulett granted a lease of a herd of dairy cows for three years, undertaking once a year to provide transport for a load of butter to Weymouth.[67] In 1778 the titheable stock in the parish included at least 61 cows and 490 sheep, excluding the stock of two farmers who paid by composition.[68] Hill farm supported 19 cows and 120 sheep.

Grassland thus accounted for most of the land in the parish in 1778, and the leading crops from the remaining arable were wheat and barley. There were also some 26 a. of oats, 11 a. of flax, and very small areas of peas, beans, and potatoes. Between 50 and 60 hogsheads of cider were also produced.[69] In 1786 the relative acreages were 371 a. of pasture, 148 a. of meadow, and 234 a. of arable. The arable was then described as 'cold and rather unfruitful', some of the pasture 'cold, bad land'.[70]

Woodland was also of significance in the parish. 'Holcombewode' formed part of Eleanor Daubeney's dower in 1386.[71] In 1699 Lord Ailesbury's tenant of land called Holcombe undertook to plant three oak, ash, or elm trees each year.[72] This policy permitted the Pouletts to allow the tenant of the dairy 220 faggots in 1754.[73] In 1786 and 1839 there were c. 80 a. of woodland, and in 1905 73 a.[74] In 1958 Holcombe Copse and Chillington Down wood, sold with the lordship of the manor, amounted to 87 a.[75]

By 1839 the parish was divided between five substantial farms: Sheephouse (154 a.), Hill (139 a.), and Chibley (132 a.) farms were held of the Pouletts, Chillington (158 a.) and Green (73 a.) farms of the Notleys.[76] Twenty years earlier Sheephouse farm had been let with the tithes of the Notley portion of the parish.[77] By 1851 further consolidation of farms had taken place: William Poole's Manor or Chillington farm had absorbed Green farm and with land in Cudworth measured 340 a. He employed 22 labourers. Arthur Hull's Hill farm amounted to 207 a., with 5 labourers employed. Neither farm had changed in size by 1958.[78] By 1973, however, Sheephouse was being worked with Ludney farm in Kingstone.[79] Dairying developed further in the 19th century: in 1851 there were six dairymen living in the parish as well as a cheese dealer.[80] By 1905 685 a. were under grass compared with 290 a. under arable.[81] Dairying predominated in 1973.

Apart from farming gloving was the most important occupation in the parish in the 19th century, employing 43 women and girls in 1851.[82] The standard of cottages was low in the 1860s, and the village was singled out as being 'a very bad parish'. Improvements were certainly being made by 1868, but there was a shifting population, due in part to the depression in gloving.[83] Nearly a quarter of the inhabitants in 1851 had been born outside the parish.[84] By 1868 there were said to be more cottages than labourers to occupy them, including some in Clay Lane, Lower Chillington, and more in Moor Lane, Higher Chillington, each having a potato plot attached.[85]

LOCAL GOVERNMENT. Chillington normally formed a single tithing in South Petherton hundred at least from the 16th century, though there is some evidence to suggest that a tithing of Hill, possibly embracing the Poulett property in the east of the parish, existed in the 17th century if not earlier.[86] Under a lease of 1735 the tenant of Hill farm was allowed 20s. a year for holding the office of tithingman and £5 for office as hundred constable when it was his turn.[87]

Pleas and perquisites of court were received from the estate at the end of the 13th century,[88] but there was no income from that source at the end of the 15th and none accounted for in 1671 when Chillington and South Harp in South Petherton were administered together.[89] One extract from a court baron survives for Chillington and South Harp from 1692,[90] but there is no other direct evidence of a manor court. A lease of 1754 required suit and service to the manor court on summons.[91]

The parish had two overseers in 1641–2 and one

[60] S.R.O., DD/HI, box 10.
[61] S.R.O., DD/SP, inventories.
[62] Bristol R.O., DC/E/24/4.
[63] S.R.O., DD/SS, bdle. 20.   [64] Ibid., bdle. 19.
[65] Bristol R.O., DC/E/24/4.
[66] S.R.O., DD/SS, bdle. 19.
[67] S.R.O., DD/PT, box 18.   [68] Ibid., box 37.
[69] Ibid.   [70] Bristol R.O., DC/E/24/4.
[71] C 136/44/1.
[72] S.R.O., DD/SS, bdle. 19.
[73] S.R.O., DD/PT, boxes 18, 22B.
[74] Bristol R.O., DC/E/24/4; S.R.O., tithe award; statistics supplied by the then Bd. of Agric. 1905.
[75] Sale cat., University Estate.
[76] S.R.O., tithe award.
[77] S.R.O., DD/PT, box 40.
[78] H.O. 107/1928; sale cat., University Estate.

[79] Ex inf. Miss Chapman.   [80] H.O. 107/1928.
[81] Statistics supplied by the then Bd. of Agric. 1905.
[82] H.O. 107/1928.
[83] Rep. Com. on Children and Women in Agric. [4202-I] pp. 128, 698, H.C. (1868–9), xiii.
[84] H.O. 107/1928.
[85] Rep. Com. Children and Women, p. 698.
[86] S.R.S. xx. 41; S.R.O., Q/SR 212/7, 9, 217/18–20, 275/6; DD/SS, bdle. 19; DD/X/SAB (transcript of Parl. Survey, f. 201). Hill was tentatively described as a manor in 1575: S.R.O., DD/PT, box 10A.
[87] S.R.O., DD/PT, box 22B, Ld. Hinton to Draper.
[88] C 133/61/23; C 133/68/5.
[89] Bradford Central Libr., Swinton MSS; S.R.O., DD/AB 14.
[90] S.R.O., DD/SS, bdle. 20.
[91] S.R.O., DD/PT, box 21, Notley to Hill, 1776.

in 1671[92] and in the 19th century.[93] The earl of Hertford gave a site for a poorhouse which was built but not entirely paid for in 1615.[94] Six freehold cottages were used for the same purpose until 1837, when they were sold.[95] The parish became part of Chard poor-law union in 1836.

CHURCH. The church at Chillington first occurs as a dependent chapel of South Petherton at the end of the 13th century when the prior of Bruton, rector of South Petherton, was ordered to provide services there.[96] Its status was confirmed in 1400,[97] but in 1494 a burial ground there was dedicated, though the inhabitants were still required to pay mortuaries to the vicar of South Petherton and to contribute to the repair of the parish church.[98] With other chapels of South Petherton it passed after the dissolution of Bruton abbey to the newly-created chapter of Bristol in 1542.[99] Lessees of the tithes both before and after the Dissolution were responsible for providing a priest until after 1838,[1] though the patronage later reverted to the chapter.[2] In 1885, when the benefice was united with Cudworth, the patronage was transferred to the bishop of Bath and Wells.[3]

In the 1570s the curate was paid £4 a year.[4] This sum was augmented by ten marks under the will of Sir Anthony Poulett (d. 1600) for preaching four times a year.[5] Between 1651 and 1655 the curate, who also served Barrington, was paid £7 10s. a quarter.[6] In the early part of the 18th century Lord Poulett, farmer of the rectory and tithes, paid the curate £15 a year.[7] The income was augmented by grants of £200 each made by lot from Queen Anne's Bounty and Parliamentary grants made in 1750, 1810, 1811, 1817, 1824, and 1832.[8] By 1786 the farmer's contribution was £20.[9] The net income in 1831 and 1851 was £60.[10] By 1909, after the sale of some glebe, fixed payments amounted to £53 11s.[11]

Glebe was evidently purchased with augmentation money in the 18th century. In 1909 there were 12½ a. at Clayhidon (Devon) and other pieces at Stockland and Dunkeswell (Devon), the last two then 'recently' sold. There were said to have been 12 a. at Thornford (Dors.) at some date 'irregularly' exchanged for the Stockland property.[12] By 1974 all the land had been sold.[13]

There appears to have been a house for the curate in 1619.[14] John Vaigge (curate 1651–5) repaired it in 1654 and Lord Poulett paid the cost.[15] There was no house by the early 19th century.[16]

On at least three occasions during the later 16th century the chancel of the church needed repair.[17] In 1577 the rector of Dowlish Wake served the cure but 'out of due time and season' and 'without the yearly sermons'.[18] In 1611 the curate failed to read the Canons as he had 'no book in church'.[19] At least two curates, Hugh Mere (1623–37 or later) and John Vaigge (1651–5), also served Barrington.[20] During the 18th and 19th centuries the curacy was several times held by schoolmasters: Thomas Hare (d. 1762), curate by 1751, was described as a 'good scholar and poet', was headmaster of Crewkerne school and from 1758 rector of Chedington (Dors.);[21] his successor at Chillington, Robert Burnet Patch, curate 1762–78, was also his successor at Crewkerne.[22] J. P. Billing, curate 1857–61, and George Phillips, curate 1861–73, were both headmasters of Chard school.[23] Neither they nor their successors were resident in the parish.

There were six communicants in 1776.[24] In the 1840s and 1870s services were held once a Sunday, alternately morning and afternoon, with celebrations of the Holy Communion eight times a year.[25] The average afternoon congregation in 1851 was 140 with 35 Sunday-school children.[26]

In 1548 a light was maintained in the church.[27]

The church of ST. JAMES is on a knoll which bears all the traces of a prehistoric site.[28] It is built of coursed rubble and has a chancel, and a nave with north vestry, south organ chamber, and south porch. The chancel is partly of the 13th century, but predominantly of the earlier 14th, and may have been enlarged at that time. Later in the same century the nave and porch were rebuilt. The chancel arch was rebuilt in the 15th century, and bears traces of painting as well as sockets for the rood screen. Perhaps at the same time the roofs were renewed, though this may not have happened until the nave windows were altered to their present square-headed form in the later 16th century. A gallery, approached by an external stair against the porch, was put into the west end of the nave probably in the 18th century,[29] but was evidently removed in

[92] Som. Protestation Returns, ed. A. J. Howard and T. L. Stoate, 88.
[93] Dwelly, Hearth Tax, 147; S.R.O., D/PS/ilm. 14.
[94] S.R.S. xxiii. 123.
[95] S.R.O., D/PS/ilm. 16.
[96] S.R.S. viii, p. 41; the order was made by Archbishop Pecham, 1279–92. An earlier reference to Robert de Bule, parson of 'Chilton', possibly Chillington, cannot be dated: ibid. p. 37.
[97] Cal. Papal Regs. v. 326.
[98] S.R.S. iii. 193–4.
[99] L. & P. Hen. VIII, xvii, p. 638.
[1] See above, p. 130.
[2] Bristol R.O., DC/E/24/5; S.R.O., DD/PT, box 19B. Dioc. Kal.
[3] Dioc. Kal.
[4] S. & D. N. & Q. xiv. 105.
[5] S.R.O., DD/X/SAB.   [6] S.R.O., DD/PT, box 40.
[7] Proc. Som. Arch. Soc. cxii. 78; S.R.O., DD/PT, box 16.
[8] Hodgson, Queen Anne's Bounty.
[9] Bristol R.O., DC/E/24/4.
[10] Rep. Com. Eccl. Revenues, pp. 158–9; H.O. 129/318/4/3/3.

[11] Cudworth par. rec., inventory.
[12] Ibid.
[13] Ex inf. Diocesan Office.
[14] S.R.O., DD/X/SAB (transcript of Bristol Cath. Chetwynd survey f. 16).
[15] S.R.O., DD/PT, box 40.
[16] Rep. Com. Eccl. Revenues, pp. 132–3.
[17] S.R.O., D/D/Ca 22, 27, 57.
[18] Ibid. 57.
[19] Ibid. 175.
[20] S.R.O., D/D/Rr; DD/PT, box 40.
[21] S.R.O., D/D/V Dioc. bk.; R. G. Bartelot, Hist. Crewkerne School (1899), 70–1.
[22] Bartelot, Hist. Crewkerne Sch. 71.
[23] Clergy List; P.O. Dir. Som. (1866).
[24] S.R.O., D/D/V Dioc. bk.
[25] S.R.O., D/D/V returns 1840, 1843, 1870.
[26] H.O. 129/318/4/3/3.
[27] S.R.S. ii. 10.
[28] See plate facing p. 161.
[29] The porch was evidently rebuilt or repaired in 1731 (inscr.), possibly in connexion with the gallery stairs.

1909, when the 15th-century style tracery was inserted into the older opening of the west window. The vestry probably belongs to the restoration of 1842.[30] A further and extensive restoration took place in 1909, when the chancel roof was replaced, the organ chamber constructed, and the font largely renewed. The pews date from 1912 to 1935.[31] The organ came from Bickenhall in 1973.[32]

The church has two bells in its western bellcot, both by Thomas Bilbie (II) and dated 1782.[33] The plate includes a cup and cover of 1573 by 'I.P.' and a cup of 1800.[34] The registers date from 1750, but there are gaps in baptisms and burials between 1761 and 1780.[35]

NONCONFORMITY. Between 1670 and 1682 two Quakers were imprisoned for refusing tithes.[36] Two houses were licensed for worship in 1695.[37] In 1776 there were said to be 'a few' Presbyterians in the parish.[38] A group of Bible Christians began worshipping there in 1824, and a house was licensed in 1828. The cause was disbanded in 1835 but was revived between 1843 and 1851, when it finally ceased.[39]

EDUCATION. By 1835 there was a Sunday school for 36 children who paid $\frac{1}{2}d$. a week, a mistress being supported by subscriptions.[40] A day-school for 30 children had been established by 1846 and was supported by subscriptions and school pence.[41] It was affiliated to the National Society by 1861.[42] The buildings were owned by the lord of the manor, and by 1903 were also used for a Sunday school and for other meetings.[43] In 1903 there was accommodation for 41 children, and there were 31 on the books.[44] By 1938, when senior pupils had been transferred, there were 65 on the books, with an average attendance of nineteen.[45] The school was closed in 1971 and the pupils were transferred to Ilminster.[46]

CHARITIES FOR THE POOR. A charity worth £12, evidently used as a loan charity, the foundation particulars of which were unknown, ceased in 1779 when the capital was in the hands of an insolvent tradesman.[47]

CRICKET ST. THOMAS

THE PARISH of Cricket St. Thomas, taking its name from the ridge (British *cruc*) below which most of it lies, is at the south-western tip of the hundred of Crewkerne, three miles east of Chard.[1] It had an area of 875 a. until 1886 when a detached portion two miles SW. of Marshwood was transferred to Winsham, reducing the acreage to 707 a.[2] The parish is roughly T-shaped, its eastern limit marked by the Purtington brook which, from the 11th century to the late 18th, drove a succession of mills and has been the principal source of water. The Windwhistle ridge, known at successive points in the parish as Swan Down, Knoll hill, and White Down, forms much of the northern boundary.

Most of the parish lies on land sloping, in places steeply, from over 700 ft. on the top of the ridge to just over 400 ft. at the lower reaches of the Purtington brook. The higher and more level land, a mixture of clay-with-flints, calcarious grit, and chalk, was evidently the cultivated area of the parish,[3] with common pasture on the gentler slopes of the south. The Purtington brook was evidently con-trolled to create water meadows by the mid 17th century.[4] Marshwood was, by its name, ancient woodland.

The village of Cricket stood on the sloping western bank of the Purtington brook c. 200 yards below the present Cricket House. It was never large, but was removed in the early 19th century to create improved surroundings for the extended new manor-house, and by 1831 only a few cottages remained.[5] In 1851 only a gamekeeper and a labourer lived there, and by 1891 a single building occupied the site.[6] To the north of the village lay the church and the earlier manor-house.[7] The park occupies almost the whole parish, including a tree-lined avenue forming the main entrance from White Down. A medieval park may have stretched NW. up the slope from the manor-house and church.[8]

Elsewhere in the parish there was settlement at Lanscombe in the north, an ancient freehold mentioned in the 12th century, marked only by a barn in 1831,[9] and at Hollowells ('the Hollywille' in 1315), beside the brook in the south.[10] A mill

30 S.R.O., D/D/V return 1843.
31 Inscr. in ch.
32 Ex inf. the P.C.C. Treasurer.
33 S.R.O., DD/SAS CH 16.
34 *Proc. Som. Arch. Soc.* xiv, 140.
35 S.R.O., D/P/chil 2/1/1–4.
36 Besse, *Sufferings*, i. 604, 610, 621, 645; *D.N.B.* s.v. Osborn.
37 S.R.O., Q/RR.
38 S.R.O., D/D/V Dioc. bk.
39 S.R.O., D/D/Rm, box 2; D/N/spc 3, 4.
40 *Educ. Enquiry Abstract.* H.C. 62 (1835), xlii.
41 *Church Sch. Inquiry, 1846–7.*
42 *P.O. Dir. Som.* (1861).
43 S.R.O., C/E 26; *Returns of Schs.* [C. 7529] H.C. 1894), lxv.
44 S.R.O., C/E 26.
45 *Bd. of Educ., List 21, 1938* (H.M.S.O.), 346.
46 S.R.O., C/E, box 100.

47 *Char. Donations, 1787–8*, H.C. 511 (1816), xvi.
1 This article was completed in 1973.
2 *Census*, 1851; Local Govt. Bd. Order 19,582.
3 Geol. Surv. Map 1″, solid and drift, sheet 312 (1958 edn.). A lime-kiln, later a quarry, was sited in the extreme SW. of the parish, and in 1652 the lord paid £2 10s. for burning 4 lime pits (S.R.O. DD/SAS, C/212, map of Cricket, 1831; D/P/c.st.t 2/1/1; DD/HI, box 52, estate bk.).
4 S.R.O., DD/HI, box 8, deposition 10 July 1727.
5 S.R.O., DD/SAS, C/212, map, 1831.
6 H.O. 107/1928; O.S. Map 6″, Som. XCII. NW. (1891 edn.).
7 G.P.R. Pulman, *Bk. of the Axe*, 384.
8 S.R.O., DD/HI, box 52, ct. roll, *sub anno* 1481; DD/SAS, C/212, map 1831.
9 Forde Abbey, Cart. p. 465; S.R.O., DD/SAS, C/212, map 1831.
10 Forde Abbey, Cart. pp. 440–3.

was subsequently built on the latter site.[11] Marshwood was a third settlement, forming a tenement by the mid 13th century and having three cottages by 1498.[12] A dwelling-house had been built there by 1590, called Great Marshwood or Marshwood House in 1616 when it was leased in two halves.[13] A new brick house had been erected before 1771,[14] and in 1831 there were two farms called Higher and Lower Marshwood.[15] Of these Marshwood farm represented Lower Marshwood in 1973, and a barn occupied the site of Higher Marshwood.

By the 19th century there were only two principal farms in Cricket, Weston (now Manor) farm and the Home farm. Three cottages lay at Hollowells in the area of the former mill, and another was sited near the former parsonage house west of the village.[16] In the 20th century individual houses have been built at Hollowells and at the Home farm, but Cricket House, the central feature of a wild-life park since 1967,[17] continues to dominate the parish.

The principal road through the parish, linking Crewkerne and Chard, runs SW. along the ridge, following the Foss Way between Windwhistle and White Down, and marks the northern and part of the western boundary of the parish. Traffic along this route may have determined the site of the fair held on White Down from the 14th century. The road was adopted by the Chard turnpike trust in 1753 and a toll house, still standing in 1973, was built in the extreme north of the parish.[18] Until 1834 two lanes branched SW. from the Crewkerne–Chard road at White Down. One, known c. 1755 as Axminster Way,[19] probably continues the line of the Foss Way and passes through South Chard towards Axminster (Devon). The other, known as Middletons Lane in 1655 and Blind Lane in 1831,[20] curved around the south-western parish boundary to Hollowells and Winsham. Goldenhay Lane, formerly Gore Lane,[21] entered the parish in the extreme west from the Crewkerne–Chard road and ran SE. through the centre of the parish to the former Cricket village, continuing across the brook to Purtington in Winsham. Roads and footpaths in the centre of the parish were closed to public use in 1834, when virtually the whole of the area was emparked, and London, Grosvenor (now White Down), and West Port lodges were placed at the three main entrances to the park.[22]

Two alehouses in the parish were suppressed in 1726.[23] There were two publicans in Cricket in 1751 and an application to sell beer, ale, and cider was made in 1770.[24]

Cricket had 10 households in 1612[25] and a population of 69 in 1801. This latter figure rose slightly to 86 in 1831 but, as the village was progressively demolished, the numbers shrank to 66 in 1861. Increasing employment on the estate resulted in a rise to 110 in 1871 and, apart from a fall to 68 in 1921 following the First World War, continued at over 85. There were 86 inhabitants in 1961 but only 67 in 1971.[26]

MANOR AND LESSER ESTATE. The overlordship of *CRICKET* manor was held in 1086 by the count of Mortain.[27] One of his Domesday tenants elsewhere was Ralph (I) Lovel, whose descendants occur as overlords of Cricket by virtue of their tenure of the manor of Castle Cary.[28] Hugh Lovel (d. 1291), eighth in descent from Ralph, held it at his death, as did his grandson Richard (d. 1351) in 1313.[29] Richard was succeeded by his granddaughter Muriel Lovel, wife of Nicholas Seymour (d. 1361), and their descendants, lords Seymour, continued as overlords, Richard Lord Seymour (d. 1409) being succeeded by his daughter Alice, wife of William, Lord Zouche (d. 1462).[30] The Zouches and their successors as lords of Castle Cary claimed the overlordship at least until 1623.[31]

The manor was held T.R.E. by Sirewold, but before 1086 had passed to Turstin.[32] The latter was succeeded both at Cricket and at Eastham in Crewkerne by the Cricket family,[33] who may have descended from him. A certain Ralph, who probably held land in Cricket St. Thomas, was succeeded by his son William of Cricket, who held two fees in the county in 1166.[34] William's son Sir Ralph (fl. 1198–1232)[35] left issue Sir Thomas of Cricket (fl. 1242–58), the last holding two fees of Mortain in 1242–3.[36] Sir Thomas was followed in turn by his son William (d. c. 1313) and grandson Michael of Cricket, the last of whom sold the manor to Walter de Rodney in 1328–9.[37] In 1337 John of Clevedon granted the reversion of half of Rodney Stoke manor to Walter de Rodney[38] and it was possibly in return for this grant that Cricket manor passed to the Clevedons. John of Clevedon's widow

[11] S.R.O., DD/HI, box 53, lease 10 Oct. 1638.
[12] Forde Abbey, Cart. pp. 461–4; S.R.O., DD/HI, box 52, ct. roll.
[13] C 142/227/197; S.R.O., DD/HI, box 52, lease 19 Feb. 1615/16, revocation of trust 15 Mar. 1627/8.
[14] S.R.O., DD/HI, box 53, letters 14 Mar., 15 Apr. 1771.
[15] S.R.O., DD/SAS, C/212, map 1831.
[16] Ibid.; O.S. Map 6", Som. XCII. NW. (1891 edn.).
[17] P. Spence, *Some of Our Best Friends are Animals*.
[18] Chard Turnpike Act, 26 Geo. II, c. 69 (Priv. Act).
[19] S.R.O., DD/HI, box 40, survey.
[20] Ibid. box 52, estate bk.; DD/SAS, C/212, map 1831.
[21] S.R.O., D/P/c.st.t 2/1/1.
[22] S.R.O., Q/SR 474; DD/SAS, C/2273, B.14.2.
[23] S.R.O., D/P/c.st.t 13/2/1.
[24] S.R.O., Q/RL; DD/HI, box 53, petition, 29 Aug. 1770.
[25] S.R.O., DD/HI, box 9, South Petherton hundred papers.
[26] *V.C.H. Som.* ii. 348; *Census*, 1911–71.

[27] *V.C.H. Som.* i. 473.
[28] *Complete Peerage*, s.v. Lovel.
[29] *Cal. Inq. p.m.* ii, p. 489; v, p. 254.
[30] *Complete Peerage*, s.vv. St. Maur, Zouche.
[31] C 142/407/72.   [32] *V.C.H. Som.* i. 473.
[33] *Feud. Aids*, iv. 317. A Turstin of Eastham witnessed a 12th-century deed of Cricket: Forde Abbey, Cart. p. 465.
[34] Forde Abbey, Cart. p. 465; *Red Bk. Exch.* (Rolls Ser.), i. 234.
[35] Forde Abbey, Cart. p. 465; *Cur. Reg. R.* i. 43, 55; *Close R. 1231–4*, 120.
[36] Forde Abbey, Cart. pp. 511, 539; *S.R.S.* xxxvi. 4; *Bk. of Fees*, ii. 252. The fees were probably Cricket and Eastham.
[37] *Cal. Inq. p.m.* iv, p. 334; v, p. 254; *S.R.S.* xii. 70, 133, 138. Thos. of Cricket was succeeded at Eastham before 1295–6 by John of Cricket, probably another son (*S.R.S.* vi. 296), although by 1313 that manor had also passed to Michael of Cricket (*Feud. Aids*, iv. 317).
[38] *S.R.S.* xii. 194.

Elizabeth presented to Cricket rectory between 1348 and 1353.[39] The manor subsequently passed to Elizabeth's daughter Margaret (d. 1412), wife successively of John St. Lo (d. 1375) and Sir Peter Courtenay (d. 1405).[40] Margaret was succeeded by her grandson, Sir William de Botreaux, who in 1459 received licence to alienate the manor to Bath priory.[41] Evidently this grant did not take effect, for on Sir William's death in 1462 the manor passed to his daughter Margaret, wife of Sir Robert Hungerford.[42] It was subsequently claimed that Margaret had purchased a release of her title to the manor from the prior of Bath.[43] In 1466 she sold Cricket to Stephen Preston (d. 1474) and his wife Maud (d. 1497), whose family subsequently lived on the manor.[44]

Stephen's son John (I) Preston (d. 1541) was succeeded by his son John (II) (d. 1590) and grandson Christopher (d. 1623).[45] Christopher's son John left issue a daughter and heir Margaret (d. 1672), married in 1628 to John Hippisley (d. 1664) of Ston Easton.[46] Their eldest son John died a year after his father and the manor passed to a second son Richard (d. 1672) and subsequently to his son Preston Hippisley (d. 1723).[47] Preston's daughter and heir Margaret (d. 1739) married John Coxe (d. 1717) of Basset Down and Leigh near Ashton Keynes (Wilts.).[48] Their son John Hippisley Coxe (d. 1769) was succeeded by his son Richard, who in 1775 sold Cricket for £14,000 to Alexander Hood (cr. Baron Bridport of Cricket St. Thomas in 1794, Viscount Bridport in 1800) (d. 1814).[49] Since this time the owners have usually lived on the manor. Alexander left his estate to his great-nephew Samuel, 2nd Baron Bridport (d. 1868); he was followed by his son Alexander Nelson, 3rd Baron (cr. Viscount Bridport in 1868).[50] The manor, heavily mortgaged, was sold to Francis James Fry (d. 1918), the chocolate manufacturer, in 1898, and his trustees conveyed it in 1920 to Mrs. Jane Hall (d. 1943).[51] The executors of her son, Mr. A. A. Hall, sold the property to Maj. E. P. G. Miller Mundy in 1965, from whom it was purchased by the present owners, Messrs. H. G. and W. J. D. Taylor, in 1967.[52]

A manor-house was first expressly mentioned in 1313.[53] A survey of 1709 listed on the ground floor a large hall paved with stone, a panelled parlour, a large kitchen, three beer cellars, a pantry, and a large brew-house; on the first floor three large chambers and six smaller ones; on the second floor nine garrets. Among the outbuildings at that date were a 6-bay barn, stable with threshing floor above, a dairy house with a corn store over, and a

cart house. Lands immediately adjoining the house then included the Fore Green, the Back Green, and the Dairy courts.[54] The house is said to have been demolished or burnt in the late 18th century, and has been traditionally located in the area later occupied by the kitchen garden and now by the menagerie and animal houses. It is possible, however, that the present house incorporates part of the earlier building, which may have been of half-H plan and perhaps of the 17th century.[55] The 'Admiral's Seat', a summerhouse dated 1797 on the hill to the north, has architectural fragments, including a date stone of 1595, which may have been saved from the original house. The employment of John Soane to design alterations for Sir Alexander Hood, who purchased the estate in 1775 and had been at sea for much of the intervening period, in 1786 could be taken as an indication that the house was included in the purchase. Soane was designing further alterations and additions in 1801 and this phase of the work continued until 1807 and cost a total of £8,650.[56] Before these additions the house seems to have comprised only the eastern two thirds of the present main block. The new work included a range of rooms along the west front and the refacing of the other sides so that each was more symmetrical. Internally, apart from minor alterations and the renewal of some fireplaces, the central stair hall was enlarged and remodelled and the new entrance hall and library behind the west front were decorated in typically Soane style.[57] Following the sale of the house at the end of the 19th century further alterations were carried out.[58] All traces of Soane's interior decoration were removed from the large drawing room and the library, and they were redecorated in mid-18th-century style. Minor alterations were made in the staircase hall, the conservatories were removed, and much of the stone facing of the exterior appears to have been renewed.

The existence of an ancient freehold estate at Lanscombe on the northern border of Cricket with Winsham is implied by references to Luke of Lancerecumbe in the 12th century, Henry of Lancelecumbe in the 13th, and Hugh Lancecombe in 1327.[59] Between 1459 and 1475 John Buller of Wood in Knowle St. Giles (d. 1485) held lands called Launscomb as a freehold of Cricket manor for 6d. a year and suit of court.[60] In 1509, however, it was claimed that William, son and heir of John Lanscombe, had formerly sold the lands to Robert Hull, whose son John Hull held them for 23 years before 1506–7, when they were claimed by John Buller's grandson and heir, Alexander (d. 1526).[61] John Hull certainly appeared as freeholder between

39 Ibid. ix. 579, 701–2, 711.
40 Ibid. xvii. 142–3; C 137/50/38; C 137/86/30.
41 C 137/86/30; C 143/452/30.
42 C 140/7/15.
43 S.R.S. xxvii. 47.
44 Cal. Close, 1461–8, 272, 394–5; S.R.S. xxii. 132; Cal. Inq. p.m. Hen. VII, ii, pp. 50–1.
45 C 142/64/92; C 142/227/197; C 142/407/72.
46 A. E. Hippisley and I. Fitzroy Jones, Some Notes on the Hippisley Fam. (priv. print. 1952), 27.
47 Ibid. 29–30.
48 Ibid. 30, 117.
49 Ibid. 118; S.R.O., DD/HA 8, covt. to produce deeds; DD/CAK box 5, abstract of title 1851.
50 Burke, Peerage (1937), 366.
51 S.R.O., DD/HA 9, 12, 19; M.I. in ch.

52 S.R.O., DD/HA, corresp. in accession file; ex inf. Mr. H. G. Taylor, Cricket St. Thomas.
53 C 134/33/5.
54 S.R.O., DD/HI, box 40, survey, 1709.
55 London, Sir John Soane's Mus. drawer IV, file 5, ff. 9, 10.
56 Ibid. acct. bk.
57 Ibid. drawer IV, file 5, ff. 1–8; see below, plate facing p. 144.
58 The sale cat. of 1895 has a plan and photographs of the ho. before alterations: S.R.O., DD/SAS, C/2273, 1.B.14.
59 Forde Abbey, Cart. p. 465; S.R.O., DD/HA 1; S.R.S. iii. 197.
60 S.R.O., DD/HI, box 52, ct. rolls.
61 Req. 2/4/49; C 1/286/79; C 1/290/79.

1501 and 1504, and in 1516 his daughter Joan, wife of John Creeke, was acknowledged to hold the lands.[62] By 1538 Henry Creeke (d. c. 1555–6) held the property, described as 30 a. of meadow and 40 a. of pasture called Lanscombes and Rainsley, after whose death it passed successively to his son William and Henry's brother, Robert Creeke.[63] Robert evidently sold the lands to James Downham (d. c. 1556) and his son William held them in 1589. In that year his title was disputed by Lionel Raynolds of Ashprington (Devon), whose mother Joan, wife of John Raynolds, had formerly had an interest under Henry Creeke's will.[64] The Raynolds claim was evidently unsuccessful, since a William Downham was recorded as the freeholder in 1627.[65] By the following year it had passed to Thomas Kingman, and by 1659 to John Albin of Evercreech.[66] The Albin family continued to hold the property until at least 1732; it was owned by a Mr. Martin between 1735 and 1737, between 1749 and 1771 by John Notley, and from 1773 until 1799 by the Revd. George Notley.[67] It was acquired by Lord Bridport c. 1800 and thereafter formed part of the Cricket estate.[68]

No reference to a house attached to the estate has been found. A barn on the northern parish boundary in 1831[69] may mark the site of a former farm-house.

ECONOMIC HISTORY. In 1086 Cricket gelded for 6 hides, of which 4 hides were held in demesne with 3 ploughs and 2 serfs, and 2 hides were worked by 6 villeins and 5 bordars with 3 ploughs. There was 1½ a. of meadow, and woodland measuring 7 by 2 furlongs. Stock comprised 14 head of cattle, 124 sheep, and 24 she-goats. The manor had formerly rendered annually to South Petherton manor 6 sheep with their lambs, representing a ewe and lamb for each hide, and from each freeman a bloom of iron, but these dues had been withheld by the post-Conquest tenant.[70]

The value of the manor rose from £4 in 1066 to £5 in 1086[71] but thereafter only to £5 13s. 10d. by 1313. In the last year there were still 6 villeins paying 2s., with harvest works worth 6d., and the 5 bordars of Domesday were represented by 5 cottars rendering 5s. A single free tenant, holding Lanscombe, paid 3s. There were 200 a. of arable worth 50s., 20 a. of hill meadow 20s., pasture in severalty 5s., wood 1s., and a mill producing 13s. 4d.[72] Subsequently, according to inquisitions, the manor increased in value: to £7 in 1412, £10 in 1459, and £13 6s. 8d. in 1497 and 1541.[73]

A rental of 1459 suggests both that the estate was undervalued in the inquisitions and also that much inclosure had already taken place. One freeholder and 14 tenants with 22 holdings were then rendering

£20. 0s. 11d. Among the individual properties 5 tenements and 7 cottages were mentioned and the lands were all in closes except parcels of land in 'the field' held by 3 tenants.[74] Any former open arable field system seems to have been disrupted by inclosure before the 15th century. In 1462 one tenant held land in three fields called 'Myddellond', 'Langlond', and 'Oughlond', and another in 1473 occupied plots in 'Seynt Whytfeld' (probably on White Down), 'Holewayfeld', and 'Horneclyfclos'. 'Myddellond' may be the field called 'Myddeldon' or 'Mydelton', later Middletons, along the western boundary, the ditching around which was the responsibility of all tenants. By the early 16th century a single open arable field appears to have remained, known in 1534 as the Great field and in 1546 as the Corn field. In the latter year it was agreed to inclose and allot the lands therein, two arbitrators being appointed for the lord and rector, and three for the tenants. Of the many gates whose repair features prominently in the business of the manor court, 'Holeweys' gate in 1468 and 'Townesyn' gate in 1539 were the responsibility of all the tenants.[75]

Fifteenth-century records of pasture land are generally of tenants trespassing on the lord's grazing: at 'Holemomede' and 'Overholewyll' in 1459, and at Codley and 'Bryddesmore' in 1468. In 1481 pasturing with sheep of 'Parkehyll' next the church was forbidden between Lady Day and Christmas, and in 1499 it was agreed that each tenement holder might have 42 sheep, a further 3 sheep for every acre of overland, and that every tenant might keep 2 bullocks and a mare. By the 16th century much of the pasture land had been inclosed in large units. Thus in 1539 single tenants held a close of 60 a. at Hollowells, one of 12 a. at Gorelease, and another of 30 a. at Knoll hill. In 1541 the common 'moor' was inclosed and allotted proportionally to each tenement and cottage, 2 a. being reserved to the lord to build a grain mill. Common land near the Parsonage gate was also mentioned in 1546.[76]

The principal unit of woodland in the Middle Ages was in the detached area of Marshwood, extending into Winsham parish to the east. Much of the wood was granted to Forde abbey by the lords of Cricket in the 13th century, although even by that time some inclosures had been made. By c. 1300 another curtilage lay in the east of 'the inclosure of Merswode'.[77] During the later 15th century tenants of Cricket held closes there, although the manor derived income from the sale of pannage and trees.[78] One tenant in 1498 took a lease of three cottages in Marshwood and a 'cokkerode' with two waggonloads of underwood each year.[79] There was also woodland on Windwhistle in 1504.[80] In 1592 Christopher Preston purchased a close of 70 a.

[62] S.R.O., DD/HI, boxes 5, 52, ct. rolls.
[63] Ibid.; C 142/108/122; C 2/Eliz. I/R4/56. A close called Rainsley lies on the east side of the Foss Way at Lanscombe.
[64] C 2/Eliz. I/R4/56.
[65] S.R.O., DD/HI, box 51, ct. roll.
[66] Ibid.; box 53, letter, Albin to Preston, 3 Nov. 1659.
[67] S.R.O., DD/S/CX; D/P/c.st.t 13/2/1–2.
[68] S.R.O., Q/RE, land tax assessments.
[69] S.R.O., DD/SAS, C/212, map, 1831.
[70] V.C.H. Som. i. 435, 473.
[71] Ibid. 473.
[72] C 134/33/5.
[73] C 137/86/30; C 143/452/30; C 142/12/64; C 142/64/92.
[74] S.R.O., DD/HI, box 52, ct. roll incl. rental.
[75] Ibid. boxes 5, 52, ct. rolls sub annis.
[76] Ibid.
[77] Forde Abbey, Cart. pp. 461–5.
[78] e.g. S.R.O., DD/HI, box 52, ct. rolls 25 Oct. 1459, 5 Mar. 1472/3, 4 Jan. 1478/9.
[79] S.R.O., DD/HI, box 52, ct. roll 7 May 1498.
[80] Ibid. 23 Jan. 1503/4.

called Marshwood in Cricket and Winsham, probably formerly held by Forde abbey.[81] With this acquisition the larger closes in Marshwood, known as the Ball, the Moor, Lower Wood, and Great and Little Marshwood, were subdivided and a total of 130 a., mainly pasture land, was granted to lessees in the years 1602–16. Covenants to plant 40 oak, ash, or elm trees were then imposed.[82]

Tenure on the manor during the later 15th century was usually by copy of court roll for the tenant's life, but subsequently copies were also granted for two or three lives.[83] In the late 16th century leases for lives were introduced, and in the early 17th century leases for 99 years or three lives.[84] The conversion to leasehold continued: in 1672 there were only 3 copyholders and 19 leaseholders, and by 1713 2 copyholders and 23 leaseholders.[85] These figures included the tenants of five leasehold properties in Chard, one of which had been occupied by Christopher Preston (d. 1623).[86] Holdings were generally small, 3 tenements and a cottage having only 18 a. of land in 1497,[87] and most were under 20 a. During the years 1647–55 there is evidence that much of the manor, particularly the demesne, was being let by the year for grazing at realistic rents, rising from £21 12s. 6d. in 1647 to £39 10s. in 1650, and £44 9s. 6d. in 1653. Covenants in such short-term leases imply that the lord continued to graze his own cattle and make hay on these lands and, in respect of a lease of a warren on Knoll hill, reserved the 'fewells' and coneys to himself.[88]

The rental of the manor, apparently excluding grazing rents, rose from £22 9s. 2d. in 1672[89] to £28 7s. 10d. in 1709. In the latter year the demesne totalled 435 a., half the parish, and was let with the manor-house to George Notley for £200 a year. Seventeen tenants held 118 a. in Cricket, of which four were cottagers, the remaining tenements varying in size from 23 a. to ½ a. A further nine tenants held 154 a. at Marshwood, individual holdings there varying from 37 a. to 6 a.[90] In 1717 quit-rents produced £26 17s. 8d., the demesne £271, and the whole manor and advowson were valued for sale at £9,898.[91] By c. 1755 the quit-rents had risen to £35 14s. and there were 14 tenants holding 124 a. in Cricket. Of 172 a. in Marshwood 92 a. were held by three tenants and Henry Holt Henley of Leigh in Winsham was renting the remainder.[92] The Henleys continued to farm Marshwood as part of their Winsham estate, buying the freehold from Lord Bridport in 1862.[93]

The Bridports bought the ancient freehold of Lanscombe c. 1800,[94] and by 1831, with the exception of 30 a. glebe, they owned the whole parish.

The land was then farmed in two units, one of 379 a. based on Weston farm (held with a further 22 a. glebe) and the other on Higher and Lower farms at Marshwood of 168 a. held by one tenant. Parkland and gardens attached to the manor-house accounted for 252 a. and the remainder was rented by smallholders and cottagers.[95] This pattern continued throughout the Bridport occupation and when the estate was sold in 1898 Home farm and the Parsonage comprised 314 a. (with a further 47 a. in Winsham) and Manor or Weston farm 226 a. (with a further 12 a. in Winsham). The grounds around the house totalled 26 a. and 136 a. of arable in the west of the parish was to be sold separately.[96] The unity of the estate, however, was preserved during the 20th century and in 1931 included 1,200 a. in Cricket and Winsham.[97] On the purchase of the estate by the Taylors in 1967 the grounds around and below the house were converted to a wild-life park. The farm lands of over 1,000 a., including lands in Winsham, were in 1973 operated as four dairy farms, Home and Manor farms in Cricket and London Lodge and Puthill farms in Winsham. The milk from the 400 cows on the estate was then devoted to the production of Cricketer cheese, made at Cricket Malherbie.[98]

The pattern of land use on the estate has been one of fluctuating arable. In 1313 there were 200 a. of arable to 20 a. of meadow, and an unstated amount of pasture.[99] Where cultivation is noted between the 15th and 17th centuries it appears that closes were generally devoted to meadow or pasture and the extensive demesnes to grazing. In 1607 the demesne of 346 a. comprised 310 a. of meadow and pasture and 36 a. of unspecified cultivation,[1] but by 1709 the 435 a. of demesne were farmed as 183 a. of arable, 234 a. grassland, and 18 a. wood.[2] By 1831 arable was almost entirely restricted to the extreme west and south-west of the parish, including Red Scrip and Barnards both pasture in the 17th century, and to closes in the north at Lanscombe.[3] In the early 17th century Marshwood was entirely meadow and pasture although by 1831 43 a. had been converted to arable.[4] In 1905 there were 544 a. of permanent grass, 112 a. of arable, and 20 a. of wood and plantation.[5]

The parish has always relied principally on agriculture for its support, although a sackweaver was mentioned in 1655, and weavers, fullers, and edge-tool-makers were working the fulling- and blade-mills during the 17th and 18th centuries.[6] In 1851, apart from a shoemaker and a female glover, the 69 inhabitants were all engaged in estate work and in 1868 Lord Bridport was also employing residents of Winsham.[7]

[81] Ibid. conveyance, 2 June 1599.
[82] Ibid. conveyance in trust 21 Mar. 1627/8; boxes 51–3, leases.
[83] Ibid. boxes 5, 52, ct. rolls.
[84] Ibid. boxes 51–3, leases.
[85] Ibid. box 40, survey, 1672; B.L. Add. MS. 18616.
[86] S.R.O., DD/HI, box 53, conveyance in trust 20 Jan. 1615/16.
[87] Ibid. box 52, ct. roll.   [88] Ibid. estate bk.
[89] Ibid. box 40, survey 1672.
[90] Ibid. survey 1709.
[91] Ibid. box 8, valuation 1717; B.L. Add. MS. 18616.
[92] S.R.O., DD/HI, box 40, survey c. 1755.
[93] S.R.O., DD/HA 8, conveyance 26 Dec. 1862.
[94] S.R.O., Q/RE, land tax assessments.

[95] S.R.O., DD/SAS, C/212, map 1831.
[96] Ibid. C/2273, B.14.2.
[97] T. Press, Som. Country Houses and Villages (1931–2), 92.
[98] Ex inf. Mr. H. G. Taylor, Cricket St. Thomas.
[99] C 134/33/5.
[1] S.R.O., DD/HI, box 53, marr. settl. 18 Mar. 1606/7.
[2] Ibid. box 40, survey 1709.
[3] S.R.O., DD/SAS, C/212, map 1831.
[4] S.R.O., DD/HI, box 51, marr. settl. 21 Mar. 1627/8.
[5] Statistics supplied by the then Bd. of Agric. 1905.
[6] S.R.O., DD/HI, box 53, leases 20 Jan. 1609/10, 15 May 1655.
[7] H.O. 107/1928; Rep. Com. on Children and Women in Agric. [4202–I] p. 478, H.C. (1868–9), xiii.

FAIR. A fair on White Down was established on Whit Sunday 1361, the profits being taken by Richard Cogan and Elizabeth of Clevedon, lady of Cricket manor.[8] No charter is known to have been obtained for the fair which by 1467 was being held on the two days after Whit Sunday. In 1467 Stephen Preston, having purchased Cricket manor, obtained a confirmation of the fair and extended it for a further two days after Whitsun.[9] A further confirmation was made in 1563 at the request of John Preston,[10] and it was called 'a great fair in Whitsunday week' in 1633.[11]

An account book recording sales at the fair survives for the years 1637–42 and 1646–9.[12] Between 1637 and 1649 2d. was levied on each sale of cattle, horses, leather, and sheep, the income amounting to 14s. 2d. in 1637 and falling steadily to 3s. 8d. in 1642. The total income of the fair dropped from 15s. in 1646 to 10s. in 1648, thereafter rising to 23s. 8d. in 1649. Cattle were occasionally brought from Glamorgan for sale and the fair attracted buyers from as far afield as Pensford, Ottery St. Mary (Devon), and Mappowder (Dors.).

Barnwoods, apparently a close on White Down between Axminster Way and Blind Lane, was in 1649 reserved to the lord as a Whit Monday fair ground, and the area within Knoll hill gate and on Horse close was similarly reserved in 1651 for the period from Good Friday to Whitsuntide.[13] In 1663 the tenant of Middledons covenanted to collect the fair dues and to erect the standings or tilts, and in 1664 the manor derived £1 2s. 6d. from this source.[14] In 1709 the fair was let with the manor-house and demesnes,[15] but by 1717 it was let separately for a rent given variously as £18 or £20.[16]

In 1882 it was stated that a century before there had been a 'carriage-day' when the gentry gathered from miles around and 'disported themselves, feasting and dancing on the green sward'.[17] By 1845 the fair was held on Whit Monday for the sale of horses, and on Whit Tuesday for that of sheep, bullocks, and other cattle. On the Tuesday there was also horse racing and a 'foot hurdle race'.[18] 'Wrestling, cudgel playing and single stick' contests continued until shortly before 1882. In that year the fair was held on the south side of White Down adjoining the lodge gate.[19] The fair is recorded in 1897 but had probably been discontinued by 1902.[20]

MILLS. The Purtington brook drove up to nine mills in the parish and these must have served other settlements in the neighbourhood of Cricket. In 1086 there was a mill paying 12s.,[21] probably to be identified with the demesne water-mill valued at 13s. 4d. in 1313.[22] There are no further references to a manor mill until 1541 when, at the inclosure of the common 'moor', a site was reserved to the lord to build a grain mill.[23] This mill was probably the property later known as Hollowells mills in the extreme south of the parish on the Purtington brook. In 1613 the lord held two water grist mills, including the common close on which stood a tucker's rack.[24] Suit to the custom mills with corn and grain was required of some lessees as late as 1626.[25] In 1635 Mr. Preston's miller, Bryant Langley, was killed by the fall of the mill wheel.[26] From 1638 a succession of leases of mills further upstream reserved to the lord the mill leat which drove Hollowells mills and passed over the lands held by other tenants.[27] Hollowells mills were occupied by the Osborne family from 1659 to 1729. Thomas Osborne was succeeded by his widow in 1709 and by Robert Osborne in 1715. Henry Adams evidently held them between 1736 and 1741 and William Tucker from 1745 until 1792.[28] Thereafter they were occupied by Lord Bridport as part of the demesne.[29]

A blade-mill, formerly a tucking-mill, was rented by William Hill, a Winsham smith, in 1593 and by John Cox, another smith from Winsham, in 1597.[30] The premises passed to John Palfrey, an 'edger', in 1610, when the rent was halved,[31] and to John Carver in 1653.[32] Another John Carver (d. 1726), an edge-tool-maker, leased the mill in 1691 and was still holding it in 1713.[33] By 1726 it was held with other mills by Robert Osborne but has not been traced after 1729.[34]

A tucking- or fulling-mill, with two 'stocks', and liberty to place a tucker's rack on Mill close nearby, was occupied by Thomas Casselyn until 1600, followed by Thomas Scriven the younger, Joan Scriven, widow (d. 1636),[35] and the Adams family from 1672 until c. 1755.[36]

A house, tucking- or fulling-mill, with two 'stocks', passed from Thomas to Edward Grimstead in 1607 and thereafter to Edward's son, John.[37] They were held from 1615 by Alice Woodwall alias Kinder, and assigned to her son John, a fuller, in 1634. By 1640–1 a second tucking-mill with two 'stocks' had been built on the property, known subsequently as the Upper Mill, the older one being named the Lower Mill. Both mills were assigned to Thomas Osborne, clothier, in 1654.[38] By 1703 the property had passed to Robert

[8] *Proc. Som. Arch. Soc.* xxviii. 142–3. In 1370 the fair was prejudicing an older fair at Lopen: ibid.
[9] *Cal. Chart. R.* 1427–1516, 216.
[10] S.R.O., DD/HI, box 51.
[11] *S.R.S.* xv. 69.
[12] S.R.O., DD/HI, box 53. The book is fully analysed in *Proc. Som. Arch. Soc.* cxii. 61–70.
[13] S.R.O., DD/HI, box 52, estate bk.
[14] Ibid. loose paper in estate bk.; lease 29 Jan. 1662/3.
[15] Ibid. box 40, survey 1709.
[16] Ibid. box 8, rental 1717; B.L. Add. MS. 18616.
[17] *Proc. Som. Arch. Soc.* xxviii. 144–5.
[18] S.R.O., DD/SAS, C/909, 154.
[19] *Proc. Som. Arch. Soc.* xxviii. 144–5.
[20] *Kelly's Dir. Som.* (1897, 1902).
[21] *V.C.H. Som.* i. 473.
[22] C 134/33/5.
[23] S.R.O., DD/HI, box 52, ct. roll.
[24] Ibid. box 53, lease 10 Oct. 1638.

[25] Ibid. box 51, lease 20 Sept. 1626.
[26] Ibid. box 9, inquest.
[27] Ibid. box 53, lease 10 Oct. 1638.
[28] S.R.O., DD/S/CX; D/P/c.st.t 13/2/1–2.
[29] S.R.O., D/P/c.st.t 13/2/2.
[30] S.R.O., DD/HI, box 51, leases 10 Apr. 1593, 2 Oct. 1597.
[31] Ibid. box 53, lease 8 Sept. 1610.
[32] Ibid. box 40, survey 1672.
[33] Ibid. box 51, lease 26 Mar. 1691; B.L. Add. MS. 18616.
[34] S.R.O., D/P/c.st.t 13/2/1.
[35] S.R.O., DD/HI, box 16, amercements; box 53, copy ct. roll 4 July 1600; D/P/c.st.t. 2/1/1.
[36] S.R.O., DD/HI, box 40, surveys 1672, 1709, c. 1755; D/P/c.st.t 13/2/1; B.L. Add. MS. 18616.
[37] S.R.O., DD/HI, box 9, surrender 5 July 1609.
[38] Ibid. box 51, surrender 30 Aug. 1615, lease 20 Dec. 1615; box 53, lease 29 Sept. 1658.

Osborne, a third tucking-mill with one 'stock' having been added, and by 1709 the mill-house had five lower rooms, three chambers, and an outhouse. The mills have not been traced after 1713.[39] William Tucker, a Winsham soap-boiler, took the premises in 1744 and possibly combined them with Hollowells mills which he was leasing by 1745.[40]

Owing to his 'pretended ignorance of his tucking-mill' in 1639 Thomas Atkins did not reside on this tenement, but was still holding it in 1646.[41] Two leases of Atkins's fulling-mill for two years each were made to Richard Scriven in 1649 and 1651, when he was required to 'find all timber work saving the wheel, the trough, and the sells'. After repairs made in 1650 the lord disputed Scriven's claim to a quarter of a cog wheel and the old mill-wheel arms.[42] In 1658 a new lease was made to Scriven, then described as a fuller, and in 1691 to Edmond Denslow, fuller (d. 1706), probably Scriven's grandson.[43] Denslow was succeeded by his widow Susanna, and from 1709 the mill was held by Robert Osborne, fuller, and described as a messuage with four lower rooms and four chambers, a 'burling' shop, and a mill with two stocks.[44] It was still held by Osborne in 1739, being described as Cricket mills in 1730, but in 1746 was leased as a former tucking-mill to a wheelwright.[45]

A corn mill was leased to the Adams family from 1692 to 1731.[46] In 1709 it comprised a house with three lower rooms and a chamber, two grist-mills, a stable, linhay, and outhouse.[47] The property as a single mill is traceable through the families of Tucker, Hutchings, and Chick between 1732 and 1788,[48] but has not been traced thereafter.

Saw mills were constructed on the Purtington brook south of the former village site in the mid 19th century, powered in 1895 by a 17 ft. overshot wheel.[49] These were still in operation in 1973 although driven by electricity.

LOCAL GOVERNMENT.

Manor courts rolls are extant for the years 1459–81, 1498–1504,[50] 1516, 1534, 1538–9,[51] 1540–1, 1546,[52] 1605–9, 1611, 1627–8.[53] Notes of amercements for 1625–6 and 1647,[54] and a court of survey for 1672[55] also survive.

The court was described as *curia* or *curia manerii* until the earlier 16th century, when it is generally termed *curia baronis*. No officers were appointed by the court although the lord's bailiff was often mentioned. Between 1638 and 1665 a tenement held initially by Philip Foxworthy was used for holding the courts.[56]

In 1626 and 1638 the parish had one church-warden and one sidesman.[57] There were two over-seers of the poor between 1642 and 1659, and from 1670 until the late 18th century the vestry was electing one churchwarden and one overseer.[58] A surveyor of the highways occurs in 1704 and two sidesmen in 1716. The vestry regularly supplied cake and ale to the poor at Easter during the later 18th century.[59]

A house in the village was given as a poorhouse by the lord in 1767 and in 1786 was occupied by three women, who were reputed to be sluggards. In the following year the vestry determined not to relieve poor persons living outside the parish and to oblige all that sought relief to live in the poor-house.[60] The house was still standing in 1831[61] but was demolished with the rest of the village. The parish became part of the Chard poor-law union in 1836.[62]

CHURCH.

There was a church at Cricket at least by the 12th century.[63] The living was a rectory and its patronage, held with the manor by 1325,[64] continued to descend with it. The bishop collated in 1362[65] and an enquiry into the ownership of the advowson was required in 1470 after Stephen Preston had purchased the manor.[66] Maud Bidik presented in 1483 as Preston's widow,[67] William Fry by grant of John Preston in 1522,[68] and Charles York as guardian of Preston Hippisley in 1689.[69] The lords Bridport retained the advowson when the manor was sold in 1898. Since the union of the benefice with Winsham in 1879 the bishop of Worcester has had two turns and Lord Bridport one turn.[70]

The benefice was assessed at £2 10s. in 1291,[71] and was valued at £10 7s. 8d. gross in 1535.[72] The living was augmented by £30 in 1658, and c.

---

[39] S.R.O., DD/HI, box 40, survey 1709; B.L. Add. MS. 18616.
[40] S.R.O., DD/HI, box 40, survey c. 1755.
[41] S.R.O., DD/HI, box 10, letter Preston to Poulett 30 Sept. 1639; par. rate 1646.
[42] Ibid. box 52, estate bk.
[43] Ibid. lease 24 Dec. 1658; box 51, lease 26 Mar. 1691; D/P/c.st.t 2/1/1. In 1672 Elizabeth Denslow, widow, was described as Richard Scriven's daughter: DD/HI, box 40, survey.
[44] S.R.O., DD/AL, box 1, lease 2 Mar. 1708/9.
[45] Ibid. further charge 14 Feb. 1730/1; D/P/c.st.t 13/2/1; DD/HI, box 53, lease 1 May 1746.
[46] S.R.O., DD/HI, box 8, survey c. 1700; box 40, survey 1709; D/P/c.st.t 13/2/1.
[47] S.R.O., DD/HI. box 40, survey 1709.
[48] S.R.O., D/P/c.st.t 2/1/2; 13/2/1–2; DD/HI, box 40, survey c. 1755.
[49] S.R.O., DD/SAS, C/212, map 1831; C/2273, B.14.2; O.S. Map 6″, Som. XCII. NW. (1891 edn.).
[50] S.R.O., DD/HI, box 52.
[51] Ibid. box 5.
[52] Ibid. box 52.
[53] Ibid. box 51.
[54] Ibid. box 16.
[55] Ibid. box 40.
[56] Ibid. box 51, leases 26 Sept. 1660, 24 Oct. 1665; box 53, lease 10 Oct. 1638.
[57] S.R.O., D/D/Rg 298.
[58] *Som. Protestation Returns*, ed. A. J. Howard and T. L. Stoate, 89; S.R.O., DD/S/CX; D/P/c.st.t 13/2/1–2.
[59] S.R.O., D/P/c.st.t 13/2/1.
[60] Ibid. 13/2/2.
[61] S.R.O., DD/SAS, C/212, map 1831.
[62] *Poor Law Com. 2nd Rep.* p. 547.
[63] Two chaplains occur as witnesses in the 12th century and a parson in 1289: Forde Abbey, Cart. pp. 464–5; *Cal. Close*, 1288–96, 47.
[64] *S.R.S.* i. 243.
[65] Ibid. ix, p. 772.
[66] Ibid. lii, p. 36.
[67] Ibid. p. 118.
[68] Ibid. lv, p. 24.
[69] *Som. Incumbents*, ed. Weaver.
[70] *Crockford*.
[71] *Tax Eccl.* (Rec. Com.), 199.
[72] *Valor Eccl.* (Rec. Com.), i. 167.

1668 produced £50.[73] It was worth £60 in 1717[74] and c. £125 net in 1815 and 1827,[75] falling to £106 in 1840.[76]

Tithes of sheaves and grain were valued at 31s. in 1334.[77] In 1535 predial tithes produced 72s., tithes of sheep and lambs 26s. 8d., and oblations and personal tithes 55s. 8d.[78] In 1615 John Preston took a lease from the rector of all tithes issuing from the manor-house and demesnes for £10 a year, on condition that the rector should not absent himself from the parsonage or commit any act which might lead to his deprivation.[79] In 1626 a tithe was taken of all wheat, rye, barley, oats, peas, beans, hemp, calves, pigs, lambs, wool, apples, and hay, 2d. a cow for kine white, Easter dues, and the agistments of rented grounds.[80] Tithes on 296 a. were commuted for £92 a year in 1838, although 857 a. were then stated to be subject to tithes.[81] Possibly tithes on the demesne were still subject to some private agreement between the rector and the lord of the manor. The modus of 2d. for each milch cow continued to be payable after 1838.[82]

The rector was often presented for the state of his glebe in the manor court.[83] The glebe lands were valued at 53s. 4d. in 1535[84] and in 1626 comprised 25 a. of arable and 7 a. of pasture, all in closes.[85] In 1799 the rector exchanged 7¼ a. for 8¼ a. held by Lord Bridport,[86] and in 1831 and 1838 held 30 a., including three cottages.[87]

The parsonage house had a barn, garden, orchard, and plot in 1626.[88] Under an agreement reached in 1799 Lord Bridport was to erect a new house for the rector,[89] but, although the house was described as 'fit', it was not occupied by either the rector or his curate in 1827.[90] It was in good repair in 1840 but had evidently been sold in 1843.[91] The house still stands but no subsequent provision for a resident rector has been made.

Thomas of Cricket, rector until 1315,[92] was probably related to the lords of the manor, and Walter Sprengehose, rector from 1353, was one of the scholars who precipitated the Oxford riot on St. Scholastica's day in 1355.[93] On account of his 'lack of knowledge of letters' John Hucker, rector 1463–70, was obliged to study for a year before being re-examined,[94] and no graduate rector has been traced before 1614. In 1563 Cricket was served only by an assistant curate,[95] but the earlier rectors were generally resident. John Langdale, rector 1644–62, served throughout the Interregnum, receiving £10 a year from the lord, but was deprived

for nonconformity in 1662.[96] He was preaching at Winsham, Wayford, and Merriott in 1669 and was licensed to preach at his house at Cricket and in Hinton St. George in 1672.[97]

Assistant curates occur regularly from 1751 to 1836[98] and it is unlikely that serving rectors were ever resident during that time. John Templeman, rector 1798–1835, also held Lopen, where he lived, and Buckland St. Mary. In 1827 he described himself as 'very decrepit and almost blind', and stated that his curate was receiving £40 a year and served Wambrook where he lived.[99] Robert Pearse Clark, rector 1835–46, held the rectory with the livings of Churchstanton and Otterford, and Charles James Shaw, rector 1846–78, a former usher of Westminster school and fellow of Sidney Sussex College, Cambridge, held it with Seaborough (Dors. formerly Som.).[1] Thereafter the benefice was held with Winsham where subsequent incumbents resided.

In 1554 the church lacked a canopy and in 1577 the parish had no quarterly sermons.[2] In 1606 the parishioners had no pewter pot to hold the Communion wine.[3] From 1697 until 1755 the church, situated on a main coaching route and yet relatively isolated, was evidently a popular place for the celebration of clandestine marriages. Of 154 marriages solemnized in this period 81 were between parties both of whom lived in other parishes and, in many cases, other dioceses.[4] Nine communicants were recorded in the parish in 1776, and Holy Communion was celebrated weekly and on certain holy days between 1815 and 1827.[5] There was a weekly sermon in 1840 and 1843, although celebrations of Holy Communion had been reduced to eight each year.[6] In 1851 morning service was attended by about 40 and twice that number in the afternoon, many coming 'from a distance'.[7]

The church of ST. THOMAS comprises chancel with south vestry, nave with south chapel, and west porch with western bellcot. The walls are flint faced, with Ham stone dressings. The church contains no visible features earlier than the 19th and 20th centuries and the claim that it was rebuilt by the 2nd Baron Bridport (d. 1868) is probably correct.[8] The interior is dominated by monuments of the Hood and related families, among them those of Alexander, Viscount Bridport (d. 1814) by Sir John Soane, of Viscountess Bridport (d. 1831) by Lucius Gahagan, and of the Revd. William, Earl Nelson, duke of Brontë (d. 1835).[9]

[73] Lambeth Palace MSS., COMM.VIb/2; S.R.O., D/D/Vc 24.
[74] S.R.O., DD/HI, box 8, survey 1717.
[75] S.R.O., D/D/B return 1815; D/D/V return 1827.
[76] County Gazette Dir. (1840).
[77] E 179/169/14.
[78] Valor Eccl. (Rec. Com.), i. 167.
[79] S.R.O., DD/HI, box 52, demise 24 Apr. 1615.
[80] S.R.O., D/D/Rg 298.
[81] S.R.O., tithe award.
[82] Ibid.
[83] S.R.O., DD/HI, box 52, ct. rolls, sub annis.
[84] Valor Eccl. (Rec. Com.), i. 167.
[85] S.R.O., D/D/Rg 298.
[86] S.R.O., D/D/C, petitions for faculty, 1799.
[87] S.R.O., DD/SAS (C/212), map 1831; tithe award.
[88] S.R.O., D/D/Rg 298.
[89] S.R.O., D/D/Cf, 1799.
[90] S.R.O., D/D/B return 1815; D/D/V return 1827.
[91] S.R.O., D/D/V returns 1840, 1843.

[92] S.R.S. i. 84.
[93] Ibid. ix, p. 711; Emden, Biog. Reg. Univ. Oxford.
[94] S.R.S. xlix, p. 386.
[95] B.L. Harl. MS. 594, f. 54v.
[96] Calamy Revised, ed. Matthews; S.R.O., DD/HI, box 52, estate bk., entries 1647–55; box 53, presentation 5 Dec. 1662.
[97] Calamy Revised, ed. Matthews.
[98] S.R.O., D/P/c.st.t 2/1/1–5.
[99] Venn, Alumni Cantab.; S.R.O., D/D/B return 1815; D/D/V return 1827.
[1] Venn, Alumni Cantab.
[2] S.R.O., D/D/Ca 22, 57.
[3] Ibid. 151.
[4] S.R.O., D/P/c.st.t 2/1/1.
[5] S.R.O., D/D/Dioc. bk.; D/D/B return 1815; D/D/V return 1827.
[6] S.R.O., D/D/V returns 1840, 1843.
[7] H.O. 129/318/3/3/10.
[8] History in ch.; see below, plate facing p. 161.
[9] Pevsner, South and West Som. 140–1.

A plate of 1674 may be the paten which, with a silver-handled knife, was given by Christopher Hippisley in 1683.[10] A cup and flagon of 1808 and 1809 were presented by Viscount Bridport.[11] The two bells are modern and uninscribed.[12] The registers date from 1564. Pages covering baptisms 1588–1612 and marriages and burials 1564–1612 have been removed, but the missing entries are supplied in a late transcript. There is also a hiatus for the years 1642–86.[13]

A chapel dedicated to St. White (otherwise St. Candida) stood in Chapel field on White Down. A 12th-century deed witnessed by Roger 'de Sancta Wita'[14] suggests that the chapel may have been built by that date. The fair was held on 'Saint White Down' from 1361[15] and in the late 15th century William of Worcester records a chapel of St. White 'on the plain near Crewkerne', the dedication of which was celebrated on Whit Sunday.[16] The rector of Cricket was ordered in 1504 to hedge his inclosure around the chapel[17] and it was annexed to Cricket rectory by 1535.[18] No details of chaplains serving the chapel have been found. The 'old chapel upon White Down was consumed by lightning' on 2 August 1740 'and a man killed that stood by it'.[19] No trace of the building survives.

NONCONFORMITY. In 1672 the ejected rector, John Langdale, was licensed to preach at his house in Cricket.[20] There were eleven Presbyterians living in the parish in 1776.[21]

EDUCATION. In 1819 there was a school in the parish with 4 or 5 children, and a Sunday school in 1825–6 was attended by 3 boys and 3 girls.[22] In 1835 Lady Bridport was 'about to establish' a school but, after the demolition of the village by 1846–7, there was no school for there were no children.[23] In 1902 the children of the parish attended Winsham school.[24]

CHARITIES FOR THE POOR. Hugh Preston of Cricket (d. 1595) by will left £40 in trust to his brother Christopher for life, to pay £4 a year to the use of the poor of the parish. On Christopher's death the charity was to be administered by the owner of Cricket manor-house, if descended from the donor's father.[25] No subsequent reference to this charity has been traced.

CUDWORTH

CUDWORTH, on the northern scarp of Windwhistle ridge, covered an area of 1,100 a. in 1841, and 1,125 a. by 1901.[1] From its southern boundary on the ridge just over 725 ft. above sea level, the land falls away, at first steeply and then more gently, to below 225 ft. at its northern limit. The parish was said in the 18th century to be 'an elevated and delightful spot' and 'peculiarly adapted for the site of a villa', commanding 'unbounded prospects of the surrounding country and the British and Bristol channels'.[2]

The southern boundary with Cricket St. Thomas follows in part the course of the Foss Way. The parish is divided from Chillington on the east by Stretford water, a name possibly derived from association with the Foss. The Wall brook, which runs parallel with Stretford water a little to the west, forms the boundary for a 'finger' of Cudworth pointing north into Dowlish Wake. The northern and western boundaries occasionally follow contours but appear otherwise to be irregular.

Clay-with-flints on the higher ground in the

south is followed by bands of chalk and chert. Outcrops of sand and marl occur further north.[3] Marl was dug in the 16th century,[4] and in 1841 there were at least seven quarries, mostly for chalk.[5] By 1886 there was a chalk pit and lime kiln north of Limekiln Lane east of Lidmarsh Farm, and another north of New Lane.[6] The place-names Cudworth and Worth both suggest woodland clearings. Woodland still survives along the higher slopes of the parish just below the Windwhistle ridge and evidently extended further north, where field-names and small inclosures indicate medieval cultivation.[7] Medieval settlement is also visible east of the church and former manor-house.

The main roads in the parish form an H-shaped plan. To the east Dowlish Lane runs north from the direction of Purtington and Higher Chillington to Dowlish Wake. Oldway Lane, in the west, runs north from White Down also to Dowlish Wake. They are joined by an east–west road, known as Water Lane in 1851, which extends west to Cricket Malherbie.[8] Hamlets grew up at the two junctions.

[10] S.R.O., D/P/c.st.t 2/1/1. The plate carries the initials 'K.H.' which were identified with Katherine Hippisley (Proc. Som. Arch. Soc. xlv. 142).
[11] Proc. Som. Arch. Soc. xlv. 141–2.
[12] S.R.O., DD/SAS CH 16.
[13] S.R.O., D/P/c.st.t 2/1/1–5, 2/9/1.
[14] Forde Abbey, Cart. p. 465.
[15] Proc. Som. Arch. Soc. xxvii. 142.
[16] Ibid. xxxvii. 44–59.
[17] S.R.O., DD/HI, box 52, ct. roll.
[18] Valor Eccl. (Rec. Com.), i. 167.
[19] S.R.O., D/P/c.st.t 2/1/1.
[20] Calamy Revised, ed. Matthews.
[21] S.R.O., D/D/V Dioc. bk.
[22] Digest of Returns to Sel. Cttee. on Educ. of Poor, H.C. 224 (1819), ix (2); Ann. Rep. B. & W. Dioc. Assoc.

S.P.C.K. (1825–6).
[23] Educ. Enquiry Abstract, H.C. 62 (1835), xlii; Church Sch. Inquiry, 1846–7.   [24] Kelly's Dir. Som. (1902).
[25] Prob. 11/86 (P.C.C. 69 Scott).
[1] S.R.O., tithe award; V.C.H. Som. ii. 348. This article was completed in 1973.
[2] S.R.O., DD/PT, box 24, sale partics.
[3] Geol. Surv. Map 1″, solid and drift, sheet 312 (1958 edn.).
[4] S.R.S. li, p. 150; S.R.O., DD/SS, bdles. 16, 31.
[5] S.R.O., tithe award.
[6] O.S. Map 6″, Som. LXXXVIII. SW., XCII. NW. (1886 edn.).
[7] S.R.O., D/PS/ilm, box 15.
[8] Cal. Inq. p.m. xiv, p. 392; Cal. Close, 1485–1500, 291–2; S.R.O., DD/X/JS, Vyne to Walrond, 1588.

That in the west, at Cross Tree,[9] has in association the parish church, the former prebendal house, and the site of the manor-house, together with West Farm, a dairy house, and cottages. The eastern junction had a larger settlement at least by the 18th century, when it was divided between Higher and Wear greens.[10] This may be the area known in the 16th century as Werthe or Upton, and thus in origin the secondary Domesday settlement known as Worde.[11] In the late 18th century it was known as Upper and Lower Weare.[12] The school and poor-house stood there in the 19th century, together with the substantial East Farm and buildings. There are scattered houses between the two hamlets and ancient settlements in the west of the parish at Bonner's Leaze and above Lidmarsh.

Apart from the church and former prebendal house the oldest buildings in the parish date from the 17th century. Knight's Farm has recently been modernized and reduced in size, but appears to have been of 17th-century origin with a passage entrance. Some earlier 17th-century panelling is still in the house although now reset. Bonner's Leaze is a long house of 17th-century origin with a barn at the rear dated 1870. A house in Lidmarsh, formerly known as Greystones and Combe Thatch, is a small 17th-century building enlarged and altered in the earlier 18th century, probably in 1720, the date on a stone over the former two-storeyed porch.[13] The other large farm-houses appear to date from the 18th or 19th centuries.

There was an inn in the parish by 1735 which by 1769 was known as the Black Horse.[14] The Wind-whistle inn, perhaps its successor, was so named by 1782.[15] It stands on the north side of the Crew-kerne–Chard road, on the extreme southern boundary of the parish, and incorporates a building of the 19th century.

Among the holders of the prebend of Cudworth were William Fulford (1452–75), a diocesan official, Edmund Audley (1475–80), later bishop of Rochester, Thomas Cornish (1494–1501), titular bishop of Tenos and suffragan to the bishops of Bath and Wells and Exeter, and Dr. Richard Busby (1639–95), headmaster of Westminster school 1638–95.[16]

There were 14 households in the parish in 1563 and 16 in 1601.[17] In 1801 the population was 163; it fell to 140 in 1811 but rose in thirty years to 155 and in a further decade to 181. It then fluctuated, but fell sharply from 115 in 1891 to 86 in 1901. The level remained fairly stable until after 1951, but in 1961 there were 65 and in 1971 64.[18]

Seven men were under suspicion of complicity in Monmouth's rebellion in 1685.[19]

MANOR AND OTHER ESTATES. The manor of *CUDWORTH* was held T.R.W. by Roger Arundel.[20] The overlord in 1236 was Roger Fitz-Payn,[21] and therefore the property is presumed to have descended like the manor of Charlton Mackrell with the Arundel barony of Powerstock (Dors.).[22] Roger FitzPayn (d. 1237) was succeeded by his son Sir Robert (II) (d. 1281) and by his grandson Robert (III), Lord Fitzpayn (d. 1315). Robert (IV), Lord FitzPayn, died in 1354, leaving as his heir his daughter Isabel, wife of Sir John Chidiock (I) (d. 1388).[23] Cudworth was said in 1384 to be held of Chidiock as of his manor of Chelborough (Dors.),[24] and in 1518 to be held of his heirs as of the same manor.[25]

In 1086 the tenant at Cudworth was Otes, who had succeeded three thegns holding 'in parage'.[26] No occupier is known thereafter until *c.* 1186–8, when Alan de Furneaux gave the church to Wells cathedral.[27] Alan was succeeded in other lands if not at Cudworth by his son Geoffrey in 1188.[28] The family continued in occupation in the 13th century. Alan de Furneaux was tenant in 1236,[29] and a namesake in 1284–5.[30] By 1303 the manor, which apparently included land in Knowle St. Giles, was held jointly by Matthew de Esse and Humphrey de Kail,[31] Matthew's claim deriving from his marriage in 1276 to Joan, daughter of Alan de Furneaux.[32] Matthew was still alive in 1316,[33] but was dead by 1333.[34] He was succeeded by Alan de Esse, who was probably also known as Alan of Kingston.[35] In 1377 Ralph Kingston, who had let his moiety to William Wythe and his wife for their lives, sold the reversion to his overlord, Sir John Chidiock.[36] By 1384 the moiety had passed to John Kail, occupier of the other moiety.[37]

Humphrey de Kail's moiety passed to William de Kail (d. 1348).[38] His son John proved his age in 1369,[39] and died in 1384, holding the entire manor of Cudworth of Sir John Chidiock, a tenement called 'Clyvelond' in Cudworth in chief, together with the land in Avishays in Chaffcombe and other properties.[40] A settlement on himself and his wife with remainder to his son Thomas was disputed after his death,[41] but the property seems to have passed successively to John's children Thomas (d. 1394) and to Idony (d. 1401), wife of John Poulett.[42] Idony's sons, John and Thomas Poulett, died in

[9] For the tree see G. A. Allan, 'Cudworth' (TS. in Taunton Castle).
[10] S.R.O., DD/PT, box 24.
[11] S.R.O., DD/X/JS.
[12] Collinson, *Hist. Som.* iii. 117–18.
[13] The initials of Hugh Legge and his wife appear on the datestone.
[14] S.R.O., Q/RL.
[15] S.R.O., DD/PT, box 14, lease to Camplin.
[16] Le Neve, *Fasti, 1300–1541, Bath and Wells,* 41–2; *D.N.B.*
[17] B.L. Harl. MS. 594, f. 55v.; S.R.O., DD/HI, box 9.
[18] *Census.*
[19] B.L. Add. MS. 30077, f. 35.
[20] *V.C.H. Som.* i. 494.
[21] *Bk. of Fees,* i. 581.
[22] *V.C.H. Som.* iii. 97.
[23] *Cal. Inq. p.m.* xiii, pp. 14–15; *Complete Peerage,* s.v. Fitzpayn.

[24] *Cal. Inq. p.m.* xiv, p. 391.
[25] C 142/33/30.
[26] *V.C.H. Som.* i. 494.
[27] *H.M.C. Wells,* i. 42–3.
[28] Pipe R. 1188 (P.R.S. xxxviii), 150, 151, 165.
[29] *Bk. of Fees,* i. 581.
[30] *Feud. Aids,* iv. 283.
[31] Ibid. iv. 315.
[32] *Plac. Coram Rege* (Index Libr. xix), 14.
[33] *Feud. Aids,* iv. 331.
[34] *S.R.S.* ix, p. 144.
[35] *H.M.C. Wells,* i. 485; ii. 8.
[36] *S.R.S.* xvii. 193.
[37] *Cal. Inq. p.m.* xiv, p. 391.
[38] Ibid. xiii, p. 15.
[39] Ibid. xii, pp. 252–3.
[40] Ibid. xiv, p. 391.
[41] *Cal. Close,* 1385–9, 353–4.
[42] Ibid. 1413–19, 28–9; C 136/93/33; C 137/33/42.

1413, and the property passed to John Kaynes.[43] Kaynes's feoffees held it in 1419 and 1428, but by 1431 the manor was in the hands of John Speke (I), husband of Joan, daughter of John Kaynes.[44]

The Spekes held the manor until the 18th century. John Speke (I) died in 1441,[45] and his property descended successively to John (II) (d. 1444),[46] John (III) (d. 1518),[47] and John (IV) (d. 1524).[48] Thomas Speke, son of John (IV), was succeeded in 1551 by his son Sir George (I), K.B. (d. 1584),[49] by his grandson George (II) (d. 1637)[50] and by his great-grandson George (III) (d. 1690).[51] The last was succeeded by his second son John[52] and then by his grandson George (IV) (d. 1753).[53] Under his will George Speke (IV) settled the manor of Cudworth, like Chillington, on trustees, to sell for the benefit of his daughter Mary. The trustees retained Cudworth until 1786, when they sold it to Samuel Harbour of Bridport (Dors.), later of Dowlish Wake.[54] Harbour sold it in turn to John Poulett, Earl Poulett (d. 1819) in 1791,[55] and it descended in the Poulett family through successive earls until 1913, when the estate, though not the lordship, was sold to Holliday Hartley.[56]

Matthew de Esse was resident in Cudworth in 1297,[57] and an oratory was licensed in his widow's house in 1333.[58] The site may be on the rising ground immediately south of the parish church, where a moat and other extensive earthworks remain.

Roger and Hugh de la Clive held a capital messuage and land in Lidmarsh in Chaffcombe in 1227.[59] 'Clyve' was the residence of the Kails by 1348, when it was apparently in the parish of Cudworth.[60] Land called 'Clyvelond' was certainly in the parish in 1370,[61] and its ownership descended at least until 1413 with the main manor.[62] By 1438 it had come into the possession of Sir Thomas Brook (d. 1439) and his wife.[63] The subsequent descent of the property is not traced, but in 1691 fields called 'Cliffbarrs' and 'Cleyhill' were in the possession of Hugh Legg, clerk, of Staple Fitzpaine.[64] They passed to James Marwood of Avishays in Chaffcombe in 1746,[65] and from William Warry Elton, Marwood's successor, to the Hon. Alexander Nelson Hood in 1859.[66] They formed part of lands exchanged between Hood and Earl Poulett in the following year, and thereafter descended with the Poulett estate.[67]

The prebend of Cudworth, which originated in the gift of the parsonage by Alan de Furneaux to Wells cathedral in 1186–8,[68] comprised land, tithes, and a house and barn in Cudworth, and land and tithes in Knowle St. Giles.[69] It was taxed at £6 13s. 4d. in 1291.[70] In 1535 the glebe lands were worth 25s. 6d. and the tithes £6 8s.[71] In 1571 there were about 30 a. in Cudworth, and in 1636 the same fields were estimated at over 33 a.[72] Moduses payable included 2½d. for every milking cow, 2d. for every heifer, 1d. for a garden and for the fall of a colt.[73] The income was said in 1650 to be £40 6s. 8d. from the whole prebend, and the property was thought to be worth on improvement £58.[74] 'Some years' before 1836 the prebend was valued at £257,[75] and in 1841 the rent-charge in lieu of tithes in Cudworth was established at £209. There were then 32 a. of glebe.[76]

The prebend was leased by the end of the 16th century, and from 1635 produced £10 a year.[77] During the 18th century it was held by the Dodd family of Charlton Mackrell. The Revd. William Dodd, formerly lessee, became prebendary in 1735;[78] his son-in-law Edward Cheselden, a clergyman, also of Charlton Mackrell, became lessee in 1761.[79] From 1792 at least until 1841 it was held by the Colmer family, formerly of Chard and later of Sibton (Suff.) and Askerswell (Dors.).[80] The property passed to the Ecclesiastical (now Church) Commissioners in 1855.[81] Members of the Webb family of Cricket Malherbie occupied the land as tenants from 1783 at least until 1841, and in 1809 paid £295 a year for the lands in Cudworth and Knowle together.[82]

The 'old, little thatched house' attached to the prebend was replaced c. 1636 by one then 'newly built . . . and well nigh furnished'. It was of two storeys with attics, and comprised on the ground floor a parlour, hall, kitchen, and buttery.[83] The house, which was the dwelling of the curate in the 17th century,[84] was normally occupied by the tenants of the prebendal estate. It became part of the benefice property of the vicarage of Cudworth and Chillington in 1886. It was altered then and in 1903, and it was known as the Old Prebendal House.[85]

A Domesday estate called Worde and hitherto regarded either as part of Knowle St. Giles or Chard,[86] may well have been in Cudworth. T.R.E.

43 Cal. Close, 1413–19, 28–9.
44 S.R.S. xxii. 55; Feud Aids, iv. 389, 432.
45 C 139/105/3.   46 C 139/119/31.
47 C 142/33/30.   48 C 142/44/119.
49 C 142/97/117; C 142/205/199.
50 C 142/482/126.
51 S.R.O., DD/SPK (C/1626), pedigree.
52 Alive in 1725: S.R.O., DD/CA 2.
53 S.R.O., DD/CA 2.   54 Ibid.
55 S.R.O., DD/PT, box 24.
56 Sale cat. penes Mr. L. Broad, Chard.
57 Plac. Coram Rege (Index Libr. xix), 14.
58 S.R.S. ix, p. 144.   59 Ibid. vi. 55–6.
60 Cal. Inq. p.m. xii, pp. 252–3.
61 Cal. Inq. Misc. iii, pp. 288–9.
62 Cal. Inq. p.m. xiv, pp. 391–2; Cal. Close, 1385–9, 353–4; 1413–19, 28–9.
63 S.R.S. xxii. 194; C 139/92/32.
64 S.R.O., DD/X/AD.
65 Devon R.O. 281M/T197–8.
66 S.R.O., DD/PT, box 14.   67 Ibid.
68 H.M.C. Wells, i. 42–3.

69 The barn was there by 1347: Cal. Inq. p.m. xii, pp. 252–3.
70 Tax. Eccl. (Rec. Com.), 200.
71 Valor Eccl. (Rec. Com.), i. 135.
72 S.R.O., D/D/Rg 299.   73 Ibid.
74 Lambeth Palace MSS., COMM. XIIa/1 f. 118.
75 S.R.O., D/D/Ppb 8.
76 S.R.O., tithe award.
77 Som. Wills, ed. Brown, iv. 69; Lambeth Palace MSS., COMM. XIIa/1 f. 118.
78 S.R.O., DD/CC 5103–8; H.M.C. Wells, ii. 527; B.L. Add. MS. 18616, ff. 63, 65.
79 S.R.O., DD/CC 5108.
80 Ibid. 5109–14; S.R.O., D/D/Ppb 8.
81 S.R.O., DD/SAS (C/909), 21.
82 S.R.O., DD/CC 19146–51; tithe award.
83 S.R.O., D/D/Rg 299.
84 Lambeth Palace MSS., COMM. XIIa/1 f. 118.
85 G. A. Allan, 'Cudworth' (TS. in Taunton Castle), 46–8 and appendix.
86 V.C.H. Som. i. 487 and n.; Proc. Som. Arch. Soc. cviii. 96.

it was held 'in parage' by two thegns, but by 1086 was part of Roger de Courcelles' holding, tenanted like Knowle by William de Almereio.[87] By *c.* 1186–8 the property was held, like Knowle and Cudworth, by Alan de Furneaux, and by 1249 another Alan had a villein tenant called Philip de Worth.[88] Thereafter it seems to have descended like Cudworth, and was held in 1312 by Matthew de Esse of Nicholas Pointz.[89] William de Kail (d. 1348) held some 40 a. of land at Worth and was succeeded by his son John.[90] The Kail holdings passed to John Kaynes who in 1413 was holding six houses and three carucates there.[91] From Kaynes the estate passed to the Spekes, and in 1497 George Speke leased several named units including Stokmansplace and Chapel place.[92] That same property was in 1588 sold by John Vyne of Baynton (Oxon.) to Henry Walrond of Sea, when it was described as being in 'Upton alias Werth and Cudworth'.[93] The lands have not been traced further, but Stokmansplace may be identified with the field name Stokmans Hay at Weare, which in turn suggests that Weare is the Domesday Worde.[94]

ECONOMIC HISTORY. Assuming that the present parish includes both the Domesday estates of Cudworde and Worde, the total area paying geld was 5 hides. T.R.E. the land had been held in parage by 5 thegns, but by 1086 was divided into two separate estates. There was land for 7 ploughs, and half the total area was Cudworde demesne, cultivated with 1 plough by 2 serfs. No demesne is mentioned at Worde, though the villeins there had 2½ of the 3 ploughs assigned to the property. Demesne stock at Cudworde comprised 2 head of cattle, 12 pigs, and 60 sheep. There were 4 villeins and 2 bordars at Cudworde, 10 villeins at Worde. Four acres of meadow, and pasture measuring 8 furlongs by 2 at Cudworde are to be compared with 4 a. of meadow and woodland measuring 4 furlongs by 2 at Worde. Worde was valued at 60*s.* both before and after the Conquest, Cudworde at 40*s.* T.R.E. but at 30*s.* in 1086.[95]

The division of Cudworth manor by the early 14th century[96] does not seem to have resulted in fragmentation of holdings. In 1327 John of Cudworth held nearly one third of the taxable property in the parish.[97] Other occupiers, including William le Coiner and Jordan le Sopere, do not by their surnames imply agricultural origins. From the later 14th century the parish included small holdings belonging to estates or families often living elsewhere. The Kail estate in 1385, for example, comprised lands in at least six neighbouring parishes;[98] the fraternity or chantry of St. Mary[99] and St. Katherine's chantry, both in Chard, had holdings there by 1548, the latter the origin of Bonner's Leaze farm;[1] and by the late 16th century the Bullers and the Wadhams had property there, the Wadhams being succeeded by the Wyndhams in the 17th century.[2]

Field names from the late 14th century onwards suggest well established inclosures and the suffix 'place' implies nucleated holdings.[3] Several fields were identifiable in the 19th century, including Rymes (Riam in 1385), Long Down (Langhedoune in 1385), and Stockmans Hay (Stokmansplace in 1497).[4] The last gives one of the few indications of animal husbandry; the will of an inhabitant proved in 1551 mentioned 16 sheep.[5]

At the break-up of the Speke estate on the death of George Speke (IV) in 1753 the trustees for Mary Speke, but in practice Frederick North, Lord North, later earl of Guilford (d. 1792),[6] held over 743 a. in Cudworth, somewhat more than half the parish. Some 250 a. were held on leases for lives and the remainder on rack rent. The property, 'greatly underlet to respectable tenants' and 'let remarkably low and capable of great improvements', was purchased by Earl Poulett for £12,700 in 1791, when its annual value was £664.[7] The two largest farms on the estate were then known as East or Eastern and West or Western farms. In 1787 they had measured 190 a. and 206 a. respectively, and West farm was then let for 14 years for £145.[8] By 1791 holdings had been re-arranged[9] and by 1819 both farms had been increased in size, Both were then let to the same tenant, W. H. Webb of Cricket Malherbie, who was also lessee of the prebendal estate. East farm then measured 199 a. and West farm 246 a.; they were let for £250 and £300 respectively.[10] The two farms dominated the parish in the 19th century, and in 1851 the tenant of both employed 21 labourers.[11] The remainder of the Poulett estate brought their holding to 898 a. by 1912, when it was put up for sale.[12] Only the Hull family holding of Bonner's Leaze and the Phelpses of Higher Weare lay outside the Poulett property.[13] After 1912 Knight's House farm was divided from West farm, and by 1923 the tenant concentrated on dairying. The other properties included some arable, which has subsequently decreased in area. Bingham's Lodge Stud farm was built at the southern end of the parish before 1923.[14]

More than half the inhabitants of the parish in

[87] *V.C.H. Som.* i. 487.
[88] *H.M.C. Wells,* i. 42–3; *S.R.S.* xi, pp. 367–8, 377–8.
[89] *Cal. Inq. p.m.* v, p. 196.
[90] Ibid. xiii, pp. 14–16; xiv. p. 391.
[91] *Cal. Close,* 1413–19, 28–9.
[92] Ibid. 1485–1500, 291–2.
[93] S.R.O., DD/X/JS.   [94] S.R.O., tithe award.
[95] *V.C.H. Som.* i. 494.
[96] *Feud. Aids,* iv. 315.   [97] *S.R.S.* iii. 197.
[98] *Cal. Inq. p.m.* xiv, p. 392.
[99] *S.R.S.* ii. 174; E 318/38/2075; *Cal. Pat.* 1547–8, 285.
[1] *S.R.S.* ii. 175; S.R.O., DD/SAS PR 225; DD/SAS (C/96), 3.
[2] *S.R.S.* li, pp. 70–1, 135, 150; lxvii, p. 130; S.R.O., DD/SS, bdles. 16, 31; DD/WY W/SR 1; DD/WY, boxes 2–3, 11.

[3] *Cal. Inq. p.m.* xiv, p. 392; *Cal. Close,* 1485–1500, 291–2; S.R.O., DD/X/JS, Vyne to Walrond, 1588.
[4] *Cal. Inq. p.m.* xiv, p. 392; *Cal. Close,* 1485–1500, 291–2; S.R.O., tithe award.
[5] *S.R.S.* xxi. 119.
[6] S.R.O., DD/PT, box 24, highways composition 1784.
[7] Ibid. sale partics.
[8] Ibid. leases.
[9] Ibid. sale partics.
[10] S.R.O., DD/PT, box 40.
[11] H.O. 107/1928.
[12] Sale cat. *penes* Mr. L. Broad.
[13] S.R.O., tithe award; DD/SAS (C/909), 15; DD/CA 86.
[14] Sale cat. Chaffcombe House estate, 1923, *penes* Mr. J. G. Vincent, Knowle St. Giles.

Barrington Court

Cricket St. Thomas: Cricket House, 1849

MARTOCK: THE FORMER CHAPEL AT MILTON

MARTOCK: THE TREASURER'S HOUSE

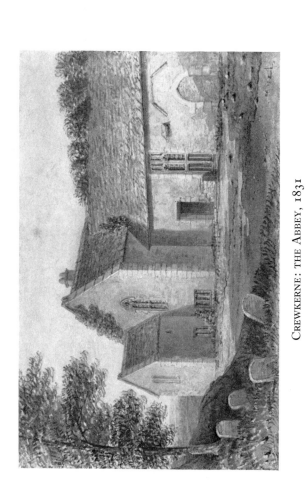

CREWKERNE: THE ABBEY, 1831

SOUTH PETHERTON: KING INA'S PALACE, 1851

1851 were not natives, as might be expected from the fluctuating population figures.[15] Apart from farm labourers there were ten glovers, two dress-makers, and two hand-loom weavers making sail-cloth.[16] Agriculture was the main occupation in the 1970s, though part of the southern portion of the parish was occupied by the Windwhistle Golf and Country Club.

Fields called Mill mead in Dowlish Wake and Mill mead and Mill hams in Cudworth, either side of the Wallbrook at the southern tip of Dowlish Wake parish, suggest the site of a water-mill.[17] Only traces of sluice-gates remain.

LOCAL GOVERNMENT. No manor court rolls are known to survive. An 18th-century conversion of a copyhold to a leasehold tenancy referred to copy of a court held in 1656,[18] but leases from 1719 onwards imply that courts were not then held, and some properties in the manor were let with the condition of suit of court to West Dowlish or Dillington should the tenants at any time be summoned.[19] Lands outside the parish, including property in Dinnington in 1370 and at Illeigh in Knowle St. Giles in 1497, were held of Cudworth manor.[20] In contrast, the property of St. Katherine's chantry, Chard, later to become Bonner's Leaze, was in 1576 held for suit of court to South Petherton manor.[21] The prebendary of Cudworth exercised a peculiar jurisdiction in the parish at least from the 16th century,[22] and a will was proved before his official in 1819.[23] His last visitation was held apparently in 1858.[24]

The parish formed a complete tithing, and the tithingman had access to the stocks in 1676.[25] There were two churchwardens, two sidesmen, a constable, and two overseers in the 17th century,[26] and in the early 19th the wardens were chosen by the ratepayers without reference to the minister, but were never sworn.[27] By 1870 one man was sole warden and overseer.[28] By 1784 there were two highway surveyors,[29] and the summary accounts for one waywarden survive for 1793–1802.[30]

In 1837 the parish possessed two unoccupied cottages, formerly used as poorhouses.[31] These were ordered to be sold, though in 1841 they were still known as the parish house.[32] They stood at Weare and in 1886 were occupied as a smithy.[33] The parish became part of the Chard poor-law union in 1836.[34]

CHURCH. About 1186–8 Alan de Furneaux, with the consent of his son Geoffrey, granted the church of Cudworth and the chapel of Knowle St. Giles to Wells cathedral to support the common fund.[35] Almost immediately the estate was converted to form the endowment of a prebend.[36] No vicarage was ordained, and the parish was served by stipendiary chaplains[37] until 1728, when the living became a perpetual curacy by a grant from Queen Anne's Bounty to meet a private benefaction.[38] The curate was occasionally described as vicar during the 19th century.[39] The benefice became a vicarage in 1886 on its union with Chillington, with an incumbent resident in the former prebendal house, given by the Ecclesiastical Commissioners.[40]

Successive curates were appointed by the pre-bendaries themselves or, from the 17th century at the latest, by the lessees of the prebendal estate, who paid their stipends. Vacancies in 1856 and 1885 were filled by the bishop of Bath and Wells, and after 1886 the united benefice of Chillington and Cudworth was in the bishop's patronage.[41]

By 1650 the curate's stipend was £10.[42] From 1728 it was augmented with £200 from Queen Anne's Bounty to meet a similar sum from Mrs. Elizabeth Palmer's legacy,[43] and from 1733 the lessee of the prebend added a further £15.[44] It was further augmented in 1809, and by 1815 was worth £40.[45] By 1851 the income was given as £58 15s., which included rent and tithes from small properties in Barton St. David and Mark, purchased with augmentation money in 1729 and 1731.[46] The Ecclesiastical Commissioners were said to have given the 'estimated' value of the prebend, excluding Knowle, to the benefice in 1886.[47] There was no glebe in the parish by 1909, and the Barton land had then recently been sold.[48]

Under a lease of 1635 the curate was to be provided with 'convenient lodging and house room' in the prebendal house.[49] Subsequent lessees of the prebend had no such obligation: there was no resident minister by 1666,[50] and the 19th-century curates lived elsewhere and served other parishes. The curate's obligation from 1635 was to preach once a quarter.[51] In 1705 the wardens asked for a service each Sunday, complained in 1716 of services only once a fortnight, and reported in 1725 that the curate was not preaching every Sunday and was neglecting his duty.[52] Leases of the prebend from 1733 onwards required the minister to hold a

[15] H.O. 107/1928.
[16] Ibid.
[17] S.R.O. tithe awards.
[18] S.R.O., DD/PT, box 24: Speke to Baker.
[19] Ibid., Speke to Hull (1719) and Speke to Salisbury (1724).
[20] Cal. Inq. Misc. iii, pp. 288–9; Cal. Inq. p.m. Hen. VII, iii, p. 553.
[21] S.R.O., DD/SAS PR 225.
[22] S.R.S. xxi. 119.
[23] S.R.O., D/D/Ppb, box 8.
[24] Ibid.
[25] S.R.O., Q/SR 131/6.
[26] S.R.O., D/D/Rg 299; Som. Protestation Returns, ed. A. J. Howard and T. L. Stoate, 89.
[27] S.R.O., D/D/Ppb, box 8.
[28] S.R.O., DD/SAS (C/909), 15.
[29] S.R.O., DD/PT, box 24.
[30] Ibid.
[31] S.R.O., D/PS/ilm, box 16.
[32] S.R.O., tithe award.
[33] O.S. Map 6″, LXXXVIII. NW. (1886 edn.).

[34] Poor Law Com. 2nd Rep. p. 547.
[35] H.M.C. Wells, i. 42.
[36] Ibid. 42–3; confirmed ibid. 44, 309, 435.
[37] See below.
[38] Hodgson, Queen Anne's Bounty.
[39] S.R.O., D/D/B return 1815; Clergy List, 1869.
[40] Proc. Som. Arch. Soc. lix. 54; Lond. Gaz. 12 Feb. 1886.
[41] Proc. Som. Arch. Soc. lix. 53.
[42] Lambeth Palace MSS., COMM. XIIa/1 f. 118.
[43] Hodgson, Queen Anne's Bounty.
[44] S.R.O., DD/CC 5103.
[45] Hodgson, Queen Anne's Bounty; S.R.O., D/D/B return 1815.
[46] H.O. 129/318/4/2/2; S.R.O., DD/CC 5111.
[47] Proc. Som. Arch. Soc. lix. 51.
[48] Cudworth par. rec. inventory, 1909.
[49] Lambeth Palace MSS., COMM. XIIa/1 f. 118.
[50] S.R.O., D/D/Ppb, box 8.
[51] Lambeth Palace MSS., COMM. XIIa/1 f. 118.
[52] S.R.O., D/D/Ppb, box 8.

service each Sunday and Holy Day, to celebrate the Holy Communion once a quarter or once a month 'if he can get sufficient communicants', catechize the children publicly twelve times a year, and preach four sermons on specified subjects, three during Lent and the fourth at Christmas.[53] By 1815 a service and sermon were held each Sunday, alternately morning and afternoon. The then minister, John Cabell, lived at Thurlbear and also served Stoke St. Mary. His assistant curate, John Hawkes Mules, served Cudworth, Dowlish Wake, and Cricket Malherbie.[54] In 1827 Cabbell's assistant was Edward Bere, who lived at Chaffcombe, which he also served.[55] On Census Sunday 1851 the single service was attended by 41 people including 15

aisle. Both could have been reset. If not then either the aisle is the original church, being older than its arcade and the present nave and chancel, or subsequent alterations have removed all traces of the main part of the early building. The existing nave and chancel appear to be of late-13th-century origin and are peculiar for the variations in the thickness of the walls and for the irregular spacing of the three bays of the arcade. Early in the 14th century new windows were put into the eastern part of the chancel and the south wall of the nave. The west wall of the nave may have been largely rebuilt in the 15th century when the doorway, the window above it, and the buttresses were constructed and in the same century one new window was let into the south wall

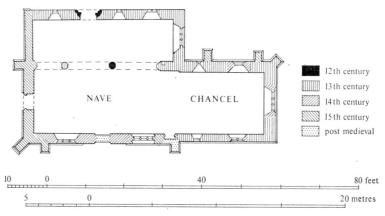

■	12th century
▦	13th century
▨	14th century
▧	15th century
▦	post medieval

THE CHURCH OF ST. MICHAEL, CUDWORTH

Sunday-school children. The average congregation was higher for the alternate afternoon services, reaching 80 people.[56] By 1858, when the cure was held by the rector of Cricket Malherbie, Holy Communion was celebrated monthly,[57] but in 1870, although there was a resident curate, Communion was again celebrated quarterly.[58]

Complaints at visitations in the 16th and 17th centuries were frequently against the prebendary about the disrepair of the chancel.[59] In 1577 the curate preached no sermons and the *Book of Homilies* had not been purchased.[60] Furnishings including the pulpit cloth and cushion needed repair or replacing in 1640 and in 1666 there were no communion rails. In 1677 the communion table was still not railed nor 'set where it ought to be', and in 1691–2 there was no cloth for the table. The general fabric of the church was poor in 1729 because of 'a vast quantity of earth and rubbish' lying against the walls.[61]

The church of *ST. MICHAEL* is built of ashlar and rubble with ashlar dressings, and has a chancel and nave with north aisle. The oldest features are the 12th-century north doorway and a small round-headed window set low down in the east wall of the

of the nave and the other was given new tracery. There is no chancel arch, but by the early 16th century there was a rood screen with a loft which was reached by a stair in a turret against the south wall. This turret and a south porch, of unknown date, have subsequently been removed and the south doorway has been blocked.[62]

The church furnishings include a large early-13th-century font with dog-tooth and cable mouldings and the remains of a mutilated 13th-century tomb top. During restoration the remains of a pre-Reformation altar top and fragments of an elaborately carved and painted statue niche were discovered. There are fragments of medieval glass in the east window of the aisle and a Jacobean pulpit. Nineteenth-century restoration[63] removed the box pews, but more extensive measures were taken in 1904. The ceiled and panelled barrel roof of the nave was restored as an open one and a new roof replaced a re-set late medieval one in the aisle. There is some good modern carving in the chancel. In the aisle is a monumental inscription to Sarah Smyth (d. 1684) whose grandfather had been exiled from Ypres by the duke of Alva.[64]

There are two bells: (i) 1607, Robert Wiseman

[53] S.R.O., DD/CC 5103.
[54] S.R.O., D/D/B return 1815.
[55] S.R.O., D/D/V return 1827.
[56] H.O. 129/318/4/2/2.
[57] S.R.O., D/D/Ppb 8; *Clergy List*, 1857.
[58] S.R.O., D/D/V return 1870.
[59] S.R.O., D/D/Ca 17 (1547), 57 (1577); D/D/Ppb 8

(1640, 1666, 1677).
[60] S.R.O., D/D/Ca 57.
[61] S.R.O., D/D/Ppb 8.
[62] G. A. Allan, 'Cudworth' (TS. in Taunton Castle).
[63] The vestry decided on total rebuilding c. 1843: Allen, 'Cudworth'.
[64] *Proc. Som. Arch. Soc.* xlix. i. 47.

of Montacute; (ii) 1678, Thomas Purdue.[65] The plate includes a cup of 1656 by 'C.P.'[66] The registers date from 1699 and appear to be complete.[67]

NONCONFORMITY. A small group of Bible Christians met for a few months in 1838.[68] Ten members were recorded in a revived group in 1861, but the cause did not survive after the end of 1862.[69]

EDUCATION. A Sunday school was opened in the parish in 1828, and by 1835 had 14 children. It was supported by subscriptions.[70] There were 17 pupils in 1846, taught by a master and a curate.[71] A school board was formed in 1875 and a day-school opened in 1877. It was a brick building, standing at Higher Weare, accommodating 30 children, with a teacher's house attached.[72] At its opening there were 23 children, including several from Chillington and Purtington.[73] There were 27 pupils in 1903[74] but numbers thereafter declined; the school was closed in 1926 and the pupils were transferred to Chillington.[75]

CHARITIES FOR THE POOR. None known.

DINNINGTON

DINNINGTON is a small parish sheltering below the 300 ft. scarp now marking the northern boundary of Hinton Park, 3 miles SW. of South Petherton. In 1839 it measured 514 a.,[1] but in 1885 this was increased to 584 a. by the absorption of detached parts of Kingstone.[2] The ancient boundaries with Kingstone to the north and west suggest a common estate and point to the ownership of both properties by Glastonbury abbey in the 10th and early 11th centuries.[3] The southern boundary, adjoining Hinton Park, is the creation of the early 18th century. Before that time Dinnington parish reached further south over the scarp to embrace the medieval warren, now a copse known as Old Warren.[4] Between 1704 and 1721 Earl Poulett created his New Park by buying out tenants both in Hinton and Dinnington,[5] and thereafter the park boundary seems to have been recognized as that of the parish. The total area lost to Dinnington may be represented by the 115 a. over which an agreement was made between Poulett and the rector.[6] A detached piece of land called the Castle Estate in the 19th century lay west of Allowenshay in Kingstone. It became part of Kingstone in 1885.[7]

Most of the present parish lies on the Yeovil Sands, the scarp of the park formed by Inferior Oolite topped with clay.[8] It is watered by a stream rising in the park towards the old warren which descends from the 300 ft. contour and drove a mill. In the 19th century a series of pools was constructed to provide power for a cheese and butter factory established at Pondhays farm by Earl Poulett.[9] Some of the buildings and sluices survived in 1973.

There were three and possibly four separate settlements in the ancient parish. Dinnington itself clustered on rising ground near the church, within a maze of deeply-cut lanes which characterize the western part of the parish. Pit Farm, on the Hinton road under the scarp, represents what remains of the hamlet of Pit, established by the 14th century, which included at least six dwellings in the 15th, and which was still a substantial cluster of cottages in the mid 19th century.[10] In the 15th century the manor also included the hamlet of Netherton, which had at least 5 tofts and 8 cottages in 1480.[11] This was probably the settlement on the lower ground beside the Foss, apparently intermixed with properties in Allowenshay manor in Kingstone, in which it formed a tithing.[12] A fourth settlement site, the detached Castle Estate west of Allowenshay, may have earlier origins. The personal name atte Castele occurs in 1327, and there was a site called Castellond in 1362, Castell place in 1568, and Castell in 1617.[13] Its elevated position above the manorial centre of Allowenshay, probably the core of the pre-Domesday estate which embraced both Dinnington and Kingstone,[14] suggests the possibility of a Saxon residence on the site.

The Foss Way runs through the parish, its course clear from the lower part of Dinnington village to the north-eastern boundary with Kingstone, but less so further south-west. Its route may have been via Nash Lane to Higher Chillington, or possibly further west.[15] Apparently a more important route in the Middle Ages, and certainly since, is the Ilminster–Crewkerne road. It was described in the 13th century as 'the way leading to St. Rayn's chapel',

[65] S.R.O., DD/SAS CH 16.
[66] Proc. Som. Arch. Soc. xlv. 18.
[67] Cudworth par. rec.
[68] S.R.O., D/N/spc 32.
[69] Ibid. 33.
[70] Educ. Enquiry Abstract, H.C. 62 (1835), xiii.
[71] Church Sch. Inquiry, 1846–7.
[72] Returns of Schs. [C. 7529], H.C. (1894), lxv.
[73] S.R.O., C/E, box 7, admission reg.
[74] Ibid. box 26.
[75] Ibid. box 7, log bk. 1903–26.
[1] S.R.O., tithe award. This article was completed in 1973.
[2] Local Govt. Bd. Prov. Orders Conf. Order (Poor Law), (No. 2), Act (1885).
[3] V.C.H. Som. iii. 203.

[4] S.R.O., DD/PT, box 40, accts. Aug. 1652, Aug. 1654.
[5] Ibid., box 25, Brice to Poulett, 1704, 1717, 1721; DD/SS, bdle. 23, Poulett to Dodge, 1708; D/D/Bg 2.
[6] S.R.O., tithe award.
[7] V.C.H. Som. iii. 203.
[8] Geol. Surv. Map 1", solid and drift, sheet 312 (1958 edn.).
[9] O.S. Map 6", Som. LXXXVIII. SE. (1904 edn.).
[10] S.R.S. iii. 197; C 140/77/81; S.R.O., tithe award.
[11] C 140/77/81.
[12] D.R.O., D54/M8, survey 1562–3.
[13] S.R.S. iii. 197; Cal. Inq. Misc. iii, p. 288; S.R.O., DD/PT, box 2; D/D/Rg 319.
[14] V.C.H. Som. iii. 203.
[15] Ibid. i. 348; I. D. Margary, Roman Roads in Britain, i. 113; see above, pp. 129, 141, and below, p. 151.

and until 1885 formed the boundary between Dinnington and Hinton at the edge of Hinton Park.[16]

In 1348 Nicholas Cadbury came to Dinnington to make a plan for building a hall for Thomas Chastelayne.[17] This house does not seem to have survived. Apart from the former parsonage house, now Parsonage Farm, the earliest buildings seem to be of the 17th century, including the Rose and Crown inn. The Orchard appears to have earlier ceiling beams but both the plan and the details of the stone work are of the early 18th century.

There was an inn at Dinnington by 1732. The several licensees named in the 18th century may have used more than one building.[18]

In 1563 there were 20 households in the parish.[19] In 1801 the population was 219 and in the next decade it reached 259. Thereafter it fluctuated until mid century and then in general fell, rapidly in the 1850s but then more gradually, reaching 69 in 1961 and 59 in 1971.[20]

MANOR. Siward the falconer held Dinnington in 1086.[21] Three virgates were held of Glastonbury abbey, what remained of the manor of Kingstone which had been lost to the count of Mortain.[22] Three hides, held by Edmar T.R.E., were held of the king's thegns. The separate identity of the Glastonbury estate survived in some degree until the late 14th century,[23] but the overlordship of the main estate became part of the honor of Gloucester. Roger de Clare had an interest in Seavington St. Michael in connexion with William the falconer c. 1201,[24] and by 1284–5 the manor was held of the earl of Gloucester.[25] It descended on the death of Gilbert de Clare in 1314 to the Despensers,[26] and from them (interrupted by forfeiture in 1400)[27] in 1439 to the Beauchamps on the death of Isabel, wife of Richard Beauchamp, earl of Warwick.[28] Through Anne (d. 1449), daughter of Henry Beauchamp, duke of Warwick, and wife of Richard Neville, earl of Warwick, the lordship passed in 1474 to Isabel (d. 1476), wife of George Plantagenet, duke of Clarence, and then to their son Edward, earl of Warwick (d. 1499).[29] On Warwick's attainder the lordship reverted to the Crown, and the manor was said in 1527 to have been held of the king as parcel of the duchy of Gloucester and of the honor of Gloucester.[30]

Siward the falconer, tenant in 1086, was apparently ancestor of the Falconer family who in the early

13th century had disputes over land in Seavington St. Michael. William the falconer occurs c. 1201,[31] followed in 1208–9 by Robert the falconer.[32] In or before 1246 the Falconer estates were divided between Avice and Joan, evidently co-heirs.[33] Dinnington was the share of Robert de la Linde, husband of Avice, to whom he was married by 1243.[34] In 1284–5 Alexander de la Linde held the manor of *DINNINGTON* in serjeanty as falconer of the earl of Gloucester.[35] Thomas de la Linde succeeded by 1314,[36] and his son Ellis in 1362.[37] Ellis died in 1386, leaving a son Alexander a minor.[38] Alexander was still alive in 1465; his son, also Alexander, died without issue in 1480, and the manor passed to his widow Edith for her life with remainder to Sir William Poulett.[39]

The manor then descended in the Poulett family like the manor of Hinton St. George. Much of the property was sold by the 8th Earl Poulett in 1941[40] and the remainder in 1968[41] but the lordship of the manor was retained by the earl at his death without heirs in 1973.[42]

The Lindes appear to have been resident at Dinnington by 1246.[43] The manor-house, no longer occupied by the lords of the manor after its acquisition by the Pouletts, was let to members of the Brice family between 1571 and 1771,[44] and thereafter to other tenants, a lease in 1790 including the right to a pew in the parish church.[45] The house ceased to be described as the capital mansion after 1811 and subsequently was known as Frog Farm.[46] In 1724 the house, on an elevated position above the church, comprised a hall, 'mattin chamber' or parlour, kitchen, cellar, and dairy room on the ground floor, and evidently originated a century earlier.[47]

ECONOMIC HISTORY. The manor of Dinnington measured 3 hides and 3 virgates in 1086, and included the small Glastonbury abbey property which was not recorded in detail. The manor proper had 2 hides in demesne, with one plough. Six villeins and 6 bordars had 2 ploughs. There were 8 a. of meadow, and pasture and wood both measuring 2 by 3 furlongs. The whole estate was worth 53s. 2d. in 1086, the larger holding having doubled in value in the previous twenty years.[48]

Between the 11th and the 16th centuries there is little evidence of economic activity in the parish. In 1387 there were said to be 60 a. of heath,[49] and the manor was extended at £15 in 1414.[50] By the early

[16] Hook Manor, Donhead St. Andrew, Arundell MSS., G 588.
[17] *Cal. Inq. p.m.* xi, pp. 292–3.
[18] S.R.O., Q/RL; DD/PT, box 25.
[19] B.L. Harl. MS. 594, f. 56.
[20] *V.C.H. Som.* ii. 348; *Census.*
[21] *V.C.H. Som.* i. 467, 523.
[22] Ibid. iii. 204.
[23] *Cal. Inq. p.m.* xvi, p. 228.
[24] *S.R.S.* xi, p. 13.
[25] *Feud. Aids*, iv. 283.
[26] *Cal. Inq. p.m.* v, p. 338.
[27] *Cal. Inq. Misc.* vii, p. 271.
[28] *Complete Peerage.*
[29] *Rot. Parl.* (Rec. Com.), vi. 160.
[30] S.R.O., DD/PT, box 1, ct. roll.
[31] *S.R.S.* xi, p. 13.
[32] *Curia Reg. R.* v, pp. 113, 214.
[33] *S.R.S.* vi. 127.

[34] Ibid. xi, p. 182.
[35] *Feud. Aids*, iv. 283.
[36] *Cal. Close, 1313–18*, 136; *Cal. Inq. p.m.* v, p. 338; *Feud. Aids*, iv. 331.
[37] *Cal. Inq. Misc.* iii, p. 288.
[38] *Cal. Inq. p.m.* xvi, p. 228.
[39] C 140/77/81.
[40] Sale cat. University Estate, 1958.
[41] Sale cat. Hinton St. George Estate, 1968.
[42] Ex inf. Mr. S. G. Lawrence, Crewkerne.
[43] *S.R.S.* vi. 127.
[44] S.R.O., DD/PT, boxes 2, 16, 25.
[45] Ibid., box 25.
[46] The property descent was traced by Mr. R. G. Gilson, Dinnington.
[47] S.R.O., DD/SP, box 15; DD/V, Chard R.D.
[48] *V.C.H. Som.* i. 467, 523.
[49] *Cal. Close 1385–9*, 365.
[50] *Cal. Inq. Misc.* vii, p. 271.

16th century there were three freeholdings on the manor, held respectively by the Viel, Ousley, and Middleton families.[51] The Ousleys had been taxed at a higher rate than the lord of the manor in 1327,[52] though the size of their holding in the 16th century is not known. John Viel and Peter Brice, successor to George Middleton by 1559,[53] were also free tenants in the adjacent manor of Allowenshay in Kingstone.[54] The Brices were evidently the most substantial family in the parish in the 16th and 17th centuries.[55] At his death in 1570–1 Peter Brice held not only the Middleton freeholding but 104 a. of barton (demesne) land by copy, including the capital mansion.[56] Hugh, his son, became armigerous from 1573;[57] Worthington Brice, grandson of Hugh, compounded for his estates in 1646,[58] and by c. 1665 three members of the family between them held nearly 170 a. of land from the manor excluding freeholds.[59] Their tomb-chests in the churchyard attest their prosperity.

The process of inclosure at Dinnington closely paralleled the pattern of its neighbour Kingstone.[60] There is evidence for seven distinct areas of common arable cultivation in the 1560s, some of which were earlier the separate furlongs of former medieval arable fields. Inclosure had already disposed of North field, between Allowenshay mead and Netherton, parts of which were under pasture by 1532. The same process had affected East field, between Pit and the Foss. Inclosure of the remaining common arable was achieved in the 1560s by committees of tenants in the manor court, appointed to measure holdings, arrange exchanges, and create closes. By this process the great western field was permanently divided, though its site remained largely arable. The common field called Vanly in the late 16th century may have lain in that part of the parish taken into Hinton Park.[61] By 1570–1 the most substantial holding in the parish contained no common arable land,[62] and by 1593–4 the perambulation was evidently abandoned because the hedges and pales impeded progress.[63] In contrast the common meadow remained uninclosed until after 1839.[64]

Conversion of copyholds to leases for lives was well advanced by the mid 17th century.[65] The Brices held nearly a third of the manor, John Brice having a farm of 116 a.[66] The farm next in size was 61 a.[67] Some of the Brices seem to have settled elsewhere at the end of the century, Worthington

(d. 1719–20) becoming a clothier at Shepton Mallet.[68] Though continuing tenants on a smaller scale,[69] and retaining occupation of the manor-house until 1771,[70] they gave place to the Easons, Hutchinses, Becks, and Donnes in the 1720s and to the Darbys in the 1750s.[71]

The manor in the 18th century was worth less than £29,[72] but between 1791 and 1819 rackrenting gave place to improved rents.[73] Pondhays farm was at first the largest holding. In 1819 it measured over 140 a., not all in the parish, and was let at £300 a year.[74] By 1851 there were five farms centred in Dinnington, the largest later known as Knott's farm. Between them they employed 10 men, 16 boys, and 3 women.[75] The parish was then equally divided between arable and grassland, with over 80 a. of wood and over 40 a. of orchards and gardens.[76] By 1905 grassland had increased, partly at the expense of wood, though dairying came later to the parish than to some of its neighbours.[77] Dinnington was largely under grass in 1973.

In 1851 flax was still grown and gave employment to six flax-dressers.[78] A flax-grower was still in business in 1871.[79] Men dealt in pigs, poultry, eggs, and potatoes, evidence of mixed farming on a small scale.[80] The village had two shops in the mid 19th century.[81] Women were employed in a variety of occupations including gloving (18), dress-making (4), and making smock frocks and straw bonnets.[82] By 1973 farming was the only occupation within the parish.

There was a water-mill at Dinnington in 1086, valued at 8d.[83] It was mentioned in 1480.[84] This mill may have been rebuilt shortly before 1566.[85] It was held by the Brice family in the 17th century and in 1653 was described as 'two water grist mills called Dinnington mills'.[86] The mill evidently stood on a site which was taken into Hinton Park in the early 18th century; its precise location is not known, but it was adjacent to the medieval warren of Dinnington, the position of which is represented by woodland called Old Warren.[87] The mill presumably ceased to exist on or before the formation of the park.

LOCAL GOVERNMENT. Extracts from court rolls survive intermittently for 1523–54 and continuously from 1559 until 1573,[88] and there are

[51] S.R.O., DD/SS, bdle. 1.
[52] S.R.S. iii. 197.
[53] S.R.O., DD/PT, box 1.
[54] D.R.O., D54/M8.
[55] S.R.S. xx. 45. See also Req. 2/30/96; Req. 2/75/42; D.R.O. D54/M8.
[56] S.R.O., DD/PT, box 2.
[57] Visit. Som. 1623 (Harl. Soc. xl), 14.
[58] Cal. Cttee. for Compounding, ii. 1128.
[59] S.R.O., DD/PT, box 46.
[60] V.C.H. Som. iii. 207.
[61] S.R.O., DD/SS, bdle. 1; DD/PT, boxes 1–2, 25.
[62] S.R.O., DD/PT, box 2, ct. roll extract 1570–1.
[63] S.R.O., D/D/Ca 98.
[64] S.R.O., tithe award.
[65] S.R.O., DD/PT, box 46, survey.
[66] Ibid.; DD/SS, bdle. 23.
[67] S.R.O., DD/PT, box 46.
[68] Som. Wills, ed. Brown, iii. 98. His brother was known in 1699 as of Crewkerne, gentleman: S.R.O., DD/SS, bdle. 23.
[69] S.R.O., DD/SS, bdle. 23, Poulett to Brice, 1719.

[70] S.R.O., DD/PT, box 25.
[71] Ibid. boxes 25, 27, 44.
[72] Ibid. box 44.
[73] Ibid. boxes 14, 44.
[74] Ibid. box 40.
[75] H.O. 107/1928.
[76] S.R.O., tithe award.
[77] Statistics supplied by the then Bd. of Agric. 1905.
[78] H.O. 107/1928.
[79] Morris & Co., Dir. Som. (1872).
[80] H.O. 107/1928.
[81] P.O. Dir. Som. (1859, 1861).
[82] H.O. 107/1928.
[83] V.C.H. Som. i. 523.
[84] C 140/77/81.
[85] S.R.O., DD/PT, box 2.
[86] S.R.O., DD/SS, bdle. 23; Som. Wills, ed. Brown, v. 18.
[87] S.R.O., DD/SS, bdle. 23.
[88] S.R.O., DD/PT, boxes 1–2; DD/SS, bdle. 1. The manor extended into the parish of Seavington St. Mary: S.R.O., DD/SS, bdle. 23.

court books for 1651–77, 1703–10, and 1715–26. Copies of court baron entries survive until 1815.[89] There were two courts annually in the 16th century, usually described as manor courts but occasionally as courts leet, apparently with no distinction of business. Apart from usual control over farming practice and local custom, the court appointed a committee to deal with inclosure in 1569 and deprived a copyholder of his land for immoral behaviour in 1533.[90] From 1566 the office of hayward was held in rotation among the tenants.[91]

No records of parish government survive, though there were two overseers in the 17th century.[92] In the 18th century there were parish poorhouses at Pit.[93] Five freehold cottages formerly used as poorhouses were sold in 1837.[94] The parish became part of the Chard poor-law union in 1836.[95]

CHURCH. A church had evidently been established in Dinnington by c. 1207.[96] Throughout the Middle Ages it was a chapel of Seavington St. Michael, though incumbents in 1254 and 1538 were described as rectors of Dinnington,[97] and the rectory house was within the chapelry. From c. 1575 the chapel was served by the rector of Hinton St. George, and was temporarily regarded as annexed to that benefice.[98] Thereafter it returned to the jurisdiction of the rectors of Seavington St. Michael who, between 1779 and 1861, were also rectors of Hinton St. George and lived there.[99] Since 1913 the chapelry has been separated from Seavington and joined with Hinton.[1]

The tithes of Dinnington were normally reckoned with those of Seavington St. Michael.[2] They were commuted to a rent-charge of £147 in 1839.[3] Just over 25 a. of benefice land lay in Dinnington in 1617, including the glebe house, two barns, two stalls, and a stable.[4] The size of the glebe remained constant until after 1635,[5] but an exchange was effected in 1709 in connexion with the extension of Hinton Park.[6] By 1839 the area of the glebe had been reduced to nearly 14 a.,[7] worth in 1851 £38.[8] In 1840 the glebe house and land were let as a small farm.[9] By 1886 it was known as Parsonage Farm, and was so named in 1973.[10] The house incorporates the remains of a medieval hall, with parlour to the south and later kitchen to the north.

In 1350, presumably because of a shortage of clergy, the rector of Seavington St. Michael was licensed for four months to celebrate mass on Sundays and feast days at Dinnington despite having done so at Seavington on the same days.[11] The rector employed a curate in 1532,[12] and by 1535 the curate enjoyed a fixed stipend of £4 13s. 4d. as chaplain of Dinnington.[13] The chapelry was served by curates from c. 1567 until c. 1575,[14] but in the early 17th century was apparently served by resident rectors. Nevertheless Edward Barret, rector 1580–1632, was in 1623 accused of failing to preach monthly sermons, not catechizing, and not reading prayers on weekdays at Dinnington.[15] The complaint about catechizing was repeated in 1629, though it may have been done by the curate from Seavington.[16] Peter Glasbroke, rector 1652–76, also served Seavington St. Mary and Lopen in 1654–5.[17] There were 17 communicants in the parish in 1776.[18] From 1779 there has been no resident clergyman, though Henry Stambury, 1789–1837, served Dinnington in person and in 1815 held a service each Sunday and celebrated the Holy Communion three times a year.[19] On Census Sunday 1851 the afternoon congregation numbered 100, besides 24 Sunday-school pupils.[20] By 1870 two services were held each Sunday.[21]

The church of ST. NICHOLAS, so dedicated by 1348,[22] is a small building of Ham stone and ashlar and has a chancel with north vestry and a nave with south porch and a western bellcot. The building was much restored in 1863 but the features appear to reproduce the original detail.[23] The small chancel was of the 14th century, the chancel arch, nave, and south porch were of the 15th, but the basic structure of the nave was probably earlier. The 13th-century font has been recut. During restoration a gallery was removed, together with a dormer window.[24] The chancel contains a large incised slab commemorating Worthington Brice (d. 1649) and the churchyard has several 17th- and 18th-century tomb-chests.

The plate includes a cup and cover by 'M.H.' dated 1574.[25] The two bells were recast in 1870 by Llewellins and James of Bristol.[26] There are registers for baptisms, marriages, and burials for 1593–1611 and 1696–1752, for baptisms and burials from 1759, and for marriages from 1754. In 1789 the marriage registers were reported 'as incomplete and mutilated as the rest'.[27]

---

[89] S.R.O., DD/PT, boxes 23, 25, 31; ct. bks. *penes* Countess Poulett, Jersey.
[90] S.R.O., DD/PT, boxes 1–2.
[91] Ibid. box 2.
[92] *S.R.S.* xxxiv. 80; *Som. Protestation Returns*, ed. A. J. Howard and T. L. Stoate, 92; Dwelly, *Hearth Tax*, 148.
[93] S.R.O., DD/PT, box 43, survey. The houses had been in hand 'for many years'.
[94] S.R.O., D/PS/ilm.
[95] *Poor Law Com. 2nd Rep.* p. 547.
[96] *Cal. Pat.* 1388–92, 149 is a reference to William, clerk of Dinnington. Dated by another witness, John de Ikeford, to 1207: *Cirencester Cart.* ed. C. D. Ross, ii. 523.
[97] *S.R.S.* xiv, p. 50; xxi. 40.
[98] *S. & D. N. & Q.* xiv. 32.
[99] See below.
[1] *Dioc. Dir.*
[2] S.R.O., D/D/Rg 319.
[3] S.R.O., tithe award.
[4] S.R.O., D/D/Rg 319.
[5] Ibid. 317.
[6] S.R.O., D/D/Bg 2.

[7] S.R.O., tithe award.
[8] H.O. 129/318/4/4/4.
[9] S.R.O., D/D/V return 1840.
[10] O.S. Map 6″, Som. LXXXVIII. NE. (1886 edn.).
[11] *S.R.S.* x, p. 635.
[12] S.R.O., D/D/Vc 20.
[13] *Valor Eccl.* (Rec. Com.) i. 164.
[14] *S. & D. N. & Q.* xiv. 32.
[15] *S.R.S.* xliii. 74–5, 112, 137.
[16] S.R.O., D/D/Ca 266.
[17] S.R.O., DD/PT, box 40.
[18] S.R.O., D/D/V Dioc. bk.
[19] S.R.O., D/D/B return 1815; D/D/V return 1827; D/P/dinn 2/1/1–2; D/P/sea. ml 2/1/1.
[20] H.O. 129/318/4/4/4.
[21] S.R.O., D/D/V return 1870.
[22] *Cal. Inq. p.m.* xi, p. 292.
[23] Dated plan in vestry.
[24] Taunton Castle, Pigott Colln.
[25] *Proc. Som. Arch. Soc.* xlv. 18.
[26] H. T. Ellacombe, *Som. Bells*, 45.
[27] S.R.O., D/P/dinn 1/1/1–5.

NONCONFORMITY. There were 10 dissenters in 1776.[28] In 1808 a house was licensed for worship, and in the following year was used by a group of Wesleyan Methodists. There were 15 members in 1810, but the cause seems to have lapsed c. 1822.[29] From 1824 until 1830 a group of Bible Christians met at Pit, and, after revival in 1838, there were 11 members in 1841.[30] On Census Sunday 1851 there were congregations of 26 in the afternoon and 46 in the evening in a room which held 35.[31] A chapel was erected c. 1873 and it continued in use by Methodists until 1956.[32] From c. 1964 it was used by a branch of the Elim Pentecostal church at Merriott.[33] The small plain building of local stone has window-frames of cast iron and retains its original fittings.

EDUCATION. In 1818 the curate had a day-school for about 20 children, who were also taught the catechism on Sundays.[34] By 1866 a day-school was held by the wife of the parish clerk and shop-keeper. It was still open in 1872.[35]

CHARITIES FOR THE POOR. None known.

DOWLISH WAKE

THE PARISH of Dowlish Wake, also called East Dowlish to distinguish it from its neighbour West Dowlish in Bulstone hundred, lies 2¼ miles south-east of Ilminster at the western end of the hundred.[1] The name Dowlish is thought to derive from the Dowlish brook which runs through the village,[2] the additional name from its early owners. The ancient parish, nearly 1¾ mile from north to south and ¾ mile from east to west, measured 794 a. until 1885 when a detached portion 1½ mile west at Bere Mills Farm was absorbed into Knowle St. Giles, leaving a total of 626 a.[3]

The main part of the parish is roughly rectangular, its boundaries following no natural feature except a stretch of the Wall brook, a feeder of Dowlish brook in the south-east, shared with Cudworth. In the north it impinges closely on Kingstone village, and at Wake Hill, also in the north, and in the east towards Ludney, it keeps to the highest ground, well over 300 ft. The boundary with West Dowlish is followed by Chard Lane[4] at its southern end. Dowlish brook, running north-west through the centre of the parish, and a smaller stream from Cudworth which joins it just west of the village, divide the parish into three parts. To the north and north-east, on the rising ground, the limestone junction beds and Yeovil Sands provided the largest area of arable and accounted for most of the known arable fields.[5] In the south-west, where the land rises more gradually towards the Windwhistle ridge, the poorer soils over the greensands and Pennards Sands were earlier inclosed for pasture from open arable; and in the south-east, on similar soils, there was a greater predominance of meadow watered by two streams.[6]

Dowlish Wake village is one of the largest in the immediate area. With the exception of 19th- and 20th-century buildings in the north at Wake Hill and close to Kingstone village, settlement is nucle-ated, largely grouped along the curving main or East Dowlish street.[7] North of the Dowlish brook in some isolation on the scarp above the village are the church and manor-house, joined in the 19th century by Parke House, the road running a tor-tuous course in a sandy hollow way evidently to avoid a direct route through the manor grounds. Further south a triangular green[8] was formed at the junction of the main street with a road to Dowlish mills and beyond; and beside it stood the dower house and a second demesne farm. Beyond the stream a further triangular area marks a second junction and the beginnings of more intensive settlement of tenants' houses and farms, the medi-eval rectory-house, and 19th-century shops, smithy, and inn. The 20th century has contributed a num-ber of bungalows and houses within this frame-work.

From the main street roads radiate somewhat indirectly, south and west to Cudworth, Chard,[9] and Oxenford (in West Dowlish), north and west to Ilminster, east to Ludney, and south-east to Chillington. Formerly more important roads cut or skirted the extremities of the parish: a section of Oldway Lane between Ludney and Cudworth marks the line either of the Foss Way or of an early deviation;[10] and the Crewkerne–Ilminster road through Kingstone, the north-eastern boundary, was turnpiked in 1759, and a stop gate and toll cottage erected on the road into Dowlish village.[11]

The earlier buildings in the parish are generally of local limestone, with thatched or tiled roofs. Higher Dowlish Farm is a substantial two-storeyed building with attics of the earlier 17th century, but has an unusual 3-roomed plan and contemporary

[28] S.R.O., D/D/V Dioc. bk.
[29] S.R.O., D/D/Rm, box 2; D/N/spc 1.
[30] S.R.O., D/N/spc 31–2.
[31] H.O. 129/318/4/4/5.
[32] S.R.O., D/N/spc 33; ex inf. the Revd. W. G. Butler, Crewkerne.
[33] Ex inf. Mr. A. J. King, Crewkerne.
[34] Digest of Returns to Sel. Cttee. on Educ. of Poor, H.C. 224 (1819), ix (2).
[35] P.O. Dir. Som. (1866, 1875); Morris & Co. Dir. Som. (1872). It was not mentioned in 1875.
[1] This article was completed in 1973.
[2] S.R.S. xiv, pp. 36–7.
[3] Local Govt. Bd. Order 16,420; Kelly's Dir. Som.

(1902). West Dowlish and Dowlish Wake were amal-gamated as a civil parish in 1933: Som. Review Order.
[4] S.R.O., DD/CN, box 11, lease 30 Sept. 1774.
[5] S.R.O., D/D/Rg 302; DD/CN, box 11; tithe award.
[6] Heathfield occurs in 1674 (S.R.O., DD/SPK 2/10); Furze hill and close in 1838 (S.R.O., tithe award).
[7] Geol. Surv. Map 1", solid and drift, sheet 312 (1958 edn.).
[8] S.R.O., DD/CN, box 11, lease 10 Oct. 1748.
[9] Ibid., lease 14 May 1747.
[10] Also occurs as Stretford Lane. See above, pp. 129, 141, 147.
[11] S.R.O., D/T/ilm 1; Ilminster Turnpike Act, 32 Geo. II, c. 39 (Priv. Act).

outshuts. Many original fittings survive and there is a cruck roof. The Dower House is dated 1674 and was leased to women of the Speke family in the later 18th century.[12] Perry's cider mill has a smoke-blackened cruck roof, but possesses no features suggesting residential use. Parke House occurs c. 1811 and Wake Hill was built by Hugh Speke before 1831.[13]

There was a licensed victualler in the parish by 1735 and three by 1751. The Horseshoe, mentioned in 1769,[14] became the New Inn between 1812 and 1822,[15] and continues under that name. The Folly, more usually called the Castle, first mentioned in 1792,[16] lay on the northern boundary in Kingstone village. It was converted to a private dwelling in 1972.[17]

The Dowlish Friendly Society was established in 1837 and dissolved in 1955. Meetings were held in the schoolroom and the feast day celebrated on Trinity Tuesday.[18] A men's club meeting at the Reading Room was founded in 1921, moved to the rectory-house in 1935, and closed in 1948. A drama group, the Dowlish Players, occurs in 1928.[19] The former school, on the west side of the church, has been converted to a village hall, renamed the Speke Hall, since 1955.[20]

The parish had 16 households in 1612.[21] From a total of 241 in 1801 its population fluctuated, rising to 380 in 1831 but falling to 319 in the next twenty years. The removal of Bere in 1885 resulted in a fall to 290 by 1891, and subsequently numbers fell to 212 in 1901,[22] and 176 in 1921. They rose slightly to 187 in 1931, and the union with West Dowlish in 1933 caused an abrupt increase to 270 in 1951. A fall to 228 in 1961 has been followed by a small rise, to 253 in 1971.[23]

John Hanning Speke (1827–64), African explorer and discoverer of the source of the Nile, is buried in the church.[24] Ludwig Petterson (1868–1934), born in Bergen, Norway, was a Klondyke pioneer in 1898. He farmed in the parish by 1927, and is buried in the churchyard.[25]

Eight parishioners were reported to have joined the Monmouth rebellion in 1685.[26]

MANOR. The manor of *DOWLISH* was held T.R.E. by Alward, but by 1086 had passed to the bishop of Coutances, under whom it was tenanted by William de Moncels.[27] The overlord in 1284–5 and 1303 was Henry de Lacy, earl of Lincoln (d. 1311),[28] and in 1348 the earl of Gloucester.[29] By 1359 the overlordship had passed to the countess of Surrey, who held it of her honor of Trowbridge,[30] and by 1361 to William Montacute, earl of Salisbury.[31] In 1420 it was stated to be held of the honor of Trowbridge, parcel of the duchy of Lancaster, and it was still so held in 1584.[32]

The manor was probably held in the later 12th century by Ralph Wake (I).[33] His widow Christine, later wife of Richard Wild (*salvagius*), received dower when her son Ralph Wake (II) succeeded in 1214.[34] A grant of land in Dowlish formerly of Ralph Wake was made by the Crown in 1216,[35] but in 1225 Ralph (II) seems still to have held land in Dowlish.[36] In 1230 his widow Hawise (d. c. 1244) recovered her dower in Dowlish and Bere,[37] and the manor passed to her son Andrew Wake.[38] Andrew (d. before 1286) was succeeded by his son Ralph (III),[39] by which time, if not before, the estate had split into the two manors of *EAST DOWLISH* or *DOWLISH WAKE* and West Dowlish, both held by the Wakes.[40] Ralph (III) was still in possession in 1290[41] but by 1303 had been followed by his son John (d. 1348).[42] Under a settlement of 1325 the manor then passed to John's eldest daughter Isabel (d. 1359), wife of John Kaynes (I),[43] and subsequently to her son Thomas (d. 1361).[44] The latter was succeeded in turn by his son John (II) (d. 1419), grandson John (III) (d. 1420),[45] and great-granddaughter Joan Kaynes (d. 1462), married successively to John Speke (I) (d. 1441) and Hugh Champernowne (d. 1482).[46]

Under a settlement made in 1448 the estate passed on Champernowne's death to William Speke (d. 1508), son of John (I), for life, and subsequently to his nephew John Speke (III) (d. 1518), son of John (II).[47] John (IV) (d. 1524), son of John (III), was succeeded by his son Sir George Speke (I) (d. 1528),[48] who left the manor to his nephew Thomas (later Sir Thomas) (d. 1551), son of John Speke (V).[49] Thereafter it descended through the Speke family with Cudworth manor until the death of George Speke in 1753, when it passed to his daughter Mary Speke of Sowton (Devon).[50] On her death the manor was inherited by her cousin William

---

[12] S.R.O., DD/CN, box 11, lease 1 Apr. 1801.
[13] See p. 155; S.R.O., Q/RE, land tax assessments.
[14] S.R.O., Q/RL.
[15] S.R.O., DD/CN, box 17, bdle. 3/1.
[16] Ibid. box 11.
[17] Local information.
[18] M. Fuller, *West-Country Friendly Socs.* 84–6, 112, 135, 151.
[19] S.R.O., DD/X/TR 3, 4.
[20] Char. Com. files.
[21] S.R.O., DD/HI, box 9.
[22] *V.C.H. Som.* ii. 348.
[23] *Census.*
[24] *D.N.B.*
[25] M.I. in chyd.; *Kelly's Dir. Som.* (1927).
[26] B.L. Add. MS. 30077, f. 35.
[27] *V.C.H. Som.* i. 445.
[28] *Feud. Aids*, iv. 283, 315; *Complete Peerage*, s.v. Lincoln.
[29] *Cal. Inq. p.m.* ix, p. 109.
[30] Ibid. x, p. 399.
[31] Ibid. xi, p. 79.
[32] *Cal. Close*, 1419–22, 78–9.

[33] *H.M.C. Wells*, i. 309; Dugdale, *Mon.* v. 26.
[34] *Pipe R.* 1214 (P.R.S. N.S. xxxv), 101; *Rot. de Ob. et Fin.* (Rec. Com.), 529, 536.
[35] *Mem. R.* 1216 (P.R.S. N.S. xxxi), 144.
[36] *S.R.S.* xi, p. 46.
[37] *Cur. Reg. R.* 1227–30, 570; *Ex. e Rot. Fin.* (Rec. Com.), i. 414.
[38] *Ex e Rot. Fin.* (Rec. Com.), i. 414; *S.R.S.* vi. 369.
[39] *S.R.S.* vi. 267; *The Genealogist*, N.S. xii. 30.
[40] *Feud. Aids*, iv. 283.
[41] *Cal. Chart. R.* 1257–1300, 349.
[42] *Feud. Aids*, iv. 315; *The Genealogist*, N.S. xii. 30; *Cal. Inq. p.m.* ix, p. 109.
[43] *Cal. Inq. p.m.* ix, p. 109; x, p. 399; *S.R.S.* xii. 104.
[44] *Cal. Inq. p.m.* x, p. 399; xi, p. 79.
[45] Ibid, xi, p. 79; C 138/42/69; C 138/51/95.
[46] *Cal. Close*, 1419–22, 78–9; *S.R.S.* xxii. 117–18, 200–1; C 140/7/13; C 140/84/32.
[47] C 140/7/13; C 142/33/30.
[48] C 142/33/30; *Visits. Som. 1531, 1573*, ed. F. W. Weaver, 4; *S.R.S.* xix. 275; C 142/44/119.
[49] C 142/50/121; C 142/97/117; *S.R.S.* xxi. 125–6.
[50] S.R.O., DD/CN, box 11.

Speke of Jordans in Ashill (d. 1839), and subsequently descended to his son William (d. 1887) and grandson William (d. 1908).[51] On the death of the last without issue the estate was left to his nephew W. H. Speke (d. 1944). The estate was subdivided and sold in 1920 but the lordship was not included in the sale,[52] and passed to Mr. P. G. H. Speke of Ashill, great-nephew and heir of W. H. Speke.

The manor-house, known as Dowlish Farm by 1688,[53] consists of only part of a larger building whose origin is suggested by a length of walling to the north of the churchyard. Between this and the existing building is a wide gateway, now blocked, which may have been the entry to a courtyard, and the range on the east side is probably of the late 15th or early 16th century. It has buttresses, mullioned windows, and in its northern part a roof, formerly open to at least the first floor, with arch-braces which terminate in pendants. Beyond this the present kitchen range is probably of slightly later date. To the north extensive farm buildings, ostensibly of the 19th century, may incorporate earlier footings.

The detached area of the parish at Bere, held with Dowlish Wake manor by 1230,[54] was described as a separate manor in the 17th and 18th centuries[55] although it continued in common ownership with the principal manor.

ECONOMIC HISTORY. The Domesday account of Dowlish as two manors probably comprehends both Dowlish Wake and West Dowlish, although the relative sizes of the two estates do not correspond with the later areas of the two parishes. Before the Conquest the larger estate of 7 hides had been held in two units of 4 and 3 hides. When combined T.R.W., the demesne was worked with 2 ploughs by 11 bordars and 2 serfs, and 11 villeins had 5 ploughs. There were then 44 a. of meadow, pasture measuring 4 by 4 furlongs and 20 a., and wood 8 by 3 furlongs and 20 a. Stock on the demesne comprised a riding-horse, 6 head of cattle, 19 swine, and 21 sheep. The smaller holding of 2¼ hides had 3 bordars and a serf with one plough on the demesne, and 3 villein tenants. Stock was 4 beasts, 7 swine, and 32 sheep. The larger estate was valued at £6 10s. and the smaller at 23s. or 24s.[56] Later valuations usually combined the manors of Dowlish Wake and West Dowlish, though in 1361 Dowlish Wake alone was worth £8,[57] and in 1482 £23 13s. 4d., a sum which included land in 'Wythele' and Bere.[58]

By the 16th century the medieval open fields had been divided into several smaller units, but some survived: Langcombe (later Kingstone or East Dowlish field), Fournecombe (later Middle field), and Leadowne occur in 1557; and Cod or Quod, Hill field, and Langforland occur c. 1600.[59] By 1674 lands had been inclosed out of Heathfield,[60] but parts were still open in 1704 though not by 1723.[61] Cod and probably Hill field were inclosed by 1772, Leadowne by 1794, and Kingstone field by 1838.[62] West mead was inclosed by 1829, Yewcrafte (Yolcraft, Yellcroft, Eel Croft) later Common mead by 1838.[63] By 1838 there were c. 400 a. of arable in the parish and 309 a. of grassland,[64] and by 1905 approximately equal quantities of arable and grass.[65]

The common change from copyhold in the 16th century to leasehold for 99 years or lives in the 17th occurs in Dowlish Wake, the units varying between cottage holdings and farms up to 35 a.[66] The largest farm was the demesne attached to the manor-house, leased to John Hanning in 1772 with 113 a. in the parish, 183 a. in West Dowlish, and 36 a. on the border between them.[67] Subsequently the amalgamation of Higher and Lower Dowlish farms created a larger unit, measuring 304 a. in 1838. The manor-house estate, known as Dowlish farm, was then 295 a., Bere Mills farm was 125 a., and Levi Wallbridge held 75 a. based on the present Wallbridge farm.[68] By 1850 the manor-house was held with 316 a., Higher and Lower Dowlish farms remained at 304 a., Bere Mills farm was 169 a., and Wallbridge farm 88 a.[69] These farms continued to be the principal ones in the parish. By the time of the sale of the Speke estate in 1920 these same units remained essentially intact, while others were small: Bryants and Dowlish mills both with 20 a. each and Churchills with 11 a.[70] The only major changes since then have been the conversions of the manor-house site to purely domestic use and of Dowlish mills to agricultural purposes as Mill farm. Dairy farming continues to predominate in the parish.

Although dependent primarily upon agriculture the parish's proximity to Ilminster evidently resulted in involvement in the cloth trade. A sergemaker occurs in 1686,[71] tailors in 1705, 1706, and 1751, and a weaver in 1706.[72] There was a canvas manufacturer between 1826 and 1829 and a succession of weavers, mostly of canvas, occur between 1821 and 1857.[73] Gloving, the most common cottage industry in the area, in 1851 occupied 40 women and girls.[74] Other varied employments pursued at various times included an attorney in 1704, a mantua maker in 1821,[75] a 'herbal doctress' in

[51] Burke, *Land. Gent.* (1914 edn.), 1752.
[52] S.R.O., DD/KW 8.
[53] S.R.O., DD/SPK, box 2, bdle. 11.
[54] *Cur. Reg. R.* xiii, p. 570.
[55] e.g. C.P. 43/349 rot. 6; C.P. 25(2)/1057/11 Geo. I Trin.
[56] *V.C.H. Som.* i. 445. 24s. in the Exchequer Domesday.
[57] C 135/159/10. But the figure may represent only assessed rents: C 138/42/69.
[58] C 140/84/32.
[59] C 3/190/6; C 2/Eliz. I/B21/44; S.R.O., D/D/Rg 302.
[60] S.R.O., DD/SPK, box 2.
[61] S.R.O., DD/SAS (C/909), 45.
[62] S.R.O., DD/CA 90; DD/CN, box 16; tithe award.

[63] S.R.O., DD/CN, box 11, lease 27 Dec. 1774, exchange 6 Oct. 1829; D/D/Rg 302; tithe award.
[64] S.R.O., tithe award.
[65] Statistics supplied by the then Bd. of Agric. 1905.
[66] S.R.O., DD/SPK, box 2, bdle. 10; DD/CN, box 11.
[67] S.R.O., DD/CA 90.
[68] S.R.O. tithe award.
[69] S.R.O., DD/SPK, box 10, bdle. 21.
[70] S.R.O., DD/KW 8.
[71] S.R.O., DD/CN, box 11.
[72] S.R.O., D/P/d.wk 2/1/1.
[73] Ibid. 2/1/4, 5; H.O. 107/1927.
[74] H.O. 107/1927.
[75] S.R.O., D/P/d.wk 2/1/1, 5.

1851,[76] a hurdlemaker in 1857, and 'factory men' in 1857 and 1873.[77]

MILLS. A water-mill granted to Monkton Farleigh priory *c.* 1200 by Ralph Wake was retained by the priory until the Dissolution.[78] There was also a corn-mill on the demesne by 1419.[79] Two millers occur at the same time in the early 18th century one of whom, Edward Symonds, worked Dowlish flour mills, later Mill Farm. His family still held the mills until after 1803.[80] In that year the miller, asked to supply additional meal in the event of invasion, pleaded scarcity of water, but promised an additional 10 qr. above his normal output if water was available.[81] Between 1826 and 1832 the mills became part of the Speke estate and were occupied by tenants who combined milling with shopkeeping until *c.* 1912, when grinding ceased.[82] The mills, on the Dowlish brook east of the village, bear the date stone 1710 and the initials of Edward Symonds and his wife. In 1920 the premises included a mill-house, a bake house with double oven to take 200 loaves, and a proving oven. The overshot wheel was removed soon afterwards, but the millstones and leat were there in 1973.[83]

Bere mills farm included fulling-mills with a drying plot in 1791.[84] On its sale in 1920 the farm had a mill-house with a grinding mill and French stones, driven by an overshot wheel[85] made by Hickey and Co. of Chard in 1889. The mill was working in 1973.

A close called Mill Mead in 1838 on the extreme south-east boundary may mark a former mill site, either there or in Cudworth.[86]

LOCAL GOVERNMENT. No court rolls have been traced for the manor, but 'Dowlish court' was being held once a year in May or June between 1815 and 1838.[87] Suit of court on two years' warning was required of a lessee as late as 1863.[88]

There were two churchwardens and two sidesmen for the parish by the late 16th century,[89] and two overseers of the poor by the late seventeenth.[90]

There was a poorhouse at the extreme south of the village in 1838.[91] This was subsequently sold to William Speke and in 1850 was occupied by

seven of his tenants.[92] The parish became part of Chard poor-law union in 1836.[93]

CHURCH. Probably from the origin of the church the advowson was held with the manor. The grant of the church to Wells cathedral by Ralph Wake (I) before 1189[94] was evidently of no effect, and ownership of manor and advowson continued to descend together in 1973. The Crown presented during wardship in 1321, 1363, and twice in 1371, and the bishop, presumably by lapse, in 1362.[95] The rectory of West Dowlish, held in plurality since the 1770s, was annexed to Dowlish Wake in 1857;[96] from 1916 it was held with Kingstone and from 1969 also with Chillington.[97]

The living was valued at £5 6s. 8d. in 1291[98] and 1334[99] and was exempted from taxation between 1440 and 1517 for poverty.[1] By 1535 the income had risen to £9[2] and by *c.* 1668 to £60.[3] In 1705 the rector complained that the patron's estate of about £80 a year 'by means of an ancient custom or pretended modus' paid only 10s. a year to the minister.[4] The value was set at £43 13s. 3¼d. *c.* 1790,[5] exceeded £150 in 1815,[6] and was £356 net in 1831.[7] It had risen to £422 by 1851.[8]

In 1334 the great tithes produced £3 6s. 8d., tithe hay 6s. 6d., and oblations and small tithes £1 5s. 6d.[9] By 1535 predial tithes were valued at £5, tithe of sheep and lambs at 10s., and oblations and personal tithes at £2 16s. 8d.[10] The tithes were commuted for a rent-charge of £392 for Dowlish Wake and West Dowlish together.[11]

Glebe was valued at 8s. a year in 1334 and at 13s. 4d. in 1535.[12] During the incumbency of Henry Kinder (1588–1619) the glebe included 5½ a. near the parsonage house and 12 a. of arable in the open fields, and in 1636 7 a. near the parsonage and 11½ a. in the fields. A small close called Poolehaye was then held by the parson from Candlemas to Lammas, and for the rest of the year by the parish.[13] In 1838 the glebe totalled 34 a.[14]

The parsonage house was held with a barn, outhouse, two gardens, and an orchard in 1636.[15] It was described in 1815 as 'a poor, mean house in which no incumbent has resided for many years', and it was not occupied by the rector nor his curate in 1827 and 1840.[16] It was subsequently bought by the Spekes and sold as a private dwelling in

[76] H.O. 107/1927.
[77] S.R.O., D/P/d.wk 2/1/5.
[78] Dugdale, *Mon.* v. 26.
[79] C 138/42/69.
[80] S.R.O., D/P/d.wk 2/1/1; S.R.O., DD/CN, box 11; Q/RE, land tax assessments; DD/X/TDR 2.
[81] *S. & D. N. & Q.* x. 169–70.
[82] S.R.O., DD/CN, box 17, 3/1; H.O. 107/1927; *P.O. Dir. Som.* (1861–75); *Kelly's Dir. Som.* (1883–1914).
[83] S.R.O., DD/KW 8; ex. inf. Mr. W. J. Sumption, Dowlish Wake.
[84] S.R.O., DD/CN, box 11.
[85] S.R.O., DD/KW 8.
[86] S.R.O., tithe award.
[87] S.R.O., DD/CN, box 17, 3/1.
[88] S.R.O., DD/SPK, box 9, bdle. 12.
[89] S.R.O., D/D/Rg 302; D/D/Rr 152.
[90] C 8/463/37.
[91] S.R.O., tithe award.
[92] S.R.O., DD/SPK, box 10, bdle. 21.
[93] *Poor Law Com. 2nd Rep.* p. 547.
[94] *H.M.C. Wells*, i. 309.

[95] *Cal. Pat.* 1317–21, 580; 1364–7, 34; 1370–4, 131, 160; *S.R.S.* x, p. 779.
[96] S.R.O., D/D/B reg 32–7.
[97] *Dioc. Dir.*
[98] *Tax Eccl.* (Rec. Com.), 199.
[99] E 179/169/14.
[1] *S.R.S.* xxxii. 250; l, p. 93; liv, pp. 172, 187.
[2] *Valor Eccl.* (Rec. Com.), i. 166.
[3] S.R.O., D/D/Vc 24.
[4] *Proc. Som. Arch. Soc.* cxii. 80.
[5] S.R.O., D/P/b. on s 23/17.
[6] S.R.O., D/D/B return 1815.
[7] *Rep. Com. Eccl. Revenues*, pp. 136–7.
[8] H.O. 129/318/1/8/10.
[9] E 179/169/14.
[10] *Valor Eccl.* (Rec. Com.), i. 166.
[11] S.R.O., tithe award.
[12] E 179/169/14; *Valor Eccl.* (Rec. Com.), i. 166.
[13] S.R.O., D/D/Rg 302.
[14] S.R.O., tithe award.
[15] S.R.O., D/D/Rg 302.
[16] S.R.O., D/D/B return 1815; D/D/V returns 1827, 1840.

1920.[17] Lying at the end of a lane west of the village, the present building contained the hall and service range of a small house of *c.* 1500 which formerly had a western wing which may have contained the parlour.[18] The roof has been largely renewed, but a pair of curved rafters, possibly crucks, are visible in the central wall. There are re-used 17th-century beams in the main room, and the whole was probably remodelled in the late 18th century when a cupboard staircase, some windows, and several doors were inserted.

Hugh Speke, rector 1827–56, had built Wake Hill house by 1831[19] where he and his successors, Benjamin Speke, rector 1857–81, and F. H. Mules, rector 1881–1908, lived.[20] The ownership of the house was evidently retained by the Speke family. Parke House, from 1972 the Old Rectory, was subsequently occupied by incumbents until 1969. A new rectory house was completed in 1972.[21]

William de Crauden, declared illiterate after institution in 1322, was ordered to find a curate to serve in his place, and was subsequently licensed to absent himself for study.[22] Thomas Austell, rector until 1486, was also canon of Salisbury and Exeter.[23] By will of 1509 he left 40s. to celebrate his obit at Dowlish for 20 years and gave a pair of vestments to the church.[24] On resignation John Williams, rector 1486–98, being 'aged and infirm' and 'suffering from poverty', was granted a pension of 4 marks a year from the rectory, half its total income.[25] John Hunt, intruded during the Interregnum, had been ejected by 1661 when the former incumbent Nicholas English was buried.[26] William Speke, rector 1759–71, and Philip Speke, rector 1771–78, were both members of the patron's family.[27] Septimus Collinson, rector 1778–1827, although resident during the early years of his incumbency, later held the benefice with the rectory of Holwell (Dors.) and was also Lady Margaret professor of divinity at Oxford, prebendary of Worcester, and Provost of the Queen's College, Oxford.[28] Hugh Speke, rector 1827–56, held the vicarage of Curry Rivel in plurality, and Benjamin Speke, rector 1857–81, combined it with the rectory of Washfield (Devon).[29] The latter caused a national sensation when he disappeared in London in 1868, and was believed to have been murdered. He was discovered at Padstow (Cornw.) seven weeks later, disguised as a bullock drover.[30]

Assistant curates were employed constantly between 1760 and 1857.[31] Many, like their rectors, were non-resident. In 1815 John Hawkes Mules was also headmaster of Ilminster grammar school, where he lived, and also served as curate of Cricket Malherbie and Cudworth.[32]

In 1554 the altar, replacing the Protestant table, was not consecrated,[33] and in 1557 the inhabitants had no quarterly sermons.[34] There were 15 communicants in 1776,[35] and in 1815 and 1827 there was a single Sunday service and sermon alternately morning and evening.[36] By 1840 there were two Sunday services, and Holy Communion was celebrated 'more than three times a year'. By 1843 there were monthly celebrations.[37] On Census Sunday 1851 there were congregations of 52 in the morning and 147 in the afternoon, while the Sunday school was attended by 57 and 48 respectively.[38] In 1870 the two Sunday services and monthly celebrations were continuing.[39]

The chapel of the chantry of John Kaynes in the parish church was mentioned in 1438,[40] although no details of its foundation have survived. By his will of 1528 Sir George Speke ordered a new aisle to be built for his burial and an unbeneficed priest employed to say mass daily for the souls of the testator and members of his family. The priest was to receive £6 a year and bread, wine, and wax in addition.[41] Two stipendiary priests were serving the church in 1532.[42]

The church of *ST. ANDREW*, so dedicated by 1349,[43] is built of Ham stone rubble and ashlar and has a chancel with north chapel, central tower, and nave with north aisle and south porch. It was much restored in 1861–2,[44] when the nave and aisle were largely rebuilt. The chancel is early-13th-century in origin, one unrestored lancet remaining in the north wall. The three-stage central tower was built into, and partly encased, its western end in the early 14th century and at about the same time one bay was added to the east. The south porch was built in the 14th century and the nave was probably earlier but was refenestrated in the 15th century. Its north aisle was a late-15th-century addition. An extension eastwards as a chantry chapel for the Kaynes family probably occurred in the earlier 15th century. Monuments in the chapel, subsequently adopted by the Spekes, include a recumbent female effigy of Ham stone *c.* 1360, identified as Isabel Wake (d. 1359), and two recumbent effigies of Doulting stone on a Ham-stone chest of a knight and his lady,[45] probably installed under the will of John Stourton (proved 1439) to commemorate John Kaynes and his wife.[46] In the same chapel stands the monument to John Hanning Speke (d. 1864) and the Norman font from the former church of West Dowlish (demolished by 1575).[47] In the mid 19th

[17] S.R.O., DD/KW 8.
[18] Taunton Castle, Som. Arch. Soc. colln., drawing by Clenell.
[19] S.R.O., Q/RE, land tax assessments.
[20] S.R.O., DD/SPK, box 9, bdle. 13; *Kelly's Dir. Som.* (1889–1902).
[21] Ex inf. the rector, the Revd. R. W. Pilgrim.
[22] *S.R.S.* i. 200; ix, p. 28.
[23] *S.R.S.* i. 135; Emden, *Biog. Reg. Univ. Oxford.*
[24] *S.R.S.* xix. 132.
[25] Ibid. liv, pp. 17, 20.
[26] *Calamy Revised,* ed. Matthews; S.R.O., D/P/d. wk 2/1/1.
[27] *Som. Incumbents,* ed. Weaver; Foster, *Alumni Oxon.*
[28] S.R.O., D/P/d. wk 2/1/2, 6; Foster, *Alumni Oxon.*
[29] Venn, *Alumni Cantab.*; Foster, *Alumni Oxon.*
[30] *Western Gazette,* 17 Jan.–28 Feb. 1868.

[31] S.R.O., D/P/d. wk 2/1/3–6.
[32] S.R.O., D/D/B return 1815.
[33] S.R.O., D/D/Ca 22.   [34] Ibid. 57.
[35] S.R.O., D/D/V Dioc. bk.
[36] S.R.O., D/D/B return 1815; D/D/V return 1827.
[37] S.R.O., D/D/V returns 1840, 1843.
[38] H.O. 129/318/1/8/10.
[39] S.R.O., D/D/V return 1870.
[40] *S.R.S.* xvi. 146.
[41] Ibid. xix. 275–6.
[42] S.R.O., D/D/Vc 20.
[43] Ibid. x, p. 584.
[44] S.R.O., D/P/d. wk 2/1/5.
[45] *Proc. Som. Arch. Soc.* lxiv. 40; lxx. 72–3; lxviii. 47–8.
[46] *S.R.S.* xvi. 146.
[47] *S. & D. N. & Q.* xiv. 33.

century the tracery of many of the windows was removed and the mullions were extended into the heads. At the restoration of 1861–2 the plan of the medieval church was retained but the nave windows were rebuilt with tracery in a 14th-century style and the north aisle was reconstructed with a pitched roof, replacing the earlier leaded flats.

There are five bells: (i) Thomas Jeffries of Bristol (d. 1545–6); (ii) 1634, T. Wroth; (iii) 1906, Taylor of Loughborough; (iv) medieval, Exeter, c. 1500; (v) 1906, Taylor.[48] The plate is modern: two cups and a salver given by the then rector in 1809.[49] The parish registers survive from 1645 and are complete.[50]

NONCONFORMITY

NONCONFORMITY. Edmund Baker, a former Methodist minister at Teddington (Mdx.), came to Dowlish Wake c. 1811 as minister of the sect of Joanna Southcott (d. 1814).[51] He had evidently converted Jane Parke and her sister Anne Gibson, both of Parke House, and they provided him with a house and chapel and a weekly salary. By 1813 he had converted over 100 people in the area. Between 1814 and 1824 Baker lived in Ilminster and drew his congregation from as far afield as Crewkerne and Taunton.[52] In 1849, evidently near death, he appointed seven male elders to superintend the congregation and left two silver-gilt cups, a bass viol, and the register of names to Mr. Churchill of Curry Rivel.[53] No subsequent reference to the sect in Dowlish has been found.

Bible Christians met once in the parish in 1824.[54]

EDUCATION

EDUCATION. An unlicensed school was discontinued in 1623.[55] In 1819 there was a Sunday school for 40 children supported by contributions.[56] Another Sunday school, started in 1822, was attended by 14 children in 1825, and 72 in 1835, and was wholly supported by the incumbent.[57]

By 1835 a National day-school for 40 children and 2 infants had been established, supported by parents, the rector, and Mrs. Jane Parke.[58] It was evidently held in a schoolroom west of the present Dower House.[59] A new school to the west of the church was built in 1840,[60] which subsequently housed both day-school and Sunday school. In 1846–7 the day-school, under one master, was attended by 16 girls and 11 infants (all boys), and the Sunday school, under one mistress, by 23 boys and 38 girls.[61] The schoolrooms were extended in 1870, and in 1894 the day-school, by then a voluntary mixed church school, had an average attendance of 57.[62] By 1903 there were 81 on the books and it was reported to be 'a good school on the whole'.[63] In 1908 there were more children from Kingstone than Dowlish Wake, and the number on the books had risen to 97.[64] In 1916 a new subscription list was drawn up to finance the school, the managers having exhausted their existing capital. It took juniors only from 1928, when the senior pupils were transferred to Ilminster.[65] This change in status reduced the number to 54 in 1938.[66] The school was closed in 1949; the children were transferred to Chillington and the building was converted to a village hall.[67]

CHARITIES FOR THE POOR. None known.

KNOWLE ST. GILES

THE PARISH of Knowle St. Giles lies on the northern scarp of Windwhistle ridge 2½ miles NE. of Chard and 2¼ miles SW. of Ilminster, and had an area estimated at 540 a. in 1842.[1] Bere Mills farm, a detached portion of Dowlish Wake, was added to the parish in 1885, increasing the area to 765 a.[2] It is irregular in shape, extending 1½ mile from E. to W. and a maximum of 1 mile from N. to S. It is bounded on the N. by Ilminster and Dowlish Wake, on the E. by Cricket Malherbie, on the S. by Chaffcombe and Chard, and on the W. by Combe St. Nicholas. In 1933 the parish was amalgamated with Cricket Malherbie in Abdick and Bulstone to form the civil parish of Knowle St. Giles, giving a total extent of 1,226 a.[3]

The parish is divided by the young river Isle and its tributaries, one of which forms part of the southern boundary at Woodhouse farm. From the gravel of their valley, which has signs of former mill-leats, the land rises gently, in the west to over 275 ft. at Clayhanger, and in the E. to over 400 ft., but sloping gently northwards. Like most of the Windwhistle ridge the soil is over Upper and Middle lias.[4]

The principal route through the parish, linking it with Ilminster and Dowlish Wake, runs across Knowle green (Middle Knowle green in 1787),[5] and at its NE. end is known as Wooley Lane. From Knowle green a second road runs eastwards over Upper Knowle green[6] at Churchills to Cricket

48 S.R.O., DD/SAS CH 16.
49 *Proc. Som. Arch. Soc.* xlv. 142–3.
50 S.R.O., D/P/d. wk 2/1/1–6.
51 Middlesex R.O., Acc. 1040/3, 64; Pulman, *Bk. of the Axe*, 195.
52 M.R.O., Acc. 1040/4, 64–5.
53 Ibid. 7.
54 S.R.O., D/N/spc 31.
55 S.R.O., D/D/Ca 235.
56 *Digest of Returns to Sel. Cttee. on Educ. of Poor*, H.C. 224 (1819), ix (2).
57 *Rep. B. & W. Dioc. Assoc. S.P.C.K.* (1825–6); *Educ. Enquiry Abstract*, H.C. 62 (1835), xiii.
58 *Educ. Enquiry Abstract*, H.C. 62 (1835), xiii.
59 S.R.O., tithe award.
60 S.R.O., C/E 26.

61 *Church Sch. Inquiry, 1846–7.*
62 S.R.O., C/E 26; *Returns of Schs.* [C. 7529] H.C. (1894), lxv.
63 S.R.O., C/E 26.
64 S.R.O., DD/X/PRY; *Bd. of Educ. List 21*, 1908 (H.M.S.O.), 411.
65 S.R.O., DD/X/PRY.
66 *Bd. of Educ., List 21, 1938* (H.M.S.O.), 347.
67 S.R.O., DD/X/PRY; Char. Com. files.
1 S.R.O., tithe award. This article was completed in 1973.
2 *Kelly's Dir. Som.* (1897); *Census,* 1901.
3 *Som. Review Order, 1933.*
4 Geol. Surv. Map 1″, drift, sheet 311 (1957 edn.).
5 M.P.E. 465, map of Knowle farm 1787.
6 Ibid.

Malherbie and Cudworth. The Chard–Ilminster road, turnpiked in 1759, formerly followed the western parish boundary, but in 1836 was diverted further east on a more direct route.[7] In 1787 a lane ran north from Knowle green to Bere Mills farm in Dowlish Wake, and another followed the northern parish boundary running from Ilminster to a cross-roads called Four Lanes on the turnpike road.[8] Both these lanes had been 'long thrown into' the adjacent fields by 1820.[9] Harford Lane (Harput Lane by 1751) has not been located but linked Knowle and Dowlish Wake and was declared to be a private road in 1676.[10]

There is no village of Knowle, but settlement was formerly greater around Upper and Middle Knowle greens. Knowle Green Dairy and Woodhouse Dairy (in 1973 the Firs) are both at Middle Knowle green, which was also the site of the manor pound.[11] The parish church appears isolated at the end of a path on the high ground in the east, where the former St. Giles's well (mentioned 1620, 1673) was sited.[12] Other settlement is in isolated farms at Illeigh, Woodhouse, and Pinkham. Widgery farm occurs in 1444 as the field-name Wygellysworthe.[13]

Chard canal, cut through the parish beside and east of the river Isle, was opened in 1842 and closed in 1867. It was succeeded by the railway to Chard via Ilminster, opened in 1866, which followed a similar course through the parish.[14]

In 1563 and 1601 Knowle had a mere ten households.[15] No further figure for its population is available until 1801, when it stood at 61. It rose to 91 in 1821, thereafter fluctuating between 90 and 110. It again rose in 1871, to 118, but, despite the extension of the civil parish in 1885, had fallen to 92 by 1891. After a brief rise to 100 in 1901[16] it fell gradually to 81 in 1931. The amalgamation with Cricket Malherbie gave a population of 127 in 1951 and 118 in 1971.[17]

Sir Amias Preston (d. ? 1617), the naval commander, leased and probably occupied Woodhouse between 1590 and 1600.[18]

In September 1644, while Charles I was at Chard, royalist forces were quartered at Knowle before moving to South Petherton.[19] Ten parishioners were accused of participating in the Monmouth rebellion of 1685.[20]

MANORS AND OTHER ESTATES. In 1066 Godric and Alvric held the manor of KNOWLE,

but by 1086 had been dispossessed and their lands granted to Roger de Courcelles.[21] The overlordship of the manor is seldom mentioned but was claimed in 1286 by Hugh Pointz[22] and in 1312 by Nicholas Pointz, when he was succeeded by his son Hugh.[23]

The Domesday tenant was William de Almereio,[24] but no occupier has been traced thereafter until c. 1186–8 when Alan de Furneaux included Knowle chapel in his grant of Cudworth church to Wells cathedral.[25] This grant was confirmed by Richard of Knowle[26] who may have had some interest in the manor or advowson. The manor was held by another Alan de Furneaux in 1286[27] and it evidently descended with Cudworth manor. Lands at Illeigh in Knowle were in 1498 held of John Speke as of his manor of Cudworth.[28]

In 1303 Hugh de Beauchamp and Ralph of Stocklinch held lands in South Illeigh and Knowle under Matthew de Esse and Humphrey de Kail.[29] This indicates an earlier subinfeudation of Knowle with Chaffcombe manor by Alan de Furneaux or Geoffrey his son to Oliver Avenel (d. c. 1226), and a subsequent descent with the halves of Chaffcombe manor through Avenel's daughters. The estate was subdivided, the Beauchamp half ultimately becoming the manor of KNOWLE ST. GILES, and the Stocklinch half comprising the farm or manor and mills of Illeigh. By 1386 two thirds of the Beauchamp lands in Knowle had been granted to John Dillington, probably in right of Elizabeth his wife, for life together with the reversion of the remaining third on Nicholas Buller's death. Thereafter the lands were to pass to Thomas and Joan Buller and their descendants.[30] When James Goodwin purchased John (VI) Buller's moiety of Chaffcombe manor in 1612 he was also offered Knowle manor for £800, but refused it.[31] In the same year Buller sold Knowle to William Powell, archdeacon of Bath (d. 1614),[32] who was succeeded by his son Samuel (I) Powell (d. 1656–7).[33] The manor then passed by successive sons to Marmaduke (d. 1682), Samuel (II) (d. 1722), Samuel (III) (d. 1738), and Samuel (IV) (d. 1739).[34] Sarah Powell (d. 1783), mother of the last, executed leases in Knowle until her second son Henry (d. 1769) came of age, and on his death she and her daughter Mary acted as joint lords.[35] Mary Powell (d. 1787) succeeded her mother and, on her death, the manor passed to her cousin the Revd. Thomas Alford (d. 1805) of Ashill, grandson of Samuel (III) Powell's sister Frances.[36] Alford agreed to sell the

[7] S.R.O., D/T/ilm 1; DD/BD 93, conveyance 30 Sept. 1836.
[8] M.P.E. 465.
[9] S.R.O., DD/PT, box 30.
[10] Ibid.; S.R.S. xxxiv. 207.
[11] S.R.O., DD/PT, box 30; tithe award.
[12] S.R.O., DD/SS, bdle. 16, leases. See also other leases of Great and Little Furzey closes: ibid. bdles. 15–16.
[13] S.R.O., DD/PT, box 1, rental 1444; DD/SS, bdle. 16.
[14] C. Hadfield, Canals of S. Eng. 230, 320; D. St. J. Thomas, Regional Hist. of Railways of G.B. i. 23–4.
[15] B.L. Harl. MS. 594, f. 55; S.R.O., DD/HI, box 9.
[16] V.C.H. Som. ii. 348.
[17] Census, 1911–71.
[18] S.R.O., DD/SS bdle. 31; D.N.B.
[19] Diary of Richard Symonds, (Camd. Soc. 1st. ser. lxxiv), 98; Proc. Som. Arch. Soc. xxviii. 58.
[20] B.L. Add. MS. 30077, f. 34v.
[21] V.C.H. Som. i. 487.   [22] Feud. Aids, iv. 283.
[23] Cal. Inq. p.m. v, p. 196.

[24] V.C.H. Som. i. 487.
[25] H.M.C. Wells, i. 42–3.
[26] Ibid. 46. Rich. of Knowle and Maud his wife granted a rent of 6s. from his lands in Knowle to Forde abbey: Forde Abbey Cart. pp. 550–1.
[27] Feud. Aids, iv. 283.
[28] Cal. Inq. p.m. Hen. VII, iii, pp. 552–3.
[29] Feud. Aids, iv. 315. 'Humphrey' is given in error for 'Hugh' de Beauchamp, husband of Idony de Lisle.
[30] S.R.S. xvii. 128.
[31] S.R.O., DD/PT, box 30, articles of agreement 27 July 1612.
[32] S.R.O., DD/AL, box 4, pardon for alienation 1614–15; H.M.C. Wells, ii. 367.
[33] C 60/468 no. 3.
[34] S.R.O., DD/AL, passim.
[35] Ibid.; DD/PT, box 30, leases.
[36] J. G. Alford and W. P. W. Phillimore, Alford Family Notes (priv. print. 1908), 153–6; S.R.O., DD/CN, box 13/3.

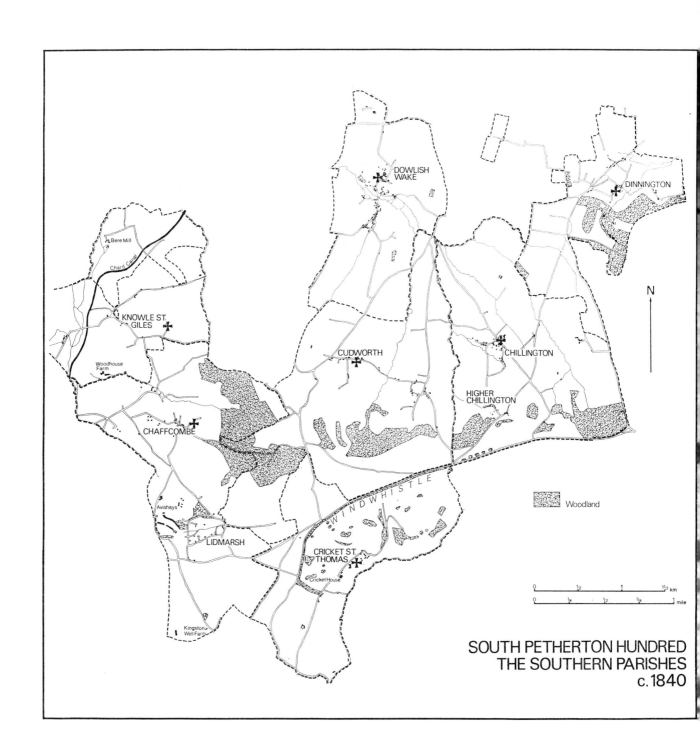

SOUTH PETHERTON HUNDRED
THE SOUTHERN PARISHES
c.1840

estate to Lord Poulett in 1797, although the sale was completed by Alford's widow Sarah, and son Edward in 1811.[37] Thereafter the manor descended through successive Earls Poulett, the lordship being omitted from the sale of the estate in 1912.[38] William John Norton was described as lord between 1927 and 1931,[39] but no subsequent reference to the manor has been traced, nor any mention of a manor-house.

The manor of *ILLEIGH* was held T.R.E. by Bruning but by 1086 had been added to Knowle manor and was held by William de Almereio under Roger de Courcelles.[40] It descended with Knowle until the division between the daughters of Oliver Avenel, when it formed the nucleus of the second half of the Knowle estate and passed with a half of Chaffcombe manor to the Noneton family and their successors. In 1303 it was held by Ralph of Stocklinch and included a carucate of land, 40 a. of meadow, 15 a. pasture, and 5 a. woodland.[41] The manorial administration was combined, like its ownership, with the Poulett moiety of Chaffcombe in the mid 16th century.[42] In 1918 Illeigh, then called Knowle farm, was sold by Lord Poulett to the tenant, E. R. Mead.[43] It passed to John Bale between 1919 and 1923[44] and under its present name, Manor farm, was sold by him in 1941 to Mr. L. Maidment, owner in 1973.[45]

The house was first mentioned in 1303[46] and was probably occupied by the Burre family, originally of Essex, who moved to Knowle from Cricket Malherbie between 1573 and 1581.[47] John Burre (d. c. 1585) was succeeded at Knowle by his son Simpson, the wealthiest inhabitant of the parish in 1628.[48] The present Manor Farm, of flint and brick with Ham stone dressings and tiled roof, has been totally modernized and has no early internal features.

The capital messuage and farm of *WOOD*, later *WOODHOUSE*, was first mentioned in the early 13th century, when John of Wood, of Knowle, held lands in Chaffcombe,[49] and Andrew of Wood held a virgate of land at Knowle in 1235.[50] John Buller (d. 1485) held Wood in fee under Knowle manor in 1444 and his family claimed to have held and occupied it from a much earlier date.[51] Thereafter it descended with the Buller half of Chaffcombe.

Alexander Buller (d. 1526) occupied the farm under Lord Daubeney, probably as lord of the hundred, and when the Bullers moved to Lillesdon they leased Wood to George Poulett in 1573.[52] There followed successive assignments of this lease to occupiers: to John Andrews alias Fry in 1582, to Amias Preston in 1590, and to Simon Courte in 1600.[53] John (VI) Buller bought the lease from Courte in 1604 and sold it with his half of Chaffcombe to James Goodwin and others in 1612, with which it passed to John Poulett, later Lord Poulett, in 1613.[54] The farm continued in the Poulett family, being occupied by John Bluet in 1701, until its sale in 1913 to J. W. Davison.[55] In 1920 he sold it to Holliday Hartley, and Hartley conveyed it in 1924 to Mr. J. G. Vincent, the owner and occupier in 1973.[56]

The medieval house was burnt down in 1806. It was thatched and included 'a spacious room open to the roof' with 'a wide fireplace, spanned over with an arched stone chimney piece'. After the fire a female skeleton was found under a paving stone and, within the wall near the oven, an infant's remains.[57] The present Ham stone house was built to the south of the original house after the fire.[58]

In 1624 Matthew Pitt of Cricket Malherbie died holding under Knowle St. Giles manor 2 houses, a cottage, 2 gardens, 3 orchards, and 145 a. of land in Knowle and Dowlish.[59] It is not known when these lands were enfranchised, but Matthew's son Benjamin (d.c. 1650) of Standerwick left leases of the property to trustees.[60] The freehold was sold in 1735 by Robert Pitt, probably grandson of Benjamin, to Nathaniel Hartley of London, under whose ownership it became known as Knowle farm.[61] Hartley died intestate without heirs in 1762 and the estate, then containing 84 a., passed to the Crown. The lands lay principally in the NE. of the parish with some 12 a. in Dowlish Wake. The farm was leased to John Vincent for 31 years in 1788 and was purchased by Lord Poulett in 1819.[62] The lands subsequently descended with the Poulett estate and were taken to form part of Pinkham farm in the early 19th century.[63] The farm-house lay at Middle Knowle green, although the lands were in a detached part of Dowlish Wake parish.[64] It had 'fallen to decay' by 1820 and was demolished soon after.[65]

---

[37] S.R.O., DD/PT, box 30, conveyance, 2 Oct. 1811; *Alford Family Notes*, 133–5.
[38] Sale cat. 1912, *penes* Mr. L. Broad, Chard.
[39] *Kelly's Dir. Som.* (1927, 1931).
[40] *V.C.H. Som.* i. 487. Wrongly identified with Eleigh Water in Combe St. Nicholas in *Domesday Geog. of SW. Eng.* 143–4.
[41] *S.R.S.* vi. 325.
[42] S.R.O., DD/SS, bdle. 1; DD/PT, boxes 1, 2.
[43] Sale cat. 1912, *penes* Mr. Broad; S.R.O., DD/X/BID, sale cat. 1941.
[44] *Kelly's Dir. Som.* (1919, 1923).
[45] S.R.O., DD/X/BID, sale cat. 1941; ex inf. Mr. J. G. Vincent, Knowle.
[46] *S.R.S.* vi. 325.
[47] *Visits. Som. 1531, 1573*, ed. Weaver, 13; S.R.O. DD/SF 3948. A small brass of Philip (d. 1584/5), seventh son of John Burre, was restored to Knowle church in 1973.
[48] *Som. Wills*, ed. Brown, iv. 69; S.R.O., DD/HI, box 53, subsidy roll.
[49] S.R.O., DD/SS, bdle. 30, lease, John of Wood to John de Stratton (n.d.). The identification of Wood with the Domesday holding of 'Worde' (*V.C.H. Som.* i. 487), has been strongly suggested in Cudworth.
[50] *S.R.S.* vi. 91.
[51] S.R.O., DD/PT, box 1, rental 1444; *Visit. Cornw. 1620* (Harl. Soc. ix), 24; *Visits. Som. 1531, 1573*, ed. Weaver, 12.
[52] C 142/45/17; S.R.O., DD/SS, bdle. 16.
[53] S.R.O., DD/SS, bdle. 31.
[54] Ibid. 30–1; *S.R.S.* li, pp. 190–1.
[55] Prob. 11/477 (P.C.C. 141 Ash); sale cat. 1923, *penes* Mr. Vincent.
[56] Ex inf. Mr. Vincent.
[57] Taunton Castle, scrapbk. newspaper cutting, 11 Feb. 1899. The burials were allegedly discovered after the sighting of a ghost by the occupier, Mrs. Vincent, and with the infant's body were found 'a lady's slipper embroidered with silver thread, a number of beads, some bone or ivory rings': ibid.
[58] Ex inf. Mr. Vincent.
[59] C 142/519/22.
[60] Prob. 11/214 (P.C.C. 186 Pembroke).
[61] S.R.O., DD/PT, box 30; DD/SAS, C/1193, 5/8, p. 238, pedigree of Pitt of Standerwick.
[62] S.R.O., DD/PT, box 30; M.P.E. 465, map of farm 1787.
[63] S.R.O., tithe award.
[64] M.P.E. 465, which includes a drawing of the house.
[65] S.R.O., DD/PT, box 30; Dowlish Wake tithe award.

ECONOMIC HISTORY. In 1086 Knowle paid geld for 1¼ hide and there was land for 2 ploughs. Three virgates and one plough were held in demesne and the remaining half hide with only a ½ plough was worked by 5 villeins and 4 bordars. Stock included 6 head of cattle and 48 sheep. Woodland measuring 4 by 2 furlongs probably represented the area later cleared to form the estate of Wood. To Knowle had been added Illeigh, evidently then a single farm, which gelded for 3 virgates and had land for 2 ploughs tilled by a single demesne plough. There were one villein, one bordar, and one serf, and no stock was recorded. The values of both estates before and after the Conquest remained unchanged at 60s. and 15s. respectively.[66]

The early medieval estates were divided by the river Isle, Illeigh on the west and Knowle on the east with Knowle's woodland lying in the south. Clearance of the woodland had probably begun by the early 13th century when the existence of Wood as a farm and freehold within Knowle manor may be inferred. The parish thus comprised two large farms and one manorial estate. Knowle manor was described in 1382 as 2 messuages, 2 mills, one carucate of land, 12 a. of meadow, 12 a. pasture, and 10s. rent,[67] and in 1386 as 2 messuages, one carucate of land, 16 a. of meadow, 20 a. pasture, 2 a. wood, 12 a. moor, and 14s. 1d. rent.[68]

In 1444 there were three freeholders paying rents of 25s. 9½d., the foremost of whom was John Buller holding Wood, a water-mill, the pasture of Old Lea (c. 40 a.),[69] and a close called 'Sherpeham'. Edward, Lord Cobham (d. 1464), held a meadow called 'Aysshilyete', and Thomas Wattes (d. 1460) owned a messuage and 40 a. in Knowle with a further 20 a. in West Dowlish,[70] apart from further customary lands in Knowle. The largest of the four customary holdings was occupied by John Fouler: a tenement, the only two cottages, 1½ a. arable, and 2 closes, and the total rental of the manor was then £4 0s. 2½d.[71] No reference has been found to the manor-house or demesne of Knowle, but the demesne of Wood is sometimes mentioned,[72] suggesting that Wood served as the manor-house and was occupied as such by the Bullers.

The value of Knowle manor had risen to £5 by 1486[73] which may be compared with an identical income from the Poulett lands at Illeigh in 1498.[74] The latter estate then comprised 100 a. of pasture, 40 a. meadow, and 2 mills.[75] In 1542 Illeigh was leased with Chaffcombe Poulett manor-house and a further 122 a. of land.[76] The demesnes attached to Wood totalled 98 a. in 1573, including a wood near the house and a green, probably Middle Knowle

green.[77] The property was then let with Chaffcombe Park (40 a.) in Chaffcombe and Marl Pit fields (50 a.) in Cudworth.[78] Leases of other lands described as former demesne of Wood were executed from 1569, including Pearse moor and Old Lea, both lying in the east of the parish.[79]

By the 15th century most of the parish seems to have been inclosed grassland[80] and there is no direct evidence for any former open field system. Unauthorized felling of ash trees in 'Knowle moor' took place after the lord's death c. 1420[81] and common of unspecified pasture occurs in the 17th century,[82] but no large tracts of open land can be located. Most of the cottages lying within the manor, which are first mentioned in the late 17th and earlier 18th century, are described as being built on the waste,[83] and settlement throughout the parish seems to have been generally by encroachments on the roadsides made during that period.

Tenure from the 16th century was mostly on leases for 99 years or 3 lives and few copyholds survived into the 17th century. The sizes of manorial holdings were small, none, apart from Old Lea of 38 a., being over 15 a.[84] In contrast Illeigh contained in 1707 141 a., all pasture and meadow, and Woodhouse had 105 a., of which 35 a. were arable.[85] In the 18th century leases for 99 years or 3 lives of these two properties were granted to members of the Poulett family, who then sublet for short terms at much higher rents.[86] The extent of Illeigh was subsequently increased by the addition of a tucking mill and 9½ a. in Knowle, and 16 a. in Chaffcombe, the whole being rented in 1786 for £162 10s.[87] With the purchases by Lord Poulett of Knowle manor from the Alfords in 1811[88] and Knowle farm from the Crown in 1819,[89] almost the whole parish, with the exception of the glebe, passed into the hands of a single owner. In 1819 Illeigh farm, the former Alford lands, and Knowle farm, totalling 296 a., were amalgamated and leased to a single tenant for £570 a year, and Woodhouse with 140 a., partly in Chaffcombe, was let for £310.[90] By 1842 the Poulett holdings of 471 a. covered 87 per cent of the parish. A new farm had been created in the east of the parish, Pinkham with 188 a., Illeigh totalled 158 a., and Woodhouse 111 a. Apart from the glebe of 36 a. there were no other tenements over 12 a. in extent.[91]

The agricultural life of the parish during the late 18th and 19th centuries was dominated by the Vincents, a large family of tenant farmers. Anthony Vincent, initially from Chard but originally from Ilminster, arrived in Knowle c. 1730.[92] His son James (d. 1801), a butcher, leased Woodhouse farm and other lands by 1771,[93] and the latter's son John

[66] V.C.H. Som. i. 487.
[67] S.R.S. xvii. 112.
[68] Ibid. 128.
[69] S.R.O., DD/PT, box 1, rental 1444.
[70] Ibid.; Cal. Pat. 1461–7, 290.
[71] S.R.O., DD/PT, box 1, rental 1444.
[72] e.g. S.R.O., DD/SS, bdle. 16, leases 3 Mar. 1597/8, 1 Nov. 1664.
[73] Cal. Inq. p.m. Hen. VII, i, p. 66.
[74] Ibid. iii, pp. 552–3.   [75] Ibid.
[76] S.R.O., DD/SS, bdle. 30.
[77] Ibid. bdle. 31, lease 23 Apr. 1582.
[78] Ibid.
[79] Ibid., lease 1 Apr. 1600; ibid. bdle. 16, leases 3 Mar. 1597/8, 1 Nov. 1664.
[80] S.R.O., DD/PT, box 1, rental 1444.

[81] S.R.O., DD/SS, bdle. 3, extr. ct. roll 1443.
[82] e.g. ibid. bdle. 16, lease 20 July 1639.
[83] S.R.O., DD/SS, bdles. 15–16; DD/PT, box 30.
[84] S.R.O., DD/SS bdles. 15–16, 31; DD/PT, box 30.
[85] S.R.O., DD/PT, box 44, survey 1707.
[86] Ibid. box 22B, lease 10 Mar. 1732/3; box 20, lease 20 Sept. 1743; box 30, lease 10 Mar. 1732/3; box 44, rental bk. 1747.
[87] Ibid. box 30, lease 30 Dec. 1786.
[88] Ibid. box 30, conveyance 2 Oct. 1811.
[89] Ibid. box 30, abstr. of title and specifications of estate 1819.
[90] Ibid. box 40.
[91] S.R.O., tithe award.
[92] Par. reg. Chard, Ilminster, Chaffcombe.
[93] S.R.O., DD/PT, box 44, rental 1771; D/P/chaf 2/1/1.

WHITESTAUNTON: MANOR-HOUSE AND CHURCH

DOWLISH WAKE: MANOR-HOUSE AND CHURCH

KNOWLE ST. GILES CHURCH FROM THE SOUTH-EAST, 1832

CHILLINGTON CHURCH FROM THE SOUTH-WEST

CRICKET ST. THOMAS CHURCH FROM THE SOUTH-EAST, 1843

BARRINGTON CHURCH FROM THE NORTH-EAST

(I) (d. 1830) rented Illeigh from 1786.[94] Of John's sons, William (d. 1856) held Woodhouse, John (II) (d. 1854) held Pinkham, and Joseph Soper (d. 1855) held Illeigh and a small farm on the western boundary, mostly in Chard.[95] The Vincents also rented lands in Chaffcombe. Robert Vincent (d. 1834), brother of John (I), and his son Robert held Chaffcombe Gate farm and another branch settled at Kingston Well.[96] Woodhouse was occupied successively by William Vincent's son and grandson, J. G. Vincent (d. 1898) and J. W. H. Vincent (d. 1929). It was held in 1973 by the son of the last, Mr. J. G. Vincent, who purchased it in 1924. In 1973 the family also held the Firs (formerly Woodhouse Dairy) in Knowle, Chaffcombe Gate, Chaffcombe Lodge, and the former glebe in Chaffcombe, and Wallscombe in Chard.[97]

When the Poulett estate was sold in 1912 Pinkham had 151 a., Illeigh (then Knowle farm) 142 a., Woodhouse 114 a. (of which 44 a. lay in Chaffcombe), Knowle Green Dairy (formerly held with Pinkham) 47 a., and Woodhouse Dairy (held with Woodhouse) 47 a.[98] The agriculture was mixed with a predominance of dairy farming. In 1905 there were 453 a. of grassland and only 155 a. of arable.[99] Only Manor farm (formerly Illeigh) had over 150 a. in 1939, and this had fallen to 113 a. by 1941.[1] By 1973 Woodhouse had increased to 126 a., while Manor farm covered 88 a. The acquisition of Pinkham farm and other lands in the eastern half of the parish by Cricket Malherbie Dairies c. 1942 had resulted in a division of the parish between them and the Vincent family.[2]

The economy of the parish has always been largely agrarian, although fulling-mills indicate links with the clothing trade, reinforced by references to two clothiers between 1682 and 1703.[3] In 1851, apart from six female glovers, the entire parish was employed in agriculture.[4]

MILLS. Gilbert atte Mulle is recorded in Knowle or Chaffcombe, probably the former, in 1327.[5] A water- and fulling-mill at Illeigh were held by Thomas Denebaud (d. 1362) under the Kail family and descended with Illeigh manor to the Pouletts.[6] In 1498 they were held with lands of 140 a. and valued at 100s.[7] In 1532 the fulling-mill, then a copyhold of Chaffcombe manor and formerly occupied by John Blackaller, was surrendered by Joan and Dorothy Morren to John Coche.[8] John Irish diverted the course of a stream flowing to the lords' mill in

1561, but as Irish held no property under the Pouletts the manorial homage could not amerce him.[9] The fulling-mill had reverted to the Morren family by 1572 when, on the death of Matilda, widow of William Morren, the mill passed to her son William.[10] In 1716 it was occupied as copyhold by Robert Morren with a mansion house, and it was leased in 1733 and 1746 to Peregrine Poulett under the name of Knowle mills.[11] By 1747 the property evidently included both the fulling- and the water grist-mill mentioned in the 14th century.[12] The mills occur in 1771[13] but cannot definitely be identified thereafter.

Another fulling-mill, owned by the Pouletts c. 1665, was then occupied by John Stone, between 1708 and 1731 by Elias Stone, and from 1731 by Jennings Darby.[14] It was leased as Willmotts mill for 42 years to Vile Miller in 1741 and excepted from a lease of Illeigh farm two years later.[15] In 1786 a seven-year lease of Illeigh farm included two water-grist-mills and two tucking-mills[16] and these were held with the farm in 1832.[17]

Two mills held by John and Joan Beauchamp in 1382 apparently lay in what became the manor of Knowle.[18] In 1444 John Buller held a water-mill in fee for a rent paid to Knowle manor.[19] A copyhold tenement with grain- and fulling-mills, occupied by John Miller, was held under the Powell manor of Knowle in 1669, the tenant having liberty to erect a cloth rack in the meadow.[20] The premises were converted to leasehold in 1681 and held by John Miller, clothier, in 1690.[21] This property may be identified with a fulling-mill, formerly occupied by William Robins, then by John Vincent, which formed part of Knowle manor conveyed to Lord Poulett in 1811.[22]

All the mills mentioned probably lay on or near the river Isle near Illeigh Farm. In 1842 fields named Millers Dry ground, Millers orchard, and Millers mead lay immediately south of the farm, and Tuckers Mill mead to the north-east.[23] The opening of Chard canal in 1842[24] may have disrupted the flow of water to some or all of these mills. None is mentioned thereafter. A mill-house and mill-leat lie at Manor (formerly Illeigh) farm, immediately west of the farm-house. The iron overshot mill-wheel was removed c. 1955.[25] It is uncertain which of the above mills this represents.

LOCAL GOVERNMENT. No court rolls have

---

94 S.R.O., DD/PT, box 30, lease 30 Dec. 1786; D/P/kn.g 2/1/1.
95 S.R.O., tithe award; par. reg. *penes* the rector.
96 S.R.O., Chaffcombe tithe award; Chaffcombe par. reg. *penes* the rector.
97 Ex inf. Mr. Vincent.
98 Sale cat. 1912, *penes* Mr. L. Board.
99 Statistics supplied by the then Bd. of Agric. 1905.
1 S.R.O., DD/X/BID, sale cat. 1941.
2 Ex inf. Mr. J. G. Vincent.
3 S.R.O., DD/SS, bdle. 15, leases 26 Dec. 1682, 26 Feb. 1686/7, 30 Oct. 1701, 21 Jan. 1701/2, 26 Feb. 1702/3.
4 H.O. 107/1927.
5 *S.R.S.* iii. 196.
6 *Cal. Inq. p.m.* xiii, pp. 14–16; C 136/66/8.
7 *Cal. Inq. p.m. Hen. VII*, iii, pp. 552–3.
8 S.R.O., DD/PT, box 1, ct. roll 10 Oct. 1532.
9 Ibid. box 2, ct. roll 30 May 1561.
10 Ibid. ct. roll 15 Apr. 1572.

11 Ibid. box 43, survey 1716; box 20, lease 10 Dec. 1746.
12 Ibid. box 44, rental 1747. The water-grist-mill was leased with Illeigh to Israel Bennett in 1743: ibid. box 20, lease 20 Sept. 1743.
13 Ibid. box 44, rental 1771.
14 Ibid. box 46, survey c. 1665; box 20, copy ct. roll 5 Mar. 1707/8; DD/SS, bdle. 29, lease 7 July 1731.
15 S.R.O., DD/PT, box 30, lease 13 July 1741; box 20, lease 20 Sept. 1743.
16 Ibid. box 30, lease 30 Dec. 1786.
17 S.R.O., Q/RE.   18 *S.R.S.* xvii. 112.
19 S.R.O., DD/PT, box 1, rental 1444.
20 S.R.O., DD/SS, bdle 15, copy ct. roll 1669.
21 Ibid. bdle. 15, lease 1 June 1681; ibid. bdle 16, lease 17 Oct. 1690.
22 S.R.O., DD/PT, box 30, conveyance 2 Oct. 1811.
23 S.R.O., tithe award.
24 C. Hadfield, *Canals of S. Eng.* 230.
25 Ex inf. Mr. L. Maidment, Knowle St. Giles.

been traced for the manor of Knowle St. Giles. The Poulett lands at Illeigh were treated as copyhold under Chaffcombe manor by 1532,[26] and courts between 1560 and 1572 were described as being held for the manors of Chaffcombe and Knowle.[27] Suit of court to the former Powell manor was demanded of a lessee as late as 1853.[28]

During the 17th and 18th centuries there were generally a single churchwarden and one assistant or sidesman, although two churchwardens occur in 1729.[29] Vestry minutes survive from 1844 and record the appointments of a churchwarden, overseer of the poor, waywarden, and (from 1857) a guardian of the poor. On occasions two or three of these offices were held by one person, and a female overseer was elected in 1874.[30]

A small cottage at 'Harput Lane' was leased by the parish in 1751 to house the poor 'in actual relief',[31] but no later reference to a poorhouse has been traced. The parish joined the Chard poor-law union in 1836.[32]

CHURCH. The chapel of Knowle is first mentioned c. 1186–8 when Alan de Furneaux granted it to Wells cathedral as part of the endowment of Cudworth prebend, upon which it was subsequently dependent.[33] There is no earlier evidence to show that it was annexed to Cudworth before that date. The cure of souls belonged directly to the prebendary and the chapel was served by assistant curates (called perpetual curates in the early 19th century)[34] nominated by him until a vacancy in the prebend in 1844. The chapel was then separated from Cudworth and the bishop assumed the appointment of perpetual curates, sometimes called vicars, at Knowle. In an exchange of patronage in 1852 the advowson was transferred to the bishop of London.[35] When a vacancy occurred at Knowle in 1908 vain efforts were made to restore Knowle to Cudworth prebend.[36] The living was united with the benefice of Cricket Malherbie in 1961 and has been held since that year in plurality with Chaffcombe.[37]

No figures for the income of Knowle distinct from that of Cudworth prebend are available until 1815, when it was valued at about £90.[38] This figure had fallen to £72 between 1831 and 1866, being composed of £60 a year from Queen Anne's Bounty and £12 10s. from the lessee of the prebendal glebe.[39] Customary tithe moduses were paid as at Cudworth, except that the tithes rendered in 1636

by the tucking-mills were assessed by mutual agreement.[40] The tithes of Knowle were commuted for a rent-charge of £65 in 1842.[41]

The glebe lands totalled 27 a. of pasture in 1571, the area of the same ground being estimated at 32 a. in 1636.[42] These fields were still held by the prebendary in 1842, although most had been converted to arable.[43] By 1894 the amount of glebe had fallen to 22 a., an acreage still held in 1923.[44]

Knowle was probably served principally by the curates of Cudworth until the mid 18th century, although a chaplain or assistant curate was recorded in 1450, 1526, and 1532.[45] From 1760 a succession of perpetual curates was licensed, all having livings or posts elsewhere. Robert Burnett Patch (curate 1778–80) was headmaster of Crewkerne grammar school[46] and Lewis Evans, F.R.S. (curate 1780–1827), the first mathematics master at the Royal Military Academy, Woolwich, London, was a noted astronomer.[47] John Allen (curate 1839–55) was headmaster of Ilminster grammar school and was succeeded in turn at Knowle by his son-in-law, Edmund Boger, and two of his sons, J. T. W. and F. E. Allen.[48] Later the living was held by three headmasters of Chard grammar school, George Phillips (curate 1873–88), W. S. Watson (curate 1889–93), and C. E. Lucette (curate 1908–17).[49] From 1893 the parish was usually held with the rectory of Cricket Malherbie, and from 1939 with that of Chaffcombe.[50] During the 19th century assistant curates were regularly employed, although these too were non-resident. In 1815 Richard Preston and in 1827 Francis Mules held the post with the curacy of Ilminster where they resided.[51]

In 1577 the prebendary was presented for not repairing the windows of Knowle chancel,[52] and his successor was also presented for dilapidations in the chancel in 1637 and 1640. The north aisle evidently belonged to the owners of Illeigh for the earls Poulett were required to mend its windows in 1637 and 1729. The wooden bell tower, in a dangerous state, and the third bell, 'cracked and useless', were repeatedly presented between 1691 and 1746. The porch, tower, and pews were out of repair in 1747.[53] The curate held one service every Sunday in 1815, for which he received £30, the surplice fees, and fees of the churchyard.[54] By 1851 there were two Sunday services, Census Sunday seeing a congregation of 39 in the morning and 75 in the afternoon, with 5 Sunday-school pupils at each.[55] The rebuilding of the chapel in 1840 had provided an additional

[26] S.R.O., DD/PT, box 1, ct. roll 10 Oct. 1532.
[27] Ibid. box 2, ct. rolls; DD/SS, bdle. 1.
[28] S.R.O., DD/LC 10/4, lease 29 Sept. 1853.
[29] S.R.O., D/D/Ppb, Cudworth and Knowle, presentments.
[30] S.R.O., D/P/kn.g 9/1/1.
[31] S.R.O., DD/PT, box 30, lease 5 Aug. 1751.
[32] Poor Law Com. 2nd. Rep. p. 547.
[33] H.M.C. Wells, i. 42–3. It may have been founded as a private chapel by Richard of Knowle or one of his family: ibid. 46.
[34] Proc. Som. Arch. Soc. lix. 50; S.R.O., D/P/kn.g 2/1/3.
[35] S. & D. N. & Q. xvii. 231–2.
[36] Ibid. 230–3; Proc. Som. Arch. Soc. lix. 45–55.
[37] Dioc. Dir.
[38] S.R.O., D/D/B return 1815.
[39] Rep. Com. Eccl. Revenues, pp. 142–3; H.O. 129/318/2/6/9; P.O. Dir. Som. (1866).
[40] S.R.O., D/D/Rg 299.
[41] S.R.O., tithe award.

[42] S.R.O., D/D/Rg 299.
[43] S.R.O., tithe award.
[44] Kelly's Dir. Som. (1923).
[45] S.R.S. xix. 249; xlix, p. 141; S.R.O., D/D/Vc 20.
[46] R. G. Bartelot, Hist. Crewkerne Sch. 71; S.R.O., D/D/V Dioc. bk.
[47] D.N.B. xviii. 70. In 1815 Evans stated 'I serve no church at all but confine myself to the important duties of the academy': S.R.O., D/D/B return 1815.
[48] P.O. Dir. Som. (1861, 1866); R. T. Graham and F. S. Carpenter, Ilminster Grammar Sch. (1949), 53–77; Venn, Alumni Cantab.; Foster, Alumni Oxon.
[49] Kelly's Dir. Som. (1883–1914); Crockford.
[50] Crockford.
[51] S.R.O., D/D/B return 1815; D/D/V return 1827.
[52] S.R.O., D/D/Ca 57.
[53] S.R.O., D/D/Ppb, Cudworth and Knowle, presentments.
[54] S.R.O., D/D/B return 1815.
[55] H.O. 129/318/2/6/9.

105 sittings, and in 1851 of 150 seats, 120 were free.[56] By 1870 there were one or two Sunday services with sermons and Holy Communion was celebrated about four times a month.[57]

In 1548 13s. 4d. was held by William Morne for the maintenance of lights within the chapel.[58]

The chapel of *ST. GILES* was totally rebuilt in 1840.[59] The old church comprised a nave with north and south porch. The nave and aisle had east windows in the 15th-century style, that in the former perhaps reset in the position of the chancel arch subsequent to the removal of the chancel whose dilapidation is mentioned above. A wooden bell tower was replaced in the 18th century by a western bellcote of stone, decorated with gothic finials.[60]

The new church by Lewis Vulliamy has a chancel with north vestry, and nave with south porch, all in a 'middle gothic' style. In the churchyard there is a 15th-century table tomb.

The plate is modern.[61] There are two bells, the first dated 1606, probably by Purdue, the second modern.[62]

The registers date from 1695 (marriages from 1696), but lack baptisms and burials for 1784–1812 and marriages for 1745–1812.[63]

NONCONFORMITY. None known.

EDUCATION. In 1819 the poor were 'without means of educating their children',[64] but by 1835 a Sunday school for 20 pupils had been started, supported chiefly by the incumbent with some assistance from three farmers.[65] A small gothic schoolroom was erected at the north corner of the churchyard c. 1840,[66] probably contemporary with the rebuilding of the church, and by 1846 the school, taught by an unpaid master, had been affiliated to the National Society. There were then only ten pupils and the school was supported by subscriptions.[67] The date at which the day-school came into being has not been traced, but it was functioning as a mixed church school in 1883 when there was an average attendance of 24.[68] By 1903 the average attendance had risen to 34, housed in two rooms which were also used for parish meetings. The children were taught by a mistress and monitress and, apart from subscriptions and grants, the school received £5 a year from an unspecified charity. The inspector in that year was particularly impressed by 'the careful and successful instruction given in gardening'.[69] Average attendance figures remained at about 35 during the early 20th century[70] and the school closed in 1920.[71] The school building was used for storage in 1973.

CHARITIES FOR THE POOR. None known.

LOPEN

THE PARISH of Lopen, little more than a mile SSW. of South Petherton and half that distance west of Stratton, occupies a roughly triangular area astride the Foss Way.[1] It was 502 a. in area in 1901.[2] It lies almost entirely on fertile Yeovil Sands and alluvium between the 250 ft. and 100 ft. contours;[3] the highest point is on the main Ilminster–Ilchester road NE. of Lopen Head, the lowest along Lopen brook, the southern boundary. A small area of oolitic limestone appears near the surface north of Lopen Farm. It was quarried there and gave the name to the common arable Stonepits field at the end of the 18th century.[4] Stone was being hauled thence in 1814,[5] and a limekiln stood there in 1838.[6] A smaller quarry was opened further north,[7] above the site of the former school, and marl was dug in the south-west of the parish.[8]

The boundaries of the southern half of the parish appear to be natural, following the Lopen brook and two tributaries. Parts of the northern limits are marked by lanes including Flower Tanners Lane opposite Seavington St. Michael, and Higgins's Grave Lane at Stratton, recalling alternatively the fate of an intrepid huntsman or of an unfortunate carpenter set upon for his money.[9] At the extreme north of the parish is Frogmary Green,[10] in the 18th century an open space with a stone in the centre, at the junction of the parishes of South Petherton, Seavington St. Michael, and Lopen.[11] Encroachments on the green had begun by 1774,[12] and it had virtually disappeared by 1838.[13]

The principal road through the village links Crewkerne with the London–Exeter road via Ilchester at Lopen Head. The line of this road, slightly

[56] Ibid.; bd. in porch.
[57] S.R.O., D/D/V return 1870.
[58] *S.R.S.* ii. 15.
[59] S.R.O., D/P/kn.g 2/1/1. During rebuilding services were held in Widgery barn.
[60] See plate facing p. 161; S.R.O., D/D/Ppb, Cudworth and Knowle, presentments.
[61] *Proc. Som. Arch. Soc.* xlv. 145.
[62] S.R.O., DD/SAS CH 16.
[63] S.R.O., D/P/kn.g 2/1/1–3; par. reg. *penes* the rector.
[64] *Digest of Returns to Sel. Cttee. on Educ. of Poor*, H.C. 224 (1819), ix (2).
[65] *Educ. Enquiry Abstract*, H.C. 62 (1835), xlii.
[66] S.R.O., C/E 27; tithe award.
[67] *Church Sch. Inquiry, 1846–7.*
[68] *Kelly's Dir. Som.* (1883).
[69] S.R.O., C/E 27.
[70] *Kelly's Dir. Som.* (1906–14).

[71] S.R.O., C/E, box 11, adm. reg.; D/P/kn.g 18/7/1.
[1] S.R.O., tithe award. This article was completed in 1974.
[2] *V.C.H. Som.* ii. 348.
[3] Geol. Surv. Map 1″, solid and drift, sheet 312 (1958 edn.).
[4] Bristol R.O., DC/E/24/4.
[5] S.R.O., DD/PT, box 50.
[6] S.R.O., tithe award.
[7] Ibid.: Quarry Orchard.
[8] Ibid.: Marlpits field.   [9] Local information.
[10] Also known as Froggelmere and Frog moor: *Cal. Inq. Misc.* iv, pp. 119–20; S.R.O., tithe award; see below, p. 205. Compare Frogenmere (c. 1150) and Freggemere (c. 1302) in Shepton Beauchamp: *S.R.S.* xxxv. 57, 64.
[11] S.R.O., maps 1774, 1796.
[12] S.R.O., DD/PT, box 45: survey 1774.
[13] S.R.O., tithe award.

broken as it crosses the Foss Way, runs south from Lopen Head between sandstone banks into the village, where it forms the main street. The importance of Lopen Head, formerly White Cross,[14] where roads from Taunton and South Petherton converged, was enhanced when the Ilchester road became part of the Western mail coach route in the early 19th century.[15] The Foss survives as a narrow metalled road stretching from Long Lane in Stratton through Broomhill and Snap or Strap Ant, and becoming known in the 18th century as Lamb Bridge Lane before leaving the parish over Lamb or Long bridge.[16]

The village developed well south of the Foss along two small lanes each side of the road to Crewkerne. Church Street, formerly Higher Street,[17] running east from Cross Tree, the site of the medieval cross and fair, leads past the parsonage barn and site of the manor-house complex, to the church and thence to the fields. Frog Street, further south, leads westwards to Lopen Farm and the nucleus of a secondary Domesday settlement, later Templar property. The street contained several substantial houses at the end of the 18th century,[18] the survivors of which are Ballarat Farm and Apple Hay. The present Court Farm and the Old Bakehouse, presumably representing the sites of the medieval court house and common bakehouse,[19] stand beside the Crewkerne road between the two streets. North of Cross Tree the main street is known as Holloway, where 18th-century cottage development on the waste included the parish poor-houses and some weaving-shops.[20]

Broomhill, on the Foss north of the village and east of the Crewkerne road, was established by the mid 18th century. At least from 1750 cottage property and the product of 42 apple trees was leased to a succession of tenants, establishing the continuity of fruit-growing from that date until the 1970s.[21] Cottages were also built on the waste at Snap Ant and at White Cross.[22]

The common arable fields covered all but the southern and south-eastern margins of the parish and the immediate settlement area. Fields such as Hangerland and Truckhay occurred under the same names in the mid 12th and the 19th centuries.[23] Ridon, later Stratton Rye Down, was so named by the late 14th century.[24] There was common pasture in the 15th and 16th centuries at Rodmoor in the east and common meadow at Worth mead and Common mead along the Lopen brook.[25]

There do not appear to be any secular buildings

earlier than the 18th century, and of the small number of that period only one or two, such as Apple Hay (dated 1747) are of traditional plan. Cross Tree House probably dates from the 18th century, but had substantial 19th-century alterations. Lopen House and Knapp Cottage belong to the early 19th century, both built between c. 1822 and 1838.[26]

There was an inn in the parish by 1735, though its position is unknown.[27] A public house and horse-changing house were established at White Cross with the coming of increased business along the London–Exeter road c. 1811.[28] There was a licensed inn there by 1813, and since 1822 it has been known as the Poulett Arms.[29] The King William inn was opened in the village by 1838 and the Crown, in Church Street, by 1840.[30] The latter survived until c. 1950.[31]

Lopen fair or play is said to have been the occasion for the young Wolsey's misbehaviour and subsequent appearance in the stocks.[32] Six Lopen men were thought to be involved in Monmouth's rebellion in 1685.[33] The local Halloween celebrations are known as Punkie Night.[34]

In 1783 there were 75 families in the parish and a total population of 285.[35] The number rose rapidly from 331 in 1811 to 425 in 1821 and 502 in 1831, but fell as rapidly to 292 by 1881.[36] In 1901 the total was 279 and in 1911 221; thereafter it remained stable, and was 230 in 1971.[37]

MANORS AND OTHER ESTATES. In 1086 there were three separate estates called Lopen. The largest, of 2 hides, had been held T.R.E. by Tofig the sheriff, and in 1086 was in the possession of a king's thegn, the Englishman Harding son of Eadnoth the staller.[38] The other two holdings, each of 1 hide, were occupied by Gerard the trencher, *fossor, fossarius* in succession to ejected Englishmen.[39]

The largest estate descended in the Meriet family like the manor of Merriott until the death of John de Meriet in 1285. His son, also John (d. 1308), succeeded as a minor and received his other lands in 1297, but Lopen, called for the first time the manor of *GREAT LOPEN*, was held in dower[40] by his mother Margaret until 1329 if not later.[41] Her successor was her grandson Sir John (d. 1369), still a minor in 1346.[42] Sir John's widow Maud,[43] held Lopen in dower until her death in 1398 when it passed under settlement jointly to William Bonville and Sir Humphrey Stafford and their

[14] S.R.O., DD/PT, map 1774.
[15] *V.C.H. Som.* iii. 182.
[16] S.R.O., DD/PT, map 1774; O.S. Map 6″, Som. LXXXVIII. NE. (1886 edn.).
[17] Local information.
[18] S.R.O., DD/PT, map 1774.
[19] The bakehouse was 'ruinous' in 1463: D.R.O., D 124, Lopen ct. roll.
[20] S.R.O., DD/PT, box 30.   [21] Ibid. boxes 30–1.
[22] S.R.O., DD/PT, maps 1774, 1796; tithe award.
[23] *S.R.S.* viii, pp. 39–40; S.R.O., tithe award.
[24] D.R.O., D 124, Lopen acct. roll 1378–9.
[25] Ibid., box 16, Lopen ct. roll 1446; S.R.O., DD/SS, bdle. 1; DD/WY, map c. 1822; DD/PT, box 30.
[26] S.R.O., DD/WY, map c. 1822; tithe award.
[27] S.R.O., Q/RL.
[28] *Proc. Som. Arch. Soc.* xxviii. 144.
[29] S.R.O., D/P/lop 2/1/4; Q/RL; D/PS/ilm. box 1.

[30] S.R.O., D/P/lop 4/1/1.
[31] Local information.
[32] *Somerset* (Wade Little Guides, 1949); G. Cavendish, *Life of Wolsey* (London 1899), 4, does not name Lopen.
[33] B.L. Add. MS. 30077, f. 35.
[34] *Somerset* (Wade Little Guides).
[35] S.R.O., D/P/lop 2/1/3.
[36] *V.C.H. Som.* ii. 348.
[37] *Census*.
[38] *V.C.H. Som.* i. 522.
[39] Ibid. 463, 474, 487–8.
[40] *Cal. Inq. p.m.* ii, pp. 341–2; *Cal. Close, 1279–88*, 321; *Proc. Som. Arch. Soc.* xxviii. 113–14.
[41] *Placita Coram Rege*, 1297, ed. Maitland (Index Libr. xix), 12; *Feud. Aids*, iv. 315.
[42] *Feud. Aids*, iv. 331, 337; *S.R.S.* iii. 198; *Proc. Som. Arch. Soc.* xxviii. 119.
[43] *S.R.S.* xvii. 84–5; D.R.O., D 124, box 15.

wives as coheirs of Sir John Meriet (d. 1391).[44] Subsequently the two joint owners agreed to a re-arrangement, Sir Humphrey Stafford acquiring the whole of Lopen and Stratton in South Petherton in exchange for his share of Merriott.[45] Sir Humphrey died in 1442 and was followed in succession by his son William (d. 1450) and his grandson Sir Humphrey (cr. Lord Stafford 1461, earl of Devon 1469, d. 1469).

The earl was succeeded at Lopen by his grand-daughter Eleanor (d. 1501), wife of Thomas Strang-ways (d. 1484) of Stinsford (Dors.).[46] From Eleanor it passed to her son Henry (d. 1504) and to Henry's widow Catherine.[47] On Catherine's death in 1505 it descended to Henry's son Sir Giles (d. 1547). His grandson and heir, also Sir Giles, sold the manor in 1555 to Sir John Sydenham of Brympton.[48] Sydenham died in 1557,[49] and his eldest son, also John, sold Lopen to another John, his younger brother (d. 1590), in 1563.[50] The latter, then de-scribed as of the Middle Temple, London, sold it to Sir Hugh Poulett in 1566.[51] The manor then de-scended through the Poulett family like the manor of Hinton St. George until 1918, when the land, amounting to 374 a., was sold. The lordship of the manor was not included in the sale, and in 1974 was vested in the executors of the last Earl Poulett (d. 1973).[52]

In 1066 Lewin held an estate called *LOPEN*. By 1086 it had been given to Roger de Courcelles, and was held by Gerard the trencher.[53] The over-lordship descended in the honor of Curry Mallet, and it is possible that the 1/5 fee held by Henry de Lopen of William Malet (I) in 1166 represents this estate.[54] It passed with one third of the Malet barony to the Pointz family c. 1216, and by 1285 was held by Hugh Pointz (II) (d. 1307).[55] The same property was held for 1/5 fee of Nicholas Pointz in 1311,[56] and the occupiers of the estate continued to pay 12d. for release of suit to the court at Curry Mallet at least until 1522.[57]

The immediate successors of Henry de Lopen as occupiers are unknown, and the earliest certain tenant is John de Meriet (d. 1285), who held it by the serjeanty of enclosing a plot of ground in Curry Mallet park.[58] The property, variously de-scribed as a hamlet and a manor,[59] seems by that time to have been absorbed into the other Meriet estate, and to have descended in the same way.

There was a 'court' at Lopen by 1285.[60] At the end of the 14th century the manor complex ap-parently included a dwelling-house, since a hall and chamber are mentioned. It also included a group of farm buildings with an ox-house, stall, dovecot, stable, and 'kyllons', together with a barton and a pond.[61] The pound and an adjoining plot called Culverhays, south-west of the church, suggest that the buildings stood near by. The barton and farm complex stood possibly in the grounds of the present Lopen House, and the dwelling-house perhaps south of the church near Court Orchard.[62]

A third estate called Lopen was held T.R.E. by one Alward and in 1086 by Gerard the trencher of the count of Mortain.[63] By the end of the 13th century the overlordship belonged to the Lovels, Hugh Lovel holding it for ½ fee of Mortain in 1295.[64] Confiscation of the Templar lands in 1312 seems to have brought the overlordship to an end. The occupiers after Gerard the trencher are unknown until some date before 1240, when Miles de Franco Quercu[65] gave a hide of land, the Domesday area, to the Knights Templar.[66] With the suppression of the Templars in 1312 the property passed to the Crown, and remained in custody until 1332 when it was granted to the Knights Hospitaller.[67] The order was suppressed in 1540 but in 1558 the lands at Lopen, part of the former preceptory of Temple Combe, were assigned to the refounded priory of St. John at Clerkenwell (Mdx.).[68] Within two years the property of this abortive priory had come into the hands of agents[69] who sold the estate, known as Lopen Temple, to John Aylworth of Wells.[70] Aylworth disposed of it to Edward Basshe of Stan-stead (Essex) in 1561, and two years later Basshe sold it to Sir Hugh Poulett.[71] Thereafter the property, known as Temple Lopen or Lopen farm, was owned by the Pouletts until 1918, when it was purchased by Somerset County Council, owners in 1974.[72]

About 1312 the only recorded building on the property was a ruined house.[73] The present farm-house was much altered in the late 19th or early 20th century, though its ground-plan may reflect that of an earlier building.[74]

By 1267 Bruton priory held 20 a. of arable and 20 a. of meadow in Lopen as part of the rectory lands of South Petherton.[75] Some of this property was exchanged for other land, also in Lopen.[76]

[44] *S.R.S.* xvii. 169–70; *Cal. Pat.* 1396–9, 175; *Cal. Close,* 1396–9, 214, 258; S.R.O., DD/SS, bdle. 27; C 136/98/5; D.R.O., D 124, box 16.
[45] *Cal. Close,* 1422–9, 93; *Cal. Fine R.* 1413–22. 396–7.
[46] C 140/32/30; D.R.O., D 124, box 17.
[47] *Cal. Pat.* 1494–1509, 543.
[48] S.R.O., DD/SS, bdle. 27.
[49] C 142/114/23; *S.R.S.* xxi. 191.
[50] S.R.O., DD/SS, bdle. 27; G. F. Sydenham, *Hist. Sydenham Family* (priv. print. 1928).
[51] S.R.O., DD/SS, bdle. 27.
[52] S.R.O., C/C (C/2586), sale cat. 1918; ex inf. Mr. S. G. Lawrence, Crewkerne.
[53] *V.C.H. Som.* i. 487.
[54] *Red Bk. Exch.* i. 227.
[55] *Cal. Inq. p.m.* ii, pp. 341–2.
[56] Ibid. v, pp. 28, 196.
[57] D.R.O., D 124, accts.
[58] *Cal. Inq. p.m.* ii, pp. 341–2.
[59] Ibid. v, p. 28; *Proc. Som. Arch. Soc.* xxviii. 111, 113–14.
[60] *Proc. Som. Arch. Soc.* xxviii. 109.

[61] D.R.O., D 124, accts., 1369–70, 1378–9. The dovecot held c. 500 pigeons: ibid. accts. 1378–9.
[62] S.R.O., tithe award. Possibly associated with a fish pond (*motam*) adjoining Little mead: D.R.O., D 124, ct. roll 1447.
[63] *V.C.H. Som.* i. 474.
[64] *Cal. Inq. p.m.* ii, pp. 489–90. Said there to be Little Lopen.
[65] Or Fraunchenney, Franckesnei.
[66] Winchester College Mun. 12843. Miles occurs 1207–17: *Sel. Cases King's Bench* (Selden Soc. lxxxiv), 23; *Bracton's Note Bk.* ed. Maitland, iii, pp. 332–3.
[67] *Cal. Close,* 1330–3, 514.
[68] *Cal. Pat.* 1557–8, 317.
[69] Ibid. 1558–60, 466–7.
[70] S.R.O., DD/SS, bdle. 27.
[71] Ibid.
[72] S.R.O., C/C, box 23.
[73] *Hospitallers in Eng.* (Camden Soc. [1st ser.], lxv), 184.
[74] S.R.O., DD/WY, plan of Lopen Fm.
[75] *S.R.S.* viii, p. 40.
[76] Ibid., pp. 39–40.

Blaise Rodbard of Bridge in South Petherton acquired 34½ a. formerly belonging to Bruton and he and James Ayshe of South Petherton sold them to Sir Hugh Poulett in 1566. One of Poulett's tenants, Andrew Denman, occupied the land involved in the 1267 exchange.[77]

The tithes attached to the chapel of Lopen were, like those of the other chapels of South Petherton, let with the rectory, from 1532 to Thomas and George Speke.[78] By 1552 Sir Hugh Poulett was in actual occupation.[79] The Pouletts retained possession as leaseholders until 1802, when they purchased the freehold, though in 1649, when their estates were under sequestration, the tithes were let to George Sanford for £50.[80] The gross value of the tithes in 1786 was nearly £76, the net value nearly £32.[81] In 1839 the tithes were commuted to a rent-charge of £200, together with a modus of ¾d. an acre on 46½ a. of meadow.[82] In 1786 the buildings on the property comprised a barn and yard, the barn being of two bays with a threshing floor.[83] It stands on the south side of Church Street.

ECONOMIC HISTORY. In 1086 the three estates called Lopen were assessed together at four hides. It is unlikely that they were all in the present parish, and probable that at least one stretched into Stratton in South Petherton, to include the medieval holding of Little Lopen.[84] The largest estate, held by Harding son of Eadnoth, amounted to half the area, and nearly three-quarters was in demesne. Of the two other estates, both occupied by Gerard the trencher, one, later absorbed into Harding's, was entirely demesne. No demesne is recorded on the third holding. The land was predominantly arable, with only 40 a. of meadow divided in the proportion of 10 a. to each hide. The recorded population of 12 included 3 serfs. Stock amounted to 1 riding-horse, 10 head of cattle, 13 pigs, and 277 sheep. All three estates had doubled in value between 1066 and 1086.[85]

Between 1210 and 1212 Nicholas de Meriet's estate was held at farm, producing a total of £13 6s. 2½d. for two years. Evidently during that period the demesne arable was let and court perquisites accounted for half the annual income.[86] By 1285 the same estate was extended at £14 9s. 11¾d. The demesne farm was then 129 a. of arable and 8 a. of meadow, representing a considerable decrease over two centuries from the 2½ hides and 3 furlongs of 1086. Rents of free and customary tenants, however, were nearly of the same value as the demesne. Customary payments including aid, larder rent, church scot, and Peter's Pence together produced 26s. 1d.[87]

By the end of the 14th century Lopen and Stratton manors were being administered together, and it is not always possible to be certain what items relate to Lopen alone. Assessed rents had certainly grown, and in 1369–70 were worth £5 18s. 2d. By 1378–9 they had increased further, and still included ancient customary rents and an additional levy at Martinmas called 'charnag' or 'chiarnag'. Very few works were commuted and chevage was paid both in cash and in blooms of iron.[88]

The demesne farm was fully exploited, between 90 a. and 100 a. being ploughed each year to raise mainly wheat, rye, and barley, but also smaller quantities of oats, hemp, beans, and peas. Pasture and meadow was limited, but the arable supported sheep, a new flock of 100 being purchased at Binegar on the Mendips in 1369–70. Some contraction in farming is suggested between 1370 and 1379 in the disappearance of five demesne workers including cow- and pig-keepers, leaving only one ploughman instead of two, a drover, a shepherd, and a carter.[89]

After the death of Maud, widow successively of Sir John Meriet and Sir Thomas Boclond, in 1398 there was no longer a resident lord in Lopen. By the mid 15th century, therefore, the demesne was divided into small units and let. One man in 1447 took 23 a. in succession to at least one previous tenant, and covenanted to build a hall of three bays and a barn of four bays.[90] Later in 1447 other parcels were let for lives including the manor pound and Court Orchard. Freeholdings in the manor were also small, John Bulling succeeding in 1463 to 10 a. of arable and 1 a. of meadow.[91] Indeed, by far the largest single unit was the former Templar estate, in the 14th century comprising 99 a. of land and 10 a. of meadow, with pasture for 100 sheep.[92] This remained the largest farm in the parish until c. 1918, and for long periods was held by members of the same family. By 1524 at least until 1574 it was occupied by the Sampfords, who had held the mill since 1461.[93] By 1601 the farm had passed to George Sampson,[94] and in 1657 another George, of Middle Lambrook, took a lease for three lives for a fine of £560.[95] Richard Sampson in 1748 took it for a fine of £250 and a slightly increased rent.[96] By 1788 the Sampsons had been succeeded by the Bartletts, Robert Bartlett having the farm for 14 years for a rent of £126.[97] At the end of the term his lease was converted to one for three lives or 99 years for a rent of £2 12s. 6d. and a fine of £640.[98]

Three copyhold farms in the parish amounted to over 50 a. each by 1601 and another to 40 a.[99] The last, held by John Chapple, probably originated in a former demesne property dating at least from

[77] S.R.O., DD/SS, bdle. 27; DD/PE, 19.
[78] S.R.O., DD/HI, box 5; DD/PE 7; DD/PT, boxes 10A, 23.
[79] S.R.O., DD/PT, boxes 10A, 23.
[80] Ibid., box 19B; DD/X/SAB, transcript of Parl. survey f. 200.
[81] Bristol R.O., DC/E/24/4.
[82] S.R.O., tithe award.
[83] Bristol R.O., DC/E/24/4.   [84] See below, p. 183.
[85] V.C.H. Som. i. 474, 487–8, 522.
[86] Pipe R. 1212 (P.R.S. N.S. xxx), 123; C 132/47/5. The undated inquisition seems to have been wrongly ascribed to Henry III's reign: Cal. Inq. p.m. i, p. 307.
[87] Proc. Som. Arch. Soc. xxviii. 111–12; Cal. Close,
1279–88, 321.
[88] D.R.O., D 124, Lopen accts. 1369–70 (box 16), 1378–9.
[89] Ibid.   [90] Ibid. box 16, Lopen ct. rolls.
[91] Ibid.
[92] Knights Hospitallers in Eng. (Camden Soc. [1st ser.] lxv), 184, 186.
[93] D.R.O., D 124, box 16, Lopen ct. roll 1461; S.R.O., DD/SS, bdles. 1, 27.
[94] S.R.O., DD/HI, box 9.
[95] S.R.O., DD/SS, bdle. 27.
[96] S.R.O., DD/PT, box 31.
[97] Ibid. box 30.
[98] Ibid.   [99] S.R.O., DD/HI, box 9.

1572 and probably from the 15th century.[1] The farm is traceable as a fairly constant unit down to 1781.[2] A similar continuity is shown by the Denman family, tenants by 1567,[3] who by 1601 had a farm of 51 a.[4] Members of the family were still substantial tenants in 1918,[5] and continued as owner-occupiers until c. 1940.[6]

The Poulett estate in the 18th century, virtually the whole parish, comprised rents of just over £30 and tithes worth in 1778 over £83 and in 1797 £109.[7] In 1814 the tithe income was £240, and between 1815 and 1818 averaged over £185.[8] During the same period the arable acreage was increased from 289 a. in 1778 to 301 a. in 1797, and to 361 a. in 1803,[9] and from 1814 the average area was c. 320 a.[10] The arable was still managed on a three-field system of two sowings and fallow, the units smaller than the original medieval fields but cultivated in strips on a large scale. The units had been reduced from eleven areas in 1566 to seven in 1786, though by that date each had relatively few unfenced strips,[11] some of which continued until after 1918.[12] Worth mead was described in 1803 as 'lately marked out for inclosure',[13] and Common mead still survived in division until after c. 1822.[14]

At the end of the 18th century the land was said to be 'exceedingly good',[15] and was enhanced in value by careful manuring. A lessee of 1781 undertook to provide 15 hogsheads of lime or 20 putts of rotten dung or good marl an acre between every three crops, or to sow with every second crop 2 bz. of 'good ever grass seed' and 10 lb. of 'good clover seed'.[16] In 1778 153½ a. were sown with wheat, but only 6 a. with barley and 3 a. with oats.[17] In 1786 119½ a. were under wheat, 48 a. under barley, and 61½ a. under Lent grain. Beans accounted for 65½ a. in 1778 and 28 a. in 1786; flax for 29 a. and 12 a. Small crops of potatoes, hemp, and peas were grown in 1778 but were replaced in 1786 by vetches.[18] During the same period grassland increased and was improved, and between 1797 and 1803 orchards had nearly doubled in size.[19] By 1838 meadow and pasture amounted to 140 a. and orchards and gardens to 46 a., as compared with 297 a. of arable.[20] In 1905 there were 279 a. of arable.[21]

Throughout the 19th century the pattern of holdings remained constant despite the steady consolidation of ancient arable strips. Apart from Lopen farm the largest unit in 1838 was that of Thomas Templeman the sailcloth manufacturer, who held

52 a. Three other farms were of c. 20 a.[22] By 1918 some change had created a 53-a. holding at Broomhill farm and a 38-a. one at Court farm.[23] Lopen farm was itself divided c. 1918 as part of Somerset County Council's smallholdings estate. By the 1970s arable had become of less importance for grain, and substantial areas were devoted to fruit and potatoes.

Although sheep were kept in large numbers from the time of Domesday if not earlier, the wool was certainly sold in the 14th century,[24] and the origin of cloth manufacture in the parish can only be traced to the late 17th century. Richard Willy, a clothier, died possessed of a shop in 1678, and in the 1690s both a silk-weaver and a flax-weaver occur.[25] At least six linen-weavers were at work between 1700 and 1742 and more later in the century, when they were joined by dowlas-weavers and yarn-washers, most if not all of whom combined their trade with small-scale farming.[26] At least two of these craftsmen, James Gummer and Thomas Arden, had links with a sailcloth maker and a shipwright at Bridport (Dors.).[27] The long outbuildings attached to several of the substantial houses in the village are witness to the concentration of the industry in the hands of a few employers by the turn of the 19th century, though at least one weaving shop survived in a cottage in Holloway in 1803.[28] By 1822 more than half the families in the parish were employed in trade and manufacture of dowlas, a time when at least five men described themselves as manufacturers.[29] By 1840 the most successful seems to have been Thomas Templeman; described as a sailcloth manufacturer, he occupied 12 a. of land called bleaching grounds, together with a building north of the mill.[30]

A wickyarn manufacturer occurs in 1841.[31] By 1861 twine was also being produced in the parish, and Sutton Brothers were established at Lopen mill as flax spinners and sailcloth manufacturers.[32] By 1883 the complex of buildings there was occupied by three firms producing sail twine, rope and twine, and sailcloth.[33] Between 1886 and 1901 a ropewalk was built.[34] Weaving continued only until the early 1890s,[35] but Denman Brothers produced rope and twine until after the First World War.[36] During the war part of the premises was taken over by the Flax Production Branch of the Board of Agriculture and Fisheries.[37] Flax was processed on a small scale by the Linen Research Association

---

[1] S.R.O., DD/PT, box 2 no. 18; D.R.O., D 124, Lopen ct. rolls.

[2] S.R.O., DD/PT, box 30.

[3] S.R.O., DD/SS, bdle. 1.

[4] S.R.O., DD/HI, box 9.

[5] S.R.O., C/C (C/2586), sale cat.

[6] Local information.

[7] S.R.O., DD/PT, boxes 37, 44.

[8] Ibid. box 31.

[9] Ibid. boxes 30, 37.

[10] Ibid. box 31.

[11] S.R.O., DD/SS, bdle. 1; Bristol R.O., DC/E/24/4.

[12] S.R.O., C/C (C/2586), sale cat.

[13] S.R.O., DD/PT, box 30.

[14] S.R.O., DD/WY, map c. 1822.

[15] Bristol R.O., DC/E/24/4.

[16] S.R.O., DD/PT, box 30, Poulett to Cable.

[17] S.R.O., DD/PT, box 37.

[18] Bristol R.O., DC/E/24/4.

[19] S.R.O., DD/PT, boxes 30, 37.

[20] S.R.O., tithe award.

[21] Statistics supplied by the then Bd. of Agric. 1905.

[22] S.R.O., tithe award.

[23] S.R.O., C/C (C/2586), sale cat.

[24] D.R.O., D 124, Lopen accts. 1369–70 (box 16), 1378–9.

[25] S.R.O., DD/SP, inventories; DD/SS, bdle. 27; Q/SR 217/7, 10.

[26] S.R.O., DD/PT, boxes 12, 30–1; DD/BD 58–9.

[27] S.R.O., DD/BD 59; DD/S/HR, box 41.

[28] S.R.O., DD/PT, box 30; DD/PT, map 1796; DD/WY, map c. 1822.

[29] C. & J. Greenwood, *Som. Delineated*; S.R.O. D/P/lop 2/1/4.

[30] S.R.O., D/P/lop 4/1/1.

[31] S.R.O., DD/S/HR, box 6, sales under inclosure.

[32] P.O. Dir. Som. (1861).

[33] *Kelly's Dir. Som.* (1883).

[34] O.S. Map 6", Som. LXXXVIII. NE. (1886, 1901 edns.).

[35] S.R.O., C/E 78.

[36] *Kelly's Dir. Som.* (1919).

[37] Ibid. (1923).

during the 1930s,[38] and a new plant was constructed by the Government during the Second World War.[39] When production ceased after the war, some of the buildings were used for grain-drying and storage, especially for rolled barley and flaked maize.[40]

There was a mill attached to the manor by 1285.[41] By the end of the 14th century it was normally let for lives,[42] and by 1381 was known as the 'nywemulle'.[43] It was still a water-grist-mill c. 1700, and may have remained exclusively so until the middle of the century.[44] James Gifford, who held the mill by 1764, was certainly a linen-weaver or linman, but grain milling continued to share water power until after 1883.[45] The original buildings were apparently abandoned soon after the First World War.[46] The mill-house, a plain brick building dating from the late 18th or early 19th century, stands next to more modern buildings which have destroyed all but a few traces of the mill-pond and leat.

FAIR. There was a fair at Lopen by 1201.[47] It was taken into Crown hands under Quo Warranto proceedings in 1280, and in 1292 was in the custody of John Tony of Crewkerne as keeper.[48] It remained in Crown custody despite petitions for its return from John de Meriet in 1303 and from George de Meriet in 1328.[49] A later petition found, evidently incorrectly, that the confiscation had taken place after the death of John de Meriet in 1308.[50] A succession of keepers or farmers continued to be appointed by the Crown. In the early 14th century the farm was 50s. a year, though in 1285 the value had been put at 40s. and in 1328 at 26s. 8d.[51] The fair, which in the 14th century was held for seven days from Whitsun, suffered after 1361 from competition from White Down Fair in Cricket St. Thomas.[52]

Later farmers paid considerably less for the fair: one in 1386 held the hamlet of Christon in addition for the same rent, and another in 1449 held two hamlets and the fair for 4d. a year.[53] In 1552 Christon and the fair were leased for £3 0s. 10d.[54] Gilbert North, appointed keeper in 1629, is the last holder of the office to have been traced.[55]

The fair survived as an entertainment until the end of the 19th century with wrestling and singlestick and cudgel-playing. About 1810, when the Exeter–London stage adopted the Ilchester route through White Cross, the 'fair' was moved to the main road. About 1880 the date of the event, known then as 'Lopen Play', was changed to Trinity Wednesday in order to avoid a clash with Somerton. By 1882 the entertainment was limited mainly to gingerbread stalls in the village street.[56]

A physical survival of the fair site is a fragment of a carved medieval cross shaft, partly buried at the foot of the Cross Tree in the centre of the village.

LOCAL GOVERNMENT. By the end of the 14th century Lopen and the Meriet estate in Stratton were administered together,[57] a practice which continued until after 1463.[58] Each property formed a tithing represented at courts held at Lopen twice, and occasionally three times, a year. Sessions were normally described as 'courts' or 'courts leet'. Rolls survive for 1442–9 and 1461–3.[59] By 1494–5 separate 'manor courts' were being held or at least recorded on the same day for each of the former tithings.[60] Court rolls for Lopen alone survive for 1511–12.[61] After 1555 the two estates were in different ownership. The Lopen court under the Pouletts continued to meet twice a year at least until 1572. It was usually described as a 'legal manor court', and its rolls survive for 1566–72.[62] There are court books for 1651–77, 1703–10, and 1715–26[63] and admissions and surrenders in the court baron have survived up to 1819.[64] A summons to 'the usual place' was addressed to the hayward in 1756.[65]

In the early 1440s the tithings of Lopen and Stratton each elected a tithingman, rent-collector, and hayward, though later in the decade the rentcollectors' appointment is not recorded. By the 1560s the haywards and tithingmen for Lopen were serving in rotation and thus occasionally by deputy.[66] In the 15th century the courts, concerned with the normal administration of agriculture and hearing cases of assize breaking, were also involved with repairs and renewals of buildings and with the levy of chevage. Both homages were fined in 1448 for 'chattering and disturbing the court'. By the 1560s most of the business concerned tenancies, though there were several attempts to enforce suit to the mill by Stratton tenants and to limit the damage done by pigs, ducks, and geese. A tumbrel and stocks were purchased in 1369–70.[67]

Court Farm, on the west side of the village street, was known in the 19th century as Court House, and may well represent the medieval court house of the manor.[68]

Active support for the poor was the principal concern of a select vestry, meeting monthly from

38 Kelly's Dir. Som. (1931); S.R.O., C/E 78.
39 O. Hallam, The N.F.U. in Som. 108.
40 Local information.
41 Proc. Som. Arch. Soc. xxviii. 109–12.
42 Cal. Pat. 1370–4, 359.
43 C 44/10/20; Cal. Fine R. 1377–83, 272; Cal. Pat. 1377–81, 615.
44 S.R.O., DD/PT, boxes 27, 31; D/P/lop 13/2/1.
45 S.R.O., DD/PT, box 31; D/P/lop 13/2/1; Kelly's Dir. Som. (1883).
46 Kelly's Dir. Som. (1919, 1923).
47 Rot. Litt. Pat. (Rec. Com.), 2; Rot. de Ob. et Fin. (Rec. Com.), 180.
48 J.I. 3/91 rot. 4d.; Rot. Parl. (Rec. Com.), ii. 13; Cal. Chanc. Wts. i. 193; Proc. Som. Arch. Soc. xxviii. 109–12.
49 Rot. Parl. (Rec. Com.), ii. 13; Cal. Chanc. Wts. i. 193; Cal. Inq. p.m. vii. pp. 144–5.
50 Proc. Som. Arch. Soc. xxvii. 142–3.

51 Cal. Close, 1318–23, 270; 1330–3, 265; Cal. Fine R. 1307–19, 76, 114; 1327–37, 163; Proc. Som. Arch. Soc. xxviii. 109–12; Cal. Inq. p.m. vii, pp. 144–5.
52 Proc. Som. Arch. Soc. xxviii. 142–3.
53 Cal. Pat. 1385–9, 135; 1446–52, 220.
54 Ibid. 1553, 379.
55 C 66/2497.
56 Proc. Som. Arch. Soc. xxviii. 142–4.
57 D.R.O., D 124, accts. 1369–70, 1378–9.
58 Ibid., ct. rolls.
59 Ibid.
60 D.R.O., D 124, accts. 1494–5, 1501–2.
61 Ibid. ct. roll.
62 S.R.O., DD/SS, bdle. 1; DD/PT, box 2, nos. 13–18.
63 Penes Countess Poulett, Jersey.
64 S.R.O., DD/PT, box 31; DD/S/HR, box 1.
65 S.R.O., DD/PT, box 31.
66 S.R.O., DD/SS, bdle. 1; DD/PT, box 2, nos. 13–18.
67 D.R.O., D 124, acct. 1369–70.
68 S.R.O., D/P/lop 4/1/1; tithe award.

the mid 18th century.[69] Regular relief for badged paupers was supplemented by the payment of house rent, repairs, and the provision of fuel and medicine. One man in 1758 was sent to hospital at Bristol. The poor-rate, administered by two overseers, was used on occasion for digging the parish ditch, employing a man to examine chimneys after two fires in 1755, repairing highways or, in 1745, celebrating the victory at Culloden with cider. By the 19th century the vestry, with slightly smaller membership, was acting as tithe collector for Lord Poulett, the lay rector.[70] By 1827 a salaried overseer was employed, and in the following year a parish mole-catcher was paid from the waywarden's rate. After 1837 the offices of overseer and waywarden were combined, and from 1849 the post was salaried.

At least by 1725 there was a house known as the parish house, which was repaired by the overseers and was probably used to house the poor.[71] By 1774 there were six poorhouses in Holloway,[72] and a further one was added in 1785.[73] These were put up for sale after the parish became part of the Chard poor-law union in 1836.[74]

CHURCH. In or before 1209 Sir Nicholas de Meriet granted the chapel of Lopen to the canons of Bruton.[75] In origin presumably a manorial foundation of the Meriets or their ancestors, it became dependent on the church of South Petherton, itself already belonging to the canons.[76] At the Dissolution[77] it passed with South Petherton to the chapter of Bristol,[78] but in 1574 acquired burial rights, severing the practical links with the mother church.[79] The chapter let the rectory of South Petherton and its chapels, and at least from 1562 the lessees were themselves required to find priests to serve them.[80] The conveyance of the tithes of Lopen from Bristol to Earl Poulett in 1802 expressly excepted the patronage, but the Pouletts retained it under an earlier unsurrendered lease until after 1838,[81] and possibly until the death of the 5th earl in 1864. Thereafter the chapter presented until 1941, when the advowson was transferred to the chapter of Wells.[82]

In the 16th century the chaplain received a stipend of £2 13s. 4d.[83] Sir Anthony Poulett (d. 1600) augmented it in return for four annual sermons.[84] During the 1650s the chaplain was paid £15 a year,[85] a sum which remained the responsibility of the farmer of the tithes, though by 1786 the lay rector was actually paying £20 a year for

duty once a Sunday.[86] The benefice was, however, augmented in 1747 by John Castleman, prebendary of Bristol and vicar of South Petherton. After a further augmentation in 1793[87] the clear value was c. £69 in 1815, £77 in 1831, and £78 in 1851.[88]

When the chapel was granted to Bruton priory in the early 13th century a portion of 'the tithes of the demesne of Meriet', formerly held by Roger, archdeacon of Winchester, was attached.[89] It is not clear whether the demesnes were in the parish of Merriott or were the Meriet demesnes in Lopen or elsewhere. Certainly the chapel possessed tithes in Kingsdon which were granted to Bruton by Hugh de Meriet (d. c. 1236).[90] Such tithes and any attached glebe thereafter formed part of the rectory estate. Land in South Petherton, amounting to 31 a., was purchased for Lopen chapel with augmentation money in 1749.[91] In 1851 it produced an income of £56,[92] but it was sold in 1920.[93]

In 1619 the curate had a house in the parish, but it was not known whether it belonged to the benefice.[94] There was no glebe house in the 19th century, though the incumbents at that time lived in the village. The last one to do so died in 1904.[95]

In 1577 John Vawdye, the curate, was described as 'unmeet' for the charge, 'being a Jersey man, not having the perfect English tongue and unlearned'.[96] The curate in 1606 held Dinnington with Lopen.[97] His successor in 1612 catechized only 'now and then' and was not licensed.[98] In the 1650s the chapel was usually served with Seavington St. Mary.[99] John Templeman, perpetual curate 1783–1835, lived in Lopen and served Cricket St. Thomas. Services at Lopen were held once every Sunday and on certain holy days.[1] Two services were held from 1827 and Templeman 'because of advanced age and infirmities' was helped by his son and eventual successor.[2] By 1851 the services were held alternately morning and evening and afternoon and evening, with average general congregations of 150 in the morning, 250 in the afternoon, and the same in the evening. Sixty Sunday-school pupils attended mornings and afternoons.[3] By 1870 the minister was reported as serving 'as well as he is able', but there was only one service each Sunday, with a sermon at nearly every one. There were then five or six celebrations of the Holy Communion each year.[4] Robert Phelps Billing, Ph.D., curate 1871–1904, who held the benefice of Kingstone from 1875, was the last resident incumbent. After his death the benefice was held by successive vicars of South Petherton until 1960,

[69] S.R.O., D/P/lop 13/2/1.
[70] Ibid. 9/1/1.
[71] Ibid. 13/2/1.
[72] S.R.O., DD/PT, map 1774.
[73] Ibid., box 30.
[74] S.R.O., D/PS/ilm. box 16; D/P/lop 9/1/1.
[75] S.R.S. viii, p. 39.
[76] See below, p. 179.
[77] Cal. Papal Regs. v. 326.
[78] L. & P. Hen. VIII, xvii, pp. 637–8.
[79] S.R.O., D/D/ol 4.
[80] S.R.O., DD/PT, box 10A.
[81] Ibid. box 19B; Bristol R.O. DC/E/24/5.
[82] Dioc. Kal.; Dioc. Dir.
[83] S. & D. N. & Q. xiv. 33.
[84] S.R.O., DD/X/SAB, transcript of Bristol Cath. Chetwynd survey f. 16.
[85] S.R.O., DD/PT, box 40.
[86] Ibid. box 16; Bristol R.O. DC/E/24/4.

[87] Hodgson, Queen Anne's Bounty.
[88] S.R.O., D/D/B return 1815; Rep. Com. Eccl. Revenues, pp. 144–5; H.O. 129/318/4/6/10.
[89] S.R.S. viii, p. 39.
[90] Ibid.
[91] S.R.O., D/P/lop 3/1/1.
[92] H.O. 129/318/4/6/10.
[93] S.R.O., D/P/lop 3/1/1.
[94] S.R.O., DD/X/SAB, Chetwynd survey f. 16.
[95] S.R.O., D/D/B return 1815, D/D/V returns 1827, 1840; Dioc. Kal.
[96] S.R.O., D/D/Ca 57.
[97] Ibid. 151.
[98] Ibid. 175.
[99] S.R.O., DD/PT, box 40.
[1] Ibid., box 27; S.R.O., D/D/B return 1815.
[2] S.R.O., D/D/V return 1827.
[3] H.O. 129/318/4/6/10.
[4] S.R.O., D/D/V return 1870.

when it was linked with Seavington St. Mary and Seavington St. Michael.[5]

The church house of Lopen, divided into two dwellings by 1700, was burnt before 1781. Its site is unknown.[6] A bier house, recently built on part of the pound, was conveyed to trustees by Earl Poulett in 1933.[7]

The church of *ALL SAINTS* is built of rubble and ashlar and has a chancel, and a nave with north transept, south porch, and western bellcot. The head of a 12th-century window is reset in the porch and it is possible that the nave and chancel may be of that date in origin, although there are no *in situ* features earlier than the 14th-century south doorway. When not entirely of the 19th century, the windows are of the 15th, but much restored. These and the contemporary chancel roof and rood stair suggest that the 15th century was a time of considerable building activity. The chancel arch may have been rebuilt in the late 16th century. The present appearance of the church owes much to major alterations in the 19th century. The north transept was added in 1833,[8] and between 1874 and 1886 part of the nave walling, including most of the windows and buttresses, and the south porch were rebuilt and the chancel restored.[9] Galleries were put up in transept (removed 1958)[10] and nave, the former approached by an external stair, and the nave was re-roofed and ceiled. The screen, designed by A. F. Erridge, was erected in 1951.[11]

There are two bells: (i) 1868; (ii) 1765, Thomas Bayley.[12] The plate includes a cup and cover of 1738.[13] Registers of baptisms date from 1693, of burials from 1694, and of marriages from 1723 and are complete.[14]

NONCONFORMITY. Two unspecified groups had licences in 1695 and one in 1707.[15] The houses of Joshua Gummer and Peter Horsey were used by Presbyterians from 1751, and in the same year Horsey's house was licensed for Anabaptists.[16] Two years later 'the workhouse at the court of Peter Horsey' was used by Methodists.[17] Horsey himself was described as a yarnwasher.[18] Later in 1753 and again in 1754 Methodists occupied other premises, and in 1759 licences were issued for both Baptists and Presbyterians. In 1760 Robert Gummer's house, previously used by both Methodists and Presbyterians, was licensed for Presbyterians and Baptists.[19] 'Some' Presbyterians were reported in 1776.[20]

The Congregationalist cause started in a private house in 1825.[21] Meetings continued in a 'small room' until 1864, when a chapel was built through the efforts of the Revd. Samuel Hebditch (1821–88), a native of Lopen and a noted preacher.[22] The building could seat 150 and cost c. £250.[23] At the end of the 19th century an evangelist stationed there worked in the surrounding villages.[24] The cause declined in the 20th century and the chapel was sold in 1952.[25] The building, of Ham stone, was used in 1974 as a store.

EDUCATION. Two schools in 1819 taught reading to 37 children.[26] A Sunday school began in 1822, the churchwardens contributing in the first year.[27] By 1826 there were 74 pupils.[28] Ten years later the Sunday school had 80 pupils, and two day-schools 28 pupils, all three supported by subscriptions.[29] The Sunday school continued to grow and by 1847 ten teachers were employed.[30]

A school board was established in 1877 and a school opened in 1879 with 74 pupils.[31] The premises comprised two rooms and a teacher's house. Average attendance rose from 48 in 1894 to 72 in 1900, and was 63 in 1902.[32] Attendance fell rapidly during the 20th century and from 1948 senior pupils were transferred to Crewkerne, leaving only 13 in 1951. The school was closed in 1952, and the children transferred to Hinton St. George.[33]

CHARITIES FOR THE POOR. None known.

SOUTH PETHERTON

THE ANCIENT parish of South Petherton, the largest in the hundred of the same name, covers 3,494 a.[1] It takes the name Petherton from the river Parrett with the addition 'South' to distinguish it from North Petherton, further down the river near Bridgwater. Roughly rectangular in shape, it is nearly 3 miles long and 2 miles wide. The boundaries follow water courses for perhaps three-quarters of

[5] S.R.O., D/P/lop 3/5/1.
[6] *Dioc. Kal.; Dioc. Dir.*
[7] S.R.O., DD/PT, box 30.
[8] S.R.O., D/P/lop 4/1/1, 6/2/1; D/D/Ca 441. The plans were drawn by George Moss of Crewkerne: DD/X/SF (C/616).
[9] S.R.O., D/P/lop 6/2/1.
[10] Ibid. 6/1/1.
[11] Ibid. 6/3/1.
[12] S.R.O., DD/SAS CH 16.
[13] *Proc. Som. Arch. Soc.* xlv. 145.
[14] S.R.O., D/P/lop 2/1/1–6. There are marriages in 1696, 1711, and 1719.
[15] S.R.O., Q/RR, meeting-house lics.
[16] Ibid.
[17] Ibid.
[18] S.R.O., DD/PT, box 31.
[19] S.R.O., Q/RR, meeting-house lics.
[20] S.R.O., D/D/V Dioc. bk. 1776.

[21] S.R.O., D/D/Rm, box 2.
[22] *Western Gazette*, 23 July 1864; Boase, *Modern English Biog.*
[23] *Rep. Som. Cong. Union* (1896).
[24] Ibid.
[25] Char. Com. file.
[26] *Digest of Returns to Sel. Cttee. on Educ. of Poor*, H.C. 224 (1819), ix (2).
[27] S.R.O., D/P/lop 4/1/1.
[28] *Rep. B. & W. Dioc. Assoc. S.P.C.K.* (1825–6).
[29] *Educ. Enquiry Abstract*, H.C. 62 (1835), xiii.
[30] *Church Sch. Inquiry, 1846–7.*
[31] S.R.O., C/E 78.
[32] Ibid., 27; *Return of Schs. 1893* [C. 7529], H.C. (1894), lxv; *Return of Schs. 1900* [Cd. 315], H.C. (1900), lv (2).
[33] S.R.O., C/E 78.
[1] *Census.* This article was completed in 1975.

their length: the Lopen brook in the south divides Petherton from Merriott; the Parrett forms the eastern limit of both parish and hundred (and also of the archdeaconry of Taunton), much of the line being opposite Martock and small lengths adjoining Stoke sub Hamdon, Norton sub Hamdon, and Chiselborough. The Lambrook, in the 19th century known as the Fish brook,[2] forms the northern boundary with Kingsbury Episcopi, and part of the division with Shepton Beauchamp. In the southwest, with part of Shepton, Lopen, and Seavington St. Michael, there is evidence of later formation: Lopen was certainly part of the ancient parish, and remained a dependent chapelry until the 20th century. The transfer of land from Seavington St. Mary to South Petherton by 1086 and the possible importance of Fouts cross as a meeting-place or market site may also account for some irregularity in the same area.[3]

Three-quarters of the parish lies on the fertile Yeovil Sands, producing the 'remarkably good' arable described in the 1780s.[4] North-east of a line drawn between Bridge, the town, and Middle Lambrook, however, is a ridge of limestone, followed by Pennard Sands and clay as the land slopes down to the alluvium of the Parrett valley. The limestone, known as Petherton stone, was quarried at Pitway in the 19th century, and bricks and tiles were manufactured on the slope of Pitway hill and along the East Lambrook road. Marl was dug in several places, including a site near Old Bridge,[5] and pits on the boundary between Compton Durville and Shepton and south of Wigborough gave their names to fields.[6]

The main settlement, in the centre of its parish, lies in a hollow, only the top stage of its church tower, capped with a spirelet, being visible from much of the surrounding land. Yet the highest point in the parish, mid-way between the town and the western boundary, is only 231 ft. above sea level, and most of the ground undulates gently a little above the 100 ft. contour. The ground falls as the boundaries are reached, except in the south-west in the slightly exposed area near Lopen Head, once a district of furze and heath.[7] The core of the town itself lies on sloping ground on the side of a stream, its church occupying a prominent position on a spur. There is some suggestion that the settlement north of this spur may at least have been defined on its western and northern sides, judging by the possibility of a ditch to the west of George Lane and by the course of Palmer Street.[8] Such a site would not have been very strong, especially in comparison with Stoodham, across the valley to the north. There the northern tip of the limestone ridge, reaching 190 ft.,

has produced evidence of occupation in the Iron Age and Romano-British periods as well as a few flint implements, though there is no evidence of any structures or fortifications, with the possible exception of a ditch above the terraces called Mere Linches.[9] The juxtaposition of two sites on each side of a stream recalls the more imposing, though still undefended, sites at Somerton and Hurcot further north.

Early occupation elsewhere in the parish has been revealed by the discovery of Bronze Age implements at Wigborough,[10] and by more extensive Roman remains. The Foss Way runs through the southern half of the parish and, although partly disused, has left its mark not only on the road pattern, but also in the place-names Stratton and Harp, the road called Harpway, and the field-names Harfurlong, Streetlands, and Netherway.[11] Confused reports of two or possibly three villas have not been authenticated, though many coins have been found over a wide area, dating mostly from the 3rd and 4th centuries.[12]

If the present settlement is more obviously of Saxon origin, yet its character is by no means uniform throughout the parish. Petherton itself lies at the centre of a group of hamlets with varying beginnings. Compton Durville seems to have originated at the centre of two, and perhaps three, pre-Domesday estates, part often associated with land in Kingsbury and also with an unidentified settlement called Clopton.[13] Traces of four common fields were apparent there at least until the end of the 18th century.[14] In the south both Wigborough and Stratton had emerged as manorial centres by the mid 11th century. The former has been suggested and rejected as the site of a battle between the Saxons of Devon and the Danes in 851, and the derivation of the place-name as 'Wicga's hill' is at variance with the gentle contours.[15] Bridge occurs as a hamlet by the end of the 12th century and is presumably named after the bridge taking the Foss over the Parrett.[16] Little Lopen occurs by 1232 and by 1386 there was a house there called the 'chapel',[17] though the position of the hamlet can only be generally indicated by the survival of Little Lopen Lane, running south near Yeabridge Farm, and by field-names. Drayton was certainly settled by 1305,[18] and judging by its name much earlier. By the end of the 13th century there was a distinction between Upper or Over and Lower or Nether Stratton, presumably originating in the two estates of the same name, the former a manorial holding linked with Lopen, the latter a member of the manor of South Petherton.[19] How far there was any distinction of settlement in a topographical sense is

[2] S.R.O., CR 141, inclosure map.
[3] V.C.H. Som. i. 473.
[4] Geol. Surv. Map 1", solid and drift, sheet 312 (1958 edn.); Bristol R.O., DC/E/24/4: survey.
[5] S.R.O., DD/PE 5: map 1773.
[6] S.R.O., tithe award.
[7] S.R.S. xvii. 121–2; Cal. Close, 1385–9, 325; S.R.O., DD/PE 19, Bacon to Cabell.
[8] The suggestion of Mr. M. Aston, Somerset County Archaeologist.
[9] V.C.H. Som. i. 366; H. Norris, South Petherton in Olden Time (2nd edn. 1913), 8–9; S. & D. N. & Q. xxvi. 171; Archaeological Review (Council for Brit. Arch., Groups 12 and 13), iii (1968), 21.
[10] O.S. Arch. recs.

[11] S.R.O., tithe award; DD/SAS (C/114), 1; D.R.O., D 124, Stratton ct. rolls; Cal. Close, 1385–9, 621–2. Harp is from Harepaeth, a military road or highway: A. H. Smith, English Place-Name Elements, i. 240, 244–5.
[12] V.C.H. Som. i. 331–2, 366; O.S. Arch. recs.
[13] For Clopton see Cur. Reg. R. vi, pp. 349, 378–9; vii, pp. 280–1.
[14] Bristol R.O., DC/E/24/4.
[15] A.-S. Chron. ed. Whitelock, Douglas, and Tucker, 42 n.; Proc. Som. Arch. Soc. xcv. 124.
[16] Rot. Cur. Reg. (Rec. Com.), ii. 209.
[17] Cur. Reg. R. xiv, pp. 437, 491; Cal. Close, 1385–9, 621–2.
[18] C 133/120/2.
[19] Feud. Aids, iv. 283.

unknown. There was a capital messuage at Little Stratton in 1506.[20] The emergence of the hamlet of Harp, probably by 1305,[21] is a further topographical puzzle, the name in the 1970s being given to two separate farms and to the road between them.

In terms of field systems in the south of the parish it seems that in the 14th century there were four common arable fields around Stratton, parts of which were attached to the manor of Wigborough.[22] By the end of the 18th century there were six near Stratton, together with common meadow in the extreme south-west of the parish, known as Yellands in the 19th century but probably part of a more extensive South mead in the Middle Ages.[23] Drayton had three fields and three separate arable furlongs in the 18th century, with a common meadow known as Drayton mead. Wigborough, then an inclosed farm, had three arable fields which may have corresponded to an earlier pattern.[24] Two other settlements in the south of the parish had widely differing origins. Yeabridge is a group of roadside cottages dating from the early 19th century, though the settlement had existed for at least the previous hundred years.[25] A much earlier development was Watergore, which occurs in 1462,[26] and which presumably owes its origin to the road junction on which it stands. The bounds of these hamlets seem to have been marked by crosses in medieval times. The *crux ville* and St. James's cross occur in 1522, and the base of a cross still surviving at the southern end of Stratton may be the remains of one of these. The dedication of a cross to St. James may suggest the existence of a chapel near by.[27]

South Petherton itself lies at the centre of a web of roads and footpaths converging on church and market-place and serving the surrounding fields. This web is most noticeable in the northern half of the parish, though there is also direct road communication with Drayton, Bridge, and South Harp, and a footpath, known as Church Path, proceeding from Stratton. The town itself, however, is not on any obviously important through route, except perhaps via Bridgeway from Petherton Bridge to Shepton Beauchamp. Indeed, by the late 18th century the only through traffic to concern the manor hayward was that along the public roads through the corn fields at the time of Petherton and Stoke fairs.[28]

South of the town, however, the parish is crossed by an east-west route which probably pre-dates the Foss Way and which since the 18th century has been part of the northern London–Exeter coach road. This road, entering the parish over Petherton Bridge, may well originally have been a prehistoric trackway linking the Iron Age fort on Ham Hill with Neroche and the Blackdowns. An ancient

bridge over the Parrett, possibly the Roman one carrying the Foss, was referred to as the 'old bridge' in *c.* 1206,[29] and gave its name to the hamlet there. The 'fair stone bridge' there in the early 17th century bore the effigies of two people, variously described as the founder and his wife and as two children drowned there.[30] The strategic importance of the bridge was evident in the Civil War, and it was broken by the Parliamentarian forces in 1645.[31] Repairs were ordered in 1648 and some were done in 1650.[32] In the early 1970s the 15th-century structure of three spans with pointed arches was replaced to take a dual carriageway, but the effigies and a direction stone have been preserved.

The road carried by this bridge diverged slightly north of the course of the Foss and at Watergore divided. Until the beginning of the 19th century the more important route, along the prehistoric course, continued to Frogmary Green. Thence it followed the parish boundary to Fouts cross. Still in the 1770s[33] this was considered the main route to Taunton via Ilford Bridges, and its importance may be gauged by the presence of inns beside it at Watergore and Fouts.[34] This route was adopted by the Ilminster turnpike trustees in 1758–9, but abandoned by them in 1802–3,[35] thus marking the end of its common use. The southern route from Watergore towards Lopen continues in use as a trunk road from London to the south-west of England.

The roads serving South Petherton itself were adopted by other turnpike trusts. The route from Fouts cross through the town to Martock was taken over by the Martock trust in 1803, perhaps in an attempt to create a through route.[36] The Langport trust adopted roads linking Fouts with Compton Durville and West Lambrook in 1824,[37] and proposals in 1830, none of which seems to have been carried out, involved the adoption of most of the roads in the town and the creation of new routes across Stoodham and Pikes Moor, south of Joyler's mill, to provide more direct access from Kingsbury southwards to Crewkerne.[38] The link towards Crewkerne was the point of a projected light railway between Martock, Petherton, and Crewkerne in 1907–8.[39] Toll houses were built at Bridge Cross, west of Petherton Bridge, and at Atkins's Gate on the Martock road, just west of the junction with the East Lambrook road.

The church and the market-place provided the focus of the medieval town of South Petherton, and the earliest reference to a street is to Cheap Street in 1443.[40] This was the name of the row of houses on the north side of the market-place, and continued in use until the 19th century.[41] In the centre of this market-place stood the market house and also a cross, said to have been removed in the 1830s or a little

20 C 142/25/26.
21 See below, p. 178.
22 *Cal. Close*, 1381–5, 579–80.
23 S.R.O., tithe award; D.R.O., D 124, boxes 13, 16, 18, Stratton ct. rolls; Bristol R.O., DC/E/24/4.
24 Bristol R.O., DC/E/24/4.
25 S.R.O., DD/SAS SX 102, *sub anno* 1710.
26 D.R.O., D 124, box 16, Stratton ct. roll.
27 Ibid.; Norris, *S. Petherton*, 51.
28 S.R.O., DD/PE 6, *sub anno* 1784.
29 *S.R.S.* viii, pp. 37–8: the spelling is 'eldebrige'.
30 *S.R.S.* xv. 111.
31 *Cal. S.P. Dom.* 1644–5, 506.
32 *S.R.S.* lxxi, pp. 22–3.
33 S.R.O., DD/PE 5: map 1773.
34 There was also the Travellers' Rest in Seavington St. Mary.
35 S.R.O., D/T/ilm.
36 Martock Turnpike Act, 43 Geo. III, c. xxvi (Local and Personal); S.R.O., Q/R deposited plan 109.
37 S.R.O. D/T/lsc 2.
38 S.R.O., Q/R deposited plan 109.
39 S.R.O., DD/PR 81.
40 *Cal. Pat.* 1441–6, 190.
41 S.R.O., DD/S/HR, box 6: Davis to Rouse 1829.

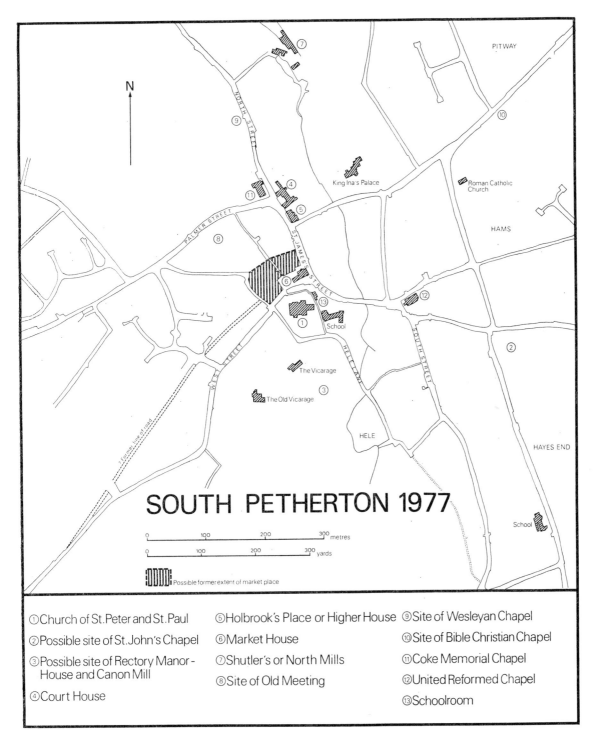

SOUTH PETHERTON 1977

0   100   200   300 metres
0   100   200   300 yards

Possible former extent of market place

① Church of St. Peter and St. Paul	⑤ Holbrook's Place or Higher House	⑨ Site of Wesleyan Chapel
② Possible site of St. John's Chapel	⑥ Market House	⑩ Site of Bible Christian Chapel
③ Possible site of Rectory Manor-House and Canon Mill	⑦ Shutler's or North Mills	⑪ Coke Memorial Chapel
④ Court House	⑧ Site of Old Meeting	⑫ United Reformed Chapel
		⑬ Schoolroom

later.[42] The steep south-eastern entrance was known as Market Hill by 1668, and as the Cornhill in the 19th century.[43]

By the 17th century the pattern of streets had taken on the present arrangement, with the market-place almost by-passed by St. James's Street and Palmer Street. Although there is no direct evidence for any planned urban development, the two lanes leading north and north-west from the market-place may represent original routes which were later made redundant either by the development of Palmer Street or by the contraction of the market-place, the latter perhaps then causing the diversion of West Street. Palmer Street was certainly by the 17th century the home of some of the wealthiest inhabitants,[44] though no. 6 is perhaps the only building to survive among some substantial 19th-century houses. The Coke Memorial Chapel replaced

[42] C. Pooley, *Old Stone Crosses of Som.*, 153. There was said to have been one in the chyd.

[43] S.R.O., Q/SR 111/60; H.O. 107/1929.
[44] S.R.O., D/P/pet.s 4/1/1, 13/2/1.

a gabled 17th-century house known as Moon's after its ownership by the Mohun family.[45] The formation of Palmer Street perhaps provided the impetus for the further development of St. James's Street which in the 19th century was the commercial centre of the town and in the 20th holds most of the shops. The origin of the name has not been traced, but the presence of Holbrook's Place (nos. 40–44) and the Court House (nos. 48–50) indicates development of the northern end by the early 16th century.[46] Most of the present building in the street is irregular, largely on the street front, but some houses lie behind gardens. Most are of the 19th and 20th centuries. Nos. 33 and 35 form a pair of thatched cottages, originally framed in timber, having at least one framed fire hood backing on the through passage. Also of the 17th century is the gabled Bell inn, dated 1622 but rebuilt in 1925. Norris House, of the 18th century, was the home of the town's doctor and historian Hugh Norris.

The expansion from the central core cannot be dated precisely. By the early 17th century there was certainly settlement at Pitway and Little Petherton, both essentially groups of waste-land cottages.[47] Both imply earlier development of West Street and Butt (Budde or Budle) Lane.[48] South and North streets occur by the 1630s.[49] The former replaced the medieval church path and Hele Lane, presumably because heavy traffic found the ford in Hele Lane inconvenient. South Street contains several substantial 18th- and 19th-century houses including Yarn Barton and Knapp House (Naphouse in 1778).[50] An earlier building is no. 25 South Street, with a jointed cruck structure.[51] No. 27, South Farm, formerly South Street Farm, was largely rebuilt on the foundations of an earlier house in 1700;[52] its gable end housed a pork butcher's shop in the 19th century.[53] Cole's House, at the southern end of the street, is an early-19th-century house of local brick.

Within these main roads a series of streets and lanes form a tight network. White, High, and Roundwell streets, Pound and Court bartons occur by the mid 17th century,[54] Prigg and Pound lanes by the mid 18th century.[55] Names apparently of 19th-century origin include Joggler's hill, Vicarage Lane, Lightgate Road, and Ebenezer Row. In the 1850s Lower St. James's Street was an alternative name for Silver Street.[56] In the 1880s there was much new building at Little Petherton and elsewhere, and 20th-century development includes dwellings at Stoodham, Hams, and Summer Shard.[57]

In the 1770s the town was said to contain 'nothing remarkable';[58] the centre was largely rebuilt in the 19th century, though on the outskirts and in the hamlets there are examples of earlier farmhouses and cottages, mostly in local stone, occasionally in brick, normally as additions. Inventories of the mid 17th century suggest that most houses had ceased to have open halls, though those of John Edmonds (1629) and John Marke (1669) seem to have been unconverted. Most were of three-roomed plan.[59] Among the surviving buildings is Hayes End Manor, divided into three dwellings. It is a 17th-century house, heightened in 1760, with a new wing added by J. W Peters. Among the associated farm buildings is a nine-bay barn, built by J. B. Edmonds in 1803, constructed on Ham stone pillars with open or weather-boarded sides, a raised floor, and a tiled roof. There is also a granary or store house of similar date, with an open cart shed on the ground floor. The construction is of Ham stone lined with brick. The top floor was used as a school in the 19th century.

Watergore includes two 17th- and one 18th-century house facing the former road to Ilford Bridges, as well as the remains of an inn. Over Stratton is virtually a single street consisting of a few 17th- and 18th-century small houses. At its southern end is Stratton Farm, a 16th-century building, originally cob walled, with a cruck-trussed roof, and an open hall in the centre. South Harp Farm, a little further south, is of three-room plan of the late 17th century with an unheated central room and a projecting semi-circular stair in the back wall. Stratton Farm has a barn of 1816 at the rear. It is partly open-sided and much of the building has an upper floor with provision for temporary joists in the main open bay. Compton Durville includes the substantial Dower House, formerly Harding's Farm, which is of 17th-century origin though with extensive additions.

By 1618 there were at least two inns in the town belonging to the main manor.[60] The earliest named is the George (1622), described as a cottage, in Cheap Street.[61] It was held by successive members of the Willy family from 1698 at least until 1761, and subsequently by Martin Pyke, from 1737 until 1786 or later.[62] It occurs until 1809.[63] By 1658 there were two other inns, the Three Cups and the Rose and Crown.[64] The latter, known as the Crown in 1635 and as the Rose and Crown in 1769–70, was more usually known as the Crown again by 1773.[65] It was the most popular house in the late 18th and early 19th centuries, being used for meetings of the vestry in 1799 and for public meetings and auction sales.[66] The present building replaced a thatched structure c. 1894.[67] The White Horse inn occurs by 1690 and

---

45 Norris, S. Petherton, 42.
46 For descriptions see below, pp. 177, 180.
47 S.R.O., D/P/pet. s 2/1/1, sub annis 1649, 1692; DD/PE 6; Hook Manor, Donhead St. Andrew, Arundell MSS., rentals and surveys 90; ibid. S. Petherton deeds 21.
48 Arundell MSS., S. Petherton deeds 23; S.R.O., DD/S/HR, box 11.
49 Arundell MSS., S. Petherton deeds 23.
50 S.R.O., DD/PE 6 sub anno.
51 Proc. Som. Arch. Soc. cxvii. 105.
52 Datestone on building.
53 Lady's Pictorial, 1 Aug. 1891, 203; ex inf. Miss C. P. R. Poole, South Petherton.
54 S.R.O., DD/PE 6. The name High St. occurs only twice.
55 S.R.O., DD/PE 6, sub annis 1749, 1771. The pound

in Pound lane occurs in 1825; DD/S/HR, box 11.
56 H.O. 107/1929: S.R.O., D/PC/pet.s 1/2/1.
57 S.R.O., D/G/Y 160.
58 New Display of the Beauties of Eng. 322.
59 S.R.O., D/D/Ct E; DD/SP, inventories; DD/S/HR, box 6.
60 Arundell MSS., ct. bk. 21 (date 21 Sept.).
61 S.R.O., D/D/Cd 57; DD/PE 6.
62 Arundell MSS., rentals and surveys 90; S.R.O., DD/PE 6; Q/RR, papists' estates; Q/RL.
63 S.R.O., D/P/pet.s 4/1/2.   64 Ibid. 13/2/1.
65 Arundell MSS., S. Petherton deeds 23; S.R.O., Q/RL; DD/PE 6.
66 Taunton Courier 7, 14 Jan. 1813.
67 Lady's Pictorial, 1 Aug. 1891, 203; Kelly's Dir. Som. (1894).

was held by the Prew family from 1751 until at least 1786; it continued until 1799 or later.[68] A house, late the White Horse inn, at Watergore, was referred to in 1866.[69] This may be a different building, or possibly a confusion with the Horseshoe or Three Horseshoes at Watergore, on the Ilford Bridges road, which occurs from 1748 at least until 1773.[70] By 1735 the Bell and by 1740 the Wheatsheaf were in business, the latter probably in Cornhill, the former in St. James's Street;[71] and by 1751 there were twelve licensed houses, including one at Compton Durville.[72] Among them was the King's Arms (by 1735) and the Running Footman (1751).[73]

In the early 19th century the principal inns were the Crown, the Castle (by 1806),[74] the Bell, and the Wheatsheaf.[75] The Castle stood next to the Crown in the market-place, but by 1851 had been converted to a shop.[76] In the 1830s new houses emerged including the Bunch of Grapes (1836) and the Plough, both at Fouts cross (1837). In 1869 the Fruiterers' Arms in Pitway was licensed, together with two beerhouses, the Royal Oak at Stratton and the New Inn.[77]

A benefit club was formed in South Petherton in 1786, to meet each year on 1 September.[78] The Labourers' Friendly Society was founded in 1852 and continued until 1918,[79] and the Female Friendly Society, established in 1874, continued until 1912.[80] A Provident Society, founded in Martock in 1883, had members from South Petherton.[81]

Leisure-time activities for the inhabitants included membership of the Literary Institute and Reading Room (founded by 1861), of the South Petherton Agricultural Society (by 1873),[82] or of the Volunteer Battalion of the Somerset Light Infantry (by 1883), which drilled at Hayes End and later in Roundwell Street.[83] By the end of the century there were many cultural groups formed to hear lectures on science and art, horticulture and hygiene, clearly the foundation of a tradition which survives into the 1970s.[84]

The four tithings of South Petherton, Over Stratton, South Harp, and Compton Durville, produced a total of 106 men at a muster in 1539,[85] and there were 154 households returned in 1563.[86] In 1656 Petherton was described as a market town of 300 families.[87] Between 1801 and 1851 the population rose rapidly from 1,674 to 2,606, and for the next forty years fluctuated by two or three hundred

a decade until 1901, when it fell to 1,997. It remained stable in the earlier 20th century, but rose in the 1960s, the total reaching 2,549 in 1971.[88]

During the Civil War cavalry under Essex visited the town in 1644 and damaged the church. They were followed by a Royalist troop including Richard Symonds, the diarist.[89] Petherton Bridge was of importance in the campaign before the battle of Langport in the following year. It was destroyed by Colonel Weldon and the Parliamentarians in May 1645, and then temporarily repaired by Goring who was in pursuit. Parliamentarians under Edward Montagu occupied the town in July after the battle.[92] The hoard of silver coins discovered in Prig Lane is assumed to have been buried by a soldier at the time of these events.[91] In 1660 a radical regiment of militia in the town demanded its pay but disappeared when its officers refused to come near.[92] During his Western Progress in 1680 Monmouth received an ovation at Petherton, and two inhabitants, Robert Sandys and Samuel Prowse, were among 24 accused of supporting him during his rebellion.[93]

Arthur Bury, D.D. (d. 1713), rector of Exeter College, Oxford, 1666–90, seems to have retired to Compton Durville, and was buried in the parish church.[94] Thomas Coke, D.C.L. (1747–1814), first superintendent and 'bishop' of the American Methodist Church, and first secretary of the Methodist Conference, was curate at the parish church from July 1772 until his summary dismissal in March 1777. He joined John Wesley but did not lose his connexion with South Petherton, and he bought a new house in St. James's Street at the end of 1778.[95] Thomas Northcote Toller (1756–1812), Nonconformist divine of Kettering (Northants.), was born in the parish.[96] Hugh Norris (1821–1910), surgeon in the town from 1852 and a noted antiquary, was first joint editor of *Somerset and Dorset Notes and Queries* 1888–90.[97] Field Marshal Lord Harding of Petherton was born in the parish in 1896.[98]

MANORS AND OTHER ESTATES. The manor of *SOUTH PETHERTON*, probably a long-standing possession of the Saxon royal house, still belonged to the Crown in 1066 and 1086.[99] Henry II gave it to Hamelin of Mayenne, a Norman, from

[68] S.R.O., DD/PE 6, *sub anno* 1769; Q/RL; DD/S/HR, box 40.
[69] Ibid. DD/S/HR, box 14.
[70] Ibid. Q/RR, papists' estates; DD/PE 5.
[71] Ibid. DD/SAS SX 102.
[72] Ibid. Q/RL.
[73] Ibid. Q/RR; DD/S/HR, box 8; DD/SAS SX 102.
[74] Ibid. D/P/pet. s 4/1/2.
[75] Ibid. Q/RL.
[76] Ibid. tithe award; H.O. 107/1929.
[77] S.R.O., D/PS/ilm, box 1.
[78] M. Fuller, *West-Country Friendly Socs.* plate II.
[79] Taunton Castle, Tite Colln.; S.R.O., D/P/pet.s 2/5/2.
[80] Taunton Castle, Tite Colln.
[81] Ibid.
[82] *P.O. Dir. Som.* (1861); S.R.O., D/P/she.b 1/7/1.
[83] *Kelly's Dir. Som.* (1883); S.R.O., D/G/Y 160.
[84] S.R.O., D/P/pet.s 17/3/2.
[85] *L. & P. Hen. VIII*, xiv (1), p. 289.
[86] B.L. Harl. MS. 594, f. 56.
[87] *Cal. S.P. Dom.* 1656–7, 198.

[88] *Census.*
[89] *Diary of Richard Symonds* (Camd. Soc. [1st. ser.], lxxiv), 98–100, 102.
[90] D. Underdown, *Som. in the Civil War and Interregnum*, 96–7, 102.
[91] *S. & D. N. & Q.* i. 177–8.
[92] Underdown, *Civil War and Interregnum*, 191.
[93] *S. & D. N. & Q.* iii. 69; B.L. Add. MS. 30077, ff. 34–34v.
[94] *D.N.B.*; *S. & D. N. & Q.* iii. 98–9; Norris, *S. Petherton*, 66. Bury had been rector of Puckington from 1649 probably until 1673, and married a South Petherton woman there in 1699: S.R.O., D/D/Vc 47; D/P/puc 2/1/1.
[95] *D.N.B.*; S.R.O., D/P/pet.s 2/1/6; DD/S/HR, box 20: Daniel to Coke 1778.
[96] Norris, *S. Petherton*, 98–9.
[97] *S. & D. N. & Q.* xii. 145; Norris, *S. Petherton*, pp. vii–xi.
[98] R. T. Graham and F. S. Carpenter, *Ilminster Grammar School*, 146–8.
[99] *V.C.H. Som.* i. 394, 435.

whom it passed to Hamelin's brother Joel.[1] Joel almost certainly rebelled against the Crown during the war in which Normandy was lost,[2] so that his English lands were seized by King John. The custody of South Petherton so seized was successively granted to Terry the German (*Teutonicus*), who held it in 1211[3] and 1212,[4] and to Philip Daubeney, a Breton, who held it by 1225.[5] In 1231 Daubeney received the manor in fee[6] and in December 1234 gave it to Ralph, his *consanguineus*.[7] Despite this Philip was able to mortgage the manor to his nephew Ralph, not certainly the same, for 7 years in February 1235[8] and by June 1235 for the same term to Jocelin, bishop of Bath.[9] By 1237 the bishop had been authorized to assign his rights as mortgagee to his steward, with remainder to the chapter of Wells.[10] How this worked out is not known, but by 1243 Ralph Daubeney (d. 1291–2), Philip's minor son, owned the manor outright.[11] Ralph was succeeded by his sons Sir Philip (d. 1294) and Ellis.[12]

Ellis was summoned to Parliament between 1295 and 1305 as Lord Daubeney. He died in 1305 leaving an infant son Ralph[13] who in 1318 succeeded to the English estates of his family.[14] Ralph Daubeney fought at Crécy, and survived at least until 1378, though he had assigned his rights in South Petherton and Barrington to his heir, Sir Giles, in 1371.[15] Sir Giles died at Barrington in 1386, his son, also Sir Giles, in 1403, and his grandson John in 1409, the estates being thus charged with double dower and farmed for five years during a minority until 1391 by Margaret Courtenay, countess of Devon.[16] By 1412, during another minority, Queen Joan farmed two-thirds of the manor while Giles, brother of John Daubeney, was under age; Margaret, widow of Sir Giles (d. 1403) held dower; and Elizabeth, John's wife, held certain specified lands. Margaret died in 1420 and Elizabeth in 1440.[17]

Sir Giles Daubeney died in 1446.[18] He was succeeded by his son William, who survived until 1461, leaving a young son Giles (later Sir Giles) as his heir.[19] The younger Giles joined Buckingham's rebellion and his lands were confiscated and given to Ralph Neville in 1484.[20] They were restored by Henry VII, who employed Sir Giles as a military commander and ambassador. He was created Baron Daubeney in 1486 and K.G. *c.* 1487. He died in 1508.

The manor then passed to his flamboyant courtier son Henry (cr. earl of Bridgwater 1538, d. 1548),

whose heavy spending forced him to sell most of his property. South Petherton was disposed of to Sir Thomas Arundell of Lanherne (Cornw.) and Wardour (Wilts.), his kinsman, in 1541 for £900, Daubeney receiving it back with Barrington in 1543 for the lives of himself and his wife.[21] Arundell, attainted in 1552, still possessed only the reversion, the manor passing to the Crown on the countess of Bridgwater's death in 1553.[22] It was then leased to Richard Gorney, Sir Thomas Arundell's widow Margaret acquiring a reversionary interest in 1554 and then apparently purchasing Gorney's lease.[23] Margaret Arundell's grant was to continue until £1,000 had been raised for the marriage portions of her two daughters; the manor was then to pass to Sir Charles Arundell, a younger son. Margaret died in 1572, apparently still in possession, and Sir Charles died without heirs in Paris in 1587.[24]

Sir Charles's heir was his brother Sir Matthew (d. 1598), and the manor then passed successively to Sir Matthew's son Thomas (cr. Lord Arundell of Wardour 1605), and to his grandson, also Thomas, in 1639.[25] Thomas, Lord Arundell, died in the royalist cause in 1643, and was succeeded by his son Henry.[26] The manor was, however, sequestrated in 1647 and again in 1651, and then in 1653 purchased for just under £4,000 by trustees headed by Humphrey Weld, of Lulworth (Dors.), like Arundell a Roman Catholic.[27] The manor was regranted to Lord Arundell in 1660[28] and descended with the barony until 1792,[29] when Henry, 8th Lord Arundell (d. 1808), sold it to John Baker Edmonds, a local landowner. Edmonds was still in possession in 1832, but it seems that after his death in 1848 the property came to John Toller Nicholetts, from whom it was transferred to William Parsons Peters, of Yeabridge House.[30] His grandson J. R. Peters of Hayes End was apparently lord of the manor in 1952 but claimed no manorial rights.

By the early 17th century Thomas Gerard found that all trace of the 'palace' of early kings had disappeared, but he was shown a spot 'something south of the church' which was the site of it.[31] Such a site certainly bears a closer relationship to the early settlement of the town than does the more widely accepted 'King Ina's Palace' (see below). The site that Gerard saw, however, may have been the capital messuage of the rectory estate which, in association with enclosures and a mill, lay between the town and Hassockmoor.[32] Subsequently the Daubeneys built a house in the valley below the

[1] *Bk. of Fees*, i. 86; for the relationship between Hamelin and Joel see *Cal. Doc. France*, ed. Round, p. 170.
[2] F. M. Powicke, *Loss of Normandy*, 176.
[3] *Pipe R.* 1211 (P.R.S. N.S. xxviii), 227.
[4] *Bk. of Fees*, i. 86.
[5] *Pat. R.* 1216–25, 513.
[6] *Cal. Chart. R.* 1226–57, 142.
[7] *Close R.* 1234–7, 25.
[8] *Cal. Pat.* 1232–47, 93.
[9] *Cal. Chart. R.* 1226–57, 202.
[10] Ibid. 226.
[11] *Bk. of Fees*, ii. 1385.
[12] *Cal. Inq. p.m.* iii, pp. 15, 111–12.
[13] Ibid. iv, p. 221.
[14] *Complete Peerage*, s.v. Daubeney.
[15] *Cal. Close*, 1370–4, 132; *Rot. Parl.* (Rec. Com.), ii. 231a.
[16] *Cal. Close*, 1389–92, 251; *Complete Peerage*.
[17] *Feud. Aids*, vi. 506; *Complete Peerage*.

[18] *Cal. Fine R.* 1452–61, 131; A. B. Connor, *Monumental Brasses of Som.*
[19] *Cal. Pat.* 1452–61, 641; 1461–7, 6, 299; *Complete Peerage*.
[20] *Cal. Pat.* 1476–85, 427.
[21] E 326/6950, 8868.
[22] C 142/97/77; *Cal. Pat.* 1553–4, 341.
[23] *Cal. Pat.* 1553–4, 341.
[24] C 142/216/89.
[25] C 142/257/83; C 142/495/17.
[26] *Complete Peerage*, s.v. Arundell.
[27] *Cal. Cttee. for Compounding*, ii. 1223; D.R.O., D 54/T 197.
[28] D.R.O., D 54/T 197.
[29] S.R.O., DD/S/HR, box 21; DD/PE 6.
[30] S.R.O., DD/S/HR, box 21; M.I. in South Petherton ch.; Norris S. Petherton, 39–40.
[31] *S.R.S.* xv. 115.
[32] Ibid. viii, p. 35.

town on its eastern side, possibly because their larger house at Barrington was in the late 14th century occupied by two dowagers.[33] The house seems to have become associated with a part of the main manor that later formed the manor of South Harp, first so called in 1475.[34] The manor passed out of Daubeney hands in 1540 and for a time the house was the manor-house of South Harp, owned until after *c.* 1633 by William Seymour, Lord Hertford (d. 1660) and let to the Sandys family from 1618.[35] The Sandyses continued as occupiers and later as owners until the death of Dr. Edwin Sandys in 1761.[36] The house then passed to Thomas Bridge and *c.* 1802 to William Gifford. By 1840 it was owned by John Batten, and in 1862 it was restored by the then owner Edmund Escourt Gale, a relative of the lord of the manor.[37] It became known as 'Old Palace' or 'King Ina's Palace' in the 19th century.[38]

The old house consisted of a main range, partly two-storeyed, partly containing a hall which extended to the roof, and at its east end a cross-wing with a decorated bay window of two storeys.[39] The hall was built probably in the later 14th century and the cross-wing added in the early sixteenth. In the mid 19th century the hall range was remodelled to give two storeys throughout, with a line of gabled windows lighting the upper floor, and attics were put into the cross-wing. Outbuildings were also added or rebuilt to the north-east to create a service wing.

In the absence of a manor-house after the sale of South Harp to Edward Seymour in 1540,[40] it seems possible that the premises known since the 19th century as the Court House were used for that purpose. The Prowse family, successors to Nicholas Saunders, a prosperous merchant, owned or occupied the house from 1675 until the 19th century.[41] It was certainly divided by 1840, and in 1974 was known as nos. 48–50 St. James's Street.

The house is in origin a 16th-century building with a main-range end on to the street and a service cross-wing beyond the entrance passage. A porch was added in the angle between the ranges in the 17th century. Early in the 18th a tall block containing two principal rooms on each floor was added next to the south gable of the cross-wing, possibly to provide accommodation for the manor court. Later in the century the main range was heightened and a two-storeyed canted bay window inserted into the gable towards the street. The fittings include a quantity of panelling of the 17th and 18th centuries.

Alward, evidently a Saxon, held T.R.E. an estate later known as the manor of *WIGBOROUGH*. By 1086 he had been succeeded by John the usher (*hostiarius*), who held the property by serjeanty as porter or usher in the king's hall.[42] This service had been commuted to a payment of 40*s.* each year by 1226,[43] and to half that sum by 1382.[44] The nominal service was still recorded in 1425, but by 1479 the manor was said to be held of William Berkeley by knight service.[45] The service of door-keeper of the king's chamber was claimed for the property in 1631.[46]

At the end of the 12th century the owner of the manor was William the usher, who was succeeded by his daughter Helen by 1207.[47] She married Eustace of Dowlish by 1219, and they were both in occupation in 1243.[48] Their son and successor, Richard of Wigborough or le Arussir, occurs in 1267 and died in 1270.[49] William of Wigborough, presumably his son, held the property in 1284–5, and one of the same name who occurs in 1306 died in 1325.[50] William was then succeeded by his brother Richard who in 1327 settled Wigborough on Richard de Cogan and his wife Mary, subject to the life interest of himself and his wife Maud.[51] Maud outlived her husband and died in 1359 when Richard (d. 1368) and Mary de Cogan succeeded.[52]

Sir William Cogan, their son, died in 1382, leaving his own son John a minor and his wife Isabel holding dower in the manor.[53] Isabel, who married Sir Robert Harington, died in or before 1408 and her property passed to the Crown during the minority of Cogan's eventual heir Fulk Fitz-Waryn (III).[54] The remainder of the manor passed on Cogan's death to his son John, who survived his father by less than a month, and was succeeded by his sister Elizabeth, wife of Sir Fulk FitzWaryn.[55] Sir Fulk died in 1391 and Elizabeth married Sir Hugh Courtenay; Hugh outlived his wife and retained her lands until his own death in 1425.[56] The heir to his FitzWaryn lands was Elizabeth, daughter of Fulk FitzWaryn (II) (d. 1407–8) and wife of Sir Richard Hankeford, who was already in possession of the remainder of the manor.

Hankeford died in 1431 leaving two young daughters, Thomasia and Elizabeth.[57] Elizabeth died in 1433 and the whole manor passed to her sister, later wife of William Bourgchier.[58] For the next hundred years the property was held by the Bourgchiers, later lords FitzWaryn and earls of Bath, the last of whom, John, married the sister of the last Daubeney to own the main manor.[59] In 1545 John Bourgchier, earl of Bath, in association with John

---

[33] C 133/68/5; C 133/120/21.
[34] *Cal. Pat.* 1467–77, 533; *Diary of Richard Symonds* (Camd. Soc. [1st ser.], lxxiv), 99.
[35] *S.R.S.* xv. 116–17; Norris, *S. Petherton*, 112.
[36] Norris, *S. Petherton*, 44.
[37] S.R.O., Q/RE; tithe award; Norris, *S. Petherton*, 40–1.
[38] S.R.O., tithe award; *P.O. Dir. Som.* (1866).
[39] See plate facing p. 145. The date 1897 and the initials 'A.M.' occur in 19th-cent. glass in the bay window.
[40] E 326/11706.
[41] S.R.O., DD/S/HK, box 20; tithe award; Norris, *S. Petherton*, 45.
[42] *V.C.H. Som.* i. 521; *Bk. of Fees*, ii. 1385; *S.R.S.* xi, p. 320.
[43] *Bk. of Fees*, i. 378.
[44] *Cal. Inq. p.m.* xv, p. 291.
[45] C 139/17/30; C 140/73/76.
[46] C 142/534/130.

[47] *S.R.S.* viii, pp. 37–8. For Clopton see B.L. Cott. MS. Tib. D. vi, f. 175.
[48] *Bk. of Fees*, i. 261, 378; ii. 1385; *S.R.S.* xi, p. 320; *Cal. Inq. p.m.* i, p. 301.
[49] *S.R.S.* viii, p. 40; xv. 111–12; *Cal. Inq. p.m.* i, pp. 244–5.
[50] *Feud. Aids*, iv. 284; *S.R.S.* vi. 346; viii, pp. 35–6; *Cal. Inq. p.m.* vi, p. 373.
[51] *S.R.S.* xii. 129. His mother had a life-interest until 1327.
[52] *Cal. Inq. p.m.* x, p. 397; xii, p. 197; *Cal. Close, 1354–60*, 368.
[53] *Cal. Inq. p.m.* xv, p. 291.
[54] B.L. Harl. Ch. 43 E 17–18.
[55] *Cal. Inq. p.m.* xvi, pp. 253–4.   [56] C 139/17/30.
[57] *Cal. Fine R.* 1430–7, 46; C 139/51/54.
[58] C 139/65/40.
[59] *Complete Peerage*, s.v. Bath.

Selwood, a Chard merchant, sold the manor to John Brome.[60] Brome died in 1558, having previously settled it on his wife Alice; his heirs were his daughter Elizabeth, wife of James Compton, and his grandchildren Brome Johnson and Alice Serrey. Alice Brome was still alive in 1559 and surrendered her interest in 1567, but survived until 1581.[61] Elizabeth Compton, owner of one third share, died in 1579 leaving her son Henry as her heir;[62] Alice Serrey, wife of William Deane, died in 1575 leaving her share to her son George;[63] and Brome Johnson died in 1586.[64]

Johnson's son Emorb in 1611 married his distant cousin Alice, daughter of Henry Compton, thus uniting two thirds of the estate.[65] The descent of the other share is not clear, but it may have been acquired by Emorb Johnson between 1596, when George Deane came of age, and his own death in 1615.[66] Emorb Johnson left three daughters Penelope, Elizabeth, and Frances. The last did not survive to majority, and the manor descended jointly to Penelope, wife of Sir Thomas Hele, and Elizabeth, wife of John Harris. Both died shortly after childbirth, the latter in 1631 and the former in 1630, but Penelope had a surviving son Thomas, who died in the lifetime of his father in 1665.[67] Sir Thomas Hele, of Flete, Holbeton (Devon), certainly occupied the house in the 1650s, and after his eldest son's death was succeeded by a younger son, Sir Henry (d. 1677), and then by a Richard Hele.[68]

Thereafter the descent of the ownership is not clear, the Gundry family being at first tenants and later owners. Nathaniel Gundry became the largest ratepayer in South Harp tithing in 1666 and the fourth largest in the whole parish.[69] He died in 1676 and was succeeded by his son Nicholas, who still occupied the property, no longer referred to as a manor, in 1696. He was followed by Thomas Gundry in 1698,[70] and a Thomas Gundry was still there in 1749.[71]

By 1762 Wigborough farm, of 216 a., was owned by Robert Hillard.[72] One of the same name held it at least until 1826, and in 1840 it was owned by his executors.[73] In 1852 Hillards' heir, Thomas Roach of Dulverton, leased the estate to George Moody;[74] Moody subsequently bought the property, and at his death in 1895 it passed to a Miss Moody.[75] In 1920 she sold the farm, then comprising 222 a., to Mr. J. G. Vaux, the tenant. In 1974 the property belonged to his son Mr. S. G. Vaux.[76]

About 1206 the prior of Bruton allowed Helen the usher to have a chantry in her oratory at Wig-borough. She and her heirs were to present a chaplain to the canons, who was to pledge himself not to take any offerings or tithes there.[77]

Buildings including the manor-house were in 1382 arranged around a courtyard. Isabel Cogan was assigned as dower two low chambers with a solar above, at the northern end of the hall, a third of the kitchen at the east end, and a third of a buttery at the south end of the courtyard, together with a chapel.[78]

Wigborough Manor now comprises the central and parlour ranges of what was probably designed as a symmetrical house, but for which there is no evidence of completion.[79] The central range contains a tall hall with screens passage and gallery above; the parlour wing also has the main staircase, adjacent to which there was a projecting garderobe turret, now removed. There is a considerable quantity of panelling, much of it reset; on one bracket is the date 1585, which may be the date of the completion of the house. There are also a number of moulded plaster ceilings of the early 17th century and one fireplace with the arms of Hele of Flete. Among the stone farm buildings is one dated 1765 with the initials of Robert Hillard and his wife.

Merlesuain the sheriff held two hides of thegnland in Stratton T.R.E. which by 1086 had become part of the manor of South Petherton.[80] By c. 1258 an estate later known as the manor of GREAT STRATTON or OVER STRATTON was held by Nicholas de Meriet of the Crown, presumably by royal grant between 1086 and the grant of the manor of South Petherton to the Daubeneys in 1225.[81] The manor, said in 1308 to be held of the Crown in free socage for 1 lb. of cumin,[82] descended like the manor of Great Lopen in Lopen to Sir Giles Strangways (d. 1562), and then to his son John, who was holding it in 1568.[83] By 1611 the manor was owned by Henry Compton (d. 1628), and from him it presumably descended through his daughter Alice to the Johnsons of Bridge and Wigborough.[84] The manor was evidently made over by William Ostler to John and George Daniel in 1755, but has not been traced further.[85]

A tenement at 'Southampton' within the manor of South Petherton occurs in 1305.[86] This may be an early reference to the hamlet of SOUTH HARP or SOUTHARP, first described as a manor in 1475.[87] The name occurs regularly as a member of the main manor from the end of the 14th century,[88] and by the mid 15th century was linked with Chillington for administrative purposes.[89] It occurs

[60] L. & P. Hen. VIII, xx (1), p. 129; xx (2), p. 455.
[61] C 142/119/153; C 142/193/88; C 142/228/55; C 142/247/74; Cal. Pat. 1558–60, 161.
[62] C 142/228/55.
[63] C 142/247/74.
[64] S.R.O., DD/X/WHM 982c; Som. Wills, ed. Brown, iv. 23.
[65] S.R.O., DD/X/WHM 834; S. & D. N. & Q. ii. 230.
[66] C 142/247/74.
[67] C 142/534/128, 130; G.E.C. Baronetage, ii. 19–20; M.I. in S. Petherton ch.
[68] S.R.O., D/P/pet.s 13/2/1.
[69] Ibid.
[70] Ibid. 2/1/2; 13/2/1; DD/SAS SX 102.
[71] S.R.O., DD/PH 131; D/P/pet.s 4/1/1.
[72] S.R.O., DD/BR/py (C/434).
[73] S.R.O., Q/REl; D/P/pet.s 4/1/2; tithe award.
[74] S.R.O., DD/S/HR, box 2.
[75] S.R.O., DD/SAS RF 1.
[76] Ibid.; ex inf. Mr. S. G. Vaux, Wigborough.
[77] S.R.S. viii, pp. 37–8.
[78] Cal. Close, 1381–5, 579–80.
[79] See plate facing p. 33.
[80] V.C.H. Som. i. 418, 435.
[81] S.R.S. xvii. 84; Cal. Inq. p.m. i, p. 163.
[82] Cal. Inq. p.m. i. p. 163; v, p. 28.
[83] Hutchins, Hist. Dors. ii. 662; C.P. 25(2)/204/10 Eliz. I East.
[84] C 142/517/70; S. & D. N. & Q. ii. 233.
[85] C.P. 25(2)/1198/28 Geo. II Hil.
[86] C 133/120/2.
[87] Cal. Pat. 1467–77, 533.
[88] C 136/44/1; Cal. Inq. p.m. xvi, pp. 259–60; Cal. Fine R. 1383–91, 153; Cal. Close, 1402–5, 98–9, 189.
[89] C 139/157/20; Cal. Fine R. 1452–61, 131.

as 'Southyngton' in 1446.[90] In 1475 it was still in the hands of the Daubeneys.[91] It passed on the death of Giles, Lord Daubeney, in 1508 to his son Henry, and in 1517 was settled jointly on Henry and his wife.[92] Henry, then earl of Bridgwater, sold the property with Chillington, subject to a life pension for himself, to Edward Seymour, earl of Hertford, in 1540.[93] On Seymour's attainder in 1552 the property passed to the Crown, which retained it until 1570 and then granted it to Thomas Wentworth, Lord Wentworth (d. 1584).[94] The Seymours, in the person of Edward, earl of Hertford (d. 1621), laid claim to the property in 1572 and finally secured it ten years later.[95]

The property then descended like the manor of Shepton Beauchamp to John Seymour, duke of Somerset who died unmarried in 1675. It then passed to Elizabeth (d. 1697), niece of John, and wife of Thomas Bruce, earl of Ailesbury (d. 1741). Lord Ailesbury held courts until 1703 and his sons Charles, Robert, and James Bruce from 1704 to 1708.[96] By 1710 they had been succeeded by John Johnson of Syon Hill, Isleworth (Mdx.), though by that time much of the land had been let on leases for lives by the Bruces.[97] By 1754, when ownership of the manor was disputed between Orlando Johnson, successor to John Johnson the younger, owner in 1726, and the Child family of Osterley Park (Heston, Mdx.), the property was apparently small.[98] Agatha, widow of the London banker Samuel Child (d. 1752), acquired the estate in 1756 in right of her late husband as creditor, and settled it together with Shepton Beauchamp, Norton sub Hamdon, and the advowson of Stocklinch Magdalen, on her elder son Francis in 1757.[99] Francis, who rebuilt Osterley Park, died without issue in 1763,[1] and was succeeded first by his brother Robert (d. 1782) and then by Robert's daughter Sarah Anne (d. 1793), wife of John Fane, earl of Westmorland (d. 1841).[2] Their only daughter, Sarah Sophia, the heir to the Child fortune, married George Villiers, later earl of Jersey, in 1804. She was to become the leader of London fashion, and occurs in two Disraeli novels.[3] Lord Jersey sold his wife's Somerset properties in 1807, the lordship of the manor of South Harp and a 'small but desirable farm' of 33 a. being bought by John Baker Edmonds for £2,000.[4] The land was then absorbed in the Edmonds estate.

The rectory estate in South Petherton, owned by the canons of Bruton from 1181–2, was presumably the hide of land Alviet the priest held in 1086.[5] By 1291 the income from lands and tithes, including the tithes from the dependent chapelries, amounted to £53 6s. 8d., the results of accumulated grants by the Daubeneys and their tenants, and earlier by Walter de Mayenne.[6] By 1334 the value was over £59 and included 36 a. of land, rents worth £4, a mill, and pasture for 8 oxen and a bull.[7] In 1511–12 the net income from the estate was just over £66, of which nearly £18 came from rents.[8]

The rectory lands, as distinct from the tithes, came into the hands of the Crown when Bruton abbey was dissolved in 1539, and in 1553 were leased with Canons mill successively to William Treasurer, William Helhouse, and Richard Radbard of Middle Lambrook. In 1563 the property, soon to be known as the lordship and manor of *SOUTH PETHERTON* alias *HELE* or simply as the manor of *HELE*, was sold to William Raven of London. He in 1566 sold his interest to Blaise Radbard of Drayton and James Ayshe of South Petherton.[9] Radbard died in 1576, leaving his share to his brother William, vicar of Somerton (d. 1581).[10] William sold a third of his share to his brother Walter, of Beer in Aller, and two thirds to his 'cousin' James Ayshe of Bucknell (Oxon.).[11] Walter in 1579 disposed of his third to Charles Arundell of Shaftesbury (Dors.), from whom it passed to Ayshe in 1582. The property thereafter descended in the Ayshe family passing from James Ayshe of Stone in Chulmleigh (Devon) to his son William in 1614. William died in 1617 leaving an heir, James, a minor. James himself died in 1626 and a long minority followed, William Ayshe coming of age c. 1642.[12] William suffered confiscation in the Civil War and died in 1657, leaving a child to succeed.[13] The heir, James, only acquired control of his property in 1679, the estate having been encumbered with debts and in the hands of trustees. He died before 1683, leaving as his heirs his sisters Mary and Elizabeth. On Elizabeth's marriage to Samuel Cabell of Buckfastleigh (Devon), Mary sold her share to Cabell for £3,500, a sum finally acknowledged in 1690.[14] Cabell died in 1699,[15] and his widow married Richard Fownes (d. 1714) of Steepleton Iwerne (Dors.) in 1701. She died in 1724.[16]

Elizabeth Fownes was succeeded by her sister Mary, wife of James Prowse of Norton Fitzwarren, who died in 1737, leaving the manor to Thomas Bowyer, vicar of Martock and her kinsman, as trustee and residuary legatee.[17] Bowyer was still in possession in 1749,[18] but by 1753 he had sold it to Henry Hele, M.D., of Salisbury.[19] Hele died in 1778 and the manor passed to Henry Stephens of Kencott (Oxon.), husband of Hele's grand-daughter Phoebe Martha, with contingent remainders to their

[90] C 139/121/26; *Cal. Fine R.* 1452–61, 131.
[91] *Cal. Pat.* 1467–77, 533.
[92] C 142/25/22; *L. & P. Hen. VIII*, ii, p. 1106.
[93] E 326/11706; C 142/115/38; Hist. MSS. Com. 58, *Bath*, iv, pp. 124–5, 180.
[94] C 142/115/38; *Cal. Pat.* 1569–72, pp. 306–7.
[95] Hist. MSS. Com. 58, *Bath*, iv. 180, 187, 189; S.R.O., DD/AB 21; T/PH/pat.
[96] S.R.O., DD/X/LT.
[97] S.R.O., DD/AB 40.
[98] S.R.O., DD/BR/py (C/492); DD/X/LT.
[99] S.R.O., DD/SAS SE 2.
[1] *V.C.H. Mdx.* iii, 109; S.R.O., DD/SAS SE 2.
[2] S.R.O., DD/SAS SE 2.
[3] She was Zenobia in *Endymion* and Lady St. Julians in *Coningsby: Complete Peerage*, s.v. Jersey.

[4] S.R.O., DD/PR 80; DD/SAS SE 22.
[5] *V.C.H. Som.* i. 471.
[6] *Tax. Eccl.* (Rec. Com.), 199; *S.R.S.* viii, pp. 34–6.
[7] E 179/169/14.
[8] S.R.O., DD/HI, box 5.
[9] *Cal. Pat.* 1563–6, p. 402; S.R.O., DD/PE 18.
[10] C 142/179/80.
[11] S.R.O., DD/PE 18.
[12] Ibid.
[13] C 142/422/33; S.R.O., DD/PE 18.
[14] S.R.O., DD/PE 21.
[15] Ibid. 18.
[16] Ibid.; D/P/puc 2/1/1.
[17] *S. & D. N. & Q.* iii. 31; *Som. Wills*, ed. Brown, v. 102–3.
[18] S.R.O., D/P/pet.s 4/1/1.
[19] S.R.O., DD/PE 8.

children and then to Hele's grandson George Jocelyn Robinson (d. 1788). In 1797–8 John Baker Edmonds of South Petherton acquired the reversion of Robinson's three sons, expectant on the death of Henry and Phoebe Stephens, and in 1822 Edmonds bought the remainder from the Revd. John Hopkins, husband of George Robinson's only daughter.[20]

The manor-house of Hele stood near Hele Lane, and was described in 1750 as 'built . . . not many years ago'. It was of Ham stone with one sashed front, perhaps added to a house elsewhere described as 'late Elizabethan, or more probably Jacobean'. There were eight rooms to each floor 'mostly well wainscotted' and it was entered from the lane 'through an arched porch forming the base of a low square turret, balustraded at the top', which betrays the earlier origin of the dwelling. Beside the house were offices, stables, a walled garden, fishponds stocked with carp, and a farm-house. The manor lands were mostly inclosed with apple trees. From the 1760s onwards the house was occupied by a farmer, and it was demolished c. 1860, its materials being incorporated in the Parrett Works in Martock.[21]

By 1511 the tithes of the parish and its dependent chapels, together with the tithe barn, were let in ten separate units, and totalled £48 10s., of which £36 13s. 4d. came from South Petherton.[22] By 1514 all the tithes were farmed by John Brett or Birte (d. 1532), who was rectory bailiff and collector of rents.[23] Isabel Brett received a lease for life of the rectory mill.[24] Elizabeth Birte held the tithes in 1562 under lease granted by Abbot Gilbert of Bruton in 1532.[25] By 1562 Hugh Poulett had already acquired an interest, and the Poulett family continued as farmers of the tithes of the whole parish under the chapter of Bristol, rendering £50 8s. a year and finding priests in the four chapels. The Pouletts continued to let the tithes in the units found in 1511.[26] The family's ascendancy in South Petherton came to an end in 1788, though they continued to lease the tithes of Lopen, Seavington, and Chillington.[27] From that date the tithes were never let as a single unit: John Eason of Bridge held the whole area south of the Foss Way except the Wigborough estate under two leases;[28] Robert Hearen of Compton Durville leased the tithes of Compton; and John Quantock of Chichester the barn, and the tithes of South Petherton and Wigborough.[29] The clear value of the tithes in the parish and its chapelries was put at £55 5s. in 1777, and at £245 19s. in 1786.[30] The tithes of Compton, lately held by Benjamin Hearen, were before 1817

divided between Burchall Peren and Vincent Stuckey, the two leading owners there.[31] The Eason interest was bought by John Weston Peters. In 1839 the tithes were commuted, the chapter of Bristol having already sold their interest as rectors to Quantock (in 1802) and Peters.[32] Frances Herne Quantock thereafter received a rent-charge of £506 2s., John Weston Peters £217, and Burchall Peren under the chapter £155.[33] The Perens continued as lessees under the chapter until 1872.[34]

In 1619 it was reported that there was no house on the rectory estate, but only a large barn,[35] 'a little distance to the south' of the church.[36] This barn, bearing the arms of two branches of the Mohun family, adopted by Bruton priory, and the arms of Abbot Gilbert, was built c. 1515,[37] and demolished in the 19th century.[38] The arms were incorporated in the then new vicarage house.

The statement about the lack of a house has been persistently denied by local tradition, which asserts that a house called 'Holbrook's Place' or 'Higher House' was the parsonage house. The name of Thomas de Holebroke occurs among the free tenants of the main manor in 1305, and the family continued as such at least until 1388.[39] By the early 17th century the house was also known as 'Higher House' to distinguish it from the present 'King Ina's Palace' both then in the hands of the Sandys family,[40] who continued to hold it at least until 1729. Its subsequent history is not known, though it was apparently acquired by the Pouletts and may have been the house let by them with the barn and tithes in 1787.[41]

The house, in 1974 divided and known as nos. 40–44 St. James's Street, has at its south end some 15th-century windows, and probably extended further to the east. The main range along St. James's Street is of 17th-century origin, and was formerly a substantial dwelling.[42]

Two Domesday estates, one of 3 hides held by Mauger de Cartrai in succession to Godric of the count of Mortain, and the other of a hide and a virgate formerly part of the manor of Martock and held by Ansger the cook, have been identified as parts of the later hamlet of Compton Durville.[43] It is possible that a third estate, called 'Contitone', held by Count Eustace, may also be identified with this Compton. This estate was held of him by Maud in succession to Ulnod.[44] The subsequent history of Compton reflects this fragmentation.

The immediate descent of these properties is not known, but a succession of disputes from 1212 onwards suggests that until that time a large estate

---

[20] S.R.O., DD/PT, box 12; DD/S/HR, box 11.
[21] *Western Flying Post*, 5 Mar. 1750; Norris, *S. Petherton*, 51, 54.
[22] S.R.O., DD/HI, box 5.
[23] S.R.O., DD/PE 7.
[24] S.C. 6/Hen. VIII/3137.
[25] S.R.O., DD/PT, box 10A.
[26] Bristol R.O., DC/E/1/2; DC/E/24/1; DC/E/24/3/4–6.
[27] Bristol R.O., DC/E/24/3/2.
[28] Bristol R.O., DC/E/24/3/1, 3.
[29] Bristol R.O., DC/D/309; DC/E/24/7.
[30] S.R.O., DD/SS, bdle. 7; Bristol R.O., DC/E/24/4: survey 1786.
[31] Bristol R.O., DC/D/309; DC/E/24/3/10–12.
[32] Bristol R.O., DC/E/24/7.
[33] S.R.O., tithe award.
[34] Bristol R.O., DC/E/24/5.

[35] S.R.O., DD/X/SAB, Chetwynd's survey f. 16.
[36] Norris, *S. Petherton*, 57.
[37] S.R.O., DD/PE 7; the account includes carriage of stone from Ham Hill.
[38] Norris, *S. Petherton*, 57. It was repaired with Ham stone tiles in the 1650s: S.R.O., DD/PT 40.
[39] C 133/120/2; C 136/44/1.
[40] Norris, *S. Petherton*, 112; S.R.O., DD/PT 36.
[41] S.R.O., DD/PT, box 12, Poulett to Griffen. The Pouletts certainly acquired the Sandys deeds of the property: DD/PT, boxes 10A, 36. It was not part of the rectory estate in 1786: Bristol R.O., DC/E/24/4.
[42] See J. H. Parker, *Glossary of Architecture*, i. 101.
[43] *V.C.H. Som.* i. 440, 474.
[44] Ibid. 472. See *Proc. Som. Arch. Soc.* xcix and c. 45; cviii. 98.

was held by the Durville family. William de Durville[45] was succeeded before 1212 by his son Eustace, and both had already subinfeudated much of their property to tenants including Reynold of Bath, the prior of Bruton, Adam le Bel, and Robert de Radwell. Subsequently, but still before 1212, two fees of the Durville estate in Compton and 'Clopton' in Kingsbury were granted by Eustace and his son William to Alice de Vaux, and these descended with her other properties in the area.[46] The remaining Durville holdings were forfeit to the Crown when Eustace was hanged for felony between 1223 and 1229.[47] Such tenants as Reynold of Bath received their holdings of the Crown by escheat.[48]

Among the early tenants of the Durvilles was Adam le Bel, granted a freeholding of 50 a. by William de Durville in the late 12th century. He was succeeded by Robert le Bel who by 1223 owed service to Alice de Vaux.[49] A Robert le Bel, either the same man or his son, died in 1256 holding ½ virgate, late Durville's, in Compton in chief, 3 virgates of Sir Alan de Furneaux, and a mill of the heirs of Sir William Malherbe alias Malet, all said to be in Compton Durville.[50] He was succeeded by his son Adam, by a grandson also Adam, and lastly by a granddaughter Isabel, wife of Reynold Funtaynes.[51] By 1280 some of the estate had been let to the Kail family.

Robert le Bel (d. 1256) leased 26 a. to Thomas Kail, whose son Humphrey was still in occupation in 1280.[52] Another Humphrey held land of the Daubeneys in 1298.[53] Kails continued to hold properties of various lords in Compton at least until the end of the 14th century, William Kail (d. 1348) having 60 a. and a rent of three separate owners, and John Kail (d. c. 1383–4) 81 a. in chief.[54] John's heir, Thomas, was a minor, and died while still under age in 1394, leaving as his heir his sister Idony, later wife of John Poulett.[55] The subsequent descent of the estate has not been traced.

The only 13th-century estate which can be linked with any certainty to the Domesday holders was that of Alice de Vaux, who in 1212 held land which descended like her manor of Seavington Vaux from Mauger de Cartrai.[56] Her son and successor, Robert de Vaux, occurs in 1223 when his mother was still alive.[57] Before 1229 part of Alice's estate, indeed perhaps all of it in Compton, was settled on her daughter Grace and William de Wydiworth on their marriage.[58] William was still in occupation in 1242–3.[59] By 1284–5 the heirs of Wythele held an estate of ½ virgate from the heirs of

Ashill, namely from the Multon family, descendants of Alice de Vaux. They in their turn held of Isabel de Forz, countess of Aumale, suggesting a descent like the manor of Seavington Vaux.[60] Henry de Wythele died in 1329 holding the same small estate, and was succeeded by his son Reynold, a minor.[61] By 1384 this property had been merged into the larger estate of Sir John Weylond, by whom it was held of Sir John Streche of Pinhoe (Devon) as of the manor of Ashill.[62]

In 1212 Reynold of Bath among other tenants of Robert son of Alice de Vaux was challenged to provide proof of right of entry to his land at Compton and 'Clopton', and claimed the right by grant of Eustace de Durville and his father.[63] Osbert of Bath, perhaps his son, was holding of the manor of South Petherton two virgates in Hassockmoor in 1232.[64] Reynold of Bath died in 1254–5 holding an estate called Radwell, in Kingsbury Episcopi, two virgates in Hassockmoor in socage of Nicholas de Meriet, lord of Merriott, and 1½ virgate lately of the fee of Eustace de Durville.[65] He was succeeded by his son Reynold, a minor.[66] Osbert of Bath held the property by 1283 and at his death in 1296 held Radwell, 80 a. of land in Compton for ⅙ fee of Mortain, and a capital messuage, rents, and 128 a. of land at Hassockmoor of the Meriets.[67] Osbert's heir was his daughter Elizabeth, wife of William de Weylond.

In 1305 William de Weylond and his wife held of her inheritance from the Daubeneys some freehold land at Hassockmoor.[68] In 1324 William, lord of Radwell, held land both at 'More', probably Hassockmoor, and at Compton.[69] Nicholas de Weylond in 1326 received a grant of free warren in his demesnes at both places,[70] but by 1331 Robert, son of William Weylond and Cecily his wife, appear to have held the land at Compton and Moor.[71] Robert was dead by 1349, though his widow survived.[72] It seems likely that the property then descended to another branch of the family, represented in 1308 by John Weylond who held land in 'Mora by South Petherton', later also called Hassockmoor, in free socage of John de Meriet.[73] A Sir John Weylond held this estate in 1373,[74] and in 1375 it was described as a carucate held for ½ fee.[75] By 1383 Sir John also held the manor of Radwell and probably also the other Weylond estate.[76] He died in 1386 holding several properties which must have originated with Alice de Vaux.[77] The estates were held jointly with his wife Burga; Peter, their son and heir, was a minor.[78] Burga

45 Cur. Reg. R. xi, pp. 53–4.
46 Ibid. vi, pp. 349, 378–9; vii, pp. 280–1; Close R. 1227–31, 169.
47 Cur. Reg. R. xi, pp. 53–4; Close R. 1227–31, 169.
48 Cal. Inq. p.m. i, p. 87.
49 Cur. Reg. R. xi, pp. 53–4.
50 Cal. Inq. p.m. i, p. 96.
51 S.R.S. xliv. 184.
52 Ibid.
53 B.L. Harl. Ch. 45 B 31.
54 V.C.H. Som. iii. 86; Cal. Close, 1385–9, 353; B.L. Harl. Ch. 53 D 3; Cal. Inq. p.m. xiii, p. 15.
55 C 136/84/26.
56 Cur. Reg. R. vi, p. 349.
57 Ibid. xi, pp. 53–4.
58 Close R. 1227–31, 169.
59 S.R.S. xi, p. 320.
60 Feud. Aids, iv. 283.
61 Cal. Inq. p.m. vii, p. 152; Cal. Fine R. 1327–37,

162; 1337–47, 74.
62 Cal. Inq. p.m. xvi, p. 181; S.R.S. xvii. 121–2.
63 Cur. Reg. R. vi, pp. 378–9.
64 Ibid. xiv, pp. 491–2.
65 Cal. Inq. p.m. i, p. 87.
66 Cal. Pat. 1247–58, 410; Close R. 1254–6, 268.
67 Cal. Inq. p.m. iii, p. 217; S.R.S. vi. 260, 266.
68 C 133/120/2.
69 B.L. Add. Ch. 15704.
70 Cal. Chart. R. 1300–26, 482.
71 S.R.S. xii. 156.
72 B.L. Harl. Ch. 48 I 23.
73 Cal. Inq. p.m. v, p. 28.
74 H.M.C. Wells, ii. 632.
75 Cal. Inq. p.m. xiv, p. 188.
76 S.R.S. xvii. 121–2.
77 Cal. Inq. p.m. xvi, p. 181.
78 Cal. Close, 1385–9, 325; S.R.O., DD/CC 110025, 12/44.

outlived her son, and at her death in 1388 the heir was Joan, daughter of Peter's sister Elizabeth.[79] A dispute ensued about the overlordship of the Hassockmoor property between the Crown as guardian of the Daubeney heir and the owners of Merriott manor.[80] Part of the property passed directly to John Streche of Ashe, Musbury (Devon), husband of Joan, Weylond's granddaughter, by 1406, when it was described as the manors of *HASSOCKMOOR, COMPTON DURVILLE,* and Radwell in a conveyance in fee to Sir Thomas Brook.[81] Streche was credited with the land in Compton and Hassockmoor in 1412,[82] but after his death his widow sold her interest to feoffees, and it is likely that the fee passed to Sir Thomas Brook.[83] Joan, Brook's widow, held property near by in 1431 which passed to her son Edward, Lord Cobham (d. 1464), to his heir John (d. 1512), and to John's younger son Thomas. In 1505 Thomas conveyed it to John Brook, gentleman.[84]

Probably this property, described as the manors of Hassockmoor and Compton Durville, was conveyed by Richard Hody, owner of land in Ash, Martock, to Griffith Meredith in 1544.[85] From Meredith Hassockmoor alone passed in 1552 to Humphrey Walrond of Sea in Ilminster (d. 1580), and then to Humphrey's son Henry (d. 1616). Humphrey, Henry's eldest son, conveyed it in 1637 to John Bonning of Atherstone in Ilminster.[86] In 1691 and 1701 the manor was held by Mrs. Mary Bacon of Harpford in Langford Budville[87] and in 1748 transferred from Thomas Westcott and John Hillard and their wives to Anne Collins, widow.[88] From her it passed to John Collins and his wife Jane of Hatch, the second of whom in 1794 sold some of the lands of the 'manor or reputed manor' to John Stuckey, to be incorporated in Compton farm.[89]

The descent of Compton Durville is difficult to trace during the 16th and 17th centuries. The Forte family, tenants of the Weylonds by the late 14th century,[90] occur as occupiers in the 16th century, and by the 17th may have lived at Rydons.[91] The Stuckeys were owners of what was called the manor in Elizabeth I's reign.[92] John Stuckey was the most substantial occupier in Compton tithing in the early 18th century, and was succeeded by his son Robert in 1741.[93] Robert's son John, of Weston in Branscombe (Devon), died in 1810 leaving his property in Compton to Vincent Stuckey of Langport.[94] On Vincent's death in 1845 it passed to John Churchill Langdon of Parrocks Lodge, Tatworth.[95] Langdon's son J. S. C. Langdon sold his holding, then known as Manor farm, to James England in 1888,

when it amounted to just over 162 a.[96] England died in 1895 and his trustees sold the property in 1909.[97] In 1919 Capt. C. P. L. Firth (d. 1955) acquired the estate from Col. A. Leggatt. In 1949 the manor-house was transferred to the Fidelity Trust for religious uses, and after Capt. Firth's death it was occupied by the Society of the Sacred Cross. In 1962 the tenancy was transferred to the present (1974) occupiers, the Community of St. Francis, which in 1964 opened a small hospital.

Compton Durville Manor is a substantial 17th-century house of three-roomed plan, with a through passage, two-storeyed porch with side entry, and a two-storeyed canted bay window. Several of the rooms contain 17th- and 18th-century panelling, the earliest brought from the present Dower House. The north end of the house was rebuilt by Capt. Firth in 1926–7 to his own designs on four floors, and incorporates a chapel. A fragment of medieval carved stone outside the chapel came from Clifton Maybank (Dors.).[98]

Opposite the house, on the site of the former stable yard and gardens, themselves replacing an earlier tithe barn, is a small hospital complex, and a chapel, designed by Royden Cooper of Yeovil and opened in 1964. A barn, formerly used as a club room for the hamlet, has since been converted into a guest-house. The bellcot over the chapel, inscribed 'J. S. 1828', came from a mill at Sandpit, near Broadwindsor (Dors.), and formerly stood on the stable block.

There was evidently a settlement at *BRIDGE* by the end of the 12th century, the family of Bruges presumably also taking its name from the bridge over the Parrett nearby. Emme de Bruges in 1200 failed in a claim for $\frac{1}{2}$ virgate in South Petherton.[99] In 1232 William de Bruges and another held $\frac{1}{2}$ virgate in Strete, probably Stratton, and other lands in Petherton and Chillington, all parcel of South Petherton manor.[1] A Hugh de Brugg was succeeded by another Hugh towards the end of the 13th century, and the family continued to hold land in the parish at least until 1330.[2] By 1305 the Daubeney demesne included a garden and a dovecot in Bridge, and by 1313 unspecified lands there, including a mill, were held by the Moleyns family.[3] The Daubeneys continued to claim lordship there linked with Great Stratton in 1388.[4]

In 1548 Robert Gerard of Sandford Orcas (Dors.) sold to William Johnson of Hinton St. George the 'farm and mansion house called Bridge' with accompanying lands for £100.[5] The property descended on William's death in 1570 to his son Brome.[6] On Brome's death in 1586 it was described

[79] *Cal. Inq. p.m.* xvi, p. 303.
[80] Ibid.; *Cal. Pat.* 1388–92, 475; *Cal. Close,* 1385–9, 581.
[81] *Reg. Chichele* (Cant. & York Soc.), ii. 140–3; *S.R.S.* xxii. 170.
[82] *Feud. Aids.* vi. 506.
[83] *S.R.S.* xxii. 181; *H.M.C. Wells,* ii. 664.
[84] *Feud. Aids,* iv. 433; *Cal. Close,* 1500–9, p. 194.
[85] Hutchins, *Hist. Dors.* ii. 233; C.P. 25(2)/36/241/35 Hen. VIII Hil.
[86] C.P. 25(2)/62/501/6 Edw. VI East.; C 142/193/41.
[87] S.R.O., DD/BK 5/9; C.P. 25(2)/480/13 Chas. I East.
[88] C.P. 25(2)/869/3 Wm. & Mary Mich.; C.P. 25(2)/1196/21 Geo. II East.; S.R.O., DD/PE 19.
[89] S.R.O., Q/RE, 1766–90; C/C, box 29.
[90] *S.R.S.* xvii. 121–4.

[91] C 1/509/39; Req. 2/27/43; Norris, *S. Petherton,* 55.
[92] C 3/157/2.
[93] S.R.O., Q/RE; D/P/pet.s 4/1/1.
[94] *S. & D. N. & Q.* iii. 250–3.
[95] Norris, *S. Petherton,* 54–5.
[96] Poole & Co., Par. Cncl. papers, Sale cat. 1909.
[97] Ibid.
[98] Ex inf. the Hon. Mrs. Firth, Compton Durville.
[99] *Cur. Reg. R.* i, p. 123.
[1] Ibid. xiv, pp. 491–2.
[2] *S.R.S.* xii. 130–1; xliv. 186, 247; *Plac. Coram Rege,* ed. Maitland, 13.
[3] *Cal. Close,* 1302–7, 267; *S.R.S.* xii. 32; *Plac. Abbrev.* (Rec. Com), 348.
[4] C 136/44/1.
[5] *S.R.S.* li, p. 35.
[6] C 142/159/63B.

as a manor and was held as of the manor of South Harp.[7] It had already been settled on his wife ten years earlier, and she retained it until after the death of her son Emorb in 1615.[8] She was dead by 1630 when the share of the property owned by Emorb's daughter Frances was divided between her two sisters, Penelope and Elizabeth.[9] The property then descended like the manor of Wigborough and in 1658 was made over to William Helyar.[10] The descent probably still followed Wigborough through the Gundry family. Thomas Gundry held Bridge in 1749 but was dead by 1752.[11] By 1766 it had passed to William Ostler, said to have been a relative.[12] Ostler was still in possession in 1782 but by 1790 was succeeded by John Eason.[13] Eason increased the size of the holding and died in 1814, leaving instructions for his burial in the plantation at the lower corner of his home close.[14] He left the estate to his sister Elizabeth (d. 1830) and then to John Weston Peters (d. 1858) of Corton Denham, provided he lived at Bridge.[15] In 1840 the estate attached to the house was 346 a.[16] The property descended to the Blake family, and in 1859 a large house was built between the older manor-house and the London road, surrounded by a small park.[17] This house was demolished c. 1950, and the park laid out for mobile homes.

Old Bridge began as a 'pretty house' built by Brome Johnson (d. 1586).[18] This seems to have been of three-roomed plan, probably with a detached kitchen, the screens passage dividing the central hall from an unheated storage room to the north. Of this house only the plan survives. Windows with ovolo mouldings were inserted in the early part of the 17th century, but these were largely replaced and a new wing added to the south in the late 17th or early 18th century.

In 1232 William de Loveney held 2 virgates in *LITTLE LOPEN* as of the manor of South Petherton.[19] The family, in the persons of Walter, Andrew, and Richard de Loveney, were successive occupiers at the end of the 13th century.[20] In 1301 William son of Walter Loveney sold property there to John de Stafford.[21] In 1305 Robert de Abindon and his wife Maud held a carucate and a house of Ellis Daubeney which Maud had purchased.[22] Maud may be identified with the Maud de Cantebrigg who died by 1332 holding land in both Little Lopen and Drayton of Ralph Daubeney. This Maud had been married to John de Stafford, and her heir was her daughter Joan, later wife of Thomas de Crauthorn.[23] The estate at Little Lopen was described as 6 bovates of arable and 2 a. of meadow.

In 1362 Joan transferred her property in the parish and elsewhere to John de Moleyns and Alice his wife, daughter of Thomas.[24] John died in 1387 holding land in Bridge, Drayton, and Little Lopen of Eleanor, widow of Sir Giles Daubeney.[25] His children were a son Nicholas, a minor, and two daughters, but the descent of the property is thereafter obscure. Land in Little Lopen was held by William Case (d. 1494), and was granted by John Case to Sir Giles Daubeney in 1505.[26] Property there was conveyed by Richard Kyrton to John Horner the younger in 1539. It was leased by Margery Chislet to John Hippisley of Ston Easton in 1576, the lease demanding suit of court to Little Lopen.[27] Later leases and sales involved small acreages there,[28] but by the mid 18th century the name referred only to closes.[29]

In 1388 Clemence, widow of John Moleyns, was assigned as part of dower a small house called the chapel at Little Lopen, with part of a garden at its north end, and a garden called Cotehay.[30]

ECONOMIC HISTORY. By 1066 there were seven separate estates in the area of the modern parish. If the whole had once been a single unit, its dissolution had begun at an early date, and one if not two properties in Compton had more recent connexions with Martock.[31] Yet the tributary holdings, the one at Stratton still a reality in 1086, the other at Cricket St. Thomas then only a memory,[32] and the status of the parish church as a minster, with daughter churches at Barrington, Seavington St. Mary, and Chillington, strongly suggests a large pre-Conquest royal estate almost certainly much greater than the Domesday manor. The minster holding was probably, like Crewkerne, carved out of the royal holding, and the later manor of Wigborough, one of several close to royal estates held by the king's usher,[33] also presumably originated in a grant from Crown land. Minor adjustments between 1066 and 1086 included the loss of $\frac{1}{2}$ hide of unidentified land and the addition of some 35 a. from Seavington St. Mary.[34]

By far the largest estate in 1086 was still the capital manor, its exact size unknown because it never paid geld. There was land for 28 ploughs, but these were only on the demesne. There were probably three estates at Compton, totalling $9\frac{1}{4}$ hides,[35] of which perhaps two thirds were in demesne.[36] Wigborough measured 2 hides, just over half in demesne, and the minster estate of

[7] C 142/214/241; *Som. Wills*, ed. Brown, iv. 23.
[8] *S.R.S.* lxvii, pp. 121–2.
[9] S.R.O., DD/X/WHM 982E; C 60/513 rot. 1d.
[10] S.R.O., DD/X/WHM 839–40.
[11] S.R.O., DD/S/HR, box 16; DD/PE 8.
[12] S.R.O., Q/RE; Norris, *S. Petherton*, 50.
[13] S.R.O., Q/RE; D/P/pet.s 4/1/2.
[14] S.R.O., DD/LC 4/2.
[15] Ibid.; Q/RE.
[16] S.R.O., tithe award.
[17] Devon R.O., 3378, sale cat. 1933. Datestone at Old Bridge.
[18] *S.R.S.* xv. 111.
[19] *Cur. Reg. R.* xiv, pp. 437, 491–2.
[20] *Cal. Close*, 1272–9, 488; *Plac. Coram Rege*, ed. Maitland, 12.
[21] *S.R.S.* vi. 313–14.

[22] C 133/120/2.
[23] *Cal. Fine R.* 1327–37, 318; *Cal. Inq. p.m.* vii, pp. 314–15; *S.R.S.* xvii. 49–50.
[24] *S.R.S.* xvii. 49–50.
[25] C 136/52/12; *Cal. Fine R.* 1383–91, 231.
[26] C.P. 25(1)/202/42/20 Hen. VII Trin.; *Cal. Inq. p.m. Hen VII*, i, p. 484.
[27] C.P. 25(2)/36/239/31 Hen. VIII East.; S.R.O., DD/HI, box 23.
[28] *S.R.S.* i. 124; S.R.O., DD/BR/py (C/492).
[29] S.R.O., DD/X/LT, survey 1754.
[30] *Cal. Close*, 1385–9, 621.
[31] *V.C.H. Som.* i. 440.   [32] Ibid. 435.
[33] Ibid. 520.   [34] Ibid. 435, 473.
[35] The Compton in ibid. 472–3, because of links with Loxton, is likely to be this one. But cf. *V.C.H. Dors.* iii. 145.
[36] *V.C.H. Som.* i. 440, 472–4.

1 hide was entirely so.[37] These holdings were predominantly arable, but there were c. 90 a. of meadow,[38] pasture measuring 4 by 2 furlongs at Compton, 10 a. of wood formerly in Seavington, and more woodland, measuring 10 by 11 furlongs, attached to the capital manor and situated locally in Neroche forest. The sheep population of 319 included 24 rendered by the occupier of Stratton. The largest flock was at Compton. The recorded population was 147, including 22 coliberts on the main manor and 10 serfs.

The subsequent development of the capital manor alone can be traced with any accuracy. There, by the end of the 13th century, most of the income was derived from rents, assessed at £40 12s. 9d. in 1291-2, and at £45 1s. 3½d. in 1305, fairly close to the £42 8s. 4d. received on the capital manor in 1086.[39] Customary works, worth 13s. 4d. in 1291-2, had not entirely disappeared by 1305,[40] but chevage, at 7s. in 1291-2, was probably not levied at the later date. The small value of such dues may be connected with unsuccessful attempts of customary tenants to avoid increased exactions demanded by Ralph Daubeney.[41]

The size of the demesne farm had not significantly changed during the same two centuries. The two carucates of 1086 were expressed as 215 a. of arable and 22 a. of meadow in 1291-2 and as 198 a. of arable and 30 a. of meadow in 1305. The Domesday wood had become 200 a. in Neroche. By 1305 the 63 villeins and 15 bordars had become 18 free tenants, 30 free tenants for life, and an unknown number of customary tenants, of whom 28 were described as cottars for life, and 15 as cottars at will.[42] The later, poorly documented, history of the capital manor suggests consolidation and growth of free tenancies into holdings of pseudo-manorial status in the hamlets of the south such as Stratton, South Harp, Bridge, Little Lopen, and Drayton.[43] By 1386 11 tenants were regarded as theoretical contributors to the Daubeney knight's fee.[44] The most substantial among these in the 14th century were Robert de Abindon, Henry de Moleyns, and Isabel Cogan. Robert de Abindon held a carucate at Little Lopen, a virgate at Drayton, and three furlongs in South Petherton in 1305,[45] Henry de Moleyns, owner of Joyler's mill, also held 1½ virgate of arable, 18 a. of meadow, and 2 a. of pasture in Bridge and Petherton by 1313.[46] His daughter-in-law was assigned substantial dower in 1388, amounting to well over 80 a. scattered in the open fields and closes throughout the parish, principally in the south.[47] Isabel Cogan held dower in Wigborough

and Stratton from 1382, including a park at Wigborough, and a number of cottages.[48]

Most of the holdings were, however, much smaller, like the farm of John Heyle or Hale, probably to be linked with the area known as Hele. John died in 1310 occupying a house, ½ virgate of arable, and 4 a. of meadow.[49] By the end of the 14th century, at least in Stratton, nativi were still present in some numbers, and in the 1460s attempts were being made to recover at least eight who had left the manor.[50]

The stock on the 50-a. estate of St. John's chapel in 1325 included 3 draught animals, a foal, 5 sheep, a lamb, a pig, and a few poultry, and crops were wheat, oats, barley, and rye, probably a fair reflexion of a primarily arable parish.[51] The rectory estate in 1334 comprised a carucate of arable, 20 a. of meadow and pasture in closes, and 16 a. of the same in common.[52] It is not known whether the proportion of inclosed to open grassland was general throughout the parish, but certainly by the 1380s it is clear that former common meadow was normally 'bounded out'.[53] The arable fields of the main manor were probably little changed from their arrangement in the 18th century: Stoodham and White fields occur in 1388,[54] Chapel field, Horse Castle, and Metlands in 1531.[55] In the south of the parish in Stratton tithing, there seem to have been four main arable fields, North, East, West, and Nether Stratton fields.[56] South mead was still grazed in common in 1462.[57]

The main settlement in the parish, a pre-Domesday mint-site[58] and minster-centre with a substantial cash-based economy, did not immediately develop additional urban characteristics. Described as a villata in 1210-11,[59] it only received a grant of a weekly market and annual fair in 1213, and these were worth only £1 together at the end of the century.[60] Ownership by the Daubeneys did not result, as far as can be traced, in any known planned urban expansion, and indeed the occupations of inhabitants in the late 13th and early 14th centuries[61] do not necessarily suggest more than a large village. By the 15th century, however, there are indications not only in the names of streets, but also in the status and occupations of some of the inhabitants, that it was something more than a village; Nicholas Davy 'husbandman alias attorney' occurs in 1447, and John Key, mercer, died in 1510.[62] John Roller, a London grocer, evidently had interests in the parish in 1471.[63] The place was of some administrative significance, for inquisitions before escheators were often conducted there,[64]

[37] V.C.H. Som. i. 471, 521.
[38] 'The 25 a. in Seavington was meadow and 'moor': ibid. 473.
[39] V.C.H. Som. i. 435; C 133/61/23; C 133/120/2.
[40] Cal. Close, 1302-7, 267.
[41] S.R.S. xli. 180; xliv. 202-4; Plac. Abbrev. (Rec. Com.), 195-6; Sel. Cases in King's Bench (Selden Soc. lv), 67-8, 80-1.
[42] C 133/120/2; much of the document is illegible.
[43] Cal. Close, 1227-31, 533; 1302-7, 267; C 133/120/2; C 136/44/1; C136/52/12; Cal. Inq. p.m. v, p. 91; Cal. Fine R. 1307-19, 69; Cal. Pat. 1307-13, 411.
[44] C 136/44/1; Cal. Close, 1385-9, 621-2.
[45] C 133/120/2.
[46] S.R.S. xii. 32; Plac. Abbrev. (Rec. Com.), 348.
[47] Cal. Close, 1385-9, 621-2.
[48] Ibid. 1381-5, 579-80.
[49] C 133/120/2.

[50] D.R.O., D 124, box 16, Stratton ct. roll.
[51] S.R.O., D/D/B reg 1, f. 226 b.
[52] E 179/169/14.
[53] Cal. Close, 1381-5, 579-80; 1385-9, 621-2.
[54] Cal. Close, 1385-9, 621-2.
[55] Glos. R.O., D 547A/M 12.
[56] Cal. Close, 1381-5, 579-80; 1385-9, 621-2.
[57] D.R.O., D 124, box 16, Stratton ct. roll.
[58] Dom. Geog. SW. Eng. ed. H. C. Darby and R. W. Finn, 213; Numismatic Circular, lxix (1961), 167.
[59] Pipe R. 1210 (P.R.S. N.S. xxvi), 57; 1211 (P.R.S. N.S. xxviii), 227.
[60] C 133/61/23.
[61] E 326/10488; S.R.S. iii. 200; Cal. Pat. 1334-8, 574.
[62] Cal. Pat. 1446-52, 105; S.R.S. xix. 145.
[63] Cal. Pat. 1467-77, 303.
[64] Cal. Inq. p.m. ii, pp. 64, 95; vi, p. 164; xii, p. 252; Cal. Inq. Misc. iv, p. 191; Cal. Pat. 1441-6, 251.

even before the 15th century when several natives were chosen for office, including William Case (d. 1494), escheator 1485–6, who lived probably in a house known in the 1640s as Cassells;[65] Cuthbert Clavelshay (coroner 1505–6), and John Brett (coroner 1505–6, escheator 1529–30).[66] Brett himself was bailiff and collector of rents for Bruton abbey and farmer of most of the tithes between 1511 and 1523.[67] He died in 1532.[68]

Accounts of South Harp, Stratton, and the rectory manors survive for the late Middle Ages. South Harp, administered with Chillington, was worth £27 5s. 9d. in rent in 1496–7.[69] Stratton rents were in 1494–5 worth a total of £13 9s. 2d., compared with rent, aid, and commuted works worth £9 5s. 3d. in 1285 and £8 15s. 5d. in 1308.[70] The total fluctuated between 1494 and 1523, rising to £14 14s. 9½d., though arrears in 1501–2 were as high as £9 11s.[71] High arrears were characteristic of the rectory estate, which included also rents from Barrington and Lopen and tithes from Lopen, Chillington, Upton in Seavington St. Mary, and Swell. The total of rents, issues, and the farm of tithes was £71 7s. 9d. in 1514–15, with arrears of over £157 stretching back 25 years.[72]

The dispersal of the Daubeney estate brought about by the financial difficulties of Henry Daubeney, earl of Bridgwater (d. 1548), and the dissolution of Bruton abbey had an important effect on the pattern of land-holding, particularly in the south of the parish, where the manors of South Harp and Stratton and the Daubeney properties were divided into small units that often fell to outside owners. The Hippisleys of Ston Easton held land in South Harp, Stratton, and Drayton by 1556,[73] the Wyndhams succeeded the Wadhams in Stratton in 1609 and still held there in 1682,[74] and the Spekes in 1680 owned a farm of 23 a. and the Wynard's house, a property which William Wynard of Exeter had bought from Richard Kympe in 1435 to endow Godshouse in Exeter.[75] The influence of these owners was small; not so that of the Pouletts, whose ownership of the great tithes on lease from the Bristol chapter made them the most substantial ratepayers in the parish for more than two centuries.[76]

There is no information about the larger landholdings until the 17th century, when a comparison is possible between the capital manor under the Arundells, Stratton under the Seymours, the former rectory manor under the Ayshes, and the slightly earlier evidence of the estate formerly belonging to St. John's chapel. In 1626 William Ayshe's holding comprised the manor of Hele, Joyler's mill, and some 34 a., some held of the Arundells and some

of the manor of Wigborough. The total value of the holding was £9.[77] By 1663 Mrs. Ayshe owned a very much larger estate, and was third in the list of parish ratepayers and the second largest owner of land.[78] Purchases continued throughout the century so that by 1699 the holding was large.[79] Lord Hertford's rent income from South Harp totalled in theory £53 3s. 10½d., more than half from customary rents, and over £13 due from the fee-farm rent of the former manor-house, let to Emanuel Sandys. Arrears, however, also amounted to over £53 at the beginning of 1650 and to over £55 at the end for South Harp and Chillington together. By the beginning of 1654 the arrears had risen to £159.[80] The income of the capital manor was just over £363 in 1631–2, rising to £381 in the next, and falling to £236 in 1633–4. Rents alone accounted for nearly £95, of which over a third were unpaid in 1642–3. Arrears in the previous year were over £92.[81] In 1653, however, the estate was valued at £3,997 when sold.[82] By 1660–1 the rent had fallen to just over £67, though contracts for leases for the year brought a profit of £1,048. The largest fine, £560, was from George Sampson, presumably for Rydon farm, and it was followed by one of £360 paid in 1661–2 by Robert Mohun.[83] By 1698 rents had fallen further, apparently amounting to £24 17s. 9d., of which £5 8s. 4d. was from the dwindling number of freeholders who had grants made 'a great many years since'.[84]

The small estate of the former St. John's chapel owned from 1558 by All Souls College, Oxford, amounted to about 80 a., and was probably typical of holdings of its size. Arable lay in 4 common fields in Petherton, 2 in Compton, 2 in Bridge, and 5 in Drayton. There was common meadow at Broadmead in the north-east of the parish, and in Drayton mead common pasture in Cowleaze in the south-west. A few closes of arable show the beginnings of the inclosure of Nether field in Petherton and of fields in Drayton. At Drayton the college was one of four estates holding both common arable and common meadow occupying strips in a fixed order 'and so keepeth that order in every furlong'.[85]

The size of the parish and the consequently large number of common fields suggest a fragmentation of holdings greater than usual in the area. The All Souls estate in James I's reign, estimated at 77 a., was held in 75 separate parcels;[86] and in 1680 George Speke's 23 a. lay in five open arable fields, though by then Petherton Nether field was partly inclosed, and Whitefield included some meadow.[87] The increasing number of closes forming the manor of Hele by 1699 and parts of Stratton South field

[65] *S.R.S.* xliii, 225; lxx, p. 74; Wedgwood, *Hist. Parl. Biogs. 1439–1509; Diary of Richard Symonds* (Camd. Soc. [1st. ser.], lxxiv,) 99.
[66] *S.R.S.* xliii. 226; *H.M.C. Wells*, ii. 191.
[67] *S.R.S.* liv, p. 92; *L. & P. Hen, VIII*, iii, p. 1143; S.R.O., DD/PE 7; DD/HI, box 5; DD/SAS PD 56.
[68] D.R.O., D 124, box 18, Stratton ct. roll; Glos. R.O., D 547A/M 12; S.R.O., DD/PT, box 10A.
[69] Bradford Central Libr., Swinton MSS.
[70] *Proc. Som. Arch. Soc.* xxxviii. 111–12, 117.
[71] D.R.O., D 124, box 11, Stratton acct.
[72] S.R.O., DD/PE 7.
[73] *S.R.S.* li, p. 55; S.R.O., DD/HI, box 4.
[74] *S.R.S.* li, pp. 71, 135; S.R.O., DD/WY, boxes 1 bdles. E, G) and 60; DD/WY W/SR 1/1.

[75] E. Devon R.O., ED/WA/5, 8–9, 12; *S.R.S.* xxii. 87; S.R.O., DD/SPK, box 7.
[76] S.R.O., DD/X/SAB, transcripts of accts. 1550–1641.
[77] S.R.O., DD/PE 18.
[78] S.R.O., D/P/pet.s 4/1/1.
[79] S.R.O., DD/PE 19.
[80] Wilts. R.O. 192/38A. 38B.
[81] Arundell MSS. receivers'-gen. accts. 16–19.
[82] Ibid. rentals and surveys 63.
[83] Wilts. R.O. 413/507.
[84] Arundell MSS. rentals and surveys 90; S.R.O., Q/RR papists' estates, 1717.
[85] Bodl. MS, DD/All Souls, 244/53; terrier 1574.
[86] Ibid. 243/28.
[87] S.R.O., DD/SPK, box 7.

'newly inclosed' by 1647 show that the process of inclosure was noticeable in the 17th century,[88] though there were certainly medieval closes in the area south-west of the village near Moor where some of the Hele property lay, and the hedge pattern suggests more ancient inclosure.[89] The estate still retained at least 56 a. in the common fields and shared in Broad and Common meads.[90]

Earlier in the century Pinson or Pinsham and Chapel fields were closed from All Saints 1633 so that Lent corn could be sown, and Ham, Ryland, and Nether fields closed at Michaelmas 1637 to prepare for winter corn. In any years when Chapel, Hams, Ryland, and Nether fields had corn, no cattle were permitted before the grain was carried, and no sheep within eight days after carrying. The common meadows, divided by merestones into doles, are less prominent because small.[91] Later in the century grazing and stinting regulations were often reiterated in the manor court, suggesting either greater pressure from increased stock or the court's ineffectiveness. Thus in 1664 all tenants were required to pay 1d. to the hayward for each acre in the grain fields. Fretting or grazing the common fields was at the rate of 2 sheep an acre up to Christmas, with a total of not more than forty. Broadmead was fretted from St. Bartholomew's Eve (23 Aug.) for three weeks with 2 beasts, a horse, 4 yearlings, or 8 calves an acre, and from then until Martinmas only with cattle belonging to inhabitants. Between Martinmas and Christmas the stint was the same as in the common fields.[92]

Farming seems generally to have been of the usual varied pattern. Tithes were payable in the 1630s on wheat, rye, barley, oats, beans, peas, vetches, hay, hemp, and flax.[93] The possessions of Alice Worth of South Harp (d. 1636) show this diversity in one holding—wheat, barley, beans, hay, hemp, cider, apples, 22 sheep, and 37 geese. Her house, typically two-storeyed with a ceiled hall, included a shop. William Edmonds (d. 1667), on the other hand, concentrated on corn-growing.[94] Thomas Parker (d. 1663), who was described as yeoman, had a flock of at least 70 sheep,[95] and John Marke (d. 1669) had forty.[96] Many farmers grew hemp.[97] Tradesmen in the 17th century included a glover in 1638,[98] a woollen-weaver in 1640, a pewterer in 1644, and a linen-weaver in 1646.[99] William Glover (d. 1644) possessed two weaver's looms, sack cloth, and yarn in his shop.[1] The market was hardly thriving in the 1630s,[2] though it was regarded as important enough to make the town an administrative centre in the 1650s.[3]

By the 17th century South Petherton was the home of a number of inter-related families including the Sandyses, Prowses, Ayshes, Mohuns, and Heles, all originating outside the parish. Emanuel Sandys was one of the most substantial freeholders by the 1640s who for some forty years had played an important role in parish affairs.[4] He lived in the former Daubeney manor-house. As constable in the 1620s he was accused of shielding a drunkard from treason charges.[5] He was also at least nineteen years in arrear with rent to the capital manor in 1631–2.[6] Many monuments in the church show the prominence of this family.[7]

Inclosure during the 18th century seems to have been slow. Rydon farm in Compton was probably consolidated by mid century if not earlier, its size having been constant from c. 1580.[8] By 1762 Wigborough farm was entirely in closes,[9] though most of the South Harp property remained scattered.[10] Elsewhere in the parish Hayes End and East fields, both in Stratton, were still entirely open in 1726.[11] Higher and Lower Bridge fields were so in 1775, though closes had by then been taken out of Hams and Chapel fields further north,[12] and individual owners were making small exchanges in the interests of consolidation.[13]

According to a tithe survey of 1786 arable and grass were evenly divided: 1,831 a. were under crop or were fallow, 1,153 a. were pasture, 449 a. were meadow, and 175 a. alternatively meadow or pasture.[14] Some 746 a. of arable were under open-field cultivation and 124 a. of meadow were held in common, mostly in Petherton mead or Petherton Broadmead. Some 677 a. were under wheat, 402 a. under beans, 159 a. under Lent grain, and 136 a. under flax. Seventy acres were sown to peas, 63 to vetches, 31 to potatoes, and 27 to barley. Clover, hemp, and turnips together were sown on 33 a. The flax seed was evidently supplied from the north, brought in by Samuel Clark, a local linen-cloth maker.[15]

Cultivation was still on a three-year system of two ploughings and fallow, and until after the turn of the century wheat was followed by beans and then by either flax or turnips and clover.[16] In 1786 wheat was grown in ten fields evenly spaced through the parish, beans in five fields, peas only in Chapel field, Lent grain only in Hayes End field, flax in Stratton Pound field. Pinson and South Compton fields were entirely fallow, Church Path and Drayton South fields were partly under flax and partly fallow. A similar rotation was used on the three fields of Wigborough.[17] In contrast to this traditional pattern, John Willy, a local farmer, won a gold medal for seed-drilling turnips in 1765.[18]

[88] S.R.O., DD/PE 19; DD/AB 36.
[89] e.g. *S.R.S.* viii, p. 35. [90] S.R.O., DD/PE 19.
[91] Arundell MSS. ct. bk. 23 (1633–9), *sub annis* 1633, 1634, 1637.
[92] S.R.O., DD/PE 6: ct. bk. 1661–1841.
[93] S.R.O., D/D/Rg 322.
[94] S.R.O., DD/SP, inventories.
[95] S.R.O., D/S/HR, box 6.
[96] S.R.O., DD/SP, inventory.
[97] Ibid. e.g. inventory of James Glover (1644).
[98] *S.R.S.* xxiv. 296.
[99] S.R.O., DD/SP, inventories.
[1] Ibid. [2] *S.R.S.* xv. 116.
[3] *Cal. S.P. Dom.* 1656–7, 198; *S.R.S.* lxxi, pp. 64–5.
[4] S.R.O., DD/HI, box 10 (1641); *S. & D. N. & Q.* iii. 66; *S.R.S.* xxiii. 276; xxiv. 164.

[5] *Cal. S.P. Dom.* 1619–23, 489.
[6] Arundell MSS. receivers'-gen. accts. 16.
[7] Norris, *S. Petherton*, 60–6.
[8] Req. 2/79/40; S.R.O., DD/HLM, boxes 2–3; DD/PE 1. [9] S.R.O., DD/BR/py (C/434).
[10] S.R.O., DD/SAS SE 13.
[11] S.R.O., DD/BR/py (C/492).
[12] S.R.O., DD/PE 1.
[13] e.g. S.R.O., DD/SAS (C/114), 1.
[14] Bristol R.O., DC/E/24/4. A survey of tithes 1778 is in S.R.O., DD/PT, box 37.
[15] *Sherborne Mercury*, 24 Mar. 1766.
[16] *Rep. Sel. Cttee. Depressed State of Agric.* H.C. 668, pp. 184–5 (1812), ix.
[17] Bristol R.O., DC/E/24/4.
[18] *Sherborne Mercury*, 26 May, 12 Oct. 1766.

Open-field farming was rapidly abandoned in the early 19th century. Already in 1786 Burns Gore field on the Lopen boundary and Drayton Little field had virtually disappeared, yet Hams field (107 a.), the largest field, still had 10 separate furlongs divided into 83 strips. Inclosure began in 1804 with Petherton mead, where about 80 a. were divided into 35 parts, mostly allotted to John Baker Edmonds.[19] The remaining open-field arable was abandoned in 1847, though by that time much more had been inclosed, and the apparent multiplicity of fields is explained by the survival of isolated furlongs.[20]

The same period of reorganization witnessed the rise of a number of individual farmers. The family of J. B. Edmonds (d. 1848) had been in the parish since the 1570s, and by the 1660s were settled at Moor.[21] He himself began his spectacular purchases with the capital manor in 1792, followed by South Harp manor in 1807, Hele farm by 1820, and the remainder of the former rectory lands in 1822.[22] By 1833 he owned just over 547 a. including Hayes End farm, where the large barn and granary that he built survive.[23] Edmonds gave evidence to the Select Committee on the Depressed State of Agriculture in 1821.[24] His son and namesake only continued as a practising farmer until 1851. Much of his land then passed to J. W. Peters (d. 1858).[25] Peters began his piecemeal purchases by 1834, and with the help of exchanges arranged as part of the inclosure award in 1847 built up a large estate based on Bridge House and later on Yeabridge House.[26] Two other prominent farmers and owners in the later 19th century were William Burchall Peren of Compton House (d. 1884) and James England (d. 1895) of Tarampa House (in 1974 the Square House), Palmer Street. Peren owned some 80 a. and leased a further 150 a.[27] His accounts and diaries suggest a model farmer.[28] In 1879, for example, he made a cash profit of nearly £1,086 but when his estate was put up for sale in 1884, during the depression, it found no buyers, but went for £9,565 in the following year.[29] His stock included 160 sheep and 20 lambs, 30 steers and heifers, and 23 horses.[30] James England, landowner rather than farmer, amassed c. 560 a. beginning in the 1850s but buying mostly in the 1880s.[31] The Blakes of Bridge House, successors to the Easons of Bridge, had a similar property based at Drayton.[32]

Tenant farms varied in size in the 1850s. Hele and Compton were the largest each with 300 a. and 30 labourers. They were followed by ones in Palmer Street (224 a. with 10 men) and Wigborough

(220 a. with 11 men, 8 boys, and 2 women). There were 2 other farms in the parish with over 100 a. and 8 with 50 a. and over.[33] Dairying was not important, only 7 adults being involved in 1851. By 1905 grassland occupied slightly over half the parish.[34] As in the previous century wartime demand for flax stimulated growth in the early 20th century, and a factory was in production at Drayton until 1931.[35] By the 1960s arable cultivation had diversified; the production of sugar beet and coarse and salad vegetables was then included, though market gardening had in fact been started by 1872.[36] In addition to cider apples, perry pears and black currants were cultivated, for the first time, in 1965,[37] and flowers and oil seed rape were among the minor crops in 1974.[38] In 1965 18 dairy herds produced up to 1,500 gallons a day, of which nearly half was used for cheese. There were then 2 permanent arable flocks.[39]

The cost of maintaining the poor during the 18th century naturally fluctuated, but a gradual rise is as usual discernible. In 1700 the cost was £76, and in 1734 £146, the number then relieved regularly being about 20 and the same number having extraordinary relief.[40] The costs rose rapidly at the end of the century, and in the most critical year, 1819, the rate levied was £1,417.[41] During the 1820s the level was always above £700 and sometimes above £800; in the spring of 1827 81 people were being permanently relieved and 24 occasionally.[42] Between 1830 and 1834 the cost was always over £800 and twice over £900, and in 1836 there were 76 regular paupers in the parish.[43] J. B. Edmonds in 1821 admitted that despite nearly full agricultural employment he felt obliged to grow hemp for the benefit of the poor, and that in bad years rather than 'letting them run about idle' he had sent 40 and more at a time to quarry stone, the loss to the parish made up out of his own pocket.[44] From 1817 a church organization, the Mother and Infants Friend Society, attempted to provide relief, and in the depressed 1860s a soup kitchen was established, dispensing 4,541 quarts between November 1860 and March 1861.[45] In 1867 there were bread riots.[46]

In 1831 264 families were engaged in agriculture and 101 in manufacturing and handcrafts.[47] By 1851 the most widespread industry was gloving, employing 434 women and children.[48] By 1871 Richard Southcombe had established a gloving factory at Watergore, which in 1965 had 16 employees.[49] A smaller factory was in production in Hele Lane in 1965.[50] The manufacture of sacking, canvas, and sailcloth involved nearly 50 people in

[19] S.R.O., CR 77.
[20] Ibid. 141.
[21] S.R.O., D/P/pet. s 2/1/1.
[22] S.R.O., DD/S/HR, boxes 11, 16.
[23] S.R.O., tithe award.
[24] Rep. Sel. Cttee. Depressed State of Agric.
[25] Taunton Courier, 7 June 1848; H.O. 107/1929.
[26] S.R.O., tithe award; DD/PLE, box 70; CR 141; DD/PE 1; DD/S/HR, box 5.
[27] S.R.O., tithe award.
[28] H.O. 107/1929; S.R.O., DD/LC, box 5.
[29] S.R.O., DD/LC, boxes 5, 21.
[30] Ibid. box 21.
[31] Sale cat. 1909, penes Poole & Co. S. Petherton.
[32] Ex inf. Mr. W. S. Blake, Old Bridge.
[33] H.O. 107/1929.
[34] Statistics supplied by the then Bd. of Agric. 1905.
[35] Ex inf. Mr. J. G. Vaux, Wigborough.
[36] S.R.O., DD/WI 39 (W.I. Scrapbk.); Morris and Co. Dir. Som. (1872).
[37] S.R.O., DD/WI 39.
[38] Ex inf. Mr. J. G. Vaux.
[39] S.R.O., DD/WI 39.
[40] S.R.O., DD/SAS SX 102.
[41] Rep. Sel. Cttee. Poor Rate Returns, H.C. 556 (1822), v.
[42] Poor Rate Returns, H.C. 83 (1830–1), xi; S.R.O., D/PC/pet. s 1/2/1.
[43] Poor Rate Returns, H.C. 44 (1835), xlvii; S.R.O., D/PC/pet. s 1/2/1.
[44] Rep. Sel. Cttee. Depressed State of Agric.
[45] S.R.O., D/P/pet.s 17/7/1, 23/1.
[46] S.R.O., DD/SF 3351.
[47] S.R.O., D/PC/pet.s 1/2/1.
[48] H.O. 107/1929.
[49] S.R.O., D/G/Y 160; DD/WI 39.
[50] S.R.O., DD/WI 39.

1851, much of the business being in the hands of Simeon Hebditch.[51] The daily conveyance from the Crown inn to Bridport, running in 1859, was probably connected with this trade.[52] Rope and twine were made at Watergore in the 1850s and 1860s, and leather knicker-bockers and gaiters in the town in the 1860s.[53] Two manufacturers of bricks and tiles were in business in 1861; one ceased c. 1889, the other soon after 1902.[54] By 1902 the Hebditch family had started to make appliances for poultry breeders, a business they later transferred to Martock.[55]

As a commercial centre South Petherton grew steadily after the 1830s. Stuckey's Bank established a branch in 1836, and by the 1850s there were a number of shops, including 8 in the market-place and others in St. James's Street. By 1859 there were at least 20, and although later in the century the number declined, there were 22 in 1965.[56] Among the professional men in the 1850s were an auctioneer, a printer and bookbinder, 2 surgeons, and 2 solicitors. One of the law firms, begun by John Toller c. 1749, was in the 1850s headed by John Toller Nicholetts, holder of numerous offices in the town and district. Nicholetts became under-sheriff for Somerset for the first time in 1847, and since 1861 his successors have continued to hold the office.[57]

MARKET AND FAIR. In 1213 King John established or confirmed a weekly market on Thursdays and a fair on Midsummer day as an endowment for the free chapel of St. John.[58] In 1294 the market was valued at 6s. 8d.[59] Leland knew South Petherton as a market town,[60] and in the 1650s it was one of six in the county where the under-sheriff issued warrants on market days.[61] 'Several' butchers including one from Langport had stalls there at the time,[62] the shambles standing above drains issuing from the two inns in the north side of the market-place.[63] From the 17th century the lord of the manor let the tolls of the market, together with the common oven.[64] In 1662 the tolls were leased for £6 13s. 4d. to Francis Venicombe,[65] who with others in 1718 conveyed either the lease or the freehold to Amos Prowse. The property then included a bake-house, land, the meat market, stallage, and tolls.[66] By 1839 the market house was held by three women, and in 1843 the market and market house were bought by the charity school trustees from John Nicholetts, either as lord of the manor or as solicitor for the owners. A new market house was then erected on the site of the old, and tolls from

butchers between August and December 1843 amounted to £9 7s. Income fell by 1849 partly as a result of the butchers' refusal to pay if they did not actually sell within the market house itself. Business thereafter declined and in 1870 the weights were removed as trading had apparently ceased. The trustees sold the house to John Seward in 1879.[67]

The market house demolished in 1843 formed the western part of a group of buildings in the market-place, the remainder being irregular half-timbered cottages and shops.[68] The new building, erected to the designs of Maurice Davis of Langport, was of one storey with open arcades. It incorporated a lock-up and housed the fire engine.[69] An upper storey was added c. 1889.[70] In 1911 Robert Blake of Yeabridge demolished the two houses at the east end of the market house and replaced them with a club house and hall in memory of his father William Blake of Bridge 'for the furtherance of the Liberal cause and principles'.[71] In the 1970s part of the premises were shared between a county library branch and the South Petherton Billiards Club.

The Midsummer fair, held in 1213 apparently on 24 June only, was extended to its eve and morrow in 1252 when it was confirmed to Ralph Daubeney.[72] In 1294 it was valued, like the market, at 6s. 8d.,[73] and in 1305 at 13s. 4d.[74] It was extended to six days in 1448.[75] Later its value declined: in 1701 it was let to George Lock, gentleman, for 6s. 8d. yearly.[76] The date of the fair changed to 5th July in 1752.[77] There was still much trade in sheep in the late 18th century, but by the end of the 19th the 'poor little fair' was 'chiefly a matter of history',[78] though entertainment and sweetmeats were still offered there.[79] Nominal tolls for standings in the market-place were levied in the 1930s 'for the sake of keeping up the old tradition'.[80]

MILLS. In 1086 there was a mill at South Petherton worth 20s., and probably one at Compton Durville worth 64d.[81] In 1214 there were certainly two mills, and millers occur throughout the 13th century.[82] John of the mill held two as of the main manor in 1305, probably the forerunners of the later Joyler's and Moleyns's or North Mills.[83] A third mill, possibly that worked in the 1280s by Jellan the miller,[84] stood on the rectory estate and became known as Canons' mill.

Joyler's or Gaylards' mill was conveyed in 1313 with land in South Petherton and Bridge by Nicholas Gaylard, parson of Babcary, to Henry son of

[51] H.O. 107/1929; P.O. Dir. Som. (1861).
[52] P.O. Dir. Som. (1859).
[53] H.O. 107/1929; P.O. Dir. Som. (1859, 1861).
[54] P.O. Dir. Som. (1861); Kelly's Dir. Som. (1889, 1902).
[55] Kelly's Dir. Som. (1902).
[56] H.O. 107/1929; P.O. Dir. Som. (1859).
[57] Ex inf. Poole and Co.
[58] Rot. Chart. (Rec. Com.), 193.
[59] C 133/68/5.
[60] Leland, Itin. ed. Toulmin Smith, iv. 122.
[61] S.R.S. lxxi, pp. 64–5.
[62] Ibid. xxviii, 325, 347.
[63] Arundell MSS. ct. bk. 23, 30 Apr. 1635.
[64] Ibid. passim.
[65] S.R.O., DD/PE 6.
[66] C.P. 25(2)/1056/4 Geo. I Trin.
[67] S.R.O., D/P/pet. s 18/3/2.
[68] Lady's Pictorial, 1 Aug. 1891, 203.

[69] S.R.O., D/P/pet. s 18/3/2.
[70] S.R.O., D/PC/pet. s 1/2/1.
[71] Char. Com. file.
[72] Cal. Chart. R. 1226–57, 377.
[73] C 133/68/5.
[74] C 133/120/2.
[75] Cal. Chart. R. 1477–1516, 100.
[76] Arundell MSS., S. Petherton deed 9.
[77] Proc. Som. Arch. Soc. xci. 73.
[78] Norris, S. Petherton, 34.
[79] Proc. Som. Arch. Soc. lxxxii. 126.
[80] Ibid.
[81] V.C.H. Som. i. 435, 473.
[82] Cur. Reg. R. vii, p. 84; xiv, p. 467; S.R.S. viii, pp. 35–6; xliv. 306–7.
[83] C 133/120/2.
[84] S.R.S. viii, pp. 35–6. The name is there spelled Tellan.

Jellan de Moleyns, with successive remainders to John de Moleyns and his son Henry.[85] The younger Henry had succeeded by 1338 to an estate of c. 50 a. with the mill.[86] John de Moleyns died in 1387 holding of the Daubeneys two mills, a dovecot, and rents in Petherton and land in Bridge, Drayton, and Little Lopen. Nicholas, a minor, was his heir to the mills.[87] The two mills were specified in 1388 as 'Jeylynesmulle' and 'Northmulle'.[88] They passed to Nicholas when he came of age in 1404, together with a holding of c. 70 a.[89] Nicholas died in 1429[90] and his son or more likely his grandson, John in 1497. The property was then described as the manors of 'Yayleris' and Gawbridge, the former comprising two mills and 36 a. of land held of the Daubeneys.[91] John's heir was his uncle Richard.[92] By 1531 both mills and the land had come to William Moleyns, who settled the 'manor' of Joylers and other property on his wife Anne.[93] After William's death in 1553 Anne married John Dauncye of Mackney (Berks.), and they together granted Joylers mill and small parcels of land first to John Walrond and in 1563 to James Ayshe of South Petherton.[94] To this in 1568 were added further lands including the dovecot near the mill.[95] The mill then descended, like the manor of Hele, to J. B. Edmonds and then to J. W. Peters, who sold it to William Blake.[96] The owner in 1975 was Mr. W. S. Blake.

Clemence, wife of John Moleyns (d. 1387), was assigned as dower part of a house attached to Joyler's mill. Her share was defined as 'all the chambers above and below, and a little chapel to the east end of the hall . . . and a third of the kitchen at the east end as far as the partition', together with part of the farm complex, and the fishery there.[97] The present buildings, comprising mill and mill-house, are of the 19th century; the mill contains an undershot wheel and a small turbine which drove three stones and supplementary dressing machinery. The wheel was driven from a leat constructed from the Parrett, but the mill now appears isolated, the leat having been filled in. Milling ceased c. 1930.[98]

The second mill, called 'Moleynsmyll' in the early 16th century,[99] passed on William Moleyns's death in 1553 to his son Anthony.[1] In 1572 Anthony conveyed or confirmed it to William Northover,[2] whose successor James sold it to Emanuel Sandys of Kingsbury in 1612.[3] His son Francis Sandys, of South Perrott (Dors.), held it in 1659 when it was described as a water-grist-mill called 'Northmills'. It was then let to Stephen England of Middle Lambrook.[4] In 1699 his son, also Stephen, of East Lambrook, conveyed his interest in the remainder

of his father's lease to William Phelips of Preston Plucknett in trust for Elizabeth Cabell, owner of Hele manor. The property passed with that manor to J. B. Edmonds, having been let for much of the 18th century to the Gould family.[5] In 1826 it comprised a dwelling-house, bakehouse, two grist mills, bolting mill, and stable.[6] By 1840 the property was owned and occupied by Joseph Bandfield; a John Bandfield was miller of 'North Street mill' in 1861.[7] Milling continued until after the Second World War.[8] The property was known in the 1970s as Shutler's mill after the last miller.

The mill-house and adjoining bakehouse seem to have been built in the early 19th century in local brick. The mill, in an earlier building, is also probably of 19th-century date, succeeding one installed by 'that ingenious millwright Mr. Thomas Apley' c. 1778. His works included two pairs of stones, capable of working more than 100 bushels of wheat in a week.[9]

By 1334 there was a mill on the rectory estate.[10] It passed to the Crown at the Dissolution and in 1546 was let to John Colthurst of London by the name of Canon mill.[11] Like the rest of the rectory lands it was leased in 1510 to Elizabeth Burt, in 1552 to William Treasorer, and then in 1554 to Thomas Reve and Giles Isham.[12] In 1563 it passed to William Raven and hence as part of the manor of Hele, to the Ayshes.[13] It was described in 1699 as Came alias Cannons mill,[14] and probably went out of use in the 18th century. The site of the mill seems to have been south of the church, where a field called Little Mill Orchard occurs in 1840.[15]

LOCAL GOVERNMENT. There are no medieval court rolls for the capital manor of South Petherton. Extents of the Daubeney manor in 1291–2 and 1293–4 refer only to the courts of the hundred, possibly implying that a distinction between manor and hundred courts was not then made, though two separate items of court perquisites were entered in an extent of 1305.[16] By 1386 a distinction was made between the foreign court of the hundred and the *intrinsecum* court with view of frankpledge.[17] In the 16th century the manor court of South Petherton seems to have been attended by tithingmen from Barrington, South Harp, and Chillington.[18]

Court books survive for 1618–19, 1633–9, and 1661–1841, and there is a copy of court roll for 1598.[19] In the early 17th century the manor court was held irregularly, but normally at least once each month, usually described as 'manor court' or 'court',

[85] Ibid. xii. 32; *Plac. Abbrev.* (Rec. Com.), 348.
[86] *S.R.S.* xii. 196–7.
[87] C 136/52/12.
[88] *Cal. Close*, 1385–9, 621–2; C 136/52/12.
[89] *Cal. Close*, 1402–5, 254.
[90] *S.R.S.* xvi. 133–4.
[91] *Cal. Inq. p.m. Hen. VII*, ii, pp. 92–3.
[92] Ibid.; C 142/13/24.
[93] C 142/108/103.
[94] S.R.O., DD/PE 19.
[95] Ibid.; DD/SH 151.
[96] S.R.O., DD/PE 18; see *Western Flying Post*, 18 Jan. 1773.
[97] *Cal. Close*, 1385–9, 621–2.
[98] Ex inf. Mr. P. W. Priddle, Joyler's Fm.
[99] S.R.O., DD/HI, box 5; DD/PE 7; DD/SH 151.
[1] C 142/108/103.
[2] C.P. 25(2)/204/14 and 15 Eliz. I Mich.

[3] C.P. 25(2)/346/10 Jas. I East.
[4] S.R.O., DD/PE 19.
[5] S.R.O., DD/S/HR, box 6.
[6] Ibid. box 1.
[7] S.R.O., tithe award; *P.O. Dir. Som.* (1861).
[8] Ex inf. Mr. A. S. Mould, Shutler's Mill.
[9] *Western Flying Post*, 16 Feb. 1778.
[10] E 179/169/14.
[11] *L. & P. Hen. VIII*, xxi(1), p. 785.
[12] S.R.O., DD/PE 18; DD/SH 151.
[13] *Cal. Pat.* 1553–4, 471.
[14] S.R.O., DD/PE 19.
[15] S.R.O., tithe award.
[16] C 133/61/23; C 133/68/5; C 133/120/2.
[17] C 136/44/1.
[18] E 134/22–3 Eliz. I Mich./11.
[19] Arundell MSS. ct. bks. 21 (1618–19), 23 (1633–9); S.R.O., DD/PE 6 (1661–1841); DD/HLM, box 2.

though in January, April, and September usually 'court leet and view of frankpledge'. The term 'court baron' was not confined to sessions devoted exclusively to admissions and surrenders. After 1661 the frequency was greatly reduced, and from 1673 meetings became annual, held in September or October and described as 'court leet, view of frankpledge, and manor court'.

Apart from the usual business of tenancy surrenders and general farming matters there were less common presentments about the lack of a cucking stool and bows and arrows in 1619, or the illegal use of a bowling alley in the same year. During the early 17th century emphasis was placed on licences to tenants to live off their holdings and on their failure to use the common oven. Orders about farming continued into the early 19th century, relating largely to common rights; the last admission of a tenant occurred in 1783. Thereafter the business of the court was confined to the appointment of officers. The last was recorded in 1841.

The earliest officer was the bailiff, either of manor or hundred, who occurs in 1280.[20] By the early 17th century the only officers were a constable and a tithingman, appointed at the Michaelmas court. By 1633 there were two grass haywards. A separate tithingman for Compton Durville was chosen in 1634. The grass haywards were in the 1660s appointed annually in April, and each tenant had to pay them 1d. an acre on St. Luke's day (18 Oct.) in the grain fields. A bailiff again emerges in the 1660s. In 1673 the tithings of Compton Durville and South Petherton each had a hayward, and in 1674 each tithing had a tithingman, a hayward, and two grass haywards. In 1684 a committee of four freeholders was set up to supervise the common grazing and to oversee the work of the hayward. Two bailiffs occur from 1685, six grass haywards, and a 'general' hayward for the two tithings in 1688, but usually thereafter there were only two for South Petherton alone, and only one from 1803. The term 'common grass hayward' was in use later for the 'general' hayward. Most of these offices were held in rotation in respect of holdings; by the end of the 18th century the constable was chosen once in five years from Compton Durville, and that tithing contributed one fifth of his expenses yearly. In the early 19th century most offices were held by deputy, and for many years between 1815 and 1841 the office of grass hayward was held by John Baker Edmonds, lord of the manor, or by his son of the same name.

After the sale of the manor-house in 1540 courts were probably held first in a house known since the 19th century as the Court House. In the 18th century the meeting-place of the manor court seems to have been the Crown inn.[21]

By 1334 courts were held for the rectory manor.[22] At the beginning of the 16th century there were usually courts leet for Michaelmas and Hockday each year, and rolls have survived for 1513–14 and 1531.[23] A halmote court met on the same day. Business included presentments for excessive tolls and the sale of bad goods as well as for repairs to buildings, breach of the peace, and control of strays. Courts were held at least until 1564.[24]

Extracts or rolls for the manor court of Stratton survive for 1461–3, 1520–3, and 1529–33.[25] Much of the business was with farming practice and the repair of roads, though in the mid 15th century there were also pleas between tenants for trespass and debt. Courts were held roughly twice a year and their orders were executed by a hayward and a tithingman, chosen annually at the Michaelmas court. In 1530 the manor possessed a common brewhouse, then out of repair.

There are no court rolls for the manor of South Harp, though copy extracts from courts baron for South Harp survive for 1647 and for the combined estate of South Harp and Chillington for 1692 and for South Harp alone for 1700.[26]

The parish in the 16th century was divided between the tithings of South Petherton, South Harp, and Stratton.[27] Compton Durville seems to have emerged as a separate tithing by 1634.[28] In the 19th century South Harp tithing was also known as Lower Stratton.[29] By the mid 17th century four overseers were in effectual control of poor-relief in the parish, which was divided into ten collecting areas. The rate itself was occasionally supplemented by interest on small loans and bequests, and was paid in cash or clothing both to regular recipients and to those in temporary distress. House repairs and rent, doctors' bills, and apprenticeship premiums were regular charges, with such irregular payments as the repair of the cucking stool and pillory in 1658, the repair of the watch house in 1660, or the provision of badges in 1696. In the late 18th and early 19th centuries patients were sent to infirmaries in Bristol and Bath, and in 1794 172 children were inoculated.[30]

General policy decisions were made by 'the men of the town' in the late 17th century or at a 'general meeting' of the parish. The poor-relief accounts, by the early 18th century compiled separately by each overseer, were normally signed by the vicar, constable, two churchwardens, and a variable number of inhabitants, by the 1730s a total of fewer than ten people. By the end of the century the vestry or 'parish meeting' was even more reduced in numbers, and a 'public vestry' in the 1820s was often attended by little more than a dozen people. By the 1840s the numbers began to rise again as the vestry took on wider interests. A salaried clerk was appointed in 1737.[31] The wardens themselves before 1719 were chosen, one for the town and the other for the parish. From that date one was nominated by the minister, the other by the vestry.[32] In 1792 the

[20] S.R.S. xliv. 13, 168.
[21] S.R.O., DD/PE 6, at end.
[22] E 179/169/14.
[23] Glos. R.O., D547A/M 6, 12. S.R.O., DD/HI, box 5, DD/PE 7, DD/SAS PD 56 are accts. recording perquisites.
[24] S.R.O., DD/PE 18.
[25] D.R.O., D 124, boxes 13, 16, 18.
[26] S.R.O., DD/AB 36; DD/SS, bdle. 20; DD/BR/py.
[27] S.R.S. xx. 36–9.

[28] S.R.O., DD/PE 6.
[29] S.R.O., DD/S/HR, box 2 (1859).
[30] S.R.O., D/P/pet.s 13/2/1 (1658–91); DD/SAS SX 102 (1695–1740); Som. County Gazette, 18 Nov. 1933 (ref. to an Order Bk. 1783–97 not traced); D/PC/pet.s 1/2/1 (1827–89).
[31] S.R.O., D/P/pet.s 4/1/2, 13/2/1; DD/SAS SX 102; D/PC/pet.s 1/2/1.
[32] S.R.O., D/P/pet.s 4/1/1.

vestry 'disavowed the indulgence' of allowing the vicar to appoint a warden unless he or his curate personally attended the Easter vestry.[33]

By the 1820s the vestry had taken control of the distribution of most charity income in the parish, and they had appointed a salaried 'perpetual or acting overseer and vestry clerk'. After the transfer of the parish to the Yeovil poor-law union in 1836 the vestry continued active, raising money in the 1840s for pauper emigration and appointing surveyors of highways. In 1865 the streets were lit with gas and a committee of nuisance was set up. A burial board was formed in 1867 and a cemetery was laid out with a lodge and two chapels, designed by J. M. Allen.[34] After some attempts to provide adequate water for the fire engine in 1868, and other drainage problems, a sewage committee was appointed in 1869. In 1876 a new drainage scheme was proposed but was voted down two years later 'considering the healthy state of the parish'. During the 1880s the prominent questions were the Guardians' antagonism to outdoor relief, the poor standard of footways in the parish, and the state of the Round well.

The vestry, led in the 1860s and 1870s by such outstanding local figures as the vicar, Henry Bond, William Blake, John Toller Nicholetts, F. G. N. Wellington, and James Patten Daniel, also played a prominent part in the establishment of a School Board and in the support for the Volunteer Fire Brigade. In 1890 the vestry had an active allotments committee. In 1895, after the formation of a parish council, all the charities of the parish were passed to it for administration.[35] Further land was purchased for allotments in 1910 and recreation fields were established first in 1897. Property at Hayes End was used from 1898 until 1917, and the present field, given by Miss Florence Blake in 1931, was extended in 1946.[36]

A parish fire engine, cared for by the sexton by 1778,[37] was normally kept in the south porch of the church. By 1823 there was another engine at Stratton. Both were sold in 1865, and a new machine was purchased by subscription for the newly-formed Volunteer Fire Brigade who received annual grants from the vestry. In 1903 the Parish Council took over the brigade, but transferred control to Yeovil R.D.C. in 1939.

At least from 1710 the parish began the policy of acquiring houses in return for relief, the first being at Yeabridge.[38] By 1783 a workhouse was established in Pitway which remained open until 1836, when the parish joined the Yeovil poor-law union. In 1841 the vestry agreed to sell it and apply the proceeds to pauper emigration.[39]

There was a watch house on Petherton Bridge in 1660[40] and a parish lock-up by the churchyard gate in the 19th century. The lock-up was removed in 1843 and another was incorporated in the newly-built market house.[41] In 1886 it was proposed to use the lock-up exclusively for the fire brigade. Three years later the plan to alter the market house involved the provision of a fire-engine house so that the lock-up could be used for the parish committee of local justices of the peace.[42]

South Petherton hospital was built in 1938 as an isolation hospital for the South Somerset area. In 1976 it had 59 beds for general cases.[43]

CHURCH. The presence of Alviet the priest holding a substantial estate in South Petherton T.R.E. and in 1086, and the subsequent appearance of several chapels dependent upon South Petherton church, is strong evidence that the church originated as a Saxon minster.[44] The church may have formed part of an abortive grant by King Stephen 1143 × 1154 when 'Perretona' and North Curry were given to Wells cathedral.[45] Late in 1181 or early in 1182 Henry II gave the church to the canons of Bruton in exchange for their church of Witham, and it remained in their possession until the Dissolution.[46]

A vicarage was ordained in the time of Archbishop Pecham (1279–92), but the patronage remained in the hands of the canons.[47] In 1542 advowson and tithes passed to the newly-created chapter of Bristol,[48] which remained patron until 1941, when its rights were transferred to the chapter of Wells.[49] Roger Hunt of London presented by grant of the Bristol chapter in 1554, Robert Millerd in 1617, the Lord Protector in 1654, and the Crown in 1660.[50]

Under the ordination the vicar received what he had when instituted, namely all offerings at the altar of the mother church and all small tithes, except tithes of mills and offerings of wax at the Purification which were the perquisites of the sacristan of Bruton priory.[51] The vicarage was valued in 1291 at £6 13s. 4d.[52] By 1535 some rearrangement of income had taken place, the vicar receiving a small amount of tithes of wool and lambs, and an annual pension from St. John's free chapel in addition to personal tithes and casuals, amounting to £24 net.[53] By the mid 17th century this figure had risen to £80, though it fell in the 1650s and was subject to augmentation.[54] About 1668 the benefice was still worth only £50.[55] By 1831 the net value was £475.[56]

The tithe income of the vicarage in 1535 amounted to £4 from wool and lambs and £19 9s. 9d. from

---

33 Ibid. 4/1/2.

34 S.R.O., D/PC/pet.s 1/2/1; *Western Gazette*, 2 June 1865.   35 *Western Chronicle*, 13 Dec. 1895.

36 S.R.O., D/PC/pet.s 1/2/2–4; par. cncl. deeds.

37 S.R.O., D/P/pet.s 4/1/2, 18/3/2; D/PC/pet.s 1/2/1, 2, 5; Char. Com. files.

38 S.R.O., DD/SAS SX 102.

39 *Som. County Gazette*, 18 Nov. 1933; S.R.O., D/PC/pet.s 1/2/1.   40 S.R.O., D/P/pet.s 13/2/1.

41 Ibid. 18/3/2.   42 S.R.O., D/PC/pet.s 1/2/1.

43 *Kelly's Dir. Som.* (1939); ex inf. Mr. S. G. Oakes, S. Petherton.

44 *V.C.H. Som.* i. 471; *Cal. Papal Letters*, v. 326.

45 *S.R.S.* viii, p. xx; xxix, p. 55; *Reg. Regum Anglo-Norm.* iii, pp. 336–7; *H.M.C. Wells*, i. 8. Perretona may,

of course, be North Petherton.

46 *S.R.S.* viii, pp. 30, 34, 102–3; *Cal. Chart. R.* 1300–26 270; *Cal. Papal Letters*, v. 326.

47 *S.R.S.* viii, p. 41.

48 *L. & P. Hen. VIII*, xvii, p. 638.

49 *Lond. Gaz.* 28 March 1941.

50 S.R.O. DD/X/SAB (grant 1550); D/D/B reg. 19, f. 2v.; Lambeth Palace MSS., COMM. III/3, p. 183; *Som. Incumbents*, ed. Weaver.

51 *S.R.S.* viii, p. 41.   52 *Tax. Eccl.* (Rec. Com.), 199.

53 *Valor Eccl.* (Rec. Com.), i. 164; *S.R.S.* ii. 10.

54 S.R.O., DD/X/SAB; *Cal. S.P. Dom.* 1655–6, 73; 1656–7, 198; 1657–8, 380; Lambeth Palace MSS., COMM. VIb/2.   55 S.R.O., D/D/Vc 24.

56 *Rep. Com. Eccl. Revenues*, pp. 148–9.

personal tithes and casuals.[57] By 1634 the sources of tithe were more closely defined: from hemp, flax, cabbages, carrots, and other garden produce; apples, pears, and other orchard fruit; hops, honey, wool, lambs, pigs, and pigeons; payments by strangers for pasturing cattle in the parish, and personal offerings.[58]

There was no glebe attached to the vicarage during the Middle Ages, and no house was expressly assigned. By 1626 the vicar claimed two gardens and an orchard adjoining the vicarage house, and in 1634 the area was *c.* 2 a.[59] In 1738 James Harcourt, vicar 1729–38, gave his successors just over an acre of land adjoining the vicarage grounds.[60] Harcourt's successor, John Castleman, acquired a house and 1¼ a. in West Street in 1753.[61] By 1839 the glebe amounted to just over 4 a. comprising the church-yard and the grounds of the vicarage house.[62]

In 1626 the vicarage house was of five bays, described as 'four field or couple of housing, sufficiently repaired'.[63] It was extended, if not rebuilt, in the 18th century, and part seems to have stood on pillars.[64] It was thought in 1815 to be 'very fit' provided the incumbent did not have a large family.[65] In 1841 it was replaced by a much larger house, built by Maurice Davis the younger for Henry Bond at a cost of over £1,670.[66] It may incorporate parts of the older house in the rear, and includes three shields in stone taken from the rectory barn.[67] Outbuildings included a stable block, stores, and a piggery. A new vicarage house in one corner of the grounds was completed in 1975.

John Wodeman, absent for study for seven years from 1395 and again in 1401 'for some time',[68] resigned the benefice and was awarded a pension in 1429. He was succeeded by John Petherton, a theologian, who, while he held South Petherton, was also rector of Hornblotton and vicar of Cheddar.[69] Of the three other graduate clergy of the century, Thomas Harrys was the most distinguished, holding administrative posts in the diocese as official of the archdeacon of Taunton by 1476 and as vicar-general in 1490 and 1493.[70]

In 1525 the patronage was temporarily ceded to trustees in order that William Gilbert, abbot of Bruton and bishop of Mayo, could be appointed vicar.[71] The appointment of Henry Bankes as vicar in 1554 suggests that his predecessor had been removed for failing to conform with the new regime. Bankes himself was in 1561 in the Fleet prison for a debt to a London mercer.[72] Thomas Seager, vicar

by 1569, was by 1612 'old and diseased and not able to travel' and so failed to go on the annual perambulation of the parish.[73] His successor, Robert Marks, vicar from 1617, also held Merriott from 1626. Although reported in 1623 for being 'often and much' absent, he claimed that he employed the curates of Lopen and Seavington when he was away.[74] Marks, an Oxford D.D. and a Royalist, was accused in 1643 of conspiring to let Prince Rupert into Bristol and of acting as a messenger for the king. He was imprisoned and deprived of his livings and of his large private income.[75] The parish was served on his removal first by Edward Bennett in 1646 and then by Benjamin Dukes between 1654 and 1660.[76] Marks himself died in 1657, and at the Restoration the Crown presented his son William to the vicarage.[77]

From the time of William Marks until 1936 most vicars had close connexions with Bristol and several held office in the cathedral.[78] During the 18th century several were absentee pluralists: Thomas Godard, vicar 1777–89, lived at Long Ashton, was vicar of Clevedon, and served as curate of Wraxall and Bourton; Francis Simpson, vicar 1813–27, lived at Tarrant Gunville (Dors.).[79] John Castleman, vicar 1738–61, was more active in parish affairs, and was accused of Anabaptism for baptising two children who had already undergone the rite at the hands of a Dissenting minister.[80]

Among the assistant curates who cared for the parish in the 18th century, the most noted was Thomas Coke, D.C.L., curate 1772–7, who was removed from office as a result of his enthusiasm, and subsequently became a leading Methodist.[81]

Endowments of lamps, obits, and a fraternity, and bequests of vestments and possession of a silver-gilt pyx suggest a prosperous church in the early 16th century.[82] By 1547, however, the new rectors, the chapter of Bristol, had failed to maintain the chancel, and there was no Bible.[83] Neither had the statue of Christ been removed, and the vicar was not preaching sermons as required.[84] There were, nevertheless, as many as 480 communicants, including those at Lopen and Chillington.[85] With the return of the old regime in 1554, the impropriators were required to find two tapers for the high altar, and it was reported that the Lord's Prayer and the Commandments had not been read in the vulgar tongue since Christmas.[86]

In 1636 the leads of the chancel were reported in decay, and the discovery of an ancient leaden coffin in the church led to its appropriation for the purpose.

[57] *Valor Eccl.* (Rec. Com.), i. 164.
[58] S.R.O., D/D/Rg 322.
[59] Ibid.
[60] S.R.O., D/P/pet.s 3/1/2.
[61] Ibid. 3/1/4.
[62] S.R.O., tithe award.
[63] S.R.O., D/D/Rg 322.
[64] S.R.O., D/P/pet.s 3/4/1.
[65] S.R.O., D/D/B return 1815.
[66] S.R.O., D/P/pet.s 3/4/2.
[67] Norris, *S. Petherton*, 57.
[68] *Cal. Papal Letters*, iv. 502; *S.R.S.* xiii, p. 16.
[69] Emden, *Biog. Reg. Univ. Oxford.*
[70] *S.R.S.* lii, pp. 64, 117, 146, 155, 161, 179. King's clerk 1487–8: *S.R.S.* liv, p. 92.
[71] *S.R.S.* lv, p. 42; S.R.O., D/D/Ca 2, p. 118.
[72] *Cal. Pat.* 1560–3, p. 56.
[73] *S. & D. N. & Q.* xiv. 32; S.R.O., D/D/Ca 175;

D/P/mart 2/1/1.
[74] S.R.O., D/D/Ca 235.
[75] *Walker Revised*, ed. Matthews.
[76] Lambeth Palace MSS., COMM. III/3, p. 183.
[77] *Cal. S.P. Dom.* 1660–1, 233.
[78] *Walker Revised*, ed. Matthews; Foster, *Alumni Oxon.*; S.R.O., D/P/pet.s 3/1/2; *Crockford.*
[79] S.R.O., D/D/BO; D/D/B return 1815.
[80] *A Letter to the Revd. Mr. Castleman . . .* (London, 2nd edn. 1751).
[81] J. Vickers, *Thomas Coke*; see below, p. 195.
[82] S.R.O., DD/X/SR; *S.R.S.* xvi. 393; xix. 145; liv, p. 68.
[83] S.R.O., D/D/Ca 17.
[84] Ibid. St. Salvator's aisle occurs in 1531: *S.R.S.* xxi. 8.
[85] *S.R.S.* ii. 10.
[86] S.R.O., D/D/Ca 22.

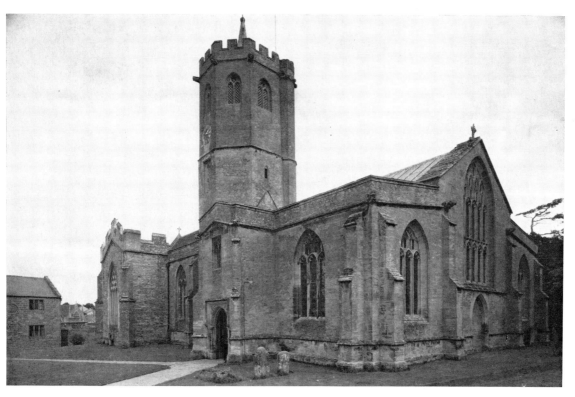

SOUTH PETHERTON CHURCH FROM THE NORTH-WEST

SHEPTON BEAUCHAMP CHURCH: THE BASE OF THE FORMER NORTH TOWER

South Petherton: Stratton Farm

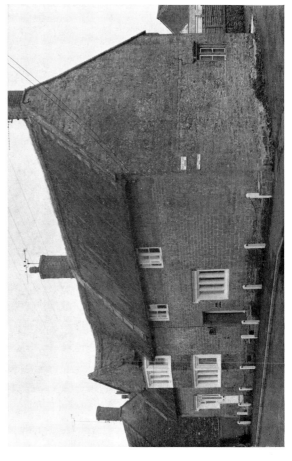

Merriott: Manor Farm

Merriott: Bow Mill

Dowlish Wake: the Dower House

A dispute ensued in which one of the church-wardens failed to do penance for his offence, a case which involved a petition to Archbishop Laud and the intervention of Bishop Piers and the Court of Arches.[87]

James Harcourt augmented the glebe in 1738 on condition that his successors catechized weekly and read prayers on Wednesdays, Fridays, and saints' days.[88] By 1776 there were usually between 70 and 90 communicants.[89] The enthusiasm which resulted in the removal of Thomas Coke as curate in 1777 seems to have shown itself in more frequent cele-brations attended by strangers as well as parishioners. Seven celebrations were usual at the end of the 18th century.[90] By 1815 two services with sermons were held each Sunday, only 'occasionally' taken by the vicar; and by 1827 there were also prayers on Wednesdays.[91] On Census Sunday 1851 the general morning congregation was 237 with 211 Sunday-school pupils, and the afternoon attendance was 403 people with 237 pupils.[92] Three services a Sunday were reported in 1870, when there was both a resident vicar and a curate, with monthly celebrations of the Holy Communion.[93] In 1876 a weekly celebration was instituted with a 'double

service' on Wednesdays and Fridays and both Morning and Evening Prayer on saints' days. Two years later daily Morning Prayer was started. A surpliced choir occurs in 1882.[94] A mission room was opened at Stratton in 1905,[95] and a chapel in Compton Durville Manor was licensed in 1927.[96]

There was a church house on the rectory estate, leased to John Brett, by 1531.[97] A church or parish house was held by the churchwardens from South Harp manor in 1650, but in 1654 it was said to be in ruins and the rent to be eight years in arrear.[98]

There was a light of Our Lady by 1503 and a High Cross light by 1538.[99] Four acres of land partly in Seavington St. Michael, given for the support of lamps and lights, passed into lay hands in 1549.[1] Our Lady candlestick is referred to in 1538 and a brotherhood of Our Lady then and in the previous year.[2]

A chantry of Our Lady was established by 1305, its endowment of ½ virgate and 2 a. held as part of the Daubeney estate. At the same date the estate supported a chaplain and two clerks.[3] In 1364 2 houses and 80 a. in South Petherton and Barrington were given by Ralph and Catherine Daubeney for a chantry before the altar of St. Catherine.[4] By 1382

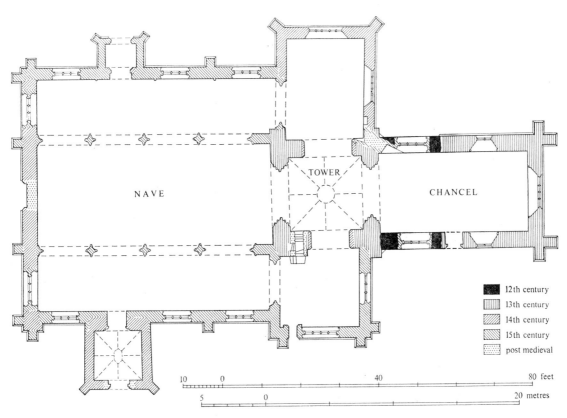

THE CHURCH OF ST. PETER AND ST. PAUL, SOUTH PETHERTON

12th century
13th century
14th century
15th century
post medieval

10   0   40   80 feet
5   0   20 metres

[87] S.R.O., D/D/Ca 310; *Cal. S.P. Dom.* 1637, 522; 1637-8, 275-6.
[88] S.R.O., D/P/pet.s 3/1/2.
[89] S.R.O., D/D/V Dioc. bk.
[90] S.R.O., D/P/pet.s 4/1/2.
[91] S.R.O., D/D/B return 1815; D/D/V return 1827.
[92] H.O. 129/319/2/4/7.
[93] S.R.O., D/D/V return 1870.

[94] S.R.O., D/P/pet.s 4/1/2.
[95] Ibid. 2/5/1.
[96] Par. rec.
[97] Glos. R.O., D547A/M12.
[98] Wilts. R.O. 192/38A, 38B.
[99] *S.R.S.* xix. 50; S.R.O., DD/X/SR.
[1] *Cal. Pat.* 1548-9, 430.
[2] S.R.O., DD/X/SR.
[3] C 133/120/2.
[4] *Cal. Pat.* 1361-4, 484.

the first was established in the Lady chapel in the south aisle, the second at a chapel in the north aisle.[5] By 1532 there appears to have been only one chantry, since only one chantry priest occurs in the parish, though there was also a stipendiary chaplain.[6] By 1548 there was certainly only one chantry, then newly established by Henry Daubeney, earl of Bridgwater, worth £6 13s. 4d.[7]

The church of *ST. PETER AND ST. PAUL* is a large building of rubble and ashlar and has a chancel, central tower with transepts, and aisled nave with north and south porches.[8] Parts of the walling of the western end of the chancel are of the 12th century, but there is no other evidence *in situ* of the form of the church at that time. This is largely the result of a major rebuilding in the later 13th and earlier 14th centuries. The chancel was extended eastwards, the tower and transepts rebuilt, and the nave, which was of similar length to the existing one of four bays, was aisled and given a south porch, the corbels and a carved panel of Sagittarius and the lion moved from an earlier doorway. The south transept and the nave were almost completely rebuilt in the 15th century when the north porch was added, and lesser works of the period included a new east window and the heightening of the central tower.

Fire-reddening over the tower arch is witness to the lights around the rood, removed with the loft and screen in Edward VI's reign. The chancel and north aisle retained their medieval glass until the 17th century, when some was broken by Parliamentary troops in 1644.[9] There is an effigy considered to be that of Sir Philip Daubeney (d. 1294),[10] and masonry fragments from a crucifixion, painted figures perhaps from a screen, and parts of a lias altar slab and a Purbeck shaft. In the south transept is a tomb with a monumental brass of Sir Giles Daubeney (d. 1446) and his first wife, together with a separate brass to his second wife (d. 1442).[11]

An organ was installed c. 1636 but was destroyed in 1644.[12] It had probably been renewed by 1715.[13] The present instrument replaced one made in 1834.[14] There is an oak altar table of 1698.

Extensive restoration began in 1859–60 with the complete reseating of church and galleries and the replacement of pulpit, reading desk, and clerk's desk. The south transept became the vestry room in place of the eastern end of the chancel, which, since 1799, had contained a grate and chimney. The work was carried out by Hicks and Isaacs of Bristol.[15] The fabric of the chancel was restored by Arthur Blomfield in 1882, the south porch in 1890, and the

tower, by J. D. Sedding and H. Wilson, in 1895.[16] The south transept was restored for use as a chapel in 1923.[17] Modern additions include the Royal Arms (1955) and figures of St. Peter and St. Paul (1974).

The church has eight bells: (i) and (ii) 1896, Mears and Stainbank; (iii) 1641, William Wiseman; (iv) 1765, Thomas Bilbie; (v) 1713, William Bilbie; (vi) 1919, Llewellins and James; (vii) 1832, W. Jefferies; (viii) 1721, William Bilbie.[18] The plate includes a cup and cover of 1573 by 'I.P.', a flagon of 1716, and a dish of 1724.[19] The registers date from 1574, but there are no entries between 1653 and 1660.[20]

In 1213 King John, then lord of the manor, granted and confirmed the endowment of a perpetual chaplain at the chapel of St. John. The endowment consisted of a weekly market and a fair on Midsummer day.[21] In 1270 Ralph Daubeney assigned rents from the manor to support services at the chapel, and the chaplain was also given oblations at the chapel from the lord and his free tenants at all times except on the four chief feasts and at Purification, when oblations were given to the vicar.[22] By 1325 the chaplain held 54½ a., and was described as rector of the free chapel.[23] By 1535 the gross value of the chapel's endowment was £5 17s. 10d., but it was subject to a pension of 14s. to the vicar of South Petherton and a rent of 2s. to the abbot of Bruton.[24] By 1548 the net income was £4 16s. 8d.[25]

At least from 1270 the patronage of the chapel belonged to the Daubeneys, lords of the manor. Queen Joan presented in 1404 during John Daubeney's minority, and again in 1415 during Giles Daubeney's.[26] Feoffees presented in 1465 and 1467.[27] The chapel was suppressed in 1548. Its goods included a bell worth 3s. 4d.[28] The chapel and its lands were granted in 1553 to agents.[29] From them it was purchased in the same year by Edward Napper of Swyre (Dors.) and Holywell (Oxf.) (d. 1558), who left it with other property to All Souls College, Oxford.[30] The devise was unsuccessfully disputed by Napper's son William when he came of age in 1575,[31] and the college retained the property at least until 1860.[32]

At least two of the rectors, Hugh Foster (1478–90) and Simon Symondes (1533–6), were graduates; Oliver, rector in 1325, and Maurice le Clerk, rector in 1327, were both foreigners. Stephen Forest, rector 1536–9, became vicar of the parish.[33]

The exact location of the chapel has not been traced, though twice in the 15th century it was said to be near the town.[34]

[5] *Cal. Inq. p.m.* xvi, pp. 259–60.
[6] S.R.O., D/D/Vc 20.
[7] *S.R.S.* ii. 9.
[8] See plate facing p. 192.
[9] *Diary of Richard Symonds* (Camd. Soc. [1st ser.], lxxiv), 98–102.
[10] *Proc. Som. Arch. Soc.* lxxv. 34–41.
[11] A. B. Connor, *Monumental Brasses of Som.*
[12] *Diary of Richard Symonds*, 102.
[13] S.R.O., D/P/pet.s 4/1/1.
[14] *Taunton Courier*, 21 May 1834.
[15] S.R.O., D/P/pet.s 6/1/2, 8/2/1. The galleries were put up by 1788 and enlarged in 1792: ibid. 4/1/1–2.
[16] Ibid. 8/2/2–4.
[17] Ibid. 8/4/1.
[18] S.R.O., DD/SAS CH 16. *The Ringing World*, lxvii. 698 (13 Aug. 1971) gives (v) as 1919 and (vi) as 1713.

[19] *Proc. Som. Arch. Soc.* xlv. 147–8.
[20] S.R.O., D/P/pet.s 2/1/1–12.
[21] *Rot. Chart.* (Rec. Com.), 193.
[22] *S.R.S.* viii, p. 75.
[23] S.R.O., D/D/B reg 1, f. 226b.
[24] *Valor Eccl.* (Rec. Com.), i. 164.
[25] *S.R.S.* ii. 8–10, 181–2.
[26] Ibid. xiii, p. 50; xxiv. 216.
[27] Ibid. lii, pp. xxii, 8.
[28] E 117/12/21; E 117/8; *S.R.S.* ii. 8–10.
[29] *Cal. Pat.* 1553, 106–7.
[30] Bodl. MS. DD/All Souls, 187/1, 13.
[31] Ibid. 22–31.   [32] D.R.O., D45/E36.
[33] *Cal. Mem. R.* 1326–7, p. 283; *S.R.S.* ii. 10; lii, p. 74; lv, pp. 68, 165; S.R.O., D/D/B reg 1, f. 226b.
[34] *S.R.S.* xlix, p. 264; lii, p. xxii. It may have stood in the field called St. John's north of Hayes End: S.R.O., tithe award.

ROMAN CATHOLICISM. In 1934 a Mass centre, served monthly from Yeovil, was opened in Knapp House, South Street. By the Second World War the house proved too small, and services were held instead in the British Legion Hall, and also in Stoke sub Hamdon. In 1961 the church of St. Michael, Lightgate Road, was opened. It was designed by Mr. A. B. Grayson of Wincanton, and is of Ham stone and cedar board, with a glass façade. Services are held each Sunday and on important feasts, and the church is served as part of the parish of Yeovil by the Missionaries of St. Francis de Sales.[35]

Knapp House was in 1974 known as St. Elizabeth's Home for Elderly Ladies.

PROTESTANT NONCONFORMITY. Edward Bennett, intruded into the vicarage c. 1646–54, returned to the parish in 1663 on the 'earnest invitation' of the parishioners to preach and to keep a school.[36] By 1672 there were two Presbyterian meeting-places in the parish, in houses in Petherton and South Harp.[37] The former was probably the successor to Bennett's cause, which was certainly Presbyterian in 1688.[38] It then had its own minister, though by 1690 its preacher came from Yeovil only fortnightly.[39] A baptism 'at the meeting house' took place in 1695.[40] A chapel, later known as the Old Meeting, was built in a garden behind a house on the south side of Palmer Street in 1705, and was licensed in 1706.[41]

In 1720 the denomination was described as Congregational or Presbyterian in a trust deed,[42] and in 1748 as Presbyterian,[43] although it seems likely that Unitarian doctrines were adopted under Henry Rutter, minister ?1726–36.[44] A second Presbyterian meeting was formed c. 1735 in the house of George Locke who, in 1750, seems to have led the secession of those against the Arianism adopted by James Kirkup, minister 1747–81. The Old Meeting continued under David Richards at least until his death in 1846, and new trustees appointed in the following year to maintain the cause included the Revds. Thomas Toller of Kettering (Northants.) and Henry Toller of Market Harborough (Leics.), and the solicitor John Nicholetts.[45] Regular services seem to have ceased c. 1843.[46]

Two groups of seceders, presumably former members of the Old Meeting, were holding services in 1752 at Stratton and in 1753 at Moor. In 1773 a group began to use a converted malthouse,[47] apparently until 1775, when a chapel was built in Roundwell Street, on the site of the present United

Reformed Church Sunday School. The cause continued Presbyterian under Richard Herdsman, a founder of the London Missionary Society, but by 1839 had become Independent.[48] On Census Sunday 1851 the general morning congregation was 200 and in the afternoon 325, with 117 Sunday-school pupils at each service. The building was then called Roundwell Street Chapel.[49] A new chapel, built in the Mid-Gothic style with rusticated masonry, at the junction of Roundwell Street and St. James's Street, was opened in 1863. A manse was erected next to it in 1868 in the Early Venetian Gothic style.[50]

At the end of the 17th century and throughout the 18th licences for other Dissenting meetings were issued, beginning with two in private houses in 1689.[51] The denominations are largely unknown, though in 1737 there was an Anabaptist meeting. The cause was continued or revived for in 1776 there were said to be 'some' Anabaptists in the parish in contrast to the 'many' Presbyterians.[52] By 1779 there were also some Independents, using a converted barn at Pitway, relicensed after alterations in 1803.[53] In 1812, 1816, and 1822 licences were issued for the use of private properties by Independents, the first two clearly involving the same group, the third sponsored by the ministers of Martock and Crewkerne.[54] By 1839 Independents were said to be using the Old Meeting, but they presumably joined the Roundwell Street meeting c. 1843. In 1851 the minister also had charge of Pound Chapel at South Harp, a small building seating 100, which on Census Sunday had an evening service attended by 50 people.[55]

Methodism came to the parish in 1753 when two houses in Stratton and one in Petherton were licensed for their use.[56] The direct influence of Dr. Thomas Coke there seems to have been slight. In 1807 a house was being used by Wesleyans, and was succeeded two years later by a chapel on the west side of North Street.[57] By 1810 there were 52 members, in 1841 95, and in 1848 84 members and 112 Sunday-school pupils.[58] On Census Sunday 1851 the general congregation was 280 in the morning and 334 in the evening, with 84 Sunday-school pupils in the morning and 120 in the afternoon.[59] The building was replaced in 1881 by the Coke Memorial Chapel, on the corner of North and Palmer streets. It is of Ham stone and slate in the early Gothic style, with a south-eastern turret and spire, and multi-gabled side elevations. It has a Sunday School at the rear and a manse, known as Coke Villa, to the west. The manse was sold c. 1970.[60]

Wesleyans met with less success elsewhere in the

---

[35] Ex inf. the Revd. Fr. D. J. Breen, M.S.F.S., parish priest.
[36] Calamy Revised, ed. Matthews.
[37] Cal. S.P. Dom. 1672, 299.
[38] Rep. Som. Cong. Union (1896).
[39] A. Gordon, Freedom after Ejection, 93; Calamy Revised, ed. Matthews.
[40] R.G. 4/4491.
[41] S.R.O., Q/RR, meeting-house lics.; Rep. Som. Cong. Union (1896).
[42] Deed penes Poole and Co., S. Petherton.
[43] Ibid.
[44] S. & D. N. & Q. i. 23–4.
[45] Deeds penes Poole and Co., S. Petherton.
[46] S. & D. N. & Q. i. 23–4.
[47] S.R.O., Q/RR, meeting-house lics.

[48] Rep. Som. Cong. Union (1896); R.G.4/2503; S.R.O., tithe award; J. Vickers, Thomas Coke, 18.
[49] H.O. 129/319/2/4/8.
[50] Rep. Som. Cong. Union (1896); datestones on buildings.
[51] S.R.O., Q/RR, meeting-house lics.
[52] S.R.O., D/D/V Dioc. bk.
[53] S.R.O., D/D/Rm, box 1; Q/RR, meeting-house lics.
[54] S.R.O., D/D/Rm, box 2.
[55] S.R.O., tithe award; H.O. 129/319/2/4/10.
[56] S.R.O., Q/RR, meeting-house lics.
[57] S.R.O., D/D/Rm, box 2.
[58] S.R.O., D/N/spc 1; E. Devon R.O. 64/2/9/1B.
[59] H.O. 129/319/2/4/11.
[60] Datestones on building; ex inf. Mr. T. Willy, S. Petherton.

parish: they supported a meeting at Stratton in 1822 for one quarter only, another at Compton for a year in 1837–8, and a third at Lower Stratton for two years from 1845.[61] More successful at Stratton were the Bible Christians, who were also active in Petherton itself. They began with a public collection at Stratton in 1826 and others in Petherton in 1831 and 1832. The Petherton cause began in 1834, and a year later there were nine members and a further 18 on trial.[62] A chapel, with a gallery, was built at Pitway in 1848–9, and was licensed in 1850.[63] On Census Sunday 1851 there was Sunday-school in the morning for 46 and services in the afternoon and evening for 163 and 149 respectively.[64] The chapel was still actively supported in 1861 but closed c. 1884.[65] The Bible Christian cause was revived at Stratton in 1859, and in 1860 there were 10 members. A chapel called Mount Calvary was built in the following year,[66] and in 1974 was still in use as part of the Crewkerne Methodist circuit. It is a small stone building in the lancet style and bears the inscription 'Bibile (sic) Christian Chapel 1861'.

EDUCATION. Licences to schoolmasters in the parish have been traced from 1575 when William Owseley was permitted to teach boys.[67] A writing school for boys was licensed under Robert Pytcher in 1586, and one for teaching Latin and English under Thomas Seager, the vicar, in 1592.[68] Thomas Bainrafe was licensed in 1605 to teach Latin and the articles of religion, though it seems likely that he moved to Martock shortly afterwards.[69] Edward Bennett, the intruded vicar, returned in 1663 partly to conduct a school.[70]

Land left to establish a school under the will of William Glanfield of Shepton Beauchamp (d. 1732) was not immediately so used, but a school was apparently open by 1735,[71] and by 1738 it was supported by offerings made on Sacrament Sundays and by subscriptions. Under the will of Mary Prowse (d. 1737) its income was augmented by the interest on £100 bequeathed to clothe and educate 20 children; in fact boys. Mary's executor paid interest to her trustees until 1748, when just over 6 a. of land was conveyed for the school.[72] Offerings continued to be given until 1759, some of which were used in 1757 to buy more property. Other benefactions included a legacy of John Lombard, interest on which for three years was paid in 1747.

By 1759 the school lands produced an income of £7 13s. 5d. and £5 15s. 6d. came from subscriptions. The master was paid £10 a year, but no money was spent on clothing between 1758 and 1772, nor after 1813. More land was bought in 1763 and in 1797, the year after subscriptions finally ceased, the income

was £20 11s. In 1843 the trustees bought the tolls of the market and the old market house for £200, and by 1850 the normal annual income was £48 10s.[73]

Under rules drawn up in 1742 the charity was administered by a treasurer and two trustees. Boys were to be chosen on the recommendation of subscribers 'in their turn', and none could be admitted 'till he can read in the Primer'. No schooling was given beyond the age of fourteen and no clothing after thirteen. All boys were required to attend church 'constantly'. The school, held by the parish clerk from 1826 until 1860,[74] had 20 pupils in 1818 and 1835.[75]

In 1876 the trustees resolved to sell assets to the value of £1,000 to buy a site for a new boys' school, provided a parish meeting pledged itself to subscribe.[76] The vestry agreed in 1877 that if the girls' school (see below) became an infants' school, then the parish would support a school for boys and girls, only provided that the management was equally divided between Churchmen and Nonconformists.[77] This plan was embodied in a Scheme of 1878, and the property of the charity school was sold for £1,378.[78]

The new school, on Cemetery Road, was opened in 1879.[79] The governors of the charity school continued to support pupils from their remaining endowment by paying school fees and providing books, despite the voluntary rate's low yield.[80] In 1893 the charity also extended the master's house. By 1895, however, the voluntary rate proved unreliable, and a School Board was established, to which the charity school governors transferred their interests.[81] In 1903 the school passed into the control of the county council.

There was accommodation for 174 boys and an average attendance of 85 in 1893, and by 1903 the average had risen to over a hundred.[82] There were then 3 teachers, and subjects included 'cottage gardening'.[83] By 1938 the average attendance was 82;[84] from 1950, when the seniors were transferred to Stoke sub Hamdon, the school took junior girls and boys, and in 1974 the extended buildings accommodated 142 children.[85]

Before the move to Cemetery Road the boys' charity school was housed from 1828 in the schoolroom on the east side of the churchyard, built by subscription in that year to house the Church Sunday-school. Much of the cost was borne by Henry Bond, the vicar, and J. B. Edmonds, who also provided the site and the stone. In 1866 the building was extended by Maurice Davis of Langport.[86]

There was at least one other charity school in 1776 attended by 10 girls.[87] By 1812 there was a Commercial and Mathematical school in the

[61] S.R.O., D/N/spc 1, 2.
[62] Ibid. 31.
[63] Ibid. 32; D/D/Rm, box 2.
[64] H.O. 129/319/2/4/9.
[65] S.R.O., D/N/spc 32–4.
[66] Ibid. 35.
[67] S.R.O., D/D/ol 4.
[68] Ibid. 9, 12.
[69] S.R.O., D/D/Vc 68.
[70] Calamy Revised, ed. Matthews.
[71] S.R.O., D/P/pet.s 17/3/1, 18/3/1.
[72] Ibid. 18/3/1.
[73] Ibid. 18/3/1–2.
[74] Ibid.
[75] Digest of Returns to Sel. Cttee. on Educ. of Poor,
H.C. 224 (1819), ix (2); Educ. Enquiry Abstract, H.C. 62 (1835), xlii.
[76] S.R.O., D/P/pet.s 18/3/2.
[77] S.R.O., D/PC/pet.s 1/2/1.
[78] S.R.O., D/P/pet.s 18/3/2.
[79] S.R.O., D/PC/pet.s 1/2/1.
[80] S.R.O., D/P/pet.s 18/3/2.
[81] Char. Com. files.
[82] Return of Schs. 1893 [C 7529], H.C. (1894), lxv; S.R.O., C/E 28.
[83] S.R.O., C/E 28.
[84] Bd. of Educ., List 21, 1938 (H.M.S.O.), 351.
[85] S.R.O., Schs. Lists.
[86] S.R.O., D/P/pet.s 18/8/1–2.
[87] S.R.O., D/D/V Dioc. bk.

town, and its master also conducted a Sunday-school for 130 children in the church. Books were suspended at different heights according to the age of the pupils, and the whole enterprise was organized on Lancasterian lines except that the Prayer Book was used.[88] By 1818 the Sunday-school had only 52 pupils, but a school of industry had been established for girls, principally supported by Dissenters, attended by c. 22 pupils.[89] The Church Sunday-school had only 45 pupils by 1825,[90] but ten years later numbers had risen to seventy-three. By that time the Wesleyans had a school for 131 in North Street chapel, the Independents for 100, probably in Roundwell Street, and the Presbyterians for 20, presumably at the Old Meeting in Palmer Street. At the same time there were 4 day schools supported by subscriptions, teaching 91 children.[91] The Church Sunday-school had since 1828 been housed in the schoolroom in the churchyard which was let on weekdays to the boys' charity school.[92]

By 1846 the church was supporting 2 day schools for a total of 68 children and 2 Sunday-schools affiliated to the National Society for 268 children. The Sunday-schools had 20 teachers, only 2 of whom were paid, and the teachers and senior children met on Sunday evenings for further study.[93]

By 1840 there were at least three private schools: a 'Commercial and Classical' boarding school for boys at Hayes End House, conducted by Joseph Billing, a girls' boarding school in Palmer Street, and a girl's day school in Silver Street.[94] The first two were still open in 1851, when there were 8 other teachers in the parish.[95] Dr. R. P. Billing's Academy continued until after 1872.[96] By 1859 there was a dame school in St. James's Street, and by 1872 3 schools in the same street and a ladies' school in Whitehall. In the same year Frederick Adolphy of Palmer Street described himself as a professor of languages.[97]

By 1859 the schoolroom in the churchyard was being used not only by the charity schoolboys but by a school for girls affiliated to the National Society. A near-by site was acquired and a subscription raised to build a new school for the girls. The architect was Maurice Davis of Langport, and half the cost was borne by the vicar, Henry Bond, and two other subscribers.[98] In 1878–9 the building was extended to accommodate infants[99] and, as South Petherton National School, had room in 1893 for 241 children, having then only 182 on the books.[1] The school retained controlled status in 1903, continuing under the management of the committee which had previously had oversight also of Stratton

school.[2] In 1908 there were 125 girls and 116 infants on the books and a total average attendance of 175 children. Twenty years later there were 202 pupils, with attendance averaging many fewer.[3] From 1950, when senior pupils were transferred to Stoke sub Hamdon, the school was restricted to infants, junior children going to South Petherton Junior School in Cemetery Road.[4] In 1953 the school, known as South Petherton C. of E. Infants School, accepted aided status.[5] In 1974 there were 102 children on the books between the ages of 5 and 7 years.[6]

In 1870 the vicar, Henry Bond, acquired a cottage in Over Stratton, on the site of which he built a school for infants, apparently opened in 1875. In 1876 it was said to be 'under good influence' and that the children were 'nicely taught'. The management of the school was under the committee of South Petherton National Schools.[7] The school was always small, having accommodation for only 68, and an average of 36 attended in 1893.[8] Dwindling numbers caused its closure in 1901.[9]

Private schools continued in the town towards the end of the 19th century, and included by 1884 a grammar school in Palmer Street under the control of N. G. Fish, at once a teacher of art and science and surveyor and sanitary inspector to the Yeovil poor-law union.[10] Another private school was conducted in the old schoolroom in the churchyard until 1906.[11] A night school was held in the boys' school by 1876,[12] science and art classes at the old schoolroom by 1892, and hygiene and horticulture lectures in the same place until 1897. Cookery and woodwork classes were organized in the early 20th century.[13]

CHARITIES FOR THE POOR. By will dated 1670 John Sandys of London, merchant, gave £100 for land, the rent to be distributed to the poor.[14] In 1681 some 6 a. of land at Hinton in Martock was bought, additional gifts or guarantees being made by Mrs. Ann Sandys and by the vicar and church-wardens to raise the purchase money to £120. Further benefactions, totalling £90, were made between 1706 and 1732 by Hugh Langley, Edmund Anstice, Samuel Gundry, and John Smart, and more land, amounting to just over 8 a., lying in different parts of South Petherton, was purchased in 1742, all producing rents to be distributed to the second poor.[15]

By 1715–16 the Poor's Ground rent, the income from the Sandys charity land at Martock parish,

[88] Taunton Courier, 16 Jan. 1812.
[89] Digest of Returns to Sel. Cttee. on Educ. of Poor, H.C. 224 (1819), ix (2).
[90] Rep. B. and W. Dioc. Assoc. S.P.C.K. (1825–6).
[91] Educ. Enquiry Abstract, H.C. 62 (1835), xlii.
[92] S.R.O., D/P/pet.s 18/8/1.
[93] Church Sch. Inquiry, 1846–7; Acct. of Church Educ. among Poor (1846).
[94] County Gazette Dir. Som. (1840).
[95] H.O. 107/1929.
[96] Morris & Co. Dir. Som. (1872).
[97] P.O. Dir. Som. (1859); Morris & Co. Dir. Som. (1872).
[98] P.O. Dir. Som. (1859); S.R.O., D/P/pet.s 4/1/2.
[99] S.R.O., D/P/pet.s 4/1/2.
[1] Return of Schs. 1893 [C. 7529], H.C. (1894), lxv.
[2] S.R.O., D/P/pet.s 18/7/2.

[3] Bd. of Educ., List 21, 1908 (H.M.S.O.), 417; ibid. 1938 (H.M.S.O.), 351.
[4] S.R.O., Schs. Lists.
[5] Som. C.C., Educ. Cttee. schs. files.
[6] S.R.O., Schs. Lists.
[7] S.R.O., D/P/pet.s 4/1/1, 18/7/1–2.
[8] Return of Schs. 1893 [C. 7529], H.C. (1894), lxv.
[9] Return of Schs. 1900 [Cd. 315] H.C. (1900), lv(2); S.R.O., D/P/pet.s 18/7/2, 23/3.
[10] Kelly's Dir. Som. (1883–97).
[11] S.R.O., D/P/pet.s 17/3/2.
[12] Ibid. 18/7/1.
[13] Ibid. 17/3/2, 18/7/2.
[14] 12th Rep. Com. Char. H.C. 358, p. 425 (1825), x; S. & D. N. & Q. iii. 68.
[15] 12th Rep. Com. Char., pp. 425–6; copy of Benefaction bd.; S.R.O., D/P/pet.s 17/3/1.

amounted to £4 10s. a year, a sum which fluctuated but was normally £5 during the earlier 18th century.[16] By 1800 it had risen to £10, and in 1830 a total of 32 recipients each had 7s.[17]

The second poor also benefited under the will of Mrs. Mary Prowse (d. 1737), who gave £100 for the maintenance of part of the north aisle of the parish church, any residue to be applied to those not receiving regular parish relief. Land was bought by her executor, Thomas Bowyer, vicar of Martock, although there was insufficient estate for the bequest. Payments were made to 43 people in 1740, 22 in 1764, 32 in 1792, and 55 in 1806.[18]

By 1828 the total of £26 5s. was in that year shared between three 'classes' of recipients, 36 in the first class receiving each 2 shares, nominally of 20d. but actually 3s. 6d. in total; 50 in the second class had 3 shares each, and 9 in the third class had 4 shares each. The surplus was distributed among 27 other recipients, one of whom was in receipt of a second-class share. In 1838 a new system divided the income between 150 people in sums varying between 2s. 6d. and 6s. Thereafter the sums tended to be larger and the number of recipients smaller, in 1876 only 44 receiving 7s. and 32 having 10s. In 1877 the distribution was made in coal, but this proved unpopular, and in 1878 cash was again given, this time in respect of age, all over 70 years receiving 10s., all over 50 years 7s., and widows and single

women over 70 years 5s., a total in that year of 90 people.[19]

In 1895 the churchwardens agreed to hand over the administration of the Prowse charity to the parish council, provided that nine old recipients should continue to receive their doles and that the north aisle should be repaired.[20]

In 1879 the governors of the free school assigned some land in trust, the rent to be applied to the 'most poor and needy inhabitants' nominated by the parish officers. The land was sold in 1895 and was added to the Second Poor charities.[21] In 1952 the South Petherton Second Poor Charity had a total income of £52, partly from land and partly from stock. Some of the land was sold in 1953. By 1965 the total income of the charity from rents and dividends was £187, of which £94 10s. was distributed to 63 people, each receiving 30s.[22]

By 1695 the overseers were distributing the interest on a capital sum of £5 given by Adam Willy to six people. The capital was evidently lent to parishioners and by 1703 payment of interest had become irregular. Distribution seems to have ceased after 1710.[23]

The William Vile Gift was established under the will of Ellen Rendall Vile of Bristol who gave £300 stock to the vicar and churchwardens by will dated 1943 for the benefit of 'poor and lonely old people'. The income of £11 10s. was so divided in 1974.[24]

SEAVINGTON ST. MARY

THE ANCIENT parish of Seavington St. Mary, about 2 miles south-west of South Petherton, is roughly L-shaped. Its ancient southern, western, and northern boundaries all followed by roads, the western forming part of the Whitelackington park bank in Park Lane and the southern part of Boxstone Hill. The northern boundary with Shepton Beauchamp and South Petherton was marked by the narrow sunken Muckleditch and Fouts lanes, until the late 18th century part of the main Ilchester–Taunton road.[1] Seavington St. Michael, which fits into the 'L' in the east is divided from Seavington St. Mary largely by hedge-boundaries and by most of Water Street, the link between the two villages. The Foss Way cuts across the south-eastern extremity of the parish at Crimbleford Knap, but in no way affects the boundary.[2] In 1875 a detached part of Ilton around Hurcott in the north-west was added to the ecclesiastical parish, and a small piece of meadow at Ilford Bridges was transferred from Seavington to Whitelackington.[3]

The parish measured 994 a. in 1841 and 1,106 a. after the inclusion of Hurcott.[4]

The southern half of the parish is dominated by the limestone ridge of Easterdown hill which rises to 249 ft. A quarry and limekiln stood just south of the village on the north side of the hill.[5] North and south of the hill bands of Yeovil Sands give way to alluvium along the Lopen brook and its tributary, forming on the south-east the largest area of meadow. North of the village, on the ground which rises to 301 ft. on Boxstone Hill, are wide bands of Pennard Sands and a junction bed of limestone. At Hurcott are the beginnings of more Yeovil Sands. The landscape in the north is characterized by large open fields divided by banks and sunken lanes.[6]

The northern half of the parish is served by two north–south roads: Boxstone Hill forms the western boundary and leads to Hurcott and Shepton Beauchamp, and a lane from Seavington St. Michael through Seavington Abbots runs to Green Lane

[16] S.R.O., D/P/pet.s 4/1/1. [17] Ibid. 4/1/2.
[18] Ibid. 4/1/2; 12th Rep. Com. Char. pp. 422–5.
[19] S.R.O., D/P/pet.s 4/1/2; D/PC/pet.s 1/2/1.
[20] Western Chronicle, 13 Dec. 1895; S.R.O., D/P/pet.s 17/3/2.
[21] Char. Com. file. Charity known as Charity of William Blake and others.
[22] Char. Com. file.
[23] S.R.O., DD/SAS SX 102: overseers' accts. 1695–1740.
[24] Char. Com. file.
[1] S.R.O., DD/PE 5, map 1773; D/P/she.b 1/7/1 sub anno 1874; O.S. Map 1″, sheet 84 (1865 edn.). This

article was completed in 1973.
[2] O.S. Map 6″, Som. LXXXI. S.E., LXXXIII. NE., NW. (1886 edn.).
[3] Ex inf. Records Officer, Church Commissioners. The transfer to the civil parish took place in 1884: Local Govt. Bd. Prov. Orders Conf. Order (Poor Law), (No. 3), Act (1884).
[4] S.R.O., tithe award; Census, 1911.
[5] S.R.O., tithe award; O.S. Map 6″, Som. LXXXVIII. NE. (1886 edn.).
[6] Geol. Surv. Map 1″, solid and drift, sheet 312 (1958 edn.).

End and thence also to Shepton. The southern part of the parish is crossed by two east–west routes, the more northerly from Seavington St. Michael to Whitelackington. From the northern end of Water Street to West Street Farm it is known as New Road, having been constructed in 1829.[7] This new route diverted the London–Exeter traffic away from Seavington St. Mary village. The village street forms the second east–west route, continuing west towards Furzey Knap, Longforward Lane, and Park (later Bread and Cheese) Lane in the extreme west of the parish on the borders with Kingstone and Whitelackington.[8] There was one minor route south of the village over Easterdown hill to Dinnington via Dark and Sawpit lanes or Rooks Meade lane. Before 1829 the parish church was isolated at the end of Church Lane north of the village street.

An interpretation of the place-name as seven settlements seems appropriate if Seavington St. Michael is included.[9] The two main settlements of the medieval period were Seavington St. Mary and Seavington Abbots or Upton. The name Oppetone Abbe occurs in the 13th century, and Seavington Upton or simply Upton in the seventeenth.[10] The name continues in Upton House. Hurcott, a mile north-west of Upton, lay until 1884 in Ilton parish. There was a settlement there by 1260.[11] There seems also to have been a small settlement in the south of the parish at Crimbleford, possibly the successor to the Roman villa overlooking the Foss.[12]

Field- and furlong-names survived to the 19th century to indicate the general position of open arable fields. Pitfurlong, on the northern boundary, Higher, Middle, Bird's Lane, and Court fields, and Middle and Stone furlongs still survived in the area north of New Road, largely farmed from Hurcott and Upton farms.[13] West and south of Seavington village in the 1840s lay Merfield, West, Rye, Middle, Harrison, Little, Southway, and Lower fields.[14] Most of this land was confined to the Seavington farms, but Upton farm had meadow in the south-east, known in the 19th century as Upton mead and in the 16th as South mead.[15]

The oldest buildings in the parish seem to date from the 17th century and include Hurcott and Upton farm-houses. Hurcott Farm probably dates from the earlier 17th century and is a substantial house of two storeys and attics. There are extensive farm buildings, some of stone and thatch, which appear to date from the 17th century and later. Upton House, another substantial stone house, appears to date from the 18th century and has later extensions. The present Rectory was until 1890

also a farm-house. Its north and west walls incorporate parts of a building of the earlier 17th century, but the house is now largely of the mid 18th century although much altered in the 19th. The roof was then heightened to provide more attic space, a service wing added on the west, and the south front re-glazed. There may also have been some internal re-planning. Subsequent alterations have included c. 1954 the demolition of the service wing. The house now lacks all its original fireplaces and ceilings.

In 1754 four men were licensed to sell beer in the parish, including Richard Upsteel in Seavington Abbots. The Travellers' Rest in Muckleditch Lane, on the Taunton road, is traceable to the mid 18th century and survived until the end of the 19th.[16] The former West Street Farm was converted to a restaurant called the Pheasant in 1971.[17]

In 1563 there were 27 households in the parish.[18] In 1801 the population was 269. In the next decade it rose rapidly, and again in the 1820s, reaching a total of 390 in 1851. During the next half century there was the normal decline for the area, and low points of 218 and 219 were reached in 1901 and 1931. The figure was 213 in 1961 and 212 in 1971.[19]

MANORS AND OTHER ESTATES. Mauger de Cartrai held an estate called Sevenehantona of the count of Morain in 1086 in succession to Alwin.[20] As in the manor of East Stoke in Stoke sub Hamdon[21] the overlordship passed by 1284–5 to Isabel de Forz, countess of Aumale, though whether through the counts of Aumale or from the Reviers family is not known.[22] From Isabel it descended to the Courtenays: Hugh, later 1st earl of Devon (d. 1340), held ½ fee there in 1303[23] and his son, also Hugh, died in 1377 possessed of 10 fees there and at Ashill.[24] The fees passed successively to Thomas Courtenay, earl of Devon (d. 1458), and then to his son and successor Thomas (d. 1461),[25] but they are not traceable thereafter. In 1431 the manor was said to be held of Lord Zouche as of Castle Cary in socage.[26]

Alice Vaux, the first known tenant of the manor of *SEAVINGTON VAUX*, occurs in the late 12th or early 13th century. Her son Robert was certainly in occupation in 1212,[27] and occurs elsewhere between 1206 and 1222.[28] Before 1236 he had been succeeded by his son Hubert, who held both Ashill and Seavington.[29] Maud, probably Hubert's daughter and wife of Thomas de Multon, succeeded by 1252[30] and retained a life interest until her death in 1293, though both manors were held from her son James from 1283.[31] James was sole occupier in 1303[32] but had died by 1316 when

[7] S.R.O., DD/BD 93.
[8] S.R.O., DD/SAS H/528, map 1829; O.S. Map 6", Som. LXXXI. SE., LXXXVIII. NE., NW. (1886 edn.).
[9] P.N. Glos. (E.P.N.S.), i. 177–8.
[10] Feud. Aids, iv. 283; S.R.O., Q/SR 113/30; DD/X/SAB transcript of Bristol Cath. MS. 49001, f. 235); S.R.S. xxiii. 263.   [11] H.M.C. Wells, i. 434.
[12] Cal. Inq. p.m. xiii, p. 16; S.R.S. xvii. 96; Cal. Close, 1385–9, 274; V.C.H. Som. i. 332.
[13] S.R.O., tithe award.
[14] Ibid. Harrison field may be so called after a family of that name in the parish in the 16th cent.: C 3/50/78.
[15] S.R.O., DD/WY, W/CR 3/2; tithe award.
[16] S.R.O., Q/RL; D/P/she.b 1/7/1.
[17] Ex inf. Mr. D. Hill, proprietor.

[18] B.M. Harl. MS. 594, f. 56.
[19] Census, 1801–1971.
[20] V.C.H. Som. i. 473.
[21] Ibid. iii. 239.
[22] Complete Peerage s.v. Aumale.
[23] Feud. Aids, iv. 315.
[24] Cal. Inq. p.m. xiv, p. 321.
[25] Cal. Close, 1422–9, 17–18; C139/169/38.
[26] C 139/51/53.
[27] Cur. Reg. R. vi, p. 378.
[28] S.R.S. xiv, p. 75.
[29] Ibid. vi. 367.
[30] Cal. Chart. R. i. 406.
[31] S.R.S. vi. 259; Feud. Aids, iv. 283.
[32] Feud. Aids, iv. 315.

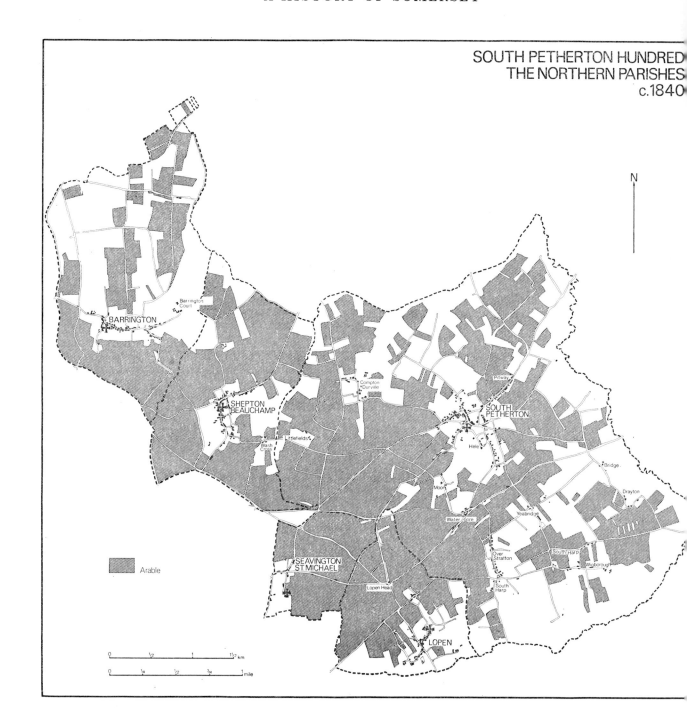

SOUTH PETHERTON HUNDRED
THE NORTHERN PARISHES
c.1840

Arable

settlement was made by his brother Thomas on his own sons John, Thomas, and James successively.[33] John succeeded *c.* 1317,[34] was apparently resident there in 1327,[35] and survived probably until after 1363.[36] By 1377, however, he had been succeeded by his son-in-law Sir John Streche, husband of his daughter Margaret.[37] Streche died in 1390 leaving two daughters as coheirs: Elizabeth, wife of Thomas Beauchamp, and Cecily, wife successively of Thomas Bonville and Sir William Cheyney of Brook, Westbury (Wilts.).[38] Cheyney occupied the manor in 1412 and died in 1420.[39] His widow survived until 1430 and, having just outlived her son Sir Edmund Cheyney, was succeeded by three young granddaughters, Elizabeth, Anne, and Cecily.[40] Cecily died six months later,[41] and the manor passed to Elizabeth, wife of Sir John Colshull (d. 1483), who herself survived at least until 1483.[42] Margaret Colshull, widow, was said to be lady of the manor in 1486,[43] but the descent is thereafter uncertain until 1542, when the manor was in the hands of Walter Willoughby, grandson of Robert, 1st Baron Willoughby de Broke, himself the eldest son of Anne Cheyney by John Willoughby.[44] Walter Willoughby made over the manor in 1542 to John Bowyer.[45] Bowyer and Sir Fulk Greville, husband of Elizabeth, Baroness Willoughby de Broke (d. 1560), were in possession in 1544–5,[46] and in 1547 Greville sold the 'manor or lordship of Seavington Vauce alias Mary Seavington' to John Thynne.[47] Before 1553 the manor had passed to Sir Edward Seymour, son of Protector Somerset, Thynne's patron; in that year Seymour sold it to the Crown in exchange for Berry Pomeroy (Devon).[48]

The manor remained in the hands of the Crown until 1574–5,[49] when it was granted to Laurence Hyde. In 1624 the property was said to be held of Robert Hyde,[50] but the manor must earlier have reverted to the Crown since in 1604 it was granted by James I to John Erskine, earl of Mar (d. 1634).[51] Mar's son, also John (d. 1653), sold it in 1652 to John Davis of Westminster and he in the following year conveyed it to Henry Dunster, a London merchant.[52] Dunster, or a son of the same name, sold it in 1680 to Simon Welman, M.D., of London.[53] Simon left the property to his brother Isaac (d. 1716), of Poundisford, in Pitminster, and it descended successively through his son Thomas (d. 1757), his grandson Isaac (d. 1782), and his

great-grandson Thomas (d. 1829) to Charles Noel Welman of Norton Fitzwarren.[54] Welman sold the property, incorrectly described as 'the manor or lordship of Seavington Abbott and Hurcott etc.' in 1876 to Vaughan Hanning Vaughan Lee, M.P., of Dillington.[55] The ownership in 1973 was vested in the Dillington Estates.

King Cnut gave to Athelney abbey between 1027 and 1032 an estate measuring two 'manses' in Seofenempton.[56] This holding measured two hides in 1086 and was still described as at Seovenamentone.[57] By 1284–5 the abbey's estate was called Oppetone Abbe and by 1260 Herdecote, both names persisting until the 19th century.[58] The abbey held the property at the Dissolution as part of its estate at Ilton,[59] and it was held by the Crown between 1539 and 1600 when it was granted, under the name of the manor or manors of *HURCOTT* and *SEVENHAMPTON ABBOT*, to William and Robert Offley.[60] Robert Offley, a London haberdasher, sold the property in 1605 to Sir George Speke of Whitelackington (d. 1637).[61] It descended in the Speke family[62] to John Speke who sold it in 1699 to Simon Welman, owner of Seavington Vaux.[63] The property was held by the Welman family until 1871 when, described as Hurcott farm and measuring 160 a., it was sold by C. N. Welman to Vaughan Hanning Lee, then of Lanelay, in Llanharan (Glam.).[64] It subsequently became part of the Dillington Estates.

In 1260 the prebendary of Ilton had a barn within the court of the abbot at Hurcott, which he exchanged for a site for a new barn further north to build another.[65]

The church of South Petherton and its dependent chapelries including Seavington St. Mary was granted by the Crown to Bruton priory at the end of the 12th century.[66] Under an ordinance of Archbishop Pecham (d. 1292) Bruton had all the great tithes in Seavington St. Mary and found a resident chaplain to serve the chapel;[67] an agreement of the early 13th century increased the priory's rights of pasturage and provided a messuage and curtilage, presumably for the chaplain and clerk to serve the church.[68] A composition made with Athelney abbey in 1285 confirmed their right to take a proportion of the crop in a specified area, presumably at Hurcott.[69] Bruton retained what was thus the rectorial estate until the Dissolution in 1539.[70] In 1542 the holding,

[33] *S.R.S.* xii. 57.   [34] *V.C.H. Som.* iii. 239.
[35] *S.R.S.* iii. 198.
[36] *Feud. Aids,* iv. 337; *Cal. Inq. Misc.* iii, p. 288.
[37] *Cal. Inq. p.m.* xiv, p. 321.
[38] Ibid. xvi, p. 416; *Cal. Pat.* 1391–6, 54, 214; *Cal. Close,* 1405–9, 419; *S. & D. N. & Q.* xiii. 9.
[39] *Feud. Aids,* vi. 506; *Cal. Close,* 1419–22, 210–11; C 138/46/46.
[40] C 139/49/42; *Cal. Close,* 1429–35, 138–9.
[41] C 139/51/53.
[42] *S.R.S.* xlix, p. 167; lii, p. 120. M.I. of Sir John in Duloe (Cornw.).
[43] *Cal. Inq. p.m. Hen. VII,* iii, p. 546.
[44] C.P. 25(2)/36/241/34 Hen. VIII Mich.; *Visit. Wilts.* 1623 (Harl Soc. cv–cvi), 217.
[45] C.P. 40/1114, Carte rot. 10.
[46] C 54/440 no. 13.
[47] C.P. 40/1132, Carte rot. 13 d.
[48] *Cal. Pat.* 1553, 76; E 318/35/1930.
[49] C 66/1132.
[50] C 142/518/162.
[51] S.R.O., DD/CA 107.

[52] Ibid. 107–8.
[53] Ibid. 107.
[54] S.R.O., DD/WN.
[55] S.R.O., DD/CA 99.
[56] *Early Charters of Wessex,* ed. Finberg, p. 149. *S.R.S.* xiv, p. 142 says 1020–25.
[57] *V.C.H. Som.* i. 469.
[58] *Feud. Aids,* iv. 283; *H.M.C. Wells,* i. 43–4.
[59] *Valor Eccl.* (Rec. Com.), i. 206.
[60] C 66/1540.
[61] C.P. 25(2)/345/3 Jas. I East.; *S.R.S.* lxvii, p. 58; S.R.O., DD/WN.
[62] See above, pp. 152–3.
[63] C.P. 25(2)/870/10 Wm. III Mich.
[64] S.R.O. DD/CA 98.
[65] *H.M.C. Wells,* i. 43–4. The agreement referred to William Pek, a former tenant, hence Peak Lane.
[66] *V.C.H. Som.* ii. 124.
[67] *S.R.S.* viii, p. 41.
[68] *Cal. Pat.* 1388–92, 149; *S.R.S.* vii, p. 37.
[69] *S.R.S.* viii, p. 37.
[70] Ibid. vii, p. 115; *Cal. Papal Regs.* v. 326.

which involved also the rectory of South Petherton and the other dependent chapelries, was granted to the chapter of Bristol.[71] It was subsequently leased by the chapter to successive members of the Poulett family for the sum of £17 a year.[72] By 1617 the real property of the rectory in Seavington was a yard of ground, known as Parsonage Plot, with a house 'near the road . . . lately built'.[73] This house replaced an earlier one apparently damaged by fire c. 1557 and later converted to a barn.[74] Sub-leases of the tithes in the parish in the late 18th century included a dwelling-house.[75] In 1842 the tithes were commuted to a rent-charge of £350, payable to Earl Poulett, lay rector since his purchase of the property from the chapter of Bristol in 1802.[76] The dwelling-house then stood on the north side of the village street at the corner of Church Lane; the site was occupied in 1973 by Allenby House.[77]

ECONOMIC HISTORY. The two estates in the parish in the 11th century were predominantly arable and measured 9 hides. The demesne on the estate of Mauger de Cartrai measured 5½ hides out of a total of 7 hides in the holding; the Athelney demesne amounted to half the property. Together the owners had 46 a. of meadow, but 10 a. of wood and 25 a. of 'moor' and meadow had been lost to South Petherton.[78] By 1349 the demesne of Hurcott, the Athelney holding, amounted to about 66 a., of which 55 a. were arable, 7 a. meadow, and 4 a. pasture. Two parts of the arable were then sown. Rents of 32s. were taken from the remainder.[79] In the 19th century this same former demesne was represented by the 100-a. Hurcott farm, and the remainder by the 106 a. which paid tithe to the prebendary of Ilton.[80] In terms of valuation, the Athelney holding was assessed at 30s. in 1086,[81] £7 6s. 3d. in 1291,[82] and £3 11s. 6d. in 1349.[83]

As many as 156 sheep were recorded on the demesne estates in 1086.[84] In the early 13th century the convent of Bruton acquired rights of common from the lord of the manor for 40 sheep and other beasts.[85] Meadow was comparatively limited. The 80-a. holding of John Kaynes in the manor in 1384 included just ½ a. of meadow, though that of John Geffereys in 1487 amounted to 60 a. of arable and 10 a. of meadow.[86] The Buller family, tenants from the 14th century, held meadow at the 'Farthyng' which they exchanged with their lord for similar property at 'Landemede' and elsewhere.[87]

The Bullers were successors to a number of sub-stantial families which held small freeholds in the parish. Walter de Thornhull had an interest in a virgate in 1268;[88] the Brooks, lords Cobham, were there in 1505,[89] and the Seymours, in the persons of Sir John and Sir Edward Seymour, between 1528 and 1560.[90] Robert Buller (d. 1506) occupied a capital messuage in Seavington Vaux manor,[91] and John Buller held it at his death in 1592.[92] Among the lesser tenants were Joan Sylvayn and Humphrey Kail, the most substantial in 1327, the latter also holding half the manor of Cudworth and land in Chaffcombe and Knowle St. Giles.[93] The Crymelford family held land in the south of the parish and in Dinnington and Allowenshay in the later 14th century.[94]

In 1553 the manor of Seavington Vaux was valued for fee farm at £29 7s. 8d., a figure which included perquisites of 25s. 8d.[95] The rent was payable after 1630 to the Whetstone Almshouses, Ilton.[96] By 1680 the manor was valued at £458.[97] The Speke property was assessed at £10 by office and £20 by certificate in 1637.[98]

In 1680 the manor acquired by Isaac Welman, amounting to some 560 a., was shared between 20 tenants holding for one, two, or three lives.[99] Most farms were of 20 a. or 40 a., though they varied much in value. The largest was the 80-a. holding of Iron Dunster, followed by Elizabeth Dunn's 60 a., and Stephen Hutchings's 52 a. Only the Hutchings family seem to have survived on a similar economic level to the 1770s, holding not only the later West Street farm, but also other lands including Kails, after the 14th-century occupier.[1] Thomas Hutchings, resident in Barrington, from 1788 shared the lease of the tithes from Lord Poulett.[2] Other prominent farmers in 1772 were Thomas Poole and Richard Bullen, with smaller properties held by non-residents such as Robert Stuckey and John Helliar.[3]

The southern part of the parish paid tithes to Lord Poulett. In 1778 tithes, moduses, and compositions together produced an income of over £113. John Poole paid £8 15s. as occupier of the inclosed Meade farm, and also held just over 100 a. elsewhere in the parish. The crops in the parish as a whole were probably reflected in the proportions in this more restricted area. Wheat (160 a.) and barley (129 a.) predominated; grassland amounted to 108 a. Other arable crops were beans (32 a.), flax (32 a.), clover (25 a.), peas (17 a.), hemp (12 a.), potatoes (11 a.), and oats (5 a.). Tithes of sheep and wool amounted to £3 16s. and of cows £1 1s. 6d.[4]

[71] L. & P. Hen. VIII, xvii, p. 638.
[72] C 2/Eliz. I/P 8/54.
[73] S.R.O., D/D/Rg 318.
[74] S.R.O., D/D/Ca 27; DD/X/SAB (transcript of Bristol Cath. Chetwynd survey f. 16).
[75] S.R.O., DD/PT, box 12.
[76] S.R.O., tithe award; DD/PT, box 19B.
[77] S.R.O., tithe award.
[78] V.C.H. Som. i. 469, 473.
[79] E 152/78/3.
[80] S.R.O., tithe awards, Ilton, Seavington St. Mary.
[81] V.C.H. Som. i. 469.
[82] Tax. Eccl. (Rec. Com.), 203.
[83] E 152/78/3.
[84] V.C.H. Som. i. 469, 473.
[85] S.R.S. viii, p. 37.
[86] Cal. Inq. p.m. xv, p. 391; Cal. Inq. p.m. Hen. VII, iii, p. 546.

[87] Cat. Anct. D. vi, C 6064.
[88] S.R.S. vi. 211.
[89] Cal. Close, 1500–9, 194.
[90] S.R.O., DD/WY W/CR 3/2.
[91] C 142/132/14.
[92] C 142/232/42.
[93] S.R.S. iii. 198.
[94] S.R.S. xvii. 96; Cal. Close, 1385–9, 274; Cal. Inq. p.m. xiii, p. 16; Cal. Inq. Misc. iii, p. 288.
[95] E 318/35/1930.
[96] S.R.S. li, p. 253.
[97] S.R.O., DD/CA 107.
[98] S.R.S. lxvii, p. 58.
[99] S.R.O., DD/CA 107.
[1] S.R.O., D/P/sea.ma 4/1/1.
[2] S.R.O., DD/PT, box 12.
[3] S.R.O., D/P/sea.ma 4/1/1.
[4] S.R.O., DD/PT, box 37.

The main farms in the early 19th century were held by the Naish, Hutchings, and Poole families.[5] By 1841 John Naish of Upton farm (171 a.) and William Naish of Home farm (173 a.) were followed by J. and W. Stephens of Hurcott (100 a.), Thomas Harding of Middlefield farm (99 a.), and Robert Poole of Meade farm (over 70 a.). West Street and Water Street farms were over 60 a. and a similar holding was based on the present Rectory.[6] By 1851 John Naish of Upton farm had 325 a. and employed 26 labourers and William Naish 190 a. with 14 workers.[7]

Traces of strip cultivation survived in the south of the parish in the 1840s in Rye, South Way, Middle, and Little fields, and in the north at Pit Furlong. Lower mead was also not permanently divided. Parts of Hurcott were inclosed by the 1520s,[8] and although Wheathill, Huish, and Bremblegaston were still open in 1560,[9] consolidation was then taking place. Final traces of strips in the south still survived into the 1880s.[10] By 1905 more than half the parish was arable,[11] and in the 1970s there was still slightly more arable than grass.

Agriculture provided most employment during the 19th century, roughly one sixth of the total population being employed as farm labourers in 1851. As many as 62 women and girls were employed as glovers in their homes.[12] Just after the turn of the century young girls found employment at a collar factory in Ilminster.[13]

Early in the 13th century Robert Vaux granted a windmill and 6 a. of land in Seavington to Montacute priory.[14] No further trace of the mill has been found.

LOCAL GOVERNMENT. The two parishes of Seavington St. Mary and Seavington St. Michael appear to have formed two tithings in the 14th century, known as Seavington Dennis and Seavington Abbots, not necessarily coterminous with parish boundaries.[15] The same division occurs in the 15th century,[16] but by 1539 there were four separate areas for musters, known as Seavington, Seavington Abbot, Seavington Dennis, and Seavington Vaux.[17] There were still three units in 1569, Seavington Mary, Seavington Abbot, and Seavington Dennis,[18] but by 1652 the 'several tithings of the three

Seavingtons' were held by one man of the Crown[19] and were thus regarded as one fiscal unit.[20] Seavington Abbot tithingman was appointed in the manor court of Hurcott,[21] and extracts of court rolls survive for 1528–9, 1542, and 1560.[22] Courts were presumably still held for Seavington Vaux in 1553[23] though no rolls have survived. There is an extract of a court baron for the manor of Seavington Mary alias Vaux for 1698.[24]

There were two overseers from the 17th century,[25] but often only one churchwarden, Thomas Hutchings holding the office alone from 1814 until 1852.[26] One warden was appointed by the parish from 1852.[27]

There was a parish house next to Parsonage Plot in 1617.[28] In 1853 the vestry agreed to the request of the Chard Union (in which the parish had been incorporated since 1836) to sell ten cottages formerly used for the poor, standing at a number of points on the waste north of the village street.[29]

CHURCH. The church of Seavington St. Mary, a dependent chapel of South Petherton, augmented if not founded by the Vaux family, occurs early in the 13th century.[30] In 1389 it acquired burial rights.[31] The canons of Bruton until 1539 and the successive tenants of the chapter of Bristol as farmers of the tithes provided curates until 1809 when the benefice became a perpetual curacy on the first vacancy after the impropriation was purchased by Earl Poulett.[32] The sale to the earl excepted the patronage[33] but he and his successors presented during most of the 19th century. The chapter resumed its rights by 1888[34] and since c. 1923, when the living was united with Seavington St. Michael, has shared the patronage.[35]

The canons of Bruton as rectors agreed to maintain a resident chaplain and clerk in the early 13th century.[36] In the 1560s the church was served by curates paid £3 a year.[37] In the early 17th century chaplains were paid £6 13s. 4d. under the will of Sir Anthony Poulett to preach four times a year,[38] presumably in addition to the £15 to serve the cure paid at least from the 1650s until the end of the 18th century.[39] The curacy was augmented by lot in sums of £200 in 1750, 1809, 1817, and 1824;[40] in 1815 it was said to be worth £43 a year, and in 1831 £50.[41] It was further augmented in 1872 by

[5] S.R.O., D/P/sea.ma 4/1/1.
[6] S.R.O., tithe award; D/P/sea.ma 4/1/1.
[7] H.O. 107/1928.
[8] S.R.O., DD/WY W/CR 3/2.
[9] Ibid.
[10] S.R.O., DD/CA 181; O.S. Map 6″, Som. LXXXVIII. NE. (1886 edn.).
[11] Statistics supplied by the then Bd. of Agric. 1905.
[12] H.O. 107/1928.
[13] See below, p. 207.
[14] S.R.S. viii, p. 150.
[15] Cal. Pat. 1388–92, 332. Hurcott was in Ilton parish until 1885.
[16] Cal. Pat. 1429–36, 466.
[17] L. & P. Hen. VIII, xiv (1), p. 289.
[18] S.R.S. xx. 36.
[19] S.R.O., DD/X/SAB (transcript of Parl. Surv. ff. 200–1).
[20] E 317/Som./11.
[21] S.R.O., DD/WY W/CR 3/2.
[22] Ibid. 3/2, 3/3.
[23] E 318/35/1930.
[24] S.R.O., DD/WN.

[25] Som. Protestation Returns, ed. A. J. Howard and T. L. Stoate, 92.
[26] S.R.O., D/P/sea.ma 4/1/1; D/D/V return 1840.
[27] S.R.O., D/P/sea.ma 4/1/1, note sub anno 1852.
[28] S.R.O., D/D/Rg 318.
[29] Poor Law Com. 2nd Rep. p. 547; S.R.O., tithe award; D/P/sea.ma 4/1/1.
[30] Cur. Reg. R. vi, p. 378; S.R.S. viii, p. 37; Cal. Pat. 1388–92, 149. John de Ikeford, a witness to the Vaux grant, occurs in 1207: Cirencester Cart. ed. C. D. Ross, 522–3.
[31] S.R.S. viii, p. 22. It seems to have had a cemetery in 1386: ibid., p. 98.
[32] S.R.O., DD/X/SAB.
[33] S.R.O., DD/PT, box 19B.
[34] Dioc. Kal.   [35] Dioc. Dir.
[36] Cal. Pat. 1388–92, 149; S.R.S. viii, p. 37.
[37] S. & D. N. & Q. xiv. 208.
[38] S.R.O., DD/PT, box 40.   [39] Ibid. box 19B.
[40] Hodgson, Queen Anne's Bounty.
[41] S.R.O., D/D/B return 1815; Rep. Com. Eccl. Revenues, pp. 150–1.

rent-charges formerly paid to the prebendaries of Ilton and Ashill, and in 1875 by a rent-charge from Hurcott when the hamlet was transferred to Seavington parish.[42]

The benefice was often held in plurality, and there was no house for the curate until 1890.[43] In 1630 Thomas Stuckey also held Seavington St. Michael and Dinnington; in the early 1650s ministers served several Poulett chapelries for a few weeks at a time.[44] Thomas Evans (curate 1809–30) was also incumbent of Chillington and lived at Shepton Beauchamp, where he was curate;[45] in 1840 the church was held with Stocklinch Ottersay,[46] in the 1850s with Whitelackington, and then with Stocklinch Ottersay again.[47] From 1871 it was always held with Seavington St. Michael.[48]

There were several complaints during the 16th century about the disrepair of the chancel,[49] there was no Bible in English in 1547,[50] and no pyx in 1554.[51] A woman 'suspected to be a sorcerer' disturbed her neighbours in church in 1577.[52] There were 6 communicants in 1776.[53] In 1815 and 1840 services were held on alternate Sundays, morning and afternoon, and in 1840 Holy Communion was celebrated eight times a year.[54] On Census Sunday 1851, during a vacancy, there was only an evening service attended by 75 people.[55] Holy Communion was celebrated nine times a year by 1853.[56] A weekly service and sermon was still the practice in 1870, with Holy Communion every six weeks.[57] A surpliced choir was introduced in 1880.[58]

In 1680 there was a church house belonging to the manor of Seavington Vaux.[59]

The church of *ST. MARY* is built of rubble with ashlar dressings and has a chancel, nave with south porch, and west tower. The nave and chancel appear to be of 13th-century origin but only the chancel arch, with its flanking recesses towards the nave, is relatively unaltered. The nave was given at least one new window in the 14th century and was otherwise refenestrated, heightened, and provided with a porch in the 15th or early 16th century. At about the same time a new east window was put into the chancel and the tower was built. The latter was heightened or the upper stage rebuilt later in the 16th century, and church and churchyard together were consecrated in 1543.[60]

The fittings include a 12th-century font, which may be evidence for an earlier building, a 14th-century aumbry, and a bier dated 1694. The church was galleried by 1816, and was restored in 1880 and 1882.[61]

There are six bells. Before 1906 there were three, all by George Purdue of Taunton and dated 1621.[62] One was recast and three new ones were added by Taylors of Loughborough.[63] There is a chalice of c. 1715 and a paten of 1851.[64] The registers of baptisms date from 1716, of burials from 1741, and of marriages from 1759.[65]

NONCONFORMITY. Claims were made by the curate of Seavington St. Mary that a conventicle had been held by a Mr. Butler in 1672,[66] and a number of those involved were fined. Licences were issued for meetings from 1689 onwards, at first without stated denomination but from 1735 for Presbyterians. Licences then and in 1752 were for houses in Seavington Abbots.[67] By 1776 there were three or four families of Presbyterians in the parish.[68] Wesleyan Methodists began worshipping in the parish in 1812 and in 1841 had 8 members.[69] The present chapel, of Ham stone standing on former waste ground beside the road, was built in 1885. Several people contributed to the Bible Christian circuit in 1829 but no formal group seems to have been created until 1834. There were 10 members in 1841 and 37 attenders and members a year later. Some of the congregation removed to Seavington St. Michael parish in 1843 but from 1846 those in Seavington St. Mary alone remained.[70] Beulah chapel was erected in Dark Lane, south of the village, in 1859. It was closed before 1929 and was known in 1973 as Beulah House.[71]

EDUCATION. In 1818 Wesleyan Methodists had a Sunday school in the parish and the curate and others supported another for c. 30 children.[72] By 1835 there was a day-school for 11 children.[73] Children attended the day-school at Seavington St. Michael from 1844 until its closure in 1968.[74] A Mrs. Butler kept a girls' school in 1875.[75]

CHARITIES FOR THE POOR. None known.

42 Ex inf. Records Officer, Church Commissioners.
43 Ibid.
44 S.R.O., D/D/Ca 274; DD/PT, box 40.
45 S.R.O., D/D/B return 1815.
46 S.R.O., D/D/V return 1840.
47 *Clergy List.*
48 Ibid.
49 S.R.O., D/D/Ca 17 (1547), 22 (1554), 27 (1557), 98 (1593–4), 235 (1623).
50 Ibid. 17.
51 Ibid. 22.   52 Ibid. 57.
53 S.R.O., D/D/V Dioc. bk.
54 S.R.O., D/D/B return 1815; D/D/V return 1840. Only four times 1806–23; S.R.O., D/P/sea. ma 4/1/1.
55 H.O. 129/318/1/5/7.
56 S.R.O., D/P/sea.ma 4/1/1.
57 S.R.O., D/D/V return 1870.
58 S.R.O., D/P/sea.ma 4/1/2.

59 S.R.O., DD/CA 107, survey.
60 *L. & P. Hen. VIII*, xviii (1), p. 121.
61 S.R.O., D/P/sea.ma 4/1/1, 4/1/2.
62 S.R.O., DD/SAS CH 16.
63 S.R.O., D/P/sea.ma 4/1/2.
64 *Proc. Som. Arch. Soc.* xlv. 146.
65 S.R.O., D/P/sea.ma 2/1/1–4.
66 *S.R.S.* xxxiv. 127, 136.
67 S.R.O., Q/RR, meeting-house lics.
68 S.R.O., D/D/V Dioc. bk.
69 S.R.O., D/D/Rm, box 2; D/N/spc 1, 2.
70 S.R.O., D/N/spc 31–2.
71 Ibid. 33–4.
72 *Digest of Returns to Sel. Cttee. on Educ. of Poor*, H.C. 224 (1819), ix (2).
73 *Educ. Enquiry Abstract*, H.C. 62 (1835), xiii.
74 See below, p. 210.
75 *P.O. Dir. Som.* (1875).

SEAVINGTON ST. MICHAEL

THE ANCIENT parish of Seavington St. Michael occupies 286 a. of the fertile Yeovil and Pennard sands in the undulating country south-west of South Petherton.[1] Most of the parish lies around the 200 ft. contour, rising to 215 ft. at Gummer's Castle[2] near the eastern boundary, and falling away gently northwards and more abruptly to the south and west. The parish is roughly square in shape, its limits following either roads or field boundaries. Part of its western boundary, shared with Seavington St. Mary, is Water Street; its eastern limit is Flower Tanner's Lane and Frogmary Lane (Froggelmere in 1383).[3] A detached area of the parish locally in Seavington St. Mary was called Devenyshemeade in the 16th century and St. Michael's mead in the nineteenth.[4]

The parish is crossed by two east–west routes radiating from Lopen Head, the more northerly dividing the former North and Middle fields and running to Shepton Beauchamp and Barrington. The other, part of the London–Exeter coach route in the 18th century, ran between Middle and Nether fields and formed the village street. One north–south route, David's Lane, joins the village street from South Petherton and is continued south as a cul-de-sac ending at the church and the possible site of the medieval manor-house.[5] The village street turned south at Buckrell's Farm to become Water Street, leading to Seavington St. Mary, though since 1829, with the creation of New Road, the main route through the two parishes has been more directly westward.[6] Beside the village street lay a pond known in the 17th century as the horse pond.[7] It was used in the 19th century for retting flax, but was subsequently filled in and is used as a car park.

Two 17th-century farm-houses survive in the parish one of which, Buckrell's Farm, was recently reduced in size by road works. An inventory of goods there in 1640 mentioned a hall with chamber over, a chamber within the hall, and a buttery.[8] Orchard Close, near the church, is a similar house with passage entry and three rooms in line. A plaster panel in the principal first-floor room is inscribed 'John Skelton May 12 1689', which probably is the date of the original building. Skelton or Skellen was then the largest ratepayer in the parish.[9] A larger house, occupied in 1667 by Richard Drewer and including a stair chamber and entry, does not appear

to have survived.[10] On a smaller scale is the 17th-century Swan Thatch, formerly the village bakery and later the post office.

An inn known as the Bell in 1770 was kept by the Hunt family from at least 1740.[11] The Volunteer Inn, on the north side of the village street, was established by 1833.[12]

The Seavington club was founded by or in 1842, when it had 141 members, presumably drawn from Seavington St. Mary and also perhaps from South Petherton. It seems to have survived at least until 1923.[13]

About 1563 there were 11 households in the parish,[14] a figure to be compared with the nine men mustered from Seavington Dennis tithing in 1539.[15] There were 12 households in 1601.[16] The population in 1801 was 103. It more than doubled in the next twenty years and reached 275 in 1841. Thereafter there was a steady decline, reaching 113 in 1961 and 104 in 1971.[17]

MANOR. The manor of *SEAVINGTON DENNIS* originated as an estate called Sevenemetone held of the king's thegns by Siward the falconer in 1086.[18] By 1284–5 it was held of the honor of Gloucester,[19] and in 1311 the earl of Gloucester presented to the living.[20] In 1383 it was said to be held of Ellis de la Linde as of his manor of Dinnington,[21] the Lindes having been mesne lords of Seavington in 1284–5.[22] Its acquisition by the Crown by 1383 extinguished the overlordship.

The suffix derives from the tenants of the manor. Adam the Dane was in occupation by 1252, when he received grant of free warren there.[23] He was also tenant of Wraxall (Dors.), which had been held by William followed by Adam the Dane in the early 13th century.[24] Adam the Dane was in occupation of Seavington in 1284–5, and held it immediately of Hamon de Bordone.[25] Adam was still alive in 1305 but Robert, Lord FitzPayn (d. 1315), his overlord at Wraxall, had by that time acquired an interest in at least some of the property[26] and probably had the remainder on the death of Adam before 1311.[27] John atte Stone was tenant in 1316,[28] and by 1327 was succeeded by Parnel de la Stone.[29] She was still there two years later, holding the manor first of Robert, Lord FitzPayn (d. 1354), and Ela his wife,[30] and then of their feoffee Jordan de Byntre.[31] The

1 S.R.O., tithe award; Geol. Surv. Map 1″, solid and drift, sheet 312 (1958 edn.). For the place-name origin see above, p. 199. This article was completed in 1973.
2 The family, also resident in Lopen, held at least one small cottage on the waste beside the London road.
3 Cal. Inq. Misc. iv, pp. 119–20.
4 Winchester Coll. Mun. 17685; S.R.O., tithe award.
5 S.R.O. tithe award.
6 S.R.O., DD/BD 93.
7 Winchester Coll. Mun. 23053.
8 S.R.O., DD/SP 1640/100.
9 S.R.O., D/P/sea.ml 4/1/1.
10 S.R.O., DD/SP inventories, 1667–8.
11 S.R.O., Q/RL.
12 S.R.O., D/PS/ilm.
13 S.R.O., D/P/sea.ml 23/5; M. Fuller, *West-Country Friendly Socs.* 133; Taunton Castle, Newspaper cuttings.
14 B.L. Harl. MS. 594, f. 56.

15 *L. & P. Hen. VIII*, xiv (1), p. 289.
16 S.R.O., DD/HI, box 9.
17 *V.C.H. Som.* ii. 348; *Census*, 1901–71
18 *V.C.H. Som.* i. 522.
19 *Feud. Aids*, iv. 283.
20 *S.R.S.* i. 44.
21 *Cal. Inq. Misc.* iv, pp. 119–20.
22 *Feud. Aids*, iv. 283.
23 *Cal. Chart. R.* 1226–57, 414.
24 Hutchins, *Hist. Dors.* ii. 201; see also Agnes of Wraxall claiming patronage in 1226: *Pat. R.* 1225–32, 83.
25 *Feud. Aids*, iv. 283; see also *S.R.S.* vi. 389.
26 *S.R.S.* vi. 394.
27 Hutchins, *Hist. Dors.* ii. 201.
28 *Feud. Aids*, iv. 331.
29 *S.R.S.* iii. 198.
30 Ibid. xii. 134.
31 Hutchins, *Hist. Dors.* ii. 201.

manor was sold in 1354 to William de Wyngham;[32] three years later Robert de Samborne, probably acting as feoffee, settled it on Richard Fitzalan, earl of Arundel and Surrey (d. 1376).[33] His son, also Richard (d. 1397), exchanged it with the Crown for other property in 1383.[34]

For the next hundred years the Crown let the manor to farm for short periods to royal servants or retainers. Sir Matthew Gournay held it between 1384 and 1390,[35] Sir Humphrey Stafford from 1399 until his death in 1413,[36] and Stafford's son, also Sir Humphrey, from 1413 until his death in 1442.[37] Thereafter a succession of keepers accounted either to the Exchequer, to Crown grantees, or to the treasurer of the Household until 1462.[38] William Milford received a grant of the manor for life in 1462,[39] and retained it until after 1468.[40] In 1481, in return for land in Dorset taken by the Crown, the manor was given to Tewkesbury abbey.[41] This grant was nullified in 1483 since the acquired land belonged to Glastonbury abbey.[42] Glastonbury therefore received the manor in the same year, and the grant was confirmed in 1489.[43] The manor was surrendered at the Dissolution in 1539, and remained in Crown hands until 1551, when it was given to Winchester college.[44] The college sold its holding, no longer described as a manor, in 1932.[45]

In 1383 the earl of Arundel's capital messuage comprised a hall, two chambers, a grange, garner, stables, byre, and piggery.[46] A field called Court Close, possibly the site of the manor-house, lies south-west of the church.[47]

ECONOMIC HISTORY. The predominance of arable in the parish has been a feature at least since Domesday, when only 8 a. of meadow are recorded compared with 3 hides of arable, most of which was in demesne, supporting 120 sheep and 10 pigs.[48] The demesne still accounted for about half the parish at the end of the 14th century. There were then only 6½ a. of meadow and apart from grazing in the open fields there was only one piece of in-closed pasture within the parish, but 24 a. outside attached to the manor, mostly at Devenysshedoune, later Moorham Down, in Lopen.[49] The whole prop-erty in 1383 was valued without stock at £13 6s. 8d.[50]

During the next century the demesne is likely to have been let by the Crown farmers. This was certainly the case before the end of the 15th century, when a rental totalling £10 11s. 2d. was divided between 8s. 7d. from the free tenants, 43s. 8d. from six customary tenants, and £7 18s. 11d. from the demesne.[51] At least from 1511 the demesnes were let by copy on one or two lives,[52] and rents from them and from the ancient copyholds were combined as assessed rents.[53] The free tenants, seven in number at the end of the 15th century and led by Sir William Poulett (d. 1488), had increased their payments to 11s. 3d. by 1535–6;[54] in 1689 the total rent was 10s. 9d. from the same number of tenants, still headed by a Poulett, in the person of John, Lord Poulett (cr. Earl Poulett 1706, d. 1743), and followed by Christopher Poole and Henry Henley.[55] All free tenants were still at this time paying relief.[56] Earl Poulett, Thomas Poole, and Henry Henley were the leading freeholders in 1732.[57] By 1815 the freeholdings amounted in area to 110 a. as compared with 178 a. copyhold.[58]

Assessed rents in 1535–6 amounted to £10 5s. 10d.[59] and by 1551 were let in seven units, representing a considerable consolidation since the late 15th century.[60] There were eight copyhold tenants in 1680 paying virtually the same amount of rent, headed by Richard Drewer.[61] By 1732 thirteen copyholders, the total rental unchanged, were headed by John Hutchings and Elizabeth Drewer.[62] During the next seventy years most of the copyhold land was combined in the hands of one lessee, but was still sub-let in smaller units. The remaining 35 a., nearly half in Lopen, were divided between four tenant farmers and some cottagers.[63] By 1932, when Winchester college sold its land in the parish, most of the estate was in one farm.[64]

The farms of the 16th century were all below 50 a., the largest that of Peter Locke, part of the former demesne and including the possible site of the manor-house at Court Close.[65] He was succeeded after 1551 by Thomas Baker, who was Glaston-bury abbey's bailiff in the manor in 1535–6.[66] By 1659 the leading occupiers were Giles Dunster, Tamsin Skellen, Richard Drewer, and John Buckerell, the last of a family who had been free-holders in the parish before the end of the 15th century, and who gave their name to a farm.[67] Giles Dunster died in 1675 aged 89, and by 1712 his family were no longer holding land in the parish.[68] They had been overtaken by the Stuckeys, who

[32] S.R.S. xvii. 27.
[33] Ibid. 36.
[34] Cal. Pat. 1381–5, 282; 1385–9, 61; Cal. Close, 1381–5, 311–12.
[35] Cal. Fine R. 1383–91, 56; Cal. Pat. 1388–92, 358.
[36] Cal. Pat. 1399–1401, 39; 1413–16, 129.
[37] Cal. Fine R. 1437–45, 257.
[38] Ibid. 1445–52, 188; 1452–61, 112, 190, 288; 1461–71, 16; Cal. Pat. 1452–61, 298.
[39] Cal. Pat. 1461–7, 210.
[40] Ibid. 1467–77, 95.
[41] Ibid. 1476–85, 273.
[42] Ibid. 336.
[43] Ibid; Cal. Pat. 1484–94, 272.
[44] L. & P. Hen. VIII, xxi (1), p. 144; Cal. Pat. 1550–3, 160.
[45] Ex inf. the Archivist, Winchester Coll.
[46] Cal. Inq. Misc. iv, pp. 119–20.
[47] S.R.O., tithe award.
[48] V.C.H. Som. i. 522.
[49] Cal. Inq. Misc. iv, pp. 119–20.
[50] Cal. Pat. 1381–5, 282.

[51] Winchester Coll. Mun. 17686. One of the freeholders was John Buller, who died in 1485: S.R.S. xlii. 61–2.
[52] Winchester Coll. Mun. 17685.
[53] S.C. 6/Hen. VIII/3104; partial copy Winchester Coll. Mun. 17689.
[54] S.C. 6/Hen. VIII/3104; Winchester Coll. Mun. 17689.
[55] Winchester Coll. Mun. 231471.
[56] Ibid.
[57] Ibid. 14058c.
[58] Ibid. 21422. This figure does not include nearly 30 a. of glebe.
[59] Winchester Coll. Mun. 17689; S.C. 6/Hen. VIII/3104.
[60] Winchester Coll. Mun. 17685.
[61] Ibid. 231471.
[62] Ibid. 14058c.
[63] Ibid. 21422.
[64] Ex inf. the Archivist, Winchester Coll.
[65] Winchester Coll. Mun. 17685.
[66] Valor Eccl. (Rec. Com.), i. 144; Winchester Coll. Mun. 17689.
[67] Winchester Coll. Mun. 17686.
[68] S.R.O., D/P/sea.ml 4/1/1–2.

appeared in 1680 and who by 1709–10 were the most substantial ratepayers.[69] The Hutchings family rose to prominence during the 1740s, and by 1776 John Hutchings held nine copyhold tenements of Winchester college which he let for about £100 a year.[70] Much of the college land was let to the Poole family by 1839.[71]

The predominantly arable parish produced for one of its substantial farmers, Henry Dunster (d. 1668), beans, peas, barley, wheat, and hay, and supported an unspecified number of sheep.[72] The frequent complaints against overstocking on stubble and fallow and against encroachments on the land-shares or baulks in the open fields emphasizes the pressure on both grazing and arable.[73] The customary stent in the common fields was two sheep to the acre and in the meadow two bullocks or a horse to the acre.[74] In the 18th and early 19th century the cultivated fields were divided between wheat and Lent grain.[75] By the end of the 18th century there was 'a deal' of flax and the parish had 'the character of good land for corn'.[76] Peas, beans, clover, 'great quantities' of potatoes, and hemp were grown besides wheat and barley.[77] In the 16th century the only timber worth recording was 80 elms 'usually lopped and "shrede" by the tenants', which was enough to maintain and repair their houses.[78] Oak, ash, and elm was valued in 1815 at over £263.[79] Incidental references to stocking and complaints in 1649 and 1650 against those who washed wool in the horse pond[80] suggest that sheep were raised.

The Winchester college surveyor in 1797 recommended that inclosure of the arable fields would add between a quarter and a third to the value of the property. Lord Poulett and Mr. Stuckey were the only other landowners mentioned and the surveyor assumed their ready consent. By this time the arable was in five fields: North, Middle, and Nether fields, Marvel Land, and Gibgaston. It was 'in a high state of cultivation', producing crops each year and having no fallow.[81] The economics of inclosure had been demonstrated forty years earlier when the value of the small amount of inclosed arable had been put at £1 an acre compared with open arable which ranged from that figure down to 8s.[82] The quality of the arable varied widely between the fields. Good husbandry, however, produced good crops where tenancies were governed by leases providing for manuring with specified quantities of lime or 'good rotten dung' and for the maintenance of the banks.[83]

There was, however, little incentive to inclose; the farmers, though holding of several different landlords, in effect worked relatively consolidated lands, and the absence of any grazing on fallow simplified cultivation. Thus in 1839 James Poole of Seavington House, the most substantial farmer, occupied 180 a. belonging to six landlords besides himself, and owned a further 6 a. which another occupied. Robert Ware of Buckrell's Farm held 45 a. of five landlords.[84] Pooles and Wares continued to farm most of the parish between them until the 1860s.[85] Inclosure had evidently not proceeded far by 1876,[86] but may have been given an impetus by the agricultural depression. Labourers were said to be 'leaving the place very fast' in 1895,[87] and farmers found the situation 'very bad'. Certainly Winchester college took the initiative in arranging exchanges in order to consolidate their own holding in 1914–15,[88] though in the former Nether field, south of Gummer's Castle, the process was still far from complete in 1932.[89] That field was still unhedged in 1973 and baulks remained forming large strips.

There are few traces of occupations other than farming. A tanner occurs in 1620,[90] one or two weavers between 1827 and 1848,[91] and a sailcloth manufacturer in 1854–5.[92] In 1851 ten people were evidently employed in canvas making at Lopen, and in the same year at least 30 women and girls worked as glovers.[93] There was a shop by 1820,[94] and two by 1859, as well as a baker and a blacksmith.[95] The presence of an emigration agent by 1875 suggests that the agricultural slump already affected the area.[96] At the turn of the century the schoolmaster was concerned at the number of girls from the village who left to work at a collar factory at Ilminster.[97]

LOCAL GOVERNMENT. Court rolls survive for the period before the accession of Winchester college in the form of extracts or copies for 1522, 1532, and 1537.[98] From 1551 to 1560 there are both rolls and extracts,[99] and thereafter proceedings were engrossed until 1925.[1] During the ownership by Glastonbury abbey there seem to have been two courts each year, described as a halmote for the Hockday session, which might be as late as July, and as *curia manerii* at other times. Under Winchester college the sessions were sometimes called simply *curia* or *curia manerii*, and sometimes courts baron, with no apparent distinction of business. Courts

[69] Ibid.
[70] Winchester Coll. Mun. 17754, 21364; S.R.O., D/P/sea.ml 4/1/2.
[71] S.R.O., tithe award.
[72] S.R.O., DD/SP 1668/49.
[73] Winchester Coll. Mun. 17685, 17688, 17701, 17706, 17713, 17715–24.
[74] Ibid. 17707 (1707).
[75] Ibid. 17712 (1725, 1728), 17716 (1809).
[76] Ibid. 21364, survey 1776; copy, ibid. 21429A.
[77] Ibid. 21367, survey 1797.
[78] Ibid. 17685.
[79] Ibid. 17702.
[80] Ibid. 23053.
[81] Ibid. 21367.
[82] Ibid. 23150A, p. 42.
[83] S.R.O., DD/PT, box 12, Poulett to Harding 1786.
[84] S.R.O., tithe award; DD/CA 103. Buckrell's fm. included land in Seavington St. Mary.
[85] P.O. Dir. Som. (1859); S.R.O., D/P/sea.ml 4/1/3; H.O. 107/1927.

[86] Winchester Coll. Mun. 17703.
[87] Ibid. corresp. Long Load and Seavington, 1882–1909.
[88] Ibid. mins. of Estate and Finance Cttee.
[89] Ex inf. the Archivist.
[90] Winchester Coll. Mun. 17690.
[91] Par. rec. bapt. reg.
[92] Winchester Coll. Mun. 23084, court 1864.
[93] H.O. 107/1927.
[94] Par. rec. bapt. reg.
[95] P.O. Dir. Som. (1859).
[96] Ibid. (1875).
[97] S.R.O., C/E 92, log bk.
[98] Winchester Coll. Mun. 17687–8, 17693C, 17695. There is a book of estreats for 1544–5: S.C. 2/200/1.
[99] Winchester Coll. Mun. 17685. Ibid. 12870 is a copy.
[1] Ibid. 23039A–23094. Notes and extracts for 1570 are ibid. 17701, for 1635–52 are ibid. 17704A–B, for 1707–28 are ibid. 17707–12, for 1718 are Hants R.O. 36 M 66/30, for 1754–1805 are Winchester Coll. Mun. 17713–17.

were held at most twice a year, during the Vernal and Autumnal Progresses of the college steward, but were usually held once a year and sometimes less often. By the 1730s sessions were more irregular, and by the end of the century were infrequent. The last presentments were made in 1806,[2] and the last formal session was held in 1868.[3] Thereafter business for admissions was completed as necessary, not in the 'usual place'[4] but at a solicitor's office in South Petherton[5] or at Winchester.[6]

A hayward was usually chosen annually at the autumn court, but the office appears to have lapsed in the 17th century. A tithingman was elected in 1552,[7] but this office too seems to have remained unfilled until the 19th century. An appointment was made in 1815,[8] and annual elections were made until 1842.[9]

From the mid 17th century the parish officers were a churchwarden and two overseers, though only one overseer accounted.[10] Wardens held office in rotation in the 17th and early 18th centuries, but by the late 18th century they and the overseers were nominated in the 'vestry or parish meeting'.[11] The warden was usually also one of the overseers in the early 18th century, and the offices were shared almost exclusively from the 1780s by the Harding and Poole families.[12] James Poole, warden 1817–53, was in 1840 described as 'churchwarden perpetual'.[13] There were usually two wardens from 1858.[14] The vestry, first referred to in 1740–1,[15] was evidently dominated by the few substantial farmers in the parish, though agreement to build a poorhouse was said to have been made by the 'inhabitants'.[16]

Badged paupers were provided with a great variety of support, apart from regular weekly payments, ranging from furniture and domestic equipment to food, clothing, nursing, house rent, and apparently work at spinning and carding. Pauper apprentices were taken by rotation. The poor were housed in the church house in 1671;[17] a 'parish house' was used for the same purpose in the 1790s, and was repaired by the overseers in 1814.[18] A new poorhouse was erected on the same site in 1817–18, though paupers' rents continued to be paid for those living elsewhere. The poorhouse, comprising three dwellings, stood in the village street opposite the present Seavington House on the west side of its junction with David's Lane.[19]

The church house probably stood at the western end of the churchyard.[20] The parish became part of the Chard poor-law union in 1836.[21]

CHURCH. The church of Seavington St. Michael first occurs in 1226.[22] Its patronage was then disputed between Simon of Dinnington and Agnes of Wraxall, evidence of the early link between Seavington and Dinnington. Dinnington, where a church had been established by c. 1207,[23] was subsequently a chapelry of Seavington, indicating the prior foundation of the principal church. The benefice was a rectory, and from the early 14th century was in the gift of the lords of Dinnington. The earl of Gloucester, the overlord, presented in 1311,[24] but by 1314–15 the advowson had passed to the Lindes, tenants of Dinnington manor.[25] The family held it until after 1465, but in 1470 the presentation was made by trustees headed by William Stourton, Lord Stourton (d. 1478), and William Poulett,[26] subsequently described as the feoffees of the late Alexander Linde.[27] Poulett succeeded under settlement in 1480,[28] and the advowson then passed to successive generations of the Poulett family until c. 1923 when, on the union of the benefice with Seavington St. Mary, the patronage was exercised alternately by Earl Poulett and the chapter of Bristol, patrons of Seavington St. Mary.[29] Earl Poulett seems to have ceded his rights to the Diocesan Board of Patronage c. 1943.[30] The inclusion of Lopen in the living in 1960 gave the Board joint rights with the chapters of Bristol and Wells.[31]

The rectory was valued in 1291 at £6 13s. 4d.,[32] and at £6 14s. 11d. clear in 1535, an earlier composition allowing £4 13s. 4d. to the chaplain at Dinnington.[33] About 1668 it was worth £30,[34] in 1815 c. £120,[35] and in 1851 £208.[36] The tithes in 1334 were worth £5 6s. 8d. and tithes and offerings together in 1535 were valued at £11.[37] A rent-charge of £145 was established in 1839,[38] though the income in 1851 was only £132.[39]

In 1535 the rector had glebe in Seavington worth 20s.[40] By 1633 this amounted to 38 a. and a barn.[41] By 1839 the glebe measured just over 26 a.,[42] and in 1851 was worth £75.[43] Until c. 1861 the rectory house for the parish was in Dinnington, the rector living either there or, after 1784, at Hinton St. George.[44] Thereafter resident rectors, from 1871 combining their living with Seavington St. Mary,

[2] Winchester Coll. Mun. 23069, 27 May 1806.
[3] Ibid. 23086, 5 Nov. 1868.
[4] Ibid. 17708, 1712.
[5] Ibid. 23087, 1881.
[6] Ibid. 23094, 1925.
[7] Ibid. 17685.
[8] Ibid. 17717.
[9] Ibid. 17724.
[10] S.R.O., D/P/sea.ml 4/1/1–3.
[11] Ibid. 13/2/1–2.
[12] Ibid. 4/1/3, 13/2/2.
[13] S.R.O. D/D/V returns 1840.
[14] S.R.O. D/P/sea.ml 4/1/3.
[15] Ibid. 4/1/2.
[16] Ibid. 13/2/2.
[17] Dwelly, *Hearth Tax*, 149.
[18] S.R.O., D/P/sea.ml 13/2/1–2.
[19] Winchester Coll. Mun. 21421; S.R.O., tithe award.
[20] It was converted to dwellings which were demolished in the 20th century.
[21] *Poor Law Com. 2nd Rep.* p. 547.
[22] *Pat. R.* 1225–32, 83.

[23] *Cal. Pat.* 1388–92, 149; *S.R.S.* xi, p. 420.
[24] *S.R.S.* i. 44.
[25] *Cal. Inq. p.m.* v, p. 338. Lysle is an error for Linde in *S.R.S.* x, p. 614.
[26] *S.R.S.* lii, p. xxi.
[27] Ibid., pp. 35, 38, 55. See also C1/31/128.
[28] C 140/77/81.
[29] *Dioc. Dir.*
[30] Ibid.
[31] Ibid.
[32] *Tax. Eccl.* (Rec. Com.) 199, 202.
[33] *Valor Eccl.* (Rec. Com.) i. 164.
[34] S.R.O., D/D/Vc 24.
[35] S.R.O., D/D/B return 1815.
[36] H.O. 129/318/1/4/6.
[37] E 179/169/14; *Valor Eccl.* (Rec. Com.) i. 164.
[38] S.R.O., tithe award.
[39] H.O. 129/318/1/4/6.
[40] *Valor Eccl.* (Rec. Com.) i. 164.
[41] S.R.O., D/D/Rg 317.
[42] S.R.O., tithe award.
[43] H.O. 129/318/1/4/6.
[44] *Clergy List.*

The Market-place with the Market House and Obelisk

The Church from the South-east

MARTOCK

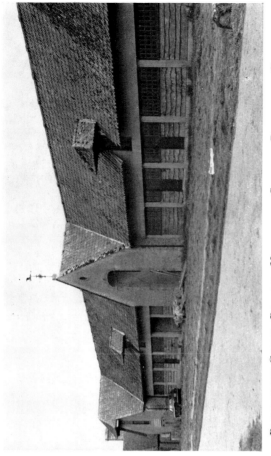

BARRINGTON COURT: BARNS IN VERNACULAR STYLE IN REINFORCED CONCRETE

SEAVINGTON ST. MARY: THE VILLAGE CARPENTER AND WHEELWRIGHT, 1903

SOUTH PETHERTON: HAYES END FARM GRANARY

lived either there[45] or later in Seavington St. Michael, at a house called the Beeches in Water Lane.[46] The present Rectory is in Seavington St. Mary.

In 1315 the rector, Thomas de Cranden, was licensed to be absent from his parish for a year in order to serve the dowager countess of Gloucester.[47] He had to provide for the *onera* of the parish, including the relief of the poor, and was evidently still in the countess's service in 1319.[48] John Attemede, appointed rector in 1321, was sent to Oxford to study for 3½ years because of insufficient education. Another priest exercised the cure, providing Attemede with 10 marks a year.[49] Thomas de Chelrye, rector from 1330, was licensed to be absent for study in 1331 and 1333.[50] Master John Poulett, rector from 1558, was also rector of Hinton St. George and *c.* 1559 was resident in Jersey, where his brother Sir Hugh was governor.[51] Edward Barret, rector 1580–1632, was also reported in 1606 to be living in Jersey.[52] Robert Clement, rector 1632–52, brother of Gregory Clement the regicide, was ejected by Parliament in 1652. He was replaced by Peter Glasbroke, presented under the Great Seal because the patron was a delinquent.[53]

During the 18th century the benefice was held by three sons of James Upton (d. 1749), headmaster successively of Ilminster and Taunton grammar schools, and himself a protégé of Lord Poulett.[54] John Upton (rector 1732–7) was followed by George (rector 1737–65) and Francis (rector 1765–78).[55] From 1779 the rectors, resident at Hinton St. George, normally employed assistant curates, who served both Seavington and Dinnington.[56] The curate in 1815 lived at South Petherton, where he occupied a similar office.[57] J. P. Billing, rector 1861–1911, served the living in person, but combined it with the curacy of Ilminster (1865–70) and with the vicarage of Seavington St. Mary from 1871.[58]

In 1412 the interdict was removed from the church after Lollard preaching had been stamped out.[59] In 1577 the rector was accused of not preaching the quarterly sermons.[60] Several complaints were made against Edward Barret, for failure to catechize and for not preaching.[61] In 1635 fringed altar and pulpit cloths had recently been provided;[62] the communion table was railed in 1677–8.[63] Holy Communion was usually celebrated four times a year during the 18th century.[64] In 1747 the 'parish meeting' determined to purchase no more special forms of prayer coming from the bishop or archdeacon, and promised to stand by the churchwarden should any trouble result.[65] By 1815 Holy Communion was celebrated three times a year and

prayers and a sermon were held once a Sunday.[66] By 1840 two services were held each Sunday, and by 1843 Holy Communion was celebrated four times a year.[67] The morning congregation on Census Sunday 1851 was 200, equally divided between adults and Sunday-school pupils. At the afternoon service there were 150 adults and 100 children.[68] By 1870 only one service with sermon was held each Sunday, but there were celebrations every six weeks.[69]

An acre of ground and a house called the church house had been given to the churchwardens to find a light in the church.[70] House and land were leased to a Crown grantee in 1571, and by 1671 the house was used to shelter the poor.[71] The land became known as 'the parish acre' or 'the clerk's acre'. In the early 18th century it was let by the churchwardens and was later allowed for the clerk's wages.[72] It continued to provide the wages of the sexton during the 19th century, but was sold *c.* 1924.[73]

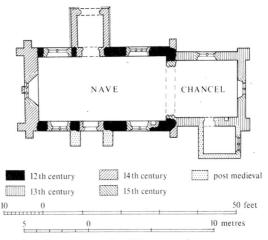

NAVE | CHANCEL

■ 12th century   ▨ 14th century   ▦ post medieval
▥ 13th century   ▧ 15th century

10   0   50 feet
5   0   10 metres

THE CHURCH OF ST. MICHAEL, SEAVINGTON
ST. MICHAEL

The church of *ST. MICHAEL* comprises a chancel with south vestry, a nave with north porch, and a western bellcot.[74] The nave is of the late 12th century and the chancel perhaps slightly later. A papal indulgence issued in 1291 to all visitors to the church[75] may be connected with the building of the porch and the heightening and refenestration of the nave. The angle buttresses were also then added, and the piscina in the chancel probably also survives from this period. Further alterations, in the 15th century, included new tracery in the older nave windows, new windows in the chancel, buttresses on the south side of the

45 S.R.O., D/D/V return 1840.
46 O.S. Map 6″, Som. LXXXVIII. NE. (1886 edn.).
47 *S.R.S.* i. 86.
48 Ibid. 22.
49 Ibid. 187.
50 Ibid. ix, pp. 46, 76, 156.
51 Cambridge, Corpus Christi Coll. MS. 97, f. 122.
52 S.R.O., D/D/Ca 151.
53 *Walker Revised* ed. Matthews.
54 *D.N.B.*
55 *Ibid.*, sub James Upton; S.R.O., D/D/V Dioc. bk.
56 S.R.O., D/P/sea.ml 2/1/1–5.
57 S.R.O., D/D/B return 1815.
58 *Crockford; Dioc. Kal.*
59 *S.R.S.* xxix, pp. 115–16.

60 S.R.O., D/D/Ca 57.
61 Ibid. 98, 175, 274.
62 *S. & D. N. & Q.* iv. 79–80.
63 S.R.O., D/P/sea.ml 4/1/1.   64 Ibid. 4/1/1–2.
65 Ibid. 4/1/2, s.d. 20 Apr. 1747.
66 S.R.O., D/D/B return 1815.
67 S.R.O., D/D/V returns 1840, 1843.
68 H.O. 129/318/1/4/6.
69 S.R.O., D/D/V return 1870.
70 E 310/23/127 no. 90.
71 *Cal. Pat.* 1569–72, p. 389; Dwelly, *Hearth Tax*, 149.
72 S.R.O., D/P/sea.ml 4/1/2.
73 S.R.O., D/D/V return 1840; Char. Com. files.
74 Taunton Castle, Pigott and Braikenridge collns.
75 *Cal. Papal Regs.* i. 539.

nave, a new chancel arch, and a rood screen. In the late 18th or early 19th century a gallery was put into the west end of the nave and the west window was remade. The nave roof was replaced in 1825, the vestry built in 1858, and the whole church reseated, with the exception of the gallery, in 1899.[76] References to a tower of stone occur frequently until the 1770s, though by 1791 there was only a wooden turret for the bells.[77] No trace of such a tower survives.

The church contains a barrel font on an octagonal shaft. In the chancel is the defaced effigy of a civilian of the late 13th century. Fragments of 15th-century glass remain in the tracery of the south-west window of the nave. Two 14th-century brackets in the form of heads were supports for the rood loft. Below the southern bracket is a trefoil-headed piscina with shelf.

There are three bells: (i) undated; (ii) 1938, Taylor and Co.; (iii) uninscribed. Two were rehung and a third added in memory of A. H. Poole (d. 1937).[78] A fourth bell, by W.S., dated 1611, lies on the floor by the font. The plate includes a cup and cover, the former inscribed with three dates between 1667 and 1671, the latter with the date-mark for 1574.[79] The baptismal registers begin in 1559, the marriages in 1562, and the burials in 1578. There are no entries between 1651 and 1654, when a civil register was appointed. Entries from 1660 until c. 1740 are incomplete.[80]

NONCONFORMITY. Three licences were issued for dissenting meetings between 1752 and 1754. Two were for a house to be used by Presbyterians, already well established in Seavington St. Mary.

The third, in 1753, was for Methodists.[81] A small group of Bible Christians appears to have broken away from the congregation in Seavington St. Mary and met at 'Higher Seavington' between 1843 and 1846. There were 22 members in 1843.[82]

EDUCATION. In 1818 there were two day-schools with 8 or 10 children in each.[83] By 1825–6 a Sunday school taught 20 boys and 27 girls.[84] This school continued at least until 1835, supported by subscriptions, and was probably that still kept in the chancel of the parish church in 1840.[85] A day-school was opened in 1833 and 17 children were taught at their parents' expense in 1835.[86] Another day-school, under Church auspices, was established in 1843, and a building adjacent to the churchyard was opened in 1844.[87] It was affiliated to the National Society.[88] The one salaried mistress was supported by subscriptions and school pence. There was accommodation in the single partitioned school-room for 100 children, and in 1893 the average attendance was 73.[89] By 1903 there were 79 pupils, with an average attendance of 58.[90] There were then two teachers. The school was also used for parish functions. By 1938 there were 80 pupils on the books, but the average attendance was only 28.[91] Numbers were increased by evacuees, mostly from London, between 1940 and 1944, and the Rectory was used as a hostel for boys not billeted.[92] Senior pupils were transferred to Ilminster in 1948, and the school closed in 1968. In 1973 the building was used as a private dwelling.

CHARITIES FOR THE POOR. None known.

SHEPTON BEAUCHAMP

THE PARISH of Shepton Beauchamp, 2 miles west of South Petherton, has an area of 841 a.[1] It is roughly rectangular in shape, nearly 2 miles from north to south and 1¼ mile from east to west, and its boundaries are largely artificial except the stream which divides it from South Petherton in the east. The southern boundary follows in part an ancient road between Ham Hill and Castle Neroche, and in the extreme south-east there is a protrusion into South Petherton, shared with Seavington St. Mary, to reach Fouts Cross.

Most of the parish lies on the Yeovil Sands, with an area of Pennard Sands beyond a fault line in the north, and alluvium in the extreme north and along the stream which forms part of the eastern

boundary.[2] Bricks and tiles were made on the north-eastern boundary in the 19th century.[3] The highest ground lies above 300 ft. in the west, from which the land falls away to below 50 ft. in the north and east. The parish is watered by a brook, known as the Mill stream in 1613 and Washwell brook in 1807,[4] which flows north-east from the village to the former mill site, and thereafter becomes the Lambrook brook.

The village street follows the shape of the contours in the centre of the parish, and is known during its course successively as Lambrook Road, North Street, Church Street, Sheepway, and Silver Street (after the former Little Silver field). In 1841 North Street was divided between Trade Street and East

[76] S.R.O., D/P/sea.ml 4/1/3, including note on inside cover.
[77] Collinson, *Hist. Som.* iii. 124.
[78] M.I. in ch.
[79] *Proc. Som. Arch. Soc.* xlv. 146; lix. 75–7.
[80] S.R.O., D/P/sea.ml 2/1/1–5.
[81] S.R.O., Q/RR.   [82] S.R.O., D/N/spc 32.
[83] *Digest of Returns to Sel. Cttee. on Educ. of Poor,* H.C. 224 (1819), ix (2).
[84] *Rep. B. & W. Dioc. Assoc. S.P.C.K.* (1825–6).
[85] *Educ. Enquiry Abstract,* H.C. 62 (1835), xiii; S.R.O., D/D/V return 1840.
[86] *Educ. Enquiry Abstract.*

[87] S.R.O., D/P/sea.ml 4/1/1, inside back; C/E 28.
[88] *Church Sch. Inquiry 1846–7*; S.R.O., C/E 28.
[89] *Return of Schs. 1893* [C. 7529], H.C. (1894), lxv.
[90] S.R.O., C/E 28.
[91] *Bd. of Educ., List 21, 1938* (H.M.S.O.), 351.
[92] S.R.O., C/E 92, log bks. 1901–68, adm. reg. 1890–1968.
[1] *Census* (1901). This article was completed in 1975.
[2] Geol. Surv. Map 1″, solid and drift, sheet 312 (1958 edn.).
[3] S.R.O., tithe award; O.S. Map 6″, Som. LXXXI. SE. (1886 edn.).
[4] S.R.O., D/D/Rg 320; DD/SAS SE 22.

Street, and Sheepway was called South Street.[5] From the cross-roads in the centre of the village, known as the Shambles, where the market was probably held, Great Lane (so called in 1747) runs west through a deep cutting to a second cross-roads, marked by an inscribed stone, no longer legible.[6] Lanes often bearing names of the furlongs run from the village to the fields.[7] In the 18th century the main route through the parish was the Taunton Higher Road, called the Mucheldich Highway where it passed through Mucheldich field. It was turnpiked in 1823 by the Ilminster trust,[8] but went out of use as a through route before the end of the 19th century.

Church and North streets seem to be the core of the settlement, with Love Lane (so called by 1807) forming a secondary medieval development off North Street and giving rear access to the eastern side of Church Street. The manor-house stood isolated to the south-west. More scattered settlement occurs by 1691 at Wash Cross; reached by Wash Way, so called in 1560.[9] Cottages on the waste both to the east and south of the village occur during the 18th century,[10] notably at Little Silver. All the older farms lay within the village, though Shells Farm, named after the medieval Shelves furlong, was a creation of the early 19th century.[11] In the 20th century there has been much building along Lambrook Road and to the east of Church Street.

Most of the houses in the centre of the village were built or reconstructed in the 19th century, and are of stone with tiled roofs. Sash windows predominate but a few houses have apparently inset stone-framed windows, and the Tudor House, although dated 1752 on the south gable, appears to be of the 17th century. A cottage in Love Lane has a thatched roof and at least one base cruck, indicating a late-medieval type. Shepton House, a gabled building in the Elizabethan style, was built c. 1850 for the rector, John Stratton Coles, by his father-in-law Vincent Stuckey, the Langport banker.[12]

The former open arable fields occupied a major portion of the parish until 1807. Parts remained open and divided until after the middle of the century, and much is without fences or hedges.[13] Meadow and pasture lay principally in the north-west at Honeymead (so called in 1485), Broomhills (Bromefelde in 1482), Bakers Croft (Oxenleaze in 1561 and 1686), and Northway (an arable field in 1540); and also east of the village at Cowleaze.[14] A

manor park, mentioned in 1485 and leased with the manor-house in 1512, lay in South Petherton parish adjacent to the eastern Shepton boundary and south of the lane from Wash Cross.[15]

A victualler was recorded in 1732, three in 1751, and four from 1754. It was probably c. 1754 that the house known by 1807 as the Duke of York was opened.[16] It formerly stood on a site immediately south of the present school in Church Street, but the landlord moved his sign to the present building at the Shambles c. 1860.[17] The Red Lion at Wash Cross was mentioned in 1754 and was recorded as the George Inn in 1839.[18] The New Inn, at the corner of Buttle Lane and Church Street, occurs in 1802; it closed c. 1960.[19] Behind it is an old fives wall with curved parapet and ball finials.[20] In 1839 the Swan inn stood in Sammys Lane and an unnamed public house on the south side of North Street.[21] Neither is mentioned thereafter. The efforts of the rector to start a temperance society in 1874 proved unsuccessful.[22]

There was a bowling green in 1602.[23] A friendly society called the Loyal Brothers was founded in 1802, when it met at the New Inn, and was re-established in 1847, meeting subsequently at the National schoolroom.[24] Club day was on Whit Wednesday until 1873 when it was changed at the rector's request to Whit Thursday.[25] The Club continued to meet until shortly before the Second World War.[26] Attempts were made in 1873 and 1874 to revive the 'Old Shepton Play' on the second Monday and Tuesday after Easter, or Hocktide, when cider was given away in the street. The rector was successful in suppressing the play, the celebration of Old Christmas Day, and a fife and drum band formed in 1873.[27] Cecil Sharp published two folk songs recorded at Shepton Beauchamp in 1905.[28]

A Reading Room and Institute had been set up in the Tudor House by 1877 and was evidently closed c. 1930.[29] The parish hall on the west side of Church Street was completed in 1933.[30]

The parish has long had an unusually large population for its area, probably as a result of its medieval market and fair, although numbers did not markedly decline either when the market ceased or during the agricultural depression of the later 19th century. The parish was described in 1868 as a 'curious place, much over-populated, nearly a person to every acre'.[31] There were 21 tax-payers

[5] H.O. 107/954.
[6] Par. rec., waywardens' accts. 1731–1802, penes the rector.
[7] Par. rec., waywardens' accts.; S.R.O., DD/X/LT, map 1755; O.S. Map 6″, Som. LXXXI. SE. (1886 edn.).
[8] Par. rec., waywardens' accts.; S.R.O., D/T/ilm. 2; DD/BD 106; DD/X/LT, map 1755.
[9] Bradford Central Libr., Swinton MSS., ct. roll; S.R.O., DD/X/LT, ct. bk.
[10] S.R.O., DD/X/LT, ct. bk.; DD/SAS SE 13.
[11] S.R.O., DD/PLE, box 104, map 1807; tithe award.
[12] V.S.S. Coles, ed. J. F. Briscoe, 32; H.O. 107/1927.
[13] S.R.O., DD/X/LT, map 1755; DD/SAS SE 13, 22; DD/PLE, box 104, map 1807; O.S. Map 6″, Som. LXXXI. SE. (1886 edn.).
[14] C 141/7/36; Bradford Central Libr. Swinton MSS., acct. 1481–2, ct. roll 1561; S.R.O., DD/X/LT, ct. bk. 1686; Longleat House, Seymour papers, vol. xii.
[15] C 141/7/36; Longleat House, Seymour papers, vol. xii; S.R.O., DD/X/LT, map 1755.
[16] S.R.O., Q/RL; DD/S/HR, box 16, assignment, 3 Dec. 1823; DD/SAS SE 22.

[17] S.R.O., tithe award; DD/EDS 2954; DD/S/HR, box 14; ex inf. Mr. E. Cornelius, Shepton Beauchamp.
[18] S.R.O., DD/X/LT, survey 1754; tithe award.
[19] F.S.1/617B/384; local information.
[20] Fives was played against the church tower in 1629: S.R.O., D/D/Ca 266.
[21] S.R.O., tithe award. In 1975 the inn in North Street had been divided into two dwellings.
[22] S.R.O., D/P/she.b 1/1/1: parish diary from 1872.
[23] S.R.O., T/PH/vch 11.
[24] F.S.1/617B/384; M. Fuller, West-Country Friendly Socs. 60, 117–18, 140, 146; Taunton Castle, Tite 95/37, rules (1909). [25] S.R.O., D/P/she.b 1/1/1.
[26] Ex inf. Mr. E. Cornelius.
[27] S.R.O., D/P/she.b 1/1/1.
[28] C. Sharp and C. L. Marson, Folk Songs from Som. 2nd ser. 69, 73. The songs were 'Tarry Trousers' and 'Midsummer Fair'.
[29] S.R.O., D/P/she.b 1/1/1, 9/1/1; Kelly's Dir. Som. (1927, 1931). [30] S.R.O., D/P/she.b 1/1/1.
[31] Rep. Com. on Children and Women in Agric. [4202–I] p. 698, H.C. (1868–9), xiii.

in 1327, a number second only to South Petherton and Barrington within the hundred, and the parish was the most populous there for its area in 1582.[32] The population was 439 in 1801, rising sharply to 559 in 1811 and to 648 in 1831. Thereafter it remained relatively constant until a further expansion to 696 in 1871. A period of fluctuation followed, after which the figures show a fall to 578 in 1931. Between 1951 and 1961 numbers declined from 579 to 533, but there was a slight increase to 545 in 1971.[33]

MANORS AND OTHER ESTATES. The manor of *SHEPTON*, later known as *SHEPTON BEAUCHAMP*, was held in 1066 by Algar, but T.R.W. passed to the count of Mortain.[34] The overlordship of Mortain is not referred to again and by the mid 12th century the terre tenant was evidently Sir Robert de Beauchamp (II).[35] The manor had thus probably been granted by the count of Mortain to Robert son of Ives with the barony of Hatch Beauchamp and passed successively to Robert de Beauchamp (I) (fl. 1092–1113) and Sir Robert (II) (fl. 1150–81).[36] Thereafter it descended in the Beauchamp family like Stoke sub Hamdon.[37]

In 1284, during the minority of John de Beauchamp (II) (Lord Beauchamp 1299, d. 1336), the manor was granted to John de Falevy who demised the custody in the same year to Robert Burnell, bishop of Bath and Wells.[38] On the death of John de Beauchamp (III) in 1361 the manor passed to his daughter and coheir Cecily Turberville (d. 1394), widow of Roger Seymour,[39] who leased it in parts, notably to Walter Clopton.[40] In 1394 the fee descended to Cicely's son Robert Seymour (d. 1413) and his wife Alice,[41] subsequently to their great-nephew Sir John Seymour (d. 1464), and thence to his grandson John Seymour (d. 1492).[42] Thereafter it evidently passed successively to Sir John Seymour (d. 1536) and his son Edward, duke of Somerset (d. 1552).[43] In 1553, during the minority of Edward's son, Edward, earl of Hertford (d. 1621), the custody of the manor was granted to John Dudley, earl of Warwick, but it was confirmed to the heir in 1581–2.[44] Edward was succeeded by his grandson William Seymour, marquess of Hertford (later duke of Somerset, d. 1660), and then by the latter's son William (d. 1671).[45] The manor passed with the dukedom to William's uncle, John Seymour

(d. 1675), and then to William's sister Elizabeth (d. 1697), wife of Thomas Bruce, earl of Ailesbury (d. 1741).[46] Elizabeth was followed by her sons Charles, Robert, and James Bruce, who apparently had sold the manor by 1710 to John Johnson of Syon Hill, Isleworth (Mdx.).[47] The property was held in 1741 by Orlando, son of John Johnson the younger, who, after heavily mortgaging the manor, sold it in 1756 to Agatha, widow of his principal creditor Samuel Child of Osterley Park, Isleworth (Mdx.). Agatha was succeeded in turn by her sons Francis (d. 1763) and Robert (d. 1782), and on Robert's death the estate descended to his daughter Sarah Ann (d. 1793), wife of John Fane, earl of Westmorland. Sarah settled it on her daughter Sarah Sophia Fane, wife of George, Viscount Villiers (later earl of Jersey).[48] The Jerseys sold the estate in 1807, the lordship and what was later known as Manor farm being purchased by Thomas Naish (d. 1813) of Seavington St. Mary.[49] Naish left his property equally between his brothers, William (d. 1830) and John (d. 1830), and his brother-in-law, John Clark of Tintinhull, and by 1845 the manor was held jointly by William Naish's sons, Thomas, William, and John.[50] Thomas Naish was described as lord from 1861 until his death in 1875, when administration of his estate was granted to John and Thomas Naish, sons of his brother John.[51] William England occurs as lord between 1889 and 1894 and the trustees of the late James England in 1897.[52] James Lean (d. 1923) of Shepton House, son-in-law of the former rector, J. S. Coles, had acquired the lordship by 1902 and was succeeded by his son James Vincent Lean, who lived at Shepton House until 1947.[53] The manor is not mentioned thereafter.

The manor-house and curtilage were worth 12*d.* a year in 1343, and in 1408 Roger and Maud Seymour were licensed to hear mass at their oratory in the house.[54] Isabel Seymour's dower there in 1485 included the principal chamber above the parlour, the 'wythdraughtis' chambers, and half the middle chamber, bakehouse, and bunting-house.[55] The house was occupied by Sir John Seymour when sheriff in 1515–16,[56] but for the remainder of the 16th century was let to the Rawe family, the tenant in 1596 collecting the lord's rents and providing lodging for up to seven of his officers twice a year.[57] In 1633 the property was said to be 'almost ruined',[58] but a lease of 'the manor-house called the farm'

[32] *S.R.S.* iii. 197–200; S.R.O., DD/SF 3948.
[33] *V.C.H. Som.* ii. 348; *Census*, 1911–71.
[34] *V.C.H. Som.* i. 474. The suffix 'Beauchamp' was first added in 1266: *S.R.S.* xiii. p. 11.
[35] *S.R.S.* xxxv. 57; Sanders, *Eng. Baronies*, 51. The manor was stated to be held in chief in 1212: *Bk. of Fees*, i. 86.
[36] Sanders, *Eng. Baronies*, 51.
[37] *V.C.H. Som.* iii. 238.
[38] *Complete Peerage*, ii. 48–9; *Cal. Pat.* 1281–92, 114–15, 119.
[39] *Complete Peerage*, ii. 49–50; *Cal. Fine R.* 1356–69, 208; *Cal. Close*, 1360–4, 449; 1381–5, 598.
[40] *Cal. Close*, 1369–74, 331; 1374–7, 109–10; 1392–6, 317; 1413–19, 41; *Cal. Pat.* 1370–4, 81; 1381–5, 97, 296; C 136/82/8.
[41] *Cal. Close*, 1392–6, 317.
[42] C 140/14/32; C 141/7/36; *Cal. Inq. p.m. Hen. VII*, i, p. 327.
[43] *Complete Peerage*, s.v. Somerset; C 142/115/38.
[44] *Cal. Pat.* 1553, 4; C 66/1218.

[45] *Complete Peerage*, s.v. Somerset; C.P. 43/262 rot. 117.
[46] *Complete Peerage*, s.vv. Somerset, Ailesbury; S.R.O., DD/X/LT, ct. bk.
[47] S.R.O., DD/X/LT, ct. bk.
[48] S.R.O., DD/PLE, box 104, abstract of title 1838; *Complete Peerage*, s.vv. Westmorland, Jersey.
[49] S.R.O., DD/SAS SE 22; DD/ED 11/173.
[50] S.R.O., DD/ED 11/173; DD/PLE, boxes 94–5.
[51] *P.O. Dir. Som.* (1861–75); *Kelly's Dir. Som.* (1883); S.R.O., DD/PLE, box 95.
[52] *Kelly's Dir. Som.* (1889–97).
[53] Ibid. (1902–39); M. Churchman, 'The Stuckeys of Somerset' (TS. in S.R.O., DD/X/Cu), 46; S.R.O., D/P/she.b 1/1/1.
[54] *S.R.S.* xxix, p. 40; xxxv. 118.   [55] C 141/7/36.
[56] S.R.O., DD/X/LT, copy custumal 1575. His children Edward, later duke of Somerset, and Jane, later Queen, may thus have lived there for a time.
[57] Longleat House, Seymour papers, vol. xii; S.R.O., DD/AB 45.   [58] *S.R.S.* xv. 118.

made in 1724 included additional rent in lieu of entertaining the lord's officers when courts were held. Abraham Atkins held the farm between 1724 and 1755 but it was subsequently leased to Edward Rowswell.[59] At the sale of the manor in 1807 the house and 98 a. of land were purchased by the occupier, William Salisbury Rowswell. The house was then 'an ancient structure in stone surrounded by venerable elms and well worthy of being created a gentleman's residence', but only part was habitable.[60] By 1839 the house and a larger holding were owned and farmed by John and William Stephens, and Mountfields House, a plain classical house with a Tuscan porch, was built soon after 1840 to the south of the old house site. Among the farm buildings, which are otherwise largely of the 19th century, are the remains of a small 16th-century barn.[61] A fish pond, called the 'great pool' in 1485, lies to the south-east of the former manor-house, beside Silver Street.[62]

In 1301–2 Alice (later Sarazin) did homage to the lord for freehold lands as cousin and heir of John Sarazin.[63] Property of about 21 a. in Shepton was granted in 1338 by William and Alice Sarazin, held in right of Alice, to John and Elizabeth Sarazin, and two years later William did homage for a messuage and 72 a. of land within the manor.[64] In 1384 the property was sold by Richard and Thomas Sarazin and Elizabeth wife of John Rogus to John Denebaud.[65] Thereafter it descended with the Denebaud manor of Hinton St. George to the Poulett family, being known in 1518 as the manor of *SHEPTON POULETT* and later as the manor of *SHEPTON*.[66] During the 16th and 17th centuries the administration of the estate was combined with the adjacent Poulett manor of Stocklinch Ottersay and by the 18th century the lands were regarded as forming part of Stocklinch manor.[67] The manor was conveyed in trust for sale in 1805 and the Shepton element was evidently split up and sold in 1809, chiefly to the Naish family, lords of the main manor of Shepton.[68]

A tenement with a dovecot, which may have been the former capital messuage of the freehold, passed in 1559 to Cuthbert Rosse on the death of Joan Seager, widow. On Cuthbert's death in 1560 it descended to Elizabeth, daughter of Nicholas Rosse, who still occupied it in 1571.[69] It was held by Elizabeth's husband, William Bonner of East Chinnock, who referred in his will, dated 1611, to the timber work and glass in his hall at Shepton Beauchamp.[70]

In 1304 Sir John de Beauchamp endowed his college at Stoke sub Hamdon with half the tithes from Shepton demesne (excepting 12 a.) and from a further 11 a., granting to the provost himself half the tithes from his court at Shepton and of those paid by the cottars in respect of their beasts.[71] In 1540 ten tenants of the manor were stated formerly to have rendered 27 bushels of rye and 4d. in money to the provost of Stoke, mainly from demesne lands then leased to them. A further 5½ bushels of barley had been payable to the prior of Bruton by five other tenants although the origin of the Bruton render has not been traced. After the Dissolution the renders were ordered to be withheld, those belonging to Stoke being valued at 66s. 8d. in 1548.[72]

Roger Trigel did homage for freehold lands in 1340 for which he rendered 4d. and service as a hayward, and in 1343 he held $\frac{1}{20}$ of a fee with John de Burgh of Shepton.[73] Other lands held by the Burgh family subsequently descended to the Denebaud family, and Trigel's holding may have merged with the later manor of Shepton Poulett.[74]

Before 1372 Cecily Turberville granted two houses and 86 a. to Richard Godscelyn and Joan his wife for their lives. In 1384–5 the property was assigned by the Godscelyns to John Rodberd of Kingsbury Episcopi and by him, in 1389, to Robert Veel and William son of Joan Fareways. Veel and Fareways subsequently acquired reversionary interests which had been granted in 1374 to Walter Clopton.[75] Veel purchased additional small quantities of land in the parish in 1400 and evidently obtained the freehold reversions from Cecily de Turberville and Robert Seymour.[76] By 1431 Robert Veel had been succeeded by his daughter Eleanor and her husband, John Coker of Worle and Mappowder (Dors.), who conveyed the estate to their son Robert (d. 1488) in 1449.[77] Robert's son John Coker (d. 1513–14) held the property by 1492 and leased it to Henry Havegod and Joan his wife in 1494.[78] By 1516 it was described as a decayed tenement called Cokers, leased to John Bowyar, and had passed to Henry Daubeney (cr. earl of Bridgwater, 1538), who held it in 1540.[79] The immediate descent has not been traced, but the property was acquired by the Rosse family, probably by purchase, and subsequently bought by Thomas Warre (d. 1682), living in Shepton by 1659.[80] The estate then descended in turn to Thomas Warre's son Thomas (d. 1685), in whose time it was still called Coker's farm, and to his grandson, also Thomas (d. 1737).[81] The last was succeeded

[59] S.R.O., DD/SAS SE 13; DD/X/LT, map 1755.
[60] S.R.O., DD/SAS SE 22.
[61] S.R.O., tithe award; DD/CA 181, sale cat. 1890. Fragments of medieval window tracery excavated in the churchyard were used to repair the barn in 1964: ex inf. Mr. J. Hallett, Shepton Beauchamp.
[62] C 141/7/36.
[63] S.R.S. xxxv. 89.
[64] Ibid. xii. 197; xxxv. 89.
[65] Ibid. xvii. 109.
[66] Cal. Inq. p.m. Hen. VII, iii, pp. 552–3; S.R.O., DD/PT, box 1.
[67] S.R.O., DD/PT, boxes 1, 2; DD/SS, bdles. 1, 26.
[68] S.R.O., DD/PT, box 13; DD/S/HR, box 16, assignment, 3 Dec. 1823; DD/PLE, box 89, covenant, 25 Sept. 1856.
[69] S.R.O., DD/PT, boxes 1, 2; DD/SS, bdle. 1.
[70] Visit. Som. 1623 (Harl. Soc. xi), 9–10; Som. Wills, ed. Brown, i. 56. Bonner entries appear in the parish register during the years 1577–1615: S.R.O., D/P/she. b 2/1/1.

[71] Collinson, Hist. Som. iii. 317.
[72] Longleat House, Seymour papers, vol. xii; S.R.S. ii. 298. In 1755 the lord of the manor was collecting for himself compositions in respect of 22½ bu. of rye and 9½ bu. of barley: S.R.O., DD/SAS SE 13.
[73] S.R.S. xxxv. 89; Cal. Inq. p.m. vii, p. 322.
[74] S.R.S. xlii. 83, 91.
[75] Cal. Inq. Misc. v, p. 198.
[76] Ibid.; S.R.S. xxii. 2.
[77] E 326/11102; S.R.S. xxii. 113; Hutchins, Hist. Dors. iii. 722–5.
[78] E 326/11102–3; Hutchins, Hist. Dors. iii. 722–5.
[79] E 326/11101; Longleat House, Seymour papers, vol. xii.
[80] S.R.S. xv. 118; E 134/3 & 4 Jas. II/Hil. 11; Som. Wills, ed. Brown, iv. 130–1.
[81] S.R.O., DD/X/LT, ct. bk. 29 Oct. 1685; E 134/3 & 4 Jas. II/Hil. 11; Som. Wills, ed. Brown, iv. 131; Burke, Peerage (1949), 2111.

by his daughter Jane (d. 1791) wife of Sir Robert Grosvenor, Bt. (d. 1755), whence it passed to Jane's second son, Thomas Grosvenor, and then to his son, Richard Erle-Drax-Grosvenor (d. 1819). Richard was followed successively by his son, Richard Edward Erle-Drax-Grosvenor (d. 1828) and daughter, Jane Frances (d. 1853), wife of J. S. W. Sawbridge (later Sawbridge-Erle-Drax) (d. 1887).[82] The property has not been traced further.

The house attached to the property was mentioned in 1494, when the tenant was charged with repairing the thatch over the hall, chambers, grange, and plastered house.[83] The building was probably occupied by the Cokers who were credited with building the north aisle of the church, where their arms could be seen in 1633.[84] The house was later occupied by the Warres, ancestors of the dukes of Westminster, and stood on the west side of Church Street, immediately north of its junction with Robins Lane. It was described as a 'large, ancient' building in 1791, was built round three sides of a courtyard open to the west, and was evidently demolished in the mid 19th century.[85]

In the mid 15th century a freehold paying 18d. rent was held by Richard Sargeant, who had been succeeded by William Sargeant before 1485.[86] In 1499 John Heyron of Langport (d. 1501) acquired lands in Shepton from William and Joan Sargeant, and on Heyron's death three houses and 50 a. of land passed to his son John (d. 1507).[87] The heirs of Heyron occur as freeholders until 1559 and it was probably this property which descended from one of the daughters of John Heyron (II) to the Rosse family, who assumed the Heyron coat of arms.[88] Cuthbert Rosse (d. 1560) was followed by his son Nicholas (d. 1562) and thereafter the premises passed through successive generations to John (d. 1617), James (I), and James (II) Rosse (d. 1670).[89] The Rosses also inherited lands in the parish from Agnes Wogan (d. 1575), a freeholder in 1560, who left them to her nephew John Rosse.[90] All the Rosse lands in Shepton were evidently sold to Thomas Warre (d. 1682),[91] and subsequently probably descended to the Grosvenors.

ECONOMIC HISTORY. The name of the parish suggests an early dependence on sheep farming,[92] although there were only 64 sheep on the demesne in 1086. In that year the manor gelded for 6 hides

and there was land for 4 ploughs. The lord held 4 hides less ½ virgate in demesne with 1½ plough worked by 3 serfs, and the remaining 2 hides and ½ virgate were occupied by 9 villeins and 3 bordars. There were 15 a. of meadow and, in addition to the sheep, stock comprised a riding-horse, 4 head of cattle, and 7 swine.

The value of the manor fell from £5 T.R.E. to £4 in 1086.[93] It was extended at £32 3s. 5d. in 1284, but by 1337 the value was £7 12s. 4d.[94] The fall may be partly explained by the creation before 1340 of three freeholds then held by William de Asshelond, Roger Trigel, and William Sarazin. Asshelond rendered only homage for his property, Trigel held his land for a rent of 4d. and service as hayward of Broadmead, and Sarazin paid 8s. rent and, besides agrarian services, had to provide an armed man to carry the lord's banner in time of war.[95] By 1343 the income from the manor had fallen still further, to £6 0s. 5d., although that figure may exclude dower. There were then 60 a. of arable, and 3 a. of pasture. Assized rents produced 62s. and customary works 14s. 11d.[96] The reversion of two houses and 86 a. of land was granted away from the manor in 1374,[97] but the estate had risen in value by 1382 when it produced £30 a year.[98]

There was little variation for the next three centuries. In 1465 the manor was worth £30 a year, less an annuity of 10 marks.[99] An undated rental of free and copyhold lands of the mid 15th century shows a total of £31 8s. 10d. being paid by 60 tenants, including customary renders of larder-silver from 19 tenants at Martinmas and chursett or church scot in chickens and hens by four tenants. There were then 16 a. of demesne leased to five tenants, and 26 cottagers.[1] In 1485 a grant of dower was valued at £6 13s. 4d., which seems to indicate a fall in the total income. The grant included 78½ a. of open arable demesne, lying in 22 named fields and leased to the tenants, four tenements of 20 a. each, four of 10 a., three of 5 a., and eleven cottagers, a total of 213½ a., with a third share in four freehold rents of £4 2s. 6d.[2] In 1492 the manor, then worth £33 6s. 8d., was subject to an annuity of 40s.[3]

The rental rose to £39 15s. 1¼d. in 1540, evidently as a result of letting the manor-house and demesne.[4] There were then 48 customary tenants and four freeholders, only John Rawe, holding the 85-a. demesne, held more than 30 a., and there were fifteen cottagers with no lands except those on

[82] Som. Wills, ed. Brown, iv. 131; Burke, Peerage (1949), 2111; Burke, Land. Gent. (1914), 557–8; S.R.O., tithe award.
[83] E 326/11102.
[84] S.R.S. xv. 118.
[85] E 134/3 & 4 Jas. II/Hil. 11; Collinson, Hist. Som. iii. 126; S.R.O. tithe award; O.S. Map 1/2,500, Som. LXXXI. 15 (1886 edn.).
[86] Bradford Central Libr., Swinton MSS., rental, n.d.; C 141/7/36.
[87] C.P. 25(1)/202/42/14 Hen. VII, East.; Cal. Inq. p.m. Hen. VII, iii, pp. 446–7; C 142/25/42.
[88] Longleat House, Seymour papers, vol. xii; S.R.O., DD/AB 8; S.R.S. xv. 118, 132. The immediate heir of the Heyrons at Shepton may have been George Sydenham, husband of another of the Heyron daughters, who was a freeholder in 1560: Bradford Central Libr., Swinton MSS., ct. roll.
[89] Visit. Som. 1623 (Harl. Soc. xi), 95; Bradford Central

Libr., Swinton MSS., ct. roll 14 Sept. 1560; S.R.O., D/P/she. b 2/1/1; DD/SAS SW 20, p. 66; Som. Wills, ed. Brown, iv. 99.
[90] Som. Wills, ed. Brown, i. 45; S.R.S. xlii. 181.
[91] Som. Wills, ed. Brown, iv. 99; S.R.O., DD/SAS SW 20.
[92] E. Ekwall, Dict. Eng. Place-Names, 416.
[93] V.C.H. Som. i. 474.
[94] Cal. Pat. 1281–92, 114–15; C 135/47/2.
[95] S.R.S. xxxv. 89.
[96] Ibid. 118; Cal. Pat. 1343–5, 123; C 135/70/7.
[97] Cal. Inq. Misc. v, p. 198.
[98] Cal. Pat. 1370–4, 81; 1381–5, 97.
[99] C 140/14/32.
[1] Bradford Central Libr., Swinton MSS. rental, n.d.
[2] C 141/7/36.
[3] Cal. Inq. p.m. Hen. VII, i, p. 327.
[4] S.C. 6/Hen. VIII/3073; Longleat House, Seymour papers, vol. xii.

which their houses stood.[5] In 1559 the income from the manor included 19*d.* paid for tenants' chimneys.[6]

The freeholders occupied nearly a quarter of the parish's total area. The lands held by the Asshelond family in 1312 comprised five cottages, 40 a. of arable, and 2 a. of meadow, worth £1 0*s.* 11*d.*[7] The Sarazin (later Poulett) holding was 72 a. in 1340 and 1498.[8] The lands later owned by the Coker family amounted to 86 a. in 1372.[9] The Heyron property comprised three houses and 50 a. of land in 1503.[10] The Rosse family as heirs of the Heyrons and Wogans owned and occupied 90 a. of land in 1602.

The income from the main manor was £44 13*s.* 7¾*d.* in 1671, of which £6 5*s.* 9*d.* represented the rent of the manor-house.[11] The rents of 73 customary tenants totalled £37 16*s.* 8¾*d.* in 1755, but a further 13 holdings which had been allowed to fall in hand were being leased at realistic rents to tenants at will and produced £141 15*s.* 6*d.* a year. The mean size of holdings was still relatively low, the consequence of a large population settled on a small acreage. The manor-house was let with nearly 90 a., two farmers held just over 60 a., two 36 a., and two over 20 a., but 62 tenants had less than 10 a. The manor was valued at £1,285 a year in 1796 when it comprised 670 a.[12] The policy of allowing lands to fall into hand was continued and had resulted in an increased rental of £991 when the manor estate of 629 a. was split up and sold in 1807.[13]

The open arable fields were being farmed on a three-year rotation in 1343,[14] although there were more than three open fields in the medieval period. Pasturage in the breached fields was calculated at two sheep per acre in 1540, when the stubble fields provided winter grazing for 778 sheep, in addition to 155 on fallow and pasture. Cowleaze accommodated 34 cows in the summer between Candlemas and Michaelmas.[15] In 1681 the stint of the stubble fields was reckoned as two sheep for every acre, an ox for every 2 a., and a horse for 4 a. This was revised in 1687 to give pasture for a bullock for every 4 a. and for a horse for every 5 a. In 1713 the breach of the fields was announced by the bailiff and grass haywards during divine service, and throughout the 18th century the overseers of the poor were responsible for maintaining certain field gates.[16] The limited pasture led to an order in 1788 limiting grazing to 25 sheep for each tenement, additional rights being granted at 4*d.* per animal.[17]

Small enclosures are recorded at an early date, and 16½ a. of demesne at Bromehill were inclosed in 1481–2,[18] but the parish was largely cultivated

in common until the 19th century. Some areas, particularly in Stankley, had been fenced by 1755, and in 1796 a surveyor commented on the advantages of inclosing. The agent had allowed some farm-houses to fall in hand for that purpose, and at the sale of the manor in 1807 the manorial lands in each open field were sold with individual farm-houses: the manor-house was disposed of with 83 a., including Little Silver, Burgaston, White, and part of Cradle common fields, Mucheldiltch field of 30 a. was sold with a farm, later the site of the Methodist chapel, and the other fields were similarly conveyed away.[19] Complete inclosure, however, was dependent on the subsequent acquisition of strips held with the Poulett and former Grosvenor estates. Mucheldiltch field, for instance, was still open to 1853, although all the former common disappeared before 1886.[20]

A new farm-house, later Shells Farm, proposed in 1796, was built between 1807 and 1832, and in 1839 was held with 104 a.[21] In 1839 the Naish family owned 247 a., most of which was farmed in three units: Thomas at the later Manor farm with 86 a., William at Home farm with 77 a., and John Naish at Draytons with 59 a. The former Grosvenor freehold was occupied by Stephen Salisbury with 72 a., Hill farm had 70 a., and the manor-house or Shepton farm, later Mountfields, 141 a. There were 620 a. of arable compared with 145 a. of meadow and pasture, and the principal crops were wheat, beans, and flax.[22] Some conversion to grassland had taken place by 1905 but arable was still predominant.[23] During the later 19th century there were usually six or seven farms. In 1851 the largest was the former manor-house farm of 300 a., although it was sold in 1890 with only 126 a.[24] The farming units continued to be relatively small and this led to the formation of the Shepton Beauchamp and District Smallholders' Association, active between 1919 and 1931.[25] Only two properties had over 150 a. between 1931 and 1939: Manor farm and the Lean family holdings (including Mountfields) attached to Shepton House.[26] Since 1939 Mountfields has developed as the largest holding in Shepton. In 1975 350 a. were farmed from there although some lay in adjacent parishes. In the parish as a whole the land was divided equally between dairy and arable farming. Both Shells farm, recently acquired by the Barrington Court estate, and Manor farm were devoted to dairying and Home farm was predominantly arable.[27]

Relief paid to the poor was supplemented in 1801 by the purchase of barley, peas, and potatoes, which were sold every Wednesday to poor families at a one-third loss. In face of general shortages the

[5] Longleat House, Seymour papers, vol. xii.
[6] S.R.O., DD/AB 9.
[7] C 134/30/7.
[8] *S.R.S.* xxxv. 89; *Cal. Inq. p.m. Hen. VII,* iii, pp. 552–3. There were 88 a. in 1755: S.R.O., DD/PT, box 46, survey of Stocklinch manor; DD/SAS SE 13.
[9] *Cal. Inq. Misc.* v, p. 198; E 326/11101.
[10] *Cal. Inq. p.m. Hen. VII,* iii, pp. 446–7.
[11] S.R.O., DD/AB 14.
[12] S.R.O., DD/SAS SE 13; DD/PLE, box 104, abstract of title, 1838.
[13] S.R.O., DD/SAS SE 22.
[14] C 135/70/7.
[15] Longleat House, Seymour papers, vol. xii.

[16] S.R.O., DD/X/LT, ct. bk.; D/P/she.b 13/2/1.
[17] S.R.O., DD/SAS SE 22.
[18] Bradford Central Libr., Swinton MSS., acct.
[19] S.R.O., DD/SAS SE 13, 22; DD/PLE, box 104, map 1807.
[20] S.R.O., DD/PLE, box 89, opinion of 1853 in deed of 6 May 1813.
[21] S.R.O., DD/SAS SE 13; Q/REr; DD/PLE, box 104, map 1807; tithe award.
[22] S.R.O., tithe award; *P.O. Dir. Som.* (1861).
[23] Statistics supplied by the then Bd. of Agric. 1905.
[24] H.O. 107/1927; S.R.O., DD/CA 181.
[25] *Kelly's Dir. Som.* (1919–31).
[26] Ibid. (1931–9).   [27] Ex inf. Mr. J. Hallett.

parishioners resolved to reduce their consumption of bread, not to use flour for making pastry, and to ration the feeding of oats to their horses.[28] The vestry agreed to apply £25 towards the emigration of the poor in 1849 and labourers were leaving the parish for South Wales and America in the 1870s.[29]

A glover was mentioned in 1708 and a glove-master, living at the eastern end of Great Lane, was active during the years 1837–47.[30] There were 126 female glovers in the parish in 1851, a number which increased to 139 in 1861 and fell to 122 in 1871 but rose soon after.[31] Gloving agents occur regularly in the late 19th century, and factories in Stoke sub Hamdon and Yeovil were both maintaining agencies in the parish by 1910.[32] The industry has been and is restricted to outwork from Yeovil and Stoke. In 1928 the trade was booming and the Shepton glovers were described as 'excellent workers'.[33] An attempt by a Martock glove company to establish a factory in Love Lane c. 1970 failed and the building was occupied by an electronics firm in 1975.[34]

Tailors were recorded at Shepton in 1625, 1657, 1668,[35] and at later dates, but there is little significant evidence of a cloth industry in the parish. A parchment-maker was mentioned in 1661, a barber in 1670, a mercer between 1734 and 1757, and a tobacconist in 1747.[36] There were weavers in Shepton by 1813, eleven of them in 1841, three in 1851, but none by 1861.[37] A variety of occupations in the mid 19th century included making straw bonnets, skirts, baskets, biscuits, collars, brushes, and mantuas.[38] The four girls who went in 1873 to work in Crewkerne were probably typical of a parish which then had insufficient employment for its high population.[39] A cycle-agent occurred in 1914, a motor-engineer and motor-cab proprietor in 1927, and a car and van-builder in 1939.[40] Shops in the village were mentioned from 1645 and there were at least nine in 1861,[41] although the number afterwards decreased to five.

In 1260 Robert de Beauchamp was granted the right to hold a Friday market and two fairs, on the eve, day, and morrow of the feasts of St. Petrock (3–5 June) and St. John the Baptist (23–5 June).[42] St. Petrock's fair survived an attempt to abolish it in 1268.[43] By 1361 the market had been altered

to Tuesday and only the St. Petrock's fair survived.[44] The rents from shambles in the market-place produced 2s. in 1482 and the tolls and customs of a fair on the feast of St. Lawrence the Martyr (10 Aug.) 3s. 4d.[45] A fair and court of pie powder were recorded in 1485 and the issues of the fair produced 10d. in 1537–8.[46] A statement in 1540 that the bailiff 'was wont' to pay 5s. a year for the profits of the fair and the shambles suggests that both fair and market had then ceased.[47] In 1575 it was mentioned that 'in time past' the first day of the fair (ascribed to St. 'Patrick's' day) had been chiefly for wool, the second day for all other wares, and that there had been a right to arrest for debt at the Tuesday markets.[48] A market stile on the south-western boundary of the manor was mentioned in 1575 and a market path in 1694.[49] The churchwardens were paying 2s. rent for the shambles by 1671 and until 1781, and repaired the premises in 1705 and 1743.[50] The area in front of the present Duke of York inn at the junction of North and Church streets is known as the Shambles and was probably the site of the medieval market and fair.

There was a water-mill worth 10s. by 1343, and it was occupied by Richard Miles in 1370.[51] It was repaired by the manor in 1481–2 and tolls went to the lord in 1485.[52] As a water grist mill it was let by copy in 1520 and passed in 1559 to Cuthbert Rosse (d. 1560) who agreed to rebuild it at his own charge.[53] In 1575 it was known as Shepton mill.[54] Thomas Forte took the mill c. 1615 and in 1621 agreed for its repair by Robert Ash and John Welchman, millwrights. Ash and Welchman, however, conspired with William Forte of South Petherton, forced the surrender of the mill to William, and engineered the imprisonment of Thomas Forte.[55] John Collins held the mill in 1669 and in 1715 it was known as Collins's mill.[56] By 1755 it was untenanted, and was valued at £3 although formerly let at £6.[57] It was held by copy[58] until the sale of the manor in 1807 when it was conveyed to James Daniel, mercer and draper, who by 1839 sub-let it.[59] Charles Best (d. 1877) occupied it as miller and baker 1861–77 and his family continued there until 1895. John Vaux was in business as miller and baker from 1902 until 1914,[60] when the mill ceased to grind, and its

[28] S.R.O., D/P/she. b 13/2/1.
[29] Ibid. 9/1/1.
[30] Par. rec., Wherriott char. accts. 1683–1851; S.R.O., D/P/she. b 2/1/5–6; tithe award; H.O. 107/954.
[31] H.O. 107/1927; R.G. 9/1633; R.G. 10/2402; S.R.O., D/P/she. b 1/1/1, 26 May 1873.
[32] S.R.O., D/P/she. b 2/1/5–6; Kelly's Dir. Som. (1910–39).
[33] Western Gazette, 31 May 1928.
[34] Local information.
[35] S.R.O., D/P/she. b 2/1/1; DD/SP, inventory of John Manninge, 1668.
[36] S.R.O., DD/SFR 8/1, f. 7; D/P/she. b 2/1/1 (1670); DD/SAS, C/114, 4; Q/jurors' bks. 1748–57; release 31 Oct. 1747, penes W. Smith, the Manor Mill, Honiton (Devon).
[37] S.R.O., D/P/she. b 2/1/5; H.O. 107/954; H.O. 107/1927; R.G. 9/1633.
[38] H.O. 107/954; H.O. 107/1927; R.G. 9/1633; S.R.O., D/P/she. b. 2/1/5–6.
[39] S.R.O., D/P/she. b 1/1/1.
[40] Kelly's Dir. Som. (1914–39).
[41] S.R.O., DD/SP, inventory of Mary Conent, 1645; P.O. Dir. Som. (1861).
[42] Cal. Chart. R. 1257–1300, 26.

[43] S.R.S. xxxvi. 27, 47, 72, 88.
[44] Cal. Inq. p.m. xi, p. 21.
[45] Bradford Central Libr., Swinton MSS., acct.
[46] C 141/7/36; S.C. 6/Hen. VIII/3073.
[47] Longleat House, Seymour papers, vol. xii.
[48] S.R.O., DD/X/LT, copy custumal 1575.
[49] Ibid.; ct. bk. 3 Aug. 1694.
[50] S.R.O., DD/AB 14; D/P/she. b 4/1/1.
[51] S.R.S. xxxv. 118; Cal. Close, 1369–74, 331; Cal. Pat. 1370–4, 81.
[52] Bradford Central Libr., Swinton MSS., acct. 1481–2; C 141/7/36.
[53] Longleat House, Seymour papers, vol. xii; S.R.O., DD/AB 8.
[54] Bradford Central Libr., Swinton MSS., ct. roll; S.R.O., DD/X/LT, copy custumal.
[55] C 3/350/6.
[56] S.R.O., DD/X/LT, ct. bk.; DD/SS, bdle. 26.
[57] S.R.O., DD/SAS SE 13.
[58] Ibid. 22.
[59] Ibid.; S.R.O., D/P/she. b 2/1/5–6; tithe award; H.O. 107/1927.
[60] P.O. Dir. Som. (1861–75); M.I. to Charles Best in chyd.; Kelly's Dir. Som. (1883–1914); R.G. 9/1633.

land and site were merged into Home farm.[61] The mill, on the eastern boundary of the parish, NE. from the village, was worked by an overshot wheel. The stones and wheel were removed *c.* 1928.[62] Ham stone footings and a small brick building marked the site in 1975.

LOCAL GOVERNMENT. Court rolls and books have been traced for the main manor for the years 1559–61, 1637, and 1681–1721, with a series of presentments for 1773–88.[63] The lord was holding two lawdays in 1340, and two lawdays with hal-mote at Michaelmas and Hockday and two other courts in 1481–2.[64] Between 1559 and 1561 the courts, held twice or three times each year, were described as *curie manerii* with a view of frankpledge on four occasions. In 1575 the lord was stated to have a lawday and court baron[65] and from 1637 the courts were called either *curie baronis* or *visus frankplegii cum curia baronis* and held once or twice each year. Business dealt with included the control of brewers, bakers, and millers, breaches of grazing customs, the repair of buildings, hedges, and ditches, taking felons' goods (1560), and cases of debt and trespass (1561).

In 1340 one of the free tenants, wearing white gloves and carrying a white rod, was required to superintend the mowing and stacking of hay in Broadmead.[66] Both steward and hayward were mentioned in 1481–2, the latter occupying his tenement rent free in return for his services. A tithingman was being elected by the court in 1560. The hayward (two in 1694) continued to be elected until at least 1788. Two grass haywards, called surveyors of the common fields in 1695, were appointed from 1682, increased to three in 1704, to four in 1714, and reduced to three in 1720 and 1721. Four were appointed from 1773, six between 1781 and 1785, and two in 1788.

Court rolls for the manor of Shepton or Shepton Poulett survive for 1518–19, 1523–4, 1532, 1552–4, 1559–73,[67] and 1651.[68] Courts were held for Shepton alone in 1518–19, 1532, 1566, and 1570, and at other times jointly twice a year with those for the adjacent Poulett manor of Stocklinch Ottersay.[69] When joint courts were held a separate homage jury continued to present for Shepton, and the court was said to be for Stocklinch Ottersay with Shepton in 1703. Thereafter courts were held at and for Stocklinch alone, although suit of court was demanded of Shepton tenants until at least 1767.[70]

No manorial officers for Shepton were appointed by the court.

There were two churchwardens in 1540, one chosen by the rector and the other by the parish in 1669. Two overseers of the poor held office by 1635 and two waywardens by 1657. The parish register appointed during the Interregnum was replaced in 1656 for being 'negligent in his office'.[71] The 19th-century vestry appointed two church-wardens, two overseers, one waywarden (two 1843–6), a guardian, and a salaried assistant overseer from 1849. The appointment of a hayward to keep the pound was proposed in 1880.[72]

Half the former church house was in the hands of the parish by 1703, and probably much earlier, and the whole came to be used as an alms- or poor-house.[73] By 1665 the overseers had acquired land formerly given to maintain church lights and the income was used in the 18th century to repair the building.[74] Most of the land was sold in 1887 and the house itself, divided into six cottages, was declared to be 'ripe for demolition' in 1934. It was sold in the following year and pulled down.[75] The cob and thatch building stood on the west side of Church Street.[76] The parish rented a house at Wash Cross between 1779 and 1806, probably for use as an additional poorhouse.[77] Shepton became part of the Chard poor-law union in 1836.[78]

CHURCH. The church was first mentioned in 1243 and the benefice was a rectory by 1254.[79] The advowson was probably held with the manor by 1304 and the patronage was so linked in 1325.[80] In 1348–9 the Crown presented five times during the minority of the lord, again in 1355, and, on the death of John de Beauchamp (III) in 1361, seized the advowson and assigned it in dower to his widow Alice.[81] She granted it to her brother-in-law, William de Beauchamp, and others in trust and William presented before 1373.[82] In 1374 the advow-son was conveyed to Matthew de Gournay, second husband of Alice, and his wife, one half in tail, and the other half for the life of Alice.[83] On Alice's death in 1383 the advowson was divided between William Beauchamp and Cecily Turberville, sister of John de Beauchamp (III).[84] The Crown unlaw-fully presented in 1391 but two years later Cecily secured the whole advowson and a revocation of that presentation.[85] Subsequently the patronage de-scended with the manor. Alexander Linde, who held a rent of 10 marks issuing from the manor and

[61] Sale cat. 1919, *penes* Mr. D. Eames, Wambrook Fm., Wambrook.

[62] Ex inf. Mr. E. Rowswell, Shepton Beauchamp.

[63] S.R.O., DD/AB 8; DD/X/LT; DD/SAS SE 22; Bradford Central Libr., Swinton MSS., ct. rolls 1560–1, ct. bk. 1637.

[64] *S.R.S.* xxxv. 89–90; Bradford Central Libr., Swinton MSS., acct. 1481–2.

[65] S.R.O., DD/X/LT, copy custumal 1575.

[66] *S.R.S.* xxxv. 89–90.

[67] S.R.O., DD/PT, boxes 1 and 2; DD/SS, bdle. 1.

[68] Ct. bks. *penes* Countess Poulett, Jersey, which also include Stocklinch courts covering Shepton manor for the years 1653–77, 1703–10, 1715–26.

[69] S.R.O., DD/SS, bdle. 26, copy ct. roll 24 Feb. 1702/3.

[70] Ibid. copy ct. roll 24 Feb. 1702/3; leases 1692–1767.

[71] Longleat House, Seymour papers, vol. xii; S.R.O., D/D/Rg 320; D/P/she. b 2/1/1, 4/1/1, 13/2/1; par rec.,

waywardens' accts. 1731–1802.

[72] S.R.O., D/P/she. b 9/1/1.

[73] S.R.O., DD/X/LT, ct. bk. *sub annis* 1707, 1718; par. rec., ch. ho. accts.

[74] *S.R.S.* ii. 16, 186; S.R.O., D/P/she. b 2/1/1; par. rec., ch. ho. accts.

[75] Char. Com. files.

[76] Ex inf. Mr. E. Cornelius.

[77] Par. rec., ch. ho. accts.

[78] *Poor Law Com. 2nd Rep.* p. 548.

[79] *S.R.S.* xi, p. 318; xiv, p. 50.

[80] Collinson, *Hist. Som.* iii. 317; *S.R.S.* i. 243.

[81] *Cal. Pat.* 1348–50, 9, 291, 338, 364, 394; 1391–6, 287; *S.R.S.* x, pp. 549, 567.

[82] *Cal. Close,* 1381–5, 598; *Cal. Pat.* 1391–6, 287.

[83] *Cal. Pat.* 1374–7, 35.

[84] *Cal. Inq. p.m.* xv, p. 385; *Cal. Fine R.* 1383–91, 36–7, 140–1.

[85] *Cal. Pat.* 1391–6, 287.

advowson, was patron in 1425 and 1426.[86] The Crown again presented during a minority in 1555 and John Clifton, after a disputed collation, in 1570.[87] James Aysshe and Roger Forte were patrons in 1576 by grant for a single turn, as were Margaret, widow of Edward Kyrton of Castle Cary, in 1661 and the executors of the Revd. Simon Paget in 1723.[88] In 1807 the advowson was sold for £2,000 to Thomas Naish (d. 1813), also purchaser of the manor, and left by him to his brothers William (d. 1830) and John Naish (d. 1830) and his brother-in-law John Clark of Tintinhull. John Naish left his share to his nephew, the Revd. William Clark, and William Naish devised his equally between his four sons.[89] One turn was exercised in 1836 by the Revd. W. G. Parks Smith, of Bovey Tracey (Devon), and his wife Elizabeth, related to the former rector, Joseph Domett (d. 1835), and the families of Naish and Clark were still joint patrons in 1840.[90] The advowson was acquired before 1861 by the then rector, James Stratton Coles (d. 1872), left by him to his widow Eliza (d. 1897), and by her to her son V. S. S. Coles, the former rector.[91] In 1913 the last gave it to the Community of the Resurrection, Mirfield (Yorks. W.R.), the patrons in 1975.[92]

The church had an income of £5 6s. 8d. in 1291, which rose to £15 in 1535.[93] It was worth £14 in 1605 and was possibly over-valued at £120 c. 1668.[94] From a figure of between £50 and £60 in 1705 the value rose to £130 in 1755, c. £360 in 1807, and £373 net in 1831.[95] By 1481 the rector was receiving 4 bushels of rye from the lord of the manor for church scot. The payment was charged on a tenement held by the Cogan family between 1613 and 1635 and on the manor-house in 1807.[96]

Tithes on lambs, wool, and sheaves payable to the rector were valued in 1334 at £4 and those on hay with oblations and the glebe at 53s. 4d.[97] By 1535 predial tithes were worth £7 15s. 8d., tithes of sheep and lambs £1 4s. 4d., and oblations and personal tithes £5 7s. 2½d.[98] In 1613 a tithe modus of 3s. 4d. at Easter was payable from the mill. Tithes were assessed in 1635 on corn, hemp, hay, wool, lambs, calves, pigs, apples, and dovecots, when 2d. was paid for a cow, and 1d. for a heifer and for the fall of a colt.[99] The tithes were valued at c. £360 in 1807 and were redeemed for a rent-charge of £373 in 1839.[1] A tithe dinner was being held at Shepton House in 1873.[2]

In the 13th century the lord of Shepton held 5 a. of land at Compton Durville in South Petherton from Shepton church.[3] The glebe lands were valued at 12s. 9½d. in 1535 and comprised 16¼ a. in 1571 and 21¼ a. between 1613 and 1635.[4] The extent had dropped to 13½ a. between 1755 and 1807, rose slightly to 17 a. in 1839, and continued at about that area until at least 1883, the land being valued at £40 a year in 1851.[5] Between 1889 and 1931 there were 10½ a. and 8 a. between 1935 and 1939.[6] In 1975 there were nearly 7 a. of glebe, including the site of the parsonage house.[7]

The rectory house in 1571 had a barn, stable, and dovecot. In 1613 the house comprised a parlour, hall, buttery, kitchen, brewhouse, and six chambers. The dovecot was mentioned in 1635 but not thereafter.[8] The house stands on the north side of North Street and continued as the parsonage until 1874. Under the name of St. Michael's Home and Penitentiary it was used by Julia M. Coles from 1886 as a home for young girls employed in laundry and housework. It was still so used in 1914 but had closed by 1919.[9] It has since been a private house known as St. Michael's. The south block, probably the original parlour with a great chamber above, is of the 16th century and has an open timber roof of three bays. The north range, formerly containing the hall, may be of earlier origin, but is not certainly older than the 17th century and additions in traditional style were made c. 1939. The 19th-century service accommodation to the north has been made into a separate house.

In 1874 a large rectory, designed by R. W. Drew of London, was built west of Church Street by V. S. S. Coles as a clergy house for the rector, the vicar of Barrington, and visiting priests and students. It was described as 'rather plain and gaunt, with a central hall for meals, and an oratory without an altar but with a great crucifix and sacred pictures; where the "lesser hours" are said and confessions sometimes heard'.[10] The house was sold in 1938 and was used for a time after 1948 as a religious guest house. It was known successively as St. Raphael, Holy Cross House, and the Old Rectory, and in 1975 was occupied as two dwellings called Beauchamp Manor.[11]

[86] *S.R.S.* xxxi, pp. 8–9; C 140/14/32.
[87] *S.R.S.* lv, p. 136; S.R.O., D/D/B reg. 15, ff. 27, 28v. Clifton had probably purchased a single presentation to the living.
[88] *Som. Incumbents*, ed. Weaver; S.R.O., D/D/B reg. 25, ff. 92, 92v. James Dugdale, rector (d. 1661), left his interest in the advowson to his son-in-law, Joseph Barker, who was presented in 1661, as above: *Som. Wills*, ed. Brown, iv. 48.
[89] S.R.O., DD/SAS SE 22; DD/ED 11/173; DD/PLE box 94, probate of John Naish; box 95, probate of William Naish.
[90] S.R.O. D/D/B reg. 34, f. 185; *County Gazette Dir.* (1840).
[91] *P.O. Dir. Som.* (1861, 1875); *Kelly's Dir. Som.* (1883–1927); M. Churchman, 'The Stuckeys of Somerset' (TS. in S.R.O., DD/X/CU).
[92] Community of the Resurrection, Mirfield, Greater Chapter mins. Apr. 1913; ex inf. the Librarian.
[93] *Tax. Eccl.* (Rec. Com.), 202; *Valor Eccl.* (Rec. Com), i. 165.
[94] S.R.O. D/D/Vc, Clergy bk. 1605; D/D/Vc 24.
[95] *Proc. Som. Arch. Soc.* cxii. 88; S.R.O., DD/SAS SE 13, 22; *Rep. Com. Eccl. Revenues*, pp. 152–3.
[96] Bradford Central Libr., Swinton MSS., acct. 1481–2; S.R.O., D/D/Rg 320; DD/SAS SE 22.
[97] E 179/169/14.
[98] *Valor Eccl.* (Rec. Com.), i. 165.
[99] S.R.O., D/D/Rg 320.
[1] S.R.O., DD/SAS SE 22; tithe award.
[2] S.R.O., D/P/she. b 1/1/1, 20 Feb. 1873.
[3] *Cal. Inq. p.m.* i, p. 295.
[4] *Valor Eccl.* (Rec. Com.), i. 165; S.R.O., D/D/Rg 320.
[5] S.R.O., DD/SAS SE 13, 22; tithe award; *P.O. Dir. Som.* (1861–75); *Kelly's Dir. Som.* (1883); H.O. 129/318/1/1/1.
[6] *Kelly's Dir. Som.* (1889–1939).
[7] Ex inf. the rector, Canon W. R. Haw.
[8] S.R.O., D/D/Rg 320.
[9] S.R.O., D/D/she. b 1/1/1; *Kelly's Dir. Som.* (1894–1919).
[10] S.R.O., D/P/she. b 1/1/1; *V. S. S. Coles*, ed. Briscoe, 32; see above, plate facing p. 65.
[11] S.R.O., D/P/she. b 1/1/1; deeds *penes* Mr. C. S. Sweeney, Shepton Beauchamp.

St. Mary's Cottage in Church Street, the former home of Miss Julia M. Coles, was used as the rectory house from 1939.[12]

Of the early rectors, Benedict de la Lade, rector by 1254 until at least 1266, had licence to study in 1266 and farm his church.[13] Pain FitzWarin, rector 1318–19, only a subdeacon when instituted, received a licence to study for a year, renewed for a further twelve months in 1319.[14] Robert de Upton, rector 1320–5, because of 'parochial strife' for which he was not responsible, in 1323 leased and two years later exchanged the living with Walter de Hulle, rector 1325–35, then rector of Binegar, from 1324 rector of Cricket St. Thomas, and later commissary-general to the bishop and subdean of Wells.[15] Hulle's successor, John de Middleton, rector 1335–7, was also commissary to the bishop.[16] Henry de Shelford, rector from 1391 until at least 1395, was described as a king's clerk in 1393.[17] John Champernon or Champney, rector 1511–31, held the living in plurality, first with Kingsbury Episcopi and later with Orchardleigh.[18] Thomas Rawe, rector 1532–54, was deprived of his benefice on Mary's accession;[19] William Owsley, rector 1577–1630, founded exhibitions at Oxford in 1626 for boys from Crewkerne grammar school.[20] James Dugdale, D.D., rector 1630–45, 1660–1, held the living in plurality with Evercreech and, as chaplain to the marquess of Hertford, lord of the manor and leader of the royalist forces in Somerset, he was involved in a skirmish at Witham House in September 1642. Taken prisoner, he was brought before the House of Commons and imprisoned. The marchioness of Hertford (later duchess of Somerset) procured his release as her chaplain and he was living at Oxford when it surrendered in 1646. His benefices were sequestrated and he was persecuted during the Interregnum.[21] James Eliot occurs as parson between 1645–6 and 1659 and witnessed the Presbyterian *Attestation* of 1648 as of Shepton, although he was not presented until 1651.[22] Robert Rowswell was recorded as a minister in the parish on his marriage in 1656 to Ann Eliot, probably related to the intruded rector.[23] Joseph Barker, rector 1661, Dugdale's son-in-law, was also chaplain to the duchess of Somerset.[24] John Paget, rector 1698–1723, Henry Newman, rector 1753–98, and Joseph Domett, rector 1798–1835, were pluralists, the last living at Bovey Tracey (Devon).[25] James Stratton Coles, rector 1836–72, was succeeded by his son Vincent Stuckey Stratton Coles, rector 1872–84, a leader of the Tractarian movement, subsequently librarian and principal of Pusey Hall, Oxford, and a hymn-writer. Coles maintained his

links with the parish, retiring there to live until his death in 1929.[26]

In 1540, and probably by 1474, ½ a. of empty ground, probably in the open fields, was devoted to maintaining 'the church sport', possibly the 'old Shepton play' at Hocktide whose revival was attempted in 1873 and 1874.[27] In 1554 there was no pyx and the stone altar, removed *c*. 1547, was withheld.[28] Holy Communion was administered three or four times a year between 1706 and 1785. One sermon was preached each Sunday in 1815 and two by 1827, and Holy Communion was celebrated once every six weeks and on feast days by 1843.[29] On Census Sunday 1851 there were congregations of 129 in the morning and 184 in the afternoon, with Sunday school attendances of 85 and 86 respectively.[30] On the arrival of James Stratton Coles as rector in 1836 there were only five regular communicants and confirmation had been administered in the area only once in seven years. Coles introduced hymns, frequent celebrations of the Holy Communion, daily Matins, weekday sermons, and coloured altar frontals for the different feasts.[31] When V. S. S. Coles succeeded his father as rector in 1872 he introduced weekly Communion services, daily Evensong, and the use of linen vestments for the Eucharist, but held separate communicant meetings for the wives of tradesmen and for those of labourers, and would not recognize a couple as farmers by sharing their wedding breakfast. There was opposition to Coles's introduction of confessions and complaints were made to the bishop in 1873 about the change to high church ritual. In the same year he founded the guild of St. Gabriel, still meeting in 1928, to encourage regular attendance at Holy Communion, and attempted to start a lodging house for young single men of the parish. The high church tradition was continued by the former curate, Arthur Lethbridge, rector from 1884, who met with opposition in 1904 over the use of silk chasubles, the wearing of red cassocks by the servers, the over-frequent celebrations of Holy Communion, and the emphasis placed on choral eucharists and the confessional. The bishop ordered a temporary return to white vestments. 'A Protestant spy' from the Royal Commission on Disorders in the Church attended at a Celebration in the same year, and the Kensitites held a meeting in the Shambles in 1905. An apparently unsolicited petition from 198 communicants in 1907 led the bishop to withdraw his objections to coloured vestments.[32]

In the mid 15th century the churchwardens held a brewhouse from the manor.[33] This may be identified with the church house held by the

[12] S.R.O., D/P/she. b 1/1/1.
[13] *S.R.S.* xiii, p. 11.
[14] *S.R.S.* i. 10, 21.
[15] Ibid. 139, 219, 243; ix, pp. 17, 26, 69, 116, 143, 172, 184.
[16] Ibid. ix, pp. 189, 242, 313; *H.M.C. Wells*, i. 239, 548; *Proc. Som. Arch. Soc.* lxxi. 77–9.
[17] *Cal. Pat.* 1388–92, 469; 1391–6, 302; 1396–9, 146.
[18] *Som. Incumbents*, ed. Weaver.
[19] *V.C.H. Som.* ii. 66.
[20] R. G. Bartelot, *Hist. Crewkerne School*, 33–8.
[21] J. Walker, *Sufferings of the Clergy*; *Walker Revised*, ed. Matthews; *Certain and True Newes of Somersetshire* (1642); *Cal. Cttee. for Compounding*, ii. 1521.
[22] S.R.O., D/P/she. b 2/1/1; *Calamy Revised*, ed. Matthews.

[23] S.R.O., D/P/she. b 2/1/2.
[24] *Som. Wills*, ed. Brown, iv. 48; Foster, *Alumni Oxon.*
[25] Foster, *Alumni Oxon*; Venn, *Alumni Cantab.*; S.R.O., D/D/B return 1815; D/D/V return 1827.
[26] *V. S. S. Coles*, ed. Briscoe; *D.N.B.* 1922–30.
[27] Longleat House, Seymour papers, vol. xii; S.R.O., D/P/she. b 1/1/1.
[28] S.R.O., D/D/Ca 17, 22.
[29] S.R.O., D/P/she. b 4/1/1, 9/1/1; D/D/B return 1815; D/D/V return 1827.
[30] H.O. 129/318/1/1/1.
[31] *V. S. S. Coles*, ed. Briscoe, 36–7, 39.
[32] S.R.O., D/P/she. b 1/1/1, 9/1/1; *Studies in Church Hist.* xi. 303–4.
[33] Bradford Central Libr., Swinton MSS., rental n.d.

churchwardens in 1540 and by the parishioners in 1548. Also in 1548 there were 2½ a. of land given to maintain lights.[34] Both these properties were confiscated by Edward VI's commissioners and in 1553 sold to London agents.[35] The church house was later used as an alms- or poorhouse until its demolition in 1935.[36]

The church of *ST. MICHAEL*[37] stands on a slight rise east of Church Street close to its junc-

Perpendicular style. The north chapel, in the angle between the chancel and the tower base, is probably contemporary with the aisle wall. The restoration of 1865 by G. E. Street involved the rebuilding of the south aisle with an increase in width of 6 ft., the reconstruction of the south arcade, the heightening and refenestration of the clerestories, the installation of new roofs to all but the north aisle, and the rebuilding of the chancel arch. The floors were tiled,

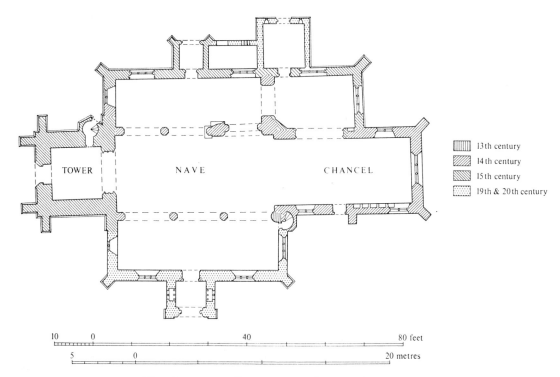

	13th century
	14th century
	15th century
	19th & 20th century

TOWER   NAVE   CHANCEL

THE CHURCH OF ST. MICHAEL, SHEPTON BEAUCHAMP

tion with North Street. It is built of lias and Ham stone and has a chancel with north chapel and vestry, aisled and clerestoreyed nave with north and south porches, and west tower. No part of the fabric can be ascribed with certainty to a date before the end of the 13th century, but it is probable that the nave preserves the outline of the building which then existed. A transeptal tower was built against its north side *c.* 1300 marking the first stage of a relatively short but important period of rebuilding. Next a south transeptal chapel was added, then the chancel was rebuilt, and finally aisles were added to the nave. In the earlier 16th century a tall and richly-decorated west tower was added. Whether it was the west tower or the old north tower which was presented as being in ruinous state in 1547[38] is not certain. The latter is perhaps more likely, for the scars of its demolition are still visible and the rebuilt north wall and porch are in a very late

new furniture was provided throughout the church, and a new organ was inserted in the north chapel.[39]

There are eight bells: (i and ii) 1905, Mears and Stainbank; (iii) 1798, J. Kingston of Bridgwater; (iv) 1738; (v) blank; (vi) 1738, Bilbie; (vii) blank; (viii) 1738, Bilbie, inscribed 'Hang me right and ring me well, they'll hear me sound at Hamdon Hill'.[40] The plate includes an Elizabethan cup and cover of 1573 by 'I.P.', and a chalice designed by G. E. Street in 1874.[41] The registers date from 1558 but lack baptisms for 1775–83, marriages for 1693–1701, 1753–4, and burials for 1679–94, 1778–83.[42] During the Interregnum marriages were usually solemnized at Middle Lambrook in Kingsbury Episcopi, and on one occasion in 1655 banns were called in South Petherton market.[43]

NONCONFORMITY. Henry Pope, a Quaker of

[34] Longleat House, Seymour papers, vol. xii; *S.R.S.* ii. 16, 186.
[35] *Cal. Pat.* 1553, 161.   [36] Char. Com. files.
[37] The dedication took place on 7 Feb.: *S.R.S.* xlii. 179; see above, plate facing p. 192.
[38] S.R.O., D/D/Ca 17.
[39] *Western Gazette*, 2 June 1865.
[40] S.R.O., DD/SAS CH 16; D/P/she. b 1/1/1, 4/1/1.
[41] *Proc. Som. Arch. Soc.* xlv. 159.
[42] S.R.O., D/P/she. b 2/1/1–10.   [43] Ibid. 2/1/1.

the parish, was imprisoned in 1661 for refusing the oath of allegiance.[44] Private houses were licensed for dissenting worship in 1691, 1695, 1703, and 1789, and there were two or three Presbyterian families in the parish *c.* 1776.[45] In 1776 Thomas Coke, curate of South Petherton and an avowed Methodist, was refused the use of the church, and preached in a private house. There followed a 'nocturnal broil' between his supporters and their opponents, and a critical pamphlet was published by John Thomas, the Shepton curate.[46]

The Wesleyans were meeting in the parish by 1812, probably registering the houses in that year and in 1820.[47] A Methodist chapel, owned by John Naish, was licensed in 1828, and was replaced by a second chapel built 1833–4.[48] There were attendances there of 48 in the morning and 40 in the evening on Census Sunday 1851, with a Sunday school of 20 in the morning and 25 in the afternoon.[49] A series of 'special sermons' at the chapel reduced parish church attendances in 1873, but chapel congregations subsequently decreased and the last service was held in 1940.[50] The small chapel, at the corner of Buttle Lane and Church Street, was being used as a store in 1975.

The house of James Tolman was licensed by dissenters in 1816, and that of James Rowsell, the 'housekeeper and minister,' by Calvinists in 1836.[51]

EDUCATION. Thomas Stuckey was licensed to teach grammar in the parish in 1586.[52]

In 1723 Thomas Rich left 6 a. of land in Merriott, 5s. of the income for cakes for twelve poor boys on St. Thomas's day and the residue for teaching the same children reading and the catechism. Two of the twelve were to be taught to write and cast accounts, and any surplus was to be spent on books. In 1751 Elizabeth Morgan, in accordance with the wishes of her deceased sister Anne Warre, gave £200 in trust, the interest to teach six boys, born and living in the parish, reading, writing, and arithmetic, to apprentice them, and provide 10s. for books. Parents were not to be in receipt of poor-relief and the pupils were only admitted when aged 8 or over and when they had learnt their primer.[53] William Mannin, schoolmaster, who died in 1785, probably taught under those charities.[54] In 1819 an income of £20 from both sources was paid to a parish schoolmaster, but the school was 'very badly attended, in consequence of

the misconduct of the master'.[55] In 1835 there were 27 children in the school, the charity income being augmented by parental contributions.[56]

A small schoolroom was built on the SE. corner of Love Lane and North Street in 1838.[57] In 1846 this housed three schools, the infants there having 'been taught to think, but not too much'.[58]

A National school was built nearly opposite the church in 1856.[59] In 1868 there were 100 on the register, all under 10, with an average attendance of ninety.[60] In 1873 the rector's sister converted St. Gabriel's Cottage in North Street into a teachers' house, which was also used until 1899 for training girls of the parish for domestic service.[61] The National school had an average attendance of 117 in 1894.[62] By 1903 numbers on the register had risen to 155 and pressure on the limited space available resulted in the addition of a further room in 1909–10.[63] Gardening was added to the curriculum in 1912. The practice of taking children under 5 to relieve mothers engaged in gloving out-work was criticized in 1927 and the provision of a crèche suggested.[64] By 1938 numbers stood at 146, of which 41 were infants.[65] The income from the Rich and Morgan charities continued to be paid to the school until 1886 when, under a Scheme consolidating all the parish charities, between £12 and £25 was allotted to the advancement of education of Shepton children in the school, for the school's general maintenance, for rewards and prizes, or in paying a capitation grant of 2s. 6d. for each child.[66] The old custom of egg shackling, recorded at the school in 1891, was continuing in 1975.[67]

Efforts made by the curate to establish a Sunday school in 1818 were unsuccessful, although one with 100 pupils had 'recently' started in 1835, evidently held in the day-school room. The Wesleyans also then had a school.[68]

By 1868 two night schools for boys and girls, started by the rector's daughter, Julia Coles, were held in winter; reading, writing, the Bible, and the catechism were taught.[69] In 1872 Miss Coles and her brother, then rector, began four night schools for men, older and younger boys, and girls, and in 1873 a master from Bath was engaged for them and the Sunday schools. A night school for younger boys was revived in 1874 but discontinued in 1876 because of poor attendances.[70]

In 1818 there were one or two dame schools and a school for girls.[71] A private girls' school for four

[44] S.R.O., DD/SFR 8/1, f. 7.
[45] S.R.O., Q/RR, meeting-house lics.; D/D/V Dioc. bk. 1776.
[46] J. Vickers, *Thomas Coke*, 34; J. Thomas, *Two Letters to the Revd. Thomas Coke* (1777), 1 sqq.
[47] S.R.O., D/N/spc 1; D/D/Rm 2.
[48] S.R.O., D/D/Rm 2; H.O. 129/318/1/1/2; E. Devon R.O. 64/2/9/1B; ex inf. the Revd. W. G. Butler, Crewkerne.
[49] H.O. 129/318/1/1/2.
[50] S.R.O., D/P/she. b 1/1/1; D/N/spc box 3.
[51] S.R.O., D/D/Rm 2.   [52] S.R.O., D/D/ol 9.
[53] *12th Rep. Com. Char.* H.C. 358, pp. 428–9, 431–2 (1825), x; S.R.O., D/P/she. b 2/1/3, extract from will of Thomas Rich.   [54] S.R.O. D/P/she. b 2/1/4.
[55] *Digest of Returns to Sel. Cttee. on Educ. of Poor,* H.C. 224 (1819), ix (2).
[56] *Educ. Enquiry Abstract,* H.C. 62 (1835), xlii.
[57] Tablet on building. There is a reference to the 'new school house' there in November 1837: S.R.O., D/P/she. b 9/1/1.   [58] *Church Sch. Inquiry, 1846–7.*
[59] S.R.O., DD/EDS 2954; C/E 28. The date of 1865

is sometimes given in error: *Kelly's Dir. Som.* (1883).
[60] *Rep. Com. on Children and Women in Agric.* [4202-1], p. 699, H.C. (1868–9), xiii; S.R.O., D/P/she. b 1/1/1.
[61] S.R.O., D/P/she. b 1/1/1.
[62] School log bk. 1890–1929, *penes* the headmaster; *Return of Schs.* [C. 7529] H.C. (1894), lxv.
[63] S.R.O., C/E 28; school log bk. 1890–1929.
[64] School log bk. 1890–1929.
[65] *Bd. of Educ., List 21, 1938* (H.M.S.O.), 351.
[66] Char. Com. files.
[67] School log bk. 1890–1929; local information. For egg shackling see Ruth L. Tongue, *Som. Folklore,* ed. K. M. Briggs, 157.
[68] *Digest of Returns to Sel. Cttee. on Educ. of Poor,* H.C. 224 (1819), ix (2); *Educ. Enquiry Abstract,* H.C. 62 (1835), xlii.
[69] *Rep. Com. on Children and Women in Agric.* [4202-1], p. 699, H.C. (1868–9), xiii.
[70] S.R.O., D/P/she. b 1/1/1.
[71] *Digest of Returns to Sel. Cttee. on Educ. of Poor,* H.C. 224 (1819), ix (2).

boarders was being run by a clergyman's daughters in 1851.[72]

CHARITIES FOR THE POOR. In 1481–2 the reeve of the manor bought bread for 'the charity of St. Nicholas' with rent of a piece of land.[73] No other reference to the charity has been noted.

William Owsley, rector of Shepton (d. 1630), left £45 to buy ½ a. and build a hospital at Shepton for four poor men.[74] The charity is not mentioned thereafter but the bequest may have led to the use of the former church house as an alms- or poorhouse.

In the early 17th century William Drew and John Cogan purchased an annuity of £3 from the manor of Chedington (Dors.), then held by William Owsley, evidently for charitable purposes. From 1625 the annuity was distributed annually to the poor before Christmas Day. It was being paid to the second poor c. 1776.[75]

In 1641 the inhabitants of Shepton, having £160 for the poor, bought a rent-charge of £8 4s. 4d. from an estate in Curry Rivel. In 1824 the income was distributed to the second poor.[76]

Henry Wherriott of Shepton Beauchamp left £100 for apprenticing or to be distributed to the poor of the parish. The money was lent out to individuals and income of £6 was distributed to the poor in 1683. During the late 17th century £3 was usually given with each apprentice and the last distribution to the poor, for want of an apprentice, was made in 1695. In 1733 an annuity of £4 a year was purchased from an estate in South Petherton. The annuity was apparently not paid between 1755 and 1786, but after Chancery proceedings, the income continued to be used for apprentices.[77]

William Glanfield (d. 1732) left 9 a. of land in South Petherton in trust, the profits to be spent after his wife's death, which occurred in 1745, in binding poor boys as apprentices. In 1787 the income was £12 18s. 8d., subsequently rising to £24 c. 1800. The charity was misspent before 1824 'by binding out the worthless portion of the children ... in the neighbouring parishes in order to get rid of the burthen'. At the same time there was nearly £262 in hand, more than half held by an insolvent trustee who could only pay 4s. in the pound. It was then suggested that any surplus from the charity might be devoted to the education of the poor. In 1881 the income stood at £23 a year.[78]

The charities had a long history of maladministration, the curate stating in 1819 that they were 'most flagrantly abused, as the feoffees embezzle the profits to the amount of a great many hundred pounds'.[79] In 1881 the charities together were producing an income of £45 9s. 4d. including bequests for education and £7 5s. used for the maintenance of the church house. Under a Scheme of 1886 all existing sources of income were consolidated under the title of the Shepton Beauchamp charities. From the income, £12 to £25 was reserved for education, up to £15 was to be spent on the deserving poor, and the residue used to apprentice poor children and to outfit those under 21 entering any trade or service. The church house was sold in 1935. The rent-charge on lands in South Petherton was redeemed in 1959, and land was sold in 1887, 1967, and 1969. In 1966 the income from investments and land totalled £85 19s. 8d. In that year £5 was granted for education, £15 for apprenticing, and £30 distributed to the poor at Christmas.[80]

Under the will of F. W. G. D. Robins (d. 1934) £200 was left to his trustees to pay £4 to the bell-ringers for a muffled peal on All Souls Day, to provide sweets for the infants of the parish on their birthdays, and for egg shackling, the residue to be devoted to general charitable purposes within the parish.[81] Surplus revenue from the charity, known as the Robins Trust, was used in 1953 to install electric lighting in the village streets.[82] The donor's intentions were being fulfilled in 1975.

WAMBROOK

THE PARISH of Wambrook had an area of 1,867 a. in 1901.[1] In 1966 573 a. were transferred to the civil parish from that of Chardstock (Devon, formerly Dors.).[2] Wambrook lies 1¼ mile WSW. from Chard, extending for 2¾ miles east to west and 1¼ mile north to south. Formerly in Dorset, the civil parish was transferred to Somerset in 1896.[3] It was included in Beaminster hundred by 1286, in Sherborne hundred in 1346, and by 1428 again in Beaminster, known as the hundred of Beaminster and Redborne in the 19th century.[4] Its northern boundary, once that of Somerset, marches with Whitestaunton and Weston, a detached area of Combe St. Nicholas. To the east it is bounded by Chard, to the south and south-east by Chardstock, and to the west by Membury (Devon).

The parish is divided in two by a north–south ridge which rises to over 825 ft. in the north, and formed the northern end of Bewley down. To the east the land falls away to a valley lying along a fault line on the sides of which lie the two principal settlements of Higher Wambrook and Lower Wambrook, the lowest point being at 350 ft. on the SE. boundary at Castle wood. Further east the ground rises again to over 700 ft. West of the ridge, in the NW. part of the parish, lie the settlement of Wortheal, Bickham wood, and another valley, at the foot of which the land drops to 400 ft. Most of the higher

[72] H.O. 107/1927.
[73] Bradford Central Libr., Swinton MSS., acct. 1481–2.
[74] Prob. 11/157 (P.C.C. 59 Scroope).
[75] *12th Rep. Com. Char.* H.C. 358, pp. 426–7 (1825), x; S.R.O., D/D/V Dioc. bk. 1776.
[76] *12th Rep. Com. Char.* 427–8.
[77] Ibid. 431; par. rec., acct. bk. Wherriott's char. 1683–1843.
[78] *12th Rep. Com. Char.* 429–30; *Char. Donations, 1787–8,* H.C. 511 (1816), xvi; Char. Com. files.

[79] *Digest of Returns to Sel. Cttee. on Educ. of Poor,* H.C. 224 (1819), ix (2). [80] Char. Com. files.
[81] Ibid. [82] S.R.O., D/P/she. b 1/1/1.
[1] *Census* (1901). This article was completed in 1975.
[2] *Census* (1971).
[3] Local Govt. Order P. 1164.
[4] *Feud. Aids,* ii. 7, 59, 79; *L. & P. Hen. VIII,* xvii, p. 494; *Kelly's Dir. Som.* (1897). The parish was entered under both Beaminster and Sherborne hundreds in 1428: *Feud. Aids,* ii. 75, 70.

ground is clay, the two valleys lying on bands of Upper Greensand over Lower Lias. There are also outcrops of chalk between the 500 and 600 ft. contours on the east side of the parish, and on the lias and chalk both stone and marl were dug from the 13th century.[5] Arable land lies principally on the high ground in the NE., and the upper slopes of both valleys together with the area around Wortheal are well wooded.

The principal road through Wambrook enters from Chard in the NE. along the parish boundary before turning SW. across Bewley down and leaving the parish in the SW. for Stockland and ultimately Honiton (Devon). This road was adopted by the Chard turnpike trust as the main route to Honiton in 1776.[6] Another road, also from Chard and known as Haselcombe Lane in 1509,[7] enters from the east, running SW. through Lower Wambrook and then west to Linnington before turning north to Lancin to link with the old turnpike road. The present main road from Chard to Honiton followed the same course through the north-west of the parish at the beginning of the 19th century and, under the Chard turnpike trust, became the main route to Honiton in 1811. Two variations in its line through Bickham wood were introduced in 1813 and 1814. The road had reverted to its former course by 1828.[8] Bewley down was a maze of tracks before inclosure in 1816 and in the early 19th century a lane ran north from the Cotley inn at Lower Wambrook following the contour to fields in the NE. of the parish. Higher and Lower Wambrook are linked by a lane from north to south past the church and other lanes link the parish with hamlets in Whitestaunton, Membury, and Chardstock. Palfrey's Lane, evidently named from a 17th-century yeoman family of Wambrook, runs NW. through the eastern corner of the parish and crosses the northern boundary at Cockcrow or Cockcrowing Stone, so called in 1765.[9]

The original settlement was probably in the area of the church, north of which lay the manor-house. Immediately south and SE. lies Lower Wambrook, known as Haselcombe by the 13th century, which includes Dinnetts Farm, named after another 17th-century family.[10] The second, and possibly later, hamlet of Higher Wambrook occurs as 'Higher Wambrook next the rectory' in 1533,[11] and includes Drakes, Wilmington, and Wambrook farms. The parish also includes several scattered and early farm sites. Linnington, SW. of Lower Wambrook, takes its name from 'the hill called Lullindone', mentioned c. 1200 (Lyllyngedoone in 1520), and Box Cottage there is called the Box, presumably from its hedged enclosure, in the 13th century.[12]

In the extreme south of the parish Castle wood is recorded in 1422, probably the home of Laurence du Chastel in 1311.[13] Lancin farm in the centre of the parish occurs as Londenesham or Londesham in the 13th century (Lansham in 1517) and Wortheal in the NW. as Wrthiale or Wurthihale c. 1200.[14] A circular embanked and ditched enclosure, with associated field system, has been traced SW. of Wortheal farm-house, possibly of pre-Roman Iron Age date.[15] Also in the NW. are Loomcroft, found as a field-name in 1550, the site of Colemans, mentioned in 1517, and Coombes farm, purchased by the Combe family in 1567.[16] Dearhams on the SW. boundary was referred to as Dorham in the 13th century.[17] The other farms in the parish were generally established in the 19th century on lands inclosed from Bewley down. Mancroft takes its name from fields called Mannecrofts inclosed in 1421–2, Salt Box was mentioned in 1838 and is now known as Mounters Hill, and Shaggs Flood is so called from the Segge or Shegge family, living in the parish by 1509.[18] Oatlands, Downlands, and Broad Oak are all mid-19th-century creations. Broad Oak was probably built c. 1850 by Brian Charles Bordes, purchased c. 1862 by Thomas Palmer Deane (d. 1873), and has since been held by members of the Eames family.[19] Beulah Cottage at Higher Wambrook, which occurs as Balah Cottage in 1865,[20] is a corruption of Bewley. Houses of 17th-century origin are Loomcroft, Lancin (two on either side of the road), Dinnetts, and Drakes farms. Apart from these, most of the buildings are 19th century.

There were two licensed victuallers in the parish in 1720 and two inns there in 1753, the Old inn and the Royal Oak, both held by members of the Seaward family, innkeepers by 1723. The Old inn evidently changed its name to the Hare and Hounds between 1754 and 1757, being last recorded in 1760, and the Royal Oak was mentioned until 1759. References to other inns include the Rose and Crown (1761–70), the Red Lion (1762, later the White Hart, 1764), and the Bell (1765).[21] The New inn at Lower Wambrook, referred to in 1867, was known as the Cotley inn in 1975.[22]

The Cotley harriers, formed c. 1796 at Cotley in Chardstock by Thomas Deane, passed to his son Thomas Palmer Deane of Broad Oak in 1855. The hounds were subsequently kennelled at Broad Oak, the master in 1974 being Lt.-Col. R. F. P. Eames of Cotley, great-great-grandson of the founder.[23]

There were about 60 communicants in the parish c. 1600.[24] The population stood at 138 in 1801, rose sharply to 174 in 1811 and 201 in 1821, and

[5] University of Nottingham, MiD 2139/1.
[6] Chard Turnpike Act, 17 Geo. III, c. 89 (Priv. Act).
[7] Univ. of Nott., Mi 5/166/31.
[8] Chard Turnpike Act, 55 Geo. III, c. lx (Local and Personal); S.R.O., D.P. 42, 48, 95.
[9] O.S. Map 1", sheet 21 (1809 edn.); S.R.O. DD/EM, conveyance, 22 Nov. 1619; I. Taylor, *Map of Dors.* (1765).
[10] Univ. of Nott., MiD 2137/4; *S. & D. N. & Q.* xiii. 211–12.   [11] Univ. of Nott., MiD 5/164/32.
[12] Ibid. 2137/3; 5/166/35.
[13] C.P. 40/189 rot. 184; Univ. of Nott., Mi 6/170/11.
[14] Univ. of Nott., MiD 2137/2, 4; 3849/1; 5/166/33.
[15] Ex inf. Mr. M. Aston from investigation by Mr. Roger Carter, Chard.

[16] Univ. of Nott., MiM 223; Mi 5/166/33; S.R.O., DD/BR/gm 3.
[17] Univ. of Nott., MiD 2137/2.
[18] Ibid. Mi 5/166/30, 6/170/11; par. rec. chwdns. accts. 1838–1951.
[19] Par. rec., chwdns. accts. 1838–1951; ex inf. Miss M. Parmiter, Chardstock.
[20] J. G. Harrod and Co. *Postal and Commercial Dir. Dors.* (1865).
[21] D.R.O., Q.S. alehouse lics. and regs.
[22] *P.O. Dir. Dors.* (1867); *Kelly's Dir. Dors.* (1880); *Kelly's Dir. Som.* (1897–1939).
[23] *V.C.H. Som.* ii. 590; *The Field*, 22 Mar. 1962; ex inf. Mr. D. Eames, Wambrook.
[24] Salisbury Dioc. R.O., Dean's presentments, 1558–1603.

then more gradually to 291 in 1871. Thereafter it declined to 201 in 1901, remaining fairly stable until a further drop to 174 in 1931. There was a slight increase to 177 in 1951 and numbers stood at 142 in 1961 and 167 (including the area transferred from Chardstock) in 1971.[25]

Sir Simonds D'Ewes (1602–50), antiquarian writer, born in Chardstock, was educated between 1611 and 1614 by Christopher Marraker, rector of Wambrook 1591–1621.[26]

MANOR AND OTHER ESTATES. An estate of four hides at 'Awanbruth' was granted to the monastery of Sherborne (Dors.) between 802 and 839 by Egbert, king of the West Saxons.[27] The grant is probably to be linked with *WAMBROOK*, subsequently held with Chardstock manor, which had evidently been conveyed to Sherborne by King Cynewulf in the 8th century.[28] The possessions of Sherborne, formerly seat of a bishopric, were taken to endow the new see of Salisbury established in the 11th century, and Wambrook was probably included in the twelve hides assigned to Chardstock in 1086, when it was held by the bishop of Salisbury.[29] The bishop continued as overlord of the manor until at least 1540.[30]

The manor may have been held in 1086 by one of two knights, William and Walter, entered in Domesday under Chardstock.[31] It had been sub-infeudated by the mid 12th century when the fee of Nicholas Oliver of Wambrook was quitclaimed to the bishop by Baldwin, earl of Exeter (d. 1155).[32] Jordan Oliver was holding one fee under the bishop of Salisbury in 1166 and the manor evidently continued in the Oliver family as a second Jordan Oliver was holding lands in Wambrook in the early 13th century.[33] The latter may probably be identified with Sir Jordan Oliver of Dorset, husband of Sibyl de Aumale, who was evidently succeeded by Jordan Oliver (III), a justice in eyre and sheriff of Somerset and Dorset 1239–40, who probably lived in the parish.[34] The latter was probably followed by his son Walter Oliver (fl. 1240–83).[35] The manor had passed by 1280 to an heiress, Sibyl Oliver, wife of Humphrey de Beauchamp of Ryme (Dors.), from whom she was divorced between 1287 and 1290.[36] By 1292 Sibyl had carried

the manor to her second husband John de Aldham and in the following year Cecily, widow of John Beauchamp, Lord Beauchamp of Hatch, whose husband had acted as trustee for his brother Humphrey, unsuccessfully claimed dower in the estate.[37] In 1306 Sibyl Oliver granted the advowson and the reversion of the manor to John de Hertrugge and Nichole his wife, with a reservation for life to Sibyl's son William, and John and Nichole secured a quitclaim of the manor from Humphrey de Beauchamp two years later.[38] John de Hertrugge died in 1309 leaving a daughter Elizabeth, although Nichole retained her life-interest and was still holding the manor in 1330.[39] Sir John Streche (d. 1355) occurs as lord in 1346, possibly holding the manor at farm, and his son was born at Wambrook in 1341.[40] By 1354, however, the manor was held by John de Farnebergh and Elizabeth his wife, possibly daughter of John de Hertrugge, in which year they sold it to William son of John de Percy and Mary daughter of William Filoll (I) of Woodlands (Dors.) on their marriage, with remainder failing issue to the heirs of Willaim Filoll.[41] In 1390 the manor was quitclaimed to William Percy and Walter Clopton, Percy's tenant for life, by Thomas Beauchamp of Ryme, great-grandson of Humphrey, but Percy died in 1407 without issue.[42] Percy's widow Mary married secondly Richard Bannebury and in 1411 they granted the manor during Mary's life to William Filoll (II), grandson of William (I), for £20 a year.[43] William (II) and his wife Joan received a grant of the reversion from William's father John Filoll, and Joan entered on the manor after the death of Mary Bannebury.[44] Joan married secondly Sir William Cheyne and died in 1434, the manor descending on her death to her son John Filoll (d. 1468).[45] John's widow Margaret, who married secondly John Wroughton, evidently held a life-interest and in 1497 conveyed the lordship to her son William (later Sir William) Filoll (III).[46]

Sir William (d. 1527) left two daughters and coheirs, Anne wife of Sir Edward Willoughby and Catherine wife of Edward Seymour later duke of Somerset.[47] Catherine was 'repudiated' by her husband c. 1530, her children were disinherited, and the whole manor passed to Sir Edward Willoughby (d. 1540) and his wife.[48] Sir Edward's son Henry was succeeded by his son Sir Francis Willoughby.[49]

[25] *Census*, 1801–1971.
[26] *D.N.B.*
[27] H. P. R. Finberg, *Early Charters of Wessex*, 121.
[28] Ibid. 180. The identification of Chardstock with six hides at 'Snarstock' is not made by Finberg.
[29] Dugdale, *Mon.* i. 333; vi. 1292; *V.C.H. Dors.* iii. 72.
[30] Univ. of Nott., Mi 6/175/37.
[31] *V.C.H. Dors.* iii. 72.
[32] *Sarum Chart. and Doc.* (Rolls Ser.), 20–1.
[33] *Red Bk. Exch.* (Rolls Ser.), i. 236; Univ. of Nott., MiD 2137/2, 3; MiD 3849/1.
[34] *Cur. Reg. R.* iii, pp. 29, 260; iv, pp. 19, 65, 155; S. W. Rawlins, *Sheriffs of Som.* 9.
[35] *Bk. of Fees*, ii. 1378; *Cal. Close*, 1279–88, 246.
[36] *Feet of Fines, Dors. 1195–1327*, ed. E. A. and G. S. Fry, 188, 192–3; *Feud. Aids*, ii. 7; C.P. 40/67 rot. 39; C.P. 40/86 rot. 38d.; C.P. 40/100 rot. 31.
[37] C.P. 40/92 rot. 181; C.P. 40/100 rot. 31; *Feet of Fines, Dors. 1195–1327*, 188, 215. The John 'Abadam' who occurs as lord in 1303 is evidently a misreading for John Aldham: *Feud. Aids*, ii. 36. Ralph de Aldham unsuccess-

fully claimed lands in Wambrook in 1316: J.I. 1/1370 rot. 14d.
[38] *Feet of Fines, Dors. 1195–1327*, 234–5; C.P. 40/161 rot. 82; Univ. of Nott., MiD 2141.
[39] *Cal. Inq. p.m.* v, pp. 111–12; *Feud. Aids*, ii. 41; Univ. of Nott., MiD 2143, 2438.
[40] *Feud. Aids*, ii. 59; *Cal. Inq. p.m.* x, pp. 207–8; xi, pp. 302–3.
[41] *Feet of Fines, Dors. 1327–1485*, ed. E. A. and G. S. Fry, 88–9.
[42] *Cal. Close*, 1389–92, 188, 279; Hist. MSS. Com. 69, *Middleton*, p. 617.
[43] Univ. of Nott., MiD 2144; Hutchins, *Hist. Dors.* iii. 152.
[44] *S. & D. N. & Q.* xiii. 99; xvi. 279; *Cal. Close*, 1413–19, 305–6.
[45] *S. & D. N. & Q.* xiii. 99; xvii. 33–5; *Feud. Aids*, ii. 108.
[46] Hutchins, *Hist. Dors.* iii. 152; iv. 113; Univ. of Nott., MiD 2146–7.   [47] C 142/46/25.
[48] *Complete Peerage*, s.v. Seymour.
[49] Univ. of Nott., MiD 2149, 2150.

In 1588 the latter sold the manor to Henry and George Drake of London to finance the building of Wollaton Hall (Notts.).[50] In the same year the Drakes, as a condition of their purchase, sold certain estates to nominees of Sir Francis, and in 1619 enfranchised most, if not all, of the lands within the manor.[51] Subsequently certain fractions of the lordship were claimed by the representatives of some of those purchasers.

A quarter of the manor was held by the Revd. Gamaliel Chase of Yarcombe (Devon) in 1677, when it was settled on his son, the Revd. John Chase, and the latter's wife Margaret for their lives with remainder to John's son Gideon.[52] It is not mentioned thereafter but probably descended with the advowson.[53]

A further quarter was evidently held by John Woolmington of Wambrook and Dorchester (d. 1717) and was divided between his daughters and coheirs, Frances and Mary. Frances married the Revd. Henry Hooton of Moreton (Dors.) who, with his daughter Frances wife of Thomas Hyde, conveyed his lands in trust for sale in 1768, when they passed to Sir Richard Glyn of London, Bt. Mary, the second daughter, married Robert Wadham of Poole (Dors.). Wadham was declared bankrupt in 1737 and his brother and assignee, Martin Wadham, disposed of the other moiety to Sir Richard Glyn, thus reuniting the quarter lordship.[54] Glyn (d. 1773) was succeeded in turn by his son Sir Richard Carr Glyn of Gaunts (d. 1838) and grandson Sir Richard Plumptre Glyn (d. 1868).[55] In the earlier 19th century this quarter is referred to as a moiety of the manor.[56] In 1881 Sir Richard George Glyn, nephew of Sir R. P. Glyn, sold his quarter to Sarah West, Richard Bowerman West, Richard John Bowerman, and Thomas Palmer Eames.[57] Evidently by virtue of this grant Richard B. T. West (d. 1900) occurs as lord in 1897 and his first cousin, Thomas Deane Eames (d. 1936), from 1902 to 1914.[58] This quarter was probably held in 1974 by the latter's nephew, Lt.-Col. R. F. P. Eames of Cotley, Chardstock.[59]

John Beviss (I) (d. c. 1791) was purchasing lands in Wambrook between 1764 and 1789 and acquired a share in the manor, termed a moiety in the earlier 19th century. He was succeeded in turn by his son John (II) (d. 1809) and grandson John (III) (d. 1840). The last left four sons between whom his lands and, presumably, his share of the manor was divided.[60] Manorial rights were claimed by the representatives of John Beviss at least until 1939.[61]

The manor-house and fruit and herbage of its garden were mentioned in 1309.[62] Repairs were made in 1421–2 to the chamber and hall of what was evidently the manor-house, and in 1508–9 and 1509–10 sums were spent on rethatching the court-house.[63] In 1529 the churchwardens took a 60-year lease of the capital messuage and court barton for 4d. a year, and were ordered to repair their 'church house' in 1543.[64] A watercourse running to the court-house was mentioned in 1570, and a lease of the court-house to four persons was excepted from the sale of the manor in 1588.[65] When the manor was enfranchised the church house and Pounds Barton were sold with Drakes farm and continued to be mentioned at least until 1666.[66] The house evidently stood on part of Court mead north of the church.

On the break-up of the manor Drakes House, later Drakes farm, was sold in 1619 by Henry Drake to Simon Mathew of East Budleigh (Devon). Mathew settled the property on trustees for his granddaughters Honor, later wife of John Bowditch of Hawkchurch (Devon), and Mary, children of John and Agnes Drake. They, with their grandfather, sold the farm to Simon's daughter Honor Westcott in 1654, who conveyed it to her son Philip Westcott of Wambrook in 1661. Westcott sold in 1666 to Richard Tirrel, a Chard sheargrinder.[67] By will proved in 1705 Tirrel left the farm to his granddaughter Rebecca, widow of John Smith of Honiton (Devon), subject to remainders in favour of the family of his nephew Michael Tirrel of Minehead. On Rebecca's death c. 1758 the property fell into moieties between John Hossem (d. 1778), a Dunster cabinet-maker and great-grandson of Michael Tirrel, and Thomas Warren, a Dunster carpenter and wheelwright, grandson of Michael Tirrel. The two moieties were purchased by Sir Richard Carr Glyn in 1796 from John Hossem's son John and from Thomas Warren,[68] and sold by Sir Richard George Glyn with his quarter of the manor in 1881.

In accordance with the wishes of Sir Francis Willoughby, Henry and George Drake conveyed two tenements called Haselcombe and Linnington with 160 a. of land to Thomas Estmond (d. 1607) of Lodge, Chardstock, in 1588. The lands passed from Thomas to his son Nicholas Estmond and thence to his granddaughter Mary, wife of Humphrey Coffin.[69] The estate was sequestered during the Interregnum for Humphrey's recusancy.[70] Mary Coffin conveyed the premises to her son John Coffin of Wambrook in 1670, who sold them to Robert Smith of Hawkchurch (Devon), later of Salisbury, M.D. In 1690 Dr. Smith (d. 1694) settled the estate with some lands in Chardstock on himself and wife for their lives with remainder to Wadham College, Oxford. The first £20 of the

---

[50] P. A. Crowther, 'The Woodlands Estate, 1357–1527' (Nott. Univ. M.A. thesis, 1968), 20; Univ. of Nott., MiD 5/167/191.
[51] Wadham Coll. Oxf., Wambrook and Chardstock deeds 42/4, 5; S.R.O., DD/EM, deeds 16 Apr. 1588, 22 Nov. 1619; DD/BR/gm 4; D.R.O. 2698.
[52] D.R.O. 8375.
[53] D.R.O. 8377–81, 8548.
[54] Par. reg. burial of Mr. John Woolmington, 17 Apr. 1717; S.R.O., DD/BR/gm.
[55] Burke, Peerage (1949), 835–6.
[56] Hutchins, Hist. Dors. ii. 151.
[57] D.R.O. 2024.
[58] Kelly's Dir. Som. (1902–14); ex inf. Miss Parmiter.
[59] Ex inf. Miss Parmiter.

[60] S.R.O., DD/EM; Hutchins, Hist. Dors. ii. 151.
[61] Kelly's Dir. Som. (1939).
[62] C 134/16/7.
[63] Univ. of Nott., Mi 5/167/85; Mi 6/170/11.
[64] Ibid. Mi 5/166/38, 41.
[65] Ibid. Mi 5/167/191; Mi 6/179/17.
[66] D.R.O. 2698–2708.
[67] Ibid. The farm probably took its name from a family called Drake living in the parish by 1532: Univ. of Nott., MiM 223.
[68] S.R.O., DD/BR/gm 7, 18.
[69] Wadham Coll. Oxf., deeds of Wambrook and Chardstock, 42/4–13; 10/2/3/1; S. & D. N. & Q. xiii. 210–11.
[70] Cal. Cttee. for Compounding, iii. 2064; iv. 2635.

income was to be paid to the college chaplains and the residue to the moderators. The college retained the property until 1875 when it was sold. It then comprised 185 a. in Wambrook and Chardstock based on Linnington Barton.[71]

ECONOMIC HISTORY. In 1309 the manor was valued at £6 1s. 11½d. a year, and the demesne included 180 a. of arable, 8 a. of meadow, several pasture worth 3s. 4d., wood and underwood worth 3s., and a water-mill.[72] A number of freeholds had been created in the previous century and more, at Wortheal before c. 1200, Lancin and Haselcombe, and by 1309 7 freehold tenants paid 20s. 0½d., while there were 17 villeins, 2 cottars, and 4 tenants rendering chevage (capitagiarii), paying total rents of 43s. 3d.[73]

Demesne leasing from 1421–2 increased the income of the manor from £15 2s. in 1416 to £25 13s. 5d., but by 1435 the value had fallen to £14 2s. The demesne holding in 1435 was 200 a. of arable, 12 a. of meadow, 20 a. of inclosed pasture, and 200 a. of hill pasture.[74] The value fell slightly in 1468, to £13 6s. 8d., but had returned to its earlier level by 1508–9, when the income was £21 13s. 11d. based on a rental of £20 13s. 6d.[75] The rental remained constant until 1573–4, in which year entry fines totalled £430.[76] After 1574 the income cannot be ascertained. Sir Edward Willoughby (d. 1540) called Wambrook 'the best manor that I have by my wife' and the family sold it for £2,400 in 1588.[77]

In 1550 the number of freeholders had fallen to two (Wortheal, and Mangerton in Netherbury, Dors.)[78] and there were 18 customary tenants sharing the demesne. The largest holding was 150 a., 5 tenants held between 50 a. and 70 a., 3 between 25 a. and 50 a., and 7 under 25 a. There were 15 a. of copyhold land at Yarcombe, part called Olyver's mead taking its name from the medieval lords.[79] There was by 1550 no indication of open fields, though field-names included North, South, East, West, and Middle fields, probably existing in the north-east of the parish before the 15th century.[80] That area was also the site of Langland where in 1570 the tenants of Higher Wambrook were required to repair the way 'used for carrying grain from the fields' and not to use the way after grain had been sown or before it was harvested. There were three customary tenants holding arable in Langland in 1550.[81]

Woodland provided a small but constant income for the manor.[82] Tenants were forbidden to cut underwood in Bickham wood in 1517 and one was fined for shrouding and lopping ash trees there in 1566.[83] Castle wood had been partly leased by 1530, comprised 45 a. held by two tenants in 1567–8, and by 1606 had been developed as the site of Castle Wood farm.[84] Bere wood had shrunk from 26 a. to 22 a. by 1567–8 and was later converted to pasture. By 1619 the northern part was held with Drakes farm, and by 1667 the southern section had passed to Wilmington farm.[85] Bickham wood was common to the tenants by 1517 and contained 60 a. with 100 oaks, ashes, and alders in 1550, when John Drake had the right to cut holly there. It had fallen to 40 a. by 1567–8, continued as common until the 1816 inclosure, and in 1975 formed the principal area of woodland in the parish.[86]

Bewley down, the largest area of common land within the manor, was pastured by all the tenants. By 1509 the lord had leased common pasture there to three residents of Southay in Whitestaunton.[87] In 1561 the tenant of Wortheal was illegally stocking the lord's common and Chardstock tenants had over-stocked it.[88] The hedge forming the northern boundary with Whitestaunton and Whitestaunton gate there were constantly out of repair in the 16th century.[89] The common contained 524 a. of furze and heath in 1567–8 and, with Bickham wood, 680 a. when inclosed by Act of Parliament in 1816.[90] In 1513 intercommoning with Whitestaunton tenants was practised on Southay hill, and in 1772 the vestry agreed to prosecute any person carrying furze, fern, or turf out of the commons.[91]

Of the early freeholds Wortheal had 70 a. and was valued at 32s. a year in 1541 when it passed from John Hody to his son John.[92] When the tenements were enfranchised at the break-up of the manor, John Legg acquired 120 a. at Haselcombe, Lancin, and Linnington in 1588 which subsequently formed Lancin farm and were still held by the Leggs in 1696.[93] The estate of 160 a. purchased in the same year by Thomas Estmond, of Lodge in Chardstock, included Castle Wood farm of c. 40 a. which descended to his grandson, Christopher Estmond of Gillingham (Dors.).[94] In 1701 Estmond sold the lands to John Deane whose family retained Castle Wood until its conveyance to John Tanner in 1814. The Tanners still held the farm in 1869.[95] John de Wolminton was witnessing Wambrook deeds in the early 13th century, and the Woolmington family had acquired lands of 90 a. by 1667

[71] Wadham Coll. Oxf., deeds of Wambrook and Chardstock, 42/15–41.   [72] C 134/16/7.
[73] Ibid.; Univ. of Nott., MiD 2037, 2137/4, 2138–40.
[74] S. & D. N. & Q. xiii. 99; Univ. of Nott., Mi 6/170/11; C 139/65/39.   [75] Univ. of Nott., Mi 5/167/85.
[76] Ibid. MiM 152, 154–6, 156/1–2; Mi 5/167/86, 88; Mi 5/169b/27; Mi 6/170/22–3, 27, 33.
[77] Notts. Misc. iv. (Thoroton Soc. Rec. Ser. xxiv), 48; Univ. of Nott. Mi 5/167/191.
[78] Lands at Mangerton were held with the manor by 1306; Feet of Fines, Dors. 1195–1327, 234–5.
[79] Univ. of Nott., MiM 223; MiD 2140. The manor also included a burgage tenement in Dorchester, held by a tenant at will, in 1567–8: ibid. Mi 6/179/17.
[80] Ibid. MiM 223.   [81] Ibid.; Mi 6/179/17.
[82] e.g. ibid. Mi 5/167/85.
[83] Ibid. MiM 112/10; Mi 5/164/33.
[84] Ibid. Mi 6/170/11; Mi 5/166/40; Mi 6/179/17; C 6/230. The two divisions of Castle wood were called

Bucknoll's and Crandon's after their respective tenants.
[85] Univ. of Nott., Mi 6/179/17; D.R.O. 2698; S.R.O., DD/BR/gm 3.
[86] Univ. of Nott., MiM 112/10; Mi 6/179/17; S.R.O., inclosure award.
[87] Univ. of Nott., Mi 5/166/31; Mi 6/179/10, 17.
[88] Ibid. Mi 6/174/41.
[89] e.g. ibid. Mi 5/166/30; Mi 6/179/17, cts. 12 Sept. 1569, 18 Oct. 1571.
[90] Ibid. Mi 6/179/17; S.R.O., inclosure award.
[91] Univ. of Nott., Mi 6/179/17; par. rec., chwdns.' accts. 1736–1837.
[92] C 142/62/88; C 142/64/183.
[93] S.R.O., DD/EM, enfranchisement 20 Aug. 1588; conveyance 4 Nov. 1696.
[94] Wadham College, Oxf., Wambrook deeds, 42/5; C 6/230.
[95] C.P. 25(2)/826/12 Wm. III Hil.; S.R.O., DD/PTR, box 4, deeds of Castle Wood fm.

which eventually became known as Wilmington farm. John Woolmington (d. 1640–1) at his death had 80 sheep, 13 head of cattle, and 3 horses.[96] Combe farm, purchased by John Combe of Chardstock in 1667, was sold by his grandson in 1735 to Henry Hooton of Moreton (Dors.). Wilmington, Coombes, and Drakes farms, a total of 280 a., were acquired in the late 18th century by Sir Richard Carr Glyn.[97] John Beviss, of Weston in Combe St. Nicholas, was from 1764 purchasing lands in Wambrook amounting to over 300 a. in all, the largest holding being 145 a. bought in 1789 from the heirs of Le Roy White (d. 1777).[98]

By 1844 the largest landowners in the parish were the Beviss family with 306 a., including the newly-created Wambrook farm, and Sir Richard Glyn with 282 a. Thomas Deane held 228 a. based on Dinnetts and Box, and John Deane 119 a. at Lancin. Wadham College, Oxford, had 185 a. at Linnington, James Benjamin Coles 181 a., including Wortheal, Thomas Mallock 120 a. at Dearhams, and the rector 103 a. including Shaggs Flood and Downlands. The largest farming units were then Wortheal with 170 a., Linnington with 161 a., Wambrook farm with 152 a., Dinnetts with 140 a., and three others, Drakes, Wilmington, and Lancin, with over 100 a. each. The parish then comprised 822 a. of grassland, 800 a. of arable, and 130 a. of coppice and woodland.[99] The principal 19th-century crops were wheat, barley, oats, and apples; flax dressers occur in 1791 and 1795 and a flax merchant, Joel Dampier of Loomcroft, in 1817.[1] The farming units continued relatively unchanged in 1975, although some of the larger holdings, such as at Wortheal, 218 a. in 1975,[2] had been extended.

A lease of a tenement in 1285 included licence to burn lime on the hill at Haselcombe.[3] Robert Pinney paid 8d. a year from 1547 until at least 1576 to dig stone at Whiteland on the waste of the lord and to build lime kilns there.[4] There are repeated references to four common marl pits in the manor from 1588, one of which lay in a close called Charlepitt in 1619,[5] and the scars left by quarrying operations and former lime kilns can be seen north-east of Lower Wambrook on either side of the road to Chard there, on the southern boundary of the parish near Oatlands, in the field called Whiteland on the northern boundary, in fields called Brookland east of Higher Wambrook, and in those called Snowdon on the north-western boundary. A further source of limestone lay in Haselcombe mead immediately south of Dinnetts farm in Chardstock parish. Chardstock had fewer sources of limestone

than Wambrook and that may explain the tortuous nature of the parish boundary near Lower Wambrook.[6]

Being close to Chard, Wambrook had links with the cloth trade. A weaver occurs in 1551, and in 1561 Roger Glade, a yeoman, left his broad looms to his son John.[7] A John Glade, weaver, was mentioned in 1589 and it was probably he who was described as a coverlet-weaver at his death in 1626. He then possessed a pair of coverlet looms and two pairs of cloth looms.[8] A hosier occurs in 1663, a tailor in 1764, and there were four dressmakers in the parish in 1851.[9] With those exceptions the parishioners were almost wholly engaged in agriculture.

The manor included a water-mill worth 6s. 8d. a year in 1309 but the mill was not mentioned thereafter.[10] A pasture called Millewere and Courteorchard, evidently near the manor-house, was mentioned in 1513 and demesne meadow called Mylmede in 1520.[11] A lease of a way called the Milleway with the 'mill stream' was granted in 1552, and in 1841 fields called Millway lay west of the church on either side of a stream there.[12]

LOCAL GOVERNMENT. Manor court rolls survive in broken series for 1506–33, 1543, 1559–61, 1565–73.[13] Courts, described as *curie* or *curie manerii*, were usually held twice a year in April or May and September or October by 1422, and there was an isolated reference to a three-weekly court in 1414.[14] Apart from normal tenurial matters court business included repairs to buildings, common gates, and hedges, the scouring of ditches and watercourses, subletting without licence, entertaining persons of evil reputation, and the sale of pannage and windfall timber. No manorial officers were appointed by the court, which was summoned by a man serving as both bailiff and rent-collector. He was receiving a stipend of 6s. 8d. a year between 1509 and 1521, raised by 1550 to 13s. 4d. with the sale of branches of trees. A woodward occurred in 1521.[15]

There were two churchwardens from 1530 but only one from the late 17th century.[16] In addition to the wardens there were two *economi* between 1597 and 1610, possibly to be identified with the two sidesmen who occur in 1638.[17] There were also two overseers and a constable in 1642.[18] A pound-keeper was appointed by the vestry from 1772 and two 'reeves' between 1789 and 1792. From 1840 there were two churchwardens, two overseers,

[96] Univ. of Nott., MiD 2137/2, 3; S.R.O., DD/BR/gm 3; W.R.O., Dean's ct., will and invent. of John Woolmington, 1640–1.
[97] S.R.O., DD/BR/gm 1, 3.
[98] S.R.O., DD/EM.   [99] D.R.O., tithe award.
[1] P.O. Dir. Dors. (1865); Kelly's Dir. Dors. (1897); par. reg. marr. 1754–1811, bap. 1813–1909.
[2] Ex inf. Mr. F. Burrough, Wambrook.
[3] Univ. of Nott., MiD 2139/1.
[4] Ibid. MiM 155, 223; Mi 6/174/43.
[5] S.R.O., DD/EM, conveyance, 22 Nov. 1619.
[6] Ex. inf. Miss M. Parmiter. The field-name Quarry Napps is found in this area in 1816: S.R.O., inclosure award.
[7] Prob. 11/34 (P.C.C. 28 Bucke), will of William Hill; W.R.O., Dean's ct., probate reg. 2.
[8] W.R.O., Dean's ct., 5/84, will of John Glade;

Chardstock peculiar, inventory 15 July 1626.
[9] W.R.O., Dean's ct., Chardstock peculiar, will of Leonard Staple, 1663; par. reg. marr. 1754–1811; H.O. 107/1927.
[10] C 134/16/7.
[11] Univ. of Nott., Mi 6/179/9; Mi 5/166/35.
[12] Ibid. MiM 223; Mi 6/179/17; D.R.O., tithe award.
[13] Univ. of Nott., MiM 112/10; Mi 5/164/33–4, 44; Mi 5/166/16, 30–41, 43; Mi 6/170/32; Mi 6/174/41; Mi 6/179/9, 10, 12, 16, 17.
[14] Ibid. Mi 6/170/11; MiD 2145.
[15] Ibid. Mi 5/166/35; Mi 5/167/85; Mi 5/169b/27; MiM 223.
[16] Ibid. Mi 5/166/40; Salisbury Dioc. R.O., Prebend of Chardstock, presentments.
[17] Salisbury Dioc. R.O., Dean's presentments.
[18] Protestation Returns, Dors. ed. E. A. Fry, 75.

two waywardens, and a guardian. A salaried assistant overseer was appointed from 1878.[19]

In 1772 the churchwardens sold what was probably a poorhouse on Bewley down for £13 10s. and devoted the money to the use of the poor.[20] There was a poorhouse lying south of Wortheal farm by 1814 and another immediately south-west of the New Inn by 1844.[21] One of them, described as the parish house, was repaired by the churchwardens in 1841, and the poorhouse near the inn was occupied by a labourer, his family of four, and a lodger in 1851.[22] The poorhouse was repaired and rethatched in 1877–8 and the materials of an old cottage, probably the same building, were sold in 1897.[23] The parish became part of the Chard poor-law union in 1836.[24]

CHURCH. The chapel, later church, of Wambrook was first mentioned in a deed of 1215–20 by which Philip of Yarcombe, chaplain, probably the parish priest, acknowledged that the chapel was a member of the prebendal church of Chardstock. It had evidently formed part of the grant of that church to Salisbury cathedral by Gerbert de Percy before 1158.[25] As a member of the prebend the parish had to repair part of Chardstock churchyard wall in 1573 and payments for the repair of the wall and church 'hatches' there continued at least until 1811.[26] The benefice was a rectory by 1306 and so remained despite a fruitless attempt to treat it as a free chapelry and dissolve it in 1551.[27] The rectory was united with the livings of Combe St. Nicholas (where the incumbent lives) and Whitestaunton in 1974, and then transferred from the diocese of Salisbury to that of Bath and Wells.

The advowson was held with the lordship of the manor by 1306 and descended with it.[28] Rectors were presented by the Crown in 1416, presumably by lapse, and for single turns by George and John Swallow in 1555 and by William Estmond and Bernard Prince in 1591.[29] The patronage was granted to Alexander and Ann Brett of Whitestaunton in 1594, presumably for a single turn, and c. 1611 to George Thornhill of Thornhill in Stalbridge (Dors.).[30] The advowson was sold by the lord c. 1620 to John Chase of Membury (Devon) (d. 1641), who presented his son Gamaliel (rector 1621–45), when the rectory was stated to be held

of the earl of Bristol as of Sherborne Castle.[31] Chase left the rectory to Gamaliel but the patronage was exercised by the Dorset Standing Committee in 1650.[32] The advowson passed from Gamaliel Chase's son John (rector 1648–9, 1662–81) to John's son Gideon Chase of Chard and Upottery (Devon), and in 1710 Gideon's son John sold it to William Bragg, of Sadborow in Thorncombe (Devon formerly Dors.), his mortgagee since 1706.[33] William (d. 1713) was succeeded in turn by his grandsons, William (d. 1726) and John Bragg (d. 1749), and from the last the advowson passed to his son John (d. 1786), and his grandson, John Bragg, all of Sadborow.[34] John Bragg sold the patronage to Charles Edwards of Chard (d. 1813) in 1796; Martha Edwards (d. 1842) presented in 1818, and Charles's son Henry (rector 1818–50) in 1850.[35] The son of the last, Henry Edwards (rector 1850–81) apparently sold the advowson to the Revd. H. H. A. Smith (assistant curate 1857–62), patron from 1859 until at least 1880.[36] The advowson was held in 1882 and 1888 by Admiral John William Dorville of Great Malvern (Worcs.) and in 1894 by Dorville's executors. By 1901 it had passed to the Revd. Melville Russell Moore, by 1906 to the Revd. Frederick Williams, of Bettiscombe in Charmouth (Dors.), father of the rector presented in 1901, and between 1919 and 1921 to Williams's daughter, Mrs. Agnes Elsie Eames, who presented until 1948. The patron from 1952 was Mrs. Eames's son, Lt.-Col. R. F. P. Eames of Cotley, Chardstock, who became joint patron of the united benefice with the bishop of Bath and Wells in 1974.[37]

The benefice was valued in 1334 at £4 6s. 8d.[38] By 1405 an annual pension of £1 was payable by the rector to the prebendary of Chardstock, evidently in lieu of tithes, and in 1535 8d. was being paid to the vicar of Chardstock. The value of the church in the latter year rose to £8 7s. 0½d. net,[39] a total which fluctuated between £7 10s. and £9 until c. 1600.[40] The rectory was 'of mean value' in 1646 and provided £41 3s. 4d. gross in 1650.[41] Between 1831 and 1864 the living was stated to be worth £262, although the figure evidently referred only to the tithes, the gross income standing at c. £324 in 1879 and in 1883 at £317.[42] The payment of £1 a year to the owner of the great tithes of Chardstock was still continuing in 1795.[43]

[19] Par. rec., chwdns.' accts. 1736–1837, 1838–1951.
[20] Ibid. 1736–1837.
[21] S.R.O., D.P. 48; D.R.O., tithe award.
[22] Par. rec., chwdns.' accts. 1838–1951; H.O. 107/1927.
[23] Par. rec., chwdns.' accts. 1838–1951.
[24] Poor Law Com. 2nd Rep. p. 547.
[25] Sarum Chart. and Doc. (Rolls Ser.), 80; Reg. St. Osmund (Rolls Ser.), i. 205. A possible reference to a chaplain of Wambrook ('Whmberiche') occurs among witnesses to a copy deed of between 1194 and 1205: Exeter Cathedral Libr., Dean and Chapter gen. cartulary, p. 44.
[26] Salisbury Dioc. R.O., Dean's act bk. 4; par. rec., chwdns.' accts. 1736–1837.
[27] Reg. Simon de Gandavo (Cant. and York Soc. xl), 895; E 315/128, ff. 71–3.
[28] Feet of Fines, Dors. 1195–1327, 234–5; Univ. of Nott., MiD 2141; Cal. Close, 1389–92, 188; 1413–19, 306; S. & D. N. & Q. xvi. 279.
[29] Cal. Pat. 1416–22, 12; Proc. Dors. Nat. Hist. and Arch. Soc. lxxiv. 78.
[30] C.P. 25(2)/124/1569, 36 Eliz. I Hil.; C 3/306/21.

[31] C 3/306/21; C 145/521/157.
[32] C 145/521/157; Min. Bks. of the Dors. Standing Cttee. ed. C. H. Mayo, 462, 564–5.
[33] D.R.O. 8374–81. [34] D.R.O., LL 31.
[35] D.R.O. 8548A and B; M.I. in ch.
[36] P.O. Dir. Dors. (1859–75); Kelly's Dir. Dors. (1880); par. reg. One of Smith's daughters was baptized Ethel Katie Dorville, which suggests a link for the subsequent descent of the advowson.
[37] Bps. regs. penes the Diocesan Registrar, Salisbury; Kelly's Dir. Som. (1897–1939); ex inf. Miss Parmiter.
[38] Tax. Eccl. (Rec. Com.), 181; Inq. Non. (Rec. Com.), 51.
[39] Salisbury Dioc. R.O., Dean Chandler's reg. f. 19; Valor Eccl. (Rec. Com.), i. 233.
[40] Proc. Dors. Nat. Hist. and Antiq. Field Club, xxvii, 231–2; xxx. 25; Univ. of Nott., Mi 6/179/17; Salisbury Dioc. R.O., Dean's presentments 1558–1603.
[41] Min. Bks. of the Dors. Standing Cttee. 54–5; Lambeth Palace MSS., COMM. XIIa/15/451–3.
[42] Rep. Com. Eccl. Revenues, pp. 156–7; Salisbury Dioc. R.O., Visit. Queries, 1864, 1879; Mortgage 283.
[43] Par. rec., chwdns.' accts. 1736–1837.

Despite the parish's dependence on Chardstock all tithes belonged to the rector. In 1334 the tithes of mills, milk, oblations, and obventions were valued with the glebe at 27s. 10d.[44] By 1535 the income from tithes was £6 16s. 7d.[45] In 1612 the rector was claiming tithes in kind on corn, hay, wool, lambs, pigs, geese, hops, and apples, 1d. for the fall of a colt, and 4d. for a cow and calf.[46] The tithes were valued at £30 a year in 1650. Compositions agreed between 1789 and 1798 amounted to £53 6s. 6d.[47] The tithes were commuted in 1844 for a rent-charge of £264.[48]

Glebe land was mentioned in 1334, and in 1405 comprised 20 a. of arable and ½ a. of meadow.[49] Glebe rents produced 24s. 9d. in 1535, there were 17 a. of glebe in 1551, and two orchards and 24 a. of arable and pasture in 1612.[50] By 1650 there were 18¾ a. of glebe worth £11 3s. 4d. and the lands were leased for £10 a year between 1789 and 1798.[51] The rector received 12½ a. under the Inclosure Award of 1816, and in 1844 the glebe amounted to 26 a.[52] The lands were valued at £60 a year in 1879 and £48 in 1883, and comprised 27 a. in 1880.[53] Estimated at 29 a. in 1897 and 1919, the area had been reduced to 10 a. by 1923.[54]

The parsonage house was described in 1612 as having a hall, a buttery outside the entry, a chamber within the hall, a kitchen, and three chambers on the first floor. There was a barn, a stable for four horses, a stall for cattle, two gardens to the east of the hall, and two orchards west and south of the house.[55] It was called 'a handsome thatched house' in 1650 when it was valued at £2 a year.[56]

It was under repair in 1788 but was in a poor state in 1800, and in 1808 it was 'pulled down and rebuilt at very great expense by the patron Charles Edwards', so that 'but few houses belong to the church equal to it'.[57] The house, some distance from the church at Higher Wambrook and now a private dwelling called Oren, was replaced by a rectory-house built in 1907 and extended in 1932.[58]

John de Fordington, rector by 1310 until at least 1312, was ordained deacon only after his institution[59] and no rector is known to have been a graduate in the Middle Ages. Both John Loder, rector c. 1507–22, and Henry Staple, rector c. 1535 until at least 1551, served as receivers for the lord,

and John Marraker, rector 1555–91, was probably related to the manor bailiff of 1565, Hugh Marraker.[60] John Marraker was evidently unpopular with his flock. About 1570 he was accused of not catechizing and in 1576 for preaching while unlicensed 'neither having knowledge therein'; he failed to read the service clearly, and was presented for immoral behaviour with a female parishioner. Between 1582 and 1585 he still did 'not read distinctly and with a voice intelligible to all the people' and, because of his 'insufficiency', most of the parishioners did not receive Communion three times a year.[61] Gamaliel Chase, rector 1621–45 who held the living in plurality with Yarcombe (Devon), was imprisoned by the Parliamentary authorities for buying land from a royalist in 1641. Having surrendered part of the purchase money he was then imprisoned by the Royalists for so doing. On his release he fled to Exeter where he lived until its capitulation in 1646. Most of his personal effects and books at Wambrook were seized by the sequestrators and in 1646 he was fined for delinquency.[62] An appeal from Chase's wife and four children for their fifths out of his estate was denied while he continued to officiate at Yarcombe.[63] Henry Backaller, rector c. 1645–8, was allowed £12 2s. 1½d. from the rent of Chardstock manor in 1646[64] but had removed to Somerset by 1648. The Dorset Standing Committee presented John Chase, Gamaliel's son, in 1648 but he was also sequestered for delinquency in the following year and William Randall, 'an idle, sottish fellow', was presented in 1650.[65] By 1662 Randall had been ejected and John Chase restored, and the Chases continued to occupy the rectory until 1716.[66] Assistant curates occur regularly from the 17th century until c. 1882,[67] and served the parish in the absence of the rectors during the later 18th century.[68] Henry Edwards the elder, rector 1818–50, was involved in 1829 in a pamphlet battle with Richard Towers, a Roman Catholic priest of Taunton, about James II's complicity in the Bloody Assizes.[69] Edwards's son, Henry, rector 1850–81, was non-resident and held the living with Churchstanton.[70]

In 1405 the church goods included a latten cross, at least ten service books, and, among other vestments, a frontal embroidered with beasts.[71]

[44] *Inq. Non.* (Rec. Com.), 51.
[45] *Valor Eccl.* (Rec. Com.), i. 233.
[46] Salisbury Dioc. R.O., Bp. of Bristol, Dors. rec. glebe terrier.
[47] Lambeth Palace MSS., COMM. XIIa/15/451–3; par rec., chwdns.' accts. 1736–1837.
[48] D.R.O., tithe award.
[49] *Inq. Non.* (Rec. Com.), 51; Salisbury Dioc. R.O., Dean Chandler's reg. f. 20b.
[50] *Valor Eccl.* (Rec. Com.), i. 233; E 315/128, f. 72; Salisbury Dioc. R.O., Bp. of Bristol, Dors. rec. glebe terrier.
[51] Lambeth Palace MSS., COMM. XIIa/15/451–3; par rec., chwdns.' accts. 1736–1837.
[52] S.R.O., inclosure award; D.R.O., tithe award.
[53] Salisbury Dioc. R.O., Visit. Queries, 1879; Mortgage 283; *Kelly's Dir. Dors.* (1880).
[54] *Kelly's Dir. Som.* (1897–1939).
[55] Salisbury Dioc. R.O., Dean's presentments 1576; Bp. of Bristol, Dors. rec. glebe terrier.
[56] Lambeth Palace MSS., COMM. XIIa/15/451–3.
[57] Salisbury Dioc. R.O., Dean's presentments 1788, 1800, 1809.
[58] M.I. to Charles Edwards in ch.; *Par. Ch. of St. Mary the Virgin, Wambrook* (1952).

[59] *Reg. Simon de Gandavo*, 895.
[60] E 315/128, ff. 71–3; Univ. of Nott., Mi 5/167/88; Mi 6/170/22–4, 27; MiM 152; Emden, *Biog. Reg. Univ. Oxford*, iii. 1645.
[61] Salisbury Dioc. R.O., Dean's presentments, c. 1570, 1576, 1582–5; *Proc. Dors. Nat. Hist. and Arch. Soc.* lxxiv. 78.
[62] *Cal. Cttee. for Compounding*, ii. 1322; *Min. Bks. of the Dors. Standing Cttee.* 54–5.
[63] *Min. Bks. of the Dors. Standing Cttee.* 77.
[64] Ibid. 58, 460.
[65] Ibid. 462, 476–7, 542–3; *Proc. Dors. Nat. Hist. and Arch. Soc.* lxxiv. 78; J. Walker, *Sufferings of the Clergy*, 217.
[66] *Wilts. Arch. and Nat. Hist. Mag.* xlv. 477; Salisbury Dioc. R.O., Dean's presentments, 1674.
[67] e.g. Salisbury Dioc. R.O., subscr. bk. 1599–1673, *sub anno* 1632; Chardstock prebend, chwdns.' presentments, 1715; Visit. Queries, 1800, 1809, 1842, 1864, 1870; par. reg.
[68] Par. reg. marr. 1754–1811.
[69] S.R.O., DD/SAS, C/909, 176.
[70] Salisbury Dioc. R.O., Visit. Queries, 1864.
[71] Salisbury Dioc. R.O., Dean Chandler's reg. f. 20v.

By 1552 the incumbent held a silver chalice parcel gilt, two copes, and five banners (one of silk), most of them seized by Edward VI's commissioners.[72] Between 1582 and 1585 it was presented that Holy Communion was often not celebrated three times a year, that the curate had failed to administer it to a sick woman, and had refused it to one couple at Easter.[73] In 1663, after the Restoration, the Communion table needed repair, and in 1674 the church was without a Communion flagon.[74] From 1736 Holy Communion was usually administered three or four times at the major feasts and in 1743 payment was made for guarding 'a lunatic person for interrupting the congregation in time of service'.[75]

In 1842 morning and evening Sunday services were held alternately with attendances of 100–150 on summer evenings and half that number in the morning. Holy Communion was being celebrated three times a year and the average number of communicants was about fourteen. The rector then had difficulty in getting the poor to attend, as the farmers paid their labourers on Sundays and the women stayed at home to prepare meals.[76] By 1864 both morning and afternoon services with sermons were being held, with attendances of 50 in the morning and 150 in the afternoon in fine weather, the number of communicants having risen to 30. The two services attracted similar attendances in 1870 and 1879 and monthly celebrations of Holy Communion had been introduced by the former year.[77]

The former manor-house was leased to the churchwardens as a church house for 60 years in 1529 and continued to be called the church house between 1543 and 1666.[78]

The church of the *BLESSED VIRGIN MARY* was described as so dedicated in 1362;[79] in 1405 it was said to be undedicated but the principal altar was consecrated to the Virgin's honour. The church is built of Ham stone rubble with ashlar dressings and has a chancel, nave with north and south porches, and west tower. The chancel is of 13th-century origin but has been much rebuilt in the 19th century. The nave, porches, and tower were all built or rebuilt in the 15th century but are also much restored. There was a bell tower by 1405.[80] In the 1560s the roof was thatched and shingled, but it was leaded by 1613.[81] Proposals for rebuilding the church in 1860 were evidently not executed, and in 1892 a faculty was obtained for taking down the chancel, with the exception of the south wall, renewing the roof and upper part of the wall of the nave, and building a vestry room to the

north of the chancel. At the same time most of the furniture and fittings were replaced.[82]

In 1552 there were four bells in the tower, a lych bell, and two sacring bells.[83] In 1975 there were five bells: (i and ii) 1892, John Warner and Sons, London; (iii and iv) early 14th century, Bristol foundry; (v) 1509–46, Thomas Jeffries, Bristol. The first and second bells were recast from the old tenor, a 15th-century bell, probably from the Exeter foundry. The third and fourth are the earliest bells in the old county of Dorset.[84]

The plate includes a silver chalice of 1621 inscribed inside 'given to this challis by me Cristover Maricker pastor of Wambrook the some of xxxv s.'[85] The registers date from 1653 but there are gaps in the marriage register for 1715–18, 1720–30, 1734–54, and in the burial register for 1733–76.[86]

NONCONFORMITY. Two persons were presented in 1665 for not coming to church or receiving communion, and were called 'schismatical' in the following year. One of them was declared to be 'inconformable' in 1667 and continued to be presented at least until 1683. John Coffin, gentleman, was presented as a popish recusant in 1674.[87]

Bible Christians met once in the parish in 1825, and there was one Baptist in 1864, although she was also 'a regular attendant at church and communion'.[88] There were 'very few' dissenters in 1879.[89] Wesleyan Methodists met in the kitchen of Loomcroft Farm from c. 1900 and built a small chapel in 1908 in the north of the parish, west of Higher Wambrook, on the Chard road. The building, derelict in 1975, seems also to have served Whitestaunton. Services had ceased by 1961 when it was sold.[90]

EDUCATION. Christopher Marraker, rector 1591–1621, was taking private pupils in 1614. One of them commented that, although an excellent teacher and a man of learning, Marraker 'had no regard to the souls of his scholars . . . never causing them to take notes of his sermons in writing, or so much as to repeat any one note they had learned out of them'.[91]

In 1818 there was no school in the parish and the farmers were averse to a Sunday school.[92] There was a Sunday school by 1842 and a school-house had been built on a site north of the church by 1845 for a National school.[93] A new school was built on the same site c. 1862, on land given by Sir R. P. Glyn.[94] Evening schools were opened during

[72] *Proc. Dors. Nat. Hist. and Antiq. Field Club*, xxvi. 122.
[73] Salisbury Dioc. R.O., Dean's presentments, 1582–5.
[74] Ibid. 1663, 1674.
[75] Par. rec., chwdns.' accts. 1736–1837.
[76] Salisbury Dioc. R.O., Visit. Queries, 1842.
[77] Ibid. 1864, 1870, 1879.
[78] Univ. of Nott., Mi 5/166/38, 41; D.R.O. 2698–2708.
[79] *Cal. Inq. p.m.* xi, pp. 302–3.
[80] Salisbury Dioc. R.O., Dean Chandler's reg. f. 20v.
[81] Ibid. Dean's presentments, 1566–9, 1613; acct. bk. 21.
[82] Par. rec., specification, Feb. 1860; faculty, 2 June 1892.
[83] *Proc. Dors. Nat. Hist. and Antiq. Field Club*, xxvi. 122.
[84] Ibid. xix. 29, 35; xxiv. 105; xxv. 97; lx. 99; S.R.O.,

DD/SAS, CH 16.
[85] J. E. Nightingale, *Church Plate of Dors.* 37.
[86] Par. reg.
[87] Salisbury Dioc. R.O., Dean's presentments, 1665–83; prebend of Chardstock, chwdns.' presentments, 1667.
[88] S.R.O., D/N/spc 1; Salisbury Dioc. R.O., Visit. Queries, 1864.
[89] Salisbury Dioc. R.O., Visit. Queries, 1879.
[90] Ex inf. Mr. Roger Thorne, Archivist to Plymouth and Exeter District; tablet and foundation stone on chapel.
[91] *D.N.B.*
[92] *Digest of Returns to Sel. Cttee. on Educ. of Poor*, H.C. 224 (1819), ix (1).
[93] Salisbury Dioc. R.O., Visit. Queries, 1842; D.R.O., tithe award.　[94] S.R.O., C/E 28; C 54/15904.

the winter of 1863–4 and again in 1868–9, 1869–70, and 1878–9. The average attendance at the day-school was 22 in 1870, although the children were then leaving at the age of 8 or 9.[95] The buildings were enlarged in 1875, and by 1903 the average attendance had risen to 36, when there were 47 children on the books. In 1903 the school had two teachers, there was a teacher's house, two school-rooms, and an evening school was again being held.[96] Numbers on the books rose to 57 in 1918 but fell to 45 in 1928. In 1935 the school took juniors and infants; older children were transferred to Combe St. Nicholas. After the Second World War the number of pupils remained fairly steady at about fifteen. The school was closed in 1963 and children

have since attended school in Chard.[97] The buildings were unoccupied in 1975.

CHARITIES FOR THE POOR. In 1842 there were stated to be no charitable endowments, but there was 'a small and inconsiderable property', the income from which was devoted to the use of the poor.[98] Thomas Deane Eames, by will proved in 1936, left £500 in trust for the repair of the church or its general benefit and the relief of the poor. The income, which was over £22 in 1966, has been used for church repairs and other expenses, there being insufficient money to assist the poor.[99]

WHITESTAUNTON

THE PARISH of Whitestaunton, known as Staunton until the earlier 14th century,[1] lies on the southern boundary of the county, 3 miles NW. from Chard. It had an area of 1,937 a. in 1883,[2] and extends just over 2 miles from east to west and about the same from north to south. Its western boundary with Yarcombe (Devon) is formed by the river Yarty and its southern marked the division between Somerset and Dorset until Wambrook was transferred to Somerset in 1896.[3] A stream and lanes mark the northern and eastern boundaries with Combe St. Nicholas.

Whitestaunton lies in the dramatic terrain of the Devon–Somerset border, with steep-sided hills and narrow valleys, the thickly-wooded high ground affording extensive views over the surrounding district. The parish occupies the valley of a tributary of the Yarty, and stretches up to high ground on both sides, reaching over 700 ft. on Cinder hill and Longlie common in the NW., to 771 ft. on the east, and to over 825 ft. on the southern boundary. The geology is extremely varied. In the north the soil is Lower Lias, Upper Greensand, and Rhaetic Beds, in the SW. Keuper Marls with alluvium along the Yarty, in the NE. and central areas further Upper Greensand with chalk outcrops, and in the south and SE. principally clay.[4] Quarries at Longlie and south of the manor-house were formerly worked for limestone for both burning and building,[5] and the same stone may give the parish its name.

Traces of prehistoric settlement survive in an oval camp south of Howley and a barrow north of Northay in a field which was called Burrow Close in 1838.[6] A Roman villa was discovered c. 1845 near an ancient well in the grounds of the manor-house

in Whitestaunton village. The building contained hypocausts, mosaics, and painted wall plaster, but has never been satisfactorily excavated. The well, known as St. Agnes well, presumably indicates why the site was chosen for both villa and manor-house and suggests continuity of settlement. The water is slightly warm and reputedly good for sprains.[7]

Whitestaunton village and Northay lie in small coombes at the head of the dividing stream in the north-east of the parish, and Howley (Holleway in 1479)[8] is on the steep hillside above the Yarty in the south-west. Cleave and Nash both occur as settlements by 1327, and Lapse, Pyle, Brownsey, and Woodhayes by 1479, indicating scattered settlement probably originating in woodland clearings.[9] There may have been some open-field system around the village,[10] and there was a park, then a wood, to the west of the manor-house by 1479, which survived as fields called Park Hill and Horse Park in 1838.[11]

The road system is irregular, two present principal arteries bypassing all the areas of settlement. The main Chard–Honiton road runs from east to west through the south-east of the parish, while the Ilminster–Honiton road cuts off the north-west corner. From these two roads access lanes run north and south to serve the various hamlets and farms and other roads link the parish with Yarcombe (Devon), Combe St. Nicholas, and Wambrook.

The houses in 1791 were stated to be 'thinly scattered and very mean, there being many cottages or huts of only one floor and a single room for the family'.[12] At Northay two houses close to the cross-roads are of traditional 17th-century form, most of the others being of the 19th century, and ¼ m. to the west the house at Nash Hill appears to be 17th

[95] Salisbury Dioc. R.O., Visit. Queries, 1864, 1870, 1879. [96] S.R.O., C/E 28.
[97] S.R.O., C/E, box 69, log bks.
[98] Salisbury Dioc. R.O., Visit. Queries, 1842. Possibly from the sale of a house on Bewley Down, the money 'to be laid out for the use of the poor': par. rec., chwdns'. accts. 1736–1837.
[99] Char. Com. files.
[1] The form Whitestaunton is recorded in 1333: Reg. John de Grandisson, ed. F. C. Hingeston-Randolph, iii. 1297. This article was completed in 1974.
[2] S.R.O., tithe award; Kelly's Dir. Som. (1883).
[3] Local Govt. Bd. Order P.1164.
[4] Geol. Surv. Map 1″, drift, sheet 311 (1906 edn.).

[5] C 142/8/1; S.R.O., DD/CN, box 12, bdle. 4; O.S. Map 1/2,500, Som. LXXXVII. 14 (1903 edn.).
[6] S.R.O., tithe award. The enclosure north of the camp was called Castle Hill in 1838: ibid. Also see V.C.H. Som. i. 180, 182, 503.
[7] V.C.H. Som. i. 334; E. Horne, Som. Holy Wells, 33. Traces of a Roman shrine were discovered at the well c. 1882.
[8] C 142/8/1.
[9] Ibid.; S.R.S. iii. 196. Southay occurs as a personal name in 1479: C 142/8/1.
[10] See below, p. 234.
[11] C 142/8/1; S.R.O., tithe award.
[12] Collinson, Hist. Som. iii. 126.

century. At Howley, Browns Farm is a long plastered and thatched house of the 17th century[13] with later additions, and adjacent to it there are a granary on staddle stones and a farmyard partly enclosed by tall buildings with open timber fronts. Cleave Hill Cottage may also be of the 17th century, but the other houses in the southern part of the parish appear to be of 19th-century or later origin. None of the other scattered cottages and farmhouses in the parish seem earlier than the 17th century, and 20th-century development has been concentrated on Howley.

There were four licensed victuallers in 1735 one of whom, John Meacham, evidently held the Rising Sun at Howley, first mentioned by name in 1766. This has been the only licensed house in the parish since the early 19th century. There is a single reference to the Bush inn in 1770.[14]

The population of Whitestaunton was 259 in 1801 and rose to 327 in 1821, continuing fairly stable until 1841 when it was 321. Thereafter it fell to 261 in 1851, remaining at that level until a further drop to 208 in 1881 and 187 in 1901.[15] A rise to 205 in 1911 was succeeded by an abrupt decline after the First World War to 121 in 1921. Since 1931, when the population numbered 169, there has been little change, the figure in 1961 and 1971 being 164.[16]

Charles Isaac Elton (1839–1900), lawyer and antiquary, was lord of the manor and M.P. for West Somerset. He wrote a variety of monographs on archaeological, legal, and literary subjects and was founder member of the Selden Society.[17] Patrick Reynolds Mitchell, dean of Wells from 1973, was born at the manor-house in 1930.[18]

In 1644 during the Civil War while Charles I stayed at Chard the Royalist troops were housed at Whitestaunton manor-house and, presumably, in the grounds.[19] Two parishioners were suspected of complicity in the Monmouth Rebellion of 1685.[20]

MANOR. The overlordship of *WHITESTAUN-TON* manor was held in 1086 by Ansgar (I) Brito (d. c. 1092–5) under the count of Mortain.[21] It then evidently descended with the barony of Odcombe, passing in turn to Walter (I) Brito (last mentioned 1108), Ansgar (II) (fl. 1126), Roger (d. by 1157), Walter (II) (d. 1179), and to the son of the last, Walter (III) (d. 1199). On the death of Walter (III) without issue the barony was divided between his two nephews Walter Croc and John de Long-

champ, who in 1200 and 1202 surrendered their shares to Richard Briwere (d. 1215).[22] The latter's brother William Briwere (d. 1233) was said to be over-lord in 1234, and subsequently his lands were divided amongst his sisters and coheirs.[23] The Briwere heirs still held the overlordship in 1284–6, but before 1321 it had passed, possibly by descent, to Aubrey wife of John Hyngaud, who had granted it to William de Montacute (cr. earl of Salisbury 1337, d. 1344).[24] Subsequently it descended with the earldom of Salisbury, although the manor is some-times described as being held of Donyatt manor, one of the Montacute properties.[25] The overlordship was last mentioned in 1618 when it was held as of the earldom of Salisbury.[26]

A mesne lordship held by William de Percy (d. 1245) in 1234 was probably created on or after his marriage with Joan daughter of William Briwere, then overlord.[27] Their son Henry (d. 1272) was succeeded by John de Percy, whose heirs possessed the mesne lordship in 1284–6.[28] It is not mentioned thereafter.

The terre tenancy was held in 1066 by Alward, and in 1166 Robert (I) of Staunton occupied two fees of Mortain under Walter (II) Brito.[29] By 1234 the manor had passed to Robert (II) of Staunton and by 1284–6 to Sir William of Staunton (d. 1311).[30] In 1312 it was conceded by Thomas of Staunton to Sir William's son Roger (I), and Roger's heirs were in possession in 1316.[31] Robert (III) of Staunton, a minor, held it in 1321 and Roger (II) of Staunton (d. 1351) in 1344.[32] Roger's son William was probably holding the manor in 1370 but by 1397 a life interest had passed to Nicholas Rede of Pole Anthony in Tiverton (Devon) and his wife Parnel, possibly widow of William of Staunton.[33] The Redes were still holding the manor in 1433–4, but by 1438 the advowson and probably the manor were in the hands of the overlord, possibly during the minority of the heir.[34] An enquiry into the owner-ship of the advowson in 1447 stated that the manor was 'long ago' given by William of Staunton to Thomas Hugyn in tail. On Thomas's death, his son John being a minor, it was granted by the over-lord to John's mother Roberta, widow of James Harington.[35] An interest in the manor, however, had been retained by John Brett of Thorncombe in Bicknoller, cousin and heir of William Staunton,[36] and the Brett and Staunton coats of arms appear together on a tomb in Whitestaunton church. It seems likely that the Bretts and Hugyns represented coheirs of William Staunton, each with half the

[13] A re-sited datestone of 1662 with George Brown's initials suggests a date for the house.
[14] S.R.O., Q/RL; DD/CN, box 12, lease 24 Dec. 1766, to Mary daughter of John Meacham; *P.O. Dir. Som.* (1861–75); *Kelly's Dir. Som.* (1883–1939).
[15] *V.C.H. Som.* ii. 348.
[16] *Census,* 1911–71.
[17] *D.N.B.* Richard Brett (c. 1567–1637), an eminent classicist, is often claimed as a member of the Bretts of Whitestaunton although he was born in London: ibid.
[18] *Crockford*; ex inf. the Very Revd. P. R. Mitchell.
[19] *Diary of Richard Symonds* (Camd. Soc. [1st ser.], lxxiv), 36–7.
[20] B.L. Add. MS. 30077, f. 35.
[21] *V.C.H. Som.* i. 474.
[22] Sanders, *Eng. Baronies,* 132–3.
[23] Ibid.; *Bk. of Fees,* i. 398.
[24] *Feud. Aids,* iv. 284; *S.R.S.* i. 195.

[25] *Cal. Inq. p.m. Hen. VII,* i, pp. 314–16; C 142/78/83; C 142/53/14.
[26] *S.R.S.* lxvii, p. 91.
[27] *Bk. of Fees,* i. 398; Sanders, *Eng. Baronies,* 148.
[28] Sanders, *Eng. Baronies,* 148; *Feud. Aids,* iv. 284.
[29] *V.C.H. Som.* i. 474; *Red Bk. Exch.* i. 233.
[30] *Bk. of Fees,* i. 398; *Feud. Aids,* iv. 284; *S.R.S.* xiv, p. 26.
[31] *S.R.S.* xii. 27; *Feud. Aids,* iv. 331.
[32] *S.R.S.* i. 195; *Cal. Inq. p.m.* viii, p. 389; *Cal. Inq. Misc.* iii, pp. 288–9.
[33] *Cal. Inq. Misc.* iii, pp. 288–9; C 136/94/35.
[34] C 88/115/81; *S.R.S.* xxxii, p. 223.
[35] *S.R.S.* xlix, pp. 73, 76–7. John Hugyn granted the reversion of the manor to Thomas Hugyn in 1422: *S.R.S.* xxii. 58.
[36] *S.R.S.* xxii. 58. For the Bretts of Whitestaunton see *Proc. Som. Arch. Soc.* xxviii. 79–88.

manor and the alternate right of presentation to the benefice. John Hugyn and John Brett were described as joint lords of the manor in 1449 and 1473 and Brett's daughter Joan married John Hugyn's son and heir Thomas.[37] One half descended from Thomas Hugyn to his son John (d. 1485) and subsequently to his grandson John (d. 1493). The last was succeeded by his daughter Joan, then a minor, who was later probably the first wife of Simon Brett.[38]

The half held by John Brett (d. 1478) passed to his son Alexander (d. 1511) and then to Alexander's son Simon (d. 1530).[39] In 1524 Simon and his second wife Eleanor settled the reversion on Simon's uncle John Brett of South Petherton (d. 1532).[40] Both Simon and John died without issue and the property was inherited by John's brother Robert Brett (d. 1541) and, subsequently, by Robert's grandson John (d. 1588), son of Alexander Brett.[41] Efforts made by Simon's brother Robert to obtain the manor were evidently fruitless.[42] From John's son Sir Alexander Brett (d. 1609) the manor descended in turn to the latter's son Alexander (d. 1617) and grandson Sir Robert Brett (d. 1666).[43] Sir Robert inadvertently saved Whitestaunton from sequestration during the Interregnum, having settled the manor on trustees in 1636–7 to raise portions for his younger children.[44] After the Restoration he failed to secure this provision for his family and turned his eldest son Alexander out of the manor-house, disposing of much of his own furniture to pay debts. In 1669 Alexander brought an action of trespass and ejectment against his father and obtained possession of the house.[45] Alexander (d. 1671) was succeeded by his brother Robert Brett, a Jesuit, who in 1673 sold the manor to Alexander's widow, Elizabeth (d. 1713), by birth a Brett of a different family who afterwards married Dr. Henry Klee (d. 1677).[46] Elizabeth Klee settled the manor on trustees in 1697 for her niece Ann, daughter of Robert Brett of London, for Ann's husband Henry Brett (of yet another family of that name), and for their son Alexander, reserving a life interest for herself. Henry Brett sold the property to Sir Abraham Elton of Bristol, Bt., in 1718 for £11,642.[47]

On Sir Abraham's death in 1728 the manor descended to his third son Jacob (d. 1765) and thereafter in turn, during Jacob's lifetime, to his sons Abraham (d. 1762) and Isaac (I) (d. 1774).[48] It passed from Isaac (I) through successive generations to Isaac (II) of Stapleton (Glos.) (d. 1790), Isaac (III) (d. 1837), and Robert James Elton (d. 1869). The last 'unexpectedly' bequeathed the estate to his nephew Charles Isaac Elton (d. 1900), and Charles's brother Frederick (d. 1922) sold off

most of the lands in 1920.[49] The manor-house and lordship were retained by Frederick's widow who sold them in 1925 to Lt.-Col. Percy Reynolds Mitchell. They were purchased by Col. Couchman in 1945 and by the present owner, Mr. A. E. Dobell, in 1947.[50]

The manor-house was first expressly mentioned

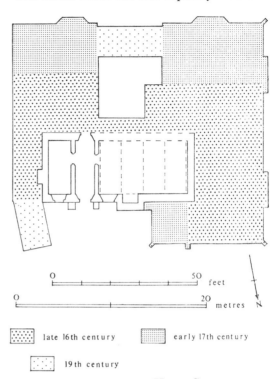

late 16th century   early 17th century

19th century

PLAN OF WHITESTAUNTON HOUSE SHOWING THE MEDIEVAL BUILDING AND ITS LATER DEVELOPMENT

in 1479, although the lords had been resident on the manor from the time of the Stauntons. Under the terms of John Hugyn's will of 1483 his widow Joan was to have a life tenancy of 'all the housing above the west end of the hall of Whitestaunton, and the occupation of the old stable, the kitchen and bakehouse to make her meat, to brew, and to bake', and underwood from the park.[51] Simon Brett (d. 1530) granted his second wife Eleanor a life interest in the house and demesnes if she continued to occupy them. On the death of John Brett in 1532 his brother and nephew, Robert and Alexander, challenged Eleanor's rights,[52] and in 1565 Alexander's son John acquired the house for a lump sum of £100 and an annuity of £40 a year, though subsequently reletting the property to her.[53] The Eltons, as successors to the Bretts, did not initially occupy the manor-house, the first Elton to be

[37] S.R.S. xlix, pp. 114, 119; C.P. 40/847 rot. 157; Cal. Inq. p.m. Hen. VII, i, pp. 314–16.

[38] Cal. Inq. p.m. Hen. VII, i, pp. 314–16; C.P. 25(2)/51/359/4 Hen. VIII Hil.

[39] S.R.O., DD/WY, box 7, Z.i.f; C 140/67/38; C 142/78/83.

[40] C142/53/14; S.R.S. xxi. 8. It was probably Simon who as 'Byrte of Whitestaunton' made unwise prophecies of future civil commotion in 1529: L. & P. Hen. VIII, iv (3), p. 2997.

[41] Cal. Pat. 1553, 322–3; C 142/223/87.

[42] Sta. Cha. 2/26/230.

[43] S.R.S. lxvii, pp. 91–2; Proc. Som. Arch. Soc. xxviii. 83–4.

[44] Cal. Cttee. for Compounding, iii. 1644.

[45] Proc. Som. Arch. Soc. xxviii. 84–5.

[46] Ibid. 86–7.

[47] S.R.O., DD/SAS, C/1193, 20, pp. 200, 202–4, quoting deeds then at Whitestaunton manor-house, since lost.

[48] Burke, Peerage (1949), 706; S.R.O., DD/CN, box 12, leases.

[49] Burke, Peerage (1949), 706–7; D.N.B. s.v. C.I. Elton; S.R.O., DD/X/SFK, sale cat. 1920.

[50] Ex inf. Mrs. A. E. Dobell, Whitestaunton.

[51] C 142/8/1.

[52] Req. 2/4/210.

[53] C 3/10/89.

buried at Whitestaunton being Abraham (d. 1762).[54] In 1785 Isaac Elton leased the manor-house, Manor farm, and 500 a. of land, to a Whitestaunton yeoman, reserving the hall, parlour, the four bed-chambers over the hall and parlour, the cellar within the parlour, a little cellar taken out of the dairy house, the parlour green, coach-house, lower stable, and joint use of the kitchen.[55] The house has been occupied by the lords of the manor from the time of R. J. Elton (d. 1869).[56]

The house lies immediately to the west of the churchyard in a small valley from which the land rises steeply on the south and west.[57] It is of ashlar and rubble with slated roofs and has been enlarged on several occasions giving it a rambling character with principal fronts to the north and west. The earliest surviving part is a relatively small house of the later 15th century containing, within a single range, a passage entry and service rooms at the east end and a ground-floor hall with a great chamber above. The chamber has an arch-braced roof of three bays which was formerly open and is elaborately decorated with mouldings and cusped wind-braces. In the later 16th century the house was more than doubled in size by the addition of a western range which contained three principal rooms on each floor and has a long symmetrical front to the garden. The panelling in the ground-floor room bears the date 1577 and the initials of members of the Brett family. At the same time as the western range was being built the old house was modernized. An entrance passage was formed across the western end of the hall and a new doorway and two-storeyed porch added to the north front and a staircase in a tower, which may in part have been older, set in the angle between the old and new ranges. The service end was extended southwards and the hall and great chamber were refenestrated, a two-storeyed oriel being constructed between the staircase tower and the extended service wing. There were internal alterations, probably of only minor character, in the 18th century but more extensive remodelling took place in the early 19th century. The roof of the hall range was raised on the south side to admit a new range of bedrooms which are partly over the oriel, and the first floor of the service end was extensively refitted. Later in the century the interior of the western range was modernized and by this time the former open court between the west and the service ranges had been largely built over for additional outbuildings.

To the east of the house, bordering the churchyard, there is a two-storeyed range of the 16th century containing stables and, added to its south end, a 19th-century building containing coach houses.

ECONOMIC HISTORY. At the time of the Conquest the manor gelded for three hides. There was land for 8 ploughs but only 5 to till it. The demesne totalled $1\frac{1}{4}$ hide with $1\frac{1}{2}$ plough and 6 serfs, and there were 18 villeins and 4 bordars with the remaining $1\frac{3}{4}$ hide and $3\frac{1}{2}$ ploughs. There were 260 a. of woodland and 50 a. of pasture which rendered 4 blooms of iron, such a customary due being recorded for only five other manors in Domesday Somerset.[58] Finds of iron slag on the Roman villa site suggest that smelting was established locally in very early times.[59] Stock in 1086 included 16 swine, 59 sheep, and 13 she-goats.[60]

A dearth of references to open fields and the hilly nature of the terrain suggest that inclosure of the low-lying areas took place early, while the higher ground remained, as at present, predominantly devoted to woodland. The parish continued almost wholly in the ownership of the lord of the manor until the 20th century. In 1479, apart from the manor-house and appurtenant closes, there were 21 tenements occupied by 15 tenants lying at Benhayes, Cleave Hill, Howley, Lapse, Pyle, Brownsey, Woodhayes, Nash, Ford, and Northay. Among the demesne lands in 1479 references to 'Bryghtfurlong', Northfields, and Southfields (and mention in 1838 of North field and Cherry Furland)[61] suggest a former arable field system around the parent settlement. In 1493 tenements were also held of the manor at Whitehall and Weston in Combe St. Nicholas, at Leigh and 'Jakettes' in Winsham and Whitestaunton, and in South Bradon.[62]

Villeins on the manor were mentioned in 1434, when two were abducted by Nicholas Cleyhill, and again in 1473.[63] Customary works are referred to as late as 1534 when every tenement holder had to weed corn for half a day, mow and 'make' one acre of meadow, and rick the grass at the manor-house; also to reap and set up 'stitches' on one acre of wheat. All tenants, including cottagers, had to work for one day at reaping corn, receiving meat and drink for their labours.[64]

The demesne was valued at 5 marks a year in 1493 and half the manor at £10 in 1511.[65] The manor continued to be valued at £20 between 1532 and 1618,[66] but when temporarily seized by the Parliamentary Committee in 1648 the leasehold and copyhold tenants were paying £130. In 1649 when let by the family trustees the rental rose to £283.[67] The last available valuation in 1674 was for about £300.[68]

In 1532 lands held with half the manor by John Brett comprised 24 messuages and gardens, 40 a. of arable, 100 a. meadow, 200 a. pasture, 200 a. woodland, and 100 a. furze and heath:[69] acreages which, while not necessarily accurate, probably reflect the land use throughout the parish. Common land is mentioned at various sites, usually on the higher ground. Howley common abutted east on the Park in 1534 (and thus evidently included most of Great Copse), when oak trees were felled

54 S.R.O., D/P/whits 2/1/1.
55 S.R.O., DD/CN, box 12, bdle. 4, lease 1 June 1785.
56 P.O. Dir. Som. (1861–75); Kelly's Dir. Som. (1883–1939); local information.
57 See plate facing p. 160.
58 Domesday Geog. of SW. Eng. ed. H. C. Darby and R. Welldon Finn, 211.
59 V.C.H. Som. i. 334; ii. 392.
60 Ibid. i. 474.
61 S.R.O., tithe award; C 142/8/1.
62 C 142/8/1.
63 C 88/115/81; C.P. 40/847 rot. 157.
64 Req. 2/4/210.
65 Cal. Inq. p.m. Hen. VII, i. p. 316; C 142/78/83.
66 C 142/53/14; C 142/223/87; S.R.S. lxvii, pp. 91–2.
67 S.P. 23/83 ff. 74–5.
68 C 10/175/151.
69 C 142/53/14.

there for house repair.[70] In 1746 the tenant of Brownseys farm covenanted not to plough the Higher common immediately west of his house, and Long lie in common in the north-west of the parish was mentioned in 1783. Land recently inclosed from Lapse common is referred to in 1796.[71] Few alterations, however, to the medieval agrarian pattern seem to have taken place and c. 1800 it was thought that the land was still 'capable of great agricultural improvement'.[72] If the 1532 figures are to be relied on, the amount of land converted to arable gradually increased. By 1838 there were 742 a. of arable, 705 a. of meadow and pasture, and 450 a. of woodland.[73] By 1905 the area devoted to grassland had risen to 881 a. while arable had fallen to 624 a. and woodland to 418 a.[74] This pattern continues relatively unchanged to the present day.

Several of the larger farms were apparently named after their tenants. Thus Brownseys may be linked with the Brownsey family, apart from the lord the wealthiest inhabitants of the parish in 1582 and 1641,[75] Browns farm with George Brown, gentleman, who kept tame deer there in 1681, and Parrisees farm with the Parris family, cousins of the Browns.[76] Tenements were usually leased for 99 years or three lives in the 17th century, but during the 18th century shorter terms at increased rents were introduced by the Eltons. A lease of Brownseys for 14 years was granted in 1746, the agreement including 500 bundles of faggots annually from the lord, and another for Woodhayes (20 a.) in 1783 for the same term.[77] Browns and Southay farms were combined in a seven-year lease in 1785, as were Pyle and Dymonds (65 a.) in the same year, and, for six years, Benhayes (27 a.) in 1787. Apart from Manor farm, which comprised 500 a. in 1785, the size of holdings was small, generally under 50 acres. The 18th-century leases often included manuring covenants. Thus at Woodhayes in 1783 the tenant agreed that on every acre in tillage he would spread 12 hogheads of lime or 180 seams of dung; and that he would not take more than two successive crops of corn or grain and thereafter sow grass seed.[78]

By 1814 the lands leased with Manor farm had shrunk to 420 a.[79] and by 1838 to 338 a., although in the latter year the lessee also occupied 53 a. of glebe. By 1838 the Eltons had extended the grounds attached to the manor-house to 434 acres. There were then, apart from Manor farm, three other farms of over 150 a., one of 84 a., and the remainder smallholdings under 50 a.[80] Redistribution of farmland to form viable units had resulted by 1851 in a five-farm parish: Manor (387 a.), Browns (250 a.),

Northay (204 a.), Parrisees (200 a.), and Elms farms (200 a.). In addition there were a further 100 a. attached to Knapp House and 40 a. to Woodhayes.[81] In 1920 when the estate was split up and sold the nine farms were principally pasture land, while the woodlands had been greatly reduced by felling during the First World War. The largest holdings were then Northay farm with 280 a., Manor farm 255 a., Browns 196 a., and Woodhayes 121 a. The estate then included not only 1,679 a. in Whitestaunton (the whole parish excepting the manor-house grounds and glebe) but a further 853 a. in the adjacent parishes of Combe St. Nicholas and Wambrook.[82] Since 1920 the farms have continued in the hands of the farmers with one exception. When sold in 1947 the manor-house had only 28 a. of ground, but purchases by the Dobells increased this to about 400 a. including Manor farm. Since 1965 much of this has been resold to other farmers or sublet.[83]

The parish had links with the cloth industry from the 16th century, probably supplying markets in Chard. Fulling mills occur in 1573,[84] two weavers in 1629 and 1668, and a tailor in 1657.[85] Thomas Ford (d. 1624) mentioned his looms in his will and bequeathed serge to provide suits and petticoats for his relations and friends.[86] John Harvie had a mill and a pair of weaver's looms in 1629.[87] A clothier occurs in 1789 and a tailor in 1813.[88] In more recent times virtually all the inhabitants have been employed in agriculture, although gloving as a cottage industry was pursued by eight women in 1851.[89]

A quarry (or quarries), presumably for the extraction of lias and limestone, were mentioned in 1479, 1513, and 1532.[90] In 1783 the tenant of Woodhayes had the right to dig limestone in several quarries on Long lie common and to burn the stone in the limekiln there.[91] The field-name Quarry close immediately north of Northay was recorded in 1838 and a second limekiln in the Warren south of the manor-house was mentioned as disused in 1903.[92] Limestone for the second kiln evidently came from closes called Lime Pits in 1838, south-west of the Warren.[93] Masons are regularly recorded in the parish in the later 18th and 19th centuries.[94] The right to take marl for Leigh tenement from a marl pit at Bromeley (located in Winsham but part of Whitestaunton manor) for half a year was granted by the lord in 1639, and another tenant received a similar licence for a marl pit in Court field in the same year. A marl pit was also recorded at Leigh in 1663.[95]

There was a mill in Whitestaunton in 1086 but it

[70] Req. 2/4/210.
[71] S.R.O., DD/CN, box 12, bdle. 4, leases.
[72] Locke, *Suppl. to Collinson*, ed. F. M. Ward, 156.
[73] S.R.O., tithe award.
[74] Statistics supplied by the then Bd. of Agric. 1905.
[75] S.R.O., DD/SF 3948; DD/HI, box 10, lay subsidy roll 1641. Stephen Brownsey held Woodhayes farm in 1644: Prob. 11/271 (P.C.C. 1657, 533).
[76] S.R.O., Q/SR 145/2, 9, 12. Thomas Parris (d. 1639) held Castle Wood and lands in Chardstock: Prob. 11/180 (P.C.C. 95 Harvey).
[77] S.R.O., DD/CN, box 12, bdle. 4, leases 1719-96.
[78] Ibid.   [79] *Taunton Courier*, 8 Sept. 1814.
[80] S.R.O., tithe award.   [81] H.O. 107/1927.
[82] S.R.O., DD/X/SFK, sale cat. 1920.
[83] Ex inf. Mrs. Dobell.

[84] See below.
[85] S.R.O., D/D/Ct H, will of John Harvie; DD/SP, inventories 1668/69; Prob. 11/268 (P.C.C. 1657, 404).
[86] Prob. 11/143 (P.C.C. 42 Byrde).
[87] S.R.O., D/D/Ct H, will and inventory of John Harvie.
[88] S.R.O., D/P/whits 2/1/5, 7.   [89] H.O. 107/1927.
[90] C 142/8/1; C.P. 25(2)/51/359/4 Hen. VIII Hil.; C 142/53/14.
[91] S.R.O., DD/CN, box 12, bdle. 4.
[92] S.R.O., tithe award; O.S. Map 1/2,500, Som. LXXXVII. 14 (1903 edn.).
[93] S.R.O., tithe award.
[94] S.R.O., D/P/whits 2/1/5, 7.
[95] S.R.O., DD/HI, box 53, lic. 20 Nov. 1639; DD/X/DF, lease 30 Dec. 1639; conveyance 23 Feb. 1662/3.

then rendered nothing as it ground solely for the manor.[96] This may possibly be identified with a blade mill held with the manor in 1513 and 1532. In 1532 John Brett also held half of another mill.[97] The manor was credited with two water-mills in 1527 and three grain-mills and three fulling mills in 1573.[98] John Brett at his death in 1588 left Howley mills to his fourth son Robert, after the death of the tenant.[99] Millers or mill-owners occur in 1615, 1619, 1629, and 1664.[1] The field-name Tucking Mill, immediately north-east of Lapse on the stream north of Howley, probably locates the site of the fulling mills once known as Howley mills. Similarly the field-names Mill Plot and Millers mead on the northern boundary along the road between Woodhayes and Northay[2] apparently indicate another mill on the same stream. Traces of a mill-leat and former buildings survive immediately south of the road there.

LOCAL GOVERNMENT. The manor court of Whitestaunton was described in 1629 as court leet with view of frankpledge and manor court, and was held twice a year in 1639.[3] No court rolls have been traced, but suit of court was demanded of a tenant in 1766.[4] No overseers' records survive but in 1812 it was evidently the custom for bread to be distributed to the poor at St. Agnes well.[5] The parish joined the Chard poor-law union in 1836.[6]

CHURCH. The church of Whitestaunton is first mentioned in 1291.[7] The living was a rectory in 1297 and the advowson was held with the lordship of the manor by 1321,[8] when the patron was Robert de Bernyll by grant of the overlord during a minority.[9] Richard Montacute, earl of Salisbury, presented as overlord in 1438, and Roberta Harington as mother and guardian of John Hugyn in 1447.[10] The patronage was exercised in 1449 by William, Lord Bonville, and William Stafford by grant of John Hugyn and John Brett as joint lords, and between 1489 and 1500 the alternate patrons were Alexander Brett and Joan Hugyn.[11] Robert Tedbury and William Cabell presented in 1517, John Alyn in 1544, and Nicholas Wootton in 1578, all by grants from the Bretts.[12] Subsequently presentations were made by the lords of the manor or their trustees until c. 1928 when the advowson

passed to Lt.-Col. William Marwood Elton (d. c. 1932–3), the lord's cousin. His widow held the patronage until her death c. 1965, when she was succeeded by her son Group Capt. N. W. D. Elton, the patron in 1974. Since 1949 the rectory has been held in plurality with Combe St. Nicholas, where the incumbent lives.[13] The united benefice of Combe St. Nicholas and Whitestaunton with Wambrook was created in 1974.

The value of the living was £5 6s. 8d. in 1291 and £14 15s. 1d. in 1535.[14] Subsequently it rose to £40 c. 1668, nearly £100 in 1727, £255 net in 1831, and £257 in 1851.[15] In 1535 predial tithes were worth £5, those of sheep and lambs £2 16s. 4d., and oblations and personal tithes £4 10s. 9d.[16] No later valuation has been found until 1838, when the tithes were commuted for a rent-charge of £222.[17] The glebe lands were valued at 47s. in 1535, and in 1617 and 1635 were extended at c. 38 a.[18] The same lands were estimated to contain 54 a. in 1838 and valued at £65 a year in 1840.[19] Their income had fallen to £50 by 1851, but the extent remained constant at 50 a. between 1861 and 1939.[20]

A rectory house was mentioned in 1534, when it was occupied by Alexander Brett, son of the lord of the manor.[21] In the 17th century it had 'an entry with a hall upon the left hand, with one house within the hall with a loft over, and on the right hand . . . two little house(s) with three little chambers over'. There was also 'a kitchen without the backer court with one other little house'. Outbuildings included a barn and stable, a little barton by the barn, two small courts, and a herb garden.[22] In 1670 the hall, study, great and little butteries, the buttery chamber, the hall chamber, and the bakehouse were named.[23] The house was described as unfit for the rector in 1815, and was not occupied by his successor in 1833.[24] The building includes the kitchen, cross-passage, and hall of the 16th-century house. The parlour and the roof were renewed in the later 1830s when W. T. Elton took up residence.[25] The old house then became the service end and the new block housed the principal rooms, entrance hall, and main staircase. It was sold c. 1967 and subsequently divided into two dwellings.[26]

Andrew de Staunton, rector in 1297, was probably related to the lords of the manor.[27] John Jordan alias Stoke, rector by 1425 until 1438, was pardoned in 1425 for having himself tonsured

[96] V.C.H. Som. i. 474.
[97] C.P. 25 (2)/51/359/4 Hen. VIII Hil.; C 142/53/14.
[98] C.P. 25(2)/35/237/19 Hen. VIII Trin.; C.P. 25(2)/ 204/15 & 16 Eliz. I Mich.
[99] Prob. 11/73 (P.C.C. 41 Leicester).
[1] S.R.O., Q/SR 21/34; D/D/Ct H, will of John Harvie; Q/SR 107/3; Prob. 11/134 (P.C.C. 96 Parker).
[2] S.R.O., tithe award.
[3] S.R.O., DD/HI, box 53, copy ct. roll 6 Apr. 1629; DD/X/DF, lease 30 Dec. 1639.
[4] S.R.O., DD/CN, box 12, bdle. 4, lease 24 Dec. 1766.
[5] Som. County Gazette, 20 Oct. 1883, p. 6.
[6] Poor Law Com. 2nd Rep. p. 547.
[7] Tax. Eccl. (Rec. Com.), 199. A reference to a rector of Staunton in 1258 may not refer to Whitestaunton: Cal. Papal Regs. i. 357.
[8] Cal. Pat. 1292–1301, 273; S.R.S. i. 195.
[9] S.R.O., D/D/B reg. 1, f. 179b.
[10] S.R.S. xxxii. 223; xlix, pp. 73, 76–7.
[11] Ibid. xlix, pp. 114, 119; lii, pp. 159, 183; liv, pp. 8, 48.

[12] Ibid. liv, p. 186; lv, p. 108; Som. Incumbents, ed. Weaver.
[13] Dioc. Dir.
[14] Tax. Eccl. (Rec. Com.), 199; Valor Eccl. (Rec. Com.), i. 167.
[15] S.R.O., D/D/Vc 24; D/D/V Dioc. bk. 1727; Rep. Com. Eccl. Revenues, pp. 152–3; H.O. 129/318/2/3/5.
[16] Valor Eccl. (Rec. Com), i. 167.
[17] S.R.O., tithe award.
[18] Valor Eccl. (Rec. Com.), i. 167; S.R.O., D/D/Rg 329.
[19] S.R.O., tithe award; County Gazette Dir. (1840).
[20] H.O. 129/318/2/3/5; P.O. Dir. Som. (1861–6); Kelly's Dir. Som. (1883–1939).
[21] Req. 2/4/210.   [22] S.R.O., D/D/Rg 329.
[23] S.R.O., DD/SP, inventory of Thomas Ballett 16 June 1670.
[24] S.R.O., D/D/B return 1815; Rep. Com. Eccl. Revenues, pp. 152–3.
[25] Coat of arms and date (last figure illegible) over porch.
[26] Ex inf. Mrs. Dobell.
[27] Cal. Pat. 1292–1301, 273.

without mentioning that he was illegitimate.[28] William Lumbard, rector 1449–89, was instituted after his deprivation at Marston Bigot and was not ordained deacon until 1450.[29] William Wyett, rector 1576–8, occupied the living while sub-rector and fellow of Exeter College, Oxford, and rector of Tawstock (Devon).[30] Joseph Greenfield, rector 1615–?51, was imprisoned during the Civil War until released by the royal Cornish army.[31] The intruded minister, Richard Smith, rector 1651–62, removed to Dinnington after his ejection.[32] John Chase, rector 1670–84, held the rectory with a fellowship at Wadham College, Oxford, and Michael Marlow, rector 1789–93, with one at St. John's College, Cambridge.[33] Joseph Attwell Small, rector 1799–1814, held the living in plurality with a number of other benefices including a chaplaincy to the King.[34] Robert Pearse Clarke, rector 1814–27, was non-resident and successively curate of Culmstock and Churchstanton.[35] W. T. Elton, rector 1827–74, was son and brother of successive lords of the manor and with his son-in-law, H. A. Cartwright, rector 1874–1909, occupied the rectory for 82 years.[36]

Thomas Snaydon, a Whitestaunton clerk also described as a thatcher, was imprisoned in 1511 for the theft of sheep.[37] An assistant minister was mentioned in 1532 and 1572–5[38] and assistant curates were regularly employed by rectors during the 17th century.[39]

A service was held each Friday in 1588, and the parishioners complained in 1612 that the Bretts had built two cross walls adjoining the chancel and tower so that they could not go about the church.[40] There were usually only 5 or 6 communicants c. 1776.[41] Single Sunday services were being held in 1815 and 1827 and, in 1843, alternately morning and afternoon.[42] Holy Communion was celebrated twice a year in 1840 and four times in 1843.[43] In 1851 the Census-Sunday congregations totalled 55 in the morning (with a further 21 Sunday-school pupils) and 76 in the afternoon.[44] By 1870 there were two Sunday services and Holy Communion was being administered six times a year.[45]

A light of the Blessed Mary was recorded in 1492 and by 1548 there was a guild of Our Lady at the church with 23s. 5½d. in the hands of two wardens. There was also a cow valued at 20s. in 1548 given to maintain obits in the church.[46]

The church of *ST. ANDREW* has walls of Ham stone ashlar and rubble and comprises chancel with north and south chapels, nave with south porch, and west tower. The walls of the narrow chancel may be in part of the 13th century; those of the nave are at least as old as the later 14th century when the two doorways and the porch were built. The whole building was refenestrated in the later 15th century, probably at about the same time as small north and south chapels were added to the chancel. The tower, of three stages with a projecting south-east stair turret, was built in the early 16th century. Also in the 16th century a rood screen, with a loft approached by a stair projecting from the north wall, was put in and the chancel arch was rebuilt. Later in the century the south chapel was widened and an external doorway was put into the west wall under the will of John Brett (d. 1588).[47] The roofs were renewed in the 19th century when the building was thoroughly restored. The fittings include a 12th-century font and some 16th-century bench ends.

There are five bells: (i) 1696, Thomas Purdue; (ii) 1695, Thomas Purdue; (iii) earlier 16th cent., Thomas Jeffries; (iv) c. 1380, Salisbury foundry; (v) 1779, T. Pike, Bridgwater.[48] Apart from modern plate there is a silver cup of 1658.[49] The registers cover baptisms from 1659 to 1666 and baptisms, marriages, and burials from 1692.[50]

NONCONFORMITY. The Brett family, lords of the manor, probably resumed the ancient faith c. 1591, on the second marriage of Sir Alexander Brett (d. 1609) with Ann daughter of John Gifford of Weston Subedge (Glos.).[51] Lady (Ann) Brett (d. 1647) occurs as a recusant at Whitestaunton in 1605.[52] She was convicted of recusancy in 1609, was heavily fined, and in 1625 was deprived of a quantity of 'old arms'.[53] John Yates alias Hopton, admitted a Jesuit in 1604, was partly educated at Whitestaunton by his uncle Alexander Brett, esq., 'a Catholic in Somerset', and Alexander Cotton, admitted a Jesuit in 1655, was the grandson of Lady (Ann) Brett and was born at Whitestaunton.[54] Of Sir Alexander's children his heir Alexander married into the Kirkhams, a recusant family at Blagdon (Devon), and two of his sisters similarly married Roman Catholic gentry. Sir Alexander's younger brother Robert Brett (d. 1665) rose to be a Benedictine prior on the Continent.[55] Some of the lands of Alexander's son, Sir Robert Brett (d. 1666), 'a papist in arms', were sequestered during the Interregnum, and in 1651 it was ordered that his children have nothing 'till it appear that they are brought up Protestants'.[56] Sir Robert's younger son Robert (d. 1678), who inherited Whitestaunton on his brother's death, was a Jesuit and was involved in the Popish plot.[57]

[28] *Cal. Papal Regs.* vii. 389.
[29] *S.R.S.* xlix, pp. 112, 114, 119; l, p. 487.
[30] Ibid. liv, pp. 8, 186; Foster, *Alumni Oxon.*
[31] *Walker Revised*, ed. A. G. Matthews.
[32] *Calamy Revised*, ed. A. G. Matthews.
[33] Foster, *Alumni Oxon*; Venn, *Alumni Cantab.*
[34] Foster, *Alumni Oxon.*
[35] S.R.O., D/D/B return 1815; D/D/V return 1827.
[36] Burke, *Land. Gent.* (1914), 606.
[37] *S.R.S.* liv, p. 147.
[38] S.R.O., D/D/Vc 20; *S. & D. N. & Q.* xiv. 32.
[39] S.R.O., D/D/Rr 464.
[40] Prob. 11/73 (P.C.C. 41 Leicester); S.R.O., D/D/Ca 175.   [41] S.R.O., D/D/V Dioc. bk. 1776.
[42] S.R.O., D/D/B return 1815; D/D/V returns 1827, 1843.

[43] S.R.O., D/D/V returns 1840, 1843.
[44] H.O. 129/318/2/3/5.
[45] S.R.O., D/D/V return 1870.
[46] *S.R.S.* ii. 14–15; xvi. 303.
[47] Prob. 11/73 (P.C.C. 41 Leicester).
[48] S.R.O., DD/SAS CH 16.
[49] *Proc. Som. Arch. Soc.* xlv. 149.
[50] S.R.O., D/P/whits 2/1/1–7.
[51] *Proc. Som. Arch. Soc.* xxviii. 83; *S.R.S.* lxvii, p. 91.
[52] S.R.O., DD/HI, box 51, subsidy roll Mar. 1604/5.
[53] C 66/1181 m.14; *Proc. Som. Arch. Soc.* xxviii. 83.
[54] *Records of the Jesuits*, ed. Foley, i. 296; iv. 616.
[55] *Proc. Som. Arch. Soc.* xxviii. 84.
[56] *Cal. Cttee. for Compounding*, iii. 1644–5.
[57] *Proc. Som. Arch. Soc.* xxviii. 87; *Records of the Jesuits*, v. 101.

The Bretts evidently attracted to their house and parish other Roman Catholics seeking refuge from persecution. In 1605 there were four recusant servants in the manor-house,[58] and Thomas Suttle, the Bretts' bailiff, and Ann his wife were repeatedly presented for recusancy from 1612 until 1626 as were other inhabitants in the parish. These included in 1623 a woman who kept a dame school and one Agnes Harvey 'lately turned a recusant'. In 1641 there were six recusants including three servants at the manor-house.[59]

The house of John Kerley and two rooms in the house of Thomas Locock were licensed for Baptist meetings in 1804.[60]

EDUCATION. Richard Parker of Whitestaunton, 'sometime schoolmaster' to Sir Alexander Brett's children, was mentioned in 1607.[61] Between 1623 and 1630 a school was kept in the parish by Mary Prescott, a recusant then living in the almshouse.[62]

In 1786 Roger Summerhayes gave £1,500 to the Royal Devon and Exeter Hospital, out of which £10 10s. a year was to be paid to a poor person to teach 11 boys and 10 girls, orphans, or other poor children of the parish or from Yarcombe (Devon).[63] This school was still open in 1819 but did not satisfy demand.[64] A Sunday school was added by the rector in 1818 and in 1835 it had 20 boys and 20 girls, attendance at the day-school having risen to 30.[65] By 1846–7 both schools were being run together in two schoolrooms taught by two mistresses who had housing provided.[66] A new school with a house for the mistress was built by the Eltons south of the churchyard in 1863–4, and by 1894 had an average attendance of 26.[67] In 1903 there were 48 children on the books and attendances averaged 37. The school had been in 'a lamentable state' but a change of teacher had caused 'a pronounced improvement'. There was then one teacher helped by a monitor and the school was supported by £14 18s. from the Summerhayes fund, with additional help from R. J. Elton and small subscriptions.[68] In 1937 children over 11 were removed to Combe St. Nicholas school leaving 15 on the books. The school was closed in 1966, the seven children remaining being transferred to Buckland St. Mary.[69] In 1974 the former school was a private dwelling called the Old Schoolhouse.

CHARITIES FOR THE POOR. John Brett (d. 1588) left £10 a year subject to a life interest from a tenement called Jacquets and lands in Yarcombe (Devon) to support four poor impotent persons in an almshouse. Until the almshouse was built Brett's heir was to continue the distribution of two loaves of bread to each of the ten poorest householders of the parish every Friday, provided that at least three attended morning service on that day each week.[70] The almshouse occurs in 1623 and 1644[71] but not thereafter.

Thomas Ford of Whitestaunton left £5 in 1624, the interest from which was to be distributed to the poor on St. Thomas's day.[72] Stephen Brownsey of Whitestaunton, by will proved in 1657, left £5 to the churchwardens and overseers for the same purposes, to be distributed 'at every year's end'.[73] Similarly Humphrey Warren of Whitestaunton, by will proved in 1648, gave £5 for the relief of the poor.[74] None of these three charities is expressly mentioned after their foundation. They may, however, be represented by an income of 10s. a year held in 1787–8 by the overseer for the benefit of the unrelieved poor.[75]

In 1786 Robert Summerhayes gave £1,500 to the Royal Devon and Exeter Hospital from the income of which £10 10s. was to be distributed weekly in seven sixpenny loaves to the unrelieved poor. The money was so used in 1926, and in 1953–5 bread was purchased for one person and 'grants' made to two others.[76]

[58] S.R.O., DD/HI, box 51, lay subsidy roll Mar. 1604/5.
[59] S.R.O., D/D/Ca 175, 235, 244, 266, 274; S.R.S. xliii. 75; S.R.O., DD/HI, box 10, lay subsidy roll 1641; box 53, lay subsidy roll 1628.
[60] S.R.O., D/D/Rm 2.
[61] S.R.O., D/D/O, registrar's correspondence, box 1.
[62] S.R.O., D/D/Ca 235, 274.
[63] Char. Com. files.
[64] Digest of Returns to Sel. Cttee. on Educ. of Poor, H.C. 224 (1819), ix (2).
[65] Educ. Enquiry Abstract (1835).
[66] Church Sch. Inquiry 1846–7.
[67] Returns of Schs. [Cd. 315] H.C. (1900), lv (2); P.O. Dir. Som. (1866).
[68] S.R.O., C/E 28.
[69] Ibid. box 90, school recs.
[70] Prob. 11/73 (P.C.C. 41 Leicester).
[71] S.R.O., D/D/Ca 235; Diary of Richard Symonds (Camd. Soc. [1st ser.], lxxiv), 36–7.
[72] Prob. 11/143 (P.C.C. 42 Byrde).
[73] Prob. 11/271 (P.C.C. 1657, 33).
[74] Prob. 11/204 (P.C.C. 81 Essex).
[75] Char. Donations, 1787–8, H.C. 511 (1816), xvi.
[76] Char. Com. files.

INDEX

NOTE. An italic page-number denotes an illustration on that page or facing it. The pages containing the substantive history of a parish or hundred are indicated by bold-face type.

Among the abbreviations used in the index the following may require elucidation: abp., archbishop; adv., advowson; agric., agriculture; Alex., Alexander; And., Andrew; Ant., Anthony; archd., archdeacon; Art., Arthur; Bart., Bartholomew; Benj., Benjamin; bp., bishop; br., bridge; cast., castle; Cath., Catherine; cent., century; ch., church(es); ch. ho., church house; chant., chantry; chap., chapel; char., charity(ies); Chas., Charles; Chris., Christopher; cncl., council; ctss., countess; ct(s)., court(s); d., died; da., daughter; Dan., Daniel; dchss., duchess; dom. archit., domestic architecture; Edm., Edmund; Edw., Edward; Eliz., Elizabeth; fam., family; fl., flourished; Geo., George; Geof., Geoffrey; Gilb., Gilbert; Hen., Henry; hosp., hospital; ho., house; Humph., Humphrey; hund., hundred; inc., inclosure; ind., industry; Jas., James; Jos., Joseph; La., Lane; m., married; man., manor; Marg., Margaret; Mat., Matthew; Mic., Michael; mkt., market; Nat., Nathaniel; Nic., Nicholas; noncof., nonconformity; par., parish; Phil., Philip; pop., population; Revd., the Reverend; Ric., Richard; rly., railway; Rob., Robert; Rom. rem., Roman remains; s., son; Sam., Samuel; sch., school; Sim., Simon; Thos., Thomas; w., wife; Wal., Walter; Wm., William.

Abbot, Ric., rector of Misterton, 67
Abdick and Bulstone, hund., 156
Abindon:
    Maud, *see* Cantebrigg
    Rob. de, 183–4
Abraham:
    Joan, 55
    Ric., rector of Chaffcombe, 127
    Sam., 55
    Susannah, w. of Sam., m. (2) Hen. Fry, 55
    Wm., 55
Adams:
    Hen., 138
    Rob. Patten, 84
    fam., 97, 138–9
Adolphy, Fred., 197
Aelfstan of Boscombe, 41
agriculture, *see* common; crop rotation; crops; customary works; dairying; demesnes; grazing; heathland; inclosure; intercommoning; milk; perambulation; planting; produce; sheep; stock; water meadows; woodland; wool
Ailesbury, earl of, *see* Bruce
Albin:
    John, 136
    fam., 136
Aldham:
    John de, 224
    Ralph, 224 *n*
    Sibyl, *see* Oliver
Alexander, John, 73
Aleyn (Alyn):
    John (fl. 1340), 70
    John (fl. 1544), 236
    and see Allen
Alford:
    Edw., 159
    Sarah, 159
    Revd. Thos., 157
    fam., 160
Alfred, king, 10
Algar, 212
Alice of the mills, 23
All Souls Coll., Oxford, 185, 194
Allen:
    F. E., curate of Knowle St. Giles, 162
    J. M., architect, 30, 32–3, 120, 128, 191
    J. T. W., curate of Knowle St. Giles, 162
    John, curate of Knowle St. Giles, 162
    and see Aleyn
Aller, 109; *and see* Beer
Allowenshay (in Kingstone), 147, 149, 202
Almereio, Wm. de, 157, 159

alms-houses, *see* Crewkerne; Hinton St. George; Ilton; Shepton Beauchamp; Whitestaunton
Alva, duke of, 146
Alviet the priest, 179, 191
Alvric, 157
Alward, 152, 165, 177, 232
Alwin, 199
Alyn, *see* Aleyn; Allen
America, 216; *and see* United States
Amesbury (Wilts.), 70
Anabaptists, 61, 106–7, 120, 128, 170, 192, 195
anchoress, 32–3
Andrews, alias Fry, John, 159
Anne, queen, 69
Ansger the cook, 180
Anstice, Edm., 197
Anston, Wm., 22
Anthony, Eliz., 51 *n*
Apley, Thos., 189
architects, *see* Allen; Benson; Bond; Blomfield; Brettingham; Carver; Cooper; Davis; Drew; Felton; Ferrey; Forbes; George; Giles; Grayson; Hicks and Isaacs; Kempthorne; Kemshead; Patch; Sedding; Soane; Street; Tate; Vialls; Vulliamy; Wilson; Wyatt; Wyatville
Arden, Thos., 167
Arminians, 108
Arthur, Prince of Wales, 10
Arundel (Arundell):
    Alex., 12
    Sir Edm., 90
    Eliz., m. (2) Sir John de Meriet, 90
    John, 12
    Sir John, and his w. Maud, 12
    Rog., 142
    Sybil, *see* Montacute
    Sir Thos., 114
    and see Arundell
Arundel, earl of, *see* Fitzalan
Arundell:
    Chas. (fl. 1579), 179
    Sir Chas. (d. 1587), 176
    Hen., Ld. Arundell (fl. 1660), 176
    Hen., Ld. Arundell (d. 1808), 176
    Marg., 176
    Sir Mat., 176
    Sir Thos., 176
    Thos., Ld. Arundell (d. 1639), 176
    Thos., Ld. Arundell (d. 1643), 176
    fam., 185
Arussir, *see* Wigborough
Asch, Pauline, *see* Boulogne; *and see* Ashe; Ayshe
Ash (Esse, in Martock), 78, 81, 83–4, 89–90, 92, 95, 97, 102, 104, 106, 108, 182

agric., 95
Ash Boulogne, 89, 95, 100–1
    ct., 89, 101
    man., 88–9
    Asshepyk, man., 89
    chap., 106
    ch., 106
    fields, 81, 95
    inc., 81, 95
    inn, 83
    man., 81, 96
    Maynes (Ashmaynes), 81
    Pykesash, 81, 95, 104
        man., 89, 97, 101
        man.-ho., 89
    sch., 106, 109
    tithing, 76, 78–9, 81, 95, 106
    vicarage, 106
Ashcombe:
    Alex. of, 71
    Alice of, m. Warresius son of Reynold, 71
    Ric. of, 71
    Warresius of, *see* Reynold
Ashcombe (in Wayford), 19, 29, 68–9, 71–2, 74–5
    man., 71
    tithing, 73
Ashe (Ash, Asshe):
    Faithful, vicar of Misterton, 67
    John de, 14–15; *and see* Henley, John de
    Rob., 216
    Rob. Hoadley, incumbent of Crewkerne and Misterton, 30, 35, 67
    Wm., 58
    Wm. (another), 65
    fam., 65
    and see Ayshe
Ashe (in Musbury, Devon), 182
Ashill, 153, 157, 181, 199, 204
    and see Jordans
Ashland, *see* Asshelond
Ashprington (Devon), 136
Ashton (Asshetone):
    John de, 12 *n*
    Rob., 86
    Sir Wm., 86
    Wm. (d. 1651), 86
    Wm. (fl. 1701), 86
    and see Asshelond
Ashton, Long, 192
    Ashton Court, 42
Ashton Keynes (Wilts.), 135
Aske (Yorks. N.R.), 67
Askerswell (Dors.), 143
Asshelond (Ashland):
    Alice, 12
    Geof. de, 12
    Ives, 12
    John de, 12 *n*

Asshelond (cont.)
Thos. (fl. 1295), 12
Thos. (fl. 14th cent.), 12
Wm. de, 12, 214
fam., 34, 56, 215
Asshetone, see Ashton
assizes of bread and ale, 2, 26, 58
Athelney, abbey, 201–2
abbot, 111 n, 201
Atherstone (in Ilminster), 182
Atkins:
Abraham, 213
Alex., vicar of Merriott, 60–1
Hugh, rector of Eastham, 34
John, 108
Thos., 139
Attemede, John, rector of Seaving-
ton St. Michael, 209
Audley:
Edm., bp. of Rochester, 142
Hugh de, earl of Gloucester, 152
Aumale:
Eliz. de, m. (1) Sir John Mau-
travers, (2) Sir Humph. Staf-
ford (d. 1442), 54, 90
Marg. de, m. Sir Wm. Bonville,
54, 90
Sibyl de, 244
Sir Wm. de, 90
Aumale, counts of, 199
ctss. of, see Forz
Austell, Thos., rector of Dowlish
Wake, 155
Austen:
Sir Edw., 114
Jane, see Strode
Rob., 114
Rob., bell-founder, 105
Avenel:
Emme, m., Jordan de Lisle, 122–3
Marg., m. (1) Warin de Noneton,
(2) Philip de Cauntelo, 122
Oliver, 122, 124 n, 157, 159
fam., 125
Awanbruth, see Wambrook
Axe, riv., 1, 4, 7, 23–4, 68–9, 71–3
Axminster (Devon), 134
Aylesbeare (Devon), 114
Aylworth, John, 165
Ayshe (Aysshe):
Eliz., m. (1) Sam. Cabell, (2) Ric.
Fownes, 179, 189
Jas. (fl. 1566), 166, 179, 189, 218
Jas. (fl. 1582), 179
Jas. (d. 1614), 179
Jas. (d. 1626), 179
Jas. (fl. 1679), 179
Wm. (d. 1617), 179
Wm. (d. 1657), 179, 185
Mrs., 185
fam., 185–6, 189

Baa, Thos. and Parnell de, 25; and see
Bath
Babcary, rector of, see Gaylard
Backaller, Hen., rector of Wambrook,
229
Backwell, 60, 122
Bacon, Mrs. Mary, 182
Baconnean, Nic., 16
Badmondesfield (in Wickhambrook,
Suff.), 16
Bagge, Jas., 58
Bainrafe, see Farnaby
Baker:
Edm., 156
H. L. P., 70
L. I., 70
Thos., 206
Bale, John, 159
Ballowe, Dan., curate of Crewkerne,
30
Bandfield:
John, 189
Jos., 189

Bankes, Hen., vicar of South Pether-
ton, 192
Bannebury:
Mary, see Filoll
Ric., 224
Baptists, 10, 35–6, 61, 67–8, 107, 170,
230, 238
Barker:
Francis, 86
Jos., rector of Shepton Beauchamp,
218 n, 219
Ralph, treasurer of Wells, 86, 103
Rob. (fl. 1701), 86
Rob. (fl. 1726), 86
Barnevill:
Ralph de, 41
Rob. de, 41, 44, 48
Barre:
Avice de la, 23
Wal. atte, 14 n
Barret, Edw., rector of Dinnington
and Seavington St. Michael, 150,
209
Barrington, 85, 107, 111–12, 113–21,
132, 176, 185, 189, 193, 202,
205, 212
adv., 118
Barrington Court, 113–17, 144, 209
canal, 113–14, 117
char., 121
ch., 113, 116, 118–20, 161, 183
plan, 119
cts., 113, 116–18
curates, 118–19; and see Combe;
Crane; Hamlet; Lethbridge;
Meacham; Mere; Smythe;
Southeye; Stevenson; Tyce;
Vaigge
dom. archit., 113, 115
factory, 117
fms., 115, 117
fields, 113, 117–18
friendly soc., 113
glebe, 119
inc., 116–17
inns, 113–14
Little Puckington, 113
man., 114–16, 120
man.-ho., 113–17, 177
mills, 117
Monmouth Rebellion, 114
Nidons, Knighton, 113
nonconf., 120
par. officers, 118
park, 114–16
poor-relief, 118
poorho., 118
pop., 114
rectors, 118
rectory, 116, 118
Rom. Cath., 120
sch., 118, 120–1
tithes, 116–18
vicar, 121, 218
Westport, 113–14, 117
wharves, 117
Bartlett:
John, 25
Rob., 166
Theo., 100 n
fam., 166
Barton St. David, 145
Basildon (Berks.), 89
Basset Down (in Lydiard Tregoze,
Wilts.), 135
Basshe, Edw., 165
Bath:
Eliz., m. Wm. de Weylond, 181
Osbert of (fl. 1232), 181
Osbert of (d. 1296), 181
Reynold of (fl. 1212), 181
Reynold of (d. 1254–5), 181
and see Baa
Bath, 27, 55, 104, 190, 221
archd. of, see Powell

bp. of, 86, 102, 118–19; and see
Jocelin
earl of, see Bourgchier
prior of, 135
priory of, 135
Bath and Wells:
bp. of, 30, 34, 48, 73–4, 103, 127,
132, 139, 142, 145, 154, 162,
219, 228; and see Burnell;
Harewell; Kidder; Montague;
Piers; Stafford
diocese of, 228
Bathealton, 74
Batten, John, 89, 177
Battiscombe:
Peter, 15
Revd. Ric., 15
Rob., 15
Rob. Chas., 15
Battlesden (Beds.), 74
Bayley (Baily, Baylie, Bayly):
John, 33
Ric., rector of Misterton, 67
Thos., bell-founder, 32, 50, 170
Zachary, 85, 93
——, 86
fam., 47
Bayley, Street, & Co., bell-founders, 50
Baynton (Oxon.), 144
beacon, 33
Beagley, Thos., 46, 52
Beaminster (Dors.), 24
(and Redborne), hund. 111, 222
Meerhay, 25
Bean:
Charlotte, m. Edw. (Whitley)
Rodbard, 54
Mary, see Rodbard
Reg. Hen., see Rodbard
Silvester Prior, 54
bear-baiting, 60
Beard (Bearde, Berd, Berde):
John, and his w., 16
Rob., curate of Misterton, 67
Rog., 37
Sam., 12
Beauchamp:
Alice, w. of John (d. 1361), m. (2)
Sir Mat. Gournay, 217
Anne, m. Ric. Neville, earl of War-
wick, 148
Cecily, w. of John (d. 1283), 224
Cecily, m. (1) Rog. Seymour, (2) —
Turberville, 212–13, 217
Eliz., see Streche
Hen., duke of Warwick, 148
Hugh de, 123, 157
Humph. de, 224
Idony, see Lisle
Isabel, see Despenser
John de, Ld. Beauchamp (d. 1283),
224
John de, Ld. Beauchamp (d. 1336),
212–13
John de (d. 1361), 212, 217
John de, and his w. Joan, 161
John de (fl. late 14th cent.), 123
John de (fl. 1420), 123
Ric., earl of Warwick, 148
Rob. de (fl. 1092–1113), 212
Sir Rob. de (fl. 1150–81), 212
Rob. de (fl. 1260), 216
Sibyl, see Oliver
Thos., 201, 224
Wm. (d. 1419–20), 123, 217
——, m. Nic. Buller, 123
fam., 125, 148, 212
Beaufort:
Edm., marquess of Dorset, duke of
Somerset, 91
Hen., earl and duke of Somerset,
85, 91
John, earl of Somerset (d. 1410), 85
John, duke of Somerset (d. 1444), 85
Marg., ctss. of Richmond, 85–6

Beaupyne, Thos., 91
Beavis:
John (d. c. 1791), 225, 227
John (d. 1809), 225
John (d. 1840), 225
fam., 227
Beck:
Ric., 40
fam., 149
Bedfordshire, see Battlesden; Pots-grove
Beer (in Aller), 179
Bel:
Adam le (late 12th cent.), 181
Adam le (fl. 1256), and his s. Adam, 181
Isabel, m. Reynold Funtaynes, 181
Rob. le (fl. 1223), 181
Rob. le (d. 1256), 181
bell-founders, see Austen; Bayley; Bayley, Street, & Co.; Bilbie; Davis; Jefferies; Kingston; Knight; Llewellins and James; Mears and Stainbank; Pike; Purdue; Taylor; W. S.; Warner; Wiseman; Wroth
bell-foundries, see Bristol; Exeter; Salisbury
Belleroche, ctss. de, 84
Beltes, Wm., 91
Bennett:
Edw., minister of South Petherton, 192, 195-6
Israel, 161 n
Benson, Chas., architect, 17, 23
Bere, Edw., assistant curate of Cudworth, 146
Bere (in Wayford), 29, 68-9, 72-4
cts., 73
man., 70-2
man.-ho., 71
Bere, see Dowlish Wake
Berengaria, queen, 84
Bergen (Norway), 152
Berkeley:
Wm. (fl. 1479), 177
Wm., see Portman
Berkshire, see Basildon; Cumnor; Hampstead Marshall; Mackney; Newbury; Windsor
Bernard, John, 70
Bernardini:
Peter, 60
Phil., rector of Merriott, 60
Bernyll, Rob. de, 236
Berry Pomeroy (Devon), 201
Best:
Chas., 216
fam., 216
Bettiscombe (in Charmouth, Dors.), 70, 74, 228
Bevyn:
John (fl. 1484), 54 n
John (? 16th cent.), 55
Bewley, Mrs. M. G., 73
Bible Christians, 35, 50, 67, 120, 128, 133, 147, 151, 156, 196, 204, 210, 230
Bickenhall, 14, 133
Bicknell:
Art., 116
Ric., 52
Wm., 116
Farmer, 116
fam., 116
Bicknoller, Thorncombe in, q.v.
Bicton (Devon), 114
Biddell, Thos., 16
Bidik, Maud, m. Stephen Preston, 135, 139
Bigod:
Maud, see Marshal
Rog., earl of Norfolk, Earl Marshal, 41, 44

Bilbie:
Thos., bell-founder, 61, 120, 133, 194, 220
Wm., bell-founder, 194
Billing:
J.P., curate of Chillington, in-cumbent of the Seavingtons, 132, 209
Jos., 197
Rob. Phelps, curate of Lopen, 169, 197
Wm., 58
Binegar, 166, 219
Bird, Rob., 21, 28, 38
bird-netting, 93
Bishops Hull, 114
Bisse, Geo., minister, 107
Blackaller, John, 161
Blackdown (in Broadwindsor, Dors.), 70
Blagdon (Devon), 237
Blake:
Florence, 191
Rob., 53, 188
W.S., 189
Wm., 188-9, 191
fam., 183, 187
Blanford:
Eleanor, m. Rob. Pauncefoot, 70
John, 70
Rob., 70
Thos., 70
Wm., and his s. Wm., 70
fam., 70
Blomfield, Art., architect, 194
Blount:
Chas., Ld. Mountjoy (d. 1545), 45
Chas., earl of Devonshire, 124
Mountjoy, Ld. Mountjoy, 124
Bluet:
Eliz., see Buckland
John (d. c. 1700), 87
John (fl. 1701), 159
Boce, Wal., 23
Boclond:
Maud, see Meriet
Sir Thos., 166
and see Buckland
Boef, Wm., 55, 58
——, Edith, w. of, see Slade
Boger, Edm., curate of Knowle, 162
Bohun, Marg. de, m. Hugh Cour-tenay, earl of Devon (d. 1377), 11, 176
Bond:
F. Bligh, architect, 32 n
Hen., vicar of South Petherton, 191-2, 196-7
Bonevile, see Crewkerne
Bonner:
Eliz., see Rosse
Wm., 213
Bonning, John, 182
Bonville:
Cath., 54
Cecily, da. of Wm., Ld. Bonville, m. (1) Thos. Grey, marquess of Dorset, (2) Hen. Stafford, earl of Wilts., 54, 88
Cecily, w. of Thos. (fl. 1390), see Streche
Eliz., m. Wm. Tailboys, 91
Guy, 16
John (d. 1427), 54
John (fl. 1454), and his w. Alice, 14
John (d. 1484), 14
John (d. 1493), 14
John (d. 1551), 14
John (fl. 1637), 14
John (fl. 1657), 10, 14
John (fl. 1667), 14
Marg., see Aumale
Ric., 14
Thos. (fl. 1390), 201
Thos. (d. 1565), 14

Sir Wm. (d. 1408), 54-5, 88, 90, 164
Wm. (d. 1412), 54
Wm., Ld. Bonville (d. 1461), 54, 88, 91, 236
fam., 1 n, 34
Bordes, Brian Chas., 223
Bordone, Hamon de, 205
Borgh, Ric. le, 18
Boscombe (Wilts.), 41
Bosworth (Leics.), 11
Botreaux:
Marg., m. Sir Rob. Hungerford, 135
Sir Wm. de, 135
Boulogne:
Joan, 88
John of, 88
Pauline of, 88
Peter of, 88
Pharamus of (d. 1183-4), 84, 88, 95
Pharamus (fl. 1270), 95 n
Ric. of, 88, 96
Sibyl, m. Ingram de Fiennes, 84
fam., 92, 95
Boulogne, counts of, see Eustace; William
Bourgchier:
John, earl of Bath, 177
Thomasia, see Hankeford
Wm., 177
fam., 177
Bovett, Ric., 91
Bovey Tracey (Devon), 218-19
Bowditch:
Honor, see Drake
John, 225
Rob., 25
Bower Hinton (Burhenton, Hanton Mertoc, in Martock), 78, 82-4, 90, 93-4, 97-8, 107-9, 197
fms., 82
fields, 82
friendly soc., 84
green, 82
inc., 94
ind., 82
inn, 83-4
sch., 108
tithing, 76, 82, 92, 109
Bowerman, Ric. John, 225
Bowes:
Sir Jerome, 54
Ralph, 54
bowling green, 42, 211
Bowyer (Bowyar):
John (fl. 1516), 213
John (fl. 1542), 201
Thos., vicar of Martock, 103, 179, 198
Boxley Abbey (Kent), 114
Bradford:
John, 79
fam., 79
Bradon, South, 60, 119, 234
Bragg (Bragge):
Eliz., 71, 75
John (17th cent.), 10
John (d. 1749), 70, 228
John (d. 1786), 70, 228
John (fl. 1796), 228
Molly, m. Claver Morris, 71
Ric. (d. 1643), 70, 73
Ric. (d. 1649), 70
Rog., 130
Wm. (d. 1702), 70, 73
Wm. (d. 1713), 70, 228
Wm. (d. 1726), 70, 73, 228
fam., 70, 72
Braine (Brayne):
Ric., 26, 34
Mr., 101
Brandon:
Chas., duke of Suffolk (d. 1545), 85
Chas., duke of Suffolk (d. 1551), 85
Hen., duke of Suffolk (d. 1551), 85

Branscombe (Devon), Weston in,
    q.v.
Bray:
    Edm., Ld. Bray, 13
    Margery, m. Wm., Ld. Sandys
        (d. 1542), 13
    Maria Sophia, m. Alex. Hood,
        Vct. Bridport, 140
    Sir Reynold, 13, 29
Brayne, see Braine
Bredy, Long (Dors.), 90
Brethren, 36, 50, 61, 108
Brett (Birte):
    Alex. (d. 1511), 233, 236
    Alex. (fl. 1532), 233, 236
    Sir Alex. (d. 1609), 228, 233, 237-8
    Alex. (d. 1617), 233, 237
    Alex. (d. 1671), 233
    Alex. (fl. 1697), 233
    Ann, w. of Sir Alex., see Gifford
    Ann, da. of Rob., of London, w. of
        Hen., 233
    Eleanor, w. of Sim., 233
    Eliz. (fl. 1562), 180
    Eliz., w. of Alex. (d. 1671), m. (2)
        Hen. Klee, 233
    Hen., 233
    Isabel, 180
    Joan, da. of John (d. 1478), m.
        Thos. Hugyn, 233
    Joan, w. of Sim., see Hugyn
    John (fl. 1449), 236
    John (d. 1478), 232-3
    John (d. 1532), escheator, coroner,
        180, 185, 193, 233-4, 236
    John (d. 1588), 233, 236-8
    Ric., 232 n
    Rob. (d. 1541), 233
    Rob. (fl. 1588), 233, 236
    Rob. (d. 1665), 237
    Sir Rob. (d. 1666), 233, 237
    Rob. (d. 1678), 237
    Rob., Jesuit, 233
    Rob., of London, 233
    Sim., 233
    fam., 233-5, 237-8
Brettingham, Mat., architect, 42
Brice:
    Hugh, 149
    John, 149
    John Hopkins, 65
    Peter, 149
    Worthington (d. 1649), 149-50
    Worthington (d. 1719-20), 149
    fam., 65, 148-9
bricks, 4, 22, 38, 42, 47, 98, 113, 171,
    188, 216
    and see tiles
Bridge, Thos., 177
Bridge (Brugg, in South Petherton),
    166, 171-2, 178, 180, 182-4,
    187-9
    man., 182-3
    man.-ho. (Old Bridge), 171, 183
Bridgwater:
    ctss. of, see Howard
    earl of, see Daubeney, Hen.
Bridgwater, 9, 32, 48, 50, 99, 170, 220
Bridport, Vct., see Hood
Bridport (Dors.), 5, 15, 20, 39, 62,
    99, 143, 167, 188
Bristol, 53, 91, 99, 169, 192, 198, 233
    abbey, 153
    bell-foundry, 67, 105, 150, 156, 230
    cath., 192
    chapter, 55, 59, 116, 118-19, 130,
        132, 169, 180, 185, 191-2, 202-
        3, 208
    prebendary, see Castleman;
        Waterland
    earl of, see Digby
    hosp., 190
Bristward, 53
Brito:
    Ansgar (d. c. 1092-5), 232

Ansgar (fl. 1126), 232
    Rog., 232
    Wal. (fl. 1108), 232
    Wal. (d. 1179), 232
    Wal. (d. 1199), 232
Briwere:
    Joan, da. of Wm., m. Wm. de
        Percy, 232
    Joan, w. of Wm., see Reviers
    Ric., 232
    Wm., 15, 28, 33, 232
Broadway, 96, 113, 117
Broadwindsor (Dors.), 16, 68-70, 182
    Drimpton, q.v.
    Netherhay, q.v.
    Sandpit, q.v.
Brome:
    Eliz., m. Jas. Compton, 178
    John, and his w. Alice, 178
Brompton (Mdx.), 57
Brontë, duke of, see Nelson
Brook:
    Edw., Ld. Cobham, 124, 160, 182
    Geo., Ld. Cobham, 124
    Hen., Ld. Cobham, 124
    John, Ld. Cobham, 124, 182
    John, 182
    Sir Thos., and his w. Joan, 124,
        143, 182
    Thos., Ld. Cobham, 124, 182
    Wm., Ld. Cobham, 124
    fam., 202
Brook (in Westbury, Wilts.), 201
Brookes
    Rebecca, see Wyke
    Thos., 54
Brotherton:
    Thos. of, 41
    Maud, da. of, dchss. of Norfolk, 41,
        44
Broughton:
    Eliz., see Pyke
    Ric., 89
Browne (Brown):
    Anne, m. John, Ld. Poulett (d.
        1665), 50
    Eliz. Adams, 61
    Geo. (d. 1677), 124
    Geo. (d. aft. 1677), 124
    Geo. (fl. 1681), 232 n, 235
    John (fl. 1559), 124
    Sir John (d. 1627), 124
    John (d. 1659), 124
    John (d. 1670), 124
    Rob., 124
    Thos., rector of Wayford, 74
    fam., 130
Browning, John, 25
Brownsey, Steph., 235 n, 238
Bruce:
    Chas., Ld. Bruce, 129, 179, 212
    Eliz., ctss. of Ailesbury, see Sey-
        mour
    Jas., 179, 212
    Rob., 179, 212
    Thos., earl of Ailesbury, 129, 131,
        179, 212
Brudenell, Sir Thos., 99
Bruges (Brugg):
    Emme de, 182
    Hugh de (late 13th cent.), 182
    Hugh de (another), 182
    Wm. de (fl. 1232), 182
    Wm. de (another), 182
    fam., 182
    and see Bridge
Brugg, see Bridge; Bruges
Bruton:
    abbey (formerly priory), 60, 112,
        130, 132, 165-6, 169, 179-80, 191,
        201-2
    abbot, 116, 194; and see Gilbert,
        Wm.
    canons, 116, 118, 169, 178-9, 191,
        203

prior, 132, 178, 181, 213
    sacristan, 191
Brympton D'Evercy, 42, 165
Buckerell, John, 206
Buckfastleigh (Devon), 179
Buckingham, duke of, see Stafford
Buckinghamshire, see Whaddon
Buckland:
    Chas., 87
    Eliz., m. John Bluet, 87
    Francis (d. 1642), 87
    Francis (fl. 1751), 58
    John (d. 1563), 87, 91
    John (d. 1678), 87
    John (fl. c. 1700), 87
    Maurice (d. 1710), 87
    Maurice (fl. 1741), 87
    Ric., 87, 91
    Thos., 87
    Thomasine, m. (1) John Buckland,
        (2) Thos. Turbeville, 91
    fam., 91
    and see Boclond
Buckland St. Mary, 100, 111, 140,
    238; and see Westcombland
Buckland Sororum, 16
Buckland, West, 35
Bucknell (Oxon.), 179
Budd:
    Thos., Quaker (d. 1670), 106-7
    Thos., minister (d. 1722), 107,
        120
    Thomasin, 120
    Wm., 38
    fam., 17
Budleigh, East (Devon), 225
Bule, Rob. de, 132 n
Bull, John, 100
bull-baiting, 60
Bullen:
    Ric., 202
    fam., 74
Buller:
    Alex., 123, 135, 159
    Joan, 157
    John (d. by 1485), 123, 160-1
    John (d. 1485), 123, 135, 159,
        206 n
    John (fl. 1526), 123, 125
    John (d. 1592), 123, 202
    John (d. 1599), 123
    John (fl. 1612), 123, 157, 159
    Nic., 123, 157
    Rob., 202
    Thos., 123, 157
    fam., 130, 144, 160, 202
Bulling, John, 166
Bulstone, hund., 151
Bund, Wm., 58
Burgh:
    John de, 213
    Maud de, m. Gilb. de Clare, earl of
        Gloucester, 209
    fam., 213
Burland:
    Claver Morris, 71
    Eliz., see Morris
    Jas. Lloyd Harris, 71
    John, 71
    Sir John, 71
    John Berkeley, 71
    John Burland (Harris), 71
    Mary Anne, 71
Burne, H. H., 55
Burnel (Burnell):
    Dorothy, 70
    Hen., 25, 70
    Isabel, 25
    John, 25, 70
    Ralph, 70
    Rob. (late 12th cent.), 70-1
    Rob. (fl. 1235), 70
    Rob., bp. of Bath and Wells, 212
    Tristram, and his w. Alice, 70
    fam., 71-2

Burre:
John, 159
Simpson, 159
fam., 159
Burrington, 120 n
Burt, Eliz., 189
Burton Bradstock (Dors.), 74
Bury, Art., rector of Exeter coll., Oxford, 175
Busby, Ric., 142
Bush, John, minister, 107
Butcher:
John, see Rodbard
Mary, see Rodbard
Wm., see Rodbard
Butler:
Hen., minister, 107, 204
Mrs., 204
Bykenhulle, John de, 14
Byntre, Jordan de, 205

Cabell:
Eliz., see Ayshe
John, curate of Cudworth, 146
Sam., 179
Wm., 236
Cable, fam., 47
Cadbury, Nic., 148
Caen (Calvados), St. Stephen's abbey, 17, 28
Calvinists, 221
Cambridge:
St. John's coll., 237
Sidney Sussex coll., 140
Canada, 55, 114
canal, see Barrington; Knowle
Cannicott, Ric., 24
Cannington, 89
Canon:
Isabel, w. of John, m. (2) Ric. Slade, 55
John, 55–6, 58
Cantebrigg:
Maud de, m. (1) John de Stafford, (2) Rob. de Abindon, 183
Joan, da. of, m. Thos. de Crauthorn, 183
Canterbury, abps. of, see Laud; Pecham
Cappes:
Eliz., see Jew
Rob., 90
Carent:
John de, 44
Leonard, 44
Wm. (d. before 1343), 44
Wm. (d. 1346), 44
Wm. (d. c. 1422), 44
Sir Wm., 44
fam., 39–40, 44–5, 47–8
Carew, fam., 55
Cartrai, Mauger de, 180–1, 199, 202
Cartwright, H. A., rector of Whitestaunton, 237
Carver:
John (fl. 1653), 138
John (d. 1726), 138
Ric., architect, 9
Cary:
Hen., 100
Thos., 100
Case:
John, 183
Wm., escheator, 183, 185
Casse:
John, 100
Mary, 100
Casselyn, Thos., 138
castle, see Chepstow; Crewkerne; Dinnington
Castle Cary, 12, 134, 199, 218
Castleman, John, vicar of South Petherton, 169, 192
Catherine of Aragon, 10, 30

Cauntelo:
Marg., see Avenel
Phil. de, 122, 125
Caversham (Oxon.), 43 n
Cecil:
Jas., earl of Salisbury, 109
Rob., earl of Salisbury, 87
Cerne Abbas (Dors.), 22
Chaffcombe, 42, 111, **121–8**, 146, 156, 162, 202
adv., 127
agric., 125–6
Avishays (Aveneleseigh, Aveneleseygh), 33, 121–2, 124, 126, 128, 130, 142–3
char., 128
ch., 121, 127–8
cts., 126
dom. archit., 123–4, 127
fms., 121, 125–6
fields, 125
fraternity, 127–8
glebe, 127, 161
inc., 121, 126
inn, 122
Kingston Well (Hecstanes, Hynkestones), 121, 124–6, 161
Lidmarsh (Libbemersa), 121–8, 142–3
man., 121–7, 157, 159, 161–2
man.-ho., 121, 123, 125, 160
minister, see Pinney; Shallett
Monmouth Rebellion, 122
nonconf., 128
Oakenhead (Okenehede), 121, 124
par. officers, 126–7
park, 121–2, 125–6, 160
poorho., 127
pop., 122
rector, 126–7; and see Abraham; Clawsey; Cox; Middleton; Penny
rectory, 127
ho., 121, 127
sch., 128
tithes, 127
tithing, 112
woodland, 125–6
Champernowne (Champernon, Champney):
Hugh, 124, 152
Joan, see Kaynes
John, rector of Shepton Beauchamp, 219
Champney, see Champernowne
Channons (Norf.), 115 n
chantry, see Crewkerne; Dowlish Wake; Hinton St. George; Martock; Petherton, South
Chapple, John, 166
charcoal, 93
Chard, 5, 7, 33–4, 45, 55, 62, 67–8, 121–2, 124, 126–8, 133–4, 137, 142–3, 151, 154, 156–7, 160–1, 178, 222–3, 225, 227–8, 230–2, 235
canal, 157, 161
chant., 144–5
curacy, 30
fraternity, 144
poor-law union, 27, 48, 59, 66, 73, 127, 132, 139, 145, 150, 154, 162, 169, 203, 208, 217, 228, 236
rural district cncl., 51
sch., 67, 132, 162
Walscombe, q.v.
Chard, South, 134
Chardstock (Devon), 222–6, 228–9
ch., 228
Cotley, 223, 225
Lodge, 226
man., 224, 229
prebendary, 228
vicar, 228

Charles I, 157, 232
Charles II, 10
Charlton Mackrell, 17, 142–3
Charmouth (Dors.), Bettiscombe, q.v.
Chase:
Gamaliel, rector of Wambrook, 225, 228–9
Gideon, 225, 228
John, rector of Wambrook and Whitestaunton, 225, 228–9, 237
John (d. 1641), 228
John (fl. 1710), 228
Marg., w. of John, rector, 225
fam., 229
chase, 11, 18, 93
Chastel, Laur. de, 223
Chastelayne, Thos., 148
Cheddar, 192
Cheddon Fitzpaine, Hestercombe, q.v.
Chedington (Dors.), 63, 132, 222
Cheeke, Edw., 86
Chelborough (Dors.), 142
Chelrye, Thos. de, rector of Seavington St. Michael, 209
Chepstow (Mon.), 41
cast., 41
Cheselden, Revd. Edw., 143
Cheshunt (Herts.), 86
chevage, 18, 166, 168, 184, 226
Cheyney (Cheyne):
Anne, m. John Willoughby, 201
Cecily, w. of Sir Wm. (d. 1420), see Streche
Cecily, da. of Sir Edm., 201
Sir Edm., 201
Eliz., m. Sir John Colshull, 201
Joan, see Filoll
Sir Wm. (d. 1420), 201
Sir Wm. (d. by 1434), 224
Chichester, John Hody, 13 n
Chichester (Suss.), 180
Chick, fam., 139
Chidiock:
Isabel, see FitzPayn
Sir John, 142
Child:
Agatha, 179, 212
Francis, 179, 212
Rob., 179, 212
Sam., 179, 212
Sarah Anne, m. John Fane, earl of Westmorland, 179, 212
Chillington, 13, 32, 72, 111, 118–19, **128–33**, 141, 143, 145, 147, 151, 154, 156, 178–9, 182, 185, 189, 192, 204
adv., 132
agric., 130–1
char., 133
Chibley (Chubbeleye), 129–30
ch., 129, 132–3, 161, 183
cts., 131, 190
curates, 132; and see Billing; Hare; Mere; Patch; Phillips; Vaigge
dom. archit., 129
fms., 130–1
fields, 129, 131
glebe, 130, 132
Higher Chillington, 129, 131, 141, 147
Hill, 51, 129, 131
man., 40, 131 n
tithing, 131
inc., 131
light, 132
Lower Chillington, 129, 131
man., 129–31, 133
man.-ho., 129–30
nonconf., 133
par. officers, 131–2
pop., 129
poorho., 132
Rom. rem., 129

Chillington (cont.)
  sch., 132–3
  tithes, 130, 132–3, 180
  tithing, 131
  vicarage, 132, 143
  woodland, 129–31
Chilthorne Domer, Oakley in, q.v.
Chinnock, East, 213
Chinnock, West, 9, 21, 52, 61, 94
Chipley (in Nynehead), 44
Chiselborough, 41, 52, 171
Chislet, Margery, 183
Cholmeley:
  Sir Ric., 114
  Ursula, m. Sir Thos. Putt, 114
Christchurch (Hants):
  prior, 18
  priory, 11, 15
Christon, 168
Chubb:
  Mat., 37
  Mistress, 37
Chudderle, John, and his w., 50
Chulmleigh (Devon), 73
  Stone in, q.v.
church house, see Crewkerne; Long
  Load; Lopen; Martock, Merriott;
  Seavington St. Mary; Seaving-
  ton St. Michael; Shepton Beau-
  champ; Wambrook
church scot (chursett), 18, 56, 92, 94,
  166, 214, 218
Churchill, Mr., 156
Churchstanton, 140, 229, 237
Chydlegh, Christine, m. Thos. Warre,
  50
Clapton:
  Alice, see Bonville
  Baldwin of, 14, 23
  Joan, see Maloisell
  John of (d. 1287), 14
  John of (fl. 1346), 14
  Ric., 14
  Rob. of (fl. 1254), 14
  Rob. of (fl. 1364), 14
  Rog. of, 14
  Wal., 14
  fam., 14
Clapton (in Crewkerne), 1 n, 4–5, 7,
  9–10, 14, 17, 19, 23–4, 30, 34–5,
  69, 75
  Clapton Court, 14, 19, 24
  inn, 10
  man., 14–15, 24
  man.-ho., 14
  mill, 14 n, 23–4, 100
  sch., 36
  tithing, 26
Clare:
  Gilb. de, earl of Gloucester (d.
    1295), 148
  Gilb. de, earl of Gloucester (d.
    1314), 122, 148
  Maud, w. of Gilb. (d. 1314), see
    Burgh
  Ric. de, earl of Gloucester, 112 n,
    122
  Ric. de, clerk, 44
  Rog. de, 148
  fam., 112
Clarence, duke of, see Plantagenet
Clarke (Clark):
  Edw., 124
  Eliz., see Sherlock
  John (fl. 1704), 26
  John (fl. 1830), 212, 218
  Rob. Pearse, rector of Cricket and
    Whitestaunton, 140, 237
  Sam., 186
  Revd. Wm., 218
  fam., 218
Clavelshay, Cuthbert, coroner, 185
Claverham, 122 n
Clawsey, John, rector of Chaffcombe,
  127

Claxton, Wm., 54 n
Clayhidon (Devon), 132
Clement:
  Gregory, 209
  Rob., rector of Seavington St.
    Michael, 209
Clerk, Maurice le, rector of St.
  John's chapel, South Petherton,
  194
Clerkenwell (Mdx.), priory, 165
Clevedon:
  Eliz. of, 134–5, 138
  John of, 134–5
  Marg., m. (1) John St. Lo, (2)
    Sir Peter Courtenay, 135
Clevedon, 115, 192
Cleyhill, Nic., 234
Clifford:
  Chas., 11
  Joan, see Courtenay
Clifton:
  Gervase, Ld. Clifton, 114
  Sir John, 114, 218
  Wm., 114–15
Clifton Maybank (Dors.), 115, 182
Clive:
  Hugh de la, 143
  Rog. de la, 143
Clopton, Wal., 212–13, 223
Clopton (? in Kingsbury Episcopi),
  171
Closworth, 128
cloth manufactures:
  canvas, 21, 98, 153, 187, 207
  cloth, 20, 57, 65, 82, 86–7, 97–8,
    111, 126, 150, 167, 186, 216,
    227, 235
  collars, 117, 203, 207, 216
  dowlas, 102, 167
  dyeing, 20–1, 72
  fuller, 20, 137, 139
  fustian, 60
  girth-webs, 21, 72; and see webbing
  lace, 22
  linen, 20–1, 46, 97, 117, 167–8
  sacking, 187
  sailcloth, 17, 21–2, 25, 47, 57, 98,
    126, 145, 167, 187, 207
  serge, 20–1, 65, 97, 153, 235
  shirts, 21
  silk, 23, 167
  stockings, 97
  weaving, 17, 20, 57, 97, 137, 164,
    167–8, 186, 207, 235
  webbing, 21, 24; and see girth-
    webs
  worsted, 21, 25, 46
  and see gloving
Cnut, king, 20, 201
Coade and Sealy, 50
coal, 79, 117
Coat (in Martock), 78, 81, 83–4, 87,
  90, 93–5, 97–8, 100–104, 107–8
  fields, 81–2
  inc., 94
  inn, 83
  man., 89–90, 96
  tithing, 76, 81–3, 92
Cobham, Ld., see Brook
Coche, John, 161
cockfighting, 9
Coffin:
  Humph., 225
  John, 225, 230
  Mary, 225
Cogan (Coggan):
  Ann, 90, 97
  Eliz., m. (1) Fulk FitzWaryn, (2)
    Sir Hugh Courtenay, 177
  Isabel, w. of Sir Wm., m. (2) Sir
    Rob. Harrington, 177–8, 184
  John (d. by 1408), 177
  John (early 17th cent.), 222
  Ric. de, 138, 177
  Thos., 90

Sir Wm., 177
  fam., 218
Coiner, Wm. le, 144
Coke, Thos., curate of South Pether-
  ton, later Methodist minister,
  107 n, 175, 192–3, 195, 221
Coker:
  Eleanor, see Veel
  John (fl. 1431), 213
  John (d. 1513–14), 213
  Rob., 213
  fam., 214–15
Coker, hund., 112
Coker, West, 54
Cole, Wm., 97
Coles:
  Eliza, 118, 218
  Jas. Benj., 227
  Jas. Stratton, rector of Shepton
    Beauchamp, curate of Bar-
    rington, 119, 211–12, 218–19,
    221
  Julia Mary, 218–19, 221
  Vincent S. S., rector of Shepton
    Beauchamp, 118–19, 218–19
Colles (Collis, Collys):
  Humph., 87
  Thos., chaplain of Long Load, 105
  Wal., rector of Crewkerne, 30
Collier:
  Ann, see Curry
  Revd. Art. (d. 1697), 64
  Revd. Art. (d. 1732), 63–4
  Genevra, 64
  Marg., 64
Collins:
  Anne, 182
  John (fl. 1669), 216
  John, and his w. Jane (late 18th
    cent.), 182
Collinson, Septimus, rector of Dow-
  lish Wake, 155
Colmer, fam., 143
Colshull:
  Eliz., see Cheyney
  Sir John, 201
  Marg., 201
Colston:
  Alice, w. of John, see Wills
  Alice, m. Rob. Merifield, 85
  John, 85
Colthurst, John, 189
Combe:
  Edw., curate of Barrington, 118–19
  John, rector of Crewkerne, 30
  John (fl. 1667), 227
Combe (in Gittisham, Devon), 90, 114
Combe Florey, 16
Combe, Higher (in Dulverton), 90
Combe St. Nicholas, 119, 156, 228,
  231, 235, 238; and see Weston;
  Whitehall
Combe Sydenham (in Stogumber),
  129
common, allotments of, 19, 117, 235
Compton:
  Alice, 178
  Eliz., see Brome
  Sir Hen., 85, 178
  Jas., 178
Compton Durville (Contitone, in
  South Petherton), 92, 111, 171–2,
  174, 180–7, 190, 196, 218
  chap., 182, 193
  fields, 171
  man., 175
  man.-ho., 182
  mill, 188
  tithes, 180
  tithing, 175, 182, 190
Compton, Over (Dors.), 85
Compton Valence (Dors.), 34
Congregationalists, 61, 107–8, 170,
  195
Contitone, see Compton Durville

Cookson, Eliz., 36
Coombe (Coombe St. Reyne, in Crewkerne), 4–5, 9, 17, 19–20, 25, 41
  mill, 25
  tithing, 26, 73
Coombs, Miss, 37
Cooper:
  Royden, architect, 182
  Wm., minister, 107
Cooth, Anne, 100
Corfield, Wm., and his w. Christian, 13
Cornish, Thos., bp. of Tenos, 142
Cornwall, 10; *and see* Duloe; Landrake; Lanherne; Padstow
  duchy of, 91, 94, 96
coroner, 185
Corton Denham, 183
Cosmo, Grand Duke of Tuscany, 42
Cossins:
  Edw., 24
  G.H., minister, 107
  Rog. (fl. 1703), 36
  Rog. (fl. 1780), 24
Cothay (in Kittisford), 88
Cotley (in Chardstock, Devon), 228
Cotton, Alex., 237
Couchman, Col., 233
Countess Marshal, *see* Brotherton
Courcelles, Rog. de, 144, 157, 159, 165
Court (Courte):
  Simon, 159
  Wm. Paris, alias, 34
Courtenay:
  Edw., earl of Devon (d. 1419), 11
  Edw., earl of Devon (d. 1556), 11
  Edw., earl of Devon (d. 1509), 11
  Edw., of Landrake, 12
  Edw. (d. 1622), 12
  Eliz., m. John Trethurf, 12
  Eliz., w. of Sir Hugh (d. 1425), *see* Cogan
  Florence, m. John Trelawney, 11
  Hen. (fl. 1461), 11
  Hen., marquess of Exeter, 11
  Sir Hugh de (d. 1292), 11
  Hugh, earl of Devon (d. 1340), 11, 18, 30, 199
  Hugh, earl of Devon (d. 1377), 11, 199
  Hugh, earl of Devon (d. 1422), 11
  Sir Hugh (d. 1425), 177
  Isabel, m. Wm. Mohun, 11
  Joan, m. (1)—Clifford, (2) Sir Wm. Knyveᵗt, 11, 33
  John (d. 1274), 11, 18, 22
  John, rector of Crewkerne, 30
  John (d. 1615), 12
  Marg., w. of Sir Peter, *see* Clevedon
  Marg., w. of Hugh, earl of Devon (d. 1377), *see* Bohun
  Marg, w. of Edw., of Landrake, *see* Trethurf
  Mary, *see* Reviers
  Maud, m. Sir John Arundel, 12
  Sir Peter (d. 1405), 135
  Peter (d. 1606), 12
  Sir Peter (fl. 1652), and his w. Alice, 12
  Phil., rector of Crewkerne, 30
  Rob. de, 1, 11, 71
  Thos., earl of Devon (d. 1458), 11, 199
  Thos., earl of Devon (d. 1461), 11, 33, 199
  Wm., and his w. Cath., 11
  fam., 1, 18, 26, 28, 30–1, 33, 66, 199
courts and franchises, *see* assizes of bread and ale; chase; cucking stool; felons' goods; frankpledge; gallows; halmote; hundred; infangthief; pillory; sheriff's tourn; shillyng stole; stocks; tumbrel; waifs and strays; warren

Cousins, Valentine, 100
Coutances, bp. of, *see* Geoffrey
Cowdrey:
  Morgan, 44
  Wm. (d. 1498), 44
  Wm., and his w. Alice, 44
Cox:
  Grace, *see* Hallett
  John, 138
  Peter, rector of Chaffcombe, 127
  R., 105
  Ric. Symes, rector of Wayford, 74
  Wm., 63
  Revd. Wm., 63
  Wm. Hody, 63
  Revd. Wm. Trevelyan, 63
  Wm. Trevelyan, 63
Coxe:
  John, 135
  John Hippisley, 135
  Marg., *see* Hippisley
  Ric. Hippisley, 135
Craft, *see* Hinton St. George
Craft St. Reyne, *see* Croft
Crane, Mr., curate of Barrington, 119
Crauden:
  Thos. de, rector of Seavington St. Michael, 209
  Wm. de, rector of Dowlish Wake, 155
Crauthorn:
  Alice, m. John de Moleyns, 183
  Joan, *see* Cantebrigg
  Thos., 183
Craven, Maj. A. E. L., 14
Creeke (Creike):
  H., 16
  Hen., 136
  Joan, *see* Hull
  John, 136
  Rob., 136
  Wm., 136
Crewkerne, *frontispiece*, 1, **4–38**, 39, 44, 52, 56, 61, 78, 85–6, 96, 107, 120, 122, 128, 134, 141–2, 147, 151, 156, 163, 168, 172, 183, 216
  Abbey, 17, *145*
  adv., 11, 28–9
  agric., 17–20
  alms-ho., 8, 37–8
  bank, 22
  Bonevile, 1
  bridewell, 27
  br., 7
  cage, 27
  cast., 5, 11
  chant., 17, 24, 27–8, 30–3, 65
  chap., 5, 12, 32–3, 147
  char., 36–8
  chase, 11, 18
  ch., 1, 4–5, 7–8, 11–12, *16*, 24, 27–34, 66, 73
    ho., 3, 27, 31
  Civil War, 10
  Clapton, q.v.
  common, 4–5, 7, 19–20
  Coombe, q.v.
  cts., 2, 18–19, 26–7
    ho., 23
  Croft, q.v.; *see also* Crewkerne, Fordscroft, Upcroft
  cross, 23, 31
  curates, 17, 29–31; *and see* Ashe; Ballowe; Forster; Fuller; Norris; Pyers; Robyns; Taggart; Toller; Tomkins
  dom. archit., 8–9, 13–17
  Eastham, q.v.
  fair, 18, 20, 22–3, 26–7
  factory, *48*
  fms., 5
  fields, 5, 19–20, 26
  Fordscroft, 19–20
  fraternity, 32

friendly socs., 10, 36
Furland, 4–5, 7, 17, 26, 52
  tithing, 26
Furringdons, 4, 19, 22, 32, 56
glebe, 29
Guyan, 1
Henley, q.v.
hermitage, 8, 33
Hewish, q.v.
hosp., 28
hund., **1–3**, 11, 26, 38, 58, 112, 133
  cts., 1–3, 26–7, 58
  officers, 3
inc., 5, 19–20
ind., 9, 21–2, 25–6, 58
inns, 9–10, 21, 28
  Angel, 21
  Antelope (or Green Dragon), 9, 21
  Bell, 9
  Cock, 21
  George, 9–10, 22
  Gun (or White Hart), 8–10, 21
  King's Arms, 9
  Labour in Vain, 21
  Lamb, 21
  Nag's Head, 9–10
  Red Lion, 8–9, 21
  Ship, 21
  Star, 21 *n*
  White Swan, 9–10, 21
  and see Clapton; Crewkerne, Roundham
justices at, 10
Laymore, 4, 16
  man., 16
Maincombe, 17, 26
man., 1, 5, 10–19, 23–4, 26, 29, 31, 33, 53, 63–5, 69, 73
  ho., 8, 12
mkt., 8, 11, 18, 20, 22–3, 26–7
mkt. pl., 7–9, 19, 22–3, 31
Merifield Ho., 8, 15–16
Merriottsford, 4 *n*
mills, 11, 17–18, 21–6, 53
minster, 4, 26, 28–9, 62, 68, 73
mint, 20
Monmouth Rebellion, 10
nonconf., 34–6, 195–6
obits, 32
par. officers, 26–7, 31
parks, 4
pillory, 27
poor-relief, 27
pop., 10
portreeve, 22, 27
Post Office, 10
public services, 9
quarry, 4 and *n*
race course, 9
rly., 5, 7
rectors, 16, 28–30, 32, 74; *and see* Collys; Combe; Courtenay, John, Phil.; Hendyman; Hoper; Kent; Lanvyan; Odelande; Plummer; Pyl; Stafford, John; Surland
rectory, 7–9, 19, 22–3, 27–32, 66, 73–4
  ho., 8, 16–17, 29
Rom. Cath., 34
Rom. rem., 5
Roundham (Rowenham), 4–5, 7, 9–10, 18–20, 39, 62, 67
  inns, 10
schs., 8–10, 27–8, 30–2, 35–7, 51, 127, 132, 162, 170, 219
seal, 28
shambles, 19, 22–3, 27–8
Sheerehall, 12
shops, 19, 22–3
Southcombe, 16
stalls, 19, 22
streets, 8
  Abbey (Carter) St., 8–9, 21, 37

Crewkerne (cont.)
Church (Scole) St., 8–9, 21, 23, 36–7
Court Barton, 8, 37
Cross (Cross Tree) St., 8
East St., 8, 15, 21, 23, 36–7
Fore St., 8, 21; and see Crewkerne, mkt. pl.; Crewkerne, streets, Market Sq.
Gould's Barton, 7, 27
Gouldsbrook Terr., 7–8, 30
Hermitage St., 8, 21, 27, 35
Lyewater, 7–8
Maiden Beech, 5 and n, 22
Market Sq., 9
Market (Sheep Market) St., 8–9, 21, 23
New Court La., 8, 29
North St., 5, 8, 21–2, 24–6, 35–6
Oxen La., 8, 36
Poples Well, 21
South St., 8–9, 21–2, 28, 33–4, 36–8
Viney Br., 8–9, 21, 24, 34
West (Almshouse, Chard) St., 8, 22–3, 35–7
theatre, 9
tithes, 4, 16–17, 28–9
tithings, 1, 5, 19, 26, 38; and see Clapton; Coombe; Eastham; Crewkerne, Furland; Hewish; Woolminstone
town clerks, 27, 30
town hall, 9, 23, 28
town house, 23
Tuncombe, 4–5
Upcroft, 19
U.D.C., 22, 38
arms, 28
vicar, 74
vicarage, 29, 74
ho., 30
Victoria Hall, 22–3
West Crewkerne, 28, 36, 38
woods, 4–5
Woolminstone, q.v.
workho., 27
Cricket:
John of, 134 n
Mic. of, 13, 134
Sir Ralph of, 134
Sir Thos. of, 134
Thos. of, rector of Cricket St. Thomas, 140
Wm. of (fl. 1166), 134
Wm. of (d. c. 1313), 12, 134
fam., 12, 34, 134
cricket, 40
Cricket Malherbie, 70, 73, 107, 121, 127, 137, 141, 143–4, 146, 155–7, 159, 161–2
Cricket St. Thomas, 12, 16, 50, 61, 111–12, 121–2, 125, 129, 133–41, 169, 183
adv., 137, 139
agric., 136–7
chap., 141
char., 141
ch., 74, 133, 136, 139–41, 161
cts., 136, 139–40
Cricket Ho., 133–4, 144
fair, 134, 138, 141, 168
fms., 134, 137
fields, 136
glebe, 137, 140
Hollowells (Hollywille), 133–4, 138
inc., 136, 138
inns, 134
Lanscombe, 133, 135–7
man., 134–5, 137–9
man.-ho., 133, 135, 137–8, 140–1
Marshwood, 133–4, 136–7
mills, 133–4, 138–9
nonconf., 140–1
par. officers, 139

park, 133–4
poorho., 139
poor-relief, 139
pop., 134
rector, 136, 139 n, 140–1, 219; and see Clark, Rob. Pearse; Cricket, Thos. of; Hucker; Langdale; Shaw; Sprengehose; Templeman, John
rectory, 135, 139, 141
ho., 134, 140
sch., 141
tithes, 140
warren, 137
White Down, 133, 136, 138, 141
woodland, 133, 136–7
Croc, Wal., 232
Croft (Craft St. Reyne, Countess's Craft, in Crewkerne), 5, 10, 18–19
cast., 5
man., 18
and see Crewkerne: Fordscroft; Upcroft
Cromwell, Oliver, 104, 191
crop rotation, 20, 45, 117, 166–7, 186, 215
crops (less common):
apples, 45, 48, 57, 66, 164, 218, 227, 229
cabbages, 57, 192
carrots, 57, 60, 192
clover, 20, 96, 167, 186, 202, 207
evergrass, 20
flax, 21, 23, 25, 46–8, 56–7, 60, 72, 87, 97, 111, 117, 131, 149, 167–8, 186–7, 192, 202, 205, 207, 215, 227
hemp, 47, 57, 60, 66, 87, 111, 117, 140, 166–7, 186–7, 192, 202, 207, 218
hops, 57, 60, 192, 229
leeks, 66
onions, 66
pears, 57
sugar beet, 187
turnips, 20, 60, 96, 103, 186
vetches, 167, 186
Crosse, John and Alice, 25
Crossley, Maj. A. A., 64
Crymelford, fam., 202
cucking stool, 112, 190
Cudworth:
Alan de (fl. 1334), 44
Alan de (d. 1361), 44
Avice, m. Stephen Derby, 44
John of, 144
Cudworth (Cudworde), 111, 121, 123–4, 127–9, 131–2, 141–7, 151, 154–5, 157, 160
adv., 145
agric., 144
ch., 141–2, 145–7, 157, 162
plan, 146
Clyve, Clyvelond, 142–3
cts., 145
curates, 145–7, 162; and see Bere; Cabell; Mules, J. H.
dom. archit., 142–3
fms., 144
glebe, 143, 145
Higher Green, 142
Higher Weare, 144, 147
inc., 144
inn, 142
man., 142–4, 152, 157, 202
man.-ho., 141–3
mill, 145
Monmouth Rebellion, 142
nonconf., 147
par. officers, 145
poorho., 142, 145
pop., 142
prebend, 143–5, 162
prebendal ho., 142–3, 145

prebendary, 142, 145–6, 162; and see Audley; Busby; Fulford; Southeye
quarries, 141
sch., 142, 146–7
tithes, 143, 145
tithing, 145
Upton, 142, 144
vicarage, 143, 145
Wear Green, 142
Weare, 142–3, 145
woodland, 141, 144
Worth (Werthe, Worde), 111, 141–4, 159 n
Cuff:
Hen., 41, 50
Wm. Fitchett, 57
Culmstock (Devon), 237
Cumnor (Berks.), 33
Curry:
Ann, m. Revd. Art. Collier, 64
Thos., 64
Wm., 64
——, m. (2) Wm. Elsdon, 64
fam., 64
Curry, North, 191; and see Lillesdon
Curry Mallet, 17, 55, 165
honor, 165
park, 165
Curry Rivel, 113, 155–6, 222
Curtis, Thos., vicar of Martock, 103
customary renders:
bakselver, 18
charnag (charniag), 166
cider, 93
eels, 93
geese, 93
gloves, 93
'greslamb', 92
Hock ewe, 64
hurdle silver, 125
iron slabs, blooms, 18, 136, 166
larder dues, rents, silver, 56, 166, 214
Lukefyne, 92
pepper, 93
Peter's Pence, 166
Plashett (Plashnett), 126
scotmust (skotmust), 18, 92
'suleacresede', 93
wax, 93
customary works (general), 18, 45, 64, 93–4, 116, 136, 166, 184, 214, 234
sheep washing, 18
sheep folding, 18
customs and services, see chevage; serjeanty, tenure by
Cutts, Ric., 16
Cynewulf, king, 224

dairying, 18, 20, 45–6, 57, 88, 130–1, 135, 137, 142, 144, 149, 153, 161, 187, 215
Dalton:
Mary, see Slade
Mary Slade, 13
Nat., 13
Damer, Edw., 107 n
Dampier, Joel, 227
Dane:
Adam the, 205
Wm. the, 205
Danger:
Frances Sarah, see Rodbard
Rob., 54
Daniel:
Geo., 178
Jas., 216
Jas. Patten, 191
John, 178
Darby:
Chas., 108

Jennings, 124, 161
fam., 149
Daubeney (Daubeny):
Cath., w. of Ralph (fl. 1378), 193
Cath., w. of Hen., see Howard
Eleanor, w. of Giles (d. 1386), 131, 183
Eliz., w. of John, see Scrope
Eliz., w. of Jas., m. (2) Wm. Keymer, 70, 73
Ellis, 116, 176, 183
Sir Giles (d. 1386), 176, 183
Sir Giles (d. 1403), 176
Sir Giles (d. 1446), 176, 194
Sir Giles, Ld. Daubeney (d. 1508), 114–15, 129, 176, 179, 183
Giles (d. 1559), 70
Giles (d. 1630), 70
Hen., earl of Bridgwater, 114–15, 117, 129, 159, 176, 179, 185, 194, 213
Hugh (d. 1565), 70
Hugh (d. 1662), and his w. Eliz., 70
Jas. (fl. 1528), 70
Jas. (d. 1613), 73, 129
John (d. 1409), 117, 176, 194
John (d. 1625), 9, 24
John (fl. 1647), 24
Marg. (?Beauchamp), w. of Giles (d. 1403), 176
Phil. (d. 1236), 111–12, 116, 176
Sir Phil. (d. 1294), 176, 194
Ralph (fl. 1234), 176
Ralph (fl. 1235, ? another), 176
Ralph (d. 1291–2), 111, 116, 176, 184, 188, 194
Ralph (fl. 1378), 176, 183, 193
Wm., 65, 176
fam., 65, 114, 129, 176–9, 181–2, 184, 186, 189, 194
Dauncye:
Anne, see Moleyns
John, 189
Davis (Davies):
Ann, see Rosewell
Geo., bell-founder, 50, 61
John (fl. 1594), 88
John (fl. 1652), 201
Mary, 37
Maurice, architect, 120 n, 188, 192, 196–7
Davison, J. W., 159
Davy, Nic., 184
Dawes, fam., 55
Deane:
Alice, see Serrey
Geo., 178
John, 226–7
Thos., 223, 227
Thos. Palmer, 223
Wm., 178
demesnes:
leasing of, 19, 55–6, 64, 93, 149, 166, 206, 214, 226
sale of, 19, 55–6, 71, 93, 96, 116
Denebaud:
Alice, see Gifford
Eliz., m. Wm. Poulett, 42, 123
Florence, 123
Hamon, 41–2, 44
Joan, see Stocklinch
John (d. 1390), 42, 123, 213
John (d. 1429), 42, 123, 125
Marg., 42, 45
Phil. (fl. 1233), 41–2
Phil. (fl. 1303), 42
Thos., 42, 44, 123, 161
Wm. (fl. mid 13th cent.), 41–2
Wm. (fl. 1303), 42, 44, 123
fam., 39, 45, 47, 50, 125, 213
Denman:
And., 166
Bros., 167

fam., 167
Dennys, Ric., 90
Denslow:
Edm., and his w. Susanna, 139
Eliz., see Scriven
Derby:
Avice, see Cudworth
Rob., 44
Steph., 44
fam., 56
Derby, earl of, see Stanley
Despenser:
Hugh le, 122
Isabel, m. Ric. Beauchamp, earl of Warwick, 148
Wal. le, and his w. Agatha, 23
fam., 148
Devereux:
Frances, m. Wm. Seymour, duke of Somerset (d. 1660), 219
Rob., earl of Essex, 10, 41, 175
Devon, ctss. of, see Forz
Devon, earls of, see Courtenay; Reviers; Stafford
Devon, 10, 30, 35, 69, 111, 171; and see Ashe; Ashprington; Axminster; Aylesbeare; Berry Pomeroy; Bicton; Blagdon; Bovey Tracey; Branscombe; Buckfastleigh; East Budleigh; Chardstock; Chulmleigh; Clayhidon; Coombe; Culmstock; Dunkeswell; Flete; Gittisham; Greenway; Halberton; Hawkchurch; Holberton; Honiton; Membury; Musbury; Otterton; Ottery St. Mary; Pinhoe; Pole Anthony; Sowton; Stockland; Stone; Tawstock; Thorncombe; Tiverton; Upottery; Washfield; Weston; Widworthy; Yarcombe
Devonshire, earl of, see Blount
D'Ewes, Sir Simonds, 224
Dewport, fam., 125
Digby, John, earl of Bristol, 228
Dillington, John, and his w. Eliz., 157
Dillington (in Ilminster), 145
Dinnett, fam., 223
Dinnington, Sim. of, 208
Dinnington, 38, 40, 49, 111, 128–9, 145, 147–51, 199, 202, 204, 208–9, 237
agric., 148–9
'cast.', 147
chaplain, 208
ch., 147–8, 150–1, 169, 208
clerk, see William
cts., 149–50
dom. archit., 148, 150
fms., 149
fields, 149
glebe, 150
inc., 149–50
inn, 148
man., 148–9, 205, 208
man.-ho., 148–9
mill, 39, 147, 149
Netherton, 147
nonconf., 151
par. officers, 150
Pit, 147, 149–50
poorho., 150
pop., 148
rectors, 40 n, 147, 150; and see Barret; Glasbroke; Stambury
rectory ho., 148, 150
sch., 151
tithes, 150
tithing, 112
Disraeli, Benj., 179
Disshe, Art., 15
Dobell:
A.E., 233
fam., 235

Dodd:
Revd. Wm., 143
fam., 143
Doddington, Leonard, 87
Dodeman, 53, 58
Domett (Dummet):
Jos., rector of Shepton Beauchamp, 218–19
Wm., 21
Dommett (in Buckland St. Mary), 111, 116
Donisthorpe:
Anna Maria Susanna, see Donne
Revd. Geo., 15
fam., 19
Donne:
Alice, w. of John (fl. 1739), see Merifield
Anna Maria Susanna, m. Revd. Geo. Donisthorpe, 15–16, 37
Benj. J. M., 15
Eliz., m. Hen. Parsons, 15
Jas., 15–16, 86
John (fl. 1739), 15, 85
John (d. 1768), 15, 85–6
John (fl. 1800), 46
fam., 149
Donyatt, 107, 119, 232
Dorchester (Dors.), 5, 37, 62–3, 225, 226 n
Dorset, marquess of, see Beaufort; Grey
Dorset, 1, 5, 7, 35, 105, 206, 224, 230–1
sheriff of, see Oliver, Jordan
Standing Committee, 228–9
and see Askerswell; Beaminster; Bettiscombe; Long Bredy; Bridport; Broadwindsor; Burton Bradstock; Cerne Abbas; Charmouth; Chedington; Chelborough; Clifton Maybank; Over Compton; Compton Valence; Dorchester; Drimpton; Evershot; Frampton; Gaunts; Gillingham; Hilton; Holwell; Hook; Iwerne Courtney; Lulworth; Lyme Regis; Maiden Newton; Mangerton; Mappowder; Meerhay; Moreton; Mosterton; Netherbury; Parnham; South Perrott; Pilsdon; Poole; North Poorton; Powerstock; Ryme Intrinseca; Sandford Orcas; Sandpit; Seaborough; Shaftesbury; Sherborne; Steepleton Iwerne; Stinsford; Stoke Abbott; Swyre; Tarrant Gunville; Thorncombe; Thornford; Whitchurch Canonicorum; Wimborne Minster; Winterborne St. Martin; Woodlands; Yetminster
Dorville, John Wm., 228
Doulting, 155
Dowding:
Eliz., m. Adolphus Kent, 55
Fred., 55
Peter, 55
Dowlish, Eustace of, and his w. Helen, 177
Dowlish Wake (East Dowlish), 25, 111, 128, 141, 143, 146, 151–6, 157
adv., 154
agric., 153
Bere, 151–4, 156–7
chant., 155
ch., 151, 154–6, 160
cts., 154
curates, 155; and see Mules, J. H.
dom. archit., 151–2, 155, 193
fms., 153
fields, 153–4
friendly soc., 152
glebe, 154

Dowlish Wake (East Dowlish) (cont.)
  inc., 153
  inns, 152
  man., 152–4
  man.-ho., 151, 153, *160*
  mills, 144, 151, 153–4
  Monmouth Rebellion, 152
  nonconf., 156
  par. officers, 154
  poorho., 154
  pop., 152
  rector, 132, 154, 156; *and see*
    Austell; Collinson; Crauden;
    English; Hunt; Kinder;
    Mules, F. H.; Speke, Benj.,
    Hugh, Phil., Wm.; Williams,
    John
  rectory ho., 151, 154–5
  sch., 156
  tithes, 154
  'Wythele', 153
Dowlish, West, 145, 151, 153–5,
    159–60
Downham:
  Jas. (d. c. 1556), 32, 136
  Jas. (fl. 1638), 25
  John (fl. 1618), 25
  ——, John, son of, 25
  Peter, 25
  Wm. (fl. 1589), 136
  Wm. (fl. 1629), 136
Downton (Wilts.), 105
Drake:
  Agnes, *see* Mathew
  Geo., 225
  Hen., 225
  Honor, m. John Bowditch, 225
  John, 225–6
  Mary, 225
  fam., 225 n
Draper:
  Chris., 91
  Jas., rector of Eastham, 34
  John (fl. 1492), 45
  John (fl. 1571), and his w. Eliz., 25
  John Gray, 22
  Wm., 22
Drayton (in South Petherton), 171,
    179, 183–5, 187, 189
  fields, 172
Drayton, 113, 119
Drew:
  R. W., architect, 218
  Wm., 222
Drewer:
  Eliz., 206
  Ric., 205–6
Drimpton (in Broadwindsor, Dors.),
    14
Dudley, John, earl of Warwick, 212
Dugdale, Jas., rector of Shepton
    Beauchamp, 218 n, 219
Dukes, Benj., minister of South
    Petherton, 192
Duloe (Cornw.), 201 n
Dulverton, 178; *and see* Higher
    Combe
Dummet, *see* Domett
Dunkeswell (Devon), 132
Dunn, Eliz., 202
Dunning, ——, 25
Dunster:
  Giles, 206
  Hen. (d. 1668), 201, 207
  Hen. (fl. 1680), 201
  Iron, 202
  fam., 206
Dunster, 225
Dunwich (Suff.), 49
Duporte, Thos., 71
Durville:
  Eustace de (fl. 1212), 14, 181
  Wm. de (late 12th cent.), 14, 181
  Wm., s. of Eustace, 181
  fam., 116, 181

Duyn, Nic. de, and his w. Alice, 15
Dyer:
  Edw., 91
  Francis, 86
  John (fl. 16th cent.), 88
  John, minister, 107
  Rob., 88, 105
  Sam., 109
  Sir Thos., 91

Eadnoth the staller, 53
  Harding, son of, *see* Harding
Eames:
  Agnes Elsie, *see* Williams
  R. F. P., 223, 225, 228
  Thos. Deane, 225, 231
  Thos. Palmer, 225
  fam., 223
Earl Marshal, 41; *and see* Bigod;
    Marshal; Mowbray
Earnshill Ho., 119
Eason:
  Eliz., 120–1, 183
  John, 180, 183
  fam., 117, 149, 180, 187
Eastham:
  John of, 12, 33
  Rog., 12
  Turstin of, 12, 134 n
Eastham (Easthams, in Crewkerne),
    4, 12, 17–19, 26–7, 29, 67, 134
  adv., 12, 34
  ch., 4, 12 n, 13, 28, 33–4
  man., 12–13, 19, 23, 34, 56, 68
  man.-ho., 13, 23
  mill, 23
  rector, 30, 33–4; *and see* Atkins;
    Draper
  tithing, 26, 34
  toll gate, 7
Ecclesiastical (Church) Commis-
    sioners, 55, 86, 92, 116, 143, 145
Eddeva, or Edith 'Swan's neck', 10
Edgar, fam., 26
Edinburgh, 73
Edith, queen, 84
Edith 'Swan's neck', *see* Eddeva
Edmar, 148
Edmonds:
  John, 174
  John Baker (d. 1848), 174, 176,
    179–80, 187, 189–90, 196
  John Baker (fl. 1851), 187, 190
  Wm., 186
Edward the Confessor, 84
Edward I, 41, 85
Edward IV, 11
Edward VI, 194, 220, 230
Edward, Black Prince, 59
Edwards:
  Chas., 228–9
  Hen. (d. 1850), rector of Wambrook,
    228–9
  Hen. (d. 1881), rector of Wam-
    brook and Churchstanton, 228–9
  Martha, 228
Egbert, king, 224
egg shackling, 221–2
Eleanor of Castile, queen, 85
Elford, John, 24
Elim Pentecostalists, 61, 151
Elizabeth I, 182
Elizabeth of York, queen, 30
Elliott (Eliot):
  Ann, 219
  Hen., 24
  Jas., 89
  Jas., minister of Shepton Beau-
    champ, 219
  John, 89
  fam., 24
Ellis, John, 87
Elsdon:
  Wm., 64
  ——, w. of, *see* Curry

Elton:
  Sir Abraham, Bt. (d. 1728), 233
  Abraham (d. 1762), 233–4
  Chas. Isaac, 232–3
  Edw., 124
  Fred., 233
  Isaac (d. 1774), 233
  Isaac (d. 1790), 233–4
  Isaac (d. 1837), 233
  Jacob, 233
  N. W. D., 236
  Rob. Jas., 233–4, 238
  W. T., rector of Whitestaunton,
    236–7
  Wm. Marwood, 235
  Wm. Warry, 124, 143
  fam., 233, 235, 238
emigration, 28, 48, 59, 102, 114, 191,
    207, 216
England:
  Jas., 182, 187, 212
  Mary, 121
  Rob., 21
  Stephen (fl. 1659), 189
  Stephen (fl. 1699), 189
  Wm., 212
Engleskevill, Theobald de, 41
English, Nic., rector of Dowlish
    Wake, 155
Erle-Drax-Grosvenor, *see* Grosvenor
Erridge, E. F., 170
Erskine:
  John, earl of Mar (d. 1634), 201
  John, earl of Mar (d. 1653), 201
escheator, 184–5
Esse:
  Alan de, 142; *and see* Kingston
  Joan, *see* Furneaux
  Mat. de, 123, 142–4, 157
  Ric. de, and his w. Alice, 14; *and see*
    Asshe
Essex, earl of, *see* Devereux
Essex, 159; *and see* Hacton; Upmin-
    ster; Stanstead
Esthalle:
  Ela, *see* Sor
  Wm. de, 122
Estmond:
  Chris., 226
  Mary, m. Humph. Coffin, 225
  Nic., 225
  Thos., 225–6
  Wm., 228
  fam., 45
Ethelred II, 20
Ethelweard, 10
Eu, counts of, 41; *and see* William
Eustace, count of Boulogne, 84, 87,
    180
  Geof., s. of, 84
  Maud, da. of, m. King Stephen,
    84
Evans:
  Lewis, curate of Knowle, 162
  Thos., curate of Seavington St.
    Mary, 204
  Wm. Bertram, and his w. Jane, 16
Evercreech, 86, 136, 219
Evershot (Dors.), 22 n, 88
Every:
  Ann, m. John Leigh, 88
  John (fl. 1600), 88–9
  John (d. 1679), 88
  Wm. (fl. 1586), 88
  Wm. (fl. 1600), 89
  Wm. (d. 1652), 88
Exeter, bps. of, 142; *and see* Neville,
    Geo.
Exeter, duke of, *see* Holand
Exeter, earl of, *see* Reviers, Baldwin
Exeter, marquess of, *see* Courtenay,
    Hen.
Exeter, 5, 27, 30, 38, 58, 67, 128,
    155–6, 163–4, 168, 172, 185,
    199, 205, 229

bell-founders, 156, 230
Godshouse, 185
Exeter College, Oxford, 175, 237

fair, *see* Crewkerne; Cricket St. Thomas; Hinton St. George; Lopen; Martock; Merriott; Petherton, South; Shepton Beauchamp
Fairfax, Sir Thos., Ld. Fairfax, 10
Falconer:
  Avice, m. Rob. de la Linde, 148
  Joan, 148
  fam., 148
falconer:
  Rob. the, *see* Robert
  Siward the, *see* Siward
  Wm. the, *see* William
Falevy, John de, 212
Fane:
  John, earl of Westmorland, 179, 212
  Sarah Anne, *see* Child
  Sarah Sophia, m. Geo. Villiers, earl of Jersey, 179, 212
Fanstone, John, 88, 105
Fareways, Joan, and her s. Wm., 213
Farnaby (Bainrafe), Thos., 84, 108, 196
Farnebergh, John de, and his w. Eliz., 224
Farnham:
  Hugh, 64
  Thos., 108
  fam., 65
Farrant, Mr., 99
Farwell:
  Art. (d. 1625), 114
  Art. (fl. 1642), 114
Fauconberg:
  Sir Peter de, 91
  Peter de, 91
  Rob. de, 91
  Wal. de, 91
  Wm. de, and his w. Maud, 91
felons' goods, 2, 26, 100
Felton, ——, 43
Fenne, Hugh de la, 91
Ferrey, Benj., architect, 60
Fidelity Trust, 182
Fiennes:
  Ingram de (d. 1189), 84
  Ingram de (d. *c.* 1270), 85, 99
  John de, 85
  Rob. de, 85
  Sibyl, *see* Boulogne
  Wm. de (fl. 1206), 84
  Wm. de (fl. 1230), 85
  Sir Wm. de (d. 1302), 11, 85
  fam., 105
Filoll:
  Anne, m. Sir Edw. Willoughby, 224
  Cath., m. Edw. Seymour, duke of Somerset, 224
  Joan, w. of Wm. (fl. 1411), m. (2) Sir Wm. Cheyne, 224
  John (fl. early 15th cent.), 224
  John (d. 1468), 224
  Marg., w. of John (d. 1468), m. (2) John Wroughton, 224
  Mary, m (1) John de Percy, (2) Ric. Bannebury, 224
  Wm. (fl. 1354), 224
  Wm. (fl. 1411), 224
  Sir Wm. (d. 1527), 224
Finchley (Mdx.), 68
Firth, Capt. C. P. L., 182
Fish, N. G., 197
fishery, 92–3, 96, 99
Fitchett, fam., 21
Fitzalan:
  Ric., earl of Arundel and Surrey (d. 1376), 206
  Ric., earl of Arundel and Surrey (d. 1397), 206

Fitzharding:
  Nic., 54
  Rob., 53
FitzPayn:
  Ela, w. of Rob. (d. 1354), 205
  Isabel, m. John Chidiock, 142
  John, 123–4
  Sir Rob. (d. 1281), 142
  Rob., Ld. FitzPayn (d. 1315), 142, 205
  Rob., Ld. FitzPayn (d. 1354), 123, 142, 205
  Rog., 142
Fitzroy, Hen., duke of Richmond, 85
FitzWaryn (FitzWarin):
  Eliz., m. Sir Ric. Hankeford, 177
  Eliz., w. of Sir Fulk, *see* Cogan
  Sir Fulk (d. 1391), 177
  Fulk (d. 1407–8), 177
  Fulk (fl. 1408), 177
  Pain, rector of Shepton Beauchamp, 219
Fivehead, 60
fives, 9, 211
forest, *see* Neroche
Flax Bourton, 192
Flemyng:
  Joan, m. Thos. Puf or Pyf, 91–2
  Rog., and his w. Christine, 91
Flete (in Holbeton, Devon), 178
Flint, Humph., 86
Foliot:
  Ellen, m. Ralph de Gorges, 69
  Rob., 69
  Thos., 69
  Wal., 69
  fam., 69
Folsham, Benet de, 85
Fone, Jasper, 24
Forbes, J. E., architect, 115
Ford:
  Jas., and his s. Rob., 25
  Thos., 235, 238
Forde (Dors.), abbey, 10, 16, 29, 33, 39, 44, 69–72, 74, 111–12, 122–4, 136–7, 157 *n*
Fordington, John de, rector of Wambrook, 229
Forest, Stephen, vicar of South Petherton and rector of St. John's chapel, 194
Forster:
  Ant., 33
  Nat., curate of Crewkerne and Misterton, 30, 66–7
Forte:
  Rog., 218
  Thos., 216
  Wm., 216
  fam., 182
Fortescue:
  John Inglett, 124
  Sarah Bridget, *see* Marwood
Forz, Isabel de (Reviers), ctss. of Aumale and Devon, 11, 15, 18, 28, 33, 181, 199
fossor, fossarius, see Gerard
Foster:
  Hugh, rector of St. John's chapel, South Petherton, 194
  fam., 21
Foston, Thos., rector of Hinton St. George, 49
Fowler (Fouler):
  Hen., 41
  John, 160
fowling, 93
Fownes:
  Eliz., *see* Ayshe
  Ric., 179
Foxworthy, Phil., 139
Frampton (Dors.), 124, 130
France, 195
Franco Quercu (Franckesnei, Fraunchenney), Miles de, 165

frankpledge, view of, 27, 58, 101, 189–90, 217, 236
fraternity (brotherhood), *see* Chaffcombe; Crewkerne; Martock; Petherton, South; Whitestaunton
Fraunceis, John (later Gwyn), 16
Fraunchenney, *see* Franco Quercu
Freke:
  Edw., 13
  Francis, 13
  John, of Crewkerne, 13, 24, 32
  John, of Hilton, 13
  Rob., 13, 16, 34
  Sir Thos., 16
  Thos., 16
  Wm., 13
  fam., 34
French:
  Jeremiah, 34
  Wm., 21
  fam., 58
friendly societies: *see* Barrington; Crewkerne; Dowlish Wake; Martock; Merriott; Misterton; Petherton, South; Seavington St. Michael; Shepton Beauchamp
fruit growing, 167; *and see* market gardening; nurseries
Fry (Frye):
  Edw., 108
  Eliz., 55
  Francis Jas., 135
  Hen., 55
  John, 90
  Nic. le, 14
  Susannah, *see* Abraham
  Wm., 139
  and see Andrews, alias Fry
Fulford, Wm., prebendary of Cudworth, 142
Fuller:
  John, curate of Crewkerne, 30
  Thos., 43 *n*
Funtaynes:
  Isabel, *see* Bel
  Reynold, 181
Furneaux:
  Alan de (fl. 1186), 122, 142–5, 157, 162
  Alan de (fl. 1236), 142, 144
  Alan de (fl. 1286), 142, 157, 181
  Geof. de, 122, 142, 145, 157
  Joan, m. Mat. de Esse, 142

Gahagan, Lucius, 140
Gale, Edm. Escourt, 177
gallows, 58
Gapper, Mary Ann, 37
Gardner:
  John, 108
  John, minister, 107
  Wm., 99
Garvys, Rog., 34
Gaunts (Dors.), 225
Gawbridge (in Kingsbury Episcopi), mill, 100
Gaylard, Nic., rector of Babcary, 188
Gear, Mary, 63
Geffereys, John, 202
Genest:
  John, 13
  Peter, 13
  Sophia, *see* Parratt
Geoffrey, bp. of Coutances, 122, 152
George, Ernest, 70
Gerard the trencher (*fossor, fossarius*). 164–6
Gerard:
  Rob., 182
  Thos., 42, 176
  fam., 45
German (Teutonicus), Terry the, 176
Gibbs:
  Gregory, 70
  Hugh Daubeney, 70

Gibson, Anne, 156
Gidley, Bart., 21–2, 24
Gifford (Giffard, Jeffard):
    Alice, m. Phil. Denebaud, 41
    Ann, m. Sir Alex. Brett, 237
    Edm., rector of Wayford, 74
    Jas., 168
    John (fl. 13th cent.), 41
    John (fl. 16th cent.), 237
    Wm., 177
Gilbert:
    Jas., 85
    Wm., bp. of Mayo and abbot of
        Bruton, 180, 192
Giles, C. E., architect, 106
Gillingham:
    Ralph (d. 1729), 65
    Ralph (d. 1802), 65
    fam., 65
Gillingham (Dors.), 226
Gilmour, D. G., 84
Gittisham (Devon), 114; and see
    Combe
Glade:
    John (fl. 1561), 227
    John (d. 1626), 227
    Rog., 227
Glamorgan, 117, 138; and see Lanelay
    (in Llanharan)
Glanfield, Wm., 196, 222
Glasbroke, Peter, rector of Seaving-
    ton St. Michael, 150, 209
Glastonbury, 25
    abbey, 60, 147–8, 206–7
Gloucester, ctss. of, see Burgh
Gloucester, earls of, see Audley;
    Clare; Monthermer
Gloucester:
    duchy, 148
    honor, 54, 112, 122, 148, 205
Gloucestershire, 122; and see Newent;
    Uley; Stapleton; Tewkesbury
Glover:
    Wm. (fl. 16th cent.), 22
    Wm. (d. 1644), 186
gloving, 20, 22 n, 47–8, 58, 82, 98,
    108, 117, 126, 131, 144, 149, 153,
    161, 186–7, 203, 207, 216, 221,
    235
Glyde:
    Ellanette, see Richards
    John, 88
    fam., 94
Glyn:
    Sir Ric., Bt., 225
    Sir Ric. Carr, Bt., 225, 227
    Sir Ric. Geo., Bt., 225
    Sir Ric. Plumptre, Bt., 225, 230
Godard, Thos., vicar of South Pether-
    ton, 192
Godric, 157, 180
Godscelyn, Ric., and his w. Joan,
    213
Godwin, 53
Godwin, earl, 17
Godwin, king's reeve, 12
Godwin, see Goodwin
Goffe, R. L., 70
Gold (Golde):
    Jas., 8
    Marg., 8, 12, 24
    Thos., 32
Goodden:
    John (d. 1722), 109
    John (d. 1883), 85
    J. R. P., 85
    Rob., 85, 97
    Wyndham, 85
    fam., 86, 99
Goodman, Rob., 91
Goodwin (Godwin):
    Jas., 157, 159
    fam., 16
Gorges:
    Ellen, see Foliot

    Ralph de, 69
    Thos., 69
    Wm., 69
Goring, Geo., Ld. Goring, 10, 175
Gorney, see Gournay
Gough:
    John, 54, 58
    Rob. (fl. 1608), 54
    Rob. (fl. 1669), 54, 61
Gould:
    Barnard, 100
    C. R., 123
    R. S. J., 123
    Thos., 99
    fam., 100, 189
Gournay (Gorney):
    Alice, w. of Sir Mat., see Beauchamp
    Sir Mat., 91, 206, 217
    Philippe, w. of Sir Mat., m. (3) Sir
        John Tiptoft, 91
    Ric., 176
Gove, Ric., rector of Hinton St.
    George, 49
Graham, Thos., 13
Gray:
    H. St. Geo., and his w., 87
    Wm., 15, 22
    and see Grey
Grayson, A. B., architect, 195
grazing, 130–1, 137
Greenfield, Jos., rector of White-
    staunton, 237
Greenham (in Wayford), 37, 68–9,
    72–3
Greenway:
    John, 20–1
    John, vicar of Merriott, 60
    Ursula, 71 n
    fam., 71
Greenway (Devon), 124
Greenwood:
    Frances, see Wyke
    Thos., 54
Gregory, Wm., rector of Misterton,
    67
Gressham, Paul, 91
Greville:
    Eliz., see Willoughby
    Sir Fulk, 201
Grey:
    Cecily, see Bonville
    Hen., marquess of Dorset, duke of
        Suffolk, 54, 58, 88, 114
    Thos., marquess of Dorset (d.
        1501), 54, 88
    Thos., marquess of Dorset (d.
        1530), 54, 88
    and see Gray
Grimstead:
    Ann, 70
    Edw., 138
    John, 138
    Thos., 138
Grosvenor:
    Jane, see Warre
    Jane Frances, m. J. S. W. Saw-
        bridge, 214
    Ric. Erle-Drax-, 214
    Ric. Edw. Erle-Drax-, 214
    Sir Rob., Bt., 214
    Thos., 214
    fam., 214
Grove, Thos., minister, 107
Gryce, Wm., 33
Guilford, earl of, see North
Gulden (Guldene):
    Hen. le, 44
    Joan, 44
    Thos., 44
    fam., 56
Gummer:
    Jas., 167
    Joshua, 170
    Rob., 170
    fam., 205 n

Gundry:
    Nat., 178
    Nic., 178
    Sam., 197
    Thos. (fl. 1698), 178
    Thos. (fl. 1749), 178, 183
    fam., 178, 183
Gunston, Percival, 67
Guppy, Thos., 24
Guyan:
    Geoffrey, 1 n
    John, 1 n
Guyan, see Crewkerne
Gwyn:
    Edw. Prideaux, 16
    Francis (d. 1734), and his w. Marg.,
        16
    Francis (d. 1752), 16
    John Fraunceis, 16

H., M., goldsmith, 128, 150
Hacton (in Upminster, Essex), 15
Haddesfeld, Wm., 11
Halberton (Devon), 116
Hale, see Heyle
Hall:
    A. A., 135
    Mrs. Jane, 135
Hallett:
    Barnaby (17th cent.), and his w.
        Kath., 63
    Barnaby (d. 1724), 63, 65
    Grace, m. Wm. Cox, 63
    John (fl. 1789), 64
    John (d. 1838), and his w. Maxi-
        milla, 64
    Merifield, 63
    Thos., and his w. Mary, 64
    Wm., and his w. Sarah, 64
    Mr., minister, 107
    fam., 63
halmote, 190, 207, 217
Halswell:
    Nic. (d. 1564), 90
    Sir Nic. (fl. 1570), 90
    Rob., 90
Hamlet, Jos., curate of Barrington,
    119
Hamlyn, fam., 97
Hampshire, see Christchurch; Stoke
    Charity; Weeke
Hampstead Marshall (Berks.), 41
Hankeford:
    Eliz., w. of Sir Ric., see FitzWaryn
    Eliz., da. of Sir Ric., 177
    Sir Ric., 177
    Thomasia, m. Wm. Bourgchier,
        177
Hanning:
    Barnaby, 50
    John, 115–17, 153
    John Lee, see Lee
    Susannah, see Harvard
    Wm., 115–16
    fam., 115
Hansford, R. B., 100
Harbour, Sam., 143
Harcourt, Jas., vicar of South Pether-
    ton, 192–3
Harding son of Eadnoth the staller,
    53–4, 56, 58, 164, 166
Harding:
    John, Field Marshal Ld. Harding,
        175
    Thos., 203
    fam., 208
Hardington Mandeville, 107
Hare, Thos., curate of Chillington, 132
Harewell, John, bp. of Bath and
    Wells, 59
Harington:
    Isabel, see Cogan
    Jas., 232
    Sir Rob., 177
    Roberta, see Hugyn

Harold II, 10
Harp, South (Southampton, Southyngton, in South Petherton), 131, 171-2, 178-9, 184, 186, 189, 195
cts., 190
man., 177-9, 183, 187, 190, 193
man.-ho., 185
tithing, 111, 175, 178, 190
Harpford (in Langford Budville), 182
Harptree, West, 87
harriers, 223
Harris (Harrys):
Eliz., see Johnson
Honoria, m. Wm. Spencer Palmer, 71
Jas. Lloyd, 71
John, 178
John Burland, see Burland
Mary Anne, see Burland
Thos., vicar of South Petherton, 192
Harrison, fam., 199 n
Hart, Art., 21
Hartley:
Holliday, 123, 127, 143, 159
Nat., 159
Harvard:
Susannah, m. John Hanning, 115
Thos., 115
Harvey (Harvie):
Agnes, 238
John, 235
Haselbury, St. Wulfric of, 32
Haselbury Plucknett, 7, 9, 34, 66
Br., 5, 7
Hastings:
Francis, earl of Huntingdon, 116
Selina, ctss. of Huntingdon, 107
Hatch Beauchamp, 182, 212
Havegod, Hen., and his w. Joan, 213
Hawkchurch (Devon), 25, 225
Hawkesley, Jane, 37
hawking, 93, 96
Hawkins, Thos., 25
Hawley, Sir Hen., and his w., 16
Haydon, Jas., 72
Hayes, John, 13, 34
Haythorn, see Kingsbury Episcopi
Hayward:
Isaac, 58
R. H., 53
Ric., 21, 25
fam., 21
Healy, John, 46
Hearen:
Benj., 180
Rob., 180
Heathfield, 61
heathland, 148, 153, 171, 234
Hebditch:
Harry, 98
Revd. Sam., 170
Simeon, 188
Wm., 61
fam., 188
Hecstanes, Wm. de, 124
Hele:
Sir Hen., 178
Dr. Hen., 15, 179-80
Penelope, see Johnson
Ric., 178
Sir Thos., 178
Thos. (d. 1665), 178
fam., 186
and see Heyle
Helen the usher, 178
Helhouse, Wm., 179
Helliar (Helyar):
John, 46, 51, 202
Wm., 183
Hendford (in Yeovil), 78
Hendyman, Thos., rector of Crewkerne, 30

Henley:
Sir And., Bt. (d. 1675), 14
Sir And., Bt. (fl. 1700), 14-15, 22
Hen. (fl. 1609), 206
Hen. (fl. 1732), 206
Hen. Holt, 137
Hen. Hoste, 124
Hen. John, 124
John de, 15
Sir Rob., 14-15
fam., 125-6
Henley (in Crewkerne), 4-5, 14-15, 20, 22, 29, 37, 62, 64
man., 14-15, 19
man.-ho., 15
Henry I, 10, 28
Henry II, 175, 191
Henry VII, 11, 85, 129, 176
Henry VIII, 30, 55, 85
Henstridge, Toomer, q.v.
Herbert:
Wm., earl of Huntingdon, 91
Sir Wm., 16
Herdsman, Ric., minister, 195
Hereford, 38
Herenden, Milicent, 99
hermit, 33
Hertfordshire, see Cheshunt
Hertrugge:
Eliz., 224
John de, 224
Nicole, 224
Hestercombe (in Cheddon Fitzpaine), 44, 61 n
Heston (Mdx.), Osterley Park, q.v.
Hewish (in Crewkerne), 4-5, 7, 9, 11, 15, 17-19, 33, 35, 38, 62
ch., 33, 37
man., 15-16, 19
mill, 25
sch., 33, 37
tithing, 26
Heyle (Hale), John, 184
Heyron:
John (d. 1501), 56, 214
John (d. 1507), 56, 214
——, m. Geo. Sydenham, 214 n
——, m. —— Rosse, 214
Hicks and Isaacs, architects, 194
Hill:
Edw., 86
John, 25
Wm., 138
Hillard:
John, 182
Rob., 178
Hillyard, fam., 97
Hilmarton (Wilts.), 41
Hilton (Dors.), 13
Hinton, Ld., see Poulett, John (d. 1764)
Hinton, Bower, see Bower Hinton
Hinton St. George, 1-2, 7-8, 15-16, 38-52, 64, 123, 140, 148, 150, 182, 208-9
adv., 44, 48
agric., 45-7
alms-ho., 51
chant., 49
char., 51-2
ch., 17, 39, 44, 48-51
Civil War, 41
cts., 47-8
Craft, Hintonscraft, Northcraft, 39-40, 44-7, 50 n
cross, 39-40
dom. archit., 40
fairs, 47
fms., 46-7
fields, 4, 39, 45
fives wall, 49
friendly soc., 40
glebe, 49
green, 39, 46, 48
Hinton Ho., 21, 32, 39-44, 47

plan, 43
hosp., 47
inc., 45
inns, 40, 48
lock-up, 48
man., 12, 15, 41-5, 148, 165, 213
man.-ho., 15
mill, 39, 47, 49
Monmouth Rebellion, 41
nonconf., 50
par. officers, 48
park, 4, 9, 17, 38-40, 45-6, 49, 147-9
poorho., 48
poor-relief, 48
pop., 41
Priory, 40, 46, 51
quarries, 38-9, 48
rectors, 48-51, 150; and see Foston; Gove; Marsley; Mercer; Peacham; Poulett, John; Stambury
rectory, 41, 44, 48
ho., 47, 49
sch., 47, 49-51, 170
tithes, 44, 48-9
Townsend, 39
warren, 9, 39, 40 n
woodland, 39-40
Hippisley:
Chris., 141
John (fl. 1576), 183
John (d. 1664), 135
John (d. 1665), 135
Marg., m. John Coxe, 135
Marg., see Preston
Preston, 135, 139
Ric., 135
fam., 185
Hitchcock:
John, 24
Rob., 24
Hodges, Wm., 24
Hody:
And. (d. 1517), 90
Eliz., see Jew
Hen., 89
Humph., 13 n
Sir John (d. 1441-2), 90
John (d. 1497), 90
John (fl. 1541), and his s. John, 226
John (fl. 1621), 89
John (fl. 1639), 25
Ric. (d. 1536), 89
Ric. (fl. 1555), 89-90, 182
Ric. (early 17th cent.), and his w. Grace, 89
Rob., 25
Wm. (d. 1535), 89
Wm. (fl. 1555), 89-90
Hoeli, 122 n
Holand, Hen., duke of Exeter, 91
Holbeton (Devon), Flete, q.v.
Holborne, Col., 10
Holebroke:
Thos. de, 180
fam., 180
Holman, Hen., 21
Holwell (Dors.), 155
Holywell (Oxf.), 194
Honiton (Devon), 18, 223, 225, 231
Hood:
Alex., Vct. Bridport, 135-6, 138, 140-1
Alex. Nelson, Vct. Bridport, 70-1, 135, 139, 143
Charlotte Mary, see Nelson
Maria Sophia, see Bray
Sam., Ld. Bridport, 70, 72, 135, 137, 140
Hook (Dors.), 100
Hooper (Hoper):
Eliz., 58
Hen., 54, 56
Jas. (fl. 1546), 58

Hooper (Hoper) (*cont.*)
  Jas. (d. 1598), 54, 61
  Wm., rector of Crewkerne, 30
  fam., 58
Hooton, Hen., 225, 227
Hope, Sarah, 86
Hoper, *see* Hooper
Hopkins:
  Eliz., 109
  Jesse, 58, 100
  John, 100
  Revd. John, 180
  Maurice Uphill, rector of Wayford, 74
  Thos., 100
  Wm., 100
  Wm. Culliford, 100
  fam., 100
Hopton, John, *see* Yates
Hornblotton, 192
Horner, John, 183
Horsey:
  Edw., 16, 29
  John de, 24
  Peter, 170
Hosegood, John, 73
Hoskins (Hoskyns):
  Revd. Chas. Thos., 34
  H. W., 13
  H. W. P., 13
  H. W. W., 13
  Revd., Hen., 13
  Thos., 34
  Wm. (d. 1813), 13
  Wm. (d. 1863), 13, 33-4
  fam., 34
Hossem:
  John (d. 1778), 225
  John (fl. 1796), 225
hostiarius, *see* John the usher
Houndsborough, hund., 112
Hounslow (Mdx.), 45
Howard:
  Cath., m. Hen. Daubeney, earl of Bridgwater, 114-15, 176
  John, duke of Norfolk, 129
  Thos., duke of Norfolk, 85
  fam., 115
Hucker, John, rector of Cricket St. Thomas, 140
Hudson, Eliz., 86
Hugyn:
  Joan, m. Sim. Brett, 233
  Joan, w. of John (d. 1485), 233, 236
  John (fl. 1422), 232 *n*
  John (fl. 1473), 232-3, 236
  John (d. 1485), 233
  John (d. 1493), 233
  Roberta, w. of Thos. (fl. 1422), m. Jas. Harington, 232, 236
  Thos. (fl. 1422), 232 and *n*
  Thos. (fl. 1473), 232
Huish Episcopi, 107; *and see* Wearne
Hull (Hulle):
  Art., 131
  Chris., minister, 107
  Joan, m. John Creeke, 136
  Ric., 24
  Rob., 25
  Rob., and his s. John, 135
  Wal. de, rector of Shepton Beauchamp, 219
  fam., 144
hundred courts, 1-3, 76-7, 111-12
Hungerford:
  Marg., *see* Botreaux
  Sir Rob., 135
  Rob., 13, 34
Hunt:
  John, minister at Dowlish Wake, 155
  Rog., 191
Huntingdon:
  ctss. of, *see* Hastings
  earl of, *see* Hastings; Herbert

Hurcott (Herdecote, in Seavington St. Mary), 111, 198-9, 201-4
  ct., 203
Hurd (Hurdd):
  Francis, 86
  Jas., 100
Hurding:
  Hen., 90
  Ralph, 90
Hurst (in Martock), 78, 82-5, 93-4, 97-8, 102, 107
  fields, 82
  Hurst Bow, 78, 82
  inc., 94
  tithing, 76, 82, 92, 109
Hussey:
  Augustus Hen., 16
  H., 16
  John, 16-17, 20, 74
  Thos., 16
  Wm., 5, 16
  fam., 19
Hutchings (Hutchins):
  Bernard, 45-6, 51, 130
  John (fl. 1732), 206
  John (fl. 1770), 207
  Thos. (fl. 1631), 10
  Thos. (fl. 1788), 202
  Thos. (fl. 1852), 203
  fam., 130, 139, 149, 202, 207
Hyde:
  Frances, *see* Woolmington
  Laurence, 32, 201
  Rob., 201
  Thos., 225
Hyngaud, John, and his w. Aubrey, 232

Ikeford, John de, 150 *n*, 203 *n*
Ilchester, earl of, *see* Strangways
Ilchester, 7, 10, 93, 96, 106, 163-4, 168, 198
Ilford Bridges (in Stocklinch Magdalen), 172, 174-5, 198
Illeigh, *see* Knowle St. Giles
Ilminster, 37, 39, 113, 121, 127-8, 130, 133, 147, 151, 153, 155-7, 160, 162-3, 172, 182, 203, 207, 209-11, 231
  sch., 162, 209
  and see Atherstone; Sea
Ilton, 198-9, 201
  alms-ho., 202
  prebend, 202
  prebendary, 201, 204
inclosure:
  of arable, 19-20, 57, 65, 72, 93-7, 117, 125, 131, 136, 149, 153, 167, 185-7, 203, 207, 215, 234
  of forest, 116-17
  of grassland, 19-20, 93-6, 117, 125-6, 131, 136, 144, 149, 160, 167, 184, 187, 206, 226, 234
  of wood, 226
Independents, 107, 120, 128, 195
infangthief, 58
intercommoning, 93-6, 226
Ireland, Job, 25
Ireland, 103
Irish, John, 161
Isham, Giles, 189
Isle, lord of, *see* Reviers, Wm.
Isle, riv., 156-7, 161
Isle Abbotts, 107
Isle Brewers, 113, 119
Isleworth (Mdx.), 212; *and see* Syon Hill
Iwerne Courtney (Dors.), 13, 16

Jakettes (in Winsham), 234
James I, 185, 201
James II, 229
James:
  Geo., 128 *n*

John, 8
Mr., 128
Jeane, Ric., 16
Jeffard, *see* Giffard
Jefferies (Jeffries):
  Thos., bell-founder, 156, 230, 237
  Wm., bell-founder, 194
Jekyll, Gertrude, 115
Jellan the miller, 188; *and see* Moleyns
Jersey, earl of, *see* Villiers
Jersey, 42, 49, 169, 209
Jesuits, 233, 237; *and see* Roman Catholicism
Jew:
  Alice, *see* Pilsdon
  Eliz., m. (1) Sir John Hody, (2) Rob. Cappes, 90
  John le, and his w. Joan, 90
  John (fl. 1336), 90
  John (d. *c.* 1416), 90
  Nic. le, 90
  Wm. le, 90
Joan of Navarre, queen, 176, 194
Jocelin, bp. of Bath, 48, 176
John, king, 41, 174, 176, 188, 194
John of the mill, 188
John the usher (*hostiarius*), 177
Johnson:
  Brome, 178, 182-3
  Eliz., m. John Harris, 178, 183
  Emorb, 178, 183
  Frances, 178, 183,
  John (fl. 1710), 179, 212
  John (fl. 1726), 179, 212
  Orlando, 179, 212
  Penelope, m. Sir Thos. Hele, 178, 183
  Wm., 15, 182
  fam., 178
Jolliffe, Geo. Slade, 37
Jordan, alias Stoke, John, rector of Whitestaunton, 236
Jordans (in Ashill), 153

Kail:
  Humph. de (fl. 1280), 181
  Humph. de (fl. early 14th cent.), 123, 142, 157, 181, 202
  Idony, m. John Poulett, 124, 142, 181
  John de, 142, 144, 181
  Thos. (fl. 1256), 181
  Thos. (d. 1394), 124, 142, 181
  Wm. de, 123, 142, 144, 181
  fam., 143-4, 161, 181, 202
Kaynes:
  Isabel, *see* Wake
  Joan, m. (1) John Speke, (2) Hugh Champernowne, 124, 143, 152
  John (fl. 1325), 152
  John (d. 1419), 144, 152, 202
  John (d. 1420), 124, 143, 152, 155
  Thos., 130, 152
  fam., 130, 155
Kempe, C. E., 120
Kempthorne, Sampson, architect, 32, 67, 106
Kemshead, J., architect, 32 *n*, 43
Kencott (Oxon.), 179
Kene:
  Ant., 89
  Hugh, and his w. Agnes, 89
  Wm., 89
Kenn, Eliz., m. John, 1st Ld. Poulett, 42
Kensitites, 219
Kent:
  Revd. Adolphus, 55
  Eliz., *see* Dowding
  Nat., 40
  Thos., rector of Crewkerne, 30
Kent, earl of, *see* Neville
Kent, *see* Boxley Abbey; Maidstone; Tenterden
Kentsford (in St. Decumans), 56

Kentwell Hall (in Long Melford, Suff.) 115 *n*
Kerley, John, 238
Kettering (Northants.), 175, 195
Key, John, 184
Keymer:
    Eliz., *see* Daubeney
    Wm., 70, 73
Kidder, Ric., bp. of Bath and Wells, 30
Kidwelly:
    Sir Morgan, 44
    fam., 56
Kilmersdon, 107
Kinder, Hen., rector of Dowlish Wake, 154
King:
    Caleb, 13, 34
    Christian, *see* Corfield
    Marg., *see* Yeatman
Kingman, Thos., 136
Kingsbury Episcopi, 78, 88, 96, 106–7, 113, 120–1, 171–2, 189, 213, 219–20
    Burrow, 120
    Clopton, 181
    Gawbridge, q.v.
    Haythorn, 92
    Lambrook, q.v.
    Radwell, 181–2
Kingsdon, 169
    Kingsdon Cary, 55
Kingsmoor (in Somerton and Long Sutton), 79, 81, 92, 96–7
Kingston:
    Alan of, 142
    John, bell-founder, 32, 50, 61, 220
    Ralph, 142
Kingstone, 39, 130–1, 147–9, 151, 154, 156, 169, 199
    and see Allowenshay; Ludney
Kirk, Col. Piercy, 10
Kirkham, fam., 237
Kirkup, Jas., minister, 195
Kittisford, *see* Cothay
Klee:
    Eliz., *see* Brett
    Hen., 233
Klondyke, 152
Knight:
    Joan, *see* Merifield
    Rob., minister, 35
    Rob., 85
    Wm., bell-founder, 128
knight:
    Wal. the, *see* Walter
    Wm. the, *see* William
Knovill, Gilb. de, 116
Knowle:
    Maud, 157 *n*
    Ric. of, 157, 162 *n*
Knowle St. Giles, 111, 121–3, 126–7, 142–4, 151, **156–63**, 202
    adv., 157, 162
    agric., 160–1
    canal, 157
    ch., 145, 157, *161*, 162–3
    Civil War, 157
    cts., 161–2
    curates, 162; *and see* Allen, F. E.; Allen, John; Allen, J. T. W.; Boger; Evans, L.; Lucette; Patch; Phillips, Geo.; Watson
    dom. archit., 159
    fms., 160–1
    fields, 160
    glebe, 160, 162
    green, 156–7, 159–60
    Illeigh, 125, 145, 157, 159–62
    Illeigh, South, 111, 157
    inc., 160
    man., 125–6, 157, 159–62
    man.-ho., 159–60
    mills, 156–7, 160–2

Monmouth Rebellion, 157
    par. officers, 162
    Pinkham, 157, 160–1
    poorho., 162
    pop., 157
    rly., 157
    sch., 163
    tithes, 143, 162
    Wood, 123, 135, 160
    woodland, 160
    Woodhouse, 125, 156–7, 159, 161
Knyvett:
    Sir Wm., 11, 33
    Joan, *see* Courtenay
Kympe, Ric., 185
Kyrton:
    Edw., 218
    Marg., 218
    Ric., 183

Lacy:
    Hen. de, earl of Lincoln, 152
    Jas., 13
    John (d. 1529), 13, 34
    Thos., 13, 34
Lade:
    Benj. de la, rector of Shepton Beauchamp, 219
    Wm. de la, 95
    Wm. de la, or the Marshal, 96 *n*
Lambert:
    Revd. Burges, 63
    John, 124
    Wm. Chas., 63–4, 67
Lambrook (in Kingsbury Episcopi):
    East, 78, 171–2, 189
    Middle, 166, 171, 179, 189, 220
    West, 172
Lancaster, duchy of, 152
Lancecombe, Lancelecumbe, Lancerecumbe, *see* Lanscombe
Landrake (Cornw.), 12
Lanelay (in Llanharan, Glam.), 201
Langdale, John, rector of Cricket St. Thomas, 50, 140–1
Langdon:
    Augustus, 89
    J. S. C., 182
    John Churchill, 182
Langford Budville, *see* Harpford
Langley:
    Bryant, 138
    Hugh, 197
Langport, 10, 29, 96, 99, 107, 118–19, 120 *n*, 172, 175, 182, 188, 196–7, 211, 214
Langton, John de, 84
Lanherne (Cornw.), 176
Lanscombe (Lancecombe, Lancelecumbe, Lancerecumbe):
    Hen. of, 135
    Hugh, 135
    John, and his s. Wm., 135
    Luke of, 135
Lansdown, battle of, 10
Lanvyan, And., rector of Crewkerne, 30
Larder, Wm., 73
Largo (Florida), 85
Latter Day Saints, 36
Laud, Wm., abp. of Canterbury, 193
Lavor:
    Joan, 88
    John, 88, 101
Lawrence, Rob., 65
Laycock, Sam., 21
Laymore, *see* Crewkerne
Layng, Hen., rector of Wayford, 74
Leach:
    Mary, 109
    Rob. (fl. 1710), 90
    Rob. (d. 1780), 90
    Rob. (d. 1837), 90
    Rob. (d. 1958), 85
    Rob. (fl. 1974), 85

Thos., 100
    Wal., 85
Leamington (Warws.), 67
Lean:
    Jas., 212
    Jas. Vincent, 212
    fam., 215
Leaves, Ann, 109
Lede, Hen., 25
Lee:
    John Lee (Hanning), 115–16
    Vaughan Hanning Vaughan, 201
    and see Leigh
Legg:
    Hugh, 143
    John, 226
    fam., 226
Leggatt, Col. A., 182
Leicester, abbot, 49
Leicestershire, *see* Loughborough; Market Harborough
Leigh (Lee):
    Ann, *see* Every
    Barnabas Eveleigh, 86, 88
    Barnaby, 86
    Eliz. (alias Reynolds), *see* Pyke
    Jas. (alias Reynolds), 89
    John (d. 1688), 88
    John (fl. early 18th cent.), 88
    John (d. 1772), 88
Leigh (in Winsham), 111, 125, 137, 234
Leigh (Wilts.), 135
Leland, John, 115, 188
L'Estre:
    Joan, *see* Paveley
    Ric. de, 14
    Wm. de (fl. 1086), 14
    Wm. de (fl. 1260), 14
Lethbridge, Art., curate of Barrington, rector of Shepton Beauchamp, 119–20, 219
Lewes (Suss.), 87
Lewin, 53, 165
Leyden, 103
Lidden, fam., 65
lights, *see* Chillington; Petherton, South; Shepton Beauchamp; Whitestaunton
Lillesdon (in North Curry), 159
limekilns, 62, 68, 113, 133 *n*, 141, 163, 198, 227, 235
Lincoln, earl of, *see* Lacy
Linde:
    Alex. de la (fl. 1285), 148
    Alex. de la (fl. 1465), 148, 208, 217–18
    Alex. de la (d. 1480), 148
    Avice, *see* Falconer
    Edith, w. of Alex. (d. 1480), m. (2) Sir Wm. Poulett, 148
    Ellis, 148, 205
    Rob. de la, 148
    Thos. de la, 148
    fam., 130, 148, 205, 208
Lisle:
    Emme, *see* Avenel
    Idony, m. Hugh de Beauchamp, 123
    John de (fl. 1272), 11, 22, 28
    John, and his w. Avice (fl. 1484), 25
    Jordan de, 123
    Wal. de, 123
    Wm. de (fl. 1249), 11, 28
    Wm. de (d. c. 1294), 123, **125**
    fam., 11
Littlecote (in Ramsbury, Wilts.), 89
Llewellins and James, bell-founders, 67, 105, 150, 194
Lo, Wm. de, 23
Load, Little (in Long Sutton), 79 *n*
Load, Long (Lade, Load St. Mary, in Martock), 78–9, 81, 84, 90, 92–3, 96–7, 100–2, 104–5, 107–8

Load, Long (*cont.*)
  agric., 94–5
  br., 78–9
  chap., 103, 105–6
  ch., 79, 103, 106
    ho., 106
  ct. ho., 101
  fms., 79
  fields, 79, 94–5
  glebe, 106
  inc., 79, 94–5
  inn, 83
  man., 83, 88, 90, 94, 100, 105–6
    ho., 88
  sch., 106, 108–9
  tithes, 106
  tithing, 76, 79, 94, 101
  vicar, 109
  wharves, 79
Locke (Lock):
  C. J. H., vicar of Misterton, 63
  Geo. (fl. 1701), 188
  Geo. (fl. 1750), 195
  Peter, 206
  fam., 58
Lockyer:
  Rob., 24
  fam., 24
Locock:
  Betty, 102
  Thos., 238
Loder, John, rector of Wambrook, 229
Lombard (Lumbard):
  John, 196
  Wm., rector of Whitestaunton, 237
  fam., 125
London, Thos. de, rector of Merriott, 60
London, 5, 10, 15, 17, 21, 32, 44–6, 50, 54, 60, 65, 67, 73, 84, 86, 89, 99, 105, 114–15, 155, 159, 163–4, 168, 172, 179, 183–4, 189, 191–2, 197, 199, 201, 205, 210, 218, 220, 225, 230, 232 *n*
  bp. of, 162
  Fleet prison, 192
  Inner Temple, 16, 24, 33
  Lincoln's Inn, 13
  Middle Temple, 16, 165
  St. Bartholomew's hosp., 44–5, 48–9
  St. Martin-in-the-Fields, q.v.
  Soho, 46
  Tower of, 30, 49
Long, Rog., 15
Longchamp, John de, 232
Longdon, Rog., 24
Lopen, Hen. de, 165
Lopen, 39, 47, 55–6, 92 *n*, 111, 140, 150, 163–70, 171–2, 187, 192, 205 *n*, 206–7
  adv., 169
  agric., 166–7
  Broomhill, 164, 167
  ch., 166, 169–70, 208
    ho., 170
  ct., 166, 168
    ho., 164, 168
  cross, 164, 168
  curate, 169, 192; *and see* Billing, Rob. Phelps; Templeman, John; Vawdye
  dom. archit., 164–5
  fair, 138 *n*, 164, 168
  fms., 167
  fields, 164, 167
  glebe, 169
  green, 163
  inc., 167
  ind., 167–8
  inns, 164
  Lopen Head, 7, 52, 163–4, 171, 205
  man., 164–6, 178
  man.-ho., 164–5

mills, 167–8
Monmouth Rebellion, 164
nonconf., 170
par. officers, 169
poorhos., 164, 169
poor-relief, 168–9
pop., 164
quarries, 163
rector, 169
rectory, 164, 169
sch., 163, 169–70
tithes, 166–7, 169, 180
tithing, 168
Lopen, Little (in South Petherton), 166, 171, 183–4
  chap., 183
Lorty, fam., 116
Loterel, Thos., 91
Lough:
  Ric., 23
  Rob., 23
Loughborough (Leics.), 120, 156, 205
Love, Benj., 47
Loveday, John, 43 *n*
Lovel:
  Hugh (d. 1291), 134
  Hugh (fl. 1295), 165
  Muriel, m. Nic. Seymour, 134
  Ralph, 134
  Ric., 134
  fam., 12
Loveney:
  And., 183
  Ric., 183
  Wal., 183
  Wm., 183
  Wm., s. of Wal. (fl. 1301), 183
Lowe, Ric., vicar of Crewkerne and Misterton, 67
Lowman:
  Hugh Perkins, 14
  John Perkins, 14
  Maria, 65
  Rob., 14
  fam., 14, 24
Loxton, 183 *n*
Lucette, C. E., curate of Knowle, 162
Lucy, Wm., 22
Ludney (in Kingstone), 151
Lufton, 55
Lulworth (Dors.), 176
Lumbard, *see* Lombard
Lumley, Ric., Vct. Lumley, 85
Lydiard Tregoze (Wilts.), *see* Basset Down
Lyle:
  Col. A. A., 115
  fam., 115
Lyme Regis (Dors.), 5, 10, 20, 22, 69
Lympsham, 127
Lyte, Thos., 55, 58

Mackney (Berks.), 189
Maiden Newton (Dors.), 100
Maidment, Mr. L., 159
Maidstone (Kent), 86
Malet, Wm., 165
Malherbe, alias Malet, Sir Wm., 181
Mallock, Thos., 227
Maloisell:
  Ralph, and his w. Joan, 14
  Wm., 14
Malvern, Great (Worcs.), 228
Mangerton (in Netherbury, Dors.), 226
Manley:
  John, 25
  fam., 25
Mannin, Wm., 221
manufactures:
  edge-tools, 137–8, 236
  engineering, 98
  hair-seating, 21
  net, 21
  plastic mouldings, 22

poultry appliances, 188
rope, 20–1, 57, 98, 111, 167, 188
smelting, 234
spinning, 25
thread, 60
tobacco-pipes, 57
tow, 25, 72
twine, 98, 167, 188
yarn, 98, 170, 186
and see cloth manufactures
Mappowder (Dors.), 138, 213
Mar, earl of, *see* Erskine
Marder, John., 22
Maricker, *see* Marraker
Mark, 145
Marke, John, 174, 186
Marker:
  Margaretta, *see* Putt
  Revd. Hen., 114
  R. J., 114
  R. R. K., 114
  Ric., 114
  Revd. T. J., 114
  market, *see* Crewkerne; Martock; South Petherton
market gardening, 52, 57, 187; *and see* fruit growing; nurseries
Market Harborough (Leics.), 195
Marks:
  Rob., vicar of Merriott and South Petherton, 60, 192
  Wm., vicar of South Petherton, 192
Marlow, Mic., rector of Whitestaunton, 237
Marraker (Maricker):
  Chris., rector of Wambrook, 224, 230
  Hugh, 229
  John, rector of Wambrook, 229
Marrowe, Thos., 91
Marsh (Marshe):
  Hen., 26
  John, 32
  Wm., 32
Marshal (Marshall):
  Anselm, 41
  Judith, 131
  Maud, m. Hugh Bigod, 41
  Ric., earl of Pembroke, 41
  fam., 41
Marsley, John, rector of Hinton St. George, 49
Marston Bigot, 237
Martin:
  Adam., 24
  Revd. Amos., 26
  Ann, *see* Sherlock
  Mr., 136
Martineau:
  G., 14
  L., 14
Martock (Mertoc), 34, 52, **78–109**, 171–2, 175, 183, 188, 196, 216
  adv., 102–3
  agric., 78, 84, 92–7
  Ash, q.v.
  Bower Hinton, q.v.
  br., 78, 83, 96–7, 101–2
  brotherhood, 104
  chant., 86, 104
  chap., 86
  char., 109
  ch., *17*, 78, 83, 86, 91, 102–6, *208*
    plan, 105
  ch. ho., 85, 93, 102
  Ch. Ho., 103
  Civil War, 78, 94
  clubs, 84
  coaches, 99
  Coat, q.v.
  cts., 100–2
    ho., 104
  cross, 99
  dom. archit., *49*, 79, 81–3, 87, 89, 91, 104

fair, 77–8, 93, 99
fms., 97
Fenn, Fenns, 83, 93, 100
    man., 101
fields, 78–9, 83, 93, 97, 109
floods, 91
friendly socs., 83–4, 108
Gawbridge Bow, 78–9, 81, 93
glebe, 103
Highway, 82, 102, 108
Hull, 90
hund., **76–7**, 92, 99–100, 111–12
    ct. ho., 77
    officers, 77, 99
Hurst, q.v.
inc., 93–4, 103, 109
ind., 78, 82–3, 97–9
inns, 83–4; George, 83–4, 98
Limbury, 82
Load, Long, q.v.
Loxhill (Lockeshull), 79, 89
    man., 89
    man.-ho., 89
    and see Ash, Pykesash
man., 76–8, 83–94, 99–101, 180
man.-ho., 85–6, 93, 108
mkt., 77–8, 83, 92–3, 99
Mkt. Ho., 93, 99, 102, 104, *208*
mills, 58, 78, 82–3, 89, 92–3, 98–
    100, 103
Milton Falconbridge, q.v.
Monmouth Rebellion, 107 *n*
Newton, q.v.
nonconf., 102, 104, 106–8, 195
par. cncl., 99, 102
par. officers, 102
Parrett Works, *48*, 83, 92, 98–100,
    180
poorho., 102, 108
poor-relief, 102, 109
pop., 84
publ. serv., 102
rly., 78, 81–4, 99
rector, 88
rectory, 86–7, 92, 101
    ho. (Treasurer's Ho.), 84, 87, *145*
river traffic, 78–9
Sayes:
    agric., 97
    man., 90–1, 100–1
    man. ho., 91
Says Bonville, man., 89 *n*, 90, 99,
    101
sch., 77, 102, 104, 107–9
    ho., *49*, 84–5, 100, 108
shambles, 99
Stapleton, q.v.
streets, 83–4, 99
tithes, 86–7, 96, 103
tithings, 78, 82–3, 92–3, 100, 109
vicar, 87, 99, 102–6, 108–9; *and see*
    Bowyer; Curtis; Salmon;
    Saunders; Southwood; Sprag-
    gett; Stevenson; Wall; Wal-
    rond
vicarage, 103, 105, 107
    ho., 103
Witcombe, q.v.
workho., 102
Marwood:
    Jas., 124, 143
    Jas. Thos. Benedictus, 124
    Mary, m. Geo. Notley, 124
    Sarah, *see* Sealy
    Sarah Bridget, m. (1) Hen. Stevens,
        (2) John Inglett Fortescue,
        124, 128
    fam., 126, 128
Mary I, queen, 219
Mary, Queen of Scots, 42
Marylebone (Mdx.), 34
Massey, Gen. Edw., 41
Masters, Hen., rector of Misterton,
    66–7
Mathers, Helen, 63

Mathew:
    Agnes, m. John Drake, 225
    Honor, m.—Westcott, 225
    Sim., 225
    and see Matthews
Matthews, Thos., 21; *and see* Mathew
Maud, 180
Maurice, Prince, 10
Mautravers:
    Eliz., *see* Aumale
    Sir John, 90
Mayenne:
    Hamelin of, 175–6
    Joel, 176
    Wal. de, 179
Mayne, Rob., 81, 95
Mayo, bp. of, *see* Gilbert, Wm.
Meacham:
    John, curate of Barrington, 119
    John, 232
Mead, E. R., 159
Mears and Stainbank, bell-founders,
    106, 128, 194–220
Melbury (Dors.), 115
Membury (Devon), 222–3, 228
Mercer, Wm. le, rector of Hinton St.
    George, 49
Mere, Hugh, curate of Barrington
    and Chillington, 119, 132
Meredith, Griffith, 182
Meriet:
    Eliz., m. Urry Seymour, 54
    Eliz., w. of Sir John (d. 1391), *see*
        Arundel
    Geo. de, 54, 56, 58, 168
    Harding de, *see* Eadnoth
    Hen. de, 54
    Hugh de, 54, 169
    John de (d. 1285), 54, 58, 164–5
    John de (d. 1308), 54, 164, 168, 181
    John de (by 1322), 54, 56
    Sir John de (d. 1327), and his w.
        Mary, 61 *n*
    Sir John de (d. 1369), 54, 164, 166
    Sir John de (d. 1391), 54–5, 59, 90,
        165
    Marg., w. of John (d. 1285), 164
    Marg., w. of John (d. 1308), 58
    Maud, w. of Sir John (d. 1369), m.
        (2) Sir Thos. Boclond, 58, 164,
        166
    Nic. de (d. by 1229), 54, 60, 166,
        169
    Nic. de (d. c. 1258), 54, 58, 178, 181
    fam., 164, 168, 181
Merifield:
    Alice, m. John Donne, 85
    Alice, w. of Rob. (d. 1686), *see*
        Colston
    Edw., 63
    Eliz., w. of Rob. (fl. 1557), 15
    Geo., 9
    Joan, w. of John (d. 1695), m. (2)
        Rob. Knight, 85
    John (d. 1581), 15
    John (d. 1623), 15
    John (d. 1666), 10, 15
    John (d. 1695), 15, 85
    Mat., 15
    Rob. (fl. 1557), 15, 24
    Rob. (d. 1608), 15, 63
    Rob. (d. 1686), 15, 85
    Rob. (d. 1739), and his w. Mary, 15
    Wm. (d. 1728), and his w. Susanna,
        15, 85
    Wm. (fl. 1752), 15, 85–6
    fam., 19, 55
Merlesuain the sheriff, 178
Merriott, 1, 4–5, 7, 17, 24–6, 32, 39,
    50–1, **52–61**, 140, 151, 169, 171,
    181, 192, 221
    adv., 55, 59
    agric., 56–7
    Ashlands, 53, 56
    Ashwell, 53

Boozer Pit, 60
Borough, 52
Bow mill, 53, 55–8, *193*
br., 52
char., 61
ch., *16*, 53, 55, 59–61
ch. ho., 60
cts., 56, 58–9
Crepe, 55
dom. archit., 52–3, 55, *193*
Eggwood, 52–3, 56–7, 60
fair, 52, 58
fms., 52–3, 55–7
fields, 52–3, 57
friendly socs., 53
glebe, 60
Green Nap, 53
inc., 57, 60
ind., 57–8, 60
inns, 53; King's Head, 53, 59
lock-up, 59
man., 53–7, 59–61, 164–5
man.-ho., 55, 57
Man. Ho., 52, 55, 57
mills, 52–3, 55–6, 58, 100
Moorlands, 53, 57, *65*
nonconf., 61
'Northton', 55
par. officers, 59
park, 56, 60
poorho., 59
poor-relief, 59, 61
pop., 53
quarry, 52
rector, 55, 59–60; *and see* Ber-
    nardini; London; Samborne
rectory, 55, 59
    ho., 56, 60
schs., 61
Shutteroaks, Schitrock, 4, 52–3
streets, 52
tithes, 55, 57, 59–60
vicar, 53, 55, 57, 59–61; *and see*
    Atkins; Greenway; Marks;
    Powell; Price; Stacy
vicarage, 55, 59
    ho., 55, 60
wood, 52–3, 57; *and see* Eggwood
Merton (Surr.), priory, 102
Methodists, 36–7, 61, 67–8, 107–8,
    156, 170, 175, 192, 195–6, 210,
    215, 221; *and see* Wesleyans
Michel, Michell, *see* Mitchell
Middlemore, Hen., 32, 67, 105 *n*, 116
Middleney, Ralph de, 99
Middlesex, *see* Clerkenwell; Heston;
    Isleworth; Marylebone; Osterley
    Park; St. Martin-in-the-Fields;
    Syon Hill; Teddington; Twic-
    kenham; Whitton
Middleton:
    Edw., rector of Chaffcombe, 127
    Geo., 149
    John de, rector of Shepton Beau-
        champ, 219
    fam., 149
Miles:
    Geo. Fred., 16
    Ric., 216
Milford, Wm., 206
milk, tithes of, 87
Miller:
    John, 161
    Vile, 161
Millerd, Rob., 191
mills, *see under parish names* s.v.
    mills
    'balling', *see* Crewkerne
    blade-, *see* Cricket St. Thomas;
        Whitestaunton
    cider, *see* Dowlish Wake
    fulling (tucking), *see* Cricket St.
        Thomas; Dowlish Wake;
        Knowle St. Giles; Martock;
        Whitestaunton

mills (*cont.*)
  horse-, *see* Martock
  malt, *see* Crewkerne; Martock
  oat-meal, *see* Crewkerne
  paper, *see* Crewkerne
  saw, *see* Cricket St. Thomas
  snuff, *see* Martock
  threshing, *see* Crewkerne
  water, *see* Barrington; Crewkerne;
      Cricket St. Thomas; Cud-
      worth; Dinnington; Dowlish
      Wake; Hinton St. George;
      Lopen; Martock; Merriott;
      Misterton; Petherton, South;
      Shepton Beauchamp; Wam-
      brook; Wayford; Whitestaun-
      ton
  wind-, *see* Crewkerne; Martock;
      Seavington St. Mary
Milton (Middleton, Milton Falcon-
    bridge, Milton Fauconberg, Mil-
    ton Fawconbridge, in Martock),
    79, 81–2, 84, 88, 91–2, 94, 100,
    102, 108
  agric., 96
  chap., 79, 91, *145*
  ct., 91
  fms., 79
  fields, 79, 96
  inc., 96
  man., 79, 91, 96, 100–1
  man.-ho., 79, 91
  tithing, 76, 78–9, 96, 106
Milverton, Torrell's Preston, q.v.
Minehead, 225
minster, 4, 26, 28–9, 62, 68, 73, 102,
    183–4, 191
mint, 184
Minterne:
  Joan, m. John Whitehead, 25
  John, 25
  Martha, 36, 38
  Ric., 25
Mirfield (Yorks. W.R.), 118,
    218
Misterton, And. of, 12
Misterton, 1, 5, 7, 15, 17–19, 24, 26,
    28–30, 33–4, 37–8, **62–8**
  adv., 66
  agric., 64–5
  br., 62
  chars., 68
  ch., 4, 28–9, 33, 62, 66–7
  ct., 64
  curate, 66, 68; *and see* Bearde;
      Vyall; Winter
  dom. archit., *33*, 62, 64
  fms., 62, 64–5
  fields, 62–3, 65
  friendly soc., 63
  glebe, 66
  hosp., 68
  inc., 65
  ind., 65
  inns, 63
  man., 11, 19, 63–4
  'Man. Ho.', 62–4
  mills, 62, 65
  Nethertown, 62, 65
  nonconf., 67–8
  Old Court, 64, 66–7
  Overtown, 62, 65
  par. cncl., 68
  par. officers, 65–6
  poorho., 66
  pop., 63
  quarries, 62
  rly., 62–3, 65
  rector, 66; *and see* Abbot; Baylie;
      Gregory; Masters; Nosse
  rectory, 67
    ho., 67
  schs., 68
  tithes, 66–7
  tithing, 26, 65

  vicars, 66; *and see* Ashe, Faithfull;
      Ashe, Rob. Hoadley; Forster;
      Locke; Lowe; Tomkins
  vicarage, 66
    ho., 67
Mitchell (Michel, Michell):
  John, 33
  John, and his w. Joan, 63
  Patrick Reynolds, dean of Wells,
      232
  Percy Reynolds, 233
  Steph., 1 *n*
  Wm., 24
Mohun:
  John, Ld. Mohun, 11
  Sir Reynold (d. 1567), 11
  Sir Reynold, Bt. (d. 1639), 11
  Rob., 185
  Warwick, Ld. Mohun, 12
  Wm., and his w. Isabel, 11
  Wm. (d. 1587), 1, 11
  fam., 174, 180, 186
Moleyns:
  Alice, *see* Crauthorn
  Anne, w. of Wm., m. (2) John
      Dauncye, 189
  Ant., 189
  Clemence, w. of John (d. 1387),
      183–4, 189
  Hen. (fl. 1313), 184, 188–9
  Hen. (fl. 1338), 189
  Jellan de (late 12th cent.), 189; *and
      see* Jellan
  Jellan de (fl. 1313), 189
  John de (fl. 1313), 189
  John de (d. 1387), 183, 189
  John (d. 1497), 189
  Nic., 183, 189
  Ric., 189
  Wm., 189
  fam., 182
Monceaux:
  Agnes de, 11, 18, 24, 28, 33
  Rob. de, 11
Moncels, Wm. de, 152
Monkton Farleigh (Wilts.), priory,
    40, 45, 154
Monkton, West, 89, 116
Monmouth, duke of, *see* Scott
Monmouth Rebellion, *see* Chaff-
    combe; Crewkerne; Cudworth;
    Hinton St. George; Knowle St.
    Giles; Lopen; Martock; Pether-
    ton, South; Whitestaunton
Montacute:
  Sibyl, m. Sir Edm. Arundel, 90
  Wm., earl of Salisbury (d. 1344),
      85, 90, 232
  Wm., earl of Salisbury (d. 1397),
      85, 152
  fam., 93
  and see Montague
Montacute, 25, 50, 106, 108, 147
  priory, 203
Montague (Montagu):
  Alice, *see* Pyke
  Edw., 175
  Jas., bp. of Bath and Wells, 49
  Rob. (fl. 1377), 15
  Rob. (fl. 1484), 15
  Wm. (d. 1484), and his w. Florence,
      15
  Wm. (d. 1489), 15, 89
Monteagle, Ld., *see* Stanley
Monthermer, Ralph de, earl of
    Gloucester, 123, 205, 208
Mont St. Michel (Manche), abbey,
    87–8, 102, 104
Moody:
  Geo., 178
  Miss, 178
Moore, Revd. Melville Russell,
    228
Morbathe, Hen., and his w. Chris-
    tine, 91

  John de, 91
  Margery, *see* Fenne
Moreton (Dors.), 225, 227
Morewell, Ric. de, 122
Morgan, Eliz., 221
Morley, Ld., *see* Parker
Morley and Monteagle, Ld., *see*
    Parker
Morne, Wm., 163; *and see* Morren
Morren (Morne, Morryn):
  Dorothy, 161
  Joan, 161
  Matilda, 161
  Rob., 161
  Wm. (d. by 1572), 127, 161
  Wm. (fl. 1572), 161
  fam., 161
Morris:
  Claver, 71
  Eliz., m. John Burland, 71
  Molly, *see* Bragg
Morryn, *see* Morren
Mortain, ct. of, *see* Robert; William
Mosterton (Dors.), 62, 75
Mountjoy, Ld., *see* Blount
Mowbray:
  Eliz., dchss. of Norfolk, 41
  John, earl of Norfolk (d. 1432), 41
  John, duke of Norfolk (d. 1476),
      41
Muchelney, 76, 78, 94–5
  abbot, 93
  abbey, 55, 59, 93, 95
Mules:
  F. H., rector of Dowlish Wake, 155
  Francis, curate of Knowle St.
      Giles, 162
  John Hawkes, curate of Cudworth,
      146, 155
Mulle, Gilb. atte, 161
Multon:
  Jas. de (d. by 1316), 199, 201
  Jas. (fl. 1316), 201
  John, 201
  Marg., m. Sir John Streche, 201
  Maud, *see* Vaux
  Thos. (fl. 1252), 199
  Thos. (fl. 1316), and his s. Thos.,
      201
  fam., 181
Mundy, E. P. G. Miller, 135
Musbury (Devon), Ashe, q.v.
Naish:
  John (d. 1830), 212, 218, 221
  John (fl. 1845), 203, 212, 215
  John (fl. 1875), 212
  Thos. (d. 1813), 212, 218
  Thos. (d. 1875), 212, 215
  Thos. (fl. 1875), 212
  Wm. (d. 1830), 212, 218
  Wm. (fl. 1845), 203, 212, 215
  fam., 203, 213, 215, 218
Napier:
  Edw. Berkeley (d. 1799), 89
  Edw. Berkeley (fl. 1835), 89
  Gerard Martin Berkeley, 89
Napper:
  And., 89
  Edw., 194
  Wm., 194
National Trust, 87, 115
Nelson:
  Charlotte Mary, m. Sam. Hood,
      Ld. Bridport, 141
  Revd. Wm., duke of Brontë, 140
Neroche:
  cast., 210
  forest, 93, 111, 113, 116–17, 172,
      184
Netherbury (Dors.), 25; *and see*
    Mangerton
Netherhay (in Broadwindsor, Dors.),
    71
Nettlecombe, 56

Neville:
  Anne, w. of Ric., earl of Warwick, *see* Beauchamp
  Anne, w. of Thos., *see* Portman
  Geo., bp. of Exeter, 11, 33
  Isabel, m. Geo. Plantagenet, duke of Clarence, 148
  Ralph, Ld. Neville, earl of Westmorland, 114, 176
  Ric., earl of Salisbury, 236
  Ric., earl of Warwick, 148
  Thos., 71
  Wm., earl of Kent, 11
New College, Oxford, 127
Newberry:
  Hen., 65
  Dr., 50
Newbury (Berks.), 73
Newent (Glos.), New Court, 71
Newfoundland, 48
Newman, Hen., rector of Shepton Beauchamp, 219
Newton, Chris., 86
Newton (in Martock), 82, 84, 93, 107
  tithing, 76, 82–3, 92
Nicholas son of Roger, 122
Nicholetts, John Toller, 176, 188, 191, 195
Nicholson, A. K., 32
nonconformists, *see* Anabaptists; Arminians; Baptists; Bible Christians; Brethren; Calvinists; Congregationalists; Elim Pentecostalists; Independents; Latter Day Saints; Methodists; Presbyterians; Quakers; Salvation Army; Southcott's followers; Unitarians; United Reformed Church; Wesleyans
Noneton:
  Baudry de, 122
  Marg., *see* Avenel
  Margery, m. Rob. de Pudele, 122
  Warin de, 122
  fam., 159
Norfolk:
  ctss. of, *see* Marshal
  dchss. of, *see* Brotherton; Mowbray
  duke of, *see* Howard; Mowbray
  earl of, *see* Bigod; Mowbray
Norfolk, *see* Channons; Norwich
Norris (Norys):
  G. R. G., rector of Wayford, 74
  Hugh, 174–5
  John, curate of Crewkerne, 30
  John (fl. 1549), 116
  John (fl. 1599), 64
  Mat., 70, 73
  Ric., 71
  Rob., 70, 73
  Wm. (fl. 1627), 70, 72–3
  Wm. (d. 1895), 68
  fam., 73
North:
  Fred., Ld. North, earl of Guilford, 144
  Gilb., 168
Northamptonshire, *see* Kettering
Northcourt (in Shorwell, I.W.), 88
Northill (Cornw.), Trebartha in, q.v.
Northover:
  Jas., 189
  Wm., 189
Norton, Wm. John, 159
Norton Fitzwarren, 179, 201
Norton sub Hamdon, 54, 171, 179
Norwich, 115
Nosse, Nat., rector of Misterton, 66–7
Notley:
  Anne, w. of Marmion, m. (2) C. F. Sweet, 130
  Geo. (fl. 1709), 137
  Revd. Geo. (d. 1768), 129–30
  Revd. Geo. (d. 1831), 124, 129, 136

Geo. (d. 1855), 129
  Jas. Thos. Benedictus (d. 1851), 129
  Jas. T. B. (d. 1872), 129
  John, 124, 130, 136
  Marmion, 130
  Marwood, 129–30
  Mary, *see* Marwood
  fam., 131
Nottinghamshire, *see* Wollaton Hall
Nurse, Stephen, 86, 108
nurseries, 46, 57; *and see* fruit growing; market gardening
Nynehead, 15; *and see* Chipley

Oakley (in Chilthorne Domer), 92
Oathill (in Wayford), 17–18, 29, 68–9, 71–4
  Grange, 71
  man., 70–1
  tithing, 73–4
obit, *see* Crewkerne
Odelande (Wodelond), John, rector of Crewkerne, 30
Odolina, anchoress, 32
Offley:
  Rob., 201
  Wm., 201
Ogle, Sir Wm., Vct. Ogle, 114
Oliver, rector of St. John's chapel, South Petherton, 194
Oliver:
  Jordan (fl. 1166), 224
  Sir Jordan (fl. early 13th cent.), 224
  Jordan (fl. 1240), sheriff of Somerset and Dorset, 224
  Nic., 224
  Sibyl, w. of Sir Jordan, *see* Aumale
  Sibyl, m. (1) Humph. de Beauchamp, (2) John de Aldham, 224
  Wal., 224
  Wm., 224
  fam., 224
Orchard, Wm., and his w. Eliz., 34
Orchard Portman, 71
Orchardleigh, 219
Osborn (Osborne):
  Elias, 129
  Rob., 138–9
  Thos., 138
  fam., 138
Osterley Park (in Heston, Mdx.), 179, 212
Ostler, Wm., 178, 183
Ostricer, Thos. le, 45
Otes, 142
Otterford, 140
Otterton (Devon), priory, 87, 102
Ottery St. Mary (Devon), 138
Ousley, *see* Owsley
Owen, Thos., 103
Owsley (Ousley, Owseley):
  Wm., rector of Shepton Beauchamp, 13 *n*, 33, 68, 219, 222
  Wm. (fl. 1575), 196
  fam., 149
Oxenford (in West Dowlish), 151
Oxford, 103, 140, 209, 219
  Holywell in, 194
Oxford University, 20, 30, 41, 47, 130
  colleges of, *see* All Souls; Exeter; New; Pusey House; Queen's; Wadham
Oxfordshire, *see* Baynton; Bucknell; Caversham; Kencott; Shiplake, Lower

P., C., goldsmith, 147
P., I., goldsmith, 120, 133, 194, 220
Padstow (Cornw.), 155
Paget:
  John, rector of Shepton Beauchamp, 219
  Revd. Simon, 218

Palfrey:
  John, 138
  fam., 223
Palmer:
  Mrs. Eliz., 145
  Hen. (fl. 1618), 65
  Hen. (d. *c.* 1715), 14
  Hen. (d. 1740), 14
  Honoria, *see* Harris
  John (fl. 1660), 24
  John (d. 1696), and his s. John, 24
  Jos., 14
  M. A., 98
  Sam., 46
  Tristram, 25
  Wm. Spencer, 71
  fam., 24, 97
Paris, 176
Paris, *see* Court
parish officers (less common):
  mole catchers, 59
  posts, 1, 58–9, 102
Parke, Jane, 156
Parker:
  Edw., Ld. Morley, 85–6
  Eliz., *see* Stanley
  Geo., 25
  Hen., Ld. Morley and Monteagle, 85, 93
  Ric., 238
  Rob., 58
  Thos., 186
  Wm., Ld. Morley and Monteagle, 85
  fam., 24, 93
parks, 4, 38–40, 45–6, 56, 60, 69, 81, 114–16, 121–2, 125–6, 133–4, 147, 149, 160, 165, 183–4, 211, 231, 233–4
  (wild life), 137
Parnham (Dors.), 115
Parratt, Jasper, and his w. Sophia, 13
Parrett, riv., 4, 52, 62, 78, 82, 111, 170–1, 182, 189
Parris, Thos., 235 *n*
Parsons:
  Ant., 86
  Eliz., *see* Donne
  Hen., 15, 64
  R. M. P., 64
  Wm., *see* Peters, Wm. Parsons
Partridge, Magdalene, 19, 33
Patch:
  John, 9
  Rob. Burnet, curate of Chillington and Knowle St. Giles, 132, 162
  fam., 58
Patten, fam., 97
Paulet, *see* Poulett
Paull, Jas., 98
Pauncefoot:
  Eleanor, *see* Blanford
  Eliz., m. Jas. Daubeney, 70
  Rob., 70
Paveley:
  Hugh, 88, 92
  John de, and his w. Eve, 14
  John de, *see* Bykenhulle
  Margery, w. of Hugh, m. (2), Roland Rake, 92
  Ric., 88
  Rob. de, and his w. Joan, 14
Payne:
  Peter Smith, 22
  Thos., 108
Peacham, Edm., rector of Hinton St. George, 49
Pecham, John, abp. of Canterbury, 132 *n*, 197, 201
Pek, Wm., 201 *n*
Pembroke, earldom of, 41; *and see* Marshal
Pendomer, 70
Penny, Chas., rector of Chaffcombe, 127

Penruddocke, John, 10
Pensford, 138
Pepys, Sam., 69
perambulation, 149
Perceval, Mrs. J., 66
Percy:
  Gerbert de, 228
  Hen., 232
  Joan, see Briwere
  John (d. by 1284), 232
  John de (fl. early 14th cent.), 224
  Mary, see Filoll
  Wm. de (d. 1245), 232
  Wm. (d. 1407), 224
Peren:
  Burchall, 180
  Wm. Burchall, 187
Perham, Rob., 22
Perkins, John, 14
Perretona, see Petherton, South
Perrott, North, 13, 33–4, 62, 66
Perrott, South (Dors.), 62–3, 115, 189
Peters:
  J. R., 176
  John Weston, 115, 174, 180, 183,
    187, 189
  W. P., 115
  Wm. Parsons, 115, 176
  fam., 117
Petherton, John, vicar of South
    Petherton, 192
Petherton, North, 170
Petherton, South (Perretona), 4, 22,
    35, 78, 111, 113, 115–16, 118,
    121, 130, 132, 157, 163–4, 170–
    98, 202, 205, 208–12, 216, 218,
    221–2
  adv., 191
  agric., 183–7, 190
  br., 172, 175, 182, 191
  Bridge, q.v.
  brotherhood, 192–3
  chant., 116, 193
  chap., 171–2, 180, 183, 189, 201;
    and see Petherton, South, St.
    John's chap.
  chaplains, 193–4
  char., 191, 196–8
  ch., 132, 169, 171–2, 175–6, 180,
    183, 186, 189, 191–4, 192,
    196–8, 201, 203
    ho., 193
    plan, 193
  Civil War, 172, 175, 194
  Compton Durville, q.v.
  cts., 112, 186, 189–90
  ct. ho., 174, 177, 190
  crosses, 172
  curates, 191, 193; and see Coke
  dom. archit., 174, 177–8, 180, 183,
    192, 193
  Drayton, q.v.
  fair, 172, 184, 188, 194
  fms., 184, 186–7, 209
  fields, 171–2, 184–7
  Fouts cross, 171–2, 174–5; and see
    Shepton Beauchamp
  friendly socs., 175
  Frogmary Green, 172; and see
    Seavington St. Michael
  Gawbridge, 189
  glebe, 192
  Harp, South, q.v.
  Hassockmoor, 176, 181–2; and see
    Petherton, South: Moor
  Hele, 179–80, 184, 187
    man., 185, 189
    man.-ho., 180
  hosp., 191
  hund., 58, 111–12, 131, 159, 170–1,
    190, 200, 212
    cts., 112, 122, 189
    officers, 112, 131, 190
  inc., 172, 185–7
  ind., 187–8

inns, 172, 174–5
  Bell, 174
  Crown, 174, 188, 190
  George, 174
  Rose and Crown, 174
  Three Cups, 174
Joylers (Yayleris), 189
King Ina's Palace, 145, 176–7,
  180
lights, 193
Little Lopen, q.v.
man., 111–12, 114, 129, 136, 145,
  171, 174–84, 188–90, 194
man.-ho., 176–7, 186, 190
mkt., 184, 188, 194, 220
  cross, 172
  ho., 172, 188, 191, 196
  pl., 172–3, 175, 188
mills, 172, 176, 179, 181, 184–5,
  188–9, 191
ministers, see Bennett, Edw.; Dukes
minster, 183, 191
mint, 184
Monmouth Rebellion, 175
Moor (Mora, More), 181, 186–7,
  195; and see Petherton, South,
  Hassockmoor
nonconf., 107, 174, 195–7
par. officers, 190
poor-relief, 187, 190–1, 197–8
pop., 175
prehist. rem., 171–2
priest, see Alviet
publ. serv., 188, 191
quarries, 171, 187
rly., 172
rector, 132
rectory, 130, 165–6, 169, 176,
  179–80, 183–5, 187, 189, 193,
  202
  ho., 180
Rom. Cath., 195
Rom. rem., 171–2
St. John's chap., 184–5, 188, 191,
  194
  rectors, 194; and see Clerk;
  Forest; Foster, Hugh; Oliver;
  Symondes
sch., 188, 196–7
shambles, 188
stalls, 188
Stoodham, 171–2, 174
Stratton, q.v.
streets, 173–4
  Cheap St., 172, 174
  Cornhill, 173, 175
  George La., 171
  Hele La., 180
  North St., 174, 195
  Palmer St., 171, 173–4, 187, 195,
    197
  Pitway, 171, 174–5, 191, 195–6
  Prig La., 175
  Roundwell St., 174–5, 195
  St. James's St., 173–5, 177, 180,
    188, 195, 197
  Silver St., 174, 197
  South St., 174, 195
  West St., 173–4, 192
tithes, 178–80, 185–6, 191–2
tithing, 112, 175, 190
vestry, 190–1, 196
vicars, 132, 169, 190–4, 197–8; and
  see Bankes; Bond, Hen.;
  Castleman; Forest; Gilbert;
  Godard; Harcourt; Harrys,
  Thos.; Marks, Rob. and Wm.;
  Petherton, John; Seager;
  Simpson, Francis; Wodeman
vicarage, 60, 191–2, 195
  ho., 180, 192
Watergore, q.v.
workho., 191
Yeabridge, q.v.
Petterson, Ludwig, 152

Phelips:
  Sir Thos. (d. 1618), 114
  Sir Thos., Bt. (d. 1625), 114
  Sir Thos., Bt. (fl. 1642), 114
  Wm., 189
Phelps:
  John, 26
  John Bryant, 14
  Thos., 22, 26
  fam., 26, 144
Phillips, Geo., curate of Chillington
  and Knowle, 132, 162
Piers, Wm., bp. of Bath and Wells,
  193
Pike, T., bell-founder, 237; and see
  Pyke
pillory, 58–9, 190
Pilsdon:
  Alice, m. John Jew, 90
  John of, 90
Pilsdon (Dors.), 89
Pincombe Trustees, 118
Pinhoe (Devon), 181
Pinney:
  Azariah, 70, 73–4
  John (fl. 1689), minister, 35
  John (d. 1771–2), 70
  John (d. 1819), 70
  John Azariah, 70
  John Fred., 70
  Rob. (fl. 1547), 227
  Rob., minister of Chaffcombe and
    Crewkerne, 34, 127
  fam., 70
Pitminster, see Poundisford
Pitney, 107
Pitt:
  Benj., 159
  Jane, 73
  John, 54, 58
  Mary, m. Thos. Sergison, 73
  Mat., 159
  Sam., 70, 73
  fam., 55
Pittard (Pittard):
  Thos., 116
  ——, 103
Pix, Nat., 86
Plantagenet:
  Edw., earl of Warwick, 148
  Geo., duke of Clarence, 11, 91, 148
  Isabel, see Neville
planting (timber), 4, 40
play, sport, 211, 219
Plummer, Chris., rector of Crew-
  kerne, 30
Plymouth (Devon), 10
Plympton (Devon), honor, 69
Pointz:
  Hugh (d. 1307), 157, 165
  Hugh (fl. 1312), 157
  Nic., 144, 157, 165
  fam., 165
Pollard:
  Sir John, 16
  Sir Ric., 16, 124
Pole Anthony (in Tiverton, Devon),
  232
Poole:
  A. H., 210
  Chris., 206
  Jas., 207–8
  John (d. c. 1715), 13
  John (fl. 1778), 202
  Mary, w. of John (d. c. 1715), 13,
    34
  Rob., 203
  Thos. (fl. 1732), 206
  Thos. (fl. 1772), 202
  Thos. (late 18th cent.), 130
  Wm., 131
  fam., 130, 207–8
Poole (Dors.), 225
Poorton, North (Dors.), 74
Pope, Hen., 220

Popham:
Alex. (d. 1669), 89
Alex. (d. 1705), 89–90
Alex. (fl. early 18th cent.), 89
Anne, 92
Francis (d. 1644), 89
Sir Francis (d. 1674), 89
Francis (fl. 1727), 89
John (fl. 1576), 89
Sir John (d. 1607), 89
Portesye:
Ric. de, 69
Scolace, see Wayford
Portman:
Anne, w. of Sir John (d. 1612), m. (2) Thos. Neville, 71
Claud Berkeley, Vct. Portman, 64, 71
Edw. Berkeley (d. 1823), 71
Edw. Berkeley, Vct. Portman (d. 1888), 63–4, 71
Sir Hen. (d. 1591), 71
Sir Hen., Bt. (d. 1622), 71
Hen. Berkeley, Vct. Portman, 71
Hen. (Seymour) (d. 1727), 71
Hen. Wm., 71
Hen. Wm. Berkeley, 71
Hen. Wm. Berkeley, Vct. Portman, 71
Sir Hugh, Bt., 71
Sir John, Bt. (d. 1612), 71
Sir John, Bt. (d. 1622), 71
Sir Wm. (d. 1557), 71
Sir Wm., Bt. (d. 1645), 71
Sir Wm., Bt. (d. 1690), 71
Wm. (Berkeley) (d. 1737), 71
fam., 72
portreeve, see Robert
Portskewet (Mon.), 41
Potsgrove (Beds.), 74
Potteford, Rob. of, 18; and see Putford
Potter, John (d. 1880), 65
Poulett:
Sir Amias (d. 1538), 42, 44–5, 50, 55, 123
Sir Amias (d. 1588), 1, 3, 12, 16, 42, 44, 123
Anne, w. of John, Ld. Poulett (d. 1665), see Browne
Anne, s. of John, Earl Poulett (d. 1743), 130–1
Sir Ant. (d. 1600), 17, 42, 118, 123, 132, 169, 203
Ant. (fl. 1660), 16
Augusta, 51
Eliz., w. of Wm., see Denebaud
Eliz., w. of John, Ld. Poulett (d. 1649), see Kenn
Eliz., m. Andrews Warner, 16
Geo., 159
Geo. Amias Fitzwarrine, Earl Poulett, 42, 47–8, 51, 159, 165, 170, 208
Hen. (d. c. 1633), and his s. Hen., 16
Sir Hugh, 15, 19, 32, 41–2, 44–5, 48–9, 116, 123, 125, 127, 130, 165–6, 180, 209
Idony, w. of John (fl. 1401), see Kail
John (fl. 1401), 124, 142, 181
John (d. 1413), 124, 142–3
John, rector of Hinton St. George, 49, 209
John, Ld. Poulett (d. 1649), 11–12, 41–2, 47, 51, 85, 123, 159
John, Ld. Poulett (d. 1665), 20, 42, 50, 118, 132
John, Ld. Poulett (d. 1679), 49
John, Earl Poulett (d. 1743), 15, 44, 132, 147, 206, 209
John, Ld. Hinton, later Earl Poulett (d. 1764), 51, 129–30
John, Earl Poulett (d. 1819), 15, 17, 22, 39, 43, 46, 49–51, 130, 143–4, 159–60, 169, 202–3, 207

John, Earl Poulett (d. 1864), 20, 25, 46–8, 51, 65, 127, 143, 159, 169, 202
Peregrine, 161
Thos. (d. 1413), 124, 142–3
Vere, Earl Poulett, 40, 46, 130
Wm. (d. 1488), 42, 123, 206, 208
Wm. Hen., Earl Poulett, 45, 50, 147
Wm. John Lydston, Earl Poulett, 41, 144
fam., 1, 3–5, 12, 15, 19–20, 22, 26, 42, 46, 48–50, 64–5, 116, 123, 125–7, 143, 148, 159–62, 165, 168–9, 180, 185, 202, 204, 208, 213
Poundisford (in Pitminster), 201
Powell (Powel, Powle):
Frances, 157
Hen., 157
Marmaduke, 157
Mary, 157
Sam. (d. 1656–7), 157
Sam. (d. 1722), 157
Sam. (d. 1738), 157
Sam. (d. 1739), 157
Sarah, 157
Theophilus, vicar of Merriott, 60
Thos., 130
Wm., archd. of Bath, 157
fam., 161–2
Powerstock (Dors.), 142
Powle, see Powell
Powtrell:
Geo., 41
John, 41
Presbyterians, 34–5, 49–50, 61, 67, 103, 107, 120, 133, 141, 170, 195, 197, 205, 210, 221
Prescott, Mary, 238
Preston:
Sir Amias, 157, 159
Chris., 135–7, 141
Hugh, 141
John (d. 1541), 135, 139
John (d. 1590), 16, 125, 135, 138
John (17th cent.), 135, 138, 140
Marg., m. John Hippisley, 135
Maud, see Bidik
Ric., assistant curate of Knowle, 162
Steph., 135, 138–9
Preston Plucknett, 189
Prew, fam., 175
Price:
Chas., 53
Thos., vicar of Merriott, 60
Priddell, John, 108
Prideaux:
Sir Edm., 10, 16
Marg., see Gwyn
Prince, Bernard, 228
produce:
butter, 22, 26, 131, 147
cheese, 18, 23, 86, 98, 130, 137, 147, 187
cider, 18, 47, 93, 103, 115, 117, 131, 134, 185
honey, 192
and see wool
provost, see Robert
Prowse:
Amos, 188
Jas., 179
Mary, see Ayshe
Sam., 175
fam., 46, 177, 186
Pruet, Ric., and his w. Alice, 23
Puckington, 113, 116, 118–19, 175 n
Pudele:
Margery, see Noneton
Rob. de, 122
Puf (Pyf):
Joan, see Flemyng
Thos., 92

Pulman (Pullman):
G. P. R., 22
Rob., 99
Purdue:
Geo., bell-founder, 204
Ric. or Rog., bell-founder, 163
Thos., bell-founder, 147, 204
Purtington (in Winsham), 55, 134, 141, 147
Pusey House, Oxford, 219
Putford, Rog. de, 24; and see Potteford
Putt:
Margaretta, m. Hen. Marker, 114
Nic., 90
Raymundo (d. 1757), 90, 114
Raymundo (d. 1812), 90, 114
Sir Thos. (d. 1686), 90, 114
Thos. (d. 1721), 90, 114
Thos. (d. 1787), 90, 114
Revd. Thos. (d. 1844), 114
Ursula, see Cholmeley
Wm., 90
fam., 114
Pyers, Wm., curate of Crewkerne, 30
Pyke:
Alice, w. of Thos., m. (2) Wm. Montague, 89
Eliz., m. (1) Ric. Broughton, (2) Jas. Leigh alias Reynolds, (3) Ant. Stracheleigh, 89
Hugh, 89
John (fl. 1356), and his w. Isabel, 89
John, the elder (d. 1520–1), 89
John, the younger (fl. 1496), 89
Martin, 174
Ric. (d. by 1309), and his w. Joan, 89
Sir Ric. (fl. 1309), 89
Ric. (fl. 1356), 89
Rob., 89
Thos. (fl. 15th cent.), 89
Thos. (d. 1555), 89
Wm., 89
and see Pike
Pyl, Rob., rector of Crewkerne, 30
Pylle, 71
Pyne:
Amy, w. of Thos., 55–6
Art., 56
Chas., 17
Christabel, m. Sir Edm. Wyndham, 56
Hugh, 56, 114
John (d. 1607), 17, 55–6
John (d. 1679), 17
John (d. 1764), 17
John (fl. 1770), 17
Thos., 17, 55–6
Pynnye, ——, 24
Pysing:
Hugh (d. 1714), 124
Hugh (fl. 1743), 124
Jeffery (d. 1706), and his w. Eliz., 124
Jeffery (d. 1735), 124
Pytcher, Rob., 196

Quakers, 34, 67, 106–7, 129, 133, 220
Quantock:
Frances Herne, 180
John, 180
quarries, 38–9, 48, 52, 62, 113, 133 n, 141, 163, 187, 198, 223, 227
Queen's College, Oxford, 155

race course, 9
Radbard, see Rodbard
Radcliffe, Sir Ric., 11
Radwell, Rob. de, 181
railway, see Crewkerne; Knowle St. Giles; Misterton
Rake:
Margery, see Paveley
Roland, 92

Ralph (fl. early 12th cent.), 134
Ralph the red, *see* Sor
Ramsbury (Wilts.), 13; *and see* Littlecote
Randall (Rendall):
  Jos., 46
  Wm., minister of Wambrook, 229
Rawe:
  John, 214
  Thos., rector of Shepton Beauchamp, 219
  fam., 212
Raynolds, *see* Reynolds
recusants, *see* Roman Catholicism
Redborne (Dors.), *see* Beaminster, hund.
Rede (Read):
  Nic., 232
  Parnel, *see* Staunton
  fam., 130
Rendall, *see* Randall
Resurrection, Community of, 218
Reviers:
  Baldwin de, earl of Devon or Exeter (d. 1155), 10, 224
  Baldwin de, earl of Devon (d. 1188), 10
  Baldwin de, 10
  Isabel de, *see* Forz
  Joan, m. Wm. Briwere, 10–11, 15, 28
  Mary, m. Rob. de Courtenay, 1, 11
  Ric. de, earl of Devon (d. 1162), 10
  Ric. de, earl of Devon (d. 1193), 10
  Wm. de, earl of Devon, 1, 10–11, 15, 28
  fam., 69, 199
Reve, Thos., 189
Reynold, Warresius, son of, and his w. Alice (of Ashcombe), 71
Reynolds (Raynolds):
  Jane, 38
  John, and his w. Joan, 136
  Lionel, 136
Rice, Wm., and his w. Barbara, 54
Rich (Riche):
  Rob., 75
  Thos., 221
Richard I, 41
Richard III, 11
Richards:
  David, minister, 195
  E. E., 88
  Ellanette, m. John Glyde, 88
  J. W., 88
  John Whitehead, 97
  Thos. (d. 1827), 88, 94, 97
  Thos. (d. 1866), 88
  W. H., 88
  Wm., 88
  Wm. Haggett, 88, 94
  fam., 94
Richmond:
  ctss. of, *see* Beaufort
  duke of, *see* Fitzroy
Roach, Thos., 178
roads:
  coach, 5, 39, 164, 168, 172, 199, 205
  Foss Way, 38–9, 78, 82–3, 111, 122, 129, 134, 141, 147, 149, 151, 163–4, 171–2, 180, 198–9
  turnpikes, 5, 7, 39, 52, 113, 134, 151, 157, 172, 211, 223
Robert, ct. of Mortain, 12, 14, 53, 134, 148, 165, 180, 199, 212, 232
Robert the falconer, 148
Robert the port reeve, 27
Robert the provost, 27
Robert son of Ives, 212
Robins (Robyns):
  F. W. G. D., 222
  Wm., rector of Eastham, 30
  Wm., 161
Robinson, Geo. Jocelyn, 180
Rochester, bp. of, *see* Audley

Rochford, Agnes de, 14 *n*
Rodbard (Radbard, Rodberd):
  Blaise, 166, 179
  Edw. (Whitley), 54
  Edw. Wm. Rodbard, 54
  Emma, 54
  Frances Sarah, m. Rob. Danger, 54
  Hen. 54
  John (fl. 1384–5), 213
  John (d. 1744), 54
  John (Butcher), 54, 59
  John Rodbard, 54
  Mary (Butcher), m. Silvester Prior Bean, 54
  Reg. Hen., 54
  Reg. Hen. (Bean), 54
  Ric., 179
  Thos., 54
  Wal., 179
  Wm., vicar of Somerton, 179
  Wm., 57
  Wm. (Butcher), 54
Rodney:
  John, 14
  Sir Ric., de, 122
  Thos., 14
  Wal. de, 134
  fam., 122
Rodney Stoke, 134
Roger, archd. of Winchester, 60, 169
Roger, Nic., son of, *see* Nicholas
Rogers:
  Ann, 89
  Sir Edw. (fl. 1555), 89–90
  Edw. (d. 1627), 89
  Sir Francis, 89
  Sir Geo., 89
  Hen., 89–90
Rogus, John, and his w. Eliz., 213
Roller, John, 184
Roman Catholicism, *see* Crewkerne; Petherton, South; Whitestaunton
Rosewell: Ann, w. of Wm. (d. 1593), m. (2) John Davies, 88
  Sir Hen., 16, 88
  Parry, 88
  Wm. (d. 1566), 16, 88
  Wm. (d. 1593), 88
Rosse:
  Cuthbert, 213–14, 216
  Eliz., m. Wm. Bonner, 213
  Jas. (fl. 1617), 214
  Jas. (d. 1670), 214
  John (fl. 1575), 214
  John (d. 1617), 214
  Nic., 213–14
  ——, and his w.—— (Heyron), 214
  fam., 56, 213–15
Rossiter, fam., 117
Row, John Wall, 21
Rowsell:
  Geo., 25 *n*
  Hen., 25
  Jas., 221
  John, 25
  Thos., 25
  and see Rowswell
Rowswell:
  Ann, *see* Eliot
  Edw., 213
  Rob., minister of Shepton Beauchamp, 219
  Wm. Salisbury, 213
  and see Rowsell
Royce:
  Wm., 116
  fam., 117
Rupert, Prince, 192
Rutter, Hen., minister, 195
Ryme Intrinseca (Dors.), 224
Rys, Adam, 23

S., F., goldsmith, 32
S., W., bell-founder, 210
Sackville, Sir Ric., 22

Sacred Cross, Society of, 182
Sadborow (in Thorncombe, Dors.), 70–1, 73, 75, 228
St. Barbe, Sir John, 90
St. Brides, Nic. de, 41
St. Clare:
  Geof. de, 87
  Ric., 88
  Sir Rob. de (d. 1195), 87
  Rob. de (fl. 1223), 87–8
  Rob. (d. bef. 1308), 87
  Rob. (d. 1308), 87–8
  Rob. (d. 1336), 87–8
  Rob. (d. 1359), 87
  Wm., 87
  fam., 92
St. Decumans, Kentsford, q.v.
St. Francis, Community of, 182
St. John of Jerusalem, Order of, 56, 88, 165
St. Lo:
  John, 135
  Marg., *see* Clevedon
St. Martin-in-the-Fields (Mdx.), 50 86
St. Reyne (Ranus), chapel of, 33
St. White (Candida), chapel of, 141
St. Wulfric of Haselbury, 32
Salisbury, Stephen, 215
Salisbury (Wilts.), 15–16, 48, 155, 179, 225
  bell-foundry, 237
  bp. of, 17, 225
  cathedral, 228
  diocese, 224, 228
  earl of, *see* Cecil; Montacute; Neville
  earldom of, 232
Salmon, E. A., vicar of Martock, 104
Salthouse, Thos., 106
salvagius, *see* Wild
Salvation Army, 36
Samborne, Rob. de, rector of Merriott, 60, 206
Sampford (Samford):
  Chris., 15, 116
  fam., 166
  and see Sanford
Sampson:
  Geo. (fl. 1601), 166
  Geo. (fl. 1657), 166, 185
  Ric., 166
Sancta Wita, Rog. de, 141
Sandford Orcas (Dors.), 182
Sandpit (in Broadwindsor, Dors.), 182
Sandys:
  Mrs. Ann, 197
  Edwin, 177
  Emanuel, 185–6, 189
  Francis, 189
  John, 197
  Margery, *see* Bray
  Rob., 175
  Wal., 13
  Wm., Ld. Sandys of the Vine (d. 1542), 13
  Wm., Ld. Sandys of the Vine (d. 1623), 13, 34
  fam., 177, 180, 186
Sanford, Geo., 166; *and see* Sampford
Sarazin:
  Alice, 213
  John, and his w. Eliz., 213
  Ric., 213
  Thos., 213
  Wm., 213–14
Sargeant:
  Joan, 214
  Ric., 214
  Wm., 214
Saunders:
  G. W., vicar of Martock, 103
  Nic., 177

Sawbridge (later Sawbridge-Erle-Drax):
  J. S. W., 214
  Jane Frances, *see* Grosvenor
Say, John de, 82, 90, 104
Sayer:
  Israel, 73
  Rob., 73
Sayes, John de, 97
Sclavine, Wm., 104
Scott:
  Jas., duke of Monmouth, 10, 40–1, 53, 69, 114, 142, 152, 157, 164, 175, 232
  John, 57
Scriven:
  Eliz., m. —— Denslow, 139 *n*
  Joan, 138
  Ric., 139
  Thos., 138
Scrope:
  Eliz., m. John Daubeney, 117, 176
  John, Ld. Scrope, 85
Sea (in Ilminster), 144, 182
Seaborough (Dors.), 1, 14 *n*, 17–18, 26, 28–9, 36–7, 62, 74, 140
  ch., 4, 28
  vicarage, 67
Seager:
  Joan, 213
  Thos., vicar of South Petherton, 192, 196
Sealy:
  Elias, 124
  John, 99
  Sam., 124
  Sarah, m. Jas. Marwood, 124, 128
  fam., 126
Seavington (Seofenempton, Seovenamentone, Sevenehantona, Sevenemetone, Sevenhampton):
Seavington Abbots (in Seavington St. Mary), 119, 198–9, 204
  man., 201; *and see* Seavington St. Mary
  tithing, 112, 203
Seavington Dennis (in Seavington St. Michael), 111
  man., 205–6
  tithing, 112, 203, 205
Seavington St. Mary, 149 *n*, 150, 171, 184, **198–204**, 205, 207 *n*, 208, *209*, 212
  adv., 203
  agric., 202–3
  chaplains, 201, 203
  ch., 169–70, 183, 201, 203–4
    ho., 204
  cts., 203
  Crimbleford, 198–9
  curates, 203–5; *and see* Evans, Thos.; Stuckey, Thos.
  dom. archit., 199
  fms., 202–3
  fields, 198–9
  Hurcott, q.v.
  inc., 203
  inns, 172 *n*, 199
  mans., 199–202; *and see* Seavington Abbots; Seavington Vaux
  man.-ho., 202
  mill, 203
  nonconf., 204, 210
  par. ho., 203
  par. officers, 203
  poorho., 203
  pop., 199
  quarry, 198
  rectors, 203
  rectory, 201–2
    ho., 199, 202–3, 209–10
  Rom. rem., 199
  sch., 204
  Seavington Abbots, q.v.
  Seavington Vaux, q.v.

tithes, 201–2
tithing, 203
Upton, q.v.
vicarage, 209
Seavington St. Michael, 49, 148, 150, 163, 170–1, 193, 198–9, 203–4, **205–10**
  adv., 208
  agric., 206–7
  ch., 205–6, 208–10
    ho., 208–9
  cts. 207–8
  curates, 192, 209
  dom. archit., 205
  fms., 206
  fields, 205, 207
  friendly soc., 205
  Froggelmere, 205
  glebe, 206 *n*, 208
  inc., 207
  ind., 207
  inns, 205
  man., 205–6; *and see* Seavington Dennis
  man.-ho., 205–6
  minister, *see* Glasbroke
  nonconf., 210
  par. officers, 208
  poorho., 208–9
  poor-relief, 208–9
  pop., 205
  rectors, 150, 208–9; *and see* Atte-mede; Barret, Edw.; Billing, J.P.; Chelrye; Clement, Rob.; Crauden; Poulett, John; Upton, Francis, Geo., John
  rectory, 208
    ho., 208–10
  sch., 204, 209–10
  tithes, 180, 208
  tithing, 203; *and see* Seavington Dennis
  warren, 205
Seavington Vaux (in Seavington St. Mary), 111, 203
  man., 181
Seaward, fam., 223
Sedding, J. D., architect, 194
Segge (Shegge), fam., 223
Selwood, John, 177–8
Seofenempton, Seovenamentone, *see* Seavington
Sergison:
  Mary, *see* Pitt
  Thos., 73
serjeanty, tenure by, 87, 148, 177, 214
Serrey (Serry):
  Alice, m. Wm. Deane, 178
  John, 23, 35
Sevenhampton, *see* Seavington
Sevenehantona, Sevenemetone, *see* Seavington
Seward, John, 188
Seymour:
  Alice, m. Wm., Ld. Zouche, 134
  Alice, w. of Rob., 212
  Cath., *see* Filoll
  Cecily, *see* Beauchamp
  Edw., earl of Hertford, duke of Somerset (d. 1552), 13, 55, 129, 177, 179, 201–2, 212, 224
  Edw., earl of Hertford (d. 1621), 129, 132, 179, 201, 212
  Eliz., w. of Urry, *see* Meriet
  Eliz., m. Thos. Bruce, earl of Ailesbury, 129, 179, 212
  Frances, *see* Devereux
  Hen., *see* Portman
  Isabel, 212
  Jane, queen, 212 *n*
  Sir John (d. 1464), 212
  John (d. 1492), 212
  Sir John (d. 1536), 202, 212
  John, duke of Somerset, 129, 212
  Muriel, *see* Lovel

  Nic., 12, 134
  Ric., Ld. Seymour, 134
  Rog. (d. by 1394), 212
  Rog., and his w. Maud (fl. 1408), 212
  Rob., 212–13
  Urry, 54
  Wm., marquess of Hertford, duke of Somerset (d. 1660), 41, 103, 129, 177, 185, 212, 219
  Wm., duke of Somerset (d. 1671), 129, 179, 212
  fam., 12, 185
Shaftesbury (Dors.), 15, 179
Shallett, Jos., minister of Chaffcombe, 127
Shapwick, 86
Sharlock, *see* Sherlock
Sharp:
  Cecil, 211
  Ric., rector of Wayford, 74
Sharpham Park (in Walton), 86
Shaw, Chas. Jas., rector of Cricket St. Thomas, 140
sheep, 7, 18–20, 22–3, 45, 56, 66, 92, 94–7, 117, 125–7, 130–1, 136, 138, 140, 144, 153–4, 160, 166–7, 184, 186–8, 202, 206–7, 214–15, 218, 227, 234, 236–7
Shelford, Hen. de, rector of Shepton Beauchamp, 219
Shepton Beauchamp, *64*, 68, 111–13, 118–19, 163 *n*, 171–2, 179, 196, 198–9, 204–5, **210–22**
  adv., 217–18
  agric., 214–15
  alms-ho., 217, 220, 222
  chars., 221–2
  ch., *192*, 214, 217–21
    ho., 217, 219–20, 222
    plan, 220
  cts., 213, 216–17
  curate, 221–2; *and see* Thomas, John
  dom. archit., 211–14, 218
  fair, 211, 216
  fms., 211, 215
  fields, 210–11, 214–15
  Fouts Cross, 210; *and see* Petherton, South
  friendly soc., 211
  glebe, 218
  hosp., 222
  inc., 215
  ind., 216
  inns, 211, 216
  lights, 217, 220
  man., 179, 212–19, 221
  man.-ho., 211–15, 218
  mkt., 211, 216
  mill, 216–18
  minister, *see* Rowswell, Rob.
  nonconf., 215, 220–1
  oratory, 212
  par. officers, 215, 217
  park, 211
  poorho., 217, 220, 222
  poor-relief, 215–16, 221
  pop., 211–12
  rector, 211, 217–18, 221; *and see* Barker; Champernowne, John; Coles, J. S. and V. S. S.; Domett; Dugdale; Eliot; Fitzwarin; Hulle, Wal. de; Lade, Benj. de la; Lethbridge; Middleton; Newman; Owsley; Paget; Rawe, Thos.; Shelford; Upton, Rob. de
  rectory, 217
    ho., *65*, 218–19
  schs., 211, 221–2
  shambles, 211, 216, 219
  streets, 210–11
  tithes, 213, 218
Shepton Mallet, 22 *n*, 85, 149

Sherborne (Dors.):
 abbey, 224
 bp., 224
 cast., 228
 hund., 222
 sch., 104
 sheriff, see Merlesuain; Tofig
 sheriff's tourn, 2, 77, 112
Sherlock (Sharlock):
 Ann, m. Amos Martin, 26
 Eliz., m. John Clarke, 26
 Ric., 25
 Rob., 23
 Wm., 38
shillyngstole, 27
Shiplake, Lower (Oxon.), 130
Shorwell (I. W.), 86
 Northcourt in, 88
Shropshire, see Stanton Lacy
Sibton (Suff.), 143
Simpson, Francis, vicar of South
 Petherton, 192
Sinclair:
 John (fl. 1377), 13
 John, the younger, 13
 John (several), 13
 Wm., and his w. Lettice, 13
 fam., 34
Sirewold, 134
Siward the falconer, 148, 205
Skellen (Skelton):
 John, 205
 Tamsin, 206
Slade:
 Ann, 85
 Edith, m. Wm. Boef, 55
 Geo. (fl. 1798), 85
 Geo. (fl. 1841), 97
 Hen., 85
 Isabel, see Canon
 John (fl. 1557), 130
 John (d. 1781), 85
 Mary, m. Nat. Dalton, 13
 Ric., 55
 fam., 93, 99
Small, Jos. Attwell, rector of White-
 staunton, 237
Smart, John, 197
Smith (Smyth, Smythe):
 A. D., 73
 Sir Edw., 64
 Ethel Katie Dorville, 228 n
 H. H. A., curate of Wambrook, 228
 John, and his w. Rebecca, 225
 John, curate of Barrington, 119
 Ric., minister of Whitestaunton,
  237
 Rob., 225
 Sarah, 146
 Revd. W. G. Parks, and his w.
  Eliz., 218
Snaydon, Thos., 237
Soane, Sir John, 42 n, 43, 135, 140
Somerset:
 duke of, see Beaufort; Seymour
 earl of, see Beaufort
Somerset, 229, 231, 237
 coroner, see Brett; Clavelshay
 County Council, 165
 escheator, see Brett; Case
 sheriff, see Oliver
 under-sheriff, 188
Somerset Trading Co., 65; and see
 Stuckey and Bagehot
Somerton, 5, 78, 81, 96, 119, 168, 171,
 179
 Hurcot, 171
 Kingsmoor, q.v.
 man., 81
 vicar, 96
Sopere, Jordan le, 144
Sor:
 Ela la, m. Wm. de Esthalle, 122
 Gwenllian, w. of Rob., m. (2) Nic. s.
  of Roger, 122

John le (fl. 1176–7), 122
John le (fl. 1194–1205), 122
John le (d. by 1255), 122
John le (d. c. 1296–7), 122
John le (fl. 1316), 123
Jordan le, 122
Otes le, 122
Ralph le, 122
Rob. le, 122
Wm. le, 122
fam., 122 and n
Southampton, see Harp, South
Southarp, see Harp, South
Southcombe, Ric., 21, 187
Southcombe, see Crewkerne
Southcott, Joanna, 35, 50, 156
 followers of, 35, 50, 156
Southeye, Wm., curate of Barrington,
 119
Southwark (Surr.), 107
Southwick (Wilts.), 90
Southwood, John, vicar of Martock,
 103
Southyngton, see Harp, South
Sowton (Devon), 152
Sparks:
 Sam., 21, 24
 Wm., 22, 33
Sparrow, Wm., 98
Speke:
 Benj., rector of Dowlish Wake, 155
 Sir Geo. (d. 1528), 144, 152, 155
 Geo. (fl. 1532), 116, 130, 166
 Sir Geo. (d. 1584), 143
 Sir Geo. (d. 1637), 116, 143, 201
 Geo. (d. 1690), 143, 185
 Geo. (d. 1753), 129, 143–4, 152
 Hugh, rector of Dowlish Wake,
  152, 155
 Joan, m. Thos. Sydenham, 124
 Joan, w. of John (d. 1441), see
  Kaynes
 John (d. 1441), 124, 143, 152
 John (d. 1444), 124, 143
 John (d. 1518), 124, 143, 152, 157
 John (d. 1524), 143, 152
 John (d. c. 1537), 124
 John (fl. 1690), 143, 201
 John Hanning, 152, 155
 Mary, 143–4, 152
 P. G. H., 153
 Phil., rector of Dowlish Wake, 155
 Thos., 124
 Sir Thos. (fl. 1532), 116, 130, 166
 Sir Thos. (d. 1551), 143, 152
 W. H., 153
 Wm. (d. 1508), 124, 130, 152
 Wm. (d. 1839), 152–4
 Wm. (d. 1887), 153
 Wm. (d. 1908), 153
 Wm., rector of Dowlish Wake, 155
 fam., 116, 152, 154–5, 201
sports, see bear-baiting; bird-netting;
 bowling green; bull-baiting;
 chase; cockfighting; cricket; egg-
 shackling; fowling; harriers;
 hawking; play; race course
Spoure:
 Digory, 63
 Hen., 63
 Phil., 63
 Thos. (fl. 15th cent.), 63
 Thos. (fl. 16th cent.), 63
 Wm., 63
 fam., 63–4
Spraggett, Geo., vicar of Martock,
 103
Sprengehose, Wal., rector of Cricket
 St. Thomas, 140
Stacy:
 Edw., 106
 John, vicar of Merriott, 60
Stafford:
 Cecily, see Bonville
 Eleanor, m. Thos. Strangways, 165

Eliz., see Aumale
Hen., duke of Buckingham (d.
 1483), 114, 129, 176
Hen., earl of Wiltshire, 54, 88
Sir Humph. (d. 1413), 90, 206
Sir Humph. (d. 1442), 54–5, 90,
 164–5, 206
Humph., duke of Buckingham, 86
Humph., Ld. Stafford, earl of
 Devon, 90, 165
John de, 183
John, bp. of Bath and Wells,
 archbp. of Canterbury, 30, 49
Wm., 165, 236
fam., 90
Stalbridge (Dors.), Thornhill, q.v.
staller, Eadnoth the, see Eadnoth
Stambury, Hen., rector of Hinton St.
 George and Dinnington, 49,
 150
Standerwick, 159
Stanley:
 Eliz., m. Edw. Parker, Ld. Morley,
  85
 Marg., see Beaufort
 Thos., earl of Derby, 85–6
 Wm., Ld. Monteagle, 85
Stanstead (Essex), 165
Stanton Lacy (Salop.), 17
Staple, Hen., rector of Wambrook,
 229
Staple Fitzpaine, 143
Stapleton (Glos.), 233
Stapleton (in Martock), 78, 81, 83–4,
 92, 100, 103, 105
 agric., 94
 chap., 88, 104
 chant., 88
 chap., 105
 ct. ho., 101, 105
 fms., 81
 fields, 81, 94
 inc., 94
 man., 86–90, 94, 100–1, 105
  ho., 81, 88, 94
 park, 81
 tithing, 76, 81, 87
Starr, Jos., 58
Staunton:
 And. de, rector of Whitestaunton,
  236
 Parnel, w. of Wm. of, m. (2) Nic.
  Rede, 232
 Rob. of (fl. 1166), 232
 Rob. of (fl. 1234), 232
 Rob. of (fl. 1321), 232
 Rog. of (fl. 1312), 232
 Rog. of (d. 1351), 232
 Thos. of, 232
 Sir Wm. of (d. 1311), 232
 Wm. of, 232
 fam., 233
Stawley, 67, 74
Steeple Langford (Wilts.), 64
Steepleton Iwerne (Dors.), 179
Stembridge:
 Agnes, 19
 Thos., 65
Stephen, king, 84, 191
Stephens:
 Hen., and his w. Phoebe Martha,
  179–80
 John, 203, 213
 Wm., 203, 213
 and see Stevens
Stevens:
 Hen., 124
 Sarah Bridget, see Marwood
Stevenson:
 Jas., vicar of Martock, 34, 103,
  106–7
 Leonard, curate of Barrington, 119
Stewkley, Sylvester, 22
Steyning (in Stogumber), 71
Stinsford (Dors.), 90, 165

stock (less common):
  geese, 56, 93–5, 168, 186, 229
  goats, 18, 136
  pigeons, 192
  turkeys, 45
  and see sheep
stocks, 28, 59, 145, 168
Stocker, Thos., 98
Stockland (Devon), 132, 223
Stocklinch:
  Joan, m. Wm. Denebaud, 123
  Ralph of, 123, 157, 159
  Rog. of, 123
Stocklinch Magdalen, 113, 179
  Ilford Bridges, q.v.
Stocklinch Ottersay, 113, 204, 213,
  217
Stogumber, Steyning in, q.v.
Stoke:
  Luke de, 44
  Wal. de, 44
  and see Jordan
Stoke Abbott (Dors.), 74
Stoke Charity (Hants), 114
Stoke St. Mary, 146
Stoke sub Hamdon, 7, 40, 83, 91, 98,
  100, 171, 195, 197, 199, 212, 216
  college, 213
  East Stoke man., 199
  fair, 172
  Ham Hill, 2, 39, 77, 112, 172, 180,
    210
  provost, 213
  sch., 196
Ston Easton, 135, 183, 185
Stone:
  Elias, 161
  John, 161
  John atte, 205
  Parnel de la, 205
Stone (in Chulmleigh, Devon), 179
Stourton:
  John, 155
  Wm., Ld. Stourton, 208
Stowell, 90
Stracheleigh:
  Ant., 89
  Eliz., *see* Pyke
Strangways:
  Cath., 165
  Eleanor, *see* Stafford
  Sir Giles (d. 1547), 90, 165
  Sir Giles (d. 1562), 90, 165, 178
  Giles Stephen Holland Fox-, earl of
    Ilchester, 54 *n*
  Hen., 90, 165
  John, 54–5, 90, 178
  Thos., 90, 165
  fam., 54 *n*, 55
Stratton, John de, 159 *n*
Stratton (Strete, in South Petherton),
  163–6, 168, 171, 174, 178, 182–5,
  191, 195–6
  ch., 193
  ct., 190
  dom. archit., *193*
  fields, 172, 186
  Great Stratton, 111, 182
  Little Stratton, 111, 172
  Lower (Nether) Stratton, 171, 190,
    196
  man., 166, 178
  Over (Upper) Stratton, 171, 174–5,
    197
  sch., 197
  tithing, 168, 175, 184, 190
Streche:
  Cecily, m. (1) Thos. Bonville, (2)
    Sir Wm. Cheyney, 201
  Eliz., m. Thos. Beauchamp, 201
  Joan, *see* Weylond
  Sir John (d. 1355), 181, 201, 224
  John (fl. 1412), 182
  Marg., *see* Multon
Street, G. E., architect, 220

Street (in Winsham), 16, 111, 124–5
Strode:
  Anne, 120
  Sir Geo., 85
  Jane, m. Rob. Austen, 114
  Wm. (d. 1666), 85, 100, 108, 114–15
  Wm. (d. 1695), 85, 114–15
  Wm. (d. 1746), 85, 93, 114, 120
  fam., 100, 114, 116
Stuckey:
  John (fl. early 18th cent.), 182
  John (d. 1810), 182, 207
  Rob., 182, 202
  Thos. (fl. 1586), 221
  Thos., curate of Seavington St.
    Mary, 204
  Vincent, 180, 182, 211
  fam., 206–7
Stuckey and Bagehot, 79, 117; *and see*
  Somerset Trading Co.
Sturtevant, Sim., 108
Suffolk, duke of, *see* Brandon; Grey
Suffolk, *see* Dunwich; Kentwell Hall;
  Sibton; Wickhambrook
Summerhayes, Rog., 238
Surland, Ric., rector of Crewkerne, 30
Surrey, ctss. of, *see* Warenne
Surrey, *see* Merton
Sussex, 41 *n*; *and see* Chichester;
  Lewes
Suttle, Thos., and his w. Ann, 238
Sutton Brothers, 167
Sutton, Long, 78, 106, 108
  Little Load, q.v.
Swallow:
  Geo., 228
  John, 228
Sweet:
  Anne, *see* Notley
  C. F., 130
Sweetland, fam., 58
Swell, 60, 116, 185
Swyre (Dors.), 194
Sydenham:
  Cath., m. Lewis Tregonwell, 90
  Geo., and his w. —— (Heyron),
    214 *n*
  Humph., and his w. Grace, 90
  Joan, *see* Speke
  Sir John (d. 1557), 165
  John (fl. 1563), 165
  John (d. 1590), 165
  Ric., 124
  St. Barbe, 90
  Thos., 124, 130
  fam., 56
Sylvayn, Joan, 202
Symonds (Symondes):
  Edw., 154
  Hen., 73
  Ric., 175
  Sim., rector of St. John's chapel,
    South Petherton, 194
  fam., 154
Syon (Mdx.), abbey, 87
Syon Hill (in Isleworth, Mdx.), 179,
  212

Taggart, Jas., curate of Crewkerne, 30
Tailboys:
  Eliz., *see* Bonville
  Wm., 91
Taile, Hubert le, 24
Tanner:
  Edw., 14
  John, 226
  fam., 226
Tarrant Gunville (Dors.), 192
Tasmania, 84, 102
Tate, ——, architect, 115
Tatworth, 182
Taunton, 5, 7, 10, 13, 21, 23, 39, 78,
  91, 97, 99, 108, 156, 164, 172,
  198–9, 204, 209, 211, 229
  archd., 31, 192

archdeaconry, 171
  sch., 209
Tawstock (Devon), 237
Taylor:
  Revd. Elias, 86
  H. G., 135
  J., bell-founders, 32, 50, 61, 120,
    156, 204, 210
  W. J. D., 135
  fam., 137
Tedbury, Rob., 236
Teddington (Mdx.), 156
Templar, Order of Knights, 28, 88,
  164–5
Temple Combe, 88, 165
Templeman:
  John (fl. 1685), 53
  John (fl. 1842), 57
  John, rector of Cricket, curate of
    Lopen, 140, 169
  Osborne, 26
  Thos. (fl. 1760), 26
  Thos. (fl. 1840), 167
Tenterden (Kent), 114
Tett, fam., 40
Teutonicus, *see* German
Tewkesbury (Glos.), abbey, 206
Thomas:
  John, curate of Shepton Beau-
    champ, 221
  Osborne, 26
  Patten, 130
  ——, 24
Thorn Coffin, 90
Thorncombe (in Bicknoller), 232
Thorncombe (Dors.), 16, 68
  Sadborow, q.v.
  sch., 71
Thorney (in Kingsbury Episcopi),
  115
Thornford (Dors.), 132
Thornhill (Thornhull):
  Geo., 228
  Wal. de, 202
Thornhill (in Stalbridge, Dors.), 228
Thurlbear, 146
Thynne, John, 201
tiles, 22, 171, 188, 216; *and see* brick
timber, 93, 207; *and see* planting;
  wood
  alder, 18, 39, 56, 226
  ash, 207, 226
  cherry, 45
  elm, 207
  holly, 226
  lime, 40
  maple, 113
  oak, 40, 207, 226, 234
  thorn, 18, 40
Tintinhull, 76, 78–9, 81, 89, 212,
  218
Tiptoft:
  Sir John, 91
  Philippe, *see* Gournay
Tirrel:
  Mic., 225
  Ric., 225
Tiverton (Devon), Pole Anthony in,
  q.v.
Tofig the sheriff, 164
Toller:
  Revd. Hen., 195
  John, curate of Crewkerne, 30
  John, 188
  Revd. Thos., 195
  Thos. Northcote, 175
Tolman, Jas., 221
Tomkins, Jacob, vicar of Misterton,
  curate of Crewkerne, 30, 67
Tony, John, 168
Toomer (in Henstridge), 44
Torrell's Preston (in Milverton), 16
Tort, Rob. le, 18
Towers, Ric., 229
Townsend, Rog., 86

trades (less common):
  gardener, 20, 57
  goldsmith, 20
  organ-maker, 20
  whittawer, 20
Treasorer, Wm., 179, 189
Trebartha (in Northill, Cornw.), 63
Tregonwell:
  Cath., see Sydenham
  Lewis Dymock Grosvenor, 90
  St. Barbe, 90
Trelawney:
  Sir Jonathan, 11
  John, and his w. Florence, 11
  John (d. 1563), 11
  John (d. 1568), 11
  John (d. 1569), 11
  John (fl. 1618), 11
  fam., 1, 26
Trelowarren (Cornw.), 12
Trenchard:
  Geo., 24
  John, 35
  Wm., 24
trencher, Gerard the, see Gerard
Trethurf:
  Eliz., m. John Vivian, 12
  John, and his w. Eliz., 12
  Marg., m. Edw. Courtenay, 12
  Thos., 12
Trevelyan:
  Sir Geo., 56
  Sir John (d. 1755), 56
  Sir John (d. 1828), 56
  Mary, m. Edm. Wyndham, 56
  fam., 59
Trigel, Rog., 213-14
Trivet:
  Thos., 24
  Wm., 24
Trowbridge (Wilts.), honor, 152
Tucker:
  Leonard, 71
  Wm., 138-9
  fam., 24, 139
tumbrel, 168
Turberville (Turbeville):
  Cecily, see Beauchamp
  Dr. Daubeney, 20, 69-70, 73, 75
  Thos., 91
  Thomasine, see Buckland
Turner, John, minister, 61, 107
Turstin, 12, 134
Twickenham (Mdx.), see Whitton
Tyce, John, curate of Barrington,
  119
Tyler, fam., 21, 99 n
Typper, Wm., 32

Uley (Glos.), 71
Ulnod, 180
Unitarians, 35-6, 195
United Reformed Church, 195
United States of America, 114; and
  see America; Largo
Upminster (Essex), 15
Upottery (Devon), 228
Upsteel, Ric., 199
Upton:
  Francis, rector of Seavington St.
    Michael, 209
  Geo., rector of Seavington St.
    Michael, 209
  Jas., 209
  John, rector of Seavington St.
    Michael, 209
  Rob. de, rector of Shepton Beau-
    champ, 219
Upton (Oppetone Abbe) (in Seaving-
  ton St. Mary), 111, 185, 199, 203
usher:
  Helen the, see Helen
  John the, see John
  Wm. the, see William
  and see Wigborough, Ric. of

Vaigge, John, curate of Barrington and
    Chillington, 119, 132
Vandruske, Col., 41
Vanner, John, 24
Vaux:
  Alice de, 14, 181, 199
  Grace, m. Wm. de Wydiworth, 181
  Hubert, 199
  J. G., 178
  John, 216
  Maud, m. Thos. de Multon, 199
  Rob. de, 14, 181, 199, 203
  S. G., 178
  Savary de, 71
  fam., 203
Vawdye, John, curate of Lopen, 169
Veel:
  Rob., 213
  Eleanor, m. John Coker, 213
  and see Viel
Venicombe, Francis, 188
Venner, Kingsford, 117
Verner, Jas., 124
Vialls, Geo., 37
Viel (Vyall):
  John, 149
  Thos., curate of Misterton, 67
  fam., 149
Vile:
  Ellen Rendall, 198
  Wm., 198
Villiers:
  Geo., earl of Jersey, 179, 212
  Sarah Sophia, see Fane
Vincent:
  Ant., 160
  Bray, 86
  J. G. (d. 1898), 161
  J. G. (fl. 1973), 159, 161
  J. W. H., 161
  Jas., 160
  John (d. 1830), 159-61
  John (d. 1854), 161
  Jos. Soper, 161
  Rob. (d. 1834), and his s. Rob., 161
  Wm., 161
  Mrs., 159 n
  fam., 126, 160-1
Vivian:
  Sir Francis, 12
  Hannibal, 12
  John (d. 1562), and his w. Eliz., 12
  John (d. 1577), 12
  Sir Ric., Bt., 12
  Sir Vyell, Bt., 12
  fam., 1, 26
Vulliamy, Lewis, architect, 163
Vyall, see Viel
Vyne, John, 144

Wadham:
  Martin, 225
  Mary, see Woolmington
  Sir Nic., 59
  Rob., 225
  fam., 144, 185
Wadham College, Oxford, 225-7, 237
waifs and strays, 2
Wake:
  And., 152
  Christine, w. of Ralph (fl. 1200), m.
    (2) Ric. Wild, 14, 152
  Isabel, m. John Kaynes, 152, 155
  John, 130, 152
  Ralph (fl. 1200), 14, 152, 154
  Ralph (fl. 1214), and his w. Hawise,
    152
  Ralph (fl. 1286), 152
Wales, 45
  South, 114, 216; and see Glamorgan
Wall, Ric., vicar of Martock, 106-7
Wallis, R. J., 57
Walrond:
  Amos, vicar of Martock, 103
  Hen., 144, 182

Humph. (d. 1580), 25, 182
Humph. (fl. 1637), 182
John, 189
Walscombe (in Chard), 126
Walter the knight, 224
Wambrook (Awanbruth, Whm-
    beriche), 111, 140, **222-31**, 235-6
  adv., 224-5, 228
  agric., 226-7
  char., 231
  ch., 227-31
    ho., 225, 230
  cts., 227
  ct. ho., 225
  curates, 229-30; and see Smith,
    H. H. A.
  dom. archit., 223
  fms., 223, 226-7
  fields, 226
  glebe, 229
  Haselcombe, 223, 225-7; and see
    Wambrook, Lower Wambrook
  Higher Wambrook, 222-3, 226-7,
    229-30
  inc., 223, 226, 229
  inns, 223, 228
  Lancin (Lansham, Londenesham,
    Londesham), 223, 226-7
  Linnington (Lyllyngedoone), 223,
    225-7
  Lower Wambrook, 222-3, 227; and
    see Wambrook, Haselcombe
  man., 223-6, 228-9
  man.-ho., 223, 225, 227, 230
  mill, 226-7, 229
  minister, see Randall
  nonconf., 230
  par. officers, 227-8
  poorho., 228
  poor-relief, 231
  pop., 223-4
  prehist. rem., 223
  priest, see Yarcombe
  quarry, 223, 227
  rectors, 227-30; and see Backaller;
    Chase, Gamaliel and John;
    Edwards, Hen. (d. 1850), and
    Hen. (d. 1881); Fordington;
    Loder; Marraker, Chris. and
    John; Randall; Staple
  rectory, 223, 228
    ho., 229
  sch., 230-1
  tithes, 228-9
  woods, 222-3, 226
  Wortheal (Wrthiale, Wurthihale),
    222-3, 226-8
Wardour (Wilts.), 176
Ware:
  Rob., 207
  fam., 207
Warenne, Joan de, ctss. of Surrey,
    152
Warner:
  Andrews, 16
  Eliz., see Poulett
  John, and Sons, bell-founders, 105,
    120, 230
Warre (Warr):
  Anne, 221
  Christine, see Chydlegh
  J. C., 36
  Jane, m. Sir Ric. Grosvenor, 214
  John (d. 1349), 44
  John (fl. 15th cent.), 44
  Mat., 44
  Ric. (fl. 1399), 44
  Ric. (d. 1465), 44
  Sir Ric. (d. c. 1482), and his w.
    Joan, 44
  Sir Ric. (d. 1532), 44
  Ric. (fl. 1568), 44
  Thos. (d. 1542), 44, 50 n
  Thos. (d. 1682), 213-14
  Thos. (d. 1685), 213

Thos. (d. 1737), 213
Wm., 44
fam., 44–5, 214
Warren:
  Humph., 238
  Thos., 225
warren, 9, 39, 40 n, 121, 125, 137, 147, 181, 205
Warry, Wm. Rob., 86–7
Warwick, earls of, see Beauchamp; Dudley; Neville; Plantagenet
Warwickshire, see Leamington
Washfield (Devon), 155
water meadows, 4, 55, 57, 131, 133
Watergore (in South Petherton), 172, 174, 187–8
  inns, 175
Waterland, Hen., 118
Watson, W.S., curate of Knowle, 162
Wattes, Thos., 160
Wayford:
  Baldwin of, and his w., 69
  Scolace of, m. Ric. de Portesye, 69–70
  Wal. of, 69
  Wm. of, and his w. Scolace, 69 and n
Wayford, 1, 5, 17–18, 20, 26, 28–9, 36, **68–75**, 140
  adv., 69–70, 73
  agric., 71–2
  Ashcombe, q.v.
  Bere, q.v.
  chap., 71
  char., 71, 75
  ch., 4, 28, 68–9, 73–5
  cts., 73
  dom. archit., 69–71
  fms., 69, 72
  fields, 69, 72
  glebe, 74
  Greenham, q.v.
  Horn Ash, 69, 72
  inc., 72
  inn, 69
  man., 68–74
  man.-ho., 33, 70–4
  mills, 72–3
  nonconf., 75
  Oathill, q.v.
  par. officers, 73
  park, 69
  poorho., 73
  pop., 69, 72
  quarries, 68
  rector, 34, 74; and see Browne; Cox; Giffard; Layng; Norris; Sharp
  rectory, 70, 73
    ho., 72, 74
  Rom. Cath., 75
  sch., 71, 75
  tithes, 71, 73–4
  tithing, 69
  Townsend, 69, 74
  woodland, 69
Wearne (in Huish Episcopi), 94, 96
Webb:
  W. H., 144
  fam., 143
Webber:
  John, 57
  W. W., 57
Weeke (Hants), 16
Welchman, John, 216
Weld, Humph., 176
Weldon, Col., 175
Wellington, F. G. N., 191
Wells, 71, 165
  cath., 50, 59, 74, 142–3, 145, 154, 157, 162, 191
  chapter, 92, 103, 169, 176, 191, 208
  dean, see Mitchell
  St. Cuthbert's ch., 103
  sub-dean, 219

treasurer, 86, 102–4; and see Barker; Langton
  vicars choral, 92, 101
Welman:
  Chas. Noel, 201
  Isaac (d. 1716), 201–2
  Isaac (d. 1782), 201
  Sim., 201
  Thos. (d. 1757), 201
  Thos. (d. 1829), 201
  fam., 201
Wentworth, Thos., Ld. Wentworth, 129, 179
Wesley (Westley):
  John (fl. 1669), minister, 34
  John (d. 1791), 175
Wesleyans, 35, 50, 108, 120, 151, 195–7, 204, 221, 230; and see Methodists
West:
  Ric. B. T., 225
  Ric. Bowerman, 225
  Rob., 130
  Sarah, 225
Westcombland (in Buckland St. Mary), 76, 92–3, 100, 103
Westcott (Westcote):
  And., 107
  Honor, see Mathew
  Phil., 225
  Thos., 182
  fam., 97
Westley, see Wesley
Westminster, dukes of, 214
Westminster, 86, 201
  Millbank, 41
  sch., 140, 142
Westmorland, earl of, see Fane
Westofer, Wm., 71
Weston (in Combe St. Nicholas), 222, 227, 234
Weston (in Branscombe, Devon), 182
Weston Subedge (Glos.), 237
Weylond:
  Burga, 181
  Eliz., sister of Peter, 181
  Eliz., w. of Wm., see Bath
  Joan, see Streche
  John (fl. 1308), 181
  Sir John (d. 1386), 181–2
  Nic. de, 181
  Peter, 181
  Rob., and his w. Cecily, 181
  Wm., 181
Weymouth (Dors.), 131
Whaddon (Bucks.), 101
Wheatley, Jas., 22
Wherriott, Hen., 222
Whitchurch Canonicorum (Dors.), 67
White:
  Le Roy, 227
  Wm., and his son Rob., 25
Whitefield, Geo., 107
Whitehall (in Combe St. Nicholas), 234
Whitehead, John, and his w. Joan, 25
Whitelackington, 64, 198–9, 201, 203
Whitelock, Carleton, 14–15, 22
Whitestaunton (Staunton), 111–12, 222–3, 226, 228, 230, **231–8**
  adv., 232, 236
  agric., 234–5
  alms-ho., 238
  char., 238
  ch., 160, 236–7
  Civil War, 232
  ct., 236
  curates, 237
  dom. archit., 231–4, 236
  fms., 235
  fields, 231, 234
  glebe, 235–6
  guild, 237
  Howley (Holleway), 231–2, 234, 236
  inc., 234–5

inns, 232
light, 237
man., 232–4, 236
man.-ho., 160, 231–5, 238
  plan, 233
mills, 235–6
minister, see Smith, Ric.
Monmouth Rebellion, 232
nonconf., 237–8
Northay, 231, 234–6
par. officers, 236, 238
park, 231, 233–4
poor-relief, 236, 238
pop., 232
prehist. rem., 231
quarries, 231, 235
rectors, 236; and see Cartwright; Chase, John; Clarke, Rob. Pearse; Elton, W. T.; Greenfield; Jordan alias Stoke; Lumbard, Wm.; Marlow; Small; Staunton, And. de; Wyett
rectory, 228, 236
  ho., 236
Rom. rem., 231, 234
St. Agnes well, 231, 236
sch., 238
tithes, 236
warren, 235
woodland, 231, 234–5
Whitley:
  Charlotte, see Bean
  Edw., see Rodbard
  Revd. H. C., 54
  H. E., 54–5
  H. H., 55
  Reg., 57
  Susannah, 57
  fam., 54–5, 57
Whitton (in Twickenham, Mdx.), 86
Whytehorne, John, 33
Wickhambrook (Suff.), Badmondesfield, q.v.
Widworthy (Devon), 124
Wigborough:
  Ric. of (or Arussir) (d. 1270), 177
  Ric. (fl. 1327), and his w. Maud, 177
  Wm. of (fl. 1284), 177
  Wm. of (d. 1324), 177
Wigborough (in South Petherton): 111, 171–2, 180, 184, 186–7
  chant., 178
  fields, 172
  inc., 172
  man., 172, 177–8, 183, 185
  man.-ho., 33, 178
  tithes, 180
Wight, Isle of, 29; and see Shorwell
Wild (salvagius):
  Christine, see Wake
  Ric., 152
William I, 10, 28
William III, 10
William IV, 53
William, clerk of Dinnington, 150
William, count of Boulogne, 84
William, count of Eu, 41
William, count of Mortain, 53
William the falconer, 148
William the knight, 224
William the usher, 177; and see Helen; Wigborough, Ric. of
Williams:
  Agnes Elsie, m. — Eames, 228
  Revd. Fred., 228
  Jas., 97
  John, rector of Dowlish Wake, 155
Willoughby:
  Anne, w. of John, see Cheyney
  Anne, w. of Sir Edw., see Filoll
  Sir Edw., 224, 226
  Eliz., Baroness Willoughby de Broke, m. Sir Fulk Greville, 201

Willoughby (*cont.*)
Sir Francis, 224–5
Hen., 224
John, 201
Rob., Ld. Willoughby de Broke, 201
Wal., 201
Wills:
Alice, m. John Colston, 85
Marianne, 38
Rob. (fl. 1633), 85, 93
Rob. (d. 1659), 85–6
Willy:
Adam, 198
John, 186
Ric., 167
fam., 174
Wilmington, F., 123
Wilson, H., architect, 194
Wiltshire, 29; *and see* Amesbury;
Ashton Keynes; Basset Down;
Boscombe; Brook; Downton;
Hilmarton; Leigh; Littlecote;
Ramsbury; Salisbury; South-
wick; Steeple Langford; Trow-
bridge; Wardour; Westbury;
Winterbourne Gunner
Wimborne Minster (Dors.), 104
Wincanton, 195
Winchester, 16, 29, 208
archd., *see* Roger
bp., 92, 102
cath., 30
chapter, 16–17, 27, 29, 66
coll., 16, 88, 90, 95, 206–8
Windsor, Agnes de, *see* Esse
Windsor (Berks.), 15
Winsham, 68–9, 74, 111, 121, 124,
133–41, 235
Bridge (Fordebrigge), 111
Jakettes, q.v.
Leigh, q.v.
Purtington, q.v.
Street, q.v.
Whatley, 111
Winter, Mark, curate of Misterton, 66
Winterborne St. Martin, Martins-
town (Dors.), 45
Winterbourne Gunner (Wilts.), 44
Wiseman:
Rob., bell-founder, 105, 146
Wm., bell-founder, 50, 194
Witcombe:
Isabel, 91
John of (fl. 1249), 95
John (d. by 1521), 89
John (d. 1527), 89, 104
John, and his w. Alice (fl. 1545), 91
Pharamus of, 95
Rob. of, 95
Wal. of, 95
Wm. (fl. 1550), 89, 91
fam., 89
Witcombe (Wythicumbe, in Mar-
tock), 79, 84, 89, 92, 97, 101
agric., 95–6
br., 79–81
fields, 81, 96
inc., 96
man., 89–90, 95–6, 101

man.-ho., 81, 90, 96
pop., 95
tithing, 76, 78, 95, 106
Witham Friary:
ch., 191
Ho., 219
Wodelond, *see* Odelande
Wodeman, John, vicar of South
Petherton, 192
Wogan, Agnes, 214
Wollaton Hall (Notts.), 225
Wolminton, *see* Woolmington
Wolsey, Thos., 164
Wood:
And. of, 159
John of, 159
Mrs. M. A., 109
Rob., 17, 24, 33, 65
Wm., 87, 97
Wm. Cole, 97
fam., 97
wood, 4, 18, 45, 47, 56, 92–3, 111,
113, 125–6, 130–1, 133, 136–7,
141, 144, 148, 160, 184, 226, 231,
234–5
and see charcoal; timber
Woodcock, Sarah, 37, 61
woodland, clearance, 57, 121, 125,
136, 160
Woodlands (Dors.), 224
Woodwall, alias Kinder:
Alice, 138
John, 138
Woodward, Miss J. L., 115
wool, 21, 57, 65, 86–7, 96, 98, 167,
207, 216
Woolmington (Wolminton):
Frances, m. Revd. Hen. Hooton, 225
John de, 226
John (d. 1640–1), 227
John (d. 1717), 225
Mary, m. Rob. Wadham, 225
fam., 226
Woolminstone (Wulureston, in Crew-
kerne), 5, 9, 15, 17–20, 24, 32–3,
35, 37–8, 55
tithing, 26
Woolwich (London), Royal Military
Academy, 162
Wootton, Nic., 235
Worcester, Wm. of, 141
Worcester, 155
bp., 139
Worcestershire, *see* Great Malvern
Worle, 213
Worth:
Alice, 186
Phil. de, 144
Wottesdone, Alex. de, 63
Wouburne, John, 12
Wraxall, Agnes of, 205 *n*, 208
Wraxall (Dors.), 205
Wraxall (Som.), 192
Wrigley, F. T., 14
Wrington, 118
Wroth, T., 156
Wroughton:
John, 224
Marg., *see* Filoll

Wyatt, Jas., architect, 43, 50
Wyatville (Wyatt), Sir Jeffry, 43
Wydiworth:
Grace, *see* Vaux
Wm., 181
Wyett, Wm., rector of Whitestaun-
ton, 237
Wyke:
Averyn, 15
Barbara, 15
Eliz., 15
Frances, m. Thos. Greenwood, 54
Hen., 15
John (d. 1517), 15
John (fl. 1517), 15
John (d. 1622), 15, 54
Rebecca, m. Thos. Brookes, 54
Ric. (d. 1590), 15
Ric. (fl. 1601), 15
Rob., 15
Thos., 15
Wm., 15
Wynard:
Wm., 185
fam., 185
Wyndham:
Christabel, *see* Pyne
Sir Edm., 56
Edm., 56
Mary, *see* Trevelyan
fam., 144, 185
Wyngham, Wm. de, 206
Wythe, Wm., and his w., 142
Wythele:
Hen. de, 181
Reynold, 181
fam., 181
Wythele, *see* Dowlish Wake

Yarcombe, Phil. of, priest of Wam-
brook, 228
Yarcombe (Devon), 225–6, 229, 231,
238
Yarty, riv., 231
Yates, alias Hopton, John, 237
Yeabridge (in South Petherton), 172,
187–8, 191
Yeatman:
Hugh, and his w. Marg., 13
Mary, *see* Dalton
Yeo, riv., 78–9
Yeovil, 17, 23, 37, 57, 67, 78, 88–91,
98–9, 107, 182, 195, 216
District, 28
poor-law union, 102, 191, 197
R.D.C., 191
Yeovilton, 91, 96, 100
Yetminster (Dors.), 65
York (Yorke):
Chas., 139
Thos., 13
Yorkshire, N.R., *see* Aske
W.R., *see* Mirfield
Ypres, 146

Zouche:
Alice, *see* Seymour
Wm., Ld. Zouche, 134, 199
fam., 134